W9-AZT-013

Educational Policy and the Law

Third Edition

Educational Policy and the Law

Third Edition

Mark G. Yudof
Dean, University of Texas
School of Law

David L. Kirp
University of California,
Berkeley

Betsy Levin
Executive Director of the
Association of American Law Schools

West Publishing Company
St. Paul New York Los Angeles San Francisco

Copyeditor: Julie Bach
Composition: Parkwood Composition

610 Opperman Drive
P.O. Box 64526
St. Paul, MN 55164–0526

Printed in the United States of America

99 98 97 96 95 7 6 5 4 3 2 1

Library of Congress Cataloging-in-Publication Data

Yudof, Mark G.
Educational policy and the law / Mark G. Yudof, David L. Kirp, Betsy Levin. — 3rd ed.
p. cm.
Rev. ed. of: Kirp & Yudof's Educational policy and the law. 2nd ed. ©1982.
Includes index.
ISBN 0-314-77299-5 (hard)
1. Educational law and legislation—United States—Cases. I. Kirp, David L. II. Levin, Betsy. III. Kirp, David L. Kirp & Yudof's Educational policy and the law. IV. Title.
KF4118.K5 1991
344.73'07—dc20
[347.3047]

91-19822
CIP

Contents

CHAPTER FIVE:

CHAPTER SIX:

Preface

From the late eighteenth century to the present, law and the legal system have played a major role in the shaping of public education in America. In the nineteenth century the law was used to justify public education, to compel attendance, and to establish a structure for its financing and governance. D. Tyack, T. James and A. Benavot, *Law and the Shaping of Public Education 1785–1954*, 7 (1987). As that century progressed, the structure of state authority became more elaborate, including state superintendents, state boards of education, provision for nonsectarian instruction, and standardization of textbooks and the curriculum. *Id.* at 55. Most of the litigation from that period involved finance and governance issues, and existing bodies of private (torts, contracts, property) and public (taxation, local government) law were applied in the school setting. *Id.* at 69.

Today, the central issues of educational policy—racial desegregation, the treatment of students with disabilities, women and minorities, school finance, religion and schooling, among others—also are important questions of law. *See* T. van Geel, *The Courts and American Education* (1987); K. Alexander and M. D. Alexander, *American Public School Law* (1985); M. Rebell and A. Block, *Educational Policy Making and the Courts* (1982). During the nearly four decades since the *Brown* decision, lawmakers have reconstituted the domain of educational policy. For one thing, decisions once made by school administrators and local boards of education have increasingly become the province of courts. *See* D. Kirp and D. Jensen (eds.), *School Days, Rule Days* (1986). For another, within the political system, initiative concerning policy has shifted from the local to the state and federal levels of government. *See generally* P. Peterson, *The Politics of School Reform 1870–1940* (1985). This transformation of political authority has been rapid and remains dynamic as different groups have pressed for educational entitlements and as legislatures have sought to improve the quality of public education. This third edition of *Educational Policy and the Law* examines both sets of changes, assessing their impact on American schooling policy and practice.

Educational Policy and the Law does not treat the law as an isolated entity but instead stresses the interplay of law and policy, legal decision and educational practice. Among the issues addressed are the relationship between schooling and the state, the nature and scope of students' and teachers' substantive and procedural rights, and the many meanings of equal educational opportunity. Questions of governance are addressed in two chapters that consider the tension among political, professional, and legal authority at the local level and the distinctive policy role of the federal government. The book borrows liberally from a range of social science sources as well as from conventional legal materials to describe and analyze how policy problems become legal matters, to canvass alternative solutions, and to specify the effects of legally mandated change.

Educational Policy and the Law should help the student of education make sense of legal decisions. It offers the law student insight into the political and policy context of legal issues. The abundant notes and references also make the book a useful reference work for lawyers or school administrators working in the field.

The first three chapters of the book take up one of the great themes of educational policy and law: the scope of liberty that students, teachers, and families have with respect to schooling. The book begins with the underlying liberty issues: Can the state compel all children to attend some school? To what extent can it regulate their education? This inquiry, which includes a discussion of alternatives to existing arrangements, identifies tensions among the interests of the state, the family, and the child in education, tensions that recur throughout the text. It also frames the background for a related set of questions, addressed in the second and third chapters: In what ways may the government regulate the lives of public school children and their teachers? The questions are, in part, substantive. What are the bounds of permissible government socialization of students? What "academic freedoms" does the public schoolteacher bring to the classroom? There is also a procedural dimension to the issue: Are students and teachers protected against arbitrary official judgment? Are they entitled to present their cause before being disciplined or discharged?

Chapter 4 reflects the tension among children, families, and the state from a different perspective. It looks at the system of government-supported schooling, focusing on that system's accountability to the wishes of the affected community. Various instruments of law and policy—collective bargaining, elections, vouchers, minimum competency requirements, restructuring, and the like—are appraised in terms of their capacity to enhance or promote the accountability of the institution. That frame has particular relevance to the treatment of the second major substantive theme of educational policy and law, the meaning of equal educational opportunity. Chapter 5 traces the evolution of the constitutional definition of equal opportunity within the racial context. While its primary emphasis is on the development of the constitutional obligation to desegregate schools, the chapter also notes the second generation of concerns that arise in the wake of desegregation and looks at other conceptions of racial equality. Chapter 6 considers equal educational opportunity in terms of school resources and student outcomes, focusing on the implications of adopting a standard of equity cast in terms of dollars, needs, or outcomes, either through legislation or judicial decision. The final chapter explores the role of the federal government in responding to other equity-based claims pressed on behalf of the educationally disadvantaged, the limited-English-speaking, women, and the handicapped. The pattern of federal involvement and the more recent diminution of federal responsibility are traced.

The casebook can be covered in its entirety in a one-semester course, meeting three hours each week, by an instructor who believes in intellectual jogging. Particular chapters or sets of chapters are rich enough for more focused courses: chapters 1 through 3, for instance, or chapters 5 and 6, or chapters 4 and 7. Instructors' views of the importance of a particular topic or its relationship to the themes being advanced in a given course also will determine how the book is used.

The format of the book deserves brief explanation. The materials have been edited to bring them within reasonable page limitations. Footnote numbers from the original source have been retained, so that readers who want to examine the original texts may easily find their way. Each major section is followed by copious notes that offer relevant supplementary information and raise questions both of law and policy.

Much has occurred in the years since 1974 when the first edition of this book appeared—the case-law has grown apace, legislative initiatives have blossomed, the social science materials are substantially richer—and all these changes are reflected here. We have also, in particular instances, revised our view of earlier materials. For that reason, relatively little of the first two editions has been carried over unchanged, and we would like to acknowledge some of the people who helped facilitate that change.

Mark G. Yudof extends his appreciation for the research assistance of Janis Herd, Jennifer Horan, Mona Hymel, and Ben Bash. Without their help, the text would have had many notable gaps and errors. Without the editorial and secretarial support of Alyce Lottman, Cetchren Nealy, Andrea Dadap, and Judy Ryser this edition might never have appeared at all.

David L. Kirp would like to thank Nina Robinson for her research assistance with chapter 7 and Rosemarie Scholtz for secretarial and proofreading assistance.

Betsy Levin thanks the following students for their help: Deanne E. Andrews, Raymond Angelo, Marilyn Averill, J. Kevin Bridston, Catherine Chaney, Sanford N. Greenberg, Bradley Hogin, Norman Frederick Kron, Jr., A. Robin Mathias, and Richard S. White.

Table of Cases

Main cases are indicated by italicized page numbers.

C

D

E

F

G

H

I

J

T

U

V

Educational Policy and the Law

Third Edition

ONE

Schooling and the State

I. THE "PIERCE COMPROMISE" AND ITS IMPLICATIONS FOR EDUCATION GOVERNANCE

In every state American children are legally obliged to attend school or to receive some minimum level of instruction in the home. The first such law was enacted in Massachusetts in 1642. Over two hundred years later Massachusetts adopted the first general compulsory attendance law, requiring children between the ages of eight and fourteen to attend school for twelve weeks each year. T. van Geel, *The Courts and American Education Law* 18 (1987). Today, most children attend publicly run schools whose policies are determined by state and local officials. In many states private schools also are governmentally regulated and home schooling is permissible in some circumstances. These facts of American schooling are familiar to most citizens. Less generally understood are such matters as how this pattern came to be; its implications for children, parents, educators, and society; the nature and scope of legitimate community and individual interests; and—most significantly for our purposes—the constitutional and statutory bases of the educational structure.

From the perspective of the late twentieth century, the present system of schooling may have the appearance of inevitability. But history tells us otherwise. *See* Tyack, "Ways of Seeing: An Essay on the History of Compulsory Schooling," 46 *Harv. Educ. Rev.* 355 (1976). The "common-school crusade" began in the mid-nineteenth century, before schooling was made compulsory by most states, but Americans—or at least white Americans—already "were probably in the vanguard in literacy and mass schooling among the peoples of the world." *Id.* at 359. In the period until 1890 Americans built a vast system of elementary education, one that attracted larger and larger numbers of children. *Id.* But it is important to note that, while schooling was increasingly made compulsory, the compulsory education laws were hotly debated on ideological grounds and poorly enforced. *Id.* Professor Tyack describes this phase in the history of compulsory education as the "symbolic" stage, the period in which Americans embraced the necessity of compelling children to go to school. *Id.*

The second stage, beginning near the turn of the twentieth century, involved the bureaucratization of American schooling. School systems grew in size and complexity. In this stage serious attention was paid to the types of bureaucratic structures necessary to implement universal and compulsory education. *Id.* Even in the South, which largely had resisted compulsory schooling, attitudes toward such schooling became more positive. *Id.* Beginning in the 1930s high school attendance increasingly became the norm, particularly as the effects of the labor surplus of the Great Depression were felt. *Id.* By the 1950s those who failed to complete high school were described as "drop-outs." In the latter half of the twentieth century, the emphasis came to be placed on equality of opportunity for all children and on advancement to higher education. Each of these stages was influenced by and in turn influenced the accompanying legal structure of education. *See* T. van Geel, *supra;* D. Tyack, T. James, A. Benavot, *Law and the Shaping of Public Education 1785–1954* (1987).

The impetus for the compulsory schooling movement has been a matter of much discussion and debate. As Professor Tyack has noted, the movement had varied roots:

> Over the long perspective of the last century and a half, both phases of compulsory school attendance may be seen as part of significant shifts in the functions of families and the status of children and youth. Households in American industrial cities became more like units of consumption than of production. . . . Advocates of compulsory schooling often argued that families—or at least some families, like those of the poor and foreign-born—were failing to carry out their traditional functions of moral and vocational training. Immigrant children in crowded cities, reformers complained, were leading disorderly lives, schooled by the street and their peers more than by Christian nurture in the home. Much of the drive for compulsory schooling reflected an animus against parents considered incompetent to train their children. Often combining fear of social unrest with humanitarian zeal, reformers used the powers of the state to intervene in families and to create alternative institutions of socialization.
>
> * * *
>
> [T]he theory of the political construction of education is powerfully suggestive, but the American historical experience raises certain anomalies. Most Americans during the early national period apparently felt no need to legitimize citizenship through formal state schooling, although that idea began to take hold by mid-nineteenth century. Until the end of the century there was considerable opposition to centralized state power, both in theory and practice.

Tyack, "Ways of Seeing," at 363, 368.

Tyack goes on to suggest that some religious and ethnic groups may have perceived that compulsory schooling would advance the values of their particular group and that progressive-era efforts to depoliticize education and leave schooling to experts and administrators may have played vital roles. *See generally* C. Glenn, *The Myth of the Common School* (1988). Others, writing from a Marxist perspective, have urged that compulsory education reflects a desire to maintain the dominance of the "ruling class" and to suppress alternatives to capitalism. *See, e.g.*, C. Persell, *Education and Inequality* (1977); S. Bowles and H. Gintis, *Schooling in Capitalist America* (1976); M. Carnoy (ed.), *Schooling in Corporate Society* (1972). *But see* Glenn, *supra*. And, "a powerful recurring argument for compulsion was that taxpayers could realize the full return on their large investment [in education] only if free schooling reached all the children; the presumption was that children who were out of school needed education the most and would become an economic burden to the community if left uneducated." Tyack, "Ways of Seeing," supra at 381–82. *See also* M. McCarthy and N. Cambron McCabe, *Public School Law* 44–5 (1988). The latter is known as the human-capital theory of education. *See* T. Schultz, *The Economic Value of Education* (1963).

The excerpt below from the work of philosopher Amy Gutmann explores the normative implications of different conceptions of education and education governance. She explains the range of theoretical choices that a society dedicated to democracy might make, and she articulates and defends her own vision of democratic education. This excerpt is followed by *Pierce v. Society of Sisters*, a landmark Supreme Court decision. *Pierce* establishes the basic constitutional framework within which the states compel and regulate schooling. The power of the state to compel attendance at a school is unquestioned, but, as the case indicates, there are limits on the authority of the state to eliminate or circumscribe educational choices. *Pierce* embodies the tensions among state, family, and child that Professor Gutmann illuminates in her essay.

"Democratic Education"

A. Gutmann, *Democratic Education*, Princeton University Press, Pages 22–26, 28–39, 41–46.

We have inherited not one but several . . . normative theories, which compete for our allegiance and account for many of our social disagreements as well as our personal uncertainties concerning the purposes of education. Three of the most distinct and distinguished of these theories can be drawn from interpretations of Plato, John Locke, and John Stuart Mill. I call them . . . the theories of the *family state*, the *state of families*, and the *state of individuals*. Despite their differences, each treats questions of education (its purposes, distributions, and authorities) as part of a principled *political* theory. . . .

The Family State

Can we speak meaningfully about a good education without knowing what a just society and a virtuous person are? Socrates poses this challenge to the Sophists in the *Protagoras*. Like most of Socrate's questions, it has remained unanswered after twenty-five centuries. But it is still worth re-asking.

In his critique of the Sophists and in the *Republic*, Plato suggests that we cannot speak about a good education without knowing what justice and virtue really are, rather than what a society assumes that they are by virtue of their shared social understandings. Justice, Socrates suggests, is the concurrent realization of individual and social good. Since the good life for individuals entails contributing to the social good, there is no necessary conflict between what is good for us and what is good for our society—provided our society is just. The defining feature of the family state is that it claims exclusive educational authority as a means of establishing a harmony—one might say, a constitutive relation—between individual and social good based on knowledge. Defenders of the family state expect to create a level of like-mindedness and camaraderie among citizens that most of us expect to find only within families (and now perhaps not even there). The purpose of education in the family state is to cultivate that unity by teaching all educable children what the (sole) good life is for them and by inculcating in them a desire to pursue the good life above all inferior ones. Citizens of a well-ordered family state learn that they cannot realize their own good except by contributing to the social good, and they are also educated to desire only what is good for themselves and their society.

One need not accept Plato's view of natural human inequality to take seriously his theoretical defense of the family state. Once we discount this view, we can find in Plato the most cogent defense of the view that state authority over education is necessary for establishing a harmony between individual virtue and social justice. Unless children learn to associate their own good with the social good, a peaceful and prosperous society will be impossible. Unless the social good that they are taught is worthy of pursuit, they will grow to be unfulfilled and dissatisfied with the society that miseducated them. All states that claim less than absolute authority over the education of children will therefore degenerate out of internal disharmony.

* * *

. . . Because a family state is at best the *artificial* parent of its citizens, it must create the conditions under which citizens are bound to honor and obey it. The moral force of parental imagery in politics (as suggested by Socrates's subsequent arguments in the *Crito* concerning the freedom available to Athenian citizens) varies either with the degree to which the wisdom of a state exceeds that of its citizens or with the fit between the goods pursued by a state and those valued by its citizens. A state that lacks wisdom or that rules against the moral convictions of most citizens cannot credibly claim parental status. Not even natural parents, moreover, may properly assert an absolute right to educate their children. . . .

The Platonic family state therefore rightly rejects the relativism of the non-Platonic family state, which would ground education on the mere opinions of state authorities, as readily as it rejects the subjectivism of Sophists, which defines a good education as one that simply satisfies the preferences of students. States that assume a parental role to educate according to false opinion are no better than Sophists who assume a professorial role to teach children virtue without knowing what virtue is. Indeed, sophistical states are worse because they wield more power.

But the Platonic family state has its own problems. The most obvious one is the difficulty of determining the best constitution for any society and the correct conception of the good for any person. . . .

The more telling criticism of the family state proceeds by accepting the possibility that someone sufficiently wise and conscientious might discover the good. She would then try to convince the rest of us that she had discovered *the* good, not just another contestable theory of the good, and the good for *us*, not just the good appropriate to some other people. It's possible that a few of us—an unusually open-minded or uncommitted few—might be convinced, but most of us (as Plato realized) would not; and we would refuse to relinquish all authority over the education of our children to the philosopher-queen (or the state).

In order to create a just family state, the philosopher therefore must wipe the social slate clean by exiling "all those in the city who happen to be older than ten; and taking over their children, . . . rear them—far away from those dispositions they now have from their parents. . . ." That is an exorbitantly high price to pay for realizing a just society. Socrates himself on behalf of the philosopher recoils from the idea. . . .

This objection to the family state is not a purely practical one—pointing to the impossibility of realizing a just society in an unjust world. Even if the philosopher-queen is right in claiming that a certain kind of life is objectively good, she is wrong in assuming that the objectively good is good for those of us who are too old or too miseducated to identify the objectively good with what is good for our own lives. "That may be the best life to which people—educated from birth in the proper manner—can aspire," we might admit, "but it's not the good life for *us*. And don't we have a claim to living a life that is good for us?" The objectively good life, defined as the life that is best for people who are rightly educated from birth, need not be the good life, or even the closest approximation of the good life, for people who have been wrongly educated. . . .

* * *

. . . As long as we differ not just in our opinions but in our moral convictions about the good life, the state's educational role cannot be defined as realizing *the* good life, objectively defined, for each of its citizens. Neither can educational authorities simply claim that a good education is whatever in their opinion is best for the state.

The family state attempts to constrain our choices among ways of life and educational purposes in a way that is incompatible with our identity as parents and citizens. In its unsuccessful attempt to do so, it successfully demonstrates that we cannot ground our conception of a good education merely on personal or political preferences. Plato presents a forceful case for resting educational authority exclusively with a centralized state, a case grounded on the principle that knowledge should be translated into political power. But even the Platonic case is not sufficiently strong to override the claims of parents and citizens to share in social reproduction, claims to which I return in defending a democratic state of education.

The State of Families

States that aspire to the moral unity of families underestimate the strength and deny the legitimacy of the parental impulse to pass values on to children. Radically opposed to the family state is the state of families, which places educational authority exclusively in the hands of parents, thereby permitting parents to predispose their children, through education, to choose a way of life consistent with their familial heritage. Theorists of the state of families typically justify placing educational authority in the hands of parents on grounds either of consequences or of rights. John Locke maintained that parents are the best protectors of their children's future interests. Some Catholic theologians, following Thomas Aquinas, claim that parents have a natural right to educational authority. Many modern-day defenders of the state of families maintain both, and add another argument: if the state is committed to the freedom of individuals, then it must cede educational authority to parents whose freedom includes the right to pass their own way of life on to their children.[19] Charles Fried, for example, argues that "the right to form one's child's values, one's child's life plan and the right to lavish attention on the child are extensions of the basic right not to be interfered with in doing these things for oneself."[20] Fried bases parental rights over children on "the facts of reproduction" and the absence of a societal right to make choices for children. Fried's denial of a societal right is based on the consequentialist judgment that parents can be relied upon to pursue the best interests of their children.

Although the appeal of the state of families is apparent upon recognizing the defects of a family state, none of these theoretical arguments justifies resting educational authority exclusively—or even primarily—in the hands of parents. It is one thing to recognize the right (and responsibility) of parents

19. For the former justification, see Milton Friedman, *Capitalism and Freedom* (Chicago: University of Chicago Press, 1962), pp. 85–107; and John E. Coons and Stephen Sugarman, *Education by Choice: The Case for Family Control* (Berkeley: University of California Press, 1978). For the latter, see Thomas Aquinas, *Supplement Summa Theologica un Divini Illius Magistri of His Holiness Pope Piux XI*, and the 1936 encyclical of the Catholic Church, where Aquinas is quoted as saying: "The child is naturally something of the father, . . . so by natural right the child before reaching the age of reason, is under the father's care. Hence it would be contrary to natural justice if any disposition were made concerning [the child] against the will of the parents." (Quoted in Francis Schrag, "The Right to Educate," *School Review*, vol. 79, no. 3 [May 1971]: 363.) . . .

20. Charles Fried, *Right and Wrong* (Cambridge, Mass.: Harvard University Press, 1978), p. 152.

to educate their children as members of a family, quite another to claim that this right of familial education extends to a right of parents to insulate their children from exposure to ways of life of thinking that conflict with their own. The consequentialist argument is surely unconvincing: parents cannot be counted upon to equip their children with the intellectual skills necessary for rational deliberation. Some parents, such as the Old Order Amish in America, are morally committed to shielding their children from all knowledge that might lead them to doubt and all worldly influences that might weaken their religious beliefs.[21] Many other parents, less radical in their rejection of modern society, are committed to teaching their children religious and racial intolerance.

To criticize the state of families, however, it is not enough to demonstrate that the perspectives of these parents are *wrong*, for we can never realistically expect any educational authority to be infallible. The strongest argument against the state of families is that neither parents nor a centralized state have a right to exclusive authority over the education of children. Because children are members of both families and states, the educational authority of parents and of policies has to be partial to be justified. We appreciate the danger of permitting a centralized state to monopolize education largely for this reason. The similar danger of placing all authority in the hands of parents may be less widely appreciated, at least in the United States, because support for parental authority over education has been associated historically with Lockean liberalism. Because the Lockean state cedes adult citizens the freedom to choose their own good, many liberals (like Fried) assume that it must also cede parents the freedom to educate their children without state interference.[22] To the worry that parents might abuse their authority, many liberals invoke a secular variant of Locke's response:

> God hath woven into the Principles of Human Nature such a tenderness for their Off-spring, that there is little fear that Parents should use their power with too much rigour; the excess is seldom on the severe side, the strong byass of Nature drawing the other way.[23]

Other liberals, more critical of the state of families, call Locke's premise into question by citing the prevalence of physical child abuse in this country. But one need not dispute Locke's claim about the direction and force of "Nature's byass" to conclude that parental instincts are an insufficient reason for resting educational authority exclusively in the family. The same principle that requires a state to grant adults personal and political freedom also commits it to assuring children an education that makes those freedoms both possible and meaningful in the future. A state makes choice possible by teaching its future citizens respect for opposing points of view and ways of life. It makes choice meaningful by equipping children with the intellectual skills necessary to evaluate ways of life different from that of their parents. History suggests that without state provision or regulation of education, children will be taught neither mutual respect among persons nor rational deliberation among ways of life. To save their children from future pain, especially the pain of eternal damnation, parents have historically shielded their children from diverse associations, convinced them that all other ways of life are sinful, and implicitly fostered (if not explicitly taught them) disrespect for people who are different. This spirit is inimical to the kind of liberal character that Locke argued that parents should teach their children. The end—moral freedom—that Locke recommends in his *Essay on Education* requires us to question the means—exclusive parental authority—that Locke defends in the *Second Treatise*, once we can assume (as Locke could not) the political possibility of dividing educational authority between families and the state. . . .

* * *

The state of families mistakenly conflates the welfare of children with the freedom of parents when it assumes that the welfare of children is best defined or secured by the freedom of parents. But the state of families rightly recognizes, as the family state does not, the value of parental freedom, at least to the extent that such freedom does not interfere with the interests of children in becoming mutually respect-

21. *See Wisconsin v. Yoder*, 406 U.S. 210–11.

22. The Lockean argument, therefore, does not depend for its force, as some critics have maintained, on the claim that children are the property of their parents, a claim that Locke himself rejected.

23. Locke, "The Second Treatise of Government," in *Two Treatises of Government*, intro. Peter Laslett (New York: Cambridge University Press, 1960), ch. 6, sec. 67, p. 355.

ful citizens of a society that sustains family life. There is no simple solution to the tension between the freedom of parents and the welfare of children. The state may not grant parents absolute authority over their children's education in the name of individual freedom, nor may it claim exclusive educational authority in the name of communal solidarity. That there is no *simple* solution, however, should not deter us from searching for a better solution than that offered by either the family state or the state of families.

The State of Individuals

"It is in the case of children," John Stuart Mill argued, "that misapplied notions of liberty are a real obstacle to the fulfillment by the State of its duties. One would almost think that a man's children were supposed to be literally, and not metaphorically, a part of himself, so jealous is opinion of the smallest interference of law with his absolute and exclusive control over them. . . ."[25] Having exposed the central flaw in the state of families, Mill defended a more liberal conception of education. "All attempts by the State to bias the conclusions of its citizens on disputed subjects are evil," Mill argued. Some contemporary liberals extend the logic of Mill's argument to defend what I call a state of individuals. They criticize all educational authorities that threaten to bias the choices of children toward some disputed or controversial ways of life and away from others. Their ideal educational authority is one that maximizes future choice without prejudicing children towards any controversial conception of the good life. The state of individuals thus responds to the weakness of both the family state and the state of families by championing the dual goals of *opportunity* for choice and *neutrality* among conceptions of the good life. A just educational authority must not bias children's choices among good lives, but it must provide every child with an opportunity to choose freely and rationally among the widest range of lives.

If neutrality is what we value, then a child must be protected from all—or at least all controversial—social prejudices. Neither parents nor states are capable of fulfilling this educational ideal. Parents are unlikely (and unwilling) to resist a strong human impulse: the desire to pass some of their particular prejudices on to their children. And even the most liberal states are bound to subvert the neutrality principle: they will try, quite understandably, to teach children to appreciate the basic (but disputed) values and the dominant (but controversial) cultural prejudices that hold their society together.

* * *

Contemporary liberal theorists often invoke the spirit of Bentham, Kant, or Mill to defend the ideal of neutrality, overlooking both its moral limitations and the substantial qualifications that each of these theorists placed on the ideal. All sophisticated liberals recognize the practical limitation of neutrality as an educational ideal: it is, in its fullest form, unrealizable. But most fail to appreciate the value of our resistance to the ideal of unprejudiced individual freedom: the value of our desire to cultivate, and allow communities to cultivate, only a select range of choice for children, to prune and weed their desires and aspirations so they are likely to choose a worthy life and sustain a flourishing society when they mature and are free to choose for themselves. . . .

[According to Professor Bruce Ackerman,] to have a rational sense of what we want to become, we need to know who we are; otherwise our choices will be endless and meaningless. We learn to speak English rather than Urdu, not by choice, but by cultural determination. And this cultural determination limits the range of our future choices, even if it does not uniquely determine who we become. Ackerman identifies this prior determination with the need for "cultural coherence," which he uses to justify the family and its nonneutral education. The need for cultural coherence, Ackerman argues, does not justify "adult pretensions to moral superiority." Neither parents nor the state may shape the character of children on the grounds that they can distinguish between better and worse moral character, yet they may shape children's character for the sake of cultural coherence, or in order to maximize their future freedom of choice.

Why, one might ask, should parents and states be free to shape children's character and guide their choices for the sake of cultural coherence but not for the sake of their leading morally good lives?

25. Mill, *On Liberty*, ch. 5, para. 12.

Sometimes the claim that we know better than children the difference between morally good and bad lives is not a pretension to moral superiority, but a reflection of our greater moral maturity. Why, then, should adults resist shaping children's character and guiding their choices on *moral* grounds?

The resistance of many contemporary liberals to one of our strongest moral impulses stems, I suspect, from formulating educational purposes and their justifications as a dichotomous choice.[34] Either we must educate children so that they are free to choose among the widest range of lives (given the constraints of cultural coherence) because freedom of choice is the paramount good, or we must educate children so that they will choose *the* life that we believe is best because leading a virtuous life is the paramount good. Let children define their own identity or define it for them. Give children liberty or give them virtue. Neither alternative is acceptable: we legitimately value education not just for the liberty but also for the virtue that it bestows on children; and the virtue that we value includes the ability to deliberate among competing conceptions of the good.[*]

* * *

Because the educational ideal of free choice commands no *special* political legitimacy, the state of individuals poses the same problem as the family state. Even if liberals could establish that, of all disputed aims of education, neutrality is singularly right, they would still have to establish why being right is a necessary or sufficient condition for ruling. The same argument that holds against the family state holds against the state of individuals: being right is not a necessary or sufficient condition because parents and citizens have a legitimate interest (independent of their "rightness") in passing some of their most salient values on to their children.

* * *

Our task therefore is to find a more inclusive ground for justifying nonneutrality in education. We disagree over the relative value of freedom and virtue, the nature of the good life, and the elements of moral character. But our desire to search for a more inclusive ground presupposes a common commitment that is, broadly speaking, political. We are committed to collectively re-creating the society that we share. Although we are not collectively committed to any particular set of educational aims, we are committed to arriving at an agreement on our educational aims (an agreement that could take the form of justifying a diverse set of educational aims and authorities). The substance of this core commitment is conscious social reproduction. As citizens, we aspire to a set of educational practices and authorities of which the following can be said: these are the practices and authorities to which we, acting collectively as a society, have consciously agreed. It follows that a society that supports conscious social reproduction must educate all educable children to be capable of participating in collectively shaping their society.

* * *

A Democratic State of Education

Cultivating character is a legitimate—indeed, an inevitable—function of education. And there are many kinds of moral character—each consistent with conscious social reproduction—that a democratic state may legitimately cultivate. Who should decide what kind of character to cultivate? I have examined and rejected three popular and philosophically forceful answers to this question. . . .

If my criticisms are correct, then these three theories are wrong. None provides an adequate foundation for educational authority. Yet each contains a partial truth. States, parents, and professional educators all have important roles to play in cultivating moral character. A democratic state of education recognizes that educational authority must be shared among parents, citizens, and professional educators even though such sharing does not guarantee that power will be wedded to knowledge, that parents can successfully pass their prejudices on to their children, or that education will be neutral among competing conceptions of the good life.

---

34. The tendency to dichotomize our moral choices is not unique to advocates of liberal neutrality. What I call the "tyranny of dualisms" is also common to communitarian critics of liberalism. See my "Communitarian Critics of Liberalism," *Philosophy and Public Affairs*, vol. 14, no. 5 (Summer 1985): 316–20.

**See also* M. Sandel, *Liberalism and the Limits of Justice* 17 (1982); J. Rawls, A Theory of Justice 264 (1971).

If a democratic state of education does not guarantee virtue based on knowledge, or the autonomy of families, or neutrality among ways of life, what is the value of its premise of shared educational authority? The broad distribution of educational authority among citizens, parents, and professional educators supports the core value of democracy: conscious social reproduction in its most inclusive form. Unlike a family state, a democratic state recognizes the value of parental education in perpetuating particular conceptions of the good life. Unlike a state of families, a democratic state recognizes the value of professional authority in enabling children to appreciate and to evaluate ways of life other than those favored by their families. Unlike a state of individuals, a democratic state recognizes the value of political education in predisposing children to accept those ways of life that are consistent with sharing the rights and responsibilities of citizenship in a democratic society. A democratic state is therefore committed to allocating educational authority in such a way as to provide its members with an education adequate to participating in democratic politics, to choosing among (a limited range of) good lives, and to sharing in the several subcommunities, such as families, that impart identity to the lives of its citizens.

A democratic state of education constrains choice among good lives not only out of necessity but out of a concern for civic virtue. Democratic states can acknowledge two reasons for permitting communities to use education to predispose children toward some ways of life and away from others. One reason is grounded on the value of moral freedom, a value not uniquely associated with democracy. All societies of self-reflective beings must admit the moral value of enabling their members to discern the difference between good and bad ways of life. Children do not learn to discern this difference on the basis of an education that strives for neutrality among ways of life. Children are not taught that bigotry is bad, for example, by offering it as one among many competing conceptions of the good life, and then subjecting it to criticism on grounds that bigots do not admit that other people's conceptions of the good are "equally" good. Children first become the kind of people who are repelled by bigotry, and then they feel the force of the reasons for their repulsion.

* * *

The second, more specifically democratic, reason for supporting the nonneutral education of states and families is that the good of children includes not just freedom of choice, but also identification with and participation in the good of their family and the politics of their society. The need for cultural coherence does not fully capture this democratic value, because it would not be enough for a centralized state to choose a set of parents and a coherent cultural orientation at random for children. People, quite naturally, value the specific cultural and political orientations of their society and family more than those of others, even if they cannot provide objective reasons for their preferences. The fact that these cultural orientations are theirs is an adequate (and generalizable) reason. Just as we love our (biological or adopted) children more than those of our friends because they are a part of *our* family, so we differentially value the cultural orientations of our country because it is *ours*. We need not claim moral superiority (or ownership) to say any of this. We need claim only that some ways of life are better than others *for us and our children* because these orientations impart meaning to and enrich the internal life of family and society. To focus exclusively on the value of freedom, or even on the value of moral freedom, neglects the value that parents and citizens may legitimately place on *partially* prejudicing the choices of children by their familial and political heritages.

[A] democratic state must aid children in developing the capacity to understand and to evaluate competing conceptions of the good life and the good society. The value of critical deliberation among good lives and good societies would be neglected by a society that inculcated in children uncritical acceptance of any particular way or ways of (personal and political) life. . . .*

To integrate the value of critical deliberation among good lives, we must defend some principled limits on political and parental authority over education,

*_See_ Yudof, "Library Book Selection and the Public Schools: The Quest for the Archimedean Point," 59 *Ind. L. J.* 527 (1984).

limits that in practice require parents and states to cede some educational authority to professional educators.

One limit is that of *nonrepression*. The principle of nonrepression prevents the state, and any group within it, from using education to restrict rational deliberation of competing conceptions of the good life and the good society. Nonrepression is not a principle of negative freedom. It secures freedom from interference only to the extent that it forbids using education to restrict *rational* deliberation or consideration of different ways of life. Nonrepression is therefore compatible with the use of education to inculcate those character traits, such as honesty, religious toleration, and mutual respect for persons, that serve as foundations for rational deliberation of differing ways of life. . . .

A second principled limit on legitimate democratic authority, which also follows from the primary value of democratic education, is *nondiscrimination*. For democratic education to support conscious *social* reproduction, all educable children must be educated. Nondiscrimination extends the logic of nonrepression, since states and families can be selectively repressive by excluding entire groups of children from schooling or by denying them an education conducive to deliberation among conceptions of the good life and the good society. . . .

Nondiscrimination can thus be viewed as the distributional complement to nonrepression. In its most general application to education, nondiscrimination prevents the state, and all groups within it, from denying anyone an educational good on grounds irrelevant to the legitimate social purpose of that good. Applied to those forms of education necessary to prepare children for future citizenship (participation in conscious social reproduction), the nondiscrimination principle becomes a principle of nonexclusion. No educable child may be excluded from an education adequate to participating in the political processes that structure choice among good lives.

Why is a theory that accepts these two principled constraints on popular (and parental) sovereignty properly considered democratic? . . .

The principles of nonrepression and nondiscrimination simultaneously support deliberative freedom and communal self-determination. The form of educational relativism acceptable under these principles is therefore democratic in a significant sense: all citizens must be educated so as to have a chance to share in self-consciously shaping the structure of their society. . . .

NOTES AND QUESTIONS

1. State of Families

What is the strongest argument against a "state of families," giving parents full control of the education of their children? May the liberties of parents and children conflict? Professor Peter Shane, for example, has urged that parental choices may "destroy our confidence in the ability of the children as adults to express their genuine preferences without unfair distortion." Shane, "Compulsory Education and the Tension Between Liberty and Equality: A Comment on Dworkin," 73 *Iowa L. Rev*. 97, 103 (1987). What is required to ensure that children are equipped "with the intellectual skills necessary to evaluate ways of life different from that of their parents"?

2. Cultivating Democratic Character

Professor Gutmann argues against the propositions that the individual choices of children should be determinative in education and that the state should be "neutral" in this process. What are the bases of her objections? Do such rights for children create conflict and adverserial relations between children and adults where there otherwise would be community and shared interest? *See* Minow, "Interpreting Rights: An Essay for Rober Cover," 96 *Yale L.J.* 1860, 1870 (1987). What does Gutmann mean when she says that "we are committed to collectively re-creating the society that we share"? If "neutrality" is not desirable or feasible, on what basis may the state "use education to predispose children toward some ways of life and away from others"? *See* Raz, "Liberalism, Skepticism, and Democracy," 74 *Iowa L. Rev*. 761, 779–86 (1989). Who should define "the difference between good and bad ways of life"? Is democratic education inherently totalitarian? *See generally* S. Arons, *Compelling Belief* 197 (1983) (Public schooling "not only deprives substantial numbers of families of the ability to participate in culture and public life, it threatens to end the process of growth altogether and to replace it with what Jung called 'the spiritual and moral darkness of state Absolutism.' ").

If "a democratic state must aid children in developing the capacity to understand and to evaluate competing conceptions of the good life and the good society," why must the state choose to embrace nonrepression and nondiscrimination? How does one distinguish between "critical deliberation" and "conscious social reproduction"? Do nonrepression and nondiscrimination flow from "conscious social reproduction" or from democratic principles?

John Dewey spoke of "education as reconstruction" as reflecting an "ideal of growth" involving a process of the "constant reorganizing or reconstructing of experience." J. Dewey, *Democracy and Education* 76 (1966). Is this what Gutmann means by "critical deliberation"?

3. *Families and Equality*

Are the aspirations of family empowerment, parental liberty, and equality in education consistent with each other? Consider these remarks by Professor James S. Fishkin:

> Suppose you were to attempt to equalize life chances while maintaining the system of meritocratic assignment. Given background conditions of inequality, it is the autonomy of families that protects the process by which advantaged families differentially affect the development of talents and other qualifications in their children. Only if this process were interfered with could both the principles of merit and of equal life chances be achieved. In other words, if equality of life chances is to be achieved, through processes consistent with the principle of merit, then conditions for the development of talents and other qualifications must be equalized. Given background conditions of inequality, this can be done only through some mechanism that systematically insulates the development of each new generation from the unequal results achieved by the last. Coercive interferences with the family would be required if advantaged parents were to be prevented, systematically, from passing on cognitive, affective, cultural, and social advantages to their children. Perhaps a massive system of collectivized child-rearing could be devised to achieve such a result. Anything short of such a large-scale alternative to the autonomous nuclear family would probably provide only an imperfect barrier between the inequalities of the parental generation and the developmental processes affecting its children.
>
> From the communal child-rearing in Plato's *Republic* to the test tube nurseries in Huxley's *Brave New World*, the replacement of the family with some alternative strategy of child-rearing has been the centerpiece of any social engineering that required complete manipulation of human development. As long as the private sphere of liberty is in place, crucial developmental factors are entrusted to the autonomous decisions of families and are, by that very fact, insulated from social control. Whether the efforts at social engineering are aimed at equalization or hierarchy, the family constitutes a crucial barrier to the manipulability of the causal factors affecting human development.
>
> * * *
>
> . . . The only strategies of intervention that might offer a hope of the required massive effects would amount to such a wholesale change in the child's environment that their obviously prohibitive expense would violate any realistic construction of the budget constraint. Hence, leveling up strategies of intervention—that leave the private sphere intact—are either prohibitive in expense or insufficient in effect. On the other hand, by making many of the children affected worse-off (those who would have been advantaged without the equalization efforts), leveling down strategies clearly violate the autonomy of families if those provisions are to be universally enforced.

J. S. Fishkin, *Justice, Equal Opportunity, and the Family* 64–66 (1983). *See generally* Becker & Murphy, "The Family and the State," 31 *J. of Law & Econ.* 1 (1988); Shane, *supra* at 104.

Pierce v. Society of Sisters

268 U.S. 510, 45 S.Ct. 571, 69 L.Ed. 1070 (1925).

Mr. Justice McReynolds delivered the opinion of the Court.

These appeals are from decrees, based upon undenied allegations, which granted preliminary orders restraining appellants from threatening or attempting to enforce the Compulsory Education Act (Ore. Gen. Laws, ch. 1, p. 9 (1923))[1] adopted November

---

1. *Be it enacted by the people of the state of Oregon:*

Section 1. That section 5259, Oregon Laws, be and the same is hereby amended so as to read as follows:

Section 5259. *Children Between the Ages of Eight and Sixteen Years.* Any parent, guardian or other person in the State of Oregon, having control or charge or custody of a child under the age of sixteen years and of the age of eight years or over at the commencement of a term of public school of the

7, 1922, under the initiative provision of her Constitution by the voters of Oregon. Judicial Code §266 (Comp. St. § 1243). . . .

The challenged Act, effective September 1, 1926, requires every parent, guardian, or other person having control or charge or custody of a child between eight and sixteen years to send him "to a public school for the period of time a public school shall be held during the current year" in the district where the child resides; and failure to do so is declared a misdemeanor. . . . The manifest purpose is to compel general attendance at public schools by normal children, between eight and sixteen, who have not completed the eighth grade. And without doubt enforcement of the statute would seriously impair, perhaps destroy, the profitable features of appellees' business and greatly diminish the value of their property.

Appellee, the Society of Sisters, is an Oregon corporation, organized in 1880, with power to care for orphans, educate and instruct the youth, establish and maintain academies or schools, and acquire necessary real and personal property. It has long devoted its property and effort to the secular and religious education and care of children, and has acquired the valuable goodwill of many parents and guardians. It conducts interdependent primary and high schools and junior colleges, and maintains orphanages for the custody and control of children between eight and sixteen. In its primary schools many children between those ages are taught the subjects usually pursued in Oregon public schools during the first eight years. Systematic religious instruction and moral training according to the tenets of the Roman Catholic Church are also regularly provided. All courses of study, both temporal and religious, contemplate continuity of training under appellee's charge; the primary schools are essential to the system and the most profitable. It owns valuable buildings, especially constructed and equipped for school purposes. The business is remunerative—the annual income from primary schools exceeds $30,000—and the successful conduct of this requires long-time contracts with teachers and parents. The Compulsory Education Act of 1922 has already caused the withdrawal from its schools of children who would otherwise continue, and their income has steadily declined. The appellants, public officers, have proclaimed their purpose strictly to enforce the statute.

After setting out the above facts, the Society's bill alleges that the enactment conflicts with the right of parents to choose schools where their children will receive appropriate mental and religious training, the right of the child to influence the parents' choice of a school, the right of schools and teachers therein to engage in a useful business or profession, and is accordingly repugnant to the Constitution and void. And, further, that unless enforcement of the measure is enjoined the corporation's business and property will suffer irreparable injury.

Appellee, Hill Military Academy, is a private corporation organized in 1908 under the laws of Oregon, engaged in owning, operating, and conducting for profit an elementary, college preparatory, and military training school for boys between the ages of five and twenty-one years. . . . It owns considerable real and personal property, some useful only

district in which said child resides, who shall fail or neglect or refuse to send such child to a public school for the period of time a public school shall be held during the current year in said district, shall be guilty of a misdemeanor and each day's failure to send such child to a public school shall constitute a separate offense; provided, that in the following cases, children shall not be required to attend public schools:

(a) *Children Physically Unable.* Any child who is abnormal, subnormal, or physically unable to attend school.

(b) *Children Who Have Completed the Eight Grade.* Any child who has completed the eighth grade, in accordance with the provisions of the state course of study.

(c) *Distance from School.* Children between the ages of eight and ten years, inclusive, whose place of residence is more than one and one-half miles, and children over ten years of age whose place of residence is more than three miles, by the nearest traveled road, from a public school; provided, however, that if transportation to and from school is furnished by the school district, this exemption shall not apply.

(d) *Private Instruction.* Any child who is being taught for a like period of time by the parent or private teacher such subjects as are usually taught in the first eight years in the public school; but before such child can be taught by a parent or a private teacher, such parent or private teacher must receive written permission from the county superintendent, and such permission shall not extend longer than the end of the current school year. Such child must report to the county school superintendent or some person designated by him at least once every three months and take an examination in the work covered. If, after such examination, the county superintendent shall determine that such child is not being properly taught then the county superintendent shall order the parent, guardian or other person, to send such child to the public school the remainder of the school year.

If any parent, guardian, or other person having control or charge or custody of any child between the ages of eight and sixteen years, shall fail to comply with any provision of this section, he shall be guilty of a misdemeanor, and shall, on conviction thereof, be subject to a fine of not less than $5, nor more than $100, or to imprisonment in the county jail not less than two nor more than thirty days, or by both such fine and imprisonment in the discretion of the court.

This Act shall take effect and be and remain in force from and after the first day of September, 1926.

for school purposes. The business and incident good will are very valuable. In order to conduct its affairs, long time contracts must be made for supplies, equipment, teachers, and pupils. Appellants, law officers of the State and County, have publicly announced that the act of November 7, 1922, is valid and have declared their intention to enforce it. By reason of the statute and threat of enforcement appellee's business is being destroyed and its property depreciated; parents and guardians are refusing to make contracts for the future instruction of their sons, and some are being withdrawn.

The Academy's bill states the foregoing facts and then alleges that the challenged Act contravenes the corporation's rights guaranteed by the Fourteenth Amendment and that unless appellants are restrained from proclaiming its validity and threatening to enforce it irreparable injury will result. The prayer is for an appropriate injunction.

No answer was interposed in either cause, and after proper notices they were heard by three judges (Judicial Code §266 [Comp. St. §1243]) on motions for preliminary injunctions upon the specifically alleged facts. The court ruled that the Fourteenth Amendment guaranteed appellees against the deprivation of their property without due process of law consequent upon the unlawful interference by appellants with the free choice of patrons, present and prospective. It declared the right to conduct schools was property and that parents and guardians, as a part of their liberty, might direct the education of children by selecting reputable teachers and places. Also, that these schools were not unfit or harmful to the public, and that enforcement of the challenged statute would unlawfully deprive them of patronage and thereby destroy their owners' business and property. Finally, that the threats to enforce the Act would continue to cause irreparable injury; and the suits were not premature.

No question is raised concerning the power of the State reasonably to regulate all schools, to inspect, supervise and examine them, their teachers and pupils; to require that all children of proper age attend some school, that teachers shall be of good moral character and patriotic disposition, that certain studies plainly essential to good citizenship must be taught, and that nothing be taught which is manifestly inimical to the public welfare.

The inevitable practical result of enforcing the Act under consideration would be destruction of appellees' primary schools, and perhaps all other private primary schools for normal children within the State of Oregon. These parties are engaged in a kind of undertaking not inherently harmful, but long regarded as useful and meritorious. Certainly there is nothing in the present records to indicate that they have failed to discharge their obligations to patrons, students, or the State. And there are no peculiar circumstances or present emergencies which demand extraordinary measures relative to primary education. . . .

[W]e think it entirely plain that the Act of 1922 unreasonably interferes with the liberty of parents and guardians to direct the upbringing and education of children under their control. As often heretofore pointed out, rights guaranteed by the Constitution may not be abridged by legislation which has no reasonable relation to some purpose within the competency of the State. The fundamental theory of liberty upon which all governments in this Union repose excludes any general power of the State to standardize its children by forcing them to accept instruction from public teachers only. The child is not the mere creature of the State; those who nurture him and direct his destiny have the right, coupled with the high duty, to recognize and prepare him for additional obligations.

Appellees are corporations, and therefore, it is said, they cannot claim for themselves the liberty which the Fourteenth Amendment guarantees. Accepted in the proper sense, this is true. . . . But they have business and property for which they claim protection. These are threatened with destruction through the unwarranted compulsion which appellants are exercising over present and prospective patrons of their schools. And this court has gone very far to protect against loss threatened by such action. . . .

The courts of the State have not construed the Act, and we must determine its meaning for ourselves. Evidently it was expected to have general application and cannot be construed as though merely intended to amend the charters of certain private corporations, as in *Berea College v. Kentucky*, 211 U.S. 45. No argument in favor of such view has been advanced.

Generally, it is entirely true, as urged by counsel, that no person in any business has such an interest in possible customers as to enable him to restrain exercise of proper power of the State upon the ground that he will be deprived of patronage. But the injunctions here sought are not against the exercise of any *proper* power. Plaintiffs asked protection against arbitrary, unreasonable, and unlawful interference with their patrons and the consequent destruction of their business and property. Their interest is clear and immediate, within the rule approved in *Truax v. Raich* [239 U.S. 33 (1915)], *Truax v. Corrigan* [257 U.S. 312 (1921)], and *Terrace v. Thompson* 263 U.S. 197 (1923)], and many other cases where injunctions have issued to protect business enterprises against interference with the freedom of patrons or customers. . . .

The suits were not premature. The injury to appellees was present and very real, not a mere possibility in the remote future. If no relief had been possible prior to the effective date of the Act, the injury would have become irreparable. Prevention of impending injury by unlawful action is a well-recognized function of courts of equity.

The decrees below are

Affirmed.

NOTES AND QUESTIONS

1. Historical Background

The requirement that Oregon's children attend public schools was unique among the American states. It had been adopted after a referendum campaign organized and promoted primarily by the Ku Klux Klan and the Oregon Scottish Rite Masons as part of a strategy to "Americanize" the schools: If the campaign was successful, a dozen other states were next in line. Bans on the teaching of Darwinism and foreign languages and requirement of teacher loyalty oaths and inoffensive textbooks were all part of a large assault on pluralism in education and society. As one Klansman noted: "Somehow these mongrel hordes must be Americanized; failing that, deportation is the only remedy." Oregon's public schoolteachers also supported the bill, apparently fearing that its rejection would be taken as a rejection of public schooling. Parochial schools were the most numerous private schools in the state, and anti-Catholicism—"religious revenge," as the Portland *Telegram* put it—helped sway voters' minds. The bill's opponents—among them churchmen who denied that "sectarianism" was "unpatriotic," businessmen fearing increased school taxes, minority groups and civil rights organizations concerned about constitutional and religious liberties—objected to state monopoly over education. But the referendum narrowly carried, splitting political party lines; one Oregon newspaper editor commented that "politics has simply gone mad." How might that background have influenced the *Pierce* decision? For a more extended discussion of the Oregon experience, see Tyack, "The Perils of Pluralism: The Background of the *Pierce* Case," 74 *Amer. Hist. Rev.* 74 (1968).

The requirement that children attend some school, public or private, was not new. The common school—locally run and financed and open without tuition to all children—had been energetically and successfully promoted by reformers such as Massachusetts' Horace Mann since the early nineteenth century. *See* C. Glenn, *The Myth of the Common School* (1988). In the view of some school officials, the taxation of property for the support of schools created a "reciprocal obligation" on the part of the state to ensure that all enjoyed the benefits of education. But the uneducated and unassimilated immigrant proletariat resisted this new venture; they badly needed the income their children's labor secured. As the Pennsylvania Board of State Charities saw the issue: "It is precisely those children whose parents or guardians are unable or indisposed to provide them with an education . . . for whom the state is most interested to provide and secure it." Education was simply too important, in the eyes of its promoters, to be left to the caprice of parental choice; it was a good imposed on the benighted by the more "enlightened" members of the community. As historian Michael Katz notes:

> If everyone was taxed for school support, if this was justified by the necessity of schooling for the preservation of urban social order, if the beneficial impact of schooling required the regular and prolonged attendance of *all* children, and finally, if persuasion and a variety of experiments had failed to bring all the children to school—then, clearly, education had to be compulsory.

M. Katz, *Class, Bureaucracy, and Schools* 48 (1971).

Massachusetts passed the first compulsory education law in 1852, requiring that all children between the ages of eight and fourteen attend school for at least twelve weeks a year, twenty-eight states passed similar legislation in the years following the Civil War. But compulsory education, although legally required, did not immediately become social fact. The resistance of some educators affords one explanation of this phenomenon. In Auburn, New York, School Superintendent B.B. Snow voiced a common sentiment: "The compulsory attendance of the element attempted to be reached by law would be detrimental to the well-being of any respectable school." In many school systems, there was insufficient space to accommodate this class of youngsters: In Illinois, for instance, school buildings could house only one-third of all eligible schoolchildren, while in New York City the average elementary school class enrolled seventy-five pupils. The insatiable demand for cheap labor continued to be satisfied by the hiring of school-age youngsters, and officials—many of whom believed that the education of workers' children was a waste of time—often ignored these violations of the law. An 1884 report drafted by Charles Peck, New York commissioner of statistics of labor, pronounced the compulsory education statute a "dead letter." In the South, compulsory attendance laws were not enforced until well into the twentieth century, and the educational needs of black children were given lowest priority.

By the end of the ninteenth century, however, the principle of compulsory schooling was generally accepted, and, by the time of the *Pierce* decision, almost every child had at least an elementary education. *See generally* D. Tyack, T. James and A. Benavot, *Law and the Shaping of Public Education, 1785–1954* (1987). State courts routinely upheld compulsory education laws. *See, e.g., State v. Hoyt*, 84 N.H. 38, 146 A. 170 (1929); *State v. Bailey*, 157 Ind. 324, 61 N.E. 730 (1901). *See also Concerned Citizens for Neighborhood Schools v. Board of Educ.*, 379 F.Supp. 1233 (E.D. Tenn. 1974). For compilations of compulsory attendance laws, *see* L. Kotin and W. Aikman, *Legal Foundations of Compulsory School Attendance* (1980); A. Steinhilber and C. Sokolowski, *State Law on Compulsory Attendance* (1966). No thorough history of compulsory schooling in America has been written; for discussion of the phenomenon, *see* E. Cubberley, *Changing Conceptions of Education* (1909); F. Ensign, *Compulsory School Attendance and Child Labor* (1921); M. S. Katz, *A History of Compulsory Education Laws* (1976); Kotin and Aikman, *supra*; D. Tyack, *The One Best System* (1974); D. Tyack, T. James and A. Benavot, *supra*; Burgess, "The Goddess, the School Book, and Compulsion," 46 *Harv. Educ. Rev.* 199 (1976); Sugarman and Kirp, "Rethinking Collective Responsibility for Education," 39 *Law & Contemp. Probs.* 144 (1975); Tyack, "Ways of Seeing: An Essay on the History of Compulsory Schooling," 46 *Harv. Educ. Rev.* 355 (1976).

2. The Constitutional Standard: Family versus State?

The *Pierce* Court could conceivably have adopted any of three standards. It could have upheld the right of the state to compel public school attendance, or it could have struck down compulsory attendance laws (an issue which was not, however, raised in the litigation), giving complete control of the child's education to the family. The formula it adopted—the third possible choice—was a compromise between these two positions: the state may compel attendance at some school, but it is the parents' right to choose between public and private schools. That result required the Court to balance the claims made by competing interests—the state, the family (speaking, at least nominally, for the child), and the private schools. Is the balance drawn correctly? Does *Pierce* embody the view of democratic education espoused by Professor Gutmann, *supra*?

From this perspective, reread the statute challenged in the *Pierce* case (reprinted in footnote 1, *supra*). Note that the county superintendent must approve of private instruction. Approval is dependent upon the county superintendent determining whether the child is being "properly taught." Given the vagaries of the standard and perhaps the self-interest of the public school officials in promoting public education, might *Pierce* be explained on the basis that the Court feared the result of such a vague delegation of authority (from the legislature) to the officials responsible for overseeing private education? Is it that state legislatures and not state administrative officials should strike the proper balance between family and state in education matters? *Cf.* Linde, "Due Process of Lawmaking," 55 *Neb. L. Rev.* 197 (1976); Tribe, "The Emerging Reconnection of Individual Rights and Institutional Design: Federalism, Bureaucracy, and Due Process of Lawmaking," 10 *Creighton L. Rev.* 433 (1977). In this respect, note that a number of state courts, reviewing statutes under state constitutions, have declared such delegations unconstitutional where the standards for regulating private schools are ambiguous and lodge what is primarily legislative authority in state educational agencies. *See, e.g., State v. Williams*, 253

N.C. 337, 117 S.E.2d 444 (1960); *Packer Collegiate Institute v. University of State of New York*, 298 N.Y. 184, 81 N.E.2d 80 (1948).

Does the actual wording of the statute before the Court in *Pierce* suggest that the Court decided an issue not properly presented to it? Why might the Court have avoided the vagueness and delegation issues? Under what constitutional provision may federal courts police the separation of powers at the state level? Or is it that the Court assumed that the discretion given county superintendents in the statute was simply a facade for abolishing private education? How could the Court know this a year before the effective date of the Act? Might the Court be acting in response to the clear anti-Catholic motivation behind the enactment of the Act?

3. *Option 1: State Monopoly over Education*

What argument might the state make to justify compulsory public schooling? *See generally* Sugarman and Kirp, *supra;* Gutmann, *supra*. For example, might the state claim that all children should be treated equally and thus receive the same education? Might the argument be made that the state has an obligation to instill certain common values, such as love of country and responsibilities of the citizen, and that this function can be performed most successfully through universal public education? *See generally* R. Weissberg, *Political Learning, Political Choice, and Democratic Citizenship* (1974). How are such assertions to be treated by a court? Are they "arbitrary, unreasonable"—the language used in *Pierce*? Consider these remarks by Professor Joseph Tussman:

> The natural right of self-preservation lies behind not only the traditionally asserted powers of war or defense, but also the universally claimed right of the community to shape its children. More fundamental and inalienable than even the war power stands the tutelary power of the state, . . . the teaching power.
>
> The *teaching power* is the inherent constitutional authority of the state to establish and direct the teaching activity and institutions needed to ensure its continuity and further its legitimate, general and special purposes. . . . The teaching power is a peer to the legislative, the executive, and the judicial powers, if it is not, indeed, the first among them.

J. Tussman, *Government and the Mind* 54 (1977). *But see* Arons, "The Separation of School and State: *Pierce* Reconsidered," 46 Harv. Educ. Rev. 76 (1976).

A century before *Pierce*, Jacksonian Frances Wright proposed that all parents be taxed for the "protective care and guardianship of the state." Their children would be registered at birth and shortly thereafter placed in public nurseries and schools where they would live, work, and study together "in pursuit of the same object—their own and each other's happiness—say! would not such a race, when arrived at manhood and womanhood, work out the reform of society, perfect the free institutions of America?" If adopted, Wright's proposal would have constricted the family's role far more than the Oregon legislation struck down in *Pierce*. Is the proposal unwise, as a matter of policy, or clearly unconstitutional, after *Pierce*? Is it relevant to either question that some societies have adopted a version of Wright's scheme with considerable success? *See, e.g.*, B. Bettelheim, *The Children of the Dream* (1969); M. Spiro, *Children of the Kibbutz* (1975).

4. *Option 2: The* "Pierce Compromise"

In examining the state's "teaching power," including the power to compel school attendance, Professor Tussman argues that the power may be asserted "in a strong or a weak form":

> The strong claim is that *the* teaching power is vested fully in the state and is to be exercised exclusively by agencies of government or, in a variation, by licensed, authorized, supervised non-governmental institutions which operate within governmentally determined policy. In the strong view, non-governmental institutions—religious, commercial, private—in the domain of education exist not by inherent right but on tolerance or out of considerations of policy.
>
> In its weak form the assertion is that the state is one of the legitimate claimants to *a* teaching power; it does not enjoy monopoly or even priority; but it may enter the field. This view would support an extensive proliferation of public education institutions, but governmental exercise of the teaching power would have to accommodate itself to the equal legitimacy and even independence of other teaching institutions. . . .
>
> The strong and weak versions pose . . . the bitter controversy between unitary sovereignty and pluralistic theories of the state . . . . [I]t may well be the weak version which is implied in our theory and practice.

J. Tussman, *Government and the Mind* 55–6 (1977). *See also* Gutmann, *supra* at 115–23.

How does the *Pierce* Court accommodate the state's interest "to the equal legitimacy" of private schools?

The Court recognizes the private schools' interest in maintaining their business and property, but how does that interest differ from the claim that any private concern (an airline not certified by the Civil Aeronautics Board, for example) might advance against particular governmental actions that limit or curtail its market? Since *Pierce*, the Court has abandoned aggressive use of the due process clause as a vehicle for overturning social and economic legislation, at least in the economic as opposed to personal liberty sphere. *See generally* McCloskey, "Economic Due Process and the Supreme Court: An Exhumation and Reburial," 1962 *Sup. Ct. Rev.* 34. "[I]f our recent decisions mean anything, they leave debatable issues as respects business, economic, and social affairs to legislative decision." *Day-Brite Lighting v. Missouri*, 342 U.S. 421, 425, 72 S.Ct. 405, 408, 96 L.Ed. 469 (1952). *See also Ferguson v. Skrupa*, 372 U.S. 726 83 S.Ct. 1028, 10 L.Ed.2d 93 (1963). In the light of such statements, do the interests of the private schools seem constitutionally persuasive today?

The *Pierce* decision is most often cited as authority for the proposition that parents have a constitutional right to educate their children in private schools:

> Reading *Pierce* as a First Amendment case and taking account of the nature of schooling suggest that *Pierce* principles reach the basic value choices on which school policy and practice are based. The result of such a reading is that it is the family and not the political majority which the Constitution empowers to make such schooling decisions.

Arons, "The Separation of School and State: *Pierce* Reconsidered," 46 *Harv. Educ. Rev.* 76, 78 (1976).

Is *Pierce* better understood as a First Amendment case? *See also* Yudof, *When Government Speaks* (1982). Why should parents have such a right? As a policy or constitutional matter, should parental values concern us more than the state's values? Does *Pierce* suggest that where the wishes of parent and child with respect to schooling conflict, the parents' view routinely prevails? Do such parental rights survive the demise of substantive due process in the economic sphere? See *Wisconsin v. Yoder*, *infra*, and subsequent notes for a more detailed discussion of this issue.

The source of this parental right is almost as difficult to fathom as its justification; some Justices have based it on the first Amendment right to freedom of speech (*see, e.g., Griswold v. Connecticut*, 381 U.S. 479, 85 S.Ct. 1678, 14 L.Ed.2d 510 (1965)), while others view the due process clause of the Fourteenth Amendment as its proper constitutional basis (*see, e.g., Abington School Dist. v. Schempp*, 374 U.S. 203, 230, 83 S.Ct. 1560, 1575, 10 L.Ed.2d 844 (1963) (Brennan, J., concurring)). Still others regard *Pierce* as a suit upholding the free exercise of religion, thus limiting its scope to issues of religious liberty (*see, e.g., Board of Education v. Allen*, 392 U.S. 236, 88 S.Ct. 1923, 20 L.Ed.2d 1060 (1968)). *See generally* Arons, *supra*. Note that *Pierce* was decided before the First Amendment was made applicable to the states through the Fourteenth Amendment. *See Fiske v. Kansas*, 274 U.S. 380, 47 S.Ct. 655, 71 L.Ed. 1108 (1927); *Whitney v. California*, 274 U.S. 357, 47 S.Ct. 641, 71 L.Ed. 1095 (1927); *Gitlow v. New York*, 268 U.S. 652, 45 S.Ct. 625, 69 L.Ed. 1138 (1925). (Assuming, *arguendo*, the applicability to the states of the freedom of expression provision of the First Amendment.)

Which textual argument seems most persuasive? What is the nexus between the constitutional right to freedom of speech and the parents' desire to educate their children in private schools? These questions are of more than lawyerly interest; the very scope of the *Pierce* compromise hinges on whether one views religion or speech as critical to the decision. John Stuart Mill's classic essay, *On Liberty*, advances a quite different compromise between state and parental interest:

> Is it not almost a self-evident axiom, that the State should require and compel the education, up to a certain standard, of every human being who is born its citizen? Yet . . . [h]ardly anyone indeed will deny that it is one of the most sacred duties of the parents . . . after summoning a human being into the world, to give to that being an education fitting him to perform his part well in life towards others and towards himself. But while this is unanimously declared to be the father's duty, scarcely anybody, in this country, will bear to hear of obliging him to perform it. . . .
>
> Were the duty of enforcing universal education once admitted there would be an end to the difficulties about what the State should teach, and how it should teach. . . . If the government would make up its mind to require for every child a good education, it might save itself the trouble of providing one. It might leave to parents to obtain the education where and how they pleased, and content itself with helping to pay the school fees of the poorer classes of children, and defraying the entire school expenses of those who have no one else to pay for them. The objections which are

> urged with reason against State education do not apply to the enforcement of education by the State, but to the State's taking upon itself to direct that education; which is a totally different thing. . . . A general State education is a mere contrivance for molding people to be exactly like one another. . . . An education established and controlled by the State should exist, if it exists at all, as one among many competing experiments, carried on for the purpose of example and stimulus, to keep the others up to a certain standard of excellence.

J. Mill, "On Liberty," in *The Utilitarians* 586–87 (1961).

Mill attempts to disentangle the question of compulsoriness from the matter of who operates schools, striking a balance of interests differing from both *Pierce* (which presumes that public schooling will be the typical, if not universal, mode of education) and the more radical education critics; his proposal is in many respects similar to the education voucher plan (discussed in chapter 4, *infra*). How would you compare its merits with, for example, Frances Wright's suggested compulsory nursery school for all American youngsters? Is Mill's approach preferable to the *Pierce* Court's alternative? To Professor Gutmann's alternative?

Does the state's interest in compelling children to attend school give rise to any rights on the part of students subject to the compulsion: Are they, for example, entitled to equitable treatment by the public schools? *See Mills v. Board of Education*, 348 F.Supp. 866, 874 (D.D.C. 1972). (For discussion of this concept, see chapters 5–7.) Note that state compulsory education laws generally make no reference to a "right" to education at public expense, albeit many state constitutions do. *See generally* L. Kotin and W.F. Aikman, *Legal Foundations of Compulsory School Attendance* 78–79 (1980). May students exercise their rights of free speech and of expression in the fullest fashion consistent with the constraint of compulsoriness? *See* chapter 2. *See generally* Note, "Freedom and Public Education: The Need for New Standards," 50 *Notre Dame Law* 530 (1975). Can those exempted from the requirement of compulsory attendance—those who, in the words of the Oregon legislation, are "abnormal, subnormal, or physically unable to attend school"—make a legal claim that they are entitled to state-provided educational services (*see* chapter 7), or does the state's interest in compelling "educable" youngsters to attend school carry with it no corollary obligations to those youngsters?

What is the relationship between the decentralization of education in America and the general acceptance of compulsory education laws? *See* R. Healey, *The French Achievement* 19 (1974).

5. Option 3: Abolishing Compulsory Education

No litigant in *Pierce* challenged Oregon's compulsory attendance law, and the Court did not seriously entertain the proposition. Indeed, not until the 1960s were any notable objections to compulsory education voiced in this country. A 1959 United Nations General Assembly "Declaration of the Rights of the Child" confirmed what had not been questioned for a century: "The child is entitled to receive education, which shall be free and *compulsory*, at least in the elementary stages." (Emphasis added.)

Leo Tolstoy's claim that "the compulsory structure of the school excludes the possibility of all progress," has been vigorously pressed by some philosophers of education. In *Compulsory Mis-Education* (1964), Paul Goodman declared: "The compulsory system has become a universal trap, and it is no good. Very many of the youth, both poor and middle class, might be better off if the system simply did not exist, even if they then had no formal schooling at all." Ivan Illich has urged that the society be "deschooled" and that "radical alternative[s] . . . the total prohibition of legislative attendance, and the transfer of control over tax funds from benevolent institutions to the individual person" be adopted. "The first article of a bill of rights for a modern, humanist society would correspond to the first Amendment of the U.S. Constitution: 'The State shall make no law with respect to the establishment of education.' There shall be no ritual obligatory for all." *See, e.g.*, Arons, *supra*; I. Illich, *Deschooling Society* (1971); E. Reiner, *School Is Dead* (1971).

These assaults on compulsory education are not merely criticisms of unhappy experiences in urban schools (for a sample of such criticisms, *see* B. Gross and R. Gross, eds., *Radical School Reform* (1969)); these are political criticisms of all required schooling, whether pleasant or oppressive. The critics reject the argument that the state can best provide for the individual's education and point to the historic failure of public schools to alter social-status relations or benefit poor and nonwhite children. *See, e.g.*, C. Greer, *The Great School Legend* (1972); E. Morgan, *Inequality in Classroom Learning* (1977).

They view as illegitimate the state's asserted interest in shaping the political and social attitudes of children through schooling, *see* Arons, *supra*. They accuse the schools of contributing "to the deterioration of domestic [family] life." *See* C. Lasch, *Haven in a Heartless World* 13 (1977).* In short, both as a matter of policy and as a matter of law, these critics prefer a pluralist educational and social system; they stress the interests of the individual and family, discounting the notion of collective or societal interests.

At this point agreement among the critics of compulsory schooling ends. Paul Goodman's preferred alternatives include " 'no school at all' for a few classes"; "decentraliz[ing] an urban school . . . into small units"; "us[ing] appropriate *unlicensed* adults of the community—the druggist, the storekeeper, the mechanic—as the proper educators . . . [emphasis added]"; and "send[ing] children to economically marginal farms for a couple of months of the year." None of those is necessarily inconsistent with general compulsory education laws. Ivan Illich's views are avowedly more political, directly linked to redistribution of other social resources. Educator John Holt views compulsoriness as but one of many restrictions on children's freedom that should be abolished; his dream is the autonomous child, not the restructured state. *See* J. Holt, *Freedom and Beyond* (1972). The National Commission on the Reform of Secondary Education (NCRSE) asserts that a lowering of the school-leaving age to fourteen would enable schools to better serve students who wish to remain in school. *See* NCRSE, *The Reform of Secondary Education: A Report to the Public and Profession* (1973).

These proposals raise questions of both policy and law. Would an end to compulsoriness be desirable in itself? What would be likely to happen if laws requiring school attendance were repealed and no other changes were made either in schools or elsewhere in the society? In other words, would the social functions presently performed by schools disappear if the requirement of school attendance disappeared? *See generally* Katz, "Compulsion and the Discourse on Compulsory Education Attendance," 27 *Educ. Theory* 179 (1977). Would alternative forms of education routinely emerge? If the response to these queries is no, does this suggest that abolishing compulsoriness would have no effect or that it would affect only those who choose—perhaps because of economic necessity—to exercise the option of not attending schools? Might such a pattern of choice actually widen disparities between rich and poor? Professor Tussman argues that "the faddish vogue of 'deschooling' would, if anyone listened, merely doom the 'disadvantaged' to permanent hopelessness." *See* J. Tussman, *Government and the Mind* 164 (1977).

Some observers have noted that the "*framework* of grades, schedules, calendar, course of study, even rituals," particularly in public high schools, is astonishingly uniform." T. Sizer, *Horace's Compromise* 6 (1984). Thus, the ultimate goal of many contemporary critics of compulsory education is the substitution of a pluralistic society (in which, in philosopher Thomas Green's terms, "there are available institutions through which people can give concrete expression to a multiplicity of different, even incompatible values") for an achievement society (in which schools function "as the channel of access for manpower and primary agency to 'fit' the human resources to the requirements of technological and military institutions"). But can changes in schools "change the social order," as educator John Dewey once hoped? Which changes first, the society or the schools? Green posits five conditions necessary to insure pluralism: (1) the society must contain institutions designed to permit, or even encourage, the expression of different value commitments in specific behavior; (2) alternative value choices must be available everywhere in the society; (3) such value choices must be available to people of roughly equal legal status and approximately equal educational opportunity; (4) the choices available to members of the society must be fundamental enough to produce significant differences between people in their attitudes and outlook on the world; and (5) those differences must not be so fundamental as to be divisive. Green, "Schools as Communities," 39 *Harv. Educ. Rev.* 221 (1969). To Green such value commitments represent political, not pedagogical, decisions; he considers them unlikely "in a society committed to mass education of a managerial type." Do you share that assessment?

* Note that in the eighteenth century education was treated in the framework of domestic relations law. *See* W. Blackstone, *Commentaries on the Laws of England*, Vol. I, 451 (Lewis, ed. 1897).

6. *Pierce and Government Expression*

In view of the alternative conceptions of *Pierce*, consider the argument by Professor Yudof that *Pierce* is a limitation on government expression, a limitation that circumscribes the ability of governments to indoctrinate a young and captive audience:

> . . . Releasing all or part of a captive audience is one effective way to counter government's persuasive powers. *Pierce v. Society of Sisters* is a superb example in the education context. . . .
>
> *Pierce* is problematic if approached entirely in terms of individual entitlements. Arguably, if the government of a state wills it, private individuals should have no more right to run educational institutions than to organize a private army to defend the nation. The doctrine of academic freedom for teachers would be twisted beyond all recognition if teachers not only had a constitutional right to make reasonable presentational decisions, but had the right to make curricular choices and to force the state to tolerate institutions within which they might make those choices. Parents historically have enjoyed great latitude in making decisions for their children, but apart from the uncertain constitutional derivation of such entitlements, it is not clear why compulsory *public* schooling is an intolerable interference with parental rights. The state frequently, and often more substantially, interferes with parental choice. Compulsory attendance laws interfere more significantly with parental autonomy than the law in *Pierce*, the decision that children must attend *some* school for eight or more years of their lives appears more consequential than the secondary decision that they must attend *public* school. Indeed, even in *Pierce*, the Court did not deny the state extensive authority to regulate the curriculum in private and public schools—presumably by requiring courses in language, history, hygiene, and civics that some parents might find objectionable. Beyond compulsory education, state regulations address intrafamily affairs by terminating parental rights because of child abuse or neglect, or abandonment; by providing compulsory vaccinations and lifesaving medical procedures for children, regardless of parental choice; by forbidding incest and fornication; by banning the sale of pornography, tobacco, and alcoholic beverages to minors, despite parental consent to their use; by regulating child labor; and by otherwise limiting the public and private rights of minors regardless of the parents' attitude toward those restrictions.[98]
>
> Thus, *Pierce* becomes intelligible only against the background of a structure limiting the power of government to indoctrinate the young. Although the Justices probably did not intend this construction, *Pierce* may be understood as telling governments that they are free to establish public schools and to make education compulsory for certain age-groups, but they are not free to eliminate competing private sector institutions that promote heterogeneity in education. It is one thing to recognize education as a legitimate enterprise for the state; it is quite another to label private education illegitimate. Similarly, it is one thing for the state to require private schools to offer English, mathematics, or civics courses, and quite another for the state to forbid them from teaching the German language, Bible study, or modern dance.
>
> A contrary decision in *Pierce* would have fostered a state monopoly in education, a monopoly that would dangerously strengthen the state's ability to mold the young. To be sure, I do not wish to overstate the case. Private schools convey many values and attitudes identical to those conveyed in public schools. Virtually all schools tend to mirror consensual values and to promote accepted norms of social behavior. Further, a requirement that students spend five or six hours a day in school, for roughly half of each year, hardly precludes socialization in the family. Radio and television, films, peer group norms and pressures, clubs, and other institutions and mechanisms for conveying messages and values greatly reduce the danger of compulsory public schooling. But in the face of indeterminacy about how the various actors and institutions contribute to socialization processes and interact with each other,[100] *Pierce* represents a reasonable, if imperfect,[101] accommodation of conflicting pressures. The state may promulgate its messages in the public school, and parents are free to choose private schools with different orientations. The state must tolerate private education, but need not fund it. The state may make some demands of private schools in satisfaction of compulsory schooling laws, but those demands may not be so excessive that they transform private schools into public schools managed and funded by the private

98. *See generally* R. Mnookin, *Child, Family, and State* (1978); Kleinfeld, "The Balance of Power Among Infants, Their Parents, and the State" (pts. 1 & 2), 4 *Fam. Law Q.* 319, 409 (1970). . . .

100. *See generally* F. Greenstein, *Children and Politics* (1965); M. K. Jennings & R. Niemi, *The Political Character of Adolescence* (1974); *Political Socialization* (R. Dawson & K. Prewitt eds. 1969); *Socialization and Society* J. Clausen ed. 1968).

101. *See* J. Coons & S. Sugarman, *Education by Choice: The Case for Family Control* (1978), in which the authors outline and defend a plan for increasing family autonomy in education. The historic criticism of *Pierce*, as it operates in fact, has been that only the religiously devout (by virtue of numbers) and the affluent (by virtue of their ability to afford expensive private schools for their children) can take advantage of the rights afforded parents by *Pierce*.

> sector. The integrity of the communications and socialization processes in private schools and families remains intact, while the state's interest in producing informed, educated, and productive citizens is preserved. Thus, a structure that limits government speech gives credence to otherwise tenuous individual rights arguments in *Pierce*.

Yudof, "When Governments Speak: Toward a Theory of Government Expression and the First Amendment," 57 *Tex. L. Rev.* 863, 888–91 (1979).

Consider how Professor Yudof's rationale for *Pierce* differs from the other First Amendment perspectives discussed above. Do you agree that there is a tenuous relationship between First Amendment freedom of expression and the historically recognized power of parents to direct the education of their children? What difference does it make whether *Pierce* is viewed as affirming the rights of parents or limiting the prerogatives of government to indoctrinate? Would these alternative rationales lead to different concepts of the scope of state and federal power to regulate private schools?

Farrington v. Tokushige

273 U.S. 284, 47 S.Ct. 406, 71 L.Ed. 646 (1927).

Mr. Justice McReynolds delivered the opinion of the Court.

The Circuit Court of Appeals affirmed [11 F.2d 710] an interlocutory decree rendered by the United States District Court of Hawaii July 21, 1925, which granted a temporary injunction forbidding petitioners—Governor, Attorney General and superintendent of Public Instruction of that Territory—from attempting to enforce the provisions of Act 30, Special Session 1920, Legislature of Hawaii, entitled, "An Act relating to foreign language schools and teachers thereof," as amended by Act 171 of 1923 and Act 152 of 1925, and certain regulations adopted by the Department of Public Instruction June 1, 1925. The interlocutory decree was granted upon the bill and affidavits presented by both sides. No answer has been filed. In these circumstances we only consider whether the judicial discretion of the trial court was improperly exercised.

Respondents claimed below and maintain here that enforcement of the challenged Act would deprive them of their liberty and property without due process of law contrary to the Fifth Amendment. Petitioners insist that the entire Act and the regulations adopted thereunder are valid; that they prescribe lawful rules for the conduct of private foreign language schools necessary for the public welfare; also that if any provision of the statute transcends the power of the Legislature it should be disregarded and the remaining ones should be enforced. . . .

There are one hundred and sixty-three foreign language schools in the Territory. Nine are conducted in the Korean language, seven in the Chinese and the remainder in the Japanese. Respondents are members of numerous voluntary unincorporated associations conducting foreign language schools for instruction of Japanese children. These are owned, maintained and conducted by upwards of five thousand persons; the property used in connection therewith is worth two hundred and fifty thousand dollars; the enrolled pupils number twenty thousand; and three hundred teachers are employed. These schools receive no aid from public funds. All children residing within the Territory are required to attend some public or equivalent school; and practically all who go to foreign language schools also attend public or such private schools. It is affirmed by counsel for petitioners that Japanese pupils in the public and equivalent private schools increased from one thousand, three hundred and twenty in 1900 to nineteen thousand, three hundred and fifty-four in 1920, and that out of a total of sixty-five thousand, three hundred and sixty-nine pupils of all races on December 31, 1924, thirty thousand, four hundred and eighty-seven were Japanese.

The challenged enactment declares that the term, "foreign language school," as used therein, "shall be construed to mean any school which is conducted in any language other than the English language or Hawaiian language, except Sabbath schools." And, as stated by the Circuit Court of Appeals, the following are its more prominent and questionable features:

> No such school shall be conducted in the territory unless under a written permit therefor from the Department of Public Instruction, nor unless the fee therefor shall have been paid as therein provided, and such permit shall be kept exposed in a prominent place at the school so as to be readily seen and read by visitors thereat.
>
> The fee prescribed is one dollar per pupil on the estimated average attendance of pupils at the school during the period during which such school was conducted during the next preceding school year, or if such school was not conducted during any part of such

preceding school year, then at the same rate at [sic] the estimated average attendance during the school year or unexpired part thereof in question, in which latter case the amount shall be adjusted to conform to the estimated average attendance during such year or part thereof. . . .

* * *

No person shall teach in a foreign language school unless and until he shall have first applied to and obtained a permit so to do from the department and this shall also be construed to include persons exercising or performing administrative powers at any school. No permit to teach in a foreign language school shall be granted unless and until the department is satisfied that the applicant for the same is possessed of the ideals of democracy; knowledge of American history and institutions, and knows how to read, write and speak the English language.

It is the declared object of the Act to fully and effectively regulate the conducting of foreign language schools and the teaching of foreign languages, in order that the Americanism of the pupils may be promoted, and the department is directed to carry out the provisions of the Act in accordance with its spirit and purpose.

Before issuing a permit to conduct a foreign language school or to teach in any such school the department shall require the applicant for such permit to sign a pledge that the applicant will, if granted a permit to teach in such a school, abide by and observe the terms of the Act, and the regulations and orders of the department, and will, to the best of his ability, so direct the minds and studies of pupils in such schools as will tend to make them good and loyal American citizens, and will not permit such students to receive instructions in any way inconsistent therewith.

No foreign language school shall be conducted in the morning before the school hours of the public schools or during the hours while the public schools are in session, nor shall any pupil attend any foreign language school for more than one hour each day, nor exceeding six hours in any one week, nor exceeding thirty-eight weeks in any school year; provided, however, the department may in its discretion and with the approval of the Governor, modify this provision.

The department shall have full power from time to time to prescribe by regulations the subjects and courses of study of all foreign language schools, and the entrance and attendance prerequisites or qualifications of education age, school attainment, demonstrated mental capacity, health and otherwise, and the textbooks used in any foreign language school.

Until otherwise provided by the department, the following regulations are in effect: Up to September 1, 1923, every pupil shall have first satisfactorily completed the American public school first grade, or a course equivalent thereto, before attending or being allowed to attend any foreign language school. Beginning September 1, 1923, and thereafter, every pupil shall have satisfactorily completed the American public school first and second grades, or courses equivalent thereto, before attending or being allowed to attend any foreign language school. Beginning September 1, 1923, and thereafter, for grades one, two and three, and beginning September 1, 1924, and thereafter, for grades four and above, all new textbooks used in elementary foreign language schools shall be based upon the principle that the pupil's normal medium of expression is English and shall contain, as far as practicable, English equivalents for foreign words and idioms.

The department is authorized to prepare, or cause to be prepared, or procure or arrange for procuring suitable textbooks for the teaching of foreign languages in the foreign language schools and to enter into an agreement or agreements for the publishing and sale of the same.

* * *

If the department shall at any time become satisfied that any holder of a permit to conduct a foreign language school or to teach therein does not possess the qualifications required by the Act, or shall have violated or failed to observe any of the provisions of the Act or of the regulations or orders of the department, the department may then and thereupon revoke the permit theretofore granted and the same shall thereupon be and become null and void.

Any person who shall conduct or participate in conducting a foreign language school or who shall teach in a foreign language school contrary to the provisions of the Act, or who shall violate or participate in violating any of the provisions thereof, or any of the regulations or orders of the department, shall be guilty of a misdemeanor, and upon conviction thereof shall be punished by a fine not to exceed twenty-five dollars, and each day's violation shall be deemed a separate offense.

* * *

On June 1, 1925, the Department of Public Instruction adopted, and the Governor approved, certain regulations which undertook to limit the pupils who might attend foreign language schools to those who regularly attended some public school or approved private school, or had completed the eighth grade, or were over fourteen years of age. Also, to designate the textbooks which foreign language schools should use in their primary grades. . . .

[T]he school Act and the measures adopted thereunder go far beyond mere regulation of privately-supported schools where children obtain instruction deemed valuable by their parents and which is not obviously in conflict with any public interest. They give affirmative direction concerning the intimate and essential details of such schools, intrust their control to public officers, and deny both owners and patrons reasonable choice and discretion in respect of teachers, curriculum and textbooks. Enforcement of the Act probably would destroy most, if not all, of them; and, certainly, it would deprive parents of fair opportunity to procure for their children instruction which they think important and we cannot say is harmful. The Japanese parent has the right to direct the education of his own child without unreasonable restrictions; the Constitution protects him as well as those who speak another tongue.

Upon the record and the arguments presented, we cannot undertake to consider the validity of each separate provision of the Act and decide whether, dissociated from the others, its enforcement would violate respondents' constitutional rights. Apparently all are parts of a deliberate plan to bring foreign language schools under a strict governmental control for which the record discloses no adequate reason. Here, the enactment has been defended as a whole. No effort has been made to discuss the validity of the several provisions. In the trial court the cause proceeded upon the theory that petitioners intended to enforce all of them.

The general doctrine touching rights guaranteed by the Fourteenth Amendment to owners, parents and children in respect of attendance upon schools has been announced in recent opinions. [Citing *Pierce v. Society of Sisters*, among other cases] . . . .

We of course appreciate the grave problems incident to the large alien population of the Hawaiian Islands. These should be given due weight whenever the validity of any governmental regulation of private schools is under consideration; but the limitations of the Constitution must not be transcended.

It seems proper to add that when petitioners present their answer the issues may become more specific and permit the cause to be dealt with in greater detail.

We find no abuse of the discretion lodged in the trial court. The decree of the Circuit Court of Appeals must be

Affirmed.

Excerpts from the *Farrington* Briefs, Summarized in the Court's Opinion

273 U.S. 285–87, 288.

Mr. William B. Lymer, Attorney General of the Territory of Hawaii, with whom *Marguerite K. Ashford*, First Deputy Attorney General, was on the brief, for the petitioners.

These laws do not violate the Constitution. *Pierce v. Society of Sisters*, 268 U.S. 510 [1925] . . . concern[s] prohibitory legislation alone, and not purely regulatory measures such as those involved in this case, which attempt rather to supervise and control than to abolish foreign language schools.

It would be a sad commentary on our system of government to hold that the Territory must stand by, impotent, and watch its foreign-born guests conduct a vast system of schools of American pupils, teaching them loyalty to a foreign country and disloyalty to their own country, and hampering them during their tender years in the learning of the home language in the public schools,—to hold that the Territory could not by mere regulatory measures even alleviate these evils to a moderate extent while not interfering in the least with the proper maintenance of these schools or the teaching of foreign languages in them, but on the contrary making them more efficient for this their declared object.

The State has authority over such schools for at least two reasons: (1) that as *parens patriae* it has extensive power with respect to infants; and (2) that it is vitally interested in quality of its citizenship . . . .

Private schools are a proper subject of regulation. *State v. Bailey*, 157 Ind. 324, [61 N.E. 730 (1901)]. Compulsory education statutes do not require attendance at public schools alone, but at either public or private schools. Necessarily, in order to meet the requirements in respect of the period of years and the field of knowledge to be covered, it must be within the power of the legislature to regulate within reasonable limits the qualifications of the teachers, the subjects to be covered, the instruction to be given and how and to what extent—within the limits of the power—other instruction should be forbidden. The right to regulate private schools in Hawaii has long been unquestioned . . . .

Mr. Joseph Lightfoot, with whom *Mr. Joseph B. Poindexter* was on the brief, for respondents.

The statute unreasonably interferes with the fundamental right of parents and guardians to direct the upbringing and education of children under their control . . . .

The Hawaiian statute . . . takes from the parent of a child attending a foreign language school, all control and direction of the education of his child. Complete control of these schools is given to the Department of Education. The effect is to make them public schools in all but the name, though the public contributes nothing to their support. They are prohibited from employing a teacher, teaching a subject, using a book, admitting a pupil, or engaging in any activity of any nature, unless approved by the Department of Education. Nor can such a school be conducted until a permit is granted and an exorbitant fee paid—a condition not imposed on any other private school in the Territory.

In the public schools all are taught the same lessons of Americanism and democratic ideals, which are considered sufficient for a majority of the pupils, yet the minority of the pupils, whose parents desire to fit them for the battle of life by teaching them a language which will be of great benefit to them in their after careers, attend the foreign language schools where they are further regulated, controlled, taxed, and this, too, in the face of the admitted fact that nothing un-American is taught in the foreign language schools, and the Americanism of the pupils is advanced, not retarded in them.

The sole purpose of the law is the Americanization of the pupils of these schools, though it is admitted that nothing un-American is taught in them. . . .

NOTES AND QUESTIONS

1. The Courts and Private School Regulation

The *Pierce* compromise leaves states free "reasonably to regulate all schools, to inspect, supervise and examine them, their teachers and pupils; require . . . that certain studies plainly essential to good citizenship must be taught, and that nothing be taught that is mainfestly inimical to the public welfare." If such regulation were not constitutionally permitted, how would the *Pierce* compromise have been affected? Could the state effectively compel the education of all children at a "school" if any private enterprise could refer to itself by that name? Alternatively, is the *Pierce* compromise too paternalistic? Professor Sacken has suggested "a renegotiation of the 'Pierce Compromise' that more explicitly restrains state intrusion on private educational alternatives." Sacken, "Regulating Nonpublic Education: A Search for Just Law and Policy," 96 *Amer. J. of Educ.* 394, 395 (1988).

Pierce gives states considerable latitude in the scope of regulation. Might a state exercise that right to adopt regulations so intrusive that they either make all private schools exactly like their public counterparts or drive nonpublic education out of business? How should the balance between competing interests be struck in this context?

2. **Meyer v. Nebraska**

In *Meyer v. Nebraska*, 262 U.S. 390, 43 S.Ct. 625, 67 L.Ed. 1042 (1923), the Supreme Court struck down a Nebraska statute that imposed criminal penalties on public or private schoolteachers who taught in any language except English or who taught languages other than English to students below high school level. The legislation in *Meyer*, as in *Farrington*, was born of the animosity against alien groups aroused by World War I; in Nebraska, the target was Germans generally and the German language in particular. *See generally* M. Janowitz, *The Reconstruction of Patriotism: Education for Civic Consciousness* (1985). The Supreme Court concluded that the legislation interfered with both the language instructor's right to engage in his profession and the parents' right to encourage such instruction. It rejected the state's claim that such legislation was needed to "promote civic development," noting that while the "desire of the legislature to foster a homogeneous people with American ideals" was understandable, the particular measure did "violence to both the letter and spirit of the Constitution." 262 U.S. at 402–03, 43 S.Ct. at 627–28.

Consider these comments by Professor Chafee on *Meyer* and *Pierce*:

> In private schools the liberty of teaching is greater, for the state cannot base its interference on its control of its own funds, but only upon the general interest of the community in the training of the young. This reason has been held by the Supreme Court not to justify the total abolition of private schools by legislation. Some governmental regulation of their curriculum will be permitted for the sake of public safety, but teaching a foreign language is not dangerous enough to be constitutionally prohibited. The Lusk Committee sought to bring private schools under strict state control through a system of licenses, but the statute was repealed before its validity was finally adjudicated in the litigation brought by the Rand School. If public school

> teaching is to be rigorously restricted by officials, the need for free private schools is all the greater. Somebody should be able to experiment. In so far as such schools are regulated, the powers and training of the public officials who supervise them become a matter of great importance.

Z. Chafee, *Free Speech in the United States* 552 (1941).

Does *Meyer* go beyond the rationale of *Pierce*? Would the result in *Meyer* be the same if Latin were forbidden? Is *Meyer* a case about the accommodation of "public safety" and the ability "to experiment"?

3. *Scope of* Farrington *and* Meyer

Farrington v. Tokushige does not indicate which provisions of the Hawaii legislation it finds objectionable. If the Hawaii legislature wished to redraft the bill to render it constitutionally acceptable, which provisions would be stricken and why? Note that by the terms of the Hawaii statute, the foreign language schools can only provide a supplementary education; they are not permitted to provide full instruction. Is that feature of the legislation constitutionally invalid? If Japanese-American students attend public or state-approved private schools during the normal school day, should the state be permitted to impose any regulations on after-school instruction? Could the state, for example, regulate the content of instruction in after-school church-run classes? Could it do so in classes run by the Communist Party? Suppose after-school instruction were structured explicitly to identify and rebut the alleged ideological bias of the public school; could such an enterprise be prohibited or regulated by the state?

Do *Farrington* and *Meyer* ultimately stand for the proposition that state statutes regulating private schools that are motivated primarily by a desire to regulate activities only of particular national origin groups are unconstitutional? Are they more equal protection than First Amendment cases? If so, do they offer much guidance as to the constitutional scope of state regulation of private schools?

Can the state permit voters in local election districts to determine whether a private school may operate in that community? *See Columbia Trust Co. v. Lincoln Institute of Kentucky*, 138 Ky. 804, 129 S.W. 113 (1910).

II. COMPULSORY SCHOOLING, PUBLIC POLICY, AND THE CONSTITUTION

Wisconsin v. Yoder

406 U.S. 205, 92 S.Ct. 1526, 32 L.Ed.2d 15 (1972).

Mr. Chief Justice Burger delivered the opinion of the Court.

On petition of the State of Wisconsin, we granted the writ of certiorari in this case to review a decision of the Wisconsin Supreme Court holding that respondents' convictions of violating the State's compulsory school attendance law were invalid under the Free Exercise Clause of the First Amendment to the United States Constitution made applicable to the States by the Fourteenth Amendment. For the reasons hereafter stated we affirm the judgment of the Supreme Court of Wisconsin.

Respondents Jonas Yoder and Wallace Miller are members of the Old Order Amish religion, and respondent Adin Yutzy is a member of the Conservative Amish Mennonite Church.* They and their families are residents of Green County, Wisconsin. Wisconsin's compulsory school-attendance law required them to cause their children to attend public or private school until reaching age 16, but the respondents declined to send their children, ages 14 and 15, to public school after they completed the eighth grade. The children were not enrolled in any private school, or within any recognized exception to the compulsory attendance law, and they are conceded to be subject to the Wisconsin statute.

On complaint of the school district administrator for the public schools, respondents were charged, tried, and convicted of violating the compulsory-attendance law in Green County Court and were

* There is some question as to the correct religious affiliation of plaintiffs Yutzy and Miller. In the Wisconsin Supreme Court report, 49 Wis.2d 430, 182 N.W.2d 539 (1971). Miller is listed as a member of the Conservative Mennonite Church, while Yutzy is labeled as Old Order Amish. These affiliations are also given in the unofficial report, 32 L.Ed.2d 15 (1971), but conflict with the official U.S. version given above.

fined the sum of $5 each.[3] Respondents defended on the ground that the application of the compulsory attendance law violated their rights under the First and Fourteenth Amendments. The trial testimony showed that respondents believed, in accordance with the tenets of the Old Order Amish communities generally, that their children's attendance at high school, public or private, was contrary to the Amish religion and way of life. They believed that by sending their children to high school, they would not only expose themselves to the danger of the censure of the church community, but, as found by the county court, endanger their own salvation and that of their children. The State stipulated that respondents' religious beliefs were sincere.

In support of their position, respondents presented as expert witnesses scholars on religion and education whose testimony is uncontradicted. They expressed their opinions on the relationship of the Amish belief concerning school attendance to the more general tenets of their religion, and described the impact that compulsory high school attendance could have on the continued survival of Amish communities as they exist in the United States today. The history of the Amish sect was given in some detail, beginning with the Swiss Anabaptists of the 16th century who rejected institutionalized churches and sought to return to the early, simple, Christian life deemphasizing material success, rejecting the competitive spirit, and seeking to insulate themselves from the modern world. As a result of their common heritage, Old Order Amish communities today are characterized by a fundamental belief that salvation requires life in a church community separate and apart from the world and worldly influence. This concept of life aloof from the world and its values is central to their faith.

A related feature of Old Order Amish communities is their devotion to a life in harmony with nature and the soil, as exemplified by the simple life of the early Christian era that continued in America during much of our early national life. Amish beliefs require members of the community to make their living by farming or closely related activities. Broadly speaking, the Old Order Amish religion pervades and determines the entire mode of life of its adherents. Their conduct is regulated in great detail by the *Ordnung*, or rules, of the church community. Adult baptism, which occurs in late adolescence, is the time at which Amish young people voluntarily undertake heavy obligations, not unlike the Bar Mitzvah of the Jews, to abide by the rules of the church community.

Amish objection to formal education beyond the eighth grade is firmly grounded in these central religious concepts. They object to the high school and higher education generally because the values they teach are in marked variance with Amish values and the Amish way of life; they view secondary school education as an impermissible exposure of their children to a "worldly" influence in conflict with their beliefs. The high school tends to emphasize intellectual and scientific accomplishments, self-distinction, competitiveness, worldly success, and social life with other students. Amish society emphasizes informal learning-through-doing; a life of "goodness," rather than a life of intellect; wisdom, rather than technical knowledge; community welfare, rather than competition; and separation from, rather than integration with, contemporary worldly society.

Formal high school education beyond the eighth grade is contrary to Amish beliefs not only because it places Amish children in an environment hostile to Amish beliefs with increasing emphasis on competition in classwork and sports and with pressure to conform to the styles, manners and ways of the peer group, but because it takes them away from their community, physically and emotionally, during the crucial and formative adolescent period of life. Dur-

3. Prior to trial, the attorney for respondents wrote the State Superintendent of Public Instruction in an effort to explore the possibilities for a compromise settlement. Among other possibilities, he suggested that perhaps the State Superintendent could administratively determine that the Amish could satisfy the compulsory attendance law by establishing their own vocational training plan similar to one that has been established in Pennsylvania . . . . Under the Pennsylvania plan, Amish children of high school age are required to attend an Amish vocational school for three hours a week, during which time they are taught such subjects as English, mathematics, health, and social studies by an Amish teacher. For the balance of the week, the children perform farm and household duties under parental supervision, and keep a journal of their daily activities. The major portion of the curriculum is home projects in agriculture and homemaking. *See generally*, J. Hostetler and G. Huntington, *Children in Amish Society* (1971); *Socialization and Community Education* c5 (1971). A similar program has been instituted in Indiana. *Ibid. See also* Iowa Code §299.24; Kansas Stats Ann. §72–1111 (Supp. 1971).

The Superintendent rejected this proposal on the ground that it would not afford Amish children "substantially equivalent education" to that offered in the schools of the area . . . .

ing this period, the children must acquire Amish attitudes favoring manual work and self-reliance and the specific skills needed to perform the adult role of an Amish farmer or housewife. They must learn to enjoy physical labor. Once a child has learned basic reading, writing, and elementary mathematics, these traits, skills, and attitudes admittedly fall within the category of those best learned through example and "doing" rather than in a classroom. And, at this time in life, the Amish child must also grow in his faith and his relationship to the Amish community if he is to be prepared to accept the heavy obligations imposed by adult baptism. In short, high school attendance with teachers who are not of the Amish faith—and may even be hostile to it—interposes a serious barrier to the integration of the Amish child into the Amish religious community. Dr. John Hostetler, one of the experts on Amish society, testified that the modern high school is not equipped, in curriculum or social environment, to impart the values promoted by Amish society.

The Amish do not object to elementary education through the first eight grades as a general proposition because they agree that their children must have basic skills in the "three Rs" in order to read the Bible, to be good farmers and citizens and to be able to deal with non-Amish people when necessary in the course of daily affairs. They view such a basic education as acceptable because it does not significantly expose their children to wordly values or interfere with their development in the Amish community during the crucial adolescent period. While Amish accept compulsory elementary education generally, wherever possible they have established their own elementary schools in many respects like the small local schools of the past. In the Amish belief higher learning tends to develop values they reject as influences that alienate man from God.

On the basis of such considerations, Dr. Hostetler testified that compulsory high school attendance could not only result in great psychological harm to Amish children, because of the conflicts it would produce, but would also, in his opinion, ultimately result in the destruction of the Old Order Amish church community as it exists in the United States today. The testimony of Dr. Donald A. Erickson, an expert witness on education, also showed that the Amish succeed in preparing their high school age children to be productive members of the Amish community. He described their system of learning through doing the skills directly relevant to their adult roles in the Amish community as "ideal" and perhaps superior to ordinary high school education. The evidence also showed that the Amish have an excellent record as law-abiding and generally self-sufficient members of society.

Although the trial court in its careful findings determined that the Wisconsin compulsory school-attendance law "does interfere with the freedom of the Defendants to act in accordance with their sincere religious belief," it also concluded that the requirement of high school attendance until age 16 was a "reasonable and constitutional" exercise of governmental power, and therefore denied the motion to dismiss the charges. The Wisconsin Circuit Court affirmed the convictions. The Wisconsin Supreme Court, however, sustained respondents' claim under the Free Exercise Clause of the First Amendment and reversed the convictions. A majority of the Court was of the opinion that the State had failed to make an adequate showing that its interest in "establishing and maintaining an education system overrides the defendants' right to the free exercise of their religion." 49 Wis2d 430, 447, 182 NW2d 539, 547 (1971).

I

There is no doubt as to the power of a State, having a high responsibility for education of its citizens, to impose reasonable regulations for the control and duration of basic education. See, e.g., *Pierce v. Society of Sisters*, 268 U.S. 510, 534 (1925). Providing public schools ranks at the very apex of the function of a State. Yet even this paramount responsibility was, in *Pierce*, made to yield to the right of parents to provide an equivalent education in a privately operated system. There the Court held that Oregon's statute compelling attendance in a public school from age eight to age 16 unreasonably interfered with the interest of parents in directing the rearing of their offspring, including their education in church-operated schools. . . . Thus, a State's interest in universal education, however highly we rank it, is not totally free from a balancing process when it impinges on fundamental rights and interests, such as those specifically protected by the Free Exercise Clause of the First Amendment, and the traditional interest of parents with respect to the religious upbringing of their children so long as they, in the words of *Pierce,* "prepare [them] for additional obligations." 268 U.S. at 535.

It follows that in order for Wisconsin to compel school attendance beyond the eighth grade against a claim that such attendance interferes with the practice of a legitimate religious belief, it must appear either that the State does not deny the free exercise of religious belief by its requirement, or that there is a state interest of sufficient magnitude to override the interest claiming protection under the Free Exercise Clause. . . .

II

We come then to the quality of the claims of the respondents concerning the alleged encroachment of Wisconsin's compulsory school-attendance statute on their rights and the rights of their children to the free exercise of the religious beliefs they and their forebears have adhered to for almost three centuries. In evaluating those claims we must be careful to determine whether the Amish religious faith and their mode of life are, as they claim, inseparable and interdependent. A way of life, however virtuous and admirable, may not be interposed as a barrier to reasonable state regulation of education if it is based on purely secular considerations; to have the protection of the Religion Clauses, the claims must be rooted in religious belief. Although a determination of what is a "religious" belief or practice entitled to constitutional protection may present a most delicate question, the very concept of ordered liberty precludes allowing every person to make his own standards on matters of conduct in which society as a whole has important interests. Thus, if the Amish asserted their claims because of their subjective evaluation and rejection of the contemporary secular values accepted by the majority, much as Thoreau rejected the social values of his time and isolated himself at Walden Pond, their claim would not rest on a religious basis. Thoreau's choice was philosophical and personal rather than religious, and such belief does not rise to the demands of the Religion Clauses.

Giving no weight to such secular considerations, however, we see that the record in this case abundantly supports the claim that the traditional way of life of the Amish is not merely a matter of personal preference, but one of deep religious conviction, shared by an organized group, and intimately related to daily living. That the Old Order Amish daily life and religious practice stems from their faith is shown by the fact that it is in response to their literal interpretation of the Biblical injunction from the Epistle of Paul to the Romans, "be not conformed to this world. . . ." This command is fundamental to the Amish faith. Moreover, for the Old Order Amish, religion is not simply a matter of theocratic belief. As the expert witnesses explained, the Old Order Amish religion pervades and determines virtually their entire way of life, regulating it with the detail of the Talmudic diet through the strictly enforced rules of the church community.

The record shows that the respondents' religious beliefs and attitude toward life, family, and home have remained constant—perhaps some would say static—in a period of unparalleled progress in human knowledge generally and great changes in education. The respondents freely concede, and indeed assert as an article of faith, that their religious beliefs and what we would today call "life-style" have not altered in fundamentals for centuries. Their way of life in a church-oriented community, separated from the outside world and "wordly" influences, their attachment to nature and the soil, is a way inherently simple and uncomplicated, albeit difficult to preserve against the pressure to conform. Their rejection of telephones, automobiles, radios, and television, their mode of dress, of speech, their habits of manual work do indeed set them apart from much of contemporary society; these customs are both symbolic and practical.

As the society around the Amish has become more populous, urban, industrialized, and complex, particularly in this century, government regulation of human affairs has correspondingly become more detailed and pervasive. The Amish mode of life has thus come into conflict increasingly with requirements of contemporary society exerting a hydraulic insistence on conformity to majoritarian standards. So long as compulsory education laws were confined to eight grades of elementary basic education imparted in a nearby rural schoolhouse, with a large proportion of students of the Amish faith, the Old Order Amish had little basis to fear that school attendance would expose their children to the worldly influence they reject. But modern compulsory secondary education in rural areas is now largely carried on in a consolidated school, often remote from the student's home and alien to his daily homelife. As the record so strongly shows, the values and programs of the modern secondary school are in sharp conflict with the fundamental mode of life mandated by the Amish religion; modern laws requiring compulsory secondary education have accordingly engendered great concern and conflict. The conclusion is inescapable that secondary schooling, by exposing Amish children to wordly influences in terms of attitudes, goals, and values contrary to beliefs, and by substantially interfering with the religious development of the Amish child and his integration into the way of life of the Amish faith community at the crucial adolescent state of development, contravenes the basic religious tenets and practice of the Amish faith, both as to the parent and the child.

The impact of the compulsory-attendance law on respondents' practice of the Amish religion is not only severe, but inescapable, for the Wisconsin law affirmatively compels them, under threat of criminal sanction, to perform acts undeniably at odds with fundamental tenets of their religious beliefs. See *Braunfeld v. Brown*, 366 U.S. 599, 605 (1961). Nor is the impact of the compulsory-attendance law confined to grave interference with important Amish religious tenets from a subjective point of view. It carries with it precisely the kind of objective danger to the free exercise of religion that the First Amendment was designed to prevent. As the record shows, compulsory school attendance to age 16 for Amish children carries with it a very real threat of undermining the Amish community and religious practice as they exist today; they must either abandon belief and be assimilated into society at large, or be forced to migrate to some other and more tolerant region.[9]

In sum, the unchallenged testimony of acknowledged experts in education and religious history, almost 300 years of consistent practice, and strong evidence of a sustained faith pervading and regulating respondents' entire mode of life support the claim that enforcement of the State's requirement of compulsory formal education after the eighth grade would gravely endanger if not destroy the free exercise of respondents' religious beliefs.

III

Neither the findings of the trial court nor the Amish claims as to the nature of their faith are challenged in this Court by the State of Wisconsin. Its position is that the State's interest in universal compulsory formal secondary education to age 16 is so great that it is paramount to the undisputed claims of respondents that their mode of preparing their youth for Amish life, after the traditional elementary education, is an essential part of their religious belief and practice. Nor does the State undertake to meet the claim that the Amish mode of life and education is inseparable from and a part of the basic tenets of their religion—indeed, as much a part of their religious belief and practices as baptism, the confessional, or a sabbath may be for others.

Wisconsin concedes that under the Religion Clauses religious beliefs are absolutely free from the State's control, but it argues that "actions," even though religiously grounded, are outside the protection of the First Amendment.[10] But our decisions have rejected the idea that religiously grounded conduct is always outside the protection of the Free Exercise Clause. . . .

Nor can this case be disposed of on the grounds that Wisconsin's requirement for school attendance to age 16 applies uniformly to all citizens of the State and does not, on its face, discriminate against religions or a particular religion, or that it is motivated by legitimate secular concerns. A regulation neutral on its face may, in its application, nonetheless offend the constitutional requirement for governmental neutrality if it unduly burdens the free exercise of religion. . . .

We turn, then, to the State's broader contention that its interest in its system of compulsory education is so compelling that even the established religious practices of the Amish must give way. Where fun-

9. Some States have developed working arrangements with the Amish regarding high school attendance. See n. 3. *supra*. However, the danger to the continued existence of an ancient religious faith cannot be ignored simply because of the assumption that its adherents will continue to be able at considerable sacrifice, to relocate in some more tolerant State or country or work out accommodations under threat of criminal prosecution. Forced migration of religious minorities was an evil that lay at the heart of the Religion Clauses. *See, e.g., Everson v. Board of Educator*, 330 U.S. 1, 9–10 (1947); J. Madison, "Memorial and Remonstrance Against Religious Assessments." 2 *Writings of James Madison* 183 (G. Hunt ed. 1901).

10. That has been the apparent ground for decision in several previous state cases rejecting claims for exemption similar to that here. *See e.g., State v. Garber*, 197 Kan. 567, 419 P.2d 896 (1966), *cert denied*, 389 U.S. 51 (1967), *State v. Hershberger*, 103 Ohio App. 188, 144 N.E.2d 693 (1955); *Commonwealth v. Beiler*, 168 Pa. Super 462, 79 A.2d 134 (1951).

damental claims of religious freedom are at stake, however, we cannot accept such a sweeping claim; despite its admitted validity in the generality of cases, we must searchingly examine the interests that the State seeks to promote by its requirement for compulsory education to age 16, and the impediment to those objectives that would flow from recognizing the claimed Amish exemption. . . .

The State advances two primary arguments in support of its system of compulsory education. It notes, as Thomas Jefferson pointed out early in our history, that some degree of education is necessary to prepare citizens to participate effectively and intelligently in our open political system if we are to preserve freedom and independence. Further, education prepares individuals to be self-reliant and self-sufficient participants in society. We accept these propositions.

However, the evidence adduced by the Amish in this case is persuasively to the effect that an additional one or two years of formal high school for Amish children in place of their long-established program of informal vocational education would do little to serve those interests. Respondents' experts testified at trial, without challenge, that the value of all education must be assessed in terms of its capacity to prepare the child for life. It is one thing to say that compulsory education for a year or two beyond the eighth grade may be necessary when its goal is the preparation of the child for life in modern society as the majority live, but it is quite another if the goal of education be viewed as the preparation of the child for life in the separated agrarian community that is the keystone of the Amish faith. . . .

The State attacks respondents' position as one fostering "ignorance" from which the child must be protected by the State. No one can question the State's duty to protect children from ignorance but this argument does not square with the facts disclosed in the record. Whatever their idiosyncrasies as seen by the majority, this record strongly shows that the Amish community has been a highly successful social unit within our society, even if apart from the conventional "mainstream." Its members are productive and very law-abiding members of society; they reject public welfare in any of its usual modern forms. The Congress itself recognized their self-sufficiency by authorizing exemption of such groups as the Amish from the obligation to pay social security taxes.

It is neither fair nor correct to suggest that the Amish are opposed to education beyond the eighth grade level. What this record shows is that they are opposed to conventional formal education of the type provided by a certified high school because it comes at the child's crucial adolescent period of religious development. Dr. Donald Erickson, for example, testified that their system of learning-by-doing was an "ideal system" of education in terms of preparing Amish children for life as adults in the Amish community, and that "I would be inclined to say they do a better job in this than most of the rest of us do." As he put it: "These people aren't purporting to be learned people, and it seems to me the self-sufficiency of the community is the best evidence I can point to—whatever is being done seems to function well."[12]

We must not forget that in the Middle Ages important values of the civilization of the Western World were preserved by members of religious orders who isolated themselves from all wordly influences against great obstacles. There can be no assumption that today's majority is "right" and the Amish and others like them are "wrong." A way of life that is odd or even erratic but interferes with no rights or interests of others is not to be condemned because it is different.

The State, however, supports its interest in providing an additional one or two years of compulsory high school education to Amish children because of the possibility that some such children will choose to leave the Amish community, and that if this occurs they will be ill-equipped for life. The State argues that if Amish children leave their church they should not be in the position of making their way in the world without the education available in the one or two additional years the State requires. However, on this record, that argument is highly speculative. There is no specific evidence of the loss of Amish adherents by attrition, nor is there any showing that upon leaving the Amish community Amish

12. Dr. Erickson had previously written: "Many public educators would be elated if their programs were as successful in preparing students for productive community life as the Amish system seems to be be. In fact, while some public schoolmen strive to outlaw the Amish approach, others are being forced to emulate many of its features." D. Erickson, "Showdown at an Amish Schoolhouse: A Description and Analysis of the Iowa Controversy," in *Public Controls for Nonpublic Schools* 15, 53 (D. Erickson ed. 1969). And see F. Littell, "Sectarian Protestantism and the Pursuit of Wisdom: Must Technological Objective Prevail?" *id.* at 61.

children, with their practical agricultural training and habits of industry and self-reliance, would become burdens on society because of educational shortcomings. Indeed, this argument of the State appears to rest primarily on the State's mistaken assumption, already noted, that the Amish do not provide any education for their children beyond the eighth grade, but allow them to grow in "ignorance." To the contrary, not only do the Amish accept the necessity for formal schooling through the eighth grade level, but continue to provide what has been characterized by the undisputed testimony of expert educators as an "ideal" vocational education for their children in the adolescent years.

There is nothing in this record to suggest that the Amish qualities of reliability, self-reliance, and dedication to work would fail to find ready markets in today's society. Absent some contrary evidence supporting the State's position, we are unwilling to assume that persons possessing such valuable vocational skills and habits are doomed to become burdens on society should they determine to leave the Amish faith, nor is there any basis in the record to warrant a finding that an additional one or two years of formal school education beyond the eighth grade would serve to eliminate any such problem that might exist.

Insofar as the State's claim rests on the view that a brief additional period of formal education is imperative to enable the Amish to participate effectively and intelligently in our democratic process, it must fall. The Amish alternative to formal secondary school education has enabled them to function effectively in their day-to-day life under self-imposed limitations on relations with the world, and to survive and prosper in contemporary society as a separate, sharply identifiable, and highly self-sufficient community for more than 200 years in this country. In itself this is strong evidence that they are capable of fulfilling the social and political responsibilities of citizenship without compelled attendance beyond the eighth grade at the price of jeopardizing their free exercise of religious belief. When Thomas Jefferson emphasized the need for education as a bulwark of a free people against tyanny, there is nothing to indicate he had in mind compulsory education through any fixed age beyond a basic education. Indeed, the Amish communities singularly parallel and reflect many of the virtues of Jefferson's ideal of the "sturdy yeoman" who would form the basis of what he considered as the ideal of a democratic society. Even their idiosyncratic separateness exemplifies the diversity we profess to admire and encourage.

The requirement for compulsory education beyond the eighth grade is a relatively recent development in our history. Less than 60 years ago, the educational requirements of almost all of the States were satisfied by completion of the elementary grades, at least where the child was regularly and lawfully employed.[15] The independence and successful social functioning of the Amish community for a period approaching almost three centuries and more than 200 years in this country are strong evidence that there is at best a speculative gain, in terms of meeting the duties of citizenship, from an additional one or two years of compulsory formal education. Against this background it would require a more particularized showing from the State on this point to justify the severe interference with religious freedom such additional compulsory attendance would entail.

We should also note that compulsory education and child labor laws find their historical origin in common humanitarian instincts, and that the age limits of both laws have been coordinated to achieve their related objectives. In the context of this case, such considerations, if anything, support rather than detract from respondents' position. The origins of

15. See [U.S.] Dep't of Interior, Bureau of Education, Bulletin No. 47, *Digest of State Laws Relating to Public Education* 527–559 (1916); *Joint Hearings on S 2475 and HR 7200 Before the Senate Committee on Education and the House Committee on Labor*, 75th Cong., 1st Sess., pt. 2, at 416.

Even today, an eighth grade education fully satisfies the educational requirements of at least six States. See Ariz. Rev. Stat. Ann. §15–321 (B)(4) (1956); Ark. Stat. Ann. §80–1504 (1947); Iowa Code §299.2 (1971); S.D. Comp. Laws Ann. §13–27–1 (1967); Wyo. Stat. Ann. §21.1–48 (Supp. 1971). Mississippi has no compulsory education law. A number of other States have flexible provisions permitting children aged 14 or having completed the eighth grade to be excused from school in order to engage in lawful employment. *E.g.*, Colo. Rev. Stat. Ann. §§ 123-20-5, 80-6-1 to 80-6-12 (1963); Conn. Gen. Stat. Rev. §§10-184, 10-189 (1964); D.C. Code Ann. §§31-202, 36-201 to 36-228 (1967); Ind. Ann. Stat. §§28-505–28-506, 28-519 (1948); Mass. Gen. Laws Ann. c.76, §1 (Supp. 1972) and c. 149, §86 (1971); Mo. Rev. Stat. §§167.031, 294.051 (1969); Nev. Rev. Stat. § 392.110 (1968); N.M. Stat. Ann. §77-10-6 (1968).

An eighth grade education satisfied Wisconsin's formal education requirements until 1933. See Wis. Laws 1927, c.425, §97; Laws 1933, c.143. (Prior to 1933, provision was made for attendance at continuation or vocational schools by working children past the eighth grade, but only if one was maintained by the community in question.) For a general discussion of the early development of Wisconsin's compulsory education and child labor laws, see F. Ensign, *Compulsory School Attendance and Child Labor* 203–230 (1921).

the requirement for school attendance to age 16, an age falling after the completion of elementary school but before completion of high school, are not entirely clear. But to some extent such laws reflected the movement to prohibit most child labor under age 16 that culminated in the provisions of the Federal Fair Labor Standards Act of 1938. It is true, then, that the 16 year child labor age limit may to some degree derive from a contemporary impression that children should be in school until that age. But at the same time, it cannot be denied that, conversely, the 16 year education limit reflects, in substantial measure, the concern that children under that age not be employed under conditions hazardous to their health, or in work that should be performed by adults.

The requirement of compulsory schooling to age 16 must therefore be viewed as aimed not merely at providing educational opportunities for children, but as an alternative to the equally undesirable consequence of unhealthful child labor displacing adult workers, or, on the other hand, forced idleness. The two kinds of statutes—compulsory school attendance and child labor laws—tend to keep children of certain ages off the labor market and in school; this regimen in turn provides opportunity to prepare for a livelihood of a higher order than that which children could pursue without education and protects their health in adolescence.

In these terms, Wisconsin's interest in compelling the school attendance of Amish children to age 16 emerges as somewhat less substantial than requiring such attendance for children generally. For, while agricultural employment is not totally outside the legitimate concerns of the child labor laws, employment of children under parental guidance and on the family farm from age 14 to age 16 is an ancient tradition that lies at the periphery of the objectives of such laws. There is no intimation that the Amish employment of their children on family farms is in any way deleterious to their health or that Amish parents exploit children at tender years. Any such inference would be contrary to the record before us. Moreover, employment of Amish children on the family farm does not present the undesirable economic aspects of eliminating jobs that might otherwise be held by adults.

IV

Finally, the State, on authority of *Prince v. Massachusetts* [321 U.S. 158 (1944)], argues that a decision exempting Amish children from the State's requirement fails to recognize the substantive right of the Amish child to a secondary education, and fails to give due regard to the power of the State as *parens patriae* to extend the benefit of secondary education to children regardless of the wishes of their parents. Taken at its broadest sweep, the Court's language in *Prince*, might be read to give support to the State's position. However, the Court was not confronted in *Prince* with a situation comparable to that of the Amish as revealed in this record; this is shown by the Court's severe characterization of the evils that it thought the legislature could legitimately associate with child labor, even when performed in the company of an adult. 321 U.S. at 169–170. The Court later took great care to confine *Prince* to a narrow scope in *Sherbert v. Verner*, when it stated:

> On the other hand, the Court has rejected challenges under the Free Exercise Clause to governmental regulation of certain overt acts prompted by religious beliefs or principles, "for even when the action is in accord with one's religious convictions, [it] is not totally free from legislative restrictions." *Braunfeld v. Brown*, 366 U.S. 599, 603 (1961). The conduct or actions so regulated have invariably posed some substantial threat to public safety, peace or order. *See, e.g., Reynolds v. U.S.*, 98 U.S. 145; *Jacobson v. Massachusetts*, 197 U.S. 11; *Prince v. Massachusetts*, 321 U.S. 158. . . . [374 U.S. 398, 402–403 (1963).]

This case, of course, is not one in which any harm to the physical or mental health of the child or to the public safety, peace, order, or welfare has been demonstrated or may be properly inferred. The record is to the contrary, and any reliance on that theory would find no support in the evidence.

Contrary to the suggestion of the dissenting opinion of Mr. Justice Douglas, our holding today in no degree depends on the assertion of the religious interest of the child as contrasted with that of the parents. It is the parents who are subject to prosecution here for failing to cause their children to attend school, and it is their right of free exercise, not that of their children, that must determine Wisconsin's power to impose criminal penalties on the parent. The dissent argues that a child who expresses a desire to attend public high school in conflict with the wishes of his parents should not be prevented from doing so. There is no reason for the Court to consider that point since it is not an issue in the case. The children are not parties to this litigation. The State has at no point tried this case on the theory that respondents were preventing their children from attending school against their expressed desires, and indeed the record is to the contrary. The State's position from the outset has been that it is empowered to apply its compulsory-attendance law to Amish parents in the same manner as to other parents—that is, without regard to the wishes of the child. That is the claim we reject today.

Our holding in no way determines the proper resolution of possible competing interests of parents, children, and the State in an appropriate state court proceeding in which the power of the State is asserted on the theory that Amish parents are preventing their minor children from attending high school despite their expressed desires to the contrary. Recognition of the claim of the State in such a proceeding would, of course, call into question traditional concepts of parental control over the religious upbringing and education of their minor children recognized in this Court's past decisions. It is clear that such an intrusion by a State into family decisions in the area of religious training would give rise to grave questions of religious freedom comparable to those raised here and those presented in *Pierce v. Society of Sisters*, 268 U.S. 510 (1925). On this record we neither reach nor decide those issues.

The State's argument proceeds without reliance on any actual conflict between the wishes of parents and children. It appears to rest on the potential that exemption of Amish parents from the requirements of the compulsory-education law might allow some parents to act contrary to the best interests of their children by foreclosing their opportunity to make an intelligent choice between the Amish way of life and that of the outside world. The same argument could, of course, be made with respect to all church schools short of college. There is nothing in the record or in the ordinary course of human experience to suggest that non-Amish parents generally consult with children up to ages 14–16 if they are placed in a church school of the parents' faith.

Indeed it seems clear that if the State is empowered, as *parens patriae*, to "save" a child from himself or his Amish parents by requiring an additional two years of compulsory formal high school education, the State will in large measure influence, if not determine, the religious future of the child. Even more markedly than in *Prince*, therefore, this case involves the fundamental interest of parents, as contrasted with that of the State, to guide the religious future and education of their children. The history and culture of Western civilization reflect a strong tradition of parental concern for the nurture and upbringing of their children. This primary role of the parents in the upbringing of their children is now established beyond debate as an enduring American tradition. . . .

However read, the Court's holding in *Pierce* stands as a charter of the rights of parents to direct the religious upbringing of their children. And, when the interests of parenthood are combined with a free exercise claim of the nature revealed by this record, more than merely a "reasonable relation to some purpose within the competency of the State" is required to sustain the validity of the State's requirement under the First Amendment. To be sure, the power of the parent, even when linked to a free exercise claim, may be subject to limitation under *Prince* if it appears that parental decisions will jeopardize the health or safety of the child, or have a potential for significant social burdens. But in this case, the Amish have introduced persuasive evidence undermining the arguments the State has advanced to support its claims in terms of the welfare of the child and society as a whole. The record strongly indicates that accommodating the religious objections of the Amish by forgoing one, or at most two, additional years of compulsory education will not impair the physical or mental health of the child, or result in an inability to be self-supporting, or to discharge the duties and responsibilities of citizenship, or in any other way materially detract from the welfare of society.

In the face of our consistent emphasis on the central values underlying the Religion Clauses in our constitutional scheme of government, we cannot accept a *parens patriae* claim of such all-encompassing scope and with such sweeping potential for broad and unforeseeable application as that urged by the State.

V

For the reasons stated we hold, with the Supreme Court of Wisconsin, that the First and Fourteenth Amendments prevent the State from compelling respondents to cause their children to attend formal high school to age 16. Our disposition of this case, however, in no way alters our recognition of the obvious fact that courts are not school boards or legislatures, and are ill-equipped to determine the "necessity" of discrete aspects of a State's program of compulsory education. This should suggest that courts must move with great circumspection in performing the sensitive and delicate task of weighing a State's legitimate social concern when faced with religious claims for exemption from generally applicable educational requirements. It cannot be overemphasized that we are not dealing with a way of life and mode of education by a group claiming to have recently discovered some "progressive" or more enlightened process for rearing children for modern life.

Aided by a history of three centuries as an identifiable religious sect and a long history as a successful and self-sufficient segment of American society, the Amish in this case have convincingly demonstrated the sincerity of their religious beliefs, the interrelationship of belief with their mode of life, the vital role that belief and daily conduct play in the continued survival of Old Order Amish communities and their religious organization, and the hazards presented by the State's enforcement of a statute generally valid as to others. Beyond this, they have carried the even more difficult burden of demonstrating the adequacy of their alternative mode of continuing informal vocational education in terms of precisely those overall interests that the State advances in support of its program of compulsory high school education. In light of this convincing showing, one that probably few other religious groups or sects could make, and weighing the minimal difference between what the State would require and what the Amish already accept, it was incumbent on the State to show with more particularity how its admittedly strong interest in compulsory education would be adversely affected by granting an exemption to the Amish. . . .

Nothing we hold is intended to undermine the general applicability of the State's compulsory school-attendance statutes or to limit the power of the State to promulgate reasonable standards that, while not impairing the free exercise of religion, provide for continuing agricultural vocational education under parental and church guidance by the Old Order Amish or others similarly situated. The States have had a long history of amicable and effective relationships with church-sponsored schools, and there is no basis for assuming that, in this related context, reasonable standards cannot be established concerning the content of the continuing vocational education of Amish children under parental guidance, provided always that state regulations are not inconsistent with what we have said in this opinion.

Affirmed. . . .

[The separate concurring opinion of Mr. Justice Stewart, joined by Mr. Justice Brennan, is omitted.]

Mr. Justice White, with whom Mr. Justice Brennan and Mr. Justice Stewart join, concurring. . . . In the present case, the State is not concerned with the maintenance of an educational system as an end in itself, it is rather attempting to nurture and develop the human potential of its children, whether Amish or non-Amish: to expand their knowledge, broaden their sensibilities, kindle their imagination, foster a spirit of free inquiry, and increase their human understanding and tolerance. It is possible that most Amish children will wish to continue living the rural life of their parents, in which case their training at home will adequately equip them for their future role. Others, however, may wish to become nuclear physicists, ballet dancers, computer programmers, or historians, and for these occupations, formal training will be necessary. There is evidence in the record that many children desert the Amish faith when they come of age. A State has a legitimate interest not only in seeking to develop the latent talents of its children but also in seeking to prepare them for the life style that they may later choose, or at least to provide them with an option other than the life they have led in the past. In the circumstances of this case, although the question is close, I am unable to say that the State has demonstrated that Amish children who leave school in the eighth grade will be intellectually stultified or unable to acquire new academic skills later. The statutory minimum school attendance age set by the State is, after all, only 16.

Decision in cases such as this and the administration of an exemption for Old Order Amish from the State's compulsory school-attendance laws will inevitably involve the kind of close and perhaps repeated scrutiny of religious practices, as is exemplified in today's opinion, which the Court has heretofore been anxious to avoid. But such entanglement does not create a forbidden establishment of religion where it is essential to implement free exercise values threatened by an otherwise neutral program instituted to foster some permissible, nonreligious state objective. I join the Court because the sincerity of the Amish religious policy here is uncontested, because the potentially adverse impact of the state requirement is great, and because the State's valid interest in education has already been largely satisfied by the eight years the children have already spent in school.

Mr. Justice Douglas, dissenting in part.

I

I agree with the Court that the religious scruples of the Amish are opposed to the education of their children beyond the grade schools, yet I disagree with the Court's conclusion that the matter is within the dispensation of parents alone. The Court's analysis assumes that the only interests at stake in the case are those of the Amish parents on the one hand, and those of the State on the other. The difficulty with this approach is that, despite the court's claim, the parents are seeking to vindicate not only their own free exercise claims, but also those of their high-school-age children.

It is argued that the right of the Amish children to religious freedom is not presented by the facts of the case, as the issue before the Court involves only the Amish parents' religious freedom to defy a state criminal statute imposing upon them an affirmative duty to cause their children to attend high school.

First, respondents' motion to dismiss in the trial court expressly asserts, not only the religious liberty of the adults, but also that of the children, as a defense to the prosecutions. It is, of course, beyond question that the parents have standing as defendants in a criminal prosecution to assert the religious interests of their children as a defense. Although the lower courts and the majority of this Court assume an identity of interest between parent and child, it is clear that they have treated the religious interest of the child as a factor in the analysis.

Second, it is essential to reach the question to decide the case, not only because the question was squarely raised in the motion to dismiss, but also because no analysis of religious-liberty claims can take place in a vacuum. If the parents in this case are allowed a religious exemption, the inevitable effect is to impose the parents' notions of religious duty upon their children. Where the child is mature enough to express potentially conflicting desires, it would be an invasion of the child's rights to permit such an imposition without canvassing his views. As in *Prince v. Massachusetts*, 321 U.S. 158 [1944], it is an imposition resulting from this very litigation. As the child has no other effective forum, it is in this litigation that his rights should be considered. And, if an Amish child desires to attend high school, and is mature enough to have that desire respected, the State may well be able to override the parents' religiously motivated objections.

Religion is an individual experience. It is not necessary, nor even appropriate, for every Amish child to express his views on the subject in a prosecution of a single adult. Crucial, however, are the views of the child whose parent is the subject of the suit. Frieda Yoder has in fact testified that her own religious views are opposed to high-school education. I therefore join the judgment of the Court as to respondent Jonas Yoder. But Frieda Yoder's views may not be those of Vernon Yutzy or Barbara Miller. I must dissent, therefore, as to respondents Adin Yutzy and Wallace Miller as their motion to dismiss also raised the question of their children's religious liberty.

II

This issue has never been squarely presented before today. Our opinions are full of talk about the power of the parents over the child's education. . . . And we have in the past analyzed similar conflicts between parent and State with little regard for the views of the child. *See Prince v. Massachusetts, supra.* Recent cases, however, have clearly held that the children themselves have constitutionally protectable interests.

These children are "persons" within the meaning of the Bill of Rights. We have so held over and over again. . . .

On this important and vital matter of education, I think the children should be entitled to be heard. While the parents, absent dissent, normally speak for the entire family, the education of the child is a matter on which the child will often have decided views. He may want to be a pianist or an astronaut or an oceanographer. To do so he will have to break from the Amish tradition.[2]

It is the future of the student, not the future of the parents, that is imperiled by today's decision. If a parent keeps his child out of school beyond the

2. A significant number of Amish children do leave the Old Order. Professor Hostetler notes that "[t]he loss of members is very limited in some Amish districts and considerable in others." *Children in Amish Society* 226. In one Pennsylvania church, he observed a defection rate of 30%. Ibid. Rates up to 50% have been reported by others. Casad, "Compulsory High School Attendance and the Old Order Amish: A Commentary on *State v. Garber*," 16 *Kan. L. Rev.* 423, 434 n.51 (1968).

grade school, then the child will be forever barred from entry into the new and amazing world of diversity that we have today. The child may decide that that is the preferred course, or he may rebel. It is the student's judgment, not his parents', that is essential if we are to give full meaning to what we have said about the Bill of Rights and of the right of students to be masters of their own destiny. If he is harnessed to the Amish way of life by those in authority over him and if his education is truncated, his entire life may be stunted and deformed. The child, therefore, should be given an opportunity to be heard before the State gives the exemption which we honor today.

The views of the two children in question were not canvassed by the Wisconsin courts. The matter should be explicitly reserved so that new hearings can be held on remand of the case.

III

I think the emphasis of the Court on the "law and order" record of this Amish group of people is quite irrelevant. A religion is a religion irrespective of what the misdemeanor or felony records of its members might be. I am not at all sure how the Catholics, Episcopalians, the Baptists, Jehovah's Witnesses, the Unitarians, and my own Presbyterians would make out if we were subjected to such a test. . . .

* * *

Action, which the Court deemed to be antisocial, could be punished even though it was grounded on deeply held and sincere religious convictions. What we do today, at least in this respect, opens the way to give organized religion a broader base than it has ever enjoyed. . . .

In another way, however, the Court retreats when in reference to Henry Thoreau it says his "choice was philosophical and personal rather than religious, and such belief does not rise to the demands of the Religion Clauses." That is contrary to what we held in *United States v. Seeger*, 380 U.S. 163, where we were concerned with the meaning of the words "religious training and belief" in the Selective Service Act, which were the basis of many conscientious objector claims. We said:

> Within that phrase would come all sincere religious beliefs which are based upon a power or being, or upon a faith, to which all else is subordinate or upon which all else is ultimately dependent. The test might be stated in these words: A sincere and meaningful belief which occupies in the life of its possessor a place parallel to that filled by the God of those admittedly qualifying for the exemption comes within the statutory definition. This construction avoids imputing to Congress an intent to classify different religious beliefs, exempting some and excluding others, and is in accord with the well-established congressional policy of equal treatment for those whose opposition to service is grounded in their religious tenets. [380 U.S. at 176.]

Welsh v. United States, 398 U.S. 333, was in the same vein, the Court saying:

> In this case, Welsh's conscientious objection to war was undeniably based in part on his perception of world politics. In a letter to his local board, he wrote: "I can only act according to what I am and what I see. And I see that the military complex wastes both human and material resources, that it fosters disregard for (what I consider a paramount concern) human needs and ends; I see that the means we employ to 'defend' our 'way of life' profoundly change that way of life. I see that in our failure to recognize the political, social, and economic realities of the world, we, *as a nation*, fail our responsibility *as a nation*." [398 U.S. at 342.]

The essence of Welsh's philosophy on the basis of which we held he was entitled to an exemption was in these words:

> I believe that human life is valuable in and of itself; in its living; therefore I will not injure or kill another human being. This belief (and the corresponding "duty" to abstain from violence toward another person) is not "superior to those arising from any human relation." On the contrary: *it is essential to every human relation*. I cannot, therefore, conscientiously comply with the government's insistence that I assume duties which I feel are immoral and totally repugnant. [398 U.S. at 343.]

I adhere to these exalted views of "religion" and see no acceptable alternative to them now that we have become a Nation of many religions and sects, representing all of the diversities of the human race. . . .

NOTES AND QUESTIONS

1. Historical Background

Conflicts between the 30,000 American Amish and the government have existed since the Amish arrived in the United States in 1727; in recent years disputes over schooling have predominated. *See generally* J. Hostetler, *Amish Society* (3d ed. 1980); A. Keim, ed., *Compulsory Education and the Amish* (1975); Hostetler, "The Amish and the Law: A Religious Minority and Its Legal Encounters," 40 *Wash. & Lee L. Rev.* 33, 40–44 (1984). The adventures of the Amish in Iowa are the best known and documented. The difficulties of the plain folk began with an effort in 1961 to unify the Hazelton and Olwein school districts. The Amish, who operated two private one-room schools in the Hazelton district, held the swing vote in the unification campaign. After high-echelon school officials promised to provide public schools tailored to their needs, the Amish voted for district reorganization. Many Hazelton residents were upset both by voter approval of the unification plan and by the Amish role in the affair. That, and a more general anti-Amish sentiment, led the school officials to renege on their promise to the Amish and to declare that the Amish schools would stay open no longer than two years and that—after fifteen years of doing so—no effort would be made to fit school instruction to Amish needs. The Amish retaliated with the announcement that they would no longer permit state-certified teachers to instruct in Amish schools. Already highly irritated, neighbors of the Amish demanded that the Amish be prosecuted for failure to send their children to schools with certified teachers. Amish fathers were accordingly fined and, when they refused to pay, sentenced to three days in jail. Newspaper pictures of Amish women visiting their jailed husbands elicited national sympathy for the plain folk and resulted in volumes of disparaging mail to Iowa officials.

After the routine of Amish fathers' driving their buggies to town to appear in court and then faithfully refusing to pay their fines grew tiresome, state and local school officials attempted, without success, to arrange a compromise with the Amish. Then they announced that the Amish children were truants and would be bused to public school. One November morning in 1965, a school bus departed for Amish country, followed by carloads of newspaper reporters. No children were to be found at their homes, but some were discovered at the local school. Before the distraught children filed out of the one-room school, the superintendent announced to the reporters that the children would board the bus and be driven to school. But it was not to be. An unidentified individual yelled "run," and the children scattered through the barbed wire fence and into the cornfields. Cameras clicked and pictures of small, frightened Amish children climbing the cornfield fence found their way into national newspapers. School officials captured one screaming six-year-old girl and a weeping thirteen-year-old boy who had been unable to keep up with their classmates.

In 1966 Governor Harold Hughes decided to intervene and push for a settlement. In its 1967 session, the state legislature, strongly influenced by outside parties, exempted the Amish from the state's minimum educational standards laws. The state Superintendent of Education was given discretion to fix educational requirements. Thus far he has allowed the Amish schools to remain open under the direction of uncertified Amish teachers. School districts west of Hazelton provide the Amish with rural schools staffed by certified teachers sympathetic to Amish ways. *See* Erickson, "Showdown in an Amish Schoolhouse," in *Public Controls for Nonpublic Schools* 53 (1969).

Pennsylvania was the first state to attempt to compel the Amish children to attend public school. After initial embarrassments not unlike those suffered by Iowa school officials, the Pennsylvania code was reinterpreted to permit the Amish to manage their own schools. The school day of the Amish school is like that of public schools, and attendance is taken. Beyond these two aspects, however, the Amish school in Pennsylvania is essentially unregulated: Teachers, for example, are not required to be certified. Eighth-grade graduates may enter "vocational high schools" where they perform farm and household chores under parental supervision and attend classes a few hours a week. *See* Hostetler, "The Amish and the Law: A Religious Minority and Its Legal Encounter," 40 *Wash. & Lee L. Rev.* 33, 41 (1984).

In Ohio, Amish schools operate in defiance of the state school code but school officials, perhaps learning from the Iowa and Pennsylvania experiences, have chosen to ignore the situation. *See State Ex. Rel. Nagle v. Olin*, 64 Ohio St.2d 341, 415 N.E.2d 279 (1980). In 1982 a newly formed Amish community left Nebraska in response to a state requirement that teachers in Amish schools must be certified. Hostetler, *supra* at 44.

2. *The Constitutional Standard*

Yoder raises the question not explicitly posed in *Pierce*: Are there constitutional interests of parents and children that outweigh the state's interest in compelling all youngsters to attend school? The question is one of extreme difficulty; as the *Yoder* decision notes, the contending interests are of the "highest order."

Parental direction of the religious upbringing of children has a "high place in our society," the Court declares. The values underlying the constitutional protections of religious freedom have been "zealously protected, sometimes even at the expense of other interests of admittedly high social importance." Compulsory education laws, the Court notes, "demonstrate our recognition of the importance of education to our democratic society." How is the Court meaningfully to evaluate and balance such imponderables? *Cf. United States v. Lee,* 455 U.S. 252, 102 S.Ct. 1051, 71 L.Ed.2d 127 (1982) (Amish employers not exempt from Social Security tax on Amish employees); *United States v. Slabaugh,* 848 F.2d 113 (8th Cir. 1988) (Amish criminal defendant not exempt from photograph requirement despite religious convictions). *See generally* Laycock, "A Survey of Religious Liberty in the United States," 47 *Ohio St. L. J.* 409, 427–31 (1986).

a. The Amish Interest in Religious Freedom. The majority opinion notes that the Amish have "convincingly demonstrated the sincerity of their religious beliefs." What factors does the Court consider in reaching that judgment? Should the Court attempt to assess religious sincerity? *See generally* Marcus, "The Forum of Conscience: Applying Standards Under the Free Exercise Clause," 1973 *Duke L. J.* 1217.

Would the result in *Yoder* have been the same had the Court not concluded that the Amish faith and mode of life are inseparable and interdependant? *See State v. Patzer,* 382 N.W.2d 631 (N.D. 1986); L. Kotin and W. F. Aikman, *Legal Foundations of Compulsory School Attendance* 252 (1980). In *Duro v. District Attorney, Second Judicial District of North Carolina,* 712 F.2d 96 (4th Cir. 1983), the court denied plaintiff's claim that North Carolina's compulsory school attendance law denied him his right of free exercise of religion. The court distinguished *Yoder* on the following grounds:

> The [parents in this case] . . . , unlike their Amish counterparts [in *Yoder*], are not members of a community which has existed for three centuries and has a long history of being a successful, self-sufficient, segment of American society. Furthermore, in *Yoder,* the Amish children attended public school through the eighth grade and then obtained informal vocational training to enable them to assimilate into the self-contained Amish community. However, in the present case, [plaintiff] . . . refuses to enroll his children in any public or nonpublic school for any length of time, but still expects them to be fully integrated and live normally in the modern world upon reaching the age of 18.

Id. at 98. *See also Burrow v. State,* 282 Ark. 479, 669 S.W.2d 441 (1984); *Delconte v. State,* 65 N.C.App. 262, 308 S.E.2d 898 (App. 1983); *State v. Riddle,* 168 W.Va. 429, 285 S.E.2d 359 (1981). The court disagreed with plaintiff's contention that the state's case was weakened by virtue of North Carolina's "deregulation of nonpublic education." (North Carolina only imposed attendance, disease immunization, and reasonable fire, health, and safety inspection requirements.) *Id.* The court also held that plaintiff had "not demonstrated that home instruction will prepare his children to be self-sufficient participants in our modern society or that these were compelling state interests. *Id.* at 99. *See generally* Lines, "Private Education Alternatives and State Regulation," 12 *J. of Law & Educ.* 189 (1983).

Does Yoder affect the result of the following cases where any infringement on religious freedom was found to be outweighed by the state's interest in compelling the child to attend public school? *Commonwealth v. Bey,* 166 Pa. Super. 136, 70 A.2d 693 (1950) (Muslim parents refused to send their child to public school on Friday, the sacred day of their religion); *In re Currence,* 42 Misc.2d 418, 248 N.Y.S.2d 251 (Fam. Ct., 1963) (parents belonging to the Ancient Divine Order of Melchizedek kept their child out of public school on a Wednesday-through-Thursday sabbath); *Commonwealth v. Renfrew,* 332 Mass. 492, 126 N.E.2d 109 (1955) (Buddhist parents who did not wish their children exposed to the tenents of the Christian faith raised their child at home); *Application of Auster,* 198 Misc. 1055, 100 N.Y.S.2d 60 (Sup. Ct. 1950), *appeal dismissed,* 342 U.S. 884, 72 S.Ct. 178, 96 L.Ed. 663 (1951) (Orthodox Jew sought to send his son to unaccredited yeshiva, believing that secular secondary education was forbidden by his religion). *Cf. Thomas v. Review Board,* 450 U.S. 707 (1981). Does *Yoder* overturn cases upholding state laws requiring immunization against diptheria and other diseases as a condition for attending public schools? *See Zucht v. King,* 260 U.S. 174, 43 S.Ct. 24, 67 L.Ed. 194 (1922); *Hanzel v. Arter,* 625 F. Supp. 1259 (S.D. Ohio 1985); *Itz v. Penick,* 493 S.W.2d 506 (Tex. 1973), *appeal dismissed,* 412 U.S. 925, 93 S.Ct. 2754, 37 L.Ed.2d 152. *See generally* T. van Geel, *The Courts and American Education* 120 (1987).

How credible is the *Yoder* assertion that "compulsory school attendance to age 16 for Amish children carries with it a very real threat of undermining the Amish community and religious practice as it exists today"? Is it critical that "the Amish people are engaged in a social discourse that requires them to build and maintain a redemptive community"? Hostetler, *supra* at 34. Consider the following comment:

> Amish parents have remarkable control over their children, and neither parents nor children, much as they might wish it to be otherwise, live entirely separate from our world. Amish children ride in cars, hear radios, read newspapers and magazines and books, perhaps even sneak off to the movies. Amish children know a great deal more of the outside world than their parents might wish; certainly, even without schools, they are exposed to it frequently. Yet the vast majority of them remain in the faith and join the church. And it may be unrealistic, as well as futile, to argue to the courts that the existence of their religion depends on judicial exemptions for their children from compulsory education laws.

Note, "The Right Not to Be Modern Men: The Amish and Compulsory Education," 53 *Va. L. Rev.* 925, 950 (1967).

Is the threat rendered more plausible by the fact that the years at issue are the child's "formative years"? How important to the decision is the fact that the Amish religion countenanced school attendance until the eighth grade? *See State v. Patzer*, 382 N.W.2d 631 (N.D. 1986); *Howell v. State*, 723 S.W.2d 755 (Tex. App. 1986); *State v. Riddle*, 168 W.Va. 429, 285 S.E.2d 359 (1981). What would be the result if only a sixth-grade education were permitted? What would be the result if a particular sect permitted no formal schooling at all, but the good citizenship and economic self-reliance of its members were unquestioned? What if the members of a religious sect, demanding no formal education after the eighth grade, held unimpeachable religious beliefs but were not always "very law abiding"?

b. Parental Rights. "However read," Chief Justice Burger states, "the Court's holding in *Pierce* stands as a charter of the rights of parents to direct the religious upbringing of their children." 406 U.S. at 233. *See generally* Friedman, "The Parental Right to Control the Religious Education of a Child," 29 *Harv. L. Rev.* 485 (1916). Is that the proposition for which *Pierce* stands? *See Lassiter v. Department of Human Services* 452 U.S. 18 (1981).

In *Prince v. Commonwealth of Massachusetts*, 321 U.S. 158, 64 S.Ct. 438, 88 L.Ed. 645 (1944), nine-year-old Betty, under the supervision of her aunt and custodian, Mrs. Prince, sold religious literature on the street in violation of Massachusetts child-labor laws. Both Betty and Mrs. Prince were Jehovah's Witnesses and believed it their religious duty to do this work. The Court held for the state; in its opinion it discussed the "harmful possibilities" that the legislature sought to prevent and then noted: "Parents may be free to become martyrs themselves. But it does not follow they are free . . . to make martyrs of their children before they have reached the age of full and legal discretion when they can make that choice for themselves." 321 U.S. at 170, 64 S.Ct. at 444. *Prince* is characterized in *Yoder* as a case in which the conduct regulated posed a substantial threat to public safety and on that basis is distinguishable from the Amish situation. *See generally* Mangrum, "Family Rights and Compulsory School Laws," 21 *Creighton L. Rev.* 1019, 1039–40 (1988). How satisfactory is that distinction? Should *Prince* have been overruled? Was the danger to the physical or mental health of the child in *Prince* any more than the danger that might be "properly inferred" in *Yoder*?

In the light of *Yoder* and *Prince*, consider these comments:

> When viewed with the common law's acceptance of parental control over the child's religious indoctrination, the *Yoder* holding, with its interpretation of the line of cases from *Pierce* through *Prince*, might be read as establishing that the first amendment's free exercise provisions vest in the parents a constitutionally-protected right to direct their child's religious upbringing in the absence of any compelling reason for state interference. Thus the common law standard of "best interest of the child," with its presumption that those interests can best be served without governmental interference, has been incorporated in the first and fourteenth amendments, with the result that the state may not circumscribe parental discretion in religious matters unless some palpable harm would otherwise befall the child.

Note, "Adjudicating What *Yoder* Left Unresolved: Religious Rights for Minor Children after *Danforth* and *Carey*," 126 *U. Pa. L. Rev.* 1135, 1145 (1978). *See also* Arons, "The Separation of School and State: *Pierce* Reconsidered," 46 *Harv. Educ. Rev.* 76 (1976); Note, "Judicial Input Into Policy Formulation: Case-Scenario Analysis and Educational Policymaking," 28 *Case West. Res. L. Rev.* 739 (1978).

Do you agree? What is the source of this constitutional entitlement? What is its scope? Note that the United Nations General Assembly in *The Universal Declaration of Human Rights* states that "parents have a prior right to choose the kind of education that shall be given to their children." G. A. Res. 217 [III], art. 26 (1948).

c. *Interests of the State.* Wisconsin suggested two justifications for compulsory education: the preparation of the child for political citizenship and the development of economic self-reliance. *See generally* Project, "Education and the Law: State Interests and Individual Rights," 74 *Mich. L. Rev.* 1373, 1384–85 (1976). Are these concerns satisfied, as the *Yoder* decision suggests, by eight years of schooling?

The answer to that query may turn on whether Amish youngsters remain in the Amish community or choose a quite different life style. As Justice White notes in his concurring opinion: "It is possible that most Amish children will wish to continue living the rural life of their parents, in which case their training at home will adequately equip them for their future role. Others, however, may wish to become nuclear physicists, ballet dancers, computer programmers, or historians, and for these occupations, formal training will be necessary." 406 U.S. at 239. Does the state have a legitimate interest in providing maximum educational opportunities to all youngsters? Does it have the right to do so by protecting a child "against the ignorance of his parents"? *See* K. Alexander and K. F. Jordan, *Legal Aspects of Educational Choice* 5 (1973).

If, in fact, few Amish youngsters deserted their community for the larger society, the interest might be dismissed as of trivial practical significance. But is that the case? Compare the discussions of Justices Burger, White, and Douglas on this point. And consider the conclusion reached by the Wisconsin Supreme Court in *Yoder*: "[T]his harm to the Amish [is not] justified because on speculation some Amish children may after reaching adulthood leave their religion. To force a worldly education on all Amish children, the majority of whom do not want or need it, in order to confer a dubious benefit on the few who might later reject their religion is not a compelling interest." *State v. Yoder*, 49 Wis.2d 430, 440, 182 N.W.2d 539, 543–44 (1971). What does that statement assume with respect to the wishes of Amish children (see d., *infra*)? Compare the position of the dissent in the same case: "The state's interest and obligation runs to each and every child in the state. In the context of the public law of the state, no child's education is below the concern of the law." 49 Wis.2d at 451, 182 N.W.2d at 549.

The state argues that the Amish faith fosters ignorance. The Court's response speaks to the "productive and very law-abiding" nature of the Amish. Does the response confront the question? The Court also notes that the Amish community provides "valuable vocational skills and habits." Just how valuable are these skills likely to be outside of the religious community? How might the black parent—or any parent, for that matter—respond if his or her child were compelled to attend a vocational school?

The last paragraph of the majority opinion suggests the state may require Amish children to attend an "Amish vocational school" or at least regulate the content of continuing vocational training provided by Amish parents. One commentator asserts: "It is not simply public school to which [the Amish] object, but *all* schooling above the eighth grade." Arons, "Compulsory Education: The Plain People Resist," *Saturday Review*, Jan. 15, 1972, at 53. If "the purpose of Amish education is not to get ahead in the world but to get to heaven," what is the likely outcome of a suit by Amish plaintiffs alleging that any type of school at all beyond the eighth grade is inconsistent with their faith? *See* S. Arons, *Compelling Belief* 138 (1983).

d. *The Interest of Amish Children.* The possibility of a clash between Amish youngsters and their parents is skirted by the Court, which notes that the children were not parties to the litigation. *See generally* Note, "The Interest of the Child in Home Education Question: *Wisconsin v. Yoder* Reexamined, 18 *Ind. L. Rev.* 711 (1985). Since children must be represented in court by an adult (typically but not necessarily by a parent or legal guardian), how might the Amish youngsters make themselves parties to the litigation? *See Buckholz v. Leveile*, 37 Mich. App. 166, 194 N.W.2d 427 (1971). *See generally* Guggenheim, "The Right to be Represented But Not Heard: Reflections on Legal Representation for Children," 59 *N.Y.U. L. Rev.* 76 (1984). The Court also denies the likelihood of a parent-child conflict, noting that "there is nothing in the record or in the ordinary course of human experience to suggest that non-Amish parents generally consult with children up to ages 14 through 16 if they are placed in a church school of their parents' faith." 406 U.S. at 232, 92 S.Ct. at 1541. Is the observation correct? Note that historically

American courts sometimes did intervene to thwart "officious intermeddlers" from interfering with parental authority over their children's religious orientation. For example, in *Prieto v. St. Alphonsus Convent of Mercy*, 52 La. Ann. 631, 27 So. 153 (1900), the Louisiana Supreme Court ordered a convent to expel a seventeen-year-old who sought to become a nun without her mother's consent. *See generally* Montana, "The Best Interest of the Child and the Constitutional Rights of Cult Member Parents: Resolution of a Conflict," 5 *N.Y. Law Sch. J. of Human Rts.* 97 (1987).

If the views of the Amish children do bear consideration, how should they be expressed? Should the Court appoint a guardian explicitly to represent the children? Should the children be canvassed, as Justice Douglas' dissent suggests? *See Henman v. Hehman*, 13 Misc.2d 318, 178 N.Y.S.2d 328 (1958). What impact would such a venture have on the Amish child and on the Amish community? Any device designed to identify the independent interest of Amish youngsters necessarily intrudes into family and community life, imposing both political and legal costs. Is the child's right to be heard of sufficient importance to justify such an intrusion? *See generally* Knudsen, "The Education of the Amish Child," 62 *Calif. L. Rev.* 1506 (1974).

The *Yoder* decision preserves the religious and community interests of the Amish, but in so doing it denies Amish children the opportunity of acquiring sufficient education to choose for themselves whether to stay in the community; a decision compelling these children to attend school would seriously affect the future viability of the Amish religion. Is there a resolution of the issues less far-reaching in its consequences than either of these alternatives? Suppose an Amish child claimed that compelled attendance at a sectarian school violated her constitutional right of free exercise of religion. How should a court treat that claim? Murphy, "Rights and Borderline Cases," 19 *Ariz. L. Rev.* 238 (1978), suggests that in some instances a child has a right to paternalistic treatment. Is this such an instance? Is there a right to compulsory education?

The rights of the child against both his or her parents and the potential role of the state as *parens patriae* have frequently presented perplexing problems to the courts. In *In re Green*, 448 Pa. 338, 292 A.2d 387 (1972), parents refused on religious grounds to permit blood transfusion preparations necessary to proceed with a spinal operation on a sixteen-year-old boy. The Pennsylvania Supreme Court found that where the situation was not one of life-or-death urgency, the state interest in the well-being of the child did not outweigh the interests of the parents in religious freedom. *See also In re Seiferth*, 309 N.Y. 80, 127 N.E.2d 820 (1955) (fourteen-year-old boy with harelip and cleft palate). The court, however, reserved its decision in the light of a possible parent–child conflict and remanded the case for a hearing to determine the child's views.

> [T]he ultimate question . . . is whether a parent's religious beliefs are paramount to the possibly adverse decision of the child. . . . It would be most anomalous to ignore [the child] in this situation when we consider the preference of an intelligent child of sufficient maturity in determining custody. . . . Moreover, we have held that a child of the same age can waive constitutional rights and receive a life sentence. . . . Indeed, minors can now bring a personal injury action in Pennsylvania against their parents. 292 A.2d at 392.

The dissent took issue with the majority's disposition of the case.

> I do not believe that sending the case back to allow Ricky to be heard is an adequate solution. We are herein dealing with a young boy who has been crippled most of his life, consequently, he has been under the direct control of his parents for that time. To now presume that he could make an independent decision as to what is best for his welfare and health is not reasonable.

292 A.2d at 395. (The child decided not to have the operation.) *See also State v. Perricone*, 37 N.J. 463, 181 A.2d 751 (1962), *cert. denied*, 371 U.S. 890, 83 S.Ct. 189, 9 L.Ed.2d 124 (1962); Raleigh Fitkin-Paul Morgan Memorial Hosp. v. Anderson, 42 N.J. 421, 201 A.2d 537 (1964), *cert. denied*, 377 U.S. 985, 84 S.Ct. 1894, 12 L.Ed.2d 1032 (1964). In many cases, however, the courts weigh the necessity of medical treatment against the parents' free exercise of religion rights, without ascertaining the wishes of the child. *See, e.g., Matter of Hamilton*, 657 S.W.2d 425 (Tenn. App. 1983) (radiation and chemotherapy ordered for twelve-year-old girl with Ewing's Sarcoma, despite religious objection of father); *People in Interest of D.L.E.*, 645 P.2d 271 (Colo. 1982). *See generally* Kessler, "Praying for Relief from *Parens Patriae*: Should A Child Be Allowed to Refuse Life-Saving Medical Treatment on Religious Grounds?," 2 *J. of Law, Ethics & Pub. Policy* 673 (1986); Note, "Parent-Child—The Right of a

State to Order Surgery on a Minor in a Nonterminal Situation Despite the Religious Objections of the Parent," 77 *Dick. L. Rev.* 693 (1973).

Can *Green* be reconciled with *Yoder*? Is the only difference between the two situations one of the foreseeability of serious injury to the child? What if the malady is not literally life threatening but may impede normal psychological development? *See In re Sampson*, 29 N.Y.2d 900, 328 N.Y.S.2d 686, 278 N.E.2d 918 (1972) (despite mother's religious objections, court ordered operation to partially correct severe facial deformity). Is this difference sufficient to justify the conclusion in *Yoder* that the education of the child is for the parents alone to determine? Note in the *Green* case that there was apparently no showing of actual conflict between parent and child. Nonetheless, the Pennsylvania court considered the child's opinion essential and thus in essence adopted the approach of Justice Douglas in *Yoder. But see In re Sampson*, 29 N.Y.2d 900, 328 N.Y.S.2d 686, 278 N.E.2d 918 (1972) (minor's consent not necessary). Consider in this context the criticism of the dissent in *Green*. Does it apply with equal validity to the opinion of Justice Douglas?

In *Planned Parenthood v. Danforth*, 428 U.S. 52, 96 S.Ct. 2831, 49 L.Ed.2d 788 (1976), the Supreme Court held that minors have a constitutionally protected right, whatever the views of their parents, to decide whether to have an abortion. *Compare City of Dallas v. Stanglin*, 49 U.S. 19, 109 S.Ct. 1591, 104 L.Ed.2d 18 (1989) (ordinance limiting use of dance halls to persons between ages fourteen and eighteen is rationally related to legitimate state purpose and does not violate Equal Protection Clause). As one commentator has stated, "[I]f children are deemed to possess independent privacy rights, is there any reason not to recognize constitutionally protected religious rights of children, even in the absence of parental support for these beliefs, or even in the face of active parental hostility?" Note, "Adjudicating What *Yoder* Left Unresolved: Religious Rights for Minor Children after *Danforth* and *Carey*," 126 *U. Pa. L. Rev.* 1135, 1138 (1978). Is *Danforth* distinguishable from *Green* and *Yoder*? Is the question the competence of the minor to make an informed decision in different contexts, or is it the nature of the state's interest that varies? *See also Carey v. Population Services International*, 431 U.S. 678, 97 S.Ct. 2010, 52 L.Ed.2d 675 (1977) (plurality opinion) (right of minors to secure contraceptives). Consider these remarks by Professor Martha Minow:

> A persistent argument against rights for children is that children lack the autonomy necessary to engage in adversarial exchange, to protect their own interests. . . . These objections grow out of a more widely accepted conception of rights, which relies on the idea that the rights-bearing person is an autonomous individual capable of exercising choice for personal ends and able to protect personal freedom from the pressure and power of others.
>
> * * *
>
> [But] . . . legal rights are interdependent and mutually defining. . . . Rights, in fact, could be understood as simply the articulation of legal consequences for particular patterns of human and institutional relationships. . . .
>
> Autonomy, then, is not a precondition for any individual's exercise of rights. The only precondition is that the community is willing to allow individuals to make claims and to participate in the shifting of boundaries.

Minow, "Interpreting Rights: An Essay for Robert Cover," 96 *Yale L. J.* 1860, 1882, 1884–5 (1987).

May a child ever assert his own interest in educational liberty? In *In re Mario*, 65 Misc.2d 708, 317 N.Y.S.2d 659 (Fam.Ct. 1971), the New York family court upheld the assignment of a thirteen-year-old boy, "beyond parental control in regard to his school attendance," to Warwick State Training School, a residential "rehabilitative" institution. The respondent asserted that such placement "imposes a restraint on his liberty." The court found the restraint constitutional

> because reasonable rehabilitative measures are justified by respondent's truancy. . . . The State has the power to perform the parental role of insuring the child's education and training, when the parent is unable to control him sufficiently to perform it. If children were permitted the same freedom of choice as adults, they might well be unequipped when they attain adulthood to exercise *any* freedom of choice—specifically, without any education or training, they would be unable to choose to work in a job for which they in fact have the potential.

317 N.Y.S.2d at 668.

Is the state's interest more compelling in *Mario* than in *Yoder*? How would the *Yoder* majority (or Justice Douglas) resolve this issue?

e. Problem. In the light of *Yoder*, consider this problem. A draftee is accorded conscientious objector status because "by reason of religious training and belief" he is opposed to participation in "war in any form." *See* 50 U.S.C. App. §465(j). The draftee completes alternative civilian service and then applies for veterans' educational benefits to defray partially the costs of attending college. Under the Veterans' Readjustment Benefits Act of 1966, 38 U.S.C.A. §101, civilian service does not qualify a draftee for such benefits. The draftee files suit in federal court alleging that the Act violates his First Amendment guarantee of religious freedom and the Fifth Amendment's guarantee of equal protection of the laws. What result? *See Johnson v. Robison*, 415 U.S. 361 (1974). Is *Yoder* distinguishable? Is it legally significant that Congress enacted the law under review rather than a state legislature? Is there a constitutional distinction between denying an educational benefit and requiring a person to accept such a benefit? How do the interests of the government differ in *Yoder* and *Johnson*? *Cf. Bowen v. Roy*, 476 U.S. 693, 707, 106 S.Ct. 2147, 2156, 90 L.Ed.2d 735 (1986) (opinion for three justices).

3. *The Scope of the* Yoder *Decision*

a. A Broad Challenge to Compulsoriness? The *Yoder* Court notes that the Amish way of life has come "into conflict increasingly with the requirements of contemporary society. . . . There can be no assumption that today's majority is 'right,' and that the Amish and others like them are 'wrong.' " 406 U.S. at 223. Are these "others" only religious sects, as the Court's opinion intimates? *See Mason v. General Brown Cent. Sch. District*, 851 F.2d 47 (2nd Cir. 1988) (belief in "genetic blueprint" not a religious belief and thus no exemption from immunization requirement for school age son). Why should the children of a contemporary Thoreau, whose objections to schooling derive not from a religion but from a philosophy of life, be forced to submit to socialization in debatable political and social values? Does freedom of religion have a higher claim to constitutional protection than freedom of expression? One commentator notes:

> The conflict of state-sponsored socialization with private values appears in bold constitutional relief when these private values can be articulated as a religion. *Yoder* holds, therefore, that state-imposed socialization is unconstitutional when it conflicts directly with religious tenets. But none of the value conflicts the Court cited—competitiveness versus cooperation, intellect versus wisdom, or disagreement over the status of manual work, for example—is necessarily religious. Any non-Amish family might be equally committed to such values and see them as threatened by state-sponsored socialization in schools. Religion provided the constitutional nexus between the plaintiff's injury and the state's policy, but the evidence the Court found compelling also supports a broader doctrine: any conflict between public schooling and a family's basic and sincerely held values interferes with the family's First Amendment rights. Thus, even though the opinion was couched in terms of religious beliefs and practices, the Chief Justice's recognition of the various elements of value inculcation, none of which is itself of religious character, has the effect of eroding the meaningfulness of the distinction between secular and religious values upon which the Court has relied so heavily.

Arons, "The Separation of School and State: *Pierce* Reconsidered," 46 *Harv. Educ. Rev.* 76, 84–85 (1976). *But cf. Mason v. General Brown Cent. Sch. District*, *supra*; *Custody of a Minor*, 375 Mass. 733, 379 N.E.2d 1053 (1978) (nonreligious parental objections to treatment of child with leukemia outweighed by need to protect child).

Does the *Yoder* opinion in fact raise this range of questions undercutting the *Pierce* premise that the state may compel children to attend some form of school? *See* T. van Geel, *The Courts and American Education* 21 (1987).

b. Compulsoriness and Equal Educational Opportunity. In re Skipwith, 14 Misc.2d 325, 180 N.Y.2d 852 (Dom. Rel. Ct. 1958), poses a quite different constitutional challenge to compulsoriness. In *Skipwith*, parents refused to send their children to ghetto schools, which they alleged were inferior to predominantly white schools. In a suit brought by the Board of Education to compel attendance, the parents introduced testimony of educators and psychologists concerning the harmful impact of racial segregation and evidence that the school in question had unlicensed teachers filling forty-three of eighty-five positions, a proportion substantially greater than the citywide average (see Chapter 5 for a discussion of racial discrimination and equal educational opportunity). Is it appropriate—as a matter either of policy or constitutional law—to keep children from school as a means of addressing the inequalities asserted by the *Skipwith* parents? *See also In re Foster*, 69 Misc.2d 400, 330 N.Y.S.2d 8 (1972); *Dobbins v. Commonwealth*, 198 Va. 697, 96 S.E.2d 154 (1957). *Compare Matter of Baum*, 382 N.Y.S.2d 672 (Fam.Ct. 1976) (allegedly racist remarks by teacher do not justify withdrawing child from public school).

4. The Demise of the Free Exercise Balancing Test? In *Employment Division, Department of Human Resources of Oregon v. Smith,* ___ U.S. ___, 110 S.Ct. 1595, 108 L.Ed. 876 (1990), the Supreme Court addressed the following question:

> [W]hether the Free Exercise Clause of the First Amendment permits the State of Oregon to include religiously inspired peyote use within the reach of its general criminal prohibition on use of that drug, and thus permits the State to deny unemployment benefits to persons dismissed from their jobs because of such religiously inspired use.

___ U.S. at ___ , 110 S.Ct. at 1597, 108 L.Ed. at 882. Justice Scalia, writing for the majority, held that Oregon's drug law did not violate the religious freedom of two members of the Native American Church who were fired from their jobs with a private drug rehabilitation organization for ingesting peyote for sacramental purposes at a religous ceremony and subsequently denied unemployment benefits. In a far-reaching decision, Justice Scalia stated that the Court had "never held that an individual's religious beliefs excuse him from compliance with an otherwise valid law prohibiting conduct that the state is free to regulate." ___ U.S. at ___ , 110 S.Ct. at 1600, 108 L.Ed. at 885. He also specifically declined to embrace a balancing test, holding that "the government's ability to enforce generally applicable prohibitions of socially harmful conduct . . . 'cannot depend on measuring the effects of a governmental action on a religious objector's spiritual development.' " ___ U.S. at ___ , 110 S.Ct. at 1603, 108 L.Ed. at 889, citing *Lyng v. Northwest Indian Cemetery Protective Association*, 485 U.S. 439, 451, 108 S.Ct. 1319, 1326, 99 L.Ed.2d 534, 548 (1988).

Is the analysis in *Smith* consistent with the Court's reasoning and result in *Yoder*? Does your answer depend on whether the failure to abide compulsory education laws is a civil or criminal offense? If it is conceded that a compulsory education law is a legitimate exercise of state authority and if there is no indication that the law was enacted to discriminate against particular religious groups, how can *Smith* and *Yoder* be distinguished? Which test is preferable? Does *Smith* eviscerate the Free Exercise Clause? Is the majority correct in its characterization of the precedents? Does *Yoder* lead to an unprincipled kind of ad hoc balancing by judges? *See* Laycock, "The Remnants of Free Exercise," 1990 Sup. Ct. Rev. ___ (publication pending).

In the *Smith* decision itself the Court distinguished *Yoder* and a number of other Free Exercise Clause precedents, asserting that those cases involved the Free Exercise Clause "in conjunction with other constitutional protections." Citing *Pierce*, it characterized *Yoder* as also involving "the right of parents . . . to direct the education of their children . . . ." Are you persuaded by this distinction? Would you advise a legislative committee to create specific exemptions from compulsory attendance for those with religous objections? What of the risk of a violation of the Establishment Clause? *See* chapter 2, *infra*.

5. Problem Multiculturalism and Compulsory Education

A state commission on minorities and the curriculum finds that African American and Hispanic students have been "victimized by intellectual and educational oppression in the curriculum of public schools" and that there is a "systematic bias in many courses toward European culture." Based on the commission's report, a group of African American children filed a law suit in federal court alleging that the state and school district in which they reside are offering a curriculum that is biased against students of non-European origin. The plaintiffs contend that the curriculum "ignores the contributions of non-Europeans in science, history, the arts, and other fields." They also allege that this systematic bias contributes to lower academic performance, higher dropout rates, and increased crime among minority children.

After *Yoder* are the plaintiffs entitled to an exemption from the compulsory attendance laws if they can prove their allegations? *Cf. Matter of McMillan*, 30 N.C.App. 235, 226 S.E.2d 693 (1976). Would the result turn on whether the parents offered a "sufficient alternative education" for the children? *See generally* S. Arons, *Compelling Belief* (1983). What would constitute an adequate alternative? Would you advise the plaintiffs to seek an alternative remedy that would remove the alleged biases from the curriculum? *See generally* chapter 2, *infra*.

III. STATE REGULATION OF NONPUBLIC SCHOOLS

Notwithstanding the landmark Supreme Court decisions in *Pierce*, *Meyer*, and *Farrington*, most states regulate private schools and require them to register and seek approval before they can operate. *See, e.g.*,

New Life Baptist Church Academy v. Town of East Longmeadow, 885 F.2d 940 (1st Cir. 1989); *State ex. rel. Douglas v. Faith Baptist Church*, 207 Neb. 802, 301 N.W.2d 571 (1981); *State v. Labarge*, 134 Vt. 276, 357 A.2d 121 (1976). *See generally* T. van Geel, *Authority to Control the School Program* 153–55 (1976); Bristow, "Private Schools in Vermont: the 'Equivalency Exception' to Compulsory Attendance in *State v. LaBarge*," 2 *Vt. L. Rev.* 205 (1977). Where registration is required or voluntary, state authorities typically have broad powers to set the standards for private schools under statutory mandates. *See, e.g., Wiley House v. Scanlon*, 502 Pa. 228, 465 A.2d 995 (1983). *See generally* Elson, "State Regulation of Nonpublic Schools: The Legal Framework," in E. Erickson (ed.), *Public Controls for Nonpublic Schools* 103 (1969). Enforcement of the standards within the framework of compulsory attendance laws often is left to local school authorities.

Some state regulation is designed to protect the public only from dangerous business, health, or building practices. *See, e.g., Manley v. Wichita Business College*, 237 Kan. 427, 701 P.2d 893 (1985); *Charton Corp. v. Brockette*, 534 S.W.2d 401 (Tex. Civ. App. 1976); *Schneider v. Pullen*, 198 Md. 64, 81 A.2d 226 (1951). *But see Katharine Gibbs, School, Inc. v. FTC*, 612 F.2d 658 (2d Cir. 1979); *State v. Williams*, 253 N.C. 337, 117 S.E.2d 444 (1960); *Packer Collegiate Institute v. University of New York*, 298 N.Y. 184, 81 N.E.2d 80 (1948). *See generally* Sacken, "Regulating Nonpublic Education: A Search for Just Law and Policy," 96 *Amer. J. of Educ.* 394 (1988); Elson, *supra* at 133. But much of it is designed to maintain minimum secular education standards and to promote democratic values in private schools. *See e.g., New Life Baptist Church Academy, supra. See generally* M. McCarthy and N. Cambron McCabe, *Public School Law* 44–47 (1988); A. Gutmann, *Democratic Education* 115–123 (1987). The excerpt later in this chapter from the work of Professor Lines discusses the modern scope of state regulation of private schools.

Note should be taken of three additional aspects of the debate over private schools. First, some fear that private "schools will siphon off the most affluent and the academically best students, leaving public schools with a student body that is disproportionately poor, economically and academically." Gutmann, *supra* at 116. The empirical support for this proposition is weak:

> The majority of private schools in the United States are religious, not secular, and a majority of these are Catholic. Two-thirds of private-school students attend Catholic schools. Although the median income of parents who send their children to parochial schools is higher than the median of public school parents, the distribution of income among private-school parents is very broad. Far from siphoning off only the best and the brightest, private schools admit students with almost as broad a range of abilities as public schools. Private schools are more segregated than public ones by religion, but not by class, race, or academic talent. . . .

Gutmann, *supra* at 117, citing J.S. Coleman, T. Hoffer and S. Kilgore, *High School Achievement: Public, Catholic, and Private Schools Compared* 16–64 (1982). Second, some advocates of private schooling argue that such schools provide competition for the public schools, thereby creating incentives for improvements in the public sector. They see private schools as "exemplars" for the public schools. Gutmann, *supra* at 116. They fear that a de facto public school monopoly would not respond adequately to student needs. *See generally* Chubb & Moe, "Politics, Markets and the Organization of Schools" 82 *Amer. Pol. Sci. Rev.* 1065 (1988).

Finally, some social scientists believe that private schools do a better job of educating the young than public schools, even when such variables as class, family background, and ethnicity are factored out. *See* Coleman, Hoffer, and Kilgore, *supra*. For example, Coleman and his colleagues found empirical support for the propositions that private schools produce higher cognitive outcomes, safer and more orderly school environments, lower student/faculty ratios, and higher self-esteem for students. *Id. See* Chubb & Moe, *supra;* Ravitch, "The Meaning of the New Coleman Report," 62 *Phi Delta Kappan* 718 (1981). Even Coleman, however, is concerned that there may be other factors in the self-selection of private school students that cannot easily be measured by social scientists and that may explain higher levels of achievement. Needless to say, there are many critics of the methodology and conclusions of the Coleman study, and some critics fear that his work will be used to support voucher systems and other efforts to privatize education. *See* Ravitch, *supra*.

"Private Education Alternatives and State Regulation"

Lines, 12 *J. Law & Education* 189, 194–97 (1983). Reprinted by permission.

State Regulation of Private Education

Traditionally, the mechanism for enforcement of minimum standards for private education has been through a state compulsory attendance law, with punitive action for parents and children, but not for those who run private schools. Typically, the basic requirement is school *attendance*, although some of those laws require education of the child. The law almost always provides for fines and jail sentences for parents who fail to comply, and often truancy charges and possible institutionalization of the child.* In almost every state the local superintendent or board, and the local prosecuting attorney are responsible for the identification of truants—that is, children who are not in an approved education program. In most states local officials also have primary responsibility for approving home instruction programs, if allowed by state law. State boards usually have the responsibility for approving private schools, although in some states, local boards may share in this task.

Acceptable ways of meeting the compulsory schooling requirements vary widely among states. Some states require certification of teachers and schools, some only approval and some only minimal evidence that schooling takes place. States like Alabama, Iowa, Nebraska, North Dakota, West Virginia and Wisconsin are at one end of the spectrum. They have obtained state court approval of at least some aspects of the state's power to regulate private educational alternatives.[21] Ohio provided even more detailed regulation, but its high court has curbed the state's regulatory system as applied to religious schools.[22]

States with more lenient statutory requirements will probably experience less litigation, *provided* that the state board does not augment the statute with stricter regulations. Such states include, for example, Connecticut, which provides a broad exception to the school attendance requirement. Parents who do not send their children to public school must educate or "cause" their children to be educated in specific subjects.[24] Other states following this model include Delaware, Idaho, New Jersey, South Dakota and Vermont. These states do not specify who must be the teacher or where instruction is to take place. Instruction apparently can be by anyone and anywhere, so long as it is equivalent to that taking place in public schools.

Some states, such as Alaska, Arizona, Georgia and Ohio give state and local school officials wide discretionary authority to excuse a child from the compulsory attendance requirement.[26] Virginia and Kentucky expressly permit exemption from compulsory school attendance where the parent has conscientious objections to such attendance.[27] In other states, in certain cases, courts have interpreted federal or state constitutional provisions in a way that permits individuals or churches to operate schools despite the state compulsory attendance law. California and Alabama permit home instruction but require the tutor to be certified by the state.[29]

Some states have consciously deregulated their private schools. These states expressly limit state administrative authority to promulgate regulations. Tennessee, for example, provides: "The state board of education and local boards of education are prohibited from regulating the selection of faculty or textbooks or the establishment of a curriculum in church related schools."[30] The law contains no hint as to whether the state can impose even minimal reporting requirements. However, private schools in Tennessee still have the option of seeking state approval.

North Carolina presents a somewhat similar option, with two 1979 laws that deregulate all private

---

* *See generally In re Michael G.*, 243 Cal. Rptr. 224, 747 P.2d 1152 (1988); *In re Ann M.*, 525 A.2d 1054 (Md. 1987).

21. *See State v. Faith Baptist Church*, 107 Neb. 802, 301 N.W.2d 571 (1981), *appeal dismissed for want of a substantial federal question*, 10 2 S.Ct. 75 (1981); *State v. Shaver*, 294 N.W.2d 883 (N.D. 1980); *State v. Kasuboski*, 87 Wis.2d 407, 275 N.W.2d 101 (Wis. App. 1978); *Hill v. State*, 381 So.2d 91 (Ala. Crim. App. 1979), *reversed on other grounds*, 381 So.2d 94 (Ala. 1980); *Hill v. State*, 410 So.2d 431 (Ala. Crim. App. 1981) (same parties; convictions upheld after procedural defects corrected); *Iowa v. Moorhead*, 308 N.W.2d 60 (Iowa 1981); *State v. Riddle*, 285 S.E.2d 359 (W. Va. 1981).

22. *State v. Whisner*, 47 Ohio St.2d 181, 351 N.E.2d 750 (1976).

24. Conn. Gen. Stat. § 10–184 (Supp. 1982) ("unless the parent . . . is able to show that the child is elsewhere receiving equivalent instruction in the studies taught in the public schools").

26. Georgia law excuses ". . . children excused from attendance in school by county and/or independent school boards of education in accordance with general policies promulgated by the State Board of Education." Ga. Code Ann. § 32-2106(b) (1980). Ohio allows a local board to excuse a child "for good and sufficient reasons . . . ." Ohio Rev. Code Ann. § 3321.04(C) (1980). . . .

27. The Kentucky constitution provides "nor shall any man be compelled to send his child to any school to which he may be conscientiously opposed . . . ." Ky. Const. § 5. *See also* Va. Const. art. VIII § 1.

29. Ala. Code §§ 16-28-3, 16-28-5 (1975); Cal. Educ. Code §§ 48224 (West 1978).

30. Tenn. Stat. Ann. §§ 49.5201-5204 (1979).

schools.[31] Prior to passage of the law, the state board had gradually expanded its regulatory framework for private schools until teachers, courses of study and textbooks had to be substantially the same as in the public schools. Under the new law, North Carolina has minimal requirements for recordkeeping (pupil attendance and disease immunization) and requires that the schools select and administer a nationally standardized test to students each year. The schools keep the tests on file and make them available to state inspectors. Eighth graders must be given a competency test. A school must meet fire, health and safety standards established in other laws.

Washington, like Tennessee and North Carolina, has consciously limited the extent to which the state board can regulate private schools.[33] The Washington law provides for stricter requirements for these schools, relative to Tennessee or North Carolina. It sets minimum standards as to school year, length of day and subjects to be taught. It expressly provides that these minimum standards shall not be altered by state agencies. However, the Washington law continues to require teacher certification except for courses in religion and other topics not taught in the public schools.[34] This requirement is a sore point with fundamentalist Christian schools and a stumbling block to many other private education alternatives. However, Washington law allows teaching by a person of "unusual competence," if supervised by a certified teacher. In practice the state may allow more flexibility than would initially appear.

Mississippi,[35] like Tennessee and North Carolina, adopts a *laissez faire* attitude, but apparently for different reasons. Mississippi abandoned its compulsory attendance law after *Brown v. Board of Education*, apparently not wishing to force children to attend desegregated schools. It has since enacted a new compulsory education law with no sanctions . . . .

Laws in about half the states permit instruction at home by a parent. In some states, such as Arizona, Ohio, Oregon and South Dakota, home instruction may be by a parent or a qualified person.[37] In Nevada and Utah, home instruction must be equivalent to that taking place in the public schools.[38] Some states allow home instruction only if the teacher is certified, ruling out most parents. In some states, courts or attorneys general have authorized home instruction by ruling that the home can qualify as a school if it meets all the requirements of a private school.[39]

Oregon's compulsory attendance law permits home instruction by a parent or anyone else. Families must formally apply to school officials for permission. To assure that education does take place, the law requires local districts to test the children periodically.

Fellowship Baptist Church v. Benton

815 F.2d 485 (8th Cir. 1987).

Before Heaney and Ross, Circuit Judges, and Larson, Senior District Judge.

Larson, Senior District Judge.

In this appeal, the Court is presented with a broad-based attack on Iowa's compulsory school laws. Plaintiffs are two fundamentalist Baptist church schools, the churches' pastors and principals, and several of the schools' teachers, parents and students. The creation of plaintiffs' church schools is a relatively recent development dating from the 1970s—a part of the growing trend towards the establishment of such schools throughout the country.

Plaintiffs' suit mirrors several previous actions involving fundamentalist groups, including one before the Iowa Supreme Court, which have generally resulted in decisions upholding the states' regulatory schemes. *See, e.g., Johnson v. Charles City Community Schools Board of Education*, 368 N.W.2d

33. Wash. Rev. Code. §§ 28A.02.201 *et seq.* and 28A.27.010 (1981).

34. Wash. Rev. Code §§ 28A.02.201 *et seq.* (1981).

35. Miss. Code Ann. § 37-13-95 (Supp. 1982).

37. *See, e.g.*, Ariz. Rev. Stat. Ann. § 15-802(B)(1) (Supp. 1982); Ohio Rev. Code § 3321.04(A)(2) (Page's 1980) (child must be taught by person "qualified to teach"); Or. Rev. Stat. § 339-020(3) (1965); S.D. Comp. Laws Ann. § 13-27-3 (1975).

38. *E.g.*, Nev. Rev. Stat. § 392.070 (1979); S.D. Comp. Laws Ann. § 13-27-3 (1975).

39. *See, e.g.*, People v. Levison, 404 Ill. 574 90 N.E.2d 213 (1950); Mich. Att. Gen. Op. No. 5579, Sept. 27, 1979. Note that where a statute provides for home instruction, parents may be precluded from seeking status for the home as a "school." *See Grigg v. Virginia*, No. 810519 (Va., Dec. 3, 1982); *State v. Bowman*, 653 P.2d 254 (Or. App. 1982) (held, parent must meet requirements for exemption to compulsory attendance law relating to "parent or private teacher," and not exemption relating to "private school"); *Gunnison Watershed School Dist. v. Funk*, No. 81-JV-3 (Colo. Dist. Ct., Gunnison County, Dec. 30, 1981). *See also* Tobak & Zirkel, *Home Instruction: An Analysis of the Statutes and Case Law*, 8 U. Dayton L. Rev. 1, 29–34, 51–53 (1982).

74 (Iowa), [(1985)] . . . . Indeed, many of plaintiffs' witnesses had testified in these other cases, including the *Charles City* case involving Iowa law, in which plaintiffs' counsel also participated.

Although many of the issues are similar to those presented to the *Charles City* Court, we of course have undertaken our own independent review of plaintiffs' challenge to the following specific requirements of Iowa law. First, principals must file annual reports with the local school districts listing their pupils' names, ages and dates of attendance, the texts used, and the names of the teachers. Iowa Code § 299.3. Second, parents of children ages 7 to 16 must place their children—until completion of the eight grade—in either a public school or a school that offers "equivalent instruction by a certified teacher." Iowa Code § 299.1. Finally, the state has determined that parents of children in the plaintiff schools are not entitled to the "Amish exemption" to the above requirements, *see* Iowa Code § 299.24, and plaintiffs argue this determination is unconstitutional. The district court found the challenged laws and their application to plaintiffs constitutional, except, following the suggestion of the *Charles City* Court, held that the term "equivalent instruction" was unconstitutionally vague "without further definition." 620 F.Supp. 308, 313–20 (S.D. Iowa 1985). . . .

* * *

I. Plantiffs' Religious Beliefs

An understanding of plaintiffs' religious beliefs and practices is essential to the proper evaluation of plaintiffs' claims. The evidence presented by plaintiffs to the district court unquestionably revealed that their religious beliefs stem from the Bible. They view Christ as the Head of their church and all of its ministries, and adhere to the doctrine of separation of church and state. Their schools were created in response to these beliefs. Neither church has a doctrine which requires members to send their children to the church school, however, and parents are not subject to discipline for removing their children from the church schools. Enrollment in the schools is not limited to those who belong to the church, and both schools have enrolled pupils whose parents are not members of the church. . . .

. . . Each school offers the basic curriculum specified in Iowa statutes with a few minor exceptions, as well as other courses, including a course in computers. Plaintiffs' witnesses admitted that there is nothing in either curriculum which forbids teaching by a certified teacher, and in fact, each school employs a teacher who is certified.

Plaintiffs believe themselves to be "in the world but not of the world," but they do not segregate themselves from modern communities. They live in ordinary residential neighborhoods and they interact with their neighbors and others not of their faith. They believe they are called by God to perform certain occupations in life, but these include ordinary occupations such as nurse, lawyer, engineer and accountant, and there is no evidence that they object to the licensing of these occupations. They own and use radios, televisions, motor vehicles and other modern conveniences and advancements. Their dress and lifestyle, while conservative, is not distinctive.

* * *

II. Reporting Requirements

Iowa's reporting requirements are very straightforward.[2] Each year, the principal of any private school in Iowa must, upon request from the secretary of the local school district, furnish the names, ages and number of days of attendance of each pupil in grades one through eight, the texts used, and the names of the teachers during the preceding year. Iowa Code § 299.3. The district court found the reporting requirements did not impinge on plaintiffs' constitutional rights, and we agree.

Administrators from other private schools confirmed that the intrusion by the state under section 299.3 is extremely limited. Once each year, the local school district sends each principal a form, which can be completed by a secretary under the principal's supervision in less than one day. The forms require nothing more of plaintiffs than that they provide the

2. Iowa does not require private schools to be approved. Private schools may choose [sic] to become approved, as for example the Catholic schools in the Keokuk School District have, or they are free to operate as nonapproved private schools. Parents may satisfy the compulsory school laws by sending their children to nonapproved private schools so long as they provide "equivalent instruction by a certified teacher." Iowa code § 299.1. No issue regarding approval of plaintiffs' schools is presented in this case.

minimal information requested, and plaintiff principals admitted that the information was readily available to them. Clearly, section 299.3 does not in any way infringe upon the content, approach or structure of plaintiffs' schools.

Plaintiff principals nonetheless argue on appeal, as they did before the district court, that the submission of the form violates their beliefs in the "Headship of Christ" and the separation of church and state. They urge that parental reporting would adequately serve the state's admittedly compelling interest in ensuring its children are receiving an adequate education, and submit that the state should be required to adopt this "least restrictive means." Plaintiff parents and children also assert that the reporting requirements violate their freedom of association, again proposing parental reporting as a "least restrictive means" of obtaining the information sought.

* * *

[W]e have no difficulty upholding the reporting requirements in this case. As the district court determined, the burden on plaintiff principals' religious beliefs—if one exists at all—is very minimal and is clearly outweighed by the states interest in receiving reliable information about where children are being educated and by whom. . . .

* * *

III. Teacher Certification

Plaintiffs also challenge the requirement in Iowa Code § 299.1 that parents of children ages 7 to 16 must send their children to public school or to a private school that utilizes certified teachers until the children complete the eighth grade. Plaintiffs allege the certification requirement violates the free exercise clause, the establishment clause, the due process clause and plaintiff teachers' freedom of expression. Plaintiffs allege these violations stem primarily from the certification requirement's interference with a teacher's calling by God to teach, the supervision of certified teachers by the Iowa Professional Teaching Practices Commission, and the "human relations" course required to obtain or maintain certification. The district court upheld the certification requirement, and plaintiffs have emphasized their free exercise objections to it on appeal, arguing that the administration of achievement tests represents the "least restrictive means" of achieving the state's interest in ensuring a quality education.

A brief outline of the provisions of Iowa law regarding certification may help to place plaintiffs' arguments in their proper context. Because section 299.1 is directed only to parents of compulsory school age children, compliance affects only teachers in grades one through eight. To obtain a certificate to teach, an applicant must have received a bachelor's degree from a recognized institution or must graduate from a nonrecognized institution and have completed not less than three courses in professional education from a recognized institution. Iowa Admin. Code 670–13.1, 13.10 to 13.12. Temporary certificates are available for those who graduate from nonrecognized institutions. *Id.* 670–13.12. In addition, each initial applicant as well as those seeking to renew their certificate must take a human relations course designed to "contribute to the development of sensitivity to and understanding of the values, beliefs, life styles and attitudes of individuals and the diverse groups found in a pluralistic society." *Id.* 670–13.18. The general components of an approved program for an elementary school level teacher include courses in liberal arts, professional education (training in teaching methods), and student teaching. *Id.* 670–15.8, 19.14 to 19.15.

* * *

Plaintiffs argue strenuously on appeal that their religious beliefs cannot be reconciled with the state having any role in the certification or approval of teachers in their schools. They urge that standardized testing be substituted for certification, asserting that many other states do not require certification.

We recognize the sincerity of plaintiffs' beliefs and the burden which they believe the certification requirement imposes upon them. We agree with the Supreme Court of Iowa, however, that plaintiffs' position is "not altogether consistent" on this matter. *Johnson v. Charles City Community Schools Board of Education*, *supra*, 368 N.W.2d at 78. Plaintiffs believe that licensure wrongfully interferes with a teacher's calling by God to teach, yet they apparently do not object to the licensure of those in their church called by God to other occupations, such as doctor or lawyer, nor do they object to obtaining a driver's license for those serving in their bus ministry, even though Pastor Jaspers testified that none of the churches' ministries could properly be regulated by government.[5]

Moreover, while plaintiffs attempt to analogize their situation to that of the Amish in the *Yoder* case, the burden the certification requirement imposes upon the plaintiffs is not nearly as great as the burden placed upon the plaintiffs in *Yoder*. . . .

Unlike the Old Order Amish in *Yoder*, plaintiffs expect and encourage their children to attend college, and have no objection to college-educated teachers per se. The certification requirement applies only to teachers in grades one through eight, and plaintiff schools in fact each employ a teacher who is certified. Iowa's certification process does not prevent teachers in plaintiff schools from teaching from a Biblical perspective nor does it prevent plaintiff schools from hiring only those teachers who meet their religious criteria. . . .

* * *

We agree on the basis of the record in this case that the state has met its burden of demonstrating that testing would not adequately serve its interests. Not only do certified teachers receive training in child development and methods of instruction, but they are also mandatory child abuse reporters and take courses on identifying those children with special needs. All of these qualities, as plaintiffs' own expert witnesses conceded, are desirable characteristics for a good teacher. Admittedly, there is a lack of empirical evidence concerning the relationship between certified teachers and a quality education, due to the difficulty of research on this issue, but there is a similar lack of empirical verification concerning plaintiffs' proposed alternative, and we do not believe such evidence is required in this case. For all of these reasons, we agree with the district court that the state's choice of certification as the best means available today to satisfy its interest in the education of its children does not violate plaintiffs' right to the free exercise of their religion.

* * *

As the district court found, . . . nothing in the certification statute or regulations requires agreement or acceptance of the beliefs or values of others. Plaintiffs' objection to the "human relations" course thus appears to be based solely upon the exposure of college-level students to viewpoints other than their own. . . . Nothing prevents a prospective teacher taking Iowa's human relations course from evaluating others' viewpoints from their own religious perspective. . . . We thus conclude the effect of the "human relations" course neither advances nor inhibits religion.

* * *

IV. Equivalent Instruction

Section 299.1 also provides that the instruction children receive from a certified teacher must be "equivalent" to that offered by the public schools. At the time of trial, the term "equivalent instruction" was not specifically defined anywhere in the Iowa Code or regulations, although the state was in the process of promulgating such regulations. Plaintiffs challenged the "equivalent instruction" requirement on vagueness grounds, and the state argued to the district court, as it does here, that other statutes sufficiently define the term. The district court rejected the state's contention, based upon statements by the Iowa Supreme Court indicating that Court's rejection of them as well. 602 F.Supp. at 317–18; *Johnson v. Charles City Community Schools Board of Education*, *supra*, 368 N.W.2d at 79–80. We agree with the district court's conclusion that the other statutes cited by the state do not cure the vagueness problem inherent in the otherwise undefined term "equivalent instruction."

In large measure as a result of the *Charles City* litigation, however, the state has recently promulgated regulations entitled "Equivalent Instruction Standards," which became effective February 6, 1986. Iowa Admin.Code 670–63.1 to 63.4. These standards specify the minimum curriculum to be offered in grades one through eight, including for example courses in English, mathematics and science. *Id.* The state argues that these regulations have effectively rendered its appeal from the district court's decision moot, but we believe the proper course is to remand this portion of the case to the district court for further consideration in light of the newly adopted standards.

5. Pastor Jaspers stated, for example, that should the church decide to open a nursing home, it too must be free from licensing or other state requirements: "The only answer I have is that I can't see any point where it will be right for the church to be regulated by the government, period."

V. The Amish Exemption

Plaintiffs' final constitutional challenge involves the state's denial of plaintiff parents' request to be exempted from the above requirements through the "Amish exemption," Iowa Code § 299.24.[7] As the district court noted, this exemption has been granted only to parents of children attending Amish schools and one conservative Mennonite school, all of which are located in distinct geographical areas of the state and which follow the style of life and religious tenets described by the Supreme Court in *Yoder*. . . .

Plaintiffs argue before this Court, as they did before the district court and before the Iowa Supreme Court, that this denial violates the equal protection clause. They further contend that granting the exemption to the Amish but not to them violates the establishment clause because the effect is to advance the Amish religion and to inhibit the plaintiffs'.

Because religion is a fundamental right, any classification of religious groups is subject to strict scrutiny. . . . That is, the state must show the classification has been precisely tailored to serve a compelling state interest. . . . Of course, this standard is substantially equivalent to the free exercise standards we have already applied to Iowa's reporting and teacher certification requirements.

* * *

Both the district court and the Iowa Supreme Court recognized that resolving plaintiffs' equal protection challenge required the court to determine whether plaintiffs and the Amish were so similarly situated that the denial of the exemption to the plaintiffs violated the constitution. Both courts analyzed the factors upon which the Supreme Court relied in *Yoder* to create an exemption to Wisconsin's compulsory attendance laws for the Amish who opposed sending their children to high school, and compared plaintiffs' position to that of the Amish. Both courts concluded that plaintiffs were properly denied the exemption. The Iowa Supreme Court stated:

> When the same factors [applied by the Supreme Court in *Yoder*] are placed in balance on this record the opposite conclusion asserts itself. Sincerity of belief is the only factor wholly common to both the Amish and these plaintiffs. The beliefs of the plaintiffs are greatly less interwoven with their daily mode of life. The Amish culture is greatly more isolated from mainstream American life. Plaintiffs' children, for all the distinctive religious convictions they will be given, will live, compete for jobs, work, and move about in a diverse and complex society. Their educational needs are plainly not as circumscribed as those of Amish children. Neither does exposure to the more general American culture pose such an immediate threat to plaintiffs' mode of living as is the case with the Amish.

Johnson v. Charles City Community Schools Board of Education, supra, 368 N.W.2d at 84.

After adopting the state court's reasoning and holding, the district court added the following observations:

> The Court is also conscious of the impact that granting these plaintiffs an exception to the compulsory education requirements could have on public education and the courts. Under *Yoder* and *Johnson* a clear line of demarcation is established that offers guidance to parents, school officials and the courts. A blurring of that line by granting an exception here would create an impossible burden upon all persons and agencies involved to decide whether minor variations of fact one way or the other entitled each individual church school to an exception. The Court is convinced that the Supreme Court intended the exception to be a narrow one.

620 F.Supp at 319. We agree with these observations. . . .

* * *

We also find no establishment clause violation on the facts of this case. As the *Yoder* Court stated, narrow exemptions such as Iowa has adopted successfully traverse the "tight rope" created by the tension between the free exercise clause and the establishment clause. *Wisconsin v. Yoder, supra*, 406 U.S. at 221, 92 S.Ct. at 1536. This narrowly drawn accommodation to one religious view does not re-

7. Iowa Code § 299.24 provides in relevant part: When members or representatives of a local congregation of a recognized church or religious denomination established for ten years or more within the state of Iowa prior to July 1, 1967, which professes principles or tenets that differ substantially from the objectives, goals, and philosophy of education embodied in standards set forth in section 257.25, and rules adopted in implementation thereof, file with the state superintendent of public instruction proof of the existence of such conflicting tenets or principles, together with a list of the names, ages, and post-office addresses of all persons of compulsory school age desiring to be exempted from the compulsory education law and the educational standards law, whose parents or guardians are members of the congregation or religious denomination, the state superintendent, subject to the approval of the state board of public instruction, may exempt the members of the congregation or religious denomination from compliance with any or all requirements of the compulsory education law and the educational standards law. . . .

quire the state, under the establishment clause, to accommodate all others. . . .

* * *

NOTES AND QUESTIONS

1. Yoder *Distinguished?*

Are you persuaded by Judge Larson that the Fellowship Baptist Church is not entitled to relief under Iowa Code Section 299.24, the "Amish exemption?" In *Johnson v. Charles City Community Schools Bd. of Educ.*, 368 N.W.2d 74 (Iowa 1985), relied upon extensively by Judge Larson, dissenting justices of the Iowa Supreme Court took issue with this conclusion:

> The majority finds that plaintiffs do not fall within the section 299.24 exception because they have not shown "that their children's educational needs are significantly different from those of other children." The statute does not address different educational needs, it is aimed at those with different educational goals. Despite the majority's conclusion to the contrary, I believe plaintiffs have established different educational goals. Thus, I believe the administrative decision was arbitrary and capricious, requiring reversal.
>
> Plaintiff's ultimate educational goal is the glorification of God. Everything taught in their school must be taught from the perspective of their religious beliefs, emphasizing the role of God and the church in their lives and in every subject taught. The children are taught to make life decisions . . . by resorting directly to God or God's word. Nowhere in section 257.25 do we find reference to a public education goal of teaching facts permeated with religion and teaching children to rely on God or God's word. . . .
>
> The majority suggest that our statute is aimed at a much smaller target than all parochial schools in the state. Although I would agree with that suggestion, I cannot agree with the implications contained in the majority opinion that places appellants in the same classification as other church groups who choose to provide a religious-oriented education. I perceive from the record that appellants are substantially different in some respects from our other private religious groups. Other parochial schools attempt to cooperate with public regulation of their schools, seeking public financial support and busing as long as the State does not interfere with their teaching of religious doctrines. The appellants, on the other hand, as a part of their ministry, insist that the exclusive right to educate belongs to the church and interpret the Bible to command their educational ministry. They share the conviction that there is no dichotomy between secular truth and sacred truth. Their educational ministry places the minister as the principal teacher. Their religious conviction that any relationship between the church and state is repugnant prevents the minister or any of the teachers from being certified by the state. . . .

Id. at 86 (Justice Schultz, dissenting).

Does Judge Larson or Justice Schultz have the more persuasive position? Does the former's view of the case fail to be sufficiently attentive to the institutional autonomy interest of religious groups? *See* Laycock, "Towards A General Theory of the Religion Clauses: The Case of Church Labor Relations and the Right to Church Autonomy," 81 *Colum. L. Rev.* 1373 (1981). If Justice Schultz is correct on the application of the Free Exercise Clause to the Baptist Fellowship Church, is he also correct in arguing that those principles would not exempt all parochial schools from state regulation? *See generally* Johnson, "Concepts and Compromise in First Amendment Doctrine," 72 *Calif. L. Rev.* 817, 842 (1984). Is a non-Amish child attending an Amish school for religious reasons entitled to an exemption? *See State ex rel. Nagle v. Olin*, 64 Ohio St.2d 341, 415 N.E.2d 279 (1980).

2. *"Equivalent Instruction"*

Is the equivalency of instruction requirement unconstitutionally vague? *See, e.g., Bangor Baptist Church v. Maine*, 549 F.Supp. 1208 (D. Me. 1982); *State v. White*, 109 Wis.2d 64, 325 N.W.2d 76 (App. 1982). *See generally* Lines, *supra* at 211–212. Did Judge Larson err in adopting "a process-oriented approach for assessing educational opportunities rather than a result orientation," i.e., educational testing? Mangrum, "Family Rights and Compulsory School Laws," 21 *Creighton L. Rev.* 1019, 1043 (1988).

3. *Reporting Requirements*

Do you agree that the reporting requirements for private schools place "a very minimal" burden on the plaintiffs' religious beliefs? *See New Life Baptist Church Academy v. Town of East Longmeadow*, 885 F.2d 940 (1st Cir. 1989). Is it the impact on beliefs or the impact on church autonomy that ought to be taken into account? *See* Laycock, *supra*. How can the "*Pierce* compromise" be implemented without reporting requirements on who is being educated and where? Are site visits preferable?

4. Teacher Certification

If "there is a lack of empirical evidence concerning the relationship between certified teachers and quality education," how can the certification requirement for private school teachers be upheld in the face of a free exercise challenge? The court argues that "Iowa's certification process does not prevent teachers in plaintiff schools from teaching from a Biblical perspective nor does it prevent plaintiff schools from hiring only those teachers who meet their religious criteria." *See also Sheridan Road Baptist Church v. Department of Education*, 426 Mich. 462, 396 N.W.2d 373 (1986). Do you agree? Consider these remarks by Professor Laycock:

> Church schools . . . are religious institutions, organized to transmit faith and values to succeeding generations. There can be no more important religious function for an institutional church; the very existence of the church depends on its success. And the employees who must carry out this function are the teachers.
>
> * * *
>
> Not every religious school can or will insist that every teacher actively promote religion. But nearly all will at least require every teacher not to interfere. . . . Thus, even the nonbelieving math teacher has some intrinsically religious responsibilities . . . Churches have strong claims to autonomy with respect to employment of teachers.

Laycock, "Towards A General Theory of the Religion Clauses: The Case of Church Labor Relations and the Right to Church Autonomy," 81 *Colum. L. Rev.* 1373, 1411 (1981). Does a teacher certification requirement impermissibly interfere with a church school's autonomy in selecting employees? Are there less onerous alternatives? Why does the court reject the standardized testing of students as an alternative? *See also New Life Baptist Church Academy v. Town of East Longmeadow*, 885 F.2d 940 (1st Cir. 1989); *Sheridan Road Baptist Church v. Department of Education, supra. See generally* Mangrum, *supra;* Banton, "State Regulation of Private Religious Schools and the State's Interest in Education," 25 *Ariz. L. Rev.* 123, 144–46 (1983).

State of Ohio v. Whisner

47 Ohio St.2d 181, 351 N.E.2d 750 (1976).

Celebrezze, Justice

This cause presents sensitive issues of paramount importance involving the power of the state to impose extensive regulations upon the structure and government of non-public education, and conversely, upon the right of these appellants to freely exercise their professed religious beliefs in the context of providing an education to their children. . . .

At the outset, we recognize that appellants do not facially attack the compulsory school attendance laws of this state as set forth, generally, in R.C. Chapter 3321. We need not now reexamine, therefore, the decision in *Parr v. State* (1927), 117 Ohio St. 23, 157 N.E. 555, upholding the constitutionality of compulsory school attendance in this state.

Nor do the appellants maintain that the state is devoid of all power to promulgate and enforce *reasonable* regulations affecting the operation of non-public schools. Numerous decisions of the Supreme Court of the United States over the years have clearly sounded the death knell with respect to any such assertion.

* * *

Appellants do contend, however, that application of Ohio's compulsory attendance laws as to them, through the medium of the Minimum Standards for Ohio Elementary Schools, prescribed by the State Board of Education pursuant to the express legislative command contained in R.C. 3321.03, infringes upon their free exercise of religion as guaranteed by the First and Fourteenth Amendments to the Constitution of the United States, and by Section 7, Article I of the Ohio Constitution.

With regard to appellants' assertion that the state's "minimum standards," as applied to them, unconstitutionally interfere with their right to freely exercise their professed religious beliefs, both the Court of Appeals and the Court of Common Pleas committed error in failing to accord the requisite judicial deference to the veracity of those beliefs. . . .

However, at this date and time in the history of our nation, it is crystal clear that neither the validity of what a person believes nor the reasons for so believing may be contested by an arm of the government. As stated in *United States v. Ballard* (1944), 322 U.S. 78, 86, . . . "Men may believe what they cannot prove. They may not be put to the proof of their religious doctrines or beliefs. Religious experiences which are as real as life to some may be incomprehensible to others." The applicable test was enunciated in *United States v. Seeger* (1965), 380 U.S. 163, 185, . . . in these words: ". . . that while the 'truth' of a belief is not open to question, there remains the significant question whether it is 'truly held.' This is the threshold question of sincerity which must be resolved in every case. It is, of course, a question of fact."

Based upon the extensive record before us, there can be no doubt but that appellants' religious beliefs are "truly held." Rev. Whisner's testimony clearly reveals that the religion in which he believes is a historical religion consisting of "born-again" Christians, who adhere to a life of separation from worldliness, and who strictly structure their lives upon a subjective interpretation of Biblical language. The uncontradicted testimony of Rev. Whisner, and that of the other defense witnesses, as documented in the foregoing statement of the case, conclusively establishes that these appellants are God-fearing people with an abiding religious conviction that Biblical training is essential to the proper inculcation of spiritual and moral values into their youth at a time when such precepts are most likely to take root—during the formative years of educational growth and physical development. In this regard, appellants' testimony unmistakenly emphasizes their collective dissatisfaction with the form of the education provided by the public schools of this state, and their total religious compulsion that their offspring be educated in the word of God according to their religious scruples. Moreover, the sincerity of appellants' religious beliefs can best be illustrated by the very fact that they were willing to subject themselves to the criminal process of this state in order to vindicate their position. No more need be said concerning the sincerity of appellants' religious beliefs, for, in our view, it has been established beyond peradventure.

* * *

Through the testimony of Rev. Whisner, appellants voiced religious objections to four of the state's denominated "minimum standards." Those standards, and appellants' objections thereto, are set forth herein as follows:

1. EDb-401-02(E)(6)—"A charter shall be granted after an inspection which determines that all standards have been met." (Appellants do not desire a charter, because acceptance of same would constitute their agreement to comply with all standards, and thereby effectively remove their ability to control the direction of the school by reposing vast powers in the hands of the State.)
2. EDb-401-02(G)—"Based on a minimum five-hour school day or one of greater length, the total instructional time allocation per week shall be:

"four-fifths—language arts, mathematics, social studies, science, health, citizenship, related directed study and self-help; optional foreign language.

"one-fifth—directed physical education, music, art, special activities and optional applied arts." (Appellants complain that this standard does not expressly allot time in which Biblical and spiritual training may be given, and, therefore, is inimicable to the fundamental purpose of a religious school in that it severely restricts the ability of the school to incorporate its religious teachings.)
3. EDb-401-02(O)—". . . All activities shall conform to policies adopted by the Board of Education." (The contention is advanced by appellants that this standard virtually provides a blank check to the public authorities to control the entire operation of their school.)
4. EDb-401-07—"Efforts toward providing quality education by the school for the community it serves shall be achieved through cooperation and interaction between the school and the community. The understanding of the roles of each and a flow of information are basic to this relationship. . . ."

* * *

. . . (Appellants maintain that a Christian school cannot seek its direction from the world or from the community it serves.)

In addition, appellants objected, upon religious grounds, to the following statements appearing in the "Interpretation and Explanatory Information" section of the publication containing the "minimum standards":

1. EDb-401-02(J)—"When a pupil transfers, within a school system or moves to a school outside of the school system, pertinent pupil information is forwarded to the principal of the receiving school. Office records of this nature are not released to parents and guardians. . . ." (Appellants contend that it is very important for a parent to be apprised of everything occurring in school relating to his or her child or children.)
2. EDb-401-03(B) (page 30 of the publication)—

"1. Common problems are solved through the consensus of thinking and action of individuals in the group.

"2. Individuals have a responsibility of authentic citizenship as a member of the school, community, state, nation and world.

"3. Citizens have a responsibility for the welfare of others and for being willing to sacrifice for the common good." (Appellants reject the idea the [sic] common problems are solved solely by the group, because they instead adhere to the belief that problems are solved by the group on their knees. In addition, appellants contend that these comments reflect a philosophy of "secular humanism" on the part of the state—a philosophy to which appellants cannot, consistent with their religious beliefs, ascribe.)

3. EDb-401-03(B) (page 48)—"Organized group life of all types must act in accordance with established rules of social relationships and a system of social controls." (Appellants against object to the "humanism" philosophy allegedly espoused herein.)

4. EDb-401-03(B) (page 60)—"The health of the child is perhaps the greatest single factor in the development of a well-rounded personality. No individual is adequately prepared for effective living unless he has a well-functioning body and can make reasonably successful adjustments to his many problems. Both are essential for facilitating learning, promoting personal efficiency, and developing successful social and family living. For these reasons health education is considered an integral part of the total education program. Its place in the curriculum becomes increasingly important as automation, population growth, changing moral standards and values, mounting pressures, and other changes in our society create new or intensify existing health problems." (Appellants contend that although man's standards may change with respect to moral values, God's does not.)

* * *

[A]s required by *Wisconsin v. Yoder*, . . . 406 U.S. 205, at page 220 . . . , we must . . . determine whether "[a] regulation neutral on its face may, in its application, nonetheless offend the constitutional requirement for governmental neutrality . . . [because] it unduly burdens the free exercise of religion." . . .

* * *

To begin with, although admittedly an admirable effort to extol the secular aims of the state in assuring that each child educated in this state obtains a quality education, we believe that these "minimum standards" overstep the boundary of *reasonable* regulation as applied to a non-public religious school.

* * *

We refer, first, to EDb-401-02(G), which allocates instructional time in the comprehensive curriculum required by R.C. 3313.60,[6] almost to the minute. Since R.C. 3313.48[7] requires a minimum school day of five hours, the requirement of EDb-401-02(G) invariably results in further control of the educational policies of a non-public religious school in a manner that we cannot say is compelled by the enabling legislation pursuant to which the "minimum standards" were adopted. R.C. 3313.48 and 3313.60, although requiring a school day of a defined length, and effectively controlling the courses of study taught non-public school children, do not further impede the ability of a religious school to incorporate the tenets of its particular faith into its required courses. We think that EDb-401-02(G) "unduly burdens the free exercise of religion" and interferes "with the rights of conscience,"[10] by requiring a set amount of time to be devoted to subjects which, by their very nature, may not easily lend

6. R.C. 3313.60 provided, in pertinent part, at the time of the trial in this cause:

"Boards of education of county, exempted village, and city school districts shall prescribe a graded course of study for all schools under their control subject to the approval of the state board of education. In such graded courses of study there shall be included the study of the following subjects:

"(A) The language arts, including reading, writing, spelling, oral and written English, and literature;

"(B) Geography, the history of the United States and of Ohio, and national, state and local government in the United States;

"(C) Mathematics;

"(D) Natural science, including instruction in the conservation of natural resources;

"(E) Health and physical education, which shall include instruction in the harmful effects, and legal restrictions against the use of drugs of abuse, alcoholic beverages, and tobacco;

"(F) The fine arts including music;

"(G) First aid, safety and fire prevention;

"Every school shall include in the requirements for promotion from the eighth grade to the ninth grade one year's course of study of American history.

* * *

The amendment to R.C. 3313.60, effective November 28, 1975, substantially changed paragraphs (B) and (E) of the foregoing to include additional curriculum requirements, and also added a separate requirement that physical education be taught.

7. R.C. 3313.48 provides, in pertinent part:

". . . Except as otherwise provided in this section, each day for grades one through six shall consist of not less than five clock hours with pupils in attendance which may include fifteen minute morning and afternoon recess periods, except in such emergency situations, including lack of classroom space, as are approved by the state board of education."

10. Section 7, Article I of the Ohio Constitution. . . .

themselves to the teaching of religious principles (*e.g.*, mathematics). We do not mean to imply that the subjects contained within EDb-401-02(G), or those contained within R.C. 3313.60, are not helpful in preparing non-public, as well as public, school children for the obligations which will eventually arise in the process of maturing into adulthood. We only emphasize that the reasonableness of the requirements contained within "minimum standard" EDb-401-02(G) wanes in the face of an attack premised upon a violation of the constitutional right of appellants to the free exercise of their chosen religion.

Secondly, in our view, EDb-401-02(O), which requires "all activities" of a non-public school to conform to policies adopted by the board of education, plainly violates appellants' right to the free exercise of their religion. If the state is to discharge its duty of remaining strictly neutral, pursuant to the establishment clause of the First Amendment, with respect to religion, how can the state constitutionally require *all activities* of a non-public religious school, which, of necessity, must include *religious activities*, to conform to the policies of a purportedly "neutral" board? . . .

* * *

Finally, EDb-401-07(B), which requires a non-public religious school to cooperate with elements of the community in which it exists, infringes upon the rights of these appellants, consistent with their religious beliefs, to engage in complete, or nearly complete, separation from community affairs. As Rev. Whisner testified, these appellants religiously adhere to the literal Biblical command that they "[b]e not conformed to this world. . . ." Upon the face of the record before us, the state may not require the contrary.

* * *

There is an additional, independent reason, ignored by the lower courts in this case, that compels upholding appellants' attack upon the state's "minimum standards." In our view, these standards are so pervasive and all-encompassing that total compliance with each and every standard by a non-public school would effectively eradicate the distinction between public and non-public education, and thereby deprive these appellants of their traditional interest as parents to direct the upbringing and education of their children. [Citing *Farrington*, *Pierce*, and *Meyer*]

In the opinion of a majority of this court, a "general education of a high quality" can be achieved by means other than the comprehensive regimentation of *all* academic centers in this state. . . .

* * *

Judgment reversed and defendants discharged.

J. J. P. Corrigan, William B. Brown and Paul W. Brown, JJ., concur.

Herbert and Stern, JJ., dissent from the syllabus and opinion, but concur in the judgment. [opinion omitted].

C. William O'Neill, C. J., not participating.

NOTES AND QUESTIONS

1. *Ultra Vires Regulations?*

Consider the Ohio statutes quoted in footnotes 6 and 7 in the court's opinion in *Whisner*. The statutes set forth the core curriculum for private schools and require a minimum of five hours of classroom instruction each day. Do the regulations promulgated by the State Board of Education exceed the requirements set forth in the statute? Are they ultra vires? What does the court mean when it states that the regulations set forth policies that are not "compelled by the enabling legislation"? Note that the regulations divide up the day into four-fifths of the day for the traditionally "academic" subjects and one-fifth of the day for physical education, music, art, and so on. Further, the regulations declare that these proportions apply to "a minimum five-hour school day *or one of greater length*" (emphasis added).

Does this suggest that the legislature left private school officials free to teach what they please beyond the minimum of five hours a day of mandated instruction while the State Board of Education did not permit this option? Does this analysis suggest that the court need not have reached the question of whether the minimum standards violate the free exercise of religion clause or that the same decision could have been reached by means of statutory construction? Is this line of analysis implicit in the objection to EDb-401-02(E)(6) in that the vague charter requirement reposes "vast powers in the hands of the state"? *But see* Comment, "Separation of Church and State: Education and Religion in Kentucky," 6 *N. Ky. L. Rev.* 125, 150–51 (1978). After *Whisner*, the State Board did not alter its regulations, and this led to a second challenge to those regulations. *State ex rel. Nagle v. Olin*, 415 N.E.2d 279 (Ohio 1980) (state minimum standards violate free exercise of religion). *See generally* Carper, "The *Whisner* Decision: A Case Study in State Regulation of Christian Day Schools," 24 *J. Church & St.* 281 (1982).

2. *Interference with Free Exercise of Religion*

In what manner do the statutes and regulations relating to private schools in Ohio infringe upon the religious rights of parents who send their children to private religious schools? *See generally* Bainton, "State Regulation of Private Religious Schools and the State's Interest in Education," 25 *Ariz. L. Rev.* 123, 134–139 (1983). Does the conclusion follow only if they are construed so as not to permit substantial religious instruction and activities beyond the minimum five hours a day of mandated instruction? Suppose the religious schools were permitted to offer seven hours of instruction each day and only five hours were stipulated by the state for specific subjects. Would this render the scheme constitutional? Is there a point at which the school day becomes so long to accommodate the minimum state curriculum and the religious orientation of the private school that the minimum itself would violate the free exercise clause?

What of the provision that "all activities shall conform to policies adopted by the board of education"? Is this clearly unconstitutional? Do you think that the provision was addressed to religious instruction and ritual? What saving construction might be given it?

Is the requirement of cooperation and interaction between the school and community anything more than hortatory? Could *community* be defined as "religious community"? Is the objection to the withholding of student records from parents an objection rooted in plaintiffs' religious beliefs?

Does the court articulate a standard to decide when state regulation of private schools intrudes upon religious belief too deeply? *See generally* Comment, "Regulation of Fundamentalist Christian Schools: Free Exercise of Religion v. The State's Interest in Quality Education," 67 *Ky. L. J.* 415 (1978–79). Is not the objection to "secular humanism" really an objection to the *Pierce* compromise? That is, if the court were to accept this objection (it did not reach it), what demands can the state constitutionally make of private, religious schools? How does *Yoder* resolve this issue? Why does the reasonableness of the state minima wane "in the face of an attack premised upon a violation of the constitutional rights of appellants to the free exercise of their chosen religion"? If Ohio's standards are presently too "pervasive and all-encompassing," what standards would pass constitutional muster? Is *Whisner* a case in which it is clear that the state sought to abolish the distinction "between public and non-public education"?

3. *Rights of Parents*

To what extent is the *Whisner* decision grounded in the rights of parents as they are thought to be embodied in *Pierce*, *Meyer*, and *Farrington*? Do those cases even begin to articulate a standard that should be applied in the context of *Whisner*? Suppose that *Whisner* had been brought by parents whose beliefs were not rooted in religion. *See State v. Kasuboski*, 275 N.W.2d 101 (Wis. Ct. App. 1978). Would the result have been the same? *See generally* Bainton, *supra*.

4. Kentucky State Board v. Rudasill

In *Kentucky State Board v. Rudasill*, 589 S.W.2d 877 (Ky. 1979), *cert. denied*, 446 U.S. 938, 100 S.Ct. 2158, 64 L.Ed.2d 792 (1980), plaintiffs successfully attacked the Kentucky rules governing private education under the free exercise clause of the Kentucky constitution. *See* Ky. Const. §5 (1891) ("No human authority shall, in any case whatever, control or interfere with the rights of conscience"). *See generally* S. Arons, *Compelling Belief* ch. 15 (1983); Comment, "Regulation of Fundamentalist Christian Schools: Free Exercise of Religion v. The State's Interest in Quality Education," 67 *Ky. L. J.* 415 (1979); Comment, "Separation of Church and State: Education and Religion in Kentucky," 6 *N. Ky. L. Rev.* 125 (1979). The objections focused, *inter alia*, on the following statutory and regulatory provisions: (1) instruction must be in the English language; (2) instruction must be offered "in the several branches of study required to be taught in the public schools"; (3) private schools may not operate for a term shorter than the public school term; (4) private schoolteachers must have a bachelor's degree in any subject; (5) textbooks must be approved by the state; (6) private and parochial schools must be accredited under state accreditation standards.

The plaintiff schools argued that few teachers who met the religious standards of the school were available and that the schools could not afford to hire teachers with college degrees. 67 *Ky. L. J.* at 422. Further, they asserted that "[S]ome of the approved texts omitted materials which their religion required them to teach, while others included material to which they were religiously opposed." *Id.* at 423. The state responded that the schools need not teach the objectionable material and that omissions could be cured by employing unapproved, supplemental texts (presumably at private and not public expense). With regard to curriculum, the required curriculum, unlike that in *State v. Whisner, supra,* left "plenty of time for religious schools to teach whatever they desire." *Id.* at 424. Plaintiffs then framed their objections in terms of the need to teach religious doctrines in the core curriculum, not limiting themselves to separate classes in religion. In the light of *Whisner,* are these rules governing private schools constitutional? *See* 6 *N. Ky. L. Rev.* at 144–49. Are rules governing health, fire, and safety in private schools distinguishable? Would a statute requiring that private religious schools administer competency tests and report the results to a state agency be constitutional? *See* 6 *N. Ky. L. Rev.* at 147–48; 67 *Ky. L. J.* at 427–29. What if students in private schools were required to pass examinations not required of public school students? *Cf. Lupert v. California State Bar,* 761 F.2d 1325 (9th Cir. 1985). *See generally* Bainton, *supra* at 144–146.

City of Sumner v. First Baptist Church of Sumner

97 Wash.2d 1, 639 P.2d 1358 (1982) (en banc).

Hicks, Justice.

This cause, certified here by the Court of Appeals, presents a conflict between the power of the state to require conformance to zoning and building code regulations on the part of a private, church-operated school, and conversely, upon the right of members of the appellant church to freely exercise their professed religious beliefs by providing Christian education for their children.

* * *

The First Baptist Church has been located at its present site in a residential section of the City of Sumner for the past 75 years. For much of that time it has operated a vacation Bible school in the church building.

Adult members of the church congregation believe their children should be educated in conformance with biblical standards and philosophies. It is asserted that a tenet of their faith and belief requires this as a convictional matter. Because the instruction their children receive in the public schools cannot comport with their belief, in September 1978, the church membership established the Washington Christian Academy which purports to offer an educational program structured to conform with scriptural principles.

The academy is claimed to be an integral and inseparable part of the educational ministry of the First Baptist Church of Sumner. At oral argument here, respondent City's counsel conceded appellants' ability to prove both the claimed tenet of faith and belief and that the school was an integral part of the educational ministry of the church, if the case was remanded for the purpose of taking evidence on those issues.

This church-operated school is housed in the basement of the church building which does not meet, for use as a school, the City of Sumner's building code and zoning ordinance. The City's building inspector, who is also its fire chief, declared that the church building, particularly the basement, failed to meet the City's building code safety standards applicable to structures used for educational purposes. The building had, however, previously passed inspection for use as a church. The City sought to enjoin use of the edifice for the church-operated school.

A limited attempt by the church was made to bring the basement into compliance with City requirements. Several safety precautions were undertaken and appellants claim a number of the purported violations noted by the City's inspector are highly technical and do not in any way endanger occupants of the building. Financial constraints, however, make unlikely any early implementation of the major structural and mechanical modifications required for full compliance with the City's demands.

* * *

I.

Under the circumstances presented here, a majority of the court believes this case raises a conflict between the fundamental rights of the congregation of the First Baptist Church of Sumner and the police power of the City of Sumner.

The congregants' right to send their children to a church-operated school is protected as a fundamental right under the United States Constitution. *Pierce v. Society of Sisters*, 268 U.S. 510, 45 S.Ct. 571, 69 L.Ed. 1070 (1925); *State v. Whisner*, 47 Ohio St.2d 181, 351 N.E.2d 750 (1976). The free exercise clause is violated by burdensome state regulation. *See generally* Bird, "Freedom From Establishment and Unneutrality in Public School Instruction and Religious School Regulation," 2 *Harv.J.L. & Pub. Pol'y* 125, 188–195 (1979). The City's police power derives from the state and its inherent power to govern. *Spokane v. J-R Distribs., Inc.*, 90 Wash.2d 722, 585 P.2d 784 (1978), and cases cited therein.

Basically, the City here attempts an evenhanded application of a regulation concerning a valid governmental interest. It may be granted that such apparent evenhanded enforcement will not *directly* adversely impact religious beliefs or prohibit religious exercise. The *indirect* effect, however, of the government regulation in this instance will profoundly impact the church and its members. This parallels *Wisconsin v. Yoder*, 406 U.S. 205 . . . (1972), and *Thomas v. Review Bd.*, 450 U.S. 707 . . . (1981), wherein it was stated:

> A regulation neutral on its face may, in its application, nonetheless offend the constitutional requirement for governmental neutrality if it unduly burdens the free exercise of religion.

Yoder, 406 U.S. at 220; . . . *Thomas*, 450 U.S. at 717. . . .

* * *

It is argued that because the regulation here involved does not impact directly a fundamental tenet of the church, it does not violate a member's First Amendment rights. Direct impact, however, has never been a requirement. It was not against a fundamental tenet of the Amish to send their children to high school; it was the incidental effects of that requirement the Amish believed to be detrimental to their faith and hence violative of their First Amendment rights. *Wisconsin v. Yoder, supra.* It was not a fundamental tenet of the Catholic faith that unionization of teachers be disallowed; yet the Supreme Court indicated that for the National Labor Relations Board to become involved regarding parochial schoolteachers could pose a significant risk of infringement on the free exercise of religion. *NLRB v. Catholic Bishop of Chicago*, 440 U.S. 490 . . . (1979).

It was not a fundamental tenet of "born again" Christians to not allow teaching of basic education 4 hours each day; yet the pernicious though incidental effect of allowing state regulation regarding mandatory subjects and allocation of classroom time has been held to violate the free exercise clause as to that religious group. *State v. Whisner, supra.* Neither is it a fundamental tenet to employ substandard teachers in a parochial school; yet it has been held that a state cannot require nonpublic schoolteachers to have "essentially equivalent" qualifications to those in public schools. *State v. LaBarge*, 134 Vt. 276, 357 A.2d 121 (1976).

So in this case, although there is no fundamental tenet against compliance with building codes or zoning ordinances, the practical effect of their uncompromising enforcement would be to close down the church-operated school. This would deny to church members the right to guide the education of their children by sending them to their church-operated school, a fundamental and constitutionally protected right. . . .

* * *

. . . [S]uch regulations will be enforced against religious schools when the state proves that the specific concerns addressed by the regulations are of sufficient magnitude to outweigh the free exercise claim, that the nonapplication of the regulations will threaten the public's health or other vital interests, and that the state's interest could not otherwise be satisfied in a way which would not infringe on religious liberty. *State v. Whisner*, 47 Ohio St.2d 181, 351 N.E.2d 750 (1976). This test ferrets out those facially neutral regulations that have an unnecessarily debilitating effect on religion.

From the record before us, it cannot be determined whether the City used the least restrictive means of achieving its compelling interest. We assume the compelling state interest in this instance is the safety of the children. The City did not develop that issue in the trial record, and the trial court did not require it to do so. The City established only that it had a building code and a zoning ordinance with which the church had not complied.

The record on appeal is, as are the trial court's findings of fact, substantially devoted to detailing code deficiencies in the church basement. That alone does not support the trial court's injunctive order.

This case concerns more than the mere routine application of a building code and a zoning ordinance.

* * *

[Parts II and III of the opinion are omitted.]

The contempt citation is vacated, the injunction dissolved, and the case is remanded for further proceedings not inconsistent with this opinion.

The foregoing opinion was prepared by Justice Floyd V. Hicks while a member of this court. It is adopted by the undersigned as the opinion of this court.

Brachtenbach, C. J., and Stafford and Dimmick, JJ., concur.

Utter, Justice (concurring).

I concur with the views stated by the majority. The parameters within which government may control religion are narrow and circumscribed by U.S.Const. amend. I and Const. art. 1, § 11.[1] Government may, under some circumstances, intervene when religious schools fail, as they allegedly did here, to meet minimum safety standards.

* * *

[Concurring opinions of Justices Williams and Dore omitted.]

Dolliver, Justice (dissenting).

This is a case which deals with the location of a parochial school and the safety of children attending that school. Because the school is operated by defendants, it has been characterized by defendants and transformed by the majority into a "freedom of religion" case under the First Amendment.

* * *

The position of the majority is that zoning regulations and building codes cannot be enforced against a litigant who claims a First Amendment right of religion unless the governmental agency can demonstrate:

> (1) a compelling governmental interest; (2) that the governmental interest outweighs appellants' First Amendment rights; (3) that the means chosen to effectuate that interest will accomplish it; and (4) that the end sought cannot be achieved by less restrictive measures.

The sweep of the majority position is breathtaking and as nearly as I have been able to determine utterly without precedent. Certainly none is cited by the majority. The cases brought to the attention of the court by defendants or cited by the majority have not the slightest reference to the position taken here. *See Kentucky State Bd. for Elementary and Secondary Educ. v. Rudasill,* 589 S.W.2d 877, 879 (Ky. 1979); Bird, "Freedom From Establishment and Unneutrality in Public School Instruction and Religious School Regulation," 2 *Harv.J. of Law and Public Policy* 125, 194 (1979).

* * *

The evidence demonstrates and the trial court found that among the numerous inadequacies of the building for use as a school are: inadequate floor space, inadequate ventilation, no approved fire alarm system, no fire extinguishers, no fire detectors, no sprinkler system, no fire-retardant walls and ceilings, no lighted exit signs, no exit signs at all, stairs that are too narrow, doors that do not open out, and stairs of inconsistent rise and run. In addition to these violations which constitute a safety hazard, there are health code violations such as inadequate restroom facilities.

The attempt by the majority to view this case as analogous to *Wisconsin v. Yoder,* 406 U.S. 205 . . . (1972), and *Thomas v. Review Bd. of Indiana Employment Sec. Div.,* 450 U.S. 707 . . . 624 (1981), is to my mind less than persuasive. In both *Yoder* and *Thorac,* the plaintiffs were left with no choice. There was no way in which the demands of the state—compulsory education to age 16 and work at a job which violated religious beliefs—could be met without a violation of a religious tenet. No such violation exists here. No bar of any kind has been raised against defendant establishing and conducting a religious school.

The majority claims "the practical effect of [the] uncompromising enforcement [of the health and safety codes] would be to close down the church-operated school." Majority opinion, at 1362. That is certainly one alternative which defendant may follow if it so chooses. The other alternative is to make the required changes to come in compliance with the code, *i.e.,* for the defendant to see to it that the children attending its school have the same fire and safety protection as other schoolchildren in the state. Before the trial court defendant made nei-

1. U.S. Const. amend. 1 provides that "Congress shall make no law respecting an establishment of religion, or prohibiting the free exercise thereof. . . ." Const. art. I, § 11 states that "no one shall be molested or disturbed in person or property on account of religion. . . ."

ther a suggestion nor a showing this could not be done.

It may be that the correction of these deficiencies would cost a substantial sum and would be a burden on the defendants. Rather than attempting to make the appropriate changes in the building, however, or to work with the city authorities to see if there is some "play in the joints," the defendants choose to assert financial inability, raise the banner of the First Amendment, and claim a violation of religious liberty. Children in a school need the protection of fire and safety codes. That they burn and hurt like anybody else and that they need to be protected does not suddenly become less just because a church is operating the school and the protections of the First Amendment are asserted. The great right of freedom of religion should not be mocked.

* * *

I would affirm the trial court and, thus, I dissent.

Rosellini, Justice (concurring in the dissent of Dolliver, J.).

NOTES AND QUESTIONS

1. **Sumner *and* Yoder**

Do you agree that *Yoder* should control the result in *Sumner*? Is compliance with the building code and fire regulations an infringement of the religious beliefs of the parents in *Sumner*? Is this akin to the modern high school in *Yoder*? Is the parents' argument that fire extinguishers violate their religious beliefs or is it that the burdens of complying with various safety and health regulations may drive the church school out of business? Should the same standard apply to state rules that undermine the autonomy of religious schools as is applied to rules that violate the beliefs of the congregants? *See* Laycock, "Towards A General Theory of the Religion Clauses: The Case of Church Labor Relations and the Right to Church Autonomy," 81 *Colum. L. Rev.* 1373 (1981). Is it generally unconstitutional to place a substantial (significant?) economic burden on religious schools? How should the line be drawn? *See Employment Division, Department of Human Resources v. Smith,* ___ U.S. ___ , 110 S.Ct. 1595, ___ L.Ed. ___ (1990). If the line cannot be drawn, what is left of the *Pierce* compromise?

2. Understanding **Sumner**

For what purpose does the court remand the case? Can *Sumner* be read as simply requiring the examination of less onerous alternatives? *Cf. McCurry v. Tesch*, 738 F.2d 271 (8th Cir. 1984). What standard should be employed in determining whether an alternative is less onerous? How much less costly must the alternative be? How much risk of health and safety injury to the children is tolerable?

3. Zoning

Suppose a local zoning ordinance forbids a church from establishing a church school, on its premises, in a residential neighborhood. The city argues that a church school in such a neighborhood would disturb the peace of the neighborhood, increasing traffic and noise levels. The church asserts that it has a First Amendment right to establish a religious school on its premises. What result? *See City of Las Cruces v. Huerta*, 102 N.M. 182, 692 P.2d 1331 (App. 1984). Would you distinguish between the regulatory burdens of zoning and the cost of compliance with health and safety codes? Do both undermine the institutional autonomy of church schools?

IV. HOME EDUCATION

The rise of the common school more than a century ago reflected, at least in part, a belief that parentally directed education was too haphazard an enterprise to guarantee educational quality and to ensure that children became productive and literate citizens. Most states, however, allow the child's formal education to take place in the home, though they usually impose specific conditions. *See generally* Sacken, "Regulating Nonpublic Education: A Search for Just Law and Home Policy," 96 *Amer.J.of Educ.* 394, 397 (1988); Lines, "An Overview of Home Instruction," *Phi Delta Kappan* 510 (March, 1987). Many parents, however, have objected to state regulation of home schooling, and this has resulted in numerous controversies and lawsuits. *See* Shepherd, "Home Schooling: Dimensions of Controversy, 1970–1984," 31 *J. of Church and State* 101 (1989). The excerpt below from an article by Alfie Kohn sets forth the framework of the national debate over home education. It is followed by three cases that examine the major legal issues that have arisen in the context.

"Home Schooling"

Alfie Kohn, *The Atlantic* 20–25 (April, 1988). Reprinted by permission.

Those who choose to educate their own children fall, roughly speaking, into two camps, each with its own ideology, newsletter, and nearly legendary standard-bearer. Holt Associates, founded by the late education critic John Holt, in Boston, is heir to the alternative-school movement. Those who receive the bi-monthly *Growing Without Schooling*, which still features reminiscences about Holt and scraps of prose by him, are likely to be skeptical of institutions. The group's libertarian inclinations are tempered by a mostly secular New Age progressivism. . . .

What Holt is to the Growers, Ray Moore is to the fundamentalist-Christian home-schoolers, who find public education unfit by virtue of its godlessness. Where Holt talks of trusting children to learn without adult interference, Moore emphasizes the importance of family values, which he believes are endangered by a socialistic state. Moore's Hewitt Research Foundation and curriculum supply center, in Washougal, Washington, puts out *The Parent Educator and Family Report*, which, like its secular New England counterpart, is filled with letters from readers. Its tone is decidedly different, though. "Are all public schools bad?" Moore asks rhetorically in one recent issue. "Hardly. Some are headed and staffed by consecrated Christians."

Partly because some home-schoolers try to lie low to avoid facing truancy charges, and partly because the movement is by its nature decentralized, no one can say with any certainty how many parents are now teaching their own children. . . .

A . . . reasonable guess comes from Patricia Lines, . . . an acknowledged expert on the subject. In a 1985–1986 survey she counted about 50,000 subscribers to various curriculum services that provide home-schoolers with teaching materials. If one assumes that this represents something like a quarter of all those learning at home . . ., which comports with the results of a poll taken by the Home School Legal Defense Association . . . then the result is a current estimate of between 200,000 and 300,000.

. . .

The estimation process is complicated by a high turnover rate. A private survey conducted in Washington state found that two thirds of all home-schooled children had been in that situation for two years or less, while a Florida survey found that only 30 percent of the students learning at home had done so during the previous year. Theoretically, such figures could simply reflect a new surge of popularity for home schooling, but the evidence available, most of it anecdotal, suggests that an interest in the practice is often short-lived. "The national average is that home-schoolers last one year," says James Prichard . . . "They find out it's not what the parents thought it was, or the parents must go back to work or something."

Bearing the sole responsibility for educating one's children—answering their questions, monitoring their progress, boning up on a range of subjects, finding appropriate texts, planning the lessons every day—can be daunting. For a working parent, it is obviously impractical; for anyone, it is likely to be more difficult than it appears. For every home-schooled child there are approximately twenty in private schools and 160 in public schools. Moreover, hardly anyone imagines that the practice will ever constitute a real threat to the jobs of professional educators.

The difficulties notwithstanding, an apparently growing number of parents keep at it. A handful of private and state-sponsored studies done in recent years offer some information about who home-schoolers are. They are far more numerous in the West and South than elsewhere. The typical home-school family is middle-class and white, and at least one of the parents has some college education. In something like nine out of ten such households the mother does most of the teaching. Boys and girls are equally likely to be taught at home.

* * *

Though many home-schoolers are disenchanted with what conventional classroom teaching offers, the members of the two camps disagree about the source of the problem. Holtians are likely to complain about rigid, autocratic, standardized procedures and a lack of opportunity for questioning and hands-on learning. Ray Moore, in contrast, speaks of parents who are "sick and tired of the teaching of evolution in the school as a cut-and-dried fact," along with other evidence of so-called secular humanism. These parents want more structure, not less. . . .

* * *

As for broader indicators of the success of home

schooling, controlled studies on achievement are in short supply. . . .

The few hard numbers that do exist—virtually all of them collected in the past few years—are uniformly positive. Studies conducted by the Departments of Education in Alaska, Washington, and Tennessee indicate that the average home-schooled student outperforms his or her traditionally schooled counterpart across the board. . . .

. . . Jon Wartes . . . sorted through the Stanford Achievement scores of all home-schooled students in the western part of the state who had taken the test in 1986, and compared those scores with national norms. With the single exception of first graders' performance in math, where home-schooled children scored in the forty-ninth percentile, those who were taught by their parents were above the 50 percent mark at every grade level and in every subject. In reading the median score of home-schooled children was at the sixty-seventh percentile, in listening-comprehension skills at the seventy-sixth. "One could speculate that home-schoolers as a group are very nurturing, caring parents," Wartes says. "Perhaps [their children] spent a lot of time being read to on their parents' laps."

Critics of home schooling are concerned about more than academic achievement, however. They fear for the social development of children deprived of the company of their peers. David Johnson, a social psychologist who teaches at the University of Minnesota, has found that children in competitive classrooms have lower self-esteem than those who learn cooperatively but that those who learn individually are in the worse shape of all. "Any kid who's isolated is in real danger," Johnson says. He pronounces home schooling a "bad idea," because it takes children away from their peer group. . . .

To this criticism home-schooling proponents have two standard responses. First, they insist that the reality of a child's social life at school is, if anything, a good argument *for* home schooling. The conservative Christians talk about the importance of being socialized by family members rather than by undesirables in the school yard. . . . Holt, in his book, *Teach Your Own*, offers a different version of the same argument: "In all but a very few of the schools I have taught in, visited, or know anything about, the social life of the children is mean-spirited, competitive, exclusive, status-seeking, snobbish . . . ."

Second, the home-schoolers reply that their children are not social isolates; they interact regularly with other children in extracurricular and recreational activities. . . .

The only research on nonachievement variables, conducted by John Wesley Taylor V in 1986, found that half of a random sample of 224 home-schooled children scored at or above the ninety-first percentile on the Piers-Harris Children's Self-Concept Scale, a psychological test that measures self-esteem, while only 10 percent were below the national average.

In place of straightforward nationwide guidelines, parents who seek permission to teach their children at home face a bewildering array of state laws, district standards, and contradictory court decisions. Home schooling is not absolutely illegal anywhere in the country, and many states have enacted legislation over the past few years that has made the practice easier to pursue legally. In Missouri a parent who files a notice of intent essentially cannot be refused permission. In North Dakota, Iowa, and Michigan, in contrast, only certified teachers can be home-schoolers. Other states require children to pass standardized achievement tests or receive instruction comparable to that in public schools. In some states home schooling is permissible if one goes through the formality of declaring one's home to be a private school.

* * *

While judges in at least five states have over the past few years cited the vagueness of home-schooling laws as grounds for striking them down, litigation on the issue has, if anything, compounded the confusion. Home-schooling advocates like to cite the 1972 Supreme Court decision *Wisconsin v. Yoder*, which allowed a religious exception to compulsory schooling after eighth grade for the Amish, but the high court has never ruled on home schooling per se. Most school districts that threaten to sue parents over the issue end up resolving the case out of court, though the record is mixed for those cases that do go before a judge. . . .

* * *

Despite the courtroom battles in which home-schoolers and their advocates often find themselves, they face no organized national opposition. Responses from the educational establishment range from indifference to low-key wariness. The idea itself is unobjectionable, educators frequently argue, but not all parents can be trusted to teach their children adequately. The right of parents to yank their kids out of school must be weighed against the state's obligation to make sure that those children are really learning something.

Care and Protection of Charles

399 Mass. 324, 504 N.E.2d 592 (1987).

Before Hennessey, C.J., and Wilkins, Nolan, Lynch and O'Connor, JJ.

Hennessey, Chief Justice.

This case concerns the education of children at home by their parents. . . . Due to religious convictions, the parents desired to educate their three children, ages eleven, eight, and six, at home during the 1985–1986 school year.[1] Although the parents instructed their children in their "home school," the school committee of Canton, on October 15, 1985, initiated truancy proceedings in Stoughton District Court, asserting a violation of G.L. c. 76, § 2. On October 16, 1985, a petition for care and protection of the children under G.L. c. 119, § 24, was filed by an attorney for the town, alleging that the three children were "without necessary and proper educational care and discipline" and that their parents were "unwilling and unable or unavailable to provide such care." At a hearing on October 25, the criminal complaints under G.L. c. 76, § 2, were dismissed. . . . On May 13, 1986, the judge issued his "findings and order," which determined that the children were in need of care and protection within the meaning of G.L. c. 119 with respect to their educational care only and ordered that the children "commence public or approved school attendance forthwith," although the children were allowed to remain in the physical and legal custody of their parents. The parents appealed this order to the Appeals Court. The judge stayed his order pending appeal. We transferred the case to this court on our own motion.

This case presents us with the question of accommodating the parents' rights under the Constitution of the United States and the Massachusetts Constitution with the governmental interest in the education of its citizens. For reasons which appear in the conclusion to this opinion, we direct that the judge's order be vacated and that the case be remanded to the lower court for further proceedings.

We summarize the relevant facts. . . . On August 21, 1985, the children's mother telephoned Dr. James C. Lynch, assistant superintendent of the Canton public schools, informing him that she and her husband intended to educate their three children at home during the 1985–1986 school year. This telephone call was followed by a letter dated September 1, 1985, which stated that: "[a]s christian parents, we are committed to introducing our children to and nurturing them in the truths of the Bible. . . . Our decision to home-school is based on the conviction that what [our children] need most is exposure to us, their parents, and a family whose foundation is the Word of God."

A meeting was held on September 4 with the parents and Drs. Lynch and Peter S. Capernaros, the superintendent of the Canton schools. At this meeting, the parents explained that they would be using a curriculum, which had yet to arrive, that was customary in "Christian Schools." In addition, they stated that the children would be involved in community activities such as gymnastics and soccer. Doctors Lynch and Capernaros determined that, although neither parent was certified to teach or had a college degree, each parent had a high school education[2] and the children's father had taken courses at the college level.

The parents attended the evening meeting of the Canton school committee on September 19 and were permitted to present their proposal in an executive session. The parents emphasized the superiority of their proposed "tutorial system" compared to the education received in public school classrooms. They stated that, although the curriculum materials still had not arrived, the curriculum would be individualized to meet each child's needs. Furthermore, they stated that they would be their children's only instructors and that the children's mother would be the primary instructor. School committee members expressed their concern about certain aspects of the

---

1. Two of the children attended Canton's Kennedy elementary School during the 1984–1985 school year; however, none of the three children named in this petition attended public school during the 1985–1986 school year. The name assigned to this case is fictitious.

2. At a subsequent school committee meeting held on September 19, the children's mother admitted that she had not graduated from high school but had only completed the eleventh grade. She subsequently obtained her high school equivalency certificate while this case was pending.

parents' proposal, including the parents' objection to school department's testing and evaluation of their children's progress. . . .

On October 2, the children's father met with Drs. Lynch and Capernaros. At this meeting, he refused, for fear of prejudice, to document his educational background and that of his wife. He also stated his unwillingness to provide the administration with the number of hours and days that would be devoted to instruction of his children and his opposition to visits by school department personnel to his home for observation of the program. He did indicate his willingness to provide the administration with copies of the table of contents of the curriculum materials when they arrived and his preference for using a particular standardized test . . . .

Although invited, the parents declined to attend the October 3 meeting of the school committee, stating that they had no additional information for the committee. The committee instructed the school superintendent to send the parents a letter informing them that their consent to the stipulations of a proposed memorandum of agreement would facilitate the committee's consideration of their proposal. On October 16, the parents returned an edited version of the agreement, unsigned, indicating the stipulations that they found unacceptable.

At the November 14 meeting of the school committee, to which the parents were invited but again declined to attend,[3] the members voted to accept the recommendation of the school superintendent to deny the parents permission to educate their children at home. The parents were informed of this vote by letter dated November 19. The letter included a memorandum which outlined the following three major objections to the parents' proposal. First, the superintendent had not been given reason to believe that the parents were competent to teach their children. Second, the parents had indicated that the children would spend less time on formal instruction than would children in public schools. Third, the parents objected to the school's efforts to monitor or observe the instructional methods used in the home school and periodically to test the children to determine whether they were making reasonable progress in their education. The superintendent indicated that, in his judgment, allowing the parents to educate their children "would be denying those children a proper education, by any reasonable standards."

* * *

The parents . . . argue that G.L. c. 76, § 1, is constitutionally deficient due to vagueness because it fails to provide any standards for the approval of a home school proposal or to provide a procedure through which this determination is to be made. The parents couple this argument with a claim that G.L. c. 76, § 1, is an unlawful delegation of legislative power to the superintendent and school committee. We have stated that the "constitutional claims of 'void for vagueness' and unlawful delegation of legislative authority are closely related. The principal question posed by both claims is whether the statute is so vague 'that men of common intelligence must necessarily guess at its meaning and differ as to its application.' . . ." *Board of Appeals of Hanover v. Housing Appeals Comm. in the Dep't of Community Affairs,* 363 Mass. 339, 363, 294 N.E.2d 393 (1973). . . . Under this standard, we conclude that G.L. c. 76, § 1, is neither void for vagueness nor an unlawful delegation of legislative authority.

. . . The purpose of G.L. c. 76, § 1, is to ensure that "all the children shall be educated. . . ." *Commonwealth v. Roberts,* 159 Mass. 372, 374, 34 N.E. 402 (1893) (interpreting a predecessor statute). In order to effectuate this purpose, the Legislature has provided a comprehensive statutory scheme setting the standards for the education of the State's youth. This statutory scheme includes standards under G.L. c. 71, §§ 1, 2, and 3, concerning the subjects that must be taught in public schools and the requirements for teacher qualification.[7] Furthermore, G.L. c. 76, § 1, specifically provides that: "For the pur-

3. The parents were represented at the meeting by counsel who addressed the committee.

7. General Laws c. 71, § 1 (1984 ed.), provides in relevant part: "Such schools shall be taught by teachers of competent ability and good morals, and shall give instruction and training in orthography, reading, writing, the English language and grammar, geography, arithmetic, drawing, music, the history and constitution of the United States, the duties of citizenship, health education, physical education and good behavior."

General Laws c. 71, § 2 (1984 ed.), provides that: "In all public elementary and high schools American history and civics, including the constitution of the United States, the declaration of independence and the bill of rights, and in all public schools the constitution of the Commonwealth and local history and government, shall be taught as required subjects for the purpose of promoting civic service and a greater knowledge thereof, and of fitting the pupils, morally and intellectually, for the duties of citizenship."

General Laws c. 71, § 3 (1984 ed.), provides, in relevant part, that: "Physical education shall be taught as a required subject in all grades for all students in the public schools for the purpose of promoting the physical well-being of such students."

poses of this section, school committees shall approve a private school when satisfied that the instruction in all the studies required by law equals in thoroughness and efficiency, and in the progress made therein, that in the public schools in the same town; but shall not withhold such approval on account of religious teaching. . . ." Our reading of this statute indicates that the Legislature intended that the approval of a home school proposal fall within the above enunciated standard for the approval of a private school. . . .

General Laws c. 76, § 1, also does not fail under the Federal standard of vagueness articulated in *Hoffman Estates v. Flipside, Hoffman Estates, Inc.*, 455 U.S. 489, 498–499, 102 S.Ct. 1186, 1193, 71 L.Ed.2d 362 (1982). . . . Furthermore, the Supreme Court indicated that the most important factor in this determination is whether the law "threatens to inhibit the exercise of constitutionally protected rights." *Id.* at 499, 102 S.Ct. at 1193. General Laws c. 76, § 1, specifically forbids the school committee from withholding approval of private schools "on account of religious teaching." Because we conclude that this legislative policy extends to home school proposals, no constitutionally protected right is implicated.

With regard to the claim that G.L. c. 76, § 1, constitutes an unlawful delegation of legislative authority, we also note that "[t]he Legislature may delegate to a board or officer the working out of the details of a policy adopted by the Legislature." . . . Although school committees do exercise broad discretion in the performance of their duties, it is not unbridled. Again, the substantial body of statutory law described above sets bounds under which the committees must act. Consequently, G.L. c. 76, § 1, does not fail as an unlawful delegation of legislative authority.

We have no doubt that the statute is constitutional. If there were any lingering doubt on this issue, it would be resolved by recognition of the guidelines which we have set out . . . [below] for the assistance of parents and school authorities. These guidelines, like the specific provisions of the statutory scheme, provide particulars through which the reasonableness of parents and public authorities may be measured.

* * *

We now examine the parents' contention that the approval process of G.L. c. 76, § 1, infringes on their right to educate their own children, a right protected by the Fourteenth Amendment to the United States Constitution. General Laws c. 76, § 1, requires that "[e]very child between the minimum and maximum ages established for school attendance by the board of education . . . attend a public day school in [the] town [where the child resides] or some other day school approved by the school committee . . . but such attendance shall not be required . . . of a child who is being otherwise instructed in a manner approved in advance by the superintendent or the school committee. . . ." The Canton school committee does not dispute the parents' right to educate their children at home. *Commonwealth v. Roberts, supra* 159 Mass. at 374, 34 N.E. 402 (allowing instruction by the parents provided "it is given in good faith and is sufficient in extent"). However, the school committee does require that the parents submit to them a home schooling proposal, outlining, among other things, the curriculum, materials to be used, and qualifications of the instructors, for its approval as required under G.L. c. 76, § 1. The parents argue that such approval infringes on their rights under the Fourteenth Amendment to control the upbringing and education of their children.[8]

The United States Supreme Court has made it clear that the liberty interests protected by the Fourteenth Amendment extend to activities involving child rearing and education. *Pierce v. Society of Sisters*, 268 U.S. 510, 535, 45 S.Ct. 571, 573, 69 L.Ed. 1070 (1925). . . .

While the parents contend, and we agree, that they possess a basic right in directing the education of their children, such a right is not absolute but must be reconciled with the substantial State interest in the education of its citizenry. . . .

8. We recognize that the parents also present arguments based on the First Amendment to the United States Constitution and art. 2 and amended art. 18 of the Declaration of Rights of the Massachusetts Constitution. Because we conclude that the parents have a basic right under the Fourteenth Amendment in directing the educational upbringing of their children subject to reasonable government regulation, we need not address these arguments. We note, however, that under the facts of this case, the free exercise of religion claims under neither the United States nor the Massachusetts Constitution would entitle the parents to any greater protection than we grant them in this opinion. See *Runyon v. McCrary*, 427 U.S. 160, 178 n. 15, 96 S.Ct. 2586, 2598 n. 15, 49 L.Ed.2d 415 (1976); *Duro v. District Attorney, Second Judicial Dist. of* N.C., 712 F.2d 96, 98 (4th Cir.1983), cert. denied, 465 U.S. 1006, 104 S.Ct. 998, 79 L.Ed.2d 230 (1984).

The Massachusetts Constitution itself proclaims the State's interest in ensuring that its citizens are educated. "Wisdom, and knowledge, as well as virtue, diffused generally among the body of the people, being necessary for the preservation of their rights and liberties; and as these depend on spreading the opportunities and advantages of education in the various parts of the country, and among the different orders of the people, it shall be the duty of Legislatures and Magistrates, in all future periods of this Commonwealth, to cherish the interests of literature and the sciences, and all seminaries of them; especially . . . public schools and grammar schools in the towns; . . . ." Mass. Const. Pt. 2, c. 5, § 2. . . .

The parents contend that, if the State has a substantial interest in this regard, the interest must be carefully defined as to its true nature. They argue that the extent of the State's interest is not in educating the children but only in knowing that the children are being educated. In the past we have had occasion to consider the State's interest under its compulsory education laws. In *Commonwealth v. Roberts, supra* 159 Mass. at 374, 34 N.E. 402, we examined the predecessor statute to G.L. c. 76, § 1, and stated that "[t]he great object of these provisions of the statutes has been that all children shall be educated, not that they shall be educated in any particular way." Consequently, we agree with the parents that the State interest in this regard lies in ensuring that the children residing within the State receive an education, not that the educational process be dictated in its minutest detail. . . .

However, in order to ensure that "all the children shall be educated," we conclude that the approval process required under G.L. c. 76, § 1, is necessary to promote effectively the State's substantial interest. *State v. McDonough*, 468 A.2d 977, 980 (Me. 1983). Without such an approval process, the State would be powerless to assert its interest in the case of a child "who is being otherwise instructed." "There is no doubt as to the power of a State, having a high responsibility for education of its citizens, to impose reasonable regulations for the control and duration of basic education." *Wisconsin v. Yoder, supra* at 213, 92 S.Ct. at 1532. Thus, the school committee may enforce, through the approval process under G.L. c. 76, § 1, certain reasonable educational requirements similar to those required for public and private schools.

* * *

Having concluded that the approval process under G.L. c. 76, § 1, is constitutionally permissible, we caution the superintendent or school committee that the approval of a home school proposal must not be conditioned on requirements that are not essential to the State interest in ensuring that "all the children shall be educated." We recognize "that courts are not school boards or legislatures, and are ill-equipped to determine the 'necessity' of discrete aspects of a State's program of compulsory education." *Wisconsin v. Yoder, supra* at 235, 92 S.Ct. at 1543. However, because we remand this case to the lower court, we offer some guidance on the extent to which approval of a home school proposal may be conditioned on certain requirements without infringing on the liberty interests of the parents under the Fourteenth Amendment.

We begin by reiterating our holding in *Commonwealth v. Renfrew*, 332 Mass. 492, 494, 126 N.E.2d 109 (1955), that "[h]ome education of their child by the defendants without the prior approval of the superintendent or the [school] committee [does] not show a compliance with the statute and bar the prosecution of the complaints." Thus, as the statute indicates, approval must be obtained *in advance*, i.e., prior to the removal of the children from the public school and to the commencement of the home schooling program. See *State v. Riddle*, 168 W.Va. 429, 285 S.E.2d 359, 364 (1981). Procedurally, the superintendent or school committee must provide the parents with an opportunity to explain their proposed plan and present witnesses on their behalf. A hearing during a school committee meeting would be sufficient to meet this requirement. In obtaining the superintendent's or the school committee's approval, the parents bear the responsibility of demonstrating that the home school proposal meets the requirements of G.L. c. 76, § 1, in that the instruction will equal "in thoroughness and efficiency, and in the progress made therein, that in the public schools in the same town. . . ." See *Matter of Kilroy*, 121 Misc.2d 98, 101, 467 N.Y.S.2d 318 (N.Y.Fam.Ct. 1983). If the home school proposal is rejected, the superintendent or the school committee must detail the reasons for the decision. The parents must then be given an opportunity to revise their proposal to remedy its inadequacies. However, if the parents commence the education of their children at home in the face of the school committee's refusal to approve the parents' home school proposal, the burden of proof under G.L. c. 119 or G.L. c. 76, § 2, shifts to the school committee to show that the instruction outlined in the home school proposal fails to equal "in thoroughness and efficiency, and in the progress made therein, that in the public schools in the same town. . . ." G.L. c. 76, § 1. See *In re Monnig*, 638 S.W.2d 782, 788 (Mo.Ct.App.1982).

The school committee of Canton presented the parents with a memorandum of agreement outlining certain requirements necessary for the parents to obtain approval for their proposal. Although we decline to address the specifics of each requirement, we recognize that certain factors may be considered by the superintendent or school committee in determining whether or not to approve a proposed home school proposal. Primary among these is the proposed curriculum and the number of hours of instruction in each of the proposed subjects. . . . General laws c. 71, §§ 1, 2, and 3, list the subjects that must be taught in schools maintained by the towns throughout the Commonwealth. Specifically, § 1 requires "instruction and training in orthography, reading, writing, the English language and grammar, geography, arithmetic, drawing, music, the history and constitution of the United States, the duties of citizenship, health education, physical education and good behavior." Under § 1, the school committee may also require other subjects considered "expedient." Furthermore, G.L. c. 71, §§ 1 and 4 and 603 Code Mass.Regs. § 27.01 (1980), require cities and towns to operate the public schools for a minimum of 180 days. The superintendent or school committee may properly consider the length of the proposed home school year and the hours of instruction in each subject. As we have stated before, "[t]he quality of education can be rendered meaningless if the quantity is subject to manipulation." . . .

The superintendent or school committee may also examine the competency of the parents to teach the children. General Laws c. 71, § 1, provides that teachers shall be "of competent ability and good morals." While we recognize that teachers in public schools must be certified, certification would not appropriately be required for parents under a home school proposal. See *State v. Riddle, supra*. 285 S.E.2d at 366 (under a statutory requirement of "persons qualified to give instruction"). But see *Hanson v. Cushman*, 490 F.Supp. 109, 112 (W.D.Mich.1980); *Jernigan v. State*, 412 So.2d 1242, 1245 (Ala.Crim.App.1982); *Grigg v. Commonwealth*, 224 Va. 356, 363–364, 297 S.E.2d 799 (1982). Nor must the parents have college or advanced academic degrees. However, the superintendent or school committee may properly inquire as to the academic credentials or other qualifications of the parent or parents who will be instructing the children.

The superintendent or school committee must also have access to the textbooks, workbooks, and other instructional aids to be used by the children and to the lesson plans and teaching manuals to be used by the parents. This access is necessary only to determine the type of subjects to be taught and the grade level of the instruction for comparison purposes with the curriculum of the public schools. The superintendent or school committee may not use this access to dictate the manner in which the subjects will be taught. This would involve the school authorities in an activity beyond the legitimate scope of the State interest involved.

Finally, the superintendent or school committee may properly require periodic standardized testing of the children to ensure educational progress and the attainment of minimum standards. . . . In consultation with the parents, the school authorities may decide where the testing is to occur and the type of testing instrument to be used. Where practical, a neutral party should administer the test. Other means of evaluating the progress of the children may be substituted for the formal testing process, such as periodic progress reports or dated work samples, subject to the approval of the parents. With appropriate testing procedures or progress reports, there may be no need for periodic on-site visits or observations of the learning environment by school authority personnel. . . .

* * *

The judge properly relied on G.L. c. 76, § 1, in determining that the children were, under G.L. c. 119, in need of care and protection with respect to their educational care. We think, also, that the judge's order finding the children in need of care and protection was warranted on the evidence. (For example, the judge found on the evidence that the parents had failed to provide documentation as to their educational qualifications and had refused to permit testing of the children.) Nevertheless, it is apparent that the parties have never confronted the issues before them in light of the legal principles and guidelines set out in this opinion. We conclude that the interests of all will be best served by the following order: the judge's order (presently stayed pending appeal) is vacated; the parties are to proceed expeditiously in a serious effort to resolve the matter by agreement; the case is remanded to the lower court where the trial judge is to have continuing jurisdiction over the case for such further proceedings as he deems necessary.

So ordered.

NOTES AND QUESTIONS

1. A Constitutional Right to Home Education?

Does *Charles* stand for the proposition that there is a constitutional right of parents, apart from their free exercise of religion, to educate children in the home? *See generally* Lupu, "Home Education, Religious Liberty, and the Separation of Powers," 67 *Bost. U. L. Rev.* 971 (1987). Or does the court simply affirm the parents' broad right to direct the education of their children in the course of examining the reasonableness of the conditions placed on home education by Massachusetts? Suppose that the court had not construed Chapter 76, Section 1, as permitting a home education exception to compulsory attendance at a public or private school. Would the statute be unconstitutional as applied to Charles and his parents? *See State v. Edgington*, 99 N.M. 715, 663 P.2d 374 (1983). *Cf. State v. Bowman*, 60 Or. App. 184, 653 P.2d 254 (1982).

Note that Chapter 76, Section 1, makes no specific reference to home schooling, home education, or parental instruction. It simply says that compulsory attendance is not required of "a child who is being otherwise instructed in a manner approved in advance by the superintendent or the school committee [of the public school district]." The statute goes on to state that "for the purposes of this section, school committees shall approve a private school when satisfied that the instruction in all the studies required by law equals in thoroughness and efficiency, and in the progress made therein, that in the public schools in the same town; but shall not withhold such approval on account of religious teaching. . . ." It further provides that pupils in private schools "shall be entitled to the same rights and privileges as to transportation to and from school as are provided by law for pupils of public schools. . . . " Does Section 1 allow for home education to satisfy the compulsory attendance law? Has the court misread the statute? Does the court's view of "otherwise instructed" reflect its wish to avoid confronting the underlying constitutional issue?

If *Pierce*, *Meyer*, and *Farrington* affirm the right of parents to send their children to regulated private schools, does it follow that there necessarily is a constitutional right to opt for home education? *See Clonlara, Inc. v. Runkel*, 722 F.Supp. 1442 (E.D. Mich. 1989). *See generally* T. van Geel, *The Courts and American Education Law* 23 (1987); Devins, "A Constitutional Right to Home Instruction?," 62 *Wash. U. L. Q.* 435 (1984). Does *Yoder* suggest this result on free exercise of religion grounds? *See* Lupu, *supra* at 976. Are there constitutionally relevant distinctions? If, as *Charles* demonstrates, it is more difficult for the state to determine compliance with minimum education standards in the home school setting, would the difficulties of oversight justify the abolition of the home school alternative? *See Delconte v. State*, 65 N.C. App. 262, 308 S.E.2d 898 (1983), *reversed on other grounds*, 313 N.C. 384, 329 S.E.2d 636 (1985). Justify it in individual cases? *See Mazanec v. North Judson-San Pierre School Corp.*, 798 F.2d 230 (7th Cir. 1986). Justify more oversight of home education than private schooling? *See Murphy v. State*, 852 F.2d 1039, 1043–44 (8th Cir. 1988); *Blount v. Department of Education*, 551 A.2d 1377 (Me. 1988).

2. Vagueness and Unlawful Delegation

Do you agree with the court that Chapter 76, Section 1, is not unconstitutionally vague and does not unlawfully delegate authority to local school officials in the context of home schooling? *See Jeffery v. O'Donnell*, 702 F.Supp. 516 (M.D.Pa. 1988); *Blackwelder v. Safnauer*, 689 F.Supp. 106 (N.D.N.Y. 1988); Lupu, *supra* at 979–82. Is the court correct in using the equality of instruction proviso, applicable on its face only to private schools, to clarify the scope of regulation of home schooling? Do you agree that "the Legislature intended that the approval of a home school proposal fall within the . . . enunciated standard for the approval of a private school?" Suppose that the standards for a private school included a minimum class size or particular grade structure. Would the court approve the application of these standards to home education? Is any impermissible vagueness or unlawful delegation cured by the court's own "guidelines" for regulating home education?

3. *The State's Interest*

The court quotes with approval the statement in *Commonwealth v. Roberts* that "[t]he great object of these provisions of the statutes has been that all children shall be educated, not that they shall be educated in any particular way." Is this consistent with Chapter 76, Section 1? That section provides for equality in terms of the "progress" made by pupils receiving instruction outside of the public schools and for equality with respect to the "thoroughness and efficiency" of the course of study. Does this language suggest that the legislature is interested in both educational process and outcomes? If the children educated at home do well enough on standardized tests, might the parents successfully argue that the state may not require any course of study or credentials for home instructors? *See* Mangrum, "Family Rights and Compulsory School Laws," 21 *Creighton L. Rev.* 1019 (1988).

4. *Procedural Due Process*

The court is insistent that certain procedural safeguards be observed in the regulation of home schooling. Are such procedures designed to protect the parents or the children or both? Consider these remarks by Professor Lupu:

> The [Massachusetts] statutes create an "entitlement" to education for the children who are the intended beneficiaries of the official and custodial duties thereby established. Children therefore possess a fourteenth amendment "property" interest in education, and a corresponding constitutional interest in a meaningful opportunity to be heard prior to the deprivation of that interest. Regardless of whether parents or school officials are the moving parties in a decision to remove children from school, the children are constitutionally entitled to some form of hearing at which the lawfulness of any such decision is tested.

Lupu, *supra* at 978. Do you agree? Has the *Charles* court creatively sought to resolve the possible conflict between the rights of parents and children that Justice Douglas noted in his dissent in *Yoder*? Has it succeeded? Are public school officials "biased" in evaluating home schooling? If so, does the absence of impartiality itself constitute a denial of due process? *See State v. Brewer*, 444 N.W.2d 923 (N.D. 1989).

Stephens v. Bongart

15 N.J. Misc. 80, 189 A. 131 (Juv. & Dom. Rel. Ct. 1937).

Siegler, Judge.

Helen Stephens, attendance officer of the school district of the town of West Orange in the county of Essex, filed her complaint against Gertrude R. Bongart and Benno Bongart, the defendants in this action, charging that they reside within the school district of the town of West Orange, and being the parents and having custody and control of William Bongart, aged twelve, and Robert Bongart, aged eleven, their children, have, since the 5th day of April, 1936, failed to cause their said children regularly to attend the public schools of the school district of the said town of West Orange; further charging said defendants having neither caused said children to attend a day school in which there is given instruction equivalent to that provided in the public schools for children of similar grades and attainments, nor have they received equivalent instruction elsewhere than at the school. . . .

The act upon which these proceedings are based, chapter 307 of the Laws of 1931 (N.J. St. Annual 1931, § 185–165c), reads as follows:

> Every parent, guardian or other person having custody and control of a child between the ages of seven and sixteen years shall cause such child regularly to attend the public schools of such district or to attend a day school in which there is given instruction equivalent to that provided in the public schools for children of similar grades and attainments or to receive equivalent instruction elsewhere than at school unless such child is above the age of fourteen years. . . . Such regular attendance shall be during all the days and hours that the public schools are in session in said school district, unless it shall be shown to the satisfaction of the Board of Education of said school district that the mental condition of the child is such that he or she cannot benefit from instruction in the school or that the bodily condition of the child is such as to prevent his or her attendance at school.

* * *

The first point raised by the defendants is that the statute under which these proceedings are brought; to wit, chapter 307 of the Laws of 1931 is invalid because it invades the Fourteenth Amendment of the United States Constitution. The problem for determination is whether the statute, as construed and applied, unreasonably infringes the liberty guaranteed to the defendants by the Fourteenth Amendment: "No State shall . . . deprive any person of life, liberty, or property, without due process of law." This statute is a legitimate exercise of the police power of the state. The object of the legislation was to create an enlightened American citizenship in sympathy with our principles and ideals, and to prevent children reared in America from remaining ignorant and illiterate. If it is within the police power of the state to regulate wages, to legislate respecting housing conditions in crowded cities, to prohibit dark rooms in tenement houses, to compel landlords to place windows in their tenements which will enable their tenants to enjoy the sunshine, it is within the police power of the state to compel every resident of New Jersey so to educate his children that the light of American ideals will permeate the life of our future citizens . . . .

The defendants rely upon the authority of . . . *Pierce v. Society of Sisters* . . . for support of their contention that the legislation under consideration is unconstitutional. The issue in the *Pierce* case . . . was not that involved here. There the court was considering property rights of the appellees; the right to engage in the business of conducting a school for the instruction of children; but throughout the whole case the question of the right of the state to require children to attend school was not challenged; this right appeared to be conceded.

* * *

In *State v. Hoyt*, 84 N.H. 38, 146 A. 170, 171 in dealing with the constitutional validity of the compulsory attendance statute, in substance like the statute in New Jersey, Chief Justice Peaslee said:

> The constitutionality of the compulsory school attendance statute . . . has not been considered to be an open question in this state . . . . "Free schooling furnished by the state is not so much a right granted to pupils as a duty imposed upon them for the public good. If they do not voluntarily attend the schools provided for them, they may be compelled to do so" . . . . The defendants' claim that the federal guaranty of liberty enables them to set at defiance any attempt of the state to prescribe the means for ascertaining the sufficiency of educational facilities furnished and to be furnished as a substitute for the public school, goes far beyond anything that has been decided to be the law.

* * *

The second point for determination is whether or not the defendants provided instruction for their children equivalent to that provided in the public schools for children of similar grades and attainments.

This necessitates an analysis of the testimony. The proof is that the defendants' children, William, twelve, and Robert, eleven, were in the sixth and fifth grades, respectively, in the Washington Street School, West Orange, until April 3, 1936. From that date, these children failed to attend a public or day school, although proper notice was served upon the defendants to return the children to a school. The defendants admit they caused the children's withdrawal from the Washington School.

Since that time, the defendants claim that they instructed their children in their own home in the subjects taught in the fifth and sixth grades. This instruction, they claim, is equivalent to that provided in the public schools for children of similar grades and attainments. The case turns on this factual situation. 2 *Words and Phrases, Second Series* 312, defines the word *equivalent* as follows: "*Equivalent* means 'equal in worth or value, force, power, effect, import and the like.' . . ."

Quite definitely, the term refers to the giving of instruction equal in value and effect to that given in a public school. In determining this question, consideration must be given, first, to the matter of the ability of the parents to provide equivalent instruction, and, secondly, to a comparison of the quality, character, and methods of teaching employed by the defendants and that of the West Orange public school system. Mrs. Bongart was graduated from the Eastern District High School, New York City, in 1911. In 1917 she was a special student at Hunter College, evening course. This required three or four evenings a week, which she carried on for only two years. She studied economics, psychology, art, portrait work, charcoal work and painting; she majored in home economics. Mrs. Bongart had no teaching experience. She was married about fifteen years ago, and her chief employment was that of housewife. Mr. Bongart is a graduate of the University of Strassbourg, in the field of electrical and mechanical engineering. He never trained for teaching, but did have employment as a teacher at the New York Aerial School, Newark Technical School, and the Newark Junior High School until recently. He taught subjects in mechanical drawing and electrical engineering. The teachers in the elementary grades of the public schools, particularly the fifth and sixth grades in the West Orange school system, must have at least a high school education and three years at an approved normal school in the state of New Jersey.

The normal school curriculum includes a type of training and education intended to qualify students to teach in the elementary class in the subjects of English, history, science, sociology, civics, mathematics, hygiene, geography, art, music, and physical education. The major aim is to give the teachers training in techniques of presentation of material to elementary school students. That involves the proper selection of material, knowledge of children, and the organization of their work, so that every teacher should know the results which must be achieved in terms of knowledge, habits, skills, attitudes, and appreciations. Her training should qualify her to develop individuality and the personality of each child under her supervision. One of the major aims of our public school today is to teach the way in which the individual must fit into the social group. The evidence establishes that the teachers in the fifth and sixth grades of Washington School possess this training and qualify in these courses.

It is clear, upon comparison, that there is a substantial variance between the training, qualifications, and experience of the defendants and those obtained in the public school system of West Orange.

Now, what was the instruction given by the defendants at their home? The children assemble, one in the dining room and the other in the front room, each morning at 9 o'clock, and continue until 12; they resume at 1 o'clock, and recess at 3 in the afternoon. They receive instruction in arithmetic, spelling, history, geography, language, and music. In the evening, the father instructs them in science between 7 and 9 o'clock.

In the study of arithmetic a textbook is used by Stone and Millis, dated 1914. There were no textbooks for spelling, language, music, civics, hygiene, and art; while the textbooks used were outmoded and outdated, the latest published in 1921 and the oldest in 1881, and all certainly of questionable value in the instruction of children. Spelling was taught without a book, the mother giving twenty words at random each week, which the children had to learn and place in a notebook. The other subjects were taught by assigning periods of 30 or 35 minutes for each. Language was largely taught through the reading of the newspapers, the Literary Digest and the Saturday Evening Post. Poetry was principally taught by the use of an occasional piece of poetry out of the Sunday Times and the New York Daily News, a tabloid newspaper. No poems were memorized. Music was taught by listening to radio concerts. There were no song books or singing exercises. Mechanical drawing and current events were given by the father in the evening. The Newark Evening News and some other periodicals were sources from which current events were drawn for discussion. The Bible was read once in a while. The flag of the country was exhibited in front of the house on patriotic occasions. The mother spoke to them about hygiene and the danger of alcoholic beverages, but no hygiene textbook was used. There were no instructions in observance of patriotic holidays, and no observance of Arbor Day. There was no physical training except that which they got outside in the ordinary course of their play. They had membership in the YMCA, but failed to attend during September and October. Of this default the parents had no knowledge.

The instruction was interrupted from time to time by the mother's household duties, occasional shopping tours, and house callers. The defendants had no definite schedule for daily instruction. The evidence indicates that the boys obtained from children in school, periodically, information as to the subjects they were studying in school, and transmitted that information to their mother, who guided herself in instructing the children, to some extent, by it. They had no marks for their work. There were no daily work papers, tests, or examinations; at least, there were none presented in evidence. In fact, the mother admits she had no standard by which to determine whether the children were absorbing the instruction she was attempting to give. There was no organized supervision over the teaching the defendants gave; the work of the children, and the results accomplished, were never submitted to any other competent authority for supervision, criticism, or approval.

A summary of the methods of instruction at the Washington School of West Orange will be useful for comparative purposes. The elementary grades are supervised by a specially trained person, who has complete supervision over the courses of study, the textbooks used, and the methods employed by the teachers in transmitting knowledge and the building and developing of the personalities of the children. The school is organized as a miniature community center, a sort of city, where each child considers himself a citizen, with duties toward the community as is required on the outside. The educational structure thus developed is in the nature of a group enterprise, where the children work together for the common good. The teacher creates the atmosphere and becomes the guiding influence. A high discipline is maintained by strict attention to the development of habits, skills and attitudes. There is group discussion. The children bring in articles from the outside. They study the biographies of great men, and discuss their achievements. In the fifth and sixth grades, reading, writing, spelling, arithmetic, English, history, geography, civics, hygiene, safety education, music, art, and penmanship are taught. The children are taught to use the dictionary. The norm for instruction may be found in several monographs on each subject, provided by the state board of education, and strict adherence is required. In the fifth grade, there are seven textbooks in daily use to cover the subjects. In the sixth grade, there are also seven textbooks, supplemented by thirteen reference and reading books used in connection with their courses, and, in addition, the school library is available to them. Every text, reading, and reference book, 26 in number, produced in evidence, is carefully selected in accordance with the regulations of the state board of education and approved by the supervisor of the elementary grades and by the board of education of West Orange. There is a student schedule for the fifth and sixth grades, which provides for instruction from 8:45 a.m. until 3 p.m. from Monday to Friday, inclusive. The curriculum provides for instruction in the development of abilities, habits, and skills. Instruction is also given by way of travel lectures, picture studies, art and music, so that every child has something to talk about. Thus, an audience situation is created for the children, where each child is required to rise and speak to the entire group. This creates self-confidence, and tends to adjust the child to the social group.

One poem a week, and appreciation for the beauties of nature and literature are taught. Besides teaching arithmetic from texts, they instruct in practical matters requiring arithmetic. Geography is taught to meet life situations by creating interest in world travel and training the children to visualize, in their reading, places that they have studied. In music, each child is allowed to develop whatever talent he may possess. In art, each child learns the harmony of color in dress, interior decoration, and everyday life. Every morning the children have a reading from the Bible and recite the Lord's Prayer. They salute the flag and sing patriotic songs. They observe Arbor Day and all patriotic holidays. A course in safety education and fire prevention is pursued. The month of June is devoted to review. They have physical education four periods each week under a special supervisor. In the civics course, the children are on the lookout for all material in current events. There are three school magazines. Washington School has a monthly newspaper, and all children are eligible to participate in its columns.

* * *

From this comparison and analysis of the evidence, I find (1) that the education, training, and equipment of the defendants are substantially inadequate, as compared with those of the public school teacher; (2) that the schedule of study and the program of activities of the defendants are irregular, uncertain, and without form, while the public school curriculum is definite and allots a specified time and, in most cases, a special teacher for every subject studied in the fifth and sixth grades; (3) that the instruction given by the defendants is without proper or modern textbooks, lacks supervision by competent authorities of pupil and teacher, lacks a method, standard, or other means of determining the progress or attainments of the child; none of which deficiencies are present in the public school; (4) that the teaching of discipline and health habits lacks plan and a trained method, fixing responsibility on the child for its execution; while, at the school, it is part of a definite program of character education; (5) that the defendants cannot provide for group or class teaching, and lack the ability to develop attitudes and create a social setting so that the children may be trained to deal with their playmates and friends as a part of a social group; (6) that the public school system provides such social groups and lays emphasis on its development, and stresses the adjustment of the child to group life and group activity and a course of living that he will be required to follow and meet as he goes out into the world.

The primary function of education is to get an understanding and interpretation of modern civilization. In the early days of the Republic, the idea that an educated citizenship lies at the very foundation of a democratic government has defined our philosophy of national development. For these reasons, the maintenance of an adequate system of public education for youth is a fundamental responsibility of any commonwealth. The public school system of New Jersey embodies the highest ideals of American democracy, and has developed a program which offers unusual opportunities to the children of our state. All citizens have a deep interest in our public schools, and should take pride in the high rank which they occupy in the nation. To deny children instruction seems as unnatural as to withhold their necessary subsistence. Education is brought, as it were, to the very door of all classes of society, and ignorance is quite inexcusable. The failure of the parents to provide the child with the benefits of that opportunity should be a matter of great concern when at issue. The education of youth is of such vast importance and of such singular utility in the journey of life that it obviously carries its own recommendation with it, for on it, in a great measure, depends all that we ever hope to be; every perfection that a generous and well-disposed mind would gladly arrive at. It is this that usually renders one man preferable to another. And, as the great end of learning is to teach man to know himself and to fit him for life, so he who knows most is enabled to practice best and to be an example for those who know but little.

The schools, whose function frequently is thought of solely in material terms, have a far more important responsibility. They must aid parents, not simply in the training of their children for the trades and professions, whose criterion of success too often is the amount of money they can make, but, rather, the training and development of men and women of character; men and women whose minds have been trained to the understanding of basic principles and ideals, with the courage and strength of will to live up to and apply them in their daily lives.

I incline to the opinion that education is no longer concerned merely with the acquisition of facts; the instilling of worthy habits, attitudes, appreciations, and skills is far more important than mere imparting of subject matter. A primary objective of education today is the development of character and good citizenship. Education must impart to the child the way to live. This brings me to the belief that, in a cosmopolitan area such as we live in, with all the complexities of life, and our reliance upon others to carry out the functions of education, it is almost impossible for a child to be adequately taught in his home. I cannot conceive how a child can receive in the home instruction and experiences in group activity and in social outlook in any manner or form comparable to that provided in the public school. To give him less than that is depriving the child of the training and development of the most necessary emotions and instincts of life. I cannot accept the theory asserted by Mr. Bongart that, "I am not interested in method, but in results." That theory is archaic, mechanical, and destructive of the finer instincts of the child. It does seem to me, too, quite unlikely that this type of instruction could produce a child with all the attributes that a person of education, refinement, and character should possess.

I have carefully observed the defendants' children in court, their demeanor, their responses under examination, and their reaction to the proceedings while in court, and there is clear evidence that it is their belief that they are on a "grand holiday," free from the restraints, discipline, and responsibility of other children in school attendance. All of this seems to me to be attributable to the course adopted and pursued by the parents. I have also carefully examined all the evidence and exhibits, and it is my opinion that the defendants have failed to give their children instruction equivalent to that provided in the public schools in the fifth and sixth grades, but, rather, have engaged in a haphazard and hit-or-miss kind of instruction, not calculated to conform with the provisions of the statute, and that both defendants actively and independently participated in causing their children not to go to the public school or a day school. I have been satisfied beyond a reasonable doubt by the evidence of the guilt of both defendants as charged. Both defendants are hereby deemed to be disorderly persons.

State v. Massa

95 N.J. Super. 382, 231 A.2d 252 (Morris County Ct. 1967).

Collins, J. C. C.

This is a trial *de novo* on appeal from the Pequannock Township Municipal Court. Defendants were charged and convicted with failing to cause their daughter Barbara, age 12, regularly to attend the public schools of the district and further for failing to either send Barbara to a private school or provide an equivalent education elsewhere than at school, contrary to the provisions of NJSA 18:14-14. The municipal magistrate imposed a fine of $2490 for both defendants.

Mr. and Mrs. Massa appeared *pro se*. Mrs. Massa conducted the case; Mr. Massa concurred.

The State presented two witnesses who testified that Barbara had been registered in the Pequannock Township School but failed to attend the 6th grade class from April 25, 1966, to June 1966 and the following school year from September 8, 1966, to November 16, 1966—a total consecutive absence of 84 days.

Mrs. Massa testified that she had taught Barbara at home for two years before September 1965. Barbara returned to school in September 1965, but began receiving her education at home again on April 25, 1966.

Mrs. Massa said her motive was that she desired the pleasure of seeing her daughter's mind develop. She felt she wanted to be with her child when the child would be more alive and fresh. She also maintained that in school much time was wasted and that at home a student can make better use of her time.

Mrs. Massa is a high school graduate. Her husband is an interior decorator. Neither holds a teacher's certificate. However, the State stipulated that a child may be taught at home and also that Mr. or Mrs. Massa need not be certified by the State of New Jersey to so teach. The sole issue in this case is one of equivalency. Have defendants provided their daughter with an education equivalent to that provided by the Pequannock Township School System?

Mrs. Massa introduced into evidence 19 exhibits. Five of these exhibits, in booklet form, are condensations of basic subjects, are concise and seem to contain all the basic subject material for the respective subjects. Mrs. Massa also introduced textbooks which are used as supplements to her own compilations as well as for test material and written problems.

Mrs. Massa introduced English, spelling and mathematics tests taken by her daughter at the Pequannock School after she had been taught for two years at home. The lowest mark on these tests was a B.

* * *

There is also a report by an independent testing service of Barbara's scores on standard achievement tests. They show that she is considerably higher than the national median except in arithmetic.

Mrs. Massa satisfied this court that she has an established program of teaching and studying. There are definite times each day for the various subjects and recreation. She evaluates Barbara's progress through testing. If Barbara has not learned something which has been taught, Mrs. Massa then reviews that particular area.

Barbara takes violin lessons and attends dancing school. She also is taught art by her father, who has taught this subject in various schools.

Mrs. Massa called Margaret Cordasco as a witness. She had been Barbara's teacher from September 1965 to April 1966. She testified basically that Barbara was bright, well behaved and not different from the average child her age except for some trouble adjusting socially.

The State called as a witness David MacMurray, the Assistant Superintendent of Pequannock Schools. He testified that the defendants were not giving Barbara an equivalent education. Most of his testimony dealt with Mrs. Massa's lack of certification and background for teaching and the lack of social development of Barbara because she is being taught alone.

He outlined procedures which Pequannock teachers perform, such as evaluation sheets, lesson plans and use of visual aids. He also stressed specialization since Pequannock schools have qualified teachers for certain specialized subjects. He did not think the defendants had the specialization necessary to teach all basic subjects. He also testified about extracurricular activity, which is available but not required.

The State placed six exhibits in evidence. These included a more recent mathematics book than is being used by defendants, a sample of teacher evaluation, a list of visual aids, sample schedules for the day and lesson plans, and an achievement testing program.

* * *

N.J.S.A. 18:14–14 provides:

> Every parent, guardian or other person having custody and control of a child between the ages of 6 and 16 years shall cause such child regularly to attend the public schools of the district or a day school in which there is given instruction equivalent to that provided

> in the public schools for children of similar grades and attainments *or to receive equivalent instruction elsewhere than at school.* (Emphasis added.)

State v. Vaughn, 44 N.J. 142, 207 a.2d 537 (1965), interpreted the above statute to permit the parent having charge and control of the child to elect to substitute one of the alternatives for public school. It is then incumbent upon the parent to introduce evidence showing one of the alternatives is being substituted. "If there is such evidence in the case, then the ultimate burden of persuasion remains with the State." . . .

N.J.S.A. 18:14–39 provides for the penalty for violation of N.J.S.A. 18:14–14:

> A parent, guardian or other person having charge or control of a child between the ages of 6 and 16 years, who shall fail to comply with any of the provisions of this article relating to his duties shall be deemed a disorderly person and shall be subject to a fine of not more than $5 for a first offense and not more than $25 for each subsequent offense, in the discretion of the court. . . .

This case presents two questions on the issue of equivalency for determination. What does the word *equivalent* mean in the context of N.J.S.A. 18:14–14? And, has the State carried the required burden of proof to convict defendants?

In *Knox v. O'Brien*, 7 N.J. Super. 608, 72 A.2d 389 (1950), the County Court interpreted the word *equivalent* to include not only academic equivalency but also the equivalency of social development. This interpretation appears untenable in the face of the language of our own statute and also the decisions in other jurisdictions.

If the interpretation in *Knox* were followed, it would not be possible to have children educated outside of school. Under the *Knox* rationale, in order for children to develop socially it would be necessary for them to be educated in a group. A group of students being educated in the same manner and place would constitute a de facto school. Our statute provides that children may receive an equivalent education elsewhere than at school. What could have been intended by the Legislature by adding this alternative?

The Legislature must have contemplated that a child could be educated alone provided the education was equivalent to the public schools. Conditions in today's society illustrate that such situations exist. Examples are the child prodigy whose education is accelerated by private tutoring, or the infant performer whose education is provided by private tutoring. If group education is required by our statute, then these examples as well as all education at home would have to be eliminated.

* * *

Faced with exiguous precedent in New Jersey and having reviewed the above cited cases in other states, this court holds that the language of the New Jersey statute, N.J.S.A. 18:14–14, providing for "equivalent education elsewhere than at school," requires only a showing of academic equivalence. As stated above, to hold that the statute requires equivalent social contact and development as well would emasculate this alternative and allow only group education, thereby eliminating private tutoring or home education. A statute is to be interpreted to uphold its validity in its entirety if possible . . . . This is the only reasonable interpretation available in this case which would accomplish this end.

Having determined the intent of the Legislature as requiring only equivalent academic instruction, the only remaining question is whether the defendants provided their daughter with an education equivalent to that available in the public schools. After reviewing the evidence presented by both the State and the defendants, this court finds that the State has not shown beyond a reasonable doubt that defendants failed to provide their daughter with an equivalent education.

The majority of testimony of the State's witnesses dealt with the lack of social development. The other point pressed by the State was Mrs. Massa's lack of teaching ability and techniques based upon her limited education and experience. However, this court finds this testimony to be inapposite to the actual issue of equivalency under the New Jersey statute and the stipulations of the State. In any case, from my observation of her while testifying and during oral argument, I am satisfied that Mrs. Massa is self-educated and well qualified to teach her daughter the basic subjects from grades one through eight.

* * *

It is the opinion of this court that defendants' daughter has received and is receiving an education equivalent to that available in the Pequannock public schools. There is no indication of bad faith or improper motive on defendants' part. Under a more definite statute with sufficient guidelines or a lesser burden of proof, this might not necessarily be the case. However, within the framework of the existing law and the nature of the stipulations by the State, this court finds the defendant not guilty and reverses the municipal court conviction. . . .

NOTES AND QUESTIONS

1. Contrasting Bongart *and* Massa

Note the curt treatment the *Bongart* court gives to the argument that New Jersey's compulsory attendance law impinges on Bongart's liberty. Is its analysis satisfactory? Does any requirement of prior governmental approval of home schooling violate the parents' rights? *See State v. McDonough*, 468 A.2d 977 (Me. 1983) (requirement upheld); *State v. Schmidt*, 505 N.E.2d 627 (Ohio 1987). What of on-site visits to the home school? *See Blackwelder v. Safnauer*, 689 F.Supp. 106 (N.D.N.Y. 1988); *Matter of Black-Welder*, 528 N.Y.S.2d 759 (S.Ct. 1988).

The *Bongart* definition of equivalency renders compulsory education synonymous with compulsory schooling. "[I]n a cosmopolitan area such as we live in . . . it is almost impossible for a child to be adequately taught in his home." Is the conclusion empirically defensible? Is it a justifiable interpretation of a statute that expressly permits equivalent instruction to take place "elsewhere than the school"? At what point do family arrangements for education become "a thinly veiled subterfuge [for] attacking compulsory school attendance?" *See In Interest of Sawyer*, 234 Kan. 436, 672 P.2d 1093 (1983).

Massa defines equivalency in a manner that permits parents to educate their own children at home. *See also Matter of Lash*, 92 Misc.2d 642, 401 N.Y.S.2d 124 (Fam. Ct. 1977); *People v. Levisen*, 404 Ill. 574, 90 N.E.2d 213 (1950). *See generally* F. Kemerer and J. Hairston, *The Educator's Guide to Texas School Law* 30–31 (2d ed. 1990). But is the process by which the court attempts to match fact situation to statutory requirement different in the two cases? How does the court in each case determine whether the parent is qualified to serve as teacher? See *People v. De Jonge*, 449 N.W.2d 899 (Mich. App. 1989); *State v. Patzer*, 382 N.W.2d 631 (N.D. 1986) (teacher certification requirement upheld); *State v. Newstrom*, 371 N.W.2d 525 (Minn. 1985) (requirement that home school teacher have "essentially equivalent" qualifications to public school teachers is unconstitutionally vague); *State v. Riddle*, 168 W.Va. 429, 285 S.E.2d 359 (1981). Whether the curriculum provided at home is adequate? *See Appeal of Pierce*, 122 N.H. 762, 451 A.2d 363 (1982) ("home-education curriculum involved limited and irregular hours of organized instruction"). How do they decide whether social as well as academic development should be treated as part of the definition of equivalency? *See* Shepherd, "Home Schooling: Dimensions of Controversy, 1970–1984," 31 *J. of Church and State* 101 (1989), *generally* Punke, "Home Instruction and Compulsory School Attendance," 5 NOLPE School L.J. 77 (1975); Comment, "Private Tutoring, Compulsory Education and the Illinois Supreme Court," 18 *U.Chi. L. Rev.* 105 (1950). In this context, is "equivalency" unconstitutionally vague? *See Ellis v. O'Hara*, 612 F.Supp. 379 (E.D.Mo. 1985) ("substantially equivalent"); *Trucke v. Erlemeier*, 657 F.Supp. 1382 (N.D.Iowa 1987) ("equivalent instruction").

The statutory "equivalency" language appears to compel the same analysis that these questions implicitly criticize. How might one draft legislation to render the task of regulating home instruction more manageable? Are the issues identical to those posed by the task of developing legislation to regulate nonpublic schools? One commentator, citing *Bongart* and *Massa*, has argued that courts frequently sidestep legislative intent in home-instruction cases: "In reaching conflicting conclusions, however, the courts have manipulated canons of statutory construction and selectively read legislative history to achieve an accommodation between state goals and individual interests that they consider appropriate." Project, "Education and the Law: State Interests and Individual Rights," 74 *Mich. L. Rev.* 1373, 1389 (1976).

2. Socialization and Association

At bottom, does *Bongart* rest on the assumption that education involves socialization to values as well as skills training and that this usually can occur only in an institutional environment with children from other families? *See also In re Davis*, 114 N.H. 242, 318 A.2d 151 (1974); *Knox v. O'Brien*, 7 N.J. Super. 608, 72 A.2d 389 (1950). If so, how does this principle conform with the accommodation reached in *Pierce? See generally* L. Kotin and W. F. Aikman, *Legal Foundations of Compulsory Attendance* 110–48 (1980); T. van Geel, *Authority to Control the School Program* 159 (1976); *Shepherd, supra.*

If a state statute or regulation refers to alternative education at a "private school," the courts may be called upon to define the meaning of school. *See Delconte v. State*, 65 N.C. App. 262, 308 S.E.2d 898 (1983). Is this but another way of raising the association and socialization issues in the context of home instruction or tutoring? *See State v. Peterman*, 32 Ind. App. 665, 70 N.E. 550 (1904); *People v. Levisen*, 404 Ill. 574, 90 N.E.2d 213 (1950). *But see State v. Hoyt*, 84 N.H. 38, 146 A. 170 (1929). *See generally* Kotin and Aiken, *supra* at 136–42, 157–66; Bumstead, "Educating Your Child at Home: The *Perchenlides* Case," *Phi Delta Kappan* 97 (1979). If the legislature provides little guidance on the meaning of the phrase "private school," is the statute unconstitutionally vague? *See Care and Protection of Charles, supra; Roemhild v. State*, 251 Ga. 569, 308 S.E.2d 154 (1983). *But see Burrow v. State*, 282 Ark. 479, 669 S.W.2d 441 (1984).

More cynically, does the requirement of an institutional education environment reflect the "fear that approving one request will lead to an exodus from school"? Bumstead, *supra* at 98–99.

3. *Too Bright Children*

The state of California compels children not otherwise excused to attend either a public or state-approved private school or to receive instruction from a tutor holding a state teaching credential. One California family, unhappy with the poor progress that its children were making in school, decided to educate them at home. The children were enrolled in a correspondence course, where they did astoundingly well: the youngsters covered as much as five years of work in eighteen months. Suit was brought against the youngsters, charging them with habitual truancy. During the trial, the state introduced a school psychologist's report that, while admitting the children were "of better than average intelligence" and "well adjusted," concluded that they would be better off "in school [where] each individual child would be in his own age group and would have a better chance to compete and to learn by hearing the others go over the same class work." The family introduced evidence of the children's academic progress. What should be the result? *See In re Shinn*, 195 Cal. App.2d 683, 16 Cal. Rptr. 165 (4th Dist. 1961). *But see State v. Peterman*, 32 Ind. App. 665, 70 N.E. 550 (1904); *Sheppard v. State*, 306 P.2d 346 (Okla. Crim. App. 1957).

4. *Other Statutory "Exemptions" from Compulsory Attendance Laws*

Strictly speaking, private schooling and home instruction are not so much "exemptions" from compulsory education laws as they are alternative methods of satisfying those laws. *See* Kotin and Aikman, *supra* at 169–70. But there are other provisions in state statutes which forgive, in whole or in part, the requirement that some children attend a school or receive instruction at home, for example, physically or mentally disabled children, those completing eight grades, expelled students, working children over a specified age, etc. *See* Kotin and Aikman, *supra* at 170–84; K. Alexander and K. F. Jordan, *Legal Aspects of Educational Choice: Compulsory Attendance and Student Assignment* 30–43 (1973). A number of these exceptions have been addressed by federal statutes or been subject to constitutional challenges. See chapters 6 and 7, *infra*. *See generally* T. van Geel, *The Courts and American Education* 127–29 (1987).

V. DISCRIMINATION AND PRIVATE EDUCATION

In recent years, there has been a growing concern and debate about the extent to which government, particularly the federal government, should be and is regulating private education. The concern has been expressed not only with regard to elementary and secondary education but also with regard to private institutions of higher learning. *See, e.g.*, W. C. Hobbs (ed.), *Government Regulation of Higher Education* (1978); A.E.D. Howard, *State Aid to Private Higher Education* (1977); Dutile, "God and Gays at Georgetown: Observations on *Gay Rights Coalition of Georgetown University Law Center v. Georgetown University*," 15 *J. of Coll. & Univ. L.* 1 (1988); O'Neil, "God and Government at Yale: The Limits of Federal Regulation of Higher Education," 44 *U. Cin. L. Rev.* 525 (1975); O'Neil, "Private Universities and Public Law," 19 *Buffalo L. Rev.* 155 (1970); Bok, "Address to Associated Harvard Alumni," *Harv. U. Gazette*, June 13, 1975, at 1, col. 2. *See generally* W. A. Kaplin, *The Law of Higher Education* (2d ed. 1985).

In the context of private elementary and secondary education, the question of the permissible scope of government regulation can arise in a number of settings. First, as discussed in earlier portions of this chapter, a state may seek to ensure a minimum quality of education and a minimum commitment to democratic principles in private schools. Second, as noted in the following section, the government can seek to condition its assistance to private schools on the meetings of specified criteria. *See Bowen v. Kendrick*, 487 U.S. 589, 108 S.Ct. 2562, 101 L.Ed.2d 520 (1988) (federal grants under Adolescent Family Life Act, 42 U.S.C.A. § 3002 *et seq.* (1982)). The danger is that there is an inevitable temptation for control to follow the dollars. *See, e.g., Roemer v. Maryland Public Works Board*, 426 U.S. 736, 96 S.Ct. 2337, 49 L.Ed.2d 179 (1976) (Justice Stevens, dissenting). *See generally* Capps and Esbeck, "The Use of Government Funding and Taxing Power to Regulate Religious Schools," 14 *J. of Law & Educ.* 553 (1985). Similarly, the tax-exempt status of a private school, and the deductibility of charitable donations, may turn on whether a school meets certain public policy or constitutional norms. *See Virginia Education Fund v. Commissioner*, 799 F.2d 903 (4th Cir. 1986). *Cf. Bob Jones University v. United States*, 461 U.S. 574, 103 S.Ct. 2017, 76 L.Ed.2d 157 (1983) (university practicing racial discrimination does not qualify as a tax-exempt organization under Section 501(c)(3) of the Internal Revenue Code of 1954)). *See generally* Shaviro, "From Big Mama Rag to National Geographic: The Controversy Regarding Exemptions for Educational Publications," 41 *Tax. L. Rev.* 693 (1986); Bittker and Kaufman, "Taxes and Civil Rights: 'Constitutionalizing' the Internal Revenue Code," 82 *Yale L. J.* 51 (1972); Note, "The Judicial Role in Attacking Racial Discrimination in Tax-Exempt Private Schools," 93 *Harv. L. Rev.* 378 (1979); Note, "Segregating Schools: The Foreseeable Consequences of Tuition Tax Credits," 89 *Yale L. J.* 168 (1979).

Third, state assistance itself may trigger a finding that the state's largesse may not be used by private schools for unconstitutional or unlawful purposes. *See, e.g., Grove City College v. Bell*, 465 U.S. 555, 104 S.Ct. 1211, 79 L.Ed.2d 516 (1984) (sex discrimination); *Norwood v. Harrison*, 413 U.S. 455, 93 S.Ct. 2804, 37 L.Ed.2d 723 (1973) (state program under which textbooks are loaned to students in public and private schools, without reference to whether any participating private school follows racially discriminatory policies, is unconstitutional)). *Cf. Bowen v. Kendrick*, 487 U.S. 589, 108 S.Ct. 2562, 101 L.Ed.2d 520 (1988). *See generally* Note, "Segregation, Academies and State Action," 82 *Yale L. J.* 1436 (1973). *Compare Norwood v. Harrison, supra*, with *Allen v. Wright*, 408 U.S. 737, 104 S.Ct. 3315, 82 L.Ed.2d 556 (1984).

Fourth, to the extent that the activities of private schools are treated as "state action" by the courts, the provisions of the federal constitution will apply to those institutions. This might mean, for example, that private schools would be held to the same standards under the establishment, equal protection, and due process clauses as public institutions. This matter is addressed briefly in chapter 2, *infra*.

Fifth, statutes of general application, for example, state and federal labor relations acts, may be applied to private schools. *See, e.g., Catholic High School Association v. Culvert*, 753 F.2d 1161 (2d Cir. 1985). *See generally* Pushaw, "Labor Relations Board Regulation of Parochial Schools: A Practical Free Exercise Accommodation," 97 *Yale L. J.* 135 (1987); Laycock, "Towards a General Theory of the Religion Clauses: The Case of Church Labor Relations and the Right to Church Autonomy," 81 *Colum. L. Rev.* 1373 (1981); Warner, "Jurisdiction Over Parochial Schools: *Catholic Bishop of Chicago v. NLRB*," 73 *Nw. U. L. Rev.* 463 (1978).

Finally, government may seek to prevent private elementary and secondary schools, including religious institutions, from engaging in racial or other forms of illegitimate discrimination. Professor van Geel has well described this development in the law and the tensions that it has created:

> Though in most respects private schools must constitutionally be allowed to set sail on their own course, does that mean they are also constitutionally protected against governmental efforts to prohibit discrimination in admissions (and other student-related matters), and employment on the basis of race, gender, religion, handicap, age, and national origin? The federal government, as well as state governments, assuming there were no constitutional obstacles, have extended a variety of antidiscrimination provisions to private education. Active governmental pursuit to eliminate private discrimination set the stage for a historical confrontation between the state and its antidiscrimination policy, and private schools claiming that these efforts infringed their rights of privacy, freedom of association and the free exercise of religion.

T. van Geel, *The Courts and American Education Law* 26 (1987). The remainder of this section largely will focus on the application of nondiscrimination laws to private schools, beginning with an excerpt from the work of Professor Laycock on government regulation and church autonomy. *See also* "Developments in the Law: Religion and the State," 100 *Harv. L. Rev.* 1606, 1750–61 (1987).

"Towards a General Theory of the Religion Clauses: The Case of Church Labor Relations and the Right to Church Autonomy"

Douglas Laycock, 81 *Colum. L. Rev.* 1373, 1374–78, 1388–92, 1398–1401 (1981).*

Secular regulation of churches has increased substantially in recent years,[1] and litigation over the constitutionality of such regulation has increased as well. Regulation of church labor relations has been a particularly prolific source of litigation. There have been challenges to the National Labor Relations Act, the Fair Labor Standards Act, the Civil Rights Act of 1964, the Federal Unemployment Tax Act, and other statutes affecting church labor policy. A wide variety of religious groups have become involved in such litigation.

Many of these cases have reached defensible results, but only a few have identified the competing interests with reasonable specificity. Most of the uncertainty results from the Supreme Court's failure to develop any coherent general theory of the religion clauses. This Article offers a start toward such a theory.

The first step is to restore the fundamental distinction between the establishment and free exercise clauses: that government support for religion is an essential element of every claim under the establishment clause. The second step is to distinguish different kinds of rights protected by the free exercise clause. One of these, the right of church autonomy, tends to be overlooked. Quite apart from whether a regulation requires a church or an individual believer to violate religious doctrine or felt moral duty, churches have a constitutionally protected interest in managing their own institutions free of government interference.

This interest, like all others under the religion clauses, may be infringed for sufficiently compelling reasons, and the third step towards a general theory is to examine how this balancing should work. Interests are not arrayed on a single continuum from important to unimportant, and the balance cannot be struck reliably without analyzing the multivariate nature of the interests on each side. Alleged state interests in regulating internal church affairs—e.g., protection of church members and church workers from exploitation—are usually illegitimate and should not count at all.

* * *

The best known series of church labor relations cases resulted from the National Labor Relations Board's decision to assert jurisdiction over religious schools.[9] Two district courts and the Seventh Circuit held the NLRA unconstitutional as applied to teachers' unions in Catholic schools, on grounds of excessive entanglement between church and state,[10] and in the Seventh Circuit case, also on the more persuasive ground that collective bargaining would interfere with ecclesiastical control of church institutions.[11] The Supreme Court affirmed the Seventh Circuit, but on statutory grounds.[12] Finding a serious risk of excessive government entanglement with religion, the Court avoided the constitutional question by requiring " ' "the affirmative intention of the Congress clearly expressed" ' " that the Act extend to such religious schools.[13] Finding no such clear expression, the Court held the Act inapplicable. Four dissenters agreed that the constitutional issue was serious, but argued that it should not be avoided by such a major distortion of the statute.[15] . . .

* *See also* Laycock and Waelbroeck, "Academic Freedom and the Free Exercise of Religion," 66 *Tex. L. Rev.* 1001 (1988).

1. Ripple, "The Entanglement Test of the Religion Clauses—A Ten Year Assessment," 27 *U.C.L.A. L. Rev.* 1195, 1230–32 (1980).

9. Henry M. Hald School Ass'n, 213 N.L.R.B. 415 (1974).

10. *Catholic Bishop v. NLRB*, 559 F.2d 1112 (7th Cir. 1977), aff'd on other grounds, 440 U.S. 490 (1979); *McCormick v. Hirsch*, 460 F.Supp. 1337 (M.D. Pa. 1978); *Caulfield v. Hirsch*, 410 F.Supp. 618 (E.D.Pa. 1976), cert. in advance of judgment denied, 436 U.S. 957 (1978).

11. 559 F.2d at 1124.

12. *NLRB v. Catholic Bishop*, 440 U.S. 490 (1979). [*See also Universidad de Bayamon v. NLRB*, 793 F.2d 383, 398–99 (1st Cir. 1985) (*en banc*) (equally divided court refused to grant NRLB's request to enforce order against university).]

13. *Id.* at 500 (quoting *McCulloch v. Sociedad Nacional de Marineros*, 372 U.S. 10, 21–22 (1963) (quoting *Benz v. Compania Naviera Hidalgo*, 353 U.S. 138, 147 (1957))). The opinion emphasized the importance of schools and teachers; the Board will undoubtedly continue to assert jurisdiction over church-owned commercial businesses.

15. *Id.* at 508. See generally Comment, NLRB Has No Jurisdiction Over Lay Teachers in Parochial Schools, 58 *Wash. U.L.Q.* 173 (1980).

Similar questions arise under antidiscrimination laws.[17] An exception to title VII of the Civil Rights Act of 1964 permits religious institutions to discriminate on the basis of religion, but not on the basis of race, sex, or national origin.[18] Some courts have criticized this statutory accommodation of religion as clumsy and unconstitutional, too broad in some ways and too narrow in others.[19] For example, the Act forbids the requirement that Catholic priests be male.[20] But two district courts have concluded that the explicit statutory exception, and rejection of amendments that would have broadened it, clearly express congressional intent to regulate the churches.[21] The Fifth Circuit reached the same conclusion,[22] but implied an exception anyway to avoid a holding of unconstitutionality.[23] The court concluded that sex discrimination against a Salvation Army officer involved "matters of church administration and government and thus, purely of ecclesiastical cognizance," and that the Act would violate the free exercise clause if applied to the case.[24] In subsequent cases involving faculty at a church college and at a seminary, this exception was limited to ministers.[25]

Other sex discrimination cases have faced the constitutional issue squarely. A district court held title VII unconstitutional as applied to a Baptist seminary that attempted to maintain what the court variously described as "a pervasively religious environment,"[26] "an atmosphere of intense piety,"[27] and "a virtually cloistral environment."[28] The church expressed no desire to discriminate on the basis of race or national origin, but said its doctrines might require it to discriminate on the basis of sex under certain circumstances. But this was not the basis of the court's decision that it was totally exempt as to all its employees.[29] Rather, the court held that the seminary was entitled to be left alone—an entitlement I will call the right of church autonomy:

> Its employment decisions, steeped in a perception of divine will and inseparable from its mission, become matters of religious prerogative and warrant the fullest protection from governmental supervision. Enforcement of Title VII claims against a seminary based on race, sex, or national origin, even in the absence of articulated doctrinal compulsion, will lead inevitably to excessive governmental entanglement with religion in the process of dissecting employment functions into religious and secular components and in divining the good faith and legitimacy of religious grounds asserted as a defense to a prima facie case of discrimination.[30]

Similar defenses were rejected in three cases involving Seventh Day Adventists. One complaint alleged sex discrimination against an employee with editorial and secretarial responsibilities in a non-

17. *See generally* Bagni, "Discrimination in the Name of the Lord: A Critical Evaluation of Discrimination by Religious Organizations," 79 *Colum. L. Rev.* 1514 (1979).

18. 42 U.S.C. § 2000e-1 (1976). [In *Corporation of Presiding Bishop v. Amos*, 483 U.S. 327, 107 S.Ct. 2862, 97 L.Ed.2d 273 (1987), the Supreme Court held that §2000e-1, exempting religious organizations from Title VII's prohibition against discrimination in employment on the basis of religion, did not violate the Establishment or Equal Protection Clauses. The Court found that the provision "is rationally related to the legitimate purpose of alleviating significant governmental interference with the ability of religious organizations to define and carry out their religious missions." 107 S.Ct. at 2870.]

19. *King's Garden, Inc. v. FCC*, 498 F.2d 51, 54–55 (D.C. Cir.), cert. denied, 419 U.S. 996 (1974); *EEOC v. Southwestern Baptist Theological Seminary*, 485 F.Supp. 255, 260 (N.D. Tex. 1980), rev'd in part, 651 F.2d 277 (5th Cir. 1981). *But see EEOC v. Mississippi College*, 626 F.2d 477, 489 (5th Cir. 1980), cert. denied, 101 S.Ct. 3143 (1981).

20. 42 U.S.C. § 2000e-1 (1976); Comment, "Title VII and the Appointment of Women Clergy: A Statutory and Constitutional Quagmire," 13 *Colum. J.L. & Soc. Probs.* 257, 260–67 (1977).

21. *Dolter v. Wahlert High School*, 483 F.Supp. 266, 268–69 (N.D. Iowa 1980); *EEOC v. Pacific Press Publ. Ass'n*, 482 F.Supp. 1291, 1302–07 (N.D. Cal. 1979). Cf. *Ritter v. Mount St. Mary's College*, 495 F.Supp. 724, 726–29 (D. Md. 1980) (relying on absence of similar exceptions in Equal Pay Act and Age Discrimination in Employment Act, and concluding that these acts do not apply to religious institutions).

22. *McClure v. Salvation Army*, 460 F.2d 553, 558 (5th Cir.), cert. denied as untimely filed, 409 U.S. 896 (1972).

23. *Id.* at 560–61.

24. *Id.* at 560.

25. *EEOC v. Southwestern Baptist Theological Seminary*, 651 F.2d 277, 283–85 (5th Cir. 1981); *EEOC v. Mississippi College*, 626 F.2d 477, 485–86 (5th Cir. 1980), cert. denied, 101 S.Ct. 3143 (1981).

26. *EEOC v. Southwestern Baptist Theological Seminary*, 485 F.Supp. 255, 258 (N.D. Tex. 1980), rev'd in part, 651 F.2d 277 (5th Cir. 1981).

27. *Id.*

28. *Id.* at 261.

29. *Id.* at 259.

30. *Id.* at 261 (footnote omitted). The Fifth Circuit affirmed with respect to the faculty, but reversed with respect to the administration and staff, 651 F.2d 277 (5th Cir. 1981). The court held that the faculty were ministers and applied its rule that the church-minister relationship is exempt from regulation, see *McClure v. Salvation Army*, 460 F.2d 553 (5th Cir.), cert. denied as untimely filed, 409 U.S. 896 (1972).

profit publishing house;[31] one alleged Equal Pay Act[32] violations in the church's schools;[33] and one charged racial discrimination against a typist-receptionist.[34] But two of these opinions indicated that the result might have been different—if the job had been "close to the heart of church administration,"[35] if there had been a "doctrinal" reason for the discrimination,[36] if the victim had been a minister or member of a religious order,[37] or if the claim had threatened continual interference with church employment practices.[38] . . .

* * *

There is also a pair of older cases rejecting challenges to key provisions of the Fair Labor Standards Act[48] and its state equivalents. The Supreme Court upheld state child labor laws against a child's claim that it was her religious duty to sell religious tracts, emphasizing the state's interest in protecting children.[49] And the Seventh Circuit upheld the minimum wage and maximum hour provisions of the FLSA as applied to employees in a church-owned printing plant, some of whom swore that they did not consider themselves "mere wage earners," but had come to the plant to help "in the work of the Lord."[50]

The most recent church labor relations issue emerged when the Secretary of Labor asserted for the first time that the Federal Unemployment Tax Act applies to church schools. The Supreme Court recently found the Act inapplicable to schools that are not separately incorporated from their sponsoring churches.[52] . . .

These labor law cases illustrate a sufficiently broad range of the constitutional questions raised by regulation of churches to make them a useful tool for analysis. The analysis offered here should be applicable, perhaps with some modifications, to other kinds of regulation, including another set of current issues: regulation of church schools in matters of curriculum,[54] teacher certification,[55] and racial discrimination.[56]

* * *

III. Free Exercise and the Right to Church Autonomy

* * *

The free exercise clause protection for religious activity includes at least three rather different kinds of rights. In each category, some claims have been accepted and others rejected; none of these rights is protected absolutely.

One category is the bare freedom to carry on religious activities: to build churches and schools, conduct worship services, pray, proselytize, and teach moral values. This is the exercise of religion in its most obvious sense.

---

31. *EEOC v. Pacific Press Publ. Ass'n*, 482 F.Supp. 1291 (N.D. Cal. 1979). [*See also EEOC v. Fremont Christian School*, 781 F.2d 1362 (9th Cir. 1986) (application of Title VII and Equal Pay Act to sex discrimination in provision of health insurance to employee does not violate Establishment or Free Exercise Clauses).]

32. 29 U.S.C. § 206(d) (1976).

33. *Marshall v. Pacific Union Conf. of Seventh-Day Adventist*, 14 Empl. Prac. Dec. 5956 (C.D. Cal. 1977).

34. *Whitney v. Greater N.Y. Corp. of Seventh-Day Adventists*, 401 F.Supp. 1363 (S.D.N.Y. 1975).

35. *Id.* at 1368.

36. *Id. Also see Ritter v. Mount St. Mary's College*, 495 F.Supp. 724, 729–30 (D.Md. 1980) (tentatively taking a similar position and denying defendant's motion for summary judgment).

37. *EEOC v. Pacific Press Publ. Ass'n*, 482 F.Supp. 1291, 1305 n.26 (N.D. Cal. 1979).

38. *Id.* at 1307–15.

48. 29 U.S.C. §§ 201–19 (1976).

49. *Prince v. Massachusetts*, 321 U.S. 158, 167–69 (1944). *See id.* at 164 (making clear that the child's rights were asserted).

50. *Mitchell v. Pilgrim Holiness Church Corp.*, 210 F.2d 879, 881, 884 (7th Cir.), cert. denied, 347 U.S. 1013 (1954).

52. *St. Martin Evangelical Lutheran Church v. South Dakota*, 101 S.Ct. 2142 (1981). [*See also Baltimore Lutheran High School Assoc. v. Employment Security Administration*, 302 Md. 649, 490 A.2d 701 (Md. 1985) (state unemployment insurance law).]

54. *Kentucky State Bd. for Elementary & Secondary Educ. v. Rudasill*, 589 S.W. 2d 877 (Ky. 1979), cert. denied, 446 U.S. 938 (1980); *State v. Whisner*, 47 Ohio St.2d 181, 351 N.E.2d 750 (1976); Comment, "Regulation of Fundamentalist Christian Schools: Free Exercise of Religion v. The State's Interest in Quality Education," 67 *Ky. L.J.* 415, 423–25 (1979).

55. *Kentucky State Bd. for Elementary & Secondary Educ. v. Rudasill*, 589 S.W.2d 877 (Ky. 1979), cert. denied, 446 U.S. 938 (1980); Comment, *supra* note 54, at 422–23.

56. *Bob Jones Univ. v. United States*, 639 F.2d 147 (4th Cir. 1980), cert. granted, 50 U.S.L.W. 3278 (U.S. Oct. 13, 1981) (No. 81-3); *Fiedler v. Marumsco Christian School*, 631 F.2d 1144 (4th Cir. 1980); *Brown v. Dade Christian Schools, Inc.*, 556 F.2d 310 (5th Cir. 1977), cert. denied, 434 U.S. 1063 (1978).

Second, and closely related, is the right of churches to conduct these activities autonomously: to select their own leaders,[129] define their own doctrines,[130] resolve their own disputes,[131] and run their own institutions.[132] Religion includes important communal elements for most believers. They exercise their religion through religious organizations, and these organizations must be protected by the clause.

Third is the right of conscientious objection to government policy. The phrase is most prominently associated with the military draft, but there has also been conscientious objector litigation with respect to war taxes, compulsory education, medical treatment and innoculations, social insurance, Sabbath observance and nonobservance, monogamy, and other requirements that conflict with the moral scruples of certain sects or individual believers. These cases are also within the clause, because one way to exercise one's religion is to follow its moral dictates.

Each of these rights has solid support in the case law, but many courts and commentators think only in terms of conscientious objection. One of the most common errors in free exercise analysis is to try to fit all free exercise claims into the conscientious objector category and reject the ones that do not fit. Under this approach, every free exercise claim requires an elaborate judicial inquiry into the conscience or doctrines of the claimant. If he is not compelled by religion to engage in the disputed conduct, he is not entitled to free exercise protection. Thus, courts have tried to decide whether activities of organized churches were required by church doctrine or were something that the churches did for nonreligious reasons.[142] Courts have even allowed schools to deny student religious groups access to schoolrooms—freely available to other student groups—on the ground that the students' religion did not require prayer and services at the disputed time and place.[143]

This approach reflects a rigid, simplistic, and erroneous view of religion. Many activities that obviously are exercises of religion are not required by conscience or doctrine. Singing in the church choir and saying the Roman Catholic rosary are two common examples. Any activity engaged in by a church as a body is an exercise of religion. This is not to say that all such activities are immune from regulation: there may be a sufficiently strong governmental interest to justify the intrusion. But neither are these activities wholly without constitutional protection. It is not dispositive that an activity is not compelled by the official doctrine of a church or the religious conscience of an individual believer. Indeed, many would say that an emphasis on rules and obligations misconceives the essential nature of some religions.[145]

Moreover, emphasis on doctrine and requirements ignores the fluidity of doctrine and the many factors that can contribute to doctrinal change. A church is a complex and dynamic organization, often including believers with a variety of views on important questions of faith, morals, and spirituality. The dominant view of what is central to the religion, and of what practices are required by the religion, may gradually change. Today's pious custom may be tomorrow's moral obligation, and vice versa.

These characteristics of doctrinal change have two consequences. One is that the officially promulgated church doctrine, on which courts too often rely, is not a reliable indication of what the faithful believe. At best the officially promulgated doctrine of a large denomination represents the dominant or most commonly held view; it cannot safely be imputed to every believer or every affiliated congregation. If an official statement of doctrine has not been revised in recent times, it may be that almost no one in the church still believes it. . . . This gap between official doctrine and rank-and-file belief means that courts

---

129. *E.g.*, *Serbian E. Orthodox Diocese v. Milivojevich*, 426 U.S. 696 (1976). . . .

130. *E.g.*, *Presbyterian Church v. Mary Elizabeth Blue Hull Memorial Presbyterian Church*, 393 U.S. 440, 449 (1969).

131. *E.g.*, *Jones v. Wolf*, 443 U.S. 595 (1979); *Maryland & Va. Eldership of the Churches of God v. Church of God*, 396 U.S. 367 (1970) (per curiam). . . .

132. *E.g.*, *NLRB v. Catholic Bishop*, 440 U.S. 490 (1979). . . .

142. *E.g.*, *Brown v. Dade Christian Schools, Inc.*, 556 F.2d 310, 311–14 (5th Cir. 1977) (en banc) (plurality opinion), cert. denied, 434 U.S. 1063 (1978); *Dolter v. Wahlert High School*, 483 F.Supp. 266, 269–70 (N.D. Iowa 1980).

143. *Brandon v. Board of Educ.*, 635 F.2d 971, 977 (2d Cir. 1980), cert. denied, 50 U.S.L.W. 3486 (U.S. Dec. 14, 1981); *Chess v. Widmar*, 480 F.Supp. 907, 917 (W.D. Mo. 1979), rev'd, 635 F.2d 1310 (8th Cir. 1980), aff'd sub nom. *Widmar v. Vincent*, 50 U.S.L.W. 4062 (U.S. Dec. 8, 1981).

145. *See, e.g.*, Galatians 3:13 ("Christ has redeemed us from the curse of the law . . . ."); 2 Corinthians 3:6 ("[T]he letter killeth, but the spirit giveth life.")

are prone to err in deciding whether activities of a local church or small group of believers are compelled by conscience.

The complex and open-ended nature of the processes that lead to doctrinal change has a second consequence that is even more important. When the state interferes with the autonomy of a church, and particularly when it interferes with the allocation of authority and influence within a church, it interferes with the very process of forming the religion as it will exist in the future. . . . In the labor relations context, it is impossible to predict the long-term effect of forcing religious leaders to share authority with a secular union, or of substituting one employee for another as a result of a discrimination charge or a union grievance. A number of such substitutions may have a cumulative effect, especially if, as seems likely, there is some bias in the process making them. Employees who are more aggressive and less deferential to authority, and therefore more litigious, are more likely to invoke remedies that result in compulsory replacement of one employee with another. Thus, any interference with church affairs may disrupt "the free development of religious doctrine."[150]

Such government-induced changes in religion are too unpredictable to be avoided on a case-by-case basis. They can be minimized only by a strong rule of church autonomy. The free exercise clause therefore forbids government interference with church operations unless there is, to use the conventional phrase, a compelling governmental interest to justify the interference. . . .

* * *

Church labor relations rather plainly fall within the right of church autonomy. Deciding who will conduct the work of the church and how that work will be conducted is an essential part of the exercise of religion. In the language of the Supreme Court's autonomy cases, labor relations are matters of "church administration"; undoubtedly, they affect "the operation of churches."

Occasionally, a labor relations law requires a church to violate its official doctrine or collective conscience. These cases present conscientious objection claims as well as church autonomy claims. But it is worth repeating that the right of church autonomy does not depend on conscientious objection.

* * *

Similarly, antidiscrimination laws initially prevent the church from deciding whether to discriminate among its employees and applicants. Many churches may wish to discriminate on the basis of religion, and some on the basis of race, sex, or national origin. Equally important, churches that do not want to discriminate at all are deprived of the chance to define discrimination. Some may oppose unequal treatment of individuals because of race, sex, or national origin, but want to be free to act on any facially neutral basis even if it has disparate impact on racial, sexual, or ethnic groups.

Even churches that accept the full scope of collective bargaining and the government's definition of discrimination may be seriously alarmed at the prospect of secular enforcement. This requires secular tribunals to review the church's comparisons of the responsibility and difficulty of jobs and of the skills, qualifications, and performance of workers; its motives for personnel decisions and the credibility of its claims to have acted for religious reasons; the religious or other necessity for employment practices that have disparate impact; even the effect on workers of its bishops' prayers and Bible readings. Similar review of church personnel decisions is required under the Federal Unemployment Tax Act.

Some of the lower court decisions and commentary give no weight at all to the loss of autonomy inherent in the enforcement process.[*] They assume that the churches' rights can be protected by determining whether a personnel action was required by church doctrine. But the distinctions required by this approach are difficult, especially for secular courts unversed in theological subtleties, and an error can result in penalizing a church for an act of conscience. More importantly, as argued above, interference in personnel matters interferes with the further development of the religion. And quite aside from these concerns about conscientious objection and the effects of interference with church labor relations, selecting and directing the employees who will carry out the work of the church is an exercise

150. *Prebyterian Church v. Mary Elizabeth Blue Hull Memorial Presbyterian Church*, 393 U.S. 440, 449 (1969). . . .

* *See Miller v. Catholic Diocese of Great Falls*, 728 P.2d 794 (Mont. 1986).

of religion, which the churches are entitled to perform freely.

* * *

Runyon v. McCrary

427 U.S. 160, 96 S.Ct. 2586, 49 L.Ed.2d 415 (1976).

Mr. Justice Stewart delivered the opinion of the Court.

The principal issue presented by these consolidated cases is whether a federal law, namely 42 U.S.C. §1981, prohibits private schools from excluding qualified children solely because they are Negroes.

I

The respondents in No. 75–62, Michael McCrary and Colin Gonzales, are Negro children. By their parents, they filed a class action against the petitioners in No. 75–62, Russell and Katheryne Runyon, who are the proprietors of Bobbe's Private School in Arlington, Va. Their complaint alleged that they had been prevented from attending the school because of the petitioners' policy of denying admission to Negroes, in violation of 42 U.S.C. § 1981[1] and Title II of the Civil Rights Act of 1964, 42 U.S.C. §2000a *et seq.*[2] They sought declaratory and injunctive relief and damages. On the same day Colin Gonzales, the respondent in No. 75–66, filed a similar complaint by his parents against the petitioner in No. 75–66, Fairfax-Brewster School, Inc., located in Fairfax County, Va. The petitioner in No. 75–278, the Southern Independent School Association, sought and was granted permission to intervene as a party defendant in the suit against the Runyons. That organization is a nonprofit association composed of six state private school associations, and represents 395 private schools. It is stipulated that many of these schools deny admission to Negroes.

The suits were consolidated for trial. The findings of the District Court, which were left undisturbed by the Court of Appeals, were as follows. Bobbe's School opened in 1958 and grew from an initial enrollment of five students to 200 in 1972. A day camp was begun in 1967 and has averaged 100 children per year. The Fairfax-Brewster School commenced operations in 1955 and opened a summer day camp in 1956. A total of 223 students were enrolled at the school during the 1972–1973 academic year, and 236 attended the day camp in the summer of 1972. Neither school has ever accepted a Negro child for any of its programs.

In response to a mailed brochure addressed "resident" and an advertisement in the "Yellow Pages" of the telephone directory, Mr. and Mrs. Gonzales telephoned and then visited the Fairfax-Brewster School in May 1969. After the visit, they submitted an application for Colin's admission to the day camp. The school responded with a form letter, which stated that the school was "unable to accommodate [Colin's] application." Mr. Gonzales telephoned the school. Fairfax-Brewster's Chairman of the Board explained that the reason for Colin's rejection was that the School was not integrated. Mr. Gonzales then telephoned Bobbe's School, from which the family had also received in the mail a brochure addressed to "resident." In response to a question concerning that school's admissions policies, he was told that only members of the Caucasian race were accepted. In August 1972, Mrs. McCrary telephoned Bobbe's School in response to an advertisement in the telephone book. She inquired about nursery school facilities for her son, Michael. She also asked if the School was integrated. The answer was no.

Upon these facts, the District Court found that the Fairfax-Brewster School had rejected Colin Gonzales' application on account of his race and that Bobbe's School had denied both children admission on racial grounds. The Court held that 42 U.S.C. § 1981 makes illegal the schools' racially discriminatory admissions policies. It therefore enjoined Fairfax-Brewster and Bobbe's School and the member schools of the Southern Independent School Association[3] from discriminating against applicants

1. 42 U.S.C. §1981 provides:

"All persons within the jurisdiction of the United States shall have the same right in every State and Territory to make and enforce contracts, to sue, be parties, give evidence, and to the full and equal benefit of all laws and proceedings for the security of persons and property as is enjoyed by white citizens, and shall be subject to like punishment, pains, penalties, taxes, licenses, and exactions of every kind, and to no other."

2. The respondents withdrew their Title II claim before trial.

3. The District Court determined that the suit could not be maintained as a class action.

for admission on the basis of race. The Court awarded compensatory relief to Mr. and Mrs. McCrary, Michael McCrary, and Colin Gonzales.[4] In a previous ruling the Court had held that the damage claim of Mr. and Mrs. Gonzales was barred by Virginia's two-year statute of limitations for personal injury actions, "borrowed" for §1981 suits filed in that State. . . .

The Court of Appeals for the Fourth Circuit, sitting en banc, affirmed the District Court's grant of equitable and compensatory relief and its ruling as to the applicable statute of limitations. . . . *McCrary v. Runyon*, 515 F.2d 1082 (1975). . . .

II

It is worth noting at the outset some of the questions that these cases do not present. They do not present any question of the right of a private social organization to limit its membership on racial or any other grounds. They do not present any question of the right of a private school to limit its student body to boys, to girls, or to adherents of a particular religious faith, since 42 U.S.C. §1981 is in no way addressed to such categories of selectivity. They do not even present the application of §1981 to private sectarian schools that practice *racial* exclusion on religious grounds.[6] Rather, these cases present only two basic questions: whether §1981 prohibits private, commercially operated, nonsectarian schools from denying admission to prospective students because they are Negroes, and, if so, whether that federal law is constitutional as so applied.

A. Applicability of §1981

It is now well established that §1 of the Civil Rights Act of 1866, 14 Stat. 27, 42 U.S.C. §1981 (1970), prohibits racial discrimination in the making and enforcements of private contracts. See *Johnson v. Railway Express Agency, Inc.*, 421 U.S. 454, 459–460; *Tillman v. Wheaton-Haven Recreation Assn.*, 410 U.S. 431, 439–440. Cf. *Jones v. Alfred H. Mayer Co.*, 392 U.S. 409, 441–443, n. 78.

In *Jones* the Court held that the portion of §1 of the Civil Rights Act of 1866 presently codified as 42 U.S.C. §1982 prohibits private racial discrimination in the sale or rental of real or personal property. Relying on the legislative history of §1, from which both §1981 and §1982 derive, the Court concluded that Congress intended to prohibit "all racial discrimination, private and public, in the sale . . . of property," 392 U.S., at 437, and that this prohibition was within Congress' power under §2 of the Thirteenth Amendment "rationally to determine what are the badges and the incidents of slavery, and . . . to translate that determination into effective legislation." *Id.*, at 440–441.

As the Court indicated in *Jones*, 392 U.S., at 441–443, n. 78, that holding necessarily implied that the portion of §1 of the 1866 Act presently codified as 42 U.S.C. §1981 likewise reaches purely private acts of racial discrimination. The statutory holding in *Jones* was that the "[1866] Act was designed to do just what its terms suggest: to prohibit all racial discrimination, whether or not under color of law, with respect to the rights enumerated therein—including the right to purchase or lease property." 392 U.S., at 436. One of the "rights enumerated" in §1 is "the same right . . . to make and enforce contracts . . . as is enjoyed by white citizens. . . ." 14 Stat. 27. Just as in *Jones* a Negro's §1 right to purchase property on equal terms with whites was violated when a private person refused to sell to the prospective purchaser solely because he was a Negro, so also a Negro's §1 right to "make and enforce contracts" is violated if a private offeror refuses to extend to a Negro, solely because he is a Negro, the same opportunity to enter into contracts as he extends to white offerees.

* * *

It is apparent that the racial exclusion practiced by the Fairfax-Brewster School and Bobbe's Private School amounts to a classic violation of §1981. The parents of Colin Gonzales and Michael McCrary sought to enter into contractual relationships with Bobbe's Private School for educational services. Colin Gonzales' parents sought to enter into a similar relationship with the Fairfax-Brewster School. Under those contractual relationships, the schools would

4. For the embarrassment, humiliation, and mental anguish which the parents and children suffered, the Court awarded Colin Gonzales $2,000 against the Fairfax-Brewster School and $500 against Bobbe's School. Michael McCrary was awarded damages of $1,000, and Mr. and Mrs. McCrary $2,000, against Bobbie's School.

6. Nothing in this record suggests that either the Fairfax-Brewster School or Bobbe's Private School excludes applicants on religious grounds, and the Free Exercise Clause of the First Amendment is thus in no way here involved.

have received payments for services rendered, and the prospective students would have received instruction in return for those payments. The educational services of Bobbe's Private School and the Fairfax-Brewster School were advertised and offered to members of the general public. But neither school offered services on an equal basis to white and nonwhite students. . . .

The petitioning schools and school association argue principally that §1981 does not reach private acts of racial discrimination. That view is wholly inconsistent with *Jones'* interpretation of the legislative history of §1 of the Civil Rights Act of 1866, an interpretation that was reaffirmed in *Sullivan v. Little Hunting Park, Inc.*, 396 U.S. 229, and again in *Tillman v. Wheaton-Haven Recreation Assn., supra*. And this consistent interpretation of the law necessarily requires the conclusion that §1981, like §1982, reaches private conduct. See *Tillman v. Wheaton-Haven Recreation Assn.*, 410 U.S., at 439–440; *Johnson v. Railway Express Agency, Inc.*, 421 U.S., at 459–460.

It is noteworthy that Congress in enacting the Equal Employment Opportunity Act of 1972, 86 Stat. 103, as amended, 42 U.S.C. §2000e *et seq.* (1970 ed. Supp. IV), specifically considered and rejected an amendment that would have repealed the Civil Rights Act of 1866, as interpreted by this Court in *Jones*, insofar as it affords private sector employees a right of action based on racial discrimination in employment. See *Johnson v. Railway Express Agency, Inc.*, 421 U.S., at 459. There could hardly be a clearer indication of congressional agreement with the view that §1981 *does* reach private acts of racial discrimination. . . . In these circumstances there is no basis for deviating from the well-settled principles of *stare decisis* applicable to this Court's construction of federal statutes. . . .

B. Constitutionality of §1981 as Applied

The question remains whether §1981, as applied, violates constitutionally protected rights of free association and privacy, or a parent's right to direct the education of his children.[13]

1. Freedom of Association. In *NAACP v. Alabama*, 357 U.S. 449, and similar decisions, the Court has recognized a First Amendment right "to engage in association for the advancement of beliefs and ideas . . . ." *Id.*, at 460. That right is protected because it promotes and may well be essential to the "[e]ffective advocacy of both public and private points of view, particularly controversial ones" that the First Amendment is designed to foster. *Id.*, at 460. . . .

From this principle it may be assumed that parents have a First Amendment right to send their children to educational institutions that promote the belief that racial segregation is desirable, and that the children have an equal right to attend such institutions. But it does not follow that the *practice* of excluding racial minorities from such institutions is also protected by the same principle. As the Court stated in *Norwood v. Harrison*, 413 U.S. 455, "the Constitution . . . places no value on discrimination," *id.*, at 469, and while "[i]nvidious private discrimination may be characterized as a form of exercising freedom of association protected by the First Amendment . . . it has never been accorded affirmative constitutional protections. And even some private discrimination is subject to special remedial legislation in certain circumstances under §2 of the Thirteenth Amendment; Congress has made such discrimination unlawful in other significant contexts." 413 U.S., at 470. In any event, as the Court of Appeals noted, "there is no showing that discontinuance of [the] discriminatory admission practices would inhibit in any way the teaching in these schools of any ideas or dogma." 515 F.2d, at 1087.

2. Parental Rights. In *Meyer v. Nebraska*, 262 U.S. 390, the Court held that the liberty protected by the Due Process Clause of the Fourteenth Amendment includes the right "to acquire useful knowledge, to marry, establish a home and bring up children," *id.*, at 399, and, concomitantly, the right to send one's children to a private school that offers specialized training—in that case, instruction in the German language. In *Pierce v. Society of Sisters*, 268 U.S. 510, the Court applied "the doctrine of *Meyer v. Nebraska*," *id.*, at 534, to hold unconstitutional an Oregon law requiring the parent, guardian, or other person having custody of a child between eight and 16 years of age to send that child to public school on pain of criminal liability. The Court thought it

13. It is clear that the schools have standing to assert these arguments on behalf of their patrons. See *Pierce v. Society of Sisters*, 268 U.S. 510, 535–536.

"entirely plain that the [statute] unreasonably interferes with the liberty of parents and guardians to direct the upbringing and education of children under their control." *Id.*, at 534–535. In *Wisconsin v. Yoder*, 406 U.S. 205, the Court stressed the limited scope of *Pierce*, pointing out that it lent "no support to the contention that parents may replace state educational requirements with their own idiosyncratic views of what knowledge a child needs to be a productive and happy member of society" but rather "held simply that while a State may posit [educational] standards, it may not preempt the educational process by requiring children to attend public schools." *Id.*, at 239. . . .

It is clear that the present application of §1981 infringes no parental right recognized in *Meyer, Pierce, Yoder*, or *Norwood*. No challenge is made to the petitioners' right to operate their private schools or the right of parents to send their children to a particular private school rather than a public school. Nor do these cases involve a challenge to the subject matter which is taught at any private school. Thus, the Fairfax-Brewster School and Bobbe's Private School and members of the intervenor association remain presumptively free to inculcate whatever values and standards they deem desirable. *Meyer* and its progeny entitle them to no more.

3. The Right of Privacy. The Court has held that in some situations the Constitution confers a right of privacy. *See Roe v. Wade*, 410 U.S. 113, 152–153; *Eisenstadt v. Baird*, 405 U.S. 438, 453; *Stanley v. Georgia*, 394 U.S. 557, 564–565; *Griswold v. Connecticut*, 381 U.S. 479, 484–485. See also *Loving v. Virginia*, 388 U.S. 1, 12; *Skinner v. Oklahoma*, 316 U.S. 535, 541.

While the application of §1981 to the conduct at issue here—a private school's adherence to a racially discriminatory admissions policy—does not represent governmental intrusion into the privacy of the home or similarly intimate setting, it does implicate parental interests. These interests are related to the procreative rights protected in *Roe v. Wade, supra*, and *Griswold v. Connecticut, supra*. A person's decision whether to bear a child and a parent's decision concerning the manner in which his child is to be educated may fairly be characterized as exercises of familial rights and responsibilities. But it does not follow that because government is largely or even entirely precluded from regulating the child-bearing decision, it is similarly restricted by the Constitution from regulating the implementation of parental decisions concerning a child's education.

The Court has repeatedly stressed that while parents have a constitutional right to send their children to private schools and a constitutional right to select private schools that offer specialized instruction, they have no constitutional right to provide their children with private school education unfettered by reasonable government regulation. *See Wisconsin v. Yoder*, 406 U.S., at 213; *Pierce v. Society of Sisters*, 268 U.S., at 534; *Meyer v. Nebraska*, 262 U.S., at 402.[15] Indeed, the Court in *Pierce* expressly acknowledged "the power of the State reasonably to regulate all schools, to inspect, supervise and examine them, their teachers and pupils. . . ." 268 U.S., at 534. See also *Prince v. Massachusetts*, 321 U.S. 158, 166.

Section 1981, as applied to the conduct at issue here, constitutes an exercise of federal legislative power under §2 of the Thirteenth Amendment fully consistent with *Meyer, Pierce*, and the cases that followed in their wake. As the Court held in *Jones v. Alfred H. Mayer Co., supra*, "[i]t has never been doubted . . . 'that the power vested in Congress to enforce [the Thirteenth Amendment] by appropriate legislation' . . . includes the power to enact laws 'direct and primary, operating upon the acts of individuals, whether sanctioned by State legislation or not.' " 392 U.S., at 438 (citation omitted). The prohibition of racial discrimination that interferes with the making and enforcement of contracts for private educational services furthers goals closely analogous to those served by §1981's elimination of racial discrimination in the making of private employment contracts and, more generally, by §1982's guarantee that "a dollar in the hands of a Negro will purchase the same thing as a dollar in the hands of a white man." *Jones v. Alfred H. Mayer Co.*, 392 U.S., at 443.

15. The *Meyer-Pierce-Yoder* "parental" right and the privacy right, while dealt with separately in this opinion, may be no more than verbal variations of a single constitutional right. See *Roe v. Wade*, 410 U.S. 113, 152–153 (*Meyer v. Nebraska, supra* and *Pierce v. Society of Sisters, supra*, cited for the proposition that this Court has recognized a constitutional right of privacy).

III

[The Court's discussion of the statute of limitations and attorneys' fees issues is omitted.]

* * *

For the reasons stated in this opinion, the judgment of the Court of Appeals is in all respects affirmed.

It is so ordered.

Mr. Justice Powell, concurring.

If the slate were clean I might well be inclined to agree with Mr. Justice White that §1981 was not intended to restrict private contractual choices. Much of the review of the history and purpose of this statute set forth in his dissenting opinion is quite persuasive. It seems to me, however, that it comes too late.

The applicability of §1981 to private contracts has been considered maturely and recently, and I do not feel free to disregard these precedents. . . .

Mr. Justice Stevens, concurring.

For me the problem in these cases is whether to follow a line of authority which I firmly believe to have been incorrectly decided.

Jones v. Alfred H. Mayer Co., 392 U.S. 409, and its progeny have unequivocally held that §1 of the Civil Rights Act of 1866 prohibits private racial discrimination. There is no doubt in my mind that construction of the statute would have amazed the legislators who voted for it. Both its language and the historical setting in which it was enacted convince me that Congress intended only to guarantee all citizens the same legal capacity to make and enforce contracts, to obtain, own and convey property, and to litigate and give evidence. Moreover, since the legislative history discloses an intent not to outlaw segregated public schools at that time, it is quite unrealistic to assume that Congress intended the broader result of prohibiting segregated private schools. Were we writing on a clean slate, I would therefore vote to reverse.

But *Jones* has been decided and is now an important part of the fabric of our law. Although I recognize the force of Mr. Justice White's argument that the construction of §1982 does not control §1981, it would be most incongruous to give those two sections a fundamentally different construction. The net result of the enactment in 1866, the re-enactment in 1870, and the codification in 1874 produced, I believe, a statute resting on the constitutional foundations provided by both the Thirteenth and Fourteenth Amendments. An attempt to give a fundamentally different meaning to two similar provisions by ascribing one to the Thirteenth and the other to the Fourteenth Amendment cannot succeed. I am persuaded, therefore, that we must either apply the rationale of *Jones* or overrule that decision.

There are two reasons which favor overruling. First, as I have already stated, my conviction that *Jones* was wrongly decided is firm. Second, it is extremely unlikely that reliance upon *Jones* has been so extensive that this Court is foreclosed from overruling it. *Compare Flood v. Kuhn*, 407 U.S. 258, 273–274, 278–279, 283. There are, however, opposing arguments of greater force.

The first is the interest in stability and orderly development of the law. As Justice Cardozo remarked, with respect to the routine work of the judiciary, "the labor of judges would be increased almost to the breaking point if every past decision could be reopened in every case, and one could not lay one's own course of bricks on the secure foundation of the courses laid by others who had gone before him."[2] Turning to the exceptional case, Justice Cardozo noted "that when a rule, after it has been duly tested by experience, has been found to be inconsistent with the sense of justice or with the social welfare, there should be less hesitation in frank disavowal and full abandonment. . . . If judges have woefully misinterpreted the *mores* of their day, or if the *mores* of their day are no longer those of ours, they ought not to tie, in helpless submission, the hands of their successors."[3] In this case, those admonitions favor adherence to, rather than departure from, precedent. For even if *Jones* did not accurately reflect the sentiments of the Reconstruction Congress, it surely accords with the prevailing sense of justice today.

The policy of the Nation as formulated by the Congress in recent years has moved constantly in the direction of eliminating racial segregation in all

2. B. Cardozo, *The Nature of Judicial Process* 149 (1921). [*See also* E. Levi, *An Introduction to Legal Reasoning* 31–33 (1949)].

3. *Id.*, at 150–152.

sectors of society.[4] This Court has given a sympathetic and liberal construction to such legislation. For the Court now to overrule *Jones* would be a significant step backwards, with effects that would not have arisen from a correct decision in the first instance. Such a step would be so clearly contrary to my understanding of the *mores* of today that I think the Court is entirely correct in adhering to *Jones*.

With this explanation, I join the opinion of the Court.

Mr. Justice White, with whom Mr. Justice Rehnquist joins, dissenting.

We are urged here to extend the meaning and reach of 42 U.S.C. §1981 so as to establish a general prohibition against a private individual or institution refusing to enter into a contract with another person because of that person's race. Section 1981 has been on the books since 1870 and to so hold for the first time would be contrary to the language of the section, to its legislative history and to the clear dictum of this Court in the Civil Rights cases, 109 U.S. 1, 16–17 (1883), almost contemporaneously with the passage of the statute, that the section reaches only discriminations imposed by state law. The majority's belated discovery of a congressional purpose which escaped this Court only a decade after the statute was passed and which escaped all other federal courts for almost 100 years is singularly unpersuasive.[2] I therefore respectfully dissent.

[Mr. Justice White's lengthy discussion of the legislative history of §1981 is omitted.]

* * *

The majority's holding that 42 U.S.C. §1981 prohibits all racially motivated contractual decisions . . . threatens to embark the judiciary on a treacherous course. Whether such conduct should be condoned or not, whites and blacks will undoubtedly choose to form a variety of associational relationships pursuant to contracts which exclude members of the other race. Social clubs, black and white, and associations designed to further the interests of blacks or whites are but two examples. Lawsuits by members of the other race attempting to gain admittance to such an association are not pleasant to contemplate. As the associational or contractual relationships become more private, the pressures to hold §1981 inapplicable to them will increase. Imaginative judicial construction of the word "contract" is foreseeable; Thirteenth Amendment limitations on Congress' power to ban "badges and incidents of slavery" may be discovered; the doctrine of the right to association may be bent to cover a given situation. In any event, courts will be called upon to balance sensitive policy considerations against each other—which considerations have never been addressed by any Congress—all under the guise of "construing a statute. This is a task appropriate for the legislature, not for the judiciary.

Such balancing of considerations as has been done by Congress in the area of racially motivated decisions not to contract with a member of the other race has led it to ban private racial discrimination in most of the job market and most of the housing market and to go no further. The judiciary should not undertake the political task of trying to decide what other areas are appropriate ones for a similar rule.

* * *

However, the majority points to language in *Johnson v. REA, Inc.*, 421 U.S. 454, stating with no discussion whatever that 42 U.S.C. §1981 supplies a cause of action for a private racially motivated refusal to contract. . . . [T]he dictum in *Johnson v. REA, Inc.*, is squarely contrary to the dictum in *The Civil Rights Cases, supra*. The issue presented in this case is too important for this Court to let the more recent of two contradictory dicta stand in the way of an objective analysis of legislative history and a correct construction of a statute passed by Congress. *Cf. Jones v. Mayer, supra*, at 420 n. 25.

Accordingly, I would reverse.

NOTES AND QUESTIONS

1. Scope of §1981

What is the nature of the dispute about the meaning of §1981? Section 1981 speaks of blacks having the

4. *See, e.g.*, The Civil Rights Act of 1964, 78 Stat. 241, as added and as amended, 28 U.S.C. § 1447 (d), 42 U.S.C. §§1971, 1975a-1975d, 2000a-2000h-6 (1970 ed. and Supp. IV); The Voting Rights Act of 1965, 79 Stat. 437, as added and as amended, 42 U.S.C. §§1973-1973bb-4; The Civil Rights Act of 1968, Titles VIII, IX, 82 Stat. 81, 89, as amended, 42 U.S.C. §3061-3631 (1970 ed. and Supp. IV).

2. I do not question at this point the power of Congress or a state legislature to ban racial discrimination in private school admissions decisions. But as I see it Congress has not yet chosen to exercise that power.

same rights as whites "to make and enforce" contracts. Does this suggest that blacks were to have an equal opportunity to enter into contracts? Or does it suggest that blacks were to have the same contractual capacity as whites and equal access to the machinery of the state to enforce their contracts? A number of distinguished commentators have viewed the legislative history of §1981 as supporting only the latter point of view. *See, e.g.*, McClellan, "The Foibles and Fables of Runyon," 67 *Wash. U.L.Q.* 13 (1989); Casper, "*Jones v. Mayer*: Clio, Bemused and Confused Muse," 1968 *Sup. Ct. Rev.* 89; Henkin, "The Supreme Court, 1967 Term," 82 *Harv. L. Rev.* 63, 96–101 (1968). Others have read the legislative history as inconclusive in itself or at least sufficiently ambiguous so as to encompass racial discrimination in the contracting process. *See, e.g.*, Hilton, "Race, Religion, and Constitutional Restraints on Private Schools," 30 *Rutgers L. Rev.* 329, 360 (1977); Note, "The Desegregation of Private Schools: Is Section 1981 the Answer?" 48 *N.Y.U. L. Rev.* 1147 (1973). One commentator has firmly endorsed the *Runyon* court's reading of the historical record. *See* Kaczorowski, "The Enforcement Provisions of the Civil Rights Act of 1866: A Legislative History in Light of *Runyon v. McCrary*," 98 *Yale L. J.* 565 (1989).

If the legislative history supporting the majority position in *Runyon* is ambiguous at best, why did not the Court construe the statute so as to avoid passing on the constitutionality of §1981 under the First Amendment? Compare *Runyon* with *NLRB v. Catholic Bishop of Chicago*, 440 U.S. 490, 99 S.Ct. 1313, 59 L.Ed.2d 533 (1979). What alternatives did the Court have if it wished to outlaw racial discrimination by private schools? Might the Court have declared that the private schools were so regulated by the state and performed such public functions that their actions should be characterized as "state action"? *But see Moose Lodge No. 107 v. Irvis*, 407 U.S. 163, 92 S.Ct. 1965, 32 L.Ed.2d 627 (1972). *See generally* Note, "Federal Power to Regulate Private Discrimination: The Revival of the Enforcement Clauses of the Reconstruction Era Amendments," 74 *Colum. L. Rev.* 449, 458–59 (1974); Note, "The Desegregation of Private Schools: Is Section 1981 the Answer?," *supra*. What are the dangers of the state action approach? Would §1981 be rendered superfluous if plaintiffs could rely on the Fourteenth Amendment and the more general provisions of §1983? What implications would such an approach have for gender or religious discrimination?

Note that all the justices appear to agree that Congress has the power under the Thirteenth Amendment to outlaw racial discrimination by private schools. Do you agree? If Congress had not enacted §1981, could the Court reach such discrimination by direct judicial enforcement of the Thirteenth Amendment?

2. Stare Decisis and Statutory Interpretation

Do you agree with Justice Stevens that the Court should construe §1981 consistent with *Jones v. Mayer* and other recent precedents—even if it is convinced that the earlier statutory constructions were erroneous? Do stability and orderly development of the law outweigh concerns about distorting the judgment of Congress with regard to so important an issue? Should *Brown* and the public policy against racial discrimination allow the Court to reinterpret §1981? *See* Frankel, "*Runyon v. McCrary* Should Not be Overruled," 67 *Wash. U.L.Q.* 1 (1989). Why? Note that while Justice Stewart considers *Runyon* to involve a "classic" violation of §1981, Justice White chastises the majority for its "belated discovery of a congressional purpose which escaped this Court only a decade after the statute was passed and which escaped all other federal courts for almost 100 years. . . ."

Amidst great controversy, the Supreme Court in *Patterson v. McLean Credit Union*, 485 U.S. 617, 109 S.Ct. 2363, 105 L.Ed.2d 132 (1989) declined to overrule *Runyon* but held that section 1981 does not apply to racial harassment, relating to the conditions of employment, which occurs after the formation of a contract and which does not interfere with the right to enforce established contract obligations. *See* Note, "*Patterson v. McLean Credit Union*: New Limitations on an Old Civil Rights Statute," 68 N.C.L. Rev. 799 (1990).

With regard to the need for consistency in statutory interpretation, consider these remarks by Professor Edward Levi:

> If legislation which is disfavored can be interpreted away from time to time, then it is not to be expected, particularly if controversy is high, that the legislature will ever act. It will always be possible to say that new legislation is not needed because the court in the future will make a more appropriate interpretation. If the court is to have freedom to reinterpret legislation, the result will be to relieve the legislature

> from pressure. The legislation needs judicial consistency. Moreover, the court's own behavior in the face of pressure is likely to be indecisive. In all likelihood it will do enough to prevent legislative revision and not much more. Therefore it seems better to say that once a decisive interpretation of legislative intent has been made, and in that sense a direction has been fixed within the gap of ambiguity, the court should take that direction as given. . . .
>
> Where legislative interpretation is concerned, therefore, it appears that legal reasoning does attempt to fix the meaning of the word. When this is done, subsequent cases must be decided upon the basis that the prior meaning remains. It must not be reworked. . . . It is a hard doctrine against which judges frequently rebel. . . .

E. Levi, *An Introduction to Legal Reasoning* 23–24 (1949).

How does Levi's analysis bear on the appropriate interpretation of §1981? Perhaps it suggests that *Jones v. Mayer* was improperly decided. But given the gloss placed on the Reconstruction Civil Rights Act in *Jones*, what is the appropriate resolution of *Runyon*? What is the significance of Congress's failure to overturn *Jones*? *See* Frankel, "*Runyon v. McCrary* Should Not Be Overruled," 67 *Wash. U.L.Q.* 1 1989).

Why is not the Court as free to reinterpret §1981 as the equal protection clause of the Fourteenth Amendment? For example, in *Plessy v. Ferguson*, 163 U.S. 537, 16 S.Ct. 1138, 41 L.Ed. 258 (1896), the Court upheld the "separate-but-equal" doctrine, thereby permitting the states to segregate the races. But in *Brown v. Board of Education*, 347 U.S. 483, 74 S.Ct. 686, 98 L.Ed. 873 (1954), the Court repudiated the doctrine in the public school context. Does this suggest that the Court has or should have more flexibility in repudiating constitutional interpretations than in rejecting earlier constructions of federal statutes? Consider again Edward Levi's view:

> Under the United States experience, contrary to what has sometimes been believed when a written constitution of a nation is involved, the court has greater freedom than it has with the application of a statute or case law. In case law, when a judge determines what the controlling similarity between the present and prior case is, the case is decided. The judge does not feel free to ignore the results of a great number of cases which he cannot explain under a remade rule. And in interpretating legislation, when the prior interpretation, even though erroneous, is determined after a comparison of facts to cover the case, the case is decided. But this is not true with a constitution. The constitution sets up the conflicting ideals of the community in certain ambiguous categories. These categories bring along with them satellite concepts covering the areas of ambiguity. It is with a set of these satellite concepts that reasoning by example must work. But no satellite concept, no matter how well developed, can prevent the court from shifting its course, not only by realigning cases which impose certain restrictions, but by going beyond realignment back to the over-all ambiguous category written into the document. The constitution, in other words, permits the court to be inconsistent. The freedom is concealed either as a search for the intention of the framers or as a proper understanding of a living instrument, and sometimes as both. . . .

Levi, *supra* at 5–6.

Do you agree with this distinction? Compare *id.* with Brest, "The Misconceived Quest for the Original Understanding," 60 *B. U. L. Rev.* 204 (1980). Does this suggest that the Court should have reinterpreted the equal protection clause to apply to racial discrimination in private schools? *See generally* Rotunda, "*Runyon v. McCrary* and the Mosaic of State Action," 67 *Wash. U. L. Q.* 47 (1989).

3. Freedom of Association, Privacy, and the Rights of Parents

On what basis does Justice Stewart conclude that the defendants' interests in freedom of association, privacy, and the rights of parents to direct the upbringing of their children are outweighed by the governmental interest in eliminating racial discrimination? *See generally* Note, "*Runyon v. McCrary* and Private School Admission Policies," 16 *J. of Fam. L.* 77 (1977). Does it answer the question to suggest that no affirmative value is attached to racial discrimination and that, indeed, an antidiscrimination principal is embedded in the Fourteenth Amendment? Does not the Constitution, at least as construed in earlier decisions, place an affirmative value on freedom of association and parental rights? *See generally* C. Rice, *Freedom of Association* (1962); Emerson, "Freedom of Association and Freedom of Expression," 74 *Yale L. J.* 1 (1964); Raggi, "An Independent Right to Freedom of Association," 12 *Harv. C. R.-C. L. L. Rev.* 1 (1977). Is a ban on racially discriminatory admissions policies in private schools akin to the reasonable regulation of private schools endorsed in *Pierce*? *See* Comment "Private School Desegregation Under Section 1981," 124

U. Pa. L. Rev. 714, 722 (1976). What is the nature of the associational interest? Is it the right to associate with other persons per se, or is it the right to join together for purposes of political and other expression? If the latter is entitled to greater constitutional protection than the former, on which side of the line does *Runyon* fall? Put somewhat differently, does *Runyon* seek to silence powerful voices advocating racial discrimination? If so, how do you distinguish *Pierce, Meyer,* and *Farrington*? Do the cases turn on the nature of the positions advocated? Is this an acceptable constitutional standard? Or is it that the Court must reconcile the First and Fourteenth Amendments and that it did so in *Runyon* by allowing advocacy of segregation but not the practice of engaging in racially discriminatory admissions? But is not the practice of segregation inextricably tied to the advocacy of that position? Is Justice Stewart persuasive when he argues that permitting the presence of blacks will not impede the socialization processes of the private schools? Or is it that, despite the unwillingness to rely on the state action doctrine, the Court is treating all education as involving substantial public interests? *See* Hilton, "Race, Religion, and Constitutional Restraints on Private Schools," 30 *Rutgers L. Rev.* 329, 369 (1977). If this is so, does this suggest that *Runyon* will not be extended to private clubs and other relationships of a less public, more intimate, nature? *See generally* Note, "The Expanding Scope of Section 1981: Assault on Private Discrimination and a Cloud on Affirmative Action," 90 *Harv. L. Rev.* 412 (1976).

Is the associational interest of the parents undercut by the fact that the schools hold themselves open to the public at large (by "yellow-page" advertisements and mass mailings) except for black applicants? *See* L. Tribe, *American Constitutional Law* 979 n. 27 (1978). Consider this argument:

> Free association has traditionally been deemed to grant only the right to join, not the right to keep others out. Indeed, the recognition of a right to exclude would impair the associational freedom of those individuals who desire to join the group.

Note, 90 *Harv. L. Rev.* at 435.

Do you find this argument persuasive?

4. *Alternative Readings of* Runyon

To what extent may it be persuasively argued that the basis of *Runyon* lies in the inferior position of blacks in the marketplace of education? One commentator has strongly urged this argument:

> If in a given case a black plaintiff proves that he was denied a contract for education on the basis of race and that because of this he was placed in an inferior position in the market for education, he has made out a far stronger case for relief than a person who asserts only a denial of contract based on race. Colin Gonzales, one of the plaintiff children in *McCrary*, in fact gained admission to another private school in the area. Although the fact of making a single contract is no more proof of good market position than is a single denial proof of a bad one, at least it demonstrates that the plaintiffs may have retained the ability to pursue desired options as effectively as most other contractors in the marketplace. If this is true, their right to contract has not been infringed in the sense under consideration. If, however, their ability to find a school to their liking is substantially inferior to that of similarly situated whites, then their right to contract for the purpose of education has been infringed.

Comment, "Private School Desegregation Under Section 1981," 124 *U. Pa. L. Rev.* 714, 750 (1976).

Is this an attempt to blend together the two interpretations of §1981: the theory of equal contractual capacity and the theory of equal opportunity to contract? Does it succeed? Suppose many or most private schools in a given locale are willing to admit blacks. Does this mean that *Runyon* then would not be applicable to any single private school that had racially discriminatory admission policies? Why should it matter? Is it that the suggested principle is more accommodating of parental rights while still broadly protecting the education choices of black parents? What of the fact that a disproportionately small number of black parents may be able to afford any private education?

Would it be better to view *Runyon* as an extension of the public school desegregation cases in which the Court sought to limit white flight to private schools? *See generally* chapter 5.

5. *Racial Motivation*

Suppose that a student's race is only one factor among several that motivated a private school to deny admission. Would such an admissions policy run afoul of *Runyon*? *See Riley v. Adirondack Southern School for Girls*, 541 F.2d 1124 (5th Cir. 1976) (en banc). *See generally* Hilton, *supra* at 372–75. What of the fact that "after *McCrary* it is unlikely that any school desiring to remain segregated would be so unsophisticated as to continue to openly rely on racial criteria for refusing to admit black pupils." *Id.* at 373. *See generally* chapter 5.

6. Cook v. Hudson

In *Cook v. Hudson,* 511 F.2d 744 (5th Cir. 1975) (per curiam), plaintiff public schoolteachers attacked the constitutionality of a county school board policy that prohibited the hiring or rehiring of any teachers whose children were enrolled in racially segregated schools. The school board, prompted by the Department of Justice, successfully defended the rule on the basis that the policy was significantly related to teacher effectiveness; black students were likely to view such teachers as rejecting them and as perceiving them as inferior. In a concurring opinion, Judge Coleman declared "the general public, who pay taxes, who keep the public school doors open, and who depend on those [public] schools to educate their children, have a right to expect undivided teacher dedication, free of any real or apparent conflict of interest." *Id.* at 749. Judge Roney also concurred separately, arguing that the policy was designed "to strengthen local support for the public schools and to effectively implement the court-ordered requirement to change from a dual segregated school system to a unitary nondiscriminatory system." *Id.* at 750. Judge Clark dissented. He urged that *Pierce* was controlling and that, "whether viewed as a part of a citizen's Fourteenth Amendment liberty or First Amendment freedom of association or a combination of both, the right plaintiffs claim is protected from state intrusion. . . ." *Id.*

The Supreme Court initially granted a writ of certiorari to review the Fifth Circuit decision, but in a per curiam opinion, the Court dismissed the writ as improvidently granted. 429 U.S. 165, 97 S.Ct. 543, 50 L.Ed.2d 373 (1976). Apparently, in the interim, the Mississippi Legislature had enacted legislation forbidding school districts from enacting and enforcing policies such as those in issue in *Cook*. *See* Miss. Code Ann. §37-9-59 (1974). Chief Justice Burger wrote a cryptic concurring opinion:

> I join in the Court's disposition of this case. In doing so, I emphasize that our decision to dismiss the writ of certiorari as improvidently granted intimates no view on the question of when, if ever, public schoolteachers—or any comparable public employees—may be required, as a condition of their employment, to enroll their children in any particular school or refrain from sending them to a school which they, as parents, in their sole discretion, consider desirable. Few familial decisions are as immune from governmental interference as parents' choice of a school for their children, so long as the school chosen otherwise meets the educational standards imposed by the State. See *Pierce v. Society of Sisters*, 268 U.S. 510 (1925); *Meyer v. Nebraska*, 262 U.S. 390 (1923); *Wisconsin v. Yoder*, 406 U.S. 205 (1972).

Id. at 166.

If Mississippi had not changed its laws, and in the light of *Runyon*, should the Court have affirmed or reversed the Circuit Court decision in *Cook? See Brantley v. Surles*, 718 F.2d 1354 (5th Cir. 1983); *Stough v. Crenshaw County Bd. of Educ.*, 744 F.2d 1479 (11th Cir. 1984).

7. *Applicability of* Runyon *to Private Religious Schools*

In *Runyon* the Court explicitly declined to comment on the applicability of its decision to sectarian as opposed to nonsectarian private schools. Should *Runyon* be extended to private religious schools? How should free exercise of religion claims be weighed against the constitutionally based (but still statutory) interest of government in outlawing racial discrimination in private schools? Only a year after *Runyon*, the Fifth Circuit was called upon to pass on this issue.

Brown v. Dade Christian Schools, Inc.

556 F.2d 310 (5th Cir. 1977) (en banc), *cert. denied*, 434 U.S. 1063, 98 S.Ct. 1235, 55 L.Ed.2d 763 (1978).

[African American parents filed suit against the Dade Christian School under 42 U.S.C. §1981 alleging that they and their children had been the victims of racial discrimination in the denial of admission to that school. Dade Christian is a sectarian school which is located on the property of and receives subsidies from the New Testament Baptist Church. "The defendant asserted that its members sincerely held a religious belief that socialization of the races would lead to racial intermarriage, and that this belief, sanctioned by the Free Exercise Clause, should prevail against private interests created by Congress." 556 F.2d at 311 (Plurality opinion of Judge Hill). The parties stipulated "that race was the sole reason for the refusal of appellant [Dade Christian School] to enroll the Brown [appellee] children." Id. The plurality declined to reach the question of the constitutionality of §1981 as applied to a religious school, holding that there was substantial evidence to support the findings of the trial judge that "defendant's policy of segregation was not the exercise of religion." 556 F.2d at 312. The plurality stated that

> [t]he absence of references to school segregation in written literature stating the church's beliefs, distributed to members of the church and the public by leaders of the church . . . , is strong evidence that school segregation is not the exercise of religion.
>
> . . . While a religious belief may be of recent vintage or formed instantaneously, the trial judge's conclusion that school segregation was nothing more than a recent policy developed in response to the growing issue of segregation and integration was amply supported by the evidence.

556 F.2d at 312, 313.

The plurality further held that where the alleged discriminatory action was taken by the institution, it was inappropriate "to scrutinize the individual religious beliefs of the parties. . . ." 556 F.2d at 313.

> In such a situation the only practical course open to a Court is to examine the corporate beliefs of the institution involved, as adopted or promulgated or carried forward as an institutional concept. To do otherwise would allow the institution to pick and choose which of its members' potentially conflicting beliefs it wished to assert at any given time. Thus, an avowedly secular school should not be permitted to interpose a free exercise defense to a §1981 action merely because it can find some of its patrons who have a sincere religiously based belief in racial segregation. Conversely, a school or church which holds racial segregation as a religious tenet should not be barred from asserting a free exercise defense to a §1981 claim merely because some of its patrons or members might individually believe racial segregation is morally wrong.

556 F.2d at 313–14.

The plurality affirmed the decision of the district court, holding the admissions policies of the Dade Christian School were in violation of §1981.]

[Concurring opinion of Chief Judge Brown omitted.]

Goldberg, Circuit Judge, specially concurring.

* * *

. . . I believe the plurality's conclusion is wrong even on its own terms. The facts do not support the view that these beliefs were merely "policy" within the plurality's distinction between "policy" and "religion." The plurality seizes upon various instances when school officials—lay persons insensitive to the overtones of their choice of language—spoke loosely of the anti-integration "policy." I believe a more balanced analysis of the record as a whole would indicate that the witnesses also repeatedly referred to the "religious" moorings of the beliefs.

Dr. Arthur E. Kreft, the school's principal, testified at his deposition that enrolling blacks in the Dade Christian school would endanger the practice of his religion. . . . He said the enrollment of blacks would alienate him from God "in the sense that I would be disobedient, according to my beliefs in the Scriptures." . . . Enrollment of blacks would erode Kreft's "religious liberties." . . . Appellees stipulated that they had no basis to impeach these statements by Kreft . . ., and I can conclude only that Kreft's beliefs are sufficiently "religious" to invoke free exercise scrutiny. I believe it incontrovertible that appellant has standing to assert the free exercise rights of its principal, Dr. Kreft. Moreover, Kreft himself was a defendant, and the district court enjoined Kreft from denying appellee students admission to Dade Christian. Kreft can certainly assert his own free exercise rights. Kreft's testimony conclusively demonstrates the necessity to address the free exercise claim on its merits.

Similar testimony came from John M. Kalapp, Dade Christian's original vice president, who left the school early in 1973. Kalapp believes that enrollment of blacks at Dade Christian would endanger his "religious beliefs" "[i]f it culminated in an intermarriage situation between the races" . . ., which he apparently believes it would. Kalapp derives these views from his "overall concept and understanding of the teaching of the entire Scriptures." . . . Appellees stipulated that they had no basis to impeach these statements. . . .

Also in evidence is a recording of remarks that Dr. Janney made to the New Testament Baptist Church congregation. Dr. Janney is the church pastor and president of Dade Christian Schools, Inc. The tape makes undeniably clear that Dr. Janney entertains religious beliefs that integrating Dade Christian would be wrong. Although he delivered the remarks after this suit was filed and in contemplation of litigation, no one questions their sincerity. The remarks were the message of a pastor to his congregation. Dr. Janney's views, derived from detailed analysis of numerous biblical passages, could hardly be characterized as anything other than "religious," even under the plurality's stringent approach. Dade Christian has standing to assert the free exercise rights of its president and founding church's pastor, and Dr. Janney's views alone should therefore take this court to the merits of the free exercise defense.

* * *

Surely a practice which is based on Biblical interpretation . . . and the contravention of which would constitute disobedience to God . . . is a "religious" practice. . . .[11]

* * *

. . . The Dade Christian leadership adopted the rule in response to religious tenets, not transient policy dictates. Knowing that it would one day face the issue, Dade Christian's board of directors undertook a discussion of "what would be the right thing scripturally to do." . . . The directors reached a decision based on "the overall concept of the teachings of the Scriptures, and such things as God's dealing with the nation of Israel, the Tower of Babel, [and] the confusion of tongues in the Book of Acts." . . . The board of directors concluded that "it was God's will that the races were made separate for a purpose." . . . Appellants stipulated that they had no basis to impeach these statements. . . . The plurality characterizes that decision, based on "God's will" as divined from the Bible, as not sufficiently "religious" even to warrant threshold consideration of the free exercise defense. I cannot agree.

* * *

There is of course more to analyzing a free exercise claim than determining whether the belief in question is "religious." We must decide whether sufficient governmental interests justify interfering with the claimant's religious practices. In his dissent, Judge Roney concludes that we should delay passing on this matter, remanding instead for the district court's initial consideration. I respectfully disagree.

* * *

I now turn to the difficult issues that I believe are unavoidable. The Supreme Court has adopted various formulations in its efforts to reconcile governmental interests with those of free exercise claimants. In *Sherbert v. Verner*, 374 U.S. 398, 403 . . . (1963) the Court said that a religious practice could be infringed only on the basis of a "compelling state interest." In *Wisconsin v. Yoder*, 406 U.S. 205, 215 . . . (1972) the Court announced that free exercise claims could be overbalanced only by "those interests of the highest importance and those not otherwise served." Whatever the precise standard, free exercise analysis requires a careful comparison of the interests on both sides of the issue.

Charting the interests of free exercise claimants requires dispassionate dedication to the principle that courts cannot question the veracity of sincerely held religious beliefs. I therefore proceed on the assumption that desegregating Dade Christian would force the principal and at least some of the teachers, students and parents to be disobedient to God. . . . Rejecting the free exercise claim would impinge upon the religious practice of maintaining racial separation in activities that constitute "socialization."

That religious practice was characterized by Mr. Kalapp as a "very minor" part of the religion. . . . Departure from the practice, although constituting disobedience to God, would not endanger salvation. While these factors do not sap the free exercise defense of vitality, they make clear that overriding that defense will not endanger the church's survival.

Nor can appellant's claim garner appreciable support from the fundamental interests of parents and students in guiding the quality and nature of the education. Allowing blacks into Dade Christian will not affect the substance of the education; the school remains free to teach any doctrine it chooses, including the merit and religious requirement of racial segregation. Dade Christian's argument that admission of blacks would itself convey an undesirable message and thereby affect educational content carries little weight. Although the school leadership's voluntary enrollment of blacks might communicate such a message, desegregation in response to a federal court's implementation of the congressional mandate of §1981 would not. Much as merchants were freed by the Civil Rights Act of 1964 from any fear that white customers would react adversely to the acceptance of black business, parents and school

11. The plurality concludes otherwise, relying on Dade Christian's printed card listing nine items which "we believe." As the plurality notes, the card does not mention racial segregation. The first belief listed, however, is that the Bible is the infallible word of God. If the "we believe" card is to be read with the exacting scrutiny we accord to legal documents, we should treat the segregative beliefs derived from the Bible as incorporated by reference.

leaders are freed by §1981 from any fear that children will interpret acceptance of blacks as an indication of church approval of the practice. The parents' right to direct the upbringing and education of their children remains intact.

Dade Christian is also unable to elicit any support from right of association principles. Here, as in *Runyon v. McCrary*, 427 U.S. 160, 175–79 . . . (1979) (rejecting association defense to §1981 action against private school), the school simply does not operate in a manner implicating associational interests. Dade Christian advertises for students in the yellow pages and concededly exercises no policy of exclusion other than its ban on blacks. . . . Dade Christian therefore can claim no constitutionally cognizable interest in the sanctity of its school community. This case on its facts simply does not implicate the interests of a church in maintaining the intimacy of its activities.

The sole basis of Dade Christian's claim is therefore the "very minor" religious practice of preserving racial segregation in activities that constitute "socialization." If such activities extended to eating in restaurants, shopping in stores, or watching the Miami Dolphins, I suppose no one would contend the religious scruples would justify segregation of the activities. The government's interest in enforcing its policy of racial equality in such areas is clearly sufficient to override any free exercise defense.[16]

Dade Christian does not, however, advance religious opposition to integration of these public activities. Rather, its grievance extends only to interracial "socialization," which it defines to include children's school attendance but to exclude the above activities with respect to which the challenge would undoubtedly fail. Dade Christian's criterion for distinguishing proscribed "socialization" from other types of interracial contact is apparently the likelihood that interracial marriage will be encouraged. . . . Thus adherents of the New Testament Baptist Church do not seek to overturn the Civil Rights Act of 1964 or to separate themselves from our integrated society; they merely seek to avoid situations that might lead to interracial marriage.

In this respect it is important to note that no one purports to use §1981 as a basis for imposing interracial marriages upon anyone. Dade Christian students, like everyone else, remain free to marry whom they choose. Dade Christian parents remain free to teach their children that interracial marriage violates religious commands. That some students may depart their parents' commands and that integrating the school might make it infinitesimally easier for them then to effectuate their disobedience are hardly prospects lending weight to Dade Christian's position. The Constitution has never guaranteed parents an opportunity simultaneously to exist in an urban environment and to exclude every possibility that children will hear and adopt ideas at odds with those of the parents.

I do not mean to suggest that the religious beliefs at issue extend only to interracial marriage. Dade Christian advances a sincere belief that integrated education violates divine command. But that belief occupies a minor position in its adherents' religion and is based largely on the prospect of interracial marriage, a prospect that no government proposes to require.

In sum, Dade Christian's interests, while not minimal, do not rise to the level that has characterized numerous free exercise claims. I find that the government's interests, in comparison, are compelling.

Most free exercise cases have involved governmental interests manifested in legislative judgments. . . .

Here, in contrast, the government's interests draw strength not only from the congressional judgment manifested in §1981 but also from the Constitution itself. The Thirteenth Amendment proscribes slavery and involuntary servitude. In ensuring blacks an equal opportunity to enter contracts, §1981 seeks to eradicate some of the badges and incidents of slavery. A more compelling governmental interest has perhaps never been enlisted in opposition to a free exercise claim.

* * *

The claim that Dade Christian advances is not one that we could recognize without inviting numerous additional claims. Opposition to integration does not die easily. Those who turned to white academies in response to public school integration will undoubtedly seek ways to avoid *Runyon v. Mc-*

16. In such cases the governmental interest in racial equality would be augmented by the interests of other customers who oppose segregation. The case at bar does not involve such interests; there is no evidence that any Dade Christian students or parents oppose segregation.

See Frankel, "*Runyon v. McCrary* Should Not Be Overruled," 67 *Wash. U.L.Q.* 1 (1989).

See generally Rotunda, "*Runyon v. McCrary* and the Mosaic of State Action,' 67 *Wash. U.L.Q.* 47 (1989).

Crary's mandate to integrate the private schools. We therefore cannot view Dade Christian's claim in isolation. We have three alternatives: recognizing Dade Christian's claim but rejecting a significant number of future claims, recognizing Dade Christian's claim and most others as well, and rejecting Dade Christian's claim.

The first alternative would commit us to a case-by-case effort to distinguish meritorious from meritless future claims. In that way we could minimize the impairment of §1981's goals but we would thrust ourselves into the troublesome course of adjudication that I have described as contrary to more fundamental religion clause values. I believe we should reject this opportunity to set ourselves up as a board of religious arbiters.

The remaining alternatives are to steel ourselves to recognize virtually all of the free exercise claims that a decision for Dade Christian would foster, or to reject Dade Christian's claim. We must choose either to recognize the free exercise defense in this and numerous cases, thus undermining to a large extent the vitality of §1981 in this area, or to override the defense and enforce §1981's constitutionally based mandate.

The appropriate result is clear. The constitutional imperative to eliminate the badges of slavery has not dimmed in the 114 years since President Lincoln issued the Emancipation Proclamation. The compelling governmental interest in moving nearer that noble goal overrides appellant's interest in preserving a "very minor" religious practice. No less restrictive alternative is available; the government cannot afford appellees their right to be free of racial discrimination in contracting without infringing appellant's opposition to such contracts. Although free exercise claims deserve the most careful consideration and the greatest deference, they cannot always prevail. When the government interest is so strong and the impact upon the religion so slight, the religious practice must yield. I concur in the judgment of affirmance.

Roney, Circuit Judge, with whom Gewin, Coleman, Ainsworth, Clark and Tjoflat, Circuit Judges, join, dissenting: [omitted]

Coleman, Circuit Judge, dissenting:

I join in the dissent filed by Judge Roney. I agree with the reasoning demonstrated in that opinion, but perhaps my views run more deeply than those there exhibited.

I do not understand that the church is operating this school as a commercial enterprise. It is a direct, intimate adjunct of church activities, conducted in the house of worship. From the earliest days, when governments were doing absolutely nothing about it, nearly all religious denominations have conducted schools, including colleges, as an integral part of their activities. If the church is to remain absolutely separate and apart from the state, then no court should have the power to compel any church to admit any student to any school operated for religious reasons.

This case may turn out to be the first step of a long, intrusive interference with the exercise of religion. I hope this does not prove to be so.

NOTES AND QUESTIONS

1. Sincerity of Religious Belief

Do you agree with the plurality that the defendant had not demonstrated that its racially exclusionary policy was a manifestation of a sincere religious belief? *See generally* "Developments in the Law: Religion and the State," 100 *Harv. L. Rev.* 1606, 1764–68 (1987) (hereinafter "Religion and the State"). Is it appropriate for the court to examine the religious literature of the church for indications of the roots of the policy? Is this consistent with *Yoder*?

Is a religious belief not reduced to writing to be ignored while the court limits itself to the written religious statements and texts of the group? Or is the plurality simply attempting to distinguish between a Christian "secular" tradition and a nonsecular tradition integrating Christian beliefs and a way of life? *See generally* Galanter, "Religious Freedoms in the United States: A Turning Point?" 1966 *Wis. L. Rev.* 217. Are the issues of religiousness and sincerity simply matters of fact to be proved at trial? If so, who should bear the burden of proof? What are the standards for evaluating those facts? *See generally* Note, "Racial Discrimination in Private Schools, Section 1981, and the Free Exercise of Religion: The Sectarian Loophole of *Runyon v. McCrary*," 48 *Col. L. Rev.* 419, 427–30 (1977). Do both the plurality and Goldberg "opinions threaten a church's right to determine its own religious doctrines"? "Religion and the State," *supra* at 1766.

Did the plurality properly take into consideration the timing of the policy in relation to pending desegregation orders? Does this suggest that recently found doctrine relating to racial separation is more likely to be treated as insincere than doctrine of greater age? Does the lack of specific Biblical references supporting defendant's position indicate that the admissions policy is not a part of a developed theology? What of the references to the Tower of Babel and the "confusion of tongues"? Despite the conventional wisdom that a court may not inquire into the truth or falsity of a religious belief, is there some point at which the logical connections are so attenuated that a court is justified in finding that the beliefs are not sincere? *But see* L. Tribe, *American Constitutional Law* §14–11 (1978) ("[I]nquiry [into sincerity] . . . can be extraordinarily dangerous. The perception of the claimant's sincerity inevitably reflects the fact-finder's view of the reasonableness of the claimant's beliefs.")

Is the plurality on sound ground when it seeks to determine the corporate beliefs of the school rather than the individual beliefs of its members and supporters? *See also Fiedler v. Marumsco Christian School*, 631 F.2d 1144 (4th Cir. 1980). Does the plurality's approach essentially require "virtual unanimity of a church's members before an institutional belief will be recognized"? "Religion and the State," *supra* at 1766. Does the Free Exercise Clause apply to corporate bodies, or do such bodies simply represent the individual beliefs of its members? Does *Yoder* support the plurality's position? Is the plurality simply raising the question of whether the school has standing to raise the interests of parents and students? Was not this issue decided in *Runyon*? In the light of the *Brown* plurality opinion, are not private nonsecular schools simply encouraged to make sure that their racially discriminatory beliefs and policies are appropriately documented in the charters of their institutions? Might this requirement in itself be a restraint on racial discrimination?

2. *Balancing Free Exercise Rights*

One commentator has summarized the balancing test under the free exercise clause as follows:

> On one side of the scale is placed the burden that is imposed on the sincere religious belief by the application of the proposed provision to the complaining group or individual. Once it is established that the religious activity is hindered in any way, the burden shifts to the government to demonstrate that there is a compelling state interest for infringing on the religious activity, that applying the statute to the religious group in question will actually further the purpose of the statute, and that there are no less restrictive means for accomplishing the same purpose.

Note, 48 *Col. L. Rev.* at 430–31. *See generally* L. Tribe, *American Constitutional Law* § 14–10 (1978); Giannella, "Religious Liberty, Nonestablishment, and Doctrinal Development—Part I: The Religious Liberty Guarantee," 80 *Harv. L. Rev.* 1381 (1967); Pfeffer, "The Supremacy of Free Exercise," 61 *Geo. L. J.* 1115 (1973); "Religion and the State," *supra*. *But see Employment Division, Department of Human Resources v. Smith*, ___U.S. ___, 110 S.Ct. 1595, 108 L.Ed. 876 (1990) (rejecting balancing test under Free Exercise Clause).

Is Judge Goldberg correct in concluding that this test favors the upholding of §1981 as it is applied to private religious schools? *Cf. Goldsboro Christian Schools, Inc. v. United States*, 436 F.Supp. 1314 (E.D. N.C. 1977). Does he ignore a religious "group's right to decide how it will be governed, how issues of religious doctrine and theology will be decided, and who will speak on behalf of the church"? "Religion and the State," *supra* at 1767; Laycock, *supra*. What about the constitutional derivation of the state interest? Is *Yoder* distinguishable in that in that case there were less onerous alternatives? *See generally* Tribe, *supra*. What of the notion that the presence of blacks does not substantially impede religious socialization? Do you agree? What of the relationship between racial intermarriage and school desegregation? Is it attenuated, unreasonable? Does the school have "less onerous" alternatives for seeking to prevent such marriages? Suppose the school expelled a white female for maintaining a romantic relationship with a black male. Would this violate §1981? *See Fiedler v. Marumsco Christian School*, 631 F.2d 1144 (4th Cir. 1980).

Is it appropriate for Judge Goldberg to classify religious beliefs into the categories of major and minor beliefs, or is this simply another way of measuring the degree of intrusion as the court performs its balancing act? Is not "a conflict which threatens the very survival of the religion or the core values of a faith . . . [a] more serious free exercise problem than . . . a conflict which merely inconveniences the faithful"? Tribe, *supra* at 862.

Is the free exercise balancing test so abstract and ill defined that it makes prediction of outcomes in particular cases nearly impossible? *See id.* at 432. Should a strong distinction be drawn between religious beliefs and acts motivated by religious beliefs? *See Employment Division, Department of Human Resources, supra; West Virginia State Board of Education v. Barnette*, 319 U.S. 624, 63 S.Ct. 1178, 87 L.Ed. 1628 (1943) (Justice Frankfurter, dissenting). *See also McDaniel v. Paty*, 435 U.S. 618, 98 S.Ct. 1322, 55 L.Ed.2d 593 (1978); *Cantwell v. Connecticut*, 310 U.S. 296, 60 S.Ct. 900, 84 L.Ed. 1213 (1940); *Hamilton v. Regents of University of* California, 293 U.S. 245, 55 S.Ct. 197, 79 L.Ed. 343 (1934).

When the Congress asserts such a "vital public goal as equality of treatment of blacks and whites," does this in itself constitute an overriding and compelling state interest? *See Hilton*, "Race, Religion, and Constitutional Restraints on Private Schools," 30 *Rutgers L. Rev*. 329, 377 (1977). But does this assertion confuse the issue? If the Thirteenth and Fourteenth Amendments would not reach racially discriminatory practices of private, nonsecular schools, then First Amendment free exercise rights are being balanced against a statutory entitlement. Why should the statutory entitlement prevail? Or is the nature of the state interest such that this is akin to enforcing antipolygamy laws against Mormons? *See United States v. Reynolds*, 98 U.S. 145, 25 L.Ed. 244 (1878). *See also Braunfeld v. Brown*, 366 U.S. 599 (1961) (Sunday closing law). But is *Yoder* distinguishable?

3. Free Exercise and the Bob Jones University *Case*

If the national interest in nondiscrimination trumps a private school's entitlement to nonprofit tax treatment, as declared in *Bob Jones University v. United States*, 461 U.S. 574, 103 S.Ct. 2017, 76 L.Ed.2d 157 (1983), does it follow that *Runyon* prevails over the free exercise claims of private, religious schools practicing racial discrimination? Does *Brown v. Dade Christian Schools* become largely irrelevant, in practical terms, after the later *Bob Jones University* decision?

Ohio Civil Rights Commission v. Dayton Christian Schools, Inc.

477 U.S. 619, 106 S.Ct. 2718, 91 L.Ed.2d 512 (1986).

Justice Rehnquist delivered the opinion of the Court.

Appellee Dayton Christian Schools, Inc. (Dayton) and various individuals brought an action in the United States District Court for the Southern District of Ohio under 42 U.S.C. § 1983, seeking to enjoin a pending state administrative proceeding brought against Dayton by appellant Ohio Civil Rights Commission (Commission). Dayton asserted that the Free Exercise and Establishment Clauses of the First Amendment prohibited the Commission from exercising jurisdiction over it or from punishing it for engaging in employment discrimination. The District Court refused to issue the injunction on grounds that any conflict between the First Amendment and the administrative proceedings was not yet ripe, and that in any case the proposed action of the Commission violated neither the Free Exercise nor the Establishment Clause of the First and Fourteenth Amendments. The Court of Appeals for the Sixth Circuit reversed, holding that the exercise of jurisdiction and the enforcement of the statute would impermissibly burden appellees' rights under the Free Exercise Clause and would result in excessive entanglement under the Establishment Clause. . . . We now conclude that we have jurisdiction, and we reverse, holding that the District Court should have abstained under our cases beginning with *Younger v. Harris*, 401 U.S. 37, 91 S.Ct. 746, 27 L.Ed.2d 669 (1971).

* * *

Linda Hoskinson was employed as a teacher at Dayton during the 1978–1979 school year. She subscribed to the Statement of Faith and expressly agreed to resolve disputes internally through the biblical chain of command. In January 1979, she informed her principal, James Rakestraw, that she was pregnant. After consulting with his superiors, Rakestraw informed Hoskinson that her employment contract would not be renewed at the end of the school year because of Dayton's religious doctrine that mothers should stay home with their preschool age children. Instead of appealing this decision internally, Hoskinson contacted an attorney who sent a letter to Dayton's Superintendent, Claude Schindler, threatening litigation based on state and federal sex discrimination laws if Dayton did not agree to rehire Hoskinson for the coming school year.

Upon receipt of this letter, Schindler informed Hoskinson that she was suspended immediately for challenging the nonrenewal decision in a manner inconsistent with the internal dispute resolution doctrine. . . .

Hoskinson filed a complaint with appellant Ohio Civil Rights Commission (Commission), alleging that Dayton's nonrenewal decision constituted sex discrimination, in violation of Ohio Rev. Code Ann. § 4112.02(A) (Supp.1985), and that its termination decision penalized her for asserting her rights, in violation of Ohio Rev.Code Ann. § 4112.02(I) (Supp.1985). . . .

* * *

While these administrative proceedings were pending, Dayton filed this action against the Commission in the United States District Court for the Southern District of Ohio under 42 U.S.C. § 1983, seeking a permanent injunction of the state proceedings on the ground that any investigation of Dayton's hiring process or any imposition of sanctions for Dayton's nonrenewal or termination decisions would violate the Religion Clauses of the First Amendment. App. 118–120. The Commission filed a motion to dismiss, arguing, *inter alia*, that the District Court should refrain from enjoining the administrative proceedings based on federal abstention doctrines. . . .

* * *

In *Younger v. Harris*, 401 U.S. 37, 91 S.Ct. 746, 27 L.Ed.2d 669 (1971), we held that a federal court should not enjoin a pending state criminal proceeding except in the very unusual situation that an injunction is necessary to prevent great and immediate irreparable injury. We justified our decision both on equitable principles, *id.*, at 43, 91 S.Ct. at 750, and on the "more vital consideration" of the proper respect for the fundamental role of States in our federal system. *Id.*, at 44, 91 S.Ct., at 750. . . .

We have since recognized that our concern for comity and federalism is equally applicable to certain other pending state proceedings. We have applied the *Younger* principle to civil proceedings in which important state interests are involved. . . .

We think the principles enunciated in these [abstention] cases govern the present one. We have no doubt that the elimination of prohibited sex discrimination is a sufficiently important state interest to bring the present case within the ambit of the cited authorities. We also have no reason to doubt that Dayton will receive an adequate opportunity to raise its constitutional claims. Dayton contends that the mere exercise of jurisdiction over it by the state administrative body violates its First Amendment rights. But we have repeatedly rejected the argument that a constitutional attack on state procedures themselves "automatically vitiates the adequacy of those procedures for purposes of the *Younger-Huffman* line of cases." . . .

Even religious schools cannot claim to be wholly free from some state regulation. *Wisconsin v. Yoder*, 406 U.S. 205, 213, 92 S.Ct. 1526, 1532, 32 L.Ed.2d 15 (1972). We therefore think that however Dayton's constitutional claim should be decided on the merits, the Commission violates no constitutional rights by merely investigating the circumstances of Hoskinson's discharge in this case, if only to ascertain whether the ascribed religious-based reason was in fact the reason for the discharge.

Dayton also contends that the administrative proceedings do not afford the opportunity to level constitutional challenges against the potential sanctions for the alleged sex discrimination. In its reply brief in this Court, the Commission cites several rulings to demonstrate that religious justifications for otherwise illegal conduct are considered by it. *See, e.g.*, *In re St. Mary of the Falls*, No. 948 (1975). Dayton in turn relies on a decision of the Supreme Court of Ohio, *Mobil Oil Corp. v. Rocky River*, 38 Ohio St.2d 23, 26, 309 N.E.2d 900, 902 (1974), in which that court held that a local zoning commission could not consider constitutional claims. But even if Ohio law is such that the Commission may not consider the constitutionality of the statute under which it operates, it would seem an unusual doctrine, and one not supported by the cited case, to say that the Commission could not construe its own statutory mandate in the light of federal constitutional principles. *Cf. NLRB v. Catholic Bishop of Chicago*, 440 U.S. 490, 99 S.Ct. 1313, 59 L.Ed.2d 533 (1979). In any event, it is sufficient . . . that constitutional claims may be raised in state court judicial review of the administrative proceeding. Section 4112.06 of Ohio Rev. Code Ann. (1980) provides that any "respondent claiming to be aggrieved by a final order of the commission . . . may obtain judicial review thereof." Dayton cites us to no Ohio authority indicating that this provision does not authorize judicial review of claims that agency action violates the United States Constitution.

The judgment of the Court of Appeals is therefore reversed and the case remanded for further proceedings consistent with this opinion.

It is so ordered.

Justice Stevens, with whom Justice Brennan, Justice Marshall, and Justice Blackmun join, concurring in the judgment [omitted].

NOTES AND QUESTIONS

1. The Decision of the Court of Appeals

The Sixth Circuit Court of Appeals, while reversing the district court's decision in favor of the defendant, affirmed the lower court's finding that the Dayton Christian Schools (DCS) had a dominant religious purpose that permeated all aspects of the educational process including teacher selection. *Dayton Christian Schools, Inc. v. Ohio Civil Rights Commission*, 766 F.2d 932, 936 (6th Cir. 1985), *reversed on other grounds*, 477 U.S. 619, 106 S.Ct. 2718, 91 L.Ed.2d 512 (1986). It quoted with favor the following passage from the district judge's opinion:

> [T]he teachers at DCS are selected because of their ability to blend their avowed religious beliefs into every lesson and school activity. Teachers are required to be born again Christians and to carry with them into their classes the religious fervor and conviction felt necessary to stimulate young minds into accepting Christ as savior . . . [T]he school demands that teachers conform both in thought and conduct to the tenets and principles felt essential to leading a Christian life. The belief system espoused by the members of DCS touches every aspect of their life: work, interpersonal relationships, family and recreational activities. Deviation in any way from what is felt to be the proper religious way of life may cast doubt on a teacher's ability to perform his or her critical role and, may, therefore, be grounds for dismissal.

766 F.2d at 938, quoting 578 F.Supp. at 1018-19. According to the testimony of the DCS superintendent, congregants believe "that the Bible teaches that even though we are equal in the sight of God, our role is different, the role of the female is different than that of the male." Citing various passages of Scriptures, he felt that God's words required that "a woman [be] . . . home with her pre-school age children." 766 F.2d at 934. Further, Ms. Hoskinson's contract with DCS provided that "all differences are to be resolved by utilizing Biblical principles—always presenting a united front." She attested that "[o]bedience to those in authority over you is clearly stated in the Bible. I believe in God's chain of command." 766 F.2d at 939.

Judge Contie, writing for the Court of Appeals, first determined that the Ohio Civil Rights Act covered religious schools, finding that statutory interpretation would not enable the court to avoid the conflict between the Ohio law and the free exercise of religion. *But see NLRB v. Catholic Bishop of Chicago*, 440 U.S. 490, 99 S.Ct. 1313, 59 L.Ed.2d 533 (1979). He also noted that while the Ohio Civil Rights Act was analogous to Title VII of the federal Civil Rights Act (42 U.S.C.A. Section 2000e *et seq.*) in forbidding discrimination on the basis of race, sex, or national origin, the federal law allowed religious educational institutions to discriminate by religion in employment practices. 766 F.2d at 941 n.18, citing 42 U.S.C.A. Sections 2000e-1 and 2000e-2(e)(2). The Ohio law contained no such exemption, and, in any event, he cited a case indicating that the Title VII exemptions for religious institutions may violate the Establishment Clause. *See King's Garden, Inc. v. FCC*, 498 F.2d 51, 55 (D.C. Cir. 1974). Two years later, however, the Supreme Court upheld the Section 2000e-1 exemption. *Corporation of Presiding Bishop v. Amos*, 483 U.S. 327, 107 S.Ct. 2862, 97 L.Ed.2d 273 (1987).

The Sixth Circuit held that the Ohio Civil rights Act, applied to the Dayton Christian Schools, violated the free exercise of religion rights of the plaintiffs and the "fundamental rights of . . . parents . . . to choose the manner in which their children will be educated, especially with regard to religious values." 766 F.2d at 947. It also found that the very assertion of jurisdiction by the Ohio Civil Rights Commission, including the use of its investigative powers and efforts to cajole a settlement, also violated the First Amendment. In this regard, Judge Contie distinguished *Bob Jones University v. United States*, 461 U.S. 574, 103 S.Ct. 2017, 76 L.Ed.2d 157 (1983):

> In *Bob Jones*, the [Supreme] Court upheld denial of tax exempt status to an institution which denied admission to those engaged in interracial dating. In weighing the school's free exercise claim, the Court observed that "[d]enial of tax benefits will inevitably have a substantial impact on the operation of private religious schools, but will not prevent those schools from observing their religious tenets." *Id.* at 603–04, 103 S.Ct. at 2034–35. In the instant case, however, appellants do not have the luxury of simply declining a public benefit. While Bob Jones University is free to continue to practice its religious beliefs free of state intervention, appellants only have the option of either conforming their religiously based employment practices to the secular guidelines promulgated in the Ohio statute or face continued harassing prosecution by the OCRC. . . .

766 F.2d at 952.

The appeals court admitted that the state's interest in eliminating sex discrimination in employment practices was "substantial and compelling," but it noted that "the state is not constitutionally compelled to enact the statute at issue here." 766 F.2d at 954. It also noted that *Runyon v. McCrary*, 427 U.S. 160, 96 S.Ct. 2586, 49 L.Ed.2d 415 (1976), did not reach the question of the constitutionality of applying Section 1981 to private sectarian schools. 766 F.2d at 954 n.40. The court concluded that the state's substantial interest in eliminating sex discrimination "does not justify such a broad and onerous limitation [on free exercise rights]. The state legislation must be 'essential,' and the least drastic means to further the state's interest":

> Accommodation of the religious beliefs in this case would not significantly interfere with the state's fulfillment of its goal of eradicating discrimination in employment. The state would still be able to regulate all employment practices of non-religious institutions except where religious belief is implicated. . . . [T]he state might further its interest in eliminating sex discrimination by conditioning receipt of [the benefits of state tax exemptions] . . . on compliance with the Ohio Civil Rights Act.

766 F.2d at 955. Finally, the court held that the assertion of jurisdiction by the Civil Rights Commission violated the entanglement aspect of the Establishment Clause, fostering a continuing and comprehensive state involvement with a religious institution. 766 F.2d at 961.

2. *Disposition in the Supreme Court*

Chief Justice Rehnquist, writing for the majority, holds that *Younger v. Harris*, 401 U.S. 37, 91 S.Ct. 746, 27 L.Ed.2d 669 (1971), is controlling and that the district court should have abstained from deciding the case during the pendency of the state administrative proceedings. In reaching this conclusion the Court finds that "the Commission violates no constitutional rights by merely investigating the circumstances of Hoskinson's discharge in this case, if only to ascertain whether the ascribed religious-based reason was in fact the reason for the discharge." Is this language consistent with the Sixth Circuit's substantive decision? What of the citation of *Yoder*? Does the majority's reasoning suggest that if the substantive issues were to reach the Supreme Court in a procedurally appropriate posture the Sixth Circuit would be reversed? *Cf. Employment Division, Department of Human Resources v. Smith*, ___U.S. ___, 110 S.Ct. 1595, 108 L.Ed. 876 (1990).

What of the Chief Justice's remarks about the importance of the state's interest in eliminating prohibited sex discrimination? Is he saying only that there will be adequate opportunity for the Dayton Christian Schools to raise constitutional issues in the state proceeding, or is he suggesting more? Why might *NLRB v. Catholic Bishop of Chicago*, 440 U.S. 490, 99 S.Ct. 1313, 59 L.Ed.2d 533 (1979) be critical to the resolution of the litigation in the state proceedings?

3. *Discrimination and the Free Exercise of Religion*

How should the courts resolve the underlying conflict between the state's interest in banning prohibited sex discrimination or other forms of discrimination in employment (or admissions) and the free exercise of religion in private sectarian schools? Do you agree with Professor Laycock, *supra*, that given the overarching religious mission of church schools such institutions should be largely autonomous with respect to the employment of teachers? Would his reasoning extend to admissions practices? *See Brown v. Dade Christian Schools, Inc.*, 556 F.2d 310, 326 (5th Cir. 1977) (Coleman, J., dissenting). Should the result turn on the type of discrimination? For example, should courts be less deferential to the free exercise of religion and church autonomy where racial discrimination is involved? Is there any principal basis for such a distinction?

What if a church school discriminates in the hiring or retention of teachers on the basis of religion? Should it matter whether the teacher teaches geography, history, theology, or hygiene? *See Maguire v. Marquette University*, 627 F.Supp. 1499 (E.D. Wis. 1986), *aff'd in part on other grounds*, 814 F.2d 1213 (7th Cir. 1987) (court upholds refusal to hire woman associate professor against a Title VII challenge; plaintiff alleged sex discrimination; defendant argued that she was rejected "because of her perceived hostility to the institutional church and its teachings.") *See* Laycock and Waelbroeck, "Academic Freedom and the Free Exercise of Religion," 66 *Tex. L. Rev.* 1001, 1009 (1988). Are the free exercise concerns more or less important in the university setting?

VI. STATE AID TO PRIVATE SCHOOLS

A. *Pierce* Extended: A Right to a State-Financed Nonpublic Education?

In the proceeding sections, discussion focused on the degree to which state and federal governments regulate nonpublic education. That inquiry was necessitated in part by the nature of the *Pierce* compromise. If parents are to have rights to send their children to private schools, private schools subject to reasonable regulation by government, then inevitably courts and legislative bodies must decide what reasonable regulation is. If government remains entirely detached from nonpublic education, taking a strongly libertarian view, there is the danger that the education provided in the private sector will not satisfy the objectives of compulsory attendance laws. If government regulates with a heavy hand, seeking to stamp out any variation from the public school program, then parental choice becomes meaningless. The question of private schools becomes even more acute where parental choices are grounded in religious convictions. As Mark DeWolfe Howe once so elegantly described *Pierce* and *Meyer*,

> In the English language case and in the case of the Society of Sisters, the Court was consciously endeavoring, for one reason or another, to find a ground for what it conceived to be a liberating decision that would do something more than set religion free. This aim seems not unlike that which Mr. Justice Jackson later sought to achieve in his flag-salute opinion [*West Virginia State Board of Education v. Barnette*, 319 U.S. 624 (1943), chapter 2, *infra*]—the aim, that is, of offering to all sincere objectors, not merely to those whose consciences were moved by religious conviction, an assurance that the Constitution provides them protection against senseless tyrannies.

M.D. Howe, *The Garden and the Wilderness* 124 (1965).

But if the goal of the *Pierce* compromise is to promote parental choice, and therefore presumably educational diversity, perhaps more than the absence of unreasonable restrictions on nonpublic education is required. That parents are free of direct regulatory restraints on securing a nonpublic education for their children does not necessarily mean that they, in fact, will have the capacity to choose; private education costs money. And parents who would choose a private school would be required to continue paying school taxes for public schools, while simultaneously absorbing the cost of private school tuition. Many parents will not be sufficiently affluent to bear this double burden; hence, economic circumstances may compel the selection of public schools. As Professor Arons has argued, the present system of public education "confronts the dissenting family with a choice between giving up its basic values and beliefs as the price of gaining a 'free' education in a government school or paying twice in order to preserve its First Amendment rights." S. Arons, *Compelling Belief* 212 (1983). Put somewhat differently, liberty may consist not only of the absence of restrictions on choice (negative liberty) but also the presence of sufficient knowledge and resources to enable the individual to select among alternative courses of action (affirmative liberty). *See generally* I. Berlin, *Four Essays on Liberty* (1969). As Professors Coons and Sugarman have cogently put the argument,

> On grounds of simple fairness children should be guaranteed reasonable access to education whatever their parents' views. . . . The humane response is that the right to education should not be limited by parental resources; parental duty [to educate] means nothing to the child if the family cannot afford to educate him. Therefore, additional collective action in necessary, and unless the child is to be taken from his parents, this requires a subsidy of the parents by the state. Only in that way can the child's hope for education be delivered from the economic limitations of his family.

J. Coons and S. Sugarman, *Education by Choice* 11 (1978).

The question of public support for private education, through subsidies to parents or private schools or otherwise, may be approached as a matter of policy, limited by applicable constitutional principles on the establishment of religion, or as a matter of constitutional entitlement. The former is taken up in the next section. See also the discussion of education vouchers, chapter 4, *infra*. The latter is the focus of attention in the present section.

A number of commentators argue that a broad reading of *Pierce* leads to the conclusion that government, if it is to remain truly neutral with regard to parental education decisions, must subsidize those decisions. *See, e.g.*, Arons, *supra*; Arons, "The Separation of School and State: *Pierce* Reconsidered," 46 *Harv. Educ. Rev.* 76, 100–01 (1976); V. Blum, *Freedom of Choice in Education* (1958); Areen, "Alternative Schools: Better Guardians than Family or State?," 81 *Sch. Rev.* 175 (1973); Areen, "The Judiciary and Education Reform: A Reassessment," 61 *Geo. L. Rev.* 1009 (1973); Areen, "Tuition Vouchers," 6 *Harv. C.R.-C.L. L. Rev.* 446 (1971); Areen, "Public Aid to Nonpublic Schools: A Breach of the Sacred Wall?," 22 *Case West L. Rev.* 230 (1971). The question of constitutionally compelled subsidization of nonpublic education rarely has been adjudicated by the courts, but in those few cases, and in dicta in other cases, the courts have responded negatively to the idea. *See Harris v. McRae*, 448

U.S. 297, 100 S.Ct. 2671, 65 L.Ed.2d 784 (1980) (dicta); *Exeter-West Greenwich Regional School District v. Pontarelli*, 460 A.2d 934 (R.I. 1983); *Brusca v. State of Missouri*, 332 F.Supp. 275 (E.D. Mo. 1971), *aff'd*, 405 U.S. 1050, 92 S.Ct. 1493, 31 L.Ed.2d 786 (1972) (per curiam). *See generally* "Developments in the Law: Religion and the State," 100 *Harv. L. Rev.* 1606, 1695–97 (1987).

Suppose parents of students in church schools argue that the failure of the state to subsidize religious schools violates the neutrality that the state is bound to follow under the religion clauses. That is, parents choosing church schools would have to pay twice—property and other taxes to support the public schools that their children did not attend and tuition to the private schools that they did attend. *Cf. Mueller v. Allen*, 463 U.S. 388, 396, 103 S.Ct. 3062, 3068, 77 L.Ed.2d 721 (1983). From this perspective, the forfeiture of the state subsidy "can plausibly be viewed as a penalty on the exercise of a constitutional right." Laycock, "A Survey of Religious Liberty in the United States," 47 *Ohio St. L.J.* 409, 444 (1986). *See Meek v. Pittenger*, 421 U.S. 349, 387, 95 S.Ct. 1753, 1174, 44 L.Ed.2d 217 (1975) (Burger, C.J., dissenting). Might such neutrality, defined in terms of equalizing the burdens for parents of children in church schools, amount to state aid of religion and hence a violation of the Establishment Clause? Which of these positions makes more sense? *See* West, "Constitutional Judgment on Nonpublic School Aid: Fresh Guidelines or New Roadblocks," 35 *Emory L.J.* 795, 815–21 (1986). Is a failure to subsidize church schools a denial of equal treatment to religion or a requirement of the Establishment Clause? *See* Laycock, *supra* at 444.

Is the state required to subsidize religious alternatives in every sphere in which it provides a state service lest it be accused of favoring its own secular program? If free exercise of religion is a protected liberty like free speech, does it follow that the state must subsidize it? Must the state subsidize private newspapers? Must it open its auditoriums and universities to private speakers? Is the implication of all this that the Free Exercise Clause embodies the concept of negative liberty, whereas the Establishment Clause forbids the state from affirmatively fostering religious liberty? *See generally* Merel, "The Protection of Individual Choice: A Consistent Understanding of Religion Under the First Amendment," 45 *U. Chi. L. Rev.* 805 (1978).

Consider these remarks by Professor Paul G. Kauper:

> The concept of religious liberty . . . should include freedom from discrimination on religious grounds in the enjoyment of legal rights, privileges, and immunities. The principle can be stated in equal protection terms, but it can also be viewed as an application of the principle of religious liberty. . . .
>
> Yet the principle that the religious factor cannot furnish the basis for discriminatory treatment is not completely unqualified . . . [S]tate consitutions commonly prohibit the use of public funds to aid sectarian schools or religious institutions or corporations. Here a policy of discrimination in the use of public funds is given express constitutional sanction. If the public policy of the state is to limit the use of educational funds to schools under public control, this involves no discrimination except the distinction between schools under public and those under private control—a distinction well recognized in our law. But if public funds are made available for all educational institutions whether public or private except those that are under the control of a religious body, it is indeed hard to avoid the conclusion that the religious factor is being used as a ground for disqualification from public benefits. It is significant that there is no sanction in our law for discrimination against an individual because of his religious belief. Discriminations based upon the religious factor have to do with activities in which the churches engage in a corporate capacity, such as the operation of schools, hospitals, and related types of institutions. These historically sanctioned discrimination must find their justification in those basic conceptions of public policy that underlie the principle of separation of church and state—whether it be the desirability of maintaining the voluntaristic character of church enterprises, the importance of protecting government against ecclesiastical demands and aggrandizement, or apprehension of disruptive social consequences that may flow from use of public funds to support church-related education programs. . . . The point I wish to emphasize here is that the general principle of freedom of religion from discriminatory classification on the basis of religion has not been fully recognized in American law.

P. Kauper, *Religion and the Constitution* 36–37 (1964).

Does Professor Kauper give sufficient attention to the possible conflict between establishment and free exercise values? Would his equal protection discrimination standard lead to the invalidation of a state law that aided only secular private schools? *Cf. Luet-*

kemeyer v. Kaufmann, 419 U.S. 888, 95 S.Ct. 167, 42 L.Ed.2d 134 (1974) (Mr. Justice White dissenting from an affirmation without opinion). Does this mean that aid to religious schools only would be unconstitutional, as would aid only to secular schools? Does the Constitution require that all private schools, subject to reasonable regulation, be aided or that none be aided? *See generally* Schwarz, "No Imposition of Religion: The Establishment Clause Value," 77 *Yale L.J.* 692 (1968).

Suppose that a state legislature sought to provide to parents direct grants or tax credits or deductions in order to enhance overall parental choice rather than for purposes of supporting religious education. *See* Laycock, "A Survey of Religious Liberty in the United States," 47 *Ohio L.J.* 409, 445 (1986); Henzke, "The Constitutionality of Federal Tuition Tax Credits," 56 *Temple L.Q.* 911 (1983); Note, "Laws Respecting An Establishment of Religion: An Inquiry Into Tuition Tax Benefits," 58 *N.Y.U.L. Rev.* 207 (1983). Would such a law be constitutional? *See Mueller v. Allen*, 463 U.S. 388, 103 S.Ct. 3062, 77 L.Ed.2d 721 (1983). Suppose a state embraced a system in which parents received vouchers to attend any public or private school (subject to reasonable state regulation). Suppose parents demanded that public schools be established that offered a program consistent with their religious beliefs. *Cf. Deerfield Hutterian Association v. Ipswich Board of Education*, 468 F.Supp. 1219 (D.S.D. 1979). Suppose they sought to enroll their children in selected school courses, on a part-time basis. Do private school students have a right to attend public school classes in subjects not offered in their private schools? *See Snyder v. Charlotte Public School District*, 421 Mich. 517, 365 N.W.2d 151 (1984). *But see Thomas v. Allegany County Bd. of Educ.*, 51 Md. App. 312, 443 A.2d 622 (1982).

B. State Aid to Private Schools and the Constitution

"The Storm Before the Lull: The Future of Private Schooling in America"

D. Doyle, in J.H. Bunzel, ed., *Challenge to American Schools* 147, 155–63 (1985).

If information about the quantity of private schooling is provisional and difficult to confirm, information about its quality is even more elusive. Indeed, until the recent publication of *High School Achievement: Public, Catholic, and Private Schools Compared*, by James Coleman and his colleagues, there was very little systematic information about the quality of private schools. . . .

* * *

. . . Coleman's research did something genuinely novel in the annals of American education: it compared private with public schools. . . .

. . . Coleman found [that] private schools are meeting their social responsibilities to poor and minority youngsters, and, other things being equal, these children do measurably better in private than in public schools. Not content just to present findings, Coleman went on to suggest that the historical exclusion of private schools from public funding might not be a sensible public policy.

* * *

In the final analysis, Coleman and his colleagues proved what the public has really known for a very long time: that some schools are better than others, that frequently the better schools are private schools, and that if money were no object, many more children would attend private schools than now do so. . . .

There is, however, no sensible or responsible way to turn education back to the private market in toto. If that were to happen, the most serious problems would ensue: the poor and the dispossessed would find themselves altogether at the mercy of a system that did not serve their interests. But the issue need not be cast in those terms.

The role of government does not have to be viewed in the stark "either–or" of the radical: the government provides education or it does not. This apocalyptic vision of government obscures the subtlety with which government intervention strategies may be designed. . . .

* * *

The classic expression of government aid to private education is typically ascribed to Adam Smith, who argued that the state had an interest in providing limited aid to the poor so that they might attend school. In the nineteenth century, John Stuart Mill insisted that state-sponsored education is

> a mere contrivance for moulding people to be exactly like one another: and as the mould in which it casts

> them is that which pleases the predominant power in the government, whether this be a monarch, a priesthood, an aristocracy, or the majority of the existing generation, in proportion as it is efficient and successful, it establishes a despotism over the mind. . . .

More recently, Albert O. Hirschman's *Exit, Voice, and Loyalty*, Charles Schultz's *The Public Use of Private Interest* and John Coons and Stephen Sugarman's *Family Choice in Education* make the case with great power that public "provision" and public support are not synonymous. Indeed, there is no a priori reason to think that the state must own and operate the means of production just because it has a substantive interest in the issue at hand. The state's interest in health and safety does not lead to state ownership of hotels, restaurants, and airlines; rather, it leads to a body of public interest regulations designed, in so far as possible, to be neutral as regards the market in which these private enterprises exist.

* * *

The most striking finding . . . [of a Gallup poll of public attitudes toward education] is in some respects the least surprising—namely, the change over time in attitudes toward public support for private schools. In 1983, for the first time since the poll was begun, a simple majority of the public supported public aid to private education.

These various issues are important to public policy analysis and public policymakers because of the new synergy they suggest. Not since the mid-nineteenth century has there been serious public funding of private elementary and secondary schools. The nativism that was then sweeping the country led to the wholesale disestablishment of private school support systems. In the nineteenth century, however, the disestablishment of private schools was the work of state legislatures, not the Supreme Court. Today, however, the roles are reversed. A number of state legislatures, particularly in states with large Catholic populations, are now interested in enacting aid schemes that will help parents enroll their children in non-public schools.

By the mid-twentieth century, however, the fate of public support schemes for private schools had been sealed by U.S. Supreme Court decisions. A series of rulings beginning in the late 1940s found that public aid represented an unconstitutional breach of the wall separating church and state. These decisions effectively closed off debate about the relation of the state to the private school, a debate that had proceeded vigorously and constructively in all other advanced democracies. . . .

In all the democracies save only America, the decision has been made to provide for some mix of control over where the child goes to school and what the child studies. As a practical matter, this means state financial support for private schools. The range is truly remarkable: the Dutch send 70 percent of their school age population to private elementary and secondary schools at state expense, while the Danes send less than 8 percent to private schools.

In Denmark, for example, the state religion is quite naturally included in the curriculum of government schools—to preserve the religious freedom of nonevangelical Lutherans, provision is made for them to start their own schools at government expense. The Danish government is explicit about this:

> The principle behind . . . large subsidies [for private schools] is that although Denmark has an efficient education system providing educational opportunities for all, it should be responsible for people to choose an alternative kind of education for their children should they wish, whether their reasons for this are ideological, political, educational, or religious.

* * *

There are, then, two major trends unfolding in American elementary and secondary education. As Coleman shows us (and by all accounts will continue to show us), private schools do a "better job" than public schools, particularly with those populations most in need of help—poor and minority youngsters. Furthermore, as Cooper points out, private school enrollments continue to grow and give every indication of further growth. The reasons for this are only surprising in the context of liberal antipathy to private schooling. The myth does die hard, but when it dies it may do so with a vegenance. . . .

Is there a larger theory to explain this change? There is, and it owes a debt to the theory offered in behalf of public schools in the days of their creation. In short form, the explanation is this: the well-to-do have always had easy access to private schools of high quality, whereas the poor, excepting only those in the most unusual circumstances, never do. The American public school, then, was first created as a school for paupers, children who could not buy in the marketplace the education they needed. Indeed, the creation of our public school system was an explicit recognition that the market did not work for the poor. The poor individual had only the most limited capacity to improve his own human capital through education. Enter public schools—they serve the interests of the individual as they serve those of the larger society. And as ever-larger numbers of children are educated in them, they lose their character as "paupers' schools" and emerge as public schools.

But today it is precisely that label that public schools in the inner city begin to wear. And they are becoming "paupers' schools" for the identical reason—market failure. Today, however, it is not the private market that is failing but the public market. Indeed, it is for reasons of public sector market failure, both real and anticipated, that a shift to the private sector is occurring. Given the size and expertise of the modern education bureaucracy, there is little choice available to the student who is interested in quality education. As Hirschman points out in his elegant and prophetic book *Exit, Voice, and Loyalty*, if "voice" is not heard, "loyalty" is exhausted, and "exit" occurs. Thus, the unresponsive public school invites quality-conscious families to leave. And leave they did in the early 1980s.

* * *

Committee for Public Education and Religious Liberty v. Nyquist

413 U.S. 756, 93 S.Ct. 2955, 37 L.Ed.2d 948 (1973).

Mr. Justice Powell delivered the opinion of the Court.

This case raises a challenge under the Establishment Clause of the First Amendment to the constitutionality of a recently enacted New York law which provides financial assistance, in several ways, to nonpublic elementary and secondary schools in that State. The case involves an intertwining of societal and constitutional issues of the greatest importance. . . .

I

The first section of the challenged enactment, entitled "Health and Safety Grants for Nonpublic School Children," provides for direct money grants from the State to "qualifying" nonpublic schools to be used for the "maintenance and repair of . . . school facilities and equipment to ensure the health, welfare and safety of enrolled pupils." A "qualifying" school is any nonpublic, nonprofit elementary or secondary school which "has been designated during the [immediately preceding] year as serving a high concentration of pupils from low-income families for purposes of Title IV of the Federal Higher Education Act of 1965 (20 U.S.C.A. § 425)." Such schools are entitled to receive a grant of $30 per pupil per year, or $40 per pupil per year if facilities are more than 25 years old. Each school is required to submit to the Commissioner of Education an audited statement of its expenditures for maintenance and repair during the preceding year, and its grant may not exceed the total of such expenses. The Commissioner is also required to ascertain the average per-pupil cost for equivalent maintenance and repair services in the public schools, and in no event may the grant to nonpublic qualifying schools exceed 50% of that figure. . . .

The remainder of the challenged legislation—§§ 2–5—is a single package captioned the "Elementary and Secondary Education Opportunity Program." It is composed, essentially, of two parts, a tuition grant program and a tax benefit program. Section 2 establishes a limited plan providing tuition reimbursements to parents of children attending elementary or secondary nonpublic schools. To qualify under this section the parent must have an annual taxable income of less than $5,000. The amount of reimbursement is limited to $50 for each grade school child and $100 for each high school child. Each parent is required, however, to submit to the Commissioner of Education a verified statement containing a receipted tuition bill, and the amount of state reimbursement may not exceed 50% of that figure. No restrictions are imposed on the use of the funds by the reimbursed parents.

This section, like § 1, is prefaced by a series of legislative findings designed to explain the impetus for the State's action. Expressing a dedication to the "vitality of our pluralistic society," the findings state that a "healthy competitive and diverse alternative to public education is not only desirable but indeed vital to a state and nation that have continually reaffirmed the value of individual differences." The findings further emphasis that the right to select among alternative educational systems "is diminished or even denied to children of lower-income families, whose parents, of all groups, have the least options in determining where their children are to be educated." Turning to the public schools, the findings state that any "precipitous decline in the number of nonpublic school pupils would cause a massive increase in public school enrollment and costs," an increase that would "aggravate an already serious fiscal crisis in public education" and would "seriously jeopardize the quality education for all children." Based on these premises, the statute asserts the State's right to relieve the financial burden of parents who send their children to nonpublic schools through this tuition reimbursement program. . . .

The remainder of the "Elementary and Secondary Education Opportunity Program," contained in §§ 3, 4, and 5 of the challenged law, is designed to provide a form of tax relief to those who fail to qualify for tuition reimbursement. Under these sections parents may subtract from their adjusted gross income for state income tax purposes a designated amount for each dependent for whom they have paid at least $50 in nonpublic school tuition. If the taxpayer's adjusted gross income is less than $9,000, he may subtract $1,000 for each of as many as three dependents. As the taxpayer's income rises, the amount he may subtract diminishes. . . . The amount of the deduction is not dependent upon how much the taxpayer actually paid for nonpublic school tuition, and is given in addition to any deductions to which the taxpayer may be entitled for other religious or charitable contributions. . . .

* * *

Although no record was developed in this case, a number of pertinent generalizations may be made about the nonpublic schools which would benefit from these enactments. . . . Some 700,000 to 800,000 students, constituting almost 20% of the State's entire elementary and secondary school population, attend over 2,000 nonpublic schools, approximately 85% of which are church affiliated. And while "all or practically all" of the 280 schools entitled to receive "maintenance and repair" grants "are related to the Roman Catholic Church and teach Catholic religious doctrine to some degree," . . . institutions qualifying under the remainder of the statute include a substantial number of Jewish, Lutheran, Episcopal, Seventh Day Adventist, and other church-affiliated schools. . . .

II

The history of the Establishment Clause has been recounted frequently and need not be repeated here. *See Everson v. Board of Education*, 330 U.S. 1 [Black, J, opinion of the Court], 28 (Rutledge, J, dissenting) (1947); *McCollum v. Board of Education*, 33 U.S. 203, 212 (1948) (Frankfurter, J, separate opinion); *McGowan v. Maryland*, 366 U.S. 420 (1961); *Engel v. Vitale*, 370 U.S. 421 (1962). It is enough to note that it is now firmly established that a law may be one "respecting the establishment of religion" even though its consequence is not to promote a "state religion," *Lemon v. Kurtzman*, 403 U.S. 602, 612 (1971), and even though it does not aid one religion more than another but merely benefits all religions alike. . . . It is equally well established, however, that not every law that confers an "indirect," "remote," or "incidental" benefit upon religious institutions is, for that reason alone, constitutionally invalid . . . *Walz v. Tax Comm'n* 397 U.S. 664, 671–672, 674–675 (1970). What our cases require is careful examination of any law challenged on establishment grounds with a view to ascertaining whether it furthers any of the evils against which that Clause protects. Primary among those evils have been "sponsorship, financial support, and active involvement of the sovereign in religious activity." . . .

Most of the cases coming to this Court raising Establishment Clause questions have involved the relationship between religion and education. Among these religion-education precedents, two general categories of cases may be identified: those dealing with religious activities within the public schools[29] and those involving public aid in varying forms to sectarian educational institutions.[30] While the New York legislation places this case in the latter category, its resolution requires consideration not only of the several aid-to-sectarian-education cases but also of our

29. *McCollum v. Board of Education, [supra]* ("release time" from public education for religious education); *Zorach v. Alauson*, 343 U.S. 306 (1952) (also a "release time" case); *Engel v. Vitale*, 370 U.S. 421 (1962) (prayer reading in public schools); *School Dist. of Abington Township v. Schempp*, 374 U.S. 203 (1963) (Bible reading in public schools); *Epperson v. Arkansas* 393 U.S. 97 (1968) (antievolutionary limitation on public school study). [*See generally* Note, "The 'Released Time' Cases Revisited: A Study of Group Decision making by the Supreme Court," 83 *Yale L.J.* 1202 (1974)].

30. *Everson v. Board of Educ. supra* (bus transportation); *Board of Educ., v. Allen*, 392 U.S. 236 (1968) (textbooks); *Lemon v. Kurtzman, supra* (teacher's salaries, textbooks, instructional materials); *Earley v. DiCenso*, 403 U.S. 602 (1971) (teachers' salaries); *Tilton v. Richardson*, 403 U.S. 672 (1971) (secular college facilities).

other education precedents and of several important noneducation cases. For the now well-defined three-part test that has emerged from our decisions is a product of considerations derived from the full sweep of the Establishment Clause cases. Taken together, these decisions dictate that to pass muster under the Establishment Clause the law in question, first, must reflect a clearly secular legislative purpose, *e.g.*, *Epperson v. Arkansas*, 393 U.S. 97 (1968), second, must have a primary effect that neither advances nor inhibits religion, *e.g.*, . . . *School District of Abington Township v. Schempp*, 374 U.S. 203 (1963), and, third, must avoid excessive government entanglement with religion. . . .

In applying these criteria to the three distinct forms of aid involved in this case, we need touch only briefly on the requirement of a "secular legislative purpose." As the recitation of legislative purposes appended to New York's law indicates, each measure is adequately supported by legitimate, nonsectarian state interests. . . . [W]e do not doubt—indeed, we fully recognize—the validity of the State's interests in promoting pluralism and diversity among its public and nonpublic schools. Nor do we hesitate to acknowledge the reality of its concern for an already overburdened public school system that might suffer in the event that a significant percentage of children presently attending nonpublic schools should abandon those schools in favor of the public schools.

But the propriety of a legislature's purposes may not immunize from further scrutiny a law which either has a primary effect that advances religion, or which fosters excessive entanglements between Church and State. Accordingly, we must weigh each of the three aid provisions challenged here against these criteria of effect and entanglement.

A

The "maintenance and repair" provisions of § 1 authorize direct payments to nonpublic schools, virtually all of which are Roman Catholic schools in low-income areas. . . . [I]t simply cannot be denied that this section has a primary effect that advances religion in that it subsidizes directly the religious activities of sectarian elementary and secondary schools. . . .

* * *

B

New York's tuition reimbursement program also fails the "effect" test. . . .

There can be no question that these grants could not, consistently with the Establishment Clause, be given directly to sectarian schools . . . In the absence of an effective means of guaranteeing that the state aid derived from public funds will be used exclusively for secular, neutral, and nonideological purposes, it is clear from our cases that direct aid in whatever form is invalid. . . . The controlling question here, then, is whether the fact that the grants are delivered to parents rather than schools is of such significance as to compel a contrary result. The State and intervenor-appellees rely on *Everson* and *Allen* for their claim that grants to parents, unlike grants to institutions, respect the "wall of separation" required by the Constitution. It is true that in those cases the Court upheld laws that provided benefits to children attending religious schools and to their parents: . . . [I]n *Everson* parents were reimbursed for bus fares paid to send children to parochial schools, and in *Allen* textbooks were loaned directly to the children. But those decisions make clear that, far from providing a *per se* immunity from examination of the substance of the State's program, the fact that aid is disbursed to parents rather than to the schools is only one among many factors to be considered.

In *Everson*, the Court found the bus fare program analogous to the provision of services such as police and fire protection, sewage disposal, highways, and sidewalks for parochial schools . . . . Such services, provided in common to all citizens, are "so separate and so indisputably marked off from the religious function," . . . that they may fairly be viewed as reflections of a neutral posture toward religious institutions. *Allen* is founded upon a similar principle. The Court there repeatedly emphasized that upon the record in that case there was no indication that textbooks would be provided for anything other than purely secular courses. "Of course books are different from buses. Most bus rides have no inherent religious significance, while religious books are common. However, the language of [the law under consideration] does not authorize the loan of religious books, and the State claims no right to distribute religious literature . . . . Absent evidence, we cannot assume that school authorities . . . are unable to distinguish between secular and religious books or that they will not honestly discharge their duties under the law." 392 U.S. at 244–45.[38]

The tuition grants here are subject to no such restrictions. There has been no endeavor "to guarantee the separation between secular and religious educational functions and to ensure that State financial aid supports only the former." . . . Indeed, it is precisely the function of New York's law to provide assistance to private schools, the great majority of which are sectarian. By reimbursing parents for a portion of their tuition bill, the State seeks to relieve their financial burdens sufficiently to assure that they continue to have the option to send their children to religion-oriented schools. And while the other purposes for that aid—to perpetuate a pluralistic educational environment and to protect the fiscal integrity of overburdened public schools—are certainly unexceptionable, the effect of the aid is unmistakably to provide desired financial support for nonpublic, sectarian institutions. . . .[39]

Although we think it clear, for the reasons above stated, that New York's tuition grant program fares no better under the "effect" test than its maintenance and repair program, in view of the novelty of the question we will address briefly the subsidiary arguments made by the state officials and intervenors in its defense.

First, it has been suggested that it is of controlling significance that New York's program calls for *reimbursement* for tuition already paid rather than for direct contributions which are merely routed through the parents to the schools, in advance of or in lieu of payment by the parents. The parent is not a mere conduit, we are told, but is absolutely free to spend the money he receives in any manner he wishes. There is no element of coercion attached to the reimbursement, and no assurance that the money will eventually end up in the hands of religious schools. The absence of any element of coercion, however, is irrelevant to questions arising under the Establishment Clause. . . . Whether the grant is labeled a reimbursement, a reward, or a subsidy, its substantive impact is still the same. . . .

* * *

Finally, the State argues that its program of tuition grants should survive scrutiny because it is designed to promote the free exercise of religion. . . . [T]his Court repeatedly has recognized that tension inevitably exists between the Free Exercise and the Establishment Clauses . . . and that it may often not be possible to promote the former without offending the latter. As a result of this tension, our cases require the State to maintain an attitude of "neutrality," neither "advancing" nor "inhibiting" religion. In its attempt to enhance the opportunities of the poor to choose between public and nonpublic education, the State has taken a step which can only be regarded as one "advancing" religion. . . .

C

Sections 3, 4, and 5 establish a system for providing income tax benefits to parents of children attending New York's nonpublic schools. . . .

[A] taxpayer's benefit under these sections is unrelated to, and not reduced by, any deductions to

38. *Allen* and *Everson* differ from the present case in a second important respect. In both cases the class of beneficiaries included *all* school children, those in public as well as those in private schools. . . . We do not agree with the suggestion in the dissent of The Chief Justice that tuition grants are an analogous endeavor to provide comparable benefits to all parents of school children whether enrolled in public or nonpublic schools. . . . The grants to parents of private school children are given in addition to the right that they have to send their children to public schools "totally at state expense." And in any event, the argument proves too much, for it would also provide a basis for approving through tuition grants the *complete subsidization* of all religious schools on the ground that such action is necessary if the State is fully to equalize the position of parents who elect such schools—a result wholly at variance with the Establishment Clause.

Because of the manner in which we have resolved the tuition grant issue, we need not decide whether the significantly religious character of the statute's beneficiaries might differentiate the present case from a case involving some form of public assistance (*e.g.*, scholarships) made available generally without regard to the sectarian-nonsectarian, or public-nonpublic nature of the institution benefitted. *See Wolman v. Essex*, 342 F.Supp. 399, 412–13 (S.D. Ohio 1972), aff'd, 409 U.S. 808 (1972). Thus, our decision today does not compel, as appellees have contended, the conclusion that the educational assistance provisions of the "GI Bill," 38 U.S.C. § 1651, impermissibly advance religion in violation of the Establishment Clause. . . .

39. Appellees, focusing on the term *principal or primary effect* which this Court has utilized in expressing the second prong of the three-part test . . . , have argued that the Court must decide in this case whether the "primary" effect of New York's tuition grant program is to subsidize religion or to promote these legitimate secular objectives. . . . We do not think that such metaphysical judgments are either possible or necessary. Our cases simply do not support the notion that a law found to have a "primary" effect to promote some legitimate end under the State's police power is immune from further examination to ascertain whether it also has the direct and immediate effect of advancing religion. . . .

Such secular objectives, no matter how desirable and irrespective whether judges might possess sufficiently sensitive calipers to ascertain whether the secular effects outweigh the sectarian benefits, cannot serve today any more than they could 200 years ago to justify such a direct and substantial advancement of religion. . . .

which he may be entitled for charitable contributions to religious institutions.[49]

In practical terms there would appear to be little difference, for purposes of determining whether such aid has the effect of advancing religion, between the tax benefit allowed here and the tuition grant allowed under § 2. The qualifying parent under either program receives the same form of encouragement and reward for sending his children to nonpublic schools. The only difference is that one parent receives an actual cash payment while the other is allowed to reduce by an arbitrary amount the sum he would otherwise be obliged to pay over to the State. . . .

Appellees . . . place their strongest reliance on *Walz v. Tax Comm'n*, in which New York's property tax exemption for religious organizations was upheld. We think that *Walz* provides no support for appellees' position. Indeed, its rationale plainly compels the conclusion that New York's tax package violates the Establishment Clause.

Tax exemptions for church property enjoyed an apparently universal approval in this country both before and after the adoption of the First Amendment. . . . We know of no historical precedent for New York's recently promulgated tax relief program. . . .

But historical acceptance without more would not alone have sufficed. . . . It was the reason underlying that long history of tolerance of tax exemptions for religion that proved controlling. A proper respect for both the Free Exercise and the Establishment Clauses compels the State to pursue a course of "neutrality" toward religion. Yet governments have not always pursued such a course, and oppression has taken many forms, one of which has been taxation of religion. Thus, if taxation was regarded as a form of "hostility" toward religion, "exemption constitute[d] a reasonable and balanced attempt to guard against those dangers. . . ." Special tax benefits, however, cannot be squared with the principle of neutrality established by the decisions of this Court. To the contrary, insofar as such benefits render assistance to parents who send their children to sectarian schools, their purpose and inevitable effect are to aid and advance those religious institutions.

Apart from its historical foundations, *Walz* is a product of the same dilemma and inherent tension found in most government-aid-to-religion controversies. To be sure, the exemption of church property from taxation conferred a benefit, albeit an indirect and incidental one. Yet that "aid" was a product not of any purpose to support or to subsidize, but of a fiscal relationship designed to minimize involvement and entanglement between Church and State. . . . The granting of the tax benefits under the New York statute, unlike the extension of an exemption, would tend to increase rather than limit the involvement between Church and State.

One further difference between tax exemptions for church property and tax benefits for parents should be noted. The exemption challenged in *Walz* was not restricted to a class composed exclusively or even predominantly of religious institutions. Instead, the exemption covered all property devoted to religious, educational, or charitable purposes. As the parties here must concede, tax reductions authorized by this law flow primarily to the parents of children attending sectarian, nonpublic schools. Without intimating whether this factor alone might have controlling significance in another context in some future case, it should be apparent that in terms of the potential divisiveness of any legislative measure the narrowness of the benefited class would be an important factor. . . .

III

Because we have found that the challenged sections have the impermissible effect of advancing religion, we need not consider whether such aid would result in entanglement of the State with religion in the sense of "[a] comprehensive, discriminating, and continuing state surveillance." *Lemon v. Kurtzman*, 403 U.S. at 619. But the importance of the competing societal interests implicated in this case prompts us to make the further observation that, apart from any specific entanglement of the State in particular religious programs, assistance of the sort here involved carries grave potential for entanglement in the broader sense of continuing political strife over aid to religion.

* * *

The Court recently addressed this issue specifically and fully in *Lemon v. Kurtzman*. After de-

49. Since the program here does not have the elements of a genuine tax deduction, such as for charitable contributions, we do not have before us, and do not decide, whether that form of tax benefit is constitutionally acceptable under the "neutrality" test in *Walz*.

scribing the political activity and bitter differences likely to result from the state programs there involved, the Court said: "The potential for political divisiveness related to religious belief and practice is aggravated in these two statutory programs by the need for continuing annual appropriations and the likelihood of larger and larger demands as costs and population grow." 403 U.S. at 623.[54]

The language of the Court applies with peculiar force to the New York statute now before us. Section 1 (grants for maintenance) and § 2 (tuition grants) will require continuing annual appropriations. Sections 3, 4, and 5 (income tax relief) will not necessarily require annual reexamination, but the pressure for frequent enlargement of the relief is predictable. . . . But we know from long experience with both Federal and State Governments that aid programs of any kind tend to become entrenched, to escalate in cost, and to generate their own aggressive constituencies. And the larger the class of recipients, the greater the pressure for accelerated increases. Moreover, the State itself, concededly anxious to avoid assuming the burden of educating children now in private and parochial schools, has a strong motivation for increasing this aid as public school costs rise and population increases. In this situation, where the underlying issue is the deeply emotional one of Church-State relationships, the potential for serious divisive political consequences needs no elaboration. And while the prospect of such divisiveness may not alone warrant the invalidation of state laws that otherwise survive the careful scrutiny required by the decisions of this Court, it is certainly a "warning signal" not to be ignored. . . .

Our examinations of New York's aid provisions, in light of all relevant considerations, compels the judgment that each, as written, has a "primary effect that advances religion" and offends the constitutional prohibition against laws "respecting the establishment of religion." We therefore affirm the three-judge court's holding as to §§ 1 and 2, and reverse as to §§ 3, 4, and 5.

It is so ordered.

Mr. Chief Justice Burger, joined in part by Mr. Justice White, and joined by Mr. Justice Rehnquist, concurring in part and dissenting in part.

I join in that part of the Court's opinion in *Committee for Public Education and Religious Liberty v. Nyquist, ante,* which holds the New York "maintenance and repair" provision unconstitutional under the Establishment Clause because it is a direct aid to religion. I disagree, however, with the Court's decisions . . . to strike down the . . . tuition grant programs and the New York tax relief provisions. I believe the Court's decisions on those statutory provisions ignore the teachings of *Everson v. Board of Educ.* 330 U.S. 1 (1947), and *Board of Education v. Allen,* 392 U.S. 236 (1968), and fail to observe what I thought the Court had held in *Walz v. Tax Comm'n,* 397 U.S. 664 (1970). . . .

While there is no straight line running through our decisions interpreting the Establishment and Free Exercise Clauses of the First Amendment, our cases do, it seems to me, lay down one solid, basic principle: that the Establishment Clause does not forbid governments, state or federal, from enacting a program of general welfare under which benefits are distributed to private individuals, even though many of those individuals may elect to use those benefits in ways that "aid" religious instruction or worship. Thus, in *Everson* the Court held that a New Jersey township could reimburse *all* parents of school-age children for bus fares paid in transporting their children to school. . . .

Twenty-one years later, in *Board of Education v. Allen* [392 U.S. 236 (1968)], the Court again upheld a state program that provided for direct aid to the parents of all school children including those in private schools. The statute there required "local public school authorities to lend textbooks free of charge to all students in grades 7 through 12; students attending private schools [were] included." Recognizing that *Everson* was the case "most nearly in point," the *Allen* Court interpreted *Everson* as holding that "the Establishment Clause does not prevent a State from extending the benefits of state laws to all citizens without regard to their religious affiliation. . . ." Applying that principle to the statute before it, the *Allen* Court stated:

> "Appellants have shown us nothing about the necessary effects of the statute that is contrary to its stated purpose. The law merely *makes available to all children*

54. The Court in *Lemon* further emphasized that political division along religious lines is to be contrasted with the political diversity expected in a democratic society: "Ordinarily political debate and division, however vigorous or even partisan, are normal and healthy manifestations of our democratic system of government, but political division along religious lines was one of the principal evils against which the First Amendment was intended to protect. Freund, Comment, "Public Aid to Parochial Schools," 82 *Harv. L. Rev.* 1680, 1692 (1969)." 403 U.S. at 622.

> the benefits of a general program to lend schoolbooks free of charge. Books are furnished at the request of the pupil and ownership remains, at least technically, in the State. *Thus no funds or books are furnished to parochial schools, and the financial benefit is to the parents and children, not to schools. . . .*"

The Court's opinions in both *Everson* and *Allen* recognized that the statutory programs at issue there may well have facilitated the decision of many parents to send their children to religious schools. . . . Notwithstanding, the Court held that such an indirect or incidental "benefit" to the religious institutions that sponsored parochial schools was not conclusive indicia of a "law respecting an establishment of religion." . . .

The essence of all these decisions, I suggest, is that government aid to individuals generally stands on an entirely different footing from direct aid to religious institutions. . . .

This fundamental principle which I see running through our prior decisions is this difficult and sensitive field of law, and which I believe governs the present cases, is premised more on experience and history than on logic. It is admittedly difficult to articulate the reasons why a State should be permitted to reimburse parents of private school children—partially at least—to take into account the State's enormous savings in not having to provide schools for those children, when a State is not allowed to pay the same benefit directly to sectarian schools on a per-pupil basis. In either case, the private individual makes the ultimate decision that may indirectly benefit church-sponsored schools; to that extent the state involvement with religion is substantially attenuated. The answer, I believe, lies in the experienced judgment of various members of this Court over the years that the balance between the policies of free exercise and establishment of religion tips in favor of the former when the legislation moves away from direct aid to religious institutions and takes on the character of general aid to individual families. This judgment reflects the caution with which we scrutinize any effort to give official support to religion and the tolerance with which we treat general welfare legislation. . . .

The tuition grant and tax relief programs now before us are, in my view, indistinguishable in principle, purpose and effect from the statutes in *Everson* and *Allen*. . . . The only discernible difference between the programs in *Everson* and *Allen* and these cases is in the method of the distribution of benefits: here the particular benefits of the Pennsylvania and New York statutes are given only to parents of private school children, while in *Everson* and *Allen* the statutory benefits were made available to parents of both public and private school children. But to regard that difference as constitutionally meaningful is to exalt form over substance. It is beyond dispute that the parents of public school children in New York and Pennsylvania presently receive the "benefit" of having their children educated totally at state expense; the statutes enacted in those States and at issue here merely attempt to equalize that "benefit" by giving to parents of private school children, in the form of dollars of tax deductions, what the parents of public school children receive in kind. It is no more than simple equity to grant partial relief to parents who support the public schools they do not use.

The Court appears to distinguish the Pennsylvania and New York statutes from *Everson* and *Allen* on the ground that here the state aid is not apportioned between the religious and secular activities of the sectarian schools attended by some recipients, while in *Everson* and *Allen* the state aid was purely secular in nature. . . . There are at present many forms of government assistance to individuals that can be used to serve religious ends, such as social security benefits or "GI Bill" payments, which are not subject to nonreligious-use restrictions. Yet, I certainly doubt that today's majority would hold those statutes unconstitutional under the Establishment Clause.

Since I am unable to discern in the Court's analysis of *Everson* and *Allen* any neutral principle to explain the result reached in these cases, I fear that the Court has in reality followed the unsupportable approach of measuring the "effect" of a law by the percentage of the recipients who choose to use the money for religious, rather than secular, education. . . .

With all due respect, I submit that such a consideration is irrelevant to a constitutional determination of the "effect" of a statute. For purposes of constitutional adjudication of that issue, it should make no difference whether 5%, 20% or 80% of the beneficiaries of an educational program of general application elect to utilize their benefits for religious purposes. The "primary effect" branch of our three-pronged test was never, at least to my understanding, intended to vary with the *number* of churches benefitted by a statute under which state aid is distributed to private citizens. . . .

Mr. Justice White joins this opinion insofar as it relates to the . . . tuition grant . . . and tax relief statute[s].

Mr. Justice White, joined in part by The Chief Justice and Mr. Justice Rehnquist, dissenting. [omitted]

Mr. Justice Rehnquist, with whom The Chief Justice and Mr. Justice White concur, dissenting in part. . . .

I find both the Court's reasoning and result all but impossible to reconcile with *Walz v. Tax Comm'n*, 397 U.S. 664 (1970), decided only three years ago. . . .

I

The opinions in *Walz* . . . make it clear that tax deductions and exemptions, even when directed to religious institutions, occupy quite a different constitutional status under the Religion Clauses of the First Amendment than do outright grants to such institutions. . . . Mr. Justice Brennan in his concurring opinion amplified the distinction between tax benefits and direct payments in these words:

> "Tax exemptions and general subsidies, however, are qualitatively different. Though both provide economic assistance, they do so in fundamentally different ways. A subsidy involves the direct transfer of public monies to the subsidized enterprise and uses resources exacted from taxpayers as a whole. An exemption, on the other hand, involves no such transfer. . . . Tax exemptions, accordingly, constitute mere passive state involvement with religion and not the affirmative involvement characteristic of outright governmental subsidy. . . ."

Here the effect of the tax benefit is trebly attenuated as compared with the outright exemption considered in *Walz*. There the result was a complete forgiveness of taxes, while here the result is merely a reduction in taxes. There the ultimate benefit was available to an actual house of worship, while here even the ultimate benefit redounds only to a religiously sponsored school. There the churches themselves received the direct reduction in the tax bill, while here it is only the parents of the children who were sent to religiously sponsored schools who receive the direct benefit.

The Court seeks to avoid the controlling effect of *Walz* by comparing its historical background to the relative recency of the challenged deduction plan; by noting that in its historical context, a property tax exemption is religiously neutral, whereas the educational cost deduction here is not; and by finding no substantive difference between a direct reimbursement from the State to parents and the State's abstention from collecting the full tax bill which the parents would otherwise have had to pay.

While it is true that the Court reached its result in *Walz* in part by examining the unbroken history of property tax exemptions for religious organizations in this country, there is no suggestion in the opinion that only those particular tax exemption schemes that have roots in pre-Revolutionary days are sustainable against an Establishment Clause challenge. . . .

[I]f long-established use of a particular tax exemption scheme leads to a holding that the scheme is constitutional, that holding should extend equally to newly devised tax benefit plans which are indistinguishable in principle from those long established.

The Court's statement that "special tax benefits, however, cannot be squared with the principle of neutrality established by decisions of this Court," . . . and that "insofar as such benefits render assistance to parents who send their children to sectarian schools, their purpose and inevitable effect are to aid and advance those religious institutions," . . . are impossible to reconcile with *Walz*. Who can doubt that the tax exemptions which that case upheld were every bit as much of a "special tax benefit" as the New York tax deduction plan here, or that the benefits resulting from the exemption in *Walz* had every bit as much tendency to "aid and advance . . . religious institutions" as did New York's plan here? . . .

NOTES AND QUESTIONS

1. Constitutional Standards

a. The "Secular Purpose" Test. The Court in *Committee for Public Education and Religious Liberty* (hereinafter *PERL*) concludes that both the voucher and tax credit legislation reflect a "clearly secular legislative purpose." Is the Court simply referring to the formal justifications for the legislation that were advanced both before its passage and during oral argument before the Court? Is it likely that the legislators had *both* a secular and religious purpose in adopting this legislation? Is that fact relevant to the Court's analysis? Why is it unconstitutional "for legislation to have the purpose or effect of assisting religious practice generally, when the Constitution itself gives a special status to religion?" Johnson, "Concepts and Compromise in First Amendment Religious Doctrine," 72 *Calif. L. Rev.* 817, 827 (1984).

b. The "Primary Effect" Test. The Court notes that "the effect of the [voucher] aid is unmistakably to provide desired financial support for nonpublic, sectarian institutions." Does that fact alone render it unconstitutional? Does the Court successfully distinguish *PERL* from *Everson v. Board of Education,* 330 U.S. 1, 67 S.Ct. 504, 91 L.Ed. 711 (1947), and *Board of Education v. Allen,* 392 U.S. 236, 88 S.Ct. 1923, 20 L.Ed.2d 1060 (1968), which upheld state aid provision of transportation and textbooks benefitting "nonpublic, sectarian institutions"? *But see Elbe v. Yankton Ind. School Dist. No. 63–3,* 372 N.W.2d 113 (S.D. 1985) (state constitution); *Fannin v. Williams,* 655 S.W.2d 480 (Ky. 1983). *See generally* Note, "Sectarian Books, the Supreme Court and the Establishment Clause," 79 *Yale L.J.* 111 (1969). Would one hundred-dollar "tuition supplements" paid to parents whose children attended public as well as private schools survive judicial scrutiny after *PERL*? What of a state law that provides for loans of textbooks to students and direct loans to the private school of films, laboratory equipment, and auxiliary services such as counseling and testing? *See Meek v. Pittenger,* 421 U.S. 349, 95 S.Ct. 1753, 44 L.Ed. 217 (1975). *See generally* Nowak, "The Supreme Court, the Religion Clauses and the Nationalization of Education," 70 *Nw. L. Rev.* 563 (1977); "The Supreme Court, 1974 Term," 89 *Harv.L.Rev.* 104–10 (1975).

In dissent, Chief Justice Burger notes: "I fear that the Court has in reality followed the insupportable approach of measuring the 'effect' of a law by the percentage of the recipients who choose to use the money for religious, rather than secular, education." Is that in fact what the *PERL* Court did? If so, is it constitutionally "insupportable"?

How does the Court reconcile its decision to strike down tax credits for nonpublic schools with *Walz v. Tax Commission,* 397 U.S. 664 (1970), which permitted states to exempt church property from taxation? Are tax credits less "neutral"—or less likely to aid sectarian institutions—than property tax exemptions? *See Public Funds for Public Schools v. Byrne,* 590 F.2d 514 (3d Cir. 1979), *aff'd,* 442 U.S. 907, 99 S.Ct. 2818, 61 L.Ed.2d 273 (1979).

c. The "Entanglement" Test. By providing vouchers and tax credits, which could be used for any public school activity, New York sought to avoid "a comprehensive, discriminating, and continuing state surveillance" of sectarian schools. *Lemon v. Kurtzman,* 403 U.S. 602, 619, 91 S.Ct. 2105, 2114, 29 L.Ed.2d 745 (1971). *See generally* Lewin, "Disentangling Myth from Reality," 3 *J. of Law & Educ.* 107 (1974); Choper, "The Establishment Clause and Aid to Parochial Schools," 56 *Calif. L. Rev.* 260, 291–303 (1968). Yet the tax credit and voucher schemes do permit public money to be spent for sectarian purposes, a factor that strongly influenced the *PERL* decision. Can one construct state legislation that avoids the Scylla of entanglement and the Charybdis of financing religion?

2. Higher versus Lower Education

In *Hunt v. McNair,* 413 U.S. 734, 93 S.Ct. 2868, 37 L.Ed.2d 923 (1973), decided the same day as *PERL,* the Supreme Court upheld state legislation that provided financial assistance for higher education construction; secular as well as sectarian institutions are eligible for the assistance. The Court thus reaffirmed a distinction, first advanced in *Tilton v. Richardson,* 403 U.S. 672, 91 S.Ct. 2091, 29 L.Ed.2d 790 (1971), between aid that benefits sectarian primary schools and aid that benefits sectarian secondary schools. *See generally* Underwood, "Public Funds for Private Schools: The Gap Between Higher and Lower Education Widens," 41 *Educ.L.Rep.* [407] (1987). The Court suggests that the former are likely to promote genuinely secular ends, while the latter seek to indoctrinate their students with religious values. Is the distinction factually correct? Is it a distinction of constitutional dimension? *See Witters v. Washington Department of Services for the Blind,* 474 U.S. 481, 106 S.Ct. 748 (1986). What if the aid to sectarian institutions of higher learning were noncategorical? Would this run afoul of *PERL* and *Meek*? *See Roemer v. Board of Maryland Public Works,* 426 U.S. 736, 96 S.Ct. 2337, 49 L.Ed.2d 179 (1976) (annual grant upheld). *See generally* Greenawalt, "Constitutional Limits on Aid to Sectarian Universities," 4 *J. Coll. & Univ. L.* 177 (1977). *But see Board of Trustees of Leland Stanford Jr. University v. Cory,* 79 Cal.App.3d 661, 145 Cal. Rptr. 136 (1978) (state constitutional ground).

3. References

The constitutional issues discussed in *PERL* have been extensively debated by commentators. *See* R. Cord, *Separation of Church and State* (1982); West, "An Economic Analysis of the Law and Politics of Nonpublic School Aid," 56 *Calif. L. Rev.* 260 (1968); Choper, "The Establishment Clause and Aid to Parochial Schools," 75 *Calif. L. Rev.* 5 (1987); "Developments in the Law: Religion and the State," 100 *Harv. L. Rev.* 1606 (1987); Giannella, "*Lemon* and *Tilton:* The Bitter and the Sweet of Church-State Entanglement," 1971 *Sup. Ct. Rev.* 147; Giannella, "Religious Liberty, Nonestablishment, and Doctrinal Development—Pt. II: The Nonestablishment Principle," 81 *Harv. L. Rev.* 513 (1968); King, "Rebuilding the 'Fallen House'—State Tuition Grants for Elementary and Secondary Education," 84 *Harv. L. Rev.* 1057 (1971); Laycock, "A Survey of Religious Liberty in the United States," 47 *Ohio St. L. J.* 409 (1986); Laycock, "Towards a General Theory of the Religion Clauses: The Case of Church Labor Relations and the Right to Church Autonomy," 81 *Colum. L. Rev.* 1373 (1981); Morgan, "The Establishment Clause and Sectarian Schools: A Final Installment?," 1973 *Sup. Ct. Rev.* 57; Powe, "Evolution to Absolutism: Justice Douglas and the First Amendment," 74 *Colum. L. Rev.* 371 (1974); Sugarman, "Family Choice: The Next Step in the Quest for Equal Educational Opportunity?," 38 *Law & Contemp. Probs.* 513 (1974).

Committee for Public Education and Religious Liberty v. Regan

444 U.S. 646, 100 S.Ct. 840, 63 L.Ed.2d 94 (1980).

Mr. Justice White delivered the opinion of the Court.

The issue in this case is the constitutionality under the First and Fourteenth Amendments of the United States Constitution of a New York statute authorizing the use of public funds to reimburse church-sponsored and secular nonpublic schools for performing various testing and reporting services mandated by state law. The District Court sustained the statute . . . [W]e now affirm the District Court's judgment.

I

In 1970 the New York Legislature appropriated public funds to reimburse both church-sponsored and secular nonpublic schools for performing various services mandated by the State. The most expensive of these services was the "administration, grading and the compiling and reporting of the results of tests and examinations." New York Laws 1970, ch. 138, §2. Covered tests included both state-prepared examinations and the more common and traditional teacher-prepared tests. Although the legislature stipulated that "[n]othing contained in this act shall be construed to authorize the making of any payment under this act for religious worship or instruction," *id.*, §8, the statute did not provide for any state audit of school financial records that would ensure that public funds were used only for secular purposes.

In *Levitt v. Committee for Public Education*, 413 U.S. 472 (1973) (*Levitt I*), the Court struck down this enactment as violative of the Establishment Clause.[1] The majority focused its concern on the statute's reimbursement of funds spent by schools on traditional teacher-prepared tests. The Court was troubled that, "despite the obviously integral role of such testing in the total teaching process, no attempt is made under the statute, and no means are available, to assure that internally prepared tests are free of religious instruction." *Id.*, at 480. It was not assumed that nonpublic school teachers would attempt in bad faith to evade constitutional requirements. Rather, the Court simply observed that "the potential for conflict 'inheres in the situation,' and because of that the State is constitutionally compelled to assure that the state-supported activity is not being used for religious indoctrination." *Id.*, quoting *Lemon v. Kurtzman*, 403 U.S. 602, 617 (1971). Because the State failed to provide the required assurance, the challenged statute was deemed to constitute an impermissible aid to religion.

The Court distinguished its earlier holdings in *Everson v. Board of Education*, 330 U.S. 1 (1947), and *Board of Education v. Allen*, 392 U.S. 236 (1968), on grounds that the state aid upheld in those cases, in the form of bus rides and loaned secular textbooks for sectarian school-children, was "of a substantially different character" from that presented

1. U.S. Const., Amdt. 1, provides that "Congress shall make no law respecting the establishment of religion . . . ." This Court has repeatedly held the Establishment Clause applicable to the States through the Fourteenth Amendment. *E.g. Meek v. Pittenger*, 421 U.S. 349, 351, (1975); *Cantwell v. Connecticut*, 310 U.S. 296, 303 (1940).

in *Levitt I*. Teacher-prepared tests were deemed by the Court to be an integral part of the teaching process. But so obviously are textbooks an integral part of the teaching process. The crucial feature that distinguished tests, according to the Court, was that, " '[i]n terms of potential for involving some aspect of fair or morals in secular subjects, a textbook's content is ascertainable, but a teacher's handling of a subject is not.' " . . . Thus the inherent teacher discretion in devising, presenting, and grading traditional tests, together with the failure of the legislature to provide for a method of auditing to ensure that public funds would be spent exclusively on secular services, disabled the enactment from withstanding constitutional scrutiny.

Almost immediately the New York Legislature attempted to eliminate these defects from its statutory scheme. A new statute was enacted in 1974,[3] and it directed New York's Commissioner of Education to apportion and to pay to nonpublic schools the actual costs incurred as a result of compliance with certain state-mandated requirements, including:

> "the requirements of the state's pupil evaluation program, the basic educational data system, regents examinations, the statewide evaluation plan, the uniform procedure for pupil attendance reporting, and other similar state prepared examinations and reporting procedures."

New York Laws 1974, ch. 507, §6. Of signal interest and importance in light of *Levitt I*, the new scheme does not reimburse nonpublic schools for the preparation, administration, or grading of teacher-prepared tests. *Ibid*. Further, the 1974 statute, unlike the 1970 version struck down in *Levitt I*, provides a means by which payments of state funds are audited, thus ensuring that only the actual costs incurred in providing the covered secular services are reimbursed out of state funds. *Id.*, §7.

Although the new statutory scheme was tailored to comport with the reasoning in *Levitt I*, the District Court invalidated the enactment with respect to both the tests and the reporting procedure. *Committee for Public Education and Religious Liberty v. Levitt*, 414 F.Supp. 1174 (1976) (*Levitt II*). The District Court understood the decision in *Meek v. Pittenger*, 421 U.S. 349 (1975), to require this result. In *Meek*, decided after *Levitt I*, this Court held unconstitutional two Pennsylvania statutes insofar as they provided auxiliary services and instructional material and equipment apart from textbooks to nonpublic schools in the State, most of which were sectarian. The Court ruled that in "religion-pervasive" institutions, secular and religious education are so "inextricably intertwined" that "[s]ubstantial aid to the educational function of such schools . . . necessarily results in aid for the sectarian school enterprise as a whole" and hence amounts to a forbidden establishment of religion. . . .

Levitt II was appealed to this Court. We vacated the District Court's judgment and remanded the case in light of our decision in *Wolman v. Walter*, 433 U.S. 229 (1977). On remand the District Court ruled that under *Wolman* "state aid may be extended to [a sectarian] school's educational activities if it can be shown with a high degree of certainty that

---

3. New York Laws 1974, ch. 507, as amended by ch. 508, provides in relevant part:

"Section 1. Legislative findings. The legislature hereby finds and declares that:

"The state has the responsibility to provide educational opportunity of a quality which will prepare its citizens for the challenges of American life in the last decades of the twentieth century.

"To fulfill this responsibility, the state has the duty and authority to evaluate, through a system of uniform state testing and reporting procedures, the quality and effectiveness of instruction to assure that those who are attending instruction, as required by law, are being adequately educated within their individual capabilities.

"In public schools these fundamental objectives are accomplished in part through state financial assistance to local school districts.

"More than seven hundred thousand pupils in the state comply with the compulsory education law by attending nonpublic schools. It is a matter of state duty and concern that such nonpublic schools be reimbursed for the actual costs which they incur in providing services to the state which they are required by law to render in connection with the state's responsibility for reporting, testing and evaluating.

* * *

"Sec. 3. Apportionment. The commissioner shall annually apportion to each qualifying school, for school years beginning on and after July first, nineteen hundred seventy-four, an amount equal to the actual cost incurred by each such school during the preceding school year for providing services required by law to be rendered to the state in compliance with the requirements of the state's pupil evaluation program, the basic educational data system, regents examinations, the statewide evaluation plan, the uniform procedure for pupil attendance reporting, and other similar state prepared examinations and reporting procedures.

"Sec. 7. Audit. No application for financial assistance under this act shall be approved except upon audit of vouchers, or other documents by the commissioner as are necessary to insure that such payments is lawful and proper."

* * *

the aid will only have secular value of legitimate interest to the State and does not present any appreciable risk of being used to aid transmission of religious views." . . . Applying this "more flexible concept," . . . the District Court concluded that New York's statutory scheme of reimbursement did not violate the Establishment Clause.

* * *

II

Under the precedents of this Court a legislative enactment does not contravene the Establishment Clause if it has a secular legislative purpose, if its principal or primary effect neither advances nor inhibits religion, and if it does not foster an excessive government entanglement with religion. See *Roemer v. Maryland Public Works Board*, 426 U.S. 736, 748 (1976); *Committee for Public Education v. Nyquist*, 413 U.S. 756, 772–73 (1973); *Lemon v. Kurtzman*, *supra*, 403 U.S., at 612–13.

In *Wolman v. Walter*, *supra*, this Court reviewed and sustained in relevant part an Ohio statutory scheme that authorized, *inter alia*, the expenditure of state funds

> "To supply for use by pupils attending nonpublic schools within the district such standardized tests and scoring services as are in use in the public schools of the state."

Ohio Rev. Code Ann. §3317.06(J). We held that this provision, which was aimed at providing the young with an adequate secular education, reflected a secular state purpose. As the opinion of Mr. Justice Blackmun stated, "[t]he State may require that schools that are utilized to fulfill the State's compulsory-education requirement meet certain standards of instruction, . . . and may examine both teachers and pupils to ensure that the State's legitimate interest is being fulfilled." *Wolman v. Walter*, *supra*, 433 U.S., at 240 . . . . Mr. Justice Blackmun further explained that under the Ohio provision the nonpublic school did not control the content of the test or its result. This "serves to prevent the use of the test as a part of religious teaching, and thus avoids that kind of direct aid to religion found present in *Levitt [I]*." *Wolman v. Walter*, *supra*, 433 U.S., at 240. The provision of testing services hence did not have the primary effect of aiding religion. . . . It was also decided that "the inability of the school to control the test eliminates the need for the supervision that gives rise to excessive entanglement." *Id.*, at 240–41. We thus concluded that the Ohio statute, insofar as it concerned examinations, passed our Establishment Clause tests.

III

We agree with the District Court that *Wolman v. Walter* controls this case. Although the Ohio statute under review in *Wolman* and the New York statute before us here are not identical, the differences are not of constitutional dimension. Addressing first the testing provisions, we note that here, as in *Wolman*, there is clearly a secular purpose behind the legislative enactment: "To provide educational opportunity of a quality which will prepare [New York] citizens for the challenges of American life in the last decades of the twentieth century." New York Laws 1974, ch. 507, § 1. Also like the Ohio statute, the New York plan calls for tests that are prepared by the State and administered on the premises by nonpublic school personnel. The nonpublic school thus has no control whatsoever over the content of the tests. The Ohio tests, however, were graded by the State; here there are three types of tests involved, one graded by the State and the other two by nonpublic school personnel, with the costs of the grading service, as well as the cost of administering all three tests, being reimbursed by the State. In view of the nature of the tests, the District Court found that the grading of the examinations by nonpublic school employees afforded no control to the school over the outcome of any of the tests.

The District Court explained that the State-prepared tests are primarily of three types: pupil evaluation program (PEP) tests, comprehensive ("end-of-the-course") achievement tests, and Regents Scholarship and College Qualifications Tests (RSCQT). . . . Each of the tests addresses a secular academic subject; none deals with religious subject matter.[4] The RSCQT

4. PEP tests are "standardized reading and mathematics achievement tests developed and published by the Educational Department and based on New York State courses of study." . . . Comprehensive tests correspond to the following subject areas: biology; bookkeeping and accounting II; business law; business mathematics; chemistry; earth science; English; French; German; Hebrew, Italian; Latin; ninth year mathematics; tenth year mathematics; eleventh year mathematics; physics; shorthand II and transcription; social studies; and Spanish. . . . The RSCQT tests are divided into two parts. Part 1 is a "test of general scholastic aptitude, containing questions intended to measure ability to think clearly and accurately." . . . Part 2 is "a test of subject matter achievement directly related to courses studied in high school." . . .

Clearly, the tests at issue are secular in character.

examinations are graded by State Education Department personnel, and the District Court correctly concluded that "the risk of [RSCQT examinations] being used for religious purposes through grading is non-existent." . . . The PEP tests, administered universally in grades three and six and optionally in grade nine, are graded by nonpublic school employees, but they "consist entirely of objective, multiple-choice questions, which can be graded by machine and, even if graded by hand, afford the schools no more control over the results than if the tests were graded by the State." . . . The comprehensive tests, based on state courses of study for use in grades nine through twelve, are also graded on the premises by school employees, but "consist largely or entirely of objective questions with multiple-choice answers." . . . Even though some of the comprehensive tests may include an essay question or two, . . . the District Court found that the chance that grading the answers to state-drafted questions in secular subjects could or would be used to gauge a student's grasp of religious ideas was "minimal," especially in light of the "complete" state procedures designed to guard against serious inconsistencies in grading and any misuse of essay questions. . . . These procedures include the submission of completed and graded comprehensive tests to the State Department of Education for review off the school premises.

We see no reason to differ with the factual or legal characterization of the testing procedure arrived at by the District Court. . . .

The District Court was also correct in its characterization of the recordkeeping and reporting services for which the State reimburses the nonpublic school. Under the New York law, "[e]ach year, private schools must submit to the State a Basic Educational Data System (BEDS) report. This report contains information regarding the student body, faculty, support staff, physical facilities, and curriculum of each school. Schools are also required to submit annually a report showing the attendance record of each minor who is a student at the school." . . . Although recordkeeping is related to the educational program, the District Court characterized it and the reporting function as "ministerial [and] lacking in ideological content or use." . . .

These tasks are not part of the teaching process and cannot "be used to foster an ideological outlook." . . . Reimbursement for the costs of so complying with state law, therefore, has primarily a secular, rather than a religious, purpose and effect.[5]

IV

The New York statute, unlike the Ohio statute at issue in *Wolman*, provides for direct cash reimbursement to the nonpublic school for administering the state-prescribed examinations and for grading two of them. We agree with the District Court that such reimbursement does not invalidate the New York statute. If the State furnished state-prepared tests, thereby relieving the nonpublic schools of the expense of preparing their own examinations, but left the grading of the tests to the schools, and if the grading procedures could be used to further the religious mission of the school, serious Establishment Clause problems would be posed under the Court's cases, for by furnishing the tests it might be concluded that the State was directly aiding religious education. But as we have already concluded, grading the secular tests furnished by the State in this case is a function that has a secular purpose and primarily a secular effect. This conclusion is not changed simply because the State pays the school for performing the grading function. As the District Court observed ". . . there does not appear to be any reason why payments to sectarian schools to cover the cost of specified activities would have the impermissible effect of advancing religion if the same activities performed by sectarian school personnel without reimbursement but with State-furnished materials have no such effect." . . .

A contrary view would insist on drawing a constitutional distinction between paying the nonpublic school to do the grading and paying state employees or some independent service to perform that task, even though the grading function is the same regardless of who performs it and would not have the primary effect of aiding religion whether or not performed by nonpublic school personnel. In either

5. The recordkeeping function, according to the parties' stipulation of facts, involves "collection of data requested from homeroom teachers, pupil personnel services staff, attendance secretaries and administrators; compilation and correlation of data; and filling out and mailing reports." . . . The attendance-taking function is described in similar ministerial terms. . . . Of interest is the District Court's finding that "[t]he lion's share of the reimbursements to private schools under the Statute would be for attendance-reporting. According to applications prepared by intervenor-defendant private schools for the 1973–1974 school year, between 85% and 95% of the total reimbursement is accounted for by the costs attributable to attendance-taking, of which all but a negligible portion represents compensation to the personnel for this service." . . .

event, the nonpublic school is being relieved of the cost of grading state-required, state-furnished examinations. We decline to embrace a formalistic dichotomy that bears so little relationship either to common sense or to the realities of school finance. None of our cases requires us to invalidate these reimbursements simply because they involve payments in cash. The Court "has not accepted the recurrent argument that all aid is forbidden because aid to one aspect of an institution frees it to spend its other resources on religious ends." *Hunt v. McNair*, 413 U.S. 734 (1973).[6] Because the recordkeeping and reporting functions also have neither a religious purpose nor a primarily religious effect, we reach the same results with respect to the reimbursements for these services.

Of course, under the relevant cases the outcome would likely be different were there no effective means for insuring that the cash reimbursements would cover only secular services. . . .

V

The District Court recognized that "[w]here a state is required in determining what aid, if any, may be extended to a sectarian school, to monitor the day-to-day activities of the teaching staff, to engage in onerous, direct oversight, or to make on-site judgments from time to time as to whether different school activities are religious in character, the risk of entanglement is too great to permit governmental involvement." . . . After examining the New York statute and its operation, however, the District Court concluded that "[t]he activities subsidized under the Statute here at issue . . . do not pose any substantial risk of such entanglement." . . .

* * *

We agree with the District Court that "[t]he services for which the private schools would be reimbursed are discrete and clearly identifiable." . . . The reimbursement process, furthermore, is straightforward and susceptible to the routinization that characterizes most reimbursement schemes. On its face, therefore, the New York plan suggests no excessive entanglement, and we are not prepared to read into the plan as an inevitability the bad faith upon which any future excessive entanglement would be predicated.[8]

VI

It is urged that the District Court judgment is unsupportable under *Meek v. Pittenger*, *supra*, which is said to have held that any aid to even secular educational functions of a sectarian school is forbidden, or more broadly still, that any aid to a sectarian school is suspect since its religious teaching is so pervasively intermixed with each and every one of its activities. Brief for Appellants 9–11. The difficulty with this position is that a majority of the Court, including the author of *Meek v. Pittenger*, upheld in *Wolman* a state statute under which the State, by preparing and grading tests in secular subjects, relieved sectarian schools of the cost of these functions, functions that they otherwise would have had to perform themselves and that were intimately connected with the educational processes. Yet the *Wolman* opinion at no point suggested that this holding was inconsistent with the decision in *Meek*. Unless the majority in *Wolman* was silently disavowing *Meek*, in whole or in part, that case was simply not understood by this Court to stand for the broad proposition urged by appellants and espoused by the District Court in *Levitt II*.

* * *

This is not to say that this case, any more than past cases, will furnish a litmus-paper test to distinguish permissible from impermissible aid to religiously oriented schools. But Establishment Clause cases are not easy; they stir deep feelings; and we are divided among ourselves, perhaps reflecting the dif-

6. As Mr. Justice Blackmun wrote in *Roemer v. Maryland Works Bd.*, 426 U.S. 736, 747 (1976) . . . , "The Court has not been blind to the fact that in aiding a religious institution to perform a secular task, the State frees the institution's resources to be put to sectarian ends. If this were impermissible, however, a church could not be protected by the police and fire departments, or have its public sidewalk kept in repair. The Court never has held that religious activities must be discriminated against in this way."

8. We find no merit whatever in appellants' argument, which was not made below, that the extent of entanglement here is sufficient to raise the danger of future political divisiveness along religious lines. Brief for Appellants 16–18. *Wolman* was decided without reference to any such potential discord. Moreover, the New York plan reimburses "actual costs." Thus it cannot be maintained that the New York system will provoke religious battles over legislative appropriations, an eventuality that could conceivably occur under a system of state aid involving direct appropriations. *Cf. Committee for Public Education v. Nyquist*, 413 U.S. 756, 794–98 (1973).

ferent views on this subject of the people of this country. What is certain is that our decisions have tended to avoid categorical imperatives and absolutist approaches at either end of the range of possible outcomes. This course sacrifices clarity and predictability for flexibility, but this promises to be the case until the continuing interaction between the courts and the States—the former charged with interpreting and upholding the Constitution and the latter seeking to provide education for their youth—produces a single, more encompassing construction of the Establishment Clause.

The judgment of the District Court is

Affirmed.

Mr. Justice Blackmun, with whom Mr. Justice Brennan and Mr. Justice Marshall join, dissenting.

The Court in this case, I fear, takes a long step backwards in the inevitable controversy that emerges when a state legislature continues to insist on providing public aid to parochial schools.

I thought that the Court's judgments in *Meek v. Pittenger*, 421 U.S. 349 (1975), and in *Wolman v. Walter*, 433 U.S. 229 (1977) (which the Court concedes . . . is the controlling authority here), at last had fixed the line between that which is constitutionally appropriate public aid and that which is not. The line necessarily was not a straight one. It could not be, when this Court, on the one hand, in *Everson v. Board of Education*, 330 U.S. 1 (1947), by a 5–4 vote, decided that there was no barrier under the First and Fourteenth Amendments to parental reimbursement of the cost of fares for the transportation of children attending parochial schools, and in *Board of Education v. Allen*, 392 U.S. 236, (1968), by a 6–3 vote, ruled that New York's lending of approved textbooks to students in private secondary schools was not violative of those Amendments, and yet, on the other hand in *Lemon v. Kurtzman*, 403 U.S. 602 (1971), struck down, as violative of the Religion Clauses, statutes that, respectively, would have supplemented nonpublic school teachers' salaries and would have authorized the "purchase" of certain "secular educational services" from nonpublic schools, and also in *Levitt v. Committee for Public Education*, 413 U.S. 472 (1973) (*Levitt I*), struck down New York's previous attempt to reimburse nonpublic schools for the expenses of tests and examinations. *See also Committee for Public Education v. Nyquist*, 413 U.S. 756 (1973), where the Court nullified New York's financial aid programs for "maintenance and repair" of facilities and equipment, a tuition reimbursement plan, and tax relief for parents who did not qualify for tuition reimbursements, and *Sloan v. Lemon*, 413 U.S. 825 (1973), where the Court ruled invalid a state plan for parental reimbursement of a portion of nonpublic school tuition expenses. . . .

But, I repeat, the line, wavering though it may be, was indeed drawn in *Meek* and in *Wolman*, albeit with different combinations of Justices, those who perceive no barrier under the First and Fourteenth Amendments and who would rule in favor of almost any aid a state legislature saw fit to provide, on the one hand, and those who perceive a broad barrier and would rule against aid of almost any kind, on the other hand, in turn joining Justices in the center on these issues to make order and a consensus out of the earlier decisions. Now, some of those who joined in *Lemon*, *Levitt I*, *Meek*, and *Wolman* in invalidating depart and validate. I am able to attribute this defection only to a concern about the continuing and emotional controversy and to a persuasion that a good-faith attempt on the part of a state legislature is worth a nod of approval.

* * *

I have no trouble in agreeing with the Court that Chapter 507 manifests a clear secular purpose. . . . I therefore would evaluate Chapter 507 under the two remaining inquiries of the three-part test.

In deciding whether Chapter 507 has an impermissible primary effect of advancing religion, or whether it fosters excessive government entanglement with sectarian affairs, one must keep in focus the nature of the assistance prescribed by the New York statute. The District Court found that \$8–10 million annually would be expended under Chapter 507, with the great majority of these funds going to sectarian schools to pay for personnel costs associated with attendance reporting. The court found that such payments would amount to from 1% to 5.4% of the personnel budget of an individual religious school receiving assistance under Chapter 507. Moreover, Chapter 507 provides direct cash payments by the State of New York to religious schools, as opposed to providing services or providing cash payments to third parties who have rendered services. And the money paid sectarian schools under Chapter 507 is designated to reimburse costs that are incurred by religious schools in order to meet basic state testing and reporting requirements, costs that would have been incurred regardless of the availability of reimbursement from the State.

This direct financial assistance provided by chapter 507 differs significantly from the types of state aid to religious schools approved by the Court in *Wolman v. Walter*. For example, in *Wolman* the Court approved that portion of the Ohio statute that provided to religious schools the standardized tests and scoring services furnished to public schools. But, unlike New York's Chapter 507, Ohio's statute provided only the tests themselves and scoring by employees of neutral testing organizations. It did not authorize direct financial aid of any type of religious schools. . . .

Similarly, the other forms of assistance upheld in *Wolman* did not involve direct cash assistance. Rather, the Court approved the State's providing sectarian school students therapeutic, remedial, and guidance programs administered by public employees on public property. It also approved certain public health services furnished by public employees to religious school pupils, even though administered in part on the sectarian premises, on the basis of its recognition in a number of cases, *see, e.g., Meek v. Pittenger*, . . . that provision of health services to all school children does not advance religion so as to contravene the Establishment Clause. . . . But beyond merely failing to approve the type of direct financial aid at issue in this case, *Wolman* reaffirmed the finding of the Court in *Meek v. Pittenger* that *direct* aid to the educational function of religious schools necessarily advances the sectarian enterprise as a whole. Thus, the Court in *Wolman* invalidated Ohio's practice of loaning instructional materials directly to sectarian schools, even though the loan ostensibly was limited to neutral and secular instructional material and equipment, [because] it inescapably had the primary effect of providing a direct and substantial advancement of the sectarian enterprise." 443 U.S., at 250. In the same vein, the Court disapproved Ohio's provision of field-trip transportation directly to religious schools as impermissible direct aid that, because of the pervasively religious nature of the schools involved, furthered the religious goals of the schools, and that also required government surveillance of expenditures to such a degree as to foster entanglement of the State in religion. *Id.*, at 252–55.

* * *

. . . To continue to function as religious schools, sectarian schools . . . are required to incur the costs outlined in § 3 of Chapter 507, or else lose accreditation by the State of New York. *See, e.g.*, N.Y. Education Law §§ 3210, 3211 (McKinney 1970). These reporting and testing requirements would be met by the schools whether reimbursement were available or not. As such, the attendance, informational, and testing expenses compensated by Chapter 507 are essential to the overall educational functioning of sectarian schools in New York in the same way instruction in secular subjects is essential. Therefore, just as direct aid for ostensibly secular purposes by provision of instructional materials or direct financial subsidy is forbidden by the Establishment Clause, so direct aid for the performance of recordkeeping and testing activities that are an essential part of the sectarian school's functioning also is interdicted. The Court stated in *Meek*, and reaffirmed in *Wolman*:

> "The very purpose of many [religious] schools is to provide an integrated secular and religious education; the teaching process is, to a large extent, devoted to the inculcation of religious values and belief. *See Lemon v. Kurtzman*, 403 U.S., at 616–17. Substantial aid to the educational function of such schools, accordingly, necessarily results in aid to the sectarian school enterprise as a whole. '[T]he secular education those schools provide goes hand in hand with the religious mission that is the only reason for the schools' existence. Within the institution, the two are inextricably intertwined.' . . ." . . . .

It is also true that the keeping of pupil attendance records is essential to the religious mission of sectarian schools. To ensure that the school is fulfilling its religious mission properly, it is necessary to provide a way to determine whether pupils are attending the sectarian classes required of them. Accordingly, Chapter 507 not only advances religion by aiding the educational mission of the sectarian school as a whole; it also subsidizes directly the religious mission of such schools. Chapter 507 makes no attempt, and none is possible, to separate the portion of the overall expense of attendance-taking attributable to the desire to ensure that students are attending religious instruction from that portion attributable to the desire to ensure that state attendance laws are complied with. This type of direct aid the Establishment Clause does not permit. *Committee for Public Education v. Nyquist* . . . .

* * *

Beyond this, Chapter 507 also fosters government entanglement with religion to an impermissible extent. Unlike *Wolman*, under Chapter 507 sectarian employees are compensated by the State for grading examinations. In some cases, such grading requires the teacher to exercise subjective judgment. For the State properly to ensure that judgment is not exercised to inculcate religion, a "comprehensive, discriminating, and continuing state surveillance will inevitably be required." *Lemon v. Kurtzman*, ...

Moreover, Chapter 507 provides for continuing reimbursement with regard to examinations in which the questions may vary from year to year, and for examinations that may be offered in the future. This will require the State continually to evaluate the examinations to ensure that reimbursement for expenses incurred in connection with their administration and grading will not offend the First Amendment. This, too, fosters impermissible government involvement in sectarian affairs, since it is likely to lead to continuing adjudication of disputes between the State and others as to whether certain questions or new examinations present such opportunities for the advancement of religion that reimbursement for administering and grading them should not be permitted. . . .

Finally, entanglement also is fostered by the system of reimbursement for personnel expenses. The State must make sure that it reimburses sectarian schools only for those personnel costs attributable to the sectarian employees' secular activities described in §3 of Chapter 507. It is difficult to see how the State adquately may discover whether the time for which reimbursement is made available was devoted only to secular activities without some type of ongoing surveillance of the sectarian employees and religious schools at issue. It is this type of extensive entanglement that the Establishment Clause forbids. . . .

* * *

I would reverse the judgment of the District Court.

Mr. Justice Stevens, dissenting.

Although I agree with Mr. Justice Blackmun's demonstration of why today's holding is not compelled by precedent, my vote also rests on a more fundamental disagreement with the Court. The Court's approval of a direct subsidy to sectarian schools to reimburse them for staff time spent in taking attendance and grading standardized tests is but another in a long line of cases making largely ad hoc decisions about what payments may or may not be constitutionally made to nonpublic schools. In groping for a rationale to support today's decision, the Court has taken a position that could equally be used to support a subsidy to pay for staff time attributable to conducting fire drills or even for constructing and maintaining fireproof premises in which to conduct classes. Though such subsidies might represent expedient fiscal policy, I firmly believe they would violate the Establishment Clause of the First Amendment.

The Court's adoption of such a position confirms my view . . . that the entire enterprise of trying to justify various types of subsidies to nonpublic schools should be abandoned. Rather than continuing with the sisyphean task of trying to patch together the "blurred, indistinct, and variable barrier" described in *Lemon v. Kurtzman* . . . , I would resurrect the "high and impregnable" wall between church and state constructed by the Framers of the First Amendment. *See Everson v. Board of Education* . . . .

NOTES AND QUESTIONS

1. **Regan** ***and Precedent***

Is *Regan* consistent with Supreme Court precedents over the previous decade? *See generally* "Developments in the Law: Religion and the State," 100 *Harv. L. Rev.* 1606, 1675–78 (1987). For example, in *Levitt v. Committee for Public Educ.[Levitt I]*, 413 U.S. 472, 93 S.Ct. 2814, 37 L.Ed.2d 736 (1973), the Court struck down a law in which the state reimbursed private schools for traditional teacher-prepared tests. Why does not *Levitt I* compel the opposite result in *Regan?* Why should it matter that the tests are prepared by the state and not by nonpublic school teachers? How do you distinguish *Meek v. Pittenger*, 421 U.S. 349, 95 S.Ct. 1753, 44 L.Ed.2d 217 (1975)? Why are the tests and record-keeping in *Regan* treated differently from auxiliary equipment and instructional material in *Meek?* Was *Meek* "silently disavowed" in *Wolman v. Walter*, 433 U.S. 229, 97 S.Ct. 2593, 53 L.Ed.2d 714 (1977) (upholding a law under which the state provided standardized tests and scoring to nonpublic schools)? Is *Wolman* consistent with *PERL?* Can *Wolman* be distinguished from *Regan?* What of the fact that two of the tests in *Regan* were to be graded by nonpublic school personnel? What of the fact that payments were made directly to the private schools, in amounts estimated to be 1 percent to 5.4 percent of personnel costs? Is it critical whether there is an objective grading sheet or whether biology is included as a subject or not?

Reconsider the primary effects and entanglement tests of *PERL*. By picking up costs that would otherwise be chargeable to nonpublic schools, is not the primary effect of the *Regan* law to advance religion? Or is the impact de minimis compared with *PERL?* What of the necessity for auditing and annual appropriations in *Regan*? Why do these requirements not violate the entanglement test?

Is Justice Stevens correct in urging that the Court's ad hoc attempts to differentiate among different types of subsidies are so unpersuasive that the Court should abandon the effort entirely? Where would this leave nonpublic schools? Should all forms of subsidies be declared unconstitutional, as Stevens suggests? Was this implicit in *PERL?* Or should all forms of subsidies, perhaps except for those explicitly directed to religious activity, be approved? Is Stevens saying that there is no intermediate ground? Is Justice Blackmun? *See* Laycock, "A Survey of Religious Liberty in the United States," 47 *Ohio St. L.J.* 409 (1986).

Is it fair to say that the Court in *Regan* and *Wolman* has significantly altered establishment clause doctrine—without expressly overruling *PERL* and other precedents? Has the scope of the *Everson* and *Allen* exceptions been expanded?

2. Regan *and State Regulation of Private Schools*

Is it significant to the *Regan* result that the state is paying the private schools for what it requires them to do under its compulsory education statute, for example, administering standardized tests? Would this lead to the conclusion that if the state requires certain secular courses in private schools, the state may (must?) pick up the tab for those courses? *Cf.* Choper, "The Establishment Clause and Aid to Parochial Schools," 56 *Cal. L. Rev.* 260 (1968). For secular private schools, is this a better accommodation of parental and state interests than the *Pierce* compromise?

3. *The Economics of the Establishment Clause*

The Court has been increasingly criticized for its efforts to make principled distinctions among different types of subsidies to private religious schools. *See, e.g.*, Choper, "The Establishment Clause and Aid to Parochial Schools," 56 *Calif. L. Rev.* 260 (1968); Schwarz, "No Imposition of Religion: The Establishment Clause Value," 77 *Yale L. J.* 692 (1968); Young, "Constitutional Validity of State Aid to Pupils in Church-Related Schools—Internal Tension Between the Establishment and Free Exercise Clauses," 38 *Ohio St. L. J.* 783 (1977). On the other hand, one commentator has stated that "despite the criticisms leveled by members of the Court and commentators against the tripartite test, the test has served at least to isolate all but the more peripheral forms of aid to parochial schools from public funding, irrespective of the ploys and feints employed to circumvent the First Amendment." Kancelbaum, "Shifting Currents in the Narrow Channel of State Aid to Parochial Schools," 38 *Ohio St. L. J.* 757, 782 (1977).

Do you agree? Is the statement still true, if it was ever true, after the *Regan* decision? If the cases seek principled resolution of the constitutionality of different forms of state aid to nonpublic schools—and not merely to eliminate all but "peripheral" forms of assistance—how much sense do the distinctions made by the Court make?

Mueller v. Allen

463 U.S. 388, 103 S.Ct. 3062, 77 L.Ed.2d 721 (1983).

Justice Rehnquist delivered the opinion of the Court.

Minnesota allows taxpayers, in computing their state income tax, to deduct certain expenses incurred in providing for the education of their children. Minn.Stat. § 290.09(22).[1] The United States Court of Appeals for the Eighth Circuit held that the Establishment Clause of the First and Fourteenth

---

1. Minn.Stat. § 290.09(22) (1982) permits a taxpayer to deduct from his or her computation of gross income the following:

"*Tuition and transportation expense.* The amount he has paid to others, not to exceed $500 for each dependent in grades K to 6 and $700 for each dependent in grades 7 to 12, for tuition, textbooks and transportation of each dependent in attending an elementary or secondary school situated in Minnesota, North Dakota, South Dakota, Iowa, or Wisconsin, wherein a resident of this state may legally fulfill the state's compulsory attendance laws, which is not operated for profit, and which adheres to the provisions of the Civil Rights Act of 1964 and chapter 363. As used in this subdivision, "textbooks" shall mean and include books and other instructional materials and equipment used in elementary and secondary schools in teaching only those subjects legally and commonly taught in public elementary and secondary schools in this state and shall not include instructional books and materials used in the teaching of religious tenets, doctrines or worship, the purpose of which is to inculcate such tenets, doctrines or worship, nor shall it include such books or materials for, or transportation to, extracurricular activities including sporting events, musical or dramatic events, speech activities, driver's education, or programs of a similar nature."

Amendments was not offended by this arrangement. Because this question was reserved in *Committee for Public Education v. Nyquist,* 413 U.S. 756 . . . (1973), and because of a conflict between the decision of the Court of Appeals for the Eighth Circuit and that of the Court of Appeals for the First Circuit in *Rhode Island Federation of Teachers v. Norberg,* 630 F.2d 855 (CA1 1980), we granted certiorari. 459 U.S. 820 (1982). We now affirm.

Minnesota, like every other state, provides its citizens with free elementary and secondary schooling. Minn.Stat. §§ 120.06, 120.72. It seems to be agreed that about 820,000 students attended this school system in the most recent school year. During the same year, approximately 91,000 elementary and secondary students attended some 500 privately supported schools located in Minnesota, and about 95 percent of these students attended schools considering themselves to be sectarian.

Minnesota, by a law originally enacted in 1955 and revised in 1976 and again in 1978, permits state taxpayers to claim a deduction from gross income for certain expenses incurred in educating their children. The deduction is limited to actual expenses incurred for the "tuition, textbooks and transportation" of dependents attending elementary or secondary schools. A deduction may not exceed $500 per dependent in grades K through six and $700 per dependent in grades seven through twelve. Minn.Stat. § 290.09.[2]

Petitioners—certain Minnesota taxpayers—sued in the United States District Court for the District of Minnesota claiming that § 290.09(22) violated the Establishment Clause by providing financial assistance to sectarian institutions. They named as respondents the Commissioner of the Department of Revenue of Minnesota and several parents who took advantage of the tax deduction for expenses incurred in sending their children to parochial schools. The District Court granted respondent's motion for summary judgment, holding that the statute was "neutral on its face and in its application and does not have a primary effect of either advancing or inhibiting religion." 514 F.Supp. 998, 1003 (D.Minn.1981). On appeal, the Court of Appeals affirmed, concluding that the Minnesota statute substantially benefited a "broad class of Minnesota citizens."

Today's case is no exception to our oft-repeated statement that the Establishment Clause presents especially difficult questions of interpretation and application. It is easy enough to quote a few words comprising that clause—"Congress shall make no law respecting an establishment of religion." It is not at all easy, however, to apply this Court's various decisions construing the Clause to governmental programs of financial assistance to sectarian schools and the parents of children attending those schools. . . .

One fixed principle in this field is our consistent rejection of the argument that "any program which in some manner aids an institution with a religious affiliation" violates the Establishment Clause. . . . For example, it is now well established that a state

2. Both lower courts found that the statute permits deduction of a range of educational expenses. The District Court found that deductible expenses included:

"1. Tuition in the ordinary sense.

2. Tuition to public school students who attend public schools outside their residence school districts.

3. Certain summer school tuition.

4. Tuition charged by a school for slow learner private tutoring services.

5. Tuition for instruction provided by an elementary or secondary school to students who are physically unable to attend classes at such school.

6. Tuition charged by a private tutor or by a school that is not an elementary or secondary school if the instruction is acceptable for credit in an elementary or secondary school.

7. Montessori School tuition for grades K through 12.

8. Tuition for driver education when it is part of the school curriculum." 514 F.Supp. at 1000.

The Court of Appeals concurred in this finding.

In addition, the District Court found that the statutory deduction for "textbooks" included not only "secular textbooks" but also:

"1. Cost of tennis shoes and sweatsuits for physical education.

2. Camera rental fees paid to the school for photography classes.

3. Ice skates rental fee paid to the school.

4. Rental fee paid to the school for calculators for mathematics classes.

5. Costs of home economics materials needed to meet minimum requirements.

6. Costs of special metal or wood needed to meet minimum requirements of shop classes.

7. Costs of supplies needed to meet minimum requirements of art classes.

8. Rental fees paid to the school for musical instruments.

9. Cost of pencils and special notebooks required for class." *Ibid.*

The Court of Appeals accepted this finding.

may reimburse parents for expenses incurred in transporting their children to school, *Everson v. Board of Education*, 330 U.S. 1 . . . (1947), and that it may loan secular textbooks to all schoolchildren within the state, *Board of Education v. Allen*, 392 U.S. 236 . . . (1968).

Notwithstanding the repeated approval given programs such as those in *Allen* and *Everson*, our decisions also have struck down arrangements resembling, in many respects, these forms of assistance. *See, e.g., Lemon v. Kurtzman*, . . . [403 U.S. 602 (1971)]; *Levitt v. Committee for Public Education*, 413 U.S. 472 . . . (1972); *Meek v. Pittenger*, 421 U.S. 349 . . . (1975); *Wolman v. Walter*, 433 U.S. 229, 237–238 . . . (1977).[3] In this case we are asked to decide whether Minnesota's tax deduction bears greater resemblance to those types of assistance to parochial schools we have approved, or to those we have struck down. Petitioners place particular reliance on our decision in *Committee for Public Education v. Nyquist, supra*, where we held invalid a New York statute providing public funds for the maintenance and repair of the physical facilities of private schools and granting thinly disguised "tax benefits," actually amounting to tuition grants, to the parents of children attending private schools. As explained below, we conclude that § 290.09(22) bears less resemblance to the arrangement struck down in *Nyquist* than it does to assistance programs upheld in our prior decisions and those discussed with approval in *Nyquist*.

The general nature of our inquiry in this area has been guided, since the decision in *Lemon v. Kurtzman*, 403 U.S. 602 . . . (1971), by the "three-part" test laid down in that case: "First, the statute must have a secular legislative purpose; second, its principal or primary effect must be one that neither advances nor inhibits religion . . .; finally, the statute must not foster 'an excessive government entanglement with religion.' " *Id.*, at 612–613. . . . While this principle is well settled, our cases have also emphasized that it provides "no more than [a] helpful signpost" in dealing with Establishment Clause challenges. *Hunt v. McNair, supra*. 413 U.S., at 741. . . . With this *caveat* in mind, we turn to the specific challenges raised against § 290.09(22) under the *Lemon* framework.

Little time need be spent on the question of whether the Minnesota tax deduction has a secular purpose. Under our prior decisions, governmental assistance programs have consistently survived this inquiry even when they have run afoul of other aspects of the *Lemon* framework. . . . This reflects, at least in part, our reluctance to attribute unconstitutional motives to the states, particularly when a plausible secular purpose for the state's program may be discerned from the face of the statute.

A state's decision to defray the cost of educational expenses incurred by parents—regardless of the type of schools their children attend—evidences a purpose that is both secular and understandable. An educated populace is essential to the political and economic health of any community, and a state's efforts to assist parents in meeting the rising cost of educational expenses plainly serves this secular purpose of ensuring that the state's citizenry is well educated. Similarly, Minnesota, like other states, could conclude that there is a strong public interest in assuring the continued financial health of private schools, both sectarian and nonsectarian. By educating a substantial number of students such schools relieve public schools of a correspondingly great burden—to the benefit of all taxpayers. In addition, private schools may serve as a benchmark for public schools, in a manner analogous to the "TVA yardstick" for private power companies. . . .

All these justifications are readily available to support § 290.09(22), and each is sufficient to satisfy the secular purpose inquiry of *Lemon*.[4]

We turn therefore to the more difficult but related question whether the Minnesota statute has "the primary effect of advancing the sectarian aims of the nonpublic schools." *Committee for Public Education v. Regan*, 444 U.S. 646, 662. . . . In concluding that it does not, we find several features of the Minnesota tax deduction particularly significant.

3. In *Lemon v. Kurtzman, supra*, the Court concluded that the state's reimbursement of nonpublic schools for the cost of teacher's salaries, textbooks, and instructional materials, and its payment of a salary supplement to teachers in nonpublic schools, resulted in excessive entanglement of church and state. In *Levitt v. Committee for Public Education, supra*, we struck down on Establishment Clause grounds a state program reimbursing nonpublic schools for the cost of teacher-prepared examinations. Finally, in *Meek v. Pittenger, supra*, and *Wolman v. Walter, supra*, we held unconstitutional a direct loan of instructional materials to nonpublic schools, while upholding the loan of textbooks to individual students.

4. Section 290.09 contains no express statements of legislative purpose, and its legislative history offers few unambiguous indications of actual intent. The absence of such evidence does not affect our treatment of the statute.

First, an essential feature of Minnesota's arrangement is the fact that § 290.09(22) is only one among many deductions—such as those for medical expenses, Minn. Stat. § 290.09(10) and charitable contributions, Minn. Stat. § 290.21—available under the Minnesota tax laws.[5] Our decisions consistently have recognized that traditionally "[l]egislatures have especially broad latitude in creating classifications and distinctions in tax statutes," *Regan v. Taxation with Representation*, 461 U.S. 540, 547 (1983), in part because the "familiarity with local conditions" enjoyed by legislators especially enables them to "achieve an equitable distribution of the tax burden." *Madden v. Kentucky*, 309 U.S. 83 . . . (1940). Under our prior decisions, the Minnesota legislature's judgment that a deduction for educational expenses fairly equalizes the tax burden of its citizens and encourages desirable expenditures for educational purposes is entitled to substantial deference.[6]

Other characteristics of § 290.09(22) argue equally strongly for the provision's constitutionality. Most importantly, the deduction is available for educational expenses incurred by *all* parents, including those whose children attend public schools and those whose children attend non-sectarian private schools or sectarian private schools. Just as in *Widmar v. Vincent*, 454 U.S. 263 . . . (1981), where we concluded that the state's provision of a forum neutrally "open to a broad class of nonreligious as well as religious speakers" does not "confer any imprimatur of State approval," so here: "the provision of benefits to so broad a spectrum of groups is an important index of secular effect."

In this respect, as well as others, this case is vitally different from the scheme struck down in *Nyquist*. There, public assistance amounting to tuition grants, was provided only to parents of children in *nonpublic* schools. This fact had considerable bearing on our decision striking down the New York statute at issue; we explicitly distinguished both *Allen* and *Everson* on the grounds that "In both cases the class of beneficiaries included *all* schoolchildren, those in public as well as those in private schools," 413 U.S., at 782, n. 38 . . . (emphasis in original). Moreover, we intimated that "public assistance (*e.g.*, scholarships) made available generally without regard to the sectarian-nonsectarian or public-nonpublic nature of the institution benefited," *ibid.*, might not offend the Establishment Clause. We think the tax deduction adopted by Minnesota is more similar to this latter type of program than it is to the arrangement struck down in *Nyquist*. Unlike the assistance at issue in *Nyquist*, § 290.09(22) permits *all* parents—whether their children attend public school or private—to deduct their children's educational expenses. As *Widmar* and our other decisions indicate, a program, like § 290.09(22), that neutrally provides state assistance to a broad spectrum of citizens is not readily subject to challenge under the Establishment Clause.

We also agree with the Court of Appeals that, by channeling whatever assistance it may provide to parochial schools through individual parents, Minnesota has reduced the Establishment Clause objections to which its action is subject. It is true, of course, that financial assistance provided to parents ultimately has an economic effect comparable to that of aid given directly to the schools attended by their children. It is also true, however, that under Minnesota's arrangement public funds become available only as a result of numerous, private choices

5. Deductions for charitable contributions, allowed by Minnesota law, Minn. Stat. § 290.21, include contributions to religious institutions, and exemptions from property tax for property used for charitable purposes under Minnesota law include property used for wholly religious purposes, Minn. Stat. § 272.02. In each case, it may be that religious institutions benefit very substantially from the allowance of such deductions. The Court's holding in *Walz v. Tax Commission*, 397 U.S. 664 . . . (1970), indicates, however, that this does not require the conclusion that such provisions of a state's tax law violate the Establishment Clause.

6. Our decision in *Nyquist* is not to the contrary on this point. We expressed considerable doubt there that the "tax benefits" provided by New York law properly could be regarded as parts of a genuine system of tax laws. Plainly, the outright grants to low-income parents did not take the form of ordinary tax benefits. As to the benefits provided to middle-income parents, the Court said:

"The amount of the deduction is unrelated to the amount of money actually expended by any parent on tuition, but is calculated on the basis of a formula contained in the statute. The formula is apparently the product of a legislative attempt to assure that each family would receive a carefully estimated net benefit, and that the tax benefit would be comparable to, and compatible with, the tuition grant for lower income families."

Indeed, the question whether a program having the elements of a "genuine tax deduction" would be constitutionally acceptable was expressly reserved in *Nyquist*, *supra*, 413 U.S. at 790, n. 49. . . . While the economic consequences of the program in *Nyquist* and that in this case may be difficult to distinguish, we have recognized on other occasions that "the form of the [state's assistance to parochial schools must be examined] for the light that it casts on the substance." *Lemon v. Kurtzman*, *supra*, 403 U.S., at 614. . . . The fact that the Minnesota plan embodies a "genuine tax deduction" is thus of some relevance, especially given the traditional rule of deference accorded legislative classifications in tax statutes.

of individual parents of school-age children. For these reasons, we recognized in *Nyquist* that the means by which state assistance flows to private schools is of some importance: we said that "the fact that aid is disbursed to parents rather than to . . . schools" is a material consideration in Establishment Clause analysis, albeit "only one among many to be considered." *Nyquist*, at 781, 93 S.Ct., at 2970. It is noteworthy that all but one of our recent cases invalidating state aid to parochial schools have involved the direct transmission of assistance from the state to the schools themselves. The exception, of course, was *Nyquist*, which, as discussed previously, is distiguishable from this case on other grounds. Where, as here, aid to parochial schools is available only as a result of decisions of individual parents no "imprimatur of State approval," *Widmar*, at 274, 102 S.Ct., at 276, can be deemed to have been conferred on any particular religion, or on religion generally.

We find it useful, in the light of the foregoing characteristics of § 290.09(22), to compare the attenuated financial benefits flowing to parochial schools from the section to the evils against which the Establishment Clause was designed to protect. These dangers are well-described by our statement that "what is at stake as a matter of policy [in Establishment Clause cases] is preventing that kind and degree of government involvement in religious life that, as history teaches us, is apt to lead to strife and frequently strain a political system to the breaking point." *Nyquist, supra*, 413 U.S., at 796 . . . quoting, *Walz v. Tax Comm'n*, 397 U.S., at 694 . . . (Harlan, J., concurring). It is important, however, to "keep these issues in perspective":

> "At this point in the 20th century we are quite far removed from the dangers that prompted the Framers to include the Establishment Clause in the Bill of Rights. . . . The risk of significant religious or denominational control over our democratic processes—or even of deep political division along religious lines—is remote, and when viewed against the positive contributions of sectarian schools, and such risk seems entirely tolerable in light of the continuing oversight of this Court."

Wolman, 433 U.S., at 263 . . . (Powell, J., concurring in part, concurring in the judgment in part, and dissenting in part).

The Establishment Clause of course extends beyond prohibition of a state church or payment of state funds to one or more churches. We do not think, however, that its prohibition extends to the type of tax deduction established by Minnesota. The historic purposes of the clause simply do not encompass the sort of attenuated financial benefit, ultimately controlled by the private choices of individual parents, that eventually flows to parochial schools from the neutrally available tax benefit at issue in this case.

Petitioners argue that, notwithstanding the facial neutrality of § 290.09(22), in application the statute primarily benefits religious institutions. Petitioners rely, as they did below, on a statistical analysis of the type of persons claiming the tax deduction. They contend that most parents of public school children incur no tuition expenses, see Minn.Stat. § 120.06, and that other expenses deductible under § 290.09(22) are negligible in value; moreover, they claim that 96 percent of the children in private schools in 1978–1979 attended religiously-affiliated institutions. Because of all this, they reason, the bulk of deductions taken under § 290.09(22) will be claimed by parents of children in sectarian schools. Respondents reply that petitioners have failed to consider the impact of deductions for items such as transportation, summer school tuition, tuition paid by parents whose children attended schools outside the school districts in which they resided, rental or purchase costs for a variety of equipment, and tuition for certain types of instruction not ordinarily provided in public schools.

We need not consider these contentions in detail. We would be loath to adopt a rule grounding the constitutionality of a facially neutral law on annual reports reciting the extent to which various classes of private citizens claimed benefits under the law. Such an approach would scarcely provide the certainty that this field stands in need of, nor can we perceive principled standards by which such statistical evidence might be evaluated. Moreover, the fact that private persons fail in a particular year to claim the tax relief to which they are entitled—under a facially neutral statute—should be of little importance in determining the constitutionality of the statute permitting such relief.

. . . If parents of children in private schools choose to take especial advantage of the relief provided by § 290.09(22), it is no doubt due to the fact that they bear a particularly great financial burden in educating their children. More fundamentally, whatever unequal effect may be attributed to the statutory classification can fairly be regarded as a rough return for the benefits, discussed above, provided to the state and all taxpayers by parents sending their children to parochial schools. In the light of all this, we believe it wiser to decline to engage in the type of empirical inquiry into those persons benefited by state law which petitioners urge.

Thus, we hold that the Minnesota tax deduction for educational expenses satisfies the primary effect inquiry of our Establishment Clause cases.

Turning to the third part of the *Lemon* inquiry, we have no difficulty in concluding that the Minnesota statute does not "excessively entangle" the state in religion. The only plausible source of the "comprehensive, discriminating, and continuing state surveillance," 403 U.S., at 619 . . ., necessary to run afoul of this standard would lie in the fact that state officials must determine whether particular textbooks qualify for a deduction. In making this decision, state officials must disallow deductions taken from "instructional books and materials used in the teaching of religious tenets, doctrines, or worship, the purpose of which is to inculcate such tenets, doctrines, or worship." Minn.Stat. § 290.09(22). Making decisions such as this does not differ substantially from making the types of decisions approved in earlier opinions of this Court. In *Board of Education v. Allen*, 392 U.S. 236 . . . (1968), for example, the Court upheld the loan of secular textbooks to parents or children attending nonpublic schools; though state officials were required to determine whether particular books were or were not secular, the system was held not to violate the Establishment Clause. . . . The same result follows in this case.[11]

For the foregoing reasons, the judgment of the Court of Appeals is

Affirmed.

Justice Marshall, with whom Justice Brennan, Justice Blackmun and Justice Stevens join, dissenting.

The Establishment Clause of the First Amendment prohibits a State from subsidizing religious education, whether it does so directly or indirectly. In my view, this principle of neutrality forbids not only the tax benefits struck down in *Committee for Public Education v. Nyquist*, 413 U.S. 756 . . . (1973), but any tax benefit, including the tax deduction at issue here, which subsidizes tuition payments to sectarian schools. I also believe that the Establishment Clause prohibits the tax deductions that Minnesota authorizes for the cost of books and other instructional materials used for sectarian purposes.

* * *

NOTES AND QUESTIONS

1. Mueller *and the* Lemon *Test*

Does the Rehnquist opinion in *Mueller* indicate "that the Court may be moving toward an effect test that concentrates on the imprimatur concern"? Note, "The Supreme Court, Effect Inquiry, and Aid to Parochial Education," 37 *Stan. L. Rev.* 219, 231–32 (1984). Is this why aid to parents is less objectionable than aid to private schools? Does the amount of the aid no longer matter? *Id.* at 232–33. Has the effects test been replaced by a balancing test? *Id.* How should the courts balance secular and religious benefits? Does balancing risk inconsistency and unpredictability of results in specific cases? *Id.* at 235. Does *Mueller* implicitly overrule *Lemon? See generally* Note, "Laws Respecting an Establishment of Religion: An Inquiry Into Tuition Tax Benefits," 58 *N.Y.U. L. Rev.* 207 (1983). Is it one more example in "a series of inconsistent and almost inexplicable decisions"? Laycock, "A Survey of Religious Liberty in the United States," 47 *Ohio L.J.* 409, 443 (1986).

2. Parental Rights

If parents have a right to send their children to private schools, "how can it be impermissible for a

11. No party to this litigation has urged that the Minnesota plan is invalid because it runs afoul of the rather elusive inquiry, subsumed under the third part of the *Lemon* test, whether the Minnesota statute partakes of the "divisive political potential" condemned in *Lemon supra*, 403 U.S., at 622, 91 S.Ct., at 2115. The argument is advanced, however, by amicus National Committee for Public Education and Religious Liberty *et al.* This variation of the "entanglement" test has been interpreted differently in different cases. . . . Since this aspect of the "entanglement" inquiry originated with *Lemon v. Kurtzman, supra*, and the Court's opinion there took pains to distinguish both *Everson v. Board of Education*, . . . *[supra]* and *Board of Education v. Allen* . . . *[supra]*, the Court in *Lemon* must have been referring to a phenomenon which, although present in that case, would have been absent in the two cases it distinguished.

The Court's language in *Lemon I* respecting political divisiveness was made in the context of Pennsylvania and Rhode Island statutes which provided for either direct payments of, or reimbursement of, a proportion of teachers' salaries in parochial schools. We think, in the light of the treatment of the point in later cases discussed above, the language must be regarded as confined to cases where direct financial subsidies are paid to parochial schools or to teachers in parochial schools.

state to make the same option available to all [regardless of wealth] by tuition tax credits, grants, or other forms of aid to private schools?" Johnson, "Concepts and Compromise in First Amendment Doctrine," 72 *Calif. L. Rev.* 817, 822–23 (1984). *But cf. Regan v. Taxation With Representation of Washington*, 461 U.S. 540, 103 S.Ct. 1997, 76 L.Ed.2d 129 (1983); *Harris v. McRae*, 448 U.S. 297, 100 S.Ct. 2671, 65 L.Ed.2d 784 (1980); *Maher v. Roe*, 432 U.S. 464, 97 S.Ct. 2376, 53 L.Ed.2d 484 (1977).

3. *Tax Deductions Under State Constitutional Law*

In *Opinion of the Justices to the Senate*, 401 Mass. 1201, 514 N.E.2d 353 (1987), the Supreme Judicial Court of Massachusetts was asked to render an advisory opinion on a state senate bill that would have provided for tax deductions for educational expenses incurred in attending public and private elementary and secondary schools. The senate bill was similar to the law upheld in *Mueller*. The Court applied Article 46, § 2 of the Amendments to the Massachusetts Constitution:

> No grant, appropriation or use of public money or property or loan of credit shall be made or authorized by the Commonwealth or any political subdivision thereof for the purpose of founding, maintaining, or aiding any infirmary, hospital, institution, primary or secondary school, or charitable or religious undertaking which is not publicly owned and under the exclusive control . . . of public officers or public agents authorized by the Commonwealth or federal authority or both. . . .

The Court held that the proposed bill violated the Massachusetts Constitution, concluding that the legislature had "an intent to aid and to maintain private schools" and that the bill "would provide 'substantial assistance' to private schools." 514 N.E.2d at 356, 357. It also held that "tax subsidies or tax expenditures of this sort are the practical equivalent of direct government grants," and thus the proposed law would violate art. 46, § 2 by lessening the financial burden on parents who choose to send their children to private schools. *Id.* at 355, 358. The Massachusetts court specifically noted its unwillingness to adhere to *Mueller*, holding that "the language of our [Massachusetts] anti-aid amendment is 'much more specific' than the First Amendment . . . and its restrictions are 'more stringent.' . . . Its prohibition is 'emphatic and comprehensive,' . . . and it 'marks no difference between 'aids,' whether religious or secular.' . . ." *Id.* at 354 n. 4. *See generally* Greenawalt, "The Concept of Religion in State Constitutions," 8 *Campbell L. Rev.* 437, 439–441 (1986).

4. *The Economics of Aid to Parochial Schools and Families With Students in Parochial Schools*

In analyzing the *Mueller* opinion, consider this economic analysis by Professor Sugarman:

"New Perspectives on 'Aid' to Private School Users"

S. Sugarman, in E. G. West, ed., *Nonpublic School Aid* 64 (1975). (Lexington, Mass.: Lexington Books, D.C. Heath and Company, Copyright 1974, D.C. Heath and Company.) Reprinted by permission.

The joint supply model which West employs* provides a helpful analogy through which the Supreme Court's treatment of the Establishment Clause in the "aid to religion" cases may be examined. The basic point of the model and analogy is that, because of the interdependency of beef (education) and hides (religion), if what society wants is beef consumption (education) and it intervenes in the market to stimulate the production or purchase of cattle, this intervention will necessarily benefit the consumers of hides (religion). Viewed in this light, the line drawing in which the Court has engaged seems rather odd to West. The Court has, by analogy, upheld schemes by which the government (1) pays for the transport of cattle to market,[2] (2) provides feed for the cattle to eat,[3] and (3) exempts from taxes that land which is used for the raising of animals.[4] Following the analogy, it also appears to be constitutional to provide ordinary municipal services to cat-

---

* Professor Sugarman's article is a response to an article by Professor West in the same volume. West, "An Economic Analysis of the Law and Politics of Nonpublic School 'Aid,' " in West, *supra* at 1.

2. *Everson v. Board of Education*, 330 U.S. 1 (1947)—reimbursement of bus transportation costs to parents sending children to private schools.
3. *Board of Education v. Allen*, 392 U.S. 236 (1968)—loaning of textbooks to children attending private schools.
4. *Walz v. Tax Commission*, 397 U.S. 664 (1970)—property tax exemption for charitable organizations, including religious organizations.

tle producers[5] and to grant tax deductions to those who donate money to nonprofit animal farms.[a] On the other hand, the Court has struck down plans which, by analogy, (1) provide money directly to cattle producers, even if earmarked for cleaning the cattle pens,[6] and (2) provide money—refunds—to buyers based upon their purchases of cattle.[7] To West these seem to be distinctions without meaningful differences, as there is a beneficial impact on users of hides in every case. This criticism of the Court's decisions is not novel, although the economics of legal commentators who have talked of each of the schemes as "freeing funds" for religion (i.e., benefiting hides) may be less elegant.[8]

Finding these differing state programs not distinguishable in terms of their basic economic effects still leaves us with the question of how they should all come out. West uses the joint supply model seemingly to suggest where he thinks the line of constitutionality should be drawn in these "aid to religion" cases. The argument has two steps: first, what ought to be seen to offend the Establishment Clause is the subsidy of religion with public tax moneys; second, the market effect on hides (religion) of government action with respect of beef (education) is not a subsidy of hides (religion). A different formulation of this "test" of constitutionality is that as long as the society is collectively subsidizing the constitutionally permissible thing—beef or literacy—that should end the inquiry, and the statute should be valid, regardless of any further market effects of that subsidy on other "products." Or, put in terms of the Court's formula for "aid to religion" cases, this approach argues that the *primary effect* of the intervention is that society obtains what it wants (say, more beef or more literacy); the fact that beef and hides (education and religion in parochial schools) are jointly supplied simply produces an unavoidable *side effect*.

With this reasoning West seems to conclude that the Court's recent decision in *Nyquist*, which struck down New York's program to provide tuition reimbursement and income tax credit to users of private schools, is unwise.

I agree that the Establishment Clause should not preclude the state from pursuing secular objectives simply because religious interests and the secular interests are interdependent. Otherwise, the very exercise of private religious beliefs would dominate and circumscribe legitimate and desired nonsectarian, collective action. Therefore, a "test" of constitutionality, in which "market effects" on religion—to use the Westian phrasing—are sufficient to strike down the statute, seems wrong. On the contrary, I think it crucial for the secular aspects of a program to be able to save it from unconstitutionality.

Let me briefly consider three "tests" which have such a focus in order to illustrate the point. (1) Surely it cannot be that legislation with *any* favorable effect on religion is unconstitutional; careful tracing could document some beneficial impact of nearly any program. (2) Nor will it do to limit the principle to laws which the legislature *knew* would benefit religion. Opponents of any bill—regardless of the basis of their opposition—would be sure to employ some of those many social scientists who ask about these days to bring such (potential) beneficial effects to the attention of the legislature. Hence, to take up West's example, a government tree-cutting program would be invalidated if it could be pointed out in advance that by generating sawdust it would, among other things, lower the price of church incense. (3) Even if the principle were limited to cases in which there was (or the legislature knew there would be) a *large* beneficial impact on religion, it would intolerably inhibit secular government action. For example, perhaps building roads and running public transportation on Sunday may be shown to have large beneficial impacts on religion. Notwithstanding this unfortunate aspect of an Establishment Clause 'test," which strikes down laws solely on the basis of their "market effects" on religion, one view of the Court's

5. No Supreme Court case actually holds that general municipal services may be furnished to religious schools, but the Court has often indicated that this is clearly allowed. Indeed, it appears permissible to provide such services to racially discriminating schools even though loaning textbooks to students at such schools is not. See *Norwood v. Harrison*, 413 U.S. 455 (1973).

a. The Supreme Court has not actually passed on the constitutionality of Section 17C of the Internal Revenue Code which allows taxpayers deductions for contributions to charitable organizations including religious organizations.

6. *Committee for Public and Religious Liberty v. Nyquist*, 413 U.S. 756 (1973)—funds earmarked for private school custodial functions. Also see *Levitt v. Committee for Public Education and Religious Liberty*, 413 U.S. 472 (1973)—funds earmarked for testing.

7. *Nyquist*, see note 6—tuition reimbursement and income tax credit for users of private schools; and *Sloan v. Lemon*, 413 U.S. 825 (1973)—tuition reimbursement for users of private schools.

8. For a discussion of this idea, see Choper, "The Establishment Clause and Aid to Parochial Schools," 56 *Calif. L. Rev.* 260, 319 (1968).

recent opinions is that this is precisely its approach. Under this view, while it is not any effect that dooms the law, the Court is nonetheless seen as finding programs unconstitutional because their market effects are rather visible. Indeed, West seems to draw this conclusion from the Court's work. As for what is "visible enough," the damning visibility may seemingly be evidenced by a variety of factors: the religious-based political alignment responsible for the passage of the bill or the religious-based nature of the political fight over the bill, the religious identity of the bill's beneficiaries, the clarity of the connection between the bill and its market effects, or perhaps simply the ease with which those market effects may be imagined. If this is what the Court is doing, society seems stuck with the result that it will be inhibited from efficiently pursuing (or perhaps pursuing at all) collective, secular objectives, whose accomplishment inevitably produces visible ties with religion because of the interdependency of religion with the particular secular objective. Whether a test of "visibility" of this sort produces any worse results than are produced by any other plausible tests is an open question which I leave to the reader to ponder after reading the remainder of the text in this section.

For me the concerns underlying the Establishment Clause could be satisfied with an affirmative answer to this hypothetical question: Would the legislature have acted as it did were there no interdependency with religion involved? If so, then I think it would be fair to say that there is no subsidy of religion, that the religious benefits are constitutionally permitted side effects. But since it is not feasible to psychoanalyze the legislators who voted for the law, and because members may be motivated to vote for a bill for a variety of reasons, in order for the courts to exercise judicial review there must be a more objective way of determining whether the "reason" for the legislation was secular—that is, whether its enactment depended upon the favorable religious impact.

And the problem with the Westian constitutional formulation, as I have thus far stated it, is that it is based on the *assumption* that the reason behind the legislative action is increased private production of secular education. But how do we know this to be the case? The legislature, too, will realize that a decision to cast a program in the form of a subsidy of the purchase of one jointly supplied good will have a market impact on the other good. Therefore, how is one to escape the possibility that the reason for the enactment was precisely to have that impact on religion, and that the legislature is not at all interested in increased private education—that is, it would not pursue this stimulation of private education but for the interdependency of religion? To be sure, this way of aiding religion may be thought clumsy, but the legislature also knows about the First Amendment, and hence realizes that open assistance is clearly unacceptable to the Supreme Court.[b] And, for this same reason it also will not suffice to rely on a legislative declaration that its purposes are secular. We must somehow go behind both the form of the law and what the legislature says about it, yet without going into the minds of its members. What objective indicia we should look for, I think, is the great issue in the "aid to religion" cases.[c]

A number of more or less objective approaches are possible. I will briefly comment on three of them. One involves examining the political position of the program's beneficiaries. For example, in a case like *Nyquist*, it may be argued that since those New Yorkers whose religious exercise is in fact aided by the subsidy are members of religious minorities (mainly Catholics), we can count on the objectives of the political majority (non-Catholics) to be secular. In many respects I find this rather convincing; what troubles me is that it is plausible that, despite the "minority" status of those directly aided, the legislative plan is part of a logrolling trade-off of aid to a minority religion in return for votes on, say, related and controversial issues such as abortion or contraception. Such logrolling might be a very sensible way to maximize individual choice in a world without the First Amendment, but ours is not that world, and thus such trading seems not allowed. And since the Court could not hope to discover accurately whether such logrolling actually occurred (if this is an important fear), such an approach is unsatisfactory. Moreover, it does not provide a helpful solution in places where Catholics are in the

b. Moreover, the form of the aid in most of the decided cases is ambiguous; although the subsidy is said to be for beef (private education), it is clear that most of those who use the subsidy are, in fact, buying the whole cow including the hide (education and religion together).

c. I do not think this problem is any way solved by the Court's willingness to concede in all these cases that the law "reflects a clearly secular purpose." That reflection does not reveal whether the law would have been enacted without the interdependencey of religion.

majority, or where the effect of the statute is to aid Protestants in the exercise of their religion—unless it is to strike down such statutes despite an interdependent and truly desired secular reason for them. That would be an unfortunate result, I think, unless there were no other way out of the dilemma.

A second approach is to try to compare the benefits of a program to religion with its secular benefits, and to hold the program unconstitutional if the religious benefits dominate. The underlying rationale for this approach would be that when the secular gains are (relatively) slight, it is unlikely that the legislature would have acted were there no religious interdependency. However, it is difficult to know on what terms such a comparison would be made, let alone how a Court could properly make the necessary calculations. One possibility is simply to identify, label, and count the beneficiaries, that is, to determine whether most or only few beneficiaries are directly aided in their religious exercise by the program. This approach may be criticized on a number of grounds, however: (1) The Court will not be able to decide whom to label as the beneficiaries of the program. (2) Clever legislative logrolling will result in packaging programs together in a way which end-runs such an approach in any event. (3) Counting and labeling beneficiaries is an unfair approximation of secular and sectarian benefits, if for no other reason than that beneficiaries aided in their religious exercise may also be aided in their secular pursuits. Moreover, this approach concedes that the pursuit of secular objectives would still be frustrated when there was no good alternative means available which did not involve largely benefiting persons in connection with their religious exercise.

Nonetheless, this count-the-numbers technique may best characterize what the Court is doing, as Chief Justice Burger claimed in his *Nyquist* dissent. In *Nyquist*, the Court plainly saw the beneficiaries of New York's tuition credit plan as those families who use private, largely religious, schools, by providing what the state claimed to be educational fairness to the child beneficiaries and financial equity to their parents. Since this is a group essentially comprised of those assisted in their exercise of religious freedom by the program, the plan would fail under the "numbers" test. Suppose, however, the Court had been made to see the plan differently—as a voluntary redemption of the child's state constitutional right to attend public school for a price to the state far below what it would have cost to provide that education. In that event, the beneficiaries, or certainly most of them, would be taxpayers who are not especially aided in their religious exercise, and the plan would be valid under the "numbers" test. The same result would follow if the Court had been made to see the plan as encompassing the state's whole school finance scheme, for public and private schools alike. But how is the Court to decide how to "see" it? And what about the fact that financially assisted religious school users in either case are directly helped with secular objectives? This example may be enough to convince some that choosing a proper class of beneficiaries to be counted and labeled is a misguided and unprincipled task.

A third approach is to concentrate only on the secular purposes the legislature claims to be advancing and then to make a judgment about whether the "deal" the state claims to have made is bona fide. One way to do that is to ask whether the state is getting its money's worth in secular benefits.[13] For example, under this approach it would be all right for the state to acquire fruitcakes from a monastery if it paid the market price, but it would be unconstitutional to pay an inflated price.

There are two main difficulties with this approach. First, how do we know the state would want fruitcakes at any price were they not made and sold by the monastery? If the product were acquired through competitive bidding, we probably could be confident that the nature of the seller was irrelevant to the government. But in the absence of competitive bids—and there were none in the "aid to religion" cases—we are forced either to assume the state wants fruitcakes or to conclude that as long as the state is obtaining full value in secular products or services for its money, it is no poorer, and then taxpayers simply cannot complain that government resources have been diverted for religious purposes. These both are rather unsatisfactory responses to what I have characterized as the central underlying question: Would the transaction have occurred in the absence of the religious interdependency?

13. My description of this approach is a generalized version, with some modification of my own, of that recommended by Choper. His test is this: "Governmental financial aid may be extended directly or indirectly to support parochial schools without violation of the establishment clause so long as such aid does not exceed the value of the secular educational service rendered by the school." 56 *Calif. L. Rev.* at 465–66.

The more serious problem with this approach involves valuing what the state obtains. One cannot say simply that since the state paid, it must have gained what it wanted, for this would empty this test of any content other than unbridled deference to the legislature. This means that the Court will have to decide whether the state obtains value for money, and I assume that will mean an "objective" valuation. But I have serious doubts about the competence of the Court to make such valuation, for it involves deciding terribly difficult empirical questions. Take the *Nyquist* situation, for example. Seemingly the Court would at least have to inquire into how much additional private secular education was provided as a result of the plan and how much that is worth to the state. But how can it determine that? Moreover, is the Court also to determine how many children did not transfer into public schools as a result of the program and how much that is worth?

While Choper realizes that he may be open to attack on the grounds that these empirical issues may be very difficult to determine, he takes refuge in the fact that under his formula there can be little doubt that the society is obtaining its money's worth when the amount of aid given is, as has been true in all the cases thus far litigated, well under half of what is spent on children in the public schools. This is true because he compares the amount paid with the *total* value of the secular education provided by religious schools. The problem I have with this method is that it is not clear why the state aid should be compared with the value of the *total secular education* provided.

Voluntarism is already creating secular benefits for which the collectivity need not pay; if what we are to envision is a process whereby the collectivity is seen to be purchasing secular education through religious schools, its agents would be rather poor negotiators if they agreed to pay for everything previously provided freely—unless that were necessary for any continued private provision at all. It is like paying for fruitcakes when you know the monastery is giving them away and would continue to do so regardless of your payment. This is not a bona fide "deal"; it is income redistribution in favor of religion.

There is yet another difficulty with this test. An objective determination of whether the state obtains value for its money, whether it is in terms of changed family or private school behavior (of an input or outcome sort), may require waiting until quite some time after the legislation has been put into effect, since the payoffs may not be immediately forthcoming. However, the Court presently is willing and accustomed to judge the "aid to religion" cases before the programs start operating—perhaps in part so as to avoid finding itself in the position of fashioning a remedy in the event of past unconstitutional payment of funds in violation of the First Amendment.

The upshot is that each of the three approaches to the Establishment Clause which I have discussed has shortcomings; and I am confident that other universal "objective" tests would as well. Thus, perhaps we should not be surprised that the Court's opinions seem to have no consistent principle and that many cases seem irreconcilable or appear to turn on whether the "aid" is thought to be inherently secular, despite West's demonstration of the economic meaninglessness of this notion.

On the other hand, perhaps the Court can do better than this—if not with a single universal test consistently applied, then at least with some general rules as to the types of considerations that are to be allowed in different kinds of cases. One approach would be to adopt rules for certain types of cases while using techniques of the *prima facie* case and shifts in the burden of proof in others. For example, in *de jure* cases, where the form of government transfer is religious in nature (such as distribution of prayerbooks or the building of churches) or where religious exercise is a condition for receiving the transfer (such as a $10 payment to those who attend church), the program might always be struck down and the state barred from arguing that the reason for the plan is the secular benefit generated by it. (Such programs might also violate the Fourteenth Amendment's equal protection clause.) Nor, perhaps, would the result differ if the scope of the distribution were expanded to include secular items; that is, prayerbooks could not be distributed along with readers, nor churches built along with gymnasiums, for their inclusion would be presumed to be intended for the purpose of, and having the effect of, aiding religious exercise. Similarly, when the state acquires secular goods or services through competitive bid, perhaps all such transactions will be upheld and opponents not permitted to argue that the reason for the purchase was the government's wish to benefit religious-group-owned suppliers. So too, when unrestricted cash is distributed to persons on the basis of formal criteria unrelated to religion or religious exercise, such as welfare or social security, perhaps no challenge arising out of alleged religious uses of the money will be entertained. In short, in these cases, at both ends of the spectrum, judicial inquiry into reasons or effects would be minimal.

By contrast, in other cases the Court might be willing to look closely at both reasons and effects with the burden of proof assigned on the basis of *prima facie* characteristics of the program. For example, perhaps in cases in which the bulk of those who receive a government transfer conditioned on some secular behavior (or the bulk of any identified subclas established by a statute) can be shown to be pursuing religious objectives through that behavior, the Court will closely scrutinize the program's effects with the burden falling on the state to demonstrate objectively that the new secular benefits obtained are worth the funds transferred. This should induce the legislature, in cases such as Nyquist, to leave a clear and convincing trail as to both reasons and anticipated impacts, if it can. What it would take to convince the Court, of course, is a difficult question. But at least in *Nyquist* the following arguments could be made and would have to be addressed by the state: (1) If the legislature is interested in children's educational equity, and not religious education, why did it not demand higher standards from private schools? (2) Unless it is to assist religious education, why were parents who mainly use religious schools singled out for relief from paying for public schools when single people and the childless were not relieved?

On the other hand, when the bulk of the recipients of a conditioned transfer are evidently not pursuing religious objectives through the conduct required for the benefit, the burden might be put on challengers to prove that nonetheless the state is not obtaining fair value in secular benefits (or perhaps that religious effects outweigh secular effects after which the burden would be shifted back to the state to justify the expenditure by the secular benefits obtained). This kind of rule would be applied, for example, in the case of tax deductions for day-care expenditures where opponents protest the placement of children by some families in church facilities where religious indoctrination accompanies the day-care service.

Actually selecting the appropriate classes of cases for the appropriate per se or *prima facie* case rule would require a nice exercise of judgment, as would fitting ambiguous cases into the proper category. At least, however, there could be established a consistent pattern of judicial review in which twin concerns which seem to go toward uncovering the reason for the enactment—are the beneficiaries using the government aid for religious purposes, and what kind of secular advantage is the state really obtaining?—would both be brought to bear in an intuitively sensible manner. It also avoids forcing the Court to decide in each case for itself what is the value of the secular benefits generated by the legislation under scrutiny.

* * *

NOTES AND QUESTIONS

1. Joint Supply Curves and the Establishment Clause

If it is true that it is economically impossible for the state to subsidize secular education in religious schools without also subsidizing religious education, what is left of the myriad of distinctions drawn by the Court from *Everson* and *Allen* through *Mueller* and *Regan?* What of Professor Sugarman's suggestion that the relevant question is whether the legislature would have acted as it did "were there no interdependency with religion involved"? This is somewhat like the test developed in the racial discrimination context: would the government have acted as it did "but for" racial prejudice? *See generally* chapter 5. Professor Sugarman finds this question exceedingly difficult to answer. But would not the mode of decision making be more principled than the mode evinced in recent Supreme Court decisions—even if the Court made some errors in the application of its rule? Is *Regan* rightly decided under the Sugarman test? Is *Mueller*? What is wrong with looking to the impact of the law on advancing religion; that is, holding legislators accountable for the foreseeable consequences of their actions? What of Professor Choper's position, amplified by Sugarman, that one might look to whether the state was getting a "good deal" in terms of secular education—even though in some respects it had advanced religion? Why cannot one measure the value of secular education in nonpublic schools as Professor Choper suggests? Is it relevant that a legislature might not have chosen to subsidize private schools except for their religious nature?

2. Balancing

Is it sufficient to ask whether private schools or parents are using state funds for religious purposes and whether the state is obtaining a secular advantage? What purpose does the former requirement serve—a largely symbolic one? Does the secular-advantage-standard test largely affirm the Court's work over the last decade? What if the evidence shows that the private schools would have offered the programs, materials, and services funded by the state even if the state had not agreed to pay their costs? Does the use of the *prima facie* case help in resolving these problems?

C. State Aid to Needy Children in Religious Schools

The Entanglement Prong of the Establishment Clause and the Needy Child in the Private School: Is Distributive Justice Possible?

Patricia M. Lines, 17 *J. of Law & Educ.* 1, 12–19, 28–29 (1988). Reprinted by permission.

Of all the programs that have extended assistance to needy children in private schools that have been reviewed by the Court, only one permitted services to be rendered to these children while they remained in their own schools. In *Wolman v. Walter*, the Court upheld diagnostic speech and hearing services provided on premises.[63] The Court stressed the brief time diagnosis would take, and distinguished it from teaching and counseling, where public school personnel might enter into a close relationship with a student in a sectarian environment.

Examination of the four most recent Court decisions in this area illustrate the point in detail. Two of these, decided on the same day in 1985—*Grand Rapids v. Ball*[64] and *Aguilar v. Felton*[65]—illustrate the difficulty of designing constitutional programs to assist needy children in private schools. The other two recent cases—*Mueller v. Allen*,[66] decided in 1983, and *Witters v. Washington Department of Services for the Blind*,[67] decided in 1986—illustrate the ease of designing a program to assist individuals if the legislative body is willing to trust the individual with control over the funds allocated to the task.

In *Ball* the Court reviewed the policy of Grand Rapids, Mich., of sending public school teachers to classrooms located in and leased from nonpublic schools. Called Shared Time, the program benefited students needing remedial and enrichment courses in mathematics, reading, art, music and physical education. Typically, the city's eligible nonpublic school student would be in a Shared Time class once or twice a week, or ten percent of his or her time. About ten percent of the Shared Time teachers had previously taught in nonpublic schools; some of these had taught in the same building when they were nonpublic school teachers.

Nonpublic school administrators select classrooms, and public administrators would inspect them. On approval, the public school would pay the nonpublic school a rental of six dollars per classroom per week. Rooms had to be free of religious symbols or artifacts and had to be posted as a "public school classroom." The classes were officially open to public school students, but only nonpublic school students attended. Of forty-one nonpublic schools participating in the programs, forty were sectarian schools. For most, religious goals permeated their education program.

In an opinion prepared by Justice Brennan, and endorsed by Justices Blackmun, Marshall, Powell and Stevens, the Court found Shared Time unconstitutional. As is typical for such cases, the program passed the first test. Justice Brennan found that the program had a valid secular purpose. The plan fell on application of the second test; its effect was to advance religion. Brennan outlined the reasons (indicating clearly that by effects, the Court meant *possible* effects; not proven effects):

> Given that 40 of the 41 schools in this case are . . . "pervasively sectarian," the challenged public-school programs operating in the religious schools may impermissibly advance religion in three different ways. First, the teachers participating in the programs may become involved in intentionally or inadvertently inculcating particular religious tenets or beliefs. Second, the programs may provide a crucial symbolic link between government and religion, thereby enlisting—at

63. *Wolman*, 433 U.S. at 241.
64. 105 S.Ct. 3216
65. 105 S.Ct. 3232.
66. 463 U.S. 388.
67. 106 S.Ct. 748 (1986).

> least in the eyes of impressionable youngsters—the powers of government to the support of the religious denomination operating the school. Third, the programs may have the effect of directly promoting religion by impermissibly providing a subsidy to the primary religious mission of the institutions affected.[70]

The court relied heavily on *Meek v. Pittenger*,[71] where it had struck down a loan of state-paid professional staff to provide remedial and accelerated instruction, guidance counseling, testing and other services on nonpublic school premises. The Court observed that without monitoring, the risk was too great that public school personnel would advance the religious mission of the school where their classrooms were located. The Court did not find it important that the Shared Time teachers were full-time employees hired by the public schools.

In *Aguilar*, New York City had sought to use federal funds for disadvantaged children to send public school teachers into nonpublic school buildings to provide remedial instruction to these children. The law, Title I of the Elementary and Secondary Education Act, as it was in effect at the time of the New York program (and now), was targeted on children who are educationally deprived and who live in low-income areas, regardless of whether they attended public or nonpublic schools. It was to be used for supplemental instruction only.[73]

About 13.2 percent of the children found eligible in New York City attended private schools; of these 84 percent were in Roman Catholic schools and 8 percent were in Hebrew day schools. Religious considerations played a key role in selection of students and teachers, and in operation of these schools. Public school personnel instructed the children in remedial reading, remedial mathematics, and English as a second language, and offered guidance services. The amount of time a professional public employee spent on the private school premises depended on the number of students in the program. Monitoring was routine. Supervisors made at least one unannounced visit each month, and program coordinators also made occasional unannounced visits. Public school professionals in the program were instructed to avoid religious involvement with any on-site religious activities, and to keep contact with private school staff at a minimum. Public school personnel had sole responsibility for identifying students for the program. All classrooms were to be free of religious symbols.

The Court, in an opinion prepared by Justice Brennan, and endorsed by the same four justices who formed the majority in *Ball*, held that the monitoring ran afoul of the third prong of the three-part test—entanglement.

> The principle that the state should not become too closely entangled with the church in the administration of assistance is rooted in two concerns. When the state becomes enmeshed with a given denomination in matters of religious significance, the freedom of religious belief of those who are not adherents of that denomination suffers, even when the governmental purpose underlying the involvement is largely secular. In addition, the freedom of even the adherents of the denomination is limited by the government intrusion into sacred matters.[74]

Justice Brennan, stressing this point, noted that the school, "which has as a primary purpose the advancement and preservation of a particular religion must endure the ongoing presence of the state personnel whose primary purpose is to monitor teachers and students in an attempt to guard against the infiltration of religious thought."[75] Brennan cited *Lemon*, where the Court has exercised considerable imagination to paint a "picture of the state inspectors prowling the halls of parochial schools and auditing classroom instruction . . . ."[76] No part of the evidentary record in either *Aguilar or Lemon* ever suggested that anything of this sort had happened, but the majority apparently felt it possible, and that was fatal. Brennan also expressed concern that public and nonpublic personnel must work together to resolve schedules, classroom assignments, problems of implementation, requests for additional services, and dissemination of information about the program.[77]

70. *Id.* at 3223–33.
71. 421 U.S. 349.
73. 20 U.S.C. §§ 3804(a), 3805(b) & 3807(b) (1982).
74. *Aguilar*, 105 S.Ct. at 3237.
75. *Id.* at 3239.
76. *Aguilar*, 105 S.Ct. at 3239, quoting *Lemon*, 403 U.S. at 650.
77. *Aguilar*, 105 S.Ct. at 3242.

Chief Justice Burger dissented in *Aguilar* and in *Ball* (as it affected Shared Time only[78]), arguing that the majority had failed to demonstrate how the interaction of public and sectarian officials "presents any threat to the values underlying the Establishment Clause."[79] Justice O'Connor also dissented in *Aguilar* and in part in *Ball* (on Shared Time only). She would require evidence that the public school teachers actually attempted to proselytize their students.[80] Justices White and Rehnquist dissented in both cases (including both programs in *Ball*).[81]

Justice Powell, considered a "swing vote" by many observers, wrote a separate concurring opinion. He concluded:

> The constitutional defect in the Title I program . . . is that it provides a direct financial subsidy to be administered in significant part by public school teachers within parochial schools—resulting in both the advancement of religion and forbidden entanglement. If, for example, Congress could fashion a program of evenhanded financial assistance to both public and private schools that could be administered, without governmental supervision in the private schools, so as to prevent the diversion of the aid from secular purposes, we would be presented with a different question.[82]

Together *Ball* and *Aguilar* illustrate the difficulty of meeting the two prongs of entanglement and effects in the three-part test. *Ball* failed for lack of monitoring; *Aguilar* failed for too much monitoring. In both cases, the Court assumed ill effects without requiring evidence to support them. In *Aguilar* the Court described an unlikely scenario of public school monitors roaming the halls of private school, ready to condemn any possible sympathetic gesture to the religious mission of the school on the part of the federally funded public school teachers.[83]

Although the Court has created a near impossible set of rules for on-premises programs operated by the public school, it has permitted easy circumnavigation of the difficulties between the effects and entanglement tests in *Mueller v. Allen*,[85] and *Witters v. Washington Department of Services for the Blind*.[86] The key, however, is to provide individuals with resources, enabling them to purchase private education.

In *Mueller* a five-member majority upheld Minnesota's law granting income tax deductions for the cost of tuition and related expenses for education. Under the Minnesota law, these expenses are deductible regardless of whether the child attends public, nonpublic parochial or nonpublic secular school.[87] The Court applied the three-part test, and easily concluded that Minnesota's purpose was secular—to ensure a well-educated citizenry and to relieve the burden on public schools.[88] The Court found no direct impact on private school finances, noting only "attenuated financial benefits flowing to parochial schools" from the neutrally available tax benefits granted to individuals. The only part of the Minnesota policy that could plausibly raise a problem of entanglement was a state review of textbooks, done to determine eligibility for the tax deduction. (They had to be secular.) The majority found this insufficient to create excessive church-state entanglement.

A key element in *Mueller* was the theoretical availability of the tax benefit to parents sending children to either public or private schools. By structuring the benefit in this way, Minnesota made it more closely resemble universally available social programs, such as police and fire protection, or income maintenance programs—the kind of program where the principle of neutrality might be violated were the benefit denied because of religious affiliation of the potential beneficiary.

A second key element was individual control over how the benefit was to be used. The government had relatively little to say about which institution would enjoy whatever secondary benefits flowed from the program. . . .

78. He agreed that the community education program was invalid.

79. *Aguilar*, 105 S.Ct. at 3242 (Burger, J., dissenting).

80. *Id.* 105 S.Ct. at 3243–48 (O'Connor, J., dissenting); *Ball*, 105 S.Ct. at 3231 (O'Connor, J., dissenting).

81. *Aguilar*, 105 S.Ct. at 3248–59 (White, J., dessenting), *Id.* at 3243–46 (Rehnquist, J., dissenting); *Ball*, 105 S.Ct. at 3231–32 (Rehnquist, J., dissenting).

82. *Aguilar*, 105 S.Ct. at 3242 (Powell, J., concurring).

83. *Id.* at 3238–39.

85. 463 U.S. 388.

86. 106 S.Ct. 748.

87. Minn. Stat. Ann. § 290.09(22) (Supp. 1983) (reference to law at time of decision).

88. *Mueller*, 463 U.S. at 394–95.

* * *

The majority saw no reason to inquire very far into effects because the benefit was, on its face, available to all, and the way in which the benefit was to be used was subject to numerous, private choices. The significance of these principles became more obvious in *Witters*.[100] Witters, a blind student at a private Christian college, sought vocational rehabilitation assistance under a state law,[101] to permit him to continue his studies, and ultimately to become a pastor, missionary or youth director. Although he qualified for assistance, the state agency denied it, on grounds that it would be used for religious instruction and, as such, was prohibited under the state constitution.[102] Witters appealed to the state courts, which affirmed the agency decision. The state supreme court declined to rest its decision on state constitutional grounds, however, finding that the aid would violate the federal Constitution. The state court applied the federal tripartite test, and ruled that aid to the student would violate the second test; it had the forbidden primary effect of aiding religion. The Supreme Court reversed, in a unanimous decision.

Justice Thurgood Marshall, author of the dissenting opinion in *Mueller* wrote the opinion for the Court in *Witters*. Marshall drew an analogy between the state aid under review and a salary paid to state employees. Of course, "a State may issue a paycheck to one of its employees, who may then donate all or part of that paycheck to a religious institution, all without constitutional barrier. . . ."[103] Of course, it doesn't matter if the state knows that this is the way the check is spent. "[T]he fact that aid goes to individuals means that the decision to support religious education is made by the individual, not by the State."[104] The Court noted the following elements of the aid plan as "central" to the issue: (1) the money was paid to individual recipients, not to institutions; (2) the money flowed to religious institutions only as a result of "genuinely independent and private choices"; (3) the program was available for use in public and private institutions without distinction; (4) there was no financial incentive to choose a sectarian education; (5) only a small number of eligible institutions were sectarian.[105] The Court did not indicate whether all of these elements had to be present. Likewise, it remained silent on whether the program might violate the entanglement prong of its three-part test. Finally, it declined to comment on the argument that to deny Witters aid would violate the guarantee of religious free exercise in the first amendment, by penalizing those who wished to use their aid for training for a religious career. Five justices wrote brief concurring opinions, indicating that they did not agree with the more limiting language of the decision.[106]

* * *

For whatever reason, participation by private school children in Chapter 1 declined precipitously following *Aguilar*. Many parents declined special education services for their eligible children because they were reluctant to authorize a walk or bus ride to a neutral site. According to estimates from the United States Department of Education, the number of private school children served under Chapter 1 declined from 176,000 prior to *Aguilar*, to 125,000 in the 1985–86 school year, to 130,600 at the beginning of the 1986–87 school year, and to an estimated 150,000 by the spring of 1987.

The first year after *Aguilar* was the most difficult. No school district found a truly satisfactory solution to the problem. . . .

NOTES AND QUESTIONS

1. The Aftermath of Aguilar v. Felton

After the Supreme Court's decision in *Aguilar v. Felton*, the City of New York successfully obtained a one-year stay of the judgment declaring unconstitutional its Title I program in private schools. *Felton v. Secretary United States Dept. of Educ.*,

---

100. 106 S.Ct. 748.
101. Wash. Rev. Code § 74.16.181 (1981) (reference at time of decision).
102. Wash. Const., art. 1, §§ 4 & 11.
103. *Witters*, 106 S.Ct. at 751–52.
104. *Id.* at 752.
105. *Id.* at 753, n. 5.
106. *Id.* at 753 (White, J., concurring); *id.* at 753–55 (Rehnquist, J., concurring, with Justices Burger and Rehnquist joining in the opinion); *id.* at 755 (O'Connor, J., concurring).

787 F.2d 35 (2d Cir. 1986). It also adopted a plan to conduct Title I remedial education classes for nonpublic school students on the premises of public schools. This plan occasioned additional litigation. *See Parents' Ass'n of P.S. 16 v. Quinones*, 803 F.2d 1235 (2d Cir. 1986).

P.S. 16 is a public elementary school located in the Williamsburg section of Brooklyn, serving mostly Hispanic boys and girls. Beth Rachel, located only four blocks away from P.S. 16, is a private elementary school affiliated with the Satmar Hasidic Jewish Sect. All of its students are girls, reflecting Orthodox Jewish beliefs about the separation of the sexes. In order to induce Beth Rachel administrators to send their pupils to the remedial education classes offered at P.S. 16, a number of adjustments were made in the program: (1) the nine classrooms dedicated to the use of Beth Rachel students were closed off from the rest of the school; (2) all of the teachers were women and Yiddish-speaking; (3) English would be taught as a second language; and (4) a reading method used at Beth Rachel ("Distar"), which was tried and rejected for P.S. 16 students, would be used.

Parents of the Hispanic students in P.S. 16 brought suit, contending that the plan for Beth Rachel students violated the Establishment Clause. *Parents' Ass'n of P.S. 16 v. Quinones, supra*. They objected to the English as a Second Language (ESL) program since such programs were not available to P.S. 16 Hispanic students. They also argued that "the enforced separation of the two groups gave at least the appearance that the City was endorsing the tenets of the Hasidic religious sect." 803 F.2d at 1238. They feared that "the City's Plan 'suggested the cruel and false idea that [their Hispanic] children are inferior and/or dangerous to the Hasidic children' . . . and that it is their 'children's sense that the walls are there to keep them out and that there are people who consider them undesirable.' . . ." *Id.* The City responded that its plan "was not intended to discriminate on a racial or religious basis" and that the Beth Rachel students would not participate in remedial classes that included P.S. 16 students. *Id.*

The District Court denied plaintiffs' motion for a preliminary injunction; the Court of Appeals reversed:

> [The] principles [of *Grand Rapids School District v. Ball*] were apparently ignored by the district court, which did not cite *Grand Rapids* or any of the concerns there addressed. Yet the City's Plan seems plainly to create a symbolic link between the state and the Hasidic sect that is likely to have a magnified negative impact on the minds of the youngsters attending P.S. 16.
>
> . . . The lengths to which the City has gone to cater to these religious views, which are inherently divisive, are plainly likely to be perceived, by the Hasidim and others, as governmental support for the separatist tenets of the Hasidic faith. Worse still, to impressionable young minds, the City's plan may appear to endorse not only separatism, but the derogatory rationale for separatism expressed by some of the Hasidim.
>
> * * *
>
> . . . The Free Exercise Clause of the First Amendment . . . does not prohibit a government from forcing a choice between receipt of a public benefit and pursuit of a religious belief if it can show a compelling reason for doing so. *See Bowen v. Roy*, 476 U.S. 693, 707, 106 S.Ct. 2147, 2156, 90 L. Ed.2d 735 (1986).
>
> * * *
>
> Finally, we note that the lengths to which the City had gone to accommodate Hasidic beliefs may well lead the trial court to conclude that the Plan violates the First Amendment under the "excessive entanglement" test as well as under the "primary effect" test. . . .

803 F.2d at 1241–42. After *Quinones*, how can local school districts resolve the "undeniable tension between the Supreme Court's ruling in *Felton* and the Chapter I statutory requirement that equitable services be provided to [disadvantaged] private school students"? *See generally* Wilkie, "School Aid: Constitutional Issues After *Aguilar v. Felton*," 31 *Cath. Lawyer* 77 (1987).

2. *A Return to* Lemon?

Does *Aguilar v. Felton* represent "a forceful return to the establishment clause principles [of *Lemon*] many thought were waning?" Note, *Aguilar v. Felton: Lemon* Revisited—The Supreme Court's Tug-of-War with the Entanglement Doctrine." 39 *U. of Miami L. Rev.* 957, 966 (1985). Did *Aguilar* reverse "the *Regan* trend toward neutralizing the 'entanglement' criterion?" *Id.* at 967. Are secular and nonsecular effects separable, once again? Are *Mueller* and *Regan* distinguishable from *Aguilar* and *Lemon?* Note that in all of these cases, only Justice Powell has consistently voted with the majority.

3. *Is the* Lemon *Test Incoherent?*

In *Edwards v. Aguillard*, 482 U.S. 578, 107 S.Ct. 2573, 96 L.Ed. 2d 510 (1987), Justice Scalia, writing in dissent, urged that the *Lemon* test under the Establishment Clause be abandoned:

> In the past we have attempted to justify our embarrassing Establishment Clause jurisprudence on the ground that it "sacrifices clarity and predictability for flexibility." . . . I think it time that we sacrifice some "flexibility" for "clarity and predictability." Abandoning *Lemon's* purpose test . . . would be a good place to start.

482 U.S. at 639–40, 107 S.Ct. at 2607. *See* Note, "The Establishment Clause and Justice Scalia: What the Future Holds for Church and State," 63 *Notre Dame L. Rev.* 380, 389 *et. seq.* (1988). Do you agree? *See* Laycock, "Survey of Religious Liberty in the United States," 47 *Ohio St. L. J.* 409, 446 (1986) (Establishment Clause cases have "not produced coherent results" and have "produced distinctions that do not commend themselves to common sense").

4. Justice O'Connor's "Endorsement Test"

Justice O'Connor, in her dissenting opinion, applies the three-part *Lemon* test, albeit she expresses her reservations about the usefulness and appropriateness of the *Lemon* approach. For her the critical fact is that "an objective observer of the implementation of the Title I program in New York would hardly view it as endorsing the tenets of the participating parochial schools." This state "endorsement" or "imprimatur" test is one that Justice O'Connor has advocated in a number of Establishment Clause cases. *See Wallace v. Jaffree*, 472 U.S. 38, 105 S.Ct. 2479, 2496–2505, 86 L.Ed. 2d 29 (1985) (O'Connor, J., concurring); *Lynch v. Donnelly*, 465 U.S. 668, 687–94, 104 S.Ct. 1355, 1366–70, 79 L.Ed.2d 604 (1984) (O'Connor, J., concurring). What is the relationship between the "endorsement" test and the *Lemon* formulation of intent, effects, and entanglement? Has Justice O'Connor refined *Lemon* or has she abandoned it? *See* Comment, "*Lemon* Reconstituted: Justice O'Connor's Proposed Modifications of the *Lemon* Test for Establishment Clause Violations," 1986 *Brig. Young U. L. Rev.* 465. *See generally* "Developments in the Law: Religion and the State," 100 *Harv. L. Rev.* 1606 (1987). What is the difference between an advancement of religion under the effects test and the endorsement of religion? Comment, "*Lemon* Reconstituted," *supra* at 471–75.

TWO

Socialization and Student and Teacher Rights

I. INTRODUCTION

A. The Socialization Dilemma

Chapter 1 focused on the legal requirement that children attend some public or private school. That requirement, virtually unchallenged in the case law, is premised on a number of asserted state interests including preparing the individual for citizenship and economic independence, inculcating values, and preserving the security of the state. If the American system of government is to survive and if the nation is to be secure, it is necessary to educate—to socialize—each new generation in those values and attitudes essential to the operation of American democracy. The schools inevitably reflect the culture and values of the larger society. But while this governmental interest is strong enough to warrant compulsory education laws and curricular and other requirements for public and private schools, the question is inevitably one of balance. The challenge is to maintain continuity, to foster knowledge, and to retain the values of the past while accommodating change, criticism, growth, and individual autonomy. *See generally* Gottlieb, "In the Name of Patriotism: The Constitutionality of 'Bending' History in the Public Secondary Schools," 62 *N.Y.U. L. Rev.* 497 (1987); Yudof, "Library Book Selection and the Public Schools: The Quest for the Archimedean Point," 59 *Ind. L. J.* 527 (1984); van Geel, "The Search for Constitutional Limits on Governmental Authority to Inculcate Youth," 62 *Tex. L. Rev.* 197 (1983). Basic attitudes, skills, and knowledge must be communicated, while giving the young "ample opportunity of making the decisions upon which these principles are based, and by which they are modified, improved, adapted to changed circumstances, or even abandoned if they become entirely unsuited to a new environment." Hare, "Decisions of Principle," in I. Scheffler, ed., *Philosophy and Education* 72, 85 (1958). *See generally* C. Lindblom, *Inquiry and Change* (1990).

The socialization dilemma is reflected in debates over authority and legal entitlements in public education. *See generally* James, "Totality in Private and Public Schooling," 97 *Amer. J. of Educ.* 1 (1988); Arons and Lawrence, "The Manipulation of Consciousness: A First Amendment Critique of Schooling," 15 *Harv. C.R. – C.L. L. Rev.* 309 (1980). In the present context, should legislatures, school boards, and administrators have exclusive control of the socialization process within the public schools, or should parents, students, and teachers have rights, and what sort of rights, to shape or resist socialization processes? What are the substantive limits, if any, within which public school systems (and perhaps also parents, students, and teachers) must operate in shaping the educational program? *See, e.g.*, Gottlieb, *supra;* Yudof, *supra;* van Geel, *supra;* Stern, "Challenging Ideological Exclusion of Curricular Material: Rights of Students and Parents," 14 *Harv. C.R.–C.L. L. Rev.* 485 (1979). Put somewhat differently, if the transmission of knowledge cannot be disentangled from socialization to values, who may or must be allowed to shape the content and methods of the education effort, and what sort of limitations, if any, are imposed by our laws and Constitution? Should courts require only "good faith" educational judgments by administrators? *See* Yudof, "Personal Speech and Government Expression," 38 *Case W. Res. L. Rev.* 671, 692–97 (1988).

The issues of limitations and the sharing of authority to shape the program of the public schools are intertwined. For example, to the extent that the First Amendment prohibits religious rituals in the public schools as a protection of the rights of parents, students, and taxpayers, parents, students, and taxpayers have a certain degree of authority to shape the content of the school program by insisting upon those rights. To the extent that parents have a right to remove their children from particular classes (*e.g.*, sex education), they have authority to limit the school's program, at least insofar as the program affects their own children. If academic freedom for teachers allows them to make a range of presentational and pedagogical decisions, then the ability of the state to inculcate common values is diminished. Indeed, these issues are closely related to those considered in chapter 4 where the issue of educational governance is taken up more explicitly: Who participates in the general decision-making processes of the public schools? By what political or market mechanisms might public schools be held accountable and accountable to whom? Accountable for what? *See generally* S. Arons, *Compelling Belief* (1983).

From yet another perspective, this chapter deals with the same theme dealt with in chapter 1—the tension among child, family, and state. But in this chapter, these issues are addressed in the context of the public school itself. Section II examines the constitutional limitations directly applicable to state and school board decisions regarding the content and methods of public schooling. Section III turns to the free speech rights of students and teachers and thus their ability to shape the overall socialization process by the exercise of rights to speak within and without the public schools.

B. State Action

With perhaps the exception of the Thirteenth Amendment, the Constitution's guarantees of individual rights generally protect individuals only from governmental action. *See NCAA v. Tarkanian*, 488 U.S. 179, 109 S.Ct. 454, 102 L.Ed.2d 469 (1988); *Runyon v. McCrary*, 427 U.S. 160, 96 S.Ct. 2586, 49 L.Ed.2d 415 (1976); *Sinn v. The Daily Nebraskan*, 829 F.2d 622 (8th Cir. 1987). Thus private schools control student and teacher behavior in ways and for reasons denied to public schools. *See, e.g.*, *Stone v. Dartmouth College*, 682 F.Supp. 106 (D.N.H. 1988). Private schools may suspend students without a hearing to determine whether a school rule has been offended. *See, e.g.*, *Bright v. Isenbarger*, 314 F.Supp. 1382 (N.D. Ind. 1970), *aff'd*, 445 F.2d 412 (7th Cir. 1971); *Blackburn v. Fisk University*, 443 F.2d 121 (6th Cir. 1971). The mere fact that a private school may be regulated by the state or that it receives governmental financial support or that it uses the name of the state in the name of the school has not been deemed sufficient involvement to conclude that the school's actions were really government action. The courts have tended to accept the position taken by Judge Friendly in *Powe v. Miles*, 407 F.2d 73, 81 (2d Cir. 1968), a case in which students attacked the disciplinary procedures of a private university:

> The contention that [there is state action in this case] overlooks the essential point—that the state must be involved not simply with some activity of the institution alleged to have inflicted injury upon a plaintiff but with the activity that caused the injury. . . . When the state bans a subject from the curriculum of a private school, as in *Meyer v. Nebraska*, 262 U.S. 390, . . . its responsibility needs no elucidation. State action would be similarly present here . . . if New York had undertaken to set policy for the control of demonstrations in all private universities. . . . But the fact that New York has exercised some regulatory powers over the standard of education offered by Alfred University does not implicate it generally in Alfred's policies toward demonstrations and discipline.

407 F.2d at 81. *See also Braden v. University of Pittsburgh*, 552 F.2d 948 (3d Cir. 1977) (en banc). *See generally* H. Friendly, *The Dartmouth College Case and the Public-Private Penumbra* (1968); O'Neill, "Private Universities and Public Law," 19 *Buffalo L. Rev.* 155 (1970); Note, "The Supreme Court—1988 Term," 103 *Harv. L. Rev.* 137, 187 (1989).

In the context of this chapter and chapter 1, the state action limitation protects diversity within the educational sector of society. For example, the absence of a state action requirement could lead to judicial decisions requiring private schools to limit teaching about or indoctrination in religion, as the public schools are obliged to do. But to the extent that private schools remain free from the limitations of the Establishment Clause, religious schooling may be free of judicial control, and the free exercise of religion may receive broader protection.

Within the context of the public schools, the state action doctrine has been interpreted in such a way that the actions of principals and teachers, even when not expressly authorized by the school board or state legislature, may be viewed as actions of the state. *Cf. Monroe v. Pape*, 365 U.S. 167 (1961).

In *Rendell-Baker v. Kohn*, 457 U.S. 830, 102 S.Ct. 2764, 73 L.Ed.2d 418 (1982), Rendell-Baker, a vocational counselor hired under a grant from the federal Law Enforcement Assistance Administration (LEAA), and five teachers were discharged by the Director of the New Perspectives School, a nonprofit institution located on privately owned property in Brookline, Massachusetts. The school specialized in serving children "who have experienced difficulty completing public high schools," including many with "drug, alcohol, or behavioral problems, or other special needs." Nearly all of the students at the New Perspectives School had been referred to it by public school districts or by the Drug Rehabilitation Division of the Massachusetts Department of Mental Health. Under applicable Massachusetts laws, school districts pay for the education of students referred to the school, and combined with funding from state and federal sources, at least 90 percent of the operating budget of the New Perspectives School came from public funds. Further, as a condition of receiving its LEAA grant, the Massachusetts Committee on Criminal Justice had to approve initial hiring decisions for vocational counselors.

Rendell-Baker and the discharged teachers filed separate suits in federal district court under 42 U.S.C. §1983, alleging that their rights under the First, Fifth, and Fourteenth Amendments to the Constitution had been violated. In essence, they asserted that they had been fired for protected speech activities and that they had been denied procedural due process. The district judge in the *Rendell-Baker* case held that "the nexus between the school and the State was not sufficiently close so that the action of the school in discharging Rendell-Baker could be considered action of the Commonwealth of Massachusetts, " and denied plaintiff any relief. Another judge in the same district, however, ruled in favor of plaintiff teachers, reaching a contrary conclusion on the state action issue. The Court of Appeals for the First Circuit consolidated the two cases, and held that the defendants had not acted under color of state law. The Supreme Court, with only two justices dissenting, affirmed the judgment of the Court of Appeals.

Chief Justice Burger, writing for the majority, reasoned that the "core issue in this case is not whether petitioners were discharged because of their speech or without adequate procedural protections, but whether the school's action in discharging them can fairly be seen as state action. If the action of the respondent is not state action, our inquiry ends:"

> The school . . . is not fundamentally different from many private corporations whose business depends primarily on contracts to build roads, bridges, dams, ships, or submarines for the government. Acts of such private contractors do not become acts of the government by reason of their significant or even total engagement in performing public contracts.
>
> * * *
>
> Here the decisions to discharge the petitioners were not compelled or even influenced by any state regulation. Indeed, in contrast to the extensive regulation of the school generally, the various regulators showed relatively little interest in the school's personnel matters. The most intrusive personnel regulation promulgated by the various government agencies was the requirement that the Committee on Criminal Justice had the power to approve persons hired as vocational counselors. Such a regulation is not sufficient to make a decision to discharge, made by private management, state action. . . .
>
> * * *
>
> There can be no doubt that the education of maladjusted high school students is a public function, but that is only the beginning of the inquiry. Chapter 766 of the Massachusetts Act of 1972 demonstrates that the State intends to provide services for such students at public expense. That legislative policy choice in no way makes these services the exclusive province of the State. Indeed, the Court of Appeals noted that until recently the State had not undertaken to provide education for students who could not be served by traditional public schools. . . . That a private entity performs a function which serves the public does not make its acts state action.

457 U.S. at 840, 102 S.Ct. at 2771. *See also NCAA v. Tarkanian*, 488 U.S. 179, 109 S.Ct. 454, 102 L.Ed.2d 469 (1988). Does the *Rendell-Baker* deci-

sion treat state action more narrowly than the test promulgated in *Powe v. Miles, supra?*

II. RELIGIOUS, POLITICAL, AND MORAL SOCIALIZATION

A. Sectarian Socialization

Questions concerning the proper place of religion in the curriculum of the public schools have been with us since the origins of the public school movement. Professor Cremin, reviewing the public school movement generally, notes that from the outset a range of positions were taken on the best way religion could be made part of the school program. The politically dominant position was one worked out as a compromise among various Protestant groups. Under this approach schools were to instruct pupils in those common values and ideals on which the Protestant sects agreed, but instruction in these values, while rooted in Christianity, would not be taught in a religious context. Instruction in specific doctrine and dogma would be left to the family, the pulpit, and the Sabbath school. The other way of providing a moral base for the teaching of the common school was the introduction of reading from the Bible without comments as part of school exercises. In different places and in different times, prayers were also introduced as part of school exercises. This approach attempted both to respect the religious diversity of the country and avoid an irreligious or nonreligious morality. L. Cremin, *The American Common School* 66–70 (1951).

Other approaches were also attempted. *See, e.g.,* C. Fairman, *Reconstruction and Reunion 1864–88* 1310–18 (1971). In New York City, the Public School Society, a quasi-public organization that operated a number of free schools supported by public funds, insisted that its schools must be and were nonsectarian, a claim the Catholic hierarchy vigorously disputed. D. Ravitch, *The Great School Wars, New York City, 1805–1973*, ch. 4 (1974). As the New York City experience suggests, the strategy of trying to avoid at least overt denominationalism met with only partial success. It was attacked as insufficiently religious by some Protestant sects, while Catholics argued that the public schools were all too sectarian. They pointed with special alarm to the use of the Protestant Bible in the public schools. Dissatisfaction with the Protestant tone of the public schools led to efforts to establish parochial schools. *See* Laycock, "A Survey of Religious Liberty in the United States," 47 *Ohio St. L. J.* 409, 418 (1986). At least in New York City, the drive for parochial schools was also premised on opposition to the notion of common schooling itself.

For much of the twentieth century, religion remained a key part of the curriculum of public schools. The prevailing attitude was aptly described in Professor Beale's classic work, *Are American Teachers Free?* (1936):

> Americans . . . generally are as determined to keep irreligion out of the schools as to exclude sectarianism. An overwhelming majority of citizens believe that teachers with at least a mild interest in religion "have a better influence" on children than those of no religion. . . . Religion makes children "better children." It gives them something that even parents who have discarded it wish them to have. . . . "Christian" in ordinary parlance is an adjective of commendation.
>
> . . . Furthermore, if the purpose of schools is to instill "patriotic" attitudes, correct economic views, and conformity to political, social, and business practices of the community . . . , why should not the community's religious beliefs also be implanted in children: agnostic attitudes where they prevail, and Catholic dogma where Catholics predominate?

Id. at 210, 217. But in the post-World War II period, the place of religion in the public schools began to change dramatically. In 1962 the Supreme Court, invoking the prohibition on the establishment of religion in the First Amendment, held that a twenty-two-word prayer used daily in New York classrooms as an invocation at the beginning of the school day was unconstitutional. *Engel v. Vitale,* 370 U.S. 421, 82 S.Ct. 1261, 8 L.Ed.2d 601 (1962). A year later the Supreme Court delivered its landmark decision on school prayer in *Abington School District v. Schempp,* 374 U.S. 203, 83 S.Ct. 1560, 10 L.Ed.2d 844 (1963).

In the *Schempp* case (and a companion case decided in the same opinion), Unitarian and atheist parents mounted a constitutional attack on public school policies requiring readings, without comment, from the Bible at the beginning of each school day. The readings were followed by a recitation of the Lord's Prayer by the students. Students were permitted to absent themselves from participation in the exercises upon a request of the parent. In an opinion by Justice Clark, the Court declared the Bible reading and school prayer to be violative of the Establishment Clause:

First, this Court has decisively settled that the First Amendment's mandate that "Congress shall make no law respecting an establishment of religion, or prohibiting the free exercise thereof" has been made wholly applicable to the States by the Fourteenth Amendment. . . .

Second, this Court has rejected unequivocally the contention that the Establishment Clause forbids only governmental preference of one religion over another. . . .

* * *

The wholesome "neutrality" of which this Court's [Establishment Clause] cases speak . . . stems from a recognition of the teachings of history that powerful sects or groups might bring about a fusion of governmental and religious functions or a concert or dependency of one upon the other to the end that official support of the State or Federal Government would be placed behind the tenets of one or of all orthodoxies. This the Establishment Clause prohibits. And a further reason for neutrality is found in the Free Exercise Clause, which recognizes the value of religious training, teaching and observance and, more particularly, the right of every person to freely choose his own course with reference thereto, free of any compulsion from the state. This the Free Exercise Clause guarantees. . . . [I]t has been consistently held that the [Establishment] [C]lause withdrew all legislative power respecting religious belief or the expression thereof. The test may be stated as follows: what are the purpose and the primary effect of the enactment? If either is the advancement or inhibition then the enactment exceeds the scope of legislative power as circumscribed by the Constitution. That is to say that to withstand the strictures of the Establishment Clause there must be a secular legislative purpose and a primary effect that neither advances nor inhibits religion. The Free Exercise Clause . . . withdraws from legislative power, state and federal, the exertion of any restraint on the free exercise of religion. Its purpose is to secure religious liberty in the individual by prohibiting any invasions thereof by civil authority. Hence it is necessary in a free exercise case for one to show the coercive effect of the enactment as it operates against him in the practice of his religion. The distinction between the two clauses is apparent—a violation of the Free Exercise Clause is predicated on coercion while the Establishment Clause violation need not be so attended. . . .

[I]n both cases the laws require religious exercises and such exercises are being conducted in direct violation of the rights of the appellees and petitioners. Nor are these required exercises mitigated by the fact that individual students may absent themselves upon parental request, for that fact furnishes no defense to a claim of unconstitutionality under the Establishment Clause. . . . Further, it is no defense to urge that the religious practices here may be relatively minor encroachments on the First Amendment. The breach of neutrality that is today a trickling stream may all too soon become a raging torrent . . . .

It is insisted that unless these religious exercises are permitted a "religion of secularism" is established in the schools. We agree of course that the State may not establish a "religion of secularism" in the sense of affirmatively opposing or showing hostility to religion, thus "preferring those who believe in no religion over those who do believe." . . . We do not agree, however, that this decision in any sense has that effect. In addition, it might well be said that one's education is not complete without a study of comparative religion or the history of religion and its relationship to the advancement of civilization. It certainly may be said that the Bible is worthy of study for its literary and historic qualities. Nothing we have said here indicates that such study of the Bible or of religion, when presented objectively as part of a secular program of education, may not be effected consistently with the First Amendment. But the exercises here do not fall into those categories. They are religious exercises, required by the States in violation of the command of the First Amendment that the Government maintain strict neutrality, neither aiding nor opposing religion.

Finally, we cannot accept that the concept of neutrality, which does not permit a State to require a religious exercise even with the consent of the majority of those affected, collides with the majority's right to free exercise of religion. While the Free Exercise Clause clearly prohibits the use of state action to deny the rights of free exercise to *anyone*, it has never meant that a majority could use the machinery of the State to practice his beliefs. . . .

In the early years after the school prayer cases, there was strong resistance to compliance, particularly in the East and South, but gradually the decisions took hold. *See* S. Wasby, *The Impact of the Supreme Court* 129–33 (1970). Subsequently, numerous groups and individuals asserted that irreligion had crept into the public schools, that public schools were hostile to religion, and, in some quarters, even that the public schools were dominated by a religion of secular humanism. *See generally* Dent, "Religious Children, Secular Schools," 61 *So. Cal. L. Rev.* 864 (1988). For example, by the late 1970s courses on the Bible as religion or literature began to disappear from the curriculum. Association for Supervision and Curriculum Development, *Re-*

ligion in the Curriculum ch. 2 (1987) (hereinafter *Religion in the Curriculum*). And a number of studies concluded that references to religion had been excised from textbooks and the curriculum. *See* O.L. Davis *et al*, *Looking at History: A Review of Major U.S. Textbooks* (1986); P. Vitz, *Censorship: Evidence of Bias in Our Children's Textbooks* (1986).

These complaints about the diminishing role of religion in the schools manifested themselves in a variety of ways. First, a number of jurisdictions enacted laws mandating "moments of silence" at the beginning of the school day as a substitute for religious exercises. *See Wallace v. Jaffree, infra*. Second, there were numerous calls for constitutional amendments, supported by popular majorities, that would have overturned the school prayer decisions. In 1982 President Reagan proposed the following constitutional amendment: "Nothing in this Constitution shall be construed to prohibit individual or group prayer in public schools or other public institutions. No person shall be required by the United States or by any State to participate in prayer." The proposed amendment was not adopted by the required two-thirds of each house of Congress. Third, lawsuits were filed by fundamentalist religious groups attacking the secular orientation of public education. *See* sections IIA1 and IIA2, *infra*. Fourth, educators began to call for the reintroduction of religion into the public schools in the limited sense of inculcating knowledge of the role of religion in history, literature, and other subjects. They argued that the public schools had overreacted to the school prayer decisions and were willing to allow a distortion of subjects in the curriculum in order to avoid controversy. *Religion in the Curriculum, supra*. As one study urged,

> [T]he quest for religious freedom that fueled the establishment of this nation receives scant treatment at best in many of the textbooks currently in use. The texts have even less to say about the profound part religious belief has played in more recent U.S. history. Students probably won't find out from their textbooks that religious groups were a vital force in the abolitionist and temperance movements of the nineteenth century or the civil rights movement of the twentieth.
>
> Nor is it only texts in American history that are affected. The critical influence of religion in world history and culture is similarly slighted in texts on political science, sociology, literature, and world history. . . .
>
> As these few examples suggest, references to religion have been all but excised from the public school curriculum. . . . This filtering of religious influences—intended as such or not . . . —is the result, in part, of concern that the constitutional wall separating church and state might be breached. It also reflects an exaggerated fear of controversy. . . . Despite the absence of teaching about religion in our schools—or perhaps because of it—some parents charge that school officials are scaling that wall by promoting "secular humanism" as a religion itself. Others demand that schools shield their children from ideas that conflict with the family's religious beliefs.

Religion in the Curriculum, supra at 7–8.

In considering the cases and materials that follow on religion and the public schools, the reader should be aware of a number of trends that may have exacerbated tensions. In reaction to the perceived breakdown of traditional values in the 1960s and the school prayer and abortion decisions, evangelical, charismatic, and fundamentalist Christian groups in America greatly gained strength while more liberal Protestant denominations gradually lost membership. The former groups were more sensitive to secular trends in public schooling and objected to the severance of the tie between morality and religion. At the same time, and partially in a misreading or exaggeration of the school prayer decisions, school officials often seemed anxious to avoid any controversy concerning religion, and they reacted by simply avoiding the subject. The latter impulse was strengthened and reinforced by a progressive privatization of religious and moral values:

> [P]ublic schools are cautious to avoid even the possibility of invading individuals' belief systems—a caution that honors the abiding American assumption of religion as private as much as it skirts constitutional issues of church and state. Moreover, distinctions among dogmas, practices, and observances in different religions are not easily drawn. This difficulty leads many schools to back away from teaching *about* religion to escape the charge that they are teaching the dogma of a particular religion.
>
> In addition, widespread confusion about the relationship of religion and morality makes shaping school policy more difficult. On the one hand, if moral education is held to be religious education, instruction about morality is constitutionally prohibited. (Indeed, many people find the very notion of a body of tenable moral positions inappropriate in a pluralistic society.) On the other hand, many people reject the assumption . . . that either individual or civic morality rests upon particular religious beliefs. Faced with the prospect of picking their way through a minefield of conflicting

opinions, educators generally assert that adherence to moral precepts is essential to a society and then leave it to individuals to decide, in the light of their own religious beliefs, what these precepts are.

Religion in the Curriculum, supra at 15.

1. School Prayer and Moments of Silence

Wallace v. Jaffree

472 U.S. 38, 105 S.Ct. 2479, 86 L.Ed.2d 29 (1985).

Justice Stevens delivered the opinion of the court.

At an early stage of this litigation, the constitutionality of three Alabama statutes was questioned: (1) § 16–1–20, enacted in 1978, which authorized a 1-minute period of silence in all public schools "for meditation";[1] (2) § 16–1–20.1, enacted in 1981, which authorized a period of silence "for meditation or voluntary prayer";[2] and (3) § 16–1–20.2, enacted in 1982, which authorized teachers to lead "willing students" in a prescribed prayer to "Almighty God . . . the Creator and Supreme Judge of the world."[3]

At the preliminary-injunction stage of this case, the District Court distinguished § 16–1–20 from the other two statutes. It then held that there was "nothing wrong" with § 16–1–20,[4] but that §§ 16–1–20.1 and 16–1–20.2 were both invalid because the sole purpose of both was "an effort on the part of the State of Alabama to encourage a religious activity." After the trial on the merits, the District Court did not change its interpretation of these two statutes, but held that they were constitutional because, in its opinion, Alabama has the power to establish a state religion if it chooses to do so.[6]

The Court of Appeals agreed with the District Court's initial interpretation of the purpose of both § 16–1–20.1 and § 16–1–20.2, and held them both unconstitutional.[7] We have already affirmed the Court of Appeals' holding with respect to § 16–1–20.2.[8] Moreover, appellees have not questioned the holding that § 16–1–20 is valid.[9] Thus, the narrow question for decision is whether § 16–1–20.1, which authorizes a period of silence for "meditation or voluntary prayer," is a law respecting the establishment of religion within the meaning of the First Amendment.

I

Appellee Ishmael Jaffree is a resident of Mobile County, Alabama. On May 28, 1982, he filed a complaint on behalf of three of his minor children; two of them were second-grade students and the third was then in kindergarten. The complaint named members of the Mobile County School Board, various school officials, and the minor plaintiffs' three teachers as defendants. The complaint alleged that the appellees brought the action "seeking principally a declaratory judgment and an injunction restraining the Defendants and each of them from maintaining or allowing the maintenance of regular religious prayer services or other forms of religious

1. Alabama Code § 16–1–20 (Supp.1984) reads as follows:

"At the commencement of the first class each day in the first through the sixth grades in all public schools, the teacher in charge of the room in which each such class is held shall announce that a period of silence, not to exceed one minute in duration, shall be observed for meditation, and during any such period silence shall be maintained and no activities engaged in."

Appellees have abandoned any claim that § 16–1–20 is unconstitutional.

2. Alabama Code § 16–1–20.1 (Supp.1984) provides:

"At the commencement of the first class of each day in all grades in all public schools the teacher in charge of the room in which each class is held may announce that a period of silence not to exceed one minute in duration shall be observed for meditation or voluntary prayer, and during any such period no other activities shall be engaged in."

3. Alabama Code § 16–1–20.2 (Supp. 1984) provides:

"From henceforth, any teacher or professor in any public educational institution within the state of Alabama, recognizing that the Lord God is one, at the beginning of any homeroom or any class, may pray, may lead willing students in prayer, or may lead the willing students in the following prayer to God:

"Almighty God, You alone are our God. We acknowledge You as the Creator and Supreme Judge of the world. May Your justice, Your truth, and Your peace abound this day in the hearts of our countrymen, in the counsels of our government, in the sanctity of our homes and in the classrooms of our schools, in the name of our Lord. Amen."

4. The court stated that it did not find any potential infirmity in § 16–1–20 because "it is a statute which prescribes nothing more than a child in school shall have the right to meditate in silence and there is nothing wrong with a little meditation and quietness." *Jaffree v. James*, 544 F.Supp. 727, 732 (SD Ala.1982).

6. *Jaffree v. Board of School Comm'rs of Mobile County*, 554 F.Supp. 1104, 1128 (SD Ala.1983).

7. 705 F.2d 1526, 1535–1536 (CA11 1983).

8. *Wallace v. Jaffree*, 466 U.S. 924, 104 S.Ct. 1704, 80 L.Ed.2d 178 (1984).

9. *See* n. 1, *supra*.

observances in the Mobile County Public Schools in violation of the First Amendment as made applicable to states by the Fourteenth Amendment to the United States Constitution." The complaint further alleged that two of the children had been subjected to various acts of religious indoctrination "from the beginning of the school year in September, 1981"; that the defendant teachers had "on a daily basis" led their classes in saying certain prayers in unison; that the minor children were exposed to ostracism from their peer group class members if they did not participate; and that Ishmael Jaffree had repeatedly but unsuccessfully requested that the devotional services be stopped. . . .

* * *

In November 1982, the District Court held a 4-day trial on the merits. The evidence related primarily to the 1981–1982 academic year—the year after the enactment of § 16–1–20.1 and prior to the enactment of § 16–1–20.2. The District Court found that during that academic year each of the minor plaintiffs' teachers had led classes in prayer activities, even after being informed of appellees' objections to these activities.[23]

In its lengthy conclusions of law, the District Court reviewed a number of opinions of this Court interpreting the Establishment Clause of the First Amendment, and then embarked on a fresh examination of the question whether the First Amendment imposes any barrier to the establishment of an official religion by the State of Alabama. After reviewing at length what it perceived to be newly discovered historical evidence, the District Court concluded that "the establishment clause of the first amendment to the United States Constitution does not prohibit the state from establishing a religion." In a separate opinion, the District Court dismissed appellees' challenge to the three Alabama statutes because of a failure to state any claim for which relief could be granted. The court's dismissal of this challenge was also based on its conclusion that the Establishment Clause did not bar the States from establishing a religion.[25]

The Court of Appeals consolidated the two cases; not surprisingly, it reversed. The Court of Appeals noted that this Court had considered and had rejected the historical arguments that the District Court found persuasive, and that the District Court had misapplied the doctrine of *stare decisis*. The Court of Appeals then held that the teachers' religious activities violated the Establishment Clause of the First Amendment.[27] With respect to § 16–1–20.1 and § 16–1–20.2, the Court of Appeals stated that "both statutes advance and encourage religious activities." The Court of Appeals then quoted with approval

23. The District Court wrote:

"Defendant Boyd, as early as September 16, 1981, led her class at E.R.Dickson in singing the following phrase:

" 'God is great, God is good,

" 'Let us thank him for our food,

" 'bow our heads we all are fed,

" 'Give us Lord our daily bread.

" 'Amen!'

"The recitation of this phrase continued on a daily basis through the 1981–82 school year.

"Defendant Pixie Alexander has led her class at Craighead in reciting the following phrase:

" 'God is great, God is good,

" 'Let us thank him for our food.'

"Further, defendant Pixie Alexander had her class recite the following, which is known as the Lord's Prayer:

" 'Our Father, which art in heaven, hallowed be Thy name. Thy kingdom come. Thy will be done on earth as it is in heaven. Give us this day our daily bread and forgive us our debts as we forgive our debtors. And lead us not into temptation but deliver us from evil, for Thine is the kingdom and the power and the glory forever. Amen.'

"The recitation of these phrases continued on a daily basis throughout the 1981–82 school year.

* * *

"Ms. Green admitted that she frequently leads her class in singing the following song:

" 'For health and strength and daily food, we praise Thy name, Oh Lord.'

"This activity continued throughout the school year, despite the fact that Ms. Green had knowledge that plaintiff did not want his child exposed to the above-mentioned song." *Jaffree v. Board of School Comm'rs of Mobile County*, 554 F.Supp., at 1107–1108.

25. *Jaffree v. James*, 554 F.Supp. 1130, 1132 (SD Ala.1983). The District Court's opinion was announced on January 14, 1983. On February 11, 1983, Justice Powell, in his capacity as Circuit Justice for the Eleventh Circuit, entered a stay which in effect prevented the District Court from dissolving the preliminary injunction that had been entered in August 1982. . . .

27. . . . This Court has denied a petition for a writ of certiorari that presented the question whether the Establishment Clause prohibited the teachers' religious prayer activities. *Board of School Comm'rs of Mobile County v. Jaffree*, 466 U.S. 926, 104 S.Ct. 1707, 80 L.Ed.2d 181 (1984).

the District Court's finding that § 16–1–20.1, and § 16–1–20.2, were efforts " 'to encourage a religious activity. Even though these statutes are permissive in form, it is nevertheless state involvement respecting an establishment of religion.' "[30]

* * *

II

Our unanimous affirmance of the Court of Appeals' judgment concerning § 16–1–20.2 makes it unnecessary to comment at length on the District Court's remarkable conclusion that the Federal Constitution imposes no obstacle to Alabama's establishment of a state religion. Before analyzing the precise issue that is presented to us, it is nevertheless appropriate to recall how firmly embedded in our constitutional jurisprudence is the proposition that the several States have no greater power to restrain the individual freedoms protected by the First Amendment than does the Congress of the United States.

As is plain from its text, the First Amendment was adopted to curtail the power of Congress to interfere with the individual's freedom to believe, to worship, and to express himself in accordance with the dictates of his own conscience.[32] Until the Fourteenth Amendment was added to the Constitution, the First Amendment's restraints on the exercise of federal power simply did not apply to the States. But when the Constitution was amended to prohibit any State from depriving any person of liberty without due process of law, that Amendment imposed the same substantive limitations on the States' power to legislate that the First Amendment had always imposed on the Congress' power. This Court has confirmed and endorsed this elementary proposition of law time and time again.

* * *

Just as the right to speak and the right to refrain from speaking are complementary components of a broader concept of individual freedom of mind, so also the individual's freedom to choose his own creed is the counterpart of his right to refrain from accepting the creed established by the majority. At one time it was thought that this right merely proscribed the preference of one Christian sect over another, but would not require equal respect from the conscience of the infidel, the atheist, or the adherent of a non-Christian faith such as Islam or Judaism.[36] But when the underlying principle has been examined in the crucible of litigation, the Court has unambiguously concluded that the individual freedom of conscience protected by the First Amendment embraces the right to select any religious faith or none at all. This conclusion derives support not only from the interest in respecting the individual's freedom of conscience, but also from the conviction that religious beliefs worthy of respect are the product of free and voluntary choice by the faithful, and

---

30. *Ibid.* After noting that the invalidity of § 16–1–20.2 was aggravated by "the existence of a government composed prayer," and that the proponents of the legislation admitted that that section "amounts to the establishment of a state religion," the court added this comment on § 16–1–20.1:

"The objective of the meditation or prayer statute (Ala.Code § 16–1–20.1) was also the advancement of religion. This fact was recognized by the district court at the hearing for preliminary relief where it was established that the intent of the statute was to return prayer to the public schools. *James*, 544 F.Supp. at 731. The existence of this fact and the inclusion of prayer obviously involves the state in religious activities. *Beck v. McElrath*, 548 F.Supp. 1161 (MD Tenn.1982). This demonstrates a lack of secular legislative purpose on the part of the Alabama Legislature. Additionally, the statute has the primary effect of advancing religion. We do not imply that simple meditation or silence is barred from the public schools; we hold that the state cannot participate in the advancement of religious activities through any guise, including teacher-led meditation. It is not the activity itself that concerns us; it is the purpose of the activity that we shall scrutinize. Thus, the existence of these elements require that we also hold section 16–1–20.1 in violation of the establishment clause." . . .

32. The First Amendment provides:

"Congress shall make no law respecting an establishment of religion, or prohibiting the free exercise thereof; or abridging the freedom of speech, or of the press; or the right of the people peaceably to assemble, and to petition the Government for a redress of grievances."

36. Thus Joseph Story wrote:

"Probably at the time of the adoption of the constitution, and of the amendment to it, now under consideration [First Amendment], the general, if not the universal sentiment in America was, that christianity ought to receive encouragement from the state, so far as was not incompatible with the private rights of conscience, and the freedom of religious worship. An attempt to level all religions, and to make it a matter of state policy to hold all in utter indifference, would have created universal disapprobation, if not universal indignation." 2 J. Story, Commentaries on the Constitution of the United States § 1874, p. 593 (1851) (footnote omitted).

In the same volume, Story continued:

"The real object of the amendment was, not to countenance, much less to advance, Mahometanism, or Judaism, or infidelity, by prostrating christianity; *but to exclude all rivalry among christian sects, and to prevent any national ecclesiastical establishment, which should give to a hierarchy the exclusive patronage of the national government. It thus cut off the means of religious persecution, (the vice and pest of former ages,) and of the subversion of the rights of conscience in matters of religion,* which had been trampled upon almost from the days of the Apostles to the present age. . . ." *Id.*, § 1877, at 594 (emphasis supplied).

from recognition of the fact that the political interest in forestalling intolerance extends beyond intolerance among Christian sects—or even intolerance among "religions"—to encompass intolerance of the disbeliever and the uncertain. As Justice Jackson eloquently stated in *West Virginia Board of Education v. Barnette*, 319 U.S. 624, 642, 63 S.Ct. 1178, 1187, 87 L.Ed. 1628 (1943):

> "If there is any fixed star in our constitutional constellation, it is that no official, high or petty, can prescribe what shall be orthodox in politics, nationalism, religion, or other matters of opinion or force citizens to confess by word or act their faith therein."

The State of Alabama, no less than the Congress of the United States, must respect that basic truth.

III

When the Court has been called upon to construe the breadth of the Establishment Clause, it has examined the criteria developed over a period of many years. Thus, in *Lemon v. Kurtzman*, 403 U.S. 602, 612–13, 91 S.Ct. 2105, 2111, 29 L.Ed.2d 745 (1971), we wrote:

> "Every analysis in this area must begin with consideration of the cumulative criteria developed by the Court over many years. Three such tests may be gleaned from our cases. First, the statute must have a secular legislative purpose; second, its principal or primary effect must be one that neither advances nor inhibits religion, *Board of Education v. Allen*, 392 U.S. 236, 243 [88 S.Ct. 1923, 1926, 20 L.Ed.2d 1060] (1968); finally the statute must not foster 'an excessive government entanglement with religion.' *Walz [v. Tax Comm'n*, 397 U.S. 664, 674 [90 S.Ct. 1409, 1414, 25 L.Ed.2d 697] (1970)]."

It is the first of these three criteria that is most plainly implicated by this case. As the District Court correctly recognized, no consideration of the second or third criteria is necessary if a statute does not have a clearly secular purpose. For even though a statute that is motivated in part by a religious purpose may satisfy the first criterion, *see, e.g., Abington School District v. Schempp*, 374 U.S. 203, 296–303, 83 S.Ct. 1560, 1610–1614, 10 L.Ed.2d 844 (1963) (Brennan, J., concurring), the First Amendment requires that a statute must be invalidated if it is entirely motivated by a purpose to advance religion.[41]

In applying the purpose test, it is appropriate to ask "whether government's actual purpose is to endorse or disapprove of religion." In this case, the answer to that question is dispositive. For the record not only provides us with an unambiguous affirmative answer, but it also reveals that the enactment of § 16–1–20.1 was not motivated by any clearly secular purpose—indeed, the statute had *no* secular purpose.

IV

The sponsor of the bill that became § 16–1–20.1, Senator Donald Holmes, inserted into the legislative record—apparently without dissent—a statement indicating that the legislation was an "effort to return voluntary prayer" to the public schools.[43] Later Senator Holmes confirmed this purpose before the District Court. In response to the question whether he had any purpose for the legislation other than returning voluntary prayer to public schools, he stated: "No, I did not have no other purpose in mind." The State did not present evidence of *any* secular purpose.[45]

---

41. *See Lynch v. Donnelly*, 465 U.S. 668, 680, 104 S.Ct. 1355, 1362–1363, 79 L.Ed.2d 604 (1984); *id.*, at 690, 104 S.Ct., at 1368 (O'Connor, J., concurring); *id.*, at 697, 104 S.Ct., at 1371–1372 (Brennan, J., joined by Marshall, Blackmun, and Stevens, JJ., dissenting); *Mueller v. Allen*, 463 U.S. 388, 394, 103 S.Ct. 3062, 3066, 77 L.Ed.2d 721 (1983); *Widmar v. Vincent*, 454 U.S., at 271, 102 S.Ct., at 275; *Stone v. Graham*, 449 U.S. 39, 40–41, 101 S.Ct. 192, 193–194, 66 L.Ed.2d 199 (1980) (*per curiam*); *Wolman v. Walter*, 433 U.S. 229, 236, 97 S.Ct. 2593, 2599, 53 L.Ed.2d 714 (1977).

43. The statement indicated, in pertinent part: "Gentlemen, by passage of this bill by the Alabama Legislature our children in this state will have the opportunity of sharing in the spiritual heritage of this state and this country. The United States as well as the State of Alabama was founded by people who believe in God. *I believe this effort to return voluntary prayer* to our public schools for its return to us to the original position of the writers of the Constitution, this local philosophies and beliefs hundreds of Alabamians have urged my continuous support for permitting school prayer. Since coming to the Alabama Senate I have worked hard *on this legislation to accomplish the return of voluntary prayer in our public schools and return to the basic moral fiber.*" . . .

45. Appellant Governor George C. Wallace now argues that § 16–1–20.1 "is best understood as a permissible accommodation of religion" and that viewed even in terms of the *Lemon* test, the "statute conforms to acceptable constitutional criteria." . . .
These arguments seem to be based on the theory that the free exercise of religion of some of the State's citizens was burdened before the statute was enacted. The United States, appearing as *amicus curiae* in support of the appellants, candidly acknowledges that "it is unlikely that in most contexts a strong Free Exercise claim could be made that time for personal prayer must be set aside during the school day." . . . There is no basis for the suggestion that § 16–1–20.1 "is a means for accommodating the religious and meditative needs of students without in any way diminishing the school's own neutrality or secular atmosphere." . . . In this case, it is undisputed that at the time of the enactment of § 16–1–20.1 there was no governmental practice impeding students from silently praying for one minute at the beginning of each schoolday; thus, there was no need to "accommodate" or to exempt individuals from any general governmental requirement because of the dictates of our cases interpreting the Free Exercise Clause. . . . What was missing in the appellants' eyes at the time of the enactment of § 16–1–20.1—and therefore what is precisely the aspect that makes the statute unconstitutional—was the State's endorsement and promotion of religion and a particular religious practice.

The unrebutted evidence of legislative intent contained in the legislative record and in the testimony of the sponsor of § 16–1–20.1 is confirmed by a consideration of the relationship between this statute and the two other measures that were considered in this case. The District Court found that the 1981 statute and its 1982 sequel had a common, nonsecular purpose. The wholly religious character of the later enactment is plainly evident from its text. When the differences between § 16–1–20.1 and its 1978 predecessor, § 16–1–20, are examined, it is equally clear that the 1981 statute has the same wholly religious character.

There are only three textual differences between § 16–1–20.1 and § 16–1–20: (1) the earlier statute applies only to grades one through six, whereas § 16–1–20.1 applies to all grades; (2) the earlier statute uses the word "shall" whereas § 16–1–20.1 uses the word "may"; (3) the earlier statute refers only to "meditation" whereas § 16–1–20.1 refers to "meditation or voluntary prayer." The first difference is of no relevance in this litigation because the minor appellees were in kindergarten or second grade during the 1981–1982 academic year. The second difference would also have no impact on this litigation because the mandatory language of § 16–1–20 continued to apply to grades one through six. Thus, the only significant textual difference is the addition of the words "or voluntary prayer."

The legislative intent to return prayer to the public schools is, of course, quite different from merely protecting every student's right to engage in voluntary prayer during an appropriate moment of silence during the schoolday. The 1978 statute already protected that right, containing nothing that prevented any student from engaging in voluntary prayer during a silent minute of meditation.[47] Appellants have not identified any secular purpose that was not fully served by § 16–1–20 before the enactment of § 16–1–20.1. Thus, only two conclusions are consistent with the text of § 16–1–20.1: (1) the statute was enacted to convey a message of state endorsement and promotion of prayer; or (2) the statute was enacted for no purpose. No one suggests that the statute was nothing but a meaningless or irrational act.

. . . The legislature enacted § 16–1–20.1, despite the existence of § 16–1–20 for the sole purpose of expressing the State's endorsement of prayer activities for one minute at the beginning of each schoolday. The addition of "or voluntary prayer" indicates that the State intended to characterize prayer as a favored practice. Such an endorsement is not consistent with the established principle that the government must pursue a course of complete neutrality toward religion.

* * *

The judgment of the Court of Appeals is affirmed.

It is so ordered.

Justice Powell, concurring.

I concur in the Court's opinion and judgment that Ala.Code § 16–1–20.1 (Supp. 1984) violates the Establishment Clause of the First Amendment. My concurrence is prompted by Alabama's persistence in attempting to institute state-sponsored prayer in the public schools by enacting three successive statutes. I agree fully with Justice O'Connor's assertion that some moment-of-silence statutes may be constitutional, a suggestion set forth in the Court's opinion as well. . . .

I write separately to express additional views and to respond to criticism of the three-pronged *Lemon* test.[3] *Lemon v. Kurtzman*, 403 U.S. 602, 91 S.Ct. 2105, 29 L.Ed.2d 745 (1971), identifies standards that have proved useful in analyzing case after case both in our decisions and in those of other courts. It is the only coherent test a majority of the Court has ever adopted. Only once since our decision in *Lemon, supra*, have we addressed an Establishment Clause issue without resort to its three-pronged test. *See Marsh v. Chambers*, 463 U.S. 783, 103 S.Ct. 3330, 77 L.Ed.2d 1019 (1983). *Lemon, supra*, has not been overruled or its test modified. Yet, continued criticism of it could encourage other courts to feel free to decide Establishment Clause cases on an ad hoc basis.

* * *

I join the opinion and judgment of the Court.

47. Indeed, for some persons meditation itself may be a form of prayer. B. Larson, Larson's Book of Cults 62–65 (1982); C. Whittier, Silent Prayer and Meditation in World Religions 1–7 (Congressional Research Service 1982).

3. Justice O'Connor asserts that the "standards announced in *Lemon* should be reexamined and refined in order to make them more useful in achieving the underlying purpose of the First Amendment." *Post*, at 2496. (concurring in judgment). Justice Rehnquist would discard the *Lemon* test entirely. *Post*, at 2518–19 (dissenting).

As I state in the text, the *Lemon* test has been applied consistently in Establishment Clause cases since it was adopted in 1971. In a word, it has been the law. Respect for *stare decisis* should require us to follow *Lemon*. . . .

Justice O'Connor, concurring in the judgment.

Nothing in the United States Constitution as interpreted by this Court or in the laws of the State of Alabama prohibits public school students from voluntarily praying at any time before, during, or after the schoolday. Alabama has facilitated voluntary silent prayers of students who are so inclined by enacting Ala.Code § 16–1–20 (Supp.1984), which provides a moment of silence in appellees' schools each day. The parties to these proceedings concede the validity of this enactment. At issue in these appeals is the constitutional validity of an additional and subsequent Alabama statute, Ala.Code § 16–1–20.1 (Supp.1984), which both the District Court and the Court of Appeals concluded was enacted solely to officially encourage prayer during the moment of silence. I agree with the judgment of the Court that, in light of the findings of the courts below and the history of its enactment, § 16–1–20.1 of the Alabama Code violates the Establishment Clause of the First Amendment. In my view, there can be little doubt that the purpose and likely effect of this subsequent enactment is to endorse and sponsor voluntary prayer in the public schools. I write separately to identify the peculiar features of the Alabama law that render it invalid, and to explain why moment of silence laws in other States do not necessarily manifest the same infirmity. I also write to explain why neither history nor the Free Exercise Clause of the First Amendment validates the Alabama law struck down by the Court today.

I

* * *

. . . Under the now familiar *Lemon* test, statutes must have both a secular legislative purpose and principal or primary effect that neither advances nor inhibits religion, and in addition they must not foster excessive government entanglement with religion. . . . Despite its initial promise, the *Lemon* test has proved problematic. The required inquiry into "entanglement" has been modified and questioned, see *Mueller v. Allen*, 463 U.S. 388, 403, n. 11, 103 S.Ct. 3062, 3071, n. 11, 77 L.Ed.2d 721 (1983), and in one case we have upheld state action against an Establishment Clause challenge without applying the *Lemon* test at all. *Marsh v. Chambers*, 463 U.S. 783, 103 S.Ct. 3330, 77 L.Ed.2d 1019 (1983). The author of *Lemon* himself apparently questions the test's general applicability. *See Lynch v. Donnelly*, 465 U.S. 668, 679, 104 S.Ct. 1355, 1362, 79 L.Ed.2d 604 (1984). Justice Rehnquist today suggests that we abandon *Lemon* entirely, and in the process limit the reach of the Establishment Clause to state discrimination between sects and government designation of a particular church as a "state" or "national" one. . . .

Perhaps because I am new to the struggle, I am not ready to abandon all aspects of the *Lemon* test. I do believe, however, that the standards announced in *Lemon* should be reexamined and refined in order to make them more useful in achieving the underlying purpose of the First Amendment. We must strive to do more than erect a constitutional "signpost," *Hunt v. McNair*, 413 U.S. 734, 741, 93 S.Ct. 2868, 2873, 37 L.Ed.2d 923 (1973), to be followed or ignored in a particular case as our predilections may dictate. Instead, our goal should be "to frame a principle for constitutional adjudication that is not only grounded in the history and language of the first amendment, but one that is also capable of consistent application to the relevant problems." Choper, Religion in the Public Schools: A Proposed Constitutional Standard, 47 Min.L.Rev. 329, 332–33 (1963) (footnotes omitted). Last Term, I proposed a refinement of the *Lemon* test with this goal in mind. *Lynch v. Donnelly*, 465 U.S., at 687–89, 104 S.Ct., at 1366–67 (concurring opinion).

The *Lynch* concurrence suggested that the religious liberty protected by the Establishment Clause is infringed when the government makes adherence to religion relevant to a person's standing in the political community. Direct government action endorsing religion or a particular religious practice is invalid under this approach because it "sends a message to nonadherents that they are outsiders, not full members of the political community, and an accompanying message to adherents that they are insiders, favored members of the political community." *Id.*, at 688, 104 S.Ct., at 1367. Under this view, *Lemon*'s inquiry as to the purpose and effect of a statute requires courts to examine whether government's purpose is to endorse religion and whether the statute actually conveys a message of endorsement.

The endorsement test is useful because of the analytic content it gives to the *Lemon*-mandated inquiry into legislative purpose and effect. In this country, church and state must necessarily operate within the same community. Because of this co-existence, it is inevitable that the secular interests of government and the religious interests of various sects and their adherents will frequently intersect, conflict, and combine. A statute that ostensibly promotes a secular interest often has an incidental or even a primary effect of helping or hindering a sectarian belief. Chaos would ensue if every such statute were invalid under the Establishment Clause. For example, the State could not criminalize murder for fear that it would thereby promote the Biblical command against killing. The task for the Court is to sort out those statutes and government practices whose purpose and effect go against the grain of religious liberty protected by the First Amendment.

The endorsement test does not preclude government from acknowledging religion or from taking religion into account in making law and policy. It does preclude government from conveying or attempting to convey a message that religion or a particular religious belief is favored or preferred. Such an endorsement infringes the religious liberty of the nonadherent, for "[w]hen the power, prestige and financial support of government is placed behind a particular religious belief, the indirect coercive pressure upon religious minorities to conform to the prevailing officially approved religion is plain." *Engel v. Vitale, supra,* 370 U.S., at 431, 82 S.Ct., at 1267. At issue today is whether state moment of silence statutes in general, and Alabama's moment of silence statute in particular, embody an impermissible endorsement of prayer in public schools.

Twenty-five states permit or require public school teachers to have students observe a moment of silence in their classrooms. A few statutes provide that the moment of silence is for the purpose of meditation alone. See Ariz.Rev.Stat.Ann. § 15–522 (1984); Conn.Gen.Stat. § 10–16a (1983); R.I.Gen.Laws § 16–12–3.1 (1981). The typical statute, however, calls for a moment of silence at the beginning of the schoolday during which students may meditate, pray, or reflect on the activities of the day. . . .

The *Engel* and *Abington* decisions are not dispositive on the constitutionality of moment of silence laws. In those cases, public school teachers and students led their classes in devotional exercises. In *Engel*, a New York statute required teachers to lead their classes in a vocal prayer. The Court concluded that "it is no part of the business of government to compose official prayers for any group of the American people to recite as part of a religious program carried on by the government." 370 U.S., at 425, 82 S.Ct., at 1264. In *Abington*, the Court addressed Pennsylvania and Maryland statutes that authorized morning Bible readings in public schools. The Court reviewed the purpose and effect of the statutes, concluded that they required religious exercises, and therefore found them to violate the Establishment Clause. 374 U.S., at 223–24, 83 S.Ct., at 1572. Under all of these statutes, a student who did not share the religious beliefs expressed in the course of the exercise was left with the choice of participating, thereby compromising the nonadherent's beliefs, or withdrawing, thereby calling attention to his or her nonconformity. The decisions acknowledged the coercion implicit under the statutory schemes, see *Engel, supra,* at 431, 82 S.Ct., at 1267, but they expressly turned only on the fact that the government was sponsoring a manifestly religious exercise.

A state-sponsored moment of silence in the public schools is different from state-sponsored vocal prayer or Bible reading. First, a moment of silence is not inherently religious. Silence, unlike prayer or Bible reading, need not be associated with a religious exercise. Second, a pupil who participates in a moment of silence need not compromise his or her beliefs. During a moment of silence, a student who objects to prayer is left to his or her own thoughts, and is not compelled to listen to the prayers or thoughts of others. For these simple reasons, a moment of silence statute does not stand or fall under the Establishment Clause according to how the Court regards vocal prayer or Bible reading. . . .

By mandating a moment of silence, a State does not necessarily endorse any activity that might occur during the period. *Cf. Widmar v. Vincent,* 454 U.S. 263, 272, n. 11, 102 S.Ct. 269, 275, n. 11, 70 L.Ed.2d 440 (1981) ("[B]y creating a forum the [State] does not thereby endorse or promote any of the particular ideas aired there"). Even if a statute specifies that a student may choose to pray silently during a quiet moment, the State has not thereby encouraged prayer over other specified alternatives. Nonetheless, it is also possible that a moment of silence statute, either as drafted or as actually implemented, could effectively favor the child who prays over the child who does not. For example, the message of endorsement would seem inescapable if the teacher exhorts children to use the designated time to pray. Similarly, the face of the statute or its legislative history may clearly establish that it seeks to encourage or promote voluntary prayer over other alternatives, rather than merely provide a quiet moment that may be dedicated to prayer by those so inclined. The crucial question is whether the State has conveyed or attempted to convey the message that children should use the moment of silence for prayer. This question cannot be answered in the abstract, but instead requires courts to examine the history, language, and administration of a particular statute to determine whether it operates as an endorsement of religion. *Lynch*, 465 U.S., at 694, 104 S.Ct., at 1370 (concurring opinion) ("Every government practice must be judged in its unique circumstances to determine whether it constitutes an endorsement or disapproval of religion").

Before reviewing Alabama's moment of silence law to determine whether it endorses prayer, some general observations on the proper scope of the inquiry are in order. First, the inquiry into the purpose of the legislature in enacting a moment of silence law should be deferential and limited. *See Everson v. Board of Education*, 330 U.S. 1, 6, 67 S.Ct. 504, 507, 91 L.Ed. 711 (1947) (courts must exercise "the most extreme caution" in assessing whether a state statute has a proper public purpose). In determining whether the government intends a moment of silence statute to convey a message of endorsement or disapproval of religion, a court has no license to psychoanalyze the legislators. *See McGowan v. Maryland*, 366 U.S. 420, 466 (1961) (opinion of Frankfurter, J.). If a legislature expresses a plausible secular purpose for a moment of silence statute in either the text or the legislative history, or if the statute disclaims an intent to encourage prayer over alternatives during a moment of silence, then courts should generally defer to that stated intent. . . .

Justice Rehnquist suggests that this sort of deferential inquiry into legislative purpose "means little," because "it only requires the legislature to express any secular purpose and omit all sectarian references." . . . It is not a trivial matter, however, to require that the legislature manifest a secular purpose and omit all sectarian endorsements from its laws. That requirement is precisely tailored to the Establishment Clause's purpose of assuring that government not intentionally endorse religion or a religious practice. It is of course possible that a legislature will enunciate a sham secular purpose for a statute. I have little doubt that our courts are capable of distinguishing a sham secular purpose from a sincere one, or that the *Lemon* inquiry into the effect of an enactment would help decide those close cases where the validity of an expressed secular purpose is in doubt. While the secular purpose requirement alone may rarely be determinative in striking down a statute, it nevertheless serves an important function. It reminds government that when it acts it should do so without endorsing a particular religious belief or practice that all citizens do not share. In this sense the secular purpose requirement is squarely based in the text of the Establishment Clause it helps to enforce.

Second, the *Lynch* concurrence suggested that the effect of a moment of silence law is not entirely a question of fact:

> "[W]hether a government activity communicates endorsement of religion is not a question of simple historical fact. Although evidentiary submissions may help answer it, the question is, like the question whether racial or sex-based classifications communicate an invidious message, in large part a legal question to be answered on the basis of judicial interpretation of social facts." 465 U.S., at 693–94, 104 S.Ct., at 1370.

The relevant issue is whether an objective observer, acquainted with the text, legislative history, and implementation of the statute, would perceive it as a state endorsement of prayer in public schools. . . .

A moment of silence law that is clearly drafted and implemented so as to permit prayer, meditation, and reflection within the prescribed period, without endorsing one alternative over the others, should pass this test.

The analysis above suggests that moment of silence laws in many States should pass Establishment Clause scrutiny because they do not favor the child who chooses to pray during a moment of silence over the child who chooses to meditate or reflect. Alabama Code § 16–1–20.1 (Supp.1984) does not stand on the same footing. However deferentially one examines its text and legislative history, however objectively one views the message attempted to be conveyed to the public, the conclusion is unavoidable that the purpose of the statute is to endorse prayer in public schools. I accordingly agree with the Court of Appeals, 705 F.2d 1526, 1535 (1983), that the Alabama statute has a purpose which is in violation of the Establishment Clause, and cannot be upheld. . . .

II

In his dissenting opinion, . . . Justice Rehnquist reviews the text and history of the First Amendment

Religion Clauses. His opinion suggests that a long line of this Court's decisions are inconsistent with the intent of the drafters of the Bill of Rights. He urges the Court to correct the historical inaccuracies in its past decisions by embracing a far more restricted interpretation of the Establishment Clause, an interpretation that presumably would permit vocal group prayer in public schools. See generally R. Cord, Separation of Church and State (1982).

The United States, in an *amicus* brief, suggests a less sweeping modification of Establishment Clause principles. In the Federal Government's view, a state-sponsored moment of silence is merely an "accommodation" of the desire of some public school children to practice their religion by praying silently. Such an accommodation is contemplated by the First Amendment's guarantee that the Government will not prohibit the free exercise of religion. Because the moment of silence implicates free exercise values, the United States suggests that the *Lemon*-mandated inquiry into purpose and effect should be modified. . . .

* * *

Justice Rehnquist does not assert, however, that the drafters of the First Amendment expressed a preference for prayer in public schools, or that the practice of prayer in public schools enjoyed uninterrupted government endorsement from the time of enactment of the Bill of Rights to the present era. The simple truth is that free public education was virtually nonexistent in the late 18th century. *See Abington*, 374 U.S., at 238, and n. 7, 83 S.Ct., at 1580 and n. 7 (Brennan, J., concurring). Since there then existed few government-run schools, it is unlikely that the persons who drafted the First Amendment, or the state legislators who ratified it, anticipated the problems of interaction of church and state in the public schools. Sky, The Establishment Clause, the Congress, and the Schools: An Historical Perspective, 52 Va.L.Rev. 1395, 1403–04 (1966). Even at the time of adoption of the Fourteenth Amendment, education in Southern States was still primarily in private hands, and the movement toward free public schools supported by general taxation had not taken hold. . . .

. . . When the intent of the Framers is unclear, I believe we must employ both history and reason in our analysis. The primary issue raised by Justice Rehnquist's dissent is whether the historical fact that our Presidents have long called for public prayers of Thanks should be dispositive on the constitutionality of prayer in public schools.[6] I think not. At the very least, Presidential Proclamations are distinguishable from school prayer in that they are received in a noncoercive setting and are primarily directed at adults, who presumably are not readily susceptible to unwilling religious indoctrination. This Court's decisions have recognized a distinction when government-sponsored religious exercises are directed at impressionable children who are required to attend school, for then government endorsement is much more likely to result in coerced religious beliefs. . . . Although history provides a touchstone for constitutional problems, the Establishment Clause concern for religious liberty is dispositive here.

The element of truth in the United States' arguments, I believe, lies in the suggestion that Establishment Clause analysis must comport with the mandate of the Free Exercise Clause that government make no law prohibiting the free exercise of religion. Our cases have interpreted the Free Exercise Clause to compel the government to exempt persons from some generally applicable government requirements so as to permit those persons to freely exercise their religion. *See, e.g., Thomas v. Review Board of the Indiana Employment Security Division*, 450 U.S. 707, 101 S.Ct. 1425, 67 L.Ed.2d 624 (1981); *Wisconsin v. Yoder*, 406 U.S. 205, 92 S.Ct. 1526, 32 L.Ed.2d 15 (1972); *Sherbert v. Verner*, 374 U.S. 398, 83 S.Ct. 1790, 10 L.Ed.2d 965 (1963). Even where the Free Exercise Clause does not compel the government to grant an exemption, the Court has suggested that the government in some circumstances may voluntarily choose to exempt religious observers without violating the Establishment Clause. *See, e.g., Gillette v. United States*, 401 U.S. 437, 453, 91 S.Ct. 828, 838, 28 L.Ed.2d 168 (1971); *Braunfeld v. Brown*, 366 U.S. 599, 81 S.Ct. 1144, 6 L.Ed.2d 563 (1961). The challenge posed by the United States' argument is how to define the proper Establishment Clause limits on voluntary government efforts to facilitate the free exercise of religion. On the one hand, a rigid application of the *Lemon* test would invalidate legislation exempting religious observers from generally applicable government ob-

6. Even assuming a taxpayer could establish standing to challenge such a practice, *see Valley Forge Christian College v. Americans United for Separation of Church and State, Inc.*, 454 U.S. 464, 102 S.Ct. 752, 70 L.Ed.2d 700 (1982), these Presidential Proclamations would probably withstand Establishment Clause scrutiny given their long history. *See Marsh v. Chambers*, 463 U.S. 783, 103 S.Ct. 3330, 77 L.Ed.2d 1019 (1983).

ligations. By definition, such legislation has a religious purpose and effect in promoting the free exercise of religion. On the other hand, judicial deference to all legislation that purports to facilitate the free exercise or religion would completely vitiate the Establishment Clause. Any statute pertaining to religion can be viewed as an "accommodation" of free exercise rights. Indeed, the statute at issue in *Lemon*, which provided salary supplements, textbooks, and instructional materials to Pennsylvania parochial schools, can be viewed as an accommodation of the religious beliefs of parents who choose to send their children to religious schools.

It is obvious that either of the two Religion Clauses, "if expanded to a logical extreme, would tend to clash with the other." *Walz*, 397 U.S., at 668–69, 90 S.Ct., at 1411. The Court has long exacerbated the conflict by calling for government "neutrality" toward religion. *See, e.g., Committee for Public Education & Religious Liberty v. Nyquist*, 413 U.S. 756, 93 S.Ct. 2955, 37 L.Ed.2d 948 (1973); *Board of Education v. Allen*, 392 U.S. 236, 88 S.Ct. 1923, 20 L.Ed.2d 1060 (1968). It is difficult to square any notion of "complete neutrality," . . . with the mandate of the Free Exercise Clause that government must sometimes exempt a religious observer from an otherwise generally applicable obligation. A government that confers a benefit on an explicitly religious basis is not neutral toward religion. . . .

The solution to the conflict between the Religion Clauses lies not in "neutrality," but rather in identifying workable limits to the government's license to promote the free exercise of religion. The text of the Free Exercise Clause speaks of laws that prohibit the free exercise of religion. On its face, the Clause is directed at government interference with free exercise. Given that concern, one can plausibly assert that government pursues Free Exercise Clause values when it lifts a government-imposed burden on the free exercise of religion. If a statute falls within this category, then the standard Establishment Clause test should be modified accordingly. It is disingenuous to look for a purely secular purpose when the manifest objective of a statute is to facilitate the free exercise of religion by lifting a government-imposed burden. Instead, the Court should simply acknowledge that the religious purpose of such a statute is legitimated by the Free Exercise Clause. I would also go further. In assessing the effect of such a statute—that is, in determining whether the statute conveys the message of endorsement of religion or a particular religious belief—courts should assume that the "objective observer" . . . is acquainted with the Free Exercise Clause and the values it promotes. Thus individual perceptions, or resentment that a religious observer is exempted from a particular government requirement, would be entitled to little weight if the Free Exercise Clause strongly supported the exemption.

While this "accommodation" analysis would help reconcile our Free Exercise and Establishment Clause standards, it would not save Alabama's moment of silence law. If we assume that the religious activity that Alabama seeks to protect is silent prayer, then it is difficult to discern any state-imposed burden on that activity that is lifted by Alabama Code § 16–1–20.1 (Supp.1984). No law prevents a student who is so inclined from praying silently in public schools. Moreover, state law already provided a moment of silence to these appellees irrespective of § 16–1–20.1. See Ala.Code § 16–1–20 (Supp.1984). Of course, the State might argue that § 16–1–20.1 protects not silent prayer, but rather group silent prayer under state sponsorship. Phrased in these terms, the burden lifted by the statute is not one imposed by the State of Alabama, but by the Establishment Clause as interpreted in *Engel* and *Abington*. In my view, it is beyond the authority of the State of Alabama to remove burdens imposed by the Constitution itself. I conclude that the Alabama statute at issue today lifts no state-imposed burden on the free exercise of religion, and accordingly cannot properly be viewed as an accommodation statute.

III

The Court does not hold that the Establishment Clause is so hostile to religion that it precludes the States from affording schoolchildren an opportunity for voluntary silent prayer. To the contrary, the moment of silence statutes of many States should satisfy the Establishment Clause standard we have here applied. The Court holds only that Alabama has intentionally crossed the line between creating a quiet moment during which those so inclined may pray, and affirmatively endorsing the particular religious practice of prayer. This line may be a fine one, but our precedents and the principles of religious liberty require that we draw it. In my view, the judgment of the Court of Appeals must be affirmed.

Chief Justice Burger, dissenting. [omitted]

Justice White, dissenting.

. . . I dissent from the Court's judgment invalidating Ala.Code § 16–1–20.1 (Supp.1984). Because I do, it is apparent that in my view the First Amendment does not proscribe either (1) statutes authorizing or requiring in so many words a moment of silence before classes begin or (2) a statute that provides, when it is initially passed, for a moment of silence for meditation or prayer. As I read the filed opinions, a majority of the Court would approve statutes that provided for a moment of silence but did not mention prayer. But if a student asked whether he could pray during that moment, it is difficult to believe that the teacher could not answer in the affirmative. If that is the case, I would not invalidate a statute that at the outset provided the legislative answer to the question "May I pray?" This is so even if the Alabama statute is infirm, which I do not believe it is, because of its peculiar legislative history.

* * *

Justice Rehnquist, dissenting.

Thirty-eight years ago this Court, in *Everson v. Board of Education*, 330 U.S. 1, 16, 67 S.Ct. 504, 512, 91 L.Ed. 711 (1947), summarized its exegesis of Establishment Clause doctrine thus:

> "In the words of Jefferson, the clause against establishment of religion by law was intended to erect 'a wall of separation between church and State.' *Reynolds v. United States*, [98 U.S. 145, 164, 25 L.Ed. 244 (1879)]."

This language from *Reynolds*, a case involving the Free Exercise Clause of the First Amendment rather than the Establishment Clause, quoted from Thomas Jefferson's letter to the Danbury Baptist Association the phrase "I contemplate with sovereign reverence that act of the whole American people which declared that their legislature should 'make no law respecting an establishment of religion, or prohibiting the free exercise thereof,' thus building a wall of separation between church and State." 8 Writings of Thomas Jefferson 113 (H. Washington ed. 1861).[1]

It is impossible to build sound constitutional doctrine upon a mistaken understanding of constitutional history, but unfortunately the Establishment Clause has been expressly freighted with Jefferson's misleading metaphor for nearly 40 years. . . .

. . . [W]hen we turn to the record of the proceedings in the First Congress leading up to the adoption of the Establishment Clause of the Constitution, including Madison's significant contributions thereto, we see a far different picture of its purpose than the highly simplified "wall of separation between church and State."

* * *

The language Madison proposed for what ultimately became the Religion Clauses of the First Amendment was this:

> "The civil rights of none shall be abridged on account of religious belief or worship, nor shall any national religion be established, nor shall the full and equal rights of conscience be in any manner, or on any pretext, infringed." . . .

On the same day that Madison proposed them, the amendments which formed the basis for the Bill of Rights were referred by the House to a Committee of the Whole, and after several weeks' delay were then referred to a Select Committee consisting of Madison and 10 others. The Committee revised Madison's proposal regarding the establishment of religion to read:

> "[N]o religion shall be established by law, nor shall the equal rights of conscience be infringed." . . .

The Committee's proposed revisions were debated in the House on August 15, 1789. The entire debate on the Religion Clauses is contained in two full columns of the "Annals," and does not seem particularly illuminating. . . .

Madison . . . spoke, and said that "he apprehended the meaning of the words to be, that Congress should not establish a religion, and enforce the legal observation of it by law, nor compel men to worship God in any manner contrary to their conscience." . . . He said that some of the state conventions had thought that Congress might rely on the Necessary and Proper Clause to infringe the rights of conscience or to establish a national religion, and "to prevent these effects he presumed the amendment was intended, and he thought it as well

1. *Reynolds* is the only authority cited as direct precedent for the "wall of separation theory." 330 U.S., at 16, 67 S.Ct., at 512. *Reynolds* is truly inapt; it dealt with a Mormon's Free Exercise Clause challenge to a federal polygamy law.

expressed as the nature of the language would admit." . . .

* * *

. . . "He believed that the people feared one sect might obtain a pre-eminence, or two combine together, and establish a religion to which they would compel others to conform. . . ."

* * *

The following week, without any apparent debate, the House voted to alter the language of the Religion Clauses to read "Congress shall make no law establishing religion, or to prevent the free exercise thereof, or to infringe the rights of conscience." . . . The floor debates in the Senate were secret, and therefore not reported in the Annals. The Senate on September 3, 1789, considered several different forms of the Religion amendment, and reported this language back to the House:

> "Congress shall make no law establishing articles of faith or a mode of worship, or prohibiting the free exercise of religion." C. Antieau, A. Downey, & E. Roberts, Freedom From Federal Establishment 130 (1964).

The House refused to accept the Senate's changes in the Bill of Rights and asked for a conference; the version which emerged from the conference was that which ultimately found its way into the Constitution as a part of the First Amendment.

> "Congress shall make no law respecting an establishment of religion, or prohibiting the free exercise thereof."

The House and the Senate both accepted this language on successive days, and the Amendment was proposed in this form.

On the basis of the record of these proceedings in the House of Representatives, James Madison was undoubtedly the most important architect among the Members of the House of the Amendments which became the Bill of Rights, but it was James Madison speaking as an advocate of sensible legislative compromise, not as an advocate of incorporating the Virginia Statute of Religious Liberty into the United State Constitution. During the ratification debate in the Virginia Convention, Madison had actually opposed the idea of any Bill of Rights. His sponsorship of the Amendments in the House was obviously not that of a zealous believer in the necessity of the Religion Clauses, but of one who felt it might do some good, could do no harm, and would satisfy those who had ratified the Constitution on the condition that Congress propose a Bill of Rights.[3] His original language "nor shall any national religion be established" obviously does not conform to the "wall of separation" between church and State idea which latter-day commentators have ascribed to him. His explanation on the floor of the meaning of his language—"that Congress should not establish a religion, and enforce the legal observation of it by law" is of the same ilk. . . .

It seems indisputable from these glimpses of Madison's thinking, as reflected by actions on the floor of the House in 1789, that he saw the Amendment as designed to prohibit the establishment of a national religion, and perhaps to prevent discrimination among sects. He did not see it as requiring neutrality on the part of government between religion and irreligion. Thus the Court's opinion in *Everson*—while correct in bracketing Madison and Jefferson together in their exertions in their home State leading to the enactment of the Virginia Statute of Religious Liberty—is totally incorrect in suggesting that Madison carried these views onto the floor of the United States House of Representatives when he proposed the language which would ultimately become the Bill of Rights.

The repetition of this error in the Court's opinion in *Illinois ex rel. McCollum v. Board of Education*, 333 U.S. 203, 68 S.Ct. 461, 92 L.Ed. 649 (1948), and *inter alia, Engel v. Vitale*, 370 U.S. 421, 82 S.Ct. 1261, 8 L.Ed.2d 601 (1962), does not make it any sounder historically. Finally, in *Abington School District v. Schempp*, 374 U.S. 203, 214, 83 S.Ct. 1560, 1567, 10 L.Ed.2d 844 (1963), the Court made the truly remarkable statement that "the views of Madison and Jefferson, preceded by Roger Williams, came to be incorporated not only in the Federal Constitution but likewise in those of most of our States" (footnote omitted). On the basis of what evidence we have, this statement is demonstrably

3. In a letter he sent to Jefferson in France, Madison stated that he did not see much importance in a Bill of Rights but he planned to support it because it was "anxiously desired by others . . . [and] it might be of use, and if properly executed could not be of disservice." 5 Writings of James Madison 271 (G. Hunt ed. 1904).

incorrect as a matter of history.[4] And its repetition in varying forms in succeeding opinions of the Court can give it no more authority than it possesses as a matter of fact; *stare decisis* may bind courts as to matters of law, but it cannot bind them as to matters of history.

None of the other Members of Congress who spoke during the August 15th debate expressed the slightest indication that they thought the language before them from the Select Committee, or the evil to be aimed at, would require that the Government be absolutely neutral as between religion and irreligion. The evil to be aimed at, so far as those who spoke were concerned, appears to have been the establishment of a national church, and perhaps the preference of one religious sect over another; but it was definitely not concerned about whether the Government might aid all religions evenhandedly. . . .

The actions of the First Congress, which reenacted the Northwest Ordinance for the governance of the Northwest Territory in 1789, confirm the view that Congress did not mean that the Government should be neutral between religion and irreligion. . . .

The Northwest Ordinance, 1 Stat. 50, reenacted the Northwest Ordinance of 1787 and provided that "[r]eligion, morality, and knowledge, being necessary to good government and the happiness of mankind, schools and the means of education shall forever be encouraged." . . . Land grants for schools in the Northwest Territory were not limited to public schools. It was not until 1845 that Congress limited land grants in the new States and Territories to nonsectarian schools. . . .

On the day after the House of Representatives voted to adopt the form of the First Amendment Religion Clauses which was ultimately proposed and ratified, Representative Elias Boudinot proposed a resolution asking President George Washington to issue a Thanksgiving Day Proclamation. Boudinot said he "could not think of letting the session pass over without offering an opportunity to all the citizens of the United States of joining with one voice, in returning to Almighty God their sincere thanks for the many blessings he had poured down upon them." . . .

Boudinot's resolution was carried in the affirmative on September 25, 1789. Boudinot and Sherman, who favored the Thanksgiving Proclamation, voted in favor of the adoption of the proposed amendments to the Constitution, including the Religion Clauses; Tucker, who opposed the Thanksgiving Proclamation, voted against the adoption of the amendments which became the Bill of Rights.

* * *

As the United States moved from the 18th into the 19th century, Congress appropriated time and again public moneys in support of sectarian Indian education carried on by religious organizations. Typical of these was Jefferson's treaty with the Kaskaskia Indians, which provided annual cash support for the Tribe's Roman Catholic priest and church. It was not until 1897, when aid to sectarian education for Indians had reached $500,000 annually, that Congress decided thereafter to cease appropriating money for education in sectarian schools. . . . This history shows the fallacy of the notion found in *Everson* that "no tax in any amount" may be levied for religious activities in any form. . . .

Joseph Story, a Member of this Court from 1811 to 1845, and during much of that time a professor at the Harvard Law School, published by far the most comprehensive treatise on the United States Constitution that had then appeared. Volume 2 of Story's Commentaries on the Constitution of the United States 630–32 (5th ed. 1891) discussed the meaning of the Establishment Clause of the First Amendment this way:

> "Probably at the time of the adoption of the Constitution, and of the amendment to it now under consideration [First Amendment], the general if not the universal sentiment in America was, that Christianity ought to receive encouragement from the State so far as was not incompatible with the private rights of conscience and the freedom of religious worship. An attempt to level all religions, and to make it a matter of state policy to hold all in utter indifference, would have created universal disapprobation, if not universal indignation.

* * *

4. State establishments were prevalent throughout the late 18th and early 19th centuries. *See* Mass. Const. of 1780, Part 1, Art. III; N.H. Const. of 1784, Art. VI; Md. Declaration of Rights of 1776, Art. XXXIII; R.I. Charter of 1633 (superseded 1842).

"The real object of the [First] [A]mendment was not to countenance, much less to advance, Mahometanism, or Judaism, or infidelity, by prostrating Christianity; but to exclude all rivalry among Christian sects, and to prevent any national ecclesiastical establishment which should give to a hierarchy the exclusive patronage of the national government. . . .

It would seem from this evidence that the Establishment Clause of the First Amendment had acquired a well-accepted meaning: it forbade establishment of a national religion, and forbade preference among religious sects or denominations. Indeed, the first American dictionary defined the word "establishment" as "the act of establishing, founding, ratifying or ordaining," such as in "[t]he episcopal form of religion, so called, in England." 1 N. Webster, American Dictionary of the English Language (1st ed. 1828). The Establishment Clause did not require government neutrality between religion and irreligion nor did it prohibit the Federal Government from providing nondiscriminatory aid to religion. There is simply no historical foundation for the proposition that the Framers intended to build the "wall of separation" that was constitutionalized in *Everson*.

Notwithstanding the absence of a historical basis for this theory of rigid separation, the wall idea might well have served as a useful albeit misguided analytical concept, had it led this Court to unified and principled results in Establishment Clause cases. The opposite, unfortunately, has been true; in the 38 years since *Everson* our Establishment Clause cases have been neither principled nor unified. Our recent opinions, many of them hopelessly divided pluralities, have with embarrassing candor conceded that the "wall of separation" is merely a "blurred, indistinct, and variable barrier," which "is not wholly accurate" and can only be "dimly perceived." *Lemon v. Kurtzman*, 403 U.S. 602, 614, 91 S.Ct. 2105, 2112, 29 L.Ed.2d 745 (1971). . . .

Whether due to its lack of historical support or its practical unworkability, the *Everson* "wall" has proved all but useless as a guide to sound constitutional adjudication. . . .

. . . The "wall of separation between church and State" is a metaphor based on bad history, a metaphor which has proved useless as a guide to judging. It should be frankly and explicitly abandoned.

The Court has more recently attempted to add some mortar to *Everson's* wall through the three-part test of *Lemon v. Kurtzman*, *supra*, 403 U.S., at 614–15, 91 S.Ct. at 2112, which served at first to offer a more useful test for purposes of the Establishment Clause than did the "wall" metaphor. Generally stated, the *Lemon* test proscribes state action that has a sectarian purpose or effect, or causes an impermissible governmental entanglement with religion.

* * *

The secular purpose prong has proven mercurial in application because it has never been fully defined, and we have never fully stated how the test is to operate. If the purpose prong is intended to void those aids to sectarian institutions accompanied by a stated legislative purpose to aid religion, the prong will condemn nothing so long as the legislature utters a secular purpose and says nothing about aiding religion. Thus the constitutionality of a statute may depend upon what the legislators put into the legislative history and, more importantly, what they leave out. The purpose prong means little if it only requires the legislature to express any secular purpose and omit all sectarian references, because legislators might do just that. . . .

However, if the purpose prong is aimed to void all statutes enacted with the intent to aid sectarian institutions, whether stated or not, then most statutes providing any aid, such as textbooks or bus rides for sectarian school children, will fail because one of the purposes behind every statute, whether stated or not, is to aid the target of its largesse. In other words, if the purpose prong requires an absence of *any* intent to aid sectarian institutions, whether or not expressed, few state laws in this area could pass the test, and we would be required to void some state aids to religion which we have already upheld. . . .

The entanglement prong of the *Lemon* test came from *Walz v. Tax Comm'n*, 397 U.S. 664, 674, 90 S.Ct. 1409, 1414, 25 L.Ed.2d 697 (1970). *Walz* involved a constitutional challenge to New York's time-honored practice of providing state property tax exemptions to church property used in worship. The *Walz* opinion . . . upheld the tax exemption. The Court examined the historical relationship between the State and church when church property was in issue, and determined that the challenged tax exemption did not so entangle New York with the church as to cause an intrusion or interference with religion. . . .

We have not always followed *Walz's* reflective inquiry into entanglement, however. . . . One of the difficulties with the entanglement prong is that when divorced from the logic of *Walz,* it creates an "insoluable paradox" in school aid cases: we have required aid to parochial schools to be closely watched lest it be put to sectarian use, yet this close supervision itself will create an entanglement. . . .

The entanglement test . . . also ignores the myriad state administrative regulations properly placed upon sectarian institutions such as curriculum, attendance, and certification requirements for sectarian schools, or fire and safety regulations for churches. Avoiding entanglement between church and State may be an important consideration in a case like *Walz,* but if the entanglement prong were applied to all state and church relations in the automatic manner in which it has been applied to school aid cases, the State could hardly require anything of church-related institutions as a condition for receipt of financial assistance.

These difficulties arise because the *Lemon* test has no more grounding in the history of the First Amendment than does the wall theory upon which it rests. The three-part test represents a determined effort to craft a workable rule from a historically faulty doctrine; but the rule can only be as sound as the doctrine it attempts to service. The three-part test has simply not provided adequate standards for deciding Establishment Clause cases, as this Court has slowly come to realize. Even worse, the *Lemon* test has caused this Court to fracture into unworkable plurality opinions, . . . depending upon how each of the three factors applies to a certain state action. . . .

* * *

The Court strikes down the Alabama statute because the State wished to "characterize prayer as a favored practice." . . . It would come as much of a shock to those who drafted the Bill of Rights as it will to a large number of thoughtful Americans today to learn that the Constitution, as construed by the majority, prohibits the Alabama Legislature from "endorsing" prayer. George Washington himself, at the request of the very Congress which passed the Bill of Rights, proclaimed a day of "public thanksgiving and prayer, to be observed by acknowledging with grateful hearts the many and signal favors of Almighty God." History must judge whether it was the Father of his Country in 1789, or a majority of the Court today, which has strayed from the meaning of the Establishment Clause.

The State surely has a secular interest in regulating the manner in which public schools are conducted. Nothing in the Establishment Clause of the First Amendment, properly understood, prohibits any such generalized "endorsement" of prayer. I would therefore reverse the judgment of the Court of Appeals.

NOTES AND QUESTIONS

1. The Constitutional Standard: The Religious Purpose Test

The majority applies the modern test for constitutionality under the Establishment Clause, asking whether the moment-of-silence statute has the purpose or effect of advancing religion and whether it fostered an excessive entanglement between government and religion. *See also Stone v. Graham,* 449 U.S. 39, 101 S.Ct. 192, 66 L.Ed.2d 199 (1980). The majority then cites evidence for the religious motivation behind the Alabama law. Does the purpose test require that the only motivation for the law be the advancement of religion? What if it is only one of a number of reasons for the law? Is a purpose test appropriate where the state claims that it is accommodating religious freedom? Is not any accommodation motivated by a desire to advance religion? *See May v. Cooperman,* 780 F.2d 240 (3d Cir. 1985), *appeal dismissed sub. nom. Karcher v. May,* 484 U.S. 72, 108 S.Ct. 388, 98 L.Ed.2d 327 (1987) (procedural grounds). *See generally* Laycock, *infra* at 62. In this regard, consider these comments by Dean Choper on the purpose test:

> As a matter of logic, the Supreme Court's approach in this area is subject to criticism. The Court's doctrine under the Establishment Clause, that any government action that has a religious purpose is unconstitutional, is in conflict with the Court's doctrine under the other religion clause of the First Amendment, the Free Exercise Clause. Under that provision, the Court has held that not only is government permitted to act for religious purposes, but at least under certain circumstances it must act for religious purposes by granting an exemption from ordinary civil regulation to people because, and only because, they hold a particular religious belief. I think the only fair way to characterize that aspect of the Supreme Court's Free Exercise Clause doctrine is to say that the Court is requiring government to act for a religious purpose. Thus, on the one hand, the Court says that under the Establishment Clause it is unconstitutional for the government to act

> for a religious purpose, but on the other hand, under the Free Exercise Clause the Court periodically holds that the government must act for a religious purpose.

Choper, "Church, State and the Supreme Court: Current Controversy," 29 *Ariz. L. Rev.* 551, 552 (1987). Has the Court been inconsistent? Or do you agree with Justice Stevens when he says that "the legislative intent to return prayer to the public schools is, of course, quite different from merely protecting every student's right to engage in voluntary prayer during an appropriate moment of silence during the schoolday"?

What is the difference, if any, between an endorsement of religion and a purpose to advance it? *See* Laycock, *infra* at 58–60.

Appellees abandoned their attack on the constitutionality of Alabama Code § 16–1–20. Why did they do so? Does the majority assume that this section is constitutional? *See* Dellinger, "The Sound of Silence: An Epistle on Prayer and the Constitution," 95 *Yale L. J.* 1631 (1986). Justice O'Connor, for example, is quite explicit on this point. Dean Choper has remarked that in *Wallace* "the separationists won the battle but lost the war in respect to silent prayer." Choper, *supra* at 555. Do you agree? Consider these comments by Professor Laycock:

> A school that sets aside a moment of silence is creating an open forum for private thought in the midst of the school day. It is not obligated to do so, but it is free to do so. Some students may think religious thoughts, or say a silent prayer. But private religious thought is even less capable of violating the establishment clause than private religious speech. Freedom of thought may be the only constitutional right that is absolutely protected.
>
> Even so, most of the cases that have invalidated moments of silence have reached the right result. Neutral moments of silence are harder to implement than equal access. . . . [I]nescapably, the teacher must introduce a moment of silence. And he must do so in the presence of the whole class. It requires careful preparation for a teacher to introduce a moment of silence without encouraging or discouraging prayer or appearing to do either. The task does not appear unmanageable in theory, but so far, it has exceeded the capacity of the schools in litigated cases. . . .

Laycock, "Equal Access and Moments of Silence: The Equal Status of Religious Speech by Private Speakers," 81 *Nw. L. Rev.* 1, 57–58 (1986). *See also* Choper, *supra* at 555. Contrast this perspective with that of Professor Gedicks:

> The most common (and plausible) of the secular purposes advanced for moment of silence laws is that the silence period signals the beginning of the school day and gives students the opportunity mentally to "shift gears" and orient themselves to the business of learning. If this is the purpose of the laws, however, it is not clear why any students should be excused from participating or why special permission should be necessary to participate, nor is it apparent why the moment of silence is prescribed only at the beginning of the school day and not after each recess or change of classrooms. In fact, evidence of a disciplinary or educational purpose rarely is evident in the legislative history of silence laws.
>
> * * *
>
> . . . Most moment of silence statutes . . . evidence an intention that an opportunity for prayer be created (1) on the public school campus, (2) in a school-sanctioned, teacher-monitored classroom setting, and (3) despite the absence of any meaningful impediment to voluntary prayer on an individual basis. The state's insistence on "accommodating" student desire to pray in school notwithstanding the absence of government impediments evidences a governmental purpose not merely to accommodate those who desire to pray but to promote prayer by the use of government influence. In the absence of controverting evidence, the laws should be found unconstitutional.

Gedicks, "Motivation, Rationality, and Secular Purpose in Establishment Clause Review," 1985 *Ariz. St. L. J.* 677, 719, 721–22. *See also* Note, "Daily Moments of Silence in Public Schools: A Constitutional Analysis," 58 *N.Y.U. L. Rev.* 364 (1983). Do you agree with Professor Laycock or Professor Gedicks? Is Professor Laycock looking at effects only and not motivation? Does Professor Gedicks apply a more stringent version of the purpose test than Justice O'Connor? Would any moment-of-silence law survive the scrutiny that Gedicks applies? Is he responding to the suspicion that legislators will articulate secular reasons for a moment-of-silence law, even if their genuine motive is to advance religion? *See* Wilkins, "One Moment Please: Private Devotion in the Public Schools," 2 *B.Y.U. J. Pub. L.* 1, 8 (1988). Is Justice O'Connor simply requiring that prayer not be mentioned in the moment-of-silence law or its legislative history? Is her approach merely cosmetic or does it reflect a reasoned view as to what constitutes government approval of religion? *See* Vieira, "School Prayer and the Principle of Uncoerced Listening," 14 *Hast. Const. L. Q.* 763 (1987). *See also* Laycock, *supra*.

2. *Voluntary Prayer*

Justice O'Connor states that "nothing in the United States Constitution as interpreted by this Court or in the laws of the State of Alabama prohibits public school students from voluntarily praying at any time before, during, or after the school day." *See also* Wilkins, *supra*. The law under review is unconstitutional only because "there can be little doubt that the purpose and likely effect of this subsequent enactment is to endorse and sponsor voluntary prayer in public schools." *See generally* Laycock, *supra*. Consider the relevance of the voluntary nature of moments of silence. Is the emphasis on voluntariness an Establishment Clause formulation or one much more concerned with the free exercise of religion? *See generally* Choper, *supra* at 555–56. In this regard, consider the evidence in *Walter v. West Virginia Bd. of Educ.*, 610 F.Supp. 1169 (S.D. W. Va. 1985):

> Q. Okay. And then the next day what happened?
> A. [Eleven-year-old Jewish Student] Well, then the next day our principal or guidance counselor read the whole sheet of guidelines to us. Then we had the moment of silence and I read a book during it.
>
> * * *
>
> Q. [Although nothing happened in the home room or in the first period, did anything happen to you in the second period?]
> A. Well, in second period, which was science, our teacher left the room . . . and one of the people who was in my home room turned around and asked me why I had been reading a book during the moment of silence. And I told him that I didn't have to pray then and I didn't want to and then he told me that I should be praying all the time and then he said something to the effect that if I prayed all the time, maybe I could go to heaven with all the Christians when Jesus came for the second time instead of, as he put it, going down with all the other Jews.
>
> * * *
>
> Q. Did anyone else participate in the conversation?
> A. Yes. There was another person who, this first boy told another boy that the Jews only used the Old Testament and they didn't use the New Testament and this other boy thought that it was really stupid . . . [T]hen the second boy said something to the effect that, why was he even trying to talk to me because the Jews weren't worth saving because they had killed Christ and that was about the end of it.
>
> * * *
>
> Q. Okay. Did you, did you talk with your teacher?
> A. No, I didn't.
> Q. Any reason that you didn't or—
> A. Well, I was afraid that the teacher either wouldn't listen or if the teacher did listen, there would be a big issue made out of it and I would be in the limelight for the wrong reasons and I was afraid that I could have a lot of bad publicity . . .

Id. at 1172–73. Given this evidence, is the moment of silence voluntary? *See* Vieira, *supra* at 765–66. Should the determination of the constitutionality of the moment of silence depend on the specific situation in each school or classroom? *See* Laycock, *supra* at 64–66. Would it be better to have a per se rule? Is the answer to require silence and not to allow reading or other activities for that time span?

Justice O'Connor emphasizes that students in public schools are "impressionable children." Why is this fact relevant to analysis under the Establishment Clause?

3. *The Dissent of Chief Justice Rehnquist*

Chief Justice Rehnquist disputes the historical basis for interpreting the Establishment Clause to require absolute government neutrality between religion and irreligion or a "wall of separation" between church and state. He succinctly states that "the 'wall of separation between church and State' is a metaphor based on bad history, a metaphor which has proved useless as a guide to judging." Are you persuaded by his arguments? *See* Smith, "Now is the Time for Reflection: *Wallace v. Jaffree* and its Legislative Aftermath," 37 *Ala. L. Rev.* 345 (1986). If the metaphor were a "useful guide" for judges, should it be retained even if it were historically wrong? What test would the Chief Justice apply in Establishment Clause cases? Note that he concludes that Madison "saw the [First] Amendment as designed to prohibit the establishment of a national religion, and perhaps to prevent discrimination among sects." From this perspective, the Establishment Clause definitely was "not concerned about whether the Government might aid all religions evenhandedly . . ." *See* Kurland, "Of Church and State and the Supreme Court," 29 *U. Chi. L. Rev.* 1 (1961). *But see* Laycock, *supra* at 3.

4. *Commencement Exercises*

In *Marsh v. Chambers*, 463 U.S. 783, 103 S.Ct. 3330, 77 L.Ed.2d 1019 (1983), the Supreme Court upheld the Nebraska Legislature's practice of opening each legislative day with a prayer by a chaplain. Emphasizing the historical tradition of legislative prayers and the absence of an "official seal of approval on one religious view," the Court noted that the prayers were nonsectarian and, after 1980, they contained no references to Christ. The Court also distinguished the school prayer cases, suggesting that the individuals claiming injury in *Marsh* were adults who were not subject to the same peer pressure as public school students. Is *Marsh v. Chambers* consistent with *Wallace v. Jaffree? See also Lynch v. Donnelly,* 465 U.S. 668, 104 S.Ct. 1355, 79 L.Ed.2d 604 (1984) (Créche included in city's Christmas display not violative of Establishment Clause).

Relying on the *Marsh* and *Lynch* decisions, one federal court of appeals held that invocations and benedictions at voluntary graduation ceremonies, as a general matter, do not violate the Establishment Clause:

> To prohibit entirely the tradition of invocations at graduation exercises while sanctioning the tradition of invocations for judges, legislators and public officials does not appear to be a consistent application of the principle of equal liberty of conscience.
>
> Furthermore, unlike classroom prayer, ceremonial invocations and benedictions present less opportunity for religious indoctrination of peer pressure. The potential for coercion in the prayer opportunity was one of the distinctions employed by the Court in *Marsh* to separate legislative prayer from classroom prayer . . . Although children are obviously attending the ceremony, the public nature of the proceeding and the usual presence of parents act as a buffer against religious coercion. In addition, the graduation context does not implicate the special nature of the teacher-student relationship—a relationship that focuses on the transmission of knowledge and values by an authority figure.

Stein v. Plainwell Community School, 822 F.2d 1406, 1409 (6th Cir. 1987). *But see Jager v. Douglas County Sch. Dist.,* 862 F.2d 824 (11th Cir. 1989) (*Marsh* inapplicable; invocations at football games violate *Lemon* test). On the other hand, the Sixth Circuit found that the specific invocations and benedictions under review did violate the *Marsh* standard:

> The invocations and benedictions . . . are framed and phrased so that they "symbolically place the government's seal of approval on one religious view"—the Christian view. They employ the language of Christian theology and prayer. Some expressly invoke the name of Jesus as the Savior. They are not the "civil" invocations or benedictions used in public legislative and judicial sessions as described in *Marsh.*

Stein, supra at 1410. *See also Weisman v. Lee,* 908 F.2d 1090 (1st Cir. 1990). *Compare Steele v. Van Buren Public School Dist.,* 845 F.2d 1492 (8th Cir. 1988) (prayers at mandatory band rehearsals and performances) and *Doe v. Aldine Independent School Dist.,* 563 F.Supp. 883 (S.D. Tex. 1982) (prayer sung to music at athletic contests, pep rallies and graduation ceremonies). *See generally* Vile, "Religious Expression in High School Valedictory Addresses: *Guidy v. Calcasieu Parish School Board,* 53 *Educ. L. Rep.* [1051] (1989).

Has the Sixth Circuit implicitly adopted the interpretation of the Establishment Clause urged by Chief Justice Rehnquist in his dissent in *Wallace*? Is it sufficient that the invocation or benediction is nondenominational and nonsectarian? What if adherents to non-Western religions are present? Is *Stein* an Establishment Clause or a Free Exercise case? Are the distinctions drawn by the *Stein* court persuasive? *See generally* Dean, "Ceremonial Invocations at Public High School Events and the Establishment Clause," 16 *Fla. St. L. Rev.* 1001 (1989).

Are the courts saying that "a little bit of . . . establishment" is fine? Laycock, *supra* at 8. Consider what Professor Laycock has to say about this approach:

> With respect to government speech, my understanding of neutrality is as rigorous as that of the most orthodox secularist. In my view, the establishment clause absolutely disables the government from taking a position for or against religion. . . .
>
> This principle explains the Supreme Court's holdings that teachers cannot lead or encourage prayer in public schools, or post the Ten Commandments on the bulletin board. The Court should have applied the same principle to its other cases. It should not have held that chaplains can open each meeting of a state legislature with prayer, or that municipalities can erect Christmas displays. These decisions are wholly unprincipled and indefensible. A little bit of government support for religion may be only a little bit of establishment, but it is still an establishment. The government should not put "In God We Trust" on coins; it should not open court sessions with "God save the United States and this honorable Court"; and it should not name a city or a naval vessel for the Body of Christ or the Queen of the Angels. Perhaps religious minorities should not waste political capital on minor violations such as these. But neither should the Supreme Court legitimate such violations.

> I mention these views to make clear that my support for the Equal Access Act and my tolerance for properly conducted moments of silence do not stem from any view that the religious right's desire for government support should be modestly indulged. The reason to allow equal access or moments of silence is not that they are acceptably small deviations from neutrality. Rather, they are strictly neutral.

Laycock *supra* at 7–9.

5. *Alternatives to Prayer and Moments of Silence*

Would it be constitutional after *Schempp* and *Wallace* "to allow a different student to begin each class with a philosophical recitation that he or she either composes or chooses," with equal dignity being given to messages affirming religion, atheism, satan worship, or secular humanism? *See*, Loewy, "School Prayer, Neutrality, and the Open Forum: Why We Don't Need a Constitutional Amendment," 61 *N. Car. L. Rev.* 141 (1982). *Cf. Jager v. Douglas County Sch. Dist.*, 862 F.2d 824, 834 (11th Cir. 1989). What if school officials prohibited the satanic messages?

Suppose a school district simply made classrooms available before or after school or during recess for various student groups of different religious, philosophical, and political orientations.

2. Evolution and Creationism. Though presaged by the work of other scientists, one of the most profound changes in scientific paradigms occurred in 1895 with the publication of Charles Darwin's *Origin of the Species*. The central concept was natural selection, the theory that "the fittest survive and spread their favored traits through populations." S.J. Gould, *Ever Since Darwin* 40 (1977). Darwin concluded that evolution had occurred and that natural selection was the mechanism by which it had occurred. *Id.* at 44. While his earlier work was suggestive, in the early 1870s he extended the theory, often called the theory of evolution, to human beings and the human mind. *Id.* at 25. *See* C. Darwin, *Descent of Man* (1871); C. Darwin, *The Expression of the Emotions in Man and Animals* (1872). By the 1880s some form of the evolution theory was accepted by nearly all American naturalists. *See* Larson, *Trial and Error* 8 (1985).

Darwin himself insisted only that "organic change led only to increasing adaptation between organisms and their own environment," but some scientists and most lay people equate evolution with biological progress, with descent from a lower, less intelligent order to a higher order. Gould, *supra* at 37. This theory of a continuity with nature—our descent from apes if you will—challenged the uniqueness of human beings and their place in the universe. As Professor Gould has stated, "the differences between adult chimps and people are not trifling, but they do not arise from any difference in kind." *Id.* at 51. Such notions were profoundly disturbing in the nineteenth century, particularly in terms of religious beliefs. They continue to be so today: "[T]he Western world has yet to make its peace with Darwin and the implications of evolutionary theory." *Id.* at 50.

There have been many efforts to reconcile post-Darwinian science with religion. *See, e.g.*, Kass, "Evolution and the Bible," *Commentary* (Nov. 1988) at 29. But most people tend to perceive a fundamental conflict between descent through natural selection and design by the Creator. *Id.* As Kass has described the conflict:

> . . . [M]ost people tend to see the first chapters of Genesis and the theory of evolution as irreconcilable. On one side, we have scientists and philosophers of science who hold that the teaching of evolution has made "plumb unbelievable" the teachings of the book of Genesis, especially about the special status of man. . . . On the other side, we have Protestant fundamentalists, who, taking the same view of the challenge, declare the teachings of evolution to be false. No longer content just citing chapter and verse, some of them would like to prove it scientifically. In recent decades, they have given birth to a new movement, so-called "creation science" or "scientific creationism," which aims both to embarrass and refute the theory of evolution and to find scientific evidence supporting the account of the origins of the world, life, and man provided by their own particular reading of Scripture.

Id. See Carter, "Evolution, Creationism, and Treating Religion as a Hobby," 1987 *Duke L. J.* 977. Professor Phillip E. Johnson has urged that the orthodox scientific attack on creationism is based on "a theory of *naturalistic* evolution which means that it absolutely rules out any miraculous or supernatural intervention at any point." Johnson, "Evolution as Dogma: The Establishment of Naturalism," *First Things*, Oct. 1990, at 15, 16. Johnson views this philosophical judgment as highly debatable. He also questions the empirical support for Darwinism, characterizing the "fossil record" as "hostile to a Darwinist interpretation" in "important respects." *Id.*

The conflict between revelation and reason has manifested itself in controversies and lawsuits over what will be taught in the public schools, for the contestants view the public schools as a primary battleground for the minds of the young. *See generally* Larson, *supra;* D. Nelkin, *Science Textbook Controversies and the Politics of Equal Time* (1977). By the 1920s, the most widely used biology textbook for high school students (Hunter, A *Civic Biology* (1914)) contained sections on heredity and evolution, and science teachers largely embraced Darwinist thinking in their biology courses. *See* Gelfand, "Of Monkeys and Men—An Atheist's Heretical View of the Constitutionality of Teaching the Disproof of a Religion in the Public Schools," 16 *J. L. & Educ.* 271, 277–78 (1987). Perhaps the most famous example is the Tennessee "monkey law," prohibiting the teaching of the theory that human beings evolved from other species. *Scopes v. State,* 154 Tenn. 105, 289 S.W. 363 (1927). *See* Kalven, "A Commemorative Case Note: *Scopes v. State,* 27 *Chi. L. Rev.* 505 (1960). John Scopes had lectured from the Hunter textbook and he was fined for violating Tennessee law. Gelfand, *supra* at 278–79. The leading protagonists in the eight-day trial—a spectacular media event—were Clarence Darrow and William Jennings Bryan. The Tennessee Supreme Court upheld the anti-evolution law, but reversed Scopes' conviction on the ground that the jury and not the judge should have imposed the $100 fine. Gelfand, *supra* at 280. *See generally* Larson, *supra.* The trial of Scopes was later turned into the widely praised dramatic film, "Inherit the Wind," starring Spencer Tracy and Frederic March.

In the years after *Scopes,* biology textbooks, particularly in the South, began to play down or omit evolution, prompting one commentator to say that "Darrow had won the battle, but the South had won the war." Gelfand, *supra* at 281. In the post-World War II period, however, textbook publishers again embraced evolution. Gelfand, *supra* at 282. Thus, more than forty years after *Scopes,* the United States Supreme Court confronted a similar state statute in *Epperson v. Arkansas,* 393 U.S. 97, 89 S.Ct. 266, 21 L.Ed.2d 228 (1968). Relying on the school prayer cases, the Court in *Epperson* declared the Arkansas anti-evolution law unconstitutional under the Establishment Clause:

> The overriding fact is that Arkansas' law selects from the body of knowledge a particular segment which it proscribes for the sole reason that it is deemed to conflict with a particular religious doctrine; that is, with a particular interpretation of the Book of Genesis by a particular religious group. . . .
>
> * * *
>
> No suggestion has been made that Arkansas' law may be justified by considerations of state policy other than the religious views of some of its citizens. It is clear that fundamentalist sectarian conviction was and is the law's reason for existence. . . .

393 U.S. at 107, 89 S.Ct. at 272. The Court declined to reach the question as to whether the teacher's alleged right to pursue his profession or to express himself in the classroom had been violated.

Justice Black concurred in the result in *Epperson* on the ground that the Arkansas law was unconstitutionally vague, but he expressed strong reservations about the majority's approach:

> A . . . question that arises for me is whether this Court's decision forbidding a State to exclude the subject of evolution from its schools infringes the religious freedom of those who consider evolution an antireligious doctrine. If the theory is considered antireligious, as the Court indicates, how can the State be bound by the Federal Constitution to permit its teachers to advocate such an "antireligious" doctrine to school children? The very cases cited by the Court as supporting its conclusion hold that the State must be neutral. . . . [D]oes not the removal of the subject of evolution leave the State in a neutral position . . . ?
>
> I am also not ready to hold that a person hired to teach school children takes with him into the classroom a constitutional right to teach sociological, economic, political, or religious subjects that the school's managers do not want discussed. . . .
>
> I question whether it is absolutely certain . . . that "academic freedom" permits a teacher to breach his contractual agreement to teach only the subjects designated by the school authorities who hired him.

393 U.S. at 113, 89 S.Ct. at 275.

Justice Stewart also concurred in the *Epperson* result, but he found a violation of the First Amendment:

> It is one thing for a State to determine that "the subject of higher mathematics, or astronomy, or biology" shall or shall not be included in its public school curriculum. It is quite another thing for a State to make it a criminal offense for a public school teacher so much as to mention the very existence of an entire system of respected human thought.

393 U.S. at 116, 89 S.Ct. at 276. *See generally* Goldstein, "The Asserted Constitutional Right of Public School Teachers to Determine What They Teach," 124 *U. Pa. L. Rev.* 1293 (1976); Van Alstyne, "The Constitutional Rights of Teachers and Professors," 1970 *Duke L. J.* 841.

Four years after *Epperson*, a federal district court confronted the question of whether the teaching of the theory of evolution in public schools, while ignoring the biblical account of human creation, itself evidenced a hostility to religion and the establishment of a religion of secular humanism. The court held that it did not:

> [T]he offending material is peripheral to the matter of religion. Science and religion necessarily deal with many of the same questions, and they may frequently provide conflicting answers. But . . . it is not the business of government to suppress real or imagined attacks upon a particular religious doctrine. . . . Teachers of science in the public schools should not be expected to avoid the discussion of every scientific issue on which some religion claims expertise.

Wright v. Houston Indep. Sch. Dist., 366 F.Supp. 1208, 1211 (S.D. Tex. 1972), *aff'd*, 486 F.2d 137 (5th Cir. 1973), *cert. denied*, 417 U.S. 969, 94 S.Ct. 3173, 41 L.Ed.2d 1140 (1974). *But see* Carter, *supra*.

Edwards v. Aguillard

482 U.S. 578, 107 S.Ct. 2573, 96 L.Ed.2d 510 (1987).

Justice Brennan delivered the opinion of the Court.

The question for decision is whether Louisiana's "Balanced Treatment for Creation-Science and Evolution-Science in Public School Instruction" Act (Creationism Act), La.Rev.Stat.Ann. §§ 17:286.1–17:286.7 (West 1982), is facially invalid as violative of the Establishment Clause of the First Amendment.

I

The Creationism Act forbids the teaching of the theory of evolution in public schools unless accompanied by instruction in "creation science." § 17:286.4A. No school is required to teach evolution or creation science. If either is taught, however, the other must also be taught. *Ibid.* The theories of evolution and creation science are statutorily defined as "the scientific evidences for [creation or evolution] and inferences from those scientific evidences." §§ 17.286.3(2) and (3).

Appellees, who include parents of children attending Louisiana public schools, Louisiana teachers, and religious leaders, challenged the constitutionality of the Act in District Court, seeking an injunction and declaratory relief.[1] Appellants, Louisiana officials charged with implementing the Act, defended on the ground that the purpose of the Act is to protect a legitimate secular interest, namely, academic freedom. Appellees attacked the Act as facially invalid because it violated the Establishment Clause. . . .

II

The Establishment Clause forbids the enactment of any law "respecting an establishment of religion." The Court has applied a three-pronged test to determine whether legislation comports with the Establishment Clause. First, the legislature must have adopted the law with a secular purpose. Second, the statute's principal or primary effect must be one that neither advances nor inhibits religion. Third, the statute must not result in an excessive entanglement of government with religion. *Lemon v. Kurtzman*, 403 U.S. 602, 612–13, 91 S.Ct. 2105, 2111, 29 L.Ed.2d 745 (1971). State action violates the Establishment Clause if it fails to satisfy any of these prongs.

* * *

The Court has been particularly vigilant in monitoring compliance with the Establishment Clause in elementary and secondary schools. Families entrust public schools with the education of their children, but condition their trust on the understanding that the classroom will not purposely be used to advance religious views that may conflict with the private beliefs of the student and his or her family. Students in such institutions are impressionable and their attendance is involuntary. . . . The State exerts great authority and coercive power through mandatory attendance requirements, and because of the

1. Appellants, the Louisiana Governor, the Attorney General, the State Superintendent, the State Department of Education and the St. Tammany Parish School Board, agreed not to implement the Creationism Act pending the final outcome of this litigation. . . .

students' emulation of teachers as role models and the children's susceptibility to peer pressure.[5] . . .

* * *

III

Lemon's first prong focuses on the purpose that animated adoption of the Act. "The purpose prong of the *Lemon* test asks whether government's actual purpose is to endorse or disapprove of religion." *Lynch v. Donnelly*, 465 U.S. 668, 690, 104 S.Ct. 1355, 1368, 79 L.Ed.2d 604 (1984) (O'Connor, J., concurring). A governmental intention to promote religion is clear when the State enacts a law to serve a religious purpose. This intention may be evidenced by promotion of religion in general, see *Wallace v. Jaffree, supra*, 472 U.S. at 52–53, 105 S.Ct., at 2488 (Establishment Clause protects individual freedom of conscience "to select any religious faith or none at all"), or by advancement of a particular religious belief, *e.g., Stone v. Graham, supra*, 449 U.S., at 41, 101 S.Ct., at 194 (invalidating requirement to post Ten Commandments, which are "undeniably a sacred text in the Jewish and Christian faiths") (footnote omitted); *Epperson v. Arkansas, supra*, 393 U.S., at 106, 89 S.Ct., at 271 (holding that banning the teaching of evolution in public schools violates the First Amendment since "teaching and learning" must not "be tailored to the principles or prohibitions of any religious sect or dogma"). If the law was enacted for the purpose of endorsing religion, "no consideration of the second or third criteria [of *Lemon*] is necessary." *Wallace v. Jaffree, supra*, 472 U.S., at 56, 105 S.Ct., at 2490. In this case, the petitioners have identified no clear secular purpose for the Louisiana Act.

True, the Act's stated purpose is to protect academic freedom. La.Rev.Stat.Ann. § 17:286.2 (West 1982). This phrase might, in common parlance, be understood as referring to enhancing the freedom of teachers to teach what they will. The Court of Appeals, however, correctly concluded that the Act was not designed to further that goal. We find no merit in the State's argument that the "legislature may not [have] use[d] the terms 'academic freedom' in the correct legal sense. They might have [had] in mind, instead, a basic concept of fairness; teaching all of the evidence." . . . Even if "academic freedom" is read to mean "teaching all of the evidence" with respect to the origin of human beings, the Act does not further this purpose. The goal of providing a more comprehensive science curriculum is not furthered either by outlawing the teaching of evolution or by requiring the teaching of creation science.

* * *

It is clear from the legislative history that the purpose of the legislative sponsor, Senator Bill Keith, was to narrow the science curriculum. During the legislative hearings, Senator Keith stated: "My preference would be that neither [creationism nor evolution] be taught." . . . Such a ban on teaching does not promote—indeed, it undermines—the provision of a comprehensive scientific education.

It is equally clear that requiring schools to teach creation science with evolution does not advance academic freedom. The Act does not grant teachers a flexibility that they did not already possess to supplant the present science curriculum with the presentation of theories, besides evolution, about the origin of life. Indeed, the Court of Appeals found that no law prohibited Louisiana public schoolteachers from teaching any scientific theory. 765 F.2d, at 1257. As the president of the Louisiana Science Teachers Association testified, "[a]ny scientific concept that's based on established fact can be included in our curriculum already, and no legislation allowing this is necessary." . . . The Act provides Louisiana schoolteachers with no new authority. Thus the stated purpose is not furthered by it.

The Alabama statute held unconstitutional in *Wallace v. Jaffree, supra*, is analogous. In *Wallace*, the State characterized its new law as one designed to provide a one-minute period for meditation. We rejected that stated purpose as insufficient, because a previously adopted Alabama law already provided for such a one-minute period. Thus, in this case, as in *Wallace*, "[a]ppellants have not identified any secular purpose that was not fully served by [existing

5. The potential for undue influence is far less significant with regard to college students who voluntarily enroll in courses. . . . Thus, for instance, the Court has not questioned the authority of state colleges and universities to offer courses on religion or theology. *See Widmar v. Vincent*, 454 U.S. 263, 271, 102 S.Ct. 269, 275, 70 L.Ed.2d 440 (1981) (Powell, J.); *id.*, at 281, 102 S.Ct., at 280 (Stevens, J., concurring in judgment).

state law] before the enactment of [the statute in question]." 472 U.S., at 59, 105 S.Ct., at 2491.

Furthermore, the goal of basic "fairness" is hardly furthered by the Act's discriminatory preference for the teaching of creation science and against the teaching of evolution.[7] While requiring that curriculum guides be developed for creation science, the Act says nothing of comparable guides for evolution. La.Rev.Stat.Ann. § 17:286.7A (West 1982). Similarly, research services are supplied for creation science but not for evolution. § 17:286.7B. Only "creation scientists" can serve on the panel that supplies the resource services. *Ibid.* The Act forbids school boards to discriminate against anyone who "chooses to be a creation-scientist" or to teach "creationism," but fails to protect those who choose to teach evolution or any other noncreation science theory, or who refuse to teach creation science. § 17:286.4C.

If the Louisiana legislature's purpose was solely to maximize the comprehensiveness and effectiveness of science instruction, it would have encouraged the teaching of all scientific theories about the origins of humankind. But under the Act's requirements, teachers who were once free to teach any and all facets of this subject are now unable to do so. Moreover, the Act fails even to ensure that creation science will be taught, but instead requires the teaching of this theory only when the theory of evolution is taught. Thus we agree with the Court of Appeals' conclusion that the Act does not serve to protect academic freedom, but has the distinctly different purpose of discrediting "evolution by counterbalancing its teaching at every turn with the teaching of creation science. . . ." 765 F.2d, at 1257.

* * *

As in *Stone* and *Abington*, we need not be blind in this case to the legislature's preeminent religious purpose in enacting this statute. There is a historic and contemporaneous link between the teachings of certain religious denominations and the teaching of evolution.[9] It was this link that concerned the Court in *Epperson v. Arkansas*, 393 U.S. 97, 89 S.Ct. 266, 21 L.Ed.2d 228 (1968), which also involved a facial challenge to a statute regulating the teaching of evolution. In that case, the Court reviewed an Arkansas statute that made it unlawful for an instructor to teach evolution or to use a textbook that referred to this scientific theory. Although the Arkansas anti-evolution law did not explicitly state its predominant religious purpose, the Court could not ignore that "[t]he statute was a product of the upsurge of 'fundamentalist' religious fervor" that has long viewed this particular scientific theory as contradicting the literal interpretation of the Bible. . . .[10] After reviewing the history of anti-evolution statutes, the Court determined that "there can be no doubt that the motivation from the [Arkansas] law was the same [as other anti-evolution statutes]: to suppress the teaching of a theory which, it was thought, 'denied' the divine creation of man." *Id.*, at 109, 89 S.Ct., at 273. The Court found that there can be no legitimate state interest in protecting particular religions from scientific views "distasteful to them," . . . and concluded "that the First Amendment does not permit the State to require that teaching and learning must be tailored to the principles or prohibitions of any religious sect or dogma," *id.*, at 106, 89 S.Ct., at 271.

These same historic and contemporaneous antagonisms between the teachings of certain religious denominations and the teaching of evolution and present in this case. The preeminent purpose of the Louisiana legislature was clearly to advance the religious viewpoint that a supernatural being created humankind.[11] The term "creation science" was defined as embracing this particular religious doctrine by those responsible for the passage of the Crea-

7. The Creationism Act's provisions appear among other provisions prescribing the courses of study in Louisiana's public schools. These other provisions, similar to those in other states, prescribe courses of study in such topics as driver training, civics, the Constitution, and free enterprise. None of these other provisions, apart from those associated with the Creationism Act, nominally mandates "equal time" for opposing opinions within a specific area of learning. *See, e.g.*, La.Rev.Stat.Ann. §§ 17:261–17:281 (West 1982 and Supp. 1987).

9. *See McLean v. Arkansas Bd. of Ed.*, 529 F.Supp. 1255, 1258–64 (ED Ark.1982) (reviewing historical and contemporary antagonisms between the theory of evolution and religious movements).

10. The Court evaluated the statute in light of a series of anti-evolution statutes adopted by state legislatures dating back to the Tennessee statute that was the focus of the celebrated *Scopes* trial in 1927. *Epperson v. Arkansas*, 393 U.S., at 98, 101, n. 8, and 109, 89 S.Ct., at 267, 269, n. 8, and 273. The Court found the Arkansas statute comparable to this Tennessee "monkey law," since both gave preference to " 'religious establishments which have as one of their tenets or dogmas the instantaneous creation of man.' " *Id.*, at 103, n. 11, 89 S.Ct., at 270, n. 11 (quoting *Scopes v. State*, 154 Tenn. 105, 126, 289 S.W. 363, 369 (1927) (Chambliss, J., concurring)).

11. While the belief in the instantaneous creation of humankind by a supernatural creator may require the rejection of every aspect of the theory of evolution, an individual instead may choose to accept some or all of this scientific theory as compatible with his or her spiritual outlook. . . .

tionism Act. Senator Keith's leading expert on creation science, Edward Boudreaux, testified at the legislative hearings that the theory of creation science included belief in the existence of a supernatural creator. . . . Senator Keith also cited testimony from other experts to support the creation-science view that "a creator [was] responsible for the universe and everything in it."[13] . . .

The legislative history therefore reveals that the term "creation science," as contemplated by the legislature that adopted this Act, embodies the religious belief that a supernatural creator was responsible for the creation of humankind.

Furthermore, it is not happenstance that the legislature required the teaching of a theory that coincided with this religious view. The legislative history documents that the Act's primary purpose was to change the science curriculum of public schools in order to provide persuasive advantage to a particular religious doctrine that rejects the factual basis of evolution in its entirety. The sponsor of the Creationism Act, Senator Keith, explained during the legislative hearings that his disdain for the theory of evolution resulted from the support that evolution supplied to views contrary to his own religious beliefs. According to Senator Keith, the theory of evolution was consonant with the "cardinal principle[s] of religious humanism, secular humanism, theological liberalism, aetheistism [*sic*]." . . . The state senator repeatedly stated that scientific evidence supporting his religious views should be included in the public school curriculum to redress the fact that the theory of evolution incidentally coincided with what he characterized as religious beliefs antithetical to his own. The legislation therefore sought to alter the science curriculum to reflect endorsement of a religious view that is antagonistic to the theory of evolution.

In this case, the purpose of the Creationism Act was to restructure the science curriculum to conform with a particular religious viewpoint. Out of many possible science subjects taught in the public schools, the legislature chose to affect the teaching of the one scientific theory that historically has been opposed by certain religious sects. As in *Epperson*, the legislature passed the Act to give preference to those religious groups which have as one of their tenets the creation of humankind by a divine creator. The "overriding fact" that confronted the Court in *Epperson* was "that Arkansas' law selects from the body of knowledge a particular segment which it proscribes for the sole reason that it is deemed to conflict with . . . a particular interpretation of the Book of Genesis by a particular religious group." 393 U.S., at 103, 89 S.Ct., at 270. Similarly, the Creationism Act is designed *either* to promote the theory of creation science which embodies a particular religious tenet by requiring that creation science be taught whenever evolution is taught *or* to prohibit the teaching of a scientific theory disfavored by certain religious sects by forbidding the teaching of evolution when creation science is not also taught. The Establishment Clause, however, "forbids *alike* the preference of a religious doctrine *or* the prohibition of theory which is deemed antagonistic to a particular dogma." *Id.*, at 106–07, 89 S.Ct., at 271 (emphasis added). Because the primary purpose of the Creationism Act is to advance a particular religious belief, the Act endorses religion in violation of the First Amendment.

We do not imply that a legislature could never require that scientific critiques of prevailing scientific theories be taught. Indeed, the Court acknowledged in *Stone* that its decision forbidding the posting of the Ten Commandments did not mean that no use could ever be made of the Ten Commandments, or that the Ten Commandments played an exclusively religious role in the history of Western Civilization. 449 U.S., at 42, 101 S.Ct., at 194. In a similar way, teaching a variety of scientific theories about the origins of humankind to schoolchildren might be validly done with the clear secular intent of enhancing the effectiveness of science instruction. But because the primary purpose of the Creationism Act is to endorse a particular religious doctrine, the Act furthers religion in violation of the Establishment Clause.

IV

Appellants contend that genuine issues of material fact remain in dispute, and therefore the District Court erred in granting summary judgment. . . .

13. Senator Keith believed that creation science embodied this view: "One concept is that a creator however you define a creator was responsible for everything that is in this world. The other concept is that it just evolved." . . . Besides Senator Keith, several of the most vocal legislators also revealed their religious motives for supporting the bill in the official legislative history. . . .

In this case, appellees' motion for summary judgment rested on the plain language of the Creationism Act, the legislative history and historical context of the Act, the specific sequence of events leading to the passage of the act, the State Board's report on a survey of school superintendents, and the correspondence between the Act's legislative sponsor and its key witnesses. Appellants contend that affidavits made by two scientists, two theologians, and an education administrator raise a genuine issue of material fact and that summary judgment was therefore barred. The affidavits define creation science as "origin through abrupt appearance in complex form" and allege that such a viewpoint constitutes a true scientific theory.

* * *

We agree with the lower courts that these affidavits do not raise a genuine issue of material fact. The existence of "uncontroverted affidavits" does not bar summary judgment. Moreover, the postenactment testimony of outside experts is of little use in determining the Louisiana legislature's purpose in enacting this statute. The Louisiana legislature did hear and rely on scientific experts in passing the bill,[17] but none of the persons making the affidavits produced by the appellants participated in or contributed to the enactment of the law or its implementation. The District Court, in its discretion, properly concluded that a Monday-morning "battle of the experts" over possible technical meanings of terms in the statute would not illuminate the contemporaneous purpose of the Louisiana legislature when it made the law. We therefore conclude that the District Court did not err in finding that appellants failed to raise a genuine issue of material fact, and in granting summary judgment.[20]

V

The Louisiana Creationism Act . . . violates the Establishment Clause of the First Amendment because it seeks to employ the symbolic and financial support of government to achieve a religious purpose. The judgment of the Court of Appeals therefore is

Affirmed.

Justice Powell, with whom Justice O'Connor joins, concurring.

I write separately to note certain aspects of the legislative history, and to emphasize that nothing in the Court's opinion diminishes the traditionally broad discretion accorded state and local school officials in the selection of the public school curriculum.

* * *

Even though I find Louisiana's Balanced Treatment Act unconstitutional, I adhere to the view "that the States and locally elected school boards should have the responsibility for determining the educational policy of the public schools." *Board of Education v. Pico,* 457 U.S. 853, 893, 102 S.Ct. 2799, 2822, 73 L.Ed.2d 435 (1982) (Powell, J., dissenting). A decision respecting the subject matter to be taught in public schools does not violate the Establishment Clause simply because the material to be taught " 'happens to coincide or harmonize with the tenets of some or all religions.' " *Harris v. McRae,* 448 U.S. 297, 319, 100 S.Ct. 2671, 2689, 65 L.Ed.2d 784 (1980) (quoting *McGowan v. Maryland,* 366 U.S. 420, 442, 81 S.Ct. 1101, 1113, 6 L.Ed.2d 393 (1961)). . . .

* * *

As a matter of history, school children can and should properly be informed of all aspects of this Nation's religious heritage. I would see no constitutional problem if school children were taught the nature of the Founding Father's religious beliefs and how these beliefs affected the attitudes of the times and the structure of our government. Courses in comparative religion of course are customary and constitutionally appropriate. In fact, since religion permeates our history, a familiarity with the nature of religious beliefs is necessary to understand many historical as well as contemporary events. In addition, it is worth noting that the Establishment Clause does not prohibit *per se* the educational use of re-

---

17. The experts, who were relied upon by the sponsor of the bill and the legislation's other supporters, testified that creation science embodies the religious view that there is a supernatural creator of the universe. . . .

20. Numerous other Establishment Clause cases that found state statutes to be unconstitutional have been disposed of without trial. *E.g., Larkin v. Grendel's Den, Inc.,* 459 U.S. 116, 103 S.Ct. 505, 74 L.Ed.2d 297 (1982); *Lemon v. Kurtzman,* 403 U.S. 602, 91 S.Ct. 2105, 29 L.Ed.2d 745 (1971); *Engel v. Vitale,* 370 U.S. 421, 82 S.Ct. 1261, 8 L.Ed.2d 601 (1962).

ligious documents in public school education. Although this Court has recognized that the Bible is "an instrument of religion," *Abington School District v. Schempp, supra,* 374 U.S., at 224, 83 S.Ct., at 1573, it also has made clear that the Bible "may constitutionally be used in an appropriate study of history, civilization, ethics, comparative religion, or the like." *Stone v. Graham,* 449 U.S., at 42, 101 S.Ct., at 194 (citing *Abington School Dist. v. Schempp, supra,* 374 U.S., at 225, 83 S.Ct., at 1572). The book is, in fact, "the world's all-time best seller" with undoubted literary and historic value apart from its religious content. The Establishment Clause is properly understood to prohibit the use of the Bible and other religious documents in public school education only when the purpose of the use is to advance a particular religious belief.

* * *

In sum, I find that the language and the legislative history of the Balanced Treatment Act unquestionably demonstrate that its purpose is to advance a particular religious belief. Although the discretion of state and local authorities over public school curricula is broad, "the First Amendment does not permit the State to require that teaching and learning must be tailored to the principles or prohibitions of any religious sect or dogma." *Epperson v. Arkansas,* 393 U.S., at 106, 89 S.Ct., at 271. Accordingly, I concur in the opinion of the Court and its judgment that the Balanced Treatment Act violates the Establishment Clause of the Constitution.

Justice White, concurring in the judgment. [Opinion omitted]

Justice Scalia, with whom the Chief Justice joins, dissenting.

Even if I agreed with the questionable premise that legislation can be invalidated under the Establishment Clause on the basis of its motivation alone, without regard to its effects, I would still find no justification for today's decision. The Louisiana legislators who passed the "Balanced Treatment for Creation-Science and Evolution-Science Act" (Balanced Treatment Act), La.Rev.Stat.Ann. §§ 17:286.1–17:286.7 (West 1982), each of whom had sworn to support the Constitution, were well aware of the potential Establishment Clause problems and considered that aspect of the legislation with great care. After seven hearings and several months of study, resulting in substantial revision of the original proposal, they approved the Act overwhelmingly and specifically articulated the secular purpose they meant it to serve. Although the record contains abundant evidence of the sincerity of that purpose (the only issue pertinent to this case), the Court today holds, essentially on the basis of "its visceral knowledge regarding what *must* have motivated the legislators," 778 F.2d 225, 227 (CA5 1985) (Gee, J., dissenting) (emphasis added), that the members of the Louisiana Legislature knowingly violated their oaths and then lied about it. I dissent. Had requirements of the Balanced Treatment Act that are not apparent on its face been clarified by an interpretation of the Louisiana Supreme Court, or by the manner of its implementation, the Act might well be found unconstitutional; but the question of its constitutionality cannot rightly be disposed of on the gallop, by impugning the motives of its supporters.

I

This case arrives here in the following posture: The Louisiana Supreme Court has never been given an opportunity to interpret the Balanced Treatment Act, State officials have never attempted to implement it, and it has never been the subject of a full evidentiary hearing. We can only guess at its meaning. We know that it forbids instruction in either "creation-science" or "evolution-science" without instruction in the other, § 17:286.4A, but the parties are sharply divided over what creation science consists of. Appellants insist that it is a collection of educationally valuable scientific data that has been censored from classrooms by an embarrassed scientific establishment. Appellees insist it is not science at all but thinly veiled religious doctrine. Both intrepretations of the intended meaning of that phrase find considerable support in the legislative history.

At least at this stage in the litigation, it is plain to me that we must accept appellants' view of what the statute means. To begin with, the statute itself *defines* "creation-science" as "the *scientific evidences* for creation and inferences from those *scientific evidences.*" § 17:286.3(2) (emphasis added). If, however, that definition is not thought sufficiently helpful, the means by which the Louisiana Supreme Court will give the term more precise content is quite clear—and again, at this stage in the litigation, favors the appellants' view. "Creation science" is unquestionably a "term of art," . . . and thus, under Louisiana law, is "to be interpreted according to [its] received meaning and acceptation with the learned in the art, trade or profession to which [it] refer[s]." La.Civ. Code Ann., Art. 15 (West 1952). The only evidence in the record of the "received meaning and acceptation" of "creation science" is found in five affidavits filed by appellants. In those affidavits, two scientists, a philosopher, a theologian, and an educator, all of whom claim extensive knowledge of creation science, swear that it is essentially a collection of scientific data supporting the theory that the physical universe and life within it appeared suddenly and have not changed substantially since appearing. . . . These experts insist that creation science is a strictly scientific concept that can be presented without religious reference. . . . At this point, then, we must assume that the Balanced Treatment Act does *not* require the presentation of religious doctrine.

Nothing in today's opinion is plainly to the contrary, but what the statute means and what it requires are of rather little concern to the Court. Like the Court of Appeals, 765 F.2d 1251, 1253, 1254 (CA5 1985), the Court finds it necessary to consider only the motives of the legislators who supported the Balanced Treatment Act . . . After examining the statute, its legislative history, and its historical and social context, the Court holds that the Louisiana Legislature acted without "a secular legislative purpose" and that the Act therefore fails the "purpose" prong of the three-part test set forth in *Lemon v. Kurtzman*, 403 U.S. 602, 612, 91 S.Ct. 2105, 2111, 29 L.Ed.2d 2105 (1971). . . . I doubt whether that "purpose" requirement of *Lemon* is a proper interpretation of the Constitution; but even if it were, I could not agree with the Court's assessment that the requirement was not satisfied here.

* * *

Nevertheless, a few principles have emerged from our cases, principles which should, but to an unfortunately large extent do not, guide the Court's application of *Lemon* today. It is clear, first of all, that regardless of what "legislative purpose" may mean in other contexts, for the purpose of the *Lemon* test it means the "actual" motives of those responsible for the challenged action. The Court recognizes this . . . as it has in the past, *see, e.g., Witters v. Washington Dept. of Services for Blind, supra*, 474 U.S., at 486, 106 S.Ct., at 751; *Wallace v. Jaffree, supra*, 472 U.S., at 56, 105 S.Ct., at 2490. Thus, if those legislators who supported the Balanced Treatment Act *in fact* acted with a "sincere" secular purpose, . . . the Act survives the first component of the *Lemon* test, regardless of whether that purpose is likely to be achieved by the provisions they enacted.

Our cases have also confirmed that when the *Lemon* Court referred to "a secular . . . purpose," 403 U.S., at 612, 91 S.Ct., at 2111, it meant "a secular purpose." The author of *Lemon*, writing for the Court, has said that invalidation under the purpose prong is appropriate when "there [is] *no question* that the statute or activity was motivated *wholly* by religious considerations." *Lynch v. Donnelly*, 465 U.S. 668, 680, 104 S.Ct. 1355, 1362, 79 L.Ed.2d 604 (1984) (Burger, C.J.) (emphasis added). . . . Thus, the majority's invalidation of the Balanced Treatment Act is defensible only if the record indicates that the Louisiana Legislature had *no* secular purpose.

It is important to stress that the purpose forbidden by *Lemon* is the purpose to "advance religion." 403 U.S., at 613, 91 S.Ct., at 2111. . . . Our cases in no way imply that the Establishment Clause forbids legislators merely to act upon their religious convictions. We surely would not strike down a law providing money to feed the hungry or shelter the homeless if it could be demonstrated that, but for the religious beliefs of the legislators, the funds would not have been approved. Also, political activism by the religiously motivated is part of our heritage. Notwithstanding the majority's implication to the contrary, . . . we do not presume that the sole purpose of a law is to advance religion merely because it was supported strongly by organized religions or by adherents of particular faiths. . . .

To do so would deprive religious men and women of their right to participate in the political process. Today's religious activism may give us the Balanced Treatment Act, but yesterday's resulted in the abolition of slavery, and tomorrow's may bring relief for famine victims.

Similarly, we will not presume that a law's purpose is to advance religion merely because it " 'happens to coincide or harmonize with the tenets of some or all religions,' " *Harris v. McRae, supra*, at 319, 100 S.Ct., at 2689 (quoting *McGowan v. Maryland*, 366 U.S. 420, 442, 81 S.Ct. 1101, 1113, 6 L.Ed.2d 393 (1961)), or because it benefits religion, even substantially. . . .

Thus, the fact that creation science coincides with the beliefs of certain religions, a fact upon which the majority relies heavily, does not itself justify invalidation of the Act.

Finally, our cases indicate that even certain kinds of governmental actions undertaken with the specific intention of improving the position of religion do not "advance religion" as that term is used in *Lemon*. 403 U.S., at 613, 91 S.Ct., at 2111. Rather, we have said that in at least two circumstances government *must* act to advance religion, and that in a third it *may* do so.

First, since we have consistently described the Establishment Clause as forbidding not only state action motivated by the desire to *advance* religion, but also that intended to "disapprove," "inhibit," or evince "hostility" toward religion. . . .

Thus, if the Louisiana Legislature sincerely believed that the State's science teachers were being hostile to religion, our cases indicate that it could act to eliminate that hostility without running afoul of *Lemon*'s purpose test.

Second, we have held that intentional governmental advancement of religion is sometimes required by the Free Exercise Clause. For example, in *Hobbie v. Unemployment Appeals Comm'n of Fla.*, 480 U.S. 136, 107 S.Ct. 1046, 94 L.Ed.2d 190 (1987); *Thomas v. Review Bd., Indiana Employment Security Div.*, 450 U.S. 707, 101 S.Ct. 1425, 67 L.Ed.2d 624 (1981); *Wisconsin v. Yoder*, 406 U.S. 205, 92 S.Ct. 1526, 32 L.Ed.2d 15 (1972); and *Sherbert v. Verner*, 374 U.S. 398, 83 S.Ct. 1790, 10 L.Ed.2d 965 (1963), we held that in some circumstances States must accommodate the beliefs of religious citizens by exempting them from generally applicable regulations. We have not yet come close to reconciling *Lemon* and our Free Exercise cases, and typically we do not really try. . . .

It is clear, however, that members of the Louisiana Legislature were not impermissibly motivated for purpose of the *Lemon* test if they believed that approval of the Balanced Treatment Act was *required* by the Free Exercise Clause.

We have also held that in some circumstances government may act to accommodate religion, even if that action is not required by the First Amendment. . . . It is well established that "[t]he limits of permissible state accommodation to religion are by no means co-extensive with the noninterference mandated by the Free Exercise Clause." *Walz v. Tax Comm'n of New York City*, 397 U.S., at 673, 90 S.Ct., at 1413; *see also Gillette v. United States*, 401 U.S. 437, 453, 91 S.Ct. 828, 838, 28 L.Ed.2d 168 (1971). We have implied that voluntary governmental accommodation of religion is not only permissible, but desirable. . . . Thus, few would contend that Title VII of the Civil Rights Act of 1964, which both forbids religious discrimination by private-sector employers, 78 Stat. 255, 42 U.S.C. § 2000e-2(a)(1), and requires them reasonably to accommodate the religious practices of their employees, § 2000e(j), violates the Establishment Clause, even though its "purpose" is, of course, to advance religion, and even though it is almost certainly not required by the Free Exercise Clause. While we have warned that at some point, accommodation may devolve into "an unlawful fostering of religion," *Hobbie v. Unemployment Appeals Comm'n of Fla., supra*, 480 U.S., at 145, 107 S.Ct., at 1051, we have not suggested precisely (or even roughly) where that point might be. It is possible, then, that even if the sole motive of those voting for the Balanced Treatment Act was to advance religion, and its passage was not actually required, or even believed to be required, by either the Free Exercise or Establishment Clauses, the Act would nonetheless survive scrutiny under *Lemon*'s purpose test.

One final observation about the application of that test: Although the Court's opinion gives no hint of it, in the past we have repeatedly affirmed "our reluctance to attribute unconstitutional motives to the States." . . . We "presume that legislatures act in a constitutional manner." . . .

With the foregoing in mind, I now turn to the purposes underlying adoption of the Balanced Treatment Act.

II

* * *

We have relatively little information upon which to judge the motives of those who supported the Act. About the only direct evidence is the statute itself and transcripts of the seven committee hearings at which it was considered. Unfortunately, several of those hearings were sparsely attended, and the legislators who were present revealed little about their motives. We have no committee reports, no floor debates, no remarks inserted into the legislative history, no statement from the Governor, and no post-enactment statements or testimony from the bill's sponsor or any other legislators. . . . Nevertheless, there is ample evidence that the majority is wrong in holding that the Balanced Treatment Act is without secular purpose.

At the outset, it is important to note that the Balanced Treatment Act did not fly through the Louisiana Legislature on wings of fundamentalist religious fervor—which would be unlikely, in any event, since only a small minority of the State's citizens belong to fundamentalist religious denominations. . . . The Act had its genesis (so to speak) in legislation introduced by Senator Bill Keith in June 1980. After two hearings before the Senate Committee on Education, Senator Keith asked that his bill be referred to a study commission composed of members of both houses of the Louisiana Legislature. He expressed hope that the joint committee would give the bill careful consideration and determine whether his arguments were "legitimate." . . . The committee met twice during the interim, heard testimony (both for and against the bill) from several witnesses, and received staff reports. Senator Keith introduced his bill again when the legislature reconvened. The Senate Committee on Education held two more hearings and approved the bill after substantially amending it (in part over Senator Keith's objection). After approval by the full Senate, the bill was referred to the House Committee on Education. That committee conducted a lengthy hearing, adopted further amendments, and sent the bill on to the full House, where it received favorable consideration. The Senate concurred in the House amendments and on July 20, 1981, the Governor signed the bill into law.

Senator Keith's statements before the various committees that considered the bill hardly reflect the confidence of a man preaching to the converted. He asked his colleagues to "keep on open mind" and not to be "biased" by misleading characterizations of creation science. . . . He also urged them to "look at this subject on its merits and not on some preconceived idea." . . .

Senator Keith's reception was not especially warm. Over his strenuous objection, the Senate Committee on Education voted 5-1 to amend this bill to deprive it of any force; as amended, the bill merely gave teachers *permission* to balance the teaching of creation science or evolution with the other. . . . The House Committee restored the "mandatory" language to the bill by a vote of only 6–5, . . . and both the full House (by vote of 52–35) . . . and full Senate (23–15) . . . had to repel further efforts to gut the bill.

The legislators understood that Senator Keith's bill involved a "unique" subject, . . . and they were repeatedly made aware of its potential constitutional problems. . . . Although the Establishment Clause, including its secular purpose requirement, was of substantial concern to the legislators, they eventually voted overwhelmingly in favor of the Balanced Treatment Act: The House approved it 71–19 (with 15 members absent), . . . the Senate 26–12 (with all members present). . . . The legislators specifically designated the protection of "academic freedom" as the purpose of the Act. La.Rev.Stat. [Ann.] § 17:286.2 (West 1982). We cannot accurately assess whether this purpose is a "sham," . . . until we first examine the evidence presented to the legislature far more carefully than the Court has done.

Before summarizing the testimony of Senator Keith and his supporters, I wish to make clear that I by no means intend to endorse its accuracy. But my views (and the views of this Court) about creation science and evolution are (or should be) beside the point. Our task is not to judge the debate about teaching the origins of life, but to ascertain what the members of the Louisiana Legislature believed. The vast majority of them voted to approve a bill which explicitly stated a secular purpose; what is crucial is not their *wisdom* in believing that purpose would be achieved by the bill, but their *sincerity* in believing it would be.

Most of the testimony in support of Senator Keith's bill came from the Senator himself and from scientists and educators he presented, many of whom enjoyed academic credentials that may have been regarded as quite impressive by members of the Louisiana Legislature. To a substantial extent, their testimony was devoted to lengthy, and, to the layman, seemingly expert scientific expositions on the origin of life. . . .

These scientific lectures touched upon, *inter alia*, biology, paleontology, genetics, astronomy, astrophysics, probability analysis, and biochemistry. The witnesses repeatedly assured committee members that "hundreds and hundreds" of highly respected, internationally renowned scientists believed in creation science and would support their testimony. . . .

Senator Keith and his witnesses testified essentially as set forth in the following numbered paragraphs:

(1) There are two and only two scientific explanations for the beginning of life—evolution and creation science. . . . Both are bona fide "sciences." . . .

Both posit a theory of the origin of life and subject that theory to empirical testing. Evolution posits that life arose out of inanimate chemical compounds and has gradually evolved over millions of years. Creation science posits that all life forms now on earth appeared suddenly and relatively recently and have changed little. Since there are only two possible explanations of the origin of life, any evidence that tends to disprove the theory of evolution necessarily tends to prove the theory of creation science, and vice versa. For example, the abrupt appearance in the fossil record of complex life, and the extreme rarity of transitional life forms in that record, are evidence for creation science. . . .

(2) The body of scientific evidence supporting creation science is as strong as that supporting evolution. In fact, it may be *stronger*. . . .

The evidence for evolution is far less compelling than we have been led to believe. Evolution is not a scientific "fact," since it cannot actually be observed in a laboratory. Rather, evolution is merely a scientific theory or "guess." . . .

It is a very bad guess at that. The scientific problems with evolution are so serious that it could accurately be termed a "myth." . . .

(3) Creation science is educationally valuable. Students exposed to it better understand the current state of scientific evidence about the origin of life. . . . Those students even have a better understanding of evolution. . . . Creation science can and should be presented to children without any religious content. . . .

(4) Although creation science is educationally valuable and strictly scientific, it is now being censored from or misrepresented in the public schools. . . . Evolution, in turn, is misrepresented as an absolute truth. . . . Teachers have been brainwashed by an entrenched scientific establishment composed almost exclusively of scientists to whom evolution is like a "religion." These scientists discriminate against creation scientists so as to prevent evolution's weaknesses from being exposed. . . .

(5) The censorship of creation science has at least two harmful effects. First, it deprives students of knowledge of one of the two scientific explanations for the origin of life and leads them to believe that evolution is proven fact; thus, their education suffers and they are wrongly taught that science has proven their religious beliefs false. Second, it violates the Establishment Clause. The United States Supreme Court has held that secular humanism is a religion. . . . Belief in evolution is a central tenet of that religion. . . .

Thus, by censoring creation science and instructing students that evolution is fact, public school teachers are *now* advancing religion in violation of the Establishment Clause. . . .

Senator Keith repeatedly and vehemently denied that his purpose was to advance a particular religious doctrine. At the outset of the first hearing on the legislation, he testified, "We are not going to say today that you should have some kind of religious instructions in our schools. . . . We are not talking about religion today. . . . I am not proposing that we take the Bible in each science class and read the first chapter of Genesis." . . . At a later hearing, Senator Keith stressed that "to . . . teach religion and disguise it as creationism . . . is not my intent. My intent is to see to it that our textbooks are not censored." . . .

We have no way of knowing, of course, how many legislators believed the testimony of Senator Keith and his witnesses. But in the absence of evidence to the contrary,[4] we have to assume that many of them did. Given that assumption, the Court today plainly errs in holding that the Louisiana Legislature passed the Balanced Treatment Act for exclusively religious purposes.

Even with nothing more than this legislative history to go on, I think it would be extraordinary to invalidate the Balanced Treatment Act for lack of a valid secular purpose. Striking down a law approved by the democratically elected representatives of the people is no minor matter. . . . If history were silent or ambiguous about the existence of a secular purpose—and here it is not—the statute should survive *Lemon*'s purpose test. But even more validation than mere legislative history is present here. The Louisiana Legislature explicitly set forth its secular purpose ("protecting academic freedom") in the very text of the Act. La.Rev.Stat. [Ann.] § 17:286.2 (West 1982). We have in the past repeatedly relied upon or deferred to such expressions. . . .

The Court seeks to evade the force of this expression of purpose by stubbornly misinterpreting it, and then finding that the provisions of the Act do not

4. Although appellees and *amici* dismiss the testimony of Senator Keith and his witnesses as pure fantasy, they did not bother to submit evidence of that to the District Court, making it difficult for us to agree with them. The State, by contrast, submitted the affidavits of two scientists, a philospher, a theologian, and an educator, whose academic credentials are rather impressive. . . .

advance that misinterpreted purpose, thereby showing it to be a sham. . . .

Had the Court devoted to this central question of the meaning of the legislatively expressed purpose a small fraction of the research into legislative history that produced its quotations of religiously motivated statements by individual legislators, it would have discerned quite readily what "academic freedom" meant: *students'* freedom from *indoctrination*. The legislature wanted to ensure that students would be free to decide for themselves how life began, based upon a fair and balanced presentation of the scientific evidence—that is, to protect "the right of each [student] voluntarily to determine what to believe (and what not to believe) free of any coercive pressures from the State." *Grand Rapids School District v. Ball*, 473 U.S., at 385, 105 S.Ct., at 3224. The legislature did not care *whether* the topic of origins was taught; it simply wished to ensure that *when* the topic was taught, students would receive " 'all of the evidence.' ". . .

As originally introduced, the "purpose" section of the Balanced Treatment Act read: "This Chapter is enacted for the purposes of protecting academic freedom . . . *of students* . . . and assisting *students* in their search for truth." . . . Among the proposed findings of fact contained in the original version of the bill was the following: "Public school instruction in only evolution-science . . . *violates the principle of academic freedom because it denies students a choice between scientific models and instead indoctrinates them in evolution science alone.*" . . .

Senator Keith unquestionably understood "academic freedom" to mean "freedom from indoctrination." . . .

If one adopts the obviously intended meaning of the statutory terms "academic freedom," there is no basis whatever for concluding that the purpose they express is a "sham." . . . To the contrary, the Act pursues that purpose plainly and consistently. . . . The Louisiana legislators had been told repeatedly that creation scientists were scorned by most educators and scientists, who themselves had an almost religious faith in evolution. It is hardly surprising, then, that in seeking to achieve a balanced, "non-indoctrinating" curriculum, the legislators protected from discrimination only those teachers whom they thought were *suffering* from discrimination. (Also, the legislators were undoubtedly aware of *Epperson v. Arkansas*, 393 U.S. 97, 89 S.Ct. 266, 21 L.Ed.2d 228 (1968), and thus could quite reasonably have concluded that discrimination against evolutionists was already prohibited.) The two provisions respecting the development of curriculum guides are also consistent with "academic freedom" as the Louisiana Legislature understood the term. Witnesses had informed the legislators that, because of the hostility of most scientists and educators to creation science, the topic had been censored from or badly misrepresented in elementary and secondary school texts. In light of the unavailability of works on creation science suitable for classroom use . . . and the existence of ample materials on evolution, it was entirely reasonable for the Legislature to conclude that science teachers attempting to implement the Act would need a curriculum guide on creation science, but not on evolution, and that those charged with developing the guide would need an easily accessible group of creation scientists. Thus, the provisions of the Act of so much concern to the Court *support* the conclusion that the Legislature acted to advance "academic freedom."

The legislative history gives ample evidence of the sincerity of the Balanced Treatment Act's articulated purpose. Witness after witness urged the legislators to support the Act so that students would not be "indoctrinated" but would instead be free to decide for themselves, based upon a fair presentation of the scientific evidence, about the origin of life. . . .

* * *

It is undoubtedly true that what prompted the Legislature to direct its attention to the misrepresentation of evolution in the schools (rather than the inaccurate presentation of other topics) was its awareness of the tension between evolution and the religious beliefs of many children. But even appellees concede that a valid secular purpose is not rendered impermissible simply because its pursuit is prompted by concern for religious sensitivities. . . . If a history teacher falsely told her students that the bones of Jesus Christ had been discovered, or a physics teacher that the Shroud of Turin had been conclusively established to be inexplicable on the basis of natural causes, I cannot believe (despite the majority's implication to the contrary . . .) that legislators or school board members would be constitutionally prohibited from taking corrective action, simply because that action was prompted by concern for the religious beliefs of the misinstructed students.

In sum, even if one concedes, for the sake of argument, that a majority of the Louisiana Legislature voted for the Balanced Treatment Act partly in order to foster (rather than merely eliminate discrimination against) Christian fundamentalist beliefs, our cases establish that that alone would not suffice to invalidate the Act, so long as there was a genuine secular purpose as well. We have, moreover, no adequate basis for disbelieving the secular purpose set forth in the Act itself, or for concluding that it is a sham enacted to conceal the legislators' violation of their oaths of office. I am astonished by the Court's unprecedented readiness to reach such a conclusion, which I can only attribute to an intellectual predisposition created by the facts and the legend of *Scopes v. State*, 154 Tenn. 105, 289 S.W. 363 (1927)—an instinctive reaction that any governmentally imposed requirements bearing upon the teaching of evolution must be a manifestation of Christian fundamentalist repression. . . .

Since the existence of secular purpose is so entirely clear, and thus dispositive, I will not go on to discuss the fact that, even if the Louisiana Legislature's purpose were exclusively to advance religion, some of the well established exceptions to the impermissibility of that purpose might be applicable—the validating intent to eliminate a perceived discrimination against a particular religion, to facilitate its free exercise, or to accommodate it. . . . I am not in any case enamored of those amorphous exceptions, since I think them no more than unpredictable correctives to what is . . . a fundamentally unsound rule. It is surprising, however, that the Court does not address these exceptions, since the context of the legislature's action gives some reason to believe they may be applicable.[6]

Because I believe that the Balanced Treatment Act had a secular purpose, which is all the first component of the *Lemon* test requires, I would reverse the judgment of the Court of Appeals and remand for further consideration.

III

I have to this point assumed the validity of the *Lemon* "purpose" test. In fact, however, I think the pessimistic evaluation that the Chief Justice made of the totality of *Lemon* is particularly applicable to the "purpose" prong: it is "a constitutional theory [that] has no basis in the history of the amendment it seeks to interpret, is difficult to apply and yields unprincipled results." *Wallace v. Jaffree*, 472 U.S., at 112, 105 S.Ct., at 2519 (Rehnquist, J., dissenting).

Our cases interpreting and applying the purpose test have made such a maze of the Establishment Clause that even the most conscientious governmental officials can only guess what motives will be held unconstitutional. We have said essentially the following: Government may not act with the purpose of advancing religion, except when forced to do so by the Free Exercise Clause (which is now and then); or when eliminating existing governmental hostility to religion (which exists sometimes); or even when merely accommodating governmentally uninhibited religious practices, except that at some point (it is unclear where) intentional accommodation results in the fostering of religion, which is of course unconstitutional. . . .

But the difficulty of knowing what vitiating purpose one is looking for is as nothing compared with the difficulty of knowing how or where to find it. For while it is possible to discern the objective "purpose" of a statute (*i.e.*, the public good at which its provisions appear to be directed), or even the formal motivation for a statute where that is explicitly set forth (as it was, to no avail, here), discerning the subjective motivation of those enacting the statute is, to be honest, almost always an impossible task. The number of possible motivations, to begin with, is not binary, or indeed even finite. In the present case, for example, a particular legislator need not have voted for the Act either because he wanted to foster religion or because he wanted to improve education. He may have thought the bill would provide jobs for his district, or may have wanted to make amends with a faction of his party he had alienated on another vote, or he may have been a close friend of the bill's sponsor, or he may have been repaying a favor he owed the Majority Leader, or he may have hoped the Governor would appreciate his vote and make a fundraising appearance

6. As the majority recognizes, . . . Senator Keith sincerely believed that "secular humanism is a bona fide religion," . . . and that "evolution is the cornerstone of that religion." . . . The Senator even told his colleagues that this Court had "held" that secular humanism was a religion. . . . (In *Torcaso v. Watkins*, 367 U.S. 488, 495, n. 11, 81 S.Ct. 1680, 1684, n. 11, 6 L.Ed.2d 982 (1961), we did indeed refer to "Secular Humanism" as a "religio[n].") Senator Keith and his supporters raised the "religion" of secular humanism *not*, as the majority suggests, to explain the source of their "disdain for the theory of evolution," . . . but to convince the Legislature that the State of Louisiana was *violating the Establishment Clause* because its teachers were misrepresenting evolution as fact and depriving students of the information necessary to question that theory. . . . The Senator repeatedly urged his colleagues to pass his bill to *remedy* this Establishment Clause violation by ensuring state neutrality in religious matters, . . . surely a permissible purpose under *Lemon*. Senator Keith's argument may be questionable, but nothing in the statute or its legislative history gives us reason to doubt his sincerity or that of his supporters.

for him, or he may have been pressured to vote for a bill he disliked by a wealthy contributor or by a flood of constituent mail, or he may have been seeking favorable publicity, or he may have been reluctant to hurt the feelings of a loyal staff member who worked on the bill, or he may have been settling an old score with a legislator who opposed the bill, or he may have been mad at his wife who opposed the bill, or he may have been intoxicated and utterly *un*motivated when the vote was called, or he may have accidentally voted "yes" instead of "no," or, of course, he may have had (and very likely did have) a combination of some of the above and many other motivations. To look for *the sole purpose* of even a single legislator is probably to look for something that does not exist.

Putting that problem aside, however, where ought we to look for the individual legislator's purpose? We cannot of course assume that every member present (if, as is unlikely, we know who or even how many they were) agreed with the motivation expressed in a particular legislator's pre-enactment floor or committee statement. Quite obviously, "[w]hat motivates one legislator to make a speech about a statute is not necessarily what motivates scores of others to enact it." *United States v. O'Brien*, 391 U.S. 367, 384, 88 S.Ct. 1673, 1683, 20 L.Ed.2d 672 (1968). Can we assume, then, that they all agree with the motivation expressed in the staff-prepared committee reports they might have read—even though we are unwilling to assume that they agreed with the motivation expressed in the very statute that they voted for? Should we consider post-enactment floor statements? Or post-enactment testimony from legislators, obtained expressly for the lawsuit? Should we consider media reports on the realities of the legislative bargaining? All of these sources, of course, are eminently manipulable. Legislative histories can be contrived and sanitized, favorable media coverage orchestrated, and post-enactment recollections conveniently distorted. Perhaps most valuable of all would be more objective indications—for example, evidence regarding the individual legislators' religious affiliations. And if that, why not evidence regarding the fervor or tepidity of their beliefs?

Having achieved, through these simple means, an assessment of what individual legislators intended, we must still confront the question (yet to be addressed in any of our cases) how *many* of them must have the invalidating intent. If a state senate approves a bill by vote of 26 to 25, and only one of the 26 intended solely to advance religion, is the law unconstitutional? What if 13 of the 26 had that intent? What if 3 of the 26 had the impermissible intent, but 3 of the 25 voting against the bill were motivated by religious hostility or were simply attempting to "balance" the votes of their impermissibly motivated colleagues? Or is it possible that the intent of the bill's sponsor is alone enough to invalidate it—on a theory, perhaps, that even though everyone else's intent was pure, what they produced was the fruit of a forbidden tree?

Because there are no good answers to these questions, this Court has recognized from Chief Justice Marshall, *see Fletcher v. Peck*, 6 Cranch 87, 130, 3 L.Ed. 162 (1810), to Chief Justice Warren, *United States v. O'Brien*, *supra*, 391 U.S. at 383–84, 88 S.Ct. at 1682–83, that determining the subjective intent of legislators is a perilous enterprise. *See also Palmer v. Thompson*, 403 U.S. 217, 224–25, 91 S.Ct. 1940, 1944–45, 29 L.Ed.2d 438 (1971); *Epperson v. Arkansas*, 393 U.S., at 113, 89 S.Ct., at 275 (Black, J., concurring). It is perilous, I might note, not just for the judges who will very likely reach the wrong result, but also for the legislators who find that they must assess the validity of proposed legislation—and risk the condemnation of having voted for an unconstitutional measure—not on the basis of what the legislation contains, nor even on the basis of what they themselves intend, but on the basis of what *others* have in mind.

Given the many hazards involved in assessing the subjective intent of governmental decisionmakers, the first prong of *Lemon* is defensible, I think, only if the text of the Establishment Clause demands it. That is surely not the case. The Clause states that "Congress shall make no law respecting an establishment of religion." One could argue, I suppose, that any time Congress acts with the *intent* of advancing religion, it has enacted a "law respecting an establishment of religion"; but far from being an unavoidable reading, it is quite an unnatural one. . . .

It is, in short, far from an inevitable reading of the Establishment Clause that it forbids all governmental action intended to advance religion; and if not inevitable, any reading with such untoward consequences must be wrong.

* * *

NOTES AND QUESTIONS

1. Religious Purpose

Was the Louisiana law requiring the balanced treatment of creationism and evolution in public schools enacted for the purpose of endorsing religion? Is there a difference between simple suppression of evolution and a requirement that creationism be taught if evolution is taught? In this regard, consider these remarks by Professor Carter:

> These [fundamentalist Christian] parents, very devout and very worried, are trying to protect the core of their own beliefs. It is not that the parents want the public schools to proselytize in their favor; it is rather that they do not want the schools to press their own children to reject what the parents believe by calling into question a central article of their faith. The response of the Christian fundamentalist to evolutionary theory may thus be more consistently viewed as a reaction to a fear of indoctrination: religion demands one intellectual position, and the state seeks to command another. . . . The creationist parents . . . deny the right of the state to tell their children that their worldview is wrong.

Carter, "Evolutionism, Creationism, and Treating Religion as a Hobby," 1987 *Duke L. J.* 977, 981. If Professor Carter is right, is the purpose of the Louisiana law to advance religion or to accommodate it? Does a purpose to accommodate itself render the law unconstitutional? *See generally* Johnson, "Concepts and Compromise in First Amendment Religious Doctrine," 72 *Calif. L. Rev.* 817 (1984). What does Justice Scalia have to say about this point?

Suppose that in *Wisconsin v. Yoder, supra* at chapter 1, the Amish parents had persuaded the Wisconsin legislature to require a course in public schools with Amish children that emphasized the evils of modern technology and the joys of the simple farm life. Would such a law violate the Establishment Clause? Does the *Yoder* decision suggest that fundamentalist Christians in Louisiana would have had a greater likelihood of success if they had simply challenged the teaching of evolution on free exercise grounds and not sought legislative approval of a balanced curriculum? *But see Mozert v. Hawkins County Board of Education, infra. But cf. Employment Division, Department of Human Resources v. Smith,* ___ U.S. ___, 110 S.Ct. 1595 (1990). Is *Yoder* inconsistent with *Epperson* and *Edwards*? *See* Gelfand, "Of Monkeys and Men—An Atheist's Heretical View of the Constitutionality of Teaching the Disproof of a Religion in the Public Schools," 16 *J. Law & Educ.* 271 (1987). What if fundamentalist parents simply had sought to exempt their children from classes in which evolution was taught? *But see Smith v. Board of School Commissioners of Mobile County, infra. See generally* Laycock, "The Remnants of Free Exercise," 1990 *Sup. Ct. Rev.*—; Gelfand, *supra*; Lines, "Scientific Creationism in the Classroom: A Constitutional Dilemma," 28 *Loy. L. Rev.* 35 (1982).

Does Justice Scalia, in his dissent, identify a secular purpose for the Louisiana statute? Or does he reject the purpose test in Establishment Clause cases? To take his examples, would laws designed to feed the hungry and house the homeless be unconstitutional if they were motivated, at least in part, by religious convictions? Laws against pornography? *See* Carter, *supra*. Is creationism distinguishable from these examples? Is Justice Scalia actually focusing on effects while the majority is focusing on purpose? Why should a law that does not significantly advance religion be unconstitutional because of the motives behind its enactment? Is the religious purpose itself a violation of the Constitution?

Justice Scalia challenges the notion that legislative motivation can be or should be determined. Is motivation difficult to discern in this case? If courts were limited to examining the face of the law only, would the balanced treatment law be constitutional under the effects test? What of the fact that the law focuses on the scientific evidence for the competing theories and not just the statement of conflicting beliefs? *See* Dhooge, "From *Scopes* to *Edwards*: The Sixty-Year Evolution of Biblical Creationism in the Public School Classroom," 22 *U. Rich. L. Rev.* 187, 210–11 (1988).

2. *Science and Religion*

Is the problem in *Edwards* that creationism is "bad science?" Carter, *supra* at 980. Is it? *See* Leedes, "Monkeying Around with the Establishment Clause and Bashing Creation-Science," 22 *U. Rich. L. Rev.* 149 (1988). If it is "bad science," does this fact strengthen the majority's conclusion that the Balanced Treatment Act was motivated by a desire to advance religion? *See* Dhooge, *supra* at 222. Or does it suggest that the Court is more concerned with preserving rational discourse, setting aside revelation masquerading as science? *See* Carter, *supra* at 984. Consider these remarks by one commentator:

> This reliance [in creation science] upon supernatural intervention is entirely different from the reliance of modern science upon principles of natural law. Explanations such as those relied upon by creation-scientists which depend upon the whimsical operation and intervention of forces external to the universe which are not guided or explainable by reference to natural law are not scientific.

Dhooge, *supra* at 223–24. Do you agree? See Johnson, "Evolution as Dogma: The Establishment of Nationalism," *First Things*, Oct. 1990, at 15. Are creation-scientists suggesting that there are forces beyond the universe? That the order of the universe is whimsical? Is the discourse of creation science irrational? *See* Carter, *supra*; Leedes, *supra*. Must Darwinists deny the possibility of supernatural intervention? Suppose Louisiana teachers were required to subject creationism and evolution to "objective, critical examination." Would that feature of the law render it constitutional? *See* Lines, *supra*. *See also* Choper, "Church, State and the Supreme Court: Current Controversy," 29 *Ariz. L. Rev.* 551, 557 (1987). May Louisiana decide that children should learn revealed truth as well as rational and reflective truth? Or, to qualify as education, must the curriculum foster "an open-minded, rigorous, and precise search for truth"? Morris, "Fundamentalism, Creationism and the First Amendment," 41 *Educ. L. Rep.* [1], [20] (1988).

Is the problem that public schools cannot be neutral as to religion while cultivating science and reason? *See generally* Laycock, "Formal, Substantive, and Disaggregated Neutrality Toward Religion," 39 *DePaul L. Rev.* 993 (1990). Is there an inconsistency between the cultivation of the analytical powers of future citizens and respect for individual autonomy with respect to religious beliefs? *See* Carter, *supra*. Why is balanced treatment of competing theories not a manifestation of neutrality? *See generally* Emerson & Haber, "The *Scopes* Case in Modern Dress, 27 *U. Chi. L. Rev.* 522, 527 (1960).

3. Academic Freedom

What did the Louisiana legislature mean when it said that the balanced treatment law advanced academic freedom? Did it mean academic freedom for the teacher or the student? Does academic freedom mean "freedom from indoctrination?" *See generally* Yudof, "Three Faces of Academic Freedom," 32 *Loy. L. Rev.* 831, 846–50 (1987). May a teacher be dismissed for devoting excessive time to creationism and too little time to evolution? *See Dale v. Board of Education*, 316 N.W.2d 108 (S.D. 1982).

4. Evolution: Truth in Packaging

Suppose a state enacted a law requiring that textbooks treating evolution insert a disclaimer that evolution is only a theory and not a scientific fact. Would such a law violate the Establishment Clause? *See Daniel v. Waters*, 515 F.2d 485 (6th Cir. 1975). *See generally* Note, "*Edwards v. Aguillard*: Creation Science and Evolution—The Fall of Balanced Treatment Acts in the Public Schools," 25 *San Diego L. Rev.* 829 (1988).

3. Secular Humanism. With the successful constitutional attacks on school prayer, moments of silence, and laws designed to prohibit the teaching of evolution or to introduce creationism, fundamentalist Christian parents perceived a rampant secularism in public schools, a secularism for which the courts were partially responsible. They initiated lawsuits that focused on the perceived hostility of public schools to their religious beliefs. *See generally* McCarthy, "Secular Humanism and Education," 19 *J. of Law & Educ.* 467 (1990); Dent, "Religious Children, Secular Schools," 61 *So. Cal. L. Rev.* 863 (1988). These plaintiffs relied on the school prayer cases: "[T]he State may not establish a 'religion of secularism' in the sense of affirmatively opposing or showing hostility to religion, thus preferring those who believe in no religion over those who do believe." *School District of Abington v. Schempp*, 374 U.S. 203, 225, 83 S.Ct. 1560, 1573, 10 L.Ed.2d 844 (1963) (quoting *Zorach v. Clauson*, 343 U.S. 306, 314, 72 S.Ct. 679, 683, 96 L.Ed. 954 (1952). *See also Epperson v. Arkansas*, 393 U.S. 97, 104, 89 S.Ct. 266, 270, 21 L.Ed.2d 228 (1968); *Engel v. Vitale*, 370 U.S. 421, 434, 82 S.Ct. 1261, 1268, 8 L.Ed.2d 601 (1962). Their arguments took two forms. First, public school authorities had violated the Establishment Clause by establishing a religion of secular humanism, for "nontheistic faiths, including Secular Humanism, can be religious for First Amendment purposes." Dent, *supra* at 867–77, citing *Torcaso v. Watkins*, 367 U.S. 488, 495, n.11, 81 S.Ct. 1680, 1684, n.11, 6 L.Ed.2d 982 (1961) (dicta). The remedy is to eliminate the texts or practices that create the unlawful establishment—just as school prayers were prohibited. *See* Dent, *supra* at 920.

Second, they argued that the dominant secular humanism in public schools manifested a hostility to religion in violation of the Free Exercise Clause. If this claim succeeded, the children of fundamentalist Christians would be exempted from reading texts or participating in activities that undermined their religious beliefs. *See* Dent, *supra* at 922. *But see* Strossen, " 'Secular Humanism' and 'Scientific Creationism': Proposed Standards for Reviewing Curricular Decisions Affecting Students' Religious

Freedom," 47 *Ohio St. L. J.* 333 (1986). *But cf. Employment Division, Department of Human Resources v. Smith,* ___ U.S. ___, 110 S.Ct. 1595 (1990). This relief would be analogous to the partial exemption granted to Amish children in *Wisconsin v. Yoder*, 406 U.S. 205, 92 S.Ct. 1526, 32 L.Ed.2d 15 (1972) and to state statutes granting exemptions from sex education courses. *See* T. van Geel, *The Courts and American Education Law* 181–185 (1987).

There is no authoritative definition of secular humanism, and many people may hold secular humanist beliefs without so identifying them. Note, "Secular Humanism, the Establishment Clause, and Public Education," 61 *N.Y.U. L. Rev.* 1149, 1153 (1986). The most commonly identified elements are these: regard for the rational individual, ethics based on individual choice, denial of the relevance of a deity, "the determination of truth through free inquiry," religious skepticism, the importance of science and technology, the need for moral education, and the separation of church and state. Note, *supra* at 1154–56 (1986). The basic conflict between the fundamentalist Christian worldview and modern secularism has been aptly described by Professor Dent in these terms:

> Fundamentalists tend to accept the literal truth of some religious text, to reject theories of evolution in favor of belief in a theistic creation, to insist that morals must derive from religion and that a person cannot be moral without religion, to believe that God dictates that fathers should be the primary family breadwinners and mothers the primary nurturers of children and that parents must discipline their children and teach them religion; and to oppose, on religious grounds, abortion, homosexuality, divorce, and premarital and extramarital sex. Modernists tend to disagree with fundamentalists on each of these issues.

Dent, *supra* at 865. The fundamentalists, relying on a number of studies, argue that the hostility to their faith in the modern public school curriculum is systemic and cumulative, not simply trivial and isolated. *But see Grove v. Mead School District No.* 354, 753 F.2d 1528 (9th Cir. 1985); *Jackson v. California*, 460 F.2d 282 (9th Cir. 1972). They assert that the family is treated simply as a "group of people," that marriage and motherhood are not celebrated, that feminist values are propounded, that protestantism is excluded, and that moral relativism is the dominant philosophy. Dent, *supra* at 867–73. In turn, these claims often have been derided in the mass media, with the fundamentalists accused of a "know-nothing alarmism." Dent, *supra* at 867, citing various articles in the *New York Times* and other national publications. The vitriolic nature of the counterattack on the fundamentalist Christians has led commentators, particularly on the left, to claim that much more than the school curriculum is at stake in Establishment Clause cases:

> [A]n incredibly broad cultural spectrum, encompassing the entire center of national self-identity, has constructed creationists as a shared enemy, an "other" through which the American mainstream can identify itself as "not them." From this vantage point, the creationist movement represents ignorance, intolerance, book-burning, religious fanaticism, and similar evils.
>
> * * *
>
> But at a deeper level, the debate . . . is the symbolic face of a broader conflict over the basic terms by which social life is understood. The creationist discourse differs from the evolutionary approach precisely because it reverses the scientific representational norms of objectivity, impersonality, and neutrality. Creationism poses subjectivity, personality and interest as the significant, and legitimate, mode for understanding the world.

Peller, "Creation, Evolution, and the New South," 2 *Tikkun* 72, 75, 76 (1987).

Smith v. Board of School Commissioners of Mobile County

827 F.2d 684 (11th Cir. 1987).

Johnson, Circuit Judge:

Appellants, Alabama State Board of Education and Wayne Teague ("Board") and Malcolm Howell, et al. ("Defendant-Intervenors") appeal the district court's order enjoining the use in Alabama public schools of forty-four textbooks approved by the Board for inclusion on the State-Adopted Textbook List, the use of which the district court found to be a violation of the establishment clause of the first amendment. We reverse.

I. Background

A. Procedural History

This case is a continuation of the Alabama school prayer cases. . . . In May 1982, Ishmael Jaffree brought an action on behalf of three of his minor children pursuant to 42 U.S.C.A. § 1983 against the Mobile County School Board, various school officials, and three teachers seeking, *inter alia*, a declaratory judgment that certain classroom prayer activities conducted in the Mobile public school system violated the establishment clause of the first amendment and an injunction against classroom prayer. By his second amended complaint, Jaffree added as defendants the Governor of Alabama and other state officials, including Appellant Board, and challenged three Alabama statutes relevant to the school prayer issue as violative of the establishment clause. Douglas T. Smith and others ("Appellees") filed a motion to intervene in the Jaffree action alleging that an injunction against religious activity in the public schools would violate their right to free exercise of religion, and the district court allowed them to intervene as defendants. Subsequently, Appellees filed a motion entitled "Request for Alternate Relief" in which Appellees requested that, if an injunction were granted in favor of Jaffree, that injunction be enforced "against the religions of secularism, humanism, evolution, materialism, agnosticism, atheism and others" or, alternatively, that Appellees be allowed to produce additional evidence showing that these religions had been established in the Alabama public schools.

The district court bifurcated the claims against the Mobile County and local defendants and the claims against state officials. The district court granted Jaffree's motion for a preliminary injunction against enforcement of two of the challenged statutes, Ala.Code Ann. §§ 16–1–20.1 and 16–1–20.2, *Jaffree v. James*, 544 F.Supp. 727, 732 (S.D.Ala.1982), but determined after trial on the merits that Jaffree was not entitled to relief in either action because the Supreme Court of the United States had erred in holding that the establishment clause of the first amendment prohibits the states from establishing a religion. . . . The district court therefore dismissed Jaffree's complaint for failure to state a claim upon which relief could be granted. . . .

This Court reversed, finding that both the school room prayer activities and sections 16–1–20.1 and 16–1–20.2 violated the establishment clause. . . . The Supreme Court denied certiorari with regard to the nonstatutory school prayer practices, *Board of School Comm'rs v. Jaffree*, 466 U.S. 926, 104 S.Ct. 1707, 80 L.Ed.2d 181 (1984), and affirmed this Court's decision with regard to the statutory provisions. *Wallace v. Jaffree*, 472 U.S. 38, 105 S.Ct. 2479, 86 L.Ed.2d 29 (1985). . . .

In its opinion denying relief in *Jaffree*, the district court had stated that "[i]f the appellate courts disagree with this Court in its examination of history and conclusion of constitutional interpretation thereof, then this Court will look again at the record in this case and reach conclusions which it is not now forced to reach." *Jaffree*, 554 F.Supp. at 1129. In a footnote, the district court indicated that the issues not reached dealt with (1) the free speech rights of teachers and students who wished to pray in school and (2) the teaching of the religion of secular humanism in the schools. *Id.* at n. 41.[1] On remand, the district court issued an order in response to Jaf-

1. With regard to the secular humanism issue, the district court stated:

> It was pointed out in the testimony that the curriculum in the public schools of Mobile County is rife with efforts at teaching or encouraging secular humanism—all without opposition from any other ethic—to such an extent that it becomes a brainwashing effort. If this Court is compelled to purge "God is great, God is good, we thank Him for our daily food" from the classroom, then this Court must also purge from the classroom those things that serve to teach that salvation is through one's self rather than through a diety.

Jaffree, 554 F.Supp. at 1129 n. 41. The district court had expressed similar views on the merits of this issue in its earlier opinion granting a preliminary injunction, which was issued before Appellees had filed their "Request for Alternate Relief":

> The case law, in the opinion of the Court, has overlooked the totality of what is religion in its consideration when deciding issues under the establishment clause of the Constitution. . . . It is apparent from a reading of the decision law that the courts acknowledge that Christianity is the religion to be proscribed. . . . The religions of atheism, materialism, agnosticism, communism and socialism have escaped the scrutiny of the courts throughout the years, and make no mistake these are to the believers religions; they are ardently adhered to and quantitatively advanced in the teachings and literature that is presented to the fertile minds of the students in the various school systems. If the courts are to involve themselves in the proscription of religious activities in the schools, then it appears to this Court that we are going to have to involve ourselves in a whole host of areas, such as censoring, that we have heretofore ignored or overlooked. An example of what the Court heard reflecting on this point is in connection with the claimed use of foul language in literature read by a fourth grader and, though it might seem innocuous to some to condemn the use of the word "Goddamn" as it is used in the writings that are required reading, it can clearly be argued that as to Christianity it is blasphemy and is the establishment of an advancement of humanism, secularism or agnosticism. If the state cannot teach or advance Christianity, how can it teach or advance the Antichrist?

Jaffree, 544 F.Supp. at 732. In that opinion, the district court stated that "[i]t is common knowledge that miscellaneous doctrines such as evolution, socialism, communism, secularism, humanism, and other concepts are advanced in the public schools." *Id.* at n. 2.

free's request for attorney's fees, finding that the relief requested by Appellees had not been fully addressed in the prior decisions in the case and, therefore, remained for consideration by the district court on remand. The district court interpreted the position of the Appellees as that "if Christianity is not a permissible subject of the curriculum of the public schools, then neither is any other religion, and under the evidence introduced it is incumbent upon this Court to strike down those portions of the curriculum demonstrated to contain other religious teachings." For the purpose of considering this issue, the district court *sua sponte* realigned the parties by making Appellees parties plaintiff, consolidated the cases, and invited the parties to submit briefs in support of their positions and to petition the Court to reopen the record for the presentation of additional evidence. The district court stated that the original plaintiffs could withdraw, if they felt their position had been "fully justified," in which case the district court would consider the attorney's fees question, or could remain in the litigation, in which event the motion for attorney's fees would be denied as premature. The original plaintiffs did withdraw, and Appellees filed a position statement in which they asserted, *inter alia*, that the curriculum in the Mobile County School System unconstitutionally advanced the religion of Humanism and unconstitutionally inhibited Christianity, and that the exclusion from the curriculum of "the existence, history, contributions and role of Christianity in the United States and the world" violated their constitutional rights of equal protection, teacher and student free speech, the student's right to receive information, and teacher and student free exercise of religion.

The twelve Defendant-Intervenors, who are parents of children currently enrolled, or soon to be enrolled, in the Mobile County School System, filed a motion to intervene as defendants in the action, which was granted by the district court. The district court certified two plaintiff classes: Class A consisting of "all those persons adhering by belief and practice to a theistic religion, who are or will be teachers in the public schools of Alabama" and Class B consisting of "all those persons adhering by belief and practice to a theistic religion, who are Alabama taxpayers and who are or will be parents of children in the public schools of Alabama." Prior to trial, defendants Governor Wallace and the Mobile County board of School Commissioners agreed to entry of a consent decree in favor of Appellees.

A bench trial was held . . . with regard to Appellees' claims. Appellees' evidence focused on elementary and secondary school textbooks in the areas of history, social studies, and home economics, which were on the Alabama State Approved Textbook List, and which Appellees argued unconstitutionally established the religion of secular humanism. The district court found that use of forty-four of these textbooks violated the establishment clause of the first amendment, and permanently enjoined the use of the textbooks in the Alabama public schools. *Smith v. Board of School Comm'rs*, 655 F.Supp. 939, 988 (S.D.Ala.1987). This appeal followed.

II. Discussion

The first amendment provides in pertinent part that "Congress shall make no law respecting an establishment of religion. . . ." The district court found that secular humanism constitutes a religion within the meaning of the first amendment and that the forty-four textbooks at issue in this case both advanced that religion and inhibited theistic faiths in violation of the establishment clause. The Supreme Court has never established a comprehensive test for determining the "delicate question" of what constitutes a religious belief for purposes of the first amendment, and we need not attempt to do so in this case, for we find that, even assuming that secular humanism is a religion for purposes of the establishment clause, Appellees have failed to prove a violation of the establishment clause through the use in the Alabama public schools of the textbooks at issue in this case.

. . . The Supreme Court has developed three criteria to serve as guidelines in determining whether this barrier has been breached by challenged government action:

> First, the statute must have a secular legislative purpose; second, its principal or primary effect must be one that neither advances nor inhibits religion; finally, the statute must not foster "an excessive government entanglement with religion."

Lemon v. Kurtzman, 403 U.S. 602, 612–13, 91 S.Ct. 2105, 2111, 29 L.Ed.2d 745 (1971) (citations omitted). . . .

* * *

The parties agree that there is no question of a religious purpose or excessive government entanglement in this case and our review of the record confirms that conclusion. Our inquiry, therefore, must center on the second *Lemon* criterion: whether use of the challenged textbooks had the primary effect of either advancing or inhibiting religion.

"The effect prong [of the *Lemon* test] asks whether, irrespective of government's actual purpose, the practice under review in fact conveys a message of endorsement or disapproval." *Jaffree*, 472 U.S. at 56 n. 42, 105 S.Ct. at 2490 n. 42 (quoting *Lynch*, 465 U.S. at 690, 104 S.Ct. at 1368 (O'Connor, J., concurring)). If government identification with religion conveys such a message of government endorsement or disapproval of religion, then "a core purpose of the Establishment Clause is violated." . . . The district court found that the home economics, history, and social studies textbooks both advanced secular humanism and inhibited theistic religion. . . .

A. Home Economics Textbooks

The district court found that the home economics textbooks required students to accept as true certain tenets of humanistic psychology, which the district court found to be "a manifestation of humanism." *Smith*, 655 F.Supp. at 987. In particular, the district court found that the books "imply strongly that a person uses the same process in deciding a moral issue that he uses in choosing one pair of shoes over another,"[5] and teach that "the student must determine right and wrong based only on his own experience, feelings and [internal] values" and that "the validity of a moral choice is only to be decided by the student." *Id.* at 986.[6] The district court stated that "[t]he emphasis and overall approach implies, and would cause any reasonable thinking student to infer, that the book is teaching that moral choices are just a matter of preferences, because, as the books say, 'you are the most important person in your life.' " *Id.* The district court stated that "[t]his highly relativistic and individualistic approach constitutes the promotion of a fundamental faith claim" that "assumes that self-actualization is the goal of every human being, that man has no supernatural attributes or component, that there are only temporal and physical consequences for man's actions, and that these results, alone, determine the morality of an action." *Id.* at 986–87. According to the district court, "[t]his belief strikes at the heart of many theistic religions' beliefs that certain actions are in and of themselves immoral, *whatever the consequences*, and that, in addition, actions will have extra-temporal consequences." *Id.* at 987 (emphasis in original). The district court stated that "some religious beliefs are so fundamental that the act of denying them will completely undermine that religion" and "[i]n addition, denial of *that* belief will result in the affirmance of a contrary belief and result in the establishment of an opposing religion." *Id.* (emphasis in original). It concluded that, while the state may teach certain moral values, such as that lying is wrong, "if, in so doing it advances a reason for the rule, the possible different reasons must be explained even-handedly" and "the state may not promote one particular reason over another in the public schools." . . .

In order to violate the primary effect prong of the *Lemon* test through advancement of religion, it is not sufficient that the government action merely accommodates religion. The constitution "affirmatively mandates accommodation, not merely tolerance, of all religions, and forbids hostility towards any." *Lynch*, 465 U.S. at 672, 104 S.Ct. at 1358. Nor is it sufficient that government conduct confers an indirect, remote or incidental benefit on a religion . . . or that its effect merely happens to coincide or harmonize with the tenets of a religion:

> [T]he Establishment Clause does not ban federal or state regulation of conduct whose reason or effect merely happens to coincide or harmonize with the tenets of some or all religions. In many instances, the Congress or state legislatures conclude that the general welfare of society, wholly apart from any religious consider-

5. In support of this statement, the district court refers to a passage in one of the home economics textbooks in which the author lists the steps in the decision-making process and states that "[a]s you can see, the steps in decision-making can be applied to something as simple as buying a new pair of shoes" and "can also be applied to more complex decisions such as those which involve religious preferences; education and career choices; the use of alcohol, tobacco and drugs; and sexual habits." F. Parnell, *Homemaking Skills for Everyday Living* 26 (1984). The book lists the steps in decision-making as (1) Define the problem; (2) Establish your goals; (3) List your goals in order of importance; (4) Look for resources; (5) Study the alternatives; (6) Make a decision; (7) Carry out the decision; (8) Evaluate the results of your decision. *Id.*

6. The district court acknowledged that the textbooks do not explicitly state that the validity of a moral choice is only to be decided by the student, but found that this conclusion was implicit in the books' repetition of statements to the effect that decisions are "yours alone," or "purely personal" or that "only you can decide." *Smith*, 655 F.Supp. at 986.

> ations, demands such regulation. Thus, for temporal purposes, murder is illegal. And the fact that this agrees with the dictates of the Judeo-Christian religions while it may disagree with others does not invalidate the regulation. So too with the questions of adultery and polygamy. The same could be said of theft, fraud, etc., because those offenses were also proscribed in the Decalogue.

McGowan v. Maryland, 366 U.S. 420, 442, 81 S.Ct. 1101, 1113–14, 6 L.Ed.2d 393 (1961). . . .

In order for government conduct to constitute an impermissible advancement of religion, the government action must amount to an endorsement of religion. . . . Examination of the contents of these textbooks, including the passages pointed out by Appellees as particularly offensive, in the context of the books as a whole and the undisputedly nonreligious purpose sought to be achieved by their use, reveals that the message conveyed is not one of endorsement of secular humanism or any religion. Rather, the message conveyed is one of a governmental attempt to instill in Alabama public school children such values as independent thought, tolerance of diverse views, self-respect, maturity, self-reliance and logical decision-making. This is an entirely appropriate secular effect. Indeed, one of the major objectives of public education is the "inculcat[ion of] fundamental values necessary to the maintenance of a democratic political system." *Bethel School Dist. No. 403 v. Fraser*, 478 U.S. 675, 106 S.Ct. 3159, 3164, 92 L.Ed.2d 549 (1986) (quoting *Ambach v. Norwick*, 441 U.S. 68, 77, 99 S.Ct. 1589, 1594, 60 L.Ed.2d 49 (1979)) (brackets in original). It is true that the textbooks contain ideas that are consistent with secular humanism; the textbooks also contain ideas consistent with theistic religion. However, as discussed above, mere consistency with religious tenets is insufficient to constitute unconstitutional advancement of religion.

Nor do these textbooks evidence an attitude antagonistic to theistic belief. The message conveyed by these textbooks with regard to theistic religion is one of neutrality: the textbooks neither endorse theistic religion as a system of belief, nor discredit it. Indeed, many of the books specifically acknowledge that religion is one source of moral values[8] and none preclude that possibility. While the Supreme Court has recognized that "the State may not establish a 'religion of secularism' in the sense of affirmatively opposing or showing hostility to religion, thus 'preferring those who believe in no religion over those who do believe,' " *Abington [v. Schempp]*. . . , that Court also has made it clear that the neutrality mandated by the establishment clause does not itself equate with hostility towards religion. . . .

It is obvious that Appellees find some of the material in these textbooks offensive. That fact, however, is not sufficient to render use of this material in the public schools a violation of the establishment clause. . . .[10]

B. History and Social Studies Textbooks

The district court's conclusion that the history and social studies textbooks violated the establishment clause was based on its finding that these books failed to include a sufficient discussion of the role of religion in history and culture. The district court found that the history books omit certain historical events with religious significance and "uniformly ignore the religious aspect of most American culture." *Smith*, 655 F.Supp. at 985. The district court found that "[r]eligion, where treated at all, is generally represented as a private matter, only influencing American public life at some extraordinary moments," and that "[t]his view of religion is one humanists have been seeking to instill for fifty years." *Id.* The district court concluded that the history books "assist that effort by perpetuating an inaccurate historical picture" and held that the books "lack so many facts as to equal ideological promotion." *Id.* The district court also found that the history books "discriminate against the very concept of religion, and theistic religions in particular, by omissions so serious that a student learning history from them would not be apprised of relevant facts about America's history."

---

8. *See, e.g.*, V. Ryder, *Contemporary Living* 52 (1985); F. Parnell, *Homemaking Skills for Everyday Living* 15 (1984); J. Kelly & E. Eubanks, *Today's Teen* 26 (1981).

10. Indeed, given the diversity of religious views in this country, if the standard were merely inconsistency with the beliefs of a particular religion there would be very little that could be taught in the public schools. As Justice Jackson has stated:

> Authorities list 256 separate and substantial religious bodies to exist in the . . . United States. . . . If we are to eliminate everything that is objectionable to any of these warring sects or inconsistent with any of their doctrines, we will leave public education in shreds. Nothing but educational confusion and a discrediting of the public school system can result. . . .

McCollum v. Board of Ed., 333 U.S. 203, 235, 68 S.Ct. 461, 477, 92 L.Ed. 649 (1948) (Jackson, J., concurring).

Id. Use of the social studies books was found unconstitutional because the books failed to integrate religion into the history of American society, ignored the importance of theistic religion as an influence in American society and contained "factual inaccuracies . . . so grave as to rise to a constitutional violation." *Id.* at 985–86.

It is clear on the record of this case that, assuming one tenet of secular humanism is to downplay the importance of religion in history and in American society, any benefit to secular humanism from the failure of the challenged history and social studies books to contain references to the religious aspects of certain historical events or to adequately integrate the place of religion in modern American society is merely incidental. There is no doubt that these textbooks were chosen for the secular purpose of education in the areas of history and social studies, and we find that the primary effect of the use of these textbooks is consistent with that stated purpose. We do not believe that an objective observer could conclude from the mere omission of certain historical facts regarding religion or the absence of a more thorough discussion of its place in modern American society that the State of Alabama was conveying a message of approval of the religion of secular humanism. Indeed, the message that reasonably would be conveyed to students and others is that the education officials, in the exercise of their discretion over school curriculum, chose to use these particular textbooks because they deemed them more relevant to the curriculum, or better written, or for some other nonreligious reason found them to be best suited to their needs. *Cf. Board of Ed. v. Pico*, 457 U.S. 853, 880, 102 S.Ct. 2799, 2815, 73 L.Ed.2d 435 (1982) (Blackmun, J., concurring). . . .

Nor can we agree with the district court's conclusion that the omission of these facts causes the books to "discriminate against the very concept of religion." *Smith*, 655 F.Supp. at 985. Just as use of these books does not convey a message of governmental approval of secular humanism, neither does it convey a message of government disapproval of theistic religions merely by omitting certain historical facts concerning them.

The district court's reliance on *Epperson v. Arkansas*, 393 U.S. 97, 89 S.Ct. 266, 21 L.Ed.2d 228 (1968), to support its conclusion that omission of certain material regarding religion in this case constituted a first amendment violation is misplaced. *Epperson* involved an Arkansas statute that made it a crime to teach the theory of evolution in the public schools. *Id.* at 98, 89 S.Ct. at 266. The Supreme Court found that the law violated the establishment clause under the purpose prong of the *Lemon* test: the state forbade the teaching of evolution because it conflicted with a particular religious doctrine. 393 U.S. at 103, 89 S.Ct. at 269. The Court stated that "the First Amendment does not permit the State to require that teaching and learning must be tailored to the principles or prohibitions of any religious sect or dogma." *Id.* at 106, 89 S.Ct. at 271. Thus, "[t]he State's undoubted right to prescribe the curriculum for its public schools does not carry with it the right to prohibit, on pain of criminal penalty, the teaching of a scientific theory or doctrine *where that prohibition is based upon reasons that violate the First Amendment.*" *Id.* at 107, 89 S.Ct. at 272 (emphasis added).

There is no question in this case that the purpose behind using these particular history and social studies books was purely secular. Selecting a textbook that omits a particular topic for nonreligious reasons is significantly different from requiring the omission of material because it conflicts with a particular religious belief.[11] Further, unlike the situation in *Epperson*, which involved total exclusion of information regarding evolution from the school curriculum, Appellees in this case merely complain that the historical treatment of religion in the challenged textbooks is inadequate. Finally, the record indicates that teachers in Alabama were free to supplement the discussion contained in the textbooks in areas they found inadequate. Thus, unlike the situation in *Epperson* where the State of Arkansas had made an attempt to teach the omitted material a criminal offense, there is no active policy on the part of Alabama that prohibits teaching historical facts about religion. There simply is nothing in this record to indicate that omission of certain facts regarding re-

11. Indeed, Justice Powell has suggested that, because "the States and locally elected school boards should have the responsibility for determining the educational policy of the public schools," interference with the curriculum decisions of these authorities "is warranted only when the *purpose* for their decisions is clearly religious." *Edwards v. Aguillard*, 482 U.S. 578, 605, 107 S.Ct. 2573, 2589, 96 L.Ed.2d 510 (1987) (Powell, J., concurring) (citations omitted) (emphasis added).

ligion from these textbooks of itself constituted an advancement of secular humanism or an active hostility towards theistic religion prohibited by the establishment clause. While these textbooks may be inadequate from an educational standpoint, the wisdom of an educational policy or its efficiency from an educational point of view is not germane to the constitutional issue of whether that policy violates the establishment clause. . . .[12]

III. Conclusion

The home economics, social studies, and history textbooks at issue in this case do not violate the establishment clause of the first amendment. The district court's conclusions to the contrary reflect a misconception of the relationship between church and state mandated by the establishment clause. What is required of the states under the establishment clause is not "comprehensive identification of state with religion," but *separation* from religion. . . . Yet implicit in the district court's opinion is the assumption that what the establishment clause actually requires is "equal time" for religion.

. . . The district court's opinion in effect turns the establishment clause requirement of "lofty neutrality" on the part of the public schools into an affirmative obligation to speak about religion. Such a result clearly is inconsistent with the requirements of the establishment clause.

The judgement of the district court is reversed and the case is remanded for the sole purpose of entry by the district court of an order dissolving the injunction and terminating this litigation.

NOTES AND QUESTIONS

1. Is Secular Humanism a Religion?

Judge Johnson asserts that the Court need not reach the question of whether secular humanism is a religion. Do you agree? If you were representing the plaintiffs, would you have agreed that there was no religious purpose in the adoption of the forty-four textbooks? How can the Court determine whether the primary effect is "neutrality" or the advancement of religion without determining whether secular humanism is a religion? Or is the Court only saying that marginal benefits to a religion do not amount to a violation of the Establishment Clause? If so, is the teaching of creationism, along with evolution, only an incidental benefit? Is there any principled way to make this determination? Would the views of secular humanists or fundamentalist Christians be determinative?

Judge Hand, the trial judge in the *Jaffree* and *Smith* cases, treated secular humanism (and atheism, communism, and other ideologies) as religions, urging that they are treated as religions by believers and that they "are ardently adhered to and quantitatively advanced in the teachings and literature." *Jaffree v. James*, 544 F. Supp. 727, 732 (S.D. Ala. 1982). *See* Whitehead & Conlan, "The Establishment of the Religion of Secular Humanism and its First Amendment Implications," 10 *Tex. Tech. L. Rev.* 1 (1978). Do you agree? Is a "religion" characterized by a belief in a deity (or more than one)? Must the beliefs be similar to those of recognized religions? Must there be rituals and prayer? A sacred text? Must the beliefs "address fundamental questions" about life, death, morality, and the place of humans in the universe? *See Malnak v. Yogi*, 592 F.2d 197, 200 (3d Cir. 1979) (Adams, J., concurring). Must it offer a "comprehensive belief system" that answers those questions? *Id.* There is an extensive literature on these questions. *See, e.g.*, McCarthy, "Secular Humanism and Education," 19 *J. of Law & Educ.* 467 (1990). Pfeffer, "The 'Religion' of Secular Humanism," 29 *J. of Ch. & St.* 495 (1987); Greenawalt, "Religion as a Concept in Constitutional Law," 72 *Calif. L. Rev.* 753 (1984); Choper, "Defining 'Religion' in the First Amendment," 1982 *U. Ill. L. Rev.* 579; Note, "Secular Humanism, the Establishment Clause, and Public Education," 61 *N.Y.U. L. Rev.* 1149, 1159–68 (1986).

With regard to whether secular humanism is a religion, consider the analysis of Judge Canby, concurring in *Grove v. Mead School District No. 354*, 753 F.2d 1528, 1535 (9th Cir. 1985):

> The analytical difficulty with plaintiffs' approach is that it tends to divide the universe of value-laden thought

---

12. Appellees assert that the district court also found that the use of the challenged textbooks violated their rights to free exercise of religion and to receive information. While the district court at one point does indicate that some of the history books affected the free exercise of religion, *see Smith*, 655 F.Supp. at 985, it is clear that the district court's holding in this case was based solely on a violation of the establishment clause. Further, we find that Appellees have failed to establish a free exercise violation or impingement upon any constitutional right to receive information.

> into only two categories—the religious and the irreligious. By adopting this dualistic social outlook, and by denominating the anti-religious half of their universe as 'secular,' plaintiffs erect an insurmountable barrier to meaningful application of the establishment clause in controversies like this one. . . . The difficulty is that plaintiffs might well concede that the primary purpose and effect was secular; indeed that is precisely their point.
>
> . . . [P]laintiffs . . . are not dealing in the same linguistic currency as the Supreme Court's establishment decisions. If the establishment clause is to have any meaning, distinctions must be drawn to recognize not simply "religious" and "anti-religious," but "nonreligious" governmental activity as well. . . .
>
> * * *
>
> Even if [the disputed work may be] viewed as representative of what can fairly be characterized as "secular humanism," it remains an autobiographical novel only tangentially concerned with religion. The work "is still far removed from a comprehensive belief system laying claim to ultimate truth and supported by a formal group," . . . which the Court was prepared to concede in *Torcaso* would constitute a religion.
>
> . . . While the Supreme Court has embraced a concept of religion in the free exercise context sufficiently expansive to encompass nontheistic views, there is much to be said for the view that the definition of religion should vary with the clause under review.

Id. at 1537 (Canby, J., concurring), citing *Malnak v. Yogi, supra* at 212 (Adams, J., concurring).

Do you agree with Judge Canby? *But see* Spiro, "The Creation of a Free Marketplace of Religious Ideas: Revisiting the Establishment Clause after the Alabama Secular Humanism Decision," 39 *Ala. L. Rev.* 1 (1987). If secularism and religion are both religions within the constitutional definition, how can public schools avoid an establishment of religion? *See* Developments in the Law, "Religion and the State," 100 *Harv. L. Rev.* 1606, 1673–74 (1987) (view that secular humanism is a religion leads to "fundamental incoherence"). Does this argument suggest that the plaintiffs' complaint in *Smith* should have been framed in terms of the Free Exercise Clause? What of Judge Canby's suggestion that "religion" may mean one thing for the Establishment Clause and something quite different for the Free Exercise Clause? *See* Tribe, *American Constitutional Law* 1186–87 (2d ed. 1988). Does such a distinction maintain neutrality between religion and nonreligion? *See* Johnson, "Concepts and Compromise in First Amendment Religion Doctrine," 72 *Calif. L. Rev.* 817 (1984).

2. *Establishment of Secular Humanism?*

Judge Johnson holds that even if secular humanism is a religion, the adoption of the textbooks and their use in class do not constitute an unconstitutional establishment. *But see* Toscano, "A Dubious Neutrality: The Establishment of Secularism in the Public Schools," 1979 *B. Y. U. L. Rev.* 177 (1979). What is his basis for this holding? Is it that the promotion of beliefs that simply coincide with those of a particular religion is not enough to constitute a constitutional violation? *See* Welch, "The State as a Purveyor of Morality," 56 *Geo. Wash. L. Rev.* 540 (1988); Dent, "Religious Children, Secular Schools," 61 *So. Cal. L. Rev.* 863, 878 (1988); Developments in the Law, "Religion and the State," 100 *Harv. L. Rev.* 1606, 1669 n.151 (1987). Would laws against murder and theft constitute an establishment of religion if the contrary view were taken? Choper, "Church, State and the Supreme Court: Current Controversies," 29 *Ariz. L. Rev.* 551, 557–58 (1987). Is Judge Johnson saying that the public schools have not endorsed secular humanism? That the advocacy of self-reliance, logical decision making, and independence of thought is not the advancement of a particular faith? *See* Developments in the Law, *supra* at 1669 n.152. Are the public schools advancing secular humanism or an "American Civil Religion"? *See* Spiro, *supra* at 3, 55–63. Does it matter?

Judge Johnson states that the "textbooks [do not] evidence an attitude antagonistic to theistic belief." *See also Williams v. Board of Educ. of Kanawha County*, 388 F. Supp. 93 (S.D. W. Va. 1975). Do you agree? Is the omission of religion from the books antagonistic? How can hostility toward religion constitute an establishment of religion?

Do you agree that plaintiffs were seeking equal time for religion and not the disestablishment of secular humanism? What is the difference? What of the claim that the books manifested a preference for the values of some religions over those of others? Should public schools be constitutionally required to expose students to a variety of religious and philosophical views on metaphysical and ethical problems? *See* Spiro, *supra* at 52, 65. In this regard, consider Professor Dent's resolution of this problem:

> Preferring certain religious beliefs in the public schools is more troubling than some other governmental actions because of the conflict with freedom of consci-

> ence and the need to teach children values. Such a preference may be desirable, however, and in any case, it is inevitable for schools to prefer some values over others, which in turn favors some religions over others. The only solution to this dilemma is to abolish public schools. So long as the public schools neither promote nor disparage any specific religious dogma they should be free to teach values, even if those values conflict with some religious beliefs.

Dent, *supra* at 879–80. Viewed from this perspective, does *Smith* stand for the proposition that some injuries to religious sensitivities must be endured if there are to be public schools? Does this formulation trivialize the concerns of the fundamentalist Christians and ignore the alleged systemic bias in the textbooks and curriculum?

3. *Accommodation or Establishment?*

If a school board, anticipating litigation similar to *Smith*, removed forty-four textbooks because of their bias in favor of secular humanism, would that action be a constitutional accommodation of freedom of religion or an unconstitutional establishment of Christian fundamentalism? *See* Dent, *supra* at 919–22.

4. *Good Faith*

Is Judge Johnson, in effect, saying that if school officials make good faith educational judgments with respect to the selection of books and the shaping of the curriculum, their decisions are largely insulated from judicial review? *See Board of Educ. v. Pico*, 457 U.S. 853, 102 S.Ct. 2799, 73 L.Ed.2d 435 (1982), *infra*. *See generally* Yudof, "Library Book Selection and the Public Schools: The Quest for the Archimedean Point," 50 *Ind. L. J.* 527 (1984).

Mozert v. Hawkins County Board of Education

827 F.2d 1058 (6th Cir. 1987).

Lively, Chief Judge.

* * *

I

A

Early in 1983 the Hawkins County, Tennessee Board of Education adopted the Holt, Rinehart and Winston basic reading series (the Holt series) for use in grades 1–8 of the public schools of the county. In grades 1–4, reading is not taught as a separate subject at a designated time in the school day. Instead, the teachers in these grades use the reading texts throughout the day in conjunction with other subjects. In grades 5–8, reading is taught as a separate subject at a designated time in each class. However, the schools maintain an integrated curriculum which requires that ideas appearing in the reading programs reoccur in other courses. By statute public schools in Tennessee are required to include "character education" in their curricula. The purpose of this requirement is "to help each student develop positive values and to improve student conduct as students learn to act in harmony with their positive values and learn to become good citizens in their school, community, and society." Tennessee Code Annotated (TCA) 49-6-1007 (1986 Supp.).

Like many school systems, Hawkins County schools teach "critical reading" as opposed to reading exercises that teach only word and sound recognition. "Critical reading" requires the development of higher order cognitive skills that enable students to evaluate the material they read, to contrast the ideas presented, and to understand complex characters that appear in reading material. Plaintiffs do not dispute that critical reading is an essential skill which their children must develop in order to succeed in other subjects and to function as effective participants in modern society. Nor do the defendants dispute the fact that any reading book will do more than teach a child how to read, since reading is instrumental in a child's total development as an educated person.

The plaintiff Vicki Frost is the mother of four children, three of whom were students in Hawkins County public schools in 1983. At the beginning of the 1983–84 school year Mrs. Frost read a story in a daughter's sixth grade reader that involved mental telepathy. Mrs. Frost, who describes herself as a "born again Christian," has a religious objection to any teaching about mental telepathy. Reading further, she found additional themes in the reader to which she had religious objections. After discussing her objections with other parents, Mrs. Frost talked with the principal of Church Hill Middle School and obtained an agreement for an alternative reading program for students whose parents objected to the assigned Holt reader. The students who elected the alternative program left their classrooms during the reading sessions and worked on assignments from an older textbook series in available office or library areas. Other students in two elementary schools were excused from reading the Holt books.

B

In November 1983 the Hawkins County School Board voted unanimously to eliminate all alternative reading programs and require every student in the public schools to attend classes using the Holt series. Thereafter the plaintiff students refused to read the Holt series or attend reading classes where the series was being used. The children of several of the plaintiffs were suspended for brief periods for this refusal. Most of the plaintiff students were ultimately taught at home, or attended religious schools, or transferred to public schools outside Hawkins County. One student returned to school because his family was unable to afford alternate schooling. Even after the board's order, two students were allowed some accommodation, in that the teacher either excused them from reading the Holt stories, or specifically noted on worksheets that the student was not required to believe the stories.

. . . [T]he plaintiffs, consisting of seven families—14 parents and 17 children—filed this action pursuant to 42 U.S.C. § 1983. In their complaint the plaintiffs asserted that they have sincere religious beliefs which are contrary to the values taught or inculcated by the reading textbooks and that it is a violation of the religious beliefs and convictions of the plaintiff students to be required to read the books and a violation of the religious beliefs of the plaintiff parents to permit their children to read the books. The plaintiffs sought to hold the defendants liable because "forcing the student-plaintiffs to read school books which teach or inculcate values in violation of their religious beliefs and convictions is a clear violation of their rights to the free exercise of religion protected by the First and Fourteenth Amendments to the United States Constitution."

C

The defendants filed a motion to dismiss or, in the alternative, for summary judgment. The district court granted the defendants' motion for summary judgment, concluding that although passages in the reading textbooks might offend sincere religious beliefs of the plaintiffs, the books appeared neutral on the subject of religion and did not violate the plaintiffs' constitutional rights. *Mozert v. Hawkins County Public Schools*, 582 F.Supp. 201 (E.D.Tenn. 1984). On appeal this court reversed and remanded for further proceedings. *Mozert v. Hawkins County Public Schools*, 765 F.2d 75 (6th Cir.1985). This court concluded that summary judgment was improper because issues of material fact were present. . . .

II

A

Following remand the Commissioner of Education of the State of Tennessee was permitted to intervene as a defendant. At a pretrial hearing the parties made certain stipulations. Counsel for the defendants stipulated that the plaintiffs' religious beliefs are sincere and that certain passages in the reading texts offend those beliefs. However, counsel steadfastly refused to stipulate that the fact that the plaintiffs found the passages offensive made the reading requirement a burden on the plaintiffs' constitutional right to the free exercise of their religion. Similarly, counsel for the plaintiffs stipulated that there was a compelling state interest for the defendants to provide a public education to the children of Hawkins County. However, counsel stipulated only to a narrow definition of the compelling state interest—one that did not involve the exclusive use of a uniform series of textbooks. These stipulations left for trial the issues of whether the plaintiffs could show a burden on their free exercise right, in a constitutional sense, and whether the defendants could show a compelling interest in requiring all students in grades 1–8 of the Hawkins County public schools to use the Holt, Rinehart and Winston basal reading textbooks. These were questions of law to be determined on the basis of evidence produced at trial.

* * *

B

Vicki Frost was the first witness for the plaintiffs and she presented the most complete explanation of the plaintiffs' position. The plaintiffs do not belong to a single church or denomination, but all consider themselves born again Christians. Mrs. Frost testified that the word of God as found in the Christian Bible "is the totality of my beliefs."

. . . There was evidence that other members of their churches, and even their pastors, do not agree with their position in this case.

Mrs. Frost testified that she had spent more than 200 hours reviewing the Holt series and had found numerous passages that offended her religious beliefs. She stated that the offending materials fell into seventeen categories which she listed. These ranged from such familiar concerns of fundamentalist Christians as evolution and "secular humanism" to less familiar themes such as "futuristic supernaturalism," pacifism, magic and false views of death.

In her lengthy testimony Mrs. Frost identified passages from stories and poems used in the Holt series that fell into each category. Illustrative is her first category, futuristic supernaturalism, which she defined as teaching "Man As God." Passages that she found offensive described Leonardo da Vinci as the human with a creative mind that "came closest to the divine touch." Similarly, she felt that a passage entitled "Seeing Beneath the Surface" related to an occult theme, by describing the use of imagination as a vehicle for seeing things not discernible through our physical eyes. She interpreted a poem, "Look at Anything," as presenting the idea that by using imagination a child can become part of anything and thus understand it better. Mrs. Frost testified that it is an "occult practice" for children to use imagination beyond the limitation of scriptural authority. She testified that the story that alerted her to the problem with the reading series fell into the category of futuristic supernaturalism. Entitled "A Visit to Mars," the story portrays thought transfer and telepathy in such a way that "it could be considered a scientific concept," according to this witness. This theme appears in the testimony of several witnesses, *i.e.*, the materials objected to "could" be interpreted in a manner repugnant to their religious beliefs.

Mrs. Frost described objectionable passages from other categories in much the same way. Describing evolution as teaching that there is no God, she identified 24 passages that she considered to have evolution as a theme. She admitted that the textbooks contained a disclaimer that evolution is a theory, not a proven scientific fact. Nevertheless, she felt that references to evolution were so pervasive and presented in such a factual manner as to render the disclaimer meaningless. After describing her objection to passages that encourage children to make moral judgments about whether it is right or wrong to kill animals, the witness stated, "I thought they would be learning to read, to have good English and grammar, and to be able to do other subject work." Asked by plaintiffs' attorney to define her objection to the textbooks, Mrs. Frost replied:

> Very basically, I object to the Holt, Rhinehart [sic] Winston series as a whole, what the message is as a whole. There are some contents which are objectionable by themselves, but my most withstanding [sic] objection would be to the series as a whole.

Another witness for the plaintiffs was Bob Mozert, father of a middle school and an elementary school student in the Hawkins County system. His testimony echoed that of Vicki Frost in large part. . . . He also found objectionable passages in the readers that dealt with magic, role reversal or role elimination, particularly biographical material about women who have been recognized for achievements outside their homes, and emphasis on one world or a planetary society. Both witnesses testified under cross-examination that the plaintiff parents objected to passages that expose their children to other forms of religion and to the feelings, attitudes and values of other students that contradict the plaintiffs' religious views without a statement that the other views are incorrect and that the plaintiffs' views are the correct ones.

C

The district court held that the plaintiffs' free exercise rights have been burdened because their "religious beliefs compel them to refrain from *exposure* to the Holt series," and the defendant school board "has effectively required that the student plaintiffs either read the offensive texts or give up their free public education." *Mozert v. Hawkins County Public Schools*, 647 F.Supp. 1194, 1200 (E.D.Tenn. 1986), (emphasis added). . . .

* * *

The [district] court entered an injunction prohibiting the defendants "from requiring the student-plaintiffs to read from the Holt series," and ordering the defendants to excuse the student plaintiffs from their classrooms "[d]uring the normal reading period" and to provide them with suitable space in the library or elsewhere for a study hall. 647 F.Supp. at 1203. . . . [T]he court awarded damages to the plaintiffs in the total amount of $51,531, largely to reimburse the plaintiff families for the costs of sending their children to alternate schools and the costs of pursuing this lawsuit.

III

A

The first question to be decided is whether a governmental requirement that a person be exposed to ideas he or she finds objectionable on religious grounds constitutes a burden on the free exercise of that person's religion as forbidden by the First Amendment. This is precisely the way the superintendent of the Hawkins County schools framed the issue in an affidavit filed early in this litigation. . . . "While it is true that these textbooks expose the student to varying values and religious backgrounds, neither the textbooks nor the teachers teach, indoctrinate, oppose or promote any particular value or religion." . . .

It is also clear that exposure to objectionable material is what the plaintiffs objected to albeit they emphasize the repeated nature of the exposure. The complaint mentioned only the textbooks that the students were required to read. It did not seek relief from any method of teaching the material and did not mention the teachers' editions. The plaintiffs did not produce a single student or teacher to testify that any student was ever required to affirm his or her belief or disbelief in any idea or practice mentioned in the various stories and passages contained in the Holt series. However, the plaintiffs appeared to assume that materials clearly presented as poetry, fiction and even "make-believe" in the Holt series were presented as facts which the students were required to believe. Nothing in the record supports this assumption.

. . . Proof that an objecting student was *required* to participate beyond reading and discussing assigned materials, or was disciplined for disputing assigned materials, might well implicate the Free Exercise Clause because the element of compulsion would then be present. But this was not the case either as pled or proved. . . .

Vicki Frost testified that an occasional reference to role reversal, pacifism, rebellion against parents, one-world government and other objectionable concepts would be acceptable, but she felt it was the repeated references to such subjects that created the burden. The district court suggested that it was a matter of balance, *id.* at 1199, apparently believing that a reading series that presented ideas with which the plaintiffs agree in juxtaposition to those with which they disagree would pass constitutional muster. While balanced textbooks are certainly desirable, there would be serious difficulties with trying to cure the omissions in the Holt series. . . .

However, the plaintiffs' own testimony casts serious doubt on their claim that a more balanced presentation would satisfy their religious views. Mrs. Frost testified that it would be acceptable for the schools to teach her children about other philosophies and religions, but if the practices of other religions were described in detail, or if the philosophy was "profound" in that it expressed a world view that deeply undermined her religious beliefs, then her children "would have to be instructed to [the] error [of the other philosophy]." It is clear that to the plaintiffs there is but one acceptable view—the Biblical view, as they interpret the Bible. Furthermore, the plaintiffs view every human situation and decision, whether related to personal belief and conduct or to public policy and programs, from a theological or religious perspective. Mrs. Frost testified that many political issues have theological roots and that there would be "no way" certain themes could be presented without violating her religious beliefs. She identified such themes as evolution, false supernaturalism, feminism, telepathy and magic as matters that could not be presented in any way without offending her beliefs. The only way to avoid conflict with the plaintiffs' beliefs in these sensitive areas would be to eliminate all references to the subjects so identified. However, the Supreme Court has clearly held that it violates the Establishment Clause to tailor a public school's curriculum to satisfy the principles or prohibitions of any religion. *Epperson v. Arkansas*, 393 U.S. 97, 106, 89 S.Ct. 266, 271, 21 L.Ed.2d 228 (1968).

. . . [Dr. Vitz] found "markedly little reference to religion, particularly Christianity, and also remarkably little to Judaism" in the Holt series. His solution would be to "beef up" the references to these two dominant religions in the United States. However, an adherent to a less widely professed religion might then object to the slighting of his or her faith. Balance in the treatment of religion lies in the eye of the beholder. Efforts to achieve the particular "balance" desired by any individual or group by the addition or deletion of religious material would lead to a forbidden entanglement of the public schools in religious matters, if done with the purpose or primary effect of advancing or inhibiting religion. . . .

B

* * *

C

. . . [T]he plaintiffs, in this court, have relied particularly upon three Supreme Court decisions. We find them all distinguishable.

The issue in *Torcaso v. Watkins*, 367 U.S. 488, 81 S.Ct. 1680, 6 L.Ed.2d 982 (1961), was whether a state could deny public office to a person solely because of the person's refusal to declare a belief in God. Quoting from its earlier decision in *Everson v. Board of Education*, 330 U.S. 1, 15, 67 S.Ct. 504, 511, 91 L.Ed. 711 (1947), the Court stated:

> We repeat and reaffirm that neither a State nor the Federal Government can constitutionally force a person "to profess a belief or disbelief in any religion."

Id. at 495, 81 S.Ct. at 1683. Since there was no evidence that the plaintiff students were ever required to profess or deny a religious belief the issue in *Torcaso* simply is not presented by the instant case.

Board of Education v. Barnette, 319 U.S. 624, 63 S.Ct. 1178, 87 L.Ed. 1628 (1943), grew out of a school board rule that required all schools to make a salute to the flag and a pledge of allegiance a regular part of their daily program. All teachers and students were required to participate in the exercise and refusal to engage in the salute was considered an act of insubordination which could lead to expulsion and possible delinquency charges for being unlawfully absent. The plaintiff was a Jehovah's Witness who considered the flag an "image" which the Bible forbids worshipping in any way. Justice Jackson, writing for the Court, stated:

> Here, . . . we are dealing with a compulsion of students to declare a belief. They are not merely made acquainted with the flag salute so that they may be informed as to what it is or even what it means.

Id. at 631, 63 S.Ct. at 1182. . . .

It is abundantly clear that the exposure to materials in the Holt series did not compel the plaintiffs to "declare a belief," "communicate by word and sign [their] acceptance" of the ideas presented, or make an "affirmation of a belief and an attitude of mind." . . .

* * *

The plaintiffs appear to contend that the element of compulsion was supplied by the requirement of class participation in the reading exercises. As we have pointed out earlier, there is no proof in the record that any plaintiff student was required to engage in role play, make up magic chants, read aloud or engage in the activity of haggling. . . . Being exposed to other students performing these acts might be offensive to the plaintiffs, but it does not constitute the compulsion described in the Supreme Court cases . . . .

D

The third Supreme Court decision relied upon by the plaintiffs is the only one that might be read to support the proposition that requiring mere exposure to materials that offend one's religious beliefs creates an unconstitutional burden on the free exercise of religion. *Wisconsin v. Yoder*, 406 U.S. 205, 92 S.Ct. 1526, 32 L.Ed.2d 15 (1972). However, *Yoder* rested on such a singular set of facts that we do not believe it can be held to announce a general rule that exposure without compulsion to act, believe, affirm or deny creates an unconstitutional burden. The plaintiff parents in *Yoder* were Old Order Amish and members of the Conservative Amish Mennonite Church, who objected to their children being required to attend either public or private schools beyond the eighth grade. Wisconsin school attendance law required them to cause their children to attend school until they reached the age of 16. Unlike the plaintiffs in the present case, the parents in *Yoder* did not want their children to attend any high school or be exposed to any part of a high school curriculum. The Old Order Amish and the Conservative Amish Mennonites separate themselves from the world and avoid assimilation into society, and attempt to shield their children from all worldly influences. The Supreme Court found from the record that—

> [C]ompulsory school attendance to age 16 for Amish children carries with it a very real threat to undermining the Amish community and religious practice as they exist today; they must either abandon belief and be assimilated into society at large, or be forced to migrate to some other and more tolerant region.

Id. at 218, 92 S.Ct. at 1534 (footnote omitted).

As if to emphasize the narrowness of its holding because of the unique 300 year history of the Old Amish Order, the Court wrote:

> It is one thing to say that compulsory education for a year or two beyond the eighth grade may be necessary when its goal is the preparation of the child for life in modern society as the majority live, but it is quite another if the goal of education be viewed as the preparation of the child for life in the separated agrarian community that is the keystone of the Amish faith.

Id. at 222, 92 S.Ct. at 1536 (citation omitted). This statement points up dramatically the difference between *Yoder* and the present case. The parents in *Yoder* were required to send their children to some school that prepared them for life in the outside world, or face official sanctions. The parents in the present case want their children to acquire all the skills required to live in modern society. They also want to have them excused from exposure to some ideas they find offensive. Tennessee offers two options to accommodate this latter desire. The plaintiff parents can either send their children to church schools or private schools, as many of them have done, or teach them at home. . . .

Yoder was decided in large part on the impossibility of reconciling the goals of public education with the religious requirement of the Amish that their children be prepared for life in a separated community. . . . No such threat exists in the present case. . . .

* * *

IV

A

The Supreme Court has recently affirmed that public schools serve the purpose of teaching fundamental values "essential to a democratic society." These values "include tolerance of divergent political and religious views" while taking into account "consideration of the sensibilities of others." *Bethel School Dist. No. 403 v. Fraser*, 478 U.S. 675, 106 S.Ct. 3159, 3164, 92 L.Ed.2d 549 (1986). The Court has noted with apparent approval the view of some educators who see public schools as an "assimilative force" that brings together "diverse and conflicting elements" in our society "on a broad but common ground." *Ambach v. Norwick*, 441 U.S. 68, 77, 99 S.Ct. 1589, 1595, 60 L.Ed.2d 49 (1979). . . .

. . . Mrs. Frost stated specifically that she objected to stories that develop "a religious tolerance that all religions are merely different roads to God."

* * *

. . . [In addition,] Mrs. Frost said, "We cannot be tolerant in that we accept other religious views on an equal basis with ours." While probably not an uncommon view of true believers in any religion, this statement graphically illustrates what is lacking in the plaintiffs' case.

The "tolerance of divergent . . . religious views" referred to by the Supreme Court is a civil tolerance, not a religious one. It does not require a person to accept any other religion as the equal of the one to which that person adheres. It merely requires a recognition that in a pluralistic society we must "live and let live." . . .

B

* * *

. . . Since we have found none of the prohibited forms of governmental compulsion in this case, we conclude that the plaintiffs failed to establish the existence of an unconstitutional burden. Having determined that no burden was shown, we do not reach the issue of the defendants' compelling interest in requiring a uniform reading series or the question, raised by the defendant, of whether awarding damages violated the Establishment Clause.

Judge Boggs concludes that the majority reverses the district court because it found the plaintiffs' claims of First Amendment protection so extreme as obviously to violate the Establishment Clause. This is not the holding of the majority. We do point out that under certain circumstances the plaintiffs, by their own testimony, would only accept accommodations that would violate the Establishment Clause. However, this is not the holding. What we do hold is that the requirement that public school students study a basal reader series chosen by the school authorities does not create an unconstitutional burden under the Free Exercise Clause when the students are not required to affirm or deny a belief or engage or refrain from engaging in a practice prohibited or required by their religion. . . .

* * *

The judgment of the district court granting injunctive relief and damages is reversed, and the case is remanded with directions to dismiss the complaint. . . .

Cornelia G. Kennedy, Circuit Judge, concurring.

I agree with Chief Judge Lively's analysis and concur in his opinion. However, even if I were to conclude that requiring the use of the Holt series or another similar series constituted a burden on appellees' free exercise rights, I would find the burden justified by a compelling state interest.

Appellants have stated that a principal educational objective is to teach the students how to think critically about complex and controversial subjects and to develop their own ideas and make judgments about these subjects. Several witnesses testified that the only way to achieve these objectives is to have the children read a basal reader, participate in class discussions, and formulate and express their own ideas and opinions about the materials presented in a basal reader. Thus, appellee students are required to read stories in the Holt series, make personal judgments about the validity of the stories, and to discuss why certain characters in the stories did what they did, or their values and whether those values were proper. . . .

. . . Teaching students about complex and controversial social and moral issues is just as essential for preparing public school students for citizenship and self-government as inculcating in the students the habits and manners of civility.

The evidence at trial demonstrated that mandatory participation in reading classes using the Holt series or some similar readers is essential to accomplish this compelling interest and that this interest could not be achieved any other way. Several witnesses for appellants testified that in order to develop critical reading skills, and therefore achieve appellants' objectives, the students must read and discuss complex, morally and socially difficult issues. Many of these necessarily will be subjects on which appellees believe the Bible states the rule or correct position. Consequently, accommodating appellees' beliefs would unduly interfere with the fulfillment of the appellants' objectives. . . . Additionally, mandatory participation in the reading program is the least restrictive means of achieving appellants' objectives. Appellees' objections would arise even if the School Board selected another basal reading textbook series since the students would be required to engage in critical reading and form their own opinions and judgments on many of the same issues.

The state and the Hawkins County School Board also have a compelling interest in avoiding disruption in the classroom. Hawkins County Schools utilize an integrated curriculum, designed to prepare students for life in a complex, pluralistic society, that reinforces skills and values taught in one subject in other areas. The Director of Elementary Education testified that teachers use every opportunity within the school day to reinforce information taught in the different subject areas. For example, the students may discuss stories in the Holt readers dealing with evolution or conservation of natural resources in the science course. This approach to learning is well-recognized and enables the students to see learning "as part of their total life, not just [as] bits and pieces." . . .

This is particularly true in grades one through four where reading is taught throughout the school day, rather than in a particular period. Appellants would be unable to utilize effectively the critical reading teaching method and accommodate appellees' religious beliefs. If the opt-out remedy were implemented, teachers in all grades would have to either avoid the students discussing objectionable material contained in the Holt readers in non-reading classes or dismiss appellee students from class whenever such material is discussed. To do this the teachers would have to determine what is objectionable to appellees. This would either require that appellees review all teaching materials or that all teachers review appellees' extensive testimony. If the teachers concluded certain material fell in the objectionable classification but nonetheless considered it appropriate to have the students discuss this material, they would have to dismiss appellee students from these classes. The dismissal of appellee students from the classes would result in substantial disruption to the public schools.

Additionally, Hawkins County Public Schools have a compelling interest in avoiding religious divisiveness. . . . The opt-out remedy would permit appellee students to be released from a core subject every day *because* of their religion. . . .

The divisiveness and disruption caused by the opt-out remedy would be magnified if the schools had to grant other exemptions. Although the District Court found that no other objections to the Hawkins County public school curriculum have been raised and the Hawkins County is homogeneous from a religious perspective, this case would create a precedent for persons from other religions to request exemptions from core subjects because of religious objections. If the school district were required to accommodate exceptions and permit other students to opt-out of the reading program and other core courses with materials others found objectionable, this would result in a public school system impossible to administer. . . .

* * *

Boggs, Circuit Judge, concurring.

I concur with my colleagues that Hawkins County is not required by the Constitution to allow plaintiffs the latitude they seek in the educational program of these children. However, I reach that result on a somewhat different view of the facts and governing principles here. It seems that the court's opinion rests first on the view that plaintiffs' objection is to any exposure to contrary ideas, and that no one's religious exercise can be burdened simply by compelled exposure. . . . Second, the opinion rests on the view that no burden can exist here because plaintiffs were not compelled to engage in any conduct prohibited by, or refrain from any practice required by, their religious beliefs. . . .

I do not believe these attempted distinctions will survive analysis. If the situation of these children is not a burden on their religious exercise, it must be because of a principle applicable to all religious objectors to public school curricula. Thus, I believe a deeper issue is present here, is implicitly decided in the court's opinion, and should be addressed openly. The school board recognizes no limitation on its power to require any curriculum, no matter how offensive or one-sided, and to expel those who will not study it, so long as it does not violate the Establishment Clause. Our opinion today confirms that right, and I would like to make plain my reasons for taking that position.

. . . For myself, I approach this case with a profound sense of sadness. At the classroom level, the pupils and teachers in these schools had in most cases reached a working accommodation. Only by the decisions of higher levels of political authority, and by more conceptualized presentations of the plaintiffs' positions, have we reached the point where we must decide these harsh questions today. . . .

* * *

Plaintiffs' requests were unusual, but a variety of accommodations in fact were made, with no evidence whatsoever of bad effects. Given the masses of speculative testimony as to the hypothetical future evils of accommodating plaintiffs in any way, had there been any evidence of bad effects from what actually occurred, the board would surely have presented it. As we ultimately decide here, on the present state of constitutional law, the school board is indeed entitled to say, "my way or the highway." But in my view the school board's decision here is certainly not required by the Establishment Clause.

. . . I believe this is a more difficult case than outlined in the court's opinion. I disagree with the first proposition in the court's opinion, that plaintiffs object to any exposure to any contrary idea. I do not believe we can define for plaintiffs their belief as to what is religiously forbidden to be so comprehensive, where both they and the district court have spoken to the contrary. A reasonable reading of plaintiffs' testimony shows they object to the overall effect of the Holt series, not simply to any exposure to any idea opposing theirs. . . .

Ultimately, I think we must address plaintiffs' claims as they actually impact their lives: it is their belief that they should not take a course of study which, on balance, to them, denigrates and opposes their religion, and which the state is compelling them to take on pain of forfeiting all other benefits of public education.

Their view may seem silly or wrong-headed to some, but it is a sincerely held religious belief. By focussing narrowly on references that make plaintiffs appear so extreme that they could never be accommodated, the court simply leaves resolution of the underlying issues here to another case, when we have plaintiffs with a more sophisticated understanding of our own and Supreme Court precedent, and a more careful and articulate presentation of their own beliefs.

Under the court's assessment of the facts, this is a most uninteresting case. It is not the test case sought, or feared, by either side. The court reviews the record and finds that the plaintiffs actually want a school system that affirmatively teaches the correctness of their religion, and prevents other students from mentioning contrary ideas. If that is indeed the case, then it can be very simply resolved. It would obviously violate the Establishment Clause for any school system to agree with such an extravagant view.

It should be noted and emphasized that if such is the holding, this decision is largely irrelevant to the national legal controversy over this case. The extent to which school systems may constitutionally require students to use educational materials that are objectionable, contrary to, or forbidden by their religious beliefs is a serious and important issue.

* * *

I also disagree with the court's view that there can be no burden here because there is no requirement of conduct contrary to religious belief. That view both slights plaintiffs' honest beliefs that studying the full Holt series would be conduct contrary to their religion, and overlooks other Supreme Court Free Exercise cases which view "conduct" that may offend religious exercise at least as broadly as do plaintiffs.

On the question of exposure to, or use of, books as conduct, we may recall the Roman Catholic Church's, "*Index Librorum Prohibitorum*." This was a list of those books the reading of which was a mortal sin, at least until the second Vatican Council in 1962.[5] I would hardly think it can be contended that a school requirement that a student engage in an act (the reading of the book) which would specifically be a mortal sin under the teaching of a major organized religion would be other than "conduct prohibited by religion," even by the court's fairly restrictive standard. Yet, in what constitutionally important way can the situation here be said to differ from that? Certainly, a religion's size or formality of hierarchy cannot determine the religiosity of beliefs. . . .

* * *

Here, plaintiffs have drawn their line as to what required school activities, what courses of study, do and do not offend their beliefs to the point of prohibition. I would hold that if they are forced over that line, they are "engaging in conduct" forbidden by their religion. The court's excellent summary of its holding on this point. . . . appears to concede that what plaintiffs were doing in school was conduct, but that there "was no evidence that the conduct required of the students was forbidden by their religion." I cannot agree. The plaintiffs provided voluminous testimony of the conflict (in their view) between reading the Holt readers and their religious beliefs, including extensive Scriptural references. The district court found that "plaintiffs' religious beliefs *compel* them to refrain from exposure to the Holt series." 647 F.Supp. at 1200 (emphasis supplied). I would think it could hardly be clearer that they believe their religion commands, not merely suggests, their course of action.

If plaintiffs did not use the exact words "reading these books is forbidden by our religion," they certainly seemed to me to make that point clearly. . . .

* * *

Thus, I believe the plaintiffs' objection is to the Holt series as a whole, and that being forced to study the books is "conduct" contrary to their beliefs. In the absence of a narrower basis that can withstand scrutiny, we must address the hard issues presented by this case: (1) whether compelling this conduct forbidden by plaintiffs' beliefs places a burden on their free exercise of their religion, in the sense of earlier Supreme Court holdings; and (2) whether *within the context of the public schools*, teaching material which offends a person's religious beliefs, but does not violate the Establishment Clause, can be a burden on free exercise. . . .

VI

* * *

Running a public school system of today's magnitude is . . . [factually distinguishable from other free exercise cases]. A constitutional challenge to the content of instruction (as opposed to participation in ritual such as magic chants, or prayers) is a challenge to the notion of a politically-controlled school system. Imposing on school boards the delicate task of satisfying the "compelling interest" test to justify failure to accommodate pupils is a significant step.[9] It is a substantial imposition on the schools to *require* them to justify each instance of not dealing with students' individual, religiously compelled, objections (as opposed to *permitting* a local, rough and ready, adjustment), and I do not see that the Su-

5. *New Catholic Encyclopedia*, Vol. 7, pp. 434–35; Vol. 2, pp. 699–701 (McGraw-Hill, 1967).

9. I do not think there is any evidence that actually accommodating pupils in practice need be as difficult as the state contends. Indeed, the state espouses a theory of rigidity (and finds alleged experts to support it) that seems a bit ludicrous in this age of individualized attention to many kinds of student language and interest. There was no evidence of actual confusion or disruption from the accommodation that did take place.

preme Court has authorized us to make such a requirement.

* * *

The average public expenditure for a pupil in Hawkins County is about 20% of the income of the average household there. Even the modest tuition in the religious schools which some plaintiffs attended here amounted to about a doubling of the state and local tax burden of the average resident. Had the Founders recognized the possibility of state intervention of this magnitude, they might have written differently. However, it is difficult for me to see that the words "free exercise of religion," at the adoption of the Bill of Rights, implied a freedom from state teaching, even of offensive material, when some alternative was legally permissible.[12]

Therefore, I reluctantly conclude that under the Supreme Court's decisions as we have them, school boards may set curricula bounded only by the Establishment Clause, as the state contends. Thus, contrary to the analogy plaintiffs suggest, pupils may indeed be expelled if they will not read from the King James Bible, so long as it is only used as literature, and not taught as religious truth. . . . Contrary to the position of *amicus* American Jewish Committee, Jewish students may not assert a burden on their religion if their reading materials overwhelmingly provide a negative view of Jews or factual or historical issues important to Jews, so long as such materials do not assert any propositions as religious truth, or do not otherwise violate the Establishment Clause.

* * *

Schools are very important, and some public schools offend some people deeply. That is one major reason private schools of many denominations—fundamentalist, Lutheran, Jewish—are growing. But a response to that phenomen is a political decision for the schools to make. . . .

NOTES AND QUESTIONS

1. Burden on Freedom of Religion

Do you agree with Chief Judge Lively that the plaintiffs in *Mozert* have not demonstrated that the use of the Holt, Rinehart & Winston basic reading series in the Hawkins County public schools is an unconstitutional burden on their free exercise of religion? Is this because exposure to views antithetical to fundamentalist Christianity is not the same thing as coercion or a compulsion to believe? *See Smith v. Ricci*, 89 N.J. 514, 446 A.2d 501, 505 (1982) and cases cited therein; Strossen, " 'Secular Humanism' and 'Scientific Creationism': Proposed Standards for Reviewing Curricular Decisions Affecting Students' Religious Freedom," 47 *Ohio St. L.J.* 333 (1986). *Cf. Employment Division, Department of Human Resources v. Smith*, ___ U.S. ___, 110 S.Ct. 1595 (1990). Because reading is not conduct? Because some offenses to one's religious beliefs must be endured? Because plaintiffs' legal position is inconsistent with the concept of public schooling?

Professor Dent has said that "at the least, most would agree that forcibly subjecting citizens to propaganda overtly hostile to their religion would violate free exercise." Dent, "Religious Children, Secular Schools," 61 *So. Cal.L.Rev.* 863, 887 (1988). Do you agree? Professor Dent cites such cases as *Schempp*, *Epperson*, and *Aguilar*. Do those precedents support his statement? How should courts determine what is "propaganda overtly hostile" to religious beliefs? Does the distinction focus on the difference between readings that convey inconsistent beliefs or fail to affirm one's own beliefs and readings that affirmatively attack one's religious beliefs? For example, the distinction between saying that evolution is right and creation science is a fraud? Does Chief Justice Lively accept the view that exposure to overtly hostile readings would violate the Free Exercise Clause? If he did, how should *Mozert* have been decided? *See* Dent at 888–94.

Wisconsin v. Yoder, *supra* at Chapter 1, is the strongest case in support of the proposition that plaintiffs' free exercise rights have been burdened by the use of the Holt, Rinehart & Winston series. In that case, Amish parents objected to any education for their children beyond the eighth grade. They did not wish their children exposed to the modern world, and they feared that such exposure would lead to the destruction of the Amish community. There is some doubt as to the continuing vitality of *Yoder*, albeit it has not been overruled. *See Employment Division v. Smith*, *supra*. *See generally* McConnell, "Free Exercise Revisionism and the *Smith* Deci-

---

12. As guaranteed by the Supreme Court's decision in *Pierce v. Society of Sisters*, 268 U.S. 510, 45 S.Ct. 571, 69 L.Ed. 1070 (1925).

sion." 57 *U.Chi. L. Rev.* 1109 (1990); Laycock, "The Remnants of Free Exercise," 1990 *S.Ct. Rev.* (this publication pending). In any event, Chief Justice Lively distinguishes *Yoder*, stressing its "singular set of facts" and the "narrowness of the holding." Is this persuasive? Is it depositive that the Amish lived in a self-contained and homogeneous community? That their religion and way of life could not be separated? That the fundamentalist Christian parents sought a remedy that extended to all grades, whereas the Amish sought relief only from public schooling after the eighth grade? That apparently no private Amish school would be acceptable to Wisconsin authorities under state law, but Tennessee would have allowed the fundamentalist Christians to achieve their objectives in private schools? Do these distinctions go to the question of burden or to the nature of the state's interest and the means by which it might be vindicated?

Consider these remarks by Professor Dent:

> The objection to exposure was qualitatively different [in *Wisconsin v. Yoder*] than in *Mozert*; in *Yoder* the very presence of the children in school burdened their religious practice. Although *Yoder* could be distinguished on this ground, it should not be. First, the Court's opinion is broad. It states that public high schools contravened the Amish faith "by exposing Amish children to worldly influences in terms of attitudes, goals, and values contrary to their beliefs, and by substantially interfering with the religious development of the Amish child and his integration into the way of life of the Amish faith community." Much the same could be said of the effect of public schools on the plaintiffs in *Mozert* and other fundamentalists.
>
> *Mozert* . . . invites trouble by distinguishing between those whose religion forbids (or requires) a practice or belief and those who consider the practices or belief merely undesirable (or desirable). . . . The Supreme Court has never adopted such a standard and has often reached contrary conclusions. . . .
>
> It does not suffice to argue that the teaching at issue in *Mozert* is not religious because it does not expressly address religion. The religion of individuals and their sects determines what matters are religious to them. . . . To rule otherwise . . . would contravene the principle of neutrality by preferring those who hold modernist or mainstream beliefs . . . over those with more fundamentalist or all-encompassing beliefs.

Dent, *supra* at 890–91.

2. The Nature of the State's Interest

Judge Kennedy concurs with Chief Judge Lively, but she argues that any burden on plaintiffs' free exercise rights is justified by the state's compelling interest in education. Is she saying that a basic mission of public education is to teach critical thinking about complex and controversial subjects and that this mission cannot be accomplished without basal readers? Why is critical thinking so important? Does it better prepare them for adult lives? If so, does not the mission of public school inevitably require a secular humanism inconsistent with fundamentalist Christianity because critical thinking refers to a way of seeing the world that is inconsistent with the fundamentalist world view? *See* Carter, "Evolutionism, Creationism, and Teaching Religion as a Hobby," 1987 *Duke L. J.* 977. Can critical thinking be taught from readers less hostile to religious beliefs? Is the problem that someone's religious sensitivities will be offended by any reader? What if the remedy were limited simply to exemption from reading the offending works?

Is Judge Kennedy suggesting that public schools need to teach democratic values and that this goal requires exposure to divergent points of view on controversial subjects? *See generally* Spiro, "The Creation of a Free Marketplace of Religious Ideas: Revisiting the Establishment Clause after the Alabama Secular Humanism Decision," 39 *Ala.L.Rev.* 1 (1987). Which views need to be canvassed and tolerated? Need the schools present the affirmative case for drug addiction or child abuse or communism? If not, does not the mission of the public schools include intolerance of some beliefs and values? *See* Arons & Lawrence, "The Manipulation of Consciousness: A First Amendment Critique of Schooling," 15 *Harv. C.R.–C.L. L. Rev.* 309 (1980). Conversely, if fundamentalist Christian children should be exposed to the idea that women may pursue professional careers outside of the home, should all students be informed that some groups believe that a woman's place is in the home? How should courts distinguish the controversial from core values that public schools may legitimately inculcate? *See* Yudof, "Library Book Selection and the Public Schools: The Quest for the Archimedean Point," 59 *Ind.L.J.* 527 (1984). Or is Judge Kennedy saying that school authorities and not judges should decide these weighty issues?

What is the state's interest in a uniform curriculum? In common schools? Would an "opt-out remedy" substantially disrupt public education? *See generally* Glenn, "Religion, Textbooks, and the Common School," 88 *The Pub. Int.* 28 (Summer 1987). Does it depend on how many groups would opt out? What does Judge Boggs have to say about this? If substantial disruption would not occur, does this suggest that there is a less onerous alternative for the state to achieve its objectives? *See Smith v. Ricci*, 89 N.J. 514, 446 A.2d 501 (N.J. 1982). That is, that the state's interest in exposing fundamentalist Christian children to the Holt, Rinehart & Winston basic reading series is not compelling?

3. Judge Boggs' Concurring Opinion

Judge Boggs, while sympathetic to the proposition that plaintiffs' free exercise of religion has been burdened, concurs on the ground that there is "no limitation on . . . [a school board's] power to require any curriculum, no matter how offensive or one-sided, and to expel those who will not study it, so long as it does not violate the Establishment Clause." Is this proposition consistent with *Yoder* and other Establishment Clause cases? *See Employment Division v. Smith, supra*. Is he improperly equating an establishment of religion with hostility toward religion? *See generally* Laycock, "Towards A General Theory of the Religion Clauses: The Case of Church Labor Relations and the Right to Church Autonomy," 81 *Colum.L.Rev.* 1373, 1380–86 (1981). Is Judge Boggs advocating a special rule only for public schools? *See generally* Yudof, *supra*; Shiffrin, "Government Speech," 27 *U.C.L.A. L. Rev.* 565, 648 (1980). Or is he saying that any good faith educational judgment with respect to curriculum should not be subject to judicial reexamination? *See Board of Educ. v. Pico*, 457 U.S. 853, 102 S.Ct. 2799, 73 L.Ed.2d 43 (1982), *infra*.

Judge Boggs argues that Chief Justice Lively and Judge Kennedy have misconstrued the facts in a way that renders a "test case" into a "most uninteresting case." That is, the other judges find that "the plaintiffs actually want a school system that affirmatively teaches the correctness of their religion, and prevents other students from mentioning contrary ideas." *See* Wood, "Religion and the Public Schools," 1986 *B.Y.U. L. Rev.* 349, 355–56 (1986). Do you agree with Judge Boggs? Have plaintiffs sought judicial intervention to establish their own religion in the public schools?

4. Selective Exemptions

Recall that the district court in *Mozert* enjoined the defendants from compelling fundamentalist Christian children to read the Holt, Rinehart & Winston series and ordered that they be excused from class during reading periods and that study space elsewhere be made available. *See generally* M. McCarthy & N. Cambron-McCabe, *Public School Law* 39–42 (1988). Presumably, the children would read alternative readings less offensive to fundamentalist Christian beliefs. If this remedy were satisfactory to the plaintiffs, does this suggest that plaintiffs did not seek to establish their own religion but only to preserve the free exercise of religion? How does the remedy sought in *Mozert* differ from the remedy sought in *Smith? See also Rosenberg v. Board of Education*, 196 Misc. 542, 92 N.Y.S.2d 344 (1949).

Can tailored exemptions be granted from various aspects of the public school program for religious reasons without significant disruption of the school and frustration of the state's educational goals? *See generally* R. O'Neil, *Classrooms in the Crossfire* ch. 8 (1981); Dent, *supra;* Hirschoff, "Parents and the Public School Curriculum: Is There a Right to Have One's Child Excused from Objectionable Instruction?" 50 *So.Cal. L. Rev.* 871 (1977). Is partial exemption preferable to a "balanced" curriculum? Suppose that the alternative readings emphasized creationism and other beliefs of fundamentalist Christians. *See* Dent, *supra* at 928. Would it be a violation of the Establishment Clause for the school district to allow fundamentalist children the time and space to read such works during school hours? *See McCollum v. Board of Educ.*, 333 U.S. 203, 68 S.Ct. 461, 92 L.Ed. 649 (1948); Dent, *supra* at 915–19, 923–27. What if the school district provided an instructor to teach from the alternative works? *See Parents Ass'n of P.S. 16 v. Quinones*, 803 F.2d 1235 (2d Cir. 1986); Dent, *supra* at 927–30. What if the alternative works were read at home and the parents took the responsibility of teaching reading skills at home? *See Zorach v. Clauson*, 343 U.S. 306, 72 S.Ct. 679, 96 L.Ed. 954 (1952); Dent, *supra* at 923–24. Does the answer depend on whether home education under state law is a permissible alternative to public schooling? *See* Dent, *supra* at 925. Does either alternative, study in another classroom or study at home, constitute state approval of religion? Preference for religion? *See* Strossen, *supra*. What if some children felt strong peer pressure to seek excusal from class? *See* Dent, *supra* at 924 n. 335.

Is there a significant distinction between a court compelling a school district to accommodate the views of the fundamentalist Christians and allowing it to accommodate those views? Between a constitutional right of accommodation and a determination that a voluntary accommodation is not unconstitutional? *See Grove v. Mead School District No.* 354, 753 F.2d 1528 (9th Cir. 1985); *Smith v. Ricci,* 89 N.J. 514, 446 A.2d 501, 505 (1982); *Citizens for Parental Rights v. San Mateo City Bd. of Educ.,* 51 Cal. App. 3d 1, 124 Cal. Rptr. 68 (1975); A. Gutmann, *Democratic Education* 122 (1987). *See generally* McCarthy & Cambron-McCabe, *supra* at 42–44.

5. *Equal Access*

In 1981, under principles of freedom of expression, the Supreme Court held that a campus religious organization could not be denied the same right as other organizations of access to facilities on a university campus. *Widmar v. Vincent,* 454 U.S. 263, 102 S.Ct. 269, 70 L.Ed.2d 440 (1981), *infra.* Three years later, Congress enacted the Equal Access Act, providing that secondary schools receiving federal assistance must not discriminate among extracurricular groups on the basis of religion, politics, or philosophy in terms of access to school facilities if they had established a "limited public forum." 20 U.S.C.A. § 4071(a) (Supp.II 1984). *See generally* Fleming and Peeler, "Mergens: The Beginning, Not the End, of Questions Arising Under the Equal Access Act," 64 *Educ. L. Rep.* [15] (1990) and Laycock, "Equal Access and Moments of Silence: The Equal Status of Religious Speech by Private Speakers," 81 *Nw. U. L. Rev.* 1, 9–57 (1986). In the light of *Smith* and *Mozert,* is the Equal Access Act unconstitutional? *See* Laycock, *supra.* Should high schools be treated differently than universities in terms of government endorsement of the religious activity of campus groups? *See Board of Education of Westside Community Schools v. Mergens, infra; Bender v. Williamsport Area School Dist.,* 741 F.2d 538 (3d Cir. 1984), *vacated on other grounds,* 475 U.S. 534, 106 S.Ct. 1326, 89 L.Ed.2d 501 (1986); *Lubbock Civil Liberties Union v. Lubbock Indep. School Dist.,* 669 F.2d 1038 (5th Cir. 1982) *cert. denied,* 459 U.S. 1155 (1983).

6. *Problem*

New York requires that all primary and secondary school students receive instruction concerning the transmission and prevention of AIDS and the avoidance of drug and alcohol abuse. The Plymouth Brethren is a religious order whose members believe that religious doctrine requires that individuals not be exposed to the "details of evil." The law allows for an exemption from classroom instruction on AIDS and substance abuse, but parents must provide assurances that they will provide suitable instruction at home. The Brethren decline to give such an assurance and file suit against the school district, claiming that their religious rights have been violated. What result? *See Ware v. Valley Stream High School Dist.,* 150 A.D.2d 14, 545 N.Y.2d 316 (1989). *Cf. Employment Division, Department of Human Services v. Smith,* ___ U.S. ___, 110 S. Ct. 1595 (1990).

B. Nonsectarian Socialization

"Library Book Selection and the Public Schools: The Quest for the Archimedean Point"

Mark G. Yudof, 59 *Ind. L. J.* 527, 527–37 (1984). Reprinted by permission.

Traditional theories of liberty and autonomy do not fit well when the subjects are children and education. For adults, democratic governments generally seek to abide by the Kantian maxim that each person should be treated as a kingdom of ends—treated with respect for his or her autonomy, rationality, and human worth—and not as a means or an instrument of another person's will. Children, however, are rightfully perceived as both ends in themselves, evolving autonomous beings, and as instruments of larger societal purposes. Those purposes include the assimilation of the child into the larger culture, for the intergenerational, exogenetic transmission of values, knowledge, language, and customs is essential to the preservation of community and to the definition of persons within community. Paradoxically, education both promotes autonomy and, in a sense, denies it by shaping and constraining present and future life choices.

The education of children, in any form, whether compulsory or not, inevitably raises conflict. Children are not born with an appreciation of literature and democratic institutions, and they, including the most precocious among them, certainly are unlikely to discover geometry, computers, or quantum mechanics without the benefit of the accumulated wisdom of the past. Professor Tawney once described children as a "new race of souls" that bursts upon us every year, who stand "on the threshold with the world at their feet, like barbarians gazing upon the time-worn plains of an ancient civilization." But, if one substitutes pejorative words like propaganda, indoctrination, and brainwashing for an acceptable word like education, one gets a sense of the conflict. Children need to be socialized to societal norms, but they also need to grow up to be relatively autonomous beings within the confines of culture. . . .

The conflict between acculturation and autonomy inevitably leads to consideration of the concept of justifiable paternalism. Education is a form of affirmative liberty. Children are socialized through subjection to coercive and persuasive measures that enable them to become autonomous as adults—that is, they are socialized for their own good. Education can expand the mind or it can contract it, and mind-expanding education facilitates adult autonomy. Upon reaching adulthood, the subjects of the earlier paternalism would express gratitude, not indignation, for their treatment. But, however justifiable the paternalism for those who have not fully matured into personhood, there remains the problem of balance. If the education is too narrow and all encompassing, then autonomous citizens will not be produced. Words like domination and constraints on choice creep into the analysis. If autonomy is stressed at the price of education, then there is a justifiable fear of loss of community, alienation, and ignorance.

* * *

The ideal education necessarily requires the location of an Archimedean point, a point positioned somewhere between critical reflection and grounding in the contingent circumstances of society. . . .

How, then, is society to account for and to achieve the Archimedean point in education? Realistically viewed, there may be no optimal, theoretical balance between basic education and an all-pervasive indoctrination. . . .

Children must be integrated into the community but they should not be stifled. The desire to create informed citizens who understand the world in which they were born and live must be tempered by the realization that much of what society achieves depends on individuals who do not or will not conform to the prevailing wisdom. As John Updike . . . expressed the point, "[o]ur artistic heroes tend to be those self-exercisers, like Picasso, and Nabokov, and Wallace Stevens, who rather defiantly kept playing past dark." Children must learn the rules of the game, but that learning must stop short of an orthodoxy that playing after dark is always forbidden.*

* * *

The problem of children and education runs deeper than a reification of the conflict between socialization and autonomy. The question cannot be whether children ought to be socialized, that is, whether their autonomy should be simultaneously constrained and nourished. To paraphrase Professor C. Edwin Baker, to the extent that adults create a reality for children, an acceptable theory must concern itself with questions of who socializes children and how.[14] A world will be created for children, for they are not born with a particular cultural orientation. The relevant question is who will write on the slates, not whether they will be written on at all. If there was no formal education in public institutions, values and beliefs would continue to be instilled by family, church, peers, and life experiences.

* * *

. . . [T]he self in the concept of autonomy is partially defined by the culture; the antithesis between autonomy and indoctrination is an oversimplification because the self has links to and is defined in the context of communicated community norms. The converse is also true. The community and its indoctrination efforts may be shaped by many selves, for there is a mutually affecting relationship between community and individual. . . . An educational system that ignored autonomy and emphasized only indoctrination to communal norms would be thoroughly totalitarian and destructive of human values.

In the context of public schooling and beyond, the key to unraveling the paradoxes of education of the young lies neither in the reification of autonomy nor in the mysticism of transcendental communities. Children are autonomous individuals, and they are members of groups. Their selves are in part defined by social relations, but social relations are also in part defined by their personalities. The self and community cannot be completely separated, but they also cannot be completely integrated. The "good" has both particular and universal aspects. Not every cultural influence or imperative constitutes domination. Cultures do and should constrain.

* *See* Alwin, "From Obedience to Autonomy: Changes in Traits Desired in Children, 1924–1978," *Pub. Opin. Q.* 33 (Spring 1988).

14. Baker, *The Scope of the First Amendment Freedom of Speech*, 25 UCLA L. Rev. 964, 1026 (1978).

A nagging problem . . . is the need to differentiate between unacceptable constraints on individuality, leading to a loss of autonomy and creativity, and acceptable communitarian constraints that reduce alienation and enhance the cultured definition of self. Unless and until the epistemological millenium is approached, wisdom lies in a pragmatic recognition of the dynamic, uncertain, and complex relationship between cultural authority and individuality. . . .

* * *

Turning from the grand abstractions to life in the trenches, what is the structure of decisionmaking on socialization issues in public schools? Who determines what is to be taught and what books are to be acquired? Who balances autonomy and acculturation? For the most part, elected representatives, school board members, school administrators, librarians, and teachers share responsibility and are, at least in theory, accountable to the citizenry for their performance. There is no necessary reason for arranging affairs this way; many have proposed alternatives that would enhance, for example, either the power of families or the power of professional librarians or teachers to make educational choices. But the basic structural decisions have already been made, and these are reflected in existing legal and institutional arrangements.

* * *

But there are risks. The power of government to make these selections, to control communications, is also the power to destroy the underpinnings of government by consent, since that consent can be manipulated out of or into existence. . . . If the reflective, informed citizen, participating in governance decisions, is a philosophical root of freedom of expression, then government domination of communications networks is potentially as destructive of that concern as government censorship of private speech. Governments, staffed by self-interested politicians and bureaucrats, may aim for self-perpetuation and uncritical acceptance of the status quo and not for the Archimedean point. Because of this danger, letting the government control education may be like letting the fox guard the henhouse. That is why the boundaries of state power need to be probed. But the denial of the power to edit [the curriculum], to determine what shall or shall not be taught and assigned, is inherently incompatible with the public schooling enterprise.

NOTES AND QUESTIONS

1. The Governmental Interest

It is widely believed that it is important for public schools to introduce students to, if not socialize them in, the basic values of the American system of government; to inform students and educate them in the operation of the existing governmental system; and to promote a sense of loyalty and patriotism. *See generally* M. Janowitz, *The Reconstruction of Patriotism: Education for Civic Consciousness* (1983). Assuming that this educational effort is legitimate, what are the limits on the methods that the state may employ to socialize students to particular values? *See generally* chapter 1. Who should decide what is to be communicated and by what criteria? Might socialization to the values of tolerance and free speech be legitimate but not socialization to racial discrimination? A. Gutmann, *Democratic Education* 41–47 (1987). Are some aspects of the state socialization effort more legitimate than other aspects, or is it all ethically relative?

How does one distinguish between the socialization that takes place in American schools and the propagandizing that allegedly occurs in schools in totalitarian countries? Gutmann, *supra* at 103 ("Democratic communities are not in principle bound to teach the truth . . . , but they must be bound *not* to teach false doctrines that threaten to undermine the future prospects of a common democratic education"). Is it simply a question of the acceptability of the means employed to accomplish the socialization objective? *See* F. Wirt and M. Kirst, *The Political Web of American Schools* 24–26 (1972). Or is it that democracy is superior to totalitarianism and hence that democratic socialization is defensible? *See generally* Gutmann, *supra*; J. Dewey, *Democracy and Education* (1966). Can socialization expand rather than contract a person's capacity to think critically and to make informed choices? Or does it inhibit inquiry and change? *See* C. Lindblom, *Inquiry and Change* (1990). Can socialization promote individual growth and self-realization? *See* Garvey, "Children and the First Amendment," 57 *Tex. L. Rev.* 321, 345 (1979). Is it true that without agreement on certain matters society would disintegrate? *See generally* C. Lindblom, *Politics and Markets* (1977); P. Wolff, *The Poverty of Liberalism* (1968). Some political scientists argue there is good evidence that shared norms and values are not a necessary condition for political support. R. Rogowski, *Rational Legitimacy* 4–17 (1974). *But see* J. Tussman, *Government and the Mind* (1977). What does one make of the fact that students attending parochial schools do not differ in their political views from students attending public schools? *See* A. M. Greeley and P. H. Rossi, *The Education of Catholic Americans* (1968). Does this evidence suggest (1) that basic American values are communicated by all schools, or (2) that differences in curriculum do not reflect differences over fundamental, underlying values? *See generally* Merelman, "Democratic Politics and the Culture of American Education," 74 *Am. Pol. Sci. Rev.* 319 (1980).

Can it be persuasively argued that the governmental interest in socialization is weak when there are data to show that public schooling does not appear to be a strong influence on the political beliefs of students, compared to parental and peer-group influences? *See* M. K. Jennings and R. G. Niemi, *The Political Character of Adolescence* 217–21 (1974). Is the governmental effort to promote political, social, and other norms simply an insurance policy that society cannot risk doing without? Or might socialization be a cumulative process, with the public schools building incrementally (and immeasurably) on the efforts of others? Is there some reason to believe that private schools would not provide the kind and quality of political education that could be considered a collective good? *See* Sugarman and Kirp, "Rethinking Collective Responsibility for Education," 39 *Law and Contemp. Probs.* 144 (1975).

2. *Constitutional Issues*

If political socialization in some form is generally regarded as legitimate, individual students, parents, teachers, and taxpayers might nonetheless object to the "majority's" imposition of values. *Cf. Crosby v. Holsinger*, 816 F.2d 162 (4th Cir. 1987) ("Johnny Reb" school logo). Various legal and moral interests may be considered here: interests in personal autonomy, freedom of belief, self-controlled political participation, educational choice, freedom of expression, and noncoercion to support beliefs inimical to one's fundamental beliefs. There are also issues of authority: How does one know when public schools speak for the "majority"? Is socialization controlled by professionals or by the electorate? What of the authority of other institutions that socialize—family, church, private associations, and so on? What of the authority of the individual over his or her own development? These interests may be embedded in legal rights, but what ought to be the scope of such rights? Would judicial or legislative affirmation of rights effectively limit the state's power to socialize? Why should a self-interested state promote these rights and hence pluralism? *See generally* E. Purcell, *Crisis of Democratic Theory* (1973).

Would direct limitations on what governments can communicate in schools be preferable to a theory grounded in vindicating individual entitlements? *See* Yudof, "When Governments Speak: Toward a Theory of Government Expression and the First Amendment," 57 *Tex. L. Rev.* 863, 897–917 (1979). What sorts of rules might one wish to impose: a rule requiring equal treatment of different points of view; a rule that prohibited "indoctrination"; a rule prohibiting an ideologically homogeneous curriculum; a rule requiring affirmative support of important minority viewpoints? *See* Gottlieb, "In the Name of Patriotism: The Constitutionality of 'Bending' History in Public Secondary Schools," 62 *N.Y.U. L. Rev.* 497 (1987). Are these or any of the many other rules one might imagine workable? What would be their constitutional basis? *See* van Geel, "The Search for Constitutional Limits on Governmental Authority to Inculcate Youth," 62 *Tex. L. Rev.* 197 (1983). Might we be better off relying on the traditional adjudication of individual constitutional rights to assure presentation of a wide range of points of view in the schools? *See* M. Yudof, *When Government Speaks* (1983). Consider here Section III, *infra*. What provisions of the Constitution would you rely upon?

3. *Socialization and "Quality Education"*

Is political socialization inconsistent with learning to think for oneself and approaching problems critically? *See* C. Lindblom, *Inquiry and Change* (1990); Janowitz, *supra*. Would you, as a matter of policy, limit schools to the task of imparting skills? Consider these comments by Michael B. Katz:

> It must be emphasized that, opinion to the contrary notwithstanding, people ask no more of schools today than they did 125 years ago. Even then the schools were asked to do the impossible. As we have seen, the purpose of the school people has been more the development of attitudes than of intellect, and this continues to be the case. It is true, and this point must be stressed, of radical reformers as well as of advocates of law and order. The latter want the schools to stop crime and check immorality by teaching obedience to authority, respect for the law, and conformity to conventional standards. The former want the schools to reform society by creating a new sense of community

through turning out warm, loving, noncompetitive people.

* * *

The moral should be clear. Educational reformers should begin to distinguish between what formal schooling can and cannot do. They must separate the teaching of skills from the teaching of attitudes, and concentrate on the former. In actual fact, it is of course impossible to separate the two; attitudes adhere in any form of practice. But there is a vast difference between leaving the formation of attitudes untended and making them the object of education.

Katz, "The Present Moment in Educational Reform," 41 *Harv. Educ. Rev.* 342, 355 (1971).

4. Meyer v. Nebraska

While most parental challenges to education have been religion-based, the landmark case concerning the rights of parents to control their children's education was not, at least ostensibly, a religion case, although it did take place in the context of a religious school. *Meyer v. Nebraska*, 262 U.S. 390, 43 S.Ct. 625, 67 L.Ed. 1042 (1923), was decided on substantive due process grounds. A teacher of German in Zion Parochial School was convicted under a Nebraska statute that prohibited teaching foreign languages to children before they had passed the eighth grade. The avowed purpose of the legislation was to "promote civic development" by ensuring that students were well-steeped in American ideals and the English language before being exposed to foreign languages and cultures.

The Court struck down the Nebraska statute, holding that it unreasonably infringed the liberty guaranteed by the Due Process Clause of the Fourteenth Amendment:

> While this court has not attempted to define with exactness the liberty thus guaranteed, the term has received much consideration, and some of the included things have been definitely stated. Without doubt, it denotes not merely freedom from bodily restraint, but also the right of the individual to contract, to engage in any of the common occupations of life, to acquire useful knowledge, to marry, establish a home and bring up children, to worship God according to the dictates of his own conscience, and, generally, to enjoy those privileges long recognized at common law as essential to the orderly pursuit of happiness by free men . . . . Mere knowledge of the German language cannot reasonably be regarded as harmful. Heretofore it has been commonly looked upon as helpful and desirable. Plaintiff in error taught this language in school as part of his occupation. His right thus to teach and the right of parents to engage him so to instruct their children, we think, are within the liberty of the Amendment.

262 U.S. at 399, 43 S.Ct. at 626. The court expressly limited this broad holding, however, noting the unquestioned power of the state to impose compulsory education, to regulate all schools (both public and private), to require instruction in the English language, and to "prescribe a curriculum for the institutions which it supports." 262 U.S. at 402, 43 S.Ct. at 628.

The continuing vitality of *Meyer* today is somewhat murky, for the Supreme Court relies infrequently on the Due Process Clause of the Fourteenth Amendment for protecting substantive as opposed to procedural rights. The major exceptions are those cases dealing with rights of privacy and control of procreation. *See Roe v. Wade*, 410 U.S. 113, 93 S.Ct. 705, 35 L.Ed.2d 147 (1973); *Griswold v. Connecticut*, 381 U.S. 479, 85 S.Ct. 1678, 14 L.Ed.2d 510 (1965). *See generally* Henkin, "Privacy and Autonomy," 74 *Colum. L. Rev.* 1410 (1974). Substantive due process, at least in the economic sphere, acquired a bad name in the New Deal era, as the Court employed the doctrine to frustrate the political will of state legislatures and Congress. *See* chapter 1. The Court has since retreated from its early heavy reliance on this clause, but it has not overruled *Meyer* and it continues to pay homage to parental rights. *See, e.g., Smith v. Organization of Foster Families*, 431 U.S. 816, 97 S.Ct. 2094, 53 L.Ed.2d 14 (1977). Some commentators believe that *Meyer* and the procreation and privacy cases rest on traditional (common law, natural law, or constitutional law) notions that adults have a fundamental right to marry, procreate (or not procreate), and rear their children. *See* Heymann and Barzelay, "The Forest and the Trees: *Roe v. Wade* and its Critics," 53 *B. U. L. Rev.* 765 (1973). *But see* Regan, "Rewriting *Roe v. Wade*," 77 *Mich. L. Rev.* 1569 (1979).

It is common for state legislatures to grant parents a right to exempt their children from health and/or sex education courses to which they may object. *See, e.g.*, Mich. Stat. Ann. § 15.41507 (4) (1979). Should the courts recognize a constitutional right of parents to make a reasonable selection from the prescribed studies offered by a public school? Do *Pierce v. Society of Sisters*, discussed in chapter 1, and *Meyer* provide a basis for claiming such a right?

Or does the constitutionally required option of private school suggest there is no such right? If such a right were to be established, what would be the origin and scope of the right? Should it apply only to whole courses or might it apply to specific topics, books, or assignments? *See Samuel Benedict Memorial School v. Bradford*, 111 Ga. 801, 36 S.E. 920 (1900), in which a father objected to his daughter's writing a specific composition. Might such a right apply to courses mandated by the state legislature as well as those mandated by the local school board? Should such a right extend to the core curriculum ("basic" courses) or ought it only extend to courses outside the core? How is the core curriculum to be defined? Is a sex-education course not within the core, despite serious public interest in providing students with information about venereal diseases and procreation?

Who should have the burden of proof in these matters? Should the state be forced to justify its educational program? Or should parents be forced to demonstrate how inimical the school's program is to their own values or the adverse impact the school's program will have on their rights as parents to control the upbringing of their child? *See* Moskowitz, "Parental Rights and State Education," 50 *Wash. L. Rev.* 623 (1975).

If some degree of parental control is to be granted, are parents' objections to be recognized, no matter how idiosyncratic they are? Consider *State ex rel. Sheibley v. School District*, 31 Neb. 552, 48 N.W. 393 (1891), in which a parent objected to his daughter's study of grammar on the ground "that said study was not taught in said school as he had been instructed when he went to school." What sorts of objections ought to be honored? Do objections gain more weight the more closely they are tied to the First Amendment? Should only religious objections be given serious consideration? *See generally* S. Arons, *Compelling Belief* (1983).

1. Ritual and Coercion of Beliefs.

West Virginia State Board of Education v. Barnette

319 U.S. 624, 63 S.Ct. 1178, 87 L.Ed. 1628 (1943).

Mr. Justice Jackson delivered the opinion of the Court.

Following the decision by this Court on June 3, 1940, in *Minersville School District v. Gobitis*, 310 U.S. 586, the West Virginia legislature amended its statutes to require all schools therein to conduct courses of instruction in history, civics, and in the Constitutions of the United States and of the State "for the purpose of teaching, fostering and perpetuating the ideals, principles and spirit of Americanism, and increasing the knowledge of the organization and machinery of the government." Appellant Board of Education was directed, with advice of the State Superintendent of Schools, to "prescribe the courses of study covering these subjects" for public schools. The Act made it the duty of private, parochial and denominational schools to prescribe courses of study "similar to those required for the public schools."

The Board of Education on January 9, 1942, adopted a resolution containing recitals taken largely from the Court's *Gobitis* opinion and ordering that the salute to the flag become "a regular part of the program of activities in the public schools," that all teachers and pupils "shall be required to participate in the salute honoring the Nation represented by the Flag; provided, however, that refusal to salute the Flag be regarded as an act of insubordination, and shall be dealt with accordingly."

The resolution originally required the "commonly accepted salute to the Flag" which it defined. Objections to the salute as "being too much like Hitler's" were raised by the Parent and Teachers Association, the Boy and Girl Scouts, the Red Cross, and the Federation of Women's Clubs. Some modification appears to have been made in deference to these objections, but no concession was made to Jehovah's Witnesses. What is now required is the "stiff-arm" salute, the saluter to keep the right hand raised with palm turned up while the following is repeated: "I pledge allegiance to the Flag of the United States of America and to the Republic for which it stands; one nation, indivisible, with liberty and justice for all."

Failure to conform is "insubordination" dealt with by expulsion. Readmission is denied by statute until compliance. Meanwhile the expelled child is "unlawfully absent" and may be proceeded against as a delinquent. His parents or guardians are liable to prosecution, and if convicted are subject to fine not exceeding $50 and jail term not exceeding thirty days.

Appellees, citizens of the United States and of West Virginia, brought suit in the United States

District Court for themselves and other similarly situated asking its injunction to restrain enforcement of these laws and regulations against Jehovah's Witnesses. The Witnesses are an unincorporated body teaching that the obligation imposed by law of God is superior to that of laws enacted by temporal government. Their religious beliefs include a literal version of Exodus, Chapter 20, verses 4 and 5, which says: "Thou shalt not make unto thee any graven image, or any likeness of anything that is in heaven above, or that is in the earth beneath, or that is in the water under the earth; thou shalt not bow down thyself to them nor serve them." They consider that the flag is an "image" within this command. For this reason they refuse to salute it.

* * *

The freedom asserted by these appellees does not bring them into collision with rights asserted by any other individual. It is such conflicts which most frequently require intervention of the State to determine where the rights of one end and those of another begin. But the refusal of these persons to participate in the ceremony does not interfere with or deny rights of others to do so. Nor is there any question in this case that their behavior is peaceable and orderly. The sole conflict is between authority and rights of the individual. The State asserts power to condition access to public education on making a prescribed sign and profession and at the same time to coerce attendance by punishing both parent and child. The latter stand on a right of self-determination in matters that touch individual opinion and personal attitude.

As the present Chief Justice said in dissent in the *Gobitis* case, the State may "require teaching by instruction and study of all in our history and in the structure and organization of our government, including the guarantees of civil liberty, which tend to inspire patriotism and love of country." 310 U.S. at 604. Here, however, we are dealing with a compulsion of students to declare a belief. They are not merely made acquainted with the flag salute so that they may be informed as to what it is or even what it means. The issue here is whether this slow and easily neglected route to aroused loyalties constitutionally may be short-cut by substituting a compulsory salute and slogan. . . .

* * *

[T]he compulsory flag salute and pledge require affirmation of a belief and an attitude of mind. It is not clear whether the regulation contemplates that pupils forego any contrary convictions of their own and become unwilling converts to the prescribed ceremony or whether it will be acceptable if they simulate assent by words without belief and by a gesture barren of meaning. It is now a commonplace that censorship or suppression of expression of opinion is tolerated by our Constitution only when the expression presents a clear and present danger of action of a kind the State is empowered to prevent and punish. It would seem that involuntary affirmation could be commanded only on even more immediate and urgent grounds than silence. But here the power of compulsion is invoked without any allegation that remaining passive during a flag salute ritual creates a clear and present danger that would justify an effort even to muffle expression. To sustain the compulsory flag salute we are required to say that a Bill of Rights which guards the individual's right to speak his own mind, left it open to public authorities to compel him to utter what is not in his mind.

Whether the First Amendment to the Constitution will permit officials to order observance of [a] ritual of this nature does not depend upon whether as a voluntary exercise we would think it to be good, bad or merely innocuous. Any credo of nationalism is likely to include what some disapprove or to omit what others think essential, and to give off different overtones as it takes on different accents or interpretations. If official power exists to coerce acceptance of any patriotic creed, what it shall contain cannot be decided by courts, but must be largely discretionary with the ordaining authority, whose power to prescribe would no doubt include power to amend. Hence validity of the asserted power to force an American citizen publicly to profess any statement of belief or to engage in any ceremony of assent to one, presents questions of power that must be considered independently of any idea we may have as to the utility of the ceremony in question.

Nor does the issue as we see it turn on one's possession of particular religious views or the sincerity with which they are held. While religion supplies appellees' motive for enduring the discomforts of making the issue in this case, many citizens who do not share these religious views hold such a compulsory rite to infringe constitutional liberty of the individual. It is not necessary to inquire whether nonconformist beliefs will exempt from the duty to salute unless we find power to make the salute a legal duty.

The *Gobitis* decision, however, *assumed*, as did the argument in that case and in this, that power exists in the State to impose the flag salute discipline upon school children in general. The Court only examined and rejected a claim based on religious beliefs of immunity from an unquestioned general rule. The question which underlies the flag salute controversy is whether such a ceremony so touching matters of opinion and political attitude may be imposed upon the individual by official authority under powers committed to any political organization under our Constitution. . . .

* * *

It was also considered in the *Gobitis* case that functions of educational officers in States, counties and school districts were such that to interfere with their authority "would in effect make us the school board for the country." [310 U.S.] at 598.

The Fourteenth Amendment, as now applied to the States, protects the citizen against the State itself and all of its creatures—Boards of Education not excepted. These have, of course, important, delicate, and highly discretionary functions, but none that they may not perform within the limits of the Bill of Rights. That they are educating the young for citizenship is reason for scrupulous protection of Constitutional freedoms of the individual, if we are not to strangle the free mind at its source and teach youth to discount important principles of our government as mere platitudes.

Such Boards are numerous and their territorial jurisdiction often small. But small and local authority may feel less sense of responsibility to the Constitution, and agencies of publicity may be less vigilant in calling it to account. The action of Congress in making flag observance voluntary and respecting the conscience of the objector in a matter so vital as raising the Army contrasts sharply with these local regulations in matters relatively trivial to the welfare of the nation. There are village tyrants as well as village Hampdens, but none who acts under color of law is beyond reach of the Constitution.

The *Gobitis* opinion reasoned that this is a field "where courts possess no marked and certainly no controlling competence," that it is committed to the legislatures as well as the courts to guard cherished liberties and that it is constitutionally appropriate to "fight out the wise use of legislative authority in the forum of public opinion and before legislative assemblies rather than to transfer such a contest to the judicial arena," since all the "effective means of inducing political changes are left free." [310 U.S.] at 597–98, 600.

The very purpose of a Bill of Rights was to withdraw certain subjects from the vicissitudes of political controversy, to place them beyond the reach of majorities and officials, and to establish them as legal principles to be applied by the courts. One's right to life, liberty, and property, to free speech, a free press, freedom of worship and assembly, and other fundamental rights may not be submitted to vote; they depend on the outcome of no elections.

* * *

Lastly, and this is the very heart of the *Gobitis* opinion, it reasons that "National unity is the basis of national security," that the authorities have "the right to select appropriate means for its attainment," and hence reaches the conclusion that such compulsory measures toward "national unity" are constitutional. [310 U.S.] at 595. Upon the verity of this assumption depends our answer in this case.

National unity as an end which officials may foster by persuasion and example is not in question. The problem is whether under our Constitution compulsion as here employed is a permissible means for its achievement.

Struggles to coerce uniformity of sentiment in support of some end thought essential to their time and country have been waged by many good as well as by evil men. Nationalism is a relatively recent phenomenon but at other times and places the ends have been racial or territorial security, support of a dynasty or regime, and particular plans for saving souls. As first and moderate methods to attain unity have failed, those bent on its accomplishment must resort to an ever-increasing severity. As governmental pressure toward unity becomes greater, so strife becomes more bitter as to whose unity it shall be. Probably no deeper division of our people could proceed from any provocation than from finding it necessary to choose what doctrine and whose program public educational officials shall compel youth to unite in embracing. . . .

The case is made difficult not because the principles of its decision are obscure but because the flag involved is our own. Nevertheless, we apply the limitations of the Constitution with no fear that freedom to be intellectually and spiritually diverse or even contrary will disintegrate the social organization. To believe that patriotism will not flourish if patriotic ceremonies are voluntary and spontaneous instead of a compulsory routine is to make an unflattering estimate of the appeal of our institutions to free minds. . . .

If there is any fixed star in our constitutional constellation, it is that no official, high or petty, can prescribe what shall be orthodox in politics, nationalism, religion, or other matters of opinion or force citizens to confess by word or act their faith therein. If there are any circumstances which permit an exception, they do not now occur to us.

We think the action of the local authorities in compelling the flag salute and pledge transcends constitutional limitations on their power and invades the sphere of intellect and spirit which it is the purpose of the First Amendment to our constitution to reserve from all official control.

Affirmed

Mr. Justice Black and Mr. Justice Douglas, concurring:

We are substantially in agreement with the opinion just read, but since we originally joined with the Court in the *Gobitis* case, it is appropriate that we make a brief statement of reasons for our change of view.

Reluctance to make the Federal Constitution a rigid bar against state regulation of conduct thought inimical to the public welfare was the controlling influence which moved us to consent to the *Gobitis* decision. Long reflection convinced us that although the principle is sound, its application in the particular case was wrong. *Jones v. Opelika*, 316 U.S. 584, 623. We believe that the statute before us fails to accord full scope to the freedom of religion secured to the appellees by the First and Fourteenth Amendments.

The statute requires the appellees to participate in a ceremony aimed at inculcating respect for the flag and for this country. The Jehovah's Witnesses, without any desire to show disrespect for either the flag or the country, interpret the Bible as commanding, at the risk of God's displeasure, that they not go through the form of a pledge of allegiance to any flag. The devoutness of their belief is evidenced by their willingness to suffer persecution and punishment, rather than make the pledge.

No well-ordered society can leave to the individuals an absolute right to make final decisions, unassailable by the State, as to everything they will or will not do. The First Amendment does not go so far. Religious faiths, honestly held, do not free individuals from responsibility to conduct themselves obediently to laws which are either imperatively necessary to protect society as a whole from grave and pressingly imminent dangers or which, without any general prohibition, merely regulate time, place or manner of religious activity. Decision as to the constitutionality of particular laws which strike at the substance of religious tenets and practices must be made by this Court. The duty is a solemn one, and in meeting it we cannot say that a failure, because of religious scruples, to assume a particular physical position and to repeat the words of a patriotic formula creates a grave danger to the nation. Such a statutory exaction is a form of test oath, and the test oath has always been abhorrent in the United States.

Words uttered under coercion are proof of loyalty to nothing but self-interest. Love of country must spring from willing hearts and free minds, inspired by a fair administration of wise laws enacted by the people's elected representatives within the bounds of express constitutional prohibitions. These laws must, to be consistent with the First Amendment, permit the widest toleration of conflicting viewpoints consistent with a society of free men.

Neither our domestic tranquillity in peace nor our martial effort in war depend on compelling little children to participate in a ceremony which ends in nothing for them but a fear of spiritual condemnation. If, as we think, their fears are groundless, time and reason are the proper antidotes for their errors. The ceremonial, when enforced against conscientious objectors, more likely to defeat than to serve its high purpose, is a handy implement for disguised religious persecution. As such, it is inconsistent with our Constitution's plan and purpose.

* * *

Mr. Justice Frankfurter, dissenting. . . .

Not so long ago we were admonished that "the only check upon our own exercise of power is our own sense of self-restraint. For the removal of unwise laws from the statute books appeal lies not to the courts but to the ballot and to the processes of democratic government. . . ."

* * *

The reason why from the beginning even the narrow judicial authority to nullify legislation has been viewed with a jealous eye is that it serves to prevent the full play of the democratic process. The fact that it may be an undemocratic aspect of our scheme of government does not call for its rejection or its disuse. But it is the best of reasons, as this Court has frequently recognized, for the greatest caution in its use.

* * *

Under our constitutional system the legislature is charged solely with civil concerns of society. If the avowed or intrinsic legislative purpose is either to promote or to discourage some religious community or creed, it is clearly within the constitutional restrictions imposed on legislatures and cannot stand. But it by no means follows that legislative power is wanting whenever a general nondiscriminatory civil regulation in fact touches conscientious scruples or religious beliefs of an individual or a group. Regard for such scruples or beliefs undoubtedly presents one of the most reasonable claims for the exertion of legislative accommodation. It is, of course, beyond our power to rewrite the State's requirement, by providing exemptions for those who do not wish to participate in the flag salute or by making some other accommodations to meet their scruples. That wisdom might suggest the making of such accommodations and that school administration would not find it too difficult to make them and yet maintain the ceremony for those not refusing to conform, is outside our province to suggest. . . .

This is no dry, technical matter. It cuts deep into one's conception of the democratic process—it concerns no less the practical differences between the means for making these accommodations that are open to courts and to legislatures. A court can only strike down. It can only say "This or that law is void." It cannot modify or qualify, it cannot make exceptions to a general requirement. And it strikes down not merely for a day. . . .

The constitutional protection of religious freedom terminated disabilities, it did not create new privileges. It gave religious equality, not civil immunity. Its essence is freedom from conformity to religious dogma, not freedom from conformity to law because of religious dogma. Religious loyalties may be exercised without hindrance from the state, not the state may not exercise that which except by leave of religious loyalties is within the domain of temporal power. Otherwise each individual could set up his own censor against obedience to laws conscientiously deemed for the public good by those whose business it is to make laws.

* * *

The essence of the religious freedom guaranteed by our Constitution is therefore this: no religion shall either receive the state's support or incur its hostility. Religion is outside the sphere of political government. This does not mean that all matters on which religious organizations or beliefs may pronounce are outside the sphere of government. Were this so, instead of the separation of church and state, there would be the subordination of the state on any matter deemed within the sovereignty of the religious conscience. Much that is the concern of temporal authority affects the spiritual interests of men. But it is not enough to strike down a nondiscriminatory law that it may hurt or offend some dissident view. It would be too easy to cite numerous prohibitions and injunctions to which laws run counter if the variant interpretations of the Bible were made the tests of obedience to law. The validity of secular laws cannot be measured by their conformity to religious doctrines. It is only in a theocratic state that ecclesiastical doctrines measure legal right or wrong.

An act compelling profession of allegiance to a religion, no matter how subtly or tenuously promoted, is bad. But an act promoting good citizenship and national allegiance is within the domain of governmental authority and is therefore to be judged by the same considerations of power and of constitutionality as those involved in the many claims of immunity from civil obedience because of religious scruples.

* * *

Parents have the privilege of choosing which schools they wish their children to attend. And the question here is whether the state may make certain requirements that seem to it desirable or important for the proper education of those future citizens who go to schools maintained by the states, or whether the pupils in those schools may be relieved from those requirements if they run counter to the consciences of their parents. Not only have parents the right to send children to schools of their own choosing, but the state has no right to bring such schools "under a strict government control" or give "affirmative direction concerning the intimate and essential details of such schools, entrust their control to public officers, and deny both owners and patrons reasonable choice and discretion in respect of teachers, curriculum, and textbooks." *Farrington v. Tokushige*, 273 U.S. 284, 298 (1926). Why should not the state likewise have constitutional power to make reasonable provisions for the proper instruction of children in schools maintained by it?

* * *

We are told that a flag salute is a doubtful substitute for adequate understanding of our institutions. The states that require such a school exercise do not have to justify it as the only means for promoting good citizenship in children, but merely as one of diverse means for accomplishing a worthy end. We may deem it a foolish measure, but the point is that this Court is not the organ of government to resolve doubts as to whether it will fulfill its purpose. Only if there be no doubt that any reasonable mind could entertain can we deny to the states the right to resolve doubts their way and not ours.

* * *

One's conception of the Constitution cannot be severed from one's conception of a judge's function in applying it. The Court has no reason for existence if it merely reflects the pressures of the day. Our system is built on the faith that men set apart for this special function, freed from the influences of immediacy and from the deflections of wordly ambition, will become able to take a view of longer range than the period of responsibility entrusted to Congress and legislatures. We are dealing with matters as to which legislators and voters have conflicting views. Are we as judges to impose our strong convictions on where wisdom lies? That which three years ago had seemed to five successive Courts to lie within permissible areas of legislation is now outlawed by the deciding shift of opinion of two Justices. What reason is there to believe that they or their successors may not have another view a few years hence? Is that which was deemed to be of so fundamental a nature as to be written into the Constitution to endure for all times to be the sport of shifting winds of doctrine? Of course, judicial opinions, even as to questions of constitutionality, are not immutable. As has been true in the past, the Court will from time to time reverse its position. But I believe that never before these Jehovah's Witnesses cases (except for minor deviations subsequently retraced) has this Court overruled decisions so as to restrict the powers of democratic government. Always heretofore, it has withdrawn narrow views of legislative authority so as to authorize what formerly it had denied.

In view of this history it must be plain that what thirteen Justices found to be within the constitutional authority of a state, legislators can not be deemed unreasonable in enacting. Therefore, in denying to the states what heretofore has received such impressive judicial sanction, some other tests of unconstitutionality must surely be guiding the Court than the absence of a rational justification for the legislation. But I know of no other test which this Court is authorized to apply in nullifying legislation.

* * *

The uncontrollable power wielded by this Court brings it very close to the most sensitive areas of public affairs. As appeal from legislation to adjudication becomes more frequent, and its consequences more far-reaching, judicial self-restraint becomes more and not less important, lest we unwarrantably enter social and political domains wholly outside our concern. I think I appreciate fully the objections to the law before us. But to deny that it presents a question upon which men might reasonably differ appears to me to be intolerance. And since men may so reasonably differ, I deem it beyond my constitutional power to assert my view of the wisdom of this law against the view of the State of West Virginia. . . .

NOTES AND QUESTIONS

1. Barnette: *A Free Exercise Case?*

Is *Barnette* a case about free exercise of religion or freedom of expression? Might the necessity to distinguish *Minersville School District v. Gobitis*, 310 U.S. 586, 60 S.Ct. 1010, 84 L.Ed. 1375 (1940), explain the majority's choice of constitutional doctrine? Do Justices Black and Douglas distinguish or repudiate *Gobitis*? Is Justice Frankfurter responding to the majority or to Black and Douglas? Viewed as a free exercise case, are the arguments in favor of the Jehovah's Witnesses stronger, or is Justice Frankfurter correct in viewing with alarm the granting of exemptions from patriotic rituals on the basis of free exercise claims? *Cf. Employment Division, Department of Human Resources v. Smith*, ___U.S. ___, 110 S.Ct. 1595 (1990). See generally Laycock, "The Remnants of Free Exercise," 1990 *Sup. Ct.* Rev. ___ ; McConnell, "Free Exercise Revisionism and the *Smith* Decision," 57 *Chi. L. Rev.* 1109 (1990). Is *Wisconsin v. Yoder*, discussed in chapter 1, consistent with Frankfurter's views? *See Sherman v. Community Consol. School Dist.*, 714 F.Supp. 932 (N.D. Ill. 1989). Is the state's interest compelling?

Does the state have "less onerous" means of inculcating patriotic values?

2. *An "Implied Political Establishment Clause"?*

Why is a voluntary patriotic ceremony, but not a voluntary religious ceremony, permitted in the public schools? Why is not coercion as much a problem in *Barnette* as in the school prayer cases? Is it that the state's interest in socializing students to patriotic values is more substantial than its interest in sectarian socialization? Or is it that the Constitution bars the establishment of religion but not the establishment of a political "religion"? What of the words in the Pledge of Allegiance about "one nation under God"? Is this an Establishment Clause violation? *See Sherman v. Community Consol. School Dist., supra.*

3. *Rights Not to Participate in a Political Demonstration?*

The majority acknowledges a right on the part of government to attempt to foster patriotism and love of country. *See* T. van Geel, *The Courts and American Education* 189 (1987). Yet it prohibits a compulsory flag salute as a way of achieving this objective. What does this distinction suggest? Might *Barnette* be viewed as forbidding the state from compelling participation in a ceremony that is tantamount to political *action*? Or can it be viewed as forbidding forced participation in a political demonstration that seeks to foster loyalty through a purely emotional appeal? *Cf.* J. P. Stern, *Hitler: The Fuhrer and the People* 37 (1975). Thus, might the case be viewed as protecting a right of nonparticipation in a patriotic ritual, or more broadly, might it protect a right not to participate in group political activities or even a right of nonassociation? *Cf. Abood v. Detroit Board of Education*, 431 U.S. 209, 97 S.Ct. 1782, 52 L.Ed.2d 261 (1977). If this is the basis of *Barnette*, why is it constitutional for the state to compel attendance in civics courses? *See* S. Arons, *Compelling Belief* 67–68 (1983). As in the school prayer cases, is the Court distinguishing between instruction about religion and patriotism and rituals designed to foster religion and patriotism?

4. *Coercion to Speak*

Is *Barnette* primarily concerned with a coerced declaration of belief? Does this mean that there is a constitutional right to remain silent? *See generally* Gaebler, "First Amendment Protection Against Government Compelled Expression and Association," 23 *B. C. L.* Rev. 995 (1982).

In *Wooley v. Maynard*, 430 U.S. 705, 97 S.Ct. 1428, 51 L.Ed.2d 752 (1977), a case involving a New Hampshire statute requiring residents' noncommercial motor vehicles to bear license plates embossed with the state motto, "Live Free or Die," the Court struck down the law at the behest of the Jehovah's Witnesses. The Court held that the right to speak and the right not to speak were "complementary components" of the First Amendment. 430 U.S. at 714, 97 S.Ct. at 1435.

What is the constitutional basis of a "right not to speak"? Is it that silence is a form of expression, or is it that a coerced confession of belief is an affront to dignity, an improper *means* of state communication and socialization? *See* T. Emerson, *The System of Freedom of Expression* 30 (1970).

In *Wooley*, the Chief Justice, writing for the majority, stated that the issue for decision was "whether the state may constitutionally require an individual to participate in the dissemination of an ideological message by displaying it on his private property in a manner and for the express purpose that it be observed and read by the public." 430 U.S. at 713, 97 S.Ct. at 1434. Was a similar issue involved in *Barnette*? Is it the compulsion to transmit the message that is critical, or is it that observers and listeners may falsely attribute the belief to the speaker? Justice Rehnquist dissented on precisely this ground in *Wooley*, arguing that reasonable people would not construe a message on a license plate as an indication of affirmation of the owner's or driver's beliefs. 430 U.S. at 719, 97 S.Ct. at 1437. Would the other students and the teachers in *Barnette* be likely to think that recital of the flag salute revealed the Jehovah's Witnesses' true beliefs? If not, is not Professor Emerson's interpretation of *Barnette* better supported than Rehnquist's view? Is it correct, then, to assert that the school prayer cases are a substantive limitation on *what* governments may say, whereas *Barnette* is a limit on *how* governments may get across a legitimate message? *Cf. Linmark Associates v. Township of Willingboro*, 431 U.S. 85, 97 S.Ct. 1614, 52 L.Ed.2d 155 (1977) (ban on posting of "For Sale" and "Sold" signs in front of residential property declared unconstitutional).

5. *Problems*

Does *Barnette* prevent public schools from requiring students to stand for the singing of the national anthem? *See Sheldon v. Fannin*, 221 F.Supp. 766 (D. Ariz. 1963). Does *Barnette* require excusing children who object to patriotic exercises that celebrate Memorial Day or Lincoln's Birthday?

Schools often close for religious or patriotic holidays. When schools close, could nonattendance be viewed as compelled affirmation of belief in violation of *Barnette* or viewed as compelled "nonassociation" in violation of *Barnette*? Would remaining open but excusing those who wish to celebrate the day provide a solution, or would this policy lead to an even greater extent to a forced affirmation of belief by the students?

6. Teachers and the Flag Salute

If a teacher refuses to participate in a salute to the flag, does *Barnette* provide the teacher with constitutional protection, or are teachers to be treated differently because they are role models and have been hired to implement the school's curriculum? *See Russo v. Central School District No. 1*, 469 F.2d 623 (2d Cir. 1972), *cert. denied*, 411 U.S. 932, 93 S.Ct. 1899, 36 L.Ed.2d 391 (1973).

Board of Education, Island Trees Union Free School District No. 26 v. Pico

457 U.S. 853, 102 S.Ct. 2799, 73 L.Ed.2d 435 (1982).

Justice Brennan announced the judgment of the Court, and delivered an opinion in which Justice Marshall and Justice Stevens joined, and in which Justice Blackmun joined except for Part II–A–(1).

The principal question presented is whether the First Amendment imposes limitations upon the exercise by a local school board of its discretion to remove library books from high school and junior high school libraries.

I

Petitioners are the Board of Education of the Island Trees Union Free School District No. 26, in New York, and Richard Ahrens, Frank Martin, Christina Fasulo, Patrick Hughes, Richard Melchers, Richard Michaels, and Louis Nessim. When this suit was brought, Ahrens was the President of the Board, Martin was the Vice-President, and the remaining petitioners were Board members. The Board is a state agency charged with responsibility for the operation and administration of the public schools within the Island Trees School District including the Island Trees High School and Island Trees Memorial Junior High School. Respondents are Steven Pico, Jacqueline Gold, Glenn Yarris, Russell Rieger, and Paul Sochinski. When this suit was brought, Pico, Gold, Yarris, and Rieger were students at the High School, and Sochinski was a student at the Junior High School.

In September 1975, petitioners Ahrens, Martin, and Hughes attended a conference sponsored by Parents of New York United (PONYU), a politically conservative organization of parents concerned about education legislation in the State of New York. At the conference these petitioners obtained lists of books described by Ahrens as "objectionable," . . . and by Martin as "improper fare for school students," . . . .[2] It was later determined that the High School library contained nine of the listed books, and that another listed book was in the Junior High School library.[3] In February 1976, at a meeting with the superintendent of schools and the principals of the High School and Junior High School, the Board gave an "unofficial direction" that the listed books be removed from the library shelves and delivered to the Board's offices, so that Board members could read them.[4] When this directive was carried out, it be-

2. The District Court noted, however, that petitioners "concede that the books are not obscene." 474 F.Supp. 387, 392 (1979).

3. The nine books in the High School library were: *Slaughter House Five*, by Kurt Vonnegut, Jr.; *The Naked Ape*, by Desmond Morris; *Down These Mean Streets*, by Piri Thomas, *Best Short Stories of Negro Writers*, edited by Langston Hughes; *Go Ask Alice*, of anonymous authorship; *Laughing Boy*, by Oliver LaFarge; *Black Boy*, by Richard Wright; *A Hero Ain't Nothin' But A Sandwich*, by Alice Childress; and *Soul on Ice*, by Eldridge Cleaver. The book in the Junior High School library was *A Reader for Writers*, edited by Jerome Archer. Still another listed book, *The Fixer*, by Bernard Malamud, was found to be included in the curriculum of a twelfth grade literature course. 474 F.Supp. 387, 389 and nn. 2–4.

4. The superintendent of schools objected to the Board's informal directive, noting that: "we already have a policy . . . designed expressly to handle such problems. It calls for the Superintendent, upon receiving an objection to a book or books, to appoint a committee to study them and make recommendations. I feel it is a good policy—and it is Board policy—and that it should be followed in this instance. Further, I think it can be followed quietly and in such a way as to reduce, perhaps avoid, the public furor which has always attended such issues in the past." . . .

The Board responded to the superintendent's objection by repeating its directive "that *all copies* of the library books in question be removed from the libraries to the Board's office." . . .

came publicized, and the Board issued a press release justifying its action. It characterized the removed books as "anti-American, anti-Christian, anti-Semitic, and just plain filthy," and concluded that "It is our duty, our moral obligation, to protect the children in our schools from this moral danger as surely as from physical and medical dangers." 474 F.Supp. 387, 390.

A short time later, the Board appointed a "Book Review Committee," consisting of four Island Trees parents and four members of the Island Trees schools staff, to read the listed books and to recommend to the Board whether the books should be retained, taking into account the books' "educational suitability," "good taste," "relevance," and "appropriateness to age and grade level." In July, the Committee made its final report to the Board, recommending that five of the listed books be retained[5] and that two others be removed from the school libraries.[6] As for the remaining four books, the Committee could not agree on two,[7] took no position on one,[8] and recommended that the last book be made available to students only with parental approval.[9] The Board substantially rejected the Committee's report later that month, deciding that only one book should be returned to the High School library without restriction,[10] that another should be made available subject to parental approval,[11] but that the remaining nine books should "be removed from elementary and secondary libraries and [from] use in the curriculum." 474 F.Supp., at 391.[12] The Board gave no reasons for rejecting the recommendations of the Committee that it had appointed.

Respondents reacted to the Board's decision by bringing the present action under 42 U.S.C. § 1983 in the United States District Court for the Eastern District of New York. They alleged that petitioners had "ordered the removal of the books from school libraries and proscribed their use in the curriculum because particular passages in the books offended their social, political and moral tastes and not because the books, taken as a whole, were lacking in educational value." . . . Respondents claimed that the Board's actions denied them their rights under the First Amendment. They asked the court for a declaration that the Board's actions were unconstitutional, and for preliminary and permanent injunctive relief ordering the Board to return the nine books to the school libraries and to refrain from interfering with the use of those books in the schools' curricula. . . .

The District Court granted summary judgment in favor of petitioners. 474 F.Supp. 387 (1979). In the court's view, "the parties substantially agree[d] about the motivation behind the board's actions," *id.*, at 391—namely, that "the board acted not on religious principles but on its conservative educational philosophy, and on its belief that the nine books removed from the school library and curriculum were irrelevant, vulgar, immoral, and in bad taste, making them educationally unsuitable for the district's junior and senior high school students." *Id.*, at 392. With this factual premise as its background, the court rejected respondents' contention that their First Amendment rights had been infringed by the Board's actions. Noting that statute, history, and precedent had vested local school boards with a broad discretion to formulate educational policy,[13] the court concluded that it should not intervene in " 'the daily operations of school systems' " unless " 'basic constitutional values' " were " 'sharply implicate[d],' "[14] and determined that the conditions for such intervention did not exist in the present case. Acknowledging that the "removal [of the books] . . . clearly

5. *The Fixer, Laughing Boy, Black Boy, Go Ask Alice,* and *Best Short Stories by Negro Writers.* . . .

6. *The Naked Ape* and *Down These Mean Streets.* . . .

7. *Soul on Ice* and *A Hero Ain't Nothin' But A Sandwich.* . . .

8. *A Reader for Writers.* . . . The reason given for this disposition was that all members of the Committee had not been able to read the book. . . .

9. *Slaughter House Five.* . . .

10. *Laughing Boy.* . . .

11. *Black Boy.* . . .

12. As a result, the nine removed books could not be assigned or suggested to students in connection with school work. *Ibid.* However, teachers were not instructed to refrain from discussing the removed books or the ideas and positions expressed in them. . . .

13. *Id.*, at 396–97, citing *Presidents Council, District 25 v. Community School Board # 25*, 457 F.2d 289 (CA2 1972); *James v. Board of Education*, 461 F.2d 566, 573 (CA2 1972); *East Hartford Educational Assn. v. Board of Education*, 562 F.2d 838, 856 (CA2 1977) (en banc).

14. 474 F.Supp., at 395–97, quoting *Presidents Council, District 25 v. Community School Board # 25, supra*, at 291 (in turn quoting *Epperson v. Arkansas*, 393 U.S. 97 . . . (1968)).

was content-based," the court nevertheless found no constitutional violation of the requisite magnitude: "The board has restricted access only to certain books which the board believed to be, in essence, vulgar. While removal of such books from a school library may . . . reflect a misguided educational philosophy, it does not constitute a sharp and direct infringement of any first amendment right." *Id.*, at 397.

A three-judge panel of the United States Court of Appeals for the Second Circuit reversed the judgment of the District Court, and remanded the action for a trial on respondents' allegations. 638 F.2d 404 (1980). Each judge on the panel filed a separate opinion. Delivering the judgment of the court, Judge Sifton treated the case as involving "an unusual and irregular intervention in the school libraries' operations by persons not routinely concerned with such matters," and concluded that petitioners were obliged to demonstrate a reasonable basis for interfering with respondents' First Amendment rights. *Id.*, at 414–15. He then determined that, at least at the summary judgment stage, petitioners had not offered sufficient justification for their action,[15] and concluded that respondents "should have . . . been offered an opportunity to persuade a finder of fact that the ostensible justifications for [petitioners'] actions . . . were simply pretexts for the suppression of free speech." *Id.*, at 417.[16] Judge Newman concurred in the result. *Id.*, at 432–38. He viewed the case as turning on the contested factual issue of whether petitioners' removal decision was motivated by a justifiable desire to remove books containing vulgarities and sexual explicitness, or rather by an impermissible desire to suppress ideas. *Id.*, at 436–37.[17] . . .

II

We emphasize at the outset the limited nature of the substantive question represented by the case before us. Our precedents have long recognized certain constitutional limits upon the power of the State to control even the curriculum and classroom. For example, *Meyer v. Nebraska*, 262 U.S. 390 . . . (1923), struck down a state law that forbade the teaching of modern foreign languages in public and private schools, and *Epperson v. Arkansas*, 393 U.S. 97 . . . (1968), declared unconstitutional a state law that prohibited the teaching of the Darwinian theory of evolution in any state-supported school. But the current action does not require us to re-enter this difficult terrain, which *Meyer* and *Epperson* traversed without apparent misgiving. For as this case is presented to us, it does not involve textbooks, or indeed any books that Island Trees students would be required to read.[18] Respondents do not seek in this Court to impose limitations upon their school board's discretion to prescribe the curricula of the Island Trees schools. On the contrary, the only books at issue in this case are *library* books, books that by their nature are optional rather than required reading. Our adjudication of the present case thus does not intrude into the classroom, or into the compulsory courses taught there. Furthermore, even as to library books, the action before us does not involve the *acquisition* of books. Respondents have not sought

15. After criticizing "the criteria for removal" employed by petitioners as "suffer[ing] from generality and overbreadth," and the procedures used by petitioners as "erratic, arbitrary and free-wheeling," Judge Sifton observed that "precision of regulation and sensitivity to First Amendment concerns" were "hardly established" by such procedures. 638 F.2d, at 416.

16. Judge Sifton stated that it could be inferred from the record that petitioners' "political views and personal taste [were] being asserted not in the interests of the children's well-being, but rather for the purpose of establishing those views as the correct and orthodox ones for all purposes in the particular community." *Id.*, at 417.

17. Judge Mansfield dissented, 638 F.2d, at 419–32, based upon a distinctly different reading of the record developed in the District Court. According to Judge Mansfield, "the undisputed evidence of the motivation for the Board's action was the perfectly permissible ground that the books were indecent, in bad taste, and unsuitable for educational purposes." *Id.*, at 430. He also asserted that in reaching its decision "the Board [had] acted carefully, conscientiously and responsibly after according due process to all parties concerned." *Id.*, at 422. Judge Mansfield concluded that "the First Amendment entitles students to reasonable freedom of expression but not to freedom from what some may consider to be excessively moralistic or conservative selection by school authorities of library books to be used as educational tools." *Id.*, at 432.

18. Four of respondents' five causes of action complained of petitioners' "resolutions ordering the removal of certain books from the school libraries of the District and prohibiting the use of those books in the curriculum." . . . The District Court concluded "that respect for the school board's substantial control over educational content . . . precludes any finding of a first amendment violation arising out of removal of any of the books from use in the curriculum." 474 F.Supp., at 397. This holding is not at issue here. Respondents' fifth cause of action complained that petitioners' "resolutions prohibiting the use of certain books in the curriculum of schools in the District" had "imposed upon teachers in the District arbitrary and unreasonable restrictions upon their ability to function as teachers in violation of principles of academic freedom." . . . The District Court held that respondents had not proved this cause of action: "before such a claim may be sustained there must at least be a real, not an imagined controversy." 474 F.Supp., at 397. Respondents have not sought review of that holding in this Court.

to compel their school board to add to the school library shelves any books that students desire to read. Rather, the only action challenged in this case is the *removal* from school libraries of books originally placed there by the school authorities, or without objection from them.

The substantive question before us is still further constrained by the procedural posture of this case. Petitioners were granted summary judgment by the District Court. The Court of Appeals reversed that judgment, and remanded the action for a trial on the merits of respondents' claims. We can reverse the judgment of the Court of Appeals, and grant petitioners' request for reinstatement of the summary judgment in their favor, only if we determine that "there is no genuine issue as to any material fact," and that petitioners are "entitled to a judgment as a matter of law." Fed. Rule Civ. Proc. 56(c). In making our determination, any doubt as to the existence of a genuine issue of material fact must be resolved against petitioners as the moving party. *Adickes v. Kress & Co.*, 398 U.S. 144, 157–59 . . . (1970). Furthermore, "on summary judgment the inferences to be drawn from the underlying facts contained . . . in the affidavits, attached exhibits, and depositions submitted below . . . must be viewed in the light most favorable to the party opposing the motion." *United States v. Diebold, Inc.*, 369 U.S. 654, 655 . . . (1962).

In sum, the issue before us in this case is a narrow one, both substantively and procedurally. It may best be restated as two distinct questions. First, does the First Amendment impose *any* limitations upon the discretion of petitioners to remove library books from the Island Trees High School and Junior High School? Second, if so, do the affidavits and other evidentiary materials before the District Court, construed most favorably to respondents, raise a genuine issue of fact whether petitioners might have exceeded those limitations? . . .

A

(1)

We have . . . acknowledged that public schools are vitally important "in the preparation of individuals for participation as citizens," and as vehicles for "inculcating fundamental values necessary to the maintenance of a democratic political system." *Ambach v. Norwick*, 441 U.S. 68, 76–77 . . . (1979). We are therefore in full agreement with petitioners that local school boards must be permitted "to establish and apply their curriculum in such a way as to transmit community values," and that "there is a legitimate and substantial community interest in promoting respect for authority and traditional values be they social, moral, or political." . . .

At the same time, however, we have necessarily recognized that the discretion of the States and local school boards in matters of education must be exercised in a manner that comports with the transcendent imperatives of the First Amendment. . . .

* * *

In short, "First Amendment rights, applied in light of the special characteristics of the school environment, are available to . . . students."

Of course, courts should not "intervene in the resolution of conflicts which arise in the daily operations of school systems" unless "basic constitutional values" are "directly and sharply implicate[d]" in those conflicts. . . . But we think that the First Amendment rights of students may be directly and sharply implicated by the removal of books from the shelves of a school library. Our precedents have focused "not only on the role of the First Amendment in fostering individual self-expression but also on its role in affording the public access to discussion, debate, and the dissemination of information and ideas." *First National Bank of Boston v. Bellotti*, 435 U.S. 765, 783 . . . (1978). And we have recognized that "the State may not, consistently with the spirit of the First Amendment, contract the spectrum of available knowledge." *Griswold v. Connecticut*, 381 U.S. 479, 482 . . . (1965). In keeping with this principle, we have held that in a variety of contexts "the Constitution protects the right to receive information and ideas." *Stanley v. Georgia*, 394 U.S. 557, 564 . . . (1969); *see Kleindienst v. Mandel*, 408 U.S. 753, 762–63 . . . (1972). This right is an inherent corollary of the rights of free speech and press that are explicitly guaranteed by the Constitution, in two senses. First, the right to receive ideas follows ineluctably from the *sender's* First Amendment right to send them: "The right of freedom of speech and press . . . embraces the right to distribute literature, . . . and necessarily protects the right to receive it." *Martin v. Struthers*, 318 U.S. 141, 143 . . . (1943) (citation omitted). "The dissemination of ideas can accomplish nothing if otherwise willing addressees are not free to receive and consider them. It would be a barren marketplace of ideas that had only sellers and no buyers." *Lamont v. Postmaster General*, 381 U.S. 301, 308 . . . (1965) (Brennan, J., concurring).

More importantly, the right to receive ideas is a necessary predicate to the *recipient's* meaningful exercise of his own rights of speech, press, and political freedom. Madison admonished us that "A popular Government, without popular information, or the means of acquiring it, is but a Prologue to a Farce or a Tragedy; or, perhaps both. Knowledge will forever govern ignorance: And a people who mean to be their own Governors, must arm themselves with the power which knowledge gives." 9 *Writings of James Madison* 103 (G. Hunt ed. 1910). . . .

. . . [J]ust as access to ideas makes it possible for citizens generally to exercise their rights of free speech and press in a meaningful manner, such access prepares students for active and effective participation in the pluralistic, often contentious society in which they will soon be adult members. Of course all First Amendment rights accorded to students must be construed "in light of the special characteristics of the school environment." *Tinker v. Des Moines School Dist.*, . . . [393 U.S. 503, 506 (1969)]. But the special characteristics of the school *library* make that environment especially appropriate for the recognition of the First Amendment rights of students.

. . . *Keyishian v. Board of Regents*, 385 U.S. 589, 87 S.Ct. 675, 17 L.Ed.2d 629 (1967), observed that "students must always remain free to inquire, to study and to evaluate, to gain new maturity and understanding." The school library is the principal locus of such freedom. As one District Court has well put it, in the school library "a student can literally explore the unknown, and discover areas of interest and thought not covered by the prescribed curriculum. . . . Th[e] student learns that a library is a place to test or expand upon ideas presented to him, in or out of the classroom." *Right to Read Defense Comm. v. School Comm.*, 454 F.Supp. 703, 715 (D.Mass. 1978). Petitioners emphasize the inculcative function of secondary education, and argue that they must be allowed *unfettered* discretion to "transmit community values" through the Island Trees schools. But that weeping claim overlooks the unique role of the school library. It appears from the record that use of the Island Trees school libraries is completely voluntary on the part of students. Their selection of books from these libraries is entirely a matter of free choice; the libraries afford them an opportunity at self-education and individual enrichment that is wholly optional. Petitioners might well defend their claim of absolute discretion in matters of *curriculum* by reliance upon their duty to inculcate community values. But we think that petitioners' reliance upon that duty is misplaced where, as here, they attempt to extend their claim of absolute discretion beyond the compulsory environment of the classroom, into the school library and the regime of voluntary inquiry that there holds sway.

(2)

In rejecting petitioners' claim of absolute discretion to remove books from their school libraries, we do not deny that local school boards have a substantial legitimate role to play in the determination of school library content. We thus must turn to the question of the extent to which the First Amendment places limitations upon the discretion of petitioners to remove books from their libraries. In this inquiry we enjoy the guidance of several precedents. *West Virginia v. Barnette* . . . stated that "If there be any fixed star in our constitutional constellation, it is that no official, high or petty, can prescribe what shall be orthodox in politics, nationalism, religion, or other matters of opinion. . . . If there are any circumstances which permit an exception, they do not now occur to us." 319 U.S. . . . [624, 642 (1943)]. This doctrine has been reaffirmed in later cases involving education. . . .

With respect to the present case, the message of these precedents is clear. Petitioners rightly possess significant discretion to determine the content of their school libraries. But that discretion may not be exercised in a narrowly partisan or political manner. If a Democratic school board, motivated by party affiliation, ordered the removal of all books written by or in favor of Republicans, few would doubt that the order violated the constitutional rights of the students denied access to those books. The same conclusion would surely apply if an all-white school board, motivated by racial animus, decided to remove all books authored by blacks or advocating racial equality and integration. Our Constitution does not permit the official suppression of *ideas*. Thus whether petitioners' removal of books from their school libraries denied respondents their First Amendment rights depends upon the motivation behind petitioners' actions. If petitioners *intended* by their removal decision to deny respondents access to ideas with which petitioners disagreed, and if this intent was the decisive factor in petitioners' decision,[22] then petitioners have exercised their discretion in violation of the Constitution. To permit such intentions to control official actions would be to encourage the precise sort of officially prescribed orthodoxy unequivocally condemned in *Barnette*. On the other hand, respondents implicitly concede that an unconstitutional motivation would *not* be demonstrated if it were shown that petitioners had decided to remove the books at issue because those books were pervasively vulgar. . . . And again, respondents concede that if it were demonstrated that the removal decision was based solely upon the "educational suitability" of the books in question, then their removal would be "perfectly permissible." . . . In other words, in respondents' view such motivations, if decisive of petitioners' actions, would not carry the danger of an official suppression of ideas, and thus would not violate respondents' First Amendment rights.

* * *

B

We now turn to the remaining question presented by this case: Do the evidentiary materials that were before the District Court, when construed most favorably to respondents, raise a genuine issue of material fact whether petitioners exceeded constitutional limitations in exercising their discretion to remove the books from the school libraries? We conclude that the materials do raise such a question, which forecloses summary judgment in favor of petitioners.

* * *

Standing alone, . . . [the] evidence respecting the substantive motivations behind petitioners' removal decision would not be decisive. This would be a very different case if the record demonstrated that petitioners had employed established, regular, and facially unbiased procedures for the review of controversial materials. But the actual record in the case before us suggests the exact opposite. Petitioners' removal procedures were vigorously challenged below by respondents, and the evidence on this issue sheds further light on the issue of petitioners' motivations. . . .

. . . [W]e cannot conclude that petitioners were "entitled to a judgment as a matter of law." The evidence plainly does not foreclose the possibility that petitioners' decision to remove the books rested decisively upon disagreement with constitutionally protected ideas in those books, or upon a desire on petitioners' part to impose upon the students of the Island Trees High School and Junior High School a political orthodoxy to which petitioners and their constituents adhered. Of course, some of the evidence before the District Court might lead a finder of fact to accept petitioners' claim that their removal decision was based upon constitutionally valid concerns. But that evidence at most creates a genuine issue of material fact on the critical question of the credibility of petitioners' justifications for their decision: On that issue, it simply cannot be said that there is no genuine issue as to any material fact.

The mandate shall issue forthwith.

Affirmed.

Justice Blackmun, concurring in part and concurring in the judgment.

While I agree with much in today's plurality opinion, and while I accept the standard laid down by the plurality to guide proceedings on remand, I write separately because I have a somewhat different perspective on the nature of the First Amendment right involved.

I

To my mind, this case presents a particularly complex problem because it involves two competing principles of constitutional stature. On the one hand, as the dissenting opinions demonstrate, and as we all can agree, the Court has acknowledged the importance of the public schools "in the prep-

22. By "decisive factor" we mean a "substantial factor" in the absence of which the opposite decision would have been reached. *See Mt. Healthy City Board of Ed. v. Doyle,* 429 U.S. . . . [274, 287 (1977)].

aration of individuals for participation as citizens, and in the preservation of values on which our society rests." *Ambach v. Norwick*, 441 U.S. 68, 76 . . . (1979). Because of the essential socializing function of schools, local education officials may attempt "to promote civic virtues," *Ambach v. Norwick*, 441 U.S., at 80, . . . and to "awake[n] the child to cultural values." *Brown v. Board of Education*, 347 U.S. 483, 493 . . . (1954). Indeed, the Constitution presupposes the existence of an informed citizenry prepared to participate in governmental affairs, and these democratic principles obviously are constitutionally incorporated into the structure of our government. It therefore seems entirely appropriate that the State use "public schools [to] . . . inculcat[e] fundamental values necessary to the maintenance of a democratic political system." *Ambach v. Norwick*, 441 U.S., at 77. . . .

On the other hand, as the plurality demonstrates, it is beyond dispute that schools and school boards must operate within the confines of the First Amendment. In a variety of academic settings the Court therefore has acknowledged the force of the principle that schools, like other enterprises operated by the State, may not be run in such a manner as to "prescribe what shall be orthodox in politics, nationalism, religion, or other matters of opinion." *West Virginia State Board of Education v. Barnette*, 319 U.S. 624, 642 . . . (1943). While none of these cases define the limits of a school board's authority to choose a curriculum and academic materials, they are based on the general proposition that "state-operated schools may not be enclaves of totalitarianism. . . . In our system, students may not be regarded as closed-circuit recipients of only that which the State chooses to communicate." *Tinker v. Des Moines School Dist.*, 393 U.S. 503, 511 . . . (1969).

The Court in *Tinker* thus rejected the view that "a State might so conduct its schools as to 'foster a homogeneous people.' " *Id.*, at 511, . . . quoting *Meyer v. Nebraska*, 262 U.S. 390, 402 . . . (1923). Similarly, *Keyishian v. Board of Regents*, 385 U.S. 589 . . . (1967)—a case that involved the State's attempt to remove "subversives" from academic positions at its universities, but that addressed itself more broadly to public education in general—held that "[t]he classroom is peculiarly the 'marketplace of ideas' "; the First Amendment therefore "does not tolerate laws that cast a pall of orthorodoxy over the classroom." *Id.*, at 603. . . . And *Barnette* is most clearly applicable here: its holding was based squarely on the view that "[f]ree public education, if faithful to the ideal of secular instruction and political neutrality, will not be partisan or enemy of any class, creed, party, or faction." The Court therefore made it clear that imposition of "ideological discipline" was not a proper undertaking for school authorities. 319 U.S., at 637. . . .

In combination with more generally applicable First Amendment rules, most particularly the central proscription of content-based regulations of speech, *see Police Department of Chicago v. Mosley*, 408 U.S. 92 . . . (1972), the cases outlined above yield a general principle: the State may not suppress exposure to ideas—for the sole *purpose* of suppressing exposure to those ideas—absent sufficiently compelling reasons. Because the school board must perform all its functions "within the limits of the Bill of Rights," *Barnette*, 319 U.S., at 637, . . . this principle necessarily applies in at least a limited way to public education. Surely this is true in an extreme case: as the plurality notes, it is difficult to see how a school board, consistent with the First Amendment, could refuse for political reasons to buy books written by Democrats or by Negroes, or books that are "anti-American" in the broadest sense of that term. Indeed, Justice Rehnquist appears "cheerfully [to] concede" this point. . . .

In my view, then, the principle involved here is both narrower and more basic than the "right to receive information" identified by the plurality. I do not suggest that the State has any affirmative obligation to provide students with information or ideas, something that may well be associated with a "right to receive." . . . And I do not believe, as the plurality suggests, that the right at issue here is somehow associated with the peculiar nature of the school library . . . if schools may be used to inculcate ideas, surely libraries may play a role in that process.[1]

1. As a practical matter, however, it is difficult to see the First Amendment right that I believe is at work here playing a role in a school's choice of curriculum. The school's finite resources—as well as the limited number of hours in the day—require that education officials make sensitive choices between subjects to be offered and competing areas of academic emphasis; subjects generally are excluded simply because school officials have chosen to devote their resources to one rather than to another subject. . . . [A] choice of this nature does not run afoul of the First Amendment. In any event, the Court has recognized that students' First Amendment rights in most cases must give way if they interfere "with the schools' work or . . . [with] the

Instead, I suggest that certain forms of state discrimination *between* ideas are improper. In particular, our precedents command the conclusion that the State may not act to deny access to an idea simply because state officials disapprove of that idea for partisan or political reasons.[2]

Certainly, the unique environment of the school places substantial limits on the extent to which official decisions may be restrained by First Amendment values. But that environment also makes it particularly important that *some* limits be imposed. The school is designed to, and inevitably will, inculate ways of thought and outlooks; if educators intentionally may eliminate all diversity of thought, the school will "strangle the free mind at its source and teach youth to discount important principles of our government as mere platitudes." *Barnette*, 319 U.S., at 637. . . . As I see it, then, the question in this case is how to make the delicate accommodation between the limited constitutional restriction that I think is imposed by the First Amendment, and the necessarily broad state authority to regulate education. In starker terms, we must reconcile the schools' "inculcative" function with the First Amendment's bar on "prescriptions of orthodoxy."

II

In my view, we strike a proper balance here by holding that school officials may not remove books for the *purpose* of restricting access to the political ideas or social perspectives discussed in them, when that action is motivated simply by the officials' disapproval of the ideas involved. It does not seem radical to suggest that state action calculated to suppress novel ideas or concepts is fundamentally antithetical to the values of the First Amendment. At a minimum, allowing a school board to engage in such conduct hardly teaches children to respect the diversity of ideas that is fundamental to the American system. In this context, then, the school board must "be able to show that its action was caused by something more than a mere desire to avoid the discomfort and unpleasantness that always accompany an unpopular viewpoint," *Tinker v. Des Moines School Dist.*, 393 U.S., at 509, . . . and that the board had something in mind in addition to the suppression of partisan or political views it did not share.

As I view it, this is a narrow principle. School officials must be able to choose one book over another, without outside interference, when the first book is deemed more relevant to the curriculum, or better written, or when one of a host of other politically neutral reasons is present. These decisions obviously will not implicate First Amendment values. And even absent space or financial limitations, First Amendment principles would allow a school board to refuse to make a book available to students because it contains offensive language, *cf. FCC v. Pacifica Foundation*, 438 U.S. 726, 757 . . . (1978) (Powell, J., concurring), or because it is psychologically or intellectually inappropriate for the age group, or even, perhaps, because the ideas it advances are "manifestly inimical to the public welfare." *Pierce v. Society of Sisters*, 268 U.S. 510, 534 . . . (1925). And, of course, school officials may choose one book over another because they believe that one subject is more important, or is more deserving of emphasis.

. . . And I believe that tying the First Amendment right to the *purposeful* suppression of ideas makes the concept more manageable than Justice Rehnquist acknowledges. Most people would recognize that refusing to allow discussion of current events in Latin class is a policy designed to "inculcate" Latin, not to suppress ideas. Similarly, removing a learned treatise criticizing American foreign policy from an elementary school library because the students would not understand it is an action unrelated to the *purpose* of suppressing ideas. In my view,

---

rights of other students to be secure and to be let alone," *Tinker v. Des Moines School Dist.*, 393 U.S. 503, 508 . . . (1969), and such interference will rise to intolerable levels if public participation in the management of the curriculum becomes commonplace. In contrast, library books on a shelf intrude not at all on the daily operation of a school.

I also have some doubt that there is a theoretical distinction between removal of a book and failure to acquire a book. But as Judge Newman observed, there is a profound practical and evidentiary distinction between the two actions: "removal, more than failure to acquire, is likely to suggest that an impermissible political motivation may be present. There are many reasons why a book is not acquired, the most obvious being limited resources, but there are few legitimate reasons why a book, once acquired, should be removed from a library not filled to capacity." 638 F.2d 404, 436 (CA2 1980) (Newman, J., concurring in the result).

2. In effect, my view presents the obverse of the plurality's analysis: while the plurality focuses on the failure to provide information, I find crucial the State's decision to single out an idea for disapproval and then deny access to it.

however, removing the same treatise because it is "anti-American" raises a far more difficult issue.

* * *

Because I believe that the plurality has derived a standard similar to the one compelled by my analysis, I join all but Part IIA(1) of the plurality opinion.

Justice White, concurring in the judgment. [Opinion omitted.]

Chief Justice Burger, with whom Justice Powell, Justice Rehnquist, and Justice O'Connor join, dissenting.

The First Amendment, as with other parts of the Constitution, must deal with new problems in a changing world. In an attempt to deal with a problem in an area traditionally left to the states, a plurality of the Court, in a lavish expansion going beyond any prior holding under the First Amendment, expresses its view that a school board's decision concerning what books are to be in the school library is subject to federal court review. Were this to become the law, this Court would come perilously close to becoming a "super censor" of school board library decisions. Stripped to its essentials, the issue comes down to two important propositions: *first*, whether local schools are to be administered by elected school boards, or by federal judges and teenage pupils; and *second*, whether the values of morality, good taste, and relevance to education are valid reasons for school board decisions concerning the contents of a school library. In an attempt to place this case within the protection of the First Amendment, the plurality suggests a new "right" that, when shorn of the plurality's rhetoric, allows this Court to impose its own views about what books must be made available to students.

* * *

Justice Powell, dissenting.

The plurality opinion today rejects a basic concept of public school education in our country: that the States and locally elected school boards should have the responsibility for determining the educational policy of the public schools. After today's decision any junior high school student, by instituting a suit against a school board or teacher, may invite a judge to overrule an educational decision by the official body designated by the people to operate the schools.

* * *

Just this term the Court held, in an opinion I joined, that the children of illegal aliens must be permitted to attend the public schools. *See Plyler v. Doe*, 467 U.S. 202 . . . (1982). Quoting from earlier opinions, the Court noted that "the public school [is] a most vital civic institution for the preservation of a democratic system of government" and that the public schools are "the primary vehicle for transmitting 'the values on which our society rests.' " *Id.*, at 221. . . . By denying to illegal aliens the opportunity "to absorb the values and skills upon which our social order rests" the law under review placed a lifelong disability upon these illegal alien children. *Ibid.*

Today the plurality drains much of the content from these apt phrases. A school board's attempt to instill in its students the ideas and values on which a democratic system depends is viewed as an impermissible suppression of other ideas and values on which other systems of government and other societies thrive. Books may not be removed because they are indecent; extoll violence, intolerance and racism; or degrade the dignity of the individual. Human history, not the least of the twentieth century, records the power and political life of these very ideas. But they are not our ideas or values. Although I would leave this educational decision to the duly constituted board, I certainly would not *require* a school board to promote ideas and values repugnant to a democratic society or to teach such values to *children*.

In different contexts and in different times, the destruction of written materials has been the symbol of depotism and intolerance. But the removal of nine vulgar or racist books from a high school library by a concerned local school board does not raise this specter. For me, today's decision symbolizes a debilitating encroachment upon the institutions of a free people.

Attached as an Appendix hereto is Judge Mansfield's summary of excerpts from the books at issue in this case.

Appendix

"The excerpts which led the Board to look into the educational suitability of the books in question are set out (with minor corrections after comparison with the text of the books themselves) below. The pagination and the underlinings are retained from the original report used by the board. In newer editions of some of the books, the quotes appear at different pages.

"1) *SOUL ON ICE* by Eldridge Cleaver

Page quote

157–58 '. . . There are white men who will pay you to fuck their wives. They approach you and say, 'How would you like to fuck a white woman?' 'What is this?' you ask. 'On the up-and-up,' he assures you. 'It's all right. She's my wife. She needs black rod, is all. She has to have it. It's like a medicine or drug to her. She has to have it. I'll pay you. It's all on the level, no trick involved. Interested?' You go with him and he drives you to their home. The three of you go into the bedroom. There is a certain type who will leave you and his wife alone and tell you to pile her real good. After it is all over, he will pay you and drive you to wherever you want to go. Then there are some who like to peep at you through a keyhole and watch you have his woman, or peep at you through a window, or lie under the bed and listen to the creaking of the bed as you work out. . . .'

"2) *A HERO AIN'T NOTHING BUT A SANDWICH* by Alice Childress

Page quote

10 'Hell, no! *Fuck the society.*'

64–65 'The hell with the junkie, the wino, the capitalist, the welfare checks, the world . . . yeah, and *fuck* you too!'

75–76 'They can have back the spread and curtains, I'm too old for them *fuckin* bunnies anyway.'

"3) *THE FIXER* by Bernard Malamud

Page quote

52 'What do you think goes on in the wagon at night: Are the drivers on their knees *fucking their mothers?*'

90 '*Fuck yourself*, said the blinker, etc.'

92 'Who else would do anything like that but a *motherfucking* Zhid?'

146 'No more noise out of you or I'll shoot your *Jew cock off.*'

189 'Also there's a lot of *fucking in the Old Testament*, so how is that religious?'

192 'You better go *fuck yourself*, Bok, said Kogin, I'm onto your Jew tricks.'

215 'Ding-dong giddyap. A *Jew's cock's* in the devil's hock.'

216 'You *cocksucker* Zhid, I ought make you lick it up off the floor.'

"4) *GO ASK ALICE* by Anonymous

Page quote

31 'I wonder if sex without acid could be so exciting, so wonderful, so indescribable. I always thought it just took a minute, or that it would be like dogs mating.'

47 'Chris and I walked into Richie and Ted's apartment to find the bastards stoned and making love to each other . . . low class queer.'

81 'shitty, goddamned, pissing, ass, goddamned beJesus, screwing life's, ass, shit. Doris was ten and had *humped* with who knows how many men in between . . . her current stepfather started having sex with her but good . . . *sonofabitch balling her*'

83 'but now when I face a girl its like facing a boy. I get all excited and turned on. *I want to screw with the girl* . . .'

84 'I'd rather screw with a guy . . . sometimes I want one of the girls to kiss me. I want her to touch me, to have her sleep under me.'

* * *

"5) *SLAUGHTERHOUSE FIVE* by Kurt Vonnegut, Jr.

Page quote

29 'Get out of the road, you dumb *motherfucker*.' The last word was still a novelty in the speech of white people in 1944. It was fresh and astonishing to Billy, who had never *fucked* anybody . . .'

32 'You stake a guy out on an anthill in the desert—see? He's facing upward, and you put *honey* all over his *balls and pecker*, and you cut off his eyelids so he has to stare at the sun till he dies.'

34 'He had a prophylactic kit containing two tough condoms 'For the prevention of disease only!' . . . He had a dirty picture of a *woman* attempting *sexual intercourse with a shetland pony*.'

94 & 95 'But the Gospels actually taught this: Before you kill somebody, make absolutely sure he isn't well connected . . . The flaw in the Christ stories, said the visitor from outer space, was that Christ who didn't look like much, was actually the son of the Most Powerful Being in the Universe. Readers understood that, so, when they came to the crucifixion, they naturally thought . . . Oh boy—they sure picked the wrong guy to lynch this time! And that thought had a brother: There are right

people to lynch. People not well connected. . . . The visitor from outer space made a gift to Earth of a new Gospel. In it, Jesus really WAS a nobody, and a pain in the neck to a lot of people with better connections then he had. . . . So the people amused themselves one day by nailing him to a cross and planting the cross in the ground. There couldn't possibly be any repercussions, the lynchers thought . . . since the new Gospel hammered home again and again what a nobody Jesus was. And then just before the nobody dies . . . the voice of God came crashing down. He told the people that he was adopting the bum as his son . . . God said this: *From this moment on, He will punish horribly anybody who torments a bum who has no connections.*'

* * *

"6) *THE BEST SHORT STORIES BY NEGRO WRITERS* Ed. by Langston Hughes

Page quote

176 'like bat's shit and camel piss,'

228 'that no-count bitch of a daughter of yours is up there up North making a whore of herself.'

237 'they made her get out and stand in front of the headlights of the car and pull down her pants and raise her dress—they said that was the only way they could be sure. And you can imagine what they said and what they did—.'

303 'You need some pussy. Come on, let's go up to the whore house on the hill.' 'Oh, these bastards, these bastards, this God damned Army and the bastards in it. The sons of bitches!'

436 'he produced a brown rag doll, looked at her again, then grabbed the doll by its legs and tore it part way up the middle. Then he jammed his finger into the rip between the doll's legs. The other men laughed. . . .'

444 'The pimps, hustlers, lesbians, and others trying to misuse me.'

* * *

"7) *BLACK BOY* by Richard Wright

Page quote

70–71 "We black children—seven or eight or nine years of age—used to run to the Jew's store and shout:

> . . . Bloody Christ Killers
> Never trust a Jew
> Bloody Christ Killers
> What won't a Jew do . . .
> Red, white and blue
> Your pa was a Jew
> Your ma a dirty dago
> What the hell is you?'

265 'Crush that nigger's nuts, nigger!' 'Hit that nigger!' 'Aw, fight, you goddam niggers!' 'Sock 'im, in his f-k-g piece!' 'Make 'im bleed!'

"8) *LAUGHING BOY* by Oliver LaFarge

Page quote

38 'I'll tell you, she is all bad; for two bits she will do the worst thing.'

258–59 'I was frightened when he wanted me to lie with him, but he made me feel all right. He knew all about how to make women forget themselves, that man.'

"9) *THE NAKED APE* by Desmond Morris

Page quote

73–74 'Also, the frontal approach provides the maximum possibility for stimulation of the female's clitoris during the pelvic thrusting of the male. It is true that it will be passively stimulated by the pulling effect of the male's thrusts, regardless of his body position in relation to the female, but in a face-to-face mating there will in addition be the direct rhythmic pressure of the male's pubic region on to the clitoral area, and this will considerably heighten the stimulation . . .' 'So it seems plausible to consider that face-to-face copulation is basic to our species. There are, of course, a number of variations that do not eliminate the frontal element: male above, female above, side by side, squatting, standing, and so on, but the most efficient and commonly used one is with both partners horizontal, the male above the female. . . .'

* * *

"10) *READER FOR WRITERS* . . ."

638 F.2d 404, 419–22 n. 1 (Mansfield, J., dissenting).

Justice Rehnquist, with whom The Chief Justice and Justice Powell join, dissenting.

Addressing only those aspects of the constitutional question which must be decided to determine whether or not the District Court was correct in granting summary judgment, I conclude that it was. I agree fully with the views expressed by The Chief Justice, and concur in his opinion. I disagree with Justice Brennan's opinion because it is largely hypothetical in character, failing to take account of the facts as admitted by the parties pursuant to local rules of the

District Court for the Eastern District of New York, and because it is analytically unsound and internally inconsistent.

I

A

* * *

Considering only the respondents' description of the factual aspects of petitioners' motivation, Justice Brennan's apparent concern that the Board's action may have been a sinister political plot "to suppress ideas" may be laid to rest. The members of the Board, in deciding to remove these books, were undoubtedly influenced by their own "personal values, morals, and tastes," just as any member of a school board is apt to be so influenced in making decisions as to whether a book is educationally suitable. Respondents essentially conceded that some excerpts of the removed books "contained profanities, some were sexually explicit, some were ungrammatical, some were anti-American, and some were offensive to racial, religious, or ethnic groups."

Respondents also agreed that, "[a]lthough the books themselves were excluded from use in the schools in any way, [petitioners] have not precluded discussion about the themes of the books or the books themselves." . . . Justice Brennan's concern with the "suppression of ideas" thus seems entirely unwarranted on this state of the record, and his creation of constitutional rules to cover such eventualities is entirely gratuitous. Though for reasons stated in part II of this opinion I entirely disagree with Justice Brennan's treatment of the constitutional issue, I also disagree with his opinion for the entirely separate reason that it is not remotely tailored to the facts presented by this case.

In the course of his discussion, Justice Brennan states:

> "Petitioners rightly possess significant discretion to determine the content of their school libraries. But that discretion may not be exercised in a narrowly partisan or political manner. If a Democratic school board, motivated by party affiliation, ordered the removal of all books written by or in favor of Republicans, few would doubt that the order violated the constitutional rights of the students. . . . The same conclusion would surely apply if an all-white school board, motivated by racial animus, decided to remove all books authored by blacks or advocating racial equality and integration. Our Constitution does not permit the official suppression of *ideas*."

I can cheerfully concede all of this, but as in so many other cases the extreme examples are seldom the ones that arise in the real world of constitutional litigation. In *this case* the facts taken most favorably to respondents suggest that nothing of this sort happened. The nine books removed undoubtedly did contain "ideas," but in the light of the excerpts from them found in the dissenting opinion of Judge Mansfield in the Court of Appeals, it is apparent that eight of them contained demonstrable amounts of vulgarity and profanity, see 638 F.2d, at 419–22 n. 1, and the ninth contained nothing that could be considered partisan or political, see *id.*, at 428 n. 6. As already demonstrated, respondents admitted as much. Petitioners did not, for the reasons stated hereafter, run afoul of the First and Fourteenth Amendments by removing these particular books from the library in the manner in which they did. I would save for another day—feeling quite confident that that day will not arrive—the extreme examples posed in Justice Brennan's opinion.

B

Considerable light is shed on the correct resolution of the constitutional question in this case by examining the role played by petitioners. Had petitioners been the members of a town council, I suppose all would agree that, absent a good deal more than is present in this record, they could not have prohibited the sale of these books by private booksellers within the municipality. But we have also recognized that the government may act in other capacities than as sovereign, and when it does the First Amendment may speak with a different voice. . . . By the same token, expressive conduct which may not be prohibited by the State as sovereign may be proscribed by the State as property owner: "The State, no less than a private owner of property, has power to preserve the property under its control for the use to which it is lawfully dedicated." *Adderley v. Florida*, 385 U.S. 39, 47 . . . (1967) (upholding state prohibition of expressive conduct on certain state property).

With these differentiated roles of government in mind, it is helpful to assess the role of government as educator, as compared with the role of government as sovereign. When it acts as an educator, at least at the elementary and secondary school level, the government is engaged in inculcating social values and knowledge in relatively impressionable young people. Obviously there are innumerable decisions to be made as to what courses should be taught, what books should be purchased, or what teachers should be employed. In every one of these areas the members of a school board will act on the basis of their own personal or moral values, will attempt to mirror those of the community, or will abdicate the making of such decisions to so-called "experts." . . . In the very course of administering the many-faceted operations of a school district, the mere decision to purchase some books will necessarily preclude the possibility of purchasing others. The decision to teach a particular subject may preclude the possibility of teaching another subject. A decision to replace a teacher because of ineffectiveness may by implication be seen as a disparagement of the subject matter taught. In each of these instances, however, the book or the exposure to the subject matter may be acquired elsewhere. The managers of the school district are not proscribing it as to the citizenry in general, but are simply determining that it will not be included in the curriculum or school library. In short, actions by the government as educator do not raise the same First Amendment concerns as actions by the government as sovereign.

II

Justice Brennan would hold that the First Amendment gives high school and junior high school students a "right to receive ideas" in the school. . . . This right is a curious entitlement. It exists only in the library of the school, and only if the idea previously has been acquired by the school in book form. It provides no protection against a school board's decision not to acquire a particular book, even though that decision denies access to ideas as fully as removal of the book from the library, and it prohibits removal of previously acquired books only if the remover "dislike[s] the ideas contained in those books," even though removal for any other reason also denies the students access to the books. . . .

But it is not the limitations which Justice Brennan places on the right with which I disagree; they simply demonstrate his discomfort with the new doctrine which he fashions out of whole cloth. It is the very existence of a right to receive information, in the junior high school and high school setting, which I find wholly unsupported by our past decisions and inconsistent with the necessarily selective process of elementary and secondary education.

A

The right described by Justice Brennan has never been recognized in the decisions of this Court and is not supported by their rationale. . . .

* * *

. . . Justice Brennan correctly characterizes the right of access to ideas as "an inherent corollary of the rights of free speech and press" which "follows ineluctably from the *sender's* First Amendment right to send them." . . . But he then fails to recognize the predicate right to speak from which the students' right to receive must follow. It would be ludicrous, of course, to contend that all authors have a constitutional right to have their books placed in junior high school and high school libraries. And yet without such a right our prior precedents would not recognize the reciprocal right to receive information. Justice Brennan disregards this inconsistency with our prior cases and fails to explain the constitutional or logical underpinnings of a right to hear ideas in a place where no speaker has the right to express them.

Justice Brennan also correctly notes that the reciprocal nature of the right to receive information derives from the fact that it "is a necessary predicate to the *recipient's* meaningful exercise of his own rights of speech, press, and political freedom." . . . But the denial of access to ideas inhibits ones own acquisition of knowledge only when that denial is relatively complete. If the denied ideas are readily available from the same source in other accessible locations, the benefits to be gained from exposure to those ideas have not been foreclosed by the State. This fact is inherent in the right-to-receive cases relied on by Justice Brennan, every one of which concerned the complete denial of access to the ideas sought. . . .

B

There are even greater reasons for rejecting Justice Brennan's analysis, however, than the significant fact that we have never adopted it in the past. "The importance of public schools in the preparation of individuals for participation as citizens, and in the preservation of the values on which our society rests, has long been recognized by our decisions." *Ambach v. Norwick*, 441 U.S. 68 . . . (1979). Public schools fulfill the vital role of teaching students the basic skills necessary to function in our society, and of "inculcating fundamental values necessary to the maintenance of a democratic political system." *Id.*, at 77. . . . The idea that such students have a right of access, *in the school*, to information other than that thought by their educators to be necessary is contrary to the very nature of an inculcative education.

Education consists of the selective presentation and explanation of ideas. The effective acquisition of knowledge depends upon an orderly exposure to relevant information. Nowhere is this more true than in elementary and secondary schools, where, unlike the broad-ranging inquiry available to university students, the courses taught are those thought most relevant to the young students' individual development. Of necessity, elementary and secondary educators must separate the relevant from the irrelevant, the appropriate from the inappropriate. Determining what information *not* to present to the students is often as important as identifying relevant material. This winnowing process necessarily leaves much information to be discovered by students at another time or in another place, and is fundamentally inconsistent with any constitutionally required eclecticism in public education.

* * *

As already mentioned, elementary and secondary schools are inculcative in nature. The libraries of such schools serve as supplements to this inculcative role. Unlike university or public libraries, elementary and secondary school libraries are not designed for free-wheeling inquiry; they are tailored, as the public school curriculum is tailored, to the teaching of basic skills and ideas. Thus, Justice Brennan cannot rely upon the nature of school libraries to escape the fact that the First Amendment right to receive information simply has no application to the one public institution which, by its very nature, is a place for the selective conveyance of ideas.

After all else is said, however, the most obvious reason that petitioners' removal of the books did not violate respondents' right to receive information is the ready availability of the books elsewhere. Students are not denied books by their removal from a school library. The books may be borrowed from a public library, read at a university library, purchased at a bookstore, or loaned by a friend. The government as educator does not seek to reach beyond the confines of the school. Indeed, following the removal from the school library of the books at issue in this case, the local public library put all nine books on display for public inspection. Their contents were fully accessible to any inquisitive student.

C

Justice Brennan's own discomfort with the idea that students have a right to receive information from their elementary or secondary schools is demonstrated by the artificial limitations which he places upon the right—limitations which are supported neither by logic nor authority and which are inconsistent with the right itself. The attempt to confine the right to the library is one such limitation, the fallacies of which have already been demonstrated.

As a second limitation, Justice Brennan distinguishes the act of removing a previously acquired book from the act of refusing to acquire the book in the first place: "[N]othing in our decision today affects in any way the discretion of a local school board to choose books to *add* to the libraries of their schools. . . . [O]ur holding today affects only the discretion to *remove* books." . . . If Justice Brennan truly has found a "right to receive ideas," . . . however, this distinction between acquisition and removal makes little sense. The failure of a library to acquire a book denies access to its contents just as effectively as does the removal of the book from the library's shelf. As a result of either action the book cannot be found in the "principal locus" of freedom discovered by Justice Brennan. . . .

The justification for this limiting distinction is said by Justice Brennan to be his concern in this case with "the suppression of ideas." . . . Whatever may be the analytical usefulness of this appealing sounding phrase, . . . the suppression of ideas surely is not the identical twin of the denial of access to information. Not every official act which denies access to an idea can be characterized as a suppression of the idea. Thus unless the "right to receive information" and the prohibition against "suppression of ideas" are each a kind of mother-hubbard catch phrase for whatever First Amendment doctrines one wishes to cover, they would not appear to be interchangeable.

* * *

The final limitation placed by Justice Brennan upon his newly discovered right is a motive requirement: the First Amendment is violated only "[i]f petitioners *intended* by their removal decision to deny respondents access to ideas with which petitioners disagreed." . . . But bad motives and good motives alike deny access to the books removed. If Justice Brennan truly recognizes a constitutional right to receive information, it is difficult to see why the reason for the denial makes any difference. Of course Justice Brennan's view is that intent matters because the First Amendment does not tolerate an officially prescribed orthodoxy. . . . But this reasoning mixes First Amendment apples and oranges. The right to receive information differs from the right to be free from an officially prescribed orthodoxy. Not every educational denial of access to information casts a pall of orthodoxy over the classroom.

It is difficult to tell from Justice Brennan's opinion just what motives he would consider constitutionally impermissible. I had thought that the First Amendment proscribes content-based restrictions on the marketplace of ideas. *See Widmar v. Vincent*, 454 U.S. 263, 269–70 (1981). Justice Brennan concludes, however, that a removal decision based solely upon the "educational suitability" of a book or upon its perceived vulgarity is " 'perfectly permissible.' " . . . But such determinations are based as much on the content of the book as determinations that the book espouses pernicious political views.

* * *

III

Accepting as true respondents' assertion that petitioners acted on the basis of their own "personal values, morals, and tastes," . . . I find the actions taken in this case hard to distinguish from the myriad choices made by school boards in the routine supervision of elementary and secondary schools. "Courts do not and cannot intervene in the resolution of conflicts which arise in the daily operation of school systems and which do not directly and sharply implicate basic constitutional values." *Epperson v. Arkansas*, 393 U.S., at 104. . . . In this case respondents' rights of free speech and expression were not infringed, and by respondents' own admission no ideas were "suppressed." I would leave to another day the harder cases.

* * *

NOTES AND QUESTIONS

1. Right to Receive Information

Justice Brennan, in his plurality opinion, relies upon a right to receive information and ideas to justify the conclusion that the removal of books from a public school library may violate the First Amendment. What is the constitutional basis for such a right? *See generally* Lee, "The Supreme Court and the Right to Receive Expression," 1987 *Sup. Ct. Rev.* 303. Does the right to acquire information and knowledge flow from a right to speak? Suppose there is no willing speaker? For example, might a student require a school library to acquire books that she wishes to read? If the "right to know" does not encompass the acquisition of books, why should it encompass decisions to remove books? If it does extend to book acquisitions, why should it not include course offerings? *See, e.g., State ex rel. Sheibley v. School Dist.*, 31 Neb. 552, 48 N.W. 393 (1891). For example, might a student seek a court order to require a school district to offer geology if no such course is currently offered? *See generally* Yudof, "Library Book Selection and the Public Schools," 59 *Ind. L. J.* 527, 545–46 (1984) (hereinafter "Library Book Selection"); Note, "State Indoctrination and the Protection of Non-State Voices in the Schools: Justifying a Prohibition of School Library Censorship," 35 *Stan. L. Rev.* 497 (1983).

Do authors, editors, and publishers have a constitutional right to have their books acquired by the state for dissemination in public schools?

Justice Brennan emphasizes the special nature of libraries as a factor in his constitutional analysis. What is so special about the library? *See* "Library Book Selection" at 546–48. Is it that a library can seek a balanced presentation of views through many books, but in the classroom a single text often is required? Or is it that each student can acquire knowledge from library books without interfering with the studies of others? That is, students may read from many books simultaneously in the library (or at home), whereas in class there is conflict if each person chooses what to learn and discuss? In effect, is he saying that the right to know, when exercised in a library, does not disrupt the educational mission of the school? In any event, what is the logical nexus between the right to know and the special characteristics of the school library?

How, if at all, would *Pico* apply to a school district's decision to remove a statue of a Confederate war hero on the ground that the statue conveys repugnant ideas about African Americans?

Would it be unconstitutional for a library to only acquire books that were directly related to the courses that formed the school's curriculum? What does Justice Rehnquist have to say about this?

If compulsory schooling is legitimate and if education inherently involves selection and judgment as to what will be studied, how coherent is a right to know in the public school setting? *See* van Geel, "The Prisoner's Dilemma and Education Policy," 3 *Notre Dame J. of Law, Eth. & Pub. Pol.* 301 (1988). If there is such a right, what is the releavance of motive? Why should it matter whether a book was removed for ideological or financial reasons? Or should the Court "have established a principle that would protect students from any effort by public schools to inculcate pupils with political ideas, attitudes, viewpoints, ideologies, values, or beliefs"? van Geel, "The Search for Constitutional Limits on Governmental Authority to Inculcate Youth, 62 *Tex. L. Rev.* 197, 239 (1983). Is this but another way of saying that public schooling is not a legitimate enterprise?

2. *Unconstitutional Motivation*

Justice Blackmun seeks to balance the inculcative or socialization mission of schools against a constitutional prohibition on the establishment of orthodoxy, and he seeks to achieve this balance through a motivation test: "I suggest that certain forms of state discrimination *between* ideas are improper. In particular, our precedents command the conclusion that the State may not act to deny access to an idea simply because state officials disapprove of the idea for partisan or political reasons." *See also Zykan v. Warsaw Community School Corp.*, 631 F.2d 1300 (7th Cir. 1980). How many of the justices accept this motivation framework for analysis—even if they disagree as to the application of the principle in *Pico*? *See* "Library Book Selection" at 549. What is the evidence that the Island Trees school board was motivated by a desire to impose a rigid political orthodoxy? Is it more difficult to justify a deacquisition decision than a decision not to acquire a book in the first place? Can books be too expensive to dust and maintain? Is the annotated list of books dispositive? What of the failure of the board to abide by established policies governing the library? *See* "Library Book Selection" at 551.

What is the difference between an illegitimate "pall of orthodoxy" and a legitimate educational effort, in good faith, to socialize students? *See generally* Ingeber, "Socialization, Indoctrination, or the 'Pall of Orthodoxy': Value Training in Public Schools," 1987 *U. Ill. L. F.* 15. Is not the flag salute law challenged in *Barnette* an attempt to create an unconstitutional pall of orthodoxy? Further, why is it unconstitutional to eliminate books written by or about Republicans or minority leaders, but constitutional to remove books that are vulgar or promote promiscuity? Are school officials not closing the minds of students to the pro-vulgarity and libertine positions? Should courts distinguish between consensual values (*e.g.*, opposition to drug abuse and sexual promiscuity, or the fostering of racial tolerance, good spelling, and patriotism) and disputed political and social questions (*e.g.*, advocacy of radical feminism, support of the New Deal, opposition to abortion)? *Cf. Arnold v. Board of Education*, 880 F.2d 305 (11th Cir. 1989) (school counselors may not "coerce" minors to refrain from consulting parents on abortion decision). Is this not a principled distinction? Is Justice Blackmun's concurrence "profoundly at odds with itself"? van Geel, *supra* at 326. Or is he attempting to define a constitutional concept of democratic education?

In the light of *Barnette*, should the definition of orthodoxy turn on how ideas are taught or promulgated and not on the content of the ideas? *See* O'Brien, "The Promise of *Pico*: A New Definition of Orthodoxy," 97 *Yale L. J.* 1805 (1988).

Might the constitutionality of a decision hinge entirely on motivation? For example, a decision not to acquire a Russian history book on the ground that Russian history is not part of the curriculum would be constitutional, but a decision based on objections to the ideas expressed in the book would be unconstitutional? *Cf. McCarthy v. Fletcher*, 207 Cal. App.3d 130, 254 Cal. Rptr. 714, 720 (1989).

What if a particular book is both ideologically objectionable to members of the school board and vulgar? If the board gives the wrong reason, is its action unconstitutional after *Pico*? Is Justice Rehnquist saying that a deacquisition decision is justifiable if the board could have acted on the basis of vulgarity—even if it did not?

Are most of the justices saying "that a school board's removal decision is legitimate if it is based on the educational suitability of the books"? *See Virgil v. School Bd. of Columbia County*, 862 F.2d 1517 (11th Cir. 1989). *See generally* "Library Book Selection" at 549. Is this tantamount to saying that school officials must act in good faith, good faith being tested against the educational mission of public schools? Would the removal of religiously oriented books be constitutional? Removal of the Bible? *See Roberts v. Madigan*, 921 F.2d 1047 (10th Cir. 1990). What of the removal of a library book because it is insulting to minority students? Is there a distinction between a library book and a school emblem? *See Crosby by Crosby v. Holsinger*, 852 F.2d 801 (4th Cir. 1988).

3. Irrevocable Delegation

If a school board has delegated decision-making power over school libraries to librarians and other officials, should it be permitted to revoke that delegation in particular cases? *See* "Library Book Selection" at 553–59. If a board is not constitutionally required to delegate authority over book selection, what is the warrant for a holding that it may not revoke a delegation when it disagrees with particular acquisition decisions? Should a board have the authority to remove books on account of their content only if the legislature expressly authorizes such actions? *See Wexner v. Anderson Union High Sch. Dist. Bd. of Trustees*, 209 Cal.App.3d 1438, 258 Cal. Rptr. 26 (1989).

4. Book Selection and Procedural Due Process

In *Loewen v. Turnipseed*, 488 F.Supp. 1138 (N.D. Miss. 1980), a "rating committee," appointed by the governor and state superintendent of education in Mississippi, approved a book entitled *Your Mississippi* for purchase by the State Textbook Purchasing Board and disapproved a book entitled *Mississippi: Conflict and Change*. The books were considered for use in ninth grade classes in Mississippi History, and apparently the state would purchase approved books for both public and parochial schools. The controversy arose because *Mississippi: Conflict and Change* allegedly emphasized the mistreatment of blacks in Mississippi, while the alternative did not. The rating committee split on the issue, with the white majority outvoting the black minority.

The court ultimately held the selection was motivated by racial discrimination, intended to perpetuate segregation, and was therefore unconstitutional. It also concluded that the rating committee's procedure for selecting the textbooks was unconstitutional. Mississippi law did not give "those adversely affected by it a voice in the matter." 488 F.Supp. at 1153. Since the publishers of the books were given an opportunity to present their positions to the committee, presumably the court had in mind the authors, students, faculty, and school districts across the state, and, indeed, they were the plaintiffs.

A governmental body is not constitutionally required to hold an adversary hearing in deciding to award, for example, a construction contract for a public building. On the other hand, governments normally are required to hold a due process hearing where their actions infringe on a protected property right or a liberty interest (see chapter 3). Should a state or local government be required to hold a hearing every time it decides to purchase some textbooks and not others?

3. Multiculturalism and the Public School Curriculum.

Crosby v. Holsinger

852 F.2d 801 (4th Cir. 1988).

Ervin, Circuit Judge:

This is the second appearance of "Johnny Reb" in this court. Johnny Reb, the former cartoon symbol of the Fairfax High School Rebels, was eliminated by defendant-appellee Harry Holsinger, the school's principal, after he received complaints from black students and parents. Students protested his decision in a number of ways before filing this action. The district court initially dismissed it as frivolous, but we reversed. 816 F.2d 162 (4th Cir.1987).* At trial, the court granted a directed verdict for Holsinger as to the broad "censorship" claim, and the jury returned a verdict for him on plaintiff-appellant Cheryl Crosby's narrower "protest restriction" claim. We affirm.

---

* Citing *Augustus v. School Board*, 507 F.2d 152, 155–56 (5th Cir. 1975); *Banks v. Muncie Community Schools*, 433 F.2d 292, 298 (7th Cir. 1970).

Holsinger acted to remove the symbol based on complaints that it offended black students and a suggestion by the school's Minority Achievement Task Force. He then allowed the students to choose a new symbol which was to be unrelated to the Confederacy.

After the elimination of Johnny Reb, the students protested by holding rallies at school, mounting a petition drive, attending a school board meeting, and displaying blue ribbons. Except for a single incident involving Crosby, Holsinger did nothing to interfere with these protests. In the one instance, he initially stopped Crosby from posting notices on school bulletin boards of the school board meeting before allowing it the next day. . . .

There is a difference between tolerating student speech and affirmatively promoting it. . . .

A school mascot or symbol bears the stamp of approval of the school itself. Therefore, school authorities are free to disassociate the school from such a symbol because of educational concerns. Here, Principal Holsinger received complaints that Johnny Reb offended blacks and limited their participation in school activities, so he eliminated the symbol based on legitimate concerns. Except to make the rough threshold judgment that this decision has an educational component, we will not interfere, and it is clear that educational concerns prompted Holsinger's decision.[2]

* * *

. . . [S]chool officials have the authority to disassociate the school from controversial speech even if it may limit student expression. Principal Holsinger was within his power to remove a school symbol that blacks found offensive.

Affirmed.

NOTES AND QUESTIONS

1. *Is Crosby Consistent with* Pico *and* Barnette?

The court holds in *Crosby* that the school principal's decision to eliminate the Johnny Reb cartoon symbol for Fairfax High School was prompted by educational concerns and that therefore there was no violation of the freedom of expression of the objecting students. On its face, the court's decision appears to be consistent with the view of most of the justices in *Pico* that good faith educational decisions regarding library book selections are not constitutionally infirm. But why is not the principal's action an example of attempting to suppress ideas, to impose a pall of orthodcxy? Is it not precisely the symbolism of the Johnny Reb cartoon, rooted in the slavery practiced in the Confederacy, that is objectionable to the Minority Achievement Task Force and Principal Holsinger? Is racial equality a consensual value akin to teaching children not to abuse drugs and alcohol? Suppose that the symbol for Fairfax High School were two clasped hands, one black and one white, and that this symbol agitated segregationists in the student body. If the principal eliminated this symbol, would the result be the same as in *Crosby* if a number of students filed suit on First Amendment grounds? If not, is the relevant distinction between good faith educational judgment and suppression of political ideas or is it between good values and bad values? *Cf. Clarke v. Board of Educ. of Sch. Dist. of Omaha*, 338 N.W.2d 272, 215 Neb. 250 (1983). Is your answer influenced by the fact that the Thirteenth Amendment abolishes slavery and the Fourteenth Amendment affords African Americans the equal protection of the laws? Is *Crosby* an affirmation of democratic education?

Are *Pico* and *Crosby* distinguishable on the ground that library books are perceived differently than a symbol or mascot for the entire school? That is, the symbol carries the "stamp of approval of the school itself," whereas no one assumes that each book in the library represents the views of the school authorities? Is the government speaking through the mascot and not through the library book collection? *See generally* Yudof, "Personal Speech and Government Expression," 38 *Case W. Res. L. Rev.* 671 (1988). Does it follow that the removal of a racist book from the library, in response to complaints from minority students and parents, would violate the First Amendment? On the other hand, if the entire school and student body is represented through the school mascot, does it follow that any student can invoke *Barnette* if he or she is required to display the symbol?

---

2. Appellants argue that Holsinger created a public forum by opening the selection process for a new symbol to outside suggestions. School facilities, however, are deemed a public forum only if opened "for indiscriminate use by the general public," while "permitting limited discourse" does not create such a forum. . . .

2. *Racially Discriminatory Motivation*

More generally, if a book selection, curricular, or other school decision involving the communication of ideas is motivated by racial discrimination, does the governmental speech violate the First Amendment (or perhaps the Fourteenth Amendment)? Should materials or books that contain racial slurs or stereotypes or that show particular racial groups in an unfavorable light give rise to constitutionally cognizable injuries? What is the nature of the harm? What is the constitutional violation? In short, can a school system violate the Constitution by what it says as well as what it does? *See Loewen v. Turnipseed, infra*. Can it incite constitutional violations? Or can it preach what it cannot do?

3. *Equal Protection: Challenges to the Rejection of Materials Proposed for Use*

In *Loewen v. Turnipseed*, 488 F.Supp. 1138 (N.D. Miss. 1980), described in note 4 after the *Pico* case, *supra*, the court's finding of a motive to discriminate in approving a textbook for adoption was based on the following evidence. The committee had split along racial lines, with five white members refusing even to rate *Mississippi: Conflict and Change* while the two black members of the committee supported its adoption. Two of the white members of the committee had said in their evaluations of the rejected book that it was "too racially oriented" and that it did not present "a true picture of the history of Mississippi." The failure of the other white members of the committee to indicate their reasons for rejection—itself a violation of their statutory duty—was a departure from normal procedure indicative of an improper motive. In the court's view, the very history of the whole statewide textbook adoption system revealed a racially discriminatory purpose in the establishment of the system, namely, a desire on the part of the legislature to insure that textbook selection reflected the predominant racial attitudes of the day. The rejected book had received favorable reviews in scholarly publications and in letters to the editors of the book from faculty members at several prominent universities. And the state failed to establish that rejection of the book had been based on alleged violations of the procedural and technical standards promulgated by the state textbook purchasing board. Thus, the court concluded that it was the treatment the book gave to controversial racial issues which led to its rejection and that this was not a justifiable reason for rejection by the committee. The court ordered that both books be eligible for consideration by local school districts. What if the court had ordered the removal of the allegedly biased book from the list of approved books? Is it appropriate or constitutional for courts to ban objectionable books from public schools? What would be the standard? Should the standard include books objectionable on grounds other than race?

4. *"Sanitized" Textbooks*

A number of commentators have suggested that modern American textbooks strive to achieve "neutrality" by eliminating all discussion of controversy, hostility to American values, or cultural differences. *See, e.g.*, J. Nelson & G. Roberts, *The Censors and the Schools*, (1977); H. Kallen, *The Education of Free Men* (1949); Krug, " 'Safe' Textbooks and Citizenship Education," 68 *Sch. Rev.* 463 (1960). *See generally* F. Fitzgerald, *America Revised* (1979). The problem is thought to be not so much that particular groups are offended by the text; rather the problem is that history, in particular, may be distorted in an attempt to please all groups. Professor Stephen E. Gottlieb has ably summarized this perspective. Gottlieb, "In the Name of Patriotism: The Constitutionality of 'Bending' History in Public Secondary Schools," 62 *N.Y.U. L.Rev.* 497, 504–08 (1987):

> The effort to pull ideology out of school is evident in battles over history textbooks. Although a few students in the best schools are exposed to better textbooks, most students read carefully censored books. The pursuit of "neutrality" often leads to censorship. The American Textbook Publishers Institute has counseled publishers "to avoid statements that might prove offensive to economic, religious, racial or social groups or any civil, fraternal, patriotic or philanthropic societies in the whole United States." Textbook manufacturers appear to have responded in some cases by deleting materials reflecting cultural differences that might have offended someone. Interest group pressures from diverse ideological camps have resulted in the deletion of materials that would undercut the perception of an American monopoly on decency, as variously defined. Business interests have occasionally attempted to intervene in textbook selection to remove materials considered hostile to the "American system." American policy is sanitized. Books rarely report questionable government action.
>
> Such apparently consistent official wisdom implies that democracy can function without a loyal opposition. Perhaps the most strikingly consistent feature of history textbooks is that they minimize the role of dis-

sent in our history. Government decisions that appear decent or beneficial are often portrayed without any of the political controversy that created them. When opposition from outside government is described, it is frequently not credited with any impact on the eventual government decision. On the issues of Vietnam and McCarthyism, for example, generally only speech by members of the executive and legislative branches is portrayed as effective. Public opinion when it does oppose government is left largely mysterious—springing without leadership or courage from the bowels of an inexplicably well-informed public.

* * *

This portrayal of democracy without disagreement or opposition is consistent in its exclusion of fundamental challenges to the social and economic system. Dissenting voices from the right as well as left are often ignored. Some conservative perspectives are simply omitted from textbooks. For example, though the right-to-work movement played a major role in shaping the Taft-Hartley Act, which continues to govern American labor relations, its activities and ideas are entirely ignored by most textbooks. In another example, the common view that President Franklin Roosevelt was too accommodating towards the Soviet Union at the end of World War II has been omitted from some textbooks.

Most conflict has been edited out of history textbooks in order to avoid affronting any group involved in textbook selection. Racial, ethnic, and sexual roles are distilled to satisfy reigning stereotypes. At one time, publishers were under pressure from the Ku Klux Klan to excise favorable references to Jews and Catholics. More recently, traditional distinctions in sex roles were simply obscured, rather than presented in a balanced light. Textbooks ignored or distorted black history and culture until the 1960s. Even now, the portrayal of the current positions of blacks and women in the textbooks omits a realistic portrayal of the battles that led to their gains. In the newer books, groups are depicted as "struggling," but it is rarely clear against whom. Farm workers, Native Americans, and Blacks are present, but growers, the Bureau of Indian Affairs, and institutionalized racism are mysteriously absent. The early development of the labor movement is similarly portrayed; industrialists are depicted as philanthropic, while skill and ethnic divisions among workers are treated as "natural" with no attempt to explain employer manipulation of such differences.

Do you agree with Professor Gottlieb? What emphasis should textbooks for students in "common schools" have? Should textbooks emphasize dissenting views or the conventional views about political culture? Or should the aspiration be objectivity and accuracy? Is that possible?

5. *Nonconstitutional Approaches*

In a nonconstitutional challenge, would the following statute, Cal. Educ. Code Ann. § 51501 (1978 Special Pamphlet), provide assistance?

> No textbook or other instructional materials shall be adopted by the state board or any governing board for use in the public schools which contains any matter reflecting adversely upon persons because of their race, sex, color, creed, national origin or ancestry.

What does the phrase "reflecting adversely upon persons because of . . ." mean? *See* Note, "California's 'Social Content' Guidelines for Textbooks," 2 *Const. Comm.* 301 (1985). Would books containing truthful statements that might be viewed adversely by the group referred to be barred by this statute? Whose opinion determines whether or not a book reflects adversely?

6. *Rights of Others*

Do the equal protection and other arguments rehearsed above conflict with the First Amendment? Might it not be argued that the First Amendment protects even racist remarks? Whose First Amendment rights would be violated by a court's adoption of one of the arguments outlined above? If a teacher or librarian selected the book, could it be argued that exclusion on the basis of the Fourteenth Amendment violated his or her free speech rights? Do teachers have such rights in the classroom? What of the First Amendment rights of publishers and textbook authors? Although a school district might choose not to buy a book on the ground that it contains racially biased passages, can it purchase the book and then remove it? Do students have a right to receive information and opinions under *Pico* that includes a right to be exposed to racist ideas?

7. *Gender Bias in the Curriculum*

While racial classifications have been declared by the Supreme Court to be "suspect" and subject to strict scrutiny, gender-based classifications, in the Court's most recent cases, have been approached under a standard of review less demanding than strict scrutiny. For a discussion of legal developments in this area see chapter 7. How should the courts respond, if at all, to books and courses that allegedly cast women in a stereotypical or inferior fashion? Should legislatures ban the use of gender-biased materials in public schools? What form should such laws take?

8. Freedom of Expression, Confederate Symbols, and Multiculturalism

The decision in *Crosby* deals with the constitutional authority of school officials to remove a school symbol repugnant to African American students, and the court holds that such a decision does not violate the First Amendment rights of students. The focus, however, is on what the school chooses to communicate and its efforts at self-censorship. A related question, addressed generally in Section III of this chapter, is whether school authorities may adopt and implement regulations to ban student expression that is offensive to minority or other students. Both questions, while presenting different constitutional issues, may be perceived as flowing from a clash of cultures, and such clashes appear to be occurring with greater frequency in the 1990s.

In early 1990, newspapers described a controversy over the wearing of Confederate flags and symbols in the Spartanburg County School District Five in South Carolina. *See* the *New York Times*, March 13, 1991, at p. A10. In 1970 a student committee at the Byrnes High School decided that "Dixie" should no longer be played at school events, that the Confederate flag should not be flown at the school, and that replicas of the Confederate flag should be removed from uniforms and school activities. The school's athletic teams, however, were to continue to be known as the "Byrnes Rebels." The compromise reflected the differing cultural views of whites and blacks in the school district. For many African Americans the symbolism of the Confederacy is one of racial hate and oppression and of slavery. For many whites, particularly those whose ancestors fought on the Confederate side in the Civil War, the Confederate flag is a vital part of their heritage, reflecting their culture and history.

Since 1980, Spartanburg schools had celebrated black history month, focusing on the achievements of African Americans. These celebrations, however, led to some tensions between black and white students, and in the spring of 1990, administrators decided to cancel the black history month celebration scheduled for early 1991. In lieu of that program, the school adopted a month-long multicultural curriculum in which the contributions of different racial and ethnic groups were studied in most of the regular courses. During that month, an assistant superintendent discovered Confederate flag decals on the back window of a truck owned by a student and demanded their removal. In relatively short order, many white students began coming to school wearing Confederate flags on their shirts or wrapped around their thighs. Some suspensions resulted, and student protests were held to voice objection to the ban on wearing the Confederate flag to school. Among other things, white students argued that "if black students are allowed to wear the red, green, and black African heritage flag and other expressions of black culture, . . . then whites should be able to wear the rebel flag." *Id.*

One question raised by the Spartanburg controversy is whether the speech rights of students wishing to wear Confederate flags to school were violated by the school district's ban. Even if *Crosby* is correctly decided, does it follow that public schools may bar individual students from displaying Confederate symbols on campus? Should the result turn on whether the wearing of the symbols results in disruption of school operations? Whether racial tensions are increased? *See* Section III, *infra*. Equally or more important, the controversy may reveal a deeper level of conflict over whether public schools are culturally biased. What to many white students may appear as a good faith effort to transmit a common culture may be viewed by minority students as biased and inattentive to the cultural achievements of groups other than the white majority. African American students may view black history month or courses dealing with multiculturalism as much-needed correctives to curricular imbalances, whereas many whites may perceive multiculturalism as a type of interest group, special pleading. The following note attempts to examine briefly the current debate on multicultural education.

Note on Multicultural Education

The multiculturalism movement has added a new dimension to the debate over the content of school curricula. Proponents of a multicultural education claim that American schools emphasize Western European culture at the expense of other cultures. They differ, however, on the extent of the problem and the remedy to be applied.

Commentators have identified two versions of multiculturalism—a weaker version and a stronger form—both of which depend on the premises that education can reshape students' values and that schools can be something more than a reflection of prevailing mores. Proponents of the weaker form seek equality for cultural groups by ensuring that the school curriculum portrays accurately and fairly the contributions of different cultures to American society. That is, the weaker version attempts to change the way people think about African American, Native American, Latino and other cultures by teaching all students more about those cultures, thus encouraging the majority to treat non-European traditions and values with dignity and respect. The weaker form of multiculturalism also finds support in sound educational practice: one cannot understand American history without understanding the contributions of African Americans, Asian Americans, Latinos, and women in building the nation. Nor can any humanities curriculum claim to be complete if it ignores Latin American poets, works by African American writers, the Koran, or Asian art. Proponents of this vision believe that to be a genuine scholar, teacher, or student, one must accept a genuine form of multiculturalism.

Whereas the weaker version of multiculturalism is a critique of educational practice, premised largely on normative concepts of democratic education, the stronger version is more a critique of Western European culture in general and American culture in particular. This version depends upon a more controversial set of ideas: (1) mere historical accuracy, inclusion of cultural perspectives that have been overlooked, and tolerance of diverse cultures are inadequate, for education should promote and maintain multiculturalism; (2) the American heritage, at least as taught in universities and public schools, is inherently racist and oppressive; (3) the social, educational, emotional, and economic plight of many members of ethnic and other minority groups is caused, at least in part, by the cultural biases of American education; and (4) the remedy is to gain control of the socialization processes in public schools. *See* Yudof, "Should We Move Beyond Tolerance?," *Texas Lawyer*, October 29, 1990 at 18 (distinguishing between the stronger and weaker forms of multiculturalism).

Professor Boateng has advocated the stronger form of multicultural education on the following grounds:

> The comparatively poor performance of African-American children in the public school system has been attributed to a variety of factors. One of the most injurious of these factors . . . is the continuous deculturalization of the African-American child and the neglect of African-American cultural values in the curriculum . . . .
>
> . . . Culture provides the blueprint that determines the way an individual thinks, feels, and behaves in society. To deculturalize African-American children is, therefore, to deprive them of that which determines the way they think, feel, and behave.
>
> * * *
>
> . . . [M]ulticultural instruction needs to be pervasive rather than supplementary. . . . Since there is a long-standing assumption that only that which is Euro-American is American, and Eurocentric curriculum cannot be changed by simply adding units or lessons here and there about African-American[s] or Chicanos. American history, literature, art, music, and culture should be taught from diverse ethnic and cultural perspectives rather than from only a Euro-American perspective. Multicultural education experts recommend using the conceptual approach in reaching this goal.
>
> In the conceptual curriculum, the understanding of such concepts as racism, acculturation, and assimilation is paramount; the cultural group selected to illustrate the concepts becomes a secondary issue. . . . However, since examples have traditionally been drawn from the Euro-American culture, there is a need to strive for a balance by selecting content from other cultures and ethnic groups.

F. Boateng, "Combatting Deculturalization of the African-American Child in the Public School System: A Multicultural Approach," in *Going to School: The African-American Experience* 73, 75 (K. Lomotey, ed. 1990).

Philosopher John Searle has been critical of this stronger version of multiculturalism. While often couched in the language of eliminating elitist practices or promoting excellence and historical accuracy, he believes that this version affirms more radical and contested assumptions:

> [First,] the history of "Western Civilization" is in large part a history of oppression. Internally, Western civilization oppressed women, various slave and serf populations, and ethnic and cultural minorities generally. In foreign affairs, the history of Western civilization is one of imperialism and colonialism. The so-called canon of Western civilization consists in the official publications of this system of oppression, and it is no accident that the authors in the "canon" are almost exclusively Western white males, because the civilization itself is ruled by a caste consisting almost entirely of Western white males. So you cannot reform education by admitting new members to the club, by opening up the canon: the whole idea of "the canon" has to be abolished. It has to be abolished in favor of something that is "multicultural" and "nonhierarchical."
>
> * * *

> . . . [Second,] in addition to having political objections to the United States and Europe, many members of the cultural left think that the primary function of teaching the humanities is political: they do not really believe that the humanities are valuable in their own right except as a means of achieving "social transformation." They (apparently) accept that in subjects like physics and mathematics there may be objective and socially independent criteria of excellence (though they do not say much about the sciences at all), but where the humanities are concerned they think that the criteria that matter are essentially political. The argument goes: since any policy in the humanities will inevitably have a political dimension, courses in the humanities might as well be explicitly and beneficially political, instead of being disguised vehicles of oppression.

J. Searle, "The Storm Over the University," *The New York Review*, December 6, 1990 at 34, 35, 36.

As Searle suggests, some proponents of the stronger version of multiculturalism movement believe that the primary value of the humanities lies in their political dimension and that education is and should be treated as a cultural form of politics. Consider the following remarks by Henry Giroux:

> How we read or define a "canonical" work may not be as important as challenging the overall function and social uses the notion of the canon has served. Within this type of discourse, the canon can be analyzed as part of a wider set of relations that connect the academic disciplines, teaching, and power to considerations defined through broader, intersecting political and cultural concerns such as race, class, gender, ethnicity, and nationalism. What is in question here is not merely a defense of a particular canon, but the issue of struggle and empowerment. In other words, the liberal arts should be defended in the interest of creating critical rather than "good" citizens. The notion of the liberal arts has to be reconstituted around a knowledge-power relationship in which the question of curriculum is seen as a form of cultural and political production grounded in a radical conception of citizenship and public wisdom.

Searle, *supra* at 36 (quoting Giroux). Many proponents of the stronger form of multiculturalism thus reject the notion that it is possible to make curricular choices or to assign readings on the basis of literary or intellectual merit. Calling such determinations elitist and hierarchical, these multiculturalists argue that books and curriculum content should be chosen on the basis of such factors as representatives, fairness, and whether they give voice to the viewpoints of traditionally underrepresented groups.

The *Baseline Essays*, written in 1982 for schools in Portland, Oregon, have provided a model for several cities incorporating the stronger version of multiculturalism into their school systems. According to the essays, the ancient Egyptians were black, Africa was the "the world center of culture and learning in antiquity," and the ancient Greeks borrowed much of their culture from Africa. The *Baseline Essays* assert that Europeans, in an attempt to obscure black achievements, "invented the theory of 'white' Egyptians who were merely browned by the sun."

Similarly, a task force on multiculturalism appointed by the New York State Commissioner of Education issued a 1989 report called A *Curriculum of Inclusion*. The task force was comprised of members from four minority groups: African American, Latinos, Asian American, and Native American. In its report, the task force noted:

> African Americans, Asian Americans, Puerto Ricans/Latinos, and Native Americans have all been the victims of an intellectual and educational oppression that has characterized the culture and institutions of the United States and the European American world for centuries. . . . [The schools of New York have a] systematic bias toward European culture and its derivatives. . . . [T]here is something vulgar and revolting in glorifying a process [such as the development of the United States Constitution] that heaped undeserved rewards on a segment of the population while oppressing the majority.

The report also states that including non-European cultures in the curriculum would, in addition to increasing minority children's self-esteem, cause children from European cultures to "have a less arrogant perspective of being part of the group that has 'done it all.' " The report occasioned much debate. For example, Professor Diane Ravitch, *infra*, argued that there is a danger that the strong version of multiculturalism would lead to the teaching of "victim history," thus stirring racial hatred.

Reacting to the more expansive brand of multiculturalism, Professor Ravitch also has described the multiculturalism movement as actually encompassing two movements—the pluralists and the particularists. According to Ravitch:

> . . . Paradoxical though it may seem, the United States has a common culture that is multicultural. . . . In a

> pluralist curriculum, we expect children to learn a broad and humane culture, to learn about the ideas and art and animating spirit of many cultures. We expect that children, whatever their color, will be inspired by the courage of people like Helen Keller, Vaclav Havel, Harriet Tubman, and Feng Lizhe. We expect that their response to literature will be determined by the ideas and images it evokes, not by the skin color of the writer. But particularists insist that children can learn only from the experiences of people from the same race.
>
> * * *
>
> Particularism can easily be carried to extremes. Students of Fredonian descent must hear that their ancestors were seminal in the development of all human civilization and without the Fredonian contribution, we would all be living in caves or trees, bereft of art, technology, and culture. To explain why Fredonians today are in modest circumstances, given their historic eminence, children are taught that somewhere, long ago, another culture stole the Fredonian's achievements, palmed them off as their own, and then oppressed the Fredonians.

D. Ravitch, "Multiculturalism: E Pluribus Plures," *The American Scholar* 337, 339, 343, 347 (Summer 1990).

Is there, as Professor Ravitch argues, a common American culture in which all ethnic groups share? Or does the "melting pot" simply neutralize the diversity of non-European cultures by assimilating them into the broader American culture? Is Professor Boateng correct in rejecting the existence of a universal American culture? If no common culture exists, does separatism in education necessarily follow? *See* M. Asante, *The Afrocentric Idea* (1987) (dismissing the idea of a universal culture and contrasting African culture with European culture); J. Sleeper, *The Closet of Strangers: Liberalism and the Politics of Race in New York* 232–239 (1990) (asserting the existence of a universal culture).

Consider the issue of multiculturalism in the light of *Wallace v. Jaffree*, *Edwards v. Aguillard*, and *Board of Education v. Pico*. These cases suggest that the Supreme Court has dodged the issue of which viewpoints must be included in the curriculum, focusing instead on the motivation of authorities who mandated a moment of silence, requiring the teaching of creationism, and removed books from the school library. *See* also *Smith v. Board of School Commissioners*, 827 F.2d 684 (11th Cir. 1987). That is, if public officials act to suppress a political ideology or to indoctrinate children to religious values, their actions may be held to violate the First Amendment. If, however, the officials make decisions in a good faith attempt to advance educational objectives, the courts have held such decisions to be virtually insulated from judicial review. *See Ambach v. Norwich*, 441 U.S. 68 (1979); *Mozert v. Hawkins County Board of Education*, 827 F.2d 1058 (6th Cir. 1987).

Suppose a group of minority students filed a lawsuit challenging a school system's "Eurocentric" curriculum on free speech and equal protection grounds. What would be the likely result? If one accepts the notions that all or nearly all curricular choices are political and that political transformation is the main purpose of teaching the humanities, could one persuasively argue that school administrators who determine curriculum content are not making good faith decisions to advance educational objectives but are instead designing the curriculum to indoctrinate children to the dominant culture. Would a court be likely to accept such an argument? After all, are not judges—like school board members, administrators, and teachers—part of the "dominant culture?" Are not cultures, by their nature, culturally biased? Is a dominant culture likely to engage in culturally self-destructive behavior? *See generally* C. Lindblom, *Inquiry and Change* (1990).

Should the school curriculum be an instrument of social change? Aspirational? Or should schools simply prepare students to function in American society as it exists—that is, with a decidedly European bent? Many schools, particularly in larger cities, enroll children of a wide variety of ethnic backgrounds. Is it possible to fairly represent in a curriculum all of the cultural backgrounds present in the particular school? Should school curricula emphasize only the cultures of enrolled students? That is, if a school has no Latinos, should the school feel free to de-emphasize teaching on the achievements of the ancient Incans or Mayans?

4. School Rules, Lifestyles, and the Hidden Curriculum. The materials in the previous sections deal with the question of constitutional limitations on the authority of the state and local school boards to shape the content of the courses of instruction. This section turns to a different means of socialization, namely, school rules that prescribe certain patterns of behavior for students and teachers—rules that are backed up with a variety of sanctions. *See generally* M. Janowitz, *The Reconstruction of Patriotism* 163–64 (1985).

These rules touch on a range of behaviors, for example, tardiness, talking back to teachers, hair and dress styles, marriage and sexual behavior, and the use of cigarettes, liquor, or drugs. The rules are instituted for a variety of overlapping reasons. Some of these rules exist simply because schools are ongoing social institutions that, like other such institutions, must establish rules and procedures for carrying out their purposes in an orderly fashion and for ensuring the safety of students and school personnel. In this respect, schools resemble hospitals, prisons, cafeterias, factories, and other public and private institutions that must create an organizational framework within which to carry out their assigned task. Other reasons for some of these rules are simply educative. The rules exist to train students in ways of behaving that will stand them in good stead as they go on to higher education and jobs. *See Felton v. Fayette School District*, 875 F.2d 191 (8th Cir. 1989) ("good citizenship" rule applied to student who stole auto parts; excluded from off-campus vocational program). These rules may be imposed in order to save students from making choices that school officials believe the students will later regret. They also exist to promote desirable behavior. *See, e.g., Clayton by Clayton v. Place*, 884 F.2d 376 (8th Cir. 1989) (prohibition of school dances on school premises does not violate Establishment Clause).

Rules governing behavior are a very important part of the life of schools. While grades for academic performance are all-pervasive and affect every student, the imposition of school sanctions for the violation of these quasi-educational and organizational rules is also frequent. Indeed, the penalties of suspension and expulsion are usually limited to enforcing these rules and not to policing academic performance. Furthermore, what students learn by conforming or not conforming to rules for conduct might become more deeply ingrained, become more a part of a person, than what is learned from reading and discussion. They involve learning by doing.

In determining the constitutionality of a school rule, courts usually begin by determining whether the student or teacher enjoys a constitutional entitlement that the rule affects. *See, e.g., Fricke v. Lunch*, 491 F.Supp. 381, 384 (D.R.I. 1980). If such a right exists, it is necessary to define more precisely its scope, the weight or importance of the right, whether the plaintiff or the defendant bears the burden of proof, and what exactly the nature of the burden is. Weight and burden of proof issues are often captured in the form of a test or judicial standard of review that guides the court. For example, the plaintiff may be required to establish that the action of the defendant had no "rational basis," did not serve a legitimate state interest, or was not necessary to serve a compelling state interest. Beneath these seemingly mechanical sets of calculations lurk a considerable number of normative, legal, and political considerations. The rules under review may attempt to conform student and teacher behavior in particular ways in order to inculcate particular values or at least to avoid the appearance of endorsing opposing values. *See, e.g., Eckmann v. Board of Educ. of Hawthorn School Dist.*, 636 F.Supp. 1214 (N.D. Ill. 1986).

Hair and Dress Codes. A variety of behaviors were associated with student unrest in the 1960s, including the adoption of what were considered to be radical hair and dress styles. One reaction on the part of a significant number of school districts around the country was to adopt hair and dress codes backed up by such sanctions as suspension or exclusion from extracurricular activities. Some of these codes were the focus of constitutional challenges by parents and students. It should be noted, however, that the controversy over hair and dress codes has largely abated, both because schools have become less rigid concerning standards of personal grooming and because students themselves have been less rebellious in recent years. Yet some attention to these cases is worthwhile: They illumine how courts resolve the tension between the interest of the state in educating pupils in a certain way and what some students and parents believe to be within the sphere of their personal autonomy.

The Supreme Court's views on the constitutionality of hair and dress codes in the public school context remain undetermined. In all school hair and dress cases, whether the lower courts granted or denied students protection from such school regulations, the Supreme Court declined to review the decisions of lower courts, leaving intact a considerable division of opinion among the circuits. Most of these cases arose prior to the Court's decision in *Kelley v. Johnson*, 425 U.S. 238, 96 S.Ct. 1440, 47 L.Ed.2d 708 (1976), in which the Court upheld the hair length regulation of a police department. In reaching its decision, the Court assumed for purposes of argument that people enjoy some liberty in matters of personal appearance, but the Court only required that the regulation not be irrational. Under this standard, the Court found the hair regulation permissible as part of an effort to make police officers readily recognizable to members of the public and as part of an effort to promote an *esprit de corps.* Whether and to what extent the decision in *Kelley* is applicable to teachers and students in schools remains a matter of speculation. Teachers are not employees in a quasi-military organization, and yet they are role models for the students. And students are analogous neither to policemen nor to teachers.

As suggested, the circuit courts are split over the regulation of student hair and dress styles. *See* Bartlett, "Hair and Dress Codes Revisited," 33 *Educ. L. Rep.* [7] (1986). The First, Second, Fourth, Seventh, and Eighth, Circuits have upheld student objections to hair and dress codes. *See, e.g., Massie v. Henry,* 455 F.2d 779 (4th Cir. 1972); *Holsapple v. Woods,* 500 F.2d (7th Cir. 1974) (per curiam), *cert. denied,* 419 U.S. 901, 95 S.Ct. 185, 42 L.Ed.2d 147 (1974); *Bishop v. Colaw,* 450 F.2d 1069 (8th Cir. 1971); *Richards v. Thurston,* 424 F.2d 1281 (1st Cir. 1970). *But see Olesen v. Board of Educ. of School Dist. No.* 228, 676 F.Supp. 820 (N.D. Ill. 1987) (Seventh Circuit cases protecting students' right to determine hair length distinguishable from school rule forbidding male students from wearing earrings). The Third, Fifth, Sixth, Ninth, Tenth, and Eleventh Circuits have rejected these constitutional claims. *See, e.g., Davenport by Davenport v. Randolph County Bd. of Educ.,* 730 F.2d 1395 (11th Cir. 1984); *Zeller v. Donegel School District,* 517 F.2d 600 (3d Cir. 1975); *Hatch v. Goerke,* 502 F.2d 1189 (10th Cir. 1974); *Karr v. Schmidt,* 460 F.2d 609 (5th Cir. 1972) (en banc), *cert. denied,* 409 U.S. 989, 93 S.Ct. 307, 34 L.Ed.2d 256 (1972); *Gfell v. Rickelman,* 441 F.2d 444 (6th Cir. 1971); *King v. Saddleback Junior College District,* 445 F.2d 932 (9th Cir. 1971), *cert. denied,* 404 U.S. 979, 92 S.Ct. 342, 30 L.Ed.2d 294 (1971).

The circuits that rejected challenges to hair codes held that a right to wear long hair did not lie in the free speech clause of the First Amendment (hair style has insufficient communicative content to warrant protection) or in notions of privacy as developed in cases such as *Griswold v. Connecticut,* 381 U.S. 479, 85 S.Ct. 1678, 14 L.Ed.2d 510 (1965) (protecting the right of married couples to use contraceptives). The more difficult task was to deal with the argument that a right to wear long hair was an element of the concept of "liberty" as protected by the Fourteenth Amendment. These courts responded by holding that the right in question was not sufficiently fundamental to warrant judicial protection. They buttressed this conclusion by noting that this kind of issue was best left to the discretion of school officials. These circuits imposed a *de minimis* standard of review in hair and dress cases. As a consequence, school officials urged successfully that such rules are necessary to prevent disruption of the educational process. This disruption allegedly has been of two sorts. Long hair is associated with disciplinary difficulties, academic failure, injuries in shop; and long hair is distracting to other students, so provocative as to be likely to produce fights.

The Tenth Circuit has also said the American Indian students who wish to wear their hair in a traditional style enjoy no special exemption from the schools' regulations. In these cases the students and their parents argued unsuccessfully that their hair style was based on religious beliefs and that parents had a right to bring up their children according to their own religious, cultural, and moral values. *Hatch v. Goerke,* 502 F.2d 1189 (10th Cir. 1974); *New Rider v. Board of Education,* 480 F.2d 699 (10th Cir. 1973), *cert. denied,* 414 U.S. 1097, 94 S.Ct. 733, 38 L.Ed.2d 556. *See Doty, "Constitutional Law: The Right to Wear a Traditional Indian Hair Style—Recognition of a Heritage,"* 4 *Am. Indian L. Rev.* 105 (1976).

Those circuits that have upheld challenges to hair and dress rules in public schools have stressed that the control of one's appearance is a fundamental right within the meaning of the Fourteenth Amendment. Only if school officials have compelling justifications for the rules should they be upheld. These courts concluded that the claims of interference with the education process were not substantiated by the evidence. To the extent that long hair on some students has proved to be provocative to other students, they suggested that the lack of self-control on the part of the student "hecklers" should not result in long-haired students being penalized.

There have been far fewer federal and state court cases dealing with hair and dress codes for teachers. In *Miller v. School District No. 167,* 495 F.2d 658 (7th Cir. 1974), the court rejected a teacher's constitutional challenge to his dismissal for sporting a Vandyke beard and sideburns. Although the Seventh Circuit had protected students from hair regulations, Judge (now Justice) Stevens concluded that the teacher's liberty interest was not of great importance and that the requirement resulted in a relatively minor deprivation. Conversely, the school board's interest in the appearance of its employees, rooted in education concerns, was strong. *See also Domico v. Rapides Parish School Bd.*, 675 F.2d 100 (5th Cir. 1982); *East Hartford Education Association v. Board of Education*, 562 F.2d 838 (2d Cir. 1977) (en banc). *But see Ramsey v. Hopkins*, 320 F.Supp. 477 (N.D. Ala. 1970); *Lucia v. Duggan*, 303 F.Supp. 112 (D. Mass. 1969); *Braxton v. Board of Public Instruction of Duval Cty.*, 303 F.Supp. 958 (M.D. Fla. 1969). Similarly, courts have upheld a school district's refusal to allow teachers to wear religious attire on campus. *See United States v. Board of Education*, 911 F.2d 882 (3rd Cir. 1990); *Cooper v. Eugene School District* No. 45, 301 Or. 358, 723 P.2d 298 (1986), *appeal dismissed*, 480 U.S. 942, 107 S.Ct. 1597, 94 L.Ed.2d 784 (1987).

Marriage, Pregnancy, and Immorality. Schools have long considered it important not merely to provide courses touching upon teenage marriage and sexual behavior, but also to try to control behavior in this area. For example, they may seek to discourage teenage marriage by excluding married students from extracurricular activities. Students who became pregnant have sometimes received similar treatment whether or not the student was married. The trend, however, lies in the direction of not penalizing students for marriage and pregnancy.

With regard to teachers, there has been a great deal of litigation over the school district's authority to restrict personal life styles. *See* M. McCarthy & N. Cambron-McCabe, Public School Law 301–04 (1988). Immoral behavior has long been a basis for dismissal, but much depends on the types of behavior encompassed by the term "immorality." *See, e.g., Chicago Board of Educ. v. Payne*, 102 Ill. App.3d 741, 58 Ill. Dec. 368, 430 N.E.2d 310 (1981) (marijuana); *Golden v. Board of Educ.*, 169 W.Va. 63, 285 S.E.2d 665 (1981) (shoplifting). The decision in *Andrews v. Drew Municipal Separate School District*, 507 F.2d 611 (5th Cir. 1975), *cert. granted*, 423 U.S. 820, 96 S.Ct. 33, 46 L.Ed.2d 37, *cert. dismissed as improvidently granted*, 425 U.S. 559, 96 S.Ct. 1752, 48 L.Ed.2d 169 (1976), is instructive. That case considered the constitutionality of a school rule that made unwed parents ineligible to be hired as teachers' aides. The appeals court agreed with the district court's argument that the status of unwed parenthood did not warrant a presumption of immorality: "A person could live an impeccable life, yet be barred as unfit for employment for an event, whether the result of indiscretion or not, occurring at any time in the past. But human experience refutes the dogmatic attitude inherent in such a policy against unwed parents." *Id.* at 615 (citing 371 F.Supp. at 33–34). As to the school district's point that unwed mothers are poor role models for students, the court said that it did not understand how the students would know of the teacher's marital status. And "the record before us contains no evidence of proselytizing of pupils by the plaintiffs. . . ." *Id.* at 616. The court also opined that it was pure speculation as to whether the hiring of such teachers would contribute to the problem of teenage pregnancies. *Id.* at 617. *See also Ponton v. Newport News Sch. Bd.*, 632 F.Supp. 1056 (E.D. Va. 1986) (compelled leave of absence for unwed, pregnant teacher violates constitutional right to privacy and Title VII of Civil Rights Act of 1964); *Reinhardt v. Board of Education of Alton Community Unit School District*, 19 Ill. App.3d 481, 311 N.E.2d 710 (1974). *See generally* Saken, "The Limits to a Teacher's Privacy Rights: *Ponton v. Newport News School Board*," 42 *Educ. L. Rep.* [19] (1987).

In other cases, the courts have upheld the dismissal of teachers for cohabitation. *Sullivan v. Meade County Independent School District*, 387 F.Supp. 1237 (D.S.D. 1975), *aff'd on other grounds*, 530 F.2d 799 (8th Cir. 1976); *contra, Fisher v. Snyder*, 346 F.Supp. 396 (D. Neb. 1972), *aff'd*, 476 F.2d 375 (8th Cir. 1973). They have also upheld the dismissal of teachers for sexual acts in public and semipublic settings. *Wishart v. McDonald*, 500 F.2d 1110 (1st Cir. 1974); *Governing Board of Mountain View School Dist. v. Metcalf*, 36 Cal.App.3d 546, 111 Cal. Rptr. 724 (1974); *Pettit v. State Board of Education*, 10 Cal.3d 29, 109 Cal. Rptr. 665, 513 P.2d 889 (1973). Sexual involvement or related conduct of teachers with pupils almost invariably is a lawful basis for dismissal. *See, e.g., Johnson v. Beaverhead City High School District*, 771 P.2d 137 (Mont. 1989); *Barcheski v. Board of Educ. of Grand Rapids Public Schools*, 162 Mich. App. 388, 412 N.W.2d 296 (Mich. Ct. App. 1987); *Mondragon v. Poudre School Dist. R–1*, 696 P.2d 831 (Colo. App. 1984); *Potter v. Kalama Pub. Sch. Dist., No. 402*, 31 Wash. App. 838, 644 P.2d 1229 (1982); *Lombardo v. Board of Education*, 100 Ill. App.2d 108, 241 N.E.2d 495 (1968). *Compare* Keller, "Consensual Amorous Relationships Between Faculty and Students: The Constitutional Right to Privacy," 15 *J. of Coll. & Univ. Law* 21 (1988) (college students and faculty). School officials also may fear that the school district will be liable to students when teachers sexually abuse them. *But see J. O. v. Alton Community School District 11*, 909 F.2d 267 (7th Cir. 1990). Sexual harassment of students or staff, not involving sexual contact, also may be a basis for dismissal. *See, e.g., Ross v. Robb*, 662 S.W.2d 257 (Mo. 1983) (*en banc*); *Downie v. Independent School Dist. No. 141*, 367 N.W.2d 913 (Minn. App. 1985). Finally, one court has held that a teacher has a fundamental right "to privacy regarding her marital status, and hence a school board may not refuse to renew the contract of a teacher because she is undergoing a divorce. *Littlejohn v. Rose*, 768 F.2d 765, 769 (6th Cir. 1985).

Homosexuality. Homosexual teachers have long been the subject of controversy. *See generally* Walden and Culverhouse, "Homosexuality and Public Education," 52 *Educ. Law Rep.* [7] (1989); "Developments in the Law—Sexual Orientation and the Law," 102 *Harv. L. Rev.* 1509, 1595–1603 (1989); Schneider-Vogel, "Gay Teachers in the Classroom: A Continuing Constitutional Debate," 15 *J. L. & Educ.* 285 (1986). As previously noted, actual sexual involvement between a teacher and a student clearly provides a sufficient basis for dismissal, whether the relationship is heterosexual or homosexual. *See, e.g., Korf v. Ball State University*, 726 F.2d 1222 (7th Cir. 1984); *Fisher v. Independent School Dist. No. 622*, 357 N.W.2d 152 (Minn. App. 1984); *Lang v. Lee*, 639 S.W.2d 111 (Mo. App. 1982). *See* Walden and Culverhouse, *supra* at [15]–[16]. Also, a public sexual act by a teacher, whether heterosexual or homosexual, normally will be grounds for dismissal. For example, the Tenth Circuit rejected a facial challenge to an Oklahoma statute providing for dismissal or suspension of teachers who engaged in public homosexual activity in *National Gay Task Force v. Board of Educ. of City of Okla. City*, 729 F.2d 1270 (10th Cir. 1984), *affirmed by an equally divided court*, 470 U.S. 903, 105 S.Ct. 1858, 84 L.Ed.2d 776 (1985). *But see Board of Educ. v. Jack M.*, 19 Cal.3d 691, 139 Cal. Rptr. 700, 566 P.2d 602 (1977). For a teacher to be disciplined or dismissed, the statute required two findings: (1) the teacher engaged in "public" homosexual activity, construed as oral or anal intercourse in an indiscreet, non-private manner; and (2) the teacher had been rendered unfit for teaching by the activity.

Factors in determining unfitness include whether the activity was likely to adversely affect students and its proximity in time and place to the teacher's duties. *See Morrison v. State Bd. of Educ.*, 1 Cal.3d 214, 82 Cal. Rptr. 175, 461 P.2d 375 (1969). For other cases concerning public homosexual acts, *see Corstvet v. Boger*, 757 F.2d 223 (10th Cir. 1985); *Ross v. Springfield Sch. Dist. No. 19*, 56 Or. App. 197, 641 P.2d 600 (1982); *Thompson v. Southwest Sch. Dist.*, 483 F.Supp. 1170 (W.D. Mo. 1980); *Kilpatrick v. Wright*, 437 F.Supp. 397 (M.D. Ala. 1977); *Moser v. State Bd. of Educ.*, 22 Cal. App.3d 988, 101 Cal. Rptr. 86 (1972).

It now appears that no broad constitutional protection exists for homosexual behavior in general, even when conducted in private between consenting adults. *See Bowers v. Hardwick*, 478 U.S. 186, 106 S.Ct. 2841, 92 L.Ed.2d 140 (1986), upholding the Georgia anti-sodomy statute. In *Bowers*, the Supreme Court declined to extend the constitutional right of privacy in marriage and family matters to homosexual behavior, citing its traditionally unprotected status. The case, however, leaves many issues concerning homosexual teachers unanswered. *See* Valente, "*Bowers v. Hardwick* and the Homosexual Teacher," 35 *Educ. L. Rep.* [1] (1986). Does the fact that states are free under the Constitution to criminalize homosexual behavior also mean that they may impose employment sanctions against a teacher, without requiring a nexus between the homosexual behavior and the teacher's performance of professional duties? Are homosexual teachers poor role models for students? *See Pryse v. Yakima School Dist. No. 7*, 30 Wash. App. 16, 632 P.2d 60 (1981); *Gaylord v. Tacoma School Dist.*, 88 Wash.2d 286, 559 P.2d 1340 (1977). *But see* Developments in the Law, *supra* at 1601–02. Should dismissal be permissible if a teacher has violated an anti-sodomy statute? *Bowers* held that community moral disapproval is a rational basis for criminalizing sodomy. Is community moral disapproval also a sufficient basis for finding a homosexual teacher unfit to teach? Several courts have said no, at least implicitly. *See Ross v. Springfield Sch. Dist. No. 19, supra*; *Burton v. Cascade School District*, 353 F.Supp. 254 (D. Or. 1973), *aff'd*, 512 F.2d 850 (9th Cir. 1975), *cert. denied*, 423 U.S. 839, 96 S.Ct. 69, 46 L.Ed.2d 59 (1975); *Morrison v. State Board of Education*, 1 Cal.3d 214, 82 Cal. Rptr. 175, 461 P.2d 375 (1969). *But see Conway v. Hampshire Cty. Bd. of Educ.*, 352 S.E.2d 739 (W.Va. 1986).

The ultimate question is whether the status of being a homosexual is sufficient reason to terminate the employment of a teacher. *See, e.g., Gaylord v. Tacoma School Dist., supra. See generally* Walden and Culverhouse, *supra*. The Supreme Court has not addressed this issue. *See Webster v. Doe*, 486 U.S. 592, 108 S.Ct. 2047, 100 L.Ed.2d (1988). *See also Padula v. Webster*, 822 F.2d 97 (D.C. Cir. 1987). One commentator has noted that school districts may require applicants for teaching positions to "reveal those associational ties that are relevant to a teacher's effectiveness" and that two courts have "interpreted this requirement to include associations with gay and lesbian organizations." Developments in the Law, *supra* at 1598, citing *Acanfora v. Board of Education*, 491 F.2d 498 (4th Cir. 1974); *McConnell v. Anderson*, 451 F.2d 193 (8th Cir. 1971). In addition, a Sixth Circuit decision may suggest that homosexual status makes a teacher unfit, at least if she or he makes public her or his sexual orientation. In *Rowland v. Mad River Loc. Sch. Dist., Montgomery Cty.*, 730 F.2d 444 (6th Cir. 1984), *cert. denied*, 470 U.S. 1009, 105 S.Ct. 1373, 84 L.Ed.2d 392 (1985), school officials requested the resignation of a non-tenured high school vocational guidance counselor who had told several other employees that she was bisexual and had a female lover. After she refused to resign, she was transferred to a position involving no student contact, and her contract was not renewed. The Sixth Circuit held that her speech was not entitled to First Amendment protection under *Connick v. Myers*, 461 U.S. 138, 103 S.Ct. 1684, 75 L.Ed.2d 708 (1983), because it did not involve a matter of public concern. *But see* Developments in the Law, *supra* at 1597–98. The court also said that her right to equal protection of the laws was not violated, since there was no evidence that heterosexual school employees who discussed their sexual preference would receive dissimilar treatment. *See generally* Walden and Culverhouse, *supra* at [21] – [24]. When the Supreme Court denied certiorari, Justices Brennan and Marshall joined in a dissent, pointing to jury findings that the employment sanctions against the teacher were imposed solely because she was bisexual and because she revealed her bisexuality. They also argued that her revelation in no way interfered with her job performance or disrupted the regular operation of the school. *See also* Developments in the Law, *supra* at 1597. The dissenters further suggested that the counselor's speech did involve a matter of public concern and that even private speech deserves constitutional protection when it does not interfere with the business of the employer. *See* Halley, "The Politics of the Closet: Towards Equal Protection for Gay, Lesbian and Bisexual Identity," 36 *U.C.L.A. L. Rev.* 915, 968–70 (1989).

National Gay Task Force v. Board of Educ. of Okla. City, supra, also addressed the issue of teachers' speech regarding sexual orientation. *See also Aumiller v. University of Delaware*, 434 F.Supp. 1273 (D. Del. 1977). While upholding the section of an Oklahoma statute sanctioning public homosexual acts by teachers, the court struck down as overbroad a section sanctioning public speech about homosexuality. *See* Halley, *supra*. The law punished "advocating, soliciting, imposing, encouraging or promoting public or private homosexual activity in a manner that creates a substantial risk that such conduct will come to the attention of school children or school employees." The court feared that the statute would deter legitimate speech by authorizing dismissal of a teacher who, for example, addressed the state legislature or appeared on television to advocate repeal of a state anti-sodomy statute. The court also said that a state's interest in regulating a teacher's speech does not justify suppression unless the teacher's speech materially or substantially disrupts normal school activities. *See United States v. Coffeeville Consol. School Dist.*, 513 F.2d 244 (5th Cir. 1975) (unauthorized class discussion of homosexuality not just cause for dismissal).

III. OPENING THE SCHOOL TO ALTERNATIVE IDEAS

This section examines the government's authority to socialize students in public schools from a somewhat different perspective than in the previous sections. Sections I and II asked if there were constitutional limits on socialization in public schools, either in terms of the substance of the messages or the methods that the school authorities might use; this section asks whether and to what extent the public schools have a constitutional obligation to tolerate ideas, often conflicting ideas, from the teachers, staff, and students who constitute the school community. *See* T. van Geel, *The Courts and American Education Law* 211–60 (1987). In a sense, the contrast is between inherent limitations on governmental powers and the assertion of rights against government by individuals under the Constitution.

But this contrast becomes murky, for it better explains the Establishment Clause cases than free exercise cases in Sections I and II. The concern here is with rights of freedom of speech and association rather than religious rights. To the extent that nongovernmental voices may be heard, they may counter or diminish the school's effectiveness in communicating its messages. *See* M. Yudof, *When Government Speaks* 224–25 (1983); Shiffrin, "Governmental Speech," 27 *U.C.L.A. L. Rev.* 565, 649–51 (1980). See generally C. Lindblom, *Inquiry and Change* (1990).

The problem may be posed in a variety of ways. What constitutional rights do students and teachers bring with them when they enter the school environment? Are public schools public forums or limited forums? Yudof, *supra* at 225–27; Garrison, "The Public School as Public Forum," 54 *Tex.L.Rev.* 90 (1975). What are the limits, if any, on the forum? *See Board of Education of Westside Community Schools v. Mergens*, ___ U.S.___ , 110 S.Ct. 2356 (1990). Do children have the same rights of expression as adults? At what point do the private voices exceed the bounds of tolerance and endanger the school's ability to carry out its educational mission? *See* Goldstein, "Reflections on Developing Trends in the Law of Student Rights," 118 *U.Pa.L.Rev.* 612 (1970). What are the limitations on the state's mission? When has the school become impermissibly dominant in drowning out other points of view? How should courts distinguish governmental speech from personal speech? *See* Yudof, "Personal Speech and Government Expression," 38 *Case Wes. Res. L. Rev.* 671 (1988). May the school engage in content regulation of student and teacher speech? What impact do rights-based court decisions have on school governance, discipline, and the student/teacher relationship? What impact do such decisions have on the socialization process itself?

A. Students Rights of Expression

Students often seek to introduce their own values, beliefs, and opinions into the public schools. They may do so informally with their peers, in classroom discussions, by disseminating materials or wearing insignia, or by other means. These communications may be within the framework of the curriculum, they may be irrelevant to the curriculum, or they may seek to counter the schools' curricular and other objectives. *See generally* Buss, "School Newspapers, Public Forum, and the First Amendment," 74 *Iowa L.Rev.* 505, 516–18 (1989). As such, the students have the capacity, however diminished by their age and maturity, to challenge the values being conveyed by school authorities. And the school authorities themselves are not able to respond with value neutrality or to embrace all student points of view. *See* Shiffrin, "Liberalism, Radicalism, and Legal Scholarship," 30 *U.C.L.A. L.Rev.* 1103, 1131–33, 1165–69 (1983). The inherent tension between school values and personal values raises substantial questions about the degree to which student expression may permissibly interfere with the accomplishment of the school's educational objectives. It also raises significant issues about the scope of freedom of expression in a complex educational environment.

One historical note is in order. *See* Friedman, "Limited Monarchy: The Rise and Fall of Student Rights," in D. Kirp and D. Jensen (eds.), *School Days, Rule Days* 238 (1986). Many of the student free speech cases discussed and cited in this section arose in the 1960s and early 1970s, when student activism was at its peak. This was the era of the civil rights revolution, protests against the Vietnam War, and draft resistance. Students today may be less concerned with public issues—or at least express their concerns in more conventional ways. This may explain the decline in the number of student free speech cases in recent years. *See generally* Friedman, *supra*; Marvell, "The Rationales for Federal Question Jurisdiction: An Empirical Examination of Student Rights Litigation," 1984 *Wisc.L.Rev.* 1315. Another likely reason for this decline is that school officials may have become more tolerant of student speech and more sophisticated in handling student unrest. Now that the broad constitutional outlines for dealing with student protest have been laid down, school officials are better acquainted with the rules under which they are to operate and are in a better position to make decisions that do not leave them vulnerable to constitutional challenges. Finally, students and their parents may be more reluctant to seek judicial remedies because they perceive the federal courts are more reticent about overturning the decisions of public school officials than they have been in the recent past. *See, e.g., Bethel School District v. Fraser*, 478 U.S. 675, 106 S.Ct. 3159, 92 L.Ed.2d 549 (1986).

1. Student Speech.

Tinker v. Des Moines Independent Community School District

393 U.S. 503, 89 S.Ct. 733, 21 L.Ed.2d 731 (1969).

Mr. Justice Fortas delivered the opinion of the Court.

Petitioner John F. Tinker, 15 years old, and petitioner Christopher Eckhardt, 16 years old, attended high schools in Des Moines, Iowa. Petitioner Mary Beth Tinker, John's sister, was a 13-year-old student in junior high school.

In December 1965, a group of adults and students in Des Moines held a meeting at the Eckhardt home. The group determined to publicize their objections to the hostilities in Vietnam and their support for a truce by wearing black armbands during the holiday season and by fasting on December 16 and New Year's Eve. Petitioners and their parents had previously engaged in similar activities, and they decided to participate in the program.

The principals of the Des Moines schools became aware of the plan to wear armbands. On December 14, 1965, they met and adopted a policy that any student wearing an armband to school would be asked to remove it and if he refused he would be suspended until he returned without the armband. Petitioners were aware of the regulation that the school authorities adopted.

On December 16, Mary Beth and Christopher wore black armbands to their schools. John Tinker wore his armband the next day. They were all sent home and suspended from school until they would come back without their armbands. They did not return to school until after the planned period for wearing armbands had expired—that is, until after New Year's Day.

This complaint was filed in the United States District Court by petitioners, through their fathers, under § 1983 of Title 42 of the United States Code. It prayed for an injunction restraining the respondent school officials and the respondent members of the board of directors of the school district from disciplining the petitioners, and it sought nominal damages. After an evidentiary hearing the District Court dismissed the complaint. It upheld the constitutionality of the school authorities' action on the ground that it was reasonable in order to prevent disturbance of school discipline. 258 F.Supp. 971 (1966). The court referred to but expressly declined to follow the Fifth Circuit's holding in a similar case that the wearing of symbols like armbands cannot be prohibited unless it "materially and substantially interfere[s] with the requirements of appropriate discipline in the operation of the school." *Burnside v. Byars*, 363 F.2d 744, 749 (1966).[1]

On appeal, the Court of Appeals for the Eighth Circuit considered the case *en banc*. The court was equally divided, and the District Court's decision was accordingly affirmed, without opinion. 383 F.2d 988 (1967). . . .

The District Court recognized that the wearing of an armband for the purpose of expressing certain views is the type of symbolic act that is within the Free Speech Clause of the First Amendment. . . . As we shall discuss, the wearing of armbands in the circumstances of this case was entirely divorced from actually or potentially disruptive conduct by those participating in it. It was closely akin to "pure speech" which, we have repeatedly held, is entitled to comprehensive protection under the First Amendment. *Cf. Cox v. Louisiana*, 379 U.S. 536, 555 (1965); *Adderley v. Florida*, 385 U.S. 39 (1966).

First Amendment rights, applied in light of the special characteristics of the school environment, are available to teachers and students. It can hardly be argued that either students or teachers shed their constitutional rights to freedom of speech or expression at the schoolhouse gate. This has been the unmistakable holding of this Court for almost 50 years. . . . On the other hand, the Court has repeatedly emphasized the need for affirming the comprehensive authority of the States and of school officials, consistent with fundamental constitutional safeguards, to prescribe and control conduct in the schools. *See Epperson v. Arkansas*, [393 U.S. 104 (1968)]; *Meyer v. Nebraska*, [262 U.S. 390, 402 (1923)]. Our problem lies in the area where students in the exercise of First Amendment rights collide with the rules of the school authorities.

1. In *Burnside*, the Fifth Circuit ordered that high school authorities be enjoined from enforcing a regulation forbidding students to wear "freedom buttons." It is instructive that in *Blackwell v. Issaquena County Board of Education*, 363 F.2d 749 (1966), the same panel on the same day reached the opposite result on different facts. It declined to enjoin enforcements of such a regulation in another high school where the students wearing freedom buttons harassed students who did not wear them and created much disturbance.

The problem posed by the present case does not relate to regulation of the length of skirts or the type of clothing, to hair style, or deportment. *Cf. Ferrell v. Dallas Independent School Dist.*, 392 F.2d 697 (5th Cir. 1968); *Pugsley v. Sellmeyer*, 158 Ark. 247, 250 S.W. 538 (1923). It does not concern aggressive, disruptive action or even group demonstrations. Our problem involves direct, primary First Amendment rights akin to "pure speech."

The school officials banned and sought to punish petitioners for a silent, passive expression of opinion, unaccompanied by any disorder or disturbance on the part of the petitioners. There is here no evidence whatever of petitioners' interference, actual or nascent, with the schools' work or of collision with the rights of other students to be secure and to be let alone. Accordingly, this case does not concern speech or action that intrudes upon the work of the schools or the rights of other students.

Only a few of the 18,000 students in the school system wore the black armbands. Only five students were suspended for wearing them. There is no indication that the work of the schools or any class was disrupted. Outside the classrooms, a few students made hostile remarks to the children wearing armbands, but there were no threats or acts of violence on the school premises.

The District Court concluded that the action of the school authorities was reasonable because it was based upon their fear of a disturbance from the wearing of the armbands. But, in our system, undifferentiated fear or apprehension of disturbance is not enough to overcome the right to freedom of expression. Any departure from absolute regimentation may cause trouble. Any variation from the majority's opinion may inspire fear. Any word spoken in class, in the lunchroom, or on the campus, that deviates from the views of another person may start an argument or cause a disturbance. But our Constitution says we must take this risk, *Terminiello v. Chicago*, 337 U.S. 1 (1949); and our history says that is this sort of hazardous freedom—this kind of openness—that is the basis of our national strength and of the independence and vigor of Americans who grow up and live in this relatively permissive, often disputatious society.

In order for the State in the person of school officials to justify prohibition of a particular expression of opinion, it must be able to show that its action was caused by something more than a mere desire to avoid the discomfort and unpleasantness that always accompany an unpopular viewpoint. Certainly where there is no finding and no showing that engaging in the forbidden conduct would "materially and substantially interfere with the requirements of appropriate discipline in the operation of the school," the prohibition cannot be sustained. *Burnside v. Byars, supra*, [363 F.2d] at 749.

In the present case, the District Court made no such finding, and our independent examination of the record fails to yield evidence that the school authorities had reason to anticipate that the wearing of the armbands would substantially interfere with the work of the school or impinge upon the rights of other students. Even an official memorandum prepared after the suspension that listed the reasons for the ban on wearing the armbands made no reference to the anticipation of such disruption.[3]

On the contrary, the action of the school authorities appears to have been based upon an urgent wish to avoid the controversy which might result from the expression, even by the silent symbol of armbands, of opposition to this Nation's part in the conflagration in Vietnam.[4] It is revealing, in this respect, that the meeting at which the school principals decided to issue the contested regulation was called in response to a student's statement to the journalism teacher in one of the schools that he wanted to write an article on Vietnam and have it published in the school paper. (The student was dissuaded.)

It is also relevant that the school authorities did not purport to prohibit the wearing of all symbols of political or controversial significance. The record

3. . . . [T]he testimony of school authorities at trial indicates that it was not fear of disruption that motivated the regulation prohibiting the armbands; the regulation was directed against "the principle of the demonstration" itself. School authorities simply felt that "the schools are no place for demonstrations," and if the students "didn't like the way our elected officials were handling things, it should be handled with the ballot box and not in the halls of our public schools."

4. The District Court found that the school authorities, in prohibiting black armbands, were influenced by the fact that "the Vietnam War and the involvement of the United States therein has been the subject of a major controversy for some time. When the armband regulation involved herein was promulgated, debate over the Vietnam War had become vehement in many localities. A protest march against the war had been recently held in Washington, D.C. A wave of draft card burning incidents protesting the war had swept the country. At that time two highly publicized draft card burning cases were pending in this Court. Both individuals supporting the war and those opposing it were quite vocal in expressing their views." 258 F. Supp. at 972–73.

shows that students in some of the schools wore buttons relating to national political campaigns, and some even wore the Iron Cross, traditionally a symbol of Nazism. The order prohibiting the wearing of armbands did not extend to these. Instead, a particular symbol—black armbands worn to exhibit opposition to this Nation's involvement in Vietnam—was singled out for prohibition. Clearly, the prohibition of expression of one particular opinion, at least without evidence that it is necessary to avoid material and substantial interference with schoolwork or discipline, is not constitutionally permissible.

In our system, state-operated schools may not be enclaves of totalitarianism. School officials do not possess absolute authority over their students. Students in school as well as out of school are "persons" under our Constitution. They are possessed of fundamental rights which the State must respect, just as they themselves must respect their obligations to the State. In our system, students may not be regarded as closed-circuit recipients of only that which the State chooses to communicate. They may not be confined to the expression of those sentiments that are officially approved. In the absence of a specific showing of constitutionally valid reasons to regulate their speech, students are entitled to freedom of expression of their views. . . .

In *Keyishian v. Board of Regents*, 385 U.S. 589 . . . Mr. Justice Brennan, speaking for the Court, said:

> "The vigilant protection of constitutional freedoms is nowhere more vital than in the community of American schools." *Shelton v. Tucker*, [364 U.S. 479], at 487. The classroom is peculiarly the "marketplace of ideas." The Nation's future depends upon leaders trained through wide exposure to that robust exchange of ideas which discovers truth "out of a multitude of tongues, [rather] than through any kind of authoritative selection."

The principle of these cases is not confined to the supervised and ordained discussion which takes place in the classroom. The principal use to which the schools are dedicated is to accommodate students during prescribed hours for the purpose of certain types of activities. Among those activities is personal intercommunication among the students.[6] This is not only an inevitable part of the process of attending school; it is also an important part of the educational process. A student's rights, therefore, do not embrace merely the classroom hours. When he is in the cafeteria, or on the playing field, or on the campus during the authorized hours, he may express his opinions, even on controversial subjects like the conflict in Vietnam, if he does so without "materially and substantially interfer[ing] with the requirements of appropriate discipline in the operation of the school" and without colliding with the rights of others. *Burnside v. Byars, supra*, [363 F.2d] at 749. But conduct by the student, in class or out of it, which for any reason—whether it stems from time, place, or type of behavior—materially disrupts classwork or involves substantial disorder or invasion of the rights of others is, of course, not immunized by the constitutional guarantee of freedom of speech. . . .

* * *

As we have discussed, the record does not demonstrate any facts which might reasonably have led school authorities to forecast substantial disruption of or material interference with school activities, and no disturbances or disorders on the school premises in fact occurred. These petitioners merely went about their ordained rounds in school. Their deviation consisted only in wearing on their sleeve a band of black cloth, not more than two inches wide. They wore it to exhibit their disapproval of the Vietnam hostilities and their advocacy of a truce, to make their views known, and, by their example, to influence others to adopt them. They neither interrupted school activities nor sought to intrude in the school affairs or the lives of others. They caused discussion outside of the classrooms, but no interference with work and no disorder. In the circumstances, our Constitution does not permit officials of the State to deny their form of expression.

We express no opinion as to the form of relief which should be granted, this being a matter for the lower courts to determine. We reverse and remand for further proceedings consistent with this opinion.

Reversed and remanded.

Mr. Justice Stewart, concurring.

---

6. In *Hammond v. South Carolina State College*, 272 F. Supp. 947 (D.S.C. 1967, District Judge Hemphill had before him a case involving a meeting on campus of 300 students to express their views on school practices. He pointed out that a school is not like a hospital or a jail enclosure. *Cf. Cox v. Louisiana*, 379 U.S. 536 (1965); *Adderley v. Florida*, 385 U.S. 39 (1966). It is a public place, and its dedication to specific uses does not imply that the constitutional rights of persons entitled to be there are to be gauged as if the premises are purely private property. . . .

Although I agree with much of what is said in the Court's opinion, and with its judgment in this case, I cannot share the Court's uncritical assumption that, school discipline aside, the First Amendment rights of children are coextensive with those of adults. Indeed, I had thought the Court decided otherwise just last term in *Ginsberg v. New York*, 390 U.S. 629. I continue to hold the view I expressed in that case: "[A] State may permissibly determine that, at least in some precisely delineated areas, a child—like someone in a captive audience—is not possessed of that full capacity for individual choice which is the presupposition of First Amendment guarantees." *Id.*, at 649–50 (concurring in result). *Cf. Prince v. Massachusetts*, 321 U.S. 158.

Mr. Justice White, concurring.

While I join the Court's opinion, I deem it appropriate to note, first, that the Court continues to recognize a distinction between communicating by words and communicating by acts or conduct which sufficiently impinges on some valid state interest; and, second, that I do not subscribe to everything the Court of Appeals said about free speech in its opinion in *Burnside v. Byars*, 363 F.2d 744, 748 (5th Cir. 1966), a case relied upon by the Court in the matter now before us.

Mr. Justice Black, dissenting.

The Court's holding in this case ushers in what I deem to be an entirely new era in which the power to control pupils by the elected "officials of state-supported public schools . . ." in the United States is in ultimate effect transferred to the Supreme Court. The Court brought this particular case here on a petition for certiorari urging that the First and Fourteenth Amendments protect the right of school pupils to express their political views all the way "from kindergarten through high school." Here the constitutional right to "political expression" asserted was a right to wear black armbands during school hours and at classes in order to demonstrate to the other students that the petitioners were mourning because of the death of United States soldiers in Vietnam and to protest that war which they were against. Ordered to refrain from wearing the armbands in school by the elected school officials and the teachers vested with state authority to do so, apparently only seven out of the school system's 18,000 pupils deliberately refused to obey the order. One defying pupil was Paul Tinker, 8 years old, who was in the second grade; another, Hope Tinker, was 11 years old and in the fifth grade; a third member of the Tinker family was 13, in the eighth grade; a fourth member of the same family was John Tinker, 15 years old, an 11th grade high school pupil. Their father, a Methodist minister without a church, is paid a salary by the American Friends Service Committee. Another student who defied the school order and insisted on wearing an armband in school was Christopher Eckhardt, an 11th grade pupil and a petitioner in this case. His mother is an official in the Women's International League for Peace and Freedom.

As I read the Court's opinion it relies upon the following grounds for holding unconstitutional the judgment of the Des Moines school officials and the two courts below. First, the Court concludes that the wearing of armbands is "symbolic speech" which is "akin to 'pure speech' " and therefore protected by the First and Fourteenth Amendments. Secondly, the Court decides that the public schools are an appropriate place to exercise "symbolic speech" as long as normal school functions are not "unreasonably" disrupted. Finally, the Court arrogates to itself, rather than to the State's elected officials charged with running the schools, the decision as to which school disciplinary regulations are "reasonable."

Assuming that the Court is correct in holding that the conduct of wearing armbands for the purpose of conveying political ideas is protected by the First Amendment, *cf. e.g., Giboney v. Empire Storage & Ice Co.*, 336 U.S. 490 (1949), the crucial remaining questions are whether students and teachers may use the schools at their whim as a platform for the exercise of free speech—"symbolic" or "pure"—and whether the courts will allocate to themselves the function of deciding how the pupils' school day will be spent. While I have always believed that under the First and Fourteeth Amendments neither the State nor the Federal Government has any authority to regulate or censor the content of speech, I have never believed that any person has a right to give speeches or engage in demonstrations where he pleases and when he pleases. . . .

While the record does not show that any of these armband students shouted, used profane language, or were violent in any manner, detailed testimony by some of them shows their armbands caused comments, warnings by other students, the poking of fun at them, and a warning by an older football player that other, nonprotesting students had better let them alone. There is also evidence that a teacher of mathematics had his lesson period practically disputes with Mary Beth Tinker, band for her "demonstration." ng of the record shows that this tudents' minds from their reg- ...ssons, and that talk, comments, etc., made John Tinker "self-conscious" in attending school with his armband. While the absence of obscene remarks or boisterous and loud disorder perhaps justifies the Court's statement that the few armband students did not actually "disrupt" the classwork, I think the record overwhelmingly shows that the armbands did exactly what the elected school officials and principals foresaw they would, that is, took the students' minds off their classwork and diverted them to thoughts about the highly emotional subject of the Vietnam War. And I repeat that if the time has come when pupils of state-supported schools, kindergartens, grammar schools, or high schools, can defy and flout orders of school officials to keep their minds on their own schoolwork, it is the beginning of a new revolutionary era of permissiveness in this country fostered by the judiciary. The next logical step, it appears to me, would be to hold unconstitutional laws that bar pupils under 21 or 18 from voting, or from being elected members of the boards of education.

***

I deny, therefore, that it has been the "unmistakable holding of this Court for almost 50 years" that "students" and "teachers" take with them into the "schoolhouse gate" constitutional rights to "freedom of speech or expression." Even *Meyer* did not hold that. It makes no reference to "symbolic speech" at all; what it did was to strike down as "unreasonable" and therefore unconstitutional a Nebraska law barring the teaching of the German language before the children reached the eighth grade. One can well agree with Mr. Justice Holmes and Mr. Justice Sutherland, as I do, that such a law was no more unreasonable than it would be to bar the teaching of Latin and Greek to pupils who have not reached the eighth grade. In fact, I think the majority's reason for invalidating the Nebraska law was that it did not like it or in legal jargon that it "shocked the Court's conscience," "offended its sense of justice, or" was "contrary to fundamental concepts of the English-speaking world," as the Court has sometimes said. . . .

In my view, teachers in state-controlled public schools are hired to teach there. Although Mr. Justice McReynolds may have intimated to the contrary in *Meyer v. Nebraska, supra*, certainly a teacher is not paid to go into school and teach subjects the State does not hire him to teach as a part of its selected curriculum. Nor are public school students sent to the schools at public expense to broadcast political or any other views to educate and inform the public. The original idea of schools, which I do not believe is yet abandoned as worthless or out of date, was that children had not yet reached the point of experience and wisdom which enabled them to teach all of their elders. It may be that the Nation has outworn the old-fashioned slogan that "children are to be seen not heard," but one may, I hope, be permitted to harbor the thought that taxpayers send children to school on the premise that at their age they need to learn, not teach. . . .

* * *

But even if the record were silent as to protests against the Vietnam war distracting students from their assigned class work, members of this Court, like all other citizens, know, without being told, that the disputes over the wisdom of the Vietnam war have disrupted and divided this country as few other issues ever have. Of course students, like other people, cannot concentrate on lesser issues when black armbands are being ostentatiously displayed in their presence to call attention to the wounded and dead of the war, some of the wounded and the dead being their friends and neighbors. It was, of course, to distract the attention of other students that some students insisted up to the very point of their own suspension from school that they were determined to sit in school with their symbolic armbands.

Change has been said to be truly the law of life but sometimes the old and the tried and true are worth holding. The schools of this Nation have undoubtedly contributed to giving us tranquility and to making us a more law-abiding people. Uncontrolled and uncontrollable liberty is an enemy to domestic peace. We cannot close our eyes to the fact that some of the country's greatest problems are crimes committed by the youth, too many of school age. School discipline, like parental discipline, is an integral and important part of training our children to be good citizens—to be better citizens. Here a very small number of students have crisply and summarily refused to obey a school order designed to give pupils who want to learn the opportunity to do so. One does not need to be a prophet or the son of a prophet to know that after the Court's holding today some students in Iowa schools and indeed in all schools will be ready, able, and willing to defy their teachers on practically all orders. This is the more unfortunate for the schools since groups of students all over the land are already running loose, conducting break-ins, sit-ins, lie-ins, and smash-ins. Many of these student groups, as is all too familiar to all who read the newspapers and watch the television news programs, have already engaged in rioting, property seizures, and destruction. They have picketed schools to force students not to cross their picket lines and have too often violently attacked earnest but frightened students who wanted an education that the pickets did not want them to get. Students engaged in such activities are apparently confident that they know far more about how to operate public school systems than do their parents, teachers, and elected school officials. It is no answer to say that the particular students here have not yet reached such high points in their demands to attend classes in order to exercise their political pressures. Turned loose with lawsuits for damages and injunctions against their teachers as they are here, it is nothing but wishful thinking to imagine that young, immature students will not soon believe it is their right to control the schools rather than the right of the States that collect taxes to hire the teachers for the benefit of the pupils. This case, therefore, wholly without constitutional reasons in my judgment, subjects all the public schools in the country to the whims and caprices of their loudest-mouthed, but maybe not their brightest, students. I, for one, am not fully persuaded that school pupils are wise enough, even with this Court's expert help from Washington, to run the 23,390 public school systems in our 50 states. I wish, therefore, wholly to disclaim any purpose on my part to hold that the Federal Constitution compels the teachers, parents, and elected school officials to surrender control of the American public school system to public school students. I dissent.

Mr. Justice Harlan, dissenting.

I certainly agree that state public school authorities in the discharge of their responsibilities are not wholly exempt from the requirements of the Fourteenth Amendment respecting the freedoms of expression and association. At the same time I am reluctant to believe that there is any disagreement between the majority and myself on the proposition that school officials should be accorded the widest authority in maintaining discipline and good order in their institutions. To translate that proposition into a workable constitutional rule, I would, in cases like this, cast upon those complaining the burden of showing that a particular school measure was motivated by other than legitimate school concerns—for example, a desire to prohibit the expression of an unpopular point of view, while permitting expression of the dominant opinion.

Finding nothing in this record which impugns the good faith of respondents in promulgating the armband regulation, I would affirm the judgment below.

NOTES AND QUESTIONS

1. Symbolic Speech

Tinker presumes that the wearing of armbands is a symbolic act, "closely akin to 'pure speech.' " Is that presumption debatable? Is Justice Black arguing that the wearing of armbands is "nonspeech?" *See generally* Ely, "Flag Desecration: A Case Study in the Roles of Categorization and Balancing in First Amendment Analysis," 88 *Harv.L.Rev.* 1482 (1975). Suppose the *Tinker* children had picketed their school. Would such "speech plus" action be entitled to constitutional protection? *See Pickens v. Okolona Mun. Separate School Dist.*, 594 F.2d 433 (5th Cir. 1979); *Karp v. Becker*, 477 F.2d 171 (9th Cir. 1973).

To the extent that symbolic speech is less articulate and persuasive than "pure speech," should the Court have afforded less protection to the message conveyed by the Tinker children? Has the Court created a rule that does not protect pure verbal expression in a class but does protect less instrusive nonverbal speech?

2. Rights of Children

Should children be afforded less extensive rights than mature adults? *See* Garvey, "Children and the First Amendment," 57 *Tex.L.Rev.* 521 (1979). Is the ability to make rational choices essential to the constitutional argument for the protection of expression? If so, should young children be entitled to less constitutional protection of their speech? Should the school's goal be the self-realization of children or their socialization to broad cultural norms? *See* Levin, "Educating Youth for Citizenship: The Conflict Between Authority and Individual Rights in Public Schools," 95 *Yale L. J.* 1647 (1986). Were the Tinker children reflecting their own views or those of their parents? If the latter, are the traditional reasons for protecting speech applicable to them? *See* Wright, "Free Speech Values, Public Schools, and the Role of Judicial Deference," 22 *New Eng.L.Rev.* 59, 62 (1987).

Do students have a right to resist state socialization processes? What does Justice Black think of this idea? Is recognition of student rights a part of socialization to democracy? *See Hazelwood School District v. Kuhlmeier, infra* (Brennan, J., dissenting). *See generally* A. Gutmann, *Democratic Education* 98 (1987); Ingber, "Rediscovering the Communal Worth of Individual Rights: The First Amendment in Institutional Contexts," 69 *Tex. L. Rev.* 1, 73–86 (1990).

3. *Rights of Teachers*

Consider *Tinker*-like claims pressed by teachers. If teachers are role models and communicators of community values, with access to an audience captured by the government, should their expression receive less protection than that of students? *Cf. Kiluma v. Wayne State University*, 72 Mich.App. 446, 250 N.W.2d 81 (1976). Are teachers, as professionals and adults, entitled to more protection of their speech than students? Should teachers be afforded the same rights as students, i.e., their speech should be subject to the substantial disruption limitation? Which view seems preferable? At least one circuit court has said that when a teacher carries out a nondisruptive protest as in *Tinker*, the teacher's expression is to be protected. In *James v. Board of Education*, 461 F.2d 566 (2d Cir. 1972), *cert. denied*, 409 U.S. 1042, 93 S.Ct. 529, 34 L.Ed.2d 491 (1972), the court overturned a teacher's dismissal for wearing a black armband to class in protest against the Vietnam War. *See also Adamian v. Lombardi*, 608 F.2d 1224 (9th Cir. 1979), *cert. denied*, 446 U.S. 938, 100 S.Ct. 2158, 64 L.Ed.2d 791 (1980).

4. *The Constitutional Basis of* Tinker

What is the rationale of *Tinker*? Is *Tinker* essentially an equal protection case, in which the constitutional wrong is that the principal discriminated against the content of the message promulgated by the Tinker children, singling out their anti-war protest while permitting other forms of expression? Would such an interpretation suggest that it is permissible to suppress all armbands, symbols, and underground newspapers? *See generally* Freeman, "The Supreme Court and First Amendment Rights of Students: A Proposed Model of Analysis," 12 *Hastings Const. L.Q.* 1 (1984).

Alternatively, might *Tinker* be viewed as a case in which the Court upheld the right of students to assert their viewpoint as citizens, despite the fact that they happened to be on public school premises? Does *Tinker* affirm the rights of parents to express themselves through their children? *See* Burt, "Developing Constitutional Rights Of, In, and For Children," 39 *Law & Contemp. Probs.* 118 (1975). Alternatively, one commentator has argued that *Tinker* rests on a particular conception of education, one that emphasizes analysis and intellectual inquiry. Goldstein, "Reflections on Developing Trends in the Law of Student Rights," 118 *U. Pa. L. Rev.* 612, 614–15 (1970). Is this view of the case supportable, and if so, was it proper for the Court to base its decision on its particular conception of educational philosophy? *See* Diamond, "The First Amendment and Public Schools: The Case Against Judicial Intervention," 59 *Tex.L.Rev.* 477 (1981). Is *Tinker* grounded in "the need to foster intellectual traits consistent with those deprived of a democratic polity . . . (emphasizing) education's role in providing a participatory forum for the exchange of ideas, a forum crucial in training future leaders"? Ingber, "Rediscovering the Communal Worth of Individual Rights: The First Amendment in Institutional Contexts," 69 *Tex. L. Rev.* 1, 81 (1990). Is this a constitutional or policy argument? Is it unconstitutional for a school to opt for a non-participatory type of education?

Might *Tinker* be seen as resting on the idea of the school as a limited public forum—a marketplace of ideas—where students and teachers with many viewpoints are allowed to express their opinions without being subject to selective regulation on the basis of the content of their messages? *See* Laycock, "Equal Access and Moments of Silence: The Equal Status of Religious Speech by Private Speakers," 81 *Nw.U.L.Rev.* 1, 47–49 (1986). Is this rationale consistent with *West Virginia State Board of Education v. Barnette*, 319 U.S. 624, 63 S.Ct. 1178, 87 L.Ed. 1628 (1943)? Alternatively, might the idea behind the public forum interpretation of *Tinker* be that it lets voices other than the potentially dominant governmental voice speak to the school's captive audience? The greater the number of voices that are allowed to speak within the school, the less the danger that the government will be able to overwhelm students with its messages. *See* Yudof, *When Gov-*

ernment Speaks 224–25 (1983); Buss, "School Newspapers, Public Forum, and the First Amendment," 74 *Iowa L.Rev.* 505, 515 (1989); Shriffin, "Government Speech," 27 *U.C.L.A. L. Rev.* 565, 649–51 (1980). Under the socialization rationale, are *Tinker* and *Pico, supra*, consistent? Is the proper test for curbing speech the good faith of the decisionmakers or the likelihood that the speech will occasion disruption of the school? Is the dissent of Justice Harlan in *Tinker* now the dominant position in *Pico?* If so, does this theory suggest that if a case such as Tinker reached the Supreme Court today, the Court would ask whether school administrators might be justifiably curtailed if the school were making a good faith effort to promote educational goals? Under the facts of *Tinker*, how should the Court answer this question?

In *Perry Education Association v. Perry Local Educators Association*, 460 U.S. 37, 103 S.Ct. 948, 74 L.Ed.2d 794 (1983), the Perry Education Association (PEA) was the duly certified exclusive representative of teachers in the Metropolitan School District of Perry Township, Indiana. Under policies of the Indiana Employment Relations Board, a school district may "provide access to communication facilities to the union selected for the discharge of the exclusive representative duties of representing the bargaining unit and its individual members without having to provide equal access to rival unions." PEA was given a right of access to teachers' mailboxes and was permitted "to use the interschool mail delivery system to the extent that the school district incurred no extra expense by such use." Under the collective bargaining agreement, however, no other union was to have access to the interschool mail system or the mailboxes. The Perry Local Educators Association (PLEA), a rival labor organization, was permitted to post notices on school bulletin boards, hold meetings on school property after school hours, and make announcements on the school's public address system (with the approval of building principals). PLEA and two of its members filed suit under 42 U.S.C.A. § 1983, contending that "PEA's preferential access to the internal mail system violates the First Amendment and the Equal Protection Clause of the Fourteenth Amendment."

Citing *Tinker* and other cases, Justice White, writing for the majority, conceded that "the First Amendment's guarantee of free speech applies to teachers' mailboxes as surely as it does elsewhere within the school. . . ." But this conclusion did not dictate "equivalent access to all parts of a school building in which some form of communication activity occurs." School mail facilities are not a traditional public forum, and "as the case comes before us, there is no indication that the school mailboxes and interschool delivery system are open for use by the general public":

> [T]he schools do allow some outside organizations such as the YMCA, Cub Scouts, and other civil and church organizations to use the facilities. This type of selective access does not transform government property into a public forum. . . .
>
> Moreover, even if we assume that by granting access to the Cub Scouts, YMCAs, and parochial schools, the school district has created a "limited" public forum, the constitutional right of access would in any event extend only to other entities of similar character. . . .

PLEA also argued that "the access policy adopted by the Perry schools favors a particular viewpoint, that of the PEA, on labor relations, and consequently must be strictly scrutinized regardless of whether a public forum is involved." Justice White rejected this contention, holding that there was "no indication that the school board intended to discourage one viewpoint and advance another."

Does *Perry* permit school districts to define criteria for a public forum "that gives access to speakers having views favored" by school authorities and to deny "access to speakers having antithetical views?" *See* Buss, *supra* at 529. *See generally Board of Education of Westside Community Schools v. Mergens*, ___U.S. ___, 110 S.Ct. 2356 (1990); Post, "Between Government and Management: The History and Theory of the Public Forum," 34 *U.C.L.A. L.Rev.* 1713 (1987). Does *Perry* alter the holding in *Tinker?* Is it necessary for the government to show material and substantial disruption if schools are limited public forums? *See* Note, "*Tinker* Revisited: *Fraser v. Bethel School District* and Regulation of Speech in the Public Schools," 1985 *Duke L. J.* 1164, 1176–77.

5. The Substantial Disruption Standard

If the First Amendment is deemed applicable to student and teacher speech, the critical issue then becomes its appropriate application "in the light of the special characteristics of the school environment." In attempting to reconcile the students' rights with the interest of government in offering a public school program, the Court in *Tinker* suggested several different standards of constitutional review. The central standard is that school officials may prohibit speech activities if they materially and substantially interfere with the operation of the school. The Court also said that speech may be banned if school officials can reasonably forecast substantial disruption or material interference with school activities.

Which of the previously stated theories of the *Tinker* case do these standards reflect? Does the substantial disruption test adequately protect the school's educational mission? *See* Diamond, *supra*. May a school discipline a student for speech not falling within the test? *See Williams v. Spencer*, 622 F.2d 1200, 1206 (4th Cir. 1980). Is the test too restrictive of free expression? Does the importance of *Tinker* lie in its articulation of a rule of law or in its signal to school officials that they do not have unfettered discretion to control student expression? *See* Denno, "Mary Beth Tinker Takes the Constitution to School," 38 *Fordham L. Rev.* 35 (1969). In this respect, is Justice Black correct in his concern about the impact of *Tinker* on authority relationships in public schools? *See also Goss v. Lopez*, 419 U.S. 565, 600 n. 22 (1975) (Powell, J., dissenting).

6. Defining "Disruption" and "Impairment"

Does the Court in *Tinker* offer any guidance concerning the meaning of "substantial disruption"? Is noise a form of disruption—disobedience, distraction, inattentiveness? Is a verbal disagreement between students, or between a student and a teacher, a substantial disruption? Is not the purpose of speech to bring the attention of listeners to the speaker's message? *See* Ladd, "Allegedly Disruptive Student Behavior and the Legal Authority of School Officials," 19 *J.Pub.Law* 209, 212–18 (1970). Should the concept of disruption vary depending on whether the institution is an elementary school, high school, or college?

In the light of the disruption standard adopted in *Tinker*, consider these excerpts from the record:

> 1. "A former student of one of our high schools was killed in Vietnam. Some of his friends are still in school, and it was felt that if any kind of demonstration existed, it might evolve into something which would be difficult to control."
> 2. "I [John Tinker] felt self-conscious about wearing the armband. . . . some of the other students talked to me about the armband and asked why I was wearing it. I told them why and some of them didn't think I should do this. . . . This discussion took place on and off during the class period."
> 3. "After gym some students were making fun of me [John Tinker] for wearing it. . . . Two or three boys made remarks in the locker room that were not very friendly. This lasted for perhaps three or four minutes. They did not threaten me with any physical harm."
> 4. "[In the lunchroom] there was one student . . . who was making smart remarks for about ten minutes. There were four to five people with him standing milling around. There were quite a few other students standing and milling around the lunchroom. To my knowledge there were no threats to hit me or anything like that. At no time was I in fear that they might attack me or hit me in the student center because there were too many people there. . . . A football player named Joe Thompson told the kids to leave me alone; that everyone had their own opinions."

Do these facts clarify the majority's concept of disruption? Could the Court have employed the disruption standard and decided the case in favor of the school authorities?

In this regard, is it relevant that the school authorities may not have been aware of the disruption standard when the protest took place? Consider these remarks made by the school principal to John Tinker at the time of his suspension: ". . . I personally felt that there were appropriate times for us to mourn our dead, including this event [Veteran's Day] and Memorial Day, and it did not seem appropriate or necessary to me to mourn them as he was doing at this time. I told him that I was a veteran of World War II and the Korean War." Brief for petitioner at 8, *Tinker v. Des Moines Independent Community School District*, 393 U.S. 503, 89 S.Ct. 733, 21 L.Ed.2d 731 (1969). With the advantage of hindsight, was this frank admission by the principal a tactical mistake? *Compare Bree v. Kahl*, 296 F.Supp. 702, 705 n. 3 (W.D.Wis. 1969), *aff'd*, 419 F.2d 1034 (7th Cir.), *cert. denied*, 398 U.S. 937, 90 S.Ct. 1836, 26 L.Ed.2d 268 (1970). Does it demonstrate "bad faith" within the meaning of *Pico*? In future student rights cases, how would you advise school officials to defend their actions? Do you have an ethical responsibility to encourage them to be truthful in describing their reasons for the disciplinary measures?

What evidence is necessary to prove a reasonable forecast of substantial disruption? Will the testimony of school officials, standing alone, suffice? Must past instances of material disruption resulting from similar speech or conduct be brought to the attention of the court? Must empirical studies be used? What about the use of expert witnesses? *See Bannister v. Paradis*, 316 F.Supp. 185 (D.N.H. 1970). Which party bears the burden of persuasion? Must the school board prove that the speech did or probably would have resulted in material disruption, or must the student prove that such consequences did not or were unlikely to occur? Does *Tinker* allow trial judges so much discretion that their personal attitudes toward public schools will be decisive? *See* Friedman, "Limited Monarchy: The Rise and Fall of Student Rights," in D. Kirp and D. Jensen (eds.), *School Days, Rule Days* 238, 250–51 (1986).

7. *The Heckler's Veto*

In order to justify limiting student speech, must the disruption arise from the student speaker's conduct? Is it sufficient if others react to the speaker's message in a disruptive fashion? *See generally* Comment, "The Supreme Court and the Decline of Students' Constitutional Rights: A Selective Analysis," 65 *Neb.L.Rev.* 161, 166–67 (1986). In *Ferrell v. Dallas Independent School Dist.*, 392 F.2d 697 (5th Cir. 1968), *cert. denied*, 393 U.S. 856, 89 S.Ct. 98, 21 L.Ed.2d 125, a case involving the suspension of male students for their failure to abide by school regulations on hair length, Judge Tuttle, in dissenting from the majority's decision in favor of the school district, addressed himself to this issue:

> These boys were not barred from school because of any actions carried out by them which were of themselves a disturbance of the peace. They were barred because it was anticipated, by reason of previous experiences, that their fellow students in some instances would disrupt the serenity or calm of the school. It is these acts which should be prohibited, not the expressions of individuality by the suspended students.

392 F.2d at 706. *See also Jones v. Board of Regents*, 436 F.2d 618, 621 (9th Cir. 1970). *See generally* Nahmod, "Controversy in the Classroom: The High School Teacher and Freedom of Expression," 39 *Geo. Wash. L. Rev.* 1032, 1039–41 (1971).

Should it ever be permissible to silence the speaker? What if a student wears a "Hinckley should have used a .44" button to a meeting of teenage Republicans in the school building? *See* Comment, *supra* at 166. Should the courts require a showing by school district officials that they attempted to control the disruption or that there were no feasible alternatives to silencing the speaker? *See* Yudof, "Student Discipline in Texas Schools," 3 *J. of Law & Educ.* 221 (1974).

8. *Litigation after* Tinker

a. Thomas Guzick, a seventeen-year-old eleventh-grade student, wore a button to school announcing an anti-war demonstration. The principal told him to remove the button, but Guzick refused; the principal suspended Guzick until he agreed to remove the button.

A school rule forbade the wearing of all buttons, badges, or scarves that identify the wearers as supporters of a cause. The genesis of the rule lay in efforts to regulate fraternities in their competition for students and with each other. The rule was thought to ease tensions between black and white students, who comprised 70 and 30 percent respectively of the school's enrollment. Under the rule, school authorities forbade students from wearing such buttons as "White is Right" and "Say it loud, Black and Proud."

School officials argue that abrogation of the rule would hinder the educational mission of the school. There was no evidence, however, that Guzick's button had any effect; indeed, Guzick had worn the button for an entire school day undetected by school authorities. Guzick claimed that the enforcement of the school rule violated his First Amendment rights as enunciated in *Tinker*. School authorities claimed that they could reasonably forecast disruption, and the court agreed. *See Guzick v. Drebus*, 431 F.2d 594 (6th Cir. 1971), *cert. denied*, 401 U.S. 948, 91 S.Ct. 941, 28 L.Ed.2d 231 (1970). Are *Guzick* and *Tinker* consistent?

b. Members of a Mexican-American students' club, devoted to promoting Mexican-American culture, wore berets to school to symbolize "Chicano Power." After repeated attempts to get the students to stop their disruptive activities—shouting in the hallways, blocking passages—the principal ordered the students to stop wearing the berets because they had become a symbol of these disruptive activities. The students claimed that *Tinker* protected their right to symbolic expression. What result? *See Hernandez v. School District No. 1*, 315 F.Supp. 289 (D.Colo. 1970).

c. Jeff Trachtman, a student, developed a sex questionnaire for distribution to students in grades nine through twelve in his high school. The twenty-five questions sought information regarding student attitudes, preferences, knowledge, and experience, and touched upon such topics as premarital sex, contraception, homosexuality, masturbation, and the extent of the student's sexual experience.

A cover letter informed the students that the questionnaire was to be filled out anonymously; it also stressed the importance of being honest and open but advised the student that "[y]ou are not required to answer any of the questions and if you feel particularly uncomfortable—don't push yourself." The aggregated results were to be published in the student newspaper.

When Trachtman sought permission to distribute the questionnaire, school authorities refused on the grounds that only a professional researcher could ask such questions and then only with the permission of the students' parents. The school asserted that Trachtman was not only communicating ideas but soliciting responses that would invade the rights of other students by subjecting them to psychological pressures that might engender significant emotional harm. Trachtman argued that *Tinker* protects his right to distribute the questionnaire. Is *Tinker* applicable and, if so, what is the result under the *Tinker* standard? *See Trachtman v. Anker*, 563 F.2d 512 (2d Cir. 1977), *cert. denied*, 435 U.S. 925, 98 S.Ct. 1491, 55 L.Ed.2d 519 (1978). *Compare id.* with *Gambino v. Fairfax County School Board*, 429 F.Supp. 731 (E.D.Va. 1977), *aff'd*, 564 F.2d 157 (4th Cir.).

d. Jane Katz wished to solicit funds from students to help pay the legal defense costs of defendants on trial in a local court. School officials, however, barred her distribution of a leaflet that requested these funds since the distribution would have violated a school rule prohibiting the solicitation of funds from pupils on school premises. Katz sought an injunction against enforcement of the rule as an interference with her right of free expression.

The school argued that solicitation was not a form of speech and that, in any event, the solicitation would disrupt the school environment. Further, school officials asserted that they sought to protect students who are compelled by law to be in school from the pressures associated with efforts to solicit funds. Solicitation could get out of hand—too many student groups could seek funds. What result? *See Katz v. McAulay*, 438 F.2d 1058 (2d Cir. 1971), *cert. denied*, 405 U.S. 933, 92 S.Ct. 930, 30 L.Ed.2d 809 (1972). *See also American Future Systems, Inc. v. Pennsylvania State University*, 618 F.2d 252 (3d Cir. 1980).

9. Student Criticism of School Officials and Their Policies

In *Tinker* the students directed their criticism toward the national government and not toward officials in their own school. Would it affect the outcome of the case if the Tinker children had been wearing their armbands in protest over, for example, the school's athletic program? *See generally* Buss, *supra* at 517. *But see* Wright, "Free Speech Values, Public Schools, and the Role of Judicial Deference," 22 *New Eng.L.Rev.* 59 (1987). The courts have generally taken the position that criticism of school officials and their policies is to be protected to the same extent as other expression. *See Scoville v. Board of Education of Joliet Township*, 425 F.2d 10 (7th cir. 1970), *cert. denied*, 400 U.S. 826, 91 S.Ct. 51, 27 L.Ed.2d 55 (1970). *But see Poling v. Murphy*, 872 F.2d 757, 759 (6th Cir. 1989) ("The administration plays tricks on your mind and they hope you won't notice."). In *Sullivan v. Houston Independent School District*, 307 F.Supp. 1328 (S.D.Tex. 1969), the court protected students from suspension for distribution of a paper on school grounds that contained critical remarks on the school's policy regarding the collection of money for various community and charitable projects and contained a satiric article on one school administrator, mocking his manner of speech and attitudes. *See also Thonen v. Jenkins*, 491 F.2d 722 (4th Cir. 1973); *Joyner v. Whiting*, 477 F.2d 456 (4th Cir. 1973).

10. Student Demonstrations

Student demonstrations directed against school policies have a greater potential for disrupting the school and hence are more likely to be punishable. *See Barker v. Hardway*, 394 U.S. 905, 89 S.Ct. 1009, 22 L.Ed.2d 217 (1969) (Justice Fortas concurring in the denial of certiorari). In *Tate v. Board of Education of Jonesboro, Arkansas*, 453 F.2d 975 (8th Cir. 1972), a group of African American students complained of the school policy of playing the song "Dixie" at pep rallies. The school responded by making attendance at the pep assemblies optional; those who did not wish to attend could report to the gymnasium. Some twenty-five black students and five white students chose not to attend the rally. But twenty-nine black students who did attend silently got up and left the rally in protest when "Dixie" was played. The program was not interrupted and apparently continued after the students left, but the students were suspended for five days. When the dispute reached the courts, school officials argued successfully that the protest constituted a disruption to the order and decorum of the school. Hence the protest was not protected by *Tinker. See also Pickens v. Okolona Mun. Separate School Dist.*, 594 F.2d 433 (5th Cir. 1979) (student and parent demonstration adjacent to public high school).

Bethel School District No. 403 v. Fraser

478 U.S. 675, 106 S.Ct. 3159, 92 L.Ed.2d 549 (1986).

Chief Justice Burger delivered the opinion of the Court.

We granted certiorari to decide whether the First Amendment prevents a school district from disciplining a high school student for giving a lewd speech at a school assembly.

I

A

On April 26, 1983, respondent Matthew N. Fraser, a student at Bethel High School in Bethel, Washington, delivered a speech nominating a fellow student for student elective office. Approximately 600 high school students, many of whom were 14-year-olds, attended the assembly. Students were required to attend the assembly or to report to the study hall. The assembly was part of a school-sponsored educational program in self-government. Students who elected not to attend the assembly were required to report to study hall. During the entire speech, Fraser referred to his candidate in terms of an elaborate, graphic, and explicit sexual metaphor.

Two of Fraser's teachers, with whom he discussed the contents of his speech in advance, informed him that the speech was "inappropriate and that he probably should not deliver it," . . . and that his delivery of the speech might have "severe consequences." . . .

During Fraser's delivery of the speech, a school counselor observed the reaction of students to the speech. Some students hooted and yelled; some by gestures graphically simulated the sexual activities pointedly alluded to in respondent's speech. Other students appeared to be bewildered and embarrassed by the speech. One teacher reported that on the day following the speech, she found it necessary to forgo a portion of the scheduled class lesson in order to discuss the speech with the class. . . .

A Bethel High School disciplinary rule prohibiting the use of obscene language in the school provides:

> "Conduct which materially and substantially interferes with the educational process is prohibited, including the use of obscene, profane language or gestures."

The morning after the assembly, the Assistant Principal called Fraser into her office and notified him that the school considered his speech to have been a violation of this rule. Fraser was presented with copies of five letters submitted by teaches, describing his conduct at the assembly; he was given a chance to explain his conduct, and he admitted to having given the speech described and that he deliberately used sexual innuendo in the speech. Fraser was then informed that he would be suspended for three days, and that his name would be removed from the list of candidates for graduation speaker at the school's commencement exercises.

Fraser sought review of this disciplinary action through the School District's grievance procedures. The hearing officer determined that the speech given by respondent was "indecent, lewd, and offensive to the modesty and decency of many of the students and faculty in attendance at the assembly." The examiner determined that the speech fell within the ordinary meaning of "obscene," as used in the disruptive conduct rule, and affirmed the discipline in its entirety. Fraser served two days of his suspension, and was allowed to return to school on the third day.

B

Respondent, by his father as guardian *ad litem*, then brought this action in the United States District Court for the Western District of Washington. Respondent alleged a violation of his First Amendment right to freedom of speech and sought both injunctive relief and monetary damages under 42 U.S.C. § 1983. The District Court held that the school's sanctions violated respondent's right to freedom of speech under the First Amendment to the United States Constitution, that the school's disruptive-conduct rule is unconstitutionally vague and overbroad, and that the removal of respondent's name from the graduation speaker's list violated the Due Process Clause of the Fourteenth Amendment because the disciplinary rule makes no mention of such removal as a possible sanction. The District Court awarded respondent $278 in damages, $12,750 in litigation costs and attorney's fees, and enjoined the School District from preventing respondent from speaking at the commencement ceremonies. Respondent, who had been elected graduation speaker by a write-in vote of his classmates, delivered a speech at the commencement ceremonies on June 8, 1983.

The Court of Appeals for the Ninth Circuit affirmed the judgment of the District Court, 755 F.2d 1356 (1985), holding that respondent's speech was indistinguishable from the protest armband in *Tinker v. Des Moines Independent Community School Dist.*, 393 U.S. 503, 89 S.Ct. 733, 21 L.Ed.2d 731 (1969). . . . We reverse.

II

* * *

The marked distinction between the political "message" of the armbands in *Tinker* and the sexual content of respondent's speech in this case seems to have been given little weight by the Court of Appeals. In upholding the students' right to engage in a nondisruptive, passive expression of a political viewpoint in *Tinker*, this Court was careful to note that the case did "not concern speech or action that intrudes upon the work of the schools or the rights of other students." . . .

* * *

III

The role and purpose of the American public school system was well described by two historians, saying "public education must prepare pupils for citizenship in the Republic. . . . It must inculcate the habits and manners of civility as values in themselves conducive to happiness and as indispensable to the practice of self-government in the community and the nation." C. Beard & M. Beard, New Basic History of the United States 228 (1968). In *Ambach v. Norwick*, 441 U.S. 68, 76–77, 99 S.Ct. 1589, 1594, 60 L.Ed.2d 49 (1979), we echoed the essence of this statement of the objectives of public education as the "inculcat[ion of] fundamental values necessary to the maintenance of a democratic political system."

These fundamental values of "habits and manners of civility" essential to a democratic society must, of course, include tolerance of divergent political and religious views, even when the views expressed may be unpopular. But these "fundamental values" must also take into account consideration of the sensibilities of others, and, in the case of a school, the sensibilities of fellow students. The undoubted freedom to advocate unpopular and controversial views in schools and classrooms must be balanced against the society's countervailing interest in teaching students the boundaries of socially appropriate behaviour. Even the most heated political discourse in a democratic society requires consideration for the personal sensibilities of the other participants and audiences.

* * *

The First Amendment guarantees wide freedom in matters of adult public discourse. A sharply divided Court upheld the right to express an antidraft viewpoint in a public place, albeit in terms highly offensive to most citizens. *See Cohen v. California*, 403 U.S. 15, 91 S.Ct. 1780, 29 L.Ed.2d 284 (1971). It does not follow, however, that simply because the use of an offensive form of expression may not be prohibited to adults making what the speaker considers a political point, that the same latitude must be permitted to children in a public school. . . . Surely it is a highly appropriate function of public school education to prohibit the use of vulgar and offensive terms in public discourse. Indeed, the "fundamental values necessary to the maintenance of a democratic political system" disfavor the use of terms of debate highly offensive or highly threatening to others. Nothing in the Constitution prohibits the states from insisting that certain modes of expression are inappropriate and subject to sanctions. The inculcation of these values is truly the "work of the schools." . . . The determination of what manner of speech in the classroom or in school assembly is inappropriate properly rests with the school board.

The process of educating our youth for citizenship in public schools is not confined to books, the curriculum, and the civics class; schools must teach by example the shared values of a civilized social order. Consciously or otherwise, teachers—and indeed the older students—demonstrate the appropriate form of civil discourse and political expression by their conduct and deportment in and out of class. Inescapably, like parents, they are role models. The schools, as instruments of the state, may determine that the essential lessons of civil, mature conduct cannot be conveyed in a school that tolerates lewd, indecent, or offensive speech and conduct such as that indulged in by this confused boy.

The pervasive sexual innuendo in Fraser's speech was plainly offensive to both teachers and students—

indeed to any mature person. By glorifying male sexuality, and in its verbal content, the speech was acutely insulting to teenage girl students. . . . The speech could well be seriously damaging to its less mature audience, many of whom were only 14 years old and on the threshold of awareness of human sexuality. Some students were reported as bewildered by the speech and the reaction of mimicry it provoked.

. . . In *Ginsberg v. New York*, 390 U.S. 629, 88 S.Ct. 1274, 20 L.Ed.2d 195 (1968), this Court upheld a New York statute banning the sale of sexually oriented material to minors, even though the material in question was entitled to First Amendment protection with respect to adults.

[A]ll Members of the Court, otherwise sharply divided, acknowledged that the school board has the authority to remove books that are vulgar. *Board of Education v. Pico*, 457 U.S. 853 . . . (1982). . . . These cases recognize the obvious concern on the part of parents, and school authorities acting *in loco parentis* to protect children—especially in a captive audience—from exposure to sexually explicit, indecent, or lewd speech.

* * *

We hold that petitioner School District acted entirely within its permissible authority in imposing sanctions upon Fraser in response to his offensively lewd and indecent speech. Unlike the sanctions imposed on the students wearing armbands in *Tinker*, the penalties imposed in this case were unrelated to any political viewpoint. . . .

* * *

IV

[The Court concludes that respondent's argument that he had no way of knowing that the speech he gave would subject him to disciplinary sanctions is "wholly without merit."]

The judgment of the Court of Appeals for the Ninth Circuit is

Reversed.

Justice Blackmun concurs in the result.

Justice Brennan, concurring in the judgment.

Respondent gave the following speech at a high school assembly in support of a candidate for student government office:

> " 'I know a man who is firm—he's firm in his pants, he's firm in his shirt, his character is firm—but most . . . of all, his belief in you, the students of Bethel, is firm.
>
> " 'Jeff Kuhlman is a man who takes his point and pounds it in. If necessary, he'll take an issue and nail it to the wall. He doesn't attack things in spurts—he drives hard, pushing and pushing until finally—he succeeds.
>
> " 'Jeff is a man who will go to the very end—even the climax, for each and every one of you.
>
> " 'So vote for Jeff for A.S.B. vice-president—he'll never come between you and the best our high school can be.' " . . .

The Court, referring to these remarks as "obscene," "vulgar," "lewd," and "offensively lewd," concludes that school officials properly punished respondent for uttering the speech. Having read the full text of respondent's remarks, I find it difficult to believe that it is the same speech the Court describes. To my mind, the most that can be said about respondent's speech—and all that need be said—is that in light of the discretion school officials have to teach high school students how to conduct civil and effective public discourse, and to prevent disruption of school educational activities, it was not unconstitutional for school officials to conclude, under the circumstances of this case, that respondent's remarks exceeded permissible limits. . . .

* * *

Justice Marshall, dissenting.

. . . I dissent from the Court's decision . . . because in my view the school district failed to demonstrate that respondent's remarks were indeed disruptive. . . .

Justice Stevens, dissenting.

"Frankly, my dear, I don't give a damn."

When I was a high school student, the use of those words in a public forum shocked the Nation. Today Clark Gable's four-letter expletive is less offensive than it was then. Nevertheless, I assume that high school administrators may prohibit the use of that word in classroom discussion and even in extracurricular activities that are sponsored by the school and held on school premises. For I believe a school faculty must regulate the content as well as the style of student speech in carrying out its educational mission. It does seem to me, however, that if a student is to be punished for using offensive speech, he is entitled to fair notice of the scope of the prohibition and the consequences of its violation. The interest in free speech protected by the First

Amendment[2] and the interest in fair procedure protected by the Due Process Clause of the Fourteenth Amendment combine to require this conclusion.

* * *

NOTES AND QUESTIONS

1. **Fraser** ***and the Substantial Disruption Test***

Is *Fraser* consistent with *Tinker? See* Ingber, "Rediscovering the Communal Worth of Individual Rights: The First Amendment in Institutional Contexts," 69 *Tex. L. Rev.* 1, 82–3 (1990). Chief Justice Burger emphasizes that Matthew Fraser's speech was greeted by hoots and yells and graphic sexual gestures by some students. Does this indicate that he believes that the *Tinker* substantial disruption test has been satisfied? What of the fact that some students felt "bewildered and embarrased" by the speech? Is this a substantial disruption? If such a response constitutes substantial disruption, has the Court modified the *Tinker* definition of disruption?

Is *Tinker* distinguishable because Fraser was addressing a school-sponsored assembly? Because the school has a substantial interest in regulating the election of student officers? *Cf. Alabama Student Party v. Student Government Association*, 867 F.2d 1344 (11th Cir. 1989). How is Fraser's speech different than wearing an armband to class? Is there a significant constitutional distinction between a student speaking as part of a school activity (electing student officers) and a student speaking on his or her own behalf apart from regular school activities and curricula? *See Board of Education of Westside Community Schools v. Mergens,* ___U.S. ___, 110 S.Ct. 2356 (1990); *Hazelwood School District v. Kuhlmeier, infra.*

2. Lewd Speech

Is *Tinker* distinguishable because it involved political speech whereas *Fraser* does not? Is this what the Chief Justice means when he says that "unlike . . . *Tinker,* the penalties imposed in this case were unrelated to any political viewpoint. . . ."? Why is a nomination speech for a school office not political speech? Is the Chief Justice suggesting that there is a distinction between the content of the message and the manner of presenting the message? *See* Comment, "Students' First Amendment Rights: Gone With the Wind?," 11 *Amer. J. of Trial Adv.* 173, 182–83 (1987); Note, "*Tinker* Revisited: *Fraser v. Bethel School District* and Regulation of Speech in the Public Schools," 1985 *Duke L. J.* 1164, 1179. If so, how is *Cohen v. California*, 403 U.S. 15, 91, S.Ct. 1780, 29 L.Ed.2d 284 (1971), distinguishable?

Is it that adults have greater latitude in matters of speech than children? That the state can go to greater lengths to protect children from vulgar speech? *See FCC v. Pacifica Foundation*, 438 U.S. 726, 98 S.Ct. 3026, 57 L.Ed.2d 1073 (1978). Would the Court have reached the same result in a case arising in a public university? *See Papish v. Board of Curators of University of Missouri*, 410 U.S. 667, 93 S.Ct. 1197, 35 L.Ed.2d 618 (1973). Is it that a public high school has a different mission than a university or courthouse? Is this why Chief Justice Burger emphasizes the socialization mission of public schools? *See* Diamond, "The First Amendment and Public Schools: The Case Against Judicial Intervention," 59 *Tex.L.Rev.* 477 (1981). *But see* Ingber, "Rediscovering the Communal Worth of Individual Rights: The First Amendment in Institutional Contexts, 69 *Tex. L. Rev.* 1, 73–86 (1990); Zirkel, Richardson and MacKenzie, "Tinkering With the First Amendment Rights of Students," 37 *Ed.Law Rep.* 433, 438–43 (1987); Note, 1985 *Duke L. J. supra* at 1185. Does the *Pico* case, *supra*, support his approach? *But see Jacobs v. Board of School Commissioners*, 490 F.2d 601 (7th Cir. 1973), *vacated as moot*, 420 U.S. 128, 95 S.Ct. 848, 43 L.Ed.2d 74 (1975). Is the *Fraser* decision "more visceral than doctrinal"? *See* Zirkel, Richardson and MacKenzie, *supra* at 445.

With regard to vulgarity or appropriateness for a student audience, should school-sponsored expression be treated identically with the personal expression of students? *See* Yudof, "Personal Speech and Government Expression," 38 *Case W. L. Rev.* 671 (1988). For example, may school officials cancel a student production of a play because of its sexual themes or vulgarity? *See Seyfried v. Walton*, 668 F.2d 214 (3d Cir. 1981) (decision to cancel *Pippin* upheld). *See generally* Faaborg, "High School Play Censorship: Are Students' First Amendment Rights Violated When Officials Cancel Theatrical Productions?," 14 *J. of Law & Educ.* 575 (1985). What if

---

2. As the Court of Appeals noted, there "is no evidence in the record indicating that any students found the speech to be offensive." . . .

a film is removed from the curriculum because of its "exaggerated and undue emphasis on violence and bloodshed"? *See Pratt v. Independent School District, No. 831*, 670 F.2d 771 (8th Cir. 1982). What if a student club, meeting after school, discusses books focusing on sexual themes or the drug culture? May school authorities forbid the club from meeting on campus? *Cf. Board of Education of Westside Community Schools v. Mergens*, ___U.S. ___, 110 S.Ct. 2356 (1990).

Should school authorities be permitted, as Justice Brennan suggests, to teach students to engage in civilized discourse—either by regulating the curriculum itself or by punishing vulgar speech by students? If so, does this mean that the *Tinker* disruption test simply is not applicable to vulgar speech? Or does it mean that such speech, by its nature, substantially interferes with the educational mission of a public school? Why is a prohibition on lewd speech not a "pall of orthodoxy" within the ambit of the plurality and Blackmun opinions in *Pico, supra?*

What if Fraser's speech contained no sexual metaphors or double entendres but simply was tasteless in the judgment of school officials? For example, what if a candidate for a school office were to use the following joke before a school assembly: "[Y]ou idiots are too darn gullible. For example, what is black and blue and wrapped in plastic? A baby in a trash bag, of course." After *Fraser* may a student be disciplined for such a speech? *See Poling v. Murphy*, 872 F.2d 757 (6th Cir. 1989).

3. Notice of Violation of the Disciplinary Rule

Fraser was disciplined for violating a school rule forbidding conduct that materially and substantially interferes with the educational process . . ., including the use of obscene, profane language or gestures." Does the wording of the rule explain Chief Justice Burger's emphasis on disruption? Did Fraser have notice that his speech would lead to his being charged with a disciplinary offense? Or do you agree with Justice Stevens? Suppose that Fraser had ample advance warning from his teachers, but a court concludes that the rule itself did not extend to a speech with clever sexual innuendos but no profane words. *See* chapter 3, *infra*.

4. Abusive Speech and Racial Harassment

Suppose that the Bethel School District adopted a rule that stated that "no person shall upbraid, insult or abuse any teacher of the public schools on the school campus in the presence of students." After *Tinker* and *Fraser*, may a student be disciplined for violating the rule even if he or she does not use profanity? *See Poling v. Murphy*, 872 F.2d 757 (6th Cir. 1989); *Gano v. School District No. 411*, 674 F.Supp. 796 (D.Idaho 1987). *Compare Klein v. Smith*, 635 F.Supp. 1440 (D.Me. 1986). What if a parent, displeased with a teacher's performance, insults a teacher in front of his child and other students? *See Commonwealth v. Ashcraft*, 691 S.W.2d 229 (Ky.App. 1985) (unconstitutionally overbroad as applied to parent).

What if the Bethel School district made it a disciplinary offense for a student to engage in speech that stigmatizes an individual on the basis of race and that has the purpose or the reasonably foreseeable effect of interfering with an individual's academic efforts or creating a demeaning or intimidating educational environment? Is such a ban on racial harassment by students a violation of the First Amendment? *See Doe v. University of Michigan*, 721 F.Supp. 852 (E.D.Mich. 1989). *See generally* Delgado, "Campus Antiracism Rules: Constitutional Narratives in Collision," 85 *Nw. L. Rev.* 343 (1991). Symposium, "Offensive and Libelous Speech," 47 *Wash. & Lee L.Rev.* 1 (1990); Strossen, "Regulating Racist Speech on Campus: A Modest Proposal?" 1990 *Duke L. J.* 484; Post, "The Constitutional Concept of Public Discourse: Outrageous Opinion, Democratic Deliberation and *Hustler Magazine v. Falwell*," 103 *Harv.L.Rev.* 601 (1990); Haviland, "Student Discriminatory Harassment," 16 *J. of Coll. & Univ. Law* 311 (1989); Delgado, "Words That Wound: A Tort Action for Racial Insults, Epithets, and Name-Calling," 17 *Harv.Civ.Rts–C.L.Rev.* 133 (1982).

What of a racial harassment rule based upon the likelihood that particular epithets would cause a fight to occur ("fighting words")? What of a rule treating racial slurs within the framework of intentional infliction of emotional distress? May racial insults create a "hostile" environment minority students akin to a hostile work environment for employees? Should the limits of expression be the same in these two contexts? *See* Note, "Racist Speech on Campus: A Title VII Solution to a Problem," 64 *So. Cal. L. Rev.* 105 (1990). What of the fact that public school students are compelled to attend school? What of the fact that they are younger and presumedly less mature than college students?

Would the display of confederate symbols by white students constitute racial harassment? If so, may school authorities discipline students for such displays?

2. Student Newspapers

Hazelwood School District v. Kuhlmeier

484 U.S. 260, 108 S.Ct. 562, 98 L.Ed.2d 592 (1988).

Justice White delivered the opinion of the Court.

This case concerns the extent to which educators may exercise editorial control over the contents of a high school newspaper produced as part of the school's journalism curriculum.

I

Petitioners are the Hazelwood School District in St. Louis County, Missouri; various school officials; Robert Eugene Reynolds, the principal of Hazelwood East High School, and Howard Emerson, a teacher in the school district. Respondents are three former Hazelwood East students who were staff members of Spectrum, the school newspaper. They contend that school officials violated their First Amendment rights by deleting two pages of articles from the May 13, 1983, issue of Spectrum.

Spectrum was written and edited by the Journalism II class at Hazelwood East. The newspaper was published every three weeks or so during the 1982–1983 school year. More than 4,500 copies of the newspaper were distributed during that year to students, school personnel, and members of the community.

The Board of Education allocated funds from its annual budget for the printing of Spectrum. These funds were supplemented by proceeds from sales of the newspaper. The printing expenses during the 1982–1983 school year totaled $4,668.50; revenue from sales was $1,166.84. The other costs associated with the newspaper—such as supplies, textbooks, and a portion of the journalism teacher's salary—were borne entirely by the Board.

The Journalism II course was taught by Robert Stergos for most of the 1982–1983 academic year. Stergos left Hazelwood East to take a job in private industry on April 29, 1983, when the May 13 edition of Spectrum was nearing completion, and petitioner Emerson took his place as newspaper adviser for the remaining weeks of the term.

The practice at Hazelwood East during the spring 1983 semester was for the journalism teacher to submit page proofs of each Spectrum issue to Principal Reynolds for his review prior to publication. On May 10, Emerson delivered the proofs of the May 13 edition to Reynolds, who objected to two of the articles scheduled to appear in that edition. One of the stories described three Hazelwood East students' experiences with pregnancy; the other discussed the impact of divorce on students at the school.

Reynolds was concerned that, although the pregnancy story used false names "to keep the identity of these girls a secret," the pregnant students still might be identifiable from the text. He also believed that the article's references to sexual activity and birth control were inappropriate for some of the younger students at the school. In addition, Reynolds was concerned that a student identified by name in the divorce story had complained that her father "wasn't spending enough time with my mom, my sister and I" prior to the divorce, "was always out of town on business or out late playing cards with the guys," and "always argued about everything" with her mother. . . . Reynolds believed that the student's parents should have been given an opportunity to respond to these remarks or to consent to their publication. He was unaware that Emerson had deleted the student's name from the final version of the article.

Reynolds believed that there was no time to make the necessary changes in the stories before the scheduled press run and that the newspaper would not appear before the end of the school year if printing were delayed to any significant extent. He concluded that his only options under the circumstances were to publish a four-page newspaper instead of the planned six-page newspaper, eliminating the two pages on which the offending stories appeared, or to publish no newspaper at all. Accordingly, he directed Emerson to withhold from publication the two pages containing the stories on pregnancy and divorce.[1] He informed his superiors of the decision, and they concurred.

1. The two pages deleted from the newspaper also contained articles on teenage marriage, runaways, and juvenile delinquents, as well as a general article on teenage pregnancy. Reynolds testified that he had no objection to these articles and that they were deleted only because they appeared on the same pages as the two objectionable articles.

* * *

II

Students in the public schools do not "shed their constitutional rights to freedom of speech or expression at the schoolhouse gate." *Tinker* [*v. Des Moines Independent Community School Dist.*]. They cannot be punished merely for expressing their personal views on the school premises—whether "in the cafeteria, or on the playing field, or on the campus during authorized hours," . . . unless school authorities have reason to believe that such expression will "substantially interfere with the work of the school or impinge upon the rights of other students." . . .

We have nonetheless recognized that the First Amendment rights of students in the public schools "are not automatically coextensive with the rights of adults in other settings," *Bethel School District No. 403 v. Fraser*. . . . A school need not tolerate student speech that is inconsistent with its "basic educational mission," . . . even though the government could not censor similar speech outside the school. Accordingly, we held in *Fraser* that a student could be disciplined for having delivered a speech that was "sexually explicit" but not legally obscene at an official school assembly, because the school was entitled to "disassociate itself" from the speech in a manner that would demonstrate to others that such vulgarity is "wholly inconsistent with the 'fundamental values' of public school education." . . . It is in this context that respondents' First Amendment claims must be considered.

A

We deal first with the question whether Spectrum may appropriately be characterized as a forum for public expression. The public schools do not possess all of the attributes of streets, parks, and other traditional public forums that "time out of mind, have been used for purposes of assembly, communicating thoughts between citizens, and discussing public questions." *Hague v. CIO*, 307 U.S. 496, 515, 59 S.Ct. 954, 964, 83 L.Ed. 1423 (1939). *Cf. Widmar v. Vincent*, 454 U.S. 263, 267–68, n. 5, 102 S.Ct. 269, 273, n. 5, 70 L.Ed.2d 440 (1981). Hence, school facilities may be deemed to be public forums only if school authorities have "by policy or by practice" opened those facilities "for indiscriminate use by the general public," *Perry Education Ass. Perry Local Educators' Assn.*, 460 U.S. 37, 47, S.Ct. 948, 956, 74 L.Ed.2d 794 (1983), or by some segment of the public, such as student organizations. . . . If the facilities have instead been reserved for other intended purposes, "communicative or otherwise," then no public forum has been created, and school officials may impose reasonable restrictions on the speech of students, teachers, and other members of the school community. . . . "The government does not create a public forum by inaction or by permitting limited discourse, but only by intentionally opening a nontraditional forum for public discourse." *Cornelius v. NAACP Legal Defense & Educational Fund, Inc., 473 U.S. 788, 802, 105 S.Ct. 3439, 3449, 87 L.Ed.2d 567 (1985).*

The policy of school officials toward Spectrum was reflected in Hazelwood School Board Policy 348.51 in the Hazelwood East Curriculum Guide. Board Policy 348.51 provided that "[s]chool sponsored publications are developed within the adopted curriculum and its educational implications in regular classroom activities." . . . The Hazelwood East Curriculum Guide described the Journalism II course as a "laboratory situation in which the students publish the school newspaper applying skills they have learned in Journalism I." . . . The lessons that were to be learned from the Journalism II course, according to the Curriculum Guide, included development of journalistic skills under deadline pressure, "the legal, moral, and ethical restrictions imposed upon journalists within the school community," and "responsibility and acceptance of criticism for articles of opinion." . . . Journalism II was taught by a faculty member during regular class hours. Students received grades and academic credit for their performance in the course.

School officials did not deviate in practice from their policy that production of Spectrum was to be part of the educational curriculum and a "regular classroom activit[y]." The District Court found that Robert Stergos, the journalism teacher during most of the 1982–1983 school year, "both had the authority to exercise and in fact exercised a great deal of control over *Spectrum*." . . . For example, Stergos selected the editors of the newspaper, scheduled publication dates, decided the number of pages for each issue, assigned story ideas to class members, advised students on the development of their stories, reviewed the use of quotations, edited stories, selected and edited the letters to the editor, and dealt with the printing company. Many of these decisions were made without consultation with the Journalism II students. The District Court thus found it "clear that Mr. Stergos was the final authority with respect to almost every aspect of the production and publication of *Spectrum*, including its content."

. . . Moreover, after each Spectrum issue had been fully approved by Stergos or his successor, the issue still had to be reviewed by Principal Reynolds prior to publication. Respondents' assertion that they had believed that they could publish "practically anything" in Spectrum was therefore dismissed by the District Court as simply "not credible." . . .

The evidence relied upon by the Court of Appeals in finding Spectrum to be a public forum . . . is equivocal at best. For example, Board Policy 348.51, which stated in part that "[s]chool sponsored student publications will not restrict free expression or diverse viewpoints within the rules of responsible journalism," also stated that such publications were "developed within the adopted curriculum and its educational implications." . . . One might reasonably infer from the full text of Policy 348.51 that school officials retained ultimate control over what constituted "responsible journalism" in a school-sponsored newspaper. Although the statement of Policy published in the September 14, 1982, issue of Spectrum declared that "*Spectrum*, as a student-press publication, accepts all rights implied by the First Amendment," this statement, understood in the context of the paper's role in the school's curriculum, suggests at most that the administration will not interfere with the students' exercise of those First Amendment rights that attend the publication of a school-sponsored newspaper. It does not reflect an intent to expand those rights by converting a curricular newspaper into a public forum.[2] Finally, that students were permitted to exercise some authority over the contents of Spectrum was fully consistent with the Curriculum Guide objective of teaching the Journalism II students "leadership responsibilities as issue and page editors." . . . A decision to teach leadership skills in the context of a classroom activity hardly implies a decision to relinquish school control over that activity. In sum, . . . school officials did not evince either "by policy or by practice," . . . any intent to open the pages of Spectrum to "indiscriminate use," . . . by its student reporters and editors, or by the student body generally. Instead, they "reserve[d] the forum for its intended purpos[e]," . . . a supervised learning experience for journalism students. Accordingly, school officials were entitled to regulate the contents of Spectrum in any reasonable manner. . . . It is this standard, rather than our decision in *Tinker*, that governs in this case.

B

The question whether the First Amendment requires a school to tolerate particular student speech—the question that we addressed in *Tinker*—is different from the question whether the First Amendment requires a school affirmatively to promote particular student speech. The former question addresses educators' ability to silence a student's personal expression that happens to occur on the school premises. The latter question concerns educators' authority over school-sponsored publications, theatrical productions, and other expressive activities that students, parents, and members of the public might reasonably perceive to bear the imprimatur of the school.

These activities may fairly be characterized as part of the school curriculum, whether or not they occur in a traditional classroom setting, so long as they are supervised by faculty members and designed to impart particular knowledge or skills to student participants and audiences.[3]

Educators are entitled to exercise greater control over this second form of student expression to assure that participants learn whatever lessons the activity is designed to teach, that readers or listeners are not exposed to material that may be inappropriate for their level of maturity, and that the views of the individual speaker are not erroneously attributed to

2. The Statement also cited *Tinker v. Des Moines Independent Community School Dist.*, 393 U.S. 503, 89 S.Ct. 733, 21 L.Ed.2d 731 (1969), for the proposition that "[o]nly speech that 'materially and substantially interferes with the requirements of appropriate discipline' can be found unacceptable and therefore be prohibited." . . . This portion of the Statement does not, of course, even accurately reflect our holding in *Tinker*. Furthermore, the Statement nowhere expressly extended the *Tinker* standard to the news and feature articles contained in a school-sponsored newspaper. The dissent apparently finds as a fact that the Statement was published annually in Spectrum; however, the District Court was unable to conclude that the Statement appeared on more than one occasion. In any event, even if the Statement says what the dissent believes that it says, the evidence that school officials never intended to designate Spectrum as a public forum remains overwhelming.

3. The distinction that we draw between speech that is sponsored by the school and speech that is not fully consistent with *Papish v. Board of Curators*, 410 U.S. 667, 93 S.Ct. 1197, 35 L.Ed.2d 618 (1973) (*per curiam*), which involved an off-campus "underground" newspaper that school officials merely had allowed to be sold on a state university campus.

the school. Hence, a school may in its capacity as publisher of a school newspaper or producer of a school play "disassociate itself," . . . not only from speech that would "substantially interfere with [its] work . . . or impinge upon the rights of other students," *Tinker*, 393 U.S., at 509, 89 S.Ct., at 738, but also from speech that is, for example, ungrammatical, poorly written, inadequately researched, biased or prejudiced, vulgar or profane, or unsuitable for immature audiences.[4] A school must be able to set high standards for the student speech that is disseminated under its auspices—standards that may be higher than those demanded by some newspaper publishers or theatrical producers in the "real" world—and may refuse to disseminate student speech that does not meet those standards. In addition, a school must be able to take into account the emotional maturity of the intended audience in determining whether to disseminate student speech on potentially sensitive topics, which might range from the existence of Santa Claus in an elementary school setting to the particulars of teenage sexual activity in a high school setting. A school must also retain the authority to refuse to sponsor student speech that might reasonably be perceived to advocate drug or alcohol use, irresponsible sex, or conduct otherwise inconsistent with "the shared values of a civilized social order," . . . or to associate the school with any position other than neutrality on matters of political controversy. . . .

* * *

This standard is consistent with our oft-expressed view that the education of the Nation's youth is primarily the responsibility of parents, teachers, and state and local school officials, and not of federal judges. *See, e.g., Board of Education of Hendrick Hudson Central School Dist. v. Rowley*, 458 U.S. 176, 208, 102 S.Ct. 3034, 3051, 73 L.Ed.2d 690 (1982); *Wood v. Strickland*, 420 U.S. 308, 326, 95 S.Ct. 992, 1003, 43 L.Ed.2d 214 (1975); *Epperson v. Arkansas*, 393 U.S. 97, 104, 89 S.Ct. 266, 270, 21 L.Ed.2d 228 (1968). It is only when the decision to censor a school-sponsored publication, theatrical production, or other vehicle of student expression has no valid educational purpose that the First Amendment is so "directly and sharply implicate[d]," . . . as to require judicial intervention to protect students' constitutional rights.[6]

III

We also conclude that Principal Reynolds acted reasonably in requiring the deletion from the May 13 issue of Spectrum of the pregnancy article, the divorce article, and the remaining articles that were to appear on the same pages of the newspaper.

The initial paragraph of the pregnancy article declared that "[a]ll names have been changed to keep the identity of these girls a secret." The principal concluded that the students' anonymity was not adequately protected, however, given the other identifying information in the article and the small number of pregnant students at the school. . . . The article did not contain graphic accounts of sexual activity. The girls did comment in the article, however, concerning their sexual histories and their use or nonuse of birth control. It was not unreasonable for the principal to have concluded that such frank talk was inappropriate in a school-sponsored publication distributed to 14-year-old freshmen and presumably taken home to be read by students' even younger brothers and sisters.

The student who was quoted by name in the version of the divorce article seen by Principal Reynolds made comments sharply critical of her father. The principal could reasonably have concluded that an individual publicly identified as an inattentive parent—indeed, as one who chose "playing cards with the guys" over home and family—was entitled to an opportunity to defend himself as a matter of journalistic fairness. . . .

4. The dissent perceives no difference between the First Amendment analysis applied in *Tinker* and that applied in *Fraser*. We disagree. The decision in *Fraser* rested on the "vulgar," "lewd," and "plainly offensive" character of a speech delivered at an official school assembly rather than on any propensity of the speech to "materially disrupt[ ] classwork or involve[ ] substantial disorder or invasion of the rights of others." . . . Indeed, the *Fraser* Court cited as "especially relevant" a portion of Justice Black's dissenting opinion in *Tinker* "disclaim[ing] any purpose . . . to hold that the Federal Constitution compels the teachers, parents and elected school officials to surrender control of the American public school system to public school students." . . . Of course, Justice Black's observations are equally relevant to the instant case.

6. We reject respondents' suggestion that school officials be permitted to exercise prepublication control over school-sponsored publications only pursuant to specific written regulations. To require such regulations in the context of a curricular activity could unduly constrain the ability of educators to educate. We need not now decide whether such regulations are required before school officials may censor publications not sponsored by the school that students seek to distribute on school grounds. *See Baughman v. Freienmuth*, 478 F.2d 1345 (CA4 1973); *Shanley v. Northwest Independent School Dist., Bexar Cty., Tex.*, 462 F.2d 960 (CA5 1972); *Eisner v. Stamford Board of Education*, 440 F.2d 803 (CA2 1971).

* * *

In sum, we cannot reject as unreasonable Principal Reynolds' conclusion that neither the pregnancy article nor the divorce article was suitable for publication in Spectrum. Reynolds could reasonably have concluded that the students who had written and edited these articles had not sufficiently mastered those portions of the Journalism II curriculum that pertained to the treatment of controversial issues and personal attacks, the need to protect the privacy of individuals whose most intimate concerns are to be revealed in the newspaper, and "the legal, moral, and ethical restrictions imposed upon journalists within [a] school community" that includes adolescent subjects and readers. Finally, we conclude that the principal's decision to delete two pages of Spectrum, rather than to delete only the offending articles or to require that they be modified, was reasonable under the circumstances as he understood them. Accordingly, no violation of First Amendment rights occurred.[9]

The judgment of the Court of Appeals for the Eighth Circuit is therefore

Reversed.

Justice Brennan, with whom Justice Marshall and Justice Blackmun join, dissenting.

When the young men and women of Hazelwood East High School registered for Journalism II, they expected a civics lesson. Spectrum, the newspaper they were to publish, "was not just a class exercise in which students learned to prepare papers and hone writing skills, it was a . . . forum established to give students an opportunity to express their views while gaining an appreciation of their rights and responsibilities under the First Amendment to the United States Constitution. . . ." 795 F.2d 1368, 1373 (CA8 1986). "[A]t the beginning of each school year," *id.*, at 1372, the student journalists published a Statement of Policy—tacitly approved each year by school authorities—announcing their expectation that "*Spectrum*, as a student-press publication, accepts all rights implied by the First Amendment. . . . Only speech that 'materially and substantially interferes with the requirements of appropriate discipline' can be found unacceptable and therefore prohibited. . . . The school board itself affirmatively guaranteed the students of Journalism II an atmosphere conducive to fostering such an appreciation and exercising the full panoply of rights associated with a free student press. "School sponsored student publications," it vowed, "will not restrict free expression or diverse viewpoints within the rules of responsible journalism." . . . (Board Policy § 348.51).

This case arose when the Hazelwood East administration breached its own promise, dashing its students' expectations. The school principal, without prior consultation or explanation, excised six articles—comprising two full pages—of the May 13, 1983, issue of Spectrum. He did so not because any of the articles would "materially and substantially interfere with the requirements of appropriate discipline," but simply because he considered two of the six "inappropriate, personal, sensitive, and unsuitable" for student consumption. 795 F.2d, at 1371.

In my view the principal broke more than just a promise. He violated the First Amendment's prohibitions against censorship of any student expression that neither disrupts classwork nor invades the rights of others, and against any censorship that is not narrowly tailored to serve its purpose.

I

* * *

Free student expression undoubtedly sometimes interferes with the effectiveness of the school's pedagogical functions. Some brands of student expression do so by directly preventing the school from pursuing its pedagogical mission: The young polemic who stands on a soapbox during calculus class to deliver an eloquent political diatribe interferes with the legitimate teaching of calculus. And the student who delivers a lewd endorsement of a student-government candidate might so extremely distract an impressionable high school audience as to interfere with the orderly operation of the school. *See Bethel School Dist. No. 403 v. Fraser*, . . . Other student speech, however, frustrates the school's le-

9. It is likely that the approach urged by the dissent would as a practical matter have far more deleterious consequences for the student press than does the approach that we adopt today. The dissent correctly acknowledges "[t]he State's prerogative to dissolve the student newspaper entirely." . . . It is likely that many public schools would do just that rather than open their newspapers to all student expression that does not threaten "materia[l] disrup[tion of] classwork" or violation of "rights that are protected by law," . . . regardless of how sexually explicit, racially intemperate, or personally insulting that expression otherwise might be.

gitimate pedagogical purposes merely by expressing a message that conflicts with the school's, without directly interfering with the school's expression of its message: A student who responds to a political science teacher's question with the retort, "Socialism is good," subverts the school's inculcation of the message that capitalism is better. Even the maverick who sits in class passively sporting a symbol of protest against a government policy, *cf. Tinker v. Des Moines Independent School Dist.*, 393 U.S. 503, 89 S.Ct. 733, 21 L.Ed.2d 731 (1969), or the gossip who sits in the student commons swapping stories of sexual escapade could readily muddle a clear official message condoning the government policy or condemning teenage sex. Likewise, the student newspaper that, like Spectrum, conveys a moral position at odds with the school's official stance might subvert the administration's legitimate inculcation of its own perception of community values.

If mere incompatibility with the school's pedagogical message were a constitutionally sufficient justification for the suppression of student speech, school officials could censor each of the students or student organizations in the foregoing hypotheticals, converting our public schools into "enclaves of totalitarianism," . . . that "strangle the free mind at its source," *West Virginia State Board of Education v. Barnette, supra*, 319 U.S., at 637, 63 S.Ct., at 1185. The First Amendment permits no such blanket censorship authority. . . .

In *Tinker*, this Court struck the balance. We held that official censorship of student expression—there the suspension of several students until they removed their armbands protesting the Vietnam War—is unconstitutional unless the speech "materially disrupts classwork or involves substantial disorder or invasion of the rights of others." . . .

This Court applied the *Tinker* test just a Term ago in *Fraser, supra*, upholding an official decision to discipline a student for delivering a lewd speech in support of a student-government candidate. The Court today casts no doubt on *Tinker*'s vitality. Instead it erects a taxonomy of school censorship, concluding that *Tinker* applies to one category and not another. On the one hand is censorship "to silence a student's personal expression that happens to occur on the school premises." . . . On the other hand is censorship of expression that arises in the context of "school-sponsored . . . expressive activities that students, parents, and members of the public might reasonably perceive to bear the imprimatur of the school." . . .

The Court does not, for it cannot, purport to discern from our precedents the distinction it creates. . . .

Nor has this Court ever intimated a distinction between personal and school-sponsored speech in any other context. Particularly telling is this Court's heavy reliance on *Tinker* in two cases of First Amendment infringement on state college campuses. *See Papish v. University of Missouri Board of Curators*, 410 U.S. 667, 671, n. 6, 93 S.Ct. 1197, 1199, n. 6, 35 L.Ed.2d 618 (1973) (*per curiam*); *Healy v. James*, 408 U.S. 169, 180, 189, and n. 18, 191, 92 S.Ct. 2338, 2345, 2350, and n. 18, 2351, 33 L.Ed.2d 266 (1972). One involved the expulsion of a student for lewd expression in a newspaper that she sold on campus pursuant to university authorization, *see Papish, supra*, 410 U.S., at 667–68, 93 S.Ct., at 1197–98, and the other involved the denial of university recognition and concomitant benefits to a political student organization, *see Healy, supra*, 408 U.S., at 174, 176, 181–82, 92 S.Ct., at 2342, 2343, 2346–47. Tracking *Tinker*'s analysis, the Court found each act of suppression unconstitutional. In neither case did this Court suggest the distinction, which the Court today finds dispositive, between school-sponsored and incidental student expression.

II

Even if we were writing on a clean slate, I would reject the Court's rationale for abandoning *Tinker* in this case. The Court offers no more than an obscure tangle of three excuses to afford educators "greater control" over school-sponsored speech than the *Tinker* test would permit: the public educator's prerogative to control curriculum; the pedagogical interest in shielding the high school audience from objectionable viewpoints and sensitive topics; and the school's need to dissociate itself from student expression. . . . None of the excuses, once disentangled, supports the distinction that the Court draws. *Tinker* fully addresses the first concern; the second is illegitimate; and the third is readily achievable through less oppressive means.

A

The Court is certainly correct that the First Amendment permits educators "to assure that participants learn whatever lessons the activity is designed to teach." . . . That is, however, the essence of the *Tinker* test, not an excuse to abandon it. Under

Tinker, school officials may censor only such student speech as would "materially disrup[t]" a legitimate curricular function. Manifestly, student speech is more likely to disrupt a curricular function when it arises in the context of a curricular activity—one that "is designed to teach" something—than when it arises in the context of a noncurricular activity. Thus, under *Tinker,* the school may constitutionally punish the budding political orator if he disrupts calculus class but not if he holds his tongue for the cafeteria. . . . That is not because some more stringent standard applies in the curricular context. (After all, this Court applied the same standard whether the Tinkers wore their armbands to the "classroom" or the "cafeteria." . . .) It is because student speech in the noncurricular context is less likely to disrupt materially any legitimate pedagogical purpose.

I fully agree with the Court that the First Amendment should afford an educator the prerogative not to sponsor the publication of a newspaper article that is "ungrammatical, poorly written, inadequately researched, biased or prejudiced," or that falls short of the "high standards for . . . student speech that is disseminated under [the school's] auspices." . . . But we need not abandon *Tinker* to reach that conclusion; we need only apply it. The enumerated criteria reflect the skills that the curricular newspaper "is designed to teach." The educator may, under *Tinker,* constitutionally "censor" poor grammar, writing, or research because to reward such expression would "materially disrup[t]" the newspaper's curricular purpose.

The same cannot be said of official censorship designed to shield the *audience* of dissociate the *sponsor* from the expression. Censorship so motivated might well serve . . . some other school purpose. But it in no way furthers the curricular purposes of a student *newspaper,* unless one believes that the purpose of the school newspaper is to teach students that the press ought never report bad news, express unpopular views, or print a thought that might upset its sponsors. Unsurprisingly, Hazelwood East claims no such pedagogical purpose.

* * *

B

The Court's second excuse for deviating from precedent is the school's interest in shielding an impressionable high school audience from material whose substance is "unsuitable for immature audiences." . . . Specifically, the majority decrees that we must afford educators authority to shield high school students from exposure to "potentially sensitive topics" (like "the particulars of teenage sexual activity") or unacceptable social viewpoints (like the advocacy of "irresponsible se[x] or conduct otherwise inconsistent with 'the shared values of a civilized social order' ") through school-sponsored student activities. . . .

Tinker teaches us that the state educator's undeniable, and undeniably vital, mandate to inculcate moral and political values is not a general warrant to act as "thought police" stifling discussion of all but state-approved topics and advocacy of all but the official position. . . .

The mere fact of school sponsorship does not, as the Court suggests, license such thought control in the high school, whether through school suppression of disfavored viewpoints or through official assessment of topic sensitivity.[2] . . . Just as a school board may not purge its state-funded library of all books that " 'offen[d] [its] social, political and moral tastes,' " . . . school officials may not, out of like motivation, discriminatorily excise objectionable ideas from a student publication. The State's prerogative to dissolve the student newspaper entirely (or to limit its subject matter) no more entitles it to dictate which viewpoints students may express on its pages, than the State's prerogative to close down the schoolhouse entitles it to prohibit the non-disruptive expression of antiwar sentiment within its gates.

Official censorship of student speech on the ground that it addresses "potentially sensitive topics" is, for related reasons, equally impermissible. I would not begrudge an educator the authority to limit the substantive scope of a school-sponsored publication to a certain, objectively definable topic, such as literary criticism, school sports, or an overview of the school year. Unlike those determinate limitations, "poten-

2. The Court quotes language in *Bethel School Dist. v. Fraser,* 478 U.S. 675, 106 S.Ct. 3159, 92 L.Ed.2d 549 (1986), for the proposition that " '[t]he determination of what manner of speech in the classroom or in school assembly is inappropriate properly rests with the school board.' " *Ante,* at 567 (quoting 478 U.S., at 685, 106 S.Ct., at 3165). As the discussion immediately preceding that quotation makes clear, however, the Court was referring only to the appropriateness of the *manner* in which the message is conveyed, not of the message's *content.* . . .

tial topic sensitivity" is a vaporous nonstandard . . . that invites manipulation to achieve ends that cannot permissibly be achieved through blatant viewpoint discrimination and chills student speech to which school officials might not object. . . .

The case before us aptly illustrates how readily school officials (and courts) can camouflage viewpoint discrimination as the "mere" protection of students from sensitive topics. Among the grounds that the Court advances to uphold the principal's censorship of one of the articles was the potential sensitivity of "teenage sexual activity." . . . Yet the District Court specifically found that the principal "did not, as a matter of principle, oppose discussion of said topi[c] in *Spectrum*." . . . That much is also clear from the same principal's approval of the "squeal law" article on the same page, dealing forthrightly with "teenage sexuality," "the use of contraceptives by teenager," and "teenage pregnancy," . . . If topic sensitivity were the true basis of the principal's decision, the two articles should have been equally objectionable. It is much more likely that the objectionable article was objectionable because of the viewpoint it expressed: It might have been read (as the majority apparently does) to advocate "irresponsible sex." . . .

C

The sole concomitant of school sponsorship that might conceivably justify the distinction that the Court draws between sponsored and nonsponsored student expression is the risk "that the views of the individual speaker [might be] erroneously attributed to the school." . . . Of course, the risk of erroneous attribution inheres in any student expression, including "personal expression" that, like the Tinkers' armbands, "happens to occur on the school premises," . . . . Nevertheless, the majority is certainly correct that indicia of school sponsorship increase the likelihood of such attribution, and that state educators may therefore have a legitimate interest in dissociating themselves from student speech.

. . . Dissociative means short of censorship are available to the school. It could, for example, require the student activity to publish a disclaimer, such as the "Statement of Policy" that *Spectrum* published each school year announcing that "[a]ll . . . editorials appearing in this newspaper reflect the opinions of the *Spectrum* staff, which are not necessarily shared by the administrators or faculty of Hazelwood East," . . . or it could simply issue its own response clarifying the official position on the matter and explaining why the student position is wrong. Yet, without so much as acknowledging the less oppressive alternatives, the Court approves of brutal censorship.

III

Since the censorship served no legitimate pedagogical purpose, it cannot by any stretch of the imagination have been designed to prevent "materia[l] disrup[tion of] classwork," *Tinker*, 393 U.S., at 513, 89 S.Ct., at 740. Nor did the censorship fall within the category that *Tinker* described as necessary to prevent student expression from "inva[ding] the rights of others," *ibid*. If that term is to have any content, it must be limited to rights that are protected by law. . . .

Finally, even if the majority were correct that the principal could constitutionally have censored the objectionable material, I would emphatically object to the brutal manner in which he did so. . . . [T]he principal used a paper shredder. He objected to some material in two articles, but excised six entire articles. He did not so much as inquire into obvious alternatives, such as precise deletions or additions (one of which had already been made), rearranging the layout, or delaying publication. Such unthinking contempt for individual rights is intolerable from any state official. It is particularly insidious from one to whom the public entrusts the task of inculcating in its youth an appreciation for the cherished democratic liberties that our Constitution guarantees.

IV

. . . The young men and women of Hazelwood East expected a civics lesson, but not the one the Court teaches them today.

I dissent.

NOTES AND QUESTIONS

1. Spectrum: Government Expression or Personal Expression?

Professor William G. Buss has written that the First Amendment right of individuals to express their views "has never been understood to create a *general* right" to use public property or resources for speech purposes. Buss, "School Newspapers, Public Forum, and the First Amendment," 74 *Iowa L. Rev.* 505, 508 (1989). While the government generally may not curtail individual speech, except in carefully delineated circumstances, it has no obligation to provide or pay for a printing press to allow an individual to reach a broader audience. *See Cornelius v. NAACP Legal Defense and Education Fund, Inc.*, 473 U.S. 788, 800, 105 S.Ct. 3439, 3447, 87 L.Ed.2d 567 (1985). *See generally* Yudof, *When Government Speaks* 235 (1983). This framework for First Amendment analysis is fully applicable in the public school setting:

> [R]ecognition that students retain their first amendment rights when they enter school property does not entail any entitlement of students to use any and all of the school's resources to communicate their views. Consequently, *Tinker* is not affected directly by the *Hazelwood* holding that students did not have a first amendment right to express their views in the official, state-funded and state-sponsored school newspaper.

Buss, *supra* at 508. *See generally* Yudof, "Personal Speech and Government Expression," 38 *Case West. L. Rev.* 671 (1988) (hereinafter "Personal Speech"). If, however, the government does subsidize private communications or provide a forum for private speech, it may be required, depending on the nature of the forum, to be evenhanded in allocating its resources among potential speakers. *See, e.g., Board of Education of Westside Community Schools v. Mergens*, ___U.S. ___, 110 S.Ct. 2356 (1990) (Equal Access Act); *Healy v. James*, 408 U.S. 169, 92 S.Ct. 2338, 33 L.Ed.2d 266 (1972); *Gay and Lesbian Students Association v. Gohn*, 850 F.2d 361 (8th Cir. 1988). *See generally* Yudof, *When Government Speaks* 234–45 (1983); Karst, "Equality as a Central Principle in the First Amendment," 43 *U. Chi. L. Rev.* 20 (1975).

The distinction between personal and governmental expression focuses on the two ways that students may attempt to counter the socialization that takes place in public schools. They may seek to counter or supplement the school's messages through their own expressive activities, or they may seek to exercise some control over the school's words to dilute or change its messages. "Personal Speech," *supra* at 683. Professor Yudof describes the distinction in these terms:

> In the former situation, students have independent constitutional rights. They may decide on what they wish to say and where they wish to say it, subject to the caveat that they have no right to unduly hamper the school's educational mission. Accordingly, they may wear black armbands to protest military activities of the national government or distribute their own newspapers; yet they may not speak on human rights in Nicaragua in the midst of a geometry class.
>
> If the expression is governmental and not personal, students generally may not interfere with the school's articulation of its own educational messages. They do not have a constitutional right to add or delete courses from the curriculum, alter the teacher's lesson plan, or scrutinize the school district's choice of textbooks. Similarly, they do not have final authority over the content of a school newspaper. The primary constitutional limitation . . . is whether the school district is carrying out its legitimate governmental functions or is acting *ultra vires.*

"Personal Speech," *supra* at 683. Does Justice White, writing for the Court in *Hazelwood*, embrace this distinction? *See Board of Education v. Mergens, supra.* If so, do you agree that there should be two distinct standards of judicial review, one for governmental speech and one for personal speech? *But see Joyner v. Whiting*, 477 F.2d 456 (4th Cir. 1973); *Quarterman v. Byrd*, 453 F.2d 54 (4th Cir. 1971). Is the distinction itself unreasonable? *See* Ingber, infra at 84.

What does Justice Brennan have to say about this issue? In this regard, consider these comments by Professor Buss:

> Plainly, these reasons [prevention of communications harmful to young students, avoidance of official endorsement of the students' points of view, and prevention of interference with the school's ability to teach its lessons] all point to important school interests. Nevertheless, the Court's discussion falls short of demonstrating how these interests are implicated uniquely by student speech published in the official school newspaper. If certain words or ideas harm other students, the harm would not seem dependent upon the forum in which they are expressed.

Buss, *supra* at 511. Do you agree with Professor Buss? Suppose that Hazelwood employed three students to write articles for *Spectrum*, and its policies were explicit that all editorial decisions were to be made by the principal on the basis of his or her best educational judgment. Would it be unconstitutional to dismiss a student for publishing unapproved views in *Spectrum*—even if there were no material disruption or other cognizable harm?

Should the government be treated differently from private publishers in the context of school newspapers? *See* "Personal Speech," *supra* at 685–86; Gottlieb, "In the Name of Patriotism: The Constitutionality of 'Bending' History in the Public Secondary Schools," 62 *N.Y.U. L. Rev.* 497, 523–24 (1987). What lesson should the students be learning? That a newspaper's owner, whether public or private, has the right to determine the content of the publication? Or have the students learned that government may censor private expression? *See* Mueller, "*Hazelwood School District v. Kuhlmeier*: Teaching Our Nation's Youth a Different Civics Lesson?," 2 *Det. C.L Rev.* 669 (1988).

Accepting this distinction, how should *Spectrum* be characterized? Clearly it is not a newspaper owned and published by students, an "underground newspaper" distributed on school premises. On the other hand, a school district can choose to delegate editorial and other authority to students, thereby opting to subsidize the students' expression. Which course did the Hazelwood School District select? Is Justice White correct in noting the managerial prerogatives of the faculty and principal? *See also Planned Parenthood v. Clark County School Dist.*, 887 F.2d 935 (9th Cir. 1989); *Burch v. Barker*, 861 F.2d 1149 (9th Cir. 1988). Or did the school district, in reality, create some form of public forum in which the students were granted the authority to express their own views in *Spectrum*? *See Gambino v. Fairfax*, 429 F.Supp. 731 (W.D. Wis. 1977), *aff'd*, 564 F.2d 157 (7th Cir.); Buss, *supra* at 509–10. If the record is unclear, should there be a presumption on one side or the other? *See Cornelius v. NAACP Legal Defense & Educ. Fund, Inc.*, 473 U.S. 788, 802, 105 S.Ct. 3439, 3449, 87 L.Ed.2d 567 (1985); *Perry Educ. Ass'n v. Perry Local Educators' Ass'n*, 460 U.S. 37, 103 S.Ct. 948, 74 L.Ed.2d 794 (1983). Which side should have the burden of proof? If the school district did delegate authority to students, is it free to retract that delegation at any time that it becomes unhappy with the students' editorial policies? *See Stanley v. McGrath*, 719 F.2d 279 (8th Cir. 1983); *Joyner v. Whiting*, 477 F.2d 456 (4th Cir. 1973).

How does the majority's emphasis on the fit between *Spectrum* and the curriculum advance the analysis? *See Nicholson v. Board of Education*, 682 F.2d 858 (9th Cir. 1982); *Seyfried v. Walton*, 668 F.2d 214 (3d Cir. 1982); *Associated Students of Western Kentucky University v. Downing*, 475 F.2d 1132 (6th Cir. 1973). Can a school newspaper be both a part of the curriculum and a limited public forum? *See* Buss, supra at 510. Is the *Hazelwood* majority emphasizing the curriculum-related nature of the speech in *Fraser*, while the dissent focuses on the discussion of disruption in that case? Which view of *Fraser* is more persuasive? What extensions of *Hazelwood*, if any, can you foresee to other areas of the curriculum?

Professor Ingber argues that "the distinction between curricular and noncurricular expression is not merely unjustified, it is dysfunctional. To teach students that they are free to speak only as long as their message is tangential to their institutional environment is to give a lesson in subservience rather than in participation and civic courage." Ingber, "Rediscovering the Cummunal Worth of Individual Rights: The First Amendment in Institutional Contexts, 69 *Tex. L.Rev.* 1, 84 (1990). Do you agree? Has Ingber misread *Hazelwood*?

2. Public Forum Analysis

Does it follow that if *Spectrum* is a limited public forum that the student editors should have the final say over editorial policy? One meaning of a limited public forum, in this context, is that *Spectrum* is limited to submissions by Hazelwood students; "outsiders" have no right to publish their views in *Spectrum*. But is the creation of a public forum the same thing as delegating decision-making authority to student editors? *See* Buss, *supra* at 512–13. Consider these remarks by Professor Yudof:

> The question is [not] . . . whether *Spectrum* has been opened by school officials to all [student] contributors, on an equal basis; the question is one of control and authority. Who is running the newspaper, the principal and instructor or the student editors? Presumably, a student editorial board would reject some articles, assign some stories and not others, and develop policies for handling sensitive material on sex, drugs, divorce, and other themes. The very power that Justice Brennan would deny the principal will be exercised by the students; there will be no public forum unless they choose to create one.

"Personal Speech," *supra* at 685. Do you agree? *See Kania v. Fordham*, 702 F.2d 475 (4th Cir. 1983); *Avins v. Rutgers*, 385 F.2d 151 (3d Cir. 1967); *Ar-*

rington v. Taylor, 380 F.Supp. 1348 (M.D.N.C. 1974), *aff'd mem.*, 526 F.2d 587 (4th Cir. 1975). How much depends on the characteristics that may be attributed to a "limited" public forum? *See Planned Parenthood v. Clark County School Dist.*, 887 F.2d 935 (9th Cir. 1989). *Cf. Lehman v. City of Shaker Heights*, 418 U.S. 298, 94 S.Ct. 2714, 41 L.Ed.2d 770 (1974). Is it meaningful to speak of a public forum only for student editors? What of a limited forum that excluded articles on sex, drugs, and divorce—or only some views on those subjects?

3. Substantial Disruption and the **Hazelwood** *Case*

If *Tinker* were applicable in *Hazelwood*, should the Court have upheld the rights of the students? Do you agree with Professor Ingber that "the Court (in *Hazelwood*) arguably has betrayed the premise of *Tinker* that schoolchildren too have fundamental first amendment rights"? Ingber, "Rediscovering the Communal Worth of Individual Rights: The First Amendment in Institutional Contexts," 69 *Tex.L.Rev.* 1, 84 (1990). What of the gloss given to *Tinker* by the *Fraser* Court? Might the principal have reasonably and foreseeably predicted a material disruption of the school environment? If vulgar student speech may be prohibited, may the principal justifiably delete the noted articles? How does Justice Brennan deal with the problem of ungrammatical student expression? Is such expression disruptive of the school's mission? Does it fall within an exception to *Tinker* akin to that for lewd speech?

Assuming that a student article was thought to be libelous, may school authorities constitutionally delete it—even if there were no reasonable forecast of a material disruption? *See Shanley v. Northeast Independent School Dist.*, 462 F.2d 960, 971 (5th Cir. 1972); *Fujishima v. Board of Education*, 460 F.2d 1355, 1359 (7th Cir. 1972).

4. Government Expression and the **Pico** *Standard*

What standard of review does the majority apply to the principal's decision to delete articles from *Spectrum*? Is it a reasonableness standard? *See Frasca v. Andrews*, 463 F.Supp. 1043 (E.D.N.Y. 1979). What would be an unreasonable decision? Should the standard be the same as for library book deselection in *Board of Education v. Pico, supra*? That is, must the decision be a good faith educational decision? *See* "Personal Speech," *supra* at 692–96. If so, what would constitute a bad faith decision?

Suppose that an external organization wished to place an advertisement in *Spectrum* that advised students about where to obtain information on birth control and pregnancy. After *Hazelwood*, may the school district decline to print the advertisement? *See Planned Parenthood v. Clark County School Dist.*, 887 F.2d 935 (9th Cir. 1989). What about an advertisement for a water pipe that often is used to smoke marijuana? *See Williams v. Spencer*, 622 F.2d 1200 (4th Cir. 1980). Would your answer depend on the district's advertising policies and their implementation? Would it matter if the students and not school officials made decisions on advertising? *See Sinn v. Daily Nebraskan*, 829 F.2d 662 (8th Cir. 1987).

What if a faculty advisor to a school newspaper fails to submit controversial articles to the principal for prior approval pursuant to school policies? May the faculty advisor be fired or removed from his or her advisory responsibilities? *See Nicholson v. Board of Education Torrance Unified School Dist.*, 682 F.2d 858 (9th Cir. 1982).

5. Advice to School Authorities and Legislative Responses to **Hazelwood**

In the light of *Tinker*, *Bethel*, *Pico*, and *Hazelwood*, what advice would you give to school authorities planning to set up and sponsor a school newspaper? *See* Buss, *supra* at 522. *See generally* Avery and Simpson, "The Constitution and Student Publications: A Comprehensive Approach," 16 *J. of Law & Educ.* 1 (1987). Is there a problem of giving the appearance of a student newspaper or public forum, while editorial authority, in reality, is retained by school officials? *See* Buss, *supra* at 526. If students are given ultimate authority over the content of a school newspaper, what is the district's risk of liability if a particular article is defamatory? *See* Mississippi Gay Alliance v. Goudelock, 536 F.2d 1073 (5th Cir. 1976).

California, Massachusetts, and Iowa enacted legislation after *Hazelwood* to guarantee freedom of expression for student editors of school newspapers, subject to limitations for obscenity, libel, encouragement to violate the law or school regulations, and the *Tinker* substantial disruption test. *See, e.g.*, *Iowa Education Code* § 280.22 (1989). The Iowa law specifically provides that school districts will not be subject to civil liability for student expression unless school employees have altered the content of the article in question. *Id.*

6. Indecency and Underground Newspapers

In *Papish v. Board of Curators of University of Mis-*

souri, 410 U.S. 667, 93 S.Ct. 1197, 35 L.Ed.2d 618 (1973), the Court held that it was unconstitutional to dismiss a graduate student for on-campus distribution of a newspaper that featured a political cartoon depicting a policeman raping the Statute of Liberty and the Goddess of Justice. The caption of the cartoon read, ". . . With Liberty and Justice for All." The paper also contained an article entitled "M----- F----- Acquitted," which discussed the trial and acquittal of a New York City youth who was a member of an organization known as "UP Against the Wall, M----- F-----." In protecting the student, the Court said that "mere dissemination of ideas—no matter how offensive to good taste—on a state university campus may not be shut off in the name alone of 'conventions of decency.' " 410 U.S. at 670, 93 S.Ct. at 1199. Does *Papish* apply to high schools? *See Jacobs v. Board of School Commissioners*, 490 F.2d 601 (7th Cir. 1973), *vacated as moot*, 420 U.S. 128, 95 S.Ct. 848, 43 L.Ed.2d 74 (1975). Is *Fraser* dispusitive? *Hazelwood?* Would *Papish* protect a high school student from dismissal for distributing a paper that included the quip, "Oral sex may cause tooth decay"? *See Scoville v. Board of Education of Joliet Township*, 425 F.2d 10 (7th Cir. 1970), *cert. denied*, 400 U.S. 826, 91 S.Ct. 51, 27 L.Ed.2d 55. *See generally* Letwin, "Administrative Censorship of the Independent Student Press—Demise of the Double Standard?," 28 *S. Car. L. Rev.* 565 (1977). Does your answer depend on whether the publication is an underground student newspaper or an official school newspaper? To what extent would *Fraser* be controlling in the former case?

B. Changing the School's Message

State and local boards of education are entrusted with the basic authority to shape the content of the school program, subject to the limitation that the program may not establish religion. *See* Section II, *supra*. The state also has an interest in selecting those teachers who are most likely to carry out the school's educational mission and in making sure that they actually do so. Those selected as teachers may seek to supplement the state's messages with their own opinions and beliefs, or they may seek to modify the message that the state and school board wish to convey. This section explores these tensions and related issues.

One way of stating the problem is to ask whether teachers may use public school resources—for example, class time, dollars, and equipment—to introduce their own curriculum materials and articles when school officials disagree with their content. Stated differently, the question is who shall control the content of the school curriculum? The more control given to the individual teacher, the greater the diversity of messages "broadcast" by the schools, and there will be less danger of the school speaking from a single ideological viewpoint. *See* Yudof, "Three Faces of Academic Freedom," 32 *Loy. L. Rev.* 831 (1987). But the more freedom given to teachers, the greater the risk of frustration of the public interest in providing a particular kind of education that the school authorities consider desirable. Teachers are not hired and appointed to proselytize at public expense, disregarding the school board's policies. This danger is exacerbated by the fact that public elementary and secondary schools have a "captive" audience, an audience that cannot easily escape a teacher's expressed values. Why should a teacher's values or academic freedom prevail over those of school boards responsible to the public? *See* Goldstein, "The Asserted Constitutional Right of Public School Teachers to Determine What They Teach," 124 *U. Pa. L. Rev.* 1293, 1342–43 (1976). But should teachers be compelled to convey only those ideas, beliefs, and opinions that have been officially approved by the school board? *See* Yudof, *supra*.

1. Academic Freedom. Concerning teachers' claim to freedom of expression in the classroom (academic freedom), the cases have not developed a coherent body of doctrine. *See generally* Byrne, "Academic Freedom: 'A Special Concern of the First Amendment,' " 99 *Yale L. J.* 251 (1989). At least one point seems reasonably well established: Teachers are not free to transform their assigned courses into something other than what the school's administration intended them to be. *Clark v. Holmes*, 474 F.2d 928 (7th Cir. 1972), *cert. denied*, 411 U.S. 972, 93 S.Ct. 2148, 36 L.Ed.2d 695 (1973); *Ahern v. Board of the School District of Grand Island*, 327 F.Supp. 1391 (D. Neb. 1971). Whether the teacher's changes constitute abandonment of the prescribed curriculum may not always be easy to decide. For example, is a change in a college drama course reducing the coverage from twenty-five plays to in-depth coverage of eleven plays an abandonment of the prescribed curriculum? *See Hetrick v. Martin*, 480 F.2d 705 (6th Cir. 1973), *cert. denied*, 414 U.S. 1075, 94 S.Ct. 592, 38 L.Ed.2d 482 (1973).

If there is a right to academic freedom within the classroom, that right is not tantamount to granting the teacher a license to do as he or she wishes. Whether a more circumscribed right should exist and what its scope should be raise difficult constitutional questions, especially in the context of elementary and secondary schools. For example, a number of courts have held that "classroom management techniques" and pedalogical methods are not constitutionally protected. *See, e.g., Bradley v. Pittsburgh Board of Education*, 910 F.2d 1172 (3rd Cir. 1990); *Adams v. Campbell County School District*, 511 F.2d 1242 (10th Cir. 1975); *Hetrick v. Martin*, 480 F.2d 705 (6th Cir. 1973).

Cary v. Board of Education

598 F.2d 535 (10th Cir. 1979).

Logan, Circuit Judge.

This is an appeal from summary judgment denying relief in a declaratory judgment action which sought enforcement of claimed rights under the First and Fourteenth Amendments to the United States Constitution. The action was brought by five high school teachers who asserted their rights were violated when the Board of Education for the Adams-Arapahoe School District in Colorado (the board) banned ten books from use in the teachers' language arts classes.

* * *

The relevant facts were stipulated; both sides sought summary judgment. All plaintiffs are tenured teachers who teach high school language arts classes in the defendant school district. The classes involved are elective courses for eleventh and twelfth grade students—Contemporary Literature, Contemporary Poetry, and American Masters—which under the board regulations were designed for elective optional reading materials chosen from classroom libraries or personal sources.

The board first adopted a policy on selection of text material in January, 1975. A High School Language Arts Text Evaluation Committee was established to review current and new materials for language arts courses. Membership was composed of representative teachers, administrators, parents and students. The committee reviewed many books which had been used or were recommended for use in these courses. It was instructed to utilize specified criteria: appropriateness to the grade level, value of the material in relation to the course objectives, and fiscal considerations. The guidelines adopted by the board required a written response, including reasons, when suggested materials were rejected.

Only one book was rejected by the majority report of the committee, with apparently 1,285 books approved. A minority report filed by three members listed nine more books they would reject. The recommended texts were on public display for twelve days. Then at a regularly scheduled public meeting of the school board, and following an open discussion, the board voted to approve a list of 1,275 books for use in language arts classes in the high schools. Ten recommended books, all of which had previously been used in those classes, were excluded from the approved list;[1] six of the ten were among those not recommended in the minority report. The majority and minority reports made reference to the specified criteria in discussing titles they rejected, but the board itself set forth no written statement of the reasons for its vote to ban the ten books. Its edict to the teachers issued after the meeting simply referenced the list of books not being approved and made the following declarations:

> Books which are not approved for instructional use will not be purchased, nor used for class assignment,

1. The banned volumes were:

a. Contemporary Literature:
   (1) *A Clockwork Orange* by Anthony Burgess;
   (2) *The Exorcist* by William P. Blatty;
   (3) *The Reincarnation of Peter Proud* by Max Ehrlich.

b. Contemporary Poetry:
   (1) *New American Poetry* by Donald Allen;
   (2) *Starting from San Francisco* by Lawrence Ferlinghetti;
   (3) *The Yage Letters* by William Burroughs and Allen Ginsberg;
   (4) *Coney Island of the Mind* by Lawrence Ferlinghetti;
   (5) *Kaddish and Other Poems* by Allen Ginsberg;
   (6) *Lunch Poems* by Frank O'Hara.

c. American Masters:
   Rosemary's Baby by Ira Levin.

nor will an individual be given credit for reading any of these books.

* * *

An unwritten board policy had permitted substitution of materials for assignments offensive to a student or his or her parents. That policy was formally adopted by the board in written form after the meeting above described.

By stipulation the parties agreed the books were not obscene, no systematic effort had been made to exclude any particular system of thought or philosophy, and a "constitutionally proper decision-maker" could decide these books were proper for high school language arts classes. It was agreed that the plaintiff teachers were subject to dismissal from their positions for insubordination for any of the following acts:

(a) adding any of the subject textbooks to the reading list of their courses;
(b) assigning the reading of any of the subject textbooks;
(c) giving any student any credit in courses for reading any of the subject textbooks;
(d) reading aloud or causing to be read aloud any of the subject textbooks in the classroom during class time; or
(e) discussing with students in the classroom during class time any of these materials at such length so as to amount to a constructive assignment of the materials.

* * *

We recognize and support the concept that "teachers [do not] shed their constitutional rights to freedom of speech or expression at the schoolhouse gate." *Tinker v. Des Moines Independent Community School Dist.*, 393 U.S. 503, 506 . . . (1969). This general commitment has been stated eloquently on occasion:

> Our Nation is deeply committed to safeguarding academic freedom, which is of transcendent value to all of us and not merely to the teachers concerned. That freedom is therefore a special concern of the First Amendment, which does not tolerate laws that cast a pall of orthodoxy over the classroom. . . . The classroom is peculiarly the "marketplace of ideas." The Nation's future depends upon leaders trained through wide exposure to that robust exchange of ideas which discovers truth "out of a multitude of tongues, [rather] than through any kind of authoritative selection." *United States v. Associated Press*, [D.C.,] 52 F.Supp. 362, 372.

Keyishian v. Board of Regents, 385 U.S. 589, 603 . . . (1967).

> To regard teachers—in our entire educational system, from the primary grades to the university—as the priests of our democracy is therefore not to indulge in hyperbole. It is the special task of teachers to foster those habits of open-mindedness and critical inquiry which alone make for responsible citizens, who, in turn, make possible an enlightened and effective public opinion. Teachers must fulfill their function by precept and practice, by the very atmosphere which they generate; they must be exemplars of open-mindedness and free inquiry. They cannot carry out their noble task if the conditions for the practice of a responsible and critical mind are denied to them.

Wieman v. Updegraff, 344 U.S. 183, 196 . . . (1952) (Frankfurter J., concurring). Most of the cases, however, have arisen at the university level, and outside the area of curricular decisions and teaching-related speech in the classroom.

* * *

Quite a number of circuit and district court decisions have involved claims of school board or school authorities' interference with teachers' First Amendment rights to conduct their classes as they see fit in exercise of their professional judgment. Most were discharge cases where the teacher was fired, or a contract not renewed, for allegedly offensive behavior, poor teaching techniques and insubordination. Conflicts over the teachers' use of dirty words in class, or assignment of reading materials containing dirty words, seeming approval of free love, drugs or rebellion against authority, were generally part of a charge of inappropriate conduct alleged to constitute good cause for discharge. The cases which held for the teachers and placed emphasis upon teachers' rights to exercise discretion in the classroom, seemed to be situations where school authorities acted in the absence of a general policy, after the fact, and had little to charge against the teacher other than the assignment with which they were unhappy. *See Sterzing v. Fort Bend Independent School Dist.*, 376 F.Supp. 657 (S.D. Tex. 1972), *vacated on remedial grounds*, 496 F.2d 92 (5th Cir. 1974); *Mailloux v. Kiley*, 436 F.2d 565 (1st Cir. 1971), *on remand*, 323 F.Supp. 1387 (D. Mass.), *aff'd on other grounds*, 448 F.2d 1242 (1st Cir. 1971); *Keefe v. Geanakos*, 418 F.2d 359 (1st Cir. 1969); *Parducci v. Rutland*, 316 F.Supp. 352 (M.D. Ala. 1979). . . . In the cases where the teachers' First Amendment claims were rejected, generally the school authorities had other good grounds supporting their discharge or nonrenewal of the teacher's contract. *Adams v. Campbell County School Dist.*, 511 F.2d 1242 (10th Cir. 1975); *Brubaker v. Board of Educ.*, 502 F.2d 973 (7th Cir. 1974), *cert. denied*, 421 U.S. 965 . . . (1975).

* * *

. . . The teachers acknowledge the right of the school board to prescribe the curriculum and the principal textbooks used in the courses. They agree the school board does not have to offer the three courses at issue here; but they say that once the courses have been approved the teachers' "right of academic freedom includes the right to use non-obscene materials electively in elective courses taught to high school students." They do not ask the board to purchase or endorse certain books; they do not seek to require a student to read materials against the student's will; but they want to be free from restrictions "based upon the personal predilections of members of the school board."

* * *

. . . We have found no law which allows a high school teacher to have the broad latitude which appellants seek.

If the board may decide that Contemporary Poetry may not be offered; if it may select the major text of the course; why may it not go further and exclude certain books from being assigned for instruction in the course? As we understand these language arts courses there is no basic text, or if there is one it is utilized only for a portion of the class study. A large part of the instructional time is review and discussion of items selected by students, with consent of the teacher, from the reading list. As adopted by the board the list contained altogether 1,275 titles approved for the three courses. Thus it can be said with some justification the texts adopted by the school board for these courses is the reading list. That, we believe, is the proper view of the situation before us; and the board was acting within its rights in omitting the books, even though the decision was a political one influenced by the personal views of the members.

We agree with the board characterization of the stipulation that it does not prohibit mention of these books in class, nor treatment by the teacher of the books as examples of contemporary poetry, literature or American masters. The ban is upon such extended reference or use in class as to constitute class assignments which in effect evade the exercise of discretion made by the board in its determination of the parameters of the courses.

. . . [T]he stipulation declares that no systematic effort was made "to exclude any particular type of thinking or book." And no objection was made that the board was not following its own standards in rejecting the books. The approved list is broad, containing 1,275 books for the three courses. No objection is made by the teachers that the exclusions prevent them from studying an entire representative group of writers. Rather the teachers want to be freed from the "personal predilections" of the board. We do not see a basis in the constitution to grant their wish.

The trial court entered judgment in favor of the defendant board and its members. Although we place our holding upon a different basis, we affirm that judgment.

William E. Doyle, Circuit Judge, concurring.

I concur in the result and in most of what appears in the opinion. I would, however, approach it somewhat differently. I would disapprove of any arbitrary selection of books that can be read and those which cannot be on the reading list. One can read the majority as, in effect, making such a ruling.

However, the court does not say it. It recognizes that the School Board has a broad right to select texts and to exclude textbooks. The approach which I prefer would be that the exclusion of books for secondary school students is not to be an arbitrary exclusion. Therefore, reasons have to be given so that there can be court review. If they are excluded because the Board member disapproves for a subjective reason, I would say that this is an unlawful and unconstitutional invasion of the classroom.

So, with the above exceptions, I concur in the submitted opinion.

NOTES AND QUESTIONS

1. Academic Freedom

Teachers' academic freedom is conventionally said to comprise freedom of inquiry and research, freedom of teaching, and freedom of extramural utterance and action. American Association of University Professors, "The 1915 Declaration of Principles," in L. Jouglin, ed., *Academic Freedom and Tenure* (1969). *See generally*, Metzger, "Profession and

Constitution: Two Definitions of Academic Freedom in America," 66 *Tex. L. Rev.* 1265 (1988). A basic premise of this right is that truth is discovered through research and inquiry and that there is no such thing as a truth not subject to question and debate. Related to this doctrine is the concept that education ideally ought to liberate students and open their minds to new and provocative ideas. *See generally* C. Lindblom, Inquiry and Change (1990). This concept of academic freedom may be applicable to universities, but should it be extended to public elementary and secondary school teachers? If, as earlier portions of this chapter indicate, one constitutionally permissible purpose of public schools is to inculcate values chosen by elected officials or administrators responsible to the community, is there is any reason to grant academic freedom to public school teachers, allowing their personal values to be pressed upon a captive audience? Goldstein, "The Asserted Constitutional Right of Public School Teachers to Determine What They Teach," 124 *U. Pa. L. Rev.* 1293, 1343 (1976). On the other hand, academic freedom would promote pluralism within the schools and diminish the danger of governmental indoctrination of students. Does this argument justify academic freedom for public school teachers? Or does the doctrine rest on the notion of the school as a marketplace of ideas?

The doctrine of academic freedom may be derived from the right of students to learn and to hear. Do students have rights of free speech derived from academic freedom? *But see* Byrne, "Academic Freedom: A 'Special Concern of the First Amendment,' " 99 *Yale L.J.* 251, 262–63 (1989) (hereinafter "Special Concern"). Is it relevant that many students and parents do not want to hear what the teacher (and other students) wish to say?

What of the need to give special protection to teachers as "priests of our democracy"? *Wieman v. Updegraff*, 344 U.S. 183, 195–96, 73 S.Ct. 215, 221, 97 L.Ed. 216 (1952) (Frankfurter, J., concurring). But who elected these "priests," and how do we know that they will proselytize democratic truths? Is Justice Frankfurter referring to a democratic process involving the free exchange of ideas and opinions? If so, is academic freedom a principle of constitutional law or an education philosophy? *See* Katz, "The First Amendment's Protection of Expressive Activity in the University Classroom: A Constitutional Myth," 16 *U. Cal.-Davis L. Rev.* 857 (1983). Is there a distinction between "academic freedom" and "constitutional academic freedom"? See "Special Concern" at 254–55. At bottom, do academic freedom for teachers and rights of expression for students rest on the supposition that public schools must instill democratic values? *See generally* Ingber, "Rediscovering the Communal Worth of Individual Rights: The First Amendment in Institutional Contexts," 69 *Tex.L.Rev.* 1, 73–86 (1990).

What definition of academic freedom would correctly balance the interest of school officials in overseeing public education with the interest of the teacher in freedom of speech? Does the position adopted by Justice Stewart in *Epperson v. Arkansas, supra*, strike a reasonable balance? That is, should the teacher be able to make reasonable pedagogical judgments within general boundaries set by the state and school board? *See Parate v. Isibor*, 868 F.2d 821 (6th Cir. 1989). *But see Carley v. Arizona Bd. of Regents*, 153 Ariz. 461, 463–65, 737 P.2d 1099, 1101–03 (App. 1987). Does *Cary* affirm this principle? Where does *Cary* draw the line between the extremes of allowing a teacher to substitute one course for another and prohibiting a teacher from deviating from the prescribed materials? *See Clark v. Holmes*, 474 F.2d 928 (7th Cir. 1972).

Does academic freedom protect the teacher's discretion in grading students? *See Parate v. Isibor, supra*; *Lovelace v. Southeastern Mass. Univ.*, 793 F.2d 419 (1st Cir. 1986).

The relevant Supreme Court cases do not involve factual situations even remotely parallel to the factual situation in the *Cary* case itself. Should a teacher have standing to attack the constitutionality of the books selected for classroom use? *See Johnson v. Stuart*, 702 F.2d 193 (9th Cir. 1983). If so, is *Hazelwood* controlling? *See Virgil v. School Board of Columbia County*, 677 F.Supp. 1547 (M.D. Fla. 1988).

2. *Academic Freedom in* Cary

Under what circumstances should the *Cary* court have concluded that the academic freedom of the teachers in the language arts courses had been violated by the exclusion of the ten books? Is it relevant that the school board declined to give reasons for the exclusions? What if the board had asserted that the books in question were inappropriate for high school students? *See Board of Education v. Pico*, 457 U.S. 853, 102 S.Ct. 2799, 73 L.Ed.2d 435 (1982). What if it took the position that the books were not good examples of the types of literature to be considered in the language arts courses? What if the board had charged that the books were vulgar, although not legally obscene? Would *Hazelwood, Fraser,* and *Pico,* be decisive? *See Virgil v. School Board, supra.* What if the board had argued that some of the books might be psychologically harmful—for example, that *Rosemary's Baby* or *The Exorcist* might frighten impressionable youngsters? Did the plaintiffs concede too much when they stipulated that a constitutionally appropriate decision maker could decide that the excluded books were appropriate? Did the parties frame the issue in such a manner that the court had little choice but to affirm the authority of the school board over book selection policies?

Is it relevant to the academic freedom issue that the public schools were not being asked to purchase the books, that there was no basic text for each course, and that teachers had over a thousand approved books from which to choose? In conjunction with the admission that there was no systematic effort to exclude any particular type of thinking, is this last point decisive of the academic freedom issue? *See Pico, supra.* If the question is one of personal taste, should the board or the teachers prevail? Consider the board's policy that allows for the substitution of other assignments when a student or parent objects to a particular book. As a matter of policy, if not constitutional law, would it be preferable to permit teachers to make the initial selections, reserving to families the right to reject specific books?

Should the *Cary* court have ordered the board to comply with its own preestablished procedures? Is the failure to abide by the procedures relevant to academic freedom? Suppose that students and parents had sued the school board for excluding the ten books. Should this change the result of *Cary*?

3. An Alternative Approach to Academic Freedom: Parducci v. Rutland

The *Cary* court distinguishes *Parducci v. Rutland,* 316 F.Supp. 352 (M.D. ala. 1970) by stating that "school authorities [there] acted in the absence of a general policy, after the fact, and had little to charge against the teacher other than the assignment with which they were unhappy." Consider these excerpts from Judge Johnson's opinion in *Parducci:*

> On April 21, 1970, plaintiff assigned as outside reading to her junior English classes a story, entitled "Welcome to the Monkey House." The story, a comic satire, was selected by plaintiff to give her students a better understanding of one particular genre of western literature—the short story. The story's author, Kurt Vonnegut, Jr., is a prominent contemporary writer who has published numerous short stories and novels, including *Cat's Cradle* and a recent best seller, *Slaughterhouse-Five.*
>
> The following morning, plaintiff was called to Principal Rutland's office for a conference with him and the Associate Superintendent of the school system. Both men expressed their displeasure with the content of the story, which they described as "literary garbage," and with the "philosophy" of the story, which they construed as condoning, if not encouraging, "the killing off of elderly people and free sex." They also expressed concern over the fact that three of plaintiff's students had asked to be excused from the assignment and that several disgruntled parents had called the school to complain. They then admonished plaintiff not to teach the story in any of her classes.
>
> Plaintiff retorted that she was bewildered by their interpretation and attitude toward the story, that she still considered it to be a good literary work, and that, while not meaning to cause any trouble, she felt that she had a professional obligation to teach the story. . . . On May 6, the School Board notified the plaintiff that she had been dismissed from her job for assigning materials which had a "disruptive" effect on the school and for refusing "the counseling and advice of the school principal." The School Board also advised the plaintiff that one of the bases for her dismissal was "insubordination" by reason of a statement that she made to the Principal and Associate Superintendent that "regardless of their counseling" she "would continue to teach the eleventh grade English class at the Jeff David High School by the use of whatever material" she wanted "and in whatever manner" she thought best.
>
> * * *
>
> At the outset, it should be made clear that plaintiff's teaching ability is not in issue. The Principal of her school has conceded that plaintiff was a good teacher and that she would have received a favorable evaluation from him at the end of the year but for the single incident which led to her dismissal.
>
> Plaintiff asserts in her complaint that her dismissal for assigning "Welcome to the Monkey House" violated her First Amendment right to academic freedom.
>
> * * *
>
> The right to academic freedom, however, like all other constitutional rights, is not absolute and must be balanced against the competing interests of society. This Court is keenly aware of the state's vital interest in protecting the impressionable minds of its young

people from *any* form of extreme propagandism in the classroom.

* * *

Thus, the first question to be answered is whether "Welcome to the Monkey House" is inappropriate reading for high school juniors. While the story contains several vulgar terms and a reference to an involuntary act of sexual intercourse, the Court, having read the story very carefully, can find nothing that would render it obscene either under the standards of *Roth v. United States* [354 U.S. 476 (1957)] or under the stricter standards for minors as set forth in *Ginsberg v. New York* [390 U.S. 629 (1968)].

The slang words are contained in two short rhymes which are less ribald than those found in many of Shakespeare's plays. The reference in the story to an act of sexual intercourse is no more descriptive than the rape scene in Pope's *Rape of the Lock*. As for the theme of the story, the Court notes that the anthology in which the story was published was reviewed by several of the popular national weekly magazines, none of which found the subject matter of any of the stories to be offensive. It appears to the Court, moreover, that the author, rather than advocating the "killing off of old people," satirizes the practice to symbolize the increasing depersonalization of man in society.

The Court's finding as to the appropriateness of the story for high school students is confirmed by the reaction of the students themselves. Rather than there being a threatened or actual substantial disruption to the educational processes of the school, the evidence reflects that the assigning of the story was greeted with apathy by most of the students. . . .

Since the defendants have failed to show either that the assignment was inappropriate reading for high school juniors, or that it created a significant disruption to the educational process of this school, this Court concludes that plaintiff's dismissal constituted an unwarranted invasion of her First Amendment right to academic freedom. 316 F.Supp. at 352 *et seq.*

How does Judge Johnson's concept of the nature and scope of academic freedom differ from that of the *Cary* court? *See* Yudof, *supra* at 844–46. Did Judge Logan accurately characterize the *Parducci* decision? Is Judge Johnson saying that teachers enjoy a right to introduce any written materials into a class as long as they are not "inappropriate reading"? What justifies the adoption of such a broad standard? Does the *Parducci* standard serve only to exclude materials that are legally obscene for minors, or does it permit a school board to punish a teacher for introduction of other sorts of materials as well? Does this standard provide useful guidance for teachers and school boards, or does the standard amount to a statement that, in effect, if the judge likes the book or materials, the teacher will be protected? Are judges to be relied upon to carry out this book-review function?

Consider these sample passages from "Welcome to the Monkey House" (1970): "The pills were so effective that you could blindfold a man who had taken one, tell him to recite the Gettysburg Address, kick him in the balls while he was doing it, and he wouldn't miss a syllable. . . ." Id. at 29. "Virgin hostess, death's recruiter, Life is cute, but you are cuter. Mourn my pecker, purple daughter—all it passed was sky-blue water." *Id.* at 35–36. Do you agree with the court's conclusion that such passages are appropriate for high school juniors? Compare *Parker v. Board of Education*, 348 F.2d 464 (4th Cir. 1965). If a parent does not wish his or her child to be exposed to such literature, why should the teacher not respect that judgment? Are judges, by virtue of their method of selection or training and experience, better able to determine the appropriateness of such literature than school officials accountable to the public?

4. *Alternative Formulations*

Would the following standard be more responsive to the academic freedom problem: Teachers may not introduce materials that effectively frustrate the legitimate interest of the school authorities in regulating the school curriculum? *See James v. Board of Educ.*, 461 F.2d 566 (2d Cir. 1972), *cert. denied*, 409 U.S. 1042, 93 S.Ct. 529, 34 L.Ed.2d 491. Alternatively, should teachers have a right to choose a teaching method and/or materials which in the view of the court serve a demonstrated educational purpose as established by the weight of opinion of the teaching profession? *See Mailloux v. Kiley*, 436 F.2d 565 (1st Cir. 1971), *after dismissal*, 323 F.Supp. 1387 (D. Mass.), *aff'd*, 448 F.2d 1242 (1st Cir. 1971) (per curiam). Or should courts examine a broad range of factors in deciding these cases: for example, was the material introduced relevant, did it have educational value, was it appropriate for the age group in question? Is the *Cary* standard preferable? *See Pratt v. Independent School District No. 831*, 670 F.2d 771 (8th Cir. 1982); *Zykan v. Warsaw Community School Corp.*, 631 F.2d 1300 (7th Cir. 1980).

5. *Problems*

a. Rosebud High School has been the center of controversy. Several students published an issue of the "Purple Albatross" using a series of explicit sexual references. They were suspended. The next morning, faculty and students found a huge sign bearing an "offensive" four letter word on the front lawn of the school. Everyone in school saw it, and the school is buzzing with conversation over its presence. Mr. Post is teaching a mathematics class, but it is clear that the students are supremely uninterested in what he is saying. Post decides to discuss the presence of the sign and the reasons for the controversy. The incident forms the basis for Post's dismissal. How should a court decide a case in which Post challenges his dismissal on constitutional grounds? Would your answer be different if Mr. Post were a civics teacher?

b. What constitutional protection, if any, should be afforded Ms. Robinson, a teacher who tells individual students out of class that it is foolish to salute the flag and that Russia has the best government and ours is the worst, who distributes to some students a pamphlet on Communism, who disparages Lincoln, who decries religion to other students, and who fails to deny to another student an accusation that she is a member of a Communist club? *See Board of Education of Eureka v. Jewett*, 21 Cal. app.2d 64, 68 P.2d 404 (1937). Would it make a difference if remarks similarly critical of the United States were made in class? *See Joyce v. Board of Education*, 325 Ill.App. 543, 60 N.E.2d 431 (1945).

6. *Institutional Academic Freedom*

Consider these remarks by Dean Yudof on institutional academic freedom:

> Thus far, I have been speaking only of the rights of teachers in public schools, for all of the cases under consideration involved state action by a public authority against allegedly miscreant instructors. The concept of academic freedom is equally applicable to private institutions, but the violation of academic freedom has a constitutional dimension only in the public sphere.[70] By contract or other arrangements, private institutions may choose to afford the personal autonomy protections of academic freedom to their teachers,[71] but the Constitution cannot plausibly be construed as requiring them to do so.[72] But there is a third face to academic freedom, a face that is turned toward private schools, that seeks to limit the power of governments to impose their will on such institutions. Consistent with the scholarly work of Professor Matthew Finkin,[73] I describe this as the institutional face of academic freedom.
>
> By way of historical background, the continental tradition of academic freedom as professorial autonomy differed substantially from the pattern of academic freedom, developed over many centuries, in Great Britain and, much later, in the United States. This tradition centered on the "legally autonomous university, chartered by the government or Parliament or the Crown," and it reposed basic institutional authority in internal, academic governing bodies. While this allocation of authority was of great consequence for individual instructors, its basic thrust was the protection of institutional or corporate autonomy and not the protection of the personal autonomy of individual professors. Professor Shils has gone so far as to state that "[l]egislators in Great Britain as on the continent did not regard the universities as falling within their jurisdiction." He hastens to add that "American state legislators did not take quite the same attitude."
>
> In varying forms and degrees, institutional academic freedom was thought to apply to both public and private universities, though the relationship between lay governing boards and academic communities in public universities has sometimes been uneasy and contentious. But it is important to note that through a curious infusion of federal constitutional law, the institutional autonomy face of academic freedom turned toward private elementary and secondary schools in the early years of this century. The leading cases are *Pierce v. Society of Sisters*,[77] and *Meyer v. Nebraska*,[78] 1920s substantive due process decisions of the United States Supreme Court. The Court in *Pierce* held that Oregon could not require all school-age children to attend public schools, and, in effect, that the institutional autonomy of private schools was constitutionally protected. In *Meyer* the justices overturned a law that forbade the teaching of German in private schools. Though the substantive due process underpinnings of *Pierce* and *Meyer* have been thoroughly repudiated over the last sixty years, interestingly enough the results have never been repudiated, and a number of justices, of varying judicial persuasions, have embraced them on one ground or other.

---

70. *See generally* . . . O'Neil "*Private Universities and Public Law*," 19 *Buffalo L. Rev.* 155 (1970).

71. *See* Finkin, "*Toward a Law of Academic Status*," 22 *Buffalo L. Rev.* 575 (1973).

72. *Cf. Rendell-Baker v. Kohn*, 457 U.S. 830 (1982). *But see* Levinson, "Princeton Versus Free Speech: A Post Mortem," in *Regulating the Intellectuals: Perspectives on Academic Freedom in the 1980s* 189 (C. Kaplan & E. Schrecker eds. 1983).

73. Finkin, "On " 'Institutional' Academic Freedom," 61 *Tex. L. Rev.* 817 (1983). *See generally* R. Hofstadter & W. Metzger, *The Development of Academic Freedom in the United States* ch. 2 (1955).

77. 268 U.S. 510 (1925). . . .

78. 262 U.S. 390 (1923).

From a constitutional perspective, *Pierce* and *Meyer* may represent a recognition of the right of parents to direct the education of their children, the right of teachers to affiliate with a private school, the right of individuals to associate with each other, or perhaps the right of religious students, parents and groups to organize their own schools. Each of these justifications is problematic, and many law review pages have been written on this engaging subject. The essential points, however, are that institutional academic freedom protects the private school from an overreaching governmental authority, and that, as in the case of the government expression face of academic freedom, the concept tends to diminish the ability of government to suppress competing ideas and ideologies. From my perspective, institutional academic freedom has less to do with the rights of private schools—and those of their operators, teachers and patrons—than it does with a limitation on the communications powers of government.

The third face of academic freedom does not always smile on individual teachers. The protection of institutional autonomy may require that private school authorities have substantial authority over who teaches and what is taught in their schools.[83] The institution will not be autonomous, a parochial school cannot convey its religious message, if it is required to allow teachers to discuss the pros and cons of abortion or birth control.[84] Indeed, institutional academic freedom does not purport to resolve disputes within a private school; it does not draw a line between the authority of the academicians and that of administrators and governing board members.

Note also that there are limits to institutional autonomy, just as there are limits to personal autonomy, and there are times when governmental regulation is entirely permissible. Private schools may not practice racial discrimination,[85] they may have to abide building and fire codes, they may be subject to various labor relations, minimum wage, and employment statutes. They also may be required to offer particular courses, to keep attendance records, and to hire qualified teachers if their students are to satisfy compulsory attendance laws.[87] In each case the compelling nature of the public policy and the limits of tolerance must balance against the specific infringement on institutional autonomy. Not surprisingly, principled results are frequently elusive.

The institutional face of academic freedom is very much in vogue, and a case raising such issues, *Dayton Christian Schools, Inc. v. Ohio Civil Rights Commission*,[88] was recently disposed of by the United States Supreme Court on abstention grounds. Bob Jones University, in a case that brought national attention, unsuccessfully argued that the Internal Revenue Service constitutionally could not require non-discriminatory treatment of minority students as a condition for being granted tax-exempt status.[90] Princeton University also invoked institutional academic freedom a few years ago in unsuccessfully seeking to bar pamphleteers from its campus.[91] Some academicians seem appalled at Princeton's effort to invoke academic freedom because of their belief that the doctrine protects individual teachers and professors and not institutions. But such a view commits the fatal error of confusing the different faces of the concept. Institutional academic freedom may well grant some protections to the managers of private schools, while affording few to faculty members. Put somewhat differently, there is no reason to assume that the personal autonomy model of academic freedom is the only acceptable one or that that model, in its constitutional formulation, should have easy application to private schools.

Yudof, "Three Faces of Academic Freedom," 32 *Loy. L. Rev.* 831, 851–54 (1987). *See also* Byrne, "Academic Freedom: A 'Special Concern' of the First Amendment," 99 *Yale L. J.* 251, 311–39 (1989).

Is institutional academic freedom not so much a free-standing right as an institutional interest to be balanced against individual assertions of right? ***See, e.g., University of Pennsylvania v. Equal Employment Opportunity Commission***, 493 U.S. 182, 110 S.Ct. 577, 107 L.Ed.2d 571 (1990); ***Regents of University of Michigan v. Ewing***, 474 U.S. 214, 106 S.Ct. 507, 88 L.Ed.2d 523 (1985); ***Regents of the University of California v. Bakke***, 438 U.S. 265, 311–19, 98 S.Ct. 2733, 2759–63, 57 L.Ed.2d 750 (1978) (Powell, J.). ***See generally*** Byrne, ***supra*** at 317. Does institutional academic freedom protect

83. *Cf. Widmar v. Vincent*, 454 U.S. 263, 277–78 (1981) (Stevens, J., concurring).

84. *See* Levinson, *supra* note 72, at 199–200.

85. *See Runyon v. McCrary*, 427 U.S. 160 (1976); *Brown v. Dade Christian Schools, Inc.*, 556 F.2d 310 (5th Cir. 1977) (en banc), *cert. denied*, 434 U.S. 1063 (1978). *Cf. Bob Jones Univ. v. United States*, 461 U.S. 574 (1983).

87. *See* T. van Geel, *Authority to Control the School Program* 153–57 (1976); Elson, "State Regulation of Nonpublic Schools: The Legal Framework," in *Public Controls for Nonpublic Schools* 103 (E. Erickson ed. 1969).

88. 766 F.2d 932 (6th Cir. 1985), *rev'd*, 106 S.Ct. 2718 (1986).

90. *Bob Jones Univ. v. United States*, 461 U.S. 574 (1983).

91. *State v. Schmid*, 84 N.J. 535, 423 A.2d 615 (1980), *appeal dismissed*, 455 U.S. 100 (1982); *see* Finkin, *supra* note 69; Levinson, *supra* note 72.

peer evaluations from discovery in a lawsuit alleging racial or sexual discrimination in tenure and promotion decisions? *See University of Pennsylvania, supra. See generally* Note, "*University of Pennsylvania v. EEOC* and *Dixon v. Rutgers:* Two Supreme Courts Speak on the Academic Freedom Privilege," 42 *Rutgers L. Rev.* 1089 (1990); Note, "Preventing Unnecessary Intrusions on University Autonomy: A Proposed Academic Freedom Privilege," 69 *Calif. L. Rev.* 1538 (1981).

2. Access to School Facilities

Board of Education of Westside Community Schools v. Mergens

493 U.S. 182, 110 S.Ct. 2356 (1990).

Justice O'Connor delivered the opinion of the Court, except as to Part III.

This case requires us to decide whether the Equal Access Act, 98 Stat. 1302, 20 U.S.C. §§ 4071–4074, prohibits Westside High School from denying a student religious group permission to meet on school premises during noninstructional time, and if so, whether the Act, so construed, violates the Establishment Clause of the First Amendment.

I

Respondents are current and former students at Westside High School, a public secondary school in Omaha, Nebraska. At the time this suit was filed, the school enrolled about 1,450 students and included grades 10 to 12; in the 1987–1988 school year, ninth graders were added. Westside High School is part of the Westside Community School system, an independent public school district. Petitioners are the Board of Education of Westside Community Schools (District 66); Wayne W. Meier, the president of the school board; James E. Findley, the principal of Westside High School; Kenneth K. Hanson, the superintendent of schools for the school district; and James A. Tangdell, the assistant superintendent of schools for the school district.

Students at Westside High School are permitted to join various student groups and clubs, all of which meet after school hours on school premises. The students may choose from approximately 30 recognized groups on a voluntary basis. A list of student groups, together with a brief description of each provided by the school, appears in the Appendix to this opinion.

School Board Policy 5610 concerning "Student Clubs and Organizations" recognizes these student clubs as a "vital part of the total education program as a means of developing citizenship, wholesome attitudes, good human relations, knowledge and skills." . . . Board Policy 5610 also provides that each club shall have faculty sponsorship and that "clubs and organizations shall not be sponsored by any political or religious organization, or by any organization which denies membership on the basis of race, color, creed, sex or political belief." . . . Board Policy 6180 on "Recognition of Religious Beliefs and Customs" requires that "[s]tudents adhering to a specific set of religious beliefs or holding to little or no belief shall be alike respected." . . . In addition, Board Policy 5450 recognizes its students' "Freedom of Expression," consistent with the authority of the Board. . . .

There is no written school board policy concerning the formation of student clubs. Rather, students wishing to form a club present their request to a school official who determines whether the proposed club's goals and objectives are consistent with school board policies and with the school district's "Mission and Goals"—a broadly worded "blueprint" that expresses the district's commitment to teaching academic, physical, civic, and personal skills and values. . . .

In January 1985, respondent Bridget Mergens met with Westside's principal, Dr. Findley, and requested permission to form a Christian club at the school. The proposed club would have the same privileges and meet on the same terms and conditions as other Westside student groups, except that the proposed club would not have a faculty sponsor. According to the students' testimony at trial, the club's purpose would have been, among other things, to permit the students to read and discuss the Bible, to have fellowship, and to pray together. Membership would have been voluntary and open to all students regardless of religious affiliation.

Findley denied the request, as did associate superintendent Tangdell. In February 1985, Findley and Tangdell informed Mergens that they had discussed the matter with superintendent Hanson and that he had agreed that her request should be denied. The school officials explained that school policy required all student clubs to have a faculty sponsor, which the proposed religious club would not or could not have, and that a religious club at the school would violate the Establishment Clause. In March 1985, Mergens appealed the denial of her request to the Board of Education, but the Board voted to uphold the denial.

Respondents, by and through their parents as next friends, then brought this suit in the United States District Court for the District of Nebraska seeking declaratory and injunctive relief. They alleged that petitioners' refusal to permit the proposed club to meet at Westside violated the Equal Access Act, 20 U.S.C. §§ 4071–4074, which prohibits public secondary schools that receive federal financial assistance and that maintain a "limited open forum" from denying "equal access" to students who wish to meet within the forum on the basis of the content of the speech at such meetings, § 4071(a). Respondents further alleged that petitioners' actions denied them their First and Fourteenth Amendment rights to freedom of speech, association, and the free exercise of religion. Petitioners responded that the Equal Access Act did not apply to Westside and that, if the Act did apply, it violated the Establishment Clause of the First Amendment and was therefore unconstitutional. The United States intervened in the action pursuant to 28 U.S.C. § 2403 to defend the constitutionality of the Act.

The District Court entered judgment for petitioners. The court held that the Act did not apply in this case because Westside did not have a "limited open forum" as defined by the Act—all of Westside's student clubs, the court concluded, were curriculum-related and tied to the educational function of the school. The court rejected respondents' constitutional claims, reasoning that Westside did not have a limited public forum as set forth in *Widmar v. Vincent*, 454 U.S. 263, 102 S.Ct. 269, 70 L.Ed.2d 440 (1981), and that Westside's denial of respondents' request was reasonably related to legitimate pedagogical concerns, see *Hazelwood School Dist. v. Kuhlmeier*, 484 U.S. 260, 273, 108 S.Ct. 562, 571, 98 L.Ed.2d 592 (1988).

The United States Court of Appeals for the Eighth Circuit reversed. 867 F.2d 1076 (1989). The Court of Appeals held that the District Court erred in concluding that all the existing student clubs at Westside were curriculum-related. The Court of Appeals noted that the "broad interpretation" advanced by the Westside school officials "would make the [Equal Access Act] meaningless" and would allow any school to "arbitrarily deny access to school facilities to any unfavored student club on the basis of its speech content," which was "exactly the result that Congress sought to prohibit by enacting the [Act]." *Id.*, at 1078. The Court of Appeals instead found that "[m]any of the student clubs at WHS, including the chess club, are noncurriculum-related." *Id.*, at 1079. Accordingly, because it found that Westside maintained a limited open forum under the Act, the Court of Appeals concluded that the Act applied to "forbi[d] discrimination against [respondents'] proposed club on the basis of its religious content." *Ibid.*

The Court of Appeals then rejected petitioners' contention that the Act violated the Establishment Clause. Noting that the Act extended the decision in *Widmar v. Vincent*, *supra*, to public secondary schools, the Court of Appeals concluded that "[a]ny constitutional attack on the [Act] must therefore be predicated on the difference between secondary school students and university students." 867 F.2d, at 1080. . . . Because "Congress considered the difference in the maturity level of secondary students and university students before passing the [Act]," the Court of Appeals held, on the basis of Congress' fact-finding, that the Act did not violate the Establishment Clause. *Ibid.*

We granted certiorari . . . and now affirm.

II

A

In *Widmar v. Vincent*, 454 U.S. 263, 102 S.Ct. 269, 70 L.Ed.2d 440 (1981), we invalidated, on free speech grounds, a state university regulation that prohibited student use of school facilities " 'for purposes of religious worship or religious teaching.' " . . . In doing so, we held that an "equal access" policy would not violate the Establishment Clause under our decision in *Lemon v. Kurtzman*, 403 U.S. 602, 612–613, 91 S.Ct. 2105, 2111, 29 L.Ed.2d 745 (1971). In particular, we held that such a policy would have a secular purpose, would not have the primary effect of advancing religion, and would not result in excessive entanglement between government and religion, *Widmar*, 454 U.S., at 271–274, 102 S.Ct., at 275–76. We noted, however, that "[u]niversity students are, of course, young adults. They are less impressionable than younger students and should be able to appreciate that the University's policy is one of neutrality toward religion." . . .

In 1984, Congress extended the reasoning of *Widmar* to public secondary schools. Under the Equal Access Act, a public secondary school with a "limited open forum" is prohibited from discriminating against students who wish to conduct a meeting within that forum on the basis of the "religious, political, philosophical, or other content of the speech at such meetings." 20 U.S.C. §§ 4071(a) and (b). Specifically, the Act provides:

> "It shall be unlawful for any public secondary school which receives Federal financial assistance and which has a limited open forum to deny equal access or a fair opportunity to, or discriminate against, any students who wish to conduct a meeting within that limited open forum on the basis of the religious, political, philosophical, or other content of the speech at such meetings." 20 U.S.C. § 4071(a).

A "limited open forum" exists whenever a public secondary school "grants an offering to or opportunity for one or more noncurriculum related student groups to meet on school premises during noninstructional time." § 4071(b). "Meeting" is defined to include "those activities of student groups which are permitted under a school's limited open forum and are not directly related to the school curriculum." § 4072(3). "Noninstructional time" is defined to mean "time set aside by the school before actual classroom instruction begins or after actual classroom instruction ends." § 4072(4). Thus, even if a public secondary school allows only one "noncurriculum related student group" to meet, the Act's obligations are triggered and the school may not deny other clubs, on the basis of the content of their speech, equal access to meet on school premises during noninstructional time.

The Act further specifies that "[s]chools shall be deemed to offer a fair opportunity to students who wish to conduct a meeting within its limited open forum" if the school uniformly provides that the meetings are voluntary and student-initiated; are not sponsored by the school, the government, or its agents or employees; do not materially and substantially interfere with the orderly conduct of educational activities within the school; and are not directed, controlled, conducted, or regularly attended by "nonschool persons." §§ 4071(c)(1), (2), (4), and (5). "Sponsorship" is defined to mean "the act of promoting, leading, or participating in a meeting. The assignment of a teacher, administrator, or other school employee to a meeting for custodial purposes does not constitute sponsorship of the meeting." § 4072(2). If the meetings are religious, employees or agents of the school or government may attend only in a "nonparticipatory capacity." § 4071(c)(3). Moreover, a State may not influence the form of any religious activity, require any person to participate in such activity, or compel any school agent or employee to attend a meeting if the content of the speech at the meeting is contrary to that person's beliefs. §§ 4071(d)(1), (2), and (3).

Finally, the Act does not "authorize the United States to deny or withhold Federal financial assistance to any school," § 4071(e), or "limit the authority of the school, its agents or employees, to maintain order and discipline on school premises, to protect the well-being of students and faculty, and to assure that attendance of students at the meetings is voluntary," § 4071(f).

B

The parties agree that Westside High School receives federal financial assistance and is a public secondary school within the meaning of the Act. App. 57–58. The Act's obligation to grant equal access to student groups is therefore triggered if Westside maintains a "limited open forum" —*i.e.*, if it permits one or more "noncurriculum related student groups" to meet on campus before or after classes.

Unfortunately, the Act does not define the crucial phrase "noncurriculum related student group." Our immediate task is therefore one of statutory interpretation. We begin, of course, with the language of the statute. . . . The common meaning of the term "curriculum" is "the whole body of courses offered by an educational institution or one of its branches." Webster's Third New International Dictionary 557 (1976); see also Black's Law Dictionary 345 (5th ed. 1979) ("The set of studies or courses for a particular period, designated by a school or branch of a school"). . . . Any sensible interpretation of "noncurriculum related student group" must therefore be anchored in the notion that such student groups are those that are not related to the body of courses offered by the school. The difficult question is the degree of "unrelatedness to the curriculum" required for a group to be considered "noncurriculum related."

The Act's definition of the sort of "meeting[s]" that must be accommodated under the statute,

§ 4071(a), sheds some light on this question. "[T]he term 'meeting' includes those activities of student groups which are . . . not *directly related* to the school curriculum." § 4072(3) (emphasis added). Congress' use of the phrase "directly related" implies that student groups directly related to the subject matter of courses offered by the school do not fall within the "noncurriculum related" category and would therefore be considered "curriculum related."

The logic of the Act also supports this view, namely, that a curriculum-related student group is one that has more than just a tangential or attenuated relationship to courses offered by the school. Because the purpose of granting equal access is to prohibit discrimination between religious or political clubs on the one hand and other noncurriculum-related student groups on the other, the Act is premised on the notion that a religious or political club is itself likely to be a noncurriculum-related student group. It follows, then, that a student group that is "curriculum related" must at least have a more direct relationship to the curriculum than a religious or political club would have.

Although the phrase "noncurriculum related student group" nevertheless remains sufficiently ambiguous that we might normally resort to legislative history . . . we find the legislative history on this issue less than helpful. Because the bill that led to the Act was extensively rewritten in a series of multilateral negotiations after it was passed by the House and reported out of committee by the Senate, the committee reports shed no light on the language actually adopted. During congressional debate on the subject, legislators referred to a number of different definitions, and thus both petitioners and respondents can cite to legislative history favoring their interpretation of the phrase. Compare 130 Cong.Rec. 19223 (1984) (statement of Sen. Hatfield) (curriculum-related clubs are those that are "really a kind of extension of the classroom"), with *ibid.* (statement of Sen. Hatfield) (in response to question whether school districts would have full authority to decide what was curriculum-related, "[w]e in no way seek to limit that discretion"). See Laycock, Equal Access and Moments of Silence: The Equal Status of Religious Speech by Private Speakers, 81 Nw.U.L.Rev. 1, 37–39 (1986).

We think it significant, however, that the Act, which was passed by wide, bipartisan majorities in both the House and the Senate, reflects at least some consensus on a broad legislative purpose. The committee reports indicate that the Act was intended to address perceived widespread discrimination against religious speech in public schools, see H.R.Rep. No. 98–710, p. 4 (1984); S.Rep. No. 98–357, pp. 10–11 (1984), and, as the language of the Act indicates, its sponsors contemplated that the Act would do more than merely validate the status quo. The committee reports also show that the Act was enacted in part in response to two federal appellate court decisions holding that student religious groups could not, consistent with the Establishment Clause, meet on school premises during noninstructional time. See H.R. Rep. No. 98–710, *supra*, at 3–6 (discussing *Lubbock Civil Liberties Union v. Lubbock Independent School Dist.*, 669 F.2d 1038, 1042–1048 (CA5 1982), cert. denied, 459 U.S. 1155–1156, 103 S.Ct. 800, 74 L.Ed.2d 1003 (1983), and *Brandon v. Guilderland Bd. of Ed.*, 635 F.2d 971 (CA2 1980), cert. denied, 454 U.S. 1123, 102 S.Ct. 970, 71 L.Ed.2d 109 (1981)); S.Rep. No. 98–357, *supra*, at 6–9, 11–14 (same). A broad reading of the Act would be consistent with the views of those who sought to end discrimination by allowing students to meet and discuss religion before and after classes.

In light of this legislative purpose, we think that the term "noncurriculum related student group" is best interpreted broadly to mean any student group that does not *directly* relate to the body of courses offered by the school. In our view, a student group directly relates to a school's curriculum if the subject matter of the group is actually taught, or will soon be taught, in a regularly offered course; if the subject matter of the group concerns the body of courses as a whole; if participation in the group is required for a particular course; or if participation in the group results in academic credit. . . .

For example, a French club would directly relate to the curriculum if a school taught French in a regularly offered course or planned to teach the subject in the near future. A school's student government would generally relate directly to the curriculum to the extent that it addresses concerns, solicits opinions, and formulates proposals pertaining to the body of courses offered by the school. If participation in a school's band or orchestra were required for the band or orchestra classes, or resulted in academic credit, then those groups would also directly relate to the curriculum. The existence of such groups at a school would not trigger the Act's obligations.

On the other hand, unless a school could show that groups such as a chess club, a stamp collecting club, or a community service club fell within our description of groups that directly relate to the curriculum, such groups would be "noncurriculum related student groups" for purposes of the Act. The existence of such groups would create a "limited open forum" under the Act and would prohibit the school from denying equal access to any other student group on the basis of the content of that group's speech. Whether a specific student group is a "noncurriculum related student group" will therefore depend on a particular school's curriculum, but such determinations would be subject to factual findings well within the competence of trial courts to make.

* * *

The dissent suggests that "an extracurricular student organization is 'noncurriculum related' if it has as its purpose (or as part of its purpose) the advocacy of partisan theological, political, or ethical views." . . . This interpretation of the Act, we are told, is mandated by Congress' intention to "track our own Free Speech Clause jurisprudence," . . . by incorporating *Widmar's* notion of a "limited public forum" into the language of the Act. . . .

This suggestion is flawed for at least two reasons. First, the Act itself neither uses the phrase "limited public forum" nor so much as hints that that doctrine is somehow "incorporated" into the words of the statute. The operative language of the statute, 20 U.S.C. § 4071(a), of course, refers to a "limited open forum," a term that is specifically defined in the next subsection, § 4071(b). Congress was presumably aware that "limited public forum," as used by the Court, is a term of art, see, *e.g.*, *Perry Ed. Assn. v. Perry Local Educators' Assn.*, 460 U.S. 37, 45–49, 103 S.Ct. 948, 954–57, 74 L.Ed.2d 794 (1983), and had it intended to import that concept into the Act, one would suppose that it would have done so explicitly. Indeed, Congress' deliberate choice to use a different term—and to define that term—can only mean that it intended to establish a standard different from the one established by our free speech cases. See Laycock, 81 Nw.U.L. Rev., at 36 ("The statutory 'limited open forum' is an artificial construct, and comparisons with the constitutional ['limited public forum'] cases can be misleading"). To paraphrase the dissent, "[i]f Congress really intended to [incorporate] *Widmar* for reasons of administrative clarity, Congress kept its intent well hidden, both in the statute and in the debates preceeding its passage." . . .

Second, and more significant, the dissent's reliance on the legislative history to support its interpretation of the Act shows just how treacherous that task can be. The dissent appears to agree with our view that the legislative history of the Act, even if relevant, is highly unreliable, . . . yet the interpretation it suggests rests solely on a few passing, general references by legislators to our decision in *Widmar* . . . The only thing that can be said with any confidence is that *some* Senators *may* have thought that the obligations of the Act would be triggered only when a school permits advocacy groups to meet on school premises during noninstructional time. That conclusion, of course, cannot bear the weight the dissent places on it.

C

The parties in the case focus their dispute on 10 of Westside's approximately 30 voluntary student clubs: Interact (a service club related to Rotary International); Chess; Subsurfers (a club for students interested in scuba diving); National Honor Society; Photography; Welcome to Westside (a club to introduce new students to the school); Future Business Leaders of America; Zonta (the female counterpart to Interact); Student Advisory Board (student government); and the Student Forum (student government). . . . Petitioners contend that all of these student activities are curriculum-related because they further the goals of particular aspects of the school's curriculum. Welcome to Westside, for example, helps "further the School's overall goal of developing effective citizens by requiring student members to contribute to their fellow students." . . . The student government clubs "advance the goals of the School's political science classes by providing an understanding and appreciation of government processes." . . . Subsurfers furthers "one of the essential goals of the Physical Education Department—enabling students to develop lifelong recreational interests." . . . Chess "supplement[s] math and science courses because it enhances students' ability to engage in critical thought processes." . . . Participation in Interact and Zonta "promotes effective citizenship, a critical goal of the WHS curriculum, specifically the Social Studies Department." . . .

To the extent that petitioners contend that "curriculum related" means anything remotely related to abstract educational goals, however, we reject that argument. To define "curriculum related" in a way that results in almost no schools having limited open fora, or in a way that permits schools to evade the Act by strategically describing existing student groups, would render the Act merely hortatory. See 130 Cong.Rec. 19222 (1984) (statement of Sen. Leahy) ("[A] limited open forum should be triggered by what a school does, not by what it says"). . . .

Rather, we think it clear that Westside's existing student groups include one or more "noncurriculum related student groups." Although Westside's physical education classes apparently include swimming, . . . counsel stated at oral argument that scuba diving is not taught in any regularly offered course at the school. . . . Based on Westside's own description of the group, Subsurfers does not directly relate to the curriculum as a whole in the same way that a student government or similar group might. . . . Moreover, participation in Subsurfers is not required by any course at the school and does not result in extra academic credit. . . . Thus, Subsurfers is a "noncurriculum related student group" for purposes of the Act. Similarly, although math teachers at Westside have encouraged their students to play chess, . . . chess is not taught in any regularly offered course at the school, . . . and participation in the chess club is not required for any class and does not result in extra credit for any class. . . . The chess club is therefore another "noncurriculum related student group" at Westside. Moreover, Westside's principal acknowledged at trial that the Peer Advocates program—a service group that works with special education classes—does not directly relate to any courses offered by the school and is not required by any courses offered by the school. . . .

Although our definition of "noncurriculum related student activities" looks to a school's actual practice rather than its stated policy, we note that our conclusion is also supported by the school's own description of its student activities. As reprinted in the Appendix to this opinion, the school states that Band "is included in our regular curriculum"; Choir "is a course offered as part of the curriculum"; Distributive Education "is an extension of the Distributive Education class"; International Club is "developed through our foreign language classes"; Latin Club is "designed for those students who are taking Latin as a foreign language"; Student Publications "includes classes offered in preparation of the yearbook (Shield) and the student newspaper (Lance)"; Dramatics "is an extension of a regular academic class"; and Orchestra "is an extension of our regular curriculum." These descriptions constitute persuasive evidence that these student clubs directly relate to the curriculum. By inference, however, the fact that the descriptions of student activities such as Subsurfers and chess do not include such references strongly suggests that those clubs do not, by the school's own admission, directly relate to the curriculum. . . .

The remaining statutory question is whether petitioners' denial of respondents' request to form a religious group constitutes a denial of "equal access" to the school's limited open forum. Although the school apparently permits respondents to meet informally after school, App. 315–316, respondents seek equal access in the form of official recognition by the school. Official recognition allows student clubs to be part of the student activities program and carries with it access to the school newspaper, bulletin boards, the public address system, and the annual Club Fair. . . . Given that the Act explicitly prohibits denial of "equal access . . . to . . . any students who wish to conduct a meeting within [the school's] limited open forum" on the basis of the religious content of the speech at such meetings, § 4071(a), we hold that Westside's denial of respondents' request to form a Christian club denies them "equal access" under the Act.

Because we rest our conclusion on statutory grounds, we need not decide—and therefore express no opinion on—whether the First Amendment requires the same result.

III

Petitioners contend that even if Westside has created a limited open forum within the meaning of the Act, its denial of official recognition to the proposed Christian club must nevertheless stand because the Act violates the Establishment Clause of the First Amendment, as applied to the States through the Fourteenth Amendment. Specifically, petitioners maintain that because the school's recognized student activities are an integral part of its educational mission, official recognition of respondents' proposed club would effectively incorporate religious activities into the school's official program, endorse participation in the religious club, and provide the club with an official platform to proselytize other students.

We disagree. In *Widmar*, we applied the three-part *Lemon* test to hold that an "equal access" policy, at the university level, does not violate the Establishment Clause. . . . We concluded that "an open-forum policy, including nondiscrimination against religious speech, would have a secular purpose," . . . and would in fact *avoid* entanglement with religion. . . . We also found that although incidental benefits accrued to religious groups who used university facilities, this result did not amount to an establishment of religion. First, we stated that a university's forum does not "confer any imprimatur of state approval on religious sects or practices." . . . Indeed, the message is one of neutrality rather than endorsement; if a State refused to let religious groups use facilities open to others, then it would demonstrate not neutrality but hostility toward religion. . . . Second, we noted that "[t]he [University's] provision of benefits to [a] broad . . . spectrum of groups"—both nonreligious and religious speakers—was "an important index of secular effect." . . .

We think the logic of *Widmar* applies with equal force to the Equal Access Act. As an initial matter, the Act's prohibition of discrimination on the basis of "political, philosophical, or other" speech as well as religious speech is a sufficient basis for meeting the secular purpose prong of the *Lemon* test. See *Edwards v. Aguillard*, 482 U.S. 578, 586, 107 S.Ct. 2573, 2579, 96 L.Ed.2d 510 (1987) (Court "is normally deferential to a [legislative] articulation of a secular purpose"). . . . Congress' avowed purpose—to prevent discrimination against religious and other types of speech—is undeniably secular. . . . Even if some legislators were motivated by a conviction that religious speech in particular was valuable and worthy of protection, that alone would not invalidate the Act, because what is relevant is the legislative *purpose* of the statute, not the possibly religious *motives* of the legislators who enacted the law. Because the Act on its face grants equal access to both secular and religious speech, we think it clear that the Act's purpose was not to " 'endorse or disapprove of religion,' " *Wallace v. Jaffree*, 472 U.S. 38, 56, 105 S.Ct. 2479, 2489, 86 L.Ed.2d 29 (1985) (quoting *Lynch v. Donnelly*, 465 U.S. 668, 690, 104 S.Ct. 1355, 1368, 79 L.Ed.2d 604 (1984) (O'Connor, J., concurring)).

Petitioners' principal contention is that the Act has the primary effect of advancing religion. Specifically, petitioners urge that, because the student religious meetings are held under school aegis, and because the state's compulsory attendance laws bring the students together (and thereby provide a ready-made audience for student evangelists), an objective observer in the position of a secondary school student will perceive official school support for such religious meetings. . . .

We disagree. First, although we have invalidated the use of public funds to pay for teaching state-required subjects at parochial schools, in part because of the risk of creating "a crucial symbolic link between government and religion, thereby enlisting—at least in the eyes of impressionable youngsters—the powers of government to the support of the religious denomination operating the school," *Grand Rapids School Dist. v. Ball*, 473 U.S. 373, 385, 105 S.Ct. 3216, 3223, 87 L.Ed.2d 267 (1985), there is a crucial difference between *government* speech endorsing religion, which the Establishment Clause forbids, and *private* speech endorsing religion, which the Free Speech and Free Exercise Clauses protect. We think that secondary school students are mature enough and are likely to understand that a school does not endorse or support student speech that it merely permits on a nondiscriminatory basis. Cf. *Tinker v. Des Moines Independent Community School Dist.*, 393 U.S. 503, 89 S.Ct. 733, 21 L.Ed.2d 731 (1969) (no danger that high school students' symbolic speech implied school endorsement); *West Virginia State Bd. of Ed. v. Barnette*, 319 U.S. 624, 63 S.Ct. 1178, 87 L.Ed. 1628 (1943) (same). . . .

Indeed, we note that Congress specifically rejected the argument that high school students are likely to confuse an equal access policy with state sponsorship of religion. See S.Rep. No. 98–357, p. 8 (1984); *id.*, at 35 ("[S]tudents below the college level are capable of distinguishing between State-initiated, school sponsored, or teacher-led religious speech on the one hand and student-initiated, student-led religious speech on the other"). . . .

Second, we note that the Act expressly limits participation by school officials at meetings of student religious groups, §§ 4071(c)(2) and (3), and that any such meetings must be held during "noninstructional time," § 4071(b). The Act therefore avoids the problems of "the students' emulation of teachers as role models" and "mandatory attendance requirement" . . . .

To be sure, the possibility of *student* peer pressure remains, but there is little if any risk of official state endorsement or coercion where no formal classroom activities are involved and no school officials actively participate. Moreover, petitioners' fear of a mistaken inference of endorsement is largely self-imposed, because the school itself has control over any impressions it gives its students. To the extent a school makes clear that its recognition of respondents' proposed club is not an endorsement of the views of the club's participants, . . . students will reasonably understand that the school's official recognition of the club evinces neutrality toward, rather than endorsement of, religious speech.

Third, the broad spectrum of officially recognized student clubs at Westside, and the fact that Westside students are free to initiate and organize additional student clubs, see App. 221–222, counteract any possible message of official endorsement of or preference for religion or a particular religious belief. . . . Under the Act, a school with a limited open forum may not lawfully deny access to a Jewish students' club, a Young Democrats club, or a philosophy club devoted to the study of Nietzsche. To the extent that a religious club is merely one of many different student-initiated voluntary clubs, students should perceive no message of government endorsement of religion. . . .

Petitioners' final argument is that by complying with the Act's requirement, the school risks excessive entanglement between government and religion. The proposed club, petitioners urge, would be required to have a faculty sponsor who would be charged with actively directing the activities of the group, guiding its leaders, and ensuring balance in the presentation of controversial ideas. Petitioners claim that this influence over the club's religious program would entangle the government in day-to-day survelliance of religion of the type forbidden by the Establishment Clause.

Under the Act, however, faculty monitors may not participate in any religious meetings, and nonschool persons may not direct, control, or regularly attend activities of student groups. §§ 4071(c)(3) and (5). Moreover, the Act prohibits school "sponsorship" of any religious meetings, § 4071(c)(2), which means that school officials may not promote, lead, or participate in any such meeting, § 4072(2). Although the Act permits "[t]he assignment of a teacher, administrator, or other school employee to the meeting for custodial purposes," *ibid.*, such custodial oversight of the student-initiated religious group, merely to ensure order and good behavior, does not impermissibly entangle government in the day-to-day surveillance or administration of religious activities. . . . Indeed, as the Court noted in *Widmar*, a denial of equal access to religious speech might well create greater entanglement problems in the form of invasive monitoring to prevent religious speech at meetings at which such speech might occur. . . .

Accordingly, we hold that the Equal Access Act does not on its face contravene the Establishment Clause. Because we hold that petitioners have violated the Act, we do not decide respondents' claims under the Free Speech and Free Exercise Clauses. For the foregoing reasons, the judgment of the Court of Appeals is affirmed.

It is so ordered.

APPENDIX

Plaintiff's Trial Exhibit 63
Student Activities

August, 1984

BAND—This activity is included in our regular curriculum. Extensions of this activity include Marching Band, Ensembles, Pep Band, and Concert Jazz Band. Performances, presentations, and programs are presented throughout the school year.

CHESS CLUB—This activity is for those interested in playing chess. Opportunities to play are held after school throughout the school year.

CHEERLEADERS—A girls sport cheerleader team is made up of a junior varsity and varsity. The boys sport cheerleaders consist of sophomores, junior varsity, and varsity. Tryouts for these spirit groups are held each spring.

CHOIR—This is a course offered as part of the curriculum. Extensions of this class include Boys and Girls Glee, Warrior Voices, and Concert and Chamber Choirs. Membership in these activities are determined by enrollment and tryouts.

CLASS OFFICERS—Voting and selection of junior and senior class officers for the following year are held each spring. Students interested in being a class officer will need to secure support, be willing to make a presentation to their class, and serve their class in an officer capacity for the following year.

DISTRIBUTIVE EDUCATION (DECA)—This is an organization that is an extension of the Distributive Education class. Membership in this activity is offered to those students involved in D.E. The club for the current year is formulated at the beginning of school each fall.

SPEECH & DEBATE—This is an activity for students interested in participating on a competitive level in both speech and debate. The season begins the first week in November and continues through March.

DRILL SQUAD & SQUIRES—These are spirit groups primarily concerned with performing at half time at football and basketball games. Selection for these squads is made in the spring of each school year. These marching units are also support groups for other athletic teams.
FUTURE BUSINESS LEADERS OF AMERICA (FBLA)—This is a club designed for students interested in pursuing the field of business. It is open to any student with an interest. Membership begins in the fall of each school year.
FUTURE MEDICAL ASSISTANTS (FMA)—This is a club designed for students with an interest in pursuing any area of medicine. The organization assists in securing blood donations from individuals at Westside High School for the Red Cross. Meetings are held to inform the membership about opportunities in the medical field. Memberships are accepted at the beginning of school each fall.
INTERACT—This is a boys volunteer organization associated with the Rotary Club of America. Its basic function is to do volunteer work within the community. They are also a support and spirit group for our athletic teams. Membership is open to 11th and 12th grade boys; with membership opportunities being available in the fall of each school year.
INTERNATIONAL CLUB—This is a club designed to help students understand people from other countries and is developed through our foreign language classes. French, German, Spanish, and Latin teachers encourage membership in this organization in the fall of each year. Sponsorship of foreign students, who attend Westside, is one of their major activities.
LATIN CLUB (Junior Classical League)—This is a club designed for those students who are taking Latin as a foreign language. This club competes in competitive situations between schools and is involved with state competition as well. Students have the opportunity to join JCL beginning in the fall of each school year.
MATH CLUB—This club is for any student interested in mathematics. Meetings are held periodically during the school year.
STUDENT PUBLICATIONS—This activity includes classes offered in preparation of the yearbook (Shield) and the student newspaper (Lance). Opportunities to learn about journalism are provided for students interested in these areas. Membership in Quill and Scroll is an extension of a student's involvement in school publications.
STUDENT FORUM—Each homeroom elects one representative as a member of the student forum. Their responsibility is to provide ideas, make suggestions, and serve as one informational group to the staff and administration for student government. Selections are made for this membership in the fall of each school year.
DRAMATICS—This activity is an extension of a regular academic class. School plays, one-act plays, and musicals are provided for students with an interest and ability in these areas. Tryouts for these productions are announced prior to the selection of individuals for these activities.
CREATIVE WRITING CLUB—This is an organization that provides students, with the interest and capability, an opportunity to do prose and poetry writing. This club meets periodically throughout the year and publishes the students' work. Any student with an interest is encouraged to become a member.
PHOTOGRAPHY CLUB—This is a club for the student who has the interest and/or ability in photography. Students have an opportunity to take photos of school activities. A dark room is provided for the students' use. Membership in this organization begins in the fall of each school year.
ORCHESTRA—This activity is an extension of our regular curriculum. Performances are given periodically throughout the year. Tryouts are held for some special groups within the orchestra. All students signed up for that class have the opportunity to try out.

* * *

SWIMMING TIMING TEAM—Offers an interested student a chance to be a part of the Timing Team that is used during the competitive swimming season. Regular season meets, invitational meets, and the metro swim meet are swimming activities at which these volunteers will work. Membership in this group is solicited prior to the beginning of the competitive season.

* * *

ZONTA CLUB (Z Club)—Is a volunteer club for girls associated with Zonta International. Approximately one hundred junior and senior girls are involved in this volunteer organization. Eleventh and twelfth grade students are encouraged to join in the fall of each school year.
SUBSURFERS—Is a club designed for students interested in learning about skin and scuba diving and other practical applications of that sport. Opportunities in the classroom and in our pool are made available for students involved in this activity. Membership is solicited in the fall and spring of each year.
WELCOME TO WESTSIDE CLUB—Is an organization for students who are interested in helping students new to District 66 and to Westside High School. Activities are held for them which are geared toward helping them become a part of our school curriculum and activities.

* * *

Justice Kennedy, with whom Justice Scalia joins, concurring in part and concurring in the judgment.

The Court's interpretation of the statutory term "noncurriculum related groups" is proper and correct, in my view, and I join Parts I and II of the Court's opinion. I further agree that the Act does not violate the Establishment Clause, and so I concur in the judgment; but my view of the analytic premise that controls the establishment question differs from that employed by the plurality. I write to explain why I cannot join all that is said in Part III of Justice O'Connor's opinion.

* * *

I agree with the plurality that a school complying with the statute by satisfying the criteria in § 4071(c) does not violate the Establishment Clause. The accommodation of religion mandated by the Act is a neutral one, and in the context of this case it suffices to inquire whether the Act violates either one of two principles. The first is that the government cannot "give direct benefits to religion in such a degree that it in fact 'establishes a [state] religion or religious faith, or tends to do so.' " *County of Allegheny v. American Civil Liberties Union, Greater Pittsburgh Chapter*, 492 U.S. 537, 109 S.Ct. 3086, 3136, 106 L.Ed.2d 472 (1989) (Kennedy, J., concurring in judgment in part and dissenting in part) (quoting *Lynch v. Donnelly*, 465 U.S. 668, 678, 104 S.Ct. 1355, 1361, 79 L.Ed.2d 604 (1984). Any incidental benefits that accompany official recognition of a religious club under the criteria set forth in the § 4071(c) do not lead to the establishment of religion under this standard. . . . The second principle controlling the case now before us, in my view, is that the government cannot coerce any student to participate in a religious activity. . . . The Act is consistent with this standard as well. Nothing on the face of the Act or in the facts of the case as here presented demonstrate that enforcement of the statute will result in the coercion of any student to participate in a religious activity. . . .

The plurality uses a different test, one which asks whether school officials, by complying with the Act, have endorsed religion. It is true that when government gives impermissible assistance to a religion it can be said to have "endorsed" religion; but endorsement cannot be the test. The word endorsement has insufficient content to be dispositive. . . . [I]ts literal application may result in neutrality in name but hostility in fact when the question is the government's proper relation to those who express some religious preference.

I should think it inevitable that a public high school "endorses" a religious club, in a common-sense use of the term, if the club happens to be one of many activities that the school permits students to choose in order to further the development of their intellect and character in an extracurricular setting. But no constitutional violation occurs if the school's action is based upon a recognition of the fact that membership in a religious club is one of many permissible ways for a student to further his or her own personal enrichment. The inquiry with respect to coercion must be whether the government imposes pressure upon a student to participate in a religious activity. This inquiry, of course, must be undertaken with sensitivity to the special circumstances that exist in a secondary school where the line between voluntary and coerced participation may be difficult to draw. No such coercion, however, has been shown to exist as a necessary result of this statute, either on its face or as respondents seek to invoke it on the facts of this case.

For these reasons, I join Parts I and II of the Court's opinion, and concur in the judgment.

Justice Marshall, with whom Justice Brennan joins, concurring in the judgment.

I agree with the majority that "noncurriculum" must be construed broadly to "prohibit schools from discriminating on the basis of the content of a student group's speech." . . . As the majority demonstrates, such a construction "is consistent with Congress' intent to provide a low threshold for triggering the Act's requirements." . . . In addition, to the extent that Congress intended the Act to track this Court's free speech jurisprudence, as the dissent argues, . . . the majority's construction is faithful to our commitment to nondiscriminatory access to open fora in public schools. . . . When a school allows student-initiated clubs not directly tied to the school's curriculum to use school facilities, it has "created a forum generally open to student groups" and is therefore constitutionally prohibited from enforcing a "content-based exclusion" of other student speech. . . .

In this respect, the Act as construed by the majority simply codifies in statute what is already constitutionally mandated: schools may not discriminate among student-initiated groups that seek access to school facilities for expressive purposes not directly related to the school's curriculum.

The Act's low threshold for triggering equal access, however, raises serious Establishment Clause concerns where secondary schools with fora that differ substantially from the forum in *Widmar* are required to grant access to student religious groups. Indeed, as applied in the present case, the Act mandates a religious group's access to a forum that is dedicated to promoting fundamental values and citizenship as defined by the school. The Establishment Clause does not forbid the operation of the Act in such circumstances, but it does require schools to change their relationship to their fora so as to dissassociate themselves effectively from religious clubs' speech. Thus, although I agree with the plurality that the Act as applied to Westside *could* withstand Establishment Clause scrutiny, . . . I write separately to emphasize the steps Westside must take to avoid appearing to endorse the Christian Club's goals. . . .

* * *

Westside currently does not recognize any student club that advocates a controversial viewpoint. Indeed, the clubs at Westside that trigger the Act involve scuba diving, chess, and counseling for special education students. . . . As a matter of school policy, Westside encourages student participation in clubs based on a broad conception of its educational mission. . . . That mission comports with the Court's acknowledgment "that public schools are vitally important 'in the preparation of individuals for participation as citizens,' and as vehicles for 'inculcating fundatmental values necessary to the maintenance of a democratic political system.' " *Board of Education, Island Trees Union Free School Dist. No. 27 v. Pico*, 457 U.S. 853, 864, 102 S.Ct. 2799, 2806, 73 L.Ed.2d 435 (1982) (plurality) quoting *Ambach v. Norwick*, 441 U.S. 68, 76–77, 99 S.Ct. 1589, 1594, 60 L.Ed.2d 49 (1979)). Given the nature and function of student clubs at Westside, the school makes no effort to disassociate itself from the activities and goals of its student clubs.

The entry of religious clubs into such a realm poses a real danger that those clubs will be viewed as part of the school's effort to inculcate fundamental values. The school's message with respect to its existing clubs is not one of toleration but one of endorsement. As the majority concedes, the program is part of the "district's commitment to teaching academic, physical, civic, and personal skills and values." . . . But although a school may permissibly encourage its students to become well-rounded as student-athletes, student-musicians, and student-tutors, the Constitution forbids schools to encourage students to become well-rounded as student-worshippers. Neutrality toward religion, as required by the Constitution, is not advanced by requiring a school that endorses the goals of some noncontroversial secular organizations to endorse the goals of religious organizations as well.

The fact that the Act, when triggered, provides access to political as well as religious speech does not ameliorate the potential threat of endorsement. The breadth of beneficiaries under the Act does suggest that the Act may satisfy the "secular purpose" requirement of the Establishment Clause inquiry we identified in *Lemon*. . . . But the crucial question is how the Act affects each school. If a school already houses numerous ideological organizations, then the addition of a religion club will most likely not violate the Establishment Clause because the risk that students will erroneously attribute the views of the religion club to the schools is minimal. To the extent a school tolerates speech by a wide range of ideological clubs, students cannot reasonably understand the school to endorse all of the groups' divergent and contradictory views. But if the religion club is the sole advocacy-oriented group in the forum, or one of a very limited number, and the school continues to promote its student-club program as instrumental to citizenship, then the school's failure to disassociate itself from the religious activity will reasonably be understood as an endorsement of that activity. That political and other advocacy-oriented groups are permitted to participate in a forum that, through school support and encouragement, is devoted to fostering a student's civic identity does not ameliorate the appearance of school endorsement unless the invitation is accepted and the forum is transformed into a forum like that in *Widmar*.

For this reason, the plurality's reliance on *Widmar* is misplaced. The University of Missouri took concrete steps to ensure "that the University's name will not 'be identified in any way with the aims, policies, programs, products, or opinions of any organization or its members,' " 454 U.S., at 274, n. 14, 102 S.Ct., at 276–77, n. 14 (quoting University of Missouri student handbook). Westside, in contrast, explicitly promotes its student clubs "as a vital part of the total education program [and] as a means of developing citizenship." App. 488. And while the

University of Missouri recognized such clubs as the Young Socialist Alliance and the Young Democrats, *Chess v. Widmar*, 635 F.2d 1310, 1312, n. 1 (CA8 1980), Westside has recognized no such political clubs, App. 488.

The different approaches to student clubs embodied in these policies reflect a significant difference, for Establishment Clause purposes, between the respective roles that Westside High School and the University of Missouri attempt to play in their students' lives. To the extent that a school emphasizes the autonomy of its students, as does the University of Missouri, there is a corresponding decrease in the likelihood that student speech will be regarded as school speech. Conversely, where a school such as Westside regards its student clubs as a mechanism for defining and transmitting fundamental values, the inclusion of a religious club in the school's program will almost certainly signal school endorsement of the religious practice.

Thus, the underlying difference between this case and *Widmar* is not that college and high school students have varying capacities to perceive the subtle differences between toleration and endorsement, but rather that the University of Missouri and Westside actually choose to define their respective missions in different ways. That high schools tend to emphasize student autonomy less than universities may suggest that high school administrators tend to perceive a difference in the maturity of secondary and university students. But the school's behavior, not the purported immaturity of high school students, is dispositive. If Westside stood apart from its club program and expressed the view, endorsed by Congress through its passage of the Act, that high school students are capable of engaging in wide-ranging discussion of sensitive and controversial speech, the inclusion of religious groups in Westside's forum would confirm the school's commitment to nondiscrimination. Here, though, the Act requires the school to permit religious speech in a forum explicitly designed to advance the school's interest in shaping the character of its students.

The comprehensiveness of the access afforded by the Act further highlights the Establishment Clause dangers posed by the Act's application to fora such as Westside's. The Court holds that "[o]fficial recognition allows student clubs to be part of the student activities program and carries with it access to the school newspaper, bulletin boards, the public address system, and the annual Club Fair." *Ante*, at 2370 (citing App. 434–435). Students would be alerted to the meetings of the religion club over the public address system; they would see religion club material posted on the official school bulletin board and club notices in the school newspaper; they would be recruited to join the religion club at the school-sponsored Club Fair. If a school has a variety of ideological clubs, as in *Widmar*, I agree with the plurality that a student is likely to understand that "a school does not endorse or support student speech that it merely permits on a nondiscriminatory basis." *Ante*, at 2372. When a school has a religion club but no other political or ideological organizations, however, that relatively fine distinction may be lost.

Moreover, in the absence of a truly robust forum that includes the participation of more than one advocacy-oriented group, the presence of a religious club could provide a fertile ground for peer pressure, especially if the club commanded support from a substantial portion of the student body. . . .

. . . When the government, through mandatory attendance laws, brings students together in a highly controlled environment every day for the better part of their waking hours and regulates virtually every aspect of their existence during that time, we should not be so quick to dismiss the problem of peer pressure as if the school environment had nothing to do with creating and fostering it. The State has structured an environment in which students holding mainstream views may be able to coerce adherents of minority religions to attend club meetings or to adhere to club beliefs. Thus, the State cannot disclaim its responsibility for those resulting pressures.

* * *

Given these substantial risks posed by the inclusion of the proposed Christian Club within Westside's present forum, Westside must redefine its relationship to its club program. . . .

Westside thus must do more than merely prohibit faculty members from actively participating in the Christian Club's meetings. It must fully disassociate itself from the Club's religious speech and avoid appearing to sponsor or endorse the Club's goals. It could, for example, entirely discontinue encouraging student participation in clubs and clarify that the clubs are not instrumentally related to the school's overall mission. Or, if the school sought to continue its general endorsement of those student clubs that did not engage in controversial speech, it could do so if it also affirmatively disclaimed any endorsement of the Christian Club.

* * *

Justice Stevens, dissenting.

The dictionary is a necessary, and sometimes sufficient, aid to the judge confronted with the task of construing an opaque act of Congress. In a case like this, however, I believe we must probe more deeply to avoid a patently bizarre result. Can Congress really have intended to issue an order to every public high school in the nation stating, in substance, that if you sponsor a chess club, a scuba diving club, or a French club—without having formal classes in those subjects—you must also open your doors to every religious, political, or social organization, no matter how controversial or distasteful its views may be? I think not. A fair review of the legislative history of the Equal Access Act (Act), 98 Stat. 1302, 20 U.S.C. §§ 4071–4074, discloses that Congress intended to recognize a much narrower forum than the Court has legislated into existence today.

* * *

. . . The Court correctly identifies three useful guides to Congress' intent. First, the text of the statute says that a school creates a limited open forum if it allows meetings on school premises by "noncurriculum related student groups," a concept that is ambiguous at best. . . . Second, because this concept is ambiguous, the statute must be interpreted by reference to its general purpose, as revealed by its overall structure and by the legislative history. . . . Third, the Act's legislative history reveals that Congress intended to guarantee student religious groups access to high school fora comparable to the college forum involved in *Widmar v. Vincent*, 454 U.S. 263, 102 S.Ct. 269, 70 L.Ed.2d 440 (1981). . . .

A fourth [guide] would seem to follow from these three. If "noncurriculum related" is an ambiguous term, and if it must therefore be interpreted in light of Congressional purpose, and if the purpose of Congress was to ensure that the rule of *Widmar* applied to high schools as it did to colleges, then the incidence of the Act in this case should depend upon whether, in light of *Widmar*, Westside would have to permit the Christian student group to meet if Westside were a college.[3] The characteristics of the college forum in *Widmar* should thus provide a useful background for interpreting the meaning of the undefined term "noncurriculum related student groups." But this step the Court does not take, and it is accordingly here that I part company with it.

* * *

To extend *Widmar* to high schools, then, would require us to pose two questions. We would first ask whether a high school had established a forum comparable under our Free Speech Clause jurisprudence to that which existed in *Widmar*. Only if this question were answered affirmatively would we then need to test the contitutionality of the Act by asking whether the Establishment Clause has different consequences when applied to a high school's open forum than when applied to a college's. I believe that in this case the first question must instead be answered in the negative, and that this answer ultimately proves dispositive under the Act just as it would were only constitutional consideration in play.

The forum at Westside is considerably different from that which existed at the University of Missouri. In *Widmar*, we held that the University had created "a generally open forum." . . . Over 100 officially recognized student groups routinely participated in that forum. . . . They included groups whose activities not only were unrelated to any specific courses, but also were of a kind that a state university could not properly sponsor or endorse. Thus, for example, they included such political organizations as the Young Socialist Alliance, the Women's Union, and the Young Democrats. . . . The University permitted use of its facilities for speakers advocating transcendental meditation and humanism. Since the University had allowed such organizations and speakers the use of campus facilities, we concluded that the University could not discriminate against a religious group on the basis of the content of its speech. The forum established by the state university accommodated participating groups that were "noncurriculum related" not only because they did not mirror the school's classroom instruction, but also because they advocated controversial positions that a state university's obligation of neutrality prevented it from endorsing.

The Court's opinion in *Widmar* left open the question whether its holding would apply to a public

3. We would, of course, then have to consider, as the Court does now, whether the Establishment Clause permits Congress to apply *Widmar's* reasoning to secondary schools.

high school that had established a similar public forum. That question has now been answered in the affirmative by the District Court, the Court of Appeals, and by this Court. I agree with that answer. Before the question was answered judicially, Congress decided to answer it legislatively in order to preclude continued unconstitutional discrimination against high school students interested in religious speech. . . . What the Court of Appeals failed to recognize, however, is the critical difference between the university forum in *Widmar* and the high school forum involved in this case. None of the clubs at the high school is even arguably controversial or partisan.

Nor would it be wise to ignore this difference. High school students may be adult enough to distinguish between those organizations that are sponsored by the school and those which lack school sponsorship even though they participate in a forum that the school does sponsor. See *ante*, at 2372. But high school students are also young enough that open fora may be less suitable for them than for college students. The need to decide whether to risk treating students as adults too soon, or alternatively to risk treating them as children too long, is an enduring problem for all educators. The youth of these students, whether described in terms of "impressionability" or "maturity," may be irrelevant to our application of the constitutional restrictions that limit educational discretion in the public schools, but it surely is not irrelevant to our interpretation of the educational policies that have been adopted. We would do no honor to Westside's administrators or the Congress by assuming that either treated casually the differences between high school and college students when formulating the policy and the statute at issue here.[6]

For these reasons, I believe that the distinctions between Westside's program and the University of Missouri's program suggest what is the best understanding of the Act : an extracurricular student organization is "noncurriculum related" if it has as its purpose (or as part of its purpose) the advocacy of partisan theological, political, or ethical views. A school that admits at least one such club has apparently made the judgment that students are better off if the student community is permitted to, and perhaps even encouraged to, compete along ideological lines. This pedagogical strategy may be defensible or even desirable. But it is wrong to presume that Congress endorsed that strategy—and dictated its nationwide adoption—simply because it approved the application of *Widmar* to high schools. And it seems absurd to presume that Westside has invoked the same strategy by recognizing clubs like Swim Timing Team and Subsurfers which, though they may not correspond directly to anything in Westside's course offerings, are no more controversial than a grilled cheese sandwich.

Accordingly, as I would construe the Act, a high school could properly sponsor a French club, a chess club, or a scuba diving club simply because their activities are fully consistent with the school's curricular mission. It would not matter whether formal courses in any of those subjects—or in directly related subjects—were being offered as long as faculty encouragement of student participation in such groups would be consistent with both the school's obligation of neutrality and its legitimate pedagogical concerns. Nothing in *Widmar* implies that the existence of a French club, for example, would create a constitutional obligation to allow student members of the Ku Klux Klan or the Communist Party to have access to school facilities. More importantly, nothing in that case suggests that the constitutional issue should turn on whether French is being taught in a formal course while the club is functioning.

Conversely, if a high school decides to allow political groups to use its facilities, it plainly cannot discriminate among controversial groups because it agrees with the positions of some and disagrees with the ideas advocated by others. Again, the fact that the history of the Republican party might be taught in a political science course could not justify a decision to allow the young Republicans to form a club while denying Communists, white supremacists, or Christian Scientists the same privilege. In my judgment, the political activities of the young Republicans are "noncurriculum related" for reasons that have nothing to do with the content of the political science course. The statutory definition of what is "noncurriculum related" should depend on the constitutional concern that motivated our decision in *Widmar*.

6. What I have said before of universities is true *a fortiori* with respect to high schools: a school's extracurricular activities constitute a part of the school's teaching mission, and the school accordingly must make "decisions concerning the content of those activities." *Widmar v. Vincent*, 454 U.S., at 278, 102 S.Ct., at 279 (Stevens, J., concurring in judgment). Absent good reason to hold otherwise, these decisions should be left to teachers. . . .

In this case, the district judge reviewed each of the clubs in the high school program and found that they are all "tied to the educational function of the institution." . . . He correctly concluded that this club system "differs dramatically from those found to create an open forum policy in *Widmar* and *Bender*." . . . I agree with his conclusion that, under a proper interpretation of the Act, this dramatic difference requires a different result.

* * *

Against all these arguments the Court interposes Noah Webster's famous dictionary. It is a massive tome but no match for the weight the Court would put upon it. The Court relies heavily on the dictionary's definition of "curriculum." . . . That word, of course, is not the Act's; moreover, the word "noncurriculum" is not in the dictionary. Neither Webster nor Congress has authorized us to assume that "noncurriculum" is a precise antonym of the word "curriculum." "Nonplus," for example, does not mean "minus" and it would be incorrect to assume that a "nonentity" is not an "entity" at all. Purely as a matter of defining a newly-coined word, the term "noncurriculum" could fairly be construed to describe either the subjects that are "not a part of the current curriculum" or the subjects that "cannot properly be included in a public school curriculum." Either of those definitions is perfectly "sensible" because both describe subjects "that are not related to the body of courses offered by the school." . . . When one considers the basic purpose of the Act, and its unquestioned linkage to our decision in *Widmar*, the latter definition surely is the more "sensible."

I respectfully dissent.

NOTES AND QUESTIONS

1. Widmar v. Vincent *and the Equal Access Act*

In 1981 the Supreme Court decided *Widmar v. Vincent*, 454 U.S. 263, 102 S.Ct. 269, 70 L.Ed.2d 440 (1981), a case involving whether a state university that makes its facilities generally available to registered student groups may deny the use of its facilities (vacant classrooms and the student center) to a student religious group. The University of Missouri argued that it had a compelling interest in avoiding the establishment of religion, urging that the use of the facilities for religious purposes by an interdenominational group of evangelical Christian students (Cornerstone) would constitute an unconstitutional establishment. The Court held that an equal access policy would not violate *Lemon v. Kurtzman*, 403 U.S. 602, 91 S.Ct. 2105, 29 L.Ed.2d 745 (1971):

> [A]n open-forum policy, including nondiscrimination against religious speech, would have a secular purpose and would avoid entanglement with religion. But the District Court concluded, and the University argues here, that allowing religious groups to share the limited public forum would have the "primary effect" of advancing religion.
>
> The University's argument misconceives the nature of this case. The question is not whether the creation of a religious forum would violate the Establishment Clause. The University has opened its facilities for use by student groups, and the question is whether it can now exclude groups because of the content of their speech. *See Healy v. James*, 408 U.S. 169 (1972). In this context we are unpersuaded that the primary effect of the public forum, open to all forms of discourse, would be to advance religion.
>
> . . . It is possible—perhaps even foreseeable—that religious groups will benefit from access to University facilities. But this Court has explained that a religious organization's enjoyment of merely "incidental" benefits does not violate the prohibition against the "primary advancement" of religion. . . .
>
> [A]n open forum in a public university does not confer any imprimatur of State approval on religious sects or practices.

454 U.S. at 721–74, 102 S.Ct. at 275–76. In the absence of an Establishment Clause justification for the denial of access, the Court held that the exclusion of Cornerstone from university facilities violated the Free Speech Clause. 454 U.S. at 289, 102 S.Ct. at 284. As Professor Laycock summarized the Court's holding:

> Regulation of speech must be content-neutral. When the government creates a forum for speech, it cannot pick and choose who can speak or what they can talk about. If students are free to discuss sex, politics, and philosophy, they must be free to discuss religion. The university let Students for a Democratic Society and the Young Socialist alliance use university facilities. It would have let those facilities be used for discussions of agnosticism, Marxism, and other doctrines hostile to religion. There was no doubt that students and faculty enjoyed an open forum in university facilities. The exclusion of religion could not be justified by any policy of neutrality, strict or otherwise. Justice Stevens noted in his concurrence that the university could control its own curriculum, and that a shortage of

> meeting rooms would require it to choose among voluntary student groups. But neither of those legitimate concerns had any relevance to the facts of *Widmar*. Rather, the university openly discriminated against religious speech.
>
> * * *
>
> With respect to the government's own speech, taking no position on religion is the most neutral practice. But with respect to private speech, protecting religious and antireligious speech equally with secular speech is far more neutral than singling [them] out . . . for special treatment.

Laycock, "Equal Access and Moments of Silence: The Equal Status of Religious Speech by Private Speakers," 81 *Nw. U. L. Rev.* 1, 10, 13–14 (1986).

Prior to the Supreme Court's decision in *Mergens*, lower federal courts divided over whether *Widmar* should be extended to public high schools. *See, e.g., Nartowicz v. Clayton County School District*, 736 F.2d 646 (11th Cir. 1984); *Lubbock Civil Liberties Union v. Lubbock Independent School District*, 669 F.2d 1038 (5th Cir. 1982). *See generally* Laycock, *supra* at 4–5. Congress entered the controversy in 1984, enacting the Equal Access Act (20 U.S.C. §§ 4071–4074 (Supp. 1985)). As interpreted by the Supreme Court, does the Act affirm or extend the holding of *Widmar*?

2. *Meaning of the Equal Access Act*

In order to trigger the application of the Equal Access Act and to establish a "limited open forum," a public secondary school receiving federal funds must have given one or more "noncurriculum related student groups" the opportunity to meet on campus during noninstructional time (before or after classroom instruction). Once a "limited open forum" has been established, then the school may not discriminate against a student group in the allocation of facilities "on the basis of the religious, political, philosophical, or other content of the speech at such meetings."

What meaning does Justice O'Connor give to "noncurriculum related"? What does it mean to say that the student clubs must have more than a "tangential or attenuated relationship to courses offered by the school"? Is a chess club curriculum related, as the *Mergens* Court suggests? Must the group and its activities be initiated by students to be noncurriculum related? What does the legislative history of the Equal Access Act show? *See generally* Strossen, "A Constitutional Analysis of the Equal Access Act's Standards Governing Public School Student Religious Meetings," 24 *Harv. J. Leg.* 117 (1987). Consider the conclusion reached by Professor Laycock:

> More than one interpretation of "curriculum related" is legitimately open to the courts. The best interpretation is the one that Senator Hatfield volunteered before he got entangled in Senator Gorton's cross-examination: curriculum related groups are those that are an extension of the classroom. That is what the statutory language seems to say, and that interpretation achieves the purposes of the sponsors and avoids the risk of abuse inherent in distinguishing between student-initiated and faculty-initiated groups. If a group is sponsored by a teacher who teaches a closely related course, and if nearly all the members of the group take that course, then the group is curriculum related, and its existence does not trigger any obligation to recognize other groups.

Laycock, *supra* at 40–41.

Does the majority in *Mergens* adopt the Laycock approach? Under the *Mergens* test, is the meeting of an athletic team curriculum related? What of the drama club? A meeting of the cast of a school play? A meeting of the student government? Board Policy 5610 refers to students clubs as a "vital part of the total education program." Why is this provision not dispositive on the issue of curriculum relatedness?

What is Justice Stevens' definition of curriculum relatedness? Is he saying that the concept of a limited open forum is not triggered by a decision to exclude clubs that engage in or teach partisan theological, ethical, or political views? Is his view supported by the legislative history of the Equal Access Act? Is it supported by the *Widmar* decision? After *Mergens*, may a school exclude a club that denies membership on the basis of race, sex, or political beliefs? What of exclusion on the basis of religious beliefs?

3. *The Constitutionality of the Equal Access Act*

Do you agree with Justice O'Connor in *Mergens* that the Equal Access Act is a constitutional extension of *Widmar*? Is *Widmar* distinguishable because high school students are more easily influenced than college students? What of the fact that high school students are required to attend school? That high school teachers may be perceived as authority figures? Do you agree with Justice Marshall that high school students are more likely to think that the meetings of religious clubs have received the imprimatur of state approval? Can they distinguish between "accommodation and endorsement"? *See* Note,

"The Constitutional Dimensions of Student-Initiated Religious Activity in Public High Schools," 92 *Yale L. J.* 499 (1983); *Clark v. Dallas Independent School District*, 671 F.Supp. 1119 (N.D. Tex. 1987). *But see* Laycock, *supra* at 14–20. Or is the primary issue, as Justice Kennedy urges, whether student participation is coerced?

If a school creates an open forum, is the opening of the facilities to religious groups motivated by an effort to advance religion or to avoid discrimination against religion? Is not every effort to accommodate religion or to put religious speech on the same level as other speech motivated by some desire to assist religion? Do you agree with Professor Laycock that "state efforts to alleviate discrimination or state-imposed burdens on religious exercise are consistent with neutrality, even though any such effort, considered in isolation, will appear to aid religion"? Laycock, *supra* at 21.

What if a school district that grudingly accepted the prohibition of school-sponsored prayer encourages students to participate in the meetings of religious clubs? Would the practice violate the Establishment Clause? *See* Laycock, *supra* at 53. What if a school district establishes an open forum because the protection of secular speech by student groups is the only constitutional way to permit prayer on school premises? *See* Note, "Student Religious Groups and the Right of Access to Public School Activity Periods," 74 *Georgetown L. J.* 205, 213 (1985). What if this were the motivation of Congress in enacting the Equal Access Act? Under such circumstances, would the extension of the open forum to student religious groups violate the secular purpose and effects parts of the *Lemon* test? *See* Teitel, "The Unconstitutionality of Equal Access Policies and Legislation Allowing Organized Student-Initiated Religious Activities in the Public High Schools: A Proposal for a Unitary First Amendment Forum Analysis," 12 *Hastings Const. L. Q.* 529, 556–59 (1985). *But see* Laycock, *supra* at 22–23.

Might the need for faculty supervision of student group activities, under some circumstances, lead to an unconstitutional entanglement of government and religion? *See Garnett v. Renton School District No. 403*, 865 F.2d 1121 (9th Cir. 1989); *Bender v. Williamsport Area School District*, 741 F.2d 538, 556–57 (3d Cir. 1984), *vacated on other grounds*, 475 U.S. 534, 106 S.Ct. 1326, 89 L.Ed.2d 501 (1986). *See generally* Laycock, *supra* at 25–27. Is this a relevant distinction between open forums in universities and in high schools?

Note that § 4071(c) of the Equal Access Act provides that noncurriculum related religious groups must be offered "a fair opportunity to meet" on the same basis as other noncurriculum related groups. Fairness requires that the meetings must be voluntary and student initiated, that nonschool persons may not regularly attend, that the meetings do not materially or substantially interfere with the school's educational mission, and that there be no school sponsorship. *See* Laycock, *supra* at 42–43. While there is some confusion as to whether these requirements apply only to religious groups or to all student groups (Laycock, *supra* at 43–45), are these limitations necessary to preserve the constitutionality of the Equal Access Act? *See* Note, "Student Religious Groups and the Right of Access to Public School Activity Periods," *supra* at 215. May school authorities allocate funds to a student religious group beyond the incidental cost of providing the space? *See* Equal Access Act § 4071(d)(1)–(7), (f).

Should a distinction be drawn between student groups that meet to discuss religion and those that meet to engage in ritual prayer and a worship service? *See Widmar v. Vincent*, 454 U.S. 263, 284–85, 102 S.Ct. 269, 282, 70 L.Ed.2d 440 (1981) (White, J., dissenting). Is the distinction intelligible? Persuasive? *See generally* Laycock, *supra* at 55–56. Professor Laycock argues that "rules that allow schools to monitor the content of religious meetings and break them up when they become 'too religious' trample the core of the free speech and free exercise clauses. They also violate the establishment clause by giving official sanction to those religious meetings that are allowed to continue." Laycock, *supra* at 57. Conversely, Professor Teitel makes the following argument:

> The Equal Access Act mandates government sponsorship of prayer in the public schools; such state sponsorship never has been given to prayer in the parks. The aegis of the school and required attendance provide state support to those wishing to gather religious adherents. This state support inevitably compromises the religious (or nonreligious) beliefs of public school students. Governmental assistance to propagation of religious beliefs through equal access . . . legislation constitutes an establishment of religion. . . .

Teitel, "When Separate is Equal: Why Organized Religious Exercises, Unlike Chess, Do Not Belong in the Public Schools," 81 *Nw. U. L. Rev.* 174, 175–176 (1987). Do you agree with Teitel or Laycock?

4. Access by Secular Student Groups

In *Healy v. James*, 408 U.S. 169, 92 S.Ct. 2338, 33 L.Ed.2d 266 (1972), students at a public university sought to organize a local chapter of the Students for a Democratic Society (SDS) and to obtain official recognition from the university. The university recognized many other student groups, including the Young Americans for Freedom, the Young Democrats, the Young Republicans, and the Liberal Party. The president of the university denied the application for three reasons: (1) "the organization's philosophy was antithetical to the school's policies"; (2) the group's independence from the national SDS was doubtful; and (3) "approval should not be granted to any group that 'openly repudiates' the College's dedication to academic freedom." The denial of official recognition meant that the SDS chapter could not announce activities and meetings in the student newspaper, it would not have access to campus bulletin boards, and most significantly, it could not use campus facilities in which to hold meetings.

Justice Powell, writing the majority opinion for the Supreme Court, held that "the mere disagreement of the President with the group's philosophy affords no reason to deny it recognition," for the First Amendment guarantees "the right of individuals to associate to further their personal beliefs." The association with the national chapter was not deemed sufficient to deny recognition in the absence of infringement of reasonable campus rules, interruption of classes, or substantial interference "with the opportunity of other students to obtain an education." The appropriate line is that between "permissible speech and impermissible conduct," and there was no "evidential basis to support the conclusion that . . . [the local SDS chapter] posed a substantial threat of material disruption in violation of" campus rules. The Court went on to state that "a college administration may impose a requirement . . . that a group affirm in advance its willingness to adhere to reasonable campus law."

Would the result in *Healy* have been different if the university had not recognized any student groups? Any noncurriculum related student groups? Is *Healy*, considered in the light of *Mergens* and *Widmar*, a disguised limited public forum case? *See* Wells, "Mandatory Student Fees: First Amendment Concerns and University Discretion," 55 *U. Chi. L. Rev.* 363, 382–85 (1988). *See generally Regents of University of California v. PERB*, 458 U.S. 589, 108 S.Ct. 1404, 99 L.Ed.2d 664 (1988); *Cornelius v. NAACP Legal Defense Fund*, 473 U.S. 788, 105 S.Ct. 3439, 87 L.Ed.2d 507 (1985); *Perry Educators' Association v. Perry Local Education Association*, 460 U.S. 37, 103 S.Ct. 948, 74 L.Ed.2d 794 (1983). *Healy* relies on the *Tinker* disruption test. Does this indicate that *Healy* is applicable to public secondary schools?

While *Healy* is primarily a freedom of association case, it also is treated as establishing the principle, affirmed by *Widmar v. Vincent* and its progeny, that school authorities may not pick and choose among student organizations on the basis of the content of their speech or ideology. *Cf. Student Coalition for Peace v. Lower Merion School, supra.* This is similar to the constitutional rules governing invitations to outside speakers on university campuses. *See generally* Wright, "The Constitution on Campus," 22 *Vand. L. Rev.* 1027 (1969). On this basis, courts have overturned denials of recognition of homosexual student groups where other student groups have received recognition. *See Gay Student Services v. Texas A & M University*, 737 F.2d 1317 (5th Cir. 1984), *cert. denied and appeal dismissed*, 471 U.S. 1001, 105 S.Ct. 1860, 85 L.Ed.2d 155 (1985); *Gay Lib. v. University of Missouri*, 558 F.2d 848 (8th Cir. 1977), *cert. denied*, 434 U.S. 1080, 98 S.Ct. 1276, 55 L.Ed.2d 789 (1978); *Gay Alliance of Students v. Matthews*, 544 F.2d 162 (4th Cir. 1976); *Gay Students Organization of University of New Hampshire v. Bonner*, 509 F.2d 652 (1st Cir. 1974); *Gay Activists Alliance v. Board of Regents*, 638 P.2d 1116 (Okla. 1981). *Cf. Gay Rights Coalition v. Georgetown University*, 536 A.2d 1 (D.C. App. 1987) (en banc). In addition, one appellate court has held that a university may not discriminate against homosexual student organizations in the allocation of university funds. *Gay and Lesbian Students Association v. Gohn*, 850 F.2d 361 (8th Cir. 1988). *Compare Cornelius v. NAACP Legal Defense and Educational Fund, supra; Regan v. Taxation With Representation*, 461 U.S. 540, 103 S.Ct. 1997, 76 L.Ed.2d 129 (1983). Judge Arnold, writing for the court in *Gohn*, made the following observation:

> It is apparent that the GLSA was denied . . . funds because of the views it espoused. Nor is there a com-

> pelling state interest justifying the Senate's denial of funds. The University provides no argument, and we can think of none. True, sodomy is illegal in Arkansas. However, the GLSA does not advocate sodomy, and, even if it did, its speech about an illegal activity would still be protected by the First Amendment. People may extol the virtues of arson or even cannibalism. They simply may not commit the acts. . . . Conduct may be prohibited or regulated, within broad limits. But government may not discriminate against people because it dislikes their ideas, not even when the ideas include advocating that certain conduct now criminal be legalized.

850 F.2d at 367–68.

Is *Gohn* consistent with *Healy*? With *Widmar*? Is it consistent with the cases dealing with homosexual teachers, discussed *supra*? Should the result be the same if a gay student organization in a public high school sought recognition? How would the *Mergens* court decide this issue? In the latter case, what is the relevance of *Hazelwood*, *Bethel*, *Pico* and other cases involving the role of the public schools in socializing students to community norms?

Would the principles of *Healy*, *Widmar*, *Mergens*, and the homosexual student organization cases apply to the recognition of alumni groups by a university or public school? *See Ad-Hoc Committee v. Bernard M. Baruch College*, 835 F.2d 980 (2d Cir. 1987). Would the banning of membership in fraternal organizations or a prohibition on their meeting on campus violate *Mergens* or the First Amendment? *See Waugh v. Board of Trustees*, 237 U.S. 589, 35 S.Ct. 720, 59 L.Ed. 1131 (1915); *Webb v. State University of New York*, 125 F.Supp. 910 (N.D.N.Y. 1954), *appeal dismissed*, 348 U.S. 867, 75 S.Ct. 113, 99 L.Ed. 683. *But see Wright v. Board of Education*, 295 Mo. 466, 246 S.W. 43 (1922). *See generally* Hauser, "Social Fraternities at Public Institutions of Higher Education: Their Rights Under the First and Fourteenth Amendments," 19 *J. of Law & Educ.* 433 (1990); Graebner, "Outlawing Teenage Populism: The Campaign Against Secret Societies in the American High School, 1900–1960," 74 *J. of Amer. Hist.* 411 (1987); Rumsey, "Legal Aspects of the Relationship Between Fraternities and Public Institutions of Higher Education: Freedom of Association and Ability to Prohibit Campus Presence or Student Membership," 11 *J. of Coll. & Univ. Law* 465 (1985).

5. Mandatory Student Fees: A Right of Nonassociation?

In *Galda v. Rutgers*, 772 F.2d 1060 (3d Cir. 1985), present and former students at Rutgers, a public university, argued that a mandatory fee of $3.50 a semester to support the Public Interest Research Group (PIRG) violated their First Amendment right not to associate with PIRG and not to be identified with ideological positions to which they objected. The New Jersey PIRG is an independent, nonprofit organization that actively engages in research, lobbying, and advocacy to promote social change, including a nuclear weapons freeze and public policies to promote consumer rights and conservation of the environment. It has both a permanent staff and student members. A student who does not wish to contribute to PIRG must request a refund, which generally occurs several months later. Plaintiffs sought to prove that PIRG was a "political action group," whereas defendants produced testimony that PIRG provided educational benefits to participating students.

The plaintiffs relied on *West Virginia State Board of Education v. Barnette*, 319 U.S. 624, 63 S.Ct. 1178, 87 L.Ed. 1628 (1943), and other Supreme Court precedents for the proposition that they "may not be compelled to contribute to an a organization which espouses and promotes ideological causes they oppose." 772 F.2d at 1063. They also relied on *Abood v. Detroit Board of Education*, 431 U.S. 209, 97 S.Ct. 1782, 52 L.Ed.2d 261 (1977), a case involving mandatory payments to a labor union, holding that employees may prevent a union from spending a portion of the service fee "to contribute to political candidates and to express political views unrelated to its duties as exclusive bargaining representative." 431 U.S. at 234, 97 S.Ct. at 1799. *See also Ellis v. Brotherhood of Railway, Airline & Steamship Clerks*, 466 U.S. 435, 104 S.Ct. 1883, 80 L.Ed.2d 428 (1984). *See generally* chapter 4, *infra*. After reviewing the precedents, the court held that the university had not shown any compelling interest that would override the plaintiffs' First Amendment rights and that the rebate procedure was "unsatisfactory." 772 F.2d at 1068. The court then enjoined the collection of the mandatory fee for PIRG.

In reaching its decision, the *Galda* court was careful to emphasize the particular facts of the case and to distinguish the mandatory fee for PIRG from a general student activity fee:

> [T]he student activity fee is used to subsidize a variety of student groups, and therefore that assessment can be "perceived broadly as providing a 'forum' for a diverse range of opinion." In contrast, "PIRG does not provide a forum for the expression of differing views"

but is a "group." . . . Moreover, the PIRG fee is segregated from other charges listed on the students' bills and supports only that "group."

* * *

. . . The elements of compulsion and payment to an outside organization with which plaintiffs disagree are the significant factors that trigger the inquiry in this case. [These factors distinguish the situation where the challenged group is part of the university community and is funded through the student activity fee.]

* * *

The education advantages described in the testimony do not differ from those that might be obtained by working with, or for, an independent organization such as the Republican or Democratic Party, or a clearly religious group which has undertaken an active and vigorous proselytizing program. . . .

PIRG's efforts are primarily devoted to changing conditions outside the University. . . . While such matters may affect that general public, those causes are not particularly germane to students of the University qua students.

* * *

Although the training PIRG members may receive is considerable, there can be no doubt that it is secondary to PIRG's stated objectives of a frankly ideological bent. To that extent the educational benefits are only "incidental." . . .

* * *

Moreover, the evidence revealed that it is impossible to isolate the "educational component" from the ideological pursuits for purposes of apportioning the expenses attributable to each.

772 F.2d at 1064–66, quoting *Galda v. Bloustein*, 686 F.2d 159 (3d Cir. 1982). *See generally* Recent Developments, "Constitutional Law: The First Amendment and Compulsory Funding of Political Advocacy," 9 *Harv. J. of Law & Pub. Pol.* 731 (1985).

Other courts have adhered to the distinction drawn in *Galda* and held that a general student activity fee, used to fund a variety of student organizations and activities, is justified under the First Amendment because it creates a forum for the expression of diverse views. *See, e.g., Kania v. Fordham*, 702 F.2d 475 (4th Cir. 1983); *Smith v. Regents of University of California*, 202 Cal.App.3d 1, 248 Cal.Rptr. 263 (1988); *Good v. Associated Students of University of Washington*, 86 Wash.2d 94, 542 P.2d 762 (1975); *Larson v. Board of Regents of University of Nebraska*, 189 Neb. 688, 204 N.W.2d 568 (1973). *See generally* Wells, "Mandatory Student Fees: First Amendment Concerns and University Discretion," 55 *U. Chi. L. Rev.* 363 (1988). In each of those cases, the courts also "regarded the activity as one which supplements classroom education by exposing the students to a variety of views on significant issues." *Smith v. Regents of University of California*, *supra* at 271.

Is the distinction between a single-purpose fee and a general student activity fee persuasive? If PIRG received a small portion of such a general fee, would the allocation be constitutional? What is the practical distinction? Would it be unconstitutional to deny funding to PIRG because of its ideological activities? *See Gay and Lesbian Students Association v. Gohn*, 850 F.2d 361 (8th Cir. 1988); Wells, *supra* at 388–95. What if a portion of the activity fee were used to fund abortions? *See Erzinger v. Regents of University of California*, 136 Cal.App.3d 1, 185 Cal.Rptr. 791 (1982), *aff'd on rehearing*, 137 Cal.App.3d 389, 187 Cal.Rptr. 164. *See generally* Antonini, "First Amendment Challenges to the Use of Mandatory Student Fees to Help Fund Student Abortions," 15 *J. of Coll. & Univ. Law* 61 (1988).

Suppose that a fee were paid only to the student government and the student government endorsed political candidates. Would it be constitutional for a university to require the student government to refrain from partisan political activities as a condition of funding through a mandatory fee? Would such a policy be consistent with *Healy* and *Widmar*? With *Hazelwood*? May a university establish a new procedure for student refunds in response to the controversial positions taken by a student organization supported by a mandatory fee? *See Stanley v. Magrath*, 719 F.2d 279 (8th Cir. 1983). Would such a step be unconstitutional censorship or a constitutional effort to protect the nonassociational rights of objecting students? *See* Wells, *supra* at 389–90.

Is the compelling distinction between fees that support student organizations and those that fund external organizations? Between a primarily educational purpose and a primarily ideological purpose? Can an external organization (e.g., the local opera company) have a primarily educational purpose for students? If a mandatory fee could be allocated between expenditures for educational and political purposes, must it be? Even if a mandatory fee is permissible, can a student be compelled to be a member of an organization to which he or she objects? *Cf. Lathrop v. Donohue*, 367 U.S. 820, 81 S.Ct. 1826, 6 L.Ed.2d 1191 (1961). Is it realistic or appropriate to associate individual students with the views of the organization as expressed through its leadership? *See Arrington v. Taylor*, 380 F.Supp. 1348 (M.D.N.C.1974). Are the university cases distinguishable from mandatory fees in public elementary and secondary schools?

Searcey v. Harris

888 F.2d 1314 (11th Cir. 1989).

Before Kravitch and Clark, Circuit Judges and Henderson, Senior Circuit Judge.

Clark, Circuit Judge:

The Atlanta Peace Alliance (APA) challenged the policy of the Atlanta School Board regarding access of military and nonmilitary groups to the Atlanta schools. The APA[1] brought suit contending that the School Board's refusal to grant the APA access to programs known as Careeer Day and Youth Motivation Day and to place information on bulletin boards and in guidance counselors' offices violated the APA members' First Amendment rights. The district court held that the denial of access to bulletin boards, guidance counselors and Career Day was unconstitutional. The Board has only appealed the district court's determination that several of the regulations concerning Career and Motivation Day are unconstitutional.

I. Facts

A major objective of the Atlanta School Board has been to improve the post-secondary opportunities available to its students, of whom 92% may be classified as "minority" and 85% classified as "poor." The Board has created programs to motivate the students to set career and educational goals and to inform the students of the opportunities that are available. The Board has involved the community in two specific programs to accomplish these goals: Youth Motivation Day and Career Day. At Youth Motivation Day, community members come into school to share their experience and to inspire students to continue their education as the best means of achieving success. At Career Day, community members speak with students about more specific job opportunities and the skills they need to attain specific jobs. A major emphasis at both programs has been stressing the importance of finishing high school and seeking further education or training after graduation. There is no set format to these programs; some schools present several Career or Motivational Days throughout the year and others combine the two programs into one event. Moreover, until the experience with the APA, the School Board only had a general policy relating to career education;[4] it was left to the discretion of each school principal to run the program as he or she saw fit. Generally, a program would include a keynote speaker at an assembly, after which the students would go to different classrooms to hear particular speakers. Often the speaker and the students would engage in a discussion in these smaller groups. Although the programs varied at each school, one constant was that there were no restrictions as to the content of the speeches or discussions. . . .

In February of 1983, the APA sent a letter to each of the Atlanta high school principals requesting permission to place literature in guidance counselors' offices, to place advertisements in school newspapers and to appear at Career Days. They submitted a plan to the Board but the Board took no action. In the meantime, two high school principals accepted the literature. In June, 1983, the APA representatives met with then Superintendent Alonzo Crim to discuss the APA's access to the school programs. Dr. Crim agreed to distribute the materials to the guidance counselors, to allow the APA to set up a table at Career Day, to make a list of APA speakers available to the high schools, and to allow the APA to place paid advertisements in the school year books.

After some publicity about Dr. Crim's agreement with the APA, on October 4, 1983, the School Board reviewed Dr. Crim's decision and directed him to deny APA all access to the schools. At the same time, the Board directed Dr. Crim to develop a policy governing Career Days. In April 1984, however, the Board had not adopted any policy regarding Career Days and still completely barred the APA from the schools. The APA then filed suit in the district court contending that the School Board was

1. APA and several individual peace activists brought an action for declaratory and injunctive relief against Dr. Alonzo Crim individually and in his official capacity as Superintendent of the Atlanta Public Schools and the Atlanta Board of Education (Board). Jerome Harris has been substituted as a party for Dr. Alonzo Crim. F.R. A.P. 43(c).

4. When the APA first sought access to Career Day, the Board's only official policy stated that career education was necessary to "enable[ ] students of all ages to examine their attitudes, interests, aptitudes, and abilities in order to relate them to career opportunities, and to make valid decisions regarding further education and future endeavors." . . .

violating their members' First Amendment rights. On August 13, 1986, the district court granted partial summary judgment in favor of the plaintiffs and entered a preliminary injunction prohibiting the Board from denying the APA an opportunity substantially equal to that afforded to the military recruiters to participate in Career Days and place information on bulletin boards and in guidance counselors offices. The Board filed an interlocutory appeal and this court affirmed in part, vacated in part, and remanded for further proceedings. The case then proceeded to trial on the issue of whether the denial of access to Career Day and bulletin boards and guidance counselor's offices was unconstitutional. The district court found that the bulletin boards and guidance counselor's offices were created public forums and that the Board had not asserted a compelling interest justifying denying the APA access. The School Board has not appealed that ruling.

Prior to trial, at the urging of the district court, the Board adopted a uniform policy relating to Career Day. The policy states that

> The Board believes that schools should provide educational programs that are pertinent to the practical aspects of post-secondary life and to the world of work. The Board therefore supports "Career Day" programs as part of the general curriculum programs for our schools. Career Day is to be a program which allows students to gain career awareness and to explore career opportunities in various fields. Participants in "Career Day" programs shall have direct knowledge of the career opportunities about which they speak and shall be limited to providing appropriate information about career fields. Participants shall not be allowed to criticize or denigrate the career opportunities provided by other participants. Written information about career opportunities may also be made available to students at school sites subject to the conditions imposed above. Restrictions may not be imposed on the types of career opportunities in such material. The Superintendent shall prepare appropriate administrative regulations for the implementation of this policy.

. . . By trial, however, the Board still had not adopted administrative regulations to interpret the policy. When the district court deferred ruling until the regulations were adopted, the Board adopted Administrative Regulations to govern Career Days. . . . The regulations require an individual or group who wishes to participate in Career Day to provide sufficient information to the school principal to show that they will communicate information in keeping with the goals of Career Day. If a school principal denies a request to participate, the individual may appeal the denial to a Central Career Day Committee. The regulations also require participants to adhere to the regulations in their presentations. In the event that a participant violates a regulation, the Central Committee is authorized to impose appropriate sanctions including barring that individual or his group from further participation in Career Days.

The regulations also expand on the general policy with respect to who may participate and what participants may say: the regulations specifically interpret the policy's requirement that participants have direct knowledge of the subject matter and present appropriate information. Regulation 9 interprets the "direct knowledge" requirement to include those individuals who by virtue of training, education or experience possess information that would be useful to students in making career choices. However, Regulation 9 also requires each presenter to have "some ***present affiliation*** or authority with that career field about which he or she is to make a presentation." (emphasis added).

In addition, the regulations define "appropriate information" as information that is helpful to students in explaining career options. Both the policy and regulations, however, specifically prohibit a participant from criticizing or denigrating the opportunities presented by other participants. The regulations specifically state that "information shall be conveyed in as positive and encouraging a manner as possible so as to be motivational to students." Reg. 10. Finally, presenters "whose primary focus or emphasis is to discourage a student's participation in a particular career field" are totally prohibited from participating in Career Day. Reg. 10, 11.

On March 4, 1988, the district court entered a written order finding that Career Day was a nonpublic forum, but that the direct knowledge requirement and prohibition on criticism violated APA's first amendment rights. The district court held that the direct knowledge, present affiliation, and no criticism regulations were unreasonable restrictions on access to Career Day. In addition, the court held that these regulations and the regulation banning groups whose primary focus is to discourage students from a particular field were unconstitutional because they were written with an intent to suppress APA's viewpoint. Thus, the court entered final judgment and a permanent injunction enjoining the Board from denying the APA "an opportunity, substantially equal to that afforded military recruiters, to present peace oriented education and career opportunities to Atlanta public school students by . . . participating in Career Days and Youth Motivation Day programs." . . . Since the APA does not challenge the district court's finding that Career Day is a non-public forum, the only issue presented on appeal is whether specific aspects of the Career Day policy and administrative regulations are valid regulations of First Amendment activity in a nonpublic forum. More specifically, the Board does not contend that it may prevent the APA from presenting information about peace oriented opportunities. Instead, the Board challenges the district court's conclusions that the direct knowledge, present affiliation, no criticism and no discouragement regulations are unconstitutional.

II. Discussion

A. The Law

The Supreme Court has explained that the type of restrictions which may be placed on First Amendment activities depends in large part on "the nature of the relevant forum." *Cornelius v. NAACP Legal Defense Fund*, 473 U.S. 788, 105 S.Ct. 3439, 3448, 87 L.Ed.2d 567 (1985). In a traditional public forum and a "created" public forum, the government may enforce content based restrictions only if necessary to serve a compelling state interest and narrowly tailored to serve that interest. The government may also enforce content neutral, *i.e.*, time, place and manner regulations, which are narrowly tailored to serve a significant interest but still leave open ample alternative means of communications. . . . In a nonpublic forum, however, the government enjoys considerably more power over the use of its property: it may impose content based restrictions which are "reasonable and [are] not an effort to suppress expression merely because public officials oppose the speaker's view." *Cornelius*, 473 U.S. at 800, 105 S.Ct. at 3448. . . . The restrictions may "be based on subject matter and speaker identity so long as the distinctions are reasonable in light of the purposes served by the forum and are viewpoint neutral." *Cornelius*, 473 U.S. at 806, 105 S.Ct. at 3451. In this case, the Board's Career Day policy and regulations will be upheld if they are reasonable in light of the purposes of the forum and were not promulgated to suppress the viewpoint of the APA.

Before undertaking this analysis, it is necessary to discuss an argument raised by the Board. The School Board argues that *Hazelwood School District v. Kuhlmeier*, 484 U.S. 260, 108 S.Ct. 562, 98 L.Ed.2d 492 (1988), changes the First Amendment analysis applied to school officials' decisions relating to curricular programs. In *Hazelwood*, students sued when the principal refused to publish several articles in a school newspaper. *Id.* at 262, 108 S.Ct. at 565. In upholding the school's actions, the Supreme Court held that educators may exercise control over student expression in a curricular program if the restrictions are "reasonably related to legitimate pedagogical concerns." 108 S.Ct. at 571. We fail to see how this standard differs from the *Cornelius* standard for non-public forums; instead it is merely an application of that standard to a curricular program. Since the purpose of a curricular program is by definition "pedagogical," the *Cornelius* standard requires that the regulations be reasonable in light of the pedagogical purposes of the particular activity. *Hazelwood* therefore does not alter the test for reasonableness in a nonpublic forum such as a school but rather provides the context in which the reasonableness of regulations should be considered.[7]

* * *

B. Reasonableness

. . . [T]he primary purpose of Career Day is informational; speakers inform the students of the career and educational opportunities available to them. The speakers may talk about the specific requirements of a certain educational program or job and/or the benefits of specific occupations.

Because Career Day and Youth Motivation Day are often combined in a single activity, the program also has a second important goal, namely motivating the students. . . .

---

7. Although the *Hazelwood* Court concluded that school officials should have great control over curricular expression, that discussion was intended to exempt student expression in a curricular activity from the more stringent standard applied to student speech in noncurricular activities enunciated in *Tinker v. Des Moines Independent School District*, 393 U.S. 503, 89 S.Ct. 733, 21 L.Ed.2d 731 (1969). . . .

Of somewhat more concern is the suggestion by the School Board that *Hazelwood* eliminates the requirement that restrictions on speech in a curricular activity be viewpoint neutral. Although the Supreme Court did not discuss viewpoint neutrality in *Hazelwood*, there is no indication that the Court intended to drastically rewrite First Amendment law to allow a school official to discriminate based on a speaker's views. As discussed, *infra*, *Hazelwood* acknowledges a school's ability to discriminate based on *content* not *viewpoint*.

1. The Direct Knowledge and Present Affiliation Requirement. . . . The district court invalidated the direct knowledge requirement because it was inserted to exclude the APA from appearing at Career Day and because the present affiliation requirement was unreasonable.

On appeal, the Board asserts that this requirement ensures that "a presenter knows what he is talking about," which in turn ensures that the speaker gives credible information and provides a credible role model for the students. In addition, the government[8] argues that the requirement is justified as a reasonable means of avoiding political debate at Career Day. Both these objectives are legitimate pedagogical concerns of the School Board. Clearly it is vital to the success of the program that the speakers provide useful information and present credible role models. In addition, school officials are entitled to prohibit political or ideological debate at Career Day. . . .

We agree with the Board that the *direct knowledge* requirement is reasonably related to ensuring that speakers present credible information and are positive role models. It was reasonable for the Board to conclude that individuals without any specific knowledge of career fields would not present appropriate information. However, as stated by the APA in its brief, "[i]f the 'direct knowledge' requirement meant only what the Board says it means, the APA would not have argued that it was unreasonable. The APA is interested in students learning the truth about military service, and therefore has no quarrel with a rule requiring presenters to know what they are talking about. The problem is that the Board's direct knowledge requirement includes the requirement that the presenter also have 'some present affiliation with that career field.' " . . . It is the *present affiliation* requirement that the district court found unreasonable. We agree.

As the district court noted, the regulation as written would exclude retired persons and professional career counselors from participation in Career Day. Since such individuals have participated in the past, the School Board has acknowledged that they may have valuable information for the students.[9] The Board advances no argument to support this regulation and thus points to no evidence in the record to explain that present affiliation requirement. Nor can we discern how this regulation is related to ensuring a successful Career Day. It is not intuitively obvious that individuals who are no longer affiliated with a career would have less information or would present a less effective role model; nor is it obvious that such an individual would be more likely to turn Career Day into a forum for his or her political views.

Although the Board offers no support for this regulation, the government argues that we must defer to the Board's decision. The government argues that although the decision to exclude retired people from Career Day may not be the wisest choice, a regulation "need only be *reasonable*; it need not be the most reasonable or the only reasonable limitation." *Cornelius*, 473 U.S. at 808, 105 S.Ct. at 3452. This argument wrongfully concludes that the regulation is reasonable and overstates the deference a court must pay to School Board decisions. Although the School Board has the discretion to choose between reasonable alternatives, there is no evidence that the Board made a *choice* in this case. There is no evidence which even arguably explains the Board's change in position; for example, there is no evidence that the Board had experienced any problems with individuals who were not affiliated with a group. We cannot *infer* the reasonableness of a regulation from a vacant record. . . . Indeed the lack of any evidence to support this regulation and the facts surrounding the adoption of the regulations support the inference that the regulation was written to specifically exclude the APA from Career Day. . . .

2. The No Criticism and No Discouragement Requirements. . . . The district court found the no criticism ban unreasonable because the school officials had acknowledged the value of both positive and negative information to students making decisions about their future. The court found the regulation prohibiting participation of those whose primary focus is to discourage students from a particular field to be reasonable in light of the motivational purposes of the forum, but since the court found that all the regulations were written in order to suppress the APA's viewpoint, even that regulation was unconstitutional.

The Board justifies both these regulations as reasonably related to motivating the students to set goals.

8. The United States intervened as a defendant in the district court on behalf of the Armed Services. . . .

9. We also note parenthetically that this regulation could totally exclude the APA from appearing at Career Day to speak about peace oriented opportunities. Thus we find the Board's representation that it has no quarrel with the APA appearing for this purpose disingenuous.

We agree that the regulation prohibiting a group whose sole purpose is discouraging students from an occupation or educational opportunity is reasonable. Discouraging students from participating in a particular field clearly detracts from the motivational purpose of the forum. It is the total banning of a group from the forum—rather than limiting what a group can say—that we find to be unreasonable.

As the district court noted, since the main purpose of Career Day is to allow students to evaluate their opportunities for the future, presenting only positive information directly conflicts with the educational purpose of the forum. The fact that speakers at previous Career Days have been able to criticize the paths urged by other speakers reflects that the policy of the Board has always been, in the words of Dr. Crim, "to provide [the students] with an optimum level of information." . . .

* * *

[W]hile avoiding controversial issues justifies prohibiting speakers from discussing the morality of war or defense spending, it does not justify excluding bona fide negative facts which are relevant to the requirements or benefits of a specific job, including one in the military. Dr. Crim acknowledged this by agreeing that the APA or any group could tell the students (if it were documented) that soldiers were underpaid. . . .

Dr. Crim was also concerned that negative information could be conveyed in a pejorative manner to discourage students from considering certain fields. . . . This concern, however, does not justify a ban of *all* critical information including the information Dr. Crim acknowledged was helpful to the students. Instead, it justifies only prohibiting the use of critical information to denigrate a profession and discourage students from that field. Finally, Dr. Crim was concerned that speakers would use negative factual information in a misleading or inaccurate manner.[14] That concern, however, does not justify banning criticism entirely. Dr. Crim's concern about perjorative information is addressed by the district court's order, which allows the schools to exclude any inaccurate or misleading information from Career Day.

Thus, the regulations banning criticism are only reasonable to the extent that they prohibit a group from denigrating the opportunities offered by a specific group. The regulations are unreasonable to the extent that they prohibit a group from presenting negative factual information about the disadvantages of specific job opportunities because such information is useful to students making decisions about careers. Moreover, the Board could not allow speakers to point out the advantages of a particular career but ban any speaker from pointing out the disadvantages of the same career. That amounts to viewpoint-based discrimination which is prohibited by the First Amendment regardless of the type of forum. We turn now to that issue.

C. Viewpoint-based Discrimination

"The existence of reasonable grounds for limiting access to a nonpublic forum, however, will not save a regulation that is in reality a facade for viewpoint-based discrimination." *Cornelius*, 473 U.S. at 811, 105 S.Ct. at 3454. In a nonpublic forum, the government may limit the subject matter discussed by all speakers in a forum but it may not distinguish between particular speakers based on their view of the approved subject matter. As the *Cornelius* Court stated "[a]lthough a speaker may be excluded from a nonpublic forum if he wishes to address a topic not encompassed within the purpose of the forum, . . . or if he is not a member of the class of speakers for whose especial benefit the forum was created, . . . the government violates the First Amendment when it denies access to a speaker solely to suppress the point of view he espouses or an otherwise includable subject." 473 U.S. at 806, 105 S.Ct. at 3451. . . . Thus, as with any other nonpublic forum, once the School Board determines that certain speech is appropriate for students, it may not discriminate between speakers who will speak on the topic merely because it disagrees with their views. . . .

The Board argues that *Hazelwood* does not prohibit school officials from engaging in viewpoint-based discrimination. We disagree. *Hazelwood* involved a content based distinction; the principal decided that the subject of teenage sexuality was inappropriate for some of the younger students. *Id.* at 274–76, 108 S.Ct. at 571–72. There was no indication that the principal was motivated by a disagreement with the views expressed in the articles. Although *Hazelwood* provides reasons for allowing a school official to discriminate based on *content*, we do not believe it offers any justification for al-

14. When asked whether a presenter could inform students that blacks and Latinos have less chances of getting a high-tech job in the military, Dr. Crim stated, "If *anyone* were to say that, and that is documented by fact, that would be useful for the student." Record, Vol. 11, at 617 (emphasis added).

lowing educators to discriminate based on viewpoint. The prohibition against viewpoint discrimination is firmly embedded in the first amendment analysis. . . . Without more explicit direction, we will continue to require school officials to make decisions relating to speech which are viewpoint neutral. *See Virgil v. School Board of Columbia County*, 862 F.2d 1517, 1522–23 & n. 6 (11th Cir. 1989) (viewpoint neutrality test applies to First Amendment claim concerning removal of books from curriculum).

In this case, the School Board has determined that the students should learn about career and educational opportunities. Having done so, the Board cannot exclude the APA solely because it disagreed with the APA's views about the career choices students should make. More specifically, the Board cannot exclude the APA because it disagreed with its views about the military. . . .

As the district court noted, there is no doubt that the Board's abrupt change in policy was caused by the APA's request for access to schools. The procedure by which the policy was adopted is an important factor in deciding whether the board engaged in viewpoint based discrimination. . . . In this case, the Board's treatment of the APA supports an inference that the Board intended to suppress the APA's views. In addition to the evidence relied on by the district court, we note two additional factors which also support the district court's finding. First, one of the Board's justifications for limiting access—avoiding debate about controversial matters—although facially reasonable is capable of concealing bias towards the approach advocated by specific speakers. If the School Board disagreed with the APA's views about careers, it could easily label them "controversial" and thus exclude them from the program. . . .

In addition, as we pointed out above, there are doubts as to the genuineness of the Board's justifications based on past practice. . . .

III. Conclusion

* * *

With respect to Regulation 9, we reverse the district court's order insofar as it struck the entire regulation. The first sentence which requires that the speakers have knowledge of the subject addressed is an appropriate content restriction. We agree with the district court that the "present affiliation" regulation is unduly restrictive and the district court's striking of the last sentence of Regulation 9 is affirmed.

The district court struck the last sentence in Regulation 10 (the no discouragement ban) and the first sentence of Regulation 11 (the no criticism, no denigration ban). We affirm the district court with some modification. . . . To the extent that a speaker is discouraging a student from entering a specific career by providing students with valid and informative disadvantages of that career, this is appropriate and allowable. To the extent a speaker discourages students from entering a specific career by denigrating that career because of its nature or purpose of the career, the administrator of the program can ban such speech. Stated another way, accurate information about a career that some might take as criticism of the career or as discouragement of students from entering that career is permissible. On the contrary, exhortative and denigrative presentations by speakers for the purpose of denouncing certain careers for the purpose which they serve may properly be banned. We do not believe the parties or any persons in the future who seek to participate in career programs can misunderstand what is and is not permissible. We affirm the district court's rulings with respect to Regulations 10 and 11, given the interpretations herein made.

* * *

Affirmed as modified.

NOTES AND QUESTIONS

1. Outside Groups and the Limited Public Forum In *Widmar* and *Mergens* the issue was whether a school may deny access to some student groups when it grants access to others. No one contended that public schools were traditional public forums akin to parks and streets, that the schools were required to open the schools to all speakers. *See Perry Educ. Ass'n v. Perry Local Educators Ass'n*, 460 U.S. 37, 103 S.Ct. 948, 74 L.Ed.2d 794 (1983); *Grayned v. Rockford*, 408 U.S. 104, 92 S.Ct. 2294, 33 L.Ed.2d 222 (1972). From this perspective, those cases address the question of content or subject discrimination where the public school already has made a decision not to close the forum to all speakers and groups. *See, e.g., City of Madison Joint School District v. Wisconsin Public Employees Relations Commissions*, 429 U.S. 167, 97 S.Ct. 421, 50 L.Ed.2d

376 (1976); *Chicago Police Department v. Mosley*, 408 U.S. 92, 92 S.Ct. 2286, 33 L.Ed.2d 212 (1972). In this sense, the cases have as much to do with notions of equality as with speech and associational rights. *See generally* Karst, "Equality as a Central Principle in the First Amendment," 43 *U.Chi.L.Rev.* 20 (1975).

But it would be incorrect to view *Healy*, *Widmar*, and their progeny as involving only equality and content discrimination. First, the forum is restricted by the identity of the speaker. The opening of the forum to student groups does not mean that the forum must be opened to outsiders. *See Cornelius v. NAACP Legal Defense and Educational Fund*, 473 U.S. 788, 806, 105 S.Ct. 3439, 3451, 87 L.Ed.2d 567 (1985); *Perry Educ. Ass'n*, 460 U.S. at 41 n. 4, 103 S.Ct. at 952 n.4. In that sense the forum is limited to participants in the schooling enterprise, those who are bound up in the mission of public education. *See Texas State Teachers Association v. Garland Independent School District*, 777 F.2d 1046 (5th Cir. 1985); Yudof, *When Government Speaks* 225 (1983). Second, "there is no general acceptance of the proposition that the state's own communications efforts may allow outsiders to successfully invoke the public-forum doctrine; rather, a right of access by outsiders is granted only when other outsiders have been afforded such a right." Yudof, *supra* at 225–26, citing *Buckel v. Prentice*, 572 F.2d 141 (6th Cir. 1978). *But see Bonner-Lyons v. School Committee*, 480 F.2d 442 (1st Cir. 1973). Third, under *Tinker* students are entitled to express themselves on campus, subject to the substantial disruption rule, and the public schools apparently may not choose to close the school to such speech. *See Tinker v. Des Moines Independent School District*, 393 U.S. 503, 89 S.Ct. 733, 21 L.Ed.2d 731 (1969). In other words, the speech rights of the students follow them into the public school; there is no need to show that the school is a public forum or a limited public forum. *See generally* Farber & Nowak, "The Misleading Nature of the Public Forum Analysis: Content and Context in First Amendment Adjudication," 70 *Va.L.Rev.* 1219 (1984).

Is the notion of the public forum consistent with the state's mission of education and socialization in public schools? *See* Shiffrin, "Government Speech," 27 *U.C.L.A. L.Rev.* 565, 579 (1980). Are *Widmar* and *Tinker* inconsistent? Does *Hazelwood* undermine *Tinker?* Is *Mergens* consistent with *Hazelwood?* What is the justification for limiting *Widmar* and *Healy* to student groups? Why did Congress limit the Equal Access Act to student groups? If there is a sense that students "belong" on campus or that they do not lose all of their speech rights at the entrance of the school, does that suggest that public forum analysis is misleading? Is it that ". . . [t]he State, no less than a private owner of property, has power to preserve the property under its control for the use to which it is lawfully dedicated"? *Adderley v. Florida*, 385 U.S. 39, 47, 87 S.Ct. 242, 247, 17 L.Ed.2d 149 (1966). *See also Greer v. Spock*, 424 U.S. 828, 96 S.Ct. 1211, 47 L.Ed.2d 505 (1976). If a school may exclude all outsiders, such as civil rights and church organizations, from school premises, why can it not decide to exclude partisan student groups? Is content discrimination between student groups more pernicious than discrimination between inside and outside groups? *See generally* Stone, "Content Regulation and the First Amendment," 25 *Wm. & Mary L.Rev.* 189 (1983). Suppose that some ideologies have no significant student constituency within the school. Is not the closing of the school to outsiders tantamont to content discrimination?

Can a limited public forum be created by accident? *Cf. Mergens, supra*. Or must the government intend, by policy or practice, to open a traditionally closed forum to speakers and groups? *See Cornelius v. NAACP Legal Defense and Educational Fund*, 473 U.S. 788, 802, 105 S.Ct. 3439, 3449, 87 L.Ed.2d 567 (1985); *Planned Parenthood v. Clark County School District*, 887 F.2d 935, 940 (9th Cir. 1989); *Student Coalition for Peace v. Lower Merion School District Board*, 776 F.2d 431 (3rd Cir. 1985).

2. Searcey v. Harris: *Limited Public Forum or Nonpublic Forum?*

Searcey v. Harris is concerned with the circumstances in which an outside group has a constitutional right of access to public schools, an issue not addressed in the prior cases in this chapter. There is no doubt but that school authorities in Atlanta have chosen to allow outside organizations access to the schools for Youth Motivation Day and Career Day, and thus the claim that the forum is limited to students and teachers has been voluntarily abandoned. If this is the case, on what basis might the district court have held that Career Day is a nonpublic forum? Why did the Atlanta Peace Alliance not challenge this finding on appeal? Has Judge Clark conflated the terms "nonpublic" and "limited public" forums? Is there not a difference between a genuine nonpublic forum, for example a mathematics class, and Career Day? Consider these remarks by Judge Wallace in *Planned Parenthood v. Clark County School District*, 887 F.2d 935 (9th Cir. 1989):

> The Constitution does not require the government to open its property to all seeking an outlet for protected expression. . . . "[T]he Court [has] identified three types of fora: the traditional public forum, the public forum created by government designation, and the nonpublic forum." . . .
>
> Traditional public fora are "streets and parks which 'have immemorially been held in trust for the use of the public and, time out of mind, have been used for purposes of assembly, communicating thoughts between citizens, and discussing public questions.' " . . . Designated public fora are created when the government opens its property " 'for indiscriminate use by the general public,' or by some segment of the public." . . . The government may also designate a forum for a limited purpose such as use by certain speakers or the discussion of specific topics.

887 F.2d at 939–40. Has the *Searcey* court improperly characterized the nature of the forum? Is the reasonableness test appropriate for Career Day? Or is it that the concept of reasonableness now includes a ban on content discrimination? But does not the mathematics class discriminate by content? Is a student constitutionally entitled to discuss foreign policy in such a class?

Judge Clark argues that *Cornelius* and *Hazelwood* are consistent, that there is no difference between a reasonableness requirement for a nonpublic forum and the standard applied to *Spectrum* "that educators may exercise control over student expression in a curricular program if the restrictions are 'reasonably related to legitimate pedagogical concerns.' " Do you agree? *But see Planned Parenthood v. Clark County School District*, 887 F.2d 935 (9th Cir. 1989). Consider this reformulation of the Atlanta school board's position. Career Day and Youth Motivation Day are extensions of the regular curriculm and are designed to acquaint students with career opportunities and to motivate the students to pursue such careers. These purposes cannot easily be achieved by the faculty, and hence some outside speakers and groups are invited to the campus to facilitate this learning process. But the forum is limited. Thus, only those with direct knowledge of a career path and with a present affiliation with the field are invited. Individuals and organizations opposed to a particular career or not affiliated with an employing organization are not invited, for the purpose of the events is not to expose the students to a robust debate over military or other careers. The purpose is only to help students qualify for and find jobs and to motivate them to do so. In this sense, the school board has created a limited public forum, one that includes only certain identifiable speakers and one that excludes subjects or points of view antithetical to its purposes. The Atlanta Peace Alliance falls outside of the limited public forum designated by school authorities, for it is not affiliated with a field and its primary purpose is to criticize careers in the military.

If a public school may refuse to allow the Atlanta Peace Alliance to address a class on world history since 1945, why must it permit that organization to participate in Career Day? How does the pedagogical purpose change as the school admits outsiders into the learning process? Should it matter whether a teacher or an invited guest sings the praises of a military career? Consider these remarks from *Planned Parenthood v. Clark County School District*, *supra* at 941:

> If a school "need not tolerate student speech that is inconsistent with its 'basic educational mission' " . . . surely this must also be true for outside speech that is equally inconsistent. To fulfill its formidable responsibility of inculcating values to our youth, a school must be able to "disassociate itself" from certain types of speech.

Do you agree? *But see San Diego Committee Against Registration and the Draft (CARD) v. Governing Board of Grossmont Union High School District*, 790 F.2d 1471 (9th Cir. 1986) (decided prior to *Hazelwood*).

If, as the court holds, the school board's rules need only be reasonable, what is unreasonable about the limitations imposed by the board? Is it sufficient that, from the perspective of school administrators, the views of the Atlanta Peace Alliance might be "controversial" and that "the school district wished to steer clear of any distractions which could impede its educational mission"? *See Planned Parenthood v. Clark County School District*, *supra* at 946; *Student Coalition for Peace v. Lower Merion School District Board*, 776 F.2d 431 (3d Cir. 1985).

Is the court saying that a nonpublic forum must be viewpoint neutral? If so, does this destroy the idea of a public forum limited by subject matter? Does it undermine the socialization functions of public schools? Is it consistent with *Hazelwood?* Or is the court only saying that viewpoint discrimination within a designated subject is impermissible? What is the difference between discrimination based on content and discrimination based on veiwpoint?

Are the concepts of limited and nonpublic forums analytically helpful to the court? If Atlanta is free to define the forum as it sees fit, then, tautologically, it can keep various subjects and speakers away from the forum. But if there are constitutional constraints on defining the forum, then is it not more meaningful to frame the issue in terms of speech rights and not public forums? Or is the court only requiring that the limitations be consistently imposed on different groups and individuals? What is Atlanta's record on that score?

3. *Illicit Motivation in* Searcey

Is the court concerned that the board's rules, which appear to be neutral on their face, are really biased and designed to exclude the Atlanta Peace Alliance? That identity rules are a subterfuge for viewpoint discrimination? *Compare Searcey with Planned Parenthood v. Clark County School District*, 887 F.2d 935, 943–44 (9th Cir. 1989). Is that why the court places so much emphasis on past practices that departed from the current rule? On the "abrupt" nature of the rule change? On the point that those with prior affiliations may have as much information as those with present affiliations? What of the purpose of providing the students with role models?

What if the board simply had adopted a rule that only speakers from employing organizations may participate in Career Day? *See Clergy and Laity Concerned v. Chicago Board of Education*, 586 F.Supp. 1408 (N.D. Ill. 1984). May a university placement office limit its facility to those actively seeking employees? Need a law school placement office allow access to the facility by those who wish to persuade law students to pursue another career?

Would the result in *Searcey* be different if the Atlanta Peace Alliance were a religious group seeking to send a priest as a representative to Career Day? *See Clergy and Laity Concerned v. Chicago Board of Education, supra.*

4. *Rental of School Facilities*

The general rule appears to be that if a school or school district rents an auditorium or other facility to private groups, it may not deny access to any particular group on the basis of the content of the group's messages. *See, e.g., Knights of the KKK v. East Baton Rouge Parish School Board*, 578 F.2d 1122 (5th Cir. 1978); *National Socialist White People's Party v. Ringers*, 473 F.2d 1010 (4th Cir 1973); *Gregoire v. Centennial School District*, 674 F.Supp. 172 (E.D. Pa. 1987). Is there any merit to the argument that a school board ought to be able to create a limited public forum that excludes private groups espousing a message (for example, racial intolerance) flatly inconsistent with the school's message? May a district exclude private religious organizations from renting a facility, fearing an establishment of religion problem? *See Gregoire v. Centennial School District, supra.*

5. *Visitors to School Campuses*

Suppose a school board adopts a policy requiring all visitors to a public school to report directly to the principal's office. The principal, then has the authority to decide whether to permit the visitation, "keeping in mind the system's obligation is to the safety, welfare, and education of children." Is such a policy constitutional? *See Hall v. Board of School Commissioners of Mobile County*, 681 F.2d 965 (5th Cir. 1982). May a public university declare a former student *persona non grata* with respect to public areas of the campus? If so, under what circumstances? *See People v. Leonard*, 62 N.Y.2d 404, 477 N.Y.S.2d 111, 465 N.E.2d 831 (1984). May parents be excluded? *Cf. Commonwealth v. Ashcraft*, 691 S.W.2d 229 (Ky.App. 1985).

The courts have tended to treat commercial speech on campus as less deserving of constitutional protection than other forms of speech, albeit most of the cases involve access to student dormitories and other university facilities. The leading case is *Board of Trustees of State Univesity of New York v. Fox*, 492 U.S. 469, 109 S.Ct. 3028, 106 L.Ed.2d 388 (1989). In that case, American Future Systems, Inc. (AFS) sought to hold "Tupperware parties" in student dormitories in order to demonstrate and sell houseware products. The university excluded AFS under a rule prohibiting commercial enterprises from operating in campus facilities. The purposes of the rule were to promote "an educational rather than commercial atmosphere on [campus], [to promote] . . . safety and security, [to prevent] . . . commercial exploitation of students, and [to preserve] . . . residential tranquility." 109 S.Ct. at 3032. The plaintiffs asserted that the rule was more expansive than necessary to promote the state's interests, i.e., that it was not the "least-restrictive means" in terms of its impact on speech. The Court upheld the campus rule, reasoning that "our decisions require a 'fit' between the legislature's end and the means chosen to accomplish those ends . . .—a fit that is not necessarily perfect, but reasonable. . . ." 109 S.Ct. at 3035. *See also Chapman v. Thomas*, 743 F.2d 1056 (4th Cir. 1984).

Does the reasoning of *Fox* apply to public elementary and secondary schools? *See Rivers v. Campbell*, 791 F.2d 837 (11th Cir. 1986); *Katz v. McAulay*, 438 F.2d 1058 (2d Cir. 1971), *cert. denied*, 405 U.S. 933, 92 S.Ct. 930, 30 L.Ed.2d 809 (1972). Would the solicitation of donations for a political organization on campus be political or commercial speech? *See Glover v. Cole*, 762 F.2d 1197 (4th Cir. 1985). *See generally Heffron v. International Society for Krishna Consciousness*, 452 U.S. 640, 101 S.Ct. 2559, 69 L.Ed.2d 298 (1981); *Village of Schaumburg v. Citizens for a Better Environment*, 444 U.S. 620, 100 S.Ct. 826, 63 L.Ed.2d 73 (1980). May a public school ban any form of solicitation of students on campus? *See Katz v. McAulay, supra*.

3. Teacher Selection. To assure that the school's message is delivered clearly and without distortion (as well as to assure pedagogical competency), legislatures, school boards, and school officials have historically focused on appropriate criteria for the selection of teachers. While there are other ways to control the message of the school program, selection of teachers who can be trusted to carry out the job they were hired to carry out is one important method. As Justice Burton, speaking for the Supreme Court in *Beilan v. Board of Education*, 357 U.S. 399, 406, 78 S.Ct. 1317, 1322, 2 L.Ed.2d 1414 (1958), stated: "We find no requirement in the federal Constitution that a teacher's classroom conduct be the sole basis for determining his fitness. Fitness for teaching depends on a broad range of factors." These factors can include such matters as college degrees, test scores, teaching certificates, experience levels, pedagogical skills, and, more controversially, personal life styles, attitudes, and beliefs.

Should attitudes and beliefs be relevant to the employment decision? If so, how are they to be determined, and what constitutes an impermissible manifestation of objectionable attitudes and beliefs? *See generally* H. Beale, *Are American Teachers Free?* (1936). Are teachers charged with "teaching social order as a dogma or an article of faith, obfuscating the question of how much order is desirable"? Do they emphasize "docility, obedience, authority, inferiority of the lower classes, piety, and faith in providence"? C. Lindblom, *Inquiry and Change* 93 (1990). If so, is the government's purpose in screening teachers a legitimate one?

The following case explores these issues in the context of state-mandated teacher hiring restrictions on resident aliens.

Ambach v. Norwick

441 U.S. 68, 99 S.Ct. 1589, 60 L.Ed.2d 49 (1979).

Mr. Justice Powell delivered the opinion of the Court.

This case presents the question whether a State, consistently with the Equal Protection Clause of the Fourteenth Amendment, may refuse to employ as elementary and secondary school teachers aliens who are eligible for United States citizenship but who refuse to seek naturalization.

New York Education Law § 3001 (3) (McKinney 1970) forbids certification as a public school teacher of any person who is not a citizen of the United States, unless that person has manifested an intention to apply for citizenship.[1] The Commissioner of Education is authorized to create exemptions from

1. The statute provides:

"No person shall be employed or authorized to teach in the public schools of the state who is:

* * *

"3. Not a citizen. The provisions of this subdivision shall not apply, however, to an alien teacher now or hereafter employed, provided such teacher shall make due application to become a citizen and thereafter within the time prescribed by law shall become a citizen. The provisions of this subdivision shall not apply after July first, nineteen hundred sixty-seven, to an alien teacher employed pursuant to regulations adopted by the commissioner of education permitting such employment." N.Y. Educ. Law § 3001 (3) (McKinney 1970).

The statute contains an exception for persons who are ineligible for United States citizenship solely because of an oversubscribed quota. § 3001-a (McKinney 1970). Because this statutory provision is in all respects narrower than the exception provided by regulation, see n. 2, *infra*, as a practical matter it has no effect.

The State does not certify the qualifications of teachers in the private schools, although it does require that such teachers be "competent." N.Y. Educ. Law § 3204 (2) (McKinney Supp. 1978–1979). Accordingly, we are not presented with the question of, and express no view as to, the permissibility of a citizenship requirement pertaining to teachers in private schools.

this prohibition, and has done so with respect to aliens who are not yet eligible for citizenship.[2] Unless a teacher obtains certification, he may not work in a public elementary or secondary school in New York.[3]

Appellee Norwick was born in Scotland and is a subject of Great Britain. She has resided in this country since 1965 and is married to a United States citizen. Appellee Dachinger is a Finnish subject who came to this country in 1966 and also is married to a United States citizen. Both Norwick and Dachinger currently meet all of the educational requirements New York has set for certification as a public school teacher, but they consistently have refused to seek citizenship in spite of their eligibility to do so. Norwick applied in 1973 for a teaching certificate covering nursery school through sixth grade, and Dachinger sought a certificate covering the same grades in 1975. Both applications were denied because of appellee's failure to meet the requirements of § 3001 (3). Norwick then filed this suit seeking to enjoin the enforcement of § 3001 (3), and Dachinger obtained leave to intervene as a plaintiff.

* * *

The decisions of this Court regarding the permissibility of statutory classifications involving aliens have not formed an unwavering line over the years. State regulation of the employment of aliens long has been subject to constitutional constraints. In *Yick Wo v. Hopkins*, 118 U.S. 356 (1886), the Court struck down an ordinance which was applied to prevent aliens from running laundries, and in *Truax v. Raich*, 239 U.S. 33 (1915), a law requiring at least 80% of the employees of certain businesses to be citizens was held to be an unconstitutional infringement of an alien's "right to work for a living in the common occupations of the community. . . ." *Id.* at 41. At the same time, however, the Court also has recognized a greater degree of latitude for the States when aliens were sought to be excluded from public employment. At the time *Truax* was decided, the governing doctrine permitted States to exclude aliens from various activities when the restriction pertained to "the regulation or distribution of the public domain, or of the common property or resources of the people of the State. . . ." *Id.*, at 39. . . .

Over time, the Court's decisions gradually have restricted the activities from which States are free to exclude aliens. . . . This process of withdrawal from the former doctrine culminated in *Graham v. Richardson, supra,* which for the first time treated classifications based on alienage as "inherently suspect and subject to close judicial scrutiny." 403 U.S., at 372. Applying *Graham*, this Court has held invalid statutes that prevented aliens from entering a State's classified civil service, *Sugarman v. Dougall*, 413 U.S. 634 (1973), practicing law, *In re Griffiths*, 413 U.S. 717 (1973), working as an engineer, *Examining Board v. Flores de Otero*, 426 U.S. 572 (1976), and receiving state educational benefits, *Nyquist v. Mauclet*, 432 U.S. 1 (1977).

Although our more recent decisions have departed substantially from the public-interest doctrine of *Truax*'s day, they have not abandoned the general principle that some state functions are so bound up with the operation of the State as a governmental entity as to permit the exclusion from those functions of all persons who have not become part of the process of self-government. In *Sugarman*, we recognized that a State could, "in an appropriately defined class of positions, require citizenship as a qualification for office." We went on to observe:

> Such power inheres in the State by virtue of its obligation, already noted above, "to preserve the basic conception of a political community." . . . And this power and responsibility of the State applies, not only to the qualifications of voters, but also to persons holding state elective or important nonelective executive, legislative, and judicial positions, for officers who participate directly in the formulation, execution, or review of broad public policy perform functions that go to the heart of representative government."

413 U.S., at 647 (citation omitted). The exclusion of aliens from such governmental positions would not invite as demanding scrutiny from this Court. *Id.*, at 648. . . .

---

2. The following regulation governs here:

"*Citizenship.* A teacher who is not a citizen of the United States or who has not declared intention of becoming a citizen may be issued a provisional certificate providing such teacher has the appropriate educational qualifications as defined in the regulations and (1) possess skills or competencies not readily available among teachers holding citizenship, or (2) is unable to declare intention of becoming a citizen for valid statutory reasons." 8 N.Y.C.R.R. § 80.2(i) (1978).

3. Certification by the Commissioner of Education is not required of teachers at state institutions of higher education and the citizenship restriction accordingly does not apply to them. . . .

Applying the rational-basis standard, we held last Term that New York could exclude aliens from the ranks of its police force. *Foley v. Connelie*, 435 U.S. 291 (1978). Because the police function fulfilled "a most fundamental obligation of government to its constituency" and by necessity cloaked policemen with substantial discretionary powers, we viewed the police force as being one of those appropriately defined classes of positions for which a citizenship requirement could be imposed. *Id.*, at 297. Accordingly, the State was required to justify its classification only "by a showing of some rational relationship between the interest sought to be protected and the limiting classification." *Id.*, at 296.

The rule for governmental functions, which is an exception to the general standards applicable to classifications based on alienage, rests on important principles inherent in the Constitution. The distinction between citizens and aliens, though ordinarily irrelevant to private activity, is fundamental to the definition and government of a State. The Constitution itself refers to the distinction no less than 11 times, *see Sugarman v. Dougall, supra*, at 651–52 (Rehnquist, J., dissenting), indicating that the status of citizenship was meant to have significance in the structure of our government. The assumption of that status, whether by birth or naturalization, denotes an association with the policy which, in a democratic republic, exercises the powers of governance. *See Foley v. Connelie, supra*, at 295. The form of this association is important: an oath of allegiance or similar ceremony cannot substitute for the unequivocal legal bond citizenship represents. It is because of this special significance of citizenship that governmental entities, when exercising the functions of government, have wider latitude in limiting the participation of noncitizens.

In determining whether, for purposes of equal protection analysis, teaching in public schools constitutes a governmental function, we look to the role of public education and to the degree of responsibility and discretion teachers possess in fulfilling that role. *See Foley v. Connelie, supra*, at 297. Each of these considerations supports the conclusion that public school teachers may be regarded as performing a task "that go[es] to the heart of representative government." *Sugarman v. Dougall, supra*, at 647.[6]

Public education, like the police function, "fulfills a most fundamental obligation of government to its constituency." *Foley, supra*, at 297. The importance of public schools in the preparation of individuals for participation as citizens, and in the preservation of the values on which our society rests, long has been recognized by our decisions. . . .

* * *

. . . Other authorities have perceived public schools as an "assimilative force" by which diverse and conflicting elements in our society are brought together on a broad but common ground. *See, e.g.*, J. Dewey, *Democracy and Education* 26 (1929); N. Edwards & H. Richey, *The School in the American Social Order* 623–24 (2d ed. 1963). These perceptions of the public schools as inculcating fundamental values necessary to the maintenance of a democratic political system have been confirmed by the observations of social scientists. *See* R. Dawson & K. Prewitt, *Political Socialization* 146–67 (1969); R. Hess & J. Torney, *The Development of Political Attitudes in Children* 114, 158–71, 217–20 (1967); V. Key, *Public Opinion and American Democracy* 323–43 (1961).[8]

Within the public school system, teachers play a critical part in developing students' attitude toward

---

6. The dissenting opinion of Mr. Justice Blackmun, in reaching an opposite conclusion, appears to apply a different analysis from that employed in our prior decisions. Rather than consider whether public school teachers perform a significant government function, the inquiry mandated by *Foley v. Connelie*, 435 U.S. 291 (1978), and *Sugarman v. Dougall*, the dissent focuses instead on the general societal importance of primary and secondary school teachers both public and private. Thus, the dissent on the one hand depreciates the importance of New York's citizenship requirement because it is not applied to private school teachers, and on the other hand argues that the role teachers perform in our society is no more significant than that filled by attorneys. This misses the point of *Foley* and *Sugarman*. New York's citizenship requirement is limited to a governmental function because it applies only to teachers employed by and acting as agents of the State. The Connecticut statute held unconstitutional in *In Re Griffiths*, 413 U.S. 717 (1973), by contrast, applied to all attorneys, most of whom do not work for the government. The exclusion of aliens from access to the bar implicated the right to pursue a chosen occupation, not access to public employment. . . .

8. The curricular requirements of New York's public school system reflect some of the ways a public school system promotes the development of the understanding that is prerequisite to intelligent participation in the democratic process. The schools are required to provide instruction "to promote a spirit of patriotic and civic service and obligation and to foster in the children of the state moral and intellectual qualities which are essential in preparing to meet the obligations of citizenship in peace or in war. . . ." N.Y. Educ. Law § 801 (1) (McKinney, 1969). Flag and other patriotic exercises also are prescribed, as loyalty is a characteristic of citizenship essential to the preservation of a country. § 802 (McKinney 1969 and Supp. 1978–1979). In addition, required courses include classes in civics, United States and New York history, and principles of American government. §§ 3204 (3)(a)(1), (McKinney 1970).

Although private schools also are bound by most of these requirements, the State has a stronger interest in ensuring that the schools it most directly controls, and for which it bears the cost, are as effective as possible in teaching these courses.

government and understanding of the role of citizens in our society. Alone among employees of the system, teachers are in direct, day-to-day contact with students both in the classrooms and in the other varied activities of a modern school. In shaping the student's experience to achieve educational goals, teachers by necessity have wide discretion over the way the course material is communicated to students. They are responsible for presenting and explaining the subject matter in a way that is both comprehensible and inspiring. No amount of standardization of teaching materials or lesson plans can eliminate the personal qualities a teacher brings to bear in achieving these goals. Further, a teacher serves as a role model for his students, exerting a subtle but important influence over their perceptions and values. Thus, through both presentation of course materials and the example he sets, a teacher has an opportunity to influence the attitudes of students toward government, the political process, and a citizen's social responsibilities.[9] This influence is crucial to the continued good health of a democracy.[10]

Furthermore, it is clear that all public school teachers, and not just those responsible for teaching the courses most directly related to government, history, and civic duties, should help fulfill the broader function of the public school system. Teachers, regardless of their specialty, may be called upon to teach other subjects, including those expressly dedicated to political and social subjects. More importantly, a State property may regard all teachers as having an obligation to promote civic virtues and understanding in their classes, regardless of the subject taught. Certainly a State also may take account of a teacher's function as an example for students, which exists independently of particular classroom subjects. In light of the foregoing considerations, we think it clear that public school teachers come well within the "governmental function" principle recognized in *Sugarman* and *Foley*. Accordingly, the Constitution requires only that a citizenship requirement applicable to teaching in the public schools bear a rational relationship to a legitimate state interest. *See Massachusetts Board of Retirement v. Murgia*, 427 U.S. 307, 314 (1976).

As the legitimacy of the State's interest in furthering the educational goals outlined above is undoubted, it remains only to consider whether §3001 (3) bears a rational relationship to this interest. The restriction is carefully framed to serve its purpose, as it bars from teaching only those aliens who have demonstrated their unwillingness to obtain United States citizenship. Appellees, and aliens similarly situated, in effect have chosen to classify themselves. They prefer to retain citizenship in a foreign country with the obligations it entails of primary duty and loyalty.[14] They have rejected the open invitation extended to qualify for eligibility to teach by applying for citizenship in this country. The people of New York, acting through their elected representatives, have made a judgment that citizenship should be a qualification for teaching the young of the State in

---

9. Although the findings of scholars who have written on the subject are not conclusive, they generally reinforce the common-sense judgment, and the experience of most of us, that a teacher exerts considerable influence over the development of fundamental social attitudes in students, including those attitudes which in the broadest sense of the term may be viewed as political. *See, e.g.*, R. Dawson & K. Prewitt, *Political Socialization* 158–167 (1969); R. Hess & J. Torney, *The Development of Political Attitudes in Children* 162–163, 217–218 (1967). *Cf.* Note, "Aliens' Right to Teach: Political Socialization and the Public Schools," 85 *Yale L.J.* 90, 99–104 (1975).

10. Appellees contend that restriction of an alien's freedom to teach in public schools is contrary to principles of diversity of thought and academic freedom embodied in the First Amendment. *See also id.*, at 106–109. We think that the attempt to draw an analogy between choice of citizenship and political expression or freedom of association is wide of the mark, as the argument would bar any effort by the State to promote particular values and attitudes toward government. Section 3001 (3) does not inhibit appellees from expressing freely their political or social views or from associating with whomever they please. *Cf. Givhan v. Western Line Consol. School Dist.*, 439 U.S. 410, 415–416 (1979); *Mt. Healthy City Board of Education v. Doyle*, 429 U.S. 274 (1977); *Pickering v. Board of Education*, 391 U.S. 563 (1968). Nor are appellees discouraged from joining with others to advance particular political ends. *Cf. Shelton v. Tucker*, 364 U.S. 479 (1960). The only asserted liberty of appellees withheld by the New York statute is the opportunity to teach in the State's schools so long as they elect not to become citizens of this country. This is not a liberty that is accorded constitutional protection.

14. As our cases have emphasized, resident aliens pay taxes, serve in the Armed Forces, and have made significant contributions to our country in private and public endeavors. *See In re Griffiths*, 413 U.S., at 722; *Sugarman v. Dougall*, 413 U.S., at 645; *Graham v. Richardson*, 403 U.S. 365, 376 (1971). No doubt many of them, and we do not exclude appellees, would make excellent public school teachers. But the legislature, having in mind the importance of education to state and local governments, *see Brown v. Board of Education*, 347 U.S. 483, 493 (1954), may determine eligibility for the key position in discharging that function on the assumption that *generally* persons who are citizens, or who have not declined the opportunity seek United States citizenship, are better qualified than are those who have elected to remain aliens. We note in this connection that regulations promulgated pursuant to § 3001 (3) do provide for situations where a particular alien's special qualifications as a teacher outweigh the policy primarily served by the statute. *See* 8 N.Y.C.R.R. § 80.2(i) (1) (1978). The appellants inform us, however, that the authority conferred by this regulation has not been exercised. . . .

the public schools, and §3001 (3) furthers that judgment.[15]

Reversed.

Mr. Justice Blackmun, with whom Mr. Justice Brennan, Mr. Justice Marshall, and Mr. Justice Stevens join, dissenting. . . .

As the Court acknowledges, . . . its decisions regarding the permissibility of statutory classifications concerning aliens "have not formed an unwavering line over the years." Thus, just last Term, in *Foley v. Connelie*, 435 U.S. 291 (1978), the Court upheld against equal protection challenge the New York statute limiting appointment of members of the state police force to citizens of the United States. . . .

On the other hand, the Court frequently has invalidated a state provision that denies a resident alien the right to engage in specified occupational activity: . . . *Sugarman v. Dougall*, *supra*, (New York statute relating to permanent positions in the "competitive class" of the state civil service); *In re Griffiths*, 413 U.S. 717 (1973) (the practice of law). . . .

Indeed, the Court has held more than once that state classifications based on alienage are "inherently suspect and subject to close judicial scrutiny." *Graham v. Richardson*, 403 U.S. 365, 372 (1971). . . .

There is thus a line, most recently recognized in *Foley v. Connelie*, between those employments that a State in its wisdom constitutionally may restrict to United States citizens, on the one hand, and those employments, on the other, that the State may not deny to resident aliens. For me, the present case falls on the *Sugarman-Griffiths-Flores de Otero-Mauclet* side of that line, rather than on the narrowly isolated *Foley* side.

We are concerned here with elementary and secondary education in the public schools of New York State. We are not concerned with teaching at the college or graduate levels. It seems constitutionally absurd, to say the least, that in these lower levels of public education a Frenchman may not teach French or, indeed, an Englishwoman may not teach the grammar of the English language. The appellees, to be sure, are resident "aliens" in the technical sense, but there is not a word in the record that either appellee does not have roots in this country or is unqualified in any way, other than the imposed requirement of citizenship, to teach. Both appellee Norwick and appellee Dachinger have been in this country for over 12 years. Each is married to a United States citizen. Each currently meets all the requirements, other than citizenship, that New York has specified for certification as a public school teacher.[4] Each is willing, if required, to subscribe to an oath to support the Constitutions of the United States and of New York. Each lives in an American community, must obey its laws, and must pay all of the taxes citizens are obligated to pay. Appellees, however, have hesitated to give up their respective British and Finnish citizenships, just as lawyer Fre Le Poole Griffiths, the subject of *In re Griffiths*, *supra*, hesitated to renounce her Netherlands citizenship, although married to a citizen of the United States and a resident of Connecticut. . . . [T]he Court holds that New York's citizenship requirement is constitutional because it bears a rational relationship to the State's interest in furthering these educational goals.

I perceive a number of difficulties along the easy road the Court takes to this conclusion:

First, the New York statutory structure itself refutes the argument. Section 3001 (3), the very statute at issue here, provides for exceptions with respect to alien teachers "employed pursuant to regulations adopted by the commissioner of education permitting such employment." Section 3001-a (McKinney 1970) provides another exception for persons ineligible for United States citizenship because of oversubscribed quotas. Also, New York is unconcerned with any citizenship qualification for teachers in the private schools of the State, even though the record

15. Appellees argue that the State cannot rationally exclude aliens from teaching positions and yet permit them to vote for and sit on certain local school boards. We note, first, that the State's legislature has not expressly endorsed this policy. Rather, appellants as an administrative matter have interpreted the statute governing New York City's unique community school boards, N.Y. Educ. Law § 2590-c (4) (McKinney Supp. 1978–1979), to permit aliens who are the parents of public school students to participate in these boards. *See* App. 27, 29. We also may assume, without having to decide, that there is a rational basis for a distinction between teachers and board members based on their respective responsibilities. Although possessing substantial responsibility for the administration of the schools, board members teach no classes, and rarely if ever are known or identified by the students.

4. Appellee Norwick is a *summa cum laude* graduate of a Massachusetts college and received an A average in full-time graduate work in the State University of New York at Albany. She has taught both in this country and in Great Britain.

Appellee Dachinger is a *cum laude* graduate, with a major in German, of Lehman College, a unit of the City University of New York, and possesses a master's degree in Early Childhood Education from that institution. She has taught at a day-care center in the Bronx.

Each appellee thus has received and excelled in educational training the State of New York itself offers.

indicates that about 18% of the pupils at the elementary and secondary levels attend private schools. The education of those pupils seems not to be inculcated with something less than what is desirable for citizenship and what the Court calls an influence "crucial to the continued good health of a democracy." . . . The State apparently, under §3001 (3), would not hesitate to employ an alien teacher while he waits to attain citizenship, even though he may fail ever to attain it.

Second, the New York statute is all-inclusive in its disqualifying provisions: "No person shall be employed or authorized to teach in the public schools of the state who is . . . [n]ot a citizen." It sweeps indiscriminately. It is "neither narrowly confined nor precise in its application," nor limited to the accomplishment of substantial state interests. *Sugarman v. Dougall*, 413 U.S., at 643. *See* Note, "Alien's Right to Teach: Political Socialization and the Public Schools," 85 *Yale L. J.* 90, 109–11 (1975).

Third, the New York classification is irrational. Is it better to employ a poor citizen teacher than an excellent resident alien teacher? Is it preferable to have a citizen who has never seen Spain or a Latin American country teach Spanish to eighth graders and to deny that opportunity to a resident alien who may have lived for 20 years in the culture of Spain or Latin America? The state will know how to select its teachers responsibly, wholly apart from citizenship, and can do so selectively and intelligently. That is the way to accomplish the desired result. An artificial citizenship bar is not a rational way. It is, instead, a stultifying provision. The route to "diverse and conflicting elements" and their being "brought together on a broad but common ground," which the Court so emphasizes, . . . is hardly to be achieved by disregarding some of the diverse elements that are available, competent, and contributory to the richness of our society and of the education it could provide.

Fourth, it is logically impossible to differentiate between this case concerning teachers and *In re Griffiths* concerning attorneys. If a resident alien *may not* constitutionally be barred from taking a state bar examination and thereby becoming qualified to practice law in the courts of a State, how is one to comprehend why a resident alien *may* constitutionally be barred from teaching in the elementary and secondary levels of a State's public schools? . . .

NOTES AND QUESTIONS

1. *Standard of Review*

As discussed more fully in chapter 5, the Court adopts a stricter standard of review than the rational-basis test if the state has employed a classification scheme that employs a "suspect classification," for example, race or religion. The Court has said that when a class of people has been saddled with political and social disabilities and subjected to a history of purposefully unequal treatment, statutes directed "against [such] discrete and insular minorities may be a special condition, which tends seriously to curtail the operation of those political processes ordinarily to be relied upon to protect minorities, and . . . [thus] may call for a correspondingly more searching judicial inquiry." *United States v. Carolene Products, Co.*, 304 U.S. 144, 152 n. 4, 58 S.Ct. 778, 783 n. 4, 82 L.Ed. 1234 (1938).

Do you agree with the Court's decision in *Graham v. Richardson*, 403 U.S. 365, 91 S.Ct. 1848, 29 L.Ed.2d 534 (1971) (cited in *Ambach*), treating classifications based on alienage as inherently suspect? *See also Bernal v. Fainter*, 467 U.S. 216, 104 S.Ct. 2312, 81 L.Ed.2d 175 (1984). Are the reasons for treating alienage as a suspect classification less salient when alienage has been used in conjunction with defining eligibility for public employment? Was the majority correct in not relying upon the strict standard of review in this case? If the majority had adhered to *Graham*, would the result in the case have been different? Is it appropriate to make the character of the classification dependent on the nature of the benefit or privilege that is denied? For example, may a state bar resident aliens from receiving state scholorships awards? *See Nyquist v. Mauclet*, 432 U.S. 1, 97 S.Ct. 2120, 53 L.Ed.2d 63 (1977).

2. *Protective Labor Legislation?*

The majority opinion and the dissent both accept the proposition that the challenged statute is designed to assure that the state's legitimate educational objectives are not frustrated by teachers who are unwilling or unable to achieve those objectives. Is this the sole or primary purpose of the law? Consider the regulation issued by the Commissioner of Education, set forth in note 2 of the opinion. Why does the law permit aliens to be hired when they "possess skills or competencies not readily available among teachers holding citizenship"? What does the availability of citizens as employees have to do with the reliability of aliens as teachers? Is this law best explained as designed to assure priority in the hiring of citizens? If so, should the Court still have ruled that the statute is constitutional? How would you distinguish *Sugarman v. Dougall*, 93 S.Ct. 2842, 37 L.Ed.2d 853, 413 U.S. 634, (1973) (discussed in *Ambach*)?

3. *Narrowing the State's Interest*

Do the majority and dissent quarrel over the teacher's socialization function, or only over whether the New York law is rational in the way it serves that purpose? *See Board of Education v. Pico*, 457 U.S. 853, 102 S.Ct. 2799, 73 L.Ed.2d 435 (1982). Is Justice Blackmun really arguing that the law is "irrational," or is he asserting that a statute could be more narrowly drawn so as to promote the socialization function without unnecessarily impinging on the ability of aliens to secure employment as public schoolteachers? Does Justice Blackmun oppose any form of exclusion of aliens? Would he accept a more narrowly drawn statute, excluding aliens from teaching only specific subjects or requiring them to sign a loyalty oath or to demonstrate their knowledge of American politics and culture? *See* T. van Geel, *The Courts and American Education Law* 216 (1987).

Why does the majority reject the dissent's argument? Might Justice Powell be concerned with federal judicial intervention in the teacher hiring process? Might he fear that adoption of the minority view could lead to other such judicial forays? How real is this fear?

4. *Political Status and the Socialization Function*

Is the status of being an alien who is eligible to apply for citizenship, but who has not done so, an adequate predictor of what that person will say and do in the classroom? Why are such people not to be trusted to follow the prescribed curriculum? Is it that they lack roots in the polity and hence the necessary knowledge? Might it plausibly be argued that not all aliens are to be distrusted on these grounds and not all citizens are to be trusted? Why cannot the state protect itself by taking action against teachers only after they have taught in such a way as to undermine the state's interest in promoting American values? Or is such an approach too risky for the state? Does it impinge upon the rights of *all* teachers since constant surveillance of teaching behavior would be required? Do schools routinely do this? If not, does this weaken or strengthen the government's case in *Ambach*?

5. *Effectiveness of Teacher Socialization*

In note 9, the majority cites social science research for the proposition that teachers have "considerable influence" on the attitudes of students. *See also* Janowitz, *The Reconstruction of Patriotism* (1983). Other research has cast some doubt on the importance of formal schooling for the development of political attitudes. *See, e.g.*, M. Jennings, and R. G. Niemi, *The Political Character of Adolescence*, 217–21 (1974). If the second body of research is correct, does this undermine the majority's argument? Should the case turn on the weight of the social science evidence or on "common-sense judgment[s]"?

6. *The Legitimacy of the State's Purpose*

The alien teachers who brought the suit argued that the New York law sought "to suppress respect for adversity and to compel standardization of ideas." Brief for Appellee at 64, *Ambach v. Norwick*. They argued that the Constitution does not tolerate "laws that cast a pall of orthodoxy over the classroom." *Keyishian v. Board of Regents*, 385 U.S. 589, 603, 87 S.Ct. 675, 684, 17 L.Ed.2d 629 (1967). *See also Board of Education v. Pico*, 457 U.S. 853, 102 S.Ct. 2799, 73 L.Ed.2d 435 (1982). They also argued that the failure to initiate naturalization is not necessarily a sign of disloyalty to the nation, and aliens may bring to the classroom different perspectives that will benefit the students. In short, they were challenging the governmental purpose of attempting to recruit a group of teachers whose job it would be to voice a set of values and to socialize youngsters in that particular set of values. *See generally* R. Battistoni, *Public Schooling and the Education of Democratic Citizens* (1985); van Geel, "The Search for Constitutional Limits on Government Authority to Inculcate Youth," 62 *Tex.L.Rev.* 197 (1983). Professor Lindblom has gone so far as to urge that teachers close the minds of students to criticism and inquiry, that their job, whether conscious or not, is to use "the school as an instrument for shutting down rather than holding a competition of ideas." C. Lindblom, *Inquiry and Change* 93 (1990). If Lindblom and the others are correct, has the court missed an opportunity to correct the situation? Are you persuaded by Justice Powell's response, in note 10 of the opinion, that the New York law does not inhibit the plaintiffs from expressing freely their political or social views or from associating with whomever they please? Did the dissent more adequately deal with this challenge? *See* Yudof, *When Government Speaks* 220–24 (1983); Gottlieb, "*In the Name of Patriotism*: The Constitutionality of 'Bending' History in Public Secondary Schools," 62 *N.Y.U. L. Rev.* 497 (1987). *See generally* C. Lindblom, *Inquiry and Change* (1990).

7. Teacher Loyalty

The majority's opinion in *Ambach* is surprising, when seen against the background of the Court's treatment of the attempts of states to exclude subversives from the teaching profession. Communists have received considerable protection from the Court, raising the question whether aliens are more dangerous than Communists in the view of the Court. The story begins with *Adler v. Board of Education*, 342 U.S. 485, 72 S.Ct. 380, 96 L.Ed. 517 (1952), which upheld a provision of the New York Civil Service Law disqualifying from the civil service and public school system any person who "advocates, advises or teaches" governmental overthrow by force or violence or who organizes or joins any group advocating such doctrine.

In the years following *Adler*, the Court's attitude toward screening out ideologically unfit teachers changed. *Cf. Sweezy v. New Hampshire*, 354 U.S. 234, 77 S.Ct. 1203, 1 L.Ed.2d 1311 (1957); *Slochower v. Board of Higher Education*, 350 U.S. 551, 76 S.Ct. 637, 100 L.Ed. 692 (1956). *Cramp v. Board of Public Instruction*, 368 U.S. 278, 82 S.Ct. 275, 7 L.Ed.2d 285 (1961), involved a Florida statute requiring public employees to swear they had never "knowingly lent their aid, support, advice, counsel or influence to the Communist Party." 368 U.S. at 285, 82 S.Ct. at 279. A refusal to take the oath meant immediate discharge. The majority, in striking down the oath requirement, stressed its "extraordinary ambiguity" and found it "completely lacking [in] terms susceptible of objective measurement." 368 U.S. at 286, 82 S.Ct. at 280. Vagueness was also the flaw in the loyalty oath requirements in *Baggett v. Bullitt*, 377 U.S. 360, 84 S.Ct. 1316, 12 L.Ed.2d 377 (1964). *Elfbrandt v. Russell*, 384 U.S. 11, 86 S.Ct. 1238, 16 L.Ed.2d 321 (1966), involved a requirement that state employees swear to support the Constitution, the laws of Arizona, and to defend them against all enemies. Anyone taking the oath who knowingly and willingly became or remained a member of the Communist Party or other organization with a purpose of overthrowing the government was subject to prosecution for perjury and to discharge. The latter provision was declared unconstitutional because it permitted the discharge of those who did not join the subversive organization with the "specific intent" to further illegal action.

In *Keyishian v. Board of Regents*, 385 U.S. 589, 87 S.Ct. 675, 17 L.Ed.2d 629 (1967), faculty members of the State University refused to sign a certificate that required them to declare that they were not Communists, or that if they had been Communists, they had communicated that fact to the President of the State University of New York. Dismissed faculty members challenged a series of related laws that disqualified people from governmental employment for utterance of seditious words, for active or inactive membership in the Communist Party, or for advocating or teaching the doctrine of the forceful overthrow of government. All these provisions were struck down for being overbroad because they imposed sanctions for active or inactive membership unaccompanied by proof of a specific intent to further the unlawful goals of the organization.

In *Connell v. Higgenbotham*, 403 U.S. 207, 91 S.Ct. 1772, 29 L.Ed.2d 418 (1971), the Court upheld an affirmative oath—"That I will support the Constitution of the United States and of the State of Florida." It invalidated a disclaimer oath—"that I do not believe in the overthrow of the Government of the United States or of the State of Florida by force or violence." In *Cole v. Richardson*, 405 U.S. 676, 92 S.Ct. 1332, 31 L.Ed.2d 593 (1972), the Court by a four to three vote upheld a two-part loyalty oath required of Massachusetts public employees. The first part required a promise to "uphold and defend" the federal and state constitutions; the second part required a promise to "oppose the overthrow of the government of the United States of America or of this Commonwealth by force, violence or by any illegal or unconstitutional method." Chief Justice Burger found the first part of the oath indistinguishable from the traditionally valid "support" oath. 405 U.S. at 682–83, 92 S.Ct. at 1336–37. As for the second part, the Chief Justice said it did not "require specific action in some hypothetical or actual situation." As he interpreted the "oppose" clause, "it is a commitment not to use illegal and constitutionally unprotected force to change the constitutional system. [It] does not expand the obligation of the first; it simply makes clear the application of the first clause to a particular issue . . . . That the second clause may be redundant is not ground to strike it down; we are not charged with correcting grammar but with enforcing a constitution." 405 U.S. at 684. For discussions of the Court's treatment of academic freedom in the loyalty cases, *see* T. Emerson, *The System of Freedom of Expression* 600–04, 616 (1970); Byrne, "Academic Freedom: A 'Special Concern of the First Amendment,' " 99 *Yale L. J.* 251, 289–98 (1989); Goldstein, "The Asserted Constitutional Right of Public School Teachers to Determine What They Teach," 124 *U.Pa.L.Rev.* 1293, 1295–98 (1976). Why does not *West Virginia State Board of Education v. Barnette,* 319 U.S. 624, 63 S.Ct. 1178, 87 L.Ed. 1628 (1943), render all loyalty oaths unconstitutional?

8. Freedom of Association

In *Shelton v. Tucker,* 364 U.S. 479, 81 S.Ct. 247, 5 L.Ed.2d 231 (1960), plaintiff, a public schoolteacher in the Little Rock Schools for twenty-five years, was a member of the national Association for the Advancement of Colored People. He was dismissed from employment when he refused to comply with the requirements of a state law that he file "annually an affidavit listing without limitation every organization to which he has belonged or regularly contributed within the preceding five years." 364 U.S. at 480, 81 S.Ct. at 248. The statute was adopted "to assist in the solution" of problems raised by the Supreme Court's decisions in school desegregation cases. In striking down the provision, Justice Stewart notes that a state may inquire into the fitness and competence of its teachers. Yet to compel a teacher to disclose his every associational tie would undermine his right of free association. "Even if there were no disclosure to the general public, the pressure upon a teacher to avoid any ties which might displease those who control his professional destiny would be constant and heavy. . . ." 364 U.S. at 485–86, 81 S.Ct. at 250–51. Under the circumstances, the Court held that the statute should be tested against the requirement that government use the least drastic means for achieving its purposes and that the unlimited and indiscriminate sweep of the statute went far beyond what might be justified in the exercise of the state's legitimate inquiry into the fitness and competency of its teachers. 364 U.S. at 488, 490, 81 S.Ct. at 252, 253. *See* Byrne, *supra* at 293–98.

Teachers and other public employees also are protected from dismissal for the sole reason of their affiliation with a particular party or candidate for public office. *Branti v. Finkel,* 445 U.S. 507, 100 S.Ct. 1287, 63 L.Ed.2d 574 (1980); *Elrod v. Burns,* 427 U.S. 347, 96 S.Ct. 2673, 49 L.Ed.2d 547 (1976); *Kercado-Melendez v. Aponte-Roque,* 829 F.2d 255 (1st Cir. 1987). How do the freedom of association and party affiliation cases alter the government's ability to socialize youngsters to particular norms? Do they suggest that the state may not seek to recruit a homogenous faculty for its public schools? If so, is *Ambach* inconsistent with these cases?

4. Teacher Rights of Expression.

Pickering v. Board of Education

391 U.S. 563, 88 S.Ct. 1731, 20 L.Ed.2d 811 (1968).

Mr. Justice Marshall delivered the opinion of the Court.

Appellant Marvin L. Pickering, a teacher in Township High School District 205, Will County, Illinois, was dismissed from his position by the appellee Board of Education for sending a letter to a local newspaper in connection with a recently proposed tax increase that was critical of the way in which the Board and the district superintendent of schools had handled past proposals to raise new revenue for the schools. Appellant's dismissal resulted from a determination by the Board, after a full hearing, that the publication of the letter was "detrimental to the efficient operation and administration of the schools of the district" and hence, under the relevant Illinois statute, Ill. Rev. Stat., c. 122, § 10-22.4 (1963), that "interests of the schools require[d] [his dismissal]."

* * *

In May of 1964 a proposed increase in the tax rate to be used for educational purposes was submitted to the voters by the Board and was defeated. Finally, on September 19, 1964, a second proposal to increase the tax rate was submitted by the Board and was likewise defeated. It was in connection with this last proposal of the School Board that appellant wrote the letter to the editor . . . that resulted in his dismissal.

Prior to the vote on the second tax increase proposal a variety of articles attributed to the District 205 Teachers' Organization appeared in the local paper. These articles urged passage of the tax increase and stated that failure to pass the increase would result in a decline in the quality of education afforded children in the district's schools. A letter from the superintendent of schools making the same point was published in the paper two days before the election and submitted to the voters in mimeographed form the following day. It was in response to the foregoing material, together with the failure of the tax increase to pass, that appellant submitted the letter in question to the editor of the local paper.

The letter constituted, basically, an attack on the School Board's handling of the 1961 bond issue proposals and its subsequent allocation of financial resources between the schools' educational and athletic programs. It also charged the superintendent of schools with attempting to prevent teachers in the district from opposing or criticizing the proposed bond issue.

The Board dismissed Pickering for writing and publishing the letter. Pursuant to Illinois law, the Board was then required to hold a hearing on the dismissal. At the hearing the Board charged that numerous statements in the letter were false and that the publication of the statements unjustifiably impugned the "motives, honesty, integrity, truthfulness, responsibility and competence" of both the Board and the school administration. The Board also charged that the false statements damaged the professional reputations of its members and of the school administrators, would be disruptive of faculty discipline, and would tend to foment "controversy, conflict, and dissension" among teachers, administrators, the Board of Education, and the residents of the district. . . .

The Illinois courts reviewed the proceedings solely to determine whether the Board's findings were supported by substantial evidence and whether, on the facts as found, the Board could reasonably conclude that appellant's publication of the letter was "detrimental to the best interests of the schools." Pickering's claim that his letter was protected by the First Amendment was rejected on the ground that his acceptance of a teaching position in the public schools obliged him to refrain from making statements about the operation of the schools "which in the absence of such position he would have an undoubted right to engage in." . . .

To the extent that the Illinois Supreme Court's opinion may be read to suggest that teachers may constitutionally be compelled to relinquish the First Amendment rights they would otherwise enjoy as citizens to comment on matters of public interest in connection with the operation of the public schools in which they work, it proceeds on the premise that has been unequivocally rejected in numerous prior decisions of this Court. *E.g.*, *Wieman v. Updegraff*, 344 U.S. 183 (1952); *Shelton v. Tucker*, 364 U.S. 479 (1960); *Keyishian v. Board of Regents*, 385 U.S. 589 (1967). "[T]he theory that public employment which may be denied altogether may be subjected to any conditions, regardless of how unreasonable, has been uniformly rejected." *Keyishian v. Board of Regents, supra*, at 605–06. At the same time it cannot be gainsaid that the State has interests as an employer in regulating the speech of its employees that differ significantly from those it possesses in connection with regulation of the speech of the citizenry in general. The problem in any case is to arrive at a balance between the interests of the teacher, as a citizen, in commenting upon matters of public concern and the interest of the State, as an employer, in promoting the efficiency of the public services it performs through its employees.

The Board contends that "the teacher by virtue of his public employment has a duty of loyalty to support his superiors in attaining the generally accepted goals of education and that, if he must speak out publicly, he should do so factually and accurately, commensurate with his education and experience." Appellant, on the other hand, argues that the test applicable to defamatory statements directed against public officials by persons having no occupational relationship with them, namely, that statements to be legally actionable must be made "with knowledge that [they were] . . . false or with reckless disregard of whether [they were] . . . false or not," *New York Times Co. v. Sullivan*, 376 U.S. 254, 280 (1964), should also be applied to public statements made by teachers. . . .

An examination of the statements in appellant's letter objected to by the Board reveals that they, like the letter as a whole, consist essentially of criticism of the Board's allocation of school funds between educational and athletic programs, and of both the

Board's and the superintendent's methods of informing, or preventing the informing of, the district's taxpayers of the real reasons why additional tax revenues were being sought for the schools. The statements are in no way directed toward any person with whom appellant would normally be in contact in the course of his daily work as a teacher. Thus no question of maintaining either discipline by immediate superiors or harmony among coworkers is presented here. Appellant's employment relationships with the Board and, to a somewhat lesser extent, with the superintendent are not the kind of close working relationships for which it can persuasively be claimed that personal loyalty and confidence are necessary to their proper functioning. Accordingly, to the extent that the Board's position here can be taken to suggest that even comments on matters of public concern that are substantially correct, . . . may furnish grounds for dismissal if they are sufficiently critical in tone, we unequivocally reject it.[3]

We next consider the statements in appellant's letter which we agree to be false. The Board's original charges included allegations that the publication of the letter damaged the professional reputations of the Board and the superintendent and would foment controversy and conflict among the Board, teachers, administrators, and the residents of the district. However, no evidence to support these allegations was introduced at the hearing. So far as the record reveals, Pickering's letter was greeted by everyone but its main target, the Board, with massive apathy and total disbelief. The Board must, therefore, have decided, perhaps by analogy with the law of libel, that the statements were *per se* harmful to the operation of the schools.

However, the only way in which the Board could conclude, absent any evidence of the actual effect of the letter, that the statements contained therein were *per se* detrimental to the interest of the schools was to equate the Board members' own interests with that of the schools. Certainly an accusation that too much money is being spent on athletics by the administrators of the school system . . . cannot reasonably be regarded as *per se* detrimental to the district schools . . . .

In addition, the fact that particular illustrations of the Board's claimed undesirable emphasis on athletic programs are false would not normally have any necessary impact on the actual operation of the schools, beyond its tendency to anger the Board. For example, Pickering's letter was written after the defeat at the polls of the second proposed tax increase. It could, therefore, have had no effect on the ability of the school district to raise necessary revenue, since there was no showing that there was any proposal to increase taxes pending when the letter was written.

More importantly, the question whether a school system requires additional funds is a matter of legitimate public concern on which the judgment of the school administration, including the School Board, cannot, in a society that leaves such questions to popular vote, be taken as conclusive. On such a question free and open debate is vital to informed decisionmaking by the electorate. Teachers are, as a class, the members of a community most likely to have informed and definite opinions as to how funds allotted to the operation of the schools should be spent. Accordingly, it is essential that they be able to speak out freely on such questions without fear of retaliatory dismissal.

In addition, the amounts expended on athletics which Pickering reported erroneously were matters of public record on which his position as a teacher in the district did not qualify him to speak with any greater authority than any other taxpayer. The Board could easily have rebutted appellant's errors by publishing the accurate figures itself, either via a letter to the same newspaper or otherwise. We are thus not presented with a situation in which a teacher has carelessly made false statements about matters so closely related to the day-to-day operations of the schools that any harmful impact on the public would be difficult to counter because of the teacher's presumed greater access to the real facts. Accordingly, we have no occasion to consider at this time whether under such circumstances a school board could rea-

---

3. It is possible to conceive of some positions in public employment in which the need for confidentiality is so great that even completely correct public statements might furnish a permissible ground for dismissal. Likewise, positions in public employment in which the relationship between superior and subordinate is of such a personal and intimate nature that certain forms of public criticism of the superior by the subordinate would seriously undermine the effectiveness of the working relationship between them can also be imagined. We intimate no views as to how we would resolve any specific instances of such situations, but merely note that significantly different considerations would be involved in such cases.

sonably require that a teacher make substantial efforts to verify the accuracy of his charges before publishing them.[4]

What we do have before us is a case in which a teacher has made erroneous public statements upon issues then currently the subject of public attention, which are critical of his ultimate employer but which are neither shown nor can be presumed to have in any way either impeded the teacher's proper performance of his daily duties in the classroom[5] or to have interfered with the regular operation of the schools generally. In these circumstances we conclude that the interest of the school administration in limiting teachers' opportunities to contribute to public debate is not significantly greater than its interest in limiting a similar contribution by any member of the general public.

* * *

In sum, we hold that, in a case such as this, absent proof or false statements knowingly or recklessly made by him,[6] a teacher's exercise of his right to speak on issues of public importance may not furnish the basis for his dismissal from public employment. Since no such showing has been made in this case regarding appellant's letter . . . his dismissal for writing it cannot be upheld and the judgment of the Illinois Supreme Court must, accordingly, be reversed and the case remanded for further proceedings not inconsistent with this opinion.

Mr. Justice White, concurring in part and dissenting in part.

The Court holds that truthful statements by a school teacher critical of the school board are within the ambit of the First Amendment. So also are false statements innocently or negligently made. The State may not fire the teacher for making either unless, as I gather it, there are special circumstances, not present in this case, demonstrating an overriding state interest, such as the need for confidentiality or the special obligations which a teacher in a particular position may owe to his superiors.[1]

The core of today's decision is the holding that Pickering's discharge must be tested by the standard of *New York Times Co. v. Sullivan*, 376 U.S. 254 (1964). To this extent I am in agreement.

The Court goes on, however, to reopen a question I had thought settled by *New York Times* and the cases that followed it, particularly *Garrison v. Louisiana*, 379 U.S. 64 (1964). The Court devotes several pages to reexamining the facts in order to reject the determination below that Pickering's statements harmed the school system, *ante*, at 570–73, when the question of harm is clearly irrelevant given the Court's determination that Pickering's statements were neither knowingly nor recklessly false and its ruling that in such circumstances a teacher may not be fired even if the statements are injurious. The Court then gratuitously suggests that when statements are found to be knowingly or recklessly false, it is an open question whether the First Amendment still protects them unless they are shown or can be presumed to have caused harm. *Ante*, at 574, n. 6. Deliberate or reckless falsehoods serve no First Amendment ends and deserve no protection under that Amendment. The Court unequivocally recognized this in *Garrison*, where after reargument the Court said that "the knowingly false statement and the false statement made with reckless disregard of the truth, do not enjoy constitutional protection." 379 U.S. at 75. The Court today neither explains nor justifies its withdrawal from the firm stand taken in *Garrison*. As I see it, a teacher may be fired without violation of the First Amendment for knowingly or recklessly making false statements regardless of their harmful impact on the schools. As the Court holds, however, in the absence of special circum-

4. There is likewise no occasion furnished by this case for consideration of the extent to which teachers can be required by narrowly drawn grievance procedures to submit complaints about the operation of the schools to their superiors for action thereon prior to bringing the complaints before the public.

5. We also note that this case does not present a situation in which a teacher's public statements are so without foundation as to call into question his fitness to perform his duties in the classroom. In such a case, of course, the statements would merely be evidence of the teacher's general competence, or lack thereof, and not an independent basis for dismissal.

6. Because we conclude that appellant's statements were not knowingly or recklessly false, we have no occasion to pass upon the additional question whether a statement that was knowingly or recklessly false would if it were neither shown nor could reasonably be presumed to have had any harmful effects, still be protected by the First Amendment. *See also* n. 5, *supra*.

1. *See ante*, at 569–70, 572 and nn. 3, 4. The Court does not elaborate upon its suggestion that there may be situations in which, with reference to certain areas of public comment, a teacher may have special obligations to his superiors. It simply holds that in this case, with respect to the particular public comment made by Pickering, he is more like a member of the general public and, apparently, too remote from the school board to require placing him into any special category. Further, as I read the Court's opinion, it does not foreclose the possibility that under the First Amendment a school system may have an enforceable rule, applicable to teachers, that public statements about school business must first be submitted to the authorities to check for accuracy.

stances he may not be fired if his statements were true or only negligently false, even if there is some harm to the school system. . . .

Nor can I join the Court in its findings with regard to whether Pickering knowingly or recklessly published false statements. Neither the State in presenting its evidence nor the state tribunals in arriving at their findings and conclusions of law addressed themselves to the elements of the new standard which the Court holds the First Amendment to require in the circumstances of this case. Indeed, the state courts expressly rejected the applicability of both *New York Times* and *Garrison*. I find it wholly unsatisfactory for this Court to make the initial determination of knowing or reckless falsehood from the cold record now before us. It would be far more appropriate to remand this case to the state courts for further proceedings in light of the constitutional standard which the Court deems applicable to this case, once the relevant facts have been ascertained in appropriate proceedings.

NOTES AND QUESTIONS

1. The Pickering *Standard*

Justice Marshall's opinion specifies the circumstances in which an employee is to be protected from dismissal for publicly voicing criticism of the school board's policies. The critical question is whether the school employee has "the kind of close working relationship, [with the board and superintendent] which . . . [requires] personal loyalty and confidence" for the employee to carry out his functions. *See Cox v. Dardanelle Public School District*, 790 F.2d 668 (8th Cir. 1986); *Derrickson v. Board of Education*, 738 F.2d 351 (8th Cir. 1984). How does the *Pickering* test differ from the *Tinker* test, discussed earlier in the chapter? May a professor's speech that substantially disrupts the educational process be the basis for dismissal or sanctions? *See, e.g., Adamian v. Jacobsen*, 523 F.2d 929 (9th Cir. 1975), *aff'd after remand sub nom. Adamian v. Lombardi*, 608 F.2d 1224 (9th Cir. 1979); *Franklin v. Leland Stanford Univ.*, 172 Cal.App.3d 322, 218 Cal.Rptr. 228 (Cal.App.1985). When is the former test applicable? Should it matter whether the employee personally criticizes individual superiors or only offers a general critique of school policies? *See Stevenson v. Lower Marion County School District No.* 3, 285 S.C. 62, 327 S.E.2d 656 (1985). Is the emphasis on loyalty a variation of the material-disruption standard of *Tinker*? Does the Court adequately accommodate the public's need for "insider" information and the school authorities' need for confidentiality and loyalty?

What would have been the outcome of the case if *Pickering* had been the assistant superintendent for academic affairs or the director of the athletic program? What if the case had involved a teacher who played an instrumental role in attempting to dismiss the school superintendent? *See Watts v. Seward School Board*, 395 P.2d 372 (Alaska 1964), *vacated*, 381 U.S. 126, 85 S.Ct. 1321, 14 L.Ed.2d 261 (1965), *on remand*, 421 P.2d 586 (Alaska 1966), *rehearing denied*, 423 P.2d 678 (Alaska 1967), *vacated*, 391 U.S. 592, 88 S.Ct. 1753, 20 L.Ed.2d 842 (1968), *on remand*, 454 P.2d 732 (Alaska 1969).

What would result if an African-American teacher criticized school policies regarding black participation in the administrative and instructional process, and was fired on the ground that for philosophical reasons the teacher and school principal could not get along; "one or the other must go"? *See Roberts v. Lake Central School Corp.*, 317 F.Supp. 63 (N.D. Ind. 1970). *See also Jordan v. Cagel*, 474 F.Supp. 1198 (N.D. Miss. 1979), *aff'd mem.*, 620 F.2d 298 (5th Cir. 1980).

Does *Pickering* provide protection for a school counselor who, concerned that children were being placed in classes for the mentally retarded because they were tested in English rather than in their native language, advised the parents of affected children to consult the local legal aid society? *See Bernasconi v. Tempe Elementary School District*, 548 F.2d 857 (9th Cir. 1977), *cert. denied*, 434 U.S. 825, 98 S.Ct. 72, 54 L.Ed.2d 82.

2. False Statements

Does the Court's test concerning false statements apply to matters of opinion? What is the difference between a matter of opinion and a matter of fact? *See D'Andrea v. Adams*, 626 F.2d 469, 473 n. 2 (5th Cir. 1980). Should a false statement ever form a constitutionally adequate basis for dismissal, in the absence of interference with working relationships? If citizens generally may utter falsehoods about the school system and school officials, why should teachers be held to a higher standard of truthfulness?

The Court leaves open the possibility that a teacher's public statements could be used by a school board as evidence of a lack of fitness to perform his or her duties in the classroom, for example, as when a mathematics teacher publishes a letter filled with computational errors. Might such public expressions be used as evidence that the teacher has character traits undesirable in an employee? *See Garza v. Rodriguez*, 559 F.2d 259 (5th Cir. 1977), *cert. denied*, 439 U.S. 877, 99 S.Ct. 215, 58 L.Ed.2d 191 (1978).

3. Speech Directed to Fellow Teachers and/or the Principal

Might teachers be dismissed for regularly voicing criticism of the principal, superintendent, and/or school board to other teachers? What sort of disruptive impact would warrant dismissal? *See McGill v. Board of Education of Pekin Elementary School*, 602 F.2d 774 (7th Cir. 1979). May a teacher circulate a questionnaire among other teachers asking their opinion of their "leaders" and their opinion of school decision-making and grievance processes? *See Lindsey v. Board of Regents*, 607 F.2d 672 (5th Cir. 1979).

4. Criticism Expressed in the Classroom or before a Student Audience

Should the *Pickering* doctrine protect teachers who voice their criticisms in the classroom? *See Clark v. Holmes*, 474 F.2d 928 (7th Cir. 1972), *cert. denied*, 411 U.S. 972, 93 S.Ct. 2148, 36 L.Ed.2d 695 (1973); *Moore v. School Board of Gulf County Florida*, 364 F.Supp. 355 (N.D. Fla. 1973). Do the standards of *Pickering, Tinker*, or *Cary* control in this situation? Should the frequency of the practice, the age group, the degree of student unrest caused, the relevance of the comments to the course, the kind of language used, and/or the salience of the issue to the lives of the students make a difference?

Cox v. Dardanelle Public School District

790 F.2d 668 (8th Cir. 1986).

Before McMillian, Circuit Judge, Henley, Senior Circuit Judge, and John R. Gibson, Circuit Judge.

John R. Gibson, Circuit Judge.

The Dardanelle Public School District and its officials, as individuals, appeal the judgment of the district court, sitting without a jury, that the school district impermissibly failed to renew the contract of appellee, Nancy Cox, in retaliation for speech and conduct protected by the first amendment, in violation of 42 U.S.C. § 1983 (1982). The appellants contend that the district court improperly concluded that appellee's activities were protected by the first amendment. They further contend that the district court erred in finding that the protected activities in which the appellee engaged were the motivating factor in the decision not to renew her teaching contract, and that but for her protected speech, she would have been rehired. . . . We affirm the judgment of the district court.

Appellee Nancy Cox was first hired by the Dardanelle Public School District to teach eighth grade English at the district's Middle School for the 1976–77 school year. Her employment contract was renewed by the School Board each of the following two years. During the first two years Cox taught at the Middle School, she established a good working relationship with the principal, Ed Bradshaw, who served as her immediate supervisor. Bradshaw gave Cox good evaluations and recommended each year that she be rehired.

At the beginning of the 1979–80 school year, the third year Cox was employed by the School District, appellant John Dillard replaced Ed Bradshaw as principal of the Middle School. During this same school year Cox became more active in the teachers local organization, the Dardanelle Education Association (DEA), and was appointed DEA representative to the Middle School for the 1979–80 school year.

The difficulties between Cox and Dillard were best illustrated by the following factual findings of the district court:

> 4. Defendant Johnny L. Dillard replaced Ed Bradshaw as Principal of the Dardanelle Middle School before the beginning of the 1979–80 school term. Defendant Dillard implemented several changes in the regulations under which the teachers had performed their duties in previous years. Plaintiff, along with a majority of the other members of the faculty of the Dardanelle Middle School, Upper Building, disagreed with some of defendant Dillard's methods.
>
> 5. Plaintiff on numerous occasions spoke out concerning the administration of the educational process at the Dardanelle Middle School, oftentimes in disagreement with defendant Dillard. On November 6, 1979, plaintiff, along with a number of the other faculty members of her school, caused a grievance to be filed with defendant Dillard concerning the educational process in their school. In that grievance, the teachers requested defendant Dillard to meet with them to discuss their dissatisfaction with the educational process then existing. Defendant Dillard instructed the teachers to file individual grievances if they wished to have their concerns addressed by him. Three teachers, Richard Johnson, Maxine Kemp and plaintiff, sub-

mitted individual grievances reflecting their names thereon to defendant Dillard. All three of the teachers submitting individual grievances were the victims of job-related sanctions from all the defendants herein. Richard Johnson was terminated in February, 1980, plaintiff was dismissed at the conclusion of the 1979–80 school term, and Maxine Kemp was placed on a probationary status for the 1980–81 school term. None of the other members of the Dardanelle Middle School Upper Building faculty suffered any job-related sanctions during or at the conclusion of the 1979–80 school term.

7. Plaintiff was informed by defendant Fugatt by letter received on or about February 29, 1980, that he was recommending to the Board of Education that her contract not be renewed for the coming school term. Later, on April 1, 1980, plaintiff received a letter from the President of the School Board specifying eleven (11) grounds for the Superintendent's nonrenewal recommendation. A hearing was held before the School Board on April 16 and 23, 1980, to consider the matter of the nonrenewal recommendation as to plaintiff's employment. After hearing considerable evidence from defendants Fugatt and Dillard, as well as plaintiff and other witnesses, the School Board voted on each of the grounds listed by the Board President in his letter to plaintiff and relied upon by defendant Fugatt. Of those eleven (11) charges, the Board voted that four (4) were false, that four (4) were true but not sufficient grounds for nonrenewal, noted that one (1) had been withdrawn by the Board's attorney, and voted that two (2) were true and constituted sufficient grounds relied upon by the Board in dismissing plaintiff were "(1) on August 30, August 31, September 4, September 7, and September 10, Mrs. Cox refused to follow directions in that she signed in for Mr. Johnson.", and "(2) on February 15, Mrs. Cox refused to follow administrative policy in that she allowed her class to be interrupted by a visitor without permission from the Principal."

Cox v. Dardanelle Public School District, No. LR-C-80-441, . . . (E.D.Ark. April 23, 1984).

The district court found that the appellants had dismissed Cox not for alleged insubordination in failing to comply with administrative directives, but because of her continued expressions of disagreement over the educational policies in force in the Middle School. The district court also found that the grounds advanced by the appellants for Cox's renewal were "pretextual and insignificant," . . . and further, that but for her criticisms, Cox's contract would have been renewed by the School Board. The court also concluded as a matter of law that Cox's expressions were protected by the first amendment. The court thereupon awarded Cox damages for the wrongful dismissal. The appellants filed the instant appeal.

Claims by public employees that they have suffered job-related sanctions as a result of speech are considered in accordance with the now familiar analysis set out by the Supreme Court in *Mt. Healthy City School District Board of Education v. Doyle*, 429 U.S. 274, 97 S.Ct. 568, 50 L.Ed.2d 471 (1977). As a threshold matter, a plaintiff must demonstrate that the speech or conduct, which she alleges as the basis of the adverse employment decision, was entitled to constitutional protection; she must then show that this protected conduct was a substantial or motivating factor in the adverse employment decision; the burden then shifts to the employer to show by a preponderance of the evidence that it would have taken the same action absent the employee's protected conduct. . . .

A

Whether a public employee's expressions are constitutionally protected involves a two-step inquiry. *Connick v. Myers*, 461 U.S. 138, 143–47, 103 S.Ct. 1684, 1688–90, 75 L.Ed.2d 708 (1983). Initially, a court must conclude that the employee's speech can be "fairly characterized as constituting speech on a matter of public concern . . ." *Id.* at 146, 103 S.Ct. at 1689; if the speech falls within this category, the court must then balance "the interest of the [employee] as a citizen, in commenting upon matters of public concern and the interests of the state, as an employer, in promoting the efficiency of the public service it performs through its employees." *Id.* at 142, 103 S.Ct. at 1687 (quoting *Pickering v. Board of Education*, 391 U.S. 563, 568, 88 S.Ct. 1731, 1734, 20 L.Ed.2d 811 (1968)).

The district court concluded that Cox's speech, for the most part, was an "expression of her own ideas concerning the educational process in the Dardanelle Middle School . . . ," . . . and therefore related to a matter of public import. Appellants contend that this conclusion is wrong as a matter of law[4] and that appellant's expressions amounted to

4. "The inquiry into the protected status of speech is one of law, not fact." *Connick*, 461 U.S. at 148 n. 7, 103 S.Ct. at 1690 n. 7; *Roberts v. Van Buren Public Schools*, 773 F.2d 949, 954 (8th Cir.1985).

no more than her "personal objections to employee work rules," . . . and thus, as expressions of private and not public concern, are not entitled to constitutional protection.

Whether a public employee's expressions relate to a matter of public concern must be considered in light of the "content, form, and context of a given statement, as revealed by the whole record." *Connick*, 461 U.S. at 147–48, 103 S.Ct. at 1690. . . . The question in each case is whether the employee's expressions can be "fairly characterized as relating to any matter of political, social, or other concern to the community . . . ." *Id.* at 146, 103 S.Ct. at 1689. Where a public employee speaks out in public or in private[5] on matters that relate solely to the employee's parochial concerns as an employee, no first amendment interests are at stake. *Id.* at 146, 103 S.Ct. at 1689. The focus is on the role the employee has assumed in advancing the particular expressions: that of a concerned public citizen, informing the public that the state institution is not properly discharging its duties, or engaged in some way in misfeasance, malfeasance or nonfeasance; or merely as an employee, concerned only with internal policies or practices which are of relevance only to the employees of that institution. . . .

Our review of the record convinces us that Cox's speech was composed of more than criticisms of internal personnel policies, but touched on matters of public concern, and was therefore entitled to constitutional protection. To begin with, not all of Cox's speech was directed at Dillard's personnel policies. The very first dispute between Cox and Dillard related to the District's decision to abandon ability grouping of students. The educational theories and practices employed by school administrators is [*sic*] clearly a question of public concern. The questions how we teach the young, what we teach them, and the environment in which we teach them are of the most central concern to every community in the nation. . . .

Additionally, we believe that much of Cox's speech directed at the school's personnel policies was not motivated solely by employment concerns, but was legitimate criticism of policies and administration which affected the educational function of the school.[6] Cox was critical in her individual grievance, and by proxy, in the general grievance, of the manner in which Dillard dealt with the faculty, and expressed the view that Dillard's administrative style had discouraged teacher input, inhibited teachers' use of different teaching techniques and classroom methods, significantly affected teacher morale at the school, and affected the students. . . .

Cox's statements on these matters were not the comments of a single employee bearing on issues unique to that employee. . . . Nor were her comments concerned solely with the immediate supervisor-employee relationship between Dillard and the faculty. They obviously touch in great measure upon the ability of Dillard and the faculty to "discharge . . . the public function of education." . . . Cox's comments are clearly attempts to inform Dillard, and ultimately his superiors, that his actions were interfering with the efficient and proper discharge of the crucial responsibilities of the faculty.[7]

We therefore conclude that a significant portion of Cox's speech was of public concern. We must now balance appellee's interest in advancing these expressions with the state's legitimate interest in the "effective and efficient fulfillment of its responsibilities to the public." *Connick*, 461 U.S. at 150, 103 S.Ct. at 1691; *Pickering*, 391 U.S. at 568, 88 S.Ct. at 1734.

An employee's interest in freely commenting on matters of public concern must generally give way

5. It is clear that an employee's right to speak out on matters of public concern is not forfeited by the choice of a private forum. *Givhan v. Western Consolidated School District*, 439 U.S. 410, 415–16, 99 S.Ct. 693, 696–97, 58 L.Ed.2d 619 (1979). Although the time, place, and manner of the speech are generally irrelevant to the inquiry into the public import of the speech, they may be relevant in striking the balance between the employee's and employer's interests. *Id.* at 415 n. 4, 99 S.Ct. at 696 n. 4; *see infra* p. 674.

6. Cox's criticism of the policies requiring teachers to sign in and out and forbidding personal use of the office phones, and her criticism regarding the timing of announcements and messages during the day all bear on internal matters relevant only to the employees of the school, and are not constitutionally protected. *Cf. Knapp v. Whitaker*, 757 F.2d at 827, 840 (7th Cir.1985) (teacher's remarks on classroom assignments and content of evaluations merely internal, personal matters, not protected speech).

7. The Court in *Connick* did not hold that criticism of the way in which one's superior administers the office or institution is always solely a question of internal concern. As Justice Brennan noted in dissent, "It is beyond doubt that personnel decisions that adversely affect discipline and morale may ultimately impair an agency's efficient performance of its duties," and comment on these decisions, therefore, is a matter of public concern as "of interest to persons seeking to develop informed opinions about the manner in which . . . an . . . official charged with managing a vital governmental agency[ ] discharges his responsibilities." 461 U.S. at 163, 103 S.Ct. at 1698 (Brennan, J., dissenting). The majority did not in principle disagree with Justice Brennan's observations, but only as they applied in the particular context—a questionnaire soliciting employees' views primarily on internal policies relating to transfers and office morale, distributed by an employee transferred against her wishes. . . .

to the state's interest in efficiently fulfilling its responsibilities where the employee's speech significantly impairs her ability to perform her duties, disrupts working relationships and harmony among co-workers, or otherwise impedes the normal operations of the institution. *McGee v. South Pemiscot School District* R–V, 712 F.2d 339, 342 (8th Cir. 1983). . . . Where the employee's comments threaten to disrupt or impair close working relationships particularly requiring personal loyalty and confidence, the state must be given an even wider degree of deference. . . . Furthermore, while the fact that an employee's comments are made to superiors in private does not strip them of constitutional protection, . . . the state is entitled to consider whether the time, place and manner of the private expression affected or threatened working relationships and the efficient operations of the institution. . . .

There is no evidence that Cox's criticisms throughout the year introduced discord into otherwise harmonious relations with her colleagues. To the contrary, the evidence indicates that this dispute was between a majority of the teachers at the Middle School and the principal. Moreover, there is no evidence that Cox's speech affected her teaching performance.[8] Nor is there evidence that Cox willfully disobeyed any directive that affected her teaching duties. . . .

Nor do we believe that any statements by Cox can fairly be said to have disrupted her relationship with Dillard. The evidence indicates that the primary source of the disruption in their relationship (indeed, the cause of disruption of the relationship between a majority of the faculty and Dillard), was Dillard's implementation and enforcement of the personnel policies, not Cox's speech. . . . Although we do not intend to minimize the importance of teacher-principal relationship, . . . it is not a "relationship between superior and subordinate . . . of such a personal and intimate nature that certain forms of [] criticism of the superior by the subordinate would seriously undermine the effectiveness of the working relationship between them . . . ." *Pickering*, 391 U.S. at 570 n. 3, 88 S.Ct. at 1735 n. 3. The teacher-principal relationship is not of such a personal and intimate nature that teachers must be precluded from filing responsible grievances. . . .

Finally, there is no allegation that the time, place or manner of appellee's speech aggravated her relationship with Dillard or impeded the normal operation of the school. Cox did not attempt to circumvent the chain of command . . . nor is there a suggestion that her individual grievance or criticisms throughout the year were intemperate, or antagonistic. . . .

B

The appellants argue that even if Cox's speech, on balance, was constitutionally protected, it was not the motivating factor in the Board's decision not to renew her contract. They contend that the Board's decision was based on Cox's repeated refusal to comply with proper administrative directives, not her criticism of those directives.

A public employee generally can be discharged for refusing to follow administrative policies and directives, even those they contend are misguided. . . . Of the eleven charges listed by the superintendent in his letter to Cox and advanced to the Board, only two were found by the Board to be true and sufficient grounds for non-renewal: Cox's violation of the sign-in policy on several occasions by signing in for a fellow teacher, Richard Johnson; and her violation of the policy forbidding unauthorized visitors in the classroom.

Whether the protected conduct of the plaintiff was a substantial or motivating factor in the adverse employment decision is question of fact. . . .

We believe that there is sufficient evidence in the record to support the district court's finding that Cox's speech motivated the Board not to renew her contract. Dillard admitted that Cox's individual grievance likely was a factor in subsequent decisions he made regarding her employment. At least three memoranda Dillard placed in Cox's personnel file, describing actions of Cox which he believed violated administrative policies or were improper, made reference to the grievance and suggested in each case that Cox's actions were not consistent with the crit-

8. The appellees have not suggested that Cox brought her criticism of Dillard's policies into the classroom. We recognize that a number of the grounds advanced by Dillard and Fugatt for the decision not to renew Cox's contract suggest that Cox's teaching was below acceptable standards. However, there is no suggestion that these putative shortcomings were connected to her protected speech. Furthermore, the School Board found all but one of these charges to be either false or an insufficient ground for nonrenewal, and the district court found these grounds to be pretexts.

icisms she had levied against him in the grievance. . . . Furthermore, the district court took explicit notice of the fact that only the three teachers who filed individual grievances were subject that year to job-related sanctions. . . . The district court's decision is not clearly erroneous.[9]

C

The appellants also argue that the district court erred in finding that the teachers did not successfully discharge the burden of demonstrating by a preponderance of the evidence that the School Board would have reached the same decision but for Cox's protected conduct. *Cf. Mt. Healthy City Board of Education*, 429 U.S. at 287, 97 S.Ct. at 576. As with the previous question of causation, this is a question of fact, and thus subject to review on the clearly erroneous standard. . . .

There is ample evidence to sustain the district court's finding. The appellants offer no reasons other than those advanced by Dillard and Fugatt and considered by the School Board to justify the employment decision. The School Board found only two of the eleven proferred charges sufficient for adverse action, and the district court concluded that these two were mere pretexts and too insignificant to support the allegations. . . .

We also reject appellants' argument that because the School Board members were unaware of Cox's grievance and other criticisms of Dillard's policies, their decision not to renew Cox's contract was not tainted by any impermissible motive. The district court could reasonably conclude that the Board would not have considered an adverse action against Cox had Dillard and Fugatt not advanced these retaliatory charges.

NOTES AND QUESTIONS

1. Matters of Public Concern and Constitutional Theory

The court relies on *Connick v. Myers* for a two-step test for determining whether Nancy Cox's speech is entitled to constitutional protection. *See generally* M. McCarthy & N. Cambion-McCabe, *Public School Law* 272–81 (1988). First, the court must decide whether the speech may be appropriately characterized as addressing "a matter of public concern." Second, if it is a matter of public concern, then the court should apply *Pickering* and determine whether the interest of the teacher in speaking as a citizen is outweighed by the state's interest in promoting efficiency in the delivery of educational services in the public schools. Does *Pickering* support this two-part test? Has *Connick* significantly altered the law applicable to public employees? What is the purpose of the "public concern" branch of the test? *See generally* Estlund, "Speech on Matters of Public Concern: The Perils of an Emerging First Amendment Category," *Geo. Wash. L. Rev.* 1 (1990); Ingber, "Rediscovering the Communal Worth of Individual Rights: The First Amendment in Institutional Contexts," 69 *Tex. L. Rev.* 1, 56–65 (1990); Allred, "From *Connick* to Confusion: The Struggle to Define Speech on Matters of Public Concern," 64 *Ind. L.J.* 43 (1988); Massaro, "Significant Silences: Freedom of Speech in the Public Sector Workplace," 61 *S. Cal. L. Rev.* 1 (1987). What does the court mean when it says that no First Amendment interests are at stake when the speech relates "solely to the employee's parochial concerns" or criticisms of "internal policies or practices which are of relevance only to the employees of that institution"? *See also Dunn & Bradstreet, Inc. v. Greenmoss Builders, Inc.*, 472 U.S. 749, 105 S.Ct. 2939, 86 L.Ed.2d 593 (1985) (plurality opinion) ("matters of purely private concern" not protected). What if Nancy Cox's speech concerned both public concerns and internal institutional policies? *See Renfroe v. Kirkpatrick*, 722 F.2d 714 (11th Cir. 1984).

How does a court know a public concern when it sees it? *See* Langvardt, "Public Concern Revisited: A New Role for an Old Doctrine in the Constitutional Law of Defamation," 21 *Va. L. Rev.* 241, 259 (1987). Does public concern or discourse refer to speech that is "substantively relevant to the processes of democratic self-governance?" *See* Post, "The Constitutional Concept of Public Discourse: Outrageous Opinion, Democratic Deliberation, and *Hustler Magazine v. Falwell*," 103 *Harv. L. Rev.*

---

9. We note, moreover, that neither violation of the administrative policies appears to have been intended as deliberate insubordination. We do not intend to imply that public employees can be sanctioned only for purposeful violations of the rules. However, the rather insignificant nature of the charges here lends support to the district court's finding that the decision not to renew Cox's contract was based not on her performance as a teacher, but upon her conduct and complaints. . . .

601, 670 (1990). Cannot every issue potentially raise the public's concern? Is not the purpose of the speech to put the matter under discussion on the public agenda? *Id.* Should the government be able to decide what is a matter of public concern? *Id. See also* Estlund, *supra*. Or does the public-concern test require "speech about issues that happen actually to interest the 'public,' which is to say 'significant number of persons.' "? *Id.* at 672, citing B. Hennessy, *Public Opinion* 8–9 (3d ed. 1975). But is not a major purpose of speech to educate the public as to matters about which it should be concerned? Or does the test require that the speech be publicly disseminated? *Id.* at 675, citing *Hustler Magazine v. Falwell*, 484 U.S. 46, 108 S.Ct. 876, 99 L.Ed.2d 41 (1988). *But see Ferrara v. Mills*, 781 F.2d 1508, 1514 (11th Cir. 1986). Is the burden of proof on the teacher or the public schools? *See Ferrara v. Mills, supra* at 1514 (burden on teacher).

According to Professor Post, "the origin of the phrase 'matters of public concern' in the first amendment doctrine . . . lies in the important 1940 decision of *Thornhill v. Alabama.*" *Id.*, citing 310 U.S. 88 (1940). *Thornhill* involved the question of whether labor picketing is constitutionally protected. Does the origin of the doctrine indicate that the purpose is to distinguish between garden-variety employee grievances and larger issues that may concern the public? *See Southside Public Schools v. Hill*, 827 F.2d 270 (8th Cir. 1987). To distinguish between speech addressed to the government as employer and speech addressed to government as policymaker? How does one tell the difference? *See* Estlund, *supra*.

Do you agree with Professor Post that the public concern doctrine "lacks internal coherence" and causes courts to examine "a wide array of particular variables inherent in specific communicative contexts"? *Id.* at 679. That "the classification of speech as public discourse" resists "expression in the form of clear, uniform, and helpful doctrinal rules"? *Id.* Consider this effort at a reformulation of the test:

> [T]he first amendment establishes a distinct domain of public discourse in order to implement our common belief in such values as neutrality, diversity, and individualism. It follows that the domain of public discourse will extend only so far as these values override other competing commitments, such as those . . . necessary [to the] exercise of community authority.

Id. at 680. Do you agree? Does the proposed test abandon *Connick* and return the course to *Pickering*?

2. *What is a Matter of Public Concern?*

Judge Gibson asserts that the ability grouping of students, school personnel policies, and the administrative style of the principal are all matters of public concern. How does he reach this conclusion? If questions of "how we teach the young," "what we teach them, and the environment in which we teach them are of the most central concern to every community in the nation," is not virtually all speech by teachers and administrators a matter of public concern? *See Rankin v. Independent School District No. I-3*, 876 F.2d 838 (10th Cir. 1989) (student discipline policies are a matter of public concern); *Anderson v. Central Point School District No. 6*, 746 F.2d 505 (9th Cir. 1984) (criticism of athletic program matter of public concern). *But see Ferrara v. Mills*, 781 F.2d 1508, 1515 (11th Cir. 1986) (rejects the argument that all speech "relating to public education" is "intrinsically" a matter "of vital public concern"); *Daniels v. Quinn*, 801 F.2d 687 (4th Cir. 1986) (criticism of late arrival of remedial reading materials not a public concern); *Saye v. Vrain Valley School District*, 785 F.2d 862 (10th Cir. 1986) (allocation of teacher aide time among teachers not a matter of public concern). On what basis does the court decline to protect criticisms of telephone and announcement policies? Is the court implicitly saying that such trivial matters do not concern the public? Should not concern the public? Has the court implicitly weighed the public's interest against the employer's interest? *See* Estlund, *supra*.

The courts have sharply divided over what constitutes a public concern in the context of speech by teachers and other public school employees. *See, e.g., Johnsen v. Independent School District No. 3*, 891 F.2d 1485 (10th Cir. 1989) (criticisms of medication policies by school nurse are matters of public concern, but speech is not protected because of disruptive impact); *Seemuller v. Fairfax County School Board*, 878 F.2d 1578 (4th Cir. 1989) (letters to newspaper, responding to allegations of sexual discrimination against female physical education students, is protected); *Berg v. Hunter*, 854 F.2d 238 (7th Cir. 1988) (unwarranted and misrepresented salary increases are matters of public concern, but speech had "decidedly adverse impact on the efficient administration of public education"); *Vukadinovich v. Bartels*, 853 F.2d 1387 (7th Cir. 1988) (statements criticizing school board's decision not to rehire plaintiff as basketball coach not protected);

Piver v. Pender County Board of Education, 835 F.2d 1076 (4th Cir. 1987) (speech favoring retention of principal is matter of public concern); *Southside Public Schools v. Hill*, 827 F.2d 270 (8th Cir. 1987) (letter to state department of education enumerating failures to implement special education program for handicapped pupils is matter of public concern); *Lewis v. Harrison School District No. 1*, 805 F.2d 310 (8th Cir. 1986) (principal's speech to school board criticizing transfer of spouse is matter of public concern); *Ferrara v. Mills*, 781 F.2d 1508 (11th Cir. 1986) (speech on collegiate registration and teacher placement did not relate to a matter of public concern); *Stevenson v. Lower Marion County School District No. 3*, 285 S.C. 62, 327 S.E.2d 656 (1985) (statement accusing superintendent of inciting student disturbances is related to personal employment dispute).

Consider the application of the public concern doctrine in *Knapp v. Whitaker*, 757 F.2d 827, 840–42 (7th Cir. 1985):

> . . . The record indicates that Knapp contacted the School Board members concerning his classroom assignment; the content of [his] . . . evaluations; the inequitable mileage allowance for . . . coaches; the liability insurance provided by [the district] . . . for coaches and volunteer parents . . . ; and the general ineffectiveness of the grievance procedure within District 150. The issues of Knapp's classroom assignment and the content of his evaluations are clearly personal matters relating solely to Knapp's employment . . . . Knapp's speech on these issues was not an attempt to inform the public that the administrators . . . were failing to discharge their governmental responsibilities. Moreover, Knapp's speech on these subjects was not aimed at uncovering a wrongdoing or breach of the public trust . . . .
>
> The issue of inequitable mileage allowance involves not only Knapp but all of the coaches . . . who travel to area high schools . . . . Knapp's speech to the School Board on the issue of mileage allowance was an attempt to inform the public and the educational policymakers of Peoria that officials in District 150 were failing in their duty to properly administer the allocation of public funds. . . .
>
> The liability insurance coverage . . . is, likewise, a matter of interest and concern to members of the Peoria community . . . .
>
> The functioning of a grievance procedure is generally an internal issue, important only to the teachers and School District employees . . . . In the present case, however, the grievance procedure was the subject of ongoing collective bargaining negotiations between the teachers' union and the administrators . . . . [W]e hold that, in the context of this case, such speech is a matter of public concern.

How do you explain the results reached by the *Knapp* court? *See also Hesse v. Board of Education*, 848 F.2d 748 (7th Cir. 1988); *Day v. South Park Independent School District*, 768 F.2d 696 (5th Cir. 1985); *Meyer v. University of Washington*, 105 Wash.2d 847, 719 P. 2d 98 (1986). Is the court balancing personal and public interests and then attaching the appropriate label? *See* Bernheim, "Free Speech for Public Employees: The Supreme Court Strikes a New Balance," 31 *Educ. Law Rep.* [7] (1986). *See generally* Estlund, *supra*. Is the court balancing interests in accordance with *Pickering* in the guise of applying *Connick*? *See also Bowman v. Pulaski County Special School District*, 723 F.2d 640 (8th Cir. 1983). *See generally Rankin v. McPherson*, 483 U.S. 378, 107 S.Ct. 2891, 97 L.Ed.2d 315 (1987). Does the public concern doctrine lead to predictable results? How would you advise a teacher planning to criticize administrative policies before a public meeting of the school board?

3. *Application of* Connick *to Classroom Speech*

Is the *Connick* public concern doctrine applicable to teacher expression in the classroom? Does it balance the same types of interests that are at issue in academic freedom cases? Is a teacher's unauthorized use of a supplemental reading list for a world history class a matter of public concern? *See Kirkland v. Northside Independent School District*, 890 F.2d 794 (5th Cir. 1989).

4. *Causation*

In teacher speech cases, the teacher has the initial burden of proving that the protected conduct "was a substantial or motivating factor" in the adverse employment or other disciplinary decision. *See Coats v. Pierce*, 890 F.2d 728 (5th Cir. 1989); *Holley v. Seminole County School District*, 755 F.2d 1492, 1500 (11th Cir. 1985). *See generally Mt. Healthy City School District Board of Education v. Doyle*, 429 U.S. 274, 97 S.Ct. 568, 50 L.Ed.2d 471 (1977). If the plaintiff meets this initial burden, the burden then shifts to the public employer "to show that the same employment decision would have been rendered absent the protected conduct." *Holley v. Seminole County School District*, *supra* at 1500. *See also Solis v. Rio Grande City Independent School*, 734 F.2d 243 (5th Cir. 1984); *Allen v. Autauga County*

Board of Education, 685 F.2d 1302, 1304 (11th Cir. 1982); *Hattisburg Municipal Separate School District v. Gates*, 461 So.2d 730, 737 (Miss. 1984). This standard of causation is generally treated as a "but for" test, i.e., the defendant must show, for example, that the plaintiff would have been dismissed even if the constitutionally protected conduct had not occurred. Do you agree with the standard of causation and the allocation of burdens of proof? Should the dismissed teacher be entitled to remedy if protected expression played any role in the dismissal? What are the perils of such a rule? What are the perils of the *Mt. Healthy* approach?

The question of causation is a fact question for the trier of fact. *See Copp v. Unified School District*, 882 F.2d 1547 (10th Cir. 1989); *Ratliff v. Wellington Exempted Village Schools Board*, 820 F.2d 792 (6th Cir. 1987); *Solis v. Rio Grande City Independent School, supra; Wells v. Hico Independent School District*, 736 F.2d 243 (5th Cir. 1984). When is it appropriate to dispose of the issue by summary judgment? *See Holley*, 755 F.2d at 1500–05. What is the standard of appellate review? *See Allen v. Autauga County Board of Education, supra* at 1305.

5. *Remedy*

A teacher who is unconstitutionally dismissed from her job because of her exercise of speech rights is entitled to back wages and other provable damages, but she may not recover for the loss of the abstract value of the constitutional right. *See Ratliff v. Wellington Exempted Village Schools Board, supra. See generally Memphis Community School District v. Stachura*, 477 U.S. 299, 106 S.Ct. 2537, 91 L.Ed.2d 249 (1986). There also is a presumptive rule that reinstatement in the position is appropriate. *See Allen v. Autauga County Board of Education, supra* at 1305–06 and cases cited therein.

6. *Profanity*

If a teacher uses profanity in addressing her supervisors and other members of the school community, may the speech still be protected as involving a matter of public concern? Or does the profanity itself provide the school district with an independent reason for dismissal or discipline? *See Ware v. Morgan County School District*, 748 P.2d 1295 (Colo. 1988) (insubordination). *Cf. Martin v. Parrish*, 805 F.2d 583 (5th Cir. 1986).

THREE

The Disciplinary Process: The Legalization of Dispute Resolution in Public Schools

I. INTRODUCTION

This chapter focuses on the discipline processes for public school students and teachers as well as the constitutional and statutory constraints that courts and legislatures impose on those processes. It takes up doctrinal issues—issues of law and policy—and questions concerning implementation, institutional competence, and the like, exploring the connection between these nominally disparate matters.

The presentation is essentially sequential, beginning with the requirements for a valid rule and proceeding through the stages of collection, presentation, and evaluation of the evidence in a disciplinary action. The chapter considers such matters as the vagueness and overbreadth doctrines as applied to school rules, limits on the gathering of evidence imposed on public officials by the Fourth Amendment (barring unreasonable searches), and the particulars of procedural due process in the school setting. It concludes with an assessment of the impact of due process decisions on schools and authority relationships within schools, recognizing the difficulties and uncertainties of implementing changes in the decisional processes of complex, bureaucratic public institutions. *See also* chapter 7, *infra*.

A recurrent theme is the degree to which courts, legislatures, and administrative bodies at the federal, state, and local levels have contributed to what could be described as the "legalization" of dispute resolution in the public schools. The term *legalization* refers to the tendency "to discover, construct, and follow rules" as a method for settling disputes and to adhere to prescribed procedures in their formulation and application. *See* J. Shklar, *Legalism* 21 (1964) ("legalism"). *See also* A. Wise, *Legislated Learning* (1979); T. Lowi, *The End of Liberalism* 297–314 (1969); P. Selznick, *Law, Society, and Industrial Justice* 11–12 (1969); Michelman, "Formal and Associational Aims in Procedural Due Process," in J.R. Pennock and J. Chapman, eds., NOMOS XVIII: *Due Process* 126 (1977).

Whatever the etiology of the legalization process, the inevitable result is a diminution or channeling of official discretion to make decisions affecting teachers and students. *See* G. Grant, *The World We Created at Hamilton High* (1988); D. Kirp and D. Jensen, eds., *School Days, Rule Days* (1986). *See generally* K. Davis, *Discretionary Justice* (1969). The formality of decision making is grounded in the supposition that the values of fairness, liberty, dignity, and participation require promulgating general rules and applying them in a uniform fashion. Critics of legalization have focused on the need to maintain authority relationships and a sense of shared community purpose in public schools, and they perceive legalization as a threat to those values. For courts and policymakers, the ultimate question is one of balance between rule and discretion, formality and informality, trusting and adversarial relationships. *See generally* Manley-Casimir, "Students' Rights," in D. Erickson and T. Reller, *The Principal in Met-*

ropolitan Schools 188 (1978). As Grant Gilmore put the matter,

> The better the society, the less law there will be. In Heaven there will be no law, and the lion will lie down with the lamb . . . . The worse the society, the more law there will be. In Hell there will be nothing but law, and due process will be meticulously observed.

G. Gilmore, *The Ages of American Law* 111 (1977).

The legalization of public education drew the fire of William Bennett, Secretary of Education during the Reagan administration. In a 1988 address to the American Bar Association entitled "The Role of Law in Education Reform," Secretary Bennett asserted that

> . . . the excessive legalization of education is inhibiting bold, innovative educators who are willing to shoulder responsibilities and to accept the consequences. Worse still is the effect education law has on school officials who prefer to avoid taking on problems. . . . Stultifying legal restrictions . . . allow them to escape responsibility for their own failings by using the law as an excuse . . . . Let's not perpetuate an environment in which the definition of an effective principal or teacher means having the agility and gall to slip around excessive legal interference. As in the military, let the men and women in the field call the shots.

As you read the materials in this chapter, you should continually ask yourself whether Secretary Bennett is right: whether the balance has been drawn appropriately, whether legalization has advanced or impeded the mission of public schools, whether teachers and students are protected too little or too much from arbitrary decisions by school authorities. *See generally* Yudof, "Legalization of Dispute Resolution, Distrust of Authority, and Organizational Theory: Implementing Due Process for Students in the Public Schools," 1981 *Wis.L.Rev.* 891; Kirp, "Proceduralism and Bureaucracy: Due Process in the School Setting," 28 (*Stan.L.Rev.* 841 (1976).

Legalization is also related to the socialization issues canvassed in chapter 2. Students learn about accepted norms by observing the actions of others, particularly as those actions have an impact on their day-to-day lives. *See generally* A. Gutmann, *Democratic Education* 88–94 (1987); T. Tapper, *Political Education and Stability* 45 (1976). *But see* Merelman, "Democratic Politics and the Culture of American Education," 74 *Am. Pol. Sci. Rev.* 319 (1980). They may develop an understanding of the relative merits of autocracy and democracy from their school experiences:

> Almost from birth people are enmeshed in complex webs of authority relationships. Every type of interpersonal activity—from learning to be a well-behaved child to sports—requires learning a relationship to established authority. In each situation, sets of acceptable behaviors, ways these rules can be modified, and penalties for infractions are acquired. Some of us learn, for example, that all rules must be obeyed regardless of one's own opinion, that authority cannot be challenged, and that disobedience brings inevitable and harsh consequences. Others learn that all regulations are flexible, rules are decided on by common consent, and punishment for wrongdoing can be negotiated. Some scholars argue that exposure to authority patterns in non-political situations creates expectations about the proper use of authority in political situations . . . . The argument suggests that where families, schools, and organizations stress unthinking acceptance of non-negotiable rules handed down by higher authorities, citizens will thus prefer a political system where decisions are similarly made and implemented. The key assumption is that people seek congruence between their personal authority experience and its relationship to broader political authority. Hence, democracy in the larger political system begins with democratic socialization (and autocratic systems similarly begin with autocratic political and non-political learning).

R. Weissberg, *Political Learning, Political Choice, and Democratic Citizenship* 17–18 (1974). *See generally* Gutmann, *supra* at ch. 3; G. Almond and S. Verba, *The Civic Culture*.

Do people seek a congruence between their own experiences with authority and their views on political authority generally? Might not students, subjected to undemocratic schools, react by seeking to reform political authority and to make it more democratic? As this book goes to press, unprecedented democratic changes are sweeping Eastern Europe. Is this an example of an incongruence between schooling experiences and views on political authority? Should policymakers and courts consider the impact of the disciplinary process in public schools on the political orientation of students—irrespective of the empirical answer to the congruence hypothesis?

II. GOVERNMENTAL REGULARITY AND SCHOOL RULES

Must school authorities act on the basis of a preexisting rule before a teacher or student may be punished for violating an institutional norm? The constitutional issue is whether the due process clause of the Fourteenth Amendment requires the prior enactment of such rules in order to assure that those in school have notice of what behavior may be subject to disciplinary sanctions. *See Bethel School District No. 403 v. Fraser,* 478 U.S. 675, 686, 106 S.Ct. 3159, 3166, 92 L.Ed.2d 549 (1986) (Stevens, J., dissenting). Even if the principle were established under the Constitution, it may be applicable only to the most severe sanctions. *Id.* (detailed rules unnecessary for two-day suspension). This is an important matter—important enough that at least one state has legislatively required that all school rules be in writing. Ind. Code Ann. § 20-8.1-5-3 (West 1985).

Courts generally have held that some behavior is so plainly disruptive of school life that those engaging in that behavior knew or should have known that they would be subject to sanctions. Moreover, courts have declared that school officials must have flexibility to respond to the unexpected. The prevailing law is that school officials generally may discipline students for conduct disruptive of the educational process or conduct that endangers the health and safety of students and school personnel without having adopted a prior rule forbidding the behavior and specifying the penalties. *See, e.g., Richards v. Thurston,* 424 F.2d 1281 (1st Cir. 1970); *Hasson v. Boothby,* 318 F.Supp. 1183 (D. Mass. 1970). *Cf. Bethel School District No. 403 v. Fraser, supra.*

If a school district promulgates written rules for student and teacher conduct, may those rules be successfully attacked on the ground that they are unconstitutionally vague? The concept of vagueness under the due process clause means that persons "of common intelligence must necessarily guess at its meaning and differ as to its application." *Connally v. General Construction Co.,* 269 U.S. 385, 391, 46 S.Ct. 126, 127, 70 L.Ed. 322 (1926). The concept has been largely limited to the criminal law, and the courts generally have declined to apply it to school rules. *See Jenkins v. Louisiana State Board of Education,* 506 F.2d 992 (5th Cir. 1975); *Esteban v. Central Missouri State College,* 415 F.2d 1077 (8th Cir. 1969), *cert. denied,* 398 U.S. 965, 90 S.Ct. 2169, 26 L.Ed.2d 548 (1970). *But see Shamloo v. Mississippi State Board,* 620 F.2d 516, 523 (5th Cir. 1980); *Soglin v. Kaufmann,* 418 F.2d 163 (7th Cir. 1969). Thus courts have upheld school disciplinary codes that broadly proscribe "willful disobedience," "intentional disruption," "student walkouts," and "vulgarity." *See, e.g., Murray v. West Baton Rouge Parish School Board,* 472 F.2d 438 (5th Cir. 1973); *Williams v. Board of Education,* 274 Ark. 530, 626 S.W.2d 361 (1982). If there were any doubts on this matter, they were put to rest by Chief Justice Burger in *Bethel School District No. 403 v. Fraser,* 478 U.S. 675, 686, 106 S.Ct. 3159, 3166, 92 L.Ed.2d 549 (1986):

> Respondent contends that the circumstances of his suspension violated due process because he had no way of knowing that the delivery of the speech in question would subject him to disciplinary sanctions. This argument is without merit. . . . Given the school's need to be able to impose disciplinary sanctions for a wide range of unanticipated conduct disruptive of the educational process, the school disciplinary rules need not be as detailed as a criminal code which imposes criminal sanctions . . . . Two days' suspension from school does not rise to the level of a penal sanction calling for the full panoply of procedural due process protections applicable to a criminal prosecution. . . . The school disciplinary rule proscribing "obscene" language and the prespeech admonition of teachers gave adequate warning to Fraser that his lewd speech could subject him to sanctions.

See also Rosa R. v. Connelly, 889 F.2d 435, 439 (2d Cir. 1989). *But see Bethel School District No. 403 v. Fraser, supra* (Stevens, J., dissenting).

Is the Court implicitly suggesting that Fraser might have been disciplined even if there were no school rule prohibiting obscene language? What if there were prior warnings from teachers but no rule? What if there were neither rules nor prior warnings? Is the standard applicable to students also applicable to teachers? If Fraser had been expelled from school for his infraction, would the vagueness doctrine have been applicable?

The overbreadth doctrine, like the vagueness doctrine, is an attack on a rule or law "on its face" as opposed to "as applied," and it is used primarily to protect expression under the First Amendment. The courts ask whether, irrespective of the plaintiff's conduct, the rule is applicable to some constitutionally protected conduct that may not be prohibited under *any* rule. That is, the rule may be unconstitutionally overbroad even though the plaintiff's conduct could have been proscribed under a properly drafted rule. While the vagueness doctrine is grounded primarily in the need for governmental regularity, the overbreadth doctrine is premised more on protecting First Amendment interests. If a rule is unconstitutionally broad, the court will strike it down to prevent the "chilling" of protected speech—even at the behest of a party who did not engage in protected activities.

Does *Fraser* close the door on overbreadth attacks on school rules? If a school need not rely on a preexisting rule when disciplining students, why should a court examine a duly enacted school rule for vagueness or overbreadth? Is it that a written rule may be more misleading? May a school district punish a student for behavior that is expressly approved in a school rule?

III. GATHERING THE EVIDENCE TO PROVE THE INFRACTION

What are the limits, if any, on the power of school officials to gather evidence that a teacher or student has violated a school rule? Once schools' concerns may have appeared to be relatively routine—a fugitive copy of *Playboy* or a can of beer in a student's locker—but the increasing presence of (and attention to) drugs and weapons on campus has made this a hotly contested area for both educational policy and law. Among the factors that make the issue legally complex are the institutional characteristics of schools, the age of students, the compulsion to attend school, the potential threat to safety, and the possibility that seized items may be used as evidence in criminal prosecutions as well as for school disciplinary purposes.

New Jersey v. T.L.O.

469 U.S. 325, 105 S.Ct. 733, 83 L.Ed.2d 720 (1985).

Justice White delivered the opinion of the Court.

* * *

I

On March 7, 1980, a teacher at Piscataway High School in Middlesex County, N.J., discovered two girls smoking in a lavatory. One of the two girls was the respondent T.L.O., who at that time was a 14-year-old high school freshman. Because smoking in the lavatory was a violation of a school rule, the teacher took the two girls to the Principal's office, where they met with Assistant Vice Principal Theodore Choplick. In response to questioning by Mr. Choplick, T.L.O.'s companion admitted that she had violated the rule. T.L.O., however, denied that she had been smoking in the lavatory and claimed that she did not smoke at all.

Mr. Choplick asked T.L.O. to come into his private office and demanded to see her purse. Opening the purse, he found a pack of cigarettes, which he removed from the purse and held before T.L.O.as he accused her of having lied to him. As he reached into the purse for the cigarettes, Mr. Choplick also noticed a package of cigarette rolling papers. In his experience, possession of rolling papers by high school students was closely associated with the use of marihuana. Suspecting that a closer examination of the purse might yield further evidence of drug use, Mr. Choplick proceeded to search the purse thoroughly. The search revealed a small amount of marihuana, a pipe, a number of empty plastic bags, a substantial quantity of money in one-dollar bills, an index card that appeared to be a list of students who owed T.L.O. money, and two letters that implicated T.L.O. in marihuana dealing.

* * *

Although we originally granted certiorari to decide the issue of the appropriate remedy in juvenile court proceedings for unlawful school searches, our doubts regarding the wisdom of deciding that question in isolation from the broader question of what limits, if any, the Fourth Amendment places on the activities of school authorities prompted us to order reargument on that question.[2] Having heard argu-

2. State and federal courts considering these questions have struggled to accommodate the interests protected by the Fourth Amendment and the interest of the States in providing a safe environment conducive to education in the public schools. Some courts have resolved the tension between these interests by giving full force to one or the other side of the balance. Thus, in a number of cases courts have held that school officials conducting in-school searches of students are private parties acting *in loco parentis* and are therefore not subject to the constraints of the Fourth Amendment. *See, e.g., D.R.C. v. State,* 646 P.2d 252 (Alaska App.1982); *In re G.,* 11 Cal.App.3d 1193, 90 Cal.Rptr. 361 (1970); *In re Donaldson,* 269 Cal. App.2d 509, 75 Cal.Rptr. 220 (1969); *R.C.M. v. State,* 660 S.W.2d 552 (Tex.App.1983); *Mercer v. State,* 450 S.W.2d 715 (Tex.Civ.App.1970). At least one court has held, on the other hand, that the Fourth Amendment applies in full to in-school searches by school officials and that a search conducted without probable cause is unreasonable, *see State v. Mora,* 307 So.2d 317 (La.), vacated, 423 U.S. 809, 96 S.Ct. 20, 46 L.Ed.2d 29 (1975), on remand, 330 So.2d 900 (La.1976); others have held or suggested that the probable-cause standard is applicable at least where the police are involved in a search, *see M. v. Board of Ed. Ball-Chatham Community Unit School Dist. No. 5,* 429 F.Supp. 288, 292 (SD Ill.1977); *Picha v. Wielgos,* 410 F.Supp. 1214, 1219–21 (ND Ill.1976); *State v. Young,* 234 Ga. 488, 498, 216 S.E.2d 586, 594 (1975); or where the search is highly intrusive, *See M.M. v. Anker,* 607 F.2d 588, 589 (CA2 1979).

ment on the legality of the search of T.L.O.'s purse, we are satisfied that the search did not violate the Fourth Amendment.[3]

II

In determining whether the search at issue in this case violated the Fourth Amendment, we are faced initially with the question whether that Amendment's prohibition on unreasonable searches and seizures applies to searches conducted by public school officials. We hold that it does.

* * *

[The] two propositions—that the Fourth Amendment applies to the States through the Fourteenth Amendment, and that the actions of public school officials are subject to the limits placed on state action by the Fourteenth Amendment—might appear sufficient to answer the suggestion that the Fourth Amendment does not proscribe unreasonable searches by school officials. On reargument, however, the State of New Jersey has argued that the history of the Fourth Amendment indicates that the Amendment was intended to regulate only searches and seizures carried out by law enforcement officers. . . .

. . . But this Court has never limited the Amendment's prohibition on unreasonable searches and seizures to operations conducted by the police. Rather, the Court has long spoken of the Fourth Amendment's strictures as restraints imposed upon "governmental action"—that is, "upon the activities of sovereign authority." . . . Accordingly, we have held the Fourth Amendment applicable to the activities of civil as well as criminal authorities. . . . Notwithstanding the general applicability of the Fourth Amendment to the activities of civil authorities, a few courts have concluded that school officials are exempt from the dictates of the Fourth Amendment by virtue of the special nature of their authority over schoolchildren. *See, e.g., R.C.M. v. State,* 660 S.W.2d 552 (Tex. App.1983). . . . Such reasoning is in tension with contemporary reality and the teachings of this Court. . . . If school authorities are state actors for purposes of the constitutional guarantees of freedom of expression and due process, it is difficult to understand why they should be deemed to be exercising parental rather than public authority when conducting searches of their students. . . .

III

To hold that the Fourth Amendment applies to searches conducted by school authorities is only to begin the inquiry into the standards governing such searches. Although the underlying command of the Fourth Amendment is always that searches and seizures be reasonable, what is reasonable depends on the context within which a search takes place. The determination of the standard of reasonableness governing any specific class of searches requires "balancing the need to search against the invasion which the search entails." . . . On one side of the balance are arrayed the individual's legitimate expectations

---

The majority of courts that have addressed the issue of the Fourth Amendment in the schools have, like the Supreme Court of New Jersey in this case, reached a middle position: the Fourth Amendment applies to searches conducted by school authorities, but the special needs of the school environment require assessment of the legality of such searches against a standard less exacting than that of probable cause. These courts have, by and large, upheld warrantless searches by school authorities provided that they are supported by a reasonable suspicion that the search will uncover evidence of an infraction of school disciplinary rules or a violation of the law. *See, e.g., Tarter v. Raybuck,* 742 F.2d 977 (CA6 1984); *Bilbrey v. Brown,* 738 F.2d 1462 (CA9 1984); *Horton v. Goose Creek Independent School Dist.,* 690 F.2d 470 (CA5 1982); *Bellnier v. Lund,* 438 F.Supp. 47 (NDNY 1977); *M. v. Board of Ed. Ball-Chatham Community Unit School Dist. No. 5, supra, In re W.,* 29 Cal.App.3d 777, 105 Cal.Rptr. 775 (1973); *State v. Baccino,* 282 A.2d 869 (Del.Super.1971); *State v. D.T.W.,* 425 So.2d 1383 (Fla.Dist.Ct.App. 1983); *State v. Young, supra; In re J.A.,* 85 Ill.App.3d 567, 40 Ill.Dec. 755, 406 N.E.2d 958 (1980); *People v. Ward,* 62 Mich.App. 46, 233 N.W.2d 180 (1975); *Doe v. State,* 88 N.M. 347, 540 P.2d 827 (App.1975); *People v. D.,* 34 N.Y.2d 483, 358 N.Y.S.2d 403, 315 N.E.2d 466 (1974); *State v. McKinnon,* 88 Wash.2d 75, 558 P.2d 781 (1977); *In re L.L.,* 90 Wis.2d 585, 280 N.W.2d 343 (App.1979).

Although few have considered the matter, courts have also split over whether the exclusionary rule is an appropriate remedy for Fourth Amendment violations committed by school authorities. The Georgia courts have held that although the Fourth Amendment applies to the schools, the exclusionary rule does not. *See, e.g., State v. Young, supra; State v. Lamb,* 137 Ga.App. 437, 224 S.E.2d 51 (1976). Other jurisdictions have applied the rule to exclude the fruits of unlawful school searches from criminal trials and delinquency proceedings. *See State v. Mora, supra; People v. D., supra.*

3. In holding that the search of T.L.O.'s purse did not violate the Fourth Amendment, we do not implicitly determine that the exclusionary rule applies to the fruits of unlawful searches conducted by school authorities. The question whether evidence should be excluded from a criminal proceeding involves two discrete inquiries: whether the evidence was seized in violation of the Fourth Amendment, and whether the exclusionary rule is the appropriate remedy for the violation. Neither question is logically antecedent to the other, for a negative answer to either question is sufficient to dispose of the case. Thus, our determination that the search at issue in this case did not violate the Fourth Amendment implies no particular resolution of the question of the applicability of the exclusionary rule.

of privacy and personal security; on the other, the government's need for effective methods to deal with breaches of public order.

. . . A search of a child's person or of a closed purse or other bag carried on her person,[5] no less than a similar search carried out on an adult, is undoubtedly a severe violation of subjective expectations of privacy.

* * *

Against the child's interest in privacy must be set the substantial interest of teachers and administrators in maintaining discipline in the classroom and on school grounds. Maintaining order in the classroom has never been easy, but in recent years, school disorder has often taken particularly ugly forms: drug use and violent crime in the schools have become major social problems. . . .

. . . It is evident that the school setting requires some easing of the restrictions to which searches by public authorities are ordinarily subject. The warrant requirement, in particular, is unsuited to the school environment: requiring a teacher to obtain a warrant before searching a child suspected of an infraction of school rules (or of the criminal law) would unduly interfere with the maintenance of the swift and informal disciplinary procedures needed in the schools. . . .

The school setting also requires some modification of the level of suspicion of illicit activity needed to justify a search. Ordinarily, a search—even one that may permissibly be carried out without a warrant—must be based upon "probable cause" to believe that a violation of the law has occurred. . . . However, "probable cause" is not an irreducible requirement of a valid search. The fundamental command of the Fourth Amendment is that searches and seizures be reasonable, and although "both the concept of probable cause and the requirement of a warrant bear on the reasonableness of a search, . . . in certain limited circumstances neither is required." . . . Thus, we have in a number of cases recognized the legality of searches and seizures based on suspicions that, although "reasonable," do not rise to the level of probable cause. . . . Where a careful balancing of governmental and private interests suggests that the public interest is best served by a Fourth Amendment standard of reasonableness that stops short of probable cause, we have not hesitated to adopt such a standard.

We join the majority of courts that have examined this issue in concluding that the accommodation of the privacy interests of schoolchildren with the substantial need of teachers and administrators for freedom to maintain order in the schools does not require strict adherence to the requirement that searches be based on probable cause to believe that the subject of the search has violated or is violating the law. Rather, the legality of a search of a student should depend simply on the reasonableness, under all the circumstances, of the search. Determining the reasonableness of any search involves a twofold inquiry: first, one must consider "whether the . . . action was justified at its inception," *Terry v. Ohio*, 392 U.S., at 20, 88 S.Ct., at 1879; second, one must determine whether the search as actually conducted "was reasonably related in scope to the circumstances which justified the interference in the first place," *ibid.* Under ordinary circumstances, a search of a student by a teacher or other school official[7] will be "justified at its inception" when there are reasonable grounds for suspecting that the search will turn up evidence that the student has violated or is violating either the law or the rules of the

---

5. We do not address the question, not presented by this case, whether a schoolchild has a legitimate expectation of privacy in lockers, desks, or other school property provided for the storage of school supplies. Nor do we express any opinion on the standards (if any) governing school officials. Compare *Zamora v. Pomeroy*, 639 F.2d 662, 670 (CA10 1981) ("Inasmuch as the school had assumed joint control of the locker it cannot be successfully maintained that the school did not have a right to inspect it"), and *People v. Overton*, 24 N.Y.2d 522, 249 N.E.2d 366, 301 N.Y.S.2d 479 (1969) (school administrators have power to consent to search of a student's locker), with *State v. Engerud*, 94 N.J. 331, 348, 463 A.2d 934, 943 (1983) ("We are satisfied that in the context of this case the student had an expectation of privacy in the contents of his locker. . . . For the four years of high school, the school locker is a home away from home. In it the student stores the kind of personal 'effects' protected by the Fourth Amendment").

7. We here consider only searches carried out by school authorities acting alone and on their own authority. This case does not present the question of the appropriate standard for assessing the legality of searches conducted by school officials in conjunction with or at the behest of law enforcement agencies, and we express no opinion on that question. *Cf. Picha v. Wielgos*, 410 F.Supp. 1214, 1219–21 (ND Ill. 1976) (holding probable cause standard applicable to searches involving the police).

school.[8] Such a search will be permissible in its scope when the measures adopted are reasonably related to the objectives of the search and not excessively intrusive in light of the age and sex of the student and the nature of the infraction.

This standard will, we trust, neither unduly burden the efforts of school authorities to maintain order in their schools nor authorize unrestrained intrusions upon the privacy of schoolchildren. By focusing attention on the question of reasonableness, the standard will spare teachers and school administrators the necessity of schooling themselves in the niceties of probable cause and permit them to regulate their conduct according to the dictates of reason and common sense. At the same time, the reasonableness standard should ensure that the interests of students will be invaded no more than is necessary to achieve the legitimate end of preserving order in the schools.

IV

There remains the question of the legality of the search in this case. . . . Our review of the facts surrounding the search leads us to conclude that the search was in no sense unreasonable for Fourth Amendment purposes.

The incident that gave rise to this case actually involved two separate searches, with the first—the search for cigarettes—providing the suspicion that gave rise to the second—the search for marihuana. Although it is the fruits of the second search that are at issue here, the validity of the search for marihuana must depend on the reasonableness of the initial search for cigarettes, as there would have been no reason to suspect that T.L.O. possessed marihuana had the first search not taken place. Accordingly, it is to the search for cigarettes that we first turn our attention. . . .

* * *

. . . The relevance of T.L.O.'s possession of cigarettes to the question whether she had been smoking and to the credibility of her denial that she smoked supplied the necessary "nexus" between the item searched for and the infraction under investigation. . . . Thus, if Mr. Choplick in fact had a reasonable suspicion that T.L.O. had cigarettes in her purse, the search was justified despite the fact that the cigarettes, if found, would constitute "mere evidence" of a violation. . . .

. . . A teacher had reported that T.L.O. was smoking in the lavatory. Certainly this report gave Mr. Choplick reason to suspect that T.L.O. was carrying cigarettes with her; and if she did have cigarettes, her purse was the obvious place in which to find them. Mr. Choplick's suspicion that there were cigarettes in the purse was not an "inchoate and unparticularized suspicion or 'hunch,' " . . . rather, it was the sort of "common-sense conclusio[n] about human behavior" upon which "practical people"—including government officials—are entitled to rely. *United States v. Cortez,* 449 U.S. 411, 418, 101 S.Ct. 690, 695, 66 L.Ed.2d 621 (1981). Of course, even if the teacher's report were true, T.L.O. *might* not have had a pack of cigarettes with her; she might have borrowed a cigarette from someone else or have been sharing a cigarette with another student. But the requirement of reasonable suspicion is not a requirement of absolute certainty . . . .

Our conclusion that Mr. Choplick's decision to open T.L.O.'s purse was reasonable brings us to the question of the further search for marihuana once the pack of cigarettes was located. The suspicion upon which the search for marihuana was founded was provided when Mr. Choplick observed a package of rolling papers in the purse as he removed the pack of cigarettes. Although T.L.O. does not dispute the

---

8. We do not decide whether individualized suspicion is an essential element of the reasonableness standard we adopt for searches by school authorities. In other contexts, however, we have held that although "some quantum of individualized suspicion is usually a prerequisite to a constitutional search or seizure[,] . . . the Fourth Amendment imposes no irreducible requirement of such suspicion." *United States v. Martinez-Fuerte,* 428 U.S. 543, 560–61, 96 S.Ct. 3074, 3084, 49 L.Ed.2d 1116 (1976). *See also Camara v. Municipal Court,* 387 U.S. 523, 87 S.Ct. 1727, 18 L.Ed.2d 930 (1967). Exceptions to the requirement of individualized suspicion are generally appropriate only where the privacy interests implicated by a search are minimal and where "other safeguards" are available "to assure that the individual's reasonable expectation of privacy is not 'subject to the discretion of the official in the field.' " *Delaware v. Prouse,* 440 U.S. 648, 654–55, 99 S.Ct. 1391, 1396–97, 59 L.Ed.2d 660 (1979). . . . Because the search of T.L.O.'s purse was based upon an individualized suspicion that she had violated school rules, *see infra,* at 745–46, we need not consider the circumstances that might justify school authorities in conducting searches unsupported by individualized suspicion.

reasonableness of Mr. Choplick's belief that the rolling papers indicated the presence of marihuana, she does contend that the scope of the search Mr. Choplick conducted exceeded permissible bounds when he seized and read certain letters that implicated T.L.O. in drug dealing. This argument, too, is unpersuasive. The discovery of the rolling papers concededly gave rise to a resonable suspicion that T.L.O. was carrying marihuana as well as cigarettes in her purse. This suspicion justified further exploration of T.L.O.'s purse, which turned up more evidence of drug-related activities: a pipe, a number of plastic bags of the type commonly used to store marihuana, a small quantity of marihuana, and a fairly substantial amount of money. Under these circumstances, it was not unreasonable to extend the search to a separate zippered compartment of the purse; and when a search of that compartment revealed an index card containing a list of "people who owe me money" as well as two letters, the inference that T.L.O. was involved in marihuana trafficking was substantial enough to justify Mr. Choplick in examining the letters to determine whether they contained any further evidence. In short, we cannot conclude that the search for marihuana was unreasonable in any respect.

Because the search resulting in the discovery of the evidence of marihuana dealing by T.L.O. was reasonable, the New Jersey Supreme Court's decision to exclude that evidence from T.L.O.'s juvenile delinquency proceedings on Fourth Amendment grounds was erroneous. Accordingly, the judgment of the Supreme Court of New Jersey is

Reversed.

Justice Powell, with whom Justice O'Connor joins, concurring.

I agree with the Court's decision, and generally with its opinion. I would place greater emphasis, however, on the special characteristics of elementary and secondary schools that make it unnecessary to afford students the same constitutional protections granted adults and juveniles in a nonschool setting.

In any realistic sense, students within the school environment have a lesser expectation of privacy than members of the population generally. They spend the school hours in close association with each other, both in the classroom and during recreation periods. The students in a particular class often know each other and their teachers quite well. Of necessity, teachers have a degree of familiarity with, and authority over, their students that is unparalleled except perhaps in the relationship between parent and child. It is simply unrealistic to think that students have the same subjective expectation of privacy as the population generally. . . .

The special relationship between teacher and student also distinguishes the setting within which school children operate. Law enforcement officers function as adversaries of criminal suspects. These officers have the responsibility to investigate criminal activity, to locate and arrest those who violate our laws, and to facilitate the charging and bringing of such persons to trial. Rarely does this type of adversarial relationship exist between school authorities and pupils. Instead, there is a commonality of interests between teachers and their pupils. The attitude of the typical teacher is one of personal responsibility for the student's welfare as well as for his education.

The primary duty of school officials and teachers, as the Court states, is the education and training of young people. A state has a compelling interest in assuring that the schools meet this responsibility. Without first establishing discipline and maintaining order, teachers cannot begin to educate their students. And apart from education, the school has the obligation to protect pupils from mistreatment by other children, and also to protect teachers themselves from violence by the few students whose conduct in recent years has prompted national concern. For me, it would be unreasonable and at odds with history to argue that the full panoply of constitutional rules applies with the same force and effect in the schoolhouse as it does in the enforcement of criminal laws.

* * *

Justice Brennan, with whom Justice Marshall joins, concurring in part and dissenting in part.

* * *

I agree that schoolteachers or principals, when not acting as agents of law enforcement authorities, generally may conduct a search of their students' belongings without first obtaining a warrant. To agree with the Court on this point is to say that school searches may justifiably be held to that extent to constitute an exception to the Fourth Amendment's warrant requirement. Such an exception, however, is not to be justified, as the Court apparently holds, by assessing net social value through application of an unguided "balancing test" in which "the individual's legitimate expectations of privacy and personal security" are weighed against "the government's need for effective methods to deal with breaches of public order." . . . Rather, some *special* governmental interest beyond the need merely to apprehend lawbreakers is necessary to justify a categorical exception to the warrant requirement. . . .

* * *

In this case, such extraordinary governmental interests do exist and are sufficient to justify an exception to the warrant requirement. Students are necessarily confined for most of the school day in close proximity to each other and to the school staff. I agree with the Court that we can take judicial notice of the serious problems of drugs and violence that plague our schools. . . . A teacher or principal could neither carry out essential teaching functions nor adequately protect students' safety if required to wait for a warrant before conducting a necessary search.

* * *

I emphatically disagree with the Court's decision to cast aside the constitutional probable-cause standard when assessing the constitutional validity of a schoolhouse search. The Court's decision jettisons the probable-cause standard—the only standard that finds support in the text of the Fourth Amendment—on the basis of its Rohrschach-like "balancing test." Use of such a "balancing test" to determine the standard for evaluating the validity of a full-scale search represents a sizable innovation in Fourth Amendment analysis. This innovation finds support neither in precedent nor policy and portends a dangerous weakening of the purpose of the Fourth Amendment to protect the privacy and security of our citizens. Moreover, even if this Court's historic understanding of the Fourth Amendment were mistaken and a balancing test of some kind were appropriate, any such test that gave adequate weight to the privacy and security interests protected by the Fourth Amendment would not reach the preordained result the Court's conclusory analysis reaches today. . . .

* * *

Considerations of the deepest significance for the freedom of our citizens counsel strict adherence to the principle that no search may be conducted where the official is not in possession of probable cause. . . . [T]he Fourth Amendment rests on the principle that a true balance between the individual and society depends on the recognition of "the right to be let alone—the most comprehesive of rights and the right most valued by civilized men." . . .

. . . For me, the finding that the Fourth Amendment applies, coupled with the observation that what is at issue is a full-scale search, is the end of the inquiry. But even if I believed that a "balancing test" appropriately replaces the judgment of the Framers of the Fourth Amendment, I would nonetheless object to the cursory and short-sighted "test" that the Court employs to justify its predictable weakening of Fourth Amendment protections. In particular, the test employed by the Court vastly overstates the social costs that a probable-cause standard entails and, though it plausibly articulates the serious privacy interests at stake, inexplicably fails to accord them adequate weight in striking the balance. . . .

* * *

A consideration of the likely operation of the probable-cause standard reinforces this conclusion. Discussing the issue of school searches, Professor LaFave has noted that the cases that have reached the appellate courts "strongly suggest that in most instances the evidence of wrongdoing prompting teachers or principals to conduct searches is sufficiently detailed and specific to meet the traditional probable cause test." 3 W. LaFave, Search and Seizure §10.11, pp. 459–60 (1978). . . .

As compared with the relative ease with which teachers can apply the probable-cause standard, the amorphous "reasonableness under all the circumstances" standard freshly coined by the Court today will likely spawn increased litigation and greater uncertainty among teachers and administrators. . . .

* * *

A legitimate balancing test whose function was something more substantial than reaching a predetermined conclusion acceptable to this Court's impressions of what authority teachers need would therefore reach rather a different result than that reached by the Court today. On one side of the balance would be the costs of applying traditional Fourth Amendment standards—the "practical" and "flexible" probable-cause standard where a full-scale intrusion is sought, a lesser standard in situations where the intrusion is much less severe and the need for greater authority compelling. Whatever costs were toted up on this side would have to be discounted by the costs of applying an unprecedented and ill-defined "reasonableness under all the circumstances" test that will leave teachers and administrators uncertain as to their authority and will encourage excessive fact-based litigation.

On the other side of the balance would be the serious privacy interests of the student, interests that the Court admirably articulates in its opinion . . . but which the Court's new ambiguous standard places in serious jeopardy. I have no doubt that a fair assessment of the two sides of the balance would necessarily reach the same conclusion that, as I have argued above, the Fourth Amendment's language compels—that school searches like that conducted in this case are valid only if supported by probable cause.

* * *

Applying the constitutional probable-cause standard to the facts of this case, I would find that Mr. Choplick's search violated T.L.O.'s Fourth Amendment rights. . . .

* * *

On my view of the case, we need not decide whether the initial search conducted by Mr. Choplick—the search for evidence of the smoking violation that was completed when Mr. Choplick found the pack of cigarettes—was valid. For Mr. Choplick at that point did not have probable cause to continue to rummage through T.L.O.'s purse. Mr. Choplick's suspicion of marihuana possession at this time was based *solely* on the presence of the package of cigarette papers. The mere presence without more of such a staple item of commerce is insufficient to warrant a person of reasonable caution in inferring both that T.L.O. had violated the law by possessing marihuana and that evidence of that violation would be found in her purse. Just as a police officer could not obtain a warrant to search a home based solely on his claim that he had seen a package of cigerette papers in that home, Mr. Choplick was not entitled to search possibly the most private possessions of T.L.O. based on the mere presence of a package of cigarette papers. Therefore, the fruits of this illegal search must be excluded. . . .

Justice Stevens, with whom Justice Marshall joins, and with whom Justice Brennan joins as to Part I, concurring in part and dissenting in part.

* * *

The majority holds that "a search of a student by a teacher or other school official will be 'justified at its inception' when there are reasonable grounds for suspecting that the search will turn up evidence *that the student has violated or is violating* either the law or *the rules of the school*." . . . This standard will permit teachers and school administrators to search students when they suspect that the search will reveal evidence of even the most trivial school regulation or precatory guideline for student behavior. The Court's standard for deciding whether a search is justified "at its inception" treats all violations of the rules of the school as though they were fungible. For the Court, a search for curlers and sunglasses in order to enforce the school dress code is apparently just as important as a search for evidence of heroin addiction or violent gang activity.

. . . A [preferable] standard . . . would permit teachers and school administrators to search a student when they have reason to believe that the search will uncover *evidence that the student is violating the law or engaging in conduct that is seriously disruptive of school order, or the educational process.*

NOTES AND QUESTIONS

1. The Constitutional Standard

T.L.O. advances a constitutional standard of reasonable suspicion, a standard weaker than the traditional probable cause standard, to determine whether a school search is permissible. Determining reasonableness, according to the Court, involves deciding first whether the search was initially justified—that is, whether there are reasonable grounds for suspecting that it will turn up evidence of a violation of the law or school rules. Second, it means determining whether the conduct of the search is reasonably related in its scope to the circumstances that initially justify the interference—that is, whether the measures taken relate reasonably to the objectives of the search and are not excessively intrusive, taking into account the student's age and sex and the nature of the alleged violation. *See generally* T. van Geel, *The Courts and American Education Law* 327–36 (1987).

Is the reasonable suspicion standard a novel standard, as the dissenters urge, or are there plausible analogies in the existing caselaw? *See also* Comment, "The Supreme Court and the Decline of Students' Constitutional Rights: A Selective Analysis," 65 *Neb.L.Rev.* 161, 178 (1986) ("an unprecedented decision in fourth amendment law"). Is the reasonable suspicion test ambiguous—more ambiguous than the traditional probable cause doctrine? *Compare T.L.O. with Illinois v. Gates*, 462 U.S. 213, 103 S.Ct. 2317, 76 L.Ed.2d 527 (1983). *See e.g.*, van Geel, "Searching of Students After *New Jersey v. T.L.O.*," in T. Jones and D. Semler, eds., *School Law Update 1986* 129 (1986); Note, "School Searches Under the Fourth Amendment: *New Jersey v. T.L.O.*," 72 *Corn.L.Rev.* 368 (1987). *But cf.* Majestic, "Search and Seizure in the Schools: Defining Reasonableness," 16:3 *School Law Bull.* 1 (1985).

a. Reasonable grounds. What does the requirement of reasonable suspicion or grounds for a search mean? Does a reasonable suspicion mean that there must be an individual suspicion that some specific person has violated school rules? *See Kuehn v. Renton School District No.* 403, 103 Wash.2d 594, 694 P.2d 1078, 1081 (1985) and cases cited therein. In footnote 8 the Court declines to reach this question, but it notes that the search of T.L.O. "was based upon an individualized suspicion that she had violated school rules." Under what circumstances may school authorities conduct a search where there is no reasonable suspicion of a specific individual? What if suspicion is focused on five or six individuals? *See In re Alexander B.*, 270 Cal.Rptr. 342 (Ct.App. 1990).

In order for a search to be justified, is it sufficient that any violation of the school's rules has occurred—talking back to a teacher, for instance—or must the school officials demonstrate the likelihood that evidence of a violation of school rules will be turned up by the search? *Cf. In re Alexander B.*, *supra*.

Is the reasonable grounds test objective or subjective? Does what is reasonable depend on the special knowledge of a school official?

What constitutes a reasonable suspicion—even if the focus is on the conduct of an individual? Professor Tyll van Geel, writing in "Searching of Students After *New Jersey v. T.L.O.*," in T. Jones and D. Semler, eds., *School Law Update 1986* 129, 134 (1986), makes the following point: "A search would be permitted if . . . any one of the following factors were present: the student makes a furtive gesture to his pocket as the teacher approaches; . . . the student flees as the teacher approaches; . . . the student is present in an area of the school where drug dealing is known to occur; . . . the student is observed placing something in a sock or shoe." Do you agree? *See also In re Alexander B.*, *supra*; *State v. Michael G.*, 106 N.M. 644, 748 P.2d 17 (App. 1987); *Tarter v. Raybuck*, 742 F.2d 977 (6th Cir. 1984), *cert. denied*, 470 U.S. 1051, 105 S.Ct. 1749, 84 L.Ed.2d 814 (1985); *Bilbrey v. Brown*, 738 F.2d 1462 (9th Cir. 1984). Might such a reading of the law frequently nab the innocent, who just happened to make what looked like a furtive gesture? If so, is that a serious constitutional problem? If the court's standard is in fact more stringent than this, in what way is it?

Does information from informants provide reasonable grounds for a search? Should the answer turn on the character or reliability of the informants? *See Commonwealth v. Carey*, 554 N.E.2d 1199 (Mass. 1990). Whether they are anonymous or known? Whether they are students, employees, or others? Whether they have provided accurate information in the past? Whether they purport to be reporting facts or rumors? *See, e.g.*, *State v. Engerud*, 94 N.J. 331, 463 A.2d 934 (1983); *Bahr v. Jenkins*, 539 F.Supp. 483 (E.D.Ky. 1982); *People v. Singletary*, 37 N.Y.2d 310, 372 N.Y.S.2d 68, 333 N.E.2d 369 (1975). Whether the informants were eyewitnesses of the possession of arms or contraband? *See Commonwealth v. Carey*, *supra* at 1203 n. 4.

Of what relevance, in assessing reasonableness, is a student's past school record and reputation?

Suppose a student, whom school officials have been watching closely for months because of a tip that he had been dealing drugs, is seen entering a restroom twice with a fellow student, leaving ten to fifteen seconds later. Are there grounds to search the student? *See People v. Scott D.*, 34 N.Y.2d 483, 358 N.Y.S.2d 403, 315 N.E.2d 466 (1974).

b. The scope of the search. The *T.L.O.* majority suggests that "the nature of the infraction," as well as the age and sex of the students involved, affect the permissible scope of the search. How so? Do expectations of privacy vary by age or sex? Would it be appropriate for a school to strip-search a class of third-graders, in response to a teacher's complaint that five dollars was missing from her desk drawer? A class of tenth-graders? A class of physical education students, all of whom are female? Or are strip searches inherently degrading and hence impermissible—even where students are suspected of secreting small quantities of hard drugs in body cavities?

Do the *T.L.O.* standards govern locker searches? *See Commonwealth v. Carey*, 554 N.E.2d 1199, 1202 (Mass. 1990). Do students have a "legitimate expectation of privacy" concerning their lockers and desks? *See Zamora v. Pomeroy*, 639 F.2d 662 (10th Cir. 1981); *State v. Joseph T.*, 336 S.E.2d 728, 736 (W.Va. 1985). Is the sniffing of students or their lockers by specially trained dogs, for the purpose of uncovering illegal drugs, a search? *See Horton v. Goose Creek Independent School District*, 690 F.2d 470 (5th cir. 1982), *cert. denied*, 463 U.S. 1207, 103 S.Ct. 3536, 77 L.Ed.2d 1387 (1983); *Zamora v. Pomeroy*, 639 F.2d 662 (10th Cir. 1981).

Under what circumstances will a court conclude that a student has voluntarily consented to a search? *See State v. Wolfer*, 39 Wash.App. 287, 693 P.2d 154 (1984); *Boynton v. Casey*, 543 F.Supp. 995 (D.Me. 1982). Under what circumstances does the interrogation of a student by a school official constitute an unreasonable seizure or arrest of the student under the Fourth Amendment? *See Edwards v. Rees*, 883 F.2d 882 (10th Cir. 1989) (twenty minute interrogation of a student by vice principal about bomb threat justified by statements made by two other students); *Coffman v. State*, 782 S.W.2d 249 (Tex.App. 1989).

c. *The probable cause standard.* How would these questions be answered if Justice Brennan had persuaded his colleagues that the familiar "probable cause" standard, rather than a reasonable suspicion test, should be applied to school-initiated searches? If Justice Stevens' distinction between serious and trivial rules infractions had prevailed?

2. *Remedies: The Exclusionary Rule and* T.L.O.

The relevance of the exclusionary rule (which makes illegally obtained evidence inadmissible in a judicial proceeding, *Mapp v. Ohio*, 367 U.S. 643, 81 S.Ct. 1684, 6 L.Ed.2d 1081 (1961)) to school searches is explicitly left undecided by the *T.L.O.* decision. The purpose of that rule is to deter official police misconduct. Should it follow that the rule also should be applied to deter overzealous school administrators? *See, e.g., Jones v. Latexo Independent School Distict*, 499 F.Supp. 223 (E.D.Tex. 1980); *Coffman v. State*, 782 S.W.2d 249 (Tex.App. 1989).

The victim of an "unreasonable" search may file a suit for damages, either for violation of privacy under state law or for a violation of civil rights under the federal statute, 42 U.S.C. § 1983. *See, e.g., Doe v. Renfrow*, 635 F.2d 582 (7th Cir. 1980). But § 1983 has been read to include a qualified immunity: If officials have acted in good faith they are not subject to liability. What would constitute a bad faith search in violation of the Fourth Amendment?

3. *Police Involvement*

A police-initiated search for purposes of obtaining evidence or a criminal prosecution against a student is typically subject to the traditional Fourth Amendment requirements applicable to police searches of adults. *See State v. McKinnon*, 88 Wash.2d 75, 558 P.2d 781 (1977). Should the Fourth Amendment requirements as applied to the police change if they work together with school officials? *See Cason v. Cook*, 810 F.2d 188 (8th Cir. 1987); *Commonwealth v. Carey*, 554 N.E.2d 1199 (Mass. 1990). What should be the standard if the police propose a search to school officials in order to obtain evidence for a criminal prosecution, and school officials actually conduct the search either alone or with the police? *See, e.g., Picha v. Wielgos*, 410 F.Supp. 1214 (N.D. Ill. 1976); *Piazzola v. Watkins*, 316 F.Supp. 624 (M.D. Ala. 1970), *aff'd*, 442 F.2d 284 (5th Cir. 1971); *People v. Overton*, 24 N.Y.2d 522, 301 N.Y.S.2d 479, 249 N.E.2d 366 (1969).

What standard should apply if the police provide a "tip" to school officials without any express understanding that if the school official finds evidence of criminal violations he or she will turn the evidence over to the police? When is a search instigated by the police? *See People in Interest of* P.E.A., 754 P.2d 382 (Colo. 1988); *State v. McKinnon, supra; see also In Re Donaldson*, 269 Cal.App.2d 509, 75 Cal.Rptr. 220 (1969); *Waters v. United States*, 311 A.2d 835 (D.C.App. 1973). What if, without any prior contact with the police, school officials voluntarily turn over incriminating evidence to the police, and a criminal or juvenile prosecution results? *See Coffman v. State*, 782 S.W.2d 249 (Tex.App. 1989). Suppose that the school official has a well-developed working relationship with the police: They meet once a week, exchange information on suspected law violators, and have in the past collaborated in sharing evidence. What would be the result? *Cf. Mercer v. State*, 450 S.W.2d 715, 721 n. 3 (Tex.Civ.App. 1970) (Hughes, J., dissenting). Should school officials be treated as police officers when they conduct a search under the suspicion that criminal misconduct has occurred? *See Piazzola v. Watkins, supra; State v. Young*, 234 Ga. 488, 510–11, 216 S.E.2d 586, 601 (1975) (Gunter, J., dissenting), *cert. denied*, 423 U.S. 1039, 96 S.Ct. 576, 46 L.Ed.2d 413 (1975).

If courts allow the police effectively to direct school searches, does that invite the police to carry out investigations that they, burdened with the need to show probable cause, would be unable to accomplish on their own?

4. Applying the Constitutional Standard: Guns, Drugs and "Just Say No"

a. War Zone High. After a gun battle in the corridors of Central High left two students wounded, school administrators decided to close all doors to the school except one and to install an airport-style metal detector at that door. Can they legally do so, or does the metal detector constitute an unwarranted general search of students? Would it matter if Central High were in California, a state with a constitutional provision guaranteeing students "the inalienable right to attend campuses which are safe, secure and peaceful?" *See In re Alexander B.*, 270 Cal.Rptr. 342, 344 (Ct.App. 1990), citing Cal.Const., Art. I, § 28.

b. Drug bust at Euphoria High. School officials at Euphoria High have seen a rash of drug-related incidents. As a result, they instituted a plan under which students were kept overtime in their first period class, while school officials accompanied by properly trained dogs went from class to class to search for drugs. Students were instructed to sit quietly at their desks with their hands and any purses placed upon their desk tops while the dog handler led the dog up and down the aisles to enable it to sniff for drugs. If the dog indicated the possibility of the presence of drugs, the student was taken from the room and searched.

Was the retention in the room for extra time a seizure (or arrest?) of the students? Was the mere entrance into the room by school officials a search? Was the use of dogs a search? Was there a reasonable suspicion that school rules had been violated? An "individualized suspicion?" Is this merely an investigation as opposed to a search, or is this a search because it is an indiscriminate intrusion into an area surrounding the body with regard to which students have an expectancy of privacy? Or does the search occur only after a dog has indicated that a particular student may have or have had illegal drugs on his or her person? *See Horton v. Goose Creek Independent School District*, 690 F.2d 470 (5th Cir. 1982), *cert. denied*, 463 U.S. 1207, 103 S.Ct. 3536, 77 L.Ed.2d 1387 (1983); *Zamora v. Pomeroy*, 639 F.2d 662 (10th Cir. 1981); *Jones v. Latexo Independent School District*, 499 F.Supp. 223 (E.D.Tex. 1980). *See generally* Gardner, "Sniffing for Drugs in the Classroom—Perspectives on Fourth Amendment Scope," 74 *Nw. U.L.Rev.* 803 (1980).

c. Drug testing at Euphoria High. In 1986, the sudden death of University of Maryland basketball star Len Bias, from heart failure resulting from a cocaine overdose, shocked the nation. It also focused popular and institutional concern on the particular problem of drug use among athletes. In response to these episodes and the "just say no" campaign to halt drug use, especially among students, a number of high schools across the country have adopted drug-testing plans.

Citing its obligation under state policy to ensure the physical fitness and safety of all of its students, the Euphoria school board requires an annual physical examination of all students, including a urinalysis to detect the presence of "controlled dangerous substances." Is that drug test "unreasonable" under *T.L.O.?* Should individual suspicion be required? Is it relevant that the board characterizes the test as a medical exam, not a search? *See Odenheim v. Carlstadt-East Rutherford Regional School District*, 211 N.J. Super. 54, 510 A.2d 709 (1985). Suppose that the school district had required medical examinations for many years, including a urinalysis, and it simply had added drug screening to the list of tests?

Is your analysis of the Euphoria High problem different if drug testing is limited to student athletes and cheerleaders? Does it matter that a positive test result means suspension from athletic events or activities? That the test is described as "educational, diagnostic and preventive, as opposed to punitive or disciplinary"? That students are not required to give the urine sample while being physically observed? That the drugs being tested for are steroids? Heroin and cocaine? *See Schaill by Kross v. Tippercanoe County School Corporation*, 864 F.2d 1309 (7th Cir. 1988); *Bally v. Northeastern University*, 532 N.E.2d 1309 (7th Cir. 1988); *Bally v. Northeastern University*, 403 Mass. 713, 532 N.E.2d 49 (1989).

On the drug-testing issue, *see generally* Bittle, Pashler, and Sernett, "Drug Testing," 36 *Educ. L. Rep.* 1067 (1986); Gillow, "Compulsory Urinalysis of Public High Students: An Unconstitutional Search and Seizure," 18 *Colum. Hum. Rts. L. Rev.* 111 (1987); Note, "An Analysis of Public College Athlete Drug Testing Programs Through the Unconstitutional Condition Doctrine and the Fourth Amendment," 60 *So. Cal.L.Rev.* 815 (1987).

d. Drug testing and school employees. Is mandatory drug testing of school employees—based on concern about a perceived "drug culture"—permissible? What if the fear is that employees are selling illegal drugs to students? Does it matter that the testing regime is confined to school bus drivers? Probationary teachers? *See Jones v. McKenzie,* 833 F.2d 335 (D.C. Cir. 1987); *Patchoque-Medford Congress of Teachers v. Board of Education,* 119 A.D.2d 35, 505 N.Y.S.2d 888 (1986).

5. T.L.O. *and the School Culture*

Justice Powell argues in his concurrence that, because of "the special characteristics of elementary and secondary schools," students should have "a lesser expectation of privacy than members of the population generally. . . . Without first establishing discipline and maintaining order, teachers cannot begin to educate their students."

Justice Stevens holds a very different view: "Schools are places where we inculcate the values essential to the meaningful exercise of rights and responsibilities by self-governing citizenry. If the nation's students can be convicted through the use of arbitrary methods destructive of personal liberty, they cannot help but feel that they have been dealt with unfairly."

Who has the better argument?

IV. PROCEDURAL DUE PROCESS

A. The Allure of Due Process

The issue of liberty within the school has partly to do with the substantive entitlements of students and teachers, their freedom to speak and act without state interference. But even where the substantive standard is clearly fixed, the rights of students and teachers also turn on the degree of assurance that the state will not act arbitrarily in particular instances. Procedural protections are intended to secure the individual against arbitrary governmental action.

Any number of devices might be designed to minimize the risk of arbitrariness. Internal monitoring of administrative behavior within the school that renders school officials bureaucratically accountable for their lapses; reliance on school-based ombudsmen, empowered to investigate student and teacher complaints; inquisitorial inquiries, in which the dispute-resolver draws on whatever information is available: these are all among the conceivable alternatives. *See, e.g.,* Boyer, "Alternatives to Administrative Trial-Type Hearings for Resolving Complex Scientific, Economic, and Social Issues," 71 *Mich.L.Rev.* 111 (1972); Mashaw, "The Management Side of Due Process: Some Theoretical and Litigation Notes on the Assurance of Accuracy, Fairness, and Timeliness in the Adjudication of Social Welfare Claims," 59 *Cornell L.Rev.* 772 (1974); Tribe, "Policy Science: Analysis or Ideology?," 2 *Philos. & Pub. Aff.* 66 (1972).

In American jurisprudence, procedural protections are routinely bound up in the notion of due process of law entailing some sort of hearing conducted by a neutral fact-finder. The equation of the hearing with procedural justice also shapes social policy; as the discussion of the rights of handicapped children to an appropriate education, discussed in chapter 7, *infra*, suggests, the hearing is increasingly regarded as an instrument for vindicating substantive rights.

The idea that government is appropriately restrained from acting arbitrarily is not a new one. In *R. v. University of Cambridge,* (1723) 1 Str. 557, the first English case to shape the terms of what in that country is called "natural justice," the court retells the Adam and Eve story as a tale of due process:

> Even God himself did not pass sentence upon Adam, before he was called upon to make his defense. "Adam," says God, "where art thou? Hast thou not eaten of the tree, whereof I commanded thee that thou shouldst not eat?" And the same question was put to Eve also.

The allure of procedural protection—specifically, some sort of hearing—has grown considerably in the intervening centuries. Only two decades ago, Warren Seavey decried the unwillingness of schools to hedge their disciplinary regimes with even rudimentary procedural safeguards. "It is shocking," he argued, "that the officials of a state educational institution . . . should not understand the elementary principles of fair play. It is equally shocking to find that a court supports them in denying to a student the protection given to a pickpocket." Seavey, "Dismissal of Students: 'Due Process'," 70 *Harv.L.Rev.* 1406, 1407 (1957). As the following excerpt suggests, things have changed considerably:

"Proceduralism and Bureaucracy: Due Process in the School Setting"

D. Kirp, 28 *Stan.L.Rev.* 841, 843–47 (1976). Reprinted by permission.

The history of public law during the past decade has been, in no small part, a history of the expansion of procedural protection. Relationships between citizens and government, traditionally shaped by administrative prerogative or legislative rule, are increasingly constrained by the command of the due process clause. Judicial decisions have dramatically altered the legal status of citizens dependent upon government largesse for such services as welfare benefits, housing, employment, and education. While these recipients were traditionally viewed as mere supplicants with few defenses against even admittedly arbitrary government actions, in the wake of the welfare rights cases and their progeny they may now advance claims based on legally cognizable rights. This constitutional claim does not guarantee some minimally adequate level of goods or services. Rather it embodies the right to impartial review of governmental actions which threaten most statutorily created substantive entitlements.

The demand for such rights is partly attributable to the vastly greater goods- and service-providing activities of government, and the resulting increased reliance upon government assistance. Coupled with this new dependency is a growing, albeit difficult to measure, distrust of the ways in which public officials exercise their delegated discretion. Such discretion ostensibly frees administrators from detailed rules which hamper enlightened management of complex social enterprises. Yet, if ever it was the prevailing belief that government, in its capacity as landlord, schoolmaster or employer, acted with consistent beneficence toward those affected by its decisions, that sense seems largely to have vanished.

Skepticism about the supposedly enlightened nature of governmental behavior has prompted critics of government programs to equate the discretion exercised by the housing authority or school principal with arbitrariness, to treat the substantial freedom delegated to welfare caseworkers as an instrument of coercion, and to perceive deviations from a norm of uniformity as favoritism. Particular individuals serving in these roles have, without doubt, abused the prerogatives of their offices. But the new perception maintains that discretionary official decisionmaking, in the context of benefits programs, not only works individual injustices but also promotes patterns of disadvantage: black children are suspended from school proportionately more frequently than whites, unwed mothers are denied access to public housing, and outspoken civil servants lose their jobs. The causes of these phenomena are said to inhere in corrupted decisionmaking devices. Given that view, the utility of due process is obvious. Constitutionally guaranteed hearings secure at least a measure of protection against governmental arbitrariness as it affects both individuals and groups, and so encourage the emergence of fair official behavior. . . .

The enduring appeal of due process justice is evident at several levels. Most obviously, it is a basic tenet of American constitutional law. Moreover, fair process has been treated as synonymous with justice, while one *particular* process—the due process hearing—is popularly thought more fair than any alternative mode of decisionmaking. . . .

These general considerations apply with particular force to the schools. For teachers, the right to a hearing has been viewed as a way of curbing the schools' capacity to dismiss them without reason. For students, the hearing has been seen as a device to combat the dramatic rise in student suspensions, estimated to affect approximately 10 percent of all junior and senior high school students. . . .

Those who urged that schools be made to conform to a regime of due process envisioned presuspension and pretermination hearings as essential in preserving the student's and teacher's rights as individuals. They hoped that such hearings would produce fairer outcomes and outcomes accepted as fair by those affected. They also anticipated that the constraint of a hearing might have salutary effects: With respect to teachers, it would encourage early evaluation and assessment of performance designed to improve practice; for students, it would reduce reliance on suspensions as a disciplinary tool, encouraging educators to seek less punitive ways of restoring authority and respect.

These aspirations treat due process as important in two distinct respects: as important in and of itself and as important for the outcomes that it generates.

Compare Professor Kirp's analysis with that of Professor Tribe:

> [As an *intrinsic* good,] the hearing may be considered both as a "mode of politics" and as an expression of the rule of law. . . . Whatever its outcome, such a hearing represents a valued human interaction in which the affected person experiences at least the satisfaction of participating in the decision . . . and perhaps the separate satisfaction of receiving an explanation of why the decision is being made in a certain way. . . . [T]hese rights to interchange express the elementary idea that to be a *person*, rather than a *thing*, is at least to be *consulted* about what is done with one. . . . A second, more *instrumental* approach . . . views the requirements of due process as constitutionally . . . valued . . . for their anticipated consequences as means of assuring that the society's agreed-upon rules of conduct, and its rules for distributing various benefits, are in fact accurately and consistently followed. . . . From this "instrumental" perspective, due process . . . ensures that a challenged action accurately reflects the substantive rules applicable to such action; its point is less to assure *participation* than to *use* participation to assure *accuracy*.

L. Tribe, *American Constitutional Law* 666–67 (2d ed. 1988) (emphasis original).

Which view do you find more persuasive as a matter of legal theory? As a description of how individuals perceive due process? Is it participation that a student threatened with suspension or a teacher faced with dismissal cares about? Is it the rightness of the decision that matters or whether he or she wins? *See* M. Tushnet, *Red, White and Blue* 241 (1988).

The introduction of due process norms into the life of the school has two other implications that bear noting. It affects the process of student socialization discussed in chapter 2. The student who perceives herself or himself as the passive recipient of whatever measure of justice school authorities make available may likely develop one view of citizenship rights and relationships with authority; a student who is listened to before discipline is meted out may form a different perception. Due process, in short, can take sides in the dispute between hierarchical and democratic norms of education. *See generally* J. Dewey, *Democracy and Education* (1966); Biber and Minuchin, "The Impact of School Philosophy and Practice on Child Development," in M. Silberman, ed., *The Experience of Schooling* 39 (1971). It also influences the internal governance structure of the school, an issue canvassed fully in chapter 4, *infra*. Teachers' due process rights, for example, supplement the rights that teachers may acquire through collective bargaining. More generally, reliance on due process legalizes dispute resolution in the school.

The next section charts the development of doctrine. While the focus is on the due process clause—specifically, on whether process is due, and if so, what process is due—the broader concern of the section is with procedural protections against allegedly arbitrary official action.

B. The Development of Constitutional Doctrine

Board of Regents v. Roth

408 U.S. 564, 92 S.Ct. 2701, 33 L.Ed.2d 548 (1972).

Mr. Justice Stewart delivered the opinion of the Court.

In 1968 the respondent, David Roth, was hired for his first teaching job as assistant professor of political science at Wisconsin State University-Oshkosh. He was hired for a fixed term of one academic year. The notice of his faculty appointment specified that his employment would begin on September 1, 1968, and would end on June 30, 1969.[1] The respondent completed that term. But he was informed that he would not be rehired for the next academic year.

The respondent had no tenure rights to continued employment. Under Wisconsin statutory law a state university teacher can acquire tenure as a "permanent" employee only after four years of year-to-year employment. Having acquired tenure, a teacher is entitled to continued employment "during efficiency and good behavior." A relatively new teacher without tenure, however, is under Wisconsin law entitled to nothing beyond his one-year appointment.[2] There are no statutory or administrative standards defining eligibility for re-employment. State law thus clearly leaves the decision whether to rehire

1. The respondent had no contract of employment. Rather, his formal notice of appointment was the equivalent of an employment contract. . . .

2. Wis. Stat. 1967, § 37.31(1), in force at the time, provided in pertinent part that: "All teachers in any state university shall initially be employed on probation. The employment shall be permanent, during efficiency and good behavior, after 4 years of continuous service in the state university system as a teacher."

a nontenured teacher for another year to the unfettered discretion of university officials.

The procedural protection afforded a Wisconsin State University teacher before he is separated from the University corresponds to his job security. As a matter of statutory law, a tenured teacher cannot be "discharged except for cause upon written charges" and pursuant to certain procedures.[3] A nontenured teacher, similarly, is protected to some extent *during* his one-year term. Rules promulgated by the Board of Regents provide that a nontenured teacher "dismissed" before the end of the year may have some opportunity for review of the "dismissal." But the Rules provide no real protection for a nontenured teacher who simply is not re-employed for the next year. He must be informed by February 1 "concerning retention or nonretention for the ensuing year." But "no reason for non-retention need be given. No review or appeal is provided in such case."[4]

In conformance with these Rules, the President of Wisconsin State University-Oshkosh informed the respondent before February 1, 1969, that he would not be rehired for the 1969–1970 academic year. He gave the respondent no reason for the decision and no opportunity to challenge it at any sort of hearing.

The respondent then brought this action in Federal District Court alleging that the decision not to rehire him for the next year infringed his Fourteenth Amendment rights. . . . First, he alleged that the true reason for the decision was to punish him for certain statements critical of the University administration, and that it therefore violated his right to freedom of speech.[5] Second, he alleged that the failure of University officials to give him notice of any reason for nonretention and an opportunity for a hearing violated his right to procedural due process of law.

The District Court granted summary judgment for the respondent on the procedural issue, ordering the university officials to provide him with reasons and a hearing. 310 F.Supp. 972. The Court of Appeals, with one judge dissenting, affirmed this partial summary judgment. 446 F.2d 806. We granted certiorari. 404 U.S. 909. The only question presented to us at this stage in the case is whether the respondent had a constitutional right to a statement of reasons and a hearing on the University's decision not to rehire him for another year.[6] We hold that he did not.

I

The requirements of procedural due process apply only to the deprivation of interests encompassed by the Fourteenth Amendment's protection of liberty and property. When protected interests are implicated, the right to some kind of prior hearing is paramount. But the range of interests protected by procedural due process is not infinite.

---

3. Wis. Stat. § 37.31(1) further provided that:

"No teacher who has become permanently employed as herein provided shall be discharged except for cause upon written charges. Within 30 days of receiving the written charges, such teacher may appeal the discharge by a written notice to the president of the board of regents of state colleges. The board shall cause the charges to be investigated, hear the case and provide such teacher with a written statement as to their decision."

4. The Rules, promulgated by the Board of Regents in 1967, provide:

"RULE I—February 1st is established throughout the State University system as the deadline for written notification of non-tenured faculty concerning retention or nonretention for the ensuing year. The President of each University shall give such notice each year on or before this date.

"RULE II—During the time a faculty member is on probation, no reason for nonretention need be given. No review or appeal is provided in such case.

"RULE III—'Dismissal' as opposed to 'Nonretention' means termination of responsibilities during an academic year. When a nontenure faculty member is dismissed he has no right under Wisconsin Statutes to a review of his case or to appeal. The President may, however, in his discretion, grant a request for a review within the institution, either by a faculty committee or by the President, or both. Any such review would be informal in nature and would be advisory only.

"RULE IV—When a non-tenure faculty member is dismissed he may request a review by or hearing before the Board of Regents. Each such request will be considered separately and the board will, in its discretion, grant or deny same in each individual case."

5. While the respondent alleged that he was not rehired because of his exercise of free speech, the petitioners insisted that the nonretention decision was based on other, constitutionally valid grounds. The District Court came to no conclusion whatever regarding the true reason for the University President's decision. "In the present case," it stated, "it appears that a determination as to the actual bases of the decision must await amplification of the facts at trial. . . . Summary judgment is inappropriate." 310 F. Supp. at 982.

6. The courts that have had to decide whether a non-tenured public employee has a right to a statement of reasons or a hearing upon nonrenewal of his contract have come to varying conclusions. Some have held that neither procedural safeguard is required. *E.g.*, *Orr v. Trinter*, 444 F.2d 128 (6th Cir.); *Jones v. Hopper*, 410 F.2d 1323 (10th Cir); *Freeman v. Gould Special School Dist.*, 405 F.2d 1153 (8th Cir). At least one court has held that there is a right to a statement of reasons but not a hearing. *Drown v. Portsmouth School Dist.*, 435 F.2d 1182 (1st Cir). And another has held that both requirements depend on whether the employee has an "expectancy" of continued employment. *Ferguson v. Thomas*, 430 F.2d 852, 856 (5th Cir.).

The District Court decided that procedural due process guarantees apply in this case by assessing and balancing the weights of the particular interests involved. It concluded that the respondent's interest in reemployment at the Wisconsin State University-Oshkosh outweighed the University's interest in denying him reemployment summarily. 310 F. Supp., at 977–79. Undeniably, the respondent's reemployment prospects were of major concern to him—concern that we surely cannot say was insignificant. And a weighing process has long been a part of any determination of the *form* of hearing required in particular situations by procedural due process.[8] But, to determine whether due process requirements apply in the first place, we must look not to the "weight" but to the *nature* of the interest at stake. . . . We must look to see if the interest is within the Fourteenth Amendment's protection of liberty and property.

"Liberty" and "property" are broad and majestic terms. They are among the "great [constitutional] concepts . . . purposely left to gather meaning from experience. . . . [T]hey relate to the whole domain of social and economic fact, and the statesmen who founded this Nation knew too well that only a stagnant society remains unchanged." *National Ins. Co. v. Tidewater Co.*, 337 U.S. 582, 646 (Frankfurter, J., dissenting). For that reason, the Court has fully and finally rejected the wooden distinction between "rights" and "privileges" that once seemed to govern the applicability of procedural due process rights.[9] The Court has also made clear that the property interests protected by procedural due process extend well beyond actual ownership of real estate, chattels, or money.[10] By the same token, the Court has required due process protection for deprivations of liberty beyond the sort of formal constraints imposed by the criminal process.[11]

Yet, while the Court has eschewed rigid or formalistic limitations on the protection of procedural due process, it has at the same time observed certain boundaries. For the words "liberty" and "property" in the Due Process of the Fourteenth Amendment must be given some meaning.

II

"While this Court has not attempted to define with exactness the liberty . . . guaranteed [by the Fourteenth Amendment], the term has received much consideration, and some of the included things have been definitely stated. Without doubt, it denotes not merely freedom from bodily restraint but also the right of the individual to contract, to engage in any of the common occupations of life, to acquire useful knowledge, to marry, establish a home and bring up children, to worship God according to the dictates of his own conscience, and generally to enjoy those privileges long recognized . . . as essential to the orderly pursuit of happiness by free men." *Meyer v. Nebraska*, 262 U.S. 390, 399 [1923]. In a Constitution for a free people, there can be no doubt that the meaning of "liberty" must be broad indeed. *See, e.g., Bolling v. Sharpe*, 347 U.S. 397, 499–500 [1954]; *Stanley v. Illinois*, 405 U.S. 645.

There might be cases in which a State refused to reemploy a person under such circumstances that interests in liberty would be implicated. But this is not such a case.

The State, in declining to rehire the respondent, did not make any charge against him that might seriously damage his standing and associations in his community. It did not base the nonrenewal of his contract on a charge, for example, that he had been guilty of dishonesty, or immorality. Had it done so, this would be a different case. For "[w]here a per-

8. "The formality and procedural requisites for the hearing can vary, depending upon the importance of the interest involved and the nature of the subsequent proceedings." *Boddie v. Connecticut*, [401 U.S. 371], 378. *See, e.g., Goldberg v. Kelly*, 397 U.S. 254, 263; *Hannah v. Larche*, 363 U.S. 420. The constitutional requirement of opportunity for *some* form of hearing before deprivation of a protected interest, of course, does not depend upon such a narrow balancing process. . . .

9. In a leading case decided many years ago, the Court of Appeals for the District of Columbia Circuit held that public employment in general was a "privilege," not a "right," and that procedural due process guarantees therefore were inapplicable. *Bailey v. Richardson*, 182 F.2d 46 (D.C. Cir. 1950), *aff'd* by an equally divided Court, 341 U.S. 918 [1951]. The basis of this holding has been thoroughly undermined in the ensuing years. For, as Mr. Justice Blackmun wrote for the Court . . ., "this Court now has rejected the concept that constitutional rights turn upon whether a governmental benefit is characterized as a 'right' or a 'privilege.' " *Graham v. Richardson*, 403 U.S. 365, 374. *See e.g., Morrissey v. Brewer*, [408 U.S. 471], 482 [1972]; *Bell v. Burson*, [402 U.S. 535], 539; *Goldberg v. Kelly*, [397 U.S. 254], 262; *Shapiro v. Thompson*, 394 U.S. 618, 627 n6; *Pickering v. Board of Educ.*, 391 U.S. 563, 568; *Sherbert v. Verner*, 374 U.S. 398, 404.

10. *See, e.g., Connell v. Higgenbotham*, 403 U.S. 207,208; *Bell v. Burson*, [402 U.S. 535]; *Goldberg v. Kelly*, [397 U.S. 254].

11. "Although the Court has not assumed to define 'liberty' [in the Fifth Amendment's Due Process Clause] with any great precision, that term is not confined to mere freedom from bodily restraint." *Bolling v. Sharpe*, 347 U.S. 497, 499. *See, e.g., Stanley v. Illinois*, 405 U.S. 645.

son's good name, reputation, honor or integrity is at stake because of what the government is doing to him, notice and an opportunity to be heard are essential." *Wisconsin v. Constantineau*, 400 U.S. 433, 437. . . . *See Cafeteria Workers v. McElroy*, 367 U.S. 886, 898. In such a case, due process would accord an opportunity to refute the charge before University officials.[12] In the present case, however, there is no suggestion whatever that the respondent's interest in his "good name, reputation, honor or integrity" is at stake.

Similarly, there is no suggestion that the State, in declining to reemploy the respondent, imposed on him a stigma or other disability that foreclosed his freedom to take advantage of other employment opportunities. The State, for example, did not invoke any regulations to bar the respondent from all other public employment in state universities. Had it done so, this, again, would be a different case. For "to be deprived not only of present government employment but of future opportunity for it certainly is no small injury. . . ." *Joint Anti-Fascist Refugee Comm. v. McGrath*, [341 U.S.] 185 (Jackson, J., concurring). *See Truax v. Raich*, 239 U.S. 33, 41.[13]

To be sure, the respondent has alleged that the nonrenewal of his contract was based on his exercise of his right to freedom of speech. But this allegation is not now before us. The District Court stayed proceedings on this issue, and the respondent has yet to prove that the decision not to rehire him was, in fact, based on his free speech activities.[14]

Hence, on the record before us, all that clearly appears is that the respondent was not rehired for one year at one university. It stretches the concept too far to suggest that a person is deprived of "liberty" when he simply is not rehired in one job but remains as free as before to seek another. *Cafeteria Workers v. McElroy*, ...

III

The Fourteenth Amendment's procedural protection of property is a safeguard of the security of interests that a person has already acquired in specific benefits. These interests—property interests—may take many forms.

Thus the Court has held that a person receiving welfare benefits under statutory and administrative standards defining eligibility for them has an interest in continued receipt of those benefits that is safeguarded by procedural due process. *Goldberg v. Kelly*, 397 U.S. 254. *See Flemming v. Nestor*, 363 U.S. 603, 611. Similarly, in the area of public employment, the Court has held that a public college professor dismissed from an office held under tenure provisions, *Slochower v. Board of Education*, 350 U.S. 551 [1956], and college professors and staff members dismissed during the terms of their con-

12. The purpose of such notice and hearing is to provide the person an opportunity to clear his name. Once a person has cleared his name at a hearing, his employer, of course, may remain free to deny him future employment for other reasons.

13. The District Court made an *assumption* "that nonretention by one university or college creates concrete and practical difficulties for a professor in his subsequent academic career." 310 F.Supp., at 979. And the Court of Appeals based its affirmance of the summary judgment largely on the premise that "the substantial adverse effect nonretention is likely to have upon the career interests of an individual professor" amounts to a limitation on future employment opportunities sufficient to invoke procedural due process guarantees. 446 F.2d at 809. But even assuming *arguendo*, that such a "substantial adverse effect" under these circumstances would constitute a state-imposed restriction on liberty, the record contains no support for these assumptions. There is no suggestion of how nonretention might affect the respondent's future employment prospects. Mere proof, for example, that his record of nonretention in one job, taken alone, might make him somewhat less attractive to some other employers would hardly establish the kind of foreclosure of opportunities amounting to a deprivation of "liberty. . . ."

14. *See* n5, *infra*. The Court of Appeals, nonetheless, argued that opportunity for a hearing and a statement of reasons were required here "as a *prophylactic* against nonretention decisions improperly motivated by exercise of protected rights." 446 F.2d at 810 (emphasis supplied). While the Court of Appeals recognized the lack of a finding that the respondent's nonretention was based on exercise of the right of free speech, it felt that the respondent's interest in liberty was sufficiently implicated here because the decision not to rehire him was made "with a background of controversy and unwelcome expressions of opinion." *Ibid.*

When a State would directly impinge upon interests in free speech or free press, this Court has on occasion held that opportunity for a fair adversary hearing must precede the action, whether or not the speech or press interest is clearly protected under substantive First Amendment standards. Thus, we have required fair notice and opportunity for an adversary hearing before an injunction is issued against the holding of rallies and public meetings. *Carroll v. Princess Anne*, 393 U.S. 175. Similarly, we have indicated the necessity of procedural safeguards before a State makes a large-scale seizure of a person's allegedly obscene books, magazines, and so forth. *A Quantity of Books v. Kansas*, 378 U.S. 205; *Marcus v. Search Warrant*, 367 U.S. 717. *See Freedman v. Maryland*, 380 U.S. 51; *Bantam Books v. Sullivan*, 372 U.S. 58. *See generally* Monaghan, "First Amendment Due Process," 83 *Harv.L.Rev.* 518.

In the respondent's case, however, the State has not directly impinged upon interests in free speech or free press in any way comparable to a seizure of books or an injunction against meetings. Whatever may be a teacher's rights of free speech, the interest in holding a teaching job at a state university, *simpliciter*, is not itself a free speech interest.

tracts, *Wieman v. Updegraff*, 344 U.S. 183 [1952], have interests in continued employment that are safeguarded by due process. Only last year, the Court held that this principle "proscribing summary dismissal from public employment without hearing or inquiry required by due process" also applied to a teacher recently hired without tenure or a formal contract, but nonetheless with a clearly implied promise of continued employment. *Connell v. Higgenbotham*, 403 U.S. 207, 208.

Certain attributes of "property" interests protected by procedural due process emerge from these decisions. To have a property interest in a benefit, a person clearly must have more than an abstract need or desire for it. He must have more than a unilateral expectation of it. He must, instead, have a legitimate claim of entitlement to it. It is a purpose of the ancient institution of property to protect those claims upon which people rely in their daily lives, reliance that must not be arbitrarily undermined. It is a purpose of the constitutional right to a hearing to provide an opportunity for a person to vindicate those claims.

Property interests, of course, are not created by the Constitution. Rather, they are created and their dimensions are defined by existing rules or understandings that stem from an independent source such as state laws—rules or understandings that secure certain benefits and that support claims of entitlement to those benefits. Thus the welfare recipients in *Goldberg v. Kelly*, 397 U.S. 254 (1970), had a claim of entitlement to welfare payments that was grounded in the statute defining eligibility for them. The recipients had not yet shown that they were, in fact, within the statutory terms of eligibility. But we held that they had a right to a hearing at which they might attempt to do so.

Just as the welfare recipients' "property" interest in welfare payments was created and defined by statutory terms, so the respondent's "property" interest in employment at the Wisconsin State University-Oshkosh was created and defined by the terms of his appointment. Those terms secured his interest in employment up to June 30, 1969. But the important fact in this case is that they specifically provided that the respondent's employment was to terminate on June 30. They did not provide for contract renewal absent "sufficient cause." Indeed, they made no provision for renewal whatsoever.

Thus the terms of the respondent's appointment secured absolutely no interest in reemployment for the next year. They supported absolutely no possible claim of entitlement to reemployment. Nor, significantly, was there any state statute or University rule or policy that secured his interest in reemployment or that created any legitimate claim to it.[16] In these circumstances, the respondent surely had an abstract concern in being rehired, but he did not have a *property* interest sufficient to require the University authorities to give him a hearing when they declined to renew his contract of employment.

IV

Our analysis of the respondent's constitutional rights in this case in no way indicates a view that an opportunity for a hearing or a statement of reasons for nonretention would, or would not, be appropriate or wise in public colleges and universities.[17] For it is a written Constitution that we apply. Our role is confined to interpretation of that Constitution.

We must conclude that the summary judgment for the respondent should not have been granted, since the respondent has not shown that he was deprived of liberty or property protected by the Fourteenth Amendment. The judgment of the Court of Appeals, accordingly, is reversed and the case is remanded for further proceedings consistent with this opinion.

It is so ordered.

Mr. Justice Powell took no part in the decision of this case.

Mr. Justice Douglas, dissenting.

Respondent Roth, like Sindermann in the companion case, had no tenure under Wisconsin law and, unlike Sindermann, he had had only one year of teaching at Wisconsin State University-Oshkosh—where during 1968–69 he had been Assistant Professor of Political Science and International Studies. Though Roth was rated by the faculty as an excellent

16. To be sure, the respondent does suggest that most teachers hired on a year-to-year basis by the Wisconsin State University-Oshkosh are, in fact, rehired. But the District Court has not found that there is anything approaching a "common law" of reemployment (*see Perry v. Sindermann*, 408 U.S. 602) so strong as to require University officials to give the respondent a statement of reasons and a hearing on their decision not to rehire him.

17. *See, e.g.*, Report of Committee A on Academic Freedom and Tenure, "Procedural Standards in the Renewal or Nonrenewal of Faculty Appointments," 56 *AAUP Bull.* No. 1, p 21 (Spring 1970).

teacher, he had publicly criticized the administration for suspending an entire group of 94 black students without determining individual guilt. He also criticized the university's regime as being authoritarian and autocratic. He used his classroom to discuss what was being done about the black episode; and one day, instead of meeting his class, he went to the meeting of the Board of Regents.

* * *

No more direct assault on academic freedom can be imagined than for the school authorities to be allowed to discharge a teacher because of his or her philosophical, political, or ideological beliefs. The same may well be true of private schools, if through the device of financing or other umbilical cords they become instrumentalities of the State. . . .

When a violation of First Amendment rights is alleged, the reasons for dismissal or for nonrenewal of an employment contract must be examined to see if the reasons given are only a cloak for activity or attitudes protected by the Constitution. A statutory analogy is present under the National Labor Relations Act, 29 U.S.C. § 151 *et. seq.* While discharges of employees for "cause" are permissible (*Fibreboard Corp. v. NLRB*, 379 U.S. 203, 217), discharges because of an employee's union activities are banned by § 8(a)(3), 29 U.S.C. § 158(a)(3). So the search is to ascertain whether the stated ground was the real one or only a pretext. *See J. P. Stevens & Co. v. NLRB*, 380 F.2d 292, 300 (1967).

In the case of teachers whose contracts are not renewed, tenure is not the critical issue. In the *Sweezy* case, the teacher, whose First Amendment rights were honored, had no tenure but was only a guest lecturer. In the *Keyishian* case, one of the petitioners (Keyishian himself) had only a "one-year-term contract" that was not renewed. 385 U.S. at 592. In *Shelton v. Tucker*, 364 U.S. 479, one of the petitioners was a teacher whose "contract for the ensuing school year was not renewed" ([364 U.S.] at 483) and two others who refused to comply were advised that it made "impossible their reemployment as teachers for the following school year." [364 U.S.] at 484. The oath required in *Keyishian* and the affidavit listing memberships required in *Shelton* were both, in our view, in violation of the First Amendment rights. Those cases mean that conditioning renewal of a teacher's contract upon surrender of First Amendment rights is beyond the power of a State.

There is sometimes a conflict between a claim for First Amendment protection and the need for orderly administration of the school system, as we noted in *Pickering v. Board of Education*, 391 U.S. 563, 569. That is one reason why summary judgments in this class of cases are seldom appropriate. Another reason is that careful factfinding is often necessary to know whether the given reason for nonrenewal of a teacher's contract is the real reason or a feigned one.

* * *

If this nonrenewal implicated the First Amendment, then Roth was deprived of constitutional rights because his employment was conditioned on a surrender of First Amendment rights; and, apart from the First Amendment, he was denied due process when he received no notice and hearing of the adverse action contemplated against him. Without a statement of the reasons for the discharge and an opportunity to rebut those reasons—both of which were refused by petitioners—there is no means short of a lawsuit to safeguard the right not to be discharged for the exercise of First Amendment guarantees. . . .

* * *

Mr. Justice Marshall, dissenting.

* * *

In my view, every citizen who applies for a government job is entitled to it unless the government can establish some reason for denying the employment. This is the "property" right that I believe is protected by the Fourteenth Amendment and that cannot be denied "without due process of law." And it is also liberty—liberty to work—which is the "very essence of the personal freedom and opportunity" secured by the Fourteenth Amendment. . . .

Employment is one of the greatest, if not the greatest, benefits that governments offer in modern-day life. When something as valuable as the opportunity to work is at stake, the government may not reward some citizens and not others without demonstrating that its actions are fair and equitable. And it is procedural due process that is our fundamental guarantee of fairness, our protection against arbitrary, capricious, and unreasonable government action.

* * *

We have often noted that procedural due process means many different things in the numerous contexts in which it applies. *See, e.g., Goldberg v. Kelly*, 397 U.S. 254 (1970); *Bell v. Burson*, 402 U.S. 535 (1971). Prior decisions have held that an applicant for admission to practice as an attorney before the United States Board of Tax Appeals may not be rejected without a statement of reasons and a chance for a hearing on disputed issues of fact;[4] that a tenured teacher could not be summarily dismissed without notice of the reasons and a hearing;[5] that an applicant for admission to a state bar could not be denied the opportunity to practice law without notice of the reasons for the rejection of his application and a hearing;[6] and even that a substitute teacher who had been employed only two months could not be dismissed merely because she refused to take a loyalty oath without an inquiry into the specific facts of her case and a hearing on those in dispute.[7] I would follow these cases and hold that respondent was denied due process when his contract was not renewed and he was not informed of the reasons and given an opportunity to respond.

It may be argued that to provide procedural due process to all public employees or prospective employees would place an intolerable burden on the machinery of government. *Cf. Goldberg v. Kelly*, *supra*. The short answer to that argument is that it is not burdensome to give reasons when reasons exist. Whenever an application for employment is denied, an employee is discharged, or a decision not to rehire an employee is made, there should be some reason for the decision. It can scarcely be argued that government would be crippled by a requirement that the reason be communicated to the person most directly affected by the government's action.

Where there are numerous applicants for jobs, it is likely that few will choose to demand reasons for not being hired. But, if the demand for reasons is exceptionally great, summary procedures can be devised that would provide fair and adequate information to all persons. As long as the government has a good reason for its actions it need not fear disclosure. It is only where the government acts improperly that procedural due process is truly burdensome. And that is precisely when it is most necessary.

It might also be argued that to require a hearing and a statement of reasons is to require a useless act, because a government bent on denying employment to one or more persons will do so regardless of the procedural hurdles that are placed in its path. Perhaps this is so, but a requirement of procedural regularity at least renders arbitrary action more difficult. Moreover, proper procedures will surely eliminate some of the arbitrariness that results, not from malice, but from innocent error. "Experience teaches . . . that the affording of procedural safeguards, which by their nature serve to illuminate the underlying facts, in itself often operates to prevent erroneous decisions on the merits from occuring." *Silver v. New York Stock Exchange*, 373 U.S. 341, 366 (1963). When the government knows it may have to justify its decisions with sound reasons, its conduct is likely to be more cautious, careful, and correct. . . .

Accordingly, I dissent.

NOTES AND QUESTIONS

1. Roth: *Scope of the Decision*

To what sources does the Court look in determining whether there exists an interest in liberty or property that would necessitate holding a hearing? Does the Court look to the Constitution itself for the proposition that "government may not adjudicate the claims of individuals by unreliable means"? Van Alstyne, "Cracks in 'The New Property': Adjudicative Due Process in the Administrative State," 62 *Corn.L.Rev.* 445, 483 (1977). Or does the Court insist upon finding some source in state law to buttress each of these interests?

Is the problem, as Justice Stewart suggests, largely definitional rather than one of balancing institutional and individual interests? Did Roth lose because his claim did not fall within acceptable definitions of *property* or *liberty?* How did Justice Douglas

4. *Goldsmith v. Board of Tax Appeals*, 270 U.S. 117 (1926).
5. *Slochower v. Board of Higher Educ.*, 350 U.S. 551 (1956).
6. *Willner v. Committee on Character*, 373 U.S. 96 (1963).
7. *Connell v. Higgenbotham*, 403 U.S. 207 (1971).

define those terms? How should they be defined? Does not the term *property* convey a myriad of legal meanings depending on the context of litigation? Might it mean a right to exclusive enjoyment over competing private interests or a right to compensation or some legal process when governmental deprivation takes place? If the latter meaning is appropriate to *Roth*, is Justice Stewart's formulation of the problem defensible? *See generally* Reich, "The New Property," 73 *Yale L. J.* 733 (1964).

2. *The* Sindermann *Case*

In *Perry v. Sindermann*, 408 U.S. 593, 92 S.Ct. 2694, 33 L.Ed.2d 570 (1972), decided the same day as *Roth*, the Supreme Court held that a professor, teaching at an institution lacking a tenure system, might nonetheless have a legitimate claim of entitlement to job tenure, entitling him to procedural due process protection. Sindermann, a professor of government at Odessa Junior College for four years, alleged that his property interest in continued employment, though not secured by a formal contractual tenure provision, was secured by a no less binding understanding fostered by the college administration. The Court declared: "the respondent has alleged the existence of rules and understandings, promulgated and fostered by state officials, that may justify his legitimate claim of entitlement to continued employment absent 'sufficient cause.' We disagree with the Court of Appeals insofar as it held that a mere subjective 'expectancy' is protected by procedural due process, but we agree that the respondent must be given an opportunity to prove the legitimacy of his claim of such entitlement in light of 'the policies and practices of the institution.' "

3. *Distinguishing* Roth *and* Sindermann

What might distinguish the *Roth* and *Sindermann* cases? Was Sindermann's dismissal more stigmatizing than Roth's? Did Sindermann have a more reasonable expectancy of reemployment than Roth? Why was the university's practice with respect to other teachers irrelevant to Roth but relevant to Sindermann? What is the difference between a contract for continued employment implied from the conduct of the parties and a reasonable expectancy of reemployment? Would a teacher's expectancy of reemployment be reasonable unless the school or university indicated its intention to continue the employment relationship? *See generally English v. Hairston*, 888 F.2d 1069 (5th Cir. 1989); *Kendall v. Board of Education*, 627 F.2d 1 (6th Cir. 1980); *Frumkin v. Board of Trustees*, 626 F.2d 19 (6th Cir. 1980).

4. *Interest-Balancing*

Applying a functional approach to the problem of hearings for nontenured teachers, what interests of the school would you take into account? A school district is not required to make public its reasons for dismissal, and the absence of reasons, by itself, does not implicate a liberty interest. *See, e.g., Hayes v. Phoenix-Talent School District*, 893 F.2d 235 (9th Cir. 1990). Does the school have an interest in secrecy? If a school dismisses a teacher for personal reasons, for example, the teacher is contentious or discourteous, are these legitimate reasons that should not be publicized? Is it adequate to argue that the teacher should have an option to demand reasons and a hearing and should bear the consequences of his or her choice? Might the formality of providing reasons and a hearing discourage educational institutions from making hard personnel decisions? Does a hearing subtly shift the burden of persuasion to the school? What of the expenses of a hearing? Should the dismissed teacher be required to pay part of the costs?

What are the interests of the dismissed teacher that you would take into account? Might the absence of reasons for dismissal lead prospective employers to think that he or she was fired for academic incompetence or immorality, even if the firing had no such cause? Will required formalities of hearing and reasons alter substantive decisions or correct arbitrary or erroneous behavior? Might a hearing requirement make schools less likely to dismiss a teacher for the exercise of First Amendment rights?

5. *Liberty, Property, and Due Process: Subsequent Developments*

> Since the latter half of the decade of the 1970's, the Supreme Court's treatment of the entitlement concept has indicated a considerable narrowing of the liberty and property interests protected by procedural due process. In *Meachum v. Fano*, for example, the Court held that the interest in "liberty" contemplated by the due process clause does not entitle "a state prisoner to a hearing when he is transferred to a prison the conditions of which are substantially less favorable to the prisoner, absent a state law or practice conditioning such transfers on proof of serious misconduct or other

events."[1] In expressly rejecting "the notion that any grievous loss visited upon a person by the state is sufficient to invoke the procedural protections of the due process clause," the Court was wary of subjecting "to judicial review a wide spectrum of discretionary actions that traditionally have been the business of prison administrations rather than of federal courts." Justice White's majority opinion concluded that "[w]hatever expectation the prisoner may have in remaining at a particular prison so long as he behaves himself, it is too ephemeral and insubstantial to trigger procedural due process protections as long as prison officials have discretion to transfer him for whatever reason or for no reason at all." . . .

A corresponding reluctance to look beyond positive state law as a source of rights protected by due process guarantees was evident in *Bishop v. Wood*, where a three and a half year veteran of the police force, classified as a "permanent employee" by a city ordinance which also provided that he could be dismissed if certain grounds were present, was fired for failure to discharge his duties properly, "without affording him a hearing to determine the sufficiency of the cause for his discharge."[8] Justice Stevens, writing for a closely divided Court, reasoned that "the sufficiency of the claim of entitlement must be decided by reference to state law," which in this case was governed by *Still v. Lance*,[10] where the North Carolina Supreme Court had held "that an enforceable expectation of continued employment in that state can exist only if the employer by statute or contract has actually granted some form of guarantee." . . .

This exclusively positivist analysis of entitlements undertaken in *Meachum, Helms* and *Bishop* presents a profoundly novel vision of procedural due process. . . . By failing to conduct "an analysis of the common practices utilized and the expectations generated by [the city], and the manner in which the local ordinance would reasonably be read" by members of the police force, the Court in *Bishop* . . . significantly retreated from its position in *Perry v. Sindermann*, where its finding that a professor arguably had a property interest in his job was based on "an unwritten common law." The practical impact of the Court's adoption of a positivist approach to the definition of "property" in *Bishop v. Wood* is that a public employee can count on procedural due process protection only if the law or contract defining the employee's job expressly provides that the employee can be discharged *only* for cause.

* * *

. . . The notion of entitlements protected by due process but stemming from independent sources "*such as* state law"* was originally introduced to provide added protection to the reasonable expectations of individuals in their relations with government over and above the rights secured by the "core" concepts of liberty and property grounded in the Constitution and in common law. In *Paul v. Davis*,[2] this new concept of entitlements seems to have been turned, for the first time, in precisely the opposite direction. Writing for a majority, Justice Rehnquist held that no interests protected by due process were implicated when the police put an individual's name on a flyer distributed to local merchants describing him as a "known" active shoplifter despite his lack of any convictions for such a crime, even though the characterization "would seriously impair his future employment opportunities." The Court first found that past cases "do not establish the proposition that reputation alone, apart from some more tangible interests such as employment, is either 'liberty' or 'property' by itself sufficient to invoke the procedural protection of the due process clause." Second, the Court looked to state law to determine whether a statutory entitlement existed, but held that "Kentucky law does not extend to respondent any legal guarantee of present enjoyment of reputation which has been altered as a result of the actions of the police, notwithstanding the protection against injury by virtue of [the state's] tort law."

In thus denying relief to a person whose reputation was seriously damaged by a state officer's action, the Court appears to have held that what previously had been recognized as a "core" interest in reputation would now be cognizable only when damage to reputation was alleged to accompany government's denial of some more tangible interest such as a specific job. Contrary to Justice Rehnquist's contention, this requirement of "reputation-plus" was a considerable departure from past precedents concerning the core interest in repu-

1. 427 U.S. 215, 216, 96 S.Ct. 2532, 2534, 49 L.Ed.2d 451 (1976). *See* Comment, "Two Views of a Prisoner's Right to Due Process: Meachum v. Fano," 12 *Harv.Civ.Rts.–Civ.Lib.L.Rev.* 405 (1977). In *Olim v. Wakinekona*, 461 U.S. 238, 244–48, 103 S.Ct. 1741, 1745–47, 75 L.Ed.2d 813 (1983), the Court extended *Meachum* to hold that no process is due when an inmate is transfered to another state's prison, "even when . . . the transfer involves long distance and an ocean crossing" (Hawaii to California), effectively separating the inmate from his family and friends.

8. 426 U.S. 341, 344, 342, 96 S.Ct. 2074, 2076, 48 L.Ed.2d 684 (1976).

10. 279 N.C. 254, 182 S.E.2d 403 (1971).

**Perry v. Sindermann*, 408 U.S. 593, 601, 92 S.Ct. 2694, 2699, 33 L.Ed.2d 576 (1972) (emphasis added).

2. 424 U.S. 693, 96 S.Ct. 1155, 47 L.Ed.2d 405 (1976).

> tation. Justice Rehnquist, for example, interpreted *Wisconsin v. Constantineau*'s[11] recognition of a liberty interest in not having one's name posted in liquor stores as a chronic drinker, as having been based on the fact that the posting "significantly altered his status as a matter of state law, and it was that alteration of legal status which, combined with the injury resulting from the defamation justified the invocation of procedural safeguards." On this view, due process was accorded in order to protect the state-conferred right to buy liquor which the posting might hinder. But the Court in *Constantineau* rested its holding *only* on the fact that "a person's good name, reputation, honor, or integrity is at stake because of what the government is doing to him." And both *Board of Regents v. Roth* and *Goss v. Lopez* reiterated this formulation of the "core" interest in reputation.

L. Tribe, *American Constitutional Law* 694–702 (2d ed. 1988).

6. *Due Process as an Intrinsic Instrumental Good*

Consider again the distinction between due process as an intrinsic good, important because it protects the interest in participation, and due process as an instrumental good whose significance inheres in the reliability of outcome that it assures. In sharply delimiting the circumstances when due process protections are required, has the Court opted for the latter position? What do you make of the argument that the Court's insistence on identifying a state-created property interest assures that there is a sufficient moral force behind the individual's entitlement claim to assure that a meaningful—that is, fully participatory—hearing is in fact held? *See* Michelman, "Formal and Associational Aims in Procedural Due Process," XVIII *Nomos* 148–53 (1977). *Compare* Tribe, "The Puzzling Persistence of Process–Based Constitutional Theories," 89 *Yale L.J.* 1063 (1980).

7. *Applying the Constitutional Standard*

In the light of *Roth*, *Sindermann*, and the subsequent decisions, how ought the following problems be analyzed:

a. A school district employee stated on his employment application that he had never been convicted of a felony. When a later school board review disclosed that he had been convicted of grand larceny, the employee was dismissed by letter. Is some type of hearing required before the discharge? *See Cleveland Board of Education v. Loudermill*, 470 U.S. 532, 105 S.Ct. 1487, 84 L.Ed.2d 494 (1985) (pre-termination hearing not required). *See also Seibert v. University of Oklahoma Health Sciences Center*, 867 F.2d 591 (10th Cir. 1989). In that particular case, the facts were not in dispute. But suppose they were—how would that affect the timing of the termination hearing?

b. The state of Dementia does not formally grant tenure. State law declares: "By May 30th of each school year, the school board shall renew the contracts of its teachers unless it is of the opinion that a teacher's contract shall not be renewed because the teacher has demonstrated a lack of professional competence, has engaged in immoral or insubordinate behavior, or has otherwise demonstrated that he or she is unfit to teach or will have an adverse impact upon the educational program of the school." Should a teacher who was not rehired in a Dementia school district be entitled to some kind of hearing? *Compare Greenholtz v. Nebraska Penal Inmates*, 442 U.S. 1 (1979); *Aggarwal v. Ponce School of Medicine*, 837 F.2d 17 (1st Cir. 1988); *Robertson v. Rogers*, 679 F.2d 1090 (4th Cir. 1982).

c. At a school board meeting, a teacher is accused by one parent of being a "sexpot" and by a student of having loaned the student a salacious book. A board member adds, "I know enough about the teacher to make me sick." The school board fails to renew the teacher's contract without making any charge or introducing findings concerning the basis of the board's actions. Should a court require a hearing? *Compare Harden v. Adams*, 841 F.2d 1091 (11th Cir. 1988); *Brandt v. Board of Co-operative Education Services*, 820 F.2d 41 (2d Cir. 1987); *Hardiman v. Jefferson County Board of Education*, 709 F.2d 635 (11th Cir. 1983); *Dennis v. S & S Consolidated Rural High School District*, 577 F.2d 338 (5th Cir. 1978); *McGhee v. Draper*, 564 F.2d 902 (10th Cir. 1977). *See also Seibert v. University of Oklahoma Health Sciences Center*, 867 F.2d 591 (10th cir. 1989).

d. Should the demotion of a department head to the status of classroom teacher require a hearing if department heads serve at the pleasure of the principal and if the principal had indicated that he thought the teacher incompetent as department head? Compare *Moore v. Otero*, 557 F.2d 435 (5th Cir. 1977); *Levitt v. University of Texas at El Paso*, 759 F.2d 1224 (5th Cir. 1985); *Skehan v. Board of Trustees*,

11. 400 U.S. 433, 91 S.Ct. 507, 27 L.Ed.2d 515 (1971). . . .

669 F.2d 142 (3d Cir. 1982). Would the transfer of a teacher to another school, under circumstances that hinted at reprimand but without reduced compensation, require a hearing? *See Sullivan v. Brown*, 544 F.2d 279 (6th Cir. 1976). Is an elementary school principal displaced because her school is closed, entitled to a hearing before being reassigned to a lesser administrative position? *See Hatcher v. Board of Public Education*, 809 F.2d 1546 (11th Cir. 1987).

e. An assistant professor is told that a tenure decision will be made no later than the beginning of the fifth year of his employment. After three years, however, his contract is not renewed. Is the assistant professor entitled to a hearing? Is he entitled to remain on the faculty until his fifth year? *See Upadhya v. Langenberg*, 834 F.2d 661 (7th Cir. 1987).

f. The contract of an untenured university lecturer is not renewed, the university stating publicly that he lacks a sufficient number of scholarly publications. Should he have a due process claim? Suppose the statement were made in a private meeting involving only the lecturer and the responsible administrator? *See Weinstein v. University of Illinois*, 811 F.2d 1091, 1096 (7th Cir. 1987): "If war is the extension of diplomacy by other means—this suit . . . is the extension of academic politics by other means."

g. A teacher is ordered, without explanation, to take a psychiatric examination. He refuses and is transferred from the classroom to the library. Is he entitled to a hearing? *See Newman v. Board of Education*, 594 F.2d 299 (2d Cir. 1979); *Stewart v. Pearce*, 484 F.2d 1031 (9th Cir. 1973).

h. A tenured high school principal is harassed by the superintendent to the point where he suffers a nervous breakdown and goes on disability leave. While on leave, he is told that his position as principal will be abolished immediately unless he returns to work within three days—which he is incapable of doing—or resigns. In fact, the post was not scheduled for abolition for some months. Days later, the principal tries to withdraw his resignation, only to be told that it has already been accepted. Is the principal entitled to a hearing? *See Giglio v. Dunn*, 732 F.2d 1133 (2d Cir. 1984).

i. A psychologist, informed by a student that he feels guilty about "something sexual" which occured with a teacher, directs the student to see a therapist. Only later, in consultation with the student and the therapist, is the incident reported to school authorities. The teacher is suspended for five days. Is he entitled to a hearing? *See Pesce v. J. Sterling Morton High School District 201*, 830 F.2d 789 (7th Cir. 1987).

j. Would the invalidation of permanent teaching certificates for all teachers in a state violate procedural or substantive due process? *See Connecticut Education Association v. Tirozzi*, 210 Conn. 286, 554 A.2d 1065 (Conn. 1989).

k. If a school dismisses tenured teachers due to financial exigency, do the dismissed teachers have a constitutional right to a hearing, at which they can challenge the existence of the alleged financial exigency? *See Johnston-Taylor v. Gannon*, 907 F.2d 1577 (6th Cir. 1990).

8. Statutory Dismissal Procedures

With few exceptions, most statutes require lengthy and detailed procedures before dismissal. Alabama's statutory provisions are typical. Ala. Code Tit. 16, §§ 16-24-1 *et.seq.* (1988). A dismissed teacher must be notified of his or her dismissal and is entitled to a statement of the reasons for the dismissal. If the dismissed teacher indicates a desire for a hearing, the school administration is required to conduct one. The hearing may be public or private at the teacher's discretion; the teacher has the right to counsel, to present evidence and witnesses, to cross-examine witnesses, and to subpoena witnesses. The hearing is held before the board of education, and a majority of the board must vote to dismiss the teacher for the removal to be effective. Provision is made for appeal to the state tenure commission, which reviews the record made before the board of education. The decision of the state commission is final.

In Colorado, the hearing is held before a three-member board, one member chosen by the teacher, one by the school board, and the third member (the chairman) chosen by the other two. In Michigan, all hearings are originally heard by the state tenure commission, composed of two classroom teachers, one school board member, one school superintendent, and one public member. Nevada provides for a hearing by a professional review committee of forty-two citizens, hearing cases in five-member panels. *See generally* National Education Association, *Teacher Tenure and Contracts* (1972). Is the majority in *Roth* and *Sindermann* open to the charge that they have chosen to protect only those who do not need protection?

Goss v. Lopez

419 U.S. 565, 95 S.Ct. 729, 42 L.Ed.2d 725 (1975).

Mr. Justice White delivered the opinion of the Court.

This appeal by various administrators of the Columbus, Ohio, Public School system (CPSS) challenges the judgment of a three-judge federal court, declaring that appellees—various high school students in the CPSS—were denied due process of law contrary to the command of the Fourteenth Amendment in that they were temporarily suspended from their high schools without a hearing either prior to suspension or within a reasonable time thereafter, and enjoining the administrators to remove all references to such suspensions from the students' records.

I

Ohio law, Rev. Code Ann. § 3313.64 (1972), provides for free education to all children between the ages of six and 21. Section 3313.66 of the Code empowers the principal of an Ohio public school to suspend a pupil for misconduct for up to 10 days or to expel him. In either case, he must notify the student's parents within 24 hours and state the reasons for his action. A pupil who is expelled, or his parents, may appeal the decision to the Board of Education and in connection therewith shall be permitted to be heard at the board meeting. The Board may reinstate the pupil following the hearing. No similar procedure is provided in § 3313.66 or any other provision of state law for a suspended student. Aside from a regulation tracking the statute, at the time of the imposition of the suspensions in this case the CPSS itself had not issued any written procedure applicable to suspensions. Nor, so far as the record reflects, had any of the individual high schools involved in this case. Each, however, had formally or informally described the conduct for which suspension could be imposed.

The nine named appellees, each of whom alleged that he or she had been suspended from public high school in Columbus for up to 10 days without a hearing pursuant to § 3313.66, filed an action under 42 U.S.C. § 1983 against the Columbus Board of Education and various administrators of the CPSS. The complaint sought a declaration that § 3313.66 was unconstitutional in that it permitted public school administrators to deprive plaintiffs of their rights to an education without a hearing of any kind, in violation of the procedural due process component of the Fourteenth Amendment. It also sought to enjoin the public school officials from issuing future suspensions pursuant to § 3313.66 and to require them to remove references to the past suspensions from the records of the students in question.

* * *

[T]he three-judge court declared that plaintiffs were denied due process of law because they were "suspended without hearing prior to suspension or within a reasonable time thereafter," and that Ohio Rev. Code Ann. § 3313.66 (1972) and regulations issued pursuant thereto were unconstitutional in permitting such suspensions. It was ordered that all references to plaintiffs' suspensions be removed from school files.

* * *

The defendant school administrators have appealed the three-judge court's decision. Because the order below granted plaintiff's request for an injunction—ordering defendants to expunge their records—this Court has jurisdiction of the appeal pursuant to 28 U.S.C. § 1253. We affirm.

II

At the outset, appellants contend that because there is no constitutional right to an education at public expense, the Due Process Clause does not protect against expulsions from the public school system. This position misconceives the nature of the issue and is refuted by prior decisions. The Fourteenth Amendment forbids the State to deprive any person of life, liberty, or property without due process of law. Protected interests in property are normally "not created by the Constitution. Rather, they are created and their dimensions are defined" by an independent source such as state statutes or rules entitling the citizen to certain benefits. *Board of Regents v. Roth*, 408 U.S. 564, 577 (1972).

* * *

Here, on the basis of state law, appellees plainly had legitimate claims of entitlement to a public education. Ohio Rev. Code Ann. §§ 3313.48 and 3313.64 (1972 and Supp. 1973) direct local authorities to provide a free education to all residents between five and 21 years of age, and a compulsory-attendance law requires attendance for a school year of not less than 32 weeks. Ohio Rev. Code Ann. § 3321.04 (1972). It is true that § 3313.66 of the Code permits school principals to suspend students for up to 10 days; but suspensions may not be imposed without any grounds whatsoever. All of the schools had their own rules specifying the grounds for expulsion or suspension. Having chosen to extend the right to an education to people of appellees' class generally, Ohio may not withdraw that right on grounds of misconduct, absent fundamentally fair procedures to determine whether the misconduct has occurred. . . .

. . . The authority possessed by the State to prescribe and enforce standards of conduct in its schools, although concededly very broad, must be exercised consistently with constitutional safeguards. Among other things, the State is constrained to recognize a student's legitimate entitlement to a public education as a property interest which is protected by the Due Process Clause and which may not be taken away for misconduct without adherence to the minimum procedures required by that Clause.

The Due Process Clause also forbids arbitrary deprivations of liberty. "Where a person's good name, reputation, honor, or integrity is at stake because of what the government is doing to him," the minimal requirements of the Clause must be satisfied. *Wisconsin v. Constantineau*, 400 U.S. 433, 437 (1971); *Board of Regents v. Roth, supra*, at 573. School authorities here suspended appellees from school for periods of up to 10 days based on charges of misconduct. If sustained and recorded, those charges could seriously damage the students' standing with their fellow pupils and their teachers as well as interfere with later opportunities for higher education and employment. It is apparent that the claimed right of the State to determine unilaterally and without process whether that misconduct has occurred immediately collides with the requirements of the Constitution.

Appellants proceed to argue that even if there is a right to a public education protected by the Due Process Clause generally, the Clause comes into play only when the State subjects a student to a "severe detriment or grievous loss." The loss of 10 days, it is said, is neither severe nor grievous and the Due Process Clause is therefore of no relevance. Appellants' argument is again refuted by our prior decisions; for in determining "whether due process requirements apply in the first place, we must look not to the 'weight' but to the *nature* of the interest at stake." *Board of Regents v. Roth, supra*, at 570–71. Appellees were excluded from school only temporarily, it is true, but the length and consequent severity of a deprivation, while another factor to weigh in determining the appropriate form of hearing, "is not decisive of the basic right" to a hearing of some kind. *Fuentes v. Shevin*, 407 U.S. 67, 86 (1972). . . .

A short suspension is, of course, a far milder deprivation than expulsion. But, "education is perhaps the most important function of state and local governments," *Brown v. Board of Education*, 347 U.S. 483, 493 (1954), and the total exclusion from the educational process for more than a trivial period, and certainly if the suspension is for 10 days, is a serious event in the life of the suspended child. Neither the property interest in educational benefits temporarily denied nor the liberty interest in reputation, which is also implicated, is so insubstantial that suspensions may constitutionally be imposed by any procedure the school chooses, no matter how arbitrary.

III

"Once it is determined that due process applies, the question remains what process is due." *Morrissey v. Brewer*, 408 U.S. at 481. We turn to that question, fully realizing as our cases regularly do that the interpretation and application of the Due Process Clause are intensely practical matters and that "[t]he very nature of due process negates any concept of inflexible procedures universally applicable to every imaginable situation." *Cafeteria Workers v. McElroy*, 367 U.S. 886, 895 (1961). We are also mindful of our own admonition:

> Judicial interposition in the operation of the public school system of the Nation raises problems requiring care and restraint. . . . By and large, public education in our Nation is committed to the control of state and local authorities."
>
> *Epperson v. Arkansas*, 393 U.S. 97, 104 (1968).

There are certain bench marks to guide us, however. *Mullane v. Central Hanover Trust Co.*, 339 U.S. 306 (1950), a case often invoked by later opinions, said that "[m]any controversies have raged about the cryptic and abstract words of the Due Process Clause but there can be no doubt that at a minimum they require that deprivation of life, liberty or property by adjudication be preceded by notice and opportunity for hearing appropriate to the nature of the case." *Id.* at 313. . . . At the very minimum, therefore, students facing suspension and the consequent interference with a protected property interest must be given *some* kind of notice and afforded *some* kind of hearing. . . .

It also appears from our cases that the timing and content of the notice and the nature of the hearing will depend on appropriate accommodation of the competing interests involved. . . . The student's interest is to avoid unfair or mistaken exclusion from the educational process, with all of its unfortunate consequences. The Due Process Clause will not shield him from suspensions properly imposed, but it disserves both his interest and the interest of the State if his suspension is in fact unwarranted. The concern would be mostly academic if the disciplinary process were a totally accurate, unerring process, never mistaken and never unfair. Unfortunately, that is not the case, and no one suggests that it is. Disciplinarians, although proceeding in utmost good faith, frequently act on the reports and advice of others; and the controlling facts and the nature of the conduct under challenge are often disputed. The risk of error is not at all trivial, and it should be guarded against if that may be done without prohibitive cost or interference with the educational process.

The difficulty is that our schools are vast and complex. Some modicum of discipline and order is essential if the educational function is to be performed. Events calling for discipline are frequent occurrences and sometimes require immediate, effective action. Suspension is considered not only to be a necessary tool to maintain order but a valuable educational device. The prospect of imposing elaborate hearing requirements in every suspension case is viewed with great concern, and many school authorities may well prefer the untrammeled power to act unilaterally, unhampered by rules about notice and hearing. But it would be a strange disciplinary system in an educational institution if no communication was sought by the disciplinarian with the student in an effort to inform him of his dereliction and to let him tell his side of the story in order to make sure that an injustice is not done. . . .[9]

We do not believe that school authorities must be totally free from notice and hearing requirements if their schools are to operate with acceptable efficiency. Students facing temporary suspension have interests qualifying for protection of the Due Process Clause, and due process requires, in connection with a suspension of 10 days or less that the student be given oral or written notice of the charges against him and, if he denies them, an explanation of the evidence the authorities have and an opportunity to present his side of the story. The Clause requires at least these rudimentary precautions against unfair or mistaken findings of misconduct and arbitrary exclusion from school.

There need be no delay between the time "notice" is given and the time of hearing. In the great majority of cases the disciplinarian may informally discuss the alleged misconduct with the student minutes after it has occurred. We hold only that, in being given an opportunity to explain his version of the facts at this discussion, the student first be told what he is accused of doing and what the basis of the accusation is. . . . Since the hearing may occur almost immediately following the misconduct, it follows that as a general rule notice and hearing should precede removal of the student from school. We agree with the District Court, however, that there are recurring situations in which prior notice and hearing cannot be insisted upon. Students whose presence poses a continuing danger to persons or property or an ongoing threat of disrupting the academic process may be immediately removed from school. In such cases, the necessary notice and ru-

9. The facts involved in this case illustrate the point. Betty Crome was suspended for conduct which did not occur on school grounds, and for which mass arrests were made—hardly guaranteeing careful individualized factfinding by the police or by the school principal. She claims to have been involved in no misconduct. However, she was suspended for 10 days without ever being told what she was accused of doing or being given an opportunity to explain her presence among those arrested. Similarly, Dwight Lopez was suspended, along with many others, in connection with a disturbance in the lunchroom. Lopez says he was not one of those in the lunchroom who was involved. However, he was never told the basis for the principal's belief that he was involved, nor was he ever given an opportunity to explain his presence in the lunchroom. The school principals who suspended Crome and Lopez may have been correct on the merits, but it is inconsistent with the Due Process Clause to have made the decision that misconduct had occurred without at some meaningful time giving Crome or Lopez an opportunity to persuade the principals otherwise.

We recognize that both suspensions were imposed during a time of great difficulty for the school administrations involved. At least in Lopez' case there may have been an immediate need to send home everyone in the lunchroom in order to preserve school order and property; and the administrative burden of providing 75 "hearings" of any kind is considerable. However, neither factor justifies a disciplinary suspension without *at any time* gathering facts relating to Lopez specifically, confronting him with them, and giving him an opportunity to explain.

dimentary hearing should follow as soon as practicable, as the District Court indicated.

In holding as we do, we do not believe that we have imposed procedures on school disciplinarians which are inappropriate in a classroom setting. Instead we have imposed requirements which are, if anything, less than a fair-minded school principal would impose upon himself in order to avoid unfair suspensions. Indeed, according to the testimony of the principal of Marion-Franklin High School, that school had an informal procedure, remarkably similar to that which we now require, applicable to suspensions generally but which was not followed in this case. Similarly, according to the most recent memorandum applicable to the entire CPSS, . . . school principals in the CPSS are now required by local rule to provide at least as much as the constitutional minimum which we have described.

We stop short of construing the Due Process Clause to require, countrywide, that hearings in connection with short suspensions must afford the student the opportunity to secure counsel, to confront and cross-examine witnesses supporting the charge, or to call his own witnesses to verify his version of the incident. Brief disciplinary suspensions are almost countless. To impose in each such case even truncated trial-type procedures might well overwhelm administrative facilities in many places and, by diverting resources, cost more than it would save in educational effectiveness. Moreover, further formalizing the suspension process and escalating its formality and adversary nature may not only make it too costly as a regular disciplinary tool but also destroy its effectiveness as part of the teaching process.

On the other hand, requiring effective notice and informal hearing permitting the student to give his version of the events will provide a meaningful hedge against erroneous action. At least the disciplinarian will be alerted to the existence of disputes about facts and arguments about cause and effect. He may then determine himself to summon the accuser, permit cross-examination, and allow the student to present his own witnesses. In more difficult cases, he may permit counsel. In any event, his discretion will be more informed and we think the risk of error substantially reduced.

Requiring that there be at least an informal give-and-take between student and disciplinarian, preferably prior to the suspension, will add little to the factfinding function where the disciplinarian himself has witnessed the conduct forming the basis for the charge. But things are not always as they seem to be, and the student will at least have the opportunity to characterize his conduct and put it in what he deems the proper context.

We should also make it clear that we have addressed ourselves solely to the short suspension, not exceeding 10 days. Longer suspensions or expulsions for the remainder of the school term, or permanently, may require more formal procedures. Nor do we put aside the possibility that in unusual situations, although involving only a short suspension, something more than the rudimentary procedures will be required.

IV

The District Court found each of the suspensions involved here to have occurred without a hearing, either before or after the suspension, and that each suspension was therefore invalid and the statute unconstitutional insofar as it permits such suspensions without notice or hearing. Accordingly, the judgment is

Affirmed.

Mr. Justice Powell, with whom The Chief Justice, Mr. Justice Blackmun, and Mr. Justice Rehnquist join, dissenting.

The Court today invalidates an Ohio statute that permits student suspensions from school without a hearing "for not more than ten days." The decision unnecessarily opens avenues for judicial intervention in the operation of our public schools that may affect adversely the quality of education. The Court holds for the first time that the federal courts, rather than educational officials and state legislatures, have the authority to determine the rules applicable to routine classroom discipline of children and teenagers in the public schools. It justifies this unprecedented intrusion into the process of elementary and secondary education by identifying a new constitutional right: the right of a student not to be suspended for as much as a single day without notice and a due process hearing either before or promptly following the suspension.

The Court's decision rests on the premise that, under Ohio law, education is a property interest protected by the Fourteenth Amendment's Due Process Clause and therefore that any suspension requires notice and a hearing. In my view, a student's interest in education is not infringed by a suspension within a limited period prescribed by Ohio law. Moreover, to the extent that there may be some arguable infringement, it is too speculative, transitory, and insubstantial to justify imposition of a *constitutional* rule.

I

In identifying property interests subject to due process protections, the Court's past opinions make clear that these interests "are created and their *dimensions are defined* by existing rules or understandings that stem from an independent source such as state law." *Board of Regents v. Roth, supra,* at 577 (emphasis supplied). The Ohio statute that creates the right to a "free" education also explicitly authorizes a principal to suspend a student for as much as 10 days. Ohio Rev. Code Ann. §§ 3313.48, 3313.64, 3313.66 (1972 and Supp. 1973). Thus the very legislation which "defines" the "dimension" of the student's entitlement, while providing a right to education generally, does not establish this right free of discipline imposed in accord with Ohio law. Rather, the right is encompassed in the entire package of statutory provisions governing education in Ohio—of which the power to suspend is one. . . .

But however one may define the entitlement to education provided by Ohio law, I would conclude that a deprivation of not more than 10 days' suspension from school, imposed as a routine disciplinary measure, does not assume constitutional dimensions. Contrary to the Court's assertion, our cases support rather than "refute" appellants' argument that "the Due Process Clause . . . comes into play only when the State subjects a student to a 'severe detriment or grievous loss.' " . . .

The Ohio suspension statute allows no serious or significant infringement of education. It authorizes only a maximum suspension of eight school days, less than 5% of the normal 180-day school year. Absences of such limited duration will rarely affect a pupil's opportunity to learn or his scholastic performance. Indeed, the record in this case reflects no educational injury to appellees. . . .

The Court also relies on a perceived deprivation of "liberty" resulting from any suspension, arguing—again without factual support in the record pertaining to these appellees—that a suspension harms a student's reputation. In view of the Court's decision in *Board of Regents v. Roth, supra,* I would have thought that this argument was plainly untenable. Underscoring the need for "serious damage" to reputation, the *Roth* Court held that a nontenured teacher who is not rehired by a public university could not claim to suffer sufficient reputational injury to require constitutional protections. Surely a brief suspension is of less serious consequence to the reputation of a teenage student.

II

In prior decisions, this Court has explicitly recognized that school authorities must have broad discretionary authority in the daily operation of public schools. This includes wide latitude with respect to maintaining discipline and good order. . . .

The Court today turns its back on these precedents. It can hardly seriously be claimed that a school principal's decision to suspend a pupil for a single day would "directly and sharply implicate basic constitutional values." . . .

Moreover, the Court ignores the experience of mankind, as well as the long history of our law, recognizing that there *are* differences which must be accommodated in determining the rights and duties of children as compared with those of adults. . . .

A

I turn now to some of the considerations which support the Court's former view regarding the comprehensive authority of the States and school officials "to prescribe and control conduct in the schools." . . . Unlike the divergent and even sharp conflict of interests usually present where due process rights are asserted, the interests here implicated—of the State through its schools and of the pupils—are essentially congruent.

The State's interest, broadly put, is in the proper functioning of its public school system for the benefit of *all* pupils and the public generally. Few rulings would interfere more extensively in the daily functioning of schools than subjecting routine discipline to the formalities and judicial oversight of due process. Suspensions are one of the traditional means—ranging from keeping a student after class to permanent expulsion—used to maintain discipline in the schools. It is common knowledge that maintaining order and reasonable decorum in school buildings and classrooms is a major educational problem, and one which has increased significantly in magnitude in recent years. Often the teacher, in protecting the rights of other children to an education (if not his or their safety), is compelled to rely on the power to suspend.

The facts set forth in the margin[10] leave little room for doubt as to the magnitude of the disciplinary problem in the public schools, or as to the extent of reliance upon the right to suspend. They also demonstrate that if hearings were required for a substantial percentage of short-term suspensions, school authorities would have time to do little else.

B

The State's generalized interest in maintaining an orderly school system is not incompatible with the individual interest of the student. Education in any meaningful sense includes the inculcation of an understanding in each pupil of the necessity of rules and obedience thereto. This understanding is no less important than learning to read and write. One who does not comprehend the meaning and necessity of discipline is handicapped not merely in his education but throughout his subsequent life. In an age when the home and church play a diminishing role in shaping the character and value judgments of the young, a heavier responsibility falls upon the schools. When an immature student merits censure for his conduct, he is rendered a disservice if appropriate sanctions are not applied or if procedures for their application are so formalized as to invite a challenge to the teacher's authority—an invitation which rebellious or even merely spirited teenagers are likely to accept.

The lesson of discipline is not merely a matter of the student's self-interest in the shaping of his own character and personality; it provides an early understanding of the relevance to the social compact of respect for the rights of others. The classroom is the laboratory in which this lesson of life is best learned. . . .

In assessing in constitutional terms the need to protect pupils from unfair minor discipline by school authorities, the Court ignores the commonality of interest of the State and pupils in the public school system. Rather, it thinks in traditional judicial terms of an adversary situation. To be sure, there will be the occasional pupil, innocent of any rule infringement who is mistakenly suspended or whose infraction is too minor to justify suspension. But, while there is no evidence indicating the frequency of unjust suspensions, common sense suggests that they will not be numerous in relation to the total number, and that mistakes or injustices will usually be righted by informal means.

C

One of the more disturbing aspects of today's decision is its indiscriminate reliance upon the judiciary, and the adversary process, as the means of resolving many of the most routine problems arising in the classroom. In mandating due process procedures the Court misapprehends the reality of the normal teacher-pupil relationship. There is an ongoing relationship, one in which the teacher must occupy many roles—educator, adviser, friend, and, at times, parent-substitute. It is rarely adversary in nature except with respect to the chronically disruptive or insubordinate pupil whom the teacher must be free to discipline without frustrating formalities.

* * *

III

No one can foresee the ultimate frontiers of the new "thicket" the Court now enters. Today's ruling appears to sweep within the protected interest in education a multitude of discretionary decisions in the educational process. Teachers and other school authorities are required to make many decisions that may have serious consequences for the pupil. They must decide, for example, how to grade the student's work, whether a student passes or fails a course, whether he is to be promoted, whether he is required to take certain subjects, whether he may be exlcuded from interscholastic athletics or other extracurricular activities, whether he may be removed from one

10. . . . .[A]n *amicus* brief submitted by several school associations in Ohio indicates that the number of suspensions is significant: in 1972–1973, 4,054 students out of a school enrollment of 81,007 were suspended in Cincinnati; 7,352 of 57,000 students were suspended in Akron; and 14,598 of 142,053 students were suspended in Cleveland. . . .

school and sent to another, whether he may be bused long distances when available schools are nearby, and whether he should be placed in a "general," "vocational," or "college-preparatory" track.

In these and many similar situations claims of impairment of one's educational entitlement identical in principle to those before the Court today can be asserted with equal or greater justification. Likewise, in many of these situations, the pupil can advance the same types of speculative and subjective injury given critical weight in this case. The District Court, relying upon generalized opinion evidence, concluded that a suspended student may suffer psychological injury. . . . The Court appears to adopt this rationale.

It hardly need be said that if a student, as a result of a day's suspension, suffers "a blow" to his "self esteem," "feels powerless," views "teachers with resentment," or feels "stigmatized by his teachers," identical psychological harms will flow from many other routine and necessary school decisions. The student who is given a failing grade, who is not promoted, who is excluded from certain extracurricular activities, who is assigned to a school reserved for children of less than average ability, or who is placed in the "vocational" rather than the "college preparatory" track, is unlikely to suffer any less psychological injury than if he were suspended for a day for a relatively minor infraction.

If, as seems apparent, the Court will now require due process procedures whenever such routine school decisions are challenged, the impact upon public education will be serious indeed. . . .

NOTES AND QUESTIONS

1. Is *Goss* Still Good Law?

Goss was decided prior to the *Meachum* and *Bishop* opinions, discussed in the excerpt from *American Constitutional Law, supra*. Does *Goss* look beyond the terms of state law in determining the nature of the student's property interest in a manner inconsistent with these cases? *Goss* rejects the argument that the statutorily created right to an education, on which the property claim rests, is properly qualified by the possibility of short suspensions as expressly permitted in the same statute. Can that position be reconciled with the subsequent decisions? Is the nature of the interest—access to education in *Goss* and prisoners rights and employment in *Meachum* and *Bishop*—constitutionally relevant here? If so, how?

What of the interest in liberty identified in *Goss*? Does it survive the *Paul* decision?

2. *Goss*: Scope of the Opinion

What is the nature of the property interest, and the liberty interest, which leads the *Goss* Court to conclude that some sort of hearing must precede short-term suspensions? In *Cleveland Board of Education v. Loudermill*, 470 U.S. 532, 105 S.Ct. 1487, 84 L.Ed.2d 494 (1985), decided nine years later, the Court held that a post-determination hearing met the requirements of due process for teachers. Is *Loudermill* now controlling?

How do the majority and dissent differ with respect to the intrinsic importance of a due process hearing; the instrumental importance of a due process hearing, that is, the possibility that such hearings will uncover errors of fact and hence prevent injustices; the impact of the decision on the governance of schools; and the appropriate role of the judiciary in setting educational policy? In this light, how do you reconcile the majority's assertion that the required procedures "are, if anything, less than a fair-minded school principal would impose upon himself" with the minority's claim that "few rulings would interfere more extensively in the daily functioning of the schools"? Do the two opinions have in mind different understandings of school governance?

3. What Kind of Hearing?

Goss speaks both to the appropriateness of providing some sort of process and to the specifics of the process that is due. The two are treated as analytically distinct, the "what" process calculus being premised on essentially utilitarian considerations. In *Mathews v. Eldridge*, 424 U.S. 319, 335, 96 S.Ct. 893, 903, 47 L.Ed.2d 18 (1976), the Court summarizes these factors: "First, the private interest that will be affected by the official action; second, the risk of an erroneous deprivation of such interest through the procedures used, and the probable value, if any, of additional substitute procedural safeguards; and finally, the Government's interest, including the function involved and the fiscal and administrative burdens that the additional or substitute procedural requirement would entail."

How well does the Court apply this utilitarian calculus to the circumstances of short-term suspensions? What do you make of the following assessment of the aspiration of the opinion?

> *By the very device of imposing minimal procedural safeguards, premised on a formal (but thin) statutory entitlement, the decision aspires to increase reliance on nonformal nonadversarial procedures,* to encourage a kind of collegiality—actual exchange and even negotiation, leading to mutually acceptable outcomes or at least shared understandings—in a system which has treated fiat as an administratively convenient rule of thumb. . . . More than . . . "*rituals* and *ceremonies*" designed to foster "courtesy and respect" are at issue here. Inherent in the creation of opportunities for colloquy is the *possibility* that both students and disciplinarians will hear each other out with something other than the patience born of legal necessity, that there exists what Kenneth Clark speaks of as the "possibility of empathy." . . . [Conversation] enables students to feel that they are being listened to and may encourage them to raise underlying grievances. It provides administrators with a relatively inexpensive vehicle for monitoring, and hence a basis for reshaping institutional relationships. The outcome of these "orderly, thoughtful" conversations may well be decisions different in their particulars from what might otherwise have been anticipated; repeated conversations which touch upon similar student grievances may ultimately lead disciplinarians to reassess whether control is so vital, and collaboration so improbable, as a means of assuring institutional order.

Kirp, "Proceduralism and Bureaucracy: Due Process in the School Setting," 28 *Stanford L. Rev.* 841, 864–66 (1976) (italics in original).

Does this analysis fairly reflect *Goss*? Does it speak to the relevance of the intrinsic value of due process in the *Goss* opinions? Does it suggest a way of distinguishing the post-*Goss* cases?

What of longer suspensions: Do the same considerations pertain? What procedural protections should be provided when a student is faced with an eleven-day suspension, a semester-long suspension, or an expulsion? At what point does it become appropriate to design the hearing to approximate a traditional due process hearing, with legal representation, a written record, a formal appeals process, and the like? *See Lamb v. Panhandle Community Unit School District* No. 2, 826 F.2d 526 (7th Cir. 1987); *McClain v. Lafayette County Board of Education*, 673 F.2d 106 (5th Cir. 1982); *Cole v. Newton Special Mun. Separate School District*, 676 F.Supp. 749 (S.D. Miss. 1987); *Darby v. School*, 544 F.Supp. 428 (W.D. Mich. 1982).

4. Applications: When is Process Due?

Should students who are suspended from a particular class and are required to spend a certain amount of time in a detention area be provided with *Goss* protections? *See Warren County Board of Education v. Wilkinson*, 500 So.2d 455 (Miss. 1986); *Jordan v. School District of City of Erie, Pennsylvania*, 583 F.2d 91 (3d Cir. 1978). Is participation in extracurricular activities a protectable property interest, deprivation of which—by keeping the star quarterback from playing, for example—properly triggers due process procedures? *See Hardy v. University Interscholastic League*, 759 F.2d 1233 (5th Cir. 1985); *Duffley v. New Hampshire Interscholastic Athletic Association*, 122 N.H. 484, 446 A.2d 462 (1982); *Kulovitz v. Illinois High School Association*, 462 F.Supp. 875 (N.D. Ill. 1978); *Dallam v. Cumberland Valley School District*, 391 F.Supp. 358 (M.D. Pa. 1975); *Braesch v. DePasquale*, 200 Neb. 726, 265 N.W.2d 842 (1978), *cert. denied*, 439 U.S. 1068, 99 S.Ct. 836, 59 L.Ed.2d 34 (1979). Is the transfer of a student from a regular school to a disciplinary school for disciplinary reasons an infringement of protected interests that should require a prior hearing? *See Madera v. Board of Education*, 386 F.2d 778 (2d Cir. 1967), *cert. denied*, 390 U.S. 1028, 88 S.Ct. 1416, 20 L.Ed.2d 284 (1968); *Everett v. Marcase*, 426 F.Supp. 397 (E.D.Pa. 1977).

5. Due Process and the Handicapped

The Education for All Handicapped Children Act, 20 U.S.C.A. §§ 1401–61 (1982), entitles disabled students to a hearing before any change in placement—even when the proposed change is premised on misconduct. *See Honig v. Doe*, 484 U.S. 305, 108 S.Ct. 592, 98 L.Ed.2d 686 (1988), discussed in chapter 7, *infra*. *See generally* Lincoln, "Disciplining Handicapped Students: Questions Unanswered in *Honig v. Doe*," 51 *Educ. Law Rep.* [1] (1989).

Ingraham v. Wright

430 U.S. 651, 97 S.Ct. 1401, 51 L.Ed.2d 711 (1977).

Mr. Justice Powell delivered the opinion of the Court.

This case presents questions concerning the use of corporal punishment in public schools: First, whether the paddling of students as a means of maintaining school discipline constitutes cruel and unusual punishment in violation of the Eighth Amendment; and second, to the extent that paddling is constitutionally permissible, whether the Due Process Clause of the Fourteenth Amendment requires prior notice and an opportunity to be heard.

I

* * *

Petitioners' evidence may be summarized briefly. In the 1970–1971 school year many of the 237 schools in Dade County used corporal punishment as a means of maintaining discipline pursuant to Florida legislation and a local school board regulation. The statute then in effect authorized limited corporal punishment by negative inference, proscribing punishment which was "degrading or unduly severe" or which was inflicted without prioı consultation with the principal or the teacher in charge of the school. . . . The regulation, Dade County School Board Policy 5144, contained explicit directions and limitations. The authorized punishment consisted of paddling the recalcitrant student on the buttocks with a flat wooden paddle measuring less than two feet long, three or four inches wide, and about one-half inch thick. The normal punishment was limited to one to five "licks" or blows with the paddle and resulted in no apparent physical injury to the student. School authorities viewed corporal punishment as a less drastic means of discipline than suspension or expulsion. Contrary to the procedural requirements of the statute and regulation, teachers often paddled students on their own authority without first consulting the principal.

Petitioners focused on Drew Junior High School, the school in which both Ingraham and Andrews were enrolled in the fall of 1970. In an apparent reference to Drew, the District Court found that "[t]he instances of punishment which could be characterized as severe, accepting the students' testimony as credible, took place in one junior high school." . . . The evidence, consisting mainly of the testimony of 16 students, suggests that the regime at Drew was exceptionally harsh. The testimony of Ingraham and Andrews, in support of their individual claims for damages, is illustrative. Because he was slow to respond to his teacher's instructions, Ingraham was subjected to more than 20 licks with a paddle while being held over a table in the principal's office. The paddling was so severe that he suffered a hematoma requiring medical attention and keeping him out of school for 11 days. Andrews was paddled several times for minor infractions. On two occasions he was struck on his arms, once depriving him of the full use of his arm for a week.

* * *

We granted certiorari, limited to the questions of cruel and unusual punishment and procedural due process. . . .

* * *

The use of corporal punishment in this country as a means of disciplining school children dates back to the colonial period. It has survived the transformation of primary and secondary education from the colonials' reliance on optional private arrangements to our present system of compulsory education and dependence on public schools. Despite the general abandonment of corporal punishment as a means of punishing criminal offenders, the practice continues to play a role in the public education of school children in most parts of the country. Professional and public opinion is sharply divided on the practice, and has been for more than a century. Yet we can discern no trend toward its elimination. . . .

Although the early cases viewed the authority of the teacher as deriving from the parents, the concept of parental delegation has been replaced by the view—more consonant with compulsory education laws—that the State itself may impose such corporal punishment as is reasonably necessary "for the proper education of the child and for the maintenance of group discipline." I F. Harper & F. James, The Law of Torts 292. All of the circumstances are to be taken into account in determining whether the punishment is reasonable in a particular case. . . .

Against this background of historical and contemporary approval of reasonable corporal punishment, we turn to the constitutional questions before us.

III

. . . An examination of the history of the amendment and the decisions of this Court construing the proscription against cruel and unusual punishment confirms that it was designed to protect those convicted of crimes. We adhere to this longstanding limitation and hold that the Eighth Amendment does not apply to the paddling of children as a means of maintaining discipline in public schools.

* * *

IV

The Fourteenth Amendment prohibits any State deprivation of life, liberty or property without due process of law. Application of this prohibition requires the familiar two-stage analysis: we must first ask whether the asserted individual interests are encompassed within the Fourteenth Amendment's protection of "life, liberty or property"; if protected interests are implicated, we then must decide what procedures constitute "due process of law." . . . Following that analysis here, we find that corporal punishment in public school implicates a constitutionally protected liberty interest, but we hold that the traditional common law remedies are fully adequate to afford due process.

A

. . . Due process is required only when a decision of the State implicates an interest within the protection of the Fourteenth Amendment. And "to determine whether due process requirements apply in the first place, we must look not to the 'weight' but to the *nature* of the interest at stake."

* * *

While the contours of this historic liberty interest in the context of our federal system of government have not been defined precisely, they always have been thought to encompass freedom from bodily restraint and punishment. *See Rochin v. California*, 342 U.S. 165 (1952). It is fundamental that the state cannot hold and physically punish an individual except in accordance with due process of law.

This constitutionally protected liberty interest is at stake in this case. There is, of course a *de minimis* level of imposition with which the Constitution is not concerned. But at least where school authorities, acting under color of state law, deliberately decided to punish a child for misconduct by restraining the child and inflicting appreciable physical pain, we hold that Fourteenth Amendment liberty interests are implicated.

B

"[T]he question remains what process is due." *Morrissey v. Brewer*, 408 U.S., at 481. Were it not for the common law privilege permitting teachers to inflict reasonable corporal punishment on children in their care, and the availability of the traditional remedies for abuse, the case for requiring advance procedural safeguards would be strong indeed. But here we deal with a punishment—paddling—within that tradition, and the question is whether the common law remedies are adequate to afford due process.

* * *

1. Because it is rooted in history, the child's liberty interest in avoiding corporal punishment while in the care of public school authorities is subject to historical limitations. . . . The concept that reasonable corporal punishment in school is justifiable continues to be recognized in the laws of most States. . . . It represents "the balance struck by this country," *Poe v. Ullman*, 367 U.S. 497, 542 (1961) (Harlan, J., dissenting), between the child's interest in personal security and the traditional view that some limited corporal punishment may be necessary in the course of a child's education. Under that long-standing accommodation of interests, there can be no deprivation of substantive rights as long as disciplinary corporal punishment is within the limits of the common law privilege.

This is not to say that the child's interest in procedural safeguards is insubstantial. The school disciplinary process is not "a totally accurate, unerring process, never mistaken and never unfair. . . ." *Goss v. Lopez*, 419 U.S. 565, 579–80 (1975). In any deliberate infliction of corporal punishment on a child who is restrained for that purpose, there is some risk that the intrusion on the child's liberty will be unjustified and therefore unlawful. In these circumstances the child has a strong interest in procedural safeguards that minimize the risk of wrongful punishment and provide for the resolution of disputed questions of justification.

We turn now to a consideration of the safeguards that are available under applicable Florida law.

2. Florida has continued to recognize, and indeed has strengthened by statute, the common law right of a child not to be subjected to excessive corporal punishment in school. Under Florida law the teacher and principal of the school decide in the first instance whether corporal punishment is reasonably necessary under the circumstances in order to discipline a child who has misbehaved. But they must exercise prudence and restraint. For Florida has pre-

served the traditional judicial proceedings for determining whether the punishment was justified. If the punishment inflicted is later found to have been excessive—not reasonably believed at the time to be necessary for the child's discipline or training—the school authorities inflicting it may be held liable in damages to the child and, if malice is shown, they may be subject to criminal penalties.

Although students have testified in this case to specific instances of abuse, there is every reason to believe that such mistreatment is an aberration. The uncontradicted evidence suggests that corporal punishment in the Dade County schools was, "[w]ith the exception of a few cases, . . . unremarkable in physical severity." . . .

In those cases where severe punishment is contemplated, the available civil and criminal sanctions for abuse—considered in light of the openness of the school environment—afford significant protection against unjustified corporal punishment. . . . Teachers and school authorities are unlikely to inflict corporal punishment unnecessarily or excessively when a possible consequence of doing so is the institution of civil or criminal proceedings against them.

It still may be argued, of course, that the child's liberty interest would be better protected if the common law remedies were supplemented by the administrative safeguards of prior notice and a hearing. We have found frequently that some kind of prior hearing is necessary to guard against arbitrary impositions on interests protected by the Fourteenth Amendment. *See, e.g., Board of Regents v. Roth*, 408 U.S., at 569–70; *Wolff v. McDonnell*, 418 U.S. 539, 557–58 (1974). . . . but where the State has preserved what "has always been the law of the land," *United States v. Barnett, supra*, the case for administrative safeguards is significantly less compelling.

* * *

3. But even if the need for advance procedural safeguards were clear, the question would remain whether the incremental benefit could justify the cost. Acceptance of petitioners' claims would work a transformation in the law governing corporal punishment in Florida and most other States. Given the impracticability of formulating a rule of procedural due process that varies with the severity of the particular imposition, the prior hearing petitioners seek would have to precede *any* paddling, however moderate or trivial.

Such a universal constitutional requirement would significantly burden the use of corporal punishment as a disciplinary measure. Hearings—even informal hearings—require time, personnel, and a diversion of attention from normal school pursuits. School authorities may well choose to abandon corporal punishment rather than incur the burdens of complying with the procedural requirements. Teachers, properly concerned with maintaining authority in the classroom, may well prefer to rely on other disciplinary measures—which they may view as less effective—rather than confront the possible disruption that prior notice and a hearing may entail. Paradoxically, such an alteration of disciplinary policy is most likely to occur in the ordinary case where the contemplated punishment is well within the common law privilege. . . . In view of the low incidence of abuse, the openness of our schools, and the common law safeguards that already exist, the risk of error that may result in violation of a schoolchild's substantive rights can only be regarded as minimal. Imposing additional administrative safeguards as a constitutional requirement might reduce that risk marginally, but would also entail a significant intrusion into an area of primary educational responsibility. We conclude that the Due Process Clause does not require notice and a hearing prior to the imposition of corporal punishment in the public schools, as that practice is authorized and limited by the common law.

* * *

Mr. Justice White, with whom Mr. Justice Brennan, Mr. Justice Marshall, and Mr. Justice Stevens join, dissenting.

Today the Court holds that corporal punishment in public schools, no matter how severe, can never be the subject of the protections afforded by the Eighth Amendment. It also holds that students in the public school systems are not constitutionally entitled to a hearing of any sort before beatings can be inflicted on them. Because I believe that these holdings are inconsistent with the prior decisions of this Court and are contrary to a reasoned analysis of the constitutional provisions involved, I respectfully dissent.

I

[The discussion of the Eighth Amendment claim is omitted.]

II

The majority concedes that corporal punishment in the public schools implicates an interest protected by the Due Process Clause—the liberty interest of the student to be free from "bodily restraint and punishment" involving "appreciable physical pain" inflicted by persons acting under color of state law. . . . The question remaining, as the majority recognizes, is what process is due.

The reason that the Constitution requires a State to provide "due process of law" when it punishes an individual for misconduct is to protect the individual from erroneous or mistaken punishment that the State would not have inflicted had it found the facts in a more reliable way. . . . In *Goss v. Lopez*, 419 U.S. 565 (1975), the Court applied this principle to the school disciplinary process, holding that a student must be given an informal opportunity to be heard before he is finally suspended from public school. . . .

The Court now holds that these "rudimentary precautions against unfair or mistaken findings of misconduct," . . . are not required if the student is punished with "appreciable physical pain" rather than with a suspension, even though both punishments deprive the student of a constitutionally protected interest. Although the respondent school authorities provide absolutely *no* process to the student before the punishment is finally inflicted, the majority concludes that the student is nonetheless given due process because he can later sue the teacher and recover damages if the punishment was "excessive."

This tort action is utterly inadequate to protect against erroneous infliction of punishment for two reasons. First, under Florida law, a student punished for an act he did not commit cannot recover damages from a teacher "proceeding in utmost good faith . . . on the reports and advice of others," p. 1423, *supra*; the student has no remedy at all for punishment imposed on the basis of mistaken facts, at least as long as the punishment was reasonable from the point of view of the disciplinarian, uninformed by any prior hearing. The "traditional common law remedies" on which the majority relies, *ante*, at 1413, thus do nothing to protect the student from the danger that concerned the Court in *Goss*—the risk of reasonable, good faith mistake in the school disciplinary process.

Second, and more important, even if the student could sue for good faith error in the infliction of punishment, the lawsuit occurs after the punishment has been finally imposed. The infliction of physical pain is final and irreparable; it cannot be undone in a subsequent proceeding. There is every reason to require, as the Court did in *Goss*, a few minutes of "informal give-and-take between student and disciplinarian" as a "meaningful hedge" against the erroneous infliction of irreparable injury. . . .

The majority's conclusion that a damage remedy for excessive corporal punishment affords adequate process rests on the novel theory that the State may punish an individual without giving him any opportunity to present his side of the story, as long as he can later recover damages from a state official if he is innocent. The logic of this theory would permit a State that punished speeding with a one-day jail sentence to make a driver serve his sentence first without a trial and then sue to recover damages for wrongful imprisonment. Similarly, the State could finally take away a prisoner's good time credits for alleged disciplinary infractions and require him to bring a damage suit after he was eventually released. There is no authority for this theory, nor does the majority purport to find any, in the procedural due process decisions of this Court. Those cases have "consistently held that *some kind of hearing is required at some time before a person is finally deprived* of his property interests . . . [and that] a person's liberty is equally protected. . . ."

[Mr. Justice Stevens' dissenting opinion has been omitted.]

NOTES AND QUESTIONS

1. Scope of the Opinion: Cruel and Unusual Punishment

The majority argues that protection against cruel and unusual punishment is properly confined to those convicted of crimes. Is this conclusion persuasive? How relevant is the fact that all of the cases in which the Court has found punishment to be cruel and unusual involved the treatment of criminals? How would the majority respond to the hypothetical case of a student who was seriously injured for being late to class? *See generally* Rosenberg, "*Ingraham v. Wright*: The Supreme Court's Whipping Boy," 78 *Colum. L. Rev.* 75 (1978).

2. *Scope of the Opinion: Due Process*

The majority and dissent agree that some process is due to students subject to corporal punishment; the disagreement concerns the nature of the process. How would you characterize that disagreement? Is it a dispute over the weight to be attached to the interests of student and school in determining the most efficacious course of action? Does it speak to the circumstances in which it is appropriate not to afford a right of prior review? Does it address the utility of the process that is in fact provided?

3. *Models of Governance Revisited*

Is the disagreement between the majority and the dissenters—in *Ingraham* as in *Goss v. Lopez*—at heart a disagreement about models of school governance and the role of courts in choosing among those models? What do you make of the discussion, in the majority opinion, of the "openness of the public school and its supervision by the community"? Is this a factually accurate portrayal? *See* Comment, "Due Process, Due Politics, and Due Respect: Three Models of Legitimate School Governance," 94 *Harv. L. Rev.* 1106 (1981). What is the constitutional relevance of the point? How does it relate to the facts of the case?

4. *Challenges to the Punishment Itself*

Ingraham deals not only with whether some procedural protections are required before a student is disciplined, but also with the permissibility of the discipline itself.

a. Corporal punishment. Might a court conclude that certain acts of corporal punishment are so excessive that they violate a student's substantive due process interest in liberty? *See Jefferson v. Ysleta Independent School District*, 817 F.2d 303 (5th Cir. 1987) (second grader tied to a chair for an entire school day and part of the next; school district asserted that an instructional technique was being employed); *Garcia v. Miera*, 817 F.2d 650 (10th Cir. 1987) (one teacher held nine-year-old female student upside down by her ankles, while a second teacher struck her with a wooden paddle five times); *Turley v. School District of Kansas City, Missouri*, 713 F.Supp. 331 (W.D.Mo. 1989) (without warning and in violation of school district policy, teacher hit students on the face, neck, shoulders, and legs with a plastic baseball bat). *Compare Wise v. Pea Ridge School District*, 855 F.2d 560 (8th Cir. 1988). *See generally* Henderson, "Constitutional Implications Involving the Use of Corporal Punishment in the Public Schools: A Comprehensive Review," 15 *J. Law and Educ.* 255 (1986). Teachers may be disciplined or dismissed for inflicting excessive force with respect to corporal punishment. *See, e.g., Burton v. Kirby*, 775 S.W.2d 834 (Tex.App. 1989).

For a discussion of the efficacy of corporal punishment in changing student behavior, *see* Bongiovanni, "A Review of Research on the Effects of Punishment: Implications for Corporal Punishment in the Schools," in *Proceedings: Conference on Corporal Punishment in the Schools: A National Debate* 35 (The National Institute of Education, February 18–20, 1977).

Should parents be permitted to determine whether the school may administer corporal punishment to their child? *See Baker v. Owen*, 395 F.Supp. 294 (M.D.N.C. 1975), *aff'd mem.*, 423 U.S. 907, 96 S.Ct. 210, 46 L.Ed.2d 137.

b. Disproportionate punishment: does the penalty fit the deed? In *Fisher v. Burkburnett Independent School District*, 419 F.Supp. 1200 (N.D. Tex. 1976), a student who took a nearly fatal overdose of drugs while in school was suspended for a term. The court rejected the argument that this punishment was so grossly excessive as to violate substantive due process. The court concluded that the suspension, while ineffective as a therapeutic measure, could reasonably be thought to deter other students from using drugs. Had plaintiff merely been found in possession of a marihuana joint, the court added, the interest in deterrence would have been insufficient to warrant the punishment, 419 F.Supp. at 1204–05. Are you persuaded by the distinction the court draws? *Compare Boykins v. Fairfield Board of Education*, 492 F.2d 697 (5th Cir. 1974), *cert. denied*, 420 U.S. 962, 95 S.Ct. 1350, 43 L.Ed.2d 438 (1975) *with Ferguson v. Thomas*, 430 F.2d 852 (5th Cir. 1970). *See generally, Mitchell v. Board of Trustees*, 625 F.2d 660 (5th Cir. 1980).

c. Grade reductions. Should it be permissible for schools to reduce students' grades or deny course credit as a punishment for unauthorized absences or misconduct? *Compare Knight v. Board of Education of Tri-Point School District*, 38 Ill. App.3d 603, 348 N.E.2d 299 (1976); *with Hamer v. Board of Education*, 66 Ill. App.3d 7, 22 Ill. Dec. 755, 383 N.E.2d 231 (1978). *See also Gutierrez v. School District R-1*, 41 Colo. App. 411, 585 P.2d 935 (1978); *Dorsey v. Bale*, 521 S.W.2d 76 (Ky. 1975); Pepe, "Student Grades and School Discipline—A

Philosophical and Legal Question," 7 *NOLPE School L. J.* 126 (1977); Liggett, "Discipline by Grade Reduction and Grade Denial Based on Attendance," in M. McGhehy, ed., *School Law in Changing Times* 40 (1982).

d. Other Forms of Control. Drugs such as Ritalin have allegedly been prescribed for students by school doctors to curb excessively aggressive behavior; this too has been viewed by some critics as an illegitimate form of control. Do you agree? Does your answer depend on the effectiveness of the drug? The side effects? Whether the parents have consented? Whether the student has consented? *See* Jackson, "The Coerced Use of Ritalin for Behavior Control in Public Schools: Legal Challenges," 10 *Clearinghouse Rev.* 181 (1976); Note, "Coercive Behavior in the Schools: Reconciling 'Individual Appropriate' Education with Damaging Changes in Educational Status," 29 *Stan. L. Rev.* 93 (1976). *See generally* M. Foucault, *Discipline and Punish* (1977).

Board of Curators of the University of Missouri v. Horowitz

435 U.S. 78, 98 S.Ct. 948, 55 L.Ed.2d 124 (1978).

Mr. Justice Rehnquist delivered the opinion of the Court.

* * *

I

Respondent was admitted with advanced standing to the Medical School in the fall of 1971. During the final years of a student's education at the school, the student is required to pursue in "rotational units" academic and clinical studies pertaining to various medical disciplines such as obstetrics-gynecology, pediatrics, and surgery. Each student's academic performance at the School is evaluated on a periodic basis by the Council on Evaluation, a body composed of both faculty and students, which can recommend various actions including probation and dismissal. The recommendations of the Council are reviewed by the Coordinating Committee, a body composed solely of faculty members, and must ultimately be approved by the Dean. Students are not typically allowed to appear before either the Council or the Coordinating Committee on the occasion of their review of the student's academic performance.

In the spring of respondent's first year of study, several faculty members expressed dissatisfaction with her clinical performance during a pediatrics rotation. The faculty members noted that respondent's "performance was below that of her peers in all clinical patient-oriented settings," that she was erratic in her attendance at clinical sessions, and that she lacked a critical concern for personal hygiene. Upon the recommendation of the Council on Evaluation, respondent was advanced to her second and final year on a probationary basis.

Faculty dissatisfaction with respondent's clinical performance continued during the following year. For example, respondent's docent, or faculty adviser, rated her clinical skills as "unsatisfactory." In the middle of the year, the Council again reviewed respondent's academic progress and concluded that respondent should not be considered for graduation in June of that year; furthermore, the Council recommended that, absent "radical improvement," respondent be dropped from the School.

Respondent was permitted to take a set of oral and practical examinations as an "appeal" of the decision not to permit her to graduate. Pursuant to this "appeal," respondent spent a substantial portion of time with seven practicing physicians in the area who enjoyed a good reputation among their peers. The physicians were asked to recommend whether respondent should be allowed to graduate on schedule and, if not, whether she should be dropped immediately or allowed to remain on probation. Only two of the doctors recommended that respondent be graduated on schedule. Of the other five, two recommended that she be immediately dropped from the school. The remaining three recommended that she not be allowed to graduate in June and be continued on probation pending further reports on her clinical progress. Upon receipt of these recommendations, the Council on Evaluation reaffirmed its prior position.

The Council met again in mid-May to consider whether respondent should be allowed to remain in school beyond June of that year. Noting that the report on respondent's recent surgery rotation rated her performance as "low-satisfactory," the Council unanimously recommended that "barring receipt of any reports that Miss Horowitz has improved radically, [she] not be allowed to re-enroll in the . . . School of Medicine." The Council delayed making its recommendation official until receiving reports on other rotations; when a report on respondent's emergency rotation also turned out to be negative, the Council unanimously reaffirmed its recommendation that respondent be dropped from the School. The Coordinating Committee and the Dean approved the recommendation and notified respondent, who appealed the decision in writing to the University's Provost for Health Sciences. The Provost sustained the School's actions after reviewing the record compiled during the earlier proceedings.

II

A

. . . [R]espondent argued that her dismissal deprived her of "liberty" by substantially impairing her opportunities to continue her medical education or return to employment in a medically related field.

* * *

B

We need not decide, however, whether respondent's dismissal deprived her of a liberty interest in pursuing a medical career. . . . Assuming the existence of a liberty or property interest, respondent has been awarded at least as much due process as the Fourteenth Amendment requires. The School fully informed respondent of the faculty's dissatisfaction with her clinical progress and the danger that this posed to timely graduation and continued enrollment. The ultimate decision to dismiss respondent was careful and deliberate. These procedures were sufficient under the Due Process Clause of the Fourteenth Amendment. We agree with the District Court that respondent

> "was afforded full procedural due process by the [school]. In fact, the Court is of the opinion, and so finds, that the school went beyond [constitutionally required] procedural due process by affording [respondent] the opportunity to be examined by seven independent physicians in order to be absolutely certain that their grading of the [respondent] in her medical skills was correct."

In *Goss v. Lopez*, 419 U.S. 565 (1975), we held that due process requires, in connection with the suspension of a student from public school for disciplinary reasons, "that the student be given oral or written notice of the charges against him and, if he denies them, an explanation of the evidence the authorities have and an opportunity to present his side of the story." . . . The Court of Appeals apparently read *Goss* as requiring some type of formal hearing at which respondent could defend her academic ability and performance. All that *Goss* required was an "informal give-and-take" between the student and the administrative body dismissing him that would, at least, give the student "the opportunity to characterize his conduct and put it in what he deems the proper context." . . . But we have frequently emphasized that "[t]he very nature of due process negates any concept of inflexible procedures universally applicable to every imaginable situation." *Cafeteria Workers v. McElroy*, 367 U.S. 886, 895 (1961). The need for flexibility is well illustrated by the significant difference between the failure of a student to meet academic standards and the violation by a student of valid rules of conduct. This difference calls for far less stringent procedural requirements in the case of an academic dismissal.

* * *

Academic evaluations of a student, in contrast to disciplinary determinations, bear little resemblance to the judicial and administrative fact-finding proceedings to which we have traditionally attached a full hearing requirement. In *Goss*, the school's decision to suspend the students rested on factual conclusions that the individual students have participated in demonstrations that had disrupted classes, attacked a police officer, or caused physical damage to school property. The requirement of a hearing, where the student could present his side of the factual issue, could under such circumstances "provide a meaningful hedge against erroneous action." The decision to dismiss respondent, by comparison, rested on the academic judgment of school officials that she did not have the necessary clinical ability to perform adequately as a medical doctor and was making insufficient progress toward that goal. Such a judgment is by its nature more subjective and evaluative than the typical factual questions presented in the average disciplinary decision. Like the decision of an individual professor as to the proper grade for a student in his course, the determination whether to dismiss a student for academic reasons requires an expert evaluation of cumulative information and is not readily adapted to the procedural tools of judicial or administrative decisionmaking.

Under such circumstances, we decline to ignore the historic judgment of educators and thereby formalize the academic dismissal process by requiring a hearing. The educational process is not by nature adversarial: instead it centers around a continuing relationship between faculty and students, "one in which the teacher must occupy many roles—educator, adviser, friend, and, at times, parent-substitute." *Goss v. Lopez*, 419 U.S. 565, 594 (1975) (Powell, J., dissenting). This is especially true as one advances through the varying regimes of the educational system, and the instruction becomes both more individualized and more specialized. In *Goss*, this Court concluded that the value of some form of hearing in a disciplinary context outweighs any resulting harm to the academic environment. Influencing this conclusion was clearly the belief that disciplinary proceedings, in which the teacher must decide whether to punish a student for disruptive or insubordinate behavior, may automatically bring an adversarial flavor to the normal student-teacher relationship. The same conclusion does not follow in the academic context. We decline to further enlarge the judicial presence in the academic community and thereby risk deterioration of many beneficial aspects of the faculty-student relationship. . . . "Judicial interposition in the operation of the public school system of the Nation raises problems requiring care and restraint. . . . By and large, public education in our Nation is committed to the control of state and local authorities." *Epperson v. Arkansas*, 393 U.S. 97, 104 (1968). We see no reason to intrude on that historic control in this case.[6]

[Concurring and dissenting opinions have been omitted.]

* * *

NOTES AND QUESTIONS

1. Horowitz: *Scope of the Decision*

The determination of how much process is due, even assuming that a liberty or property interest is at stake in *Horowitz*, turns on the majority's classification of the interest as "academic" and not "disciplinary." How persuasive do you find the distinction? What factors are relevant to making the distinction: the degree of subjectivity of the required judgment, the inaptness of a *Goss*-type exchange, the degree and type of expertise required to make the decision, the nonadversarial nature of the process? Is it the characterization of the interest or the fact and extent of the deprivation that merits attention in determining what process is due? Does the Court's standard give judges too much leeway? Precisely what sort of hearing, if any, is required after *Horowitz*, where the dispute is academic in nature? *See Board of Regents v. Tomanio*, 446 U.S. 478, 493, 100 S.Ct. 1790, 1799, 64 L.Ed.2d 440 (1980).

Was the dispute in *Horowitz* in fact academic? What is the relevance to academic performance of Ms. Horowitz's allegedly unsatisfactory personal hygiene, discussed in footnote 6 of the opinion? Is good hygiene part of "clinical competence," the ostensible basis for the school's action?

The conceptual basis for the *Horowitz* decision was later elaborated upon by the Supreme Court. In *Regents of the University of Michigan v. Ewing*, 474 U.S. 214, 106 S.Ct. 507, 88 L.Ed.2d 523 (1985), a university student challenged the constitutionality of his dismissal from a six-year program of study leading to an undergraduate and medical degree. Scott Ewing was dismissed after failing five of the seven sections of a test administered by the National Board of Medical Examiners. The dismissal decision was made by a faculty Promotion and Review Board after individual review of the student's file. Upon petition by Ewing to reconsider the matter, he was allowed to appear personally before the Board, and he argued that the test did not fairly represent his academic progress or potential. The Board then reaffirmed its decision. The Court assumed, without holding, that Ewing had a constitutionally protected property interest, but nonetheless it held that he had not been denied due process:

> The record unmistakably demonstrates . . . that the faculty's decision was made conscientiously and with

6. Respondent contends in passing that she was not dismissed because of "clinical incompetence," an academic inquiry, but for disciplinary reasons similar to those involved in *Goss*. Thus, as in *Goss*, a hearing must be conducted. In this regard, respondent notes that the school warned her that significant improvement was needed not only in the area of clinical performance but also in her personal hygiene and in keeping to her clinical schedules. The record, however, leaves no doubt that respondent was dismissed for pure academic reasons, a fact assumed without discussion by the lower courts. Personal hygiene and timeliness may be as important . . . in a school's determination of whether a student will make a good medical doctor as the student's ability to take a case history or diagnose an illness. . . .

careful deliberation, based on an evaluation of the entirety of Ewing's academic career. When judges are asked to review the substance of a genuinely academic decision, such as this one, they should show great respect for the faculty's professional judgment. Plainly, they may not override it unless it is such a substantial departure from accepted academic norms as to demonstrate that the person or committee responsible did not actually exercise professional judgment.

. . . Added to our concern for lack of standards is a reluctance to trench on the prerogatives of state and local educational institutions and our responsibility to safeguard their academic freedom, "a special concern of the First Amendment." . . . If a "federal court is not the appropriate forum in which to review the multitude of personnel decisions that are made daily by public agencies," . . . far less is it suited to evaluate the substance of the multitude of academic decisions that are made daily by faculty members of public educational institutions—decisions that require "an expert evaluation of cumulative information and [are] not readily adapted to the procedural tools of judicial or administrative decision making." . . .

. . . [T]he Regents "had good reason to dismiss Ewing from the program." . . . Before failing the [test] . . ., Ewing accumulated an unenviable record characterized by low grades, seven incompletes, and several terms during which he was on an irregular or reduced course load. Ewing's failure of his medical boards, in the words of one of his professors, "merely culminate[d] a series of deficiencies. . . . In many ways, it's the straw that broke the camel's back." . . .

474 U.S. at 224–27, 106 S.Ct. at 513–14. *See also Akins v. Board of Governors*, 840 F.2d 1371 (7th Cir. 1988); *Clements v. County of Nassau*, 835 F.2d 1000 (2d Cir. 1987); *Harris v. Blake*, 798 F.2d 419 (10th Cir. 1986); *Crook v. Baker*, 813 F.2d 88 (6th Cir. 1987); *Mauriello v. University of Medicine and Dentistry of New Jersey*, 781 F.2d 46 (3d Cir. 1986); *Spring Branch I.S.D. v. Stamos*, 695 S.W.2d 556 (Tex. 1985); *Marquez v. University of Washington*, 32 Wash. App. 302, 648 P.2d 94 (1982). *See generally* Buss, "Easy Cases Make Bad Law: Academic Expulsion and the Uncertain Law of Procedural Due Process," 65 *Iowa L. Rev.* 1 (1979).

In the light of *Ewing*, is *Horowitz* an institutional academic freedom case? Does *Ewing* indicate that nearly all cases will be characterized as involving academic rather than disciplinary dismissals? If a student is dismissed from veterinary school for cheating on examinations, is that an academic or disciplinary decision? *See Nash v. Auburn University*, 812 F.2d 655 (11th Cir. 1987). What if the student were expelled for shoplifting off campus?

2. *Horowitz* and *Stigma*

"To be dismissed from one university . . . means the student can never again be a candidate for any degree. . . . The employee may find a new job; the student cannot find a new university. . . . The economic wound inflicted by dismissal remains with the student for the rest of his life, but often the wound goes deeper. In notorious cases, universities are wont to publicize apprehensions of offending students in order to placate the university community, irrespective of the emotional distress to the student or the irreparable harm to the student's reputation. When one tallies the potential harm to a student . . . the penalty for dismissal from a university for disciplinary reasons resembles the suspended sentence a felon might receive in a criminal court." Picozzi, "University Disciplinary Process: What's Fair, What's Due, and What You Don't Get," 96 *Yale L. J.* 2132, 2138–40 (1987). If you accept the suspended sentence analogy, what should be the constitutional consequences?

3. *What Process Is Due?*

As *Goss*, *Ingraham*, and *Horowitz* reveal, the nature of the process that is due is of critical importance.

a. Notice. What constitutes adequate advance notice of the charges and the date of the hearing? Must the notice be in writing? Must the notice actually be communicated to the student or teacher? *See Mueller v. University of Minnesota*, 855 F.2d 555 (8th Cir. 1988); *Nash v. Auburn University*, 812 F.2d 655 (11th Cir. 1987); *Strickland v. Inlow*, 519 F.2d 744 (8th Cir. 1975); *Dixon v. Alabama State Board of Education*, 294 F.2d 150 (5th Cir. 1961), *cert. denied*, 368 U.S. 930, 82 S.Ct. 368, 7 L.Ed.2d 193 (1961).

b. Impartial hearing. What constitutes impartiality? Can a racially charged atmosphere for a hearing render it unfair? *See The Dartmouth Review v. Dartmouth College*, 889 F.2d 13 (1st Cir. 1989). Does prior knowledge of the case disqualify a hearing officer? *See Nash v. Auburn University*, 812 F.2d 655 (5th Cir. 1987). May the trier of fact commingle the decision-making and prosecutorial functions? Does a prior history of friendship or animosity toward the accused disqualify a trier of fact? *See Newsome v. Batavia Local School District*, 842 F.2d 920 (6th Cir. 1988); *Gorman v. University of Rhode Island*,

837 F.2d 7 (1st Cir. 1988); *Sullivan v. Houston Independent School District*, 475 F.2d 1071 (5th Cir. 1973), *cert. denied*, 414 U.S. 1032, 1077, 94 S.Ct. 461, 38 L.Ed.2d 323, *Duke v. North Texas State University*, 469 F.2d 829 (5th Cir. 1972), *cert. denied*, 412 U.S. 932, 93 S.Ct. 2760, 37 L.Ed.2d 160 (1973); Hawkins v. Coleman, 376 F.Supp. 1330 (N.D. Tex. 1974); *Warren v. National Association of Secondary School Principals*, 375 F.Supp. 1043 (N.D. Tex. 1974); Buss, "Procedural Due Process for School Discipline: Probing the Constitutional Outline," 119 *U. Pa. L. Rev.* 545, 618–30 (1971).

c. Cross-examination. Should examination and cross-examination of witnesses be required in school cases? Consider *Newsome v. Batavia Local School Dist.*, 842 F.2d 920, 924–25 (6th Cir. 1988). A student was accused by an anonymous tipster of selling marihuana cigarettes on school grounds. Denying the student's claim that he was entitled to cross-examine his accusers, or at least to know their identities, the court declared: "In this turbulent, sometimes violent, school atmosphere, it is critically important that we protect the anonymity of students who 'blow the whistle' on their classmates who engage in drug trafficking and other serious offenses. Without the cloak of anonymity, students who witness criminal activity on school property will be much less likely to notify school authorities. . . . [T]he necessity of protecting student witnesses from ostracism and reprisal outweighs the value to the truth-determining process of allowing the accused student to cross-examine his accusers." Do you agree? *Compare John A. v. San Bernardino City Unified School District*, 187 Cal. Reptr. 472, 654 P.2d 242 (1982) (under state statute, it was improper to expel student without testimony of witnesses to altercation). *See also Nash v. Auburn University*, 812 F.2d 655 (11th Cir. 1987); *Franklin v. Board of Trustees*, 626 F.2d 19 (6th Cir. 1980); *McGhee v. Draper*, 564 F.2d 902 (10th Cir. 1977); *Nitzberg v. Parks*, 525 F.2d 378 (4th Cir. 1975); *Dixon v. Alabama State Board of Education*, 294 F.2d 150 (5th Cir. 1961), *cert. denied*, 368 U.S. 930, 82 S.Ct. 368, 7 L.Ed.2d 193; *Givens v. Poe*, 346 F.Supp. 202 (W.D.N.C. 1972); *De Jesus v. Penberthy*, 344 F.Supp. 70 (D.Conn. 1972). Are the circumstances of the case decisive? Should it, for instance, be permissible to discipline a student accused of assaulting female students if the alleged victims are afraid of retaliation if they testify and will only offer unsigned written statements? *See Tibbs v. Board of Education*, 114 N.J. Super. 287, 276 A.2d 165 (1971), *aff'd*, 59 N.J. 506, 284 A.2d 179.

d. Counsel. Should the due process clause be read to permit students and teachers to be represented by legal counsel or to require appointed counsel? Does your answer depend on the severity of the potential sanction? Would your answer differ if the school case were factually intertwined with a pending criminal case? Would your answer be affected by whether or not the school district employed a lawyer to represent it? *See, e.g., Gabrilowitz v. Newman*, 582 F.2d 100 (1st Cir. 1978); *Black Coalition v. Portland School District No. 1*, 484 F.2d 1040 (9th Cir. 1973); *Linwood v. Board of Education*, 463 F.2d 763 (7th Cir. 1972), *cert. denied*, 409 U.S. 1027, 93 S.Ct. 475, 34 L.Ed.2d 320. *See generally* Blaskey, "University Students' Right to Retain Counsel for Disciplinary Proceedings," 24 *Cal. W. L. Rev.* 65 (1988).

e. Evidence. Should the technical rules of evidence be followed in school proceedings? For example, should the rules regarding the exclusion of hearsay evidence apply in these proceedings? *See Boykins v. Fairfield Board of Education*, 492 F.2d 697 (5th Cir. 1974), *cert. denied*, 420 U.S. 962, 95 S.Ct. 1350, 43 L.Ed.2d 438 (1975). What should constitute sufficient evidence to warrant action by a school board? *See Jones v. Board of Trustees*, 524 So.2d 968 (Miss. 1988). Is this a constitutional question? Is it a denial of due process if there is no relevant evidence as to a critical element of the alleged infraction? *Cf. Vachon v. New Hampshire*, 414 U.S. 478, 94 S.Ct. 664, 38 L.Ed.2d 666 (1974); *Thompson v. Louisville*, 362 U.S. 199, 80 S.Ct. 624, 4 L.Ed.2d 654 (1960).

f. Transcript. Should a school be required to provide a transcript of the hearing when the student or teacher requests one? *Compare Mills v. Board of Education*, 348 F.Supp. 866 (D.D.C. 1972) *with Wasson v. Trowbridge*, 382 F.2d 807 (2d Cir. 1967).

4. Federal Legislation: The Family Educational Rights and Privacy Act and the Hatch Amendment

In the early 1970s, a number of organizations, including the American Civil Liberties Union and the Russell Sage Foundation, began to identify abuses in the keeping of public records by public educational institutions. Public elementary and secondary school officials sometimes released student records to law enforcement agencies, creditors, prospective employers, credit card companies, and so on without obtaining students' or parents' permission. There was also grave concern about the nature and educational relevance of the information being kept in the files. *See Merriken v. Cressman*, 364 F.Supp. 913 (E.D. Pa. 1973). Horror stories were cited in which records identified parents of students as radicals, described high school students as bedwetters in their preteenage years, and presented unverified personal opinions of teachers about the psychological health of students. Concern was also expressed that parents and students might not know what was in the educational records, might be denied access to those records, and might have no opportunity to challenge harmful statements contained in the records. *Cf. Van Allen v. McCleary*, 27 Misc.2d 81, 211 N.Y.S.2d 501 (1961). These pressures and others led to the passage of the Federal Educational Rights and Privacy Act (20 U.S.C.A. §§ 1232g–1232i). *See generally* Note, "The Buckley Amendment: Opening School Files for Student and Parental Review," 24 *Cath. U. L. Rev.* 588 (1975).

The Act provides that parents (or students, for those over age 18 or in postsecondary school) have a right of access to school records and a right to request that the record be amended or altered if they believe that statements in the record are false, misleading, violate the right to privacy, or are violative of other rights. School authorities generally must permit access to the records within forty-five days of a request and must consider the parents' request for alteration. If parents and school authorities are unable to agree, the student and his parents are entitled to a hearing within a reasonable period of time. If the student does not prevail at the hearing, no corrective action need be taken by school officials. If the student does prevail, the appropriate changes in the record must be made. Even in the event of an adverse decision by the hearing officer or body, the student is entitled to append a statement to the record explaining his or her side of the story. Appeals from an adverse decision are administrative in nature, and no private right of action to sue in federal court is provided in the Act. *See Girardier v. Webster College*, 563 F.2d 1267 (8th Cir. 1977). But the statute contemplates withholding all federal funds to districts that violate the Act; and a school district may be liable, under 42 U.S.C.A. § 1983, for denying a parent access to his children's educational records. *Fay v. South Colonie Central School District*, 802 F.2d 21 (2d Cir. 1986).

The Act requires a "full and fair" hearing, including notice; the right to present evidence and to cross-examine witnesses; and the right to have an attorney or other person represent the student at the hearing. The hearing officer may be a school person or anyone who has no direct involvement in the case. A decision must be rendered within a reasonable period of time, be in writing, and summarize the evidence and the reasons for the decision. The decision may be based only upon the evidence actually received at the hearing. *See generally* Regulations for the Family Educational Rights and Privacy Act of 1974, 45 C.F.R. §§ 99.1–99.67 (1979).

Consider to what extent the Family Educational Rights and Privacy Act supplements or supplants judicially imposed due process procedures. On the face of the Act, the student and his parents may contest anything contained in the record. The only clear exception from the limited legislative history is that grades may not be challenged unless the contention is that the grade was improperly recorded—a student may not challenge the accuracy of the grade itself. *See generally* McClung, "Student Records: The Family Educational Rights and Privacy Act of 1974," 22 *Inequality in Education* 5 (1977).

The Hatch Amendment, adopted in 1978, gives parents the right to examine instructional materials in experimental programs and also requires parental consent before students participate in federally funded programs that involve psychological examination, testing, or treatment designed to unearth personal beliefs, behaviors, and family relationships. 20 U.S.C.A. § 1232(h). "A coalition of more than thirty education and civil rights organizations has asserted that the regulations [issued by the Department of Education pursuant to this amendment, in 1984] . . . provide 'inroads for conservatives aiming to gain control of local curriculum and instruction' by interpreting 'psychological treatment' as covering any subject matter that is controversial or may require a value response from students." M. McCarthy and N. Cambron-McCabe, *Public School Law: Teachers' and Students' Rights* 97 (1988).

5. State Statutes

The procedures to be followed in teacher and student discipline cases are controlled not only by constitutional requirements but also by state statutes. New

York, for example, requires that a school board provide a probationary teacher with a statement of reasons for nonrenewal if the teacher requests it. N.Y. Educ. Law Ann. § 3031 (Supp. 1979). States typically have elaborate procedures for dealing with the dismissal of tenured faculty.

Student discipline is also often governed by state statutes that show the influence of *Goss*. For example, the California Education Code permits a teacher to suspend a pupil from class for up to two days. The suspended pupil must be sent to the principal; the teacher must seek a conference with the pupil's parents or guardian as soon as possible. A school principle may suspend a pupil from school for up to five days after an informal conference between the pupil and principal or the principal's designee. At the conference, the pupil must be informed of the reason for the action and the evidence on which the action is based and must be given the opportunity to present his or her side of the story.

In an emergency, the pupil may be suspended without this conference, but one must be held within seventy-two hours of the suspension. Within twenty-four hours, the principal must inform the student's parent and seek a conference with the parent. For their part, parents may also seek a meeting with the school superintendent for purposes of reviewing the suspension. This meeting must be held within three days of the request and a decision must be rendered two days after the meeting. Expulsions or longer suspensions must be preceded by a formal trial-type of hearing. Cal. Educ. Code Ann. § 48900 et. seq. (West 1978).

C. Implementing Due Process Protections

Constitutional rights are not just declarations about doctrine. They also are shaped by efforts to put those declarations into practice. School officials who implement constitutional decisions or who ignore those decisions are thus, in a vital sense, making law. The ways in which constitutional rights are implemented have already been noted (see chapter 2); the subject is more fully treated in chapters 5 and 7.

This section looks at implementation in two contexts. It begins with damage suits brought against school officials who violate students' (or teachers') constitutional rights, and then takes up the implementation of those rights.

1. The Threat of Damage Suits as a Goad to Implementation. 42 U.S.C.A. § 1983, a Civil War-era statute, has been used to prod officials—including school officials—into enforcing constitutional rights. That law authorizes suits for damages against anyone who, acting under color of state law, deprives an individual of federal constitutional or statutory rights.

The theory was that fear of pocketbook loss, through a § 1983 lawsuit, might make prompt effectuation of substantive rights a reality. *See, e.g.*, Wilkinson, "*Goss v. Lopez*: the Supreme Court as School Superintendent," 1975 *Sup. Ct. Rev.* 25; Note, "Procedural Due Process in Public Schools: The 'Thicket' of *Goss v. Lopez*," 1976 *Wis. L. Rev.* 934. *Compare* "Symposium on Medical Malpractice," 1975 *Duke L. J.* 1177. The reality, however, has proved to be more complex.

In *Wood v. Strickland*, 420 U.S. 308, 95 S.Ct. 992, 43 L.Ed.2d 214 (1975), the Supreme Court declared that school officials were not absolutely liable if they denied students or teachers their constitutional rights. Good faith is the test, and only violations of "the basic, unquestioned constitutional rights of [an official's] charges" would lead to liability. Even that formulation worried Justice Powell, who wondered in his dissent "whether qualified persons will continue in the desired numbers to volunteer for service in public education," knowing they might be financially liable if they failed to divine the law.

The restrictive standard set out in *Wood* was subsequently refined in *Harlow v. Fitzgerald*, 457 U.S. 800, 818, 102 S.Ct. 272, 2738, 73 L.Ed.2d 396 (1982), which held that the test of liability is whether officials' conduct "violates clearly established statutory or constitutional rights of which a reasonable person would have known." *See also Davis v. Scherer*, 468 U.S. 183, 104 S.Ct. 3012, 82 L.Ed.2d 139 (1984); *Anderson v. Creighton*, 483 U.S. 635, 107 S.Ct. 3034, 97 L.Ed.2d 523 (1987). The impact of this judicial grant of limited immunity has been to eliminate the subjective test of good faith in favor of an objective test, thereby limiting the role of juries in such cases. *See generally* Kinports, "Qualified Immunity in Section 1983 Cases: The Unanswered Questions," 23 *Ga. L. Rev.* 597 (1989).

Federal judges also have imposed restrictions on damage awards under § 1983. In a suit brought by students suspended without benefit of hearing, the justices held that only compensatory damages for proven actual injury could be awarded under this section. *Carey v. Piphus*, 435 U.S. 247, 98 S.Ct. 1042, 55 L.Ed.2d 252 (1978). Subsequently, in *Memphis Community School District v. Stachura*, 477 U.S. 299, 106 S.Ct. 2537, 91 L.Ed.2d 249 (1986), a case involving a tenured junior-high science teacher suspended without a hearing for showing his class films on human sexuality, the court denied a claim for damages based on the "value" of the constitutional rights at stake. Compensatory or actual damages, said the justices, suffice to vindicate the rights protected by § 1983 and to discourage constitutional violations.

Section 1983 is complex—some would say less than coherent—judicial terrain. For discussion of these issues and other related questions, including the immunity standard and damage test to be applied in § 1983 suits against governmental units (rather than officials), *see, e.g.*, S. Nahmod, *Civil Rights and Civil Liberties Litigation*, (2d ed. 1986); M. Schwartz & J. Kirklin, *Section 1983 Litigation; Claims, Defenses and Fees* (1983); Kinports, *supra*; Collins, " 'Economic Rights,' Implied Constitutional Actions, and the Scope of Section 1983," 77 *Geo. L. J.* 1493 (1989); Shapiro, "Public Officials' Qualified Immunity in Section 1983 Actions under *Harlow v. Fitzgerald* and Its Progeny: A Critical Analysis," 22 *J. Law Reform* 249 (1989); Jeffries, "Compensation for Constitutional Torts: Reflections on the Significance of Fault," 88 *Mich. L. Rev.* 82 (1988); Love, "Damages: A Remedy for the Violation of Constitutional Rights," 67 *Calif. L. Rev.* 1242 (1979); Yudof, "Liability for Constitutional Torts and the Risk-Averse Public School Official," 49 *So. Cal. L. Rev.* 1322 (1976).

2. Implementation and Due Process: *Goss* Revisited.

"Proceduralism and Bureaucracy: Due Process in the School Setting"

D. Kirp, 28 *Stan. L. Rev.* 841, 859–64 (1976). Reprinted by permission.

. . . [School officials are fearful that the formalism of *Goss* makes likely] disruption of the relationship between students and teachers, a further erosion of the schools' authority, and a predictable dislocation of the schools' standard operating procedures. . . . The decision at times speaks of the rights of students as distinctive from and even antagonistic to the claims of the school. It applies to the schoolhouse, albeit in drastically modified form, a mode of dispute resolution once thought fit only for the courtroom. . . .

The measurable costs of this approach are considerable. The full-dress hearings which the Supreme Court will probably demand before long-term suspensions are meted out may require resource commitments of as much as $500, nearly half of what is spent for the education of an average student for an entire school year. The intangible costs are of even greater moment. To school officials, the demand for formalism which apparently inheres in *Goss* signals an erosion of the confidence which has historically been placed in the fairness (if not the rightness) of their decisions and the supplanting of a relationship based on trust with one adversarial in nature. Education journals addressed to teachers and administrators have sounded this theme. They read the court-created requirement of adversariness—as well as state educational accountability legislation, federal student records legislation and other judicial decisions—as a vote of no confidence in what the schools are about.

A. Defensive Strategies

The range of likely responses to this command can readily be imagined: *Goss* may go ignored, or few students may demand hearings, or the hearing right may be so truncated as to be rendered practically meaningless.

Some school systems, either unaware of or decidedly hostile to *Goss*, will simply ignore the decision. This has happened before, notably in the wake of Supreme Court decisions banning sectarian prayer in the public schools, and while due process seems at worst disruptive rather than godless or immoral, the educators' reaction may be similar.

In a community whose students are not so innocent of their legal rights, schools will be disabled from proceeding as if *Goss* did not exist. The Supreme Court's decision in *Wood v. Strickland*, holding school board members (and by implication responsible school officials) liable in money damages if they deny students their "basic, unquestioned constitutional rights," renders defiance literally too costly a posture, and ignorance of the law provides no excuse. Under these circumstances, *Goss*-ordered hearings would be undertaken as one of those "impossible to withstand" pressures.

Even if *Goss* is not ignored, few hearings may in fact be held. In other noncriminal law contexts where the Supreme Court has established a right to due process, the Court has not required that the hearing itself take place, but only that notice and the *opportunity* for a hearing be provided. That opportunity has been infrequently utilized by those who potentially might benefit from it. For example, a mere 6 percent of those denied welfare benefits or stricken from the welfare rolls request a hearing. Why so few individuals would exercise their constitutionally guaranteed prerogative is difficult to understand. It cannot be the case that the disappointed individual is more concerned about maintaining a good relationship with the welfare system than about vindicating particular rights, since there exists no relationship to jeopardize once benefits have been denied or terminated. Perhaps the welfare system's determination is so indisputably right that a hearing would accomplish nothing, but that hypothesis is belied by data concerning the reliability of governmental decisions. The most likely possibility is that individual claimants either do not know of, or are generally fearful of exercising, the unfamiliar right to a hearing.

Similar results can be anticipated with respect to school discipline if *Goss* too insists only upon notice and the opportunity for a hearing. Although students may be more knowledgeable than those who seek welfare assistance, they may well be discouraged from demanding their "day in court" by the threat of subtle, and judicially unreviewable, punishments from teachers and administrators, such as denigration and insistence on unusually strict rule adherence. . . .

If due process seems at once threatening and irresistible, the most predictable school system response is the conversion of the "hearing" into a perfunctory affair. This could be accomplished by altering the *substantive* bases for suspension; for example, identifying "insubordination" and not some more objective and specifiable mischief as justifiable basis for discipline would effectively disable a student from disputing the matter.[118] Alternatively, the *process* itself may be structured to allow no room for the disciplinarian to change his mind; the student would merely be permitted to explain himself before punishment is inevitably imposed.[119]

This last course of action accomplishes several things. It renders the official legally invulnerable, for a challenge to a decision based on impressions of the decisionmaker's unreceptiveness is hard to foresee; all that due process formally demands is a particular structuring of the outward forms of decisionmaking. It readily permits the routinization of the new, enabling the administrator to proceed comfortably "by the book" without actually altering the substance of his actions. It typifies what might be termed defensive bureaucratic behavior.

School personnel have behaved this way, sacrificing purpose for form, in responding to what they regarded as other externally set limits on their discretion. In the wake of damage suits brought by students injured in freakish school accidents, teachers have been instructed to keep constant watch over their charges, in order to prevent any accidents—and, incidentally, any spontaneity. The student records legislation, which enables parents to see their children's permanent school files, led initially to a massive sanitizing and shredding of those records, and now promises to promote among teachers an oral tradition rivalling that of the Navajo Nation.

Defensive behavior is epitomized by this bit of advice rendered by a school attorney after *Goss*: "If you have any doubts . . . conduct a hearing." Undoubtedly, this seems a safe, risk-minimizing course of action. However, defensiveness both subverts the values which inhere in procedural justice and forecloses the possibility that schools will take the occasion to reexamine the ways in which they function. In its treatment of the individual student, defensiveness promotes a mechanical impersonalism beneficial neither to the student nor to the school.

---

118. *See, e.g., Schwartz v. Schuker*, 298 F.Supp. 238 (E.D.N.Y. 1969) (upholding suspension for "insubordination"). Alternatively, a school might adopt a harsher code of "student rights and responsibilities," which created more—and more specific—regulations for students to follow. A sufficiently exhaustive and precise code would limit bases for student objection.

119. The relevant structural factors include the forum in which the proceeding was held, the attitude that the decisionmaker communicated to the accused student offender, the time allotted to the hearing, and the manner in which the hearing was conducted.

At the institutional level, the locus of commitment shifts from educational goals to specific rules; instead of a means, rules become an end. Defensiveness may protect the school from having to evaluate the fit between its mission and the methods relied on to accomplish that mission, but it is a costly strategy. It further erodes the strength of the school's assertion of institutional competence and the credibility of its demands for trust. In short, defensive behavior is a regrettable, if understandable, reaction in the short run, and an institutionally self-defeating response over the long run.

NOTES AND QUESTIONS

1. A Contending View

In "Legalization of Dispute Resolutions, Distrust of Authority, and Organizational Theory: Implementing Due Process for Students in the Public Schools," 1981 *Wisc. L. Rev.* 891, Mark Yudof takes issue with the argument advanced in the previous excerpt. Yudof argues that neither school board members nor administrators "are prepared to do battle over this issue" and that the public will acquiesce. Administrators may even favor due process safeguards because "due process is consistent with the bureaucratic zeal for uniformity and established routines." Teachers and principals may not be as receptive to legalization of dispute resolution, since proceduralization both undermines trusting relationships with students and threatens to take matters out of teachers' and principals' hands, thereby transferring such matters to a higher level for decision. Yet, notes Yudof, because teachers have come to rely increasingly on law to pursue their own goals—through collective bargaining, for instance—they may be growing accustomed to legalization. If so, "this could reduce their hostility toward proceduralization of disputes with students. . . ." Moreover, "legalization of dispute resolution still leaves substantial power in the hands of principals and teachers in determining when more formal procedures will be utilized," and "proceduralization could be a way for teachers to avoid taking responsibility for a particular decision. . . ." Yudof adds that teachers and principals may have sufficient commitment to the "normative force of law" to adhere to the *Goss* requirements, even though they might disagree with them.

Relevant empirical evidence comes from a 1980 survey of 58 public institutions (out of 83 contacted), 36.2 percent did not allow cross-examination by the accused student; 37.9 percent did not allow the student to have legal counsel; 55.2 percent did not guarantee the student an impartial decision maker (either a hearing officer or tribunal). Argues one dissatisfied participant of a disciplinary hearing: "The procedural game too many universities in this country play is to give students enough process to fulfill the vague dictates of *Goss*, but not enough for the student to have a fair opportunity to defend himself—not enough to keep the university, and its officials, from having their way with him. . . . There's nothing magically collegial about a university; once a student is charged, a full-fledged adversarial relationship exists, and university officials are like everyone else. They play to win." Picossi, "University Disciplinary Process: What's Fair, What's Due, and What You Don't Get," 96 *Yale L. J.* 2132, 2149–50 (1987).

2. Other Approaches—The "Safe Schools" Law

In 1982, California voters, concerned about schools becoming "blackboard jungles," adopted an amendment to the state constitution. The provision guarantees students and school staff "the inalienable right to attend campuses which are safe, secure and peaceful." That unexceptionable-sounding prose has begun to generate litigation. Is the language merely hortatory or does it offer new legal protections? Must the legislature define specifically prohibited acts? What limitations, if any—feasibility, cost—should be read into the provision? *See* Biegel, "The 'Safe Schools' Provision: Can a Nebulous Constitutional Right Be a Vehicle for Change?" 14 *Hastings Const. L. Q.* 789 (1987).

3. Principal to Legend: Joe Clark and Due Process

In the winter of 1987–88, Joe Clark, principal of Eastside High in Paterson, New Jersey, made national headlines: "The principal bounced 66 students—'leechers, drains, troublemakers, goldbrickers,' he calls them—dumping them onto the streets without an alternative educational program, without benefit of any kind of hearing, secure in the belief that, at age 17 or 18, none of them was anything other than the scum of the earth.

> " 'Hang around, sell drugs, rape people,' Clark says, reinventing the moment when I asked him about the incident. 'Oh no! You're not going to stain and besmirch this school.' This wasn't the first time Clark had cleaned house [over the years, he had similarly

> bounced several hundred students] but the newly elected school board finally decided it had had enough. It proposed disciplining, perhaps even firing, its principal for 'unbecoming conduct' and 'insubordination.'
>
> "Without the threat of firing, Joe Clark would be just another ghetto principal, struggling in obscurity. But Paterson parents packed the school board meeting, turning it into a pep rally. 'We want Joe,' they yelled. TV crews came, sensing drama, and high school students told the reporters that, if Clark went, so would they. The multiplatinum rap group Run D.M.C. showed up to pound out support, one pop icon helping to create another. Then came a book offer and a 'Nightline' appearance, generally adulatory *Time* magazine cover story, and a six-figure contract for the movie rights. Education Secretary William Bennett came to Clark's defense, and the principal was offered a policy advisor's job in the White House. By the time the Paterson school board beat a strategic retreat, it had a hero—or at least a cult figure—on its hands."

Kirp, "Education: The Movie," XIV *Mother Jones* No. 1, p. 36 (January 1989).

What does this incident suggest about the appeal—and the durability—of the values that underlie due process, at a time when for many "law and order" is the first priority for public schools?

4. Note on Further Reading

Other theoretical perspectives on these issues are offered by Manley-Casimir, "School Governance as Discretionary Justice," 82 *Sch. Rev.* 347 (1974); Mandel "Judicial Decisions and Organizational Change in Public Schools," 82 *Sch. Rev.* 327 (1974); Wilkinson, "*Goss v. Lopez:* The Supreme Court as School Superintendent," 1975 *Sup. Ct. Rev.* 25. For more general discussions of schools as organizations, *see* M. Metz, *Classrooms and Corridors* (1978); S. Sarason, *The Culture of the School and the Problem of Change* (1971); Bidwell, "The School as a Formal Organization," in J. March, ed., *Handbook of Organizations* 972 (1965); March, "American Public School Administration: A Short Analysis," 86 *Sch. Rev.* 217 (1978); Weick, "Educational Organizations as Loosely Coupled Systems," 21 *Admin. Sci. Q.* 1 (1974). On due process theory, *see* L. Tribe, *American Constitutional Law* § 10–7 (2d ed. 1988); Goforth, "A Jurisprudential Reflection Upon the Burger Court's Approach to Procedural Due Process," 42 *Ark. L. Rev.* 837 (1989); Laycock, "Due Process and the Separation of Powers: The Effort to Make the Due Process Clause Nonjusticiable," 60 *Tex. L. Rev.* 875 (1982); Mashaw, "Administrative Due Process: The Quest for a Dignitary Theory," 61 *B.U.L. Rev.* 885 (1981); Saphire, "Specifying Due Process Values: Toward a More Responsive Approach to Procedural Protection," 127 *U. Pa. L. Rev.* 110 (1978).

FOUR

Educational Governance and the Law

I. INTRODUCTION: ELECTIONS, BUREAUCRACY, AND DEMOCRATIC ACCOUNTABILITY

The issues of compulsory education and socialization in public schools canvassed in chapters 1, 2, and 3 are inextricably tied to the question of how public education is and should be governed. Underlying the dilemmas of what should be taught and to whom are basic considerations of who should decide such matters. The question of who governs is vital to the legitimacy of the entire public education enterprise. A legitimate education system must be founded upon some notions of public control of education decision making. To be sure, expertise and professionalism have their place, but ultimately there should be an ongoing process of consultation and consent that renders the exercise of expertise and professionalism acceptable. This does not assume that the majority embraces every educational decision or even that there is an informed and articulate citizenry that presses its leaders at every turn. What is at stake is the *ability* of citizens to assert control over educational institutions through elections and other political and economic means. As Robert Dahl and Charles Lindblom have noted, the question of whether the citizenry has this "last word" is a matter of degree, for there are no absolute criteria. *See* R. Dahl and C. Lindblom, *Politics, Economics, and Welfare* 278 (1953).

Democratic legitimacy is important with respect to all of the institutions, bureaucracies, and functions of the modern welfare state, but it is critical in the realm of public education. This is because public schools are the primary public institution (as opposed to family and church in the private sector, for example) for socializing the young, for bringing them into the larger culture. In a sense, public schools are responsible for inculcating the rules by which democracy survives and thrives. If this task is performed well, students learn to appreciate the ways of democracy while retaining the flexibility and critical judgment necessary to engage in a continuing process of reevaluating its premises, values, and practices. The individual's capacity for autonomous choice is increased. *See* I. Berlin, *Four Essays on Liberty* (1969). But this introduces a serious problem of circularity. Public schools are charged with communicating an understanding of the very processes by which public schools are held accountable. In this fashion, there is a mutually affecting relationship between educational governance and the socialization functions of the public schools.

The structure and processes of educational governance are also linked to the quality of education and to equality of educational opportunity, the subject of chapters 5 through 7. As in the case of any enterprise that produces goods and services for the public, the nature of the mechanisms for controlling organizational and individual behavior will determine the types and quality of the goods and services produced. This is a particularly knotty problem in the case of public schooling; for market forces, the preferences of consumers as expressed through voluntary economic transactions, currently play a marginal role in the allocation of free (and compulsory) education services. Public school systems can be looked upon as institutional devices to isolate to a large extent the distribution of school services from market forces, to provide educational opportunities irrespective of student or parental preferences or wealth. In economic jargon, education has been treated as a merit good, a good to which everyone is entitled and which one may not sell or transfer. In part, this reflects the notion that education (or educational opportunity) should be distributed equally. This further complicates the problem of educational governance. Concerns about equality are superimposed on concerns about quality and democratic accountability. Satisfaction of these concerns can overlap, but then again it may not. If people act in their own best interest (narrowly conceived), this suggests that the approximation of some criterion of equality may be a function of who governs (and to whom they feel beholden or accountable). If, for example, racial minorities are excluded from the governing processes of education (say by disenfranchisement), then one could reasonably predict that minority students will suffer for this in the distribution of educational services. This, in turn, can have profound consequences for socialization of all students to democratic norms.

This brings us to the politics of education. The tendency is to think exclusively in terms of electoral constraints on public school systems. These constraints are clearly essential, and they are discussed below. But, as Charles Lindblom notes in *Politics and Markets* (1977), there are in reality a great number of components to the "social machinery for control of authority." This chapter is devoted to exploring these different control components or mechanisms in the public education context. *See generally* J. Chubb and T. Moe, *Politics, Markets, & America's Schools* (1990). School organizations can be controlled and receive direction through rules and regulations, intergovernmental constraints (some hierarchical, some not), inducements, institutional restructuring, capacity-building, interest-group pressures, professionalism, bureaucracy, and so on. *See generally* L. McDonnell and R. Elmore, *Alternative Policy Instruments* (1987). To this array, we have added recent proposals for reintroducing market systems into education as a method of improving the performance of schools.

Before proceeding to the task of exploring the complexities of educational governance, it is first necessary to understand the legal, political, institutional, bureaucratic, and professional environment of modern public schools. *See generally* F. Wirt and M. Kirst, *The Politics of Education: Schools in Conflict* (2d ed. 1989).

"The Legal Foundation of Public Education"

M. McCarthy and N. Cambron-McCabe, *Public School Law, Teacher and Student Rights* 2–7 (1992). Reprinted by permission.

All state constitutions specifically address the legislative responsibility for establishing public schools. For example, the Arizona Constitution stipulates: "The legislature shall . . . provide for the establishment and maintenance of a general and uniform public school system. . . ." The state legislature has plenary, or absolute, power to make laws governing education. . . .

Courts have recognized the state legislature's authority to raise revenue and distribute educational funds, control teacher certification, prescribe curricular offerings, establish pupil performance standards, and regulate other specific aspects of public school operations. Legislatures are empowered to create, reorganize, consolidate, and abolish school districts, even over the objections of affected residents. . . .

* * *

Although the state legislature cannot relinquish its law-making powers, it can delegate to subordinate agencies the authority to make rules and regulations necessary to implement laws. These administrative functions must be carried out within the guidelines established by the legislature. Some states are quite liberal in delegating administrative authority, whereas other states prescribe detailed standards that must be followed by subordinate agencies. It is a widely held perception that local school boards control public education within this nation, but local boards have only those powers conferred by the state. Courts consistently have reiterated that the authority for public education is not a local one, but rather is a central power residing in the state legislature. School buildings are considered state property, local school board members are state officials, and teachers are state employees. Public school funds, regardless of where collected, are state funds.

* * *

Since it has been neither feasible nor desirable to include in statutes every minor detail governing public schools, all states have established some type of state board of education. This board typically supplies the structural details necessary to implement broad legislative mandates. In most states, members of the state board of education are elected by the citizenry or appointed by the governor, and the board usually functions immediately below the legislature in the hierarchy of educational governance.

Licensure is an important tool used by state boards to compel local school districts to abide by their directives. School districts often must satisfy state licensure or accreditation requirements as a condition of receiving state funds. Though licensure models vary among states, the most common approach involves the establishment of minimum standards in areas such as curriculum, teacher qualifications, instructional materials, and facilities. In some states, different grades of school accreditation exist, with financial incentives to encourage local schools to attain the highest licensure level.

* * *

In addition to the state board, generally considered a policy-making body, all states have designated a chief state school officer (often known as the superintendent of public instruction or commissioner of education) to function in an executive capacity. Traditionally, the duties of the chief state school officer (CSSO) have been regulatory in nature. However, other activities, such as research and long-range planning, have been added to this role. In some states, the CSSO is charged with adjudicating educational controversies, and citizens cannot invoke judicial remedies for a grievance pertaining to internal school operations until such administrative appeals have been exhausted. When considering an appeal of a CSSO's decision, courts will not judge the wisdom of the decision or overrule such a decision unless it is clearly arbitrary or against the preponderance of evidence.

Each state also has established a state department of education, consisting of educational specialists who provide consultation to the state board, chief state school officer, and local school boards. State department personnel often collect data from school districts to ensure that legislative enactments and state board policies are properly implemented. Most state departments also engage in research and development activities to improve educational practices within the state.*

* * *

Although public education is state controlled in our nation, it is for the most part locally administered. All states except Hawaii have created local school boards in addition to state education agencies and have delegated certain administrative authority over schools to these local boards. Nationwide, there are approximately 15,700 school districts, ranging from a few students to several hundred thousand. Some states, particularly those with a large number of small school districts, have established intermediate or regional administrative units that perform regulatory or service functions for several local districts.

As with the delegation of authority to state agencies, delegation of powers to local school boards is handled very differently across states. Some states with a deeply rooted tradition of local control over education (e.g., Colorado), give local boards a great deal of latitude in making operational decisions about schools. In other states that tend toward centralized control of education (e.g., Florida), local boards must function within the framework of detailed legislative directives. . . .

Local school board members usually are elected by the citizenry within the school district. The Supreme Court has recognized that the equal protection clause requires each qualified voter to be given an opportunity to participate in the election of board members, with each vote given the same weight as far as practicable. When board members are elected from geographical districts, such districts must be established to protect voting rights under the "one man, one vote" principle. If "at-large" elections result in a dilution of the minority vote, an abridgment of the federal Voting Rights Act may be found.

The state legislature can specify the qualifications, method of selection, and terms and conditions of local school board membership. Board members are

* *See generally* Murphy, "The Paradox of State Government Reform," 64 *The Public Interest* 124 (1981).

considered public school officers with sovereign power, in contrast to school employees, who are hired to implement directives. Public officers cannot hold two offices if one is subordinate to the other, cannot have an interest in contracts made by their agencies, and in some states cannot occupy more than one office for which they receive pay. Generally, statutes stipulate procedures that must be followed in removing public officers from their positions. Typical causes for removal include neglect of duty, illegal performance of duty, breach of good faith, negligence, and incapacity.

A local board must act as a body; individual board members are not empowered to make policies or perform official acts on behalf of the board. . . .

School board meetings and records must be open to the public. Most states have enacted "sunshine" or "open meeting" laws,* acknowledging that the public has a right to be fully informed regarding the actions of public agencies. What constitutes a meeting is sometimes defined by statute, and certain exceptions to open meeting requirements are usually specified. For example, in many states, school boards can meet in executive session to discuss matters that threaten public safety or pertain to pending or current litigation, personnel matters, collective bargaining, or the disposition of real property. While discussion of these matters may take place in closed meetings, statutes usually stipulate that formal action must take place in open meetings.

Local school boards hold powers specified or implied in state law and other powers considered necessary to achieve the purposes of the express powers. These delegated powers generally encompass the authority to determine the specifics of the curriculum offered within the school district, raise revenue to build and maintain schools, select personnel, and enact other policies necessary to implement the educational program pursuant to law. Courts have recognized that without specific enabling legislation local boards have discretionary authority to establish and support secondary schools, kindergartens, nongraded schools, and various school-related programs; alter school attendance zones; and close schools.

* * *

Local school boards cannot delegate their decision-making authority to other agencies or associations. In an illustrative case, a New Jersey court ruled that a school board could not relinquish to the teachers' association responsibility for determining courses of study or settling classroom controversies. Also, the Iowa Supreme Court held that a school board could not delegate its rule-making authority to a state high school athletic association.

Local boards are authorized to perform discretionary duties (i.e., involving judgment), while school employees, such as superintendents, principals, and teachers, can perform only ministerial duties necessary to carry out policies. Hence, a superintendent can recommend personnel to be hired and propose a budget to the board, but the board must make the actual decisions. Although it might appear that educators at the building level retain little decision-making authority, administrators as well as classroom teachers can enact rules and regulations, consistent with board policy and law, to ensure the efficient operation of the school or class under their supervision.

"Schools in Conflict"

F. Wirt and M. Kirst, *Schools in Conflict*, 112–119, 137–140 (1989). © McCutchan Publishing Corporation. Reprinted by permission.

Popular participation in school policymaking has traditionally taken two forms—election of officials and referendums on issues. . . . *Local* school elections operate independently of political parties. Contrary to popular impression, political parties at the *national* level have sought unsuccessfully to serve as a link between citizens and school policy. For almost a century of national party platforms, education has been among "the predominant forces in operation during election years."

Yet schools have not escaped citizen control by avoiding the clutches of national parties, for direct and indirect popular control still exists. Directly, there is the widespread practice of electing school boards at the local level and boards and superintendents at the state level. Indirectly, control exists in the election of state legislators, executives, and judges, whose broad responsibilities include authority over many aspects of public education. . . .

* * *

. . . Eighty-five percent of local school boards in this country are elective. . . . We know that these officials, five to seven on a board, almost always seek their three- or four-year terms on a nonpartisan bal-

* *See, e.g. Cox Enterprises v. Board of Trustees,* 706 S.W.2d 956 (Tex. 1986); *Braswell v. Roche,* 299 S.C. 181 (1989).

lot. We also know that the board appoints a superintendent, usually professionally trained, who operates under its general policy guides and who may also be removed by it. The exception to this pattern is the appointment method often used in our biggest cities. In the usual community, the theory of democratic control makes the board member a pivot between community demands and school operations. . . .

* * *

School board elections have little voter turnout, even less than that for other government offices. The reasons for this are not clear. Is it because of the nonpartisan myth of school politics or because school board elections are held in off years and at primary dates when turnout is low for all contests? . . . It is clear, though, that campaigning in school contests is limited, candidate visibility low, and the contest rarely based on specific policies. . . .

* * *

When the Progressive reforms of nonpartisanship in school matters finally settled into place across the nation, the large working-class membership had almost disappeared from school boards, and white middle-class members dominated everywhere. Moreover, most of these members were male, married with children in the public schools, and active in the community. From the landmark study by Counts in 1924* to a replication by the National School Boards Association almost fifty years later, all the research substantiates this finding. A test of the link between representation and the possession of resources appears with blacks. Their representation on 168 big-city boards was smaller than their resources (i.e., numbers, money, organization); at-large systems effectively widened the gap between resources and board seats.

High social status alone does not give entry to the school board, but community activity—whether civic, business, political, or educational—joined with high social status provides training for office that few of the well-off actually use. . . .

* * *

Time and again what emerges from studies of board elections is that they are little-used channels to the political system. Like arroyos in the Southwest, only rarely does intense turmoil surge through these channels. Certain occasions can, however, have the effect of flash floods through desert courses—enormous conflict followed by altered features in the immediate environment. Much more often, however, these election campaigns offer only slight variations in ideology or policy orientation. And, as noted earlier, the structure of voting, dominated by nonpartisanship, depresses turnout. These conditions make the democratic model of informed choice between significant policy options by a sizable electorate more a pleasant fiction than a hard fact. . . .

* * *

In short, political scientists have found that what applies to nonpartisanship in other aspects of the local political scene holds true for school politics. Such reforms increase the cost of citizen participation, make the bridge between representative and citizen more tenuous, and consequently muffle expression of the full range of political interests within a community. Those constrained citizens tend to be of lower socioeconomic status, so governing structures are not value free. Rather, these reforms actually encourage the access and satisfaction of another group, middle-class and higher-status people. The rhetoric of Progressivism proclaimed the expansion of democracy—"the cure for the evils of democracy is more democracy" was their standard. The reality has been otherwise, deflecting those who cannot use the cue of political party to decide among complicated public issues, including those of schooling. Such reforms ensure that—until recently at any rate—the game of school politics was played by few, and mostly by those whom fortune favored.

* * *

. . . School boards[, however,] are faced with extramural pressures they cannot control that determine what they can do. Thus, changes in the shape of the national economy—a time of boom or a bust—can drastically affect the local school budget. The oil crisis after 1973 seriously redirected school budgets away from strictly educational purposes to cover rising energy costs. In the boom time for the Sunbelt states in the 1980s, school programs expanded under the pressure of greater resources. . . . Perhaps an even greater outside influence stemmed from the state itself, as it expanded its constitutional powers under political pressures. The rise of strong teacher organizations also represents a local sign of what is

* G. Counts, *The Social Composition of Boards of Education* (1927).

in essence a national development. This group's influence in one big city's schools has led an analyst to label it "union rule in Chicago." If the state continues to extend its control and take up its share of local costs into the 1990s, teacher groups may well escalate their pressure on state legislatures to reach decisions that are binding on local districts. We know how teachers, under fiscal stress, favor instructional and personnel costs or resist merit pay schemes suddenly popular in the 1980s.

* * *

The result of all this has been an increase in the number of groups seeking to influence local school governance, in the issues that get on the school agenda, and in the resources brought to bear upon the school board. . . .

* * *

. . . One finding seems consistent: Relatively few citizens use the channels available to them to register their educational needs. Popular participation is episodic at best, providing spasms rather than a flow of demands. When finally aroused, these demands do not focus on broad policies but rather on specifics. Of late, this involvement has taken the form of an increasing failure to pass local school levies, from almost two-thirds passing in the mid-1960s to only one-third by 1980. Alongside this flood of dissatisfaction with public schools by an apathetic public are occasional waves of protest generated by a sex education course, a too-liberal textbook, student dress regulations, or some other specific causes.

Interest groups may thus be the most common form of participation, but few citizens belong to them; the difficulties PTAs have in getting members enrolled and turned out are well known. Even groups seeking wide popular authority over local schools through "community control" programs have found it hard to get "the community" to participate. And board elections are rarely enticing enough to attract more than a small minority; they are dominated by the success of incumbents in getting reelected, and the competition is negligible. The potential exists for sweeping the "school rascals" out of office and replacing them with members who have different ideas. Elections certainly can operate in this fashion—but usually they do not.

Yet to say that relatively few participate is not to say that this frees the school authorities to do whatever they wish. The power of one parent with a complaint raised against a perceived injustice is enough to agitate administrators and can, if not met, escalate into a flood of community energy. . . . While the day-to-day life of school officials or teachers is filled with simply administering past directives from the public and profession, the potential exists for new waves of citizen inputs. At any moment, the schools can be caught between the forces of popular participation and bureaucratization. . . . Over time, the latter prevails, but also through time the influence of citizen participation becomes a zone of tolerance within which school authorities must act. This does not mean that they live in ongoing hypersensitivity to community and group demands—far from it, if one accepts the continuous criticism of school bureaucracy. Nor does this mean that the authorities are so inert that they cannot change their course—the history of educational reform belies that charge.

* * *

Why is there more concern about the effectiveness of school boards at this time in our history? One major reason is the lack of attention to school boards in virtually all the major national and state reports on education from 1983–86. For example, rather than not discussing school boards, the reform reports could have said that the school board is the crucial agent for school improvement and that state reforms should be directed at strengthening the local school board's capacity to bring about and monitor change. Instead, the unstated implication of many reports is that school boards are part of the problem and have not exercised leadership and their authority to improve education. This message further implies that boards need to be circumvented, if not through direct state regulation, then certainly through vastly increased state prescriptions and monitoring. . . .

This suspicion about the inability of school boards to provide academic leadership was exacerbated by the predominant research emphasis of these reports, which was on effective schools (in contrast to effective school districts). It was the school site that was the crucial focus for improvement, and the principal was the key catalyst. . . .

* * *

The apathy and ignorance about school boards is made worse by another finding. Local boards and board members interact with general government only occasionally and seem to be isolated (in boards' and civic leaders' perceptions) from mainstream community political structures. Very little systematic communication takes place between school boards and general government, despite the fact that ever more students have learning problems associated with nonschool factors such as poor housing, lack of family support and resources, and drug dependencies. When such interaction does exist on a regular basis, it often is only through the superintendent. . . .

NOTES AND QUESTIONS

1. Further Readings

The literature on the politics of education is quite extensive. For those interested in pursuing the subject further, the following books should be considered: J. Chubb and T. Moe, *Politics, Markets & America's Schools* (1990); P. Peterson, *The Politics of School Reform 1870–1940* (1985); M. Kirst, *Who Controls the Schools? American Values in Conflict* (1984); D. Rogers and N. Chung, *110 Livingston Street Revisited: Decentralization in Action* (1983); H. Tucker and L.H. Zeigler, *Professionals Versus the Public: Attitudes, Communication, and Response in School Districts* (1980); P. Peterson, *School Politics Chicago Style* (1976); T. van Geel, *Authority to Control the School Program* (1976); P. Cistone, ed., *Understanding School Boards: Problems and Prospects* (1975); W. Boyd, *Community Status and Conflict in Surburban School Politics* (1975); L.H. Zeigler, M. Jennings, and G. Peak, *Governing American Schools: Political Interaction in Local School Districts* (1974); L.H. Zeigler and K. Johnson, *The Politics of Education in the States* (1972); L. Iannaccone, *Politics in Education* (1967); N. Gross, *Who Runs Our Schools?* (1958).

2. Elections and Public Accountability

Are Professors Wirt and Kirst suggesting that the election of members of the local school board is an ineffective way for citizens to exercise control over public education? Why is this? Is it because such elections usually are nonpartisan? Because the public, most often, is apathetic? Because of the nature of educational services? Is it because nonelected officials are not subordinate to elected leaders, or because different groups have unequal influence in the electoral process—even if all votes are equally weighted? *See generally* D. Rogers, *110 Livingston Street: Politics and Bureaucracy in the New York City School System* (1968); R. Dahl and C. Lindblom, *Politics, Economics, and Welfare* 277–78 (1953).

Does the problem lurk in the structure of school board elections? Government establishes qualifications for voting, procedures for establishing voter qualifications, candidate eligibility requirements, lines for district boundaries, rules on campaign financing, single and multi-member districts, and the like, and this structure presumably has a powerful influence on electoral outcomes. *See generally* "Developments in the Law—Elections," 88 *Harv. L. Rev.* 1111 (1975). But are not all elections marked by such structural constraints? Would it be better for school board members to be appointed by other governmental bodies? Would an appointive system be more or less protective than an elective system of the interests of racial and other minorities? *See generally Irby v. Virginia State Board of Elections*, 889 F.2d 1352 (4th Cir. 1989).

Do school boards play a greater role in legitimizing school policies than in setting and implementing them? *See generally* Kerr, "The School Board as an Agency of Legitimation," 38 *Soc. of Educ.* 35 (1964).

3. Constitutional and Federal Statutory Protection of Voting Rights

The United States Supreme Court has produced a variety of opinions protecting voting rights, including the landmark one-person, one-vote decision in *Reynolds v. Sims*, 377 U.S. 533 (1964). *See also Dunn. v. Blumstein*, 405 U.S. 330 (1972) (durational residency requirement invalidated); *Kramer v. Union Free School District*, 395 U.S. 621 (1969) (property ownership requirement invalidated); *Harper v. Virginia Board of Elections*, 383 U.S. 663 (1966) (poll tax invalidated); *Gomillion v. Lightfoot*, 364 U.S. 339 (1960) (racial gerrymandering overturned). These constitutional decisions have been supplemented by the federal Voting Rights Act of 1965 (42 U.S.C.A. §§ 1973 to 1973bb-1) (1982 & Supp. IV 1986), focusing on electoral practices that discriminate on the basis of race. *See, e.g., Solomon v. Liberty County, Florida*, 899 F.2d 1012 (11th Cir. 1990); *Brewer v. Ham*, 876 F.2d 448 (5th Cir. 1989); *League of United Latin American Citizens v. Midland Independent School District*, 829 F.2d 546 (5th Cir. 1987). The subject is complex, and there are a variety of sources the interested reader may wish to examine. *See, e.g.*, A. Thernstrom,

Whose Votes Count? Affirmative Action and Minority Voting Rights (1987); C. Chandler, *Minority Vote Dilution* (1984); T. O'Rourke, *The Impact of Reapportionment* (1980); R. Cortner, *The Apportionment Cases* (1970); R. Dixon, *Democratic Representation: Reapportionment in Law and Politics* (1968); R. McKay, *The Law and Politics of Equal Representation* (1965); Fraga, Meier, and England, "Hispanic Americans and Educational Policy: Limits to Equal Access," 48 *J. of Politics* 850 (1986); Lowenstein and Steinberg, "The Quest for Legislative Districting in the Public Interest: Elusive or Illusory?" 33 *UCLA L. Rev.* 1 (1985); Levinson, "Gerrymandering and the Brooding Omnipresence of Proportional Representation: Why Won't It Go Away?" 33 *UCLA L. Rev.* 257 (1985); "Developments in the Law—Elections," 88 *Harv. L. Rev.* 1111 (1975).

The following excerpt, written by Professor Karlan, identifies the critical issues arising in the voting rights cases. As you review her article, you should seek to determine whether the assumptions underlying these cases are consistent with the descriptions of the politics of education presented elsewhere in this chapter.

"Maps and Misreadings: The Role of Geographic Compactness in Racial Vote Dilution Litigation"

P. Karlan, 24 *Harv. C.R.–C.L. L. Rev.* 173, 176–183, 213–218 (1989). Permission granted by the Harvard CR-CL Law Review.

. . . Modern vote dilution litigation began in 1964 with *Reynolds v. Sims*,[1] in which the Supreme Court held that "the right of suffrage can be denied by a debasement or dilution of the weight of a citizen's vote just as effectively as by wholly prohibiting the free exercise of the franchise."[2] Five years later, in *Allen v. State Board of Elections*,[3] the Court relied on *Reynolds* to hold that diluting the voting strength of racial minorities would violate the Voting Rights Act of 1965, which forbade the use of electoral practices that denied the right to vote on account of race.[4] In this Article, I examine two themes that run throughout the past quarter century of vote dilution litigation: the proper role of geographic factors and the meaning of effective access to the political process.

* * *

Broadly speaking, there are two kinds of vote dilution. "Quantitative" vote dilution cases are "based solely on a mathematical analysis" that shows that the votes of persons in one district are devalued relative to the votes of persons in a less-populated district.[13] The one-person, one-vote cases involve claims of quantitative dilution.

Even in cases in which there is absolute population equality, however, vote dilution may occur if the election method impairs the political effectiveness of an identifiable subgroup of the electorate. This latter form of dilution may be termed "qualitative" because "the quality of representation" the affected group receives is adversely affected by its relative political impotence.[14]

Any theory of qualitative vote dilution necessarily requires some notion of what the "undiluted" voting strength of the plaintiff class should be.[15] In other words, courts must measure the observed results against some baseline of expected outcomes. Approaches based on geographic compactness and civic inclusion express different responses to this problem.

* * *

In many instances, ethnic minority groups are residentially segregated. This segregation is often a

1. 377 U.S. 533 (1964).
2. *Id.* at 555.
3. 393 U.S. 544, 569 (1969).
4. 42 U.S.C. §§ 1973 to 1973bb-1 (1982 & Supp. IV 1986).
13. *Nevitt v. Sides*, 571 F.2d 209, 215 (5th Cir. 1978).
14. *Whitcomb v. Chavis*, 403 U.S. 124, 142 (1971); *see Nevitt v. Sides*, 571 F.2d at 216.
Claims of gerrymandering, either racial, *e.g.*, *Gomillion*, 364 U.S. 339 (1960) (lines drawn to exclude blacks from Tuskegee, Alabama); *Kirksey v. Board of Supervisors*, 554 F.2d 139 (5th Cir.) (en banc) (lines drawn to split black community among several districts), *cert. denied*, 434 U.S. 968 (1977), or political, *e.g.*, *Davis v. Bandemer*, 478 U.S. 109 (1986) (lines drawn to increase number of representative districts in state legislature), also fall into the category of qualitative dilution.
15. *See [Thornburg] v. Gingles*, 478 U.S. [30,] 87–88 (O'Connor, J., concurring in the judgment); *Mississippi Republican Executive Committee v. Brooks*, 469 U.S. 1002, 1012 (1984) (Rehnquist, J., dissenting).

product of racial discrimination in both the private and public housing markets. In addition, residence often reflects socioeconomic status and interests. Thus, geography can serve as a proxy for a bundle of distinct political interests.

Given residential segregation and a significant minority-group population, a geographically based districting scheme is likely to produce some districts in which the electorate is composed primarily of minority-group members. In those predominantly minority districts, minority-group voters can elect candidates responsive to their needs. In assessing a claim of vote dilution, then, a court might compare the likely electoral success of the minority group under a plan using single-member districts with that group's observed success under at-large elections: if the minority would have a greater ability to elect its preferred candidates from geographically defined districts than it enjoys under at-large elections, dilution has occurred.

* * *

. . . Individuals do not become fungible when they enter the voting booth. Rather, they take with them their political, racial, ethnic and socioeconomic affiliations and interests. An approach to vote dilution based on the concept of civic inclusion builds upon this insight as well as upon the *Reynolds* majority's emphasis on equal political access for all voters. It rests on a belief in the distinctive values that inclusion in governmental decisionmaking brings: a sense of connectedness to the community and of equal political dignity; greater readiness to acquiesce in governmental decisions and hence broader consent and legitimacy; and more informed, equitable and intelligent governmental decisionmaking.[27] Thus, in deciding whether a minority's votes have been diluted, a court guided by the value of civic inclusion must necessarily embark on an intensely local appraisal of political reality in the relevant jurisdiction. It must look beyond the voting booth to the council chamber and the "voting" (decisionmaking) that occurs there.

There are two complementary ways of thinking about the level of civic inclusion, that is, about access to this broad governmental process. First, one might look at the number of minority elected officials. Elected minority representation provides a measure of direct minority participation. Second, one might look at how responsive the decisions reached by the process are to minority interests. Evaluating responsiveness provides a measure of the overall influence of the minority's views. In a society in which minorities enjoy equal access to the political process, broadly understood, one would not expect to find monochromatic legislatures enacting white supremacist legislation. An analysis based on civic inclusion does not depend on geographic baselines because it sees geography as only an imperfect and formalistic proxy for the distinctive interests of minority individuals. Some of the discrete interests of minority citizens, such as the provision of municipal services at the neighborhood level (*e.g.*, street paving, allocation of programs among neighborhood schools, or police services), will be closely correlated with geography. But many minority interests, such as fair municipal hiring or decisions about which city-wide objectives to pursue, may be relatively unconnected to whether black people live in a single neighborhood, live in several small enclaves or are spread throughout the jurisdiction. Proponents of civic inclusion realize that minorities may be totally segregated from the political process even if they are entirely integrated into the political subdivision. An approach based on civic inclusion rests in part on a principle that also drives the new civic republican-

27. *See generally* W. McWilliams, *The Idea of Fraternity in America* (1973). In this sense, the values of civic inclusion parallel the values of the "new civic republicanism," which also rest on a belief in governmental deliberation and a desire to perfect that process. *See* Fitts, *The Vices of Virtue: A Political Party Perspective on Civic Virtue Reforms of the Legislative Process*, 136 U.Pa.L.Rev. 1567, 1586–92 (1988); Sunstein, *Beyond the Republican Revival*, 97 Yale L.J. 1539 (1988) [hereinafter Sunstein, *Republican Revival*]; *Sunstein*, **Interest Groups in American Public Law**, 38 *Stan.L.Rev.* 29 *(1985) [hereinafter Sunstein*, **Interest Groups**].

The two concepts are not identical, however. Proponents of civic republicanism often seek to insulate representatives from constituent pressures, in the hope that this will induce dispassionate deliberation by legislators. *See* Sunstein, *Republican Revival*, *supra*. Taken to its ultimate end of public-regardingness, civic republicanism suggests that the identity and distinctiveness of legislators should not matter; each legislator should act according to a generalizable conception of the proper course of action. It is hardly an accident that the original civic republicans conceived of societies which, although perhaps factionalized, were not at all diverse along racial, ethnic or sexual lines. *See* Sunstein, *Interest Groups*, *supra*, at 34.

By contrast, the approach suggested here accepts the bedrock diversity of modern America and seeks to bring diverse groups into the governing circle because, quite simply, the best way to ensure that all points of view are taken into account is to create decisionmaking bodies in which all points of view are represented by people who embody them. It is not enough that there are people who can only imagine what minority interests might require.

ism: one of the functions of deliberative representative government is to enable the polity to transcend simple logrolling and special-interest bargaining among discrete groups. To tie representation to small geographic areas within a jurisdiction can impair the development of representatives concerned with the welfare of the entire community. For republicans, this insight counsels almost categorically against election from small districts precisely because of the tendency for representatives then to identify solely with the small subset that elected them. Proponents of minority inclusion, however, recognize that small districts sometimes provide the best tool for ensuring the inclusion of minorities in deliberative bodies.[33] When they do, they should be adopted. But when they do not, some other means must be used to assure the primary goal, which is representation of people, not geographic interests.

* * *

"The Voting Rights Act was designed to enable minority citizens to gain access to the political process and *to gain the influence that participation brings*." . . .

* * *

One of the central debates in voting rights law has been, at least ostensibly, over the means of assuring black civic inclusion: are blacks better off controlling completely the electoral fortunes of a few representatives or are they better off influencing the electoral prospects of a large number of candidates? The amendment of Section 2 reflects a decided preference for the former approach: "the extent to which members of a protected class have been elected to office" is the one measure of political inclusion explicitly mentioned in the statute,[170] and the Senate Report states that the "[u]nresponsiveness" of elected officials to distinctive minority concerns "is not an essential part of [a] plaintiff's case." Thus, minority influence without minority presence does not constitute the "equal access to the political process" that Section 2 was intended to secure.

The reasons for the importance of minority presence are varied. Racial diversity among elected officials makes a powerful symbolic statement of the value of civic inclusion. The presence of black council members and county commissioners, like the presence of black police on forces with a history of brutality against the black community, the presence of black teachers in school systems with histories of segregation, and the presence of black election officials at polling places in jurisdictions with a history of depressed black political participation, may help to dispel the sense that these positions are reserved for whites and may encourage greater minority participation by creating a sense of political efficacy and membership in the governing community.

Just as voting itself is more than a mere symbol of civic inclusion, so, too, the presence of nonwhites on governing bodies is more than a mere symbol. Racial diversity is necessary in the council chamber as well as in the voting booth because of the distinctive dual nature of voting in a representative democracy. Two separate groups vote, and they vote for different things: the citizenry votes to select representatives, and the representatives vote to select governmental policies. The relationship between these two groups of voters—the citizenry and the representatives—is the subject of a great deal of recent scholarship.[181] That scholarship compares, on both positive and normative grounds, an "interest group" model of politics, in which politics is the art of aggregating individual preferences and representatives reflect and translate the prepolitical wishes of their constituents into policy, with a "republican" model of politics, in which politics marks an opportunity to create communal preferences, and representatives deliberate and select among policies using their independent judgments. Under either model, racial diversity serves an important purpose.

At first glance, it may seem that an interest-group model is somewhat unpromising for the fortunes of blacks in the political process: if blacks form only a minority of the populace and hence elect only a minority of the representatives then they will presumably be outvoted regardless of the electorate among whom the voting takes place. But that view fails to recognize that voting and coalition-building among representatives differ significantly from voting and

33. Small size may provide an additional impetus for civic participation: it may encourage greater citizen involvement in the governmental process. *See* C. Pateman, *Participation and Democratic Theory* 45 (1970); Frug, "The City as a Legal Concept," 93 *Harv.L.Rev.* 1059 (1980); Sunstein, Interest Groups, *supra* note 27, at 36.

170. 42 U.S.C. § 1973(b) (1982).

181. *See* Fitts, *supra* note 27, at 1572–76 (citing sources); Sunstein, *Republican Revival, supra* note 27 (same).

coalition-building among the citizenry as a whole. To the extent that blacks are able to participate in the representative-voting process, they will be able to advance their distinctive interests in a way they cannot in the general election process. First, local representative bodies are intimate groups—they rarely contain more than two dozen members. . . . It is fairly well-established in a variety of contexts that small groups operate under a different dynamic than do larger ones. A single black legislator on a five-member body may be able to build bridges to other members of that group, particularly to the extent that its members come to have shared values (like the desire to protect incumbents) and on-going relationships.

Second, members of legislative bodies have many more voting opportunities than does the citizenry. . . . The voter cannot split his vote among candidates to reflect his particular preferences. Elected representatives, by contrast, vote on many proposals at each of many meetings. Legislative coalition-building, or logrolling, requires that there be more than one voting occasion. The fact that voting in legislative bodies, unlike voting in general elections, is not anonymous furthers this process of accommodation. Thus, if there are particular issues of distinctive concern to the minority community, a representative directly dependent on that community will have the ability to trade her vote on issues of relative indifference to her constituents for other representatives' support on those critical issues. Similarly, the presence of minority representatives may restrain particularly egregious conduct.

Third, and most important, legislative voting, as opposed to general election voting, occurs in an institutional setting that maximizes the possibilities for deliberation through debates, amendment processes and mark-ups, and hearings in which the voter/representatives participate actively. With such deliberation may come greater understanding and acceptance of minority positions and a greater willingness to compromise. It is critical to this process, however, that an advocate of the distinctive minority perspective be present to advance its views. In this sense, a strong commitment by a few persons to address these concerns is preferable to a weaker commitment by many persons.

This last contribution of racial diversity is even more important if one adopts a republican perspective, in which deliberation among legislators is supposed to take the place of crude interest-group representation. In the same way that ensuring a fair cross-section on juries contributes to the search for truth because it increases the likelihood that wisdom acquired from diverse experiences will be available during the deliberative process, so, too, ensuring diversity on governing bodies will contribute to the likelihood that wisdom acquired from diverse experiences will be available for legislative decision making. Moreover, such diversity enhances the legitimacy of that deliberative process by allaying fears that the governing body has ignored the distinctive perspective of minority groups. . . .

"Schools in Conflict"

F. Wirt and M. Kirst, *Schools in Conflict* 2/e, 177–80 (1989). © 1989 by McCutchan Publishing Corporation. Reprinted by permission.

If the community is only occasionally active and the board has strong limitations, school professionals should retain a greater influence on policy issues. Professional educators have their resources, too. They define choices, produce research, provide specific recommendations, and shape the formal agenda. Using these resources, professionals generate pressures and information that can affect, if not determine, the board's deliberations and decisions. In Easton's framework, the school superintendent and staff provide inputs to the school board and the bureaucracy. Many specific policy issues, however, may never reach the school board if the superintendent and staff act under broad discretion from the school board. Consequently, both board and superintendent are authorities seeking to gain support from the community through the use of appropriate outputs in the form of budget, curriculum, teacher selection, and so on.

The professional staff does operate under certain constraints, however. They must anticipate reactions of board members to their actions because the board does have the basic power to fire them. They also know that the ultimate power of a provoked electorate is to remove them by changing the board, as noted earlier. It is also likely that the superintendent would act in keeping with the school board's wishes on many issues even *without* the threat of job loss. It is natural to assume that board members would hire a person whose values were similar to their own. An example of this is the low rate of turnover in smaller districts, which tend to be more homogeneous in their values. In effect, the board's impact on specific decisions may be more indirect than direct, but it is nevertheless real. The superintendent operates with considerable latitude as long as he or she stays within the board's ideological zone of tolerance.

A major research question during the 1970s was whether superintendents molded school boards into suppliant agents by professional control of policymaking. One way this was thought to occur was the socialization of the new board member to professional values. . . .

The question about who controlled whom received much national attention among educational administrators with the publication of the Zeigler and Jennings study of eighty-eight school districts.[4] The authors focused on whether democratic principles were being served in the interaction between board and superintendent; their answer was an emphatic "No," although numerous qualifying conditions were given. . . . Ironically, . . . Zeigler and Jennings found that effective opposition to professional influence by the board occurred in small districts with their limited political conflict and consensual elite board. Urban boards, on the other hand, were more contentious but had only limited effect against professional power.

* * *

But an immediate and powerful critique of this finding of superintendent dominance arose. Boyd pointed out that administrator control over the board was highly contingent on other matters.[6] It varied with the kind of policy at issue and with the size and homogeneity of the district. . . .

In all this, Boyd noted, one factor of the board-administrator relation not tapped in research is the force of what political scientists term the "law of anticipated reaction." This is the capacity of the administrator to estimate the limits within which she or he could act without board concern—the "zone of tolerance" in organizational theory. In other words, superintendents inhibit their own behavior based on knowing the controls these boards may exert. Subtle and hard to measure, this influence is still a reality that superintendents will detail in endless anecdotes. . . .

"Politics, Markets & America's Schools"

J. Chubb & T. Moe, *Politics, Markets & America's Schools* 156–60, © 1990 by the Brookings Institution. Reprinted by permission.

It may be better to think of the public school principal as a lower-level manager than as a leader. In the public sector, the principal is a bureaucrat with supervisory responsibility for a public agency. Most of the important decisions about policy have been taken by higher authorities: they set the goals and the principal is expected to administer them. Many of the important structural decisions are also taken by higher authorities: the principal is bound by all sorts of formal rules and regulations that dictate aspects of internal structure. And many of the important personnel decisions are imposed from above as well: the principal is unlikely to have much control over the choice of teachers or the incentives that motivate them. The real leaders of the public school are the authorities, not the principal.

Most of the high-level rhetoric about the importance of the principal's leadership role is essentially just that. The fact is that those who succeed in exercising public authority want principals to behave more like bureaucrats than leaders. Authorities want principals to ensure that formal hierarchical directives are put into effect; they do not want principals to exercise real discretion. The public system is set up accordingly. The position of principal is a bureaucratic office in a recognized hierarchy of offices. People who desire advancement within the educational system begin as teachers—the lowliest of bureaucrats—then advance up the ladder to assistant principal, then principal, then into the district office as assistant superintendent, and so on. They are on a career track, and the principalship is one step along the way. Doing a good job as principal qualifies one for advancement.

The nature of the job and its career path inevitably generate a process of selective attraction. People who

4. L. Harmon Zeigler and M. Kent Jennings, *Governing American Schools* (North Scituate, Mass.: Duxbury, 1974), pp. 39–42, Pt. III.
6. William L. Boyd, "The Public, the Professionals, and Educational Policy-Making: Who Governs?" *Teachers College Record* 77 (1976): 556–58.

like administrative work and who desire advancement in an administrative hierarchy tend to be attracted to the job, while people who want to be genuine leaders tend to be turned off. Once in the job, moreover, the incentives promote behavior that is classically bureaucratic. Doing a good job, and thus doing what is necessary to get ahead, requires playing by the rules, implementing them as faithfully and effectively as possible—and staying out of trouble. The easiest way to get into trouble is to launch bold, aggressive, innovative moves: discretionary acts of leadership that are bound to be threatening to the interests of someone, somewhere, in a position of political power.

* * *

In the public sector, the whole thrust of democratic politics is to formalize and constrain educational practice. As public authority is captured and put to use by various interests over time, the discretionary exercise of professional judgment is systematically curtailed, and the practice of education is transformed into an exercise in administration. Because technical concerns remain important to those who make political decisions, all discretion is not eliminated. Moreover, because so much technical and operational knowledge is concentrated at the lower reaches of the organization, in people whose professional sensibilities are violated by formal constraint, hierarchical control is inevitably imperfect: teachers will subtly be able to evade some of the rules without detection or punishment.

Nonetheless, the public world of educational practice is a world of rules imposed on the schools by local, state, and federal authorities. Some of these specify what teachers are to do and how they are to do it—rules about curriculum, about instructional methods, about the design of special programs, about textbooks, about time spent on various activities, about what can and cannot be discussed. In addition, there are all sorts of rules—monitoring and reporting rules—designed to ensure that teachers are doing these things and not evading hierarchical control. Thus teachers are doubly constrained in their efforts to perform their educational tasks as they see fit. First, they are required to follow rules that cause them to depart from what they might otherwise do, and thus to behave in ways that contradict or fail to take advantage of their professional expertise and judgment. Second, they are required to spend time and effort documenting, usually through formal paperwork, that they have in fact followed these rules. The combination may leave little room for them to do the kind of teaching they think they ought to be doing.

The most formal aspects of educational practice are often imposed by federal and state authorities, who are far from the scene and thus particularly vulnerable to discretionary departures from the objectives they want schools to pursue. But local politics is an important source of formalization as well—collective bargaining agreements, for instance, may specify in detail who is to do what, when, and how. Even in the absence of formalization, moreover, local politics still puts an indelible stamp on how education gets carried out.

Consider, for instance, local practices having to do with such things as homework, academic tracking, or discipline. Districts may abstain from imposing formal rules on these scores, but this does not mean schools are truly free to adopt practices that, on professional grounds, seem most conducive to effective education. The fact is that school practices can easily become politicized when one or more groups become disgruntled and pressure the authorities for action. Were teachers to decide that most students should be academically tracked, assigned significantly more homework, and held to strict academic standards in order to pass, the size and heterogeneity of the democratic constituency virtually guarantees a fearsome political response. Similarly, were schools unable to control violence and drugs on their campuses, the political authorities would inevitably come under pressure to "do something" by imposing disciplinary policies from without.

If schools do not anticipate and defuse these political problems through their choice of practices, then, the district is likely to exercise its authority to adopt formal rules on homework, tracking, discipline, and any other school practices that excite constituents—the result of which is still more formalization and still less discretion for schools. Conversely, the absence of formal rules does not mean the schools are using their apparent discretion to adopt practices that are considered best on professional grounds. It means that they have settled practices that are politically acceptable, and thus safe from formal reprisal by the authorities.

* * *

II. PROFESSIONALISM AND COLLECTIVE BARGAINING

"The Changing Idea of a Teachers' Union"

C. Kerchner and D. Mitchell, *The Changing Idea of a Teachers' Union* 1–9 (1988). Reprinted by permission.

A new era in American education began on the morning of 11 April 1962. The events of that day signaled a permanent change in the relationship between organized teachers and their schools. That morning *The New York Times* announced 'Teachers strike today.' . . .

The teachers risked their jobs. New York's Condon-Wadlin Act made striking punishable by dismissal, and Max Rubin, President of the Board of Education, declared that the teachers 'themselves terminated their employment'. The strike was also unpopular. Newspapers editorialized against it. The city's labor unions were either silent or hostile. . . .

In twenty-four hours it was all over. Teachers returned to work the next day in the face of an injunction. No one was fired, the *Times* editorialized in favor of higher teacher salaries, and Governor Nelson Rockefeller came to the city's aid with additional finances. . . . [T]he New York strike marked a watershed in public school labor relations throughout the nation. While there had been a strike in New York City two years earlier—as well as teacher strikes in other cities dating back to the early part of the century—they had been regarded as extraordinary occurrences brought about by special circumstances. Even the adoption of a collective bargaining statute in Wisconsin in 1959 did not galvanize the attention of the press, nor did it appear to reflect any basic shift in national attitudes toward teacher rights and responsibilities. The strike of 11 April, however, has been gradually recognized as a natural, though distasteful, correlate of a permanent change in the relationship between teachers and their school district employers.

* * *

In the space of a quarter-century, teacher unions in the United States have changed public education—its governance, school organization, and even the nature of teaching work. The transformation has been as swift as, and more complete than, the massive industrial changes brought about by the National Labor Relations Act and the spread of industrial unionism in the 1930s. For schools, the impact rivals that caused by the municipal reform movement in the first quarter of the twentieth century that gave rise to the appointed superintendent and a belief in the legitimacy for technical expertise. Clearly, teacher unionism ranks alongside school desegregation and categorical funding as one of the three major structural changes in public education since World War II.

* * *

In the popular mind, and to some practitioners, unions are organizations that engage in collective bargaining. But historically and functionally unions have engaged in a much broader set of activities: protective legislation, standards setting, employee education and apprenticeship, testing and certification, and electoral politics. This expansive view of union functions allows us to extend our analysis into the pre-collective bargaining days of teacher unions and find important elements of union development during a time of administrative dominance. This view also allows us to find elements of future union development in current issues and struggles surrounding unions and educational reform.

Historically, there have been three basic elements in union development: the right to organize, the establishment of binding agreements, and the expansion of employee's legitimate interests. These elements have become apparent over the last twenty-five years as teacher unionism has evolved through three distinct stages, each characterized by different core ideas. Organizing around those ideas has created what we call 'generations' of labor relations. The essence of each generation is captured in three common phrases used to describe the relationship between teachers and school managers:

— the 'Meet-and-Confer' Generation
— the 'Good Faith Bargaining' Generation, and
— the 'Negotiated Policy' Generation.

* * *

First Generation labor relations—characterized by a 'meet-and-confer' relationship between teachers and managers—established the right of teachers to organize as workers. . . .

* * *

The Progressive/Urban Reform Movement, which swept the country during the first quarter of the twentieth century heralded the virtues of *bureaucracy* in education, arguing that organization should be built on a rational division of labor and driven by politically neutral technical expertise. But bureaucracy was to be joined by the new human relations school of management, which gave credibility to the idea of employee participation in organizational decisions. As these two concepts merged, it became easy to believe that educational programs and practices would be substantially improved if teachers were permitted, even encouraged, to organize and to express their views on a broad range of school policies. The right of teachers to choose representatives who would confer regularly with managers about working conditions, wages, and other matters of concern was relatively easily defended as a way of simultaneously increasing loyalty and meeting the social-psychological needs of the workers.

Before 1960, these meet-and-confer sessions were rarely thought to involve explicit bargaining between teachers and their employers. The difference between conferring and bargaining is, of course, partly a matter of legal definition. But even more fundamentally, it is a matter of underlying ideology or assumption. Meet-and-confer sessions are predicated on the assumption that both sides are committed to defining and solving mutual problems using educational effectiveness as the criterion for a decision. In contrast, bargaining assumes that each side has its own interests, that each defines problems differently, and that each will pursue its own interests in dealing with the other. Teacher organizations began to discard meet-and-confer assumptions in the late 1950s, and the New York strike in 1962 gave added momentum to this change. What these organizations sought were binding contractual agreements, not just a means of airing their views.

* * *

During the First Generation meet-and-confer era, the profession of education is viewed as a unitary one. School administrators are distinguished from teachers by status and job role, but their interests are seen as fundamentally the same. Both teachers and administrators are supposed to express a selfless and universal interest in 'what's good for kids', and open displays of self-interest are socially illegitimate. It is the *duty* of the institution to look after teachers' welfare. In particular, administrators are supposed to function as their advocates, and school boards, as *trustees* of the common good, are expected to see that teachers are provided for.

These relationships are, of course, normative ideals—not universal behaviors. Teachers in the First Generation do have self interests, and some of them express and act upon those interests. Some administrators openly part company with teachers and deny having a duty to represent teachers' interests. And even more frequently, school boards fail to respond disinterestedly, expressing personal or class bias in their dealings with teachers. But the idea that there are fundamental common interests is a powerful one that serves to legitimate the authority of administrators and to couch governance and organizational decision making in terms of a unitary, shared framework of belief.

Because meet-and-confer relationships are based on the premise that all educators share a common interest in educating children, teacher organizations are seen as legitimate only so long as they recognize the ultimate authority of the administration and school board and do not challenge it publicly. Teachers can form organizations, participate in a broad range of discussions, and bring their special knowledge to bear. But they must interpret their special interests in terms of the whole school system. And when their conception of the common goals diverges from those of administrators and school boards members, they are expected to defer and acquiesce.

* * *

In due time, social and political conditions change, ending the idea that teacher interests can be incorporated into school policy through First Generation meet-and-confer procedures. Conflict erupts—often quite suddenly—and a new system of labor relations becomes dominant.

The *Second Generation* is epitomized by the phrase 'good faith bargaining' because it become legitimate for teachers to represent their own welfare interests, and to explicitly bargain with management over economic and procedural due process questions.

Establishing a right to contract represented a second important milestone in history: for unions generally, for teacher unions, and for each group of teachers and their school district employers. Collective contracts replace administratively determined civil service salary schedules, and grievance adjudication replaces board policy or administrative discretion as the basis for settling disagreements over negotiated work rules.

Second Generation norms include a very strong belief that conflict is endemic to the workplace and that effective conflict management is a vitally important aspect of labor relations. When strikes and other forms of public conflict occur, they are generally viewed as breakdown of the system, the result of bad faith or lack of expertise on the part of either labor leaders or managers. Second Generation labor relations values expertise and eschews amateurism. Labor relations experts emerge quickly. Once they are established, experts view as meddlers any outsiders (citizen groups, students, or politicians) who want to use labor relations for other than the intended purpose of codifying the welfare interests of teachers.

The participants in Second Generation labor relations generally adopt the beliefs of private sector industrial unionism that labor relations can and should be separated from organizational policy: 'Boards govern, superintendents administer, teachers teach.' This belief disappears during the transition to the Third Generation. More importantly, however, a close examination of school systems reveals that this belief is fundamentally inaccurate. Changes in labor relations do transform both policy and practice in the schools; this, despite the fact that labor laws almost universally forbid bargaining over educational or organizational policy. While managers and unionists often perceive that bargaining is largely limited to wages and working conditions, the evidence from our study suggests that many important issues of school policy and program are directly affected. To a surprising extent, negotiators for both sides heatedly deny that their actions affect the flow of educational services to children. And when they do think about such effects it is usually to claim that they are helping to keep labor strife from interfering with the educational mission of the schools. As a result, the very substantial policy effects that have resulted from the adoption of Second Generation, good faith bargaining, approaches to labor relations are often *accidental by-products* rather than the intended results of the new labor relations system.

Good faith bargaining is not, however, the end of the line for public school labor relations. After some years of trying to make Second Generation labor relations work, an increasing number of school districts are finding that new tensions and conflicts have surfaced around the legitimacy of teachers engaging in substantive agreements about school policy. The essence of conflict and the subsequent movement to *Third Generation* labor relations is an explicit attempt to shape school district policy through the contract and the union rather than attempting to manage 'around the contract' or through informal accommodation with the union. Sometimes the union is the moving party pressing for a new relationship, but in other cases external school reformers—citizens groups, board candidates—are the sources of renewed political tension. Two symbolic issues surface during this second period of labor conflict. In some cases, the unions' informal role in educational matters becomes an issue, the perception being that the bilateral bargaining relationship has frozen out other participants, particularly school board members. School boards and managers set out to 'win back the keys to the store' usually by attacking the work rule clauses in the contract. In other cases, school reformers target school performance itself: declining test scores, lax discipline, and flimsy curriculum. Sometimes with strong union backing, sometimes with opposition, the reformers perceive that collective bargaining is a means toward educational reform.

The result of this renewed tension and conflict is a *Third Generation* of labor relations, the essence of which is conveyed in the phrase 'negotiated policy'. During this generation, all parties, including the public, acknowledge that teacher negotiations are substantially and directly concerned with the ways in which schools will be run; the patterns of authority and social interaction in the buildings; the definition of what will be taught, for how long, and to whom; and the determinations of who has the right to decide how planning, evaluation and supervision of instruction will be carried out. Typically, the era of negotiated policy begins with the recognition by management and the school board that they have a genuine interest in negotiating an effective and workable evaluation clause in the contract. Their affirmative interest in having particular issues placed in a written agreement represents a fundamental departure from the Second Generation ideology, in which management asserts that 'the best contract is the shortest one'.

There is no reason to expect that the Third Generation is to last forever. . . .

* * *

"Collective Bargaining in the Public Schools: Reassessing Labor Policy in an Era of Reform,"

M. Finch and T. Nagel, 1984 *Wisc. L. Rev.* 1573, 1579–90, 1598–1603, 1607–13, 1616–26.

The traditions of local control are . . . reflected in the legal structure of school labor relations. The role of state government is usually that of insuring minimum qualifications in the teaching staff, and minimum levels of employment benefits and job protection. Otherwise, labor relations remain a distinctly local phenomenon. Only in Hawaii, do teachers negotiate the terms of employment at a statewide level. In the remaining states where bargaining is permitted, it occurs at the school district level between the district board of education and the elected union representative of district teachers. As a consequence of this decentralized system of bargaining, most of the important personnel decisions in the schools remain subject to local determination.

Though highly diffuse in structure, teacher unionism and collective bargaining have experienced remarkable growth in recent decades. The task of organizing teachers was greatly facilitated by professional associations like the National Education Association (NEA) and its local affiliates, which were developed into functioning unions.[25] This process was accelerated by the emergence of the more militant American Federation of Teachers (AFT), an offshoot of the AFL-CIO, as a rival to the NEA. Since the early organizational successes of the AFT in New York City and other metropolitan school districts, the two unions have waged a continual campaign for membership.[26] Today, eighty-eight percent of the nations' school teachers belong to either the NEA or the AFT, and eighty-three percent are members of a local teachers' organization.[27] By contrast, a dwindling twenty-one percent of all private sector employees currently belong to a labor organization, a decline that has occurred simultaneously with the rise in teacher unionism.

The increase in union density among public school teachers has been accompanied by a proliferation in the number of bargaining statutes and formal bargaining agreements. Since 1959, when Wisconsin first authorized teacher collective bargaining, thirty-three states have recognized a statutory duty to bargain,[29] and eleven states have recognized some form of teacher participation in school board decision-making.[30] Only four states continue to prohibit collective bargaining by teachers.[31] The nation's teaching force, moreover, has responded swiftly to the opportunities presented by the adoption of teacher bargaining laws. Current estimates indicate that approximately seventy percent of the nation's school systems operate under the provisions of a collective bargaining agreement.

Teacher bargaining laws have usually been patterned after private sector precedent, particularly the National Labor Relations Act. Among the labor conventions borrowed from the private sector have been:

---

25. *See generally* A. Cresswell & M. Murphy, *Teachers, Unions, and Collective Bargaining in Public Education* 53–102 (1980); Gee, "The Unionization of Mr. Chips: A Survey Analysis of Collective Bargaining in the Public Schools," 15 *Willamette L. J.* 367, 374–80 (1979).

26. *See* M. Liberman & M. Moskow, *Collective Negotiations for Teachers* 55–61 (1966). . . .

27. National Education Association, *Status of the American School Teacher*, 1980–81, 67 (1982) [hereinafter cited as *Status*]. . . .

29. *See* Alaska Stat. § 14.20.550 (1975); Cal. Gov't Code § 3540 (West 1977); Conn. Gen. Stat. § 10–153a (1979); Del. Code Ann. tit. 14, § 4001 (1982); Fla. Stat. § 447.201 (1980); Hawaii Rev. Stat. § 89–1 (1982); Idaho Code § 20.9 (1978); Ill. Ann. Stat. ch. 48, ¶1701 (Smith-Hurd Supp. 1984); Ind. Code § 20-7.5-1-3 (1978); Iowa Code § 20.9 (1978); Kan. Stat. Ann. § 72-5414 (1980); Me. Rev. Stat. Ann. tit. 26, § 965 (1974); Md. Educ. Code Ann. § 6-408 (1978); Mass. Gen. Laws Ann. ch. 150E, § 2 (West 1981); Mich. Comp. Laws Ann. § 423.215 (West 1978); Minn. Stat. § 179.61 (1983); Mont. Code Ann. § 39-31-305 (1983); Neb. Rev. Stat. § 79-1292 (1981); Nev. Rev. Stat. § 288.150 (1983); N.H. Rev. Stat. Ann. § 273-A:3 (1975); N.J. Rev. Stat. § 34:13A-6 (1982); N.Y. Civ. Serv. Law § 200 (Consol. 1983); N.D. Cent. Code § 15-38.1-12 (1969); Ohio Rev. Code Ann. § 4117.04 (1983); Okla. Stat. Ann. tit. 70, § 509.2 (1982); Or. Rev. Stat. § 243.656 (1979); 43 Pa. Cons. Stat. § 1101.401 (1976); R.I. Gen. Laws § 36-11-7 (1980); S.D. Codified Laws Ann. § 3-18-2 (1983); Tenn. Code Ann. § 49-5-501 (1978); Vt. Stat. Ann. tit. 16, § 2001 (1977); Wash. Rev. Code § 41.59.140 (1983); Wis. Stat. § 111.91 (1982).

30. *See* Ala. Code § 73 (1973) (mandatory consultation); Op. Att'y Gen. No. 74.11 (Ariz. May 20, 1974) (permissive consultation); Op. Att'y Gen. (Ark. Sept. 25, 1968) (permissive collective bargaining); *Littleton Educ. Ass'n v. Arapahoe Cty. School Dist.*, 553 P.2d 793 (Col. 1976) (permissive collective bargaining); Op. Att'y Gen. (Ga. Sept. 1, 1966) (permissive consultation); Op. Att'y Gen. 65–84 (Ky. 1965) (permissive collective bargaining); Op. Att'y Gen. 74–413 (La. 1974) (permissive collective bargaining); *Peters v. Board of Educ.*, 506 S.W.2d 429 (Mo. 1974) (permissive consultation); *IBEW v. Town of Farmington*, 405 P.2d 233 (N.M. 1965) (permissive collective bargaining); Op. Att'y Gen. (S.C. Sept. 27, 1978) (permissive collective bargaining); Op. Att'y Gen. (W.Va. June 26, 1974) (permissive collective bargaining).

31. *See* N.C. Gen. Stat. § 95-98 (1959); Tex. Stat. Ann. art. 5154C (Vernon 1947); Op. Att'y Gen. 60–003 (Utah 1960); *Virginia v. County Bd. of Arlington City*, 232 S.E.2d 30 (Va. 1977).

1) recognition of a single union with exclusive power to represent local school teachers; 2) recognition of management's duty to bargain in good faith with the union representative; and 3) recognition of limitations on the scope of the duty to bargain. In defining the scope of the duty to bargain, states have often accepted the private sector distinction between mandatory and permissive subjects of bargaining. Some states have expressly enumerated the mandatory subjects of bargaining, but most states have adopted the private sector definition of the scope of the bargaining duty, which extends the duty to all "terms and conditions of employment." In these states, the task of determining the specific scope of the duty to bargain has fallen upon the parties themselves and ultimately upon the courts.

In one significant respect, teacher labor relations have departed from the private sector paradigm: teachers are denied the right to strike, and are compelled to accept in its stead one or more of a variety of conciliatory procedures. In only nine states is there recognition of a limited right to strike, and exercise of that right is usually contingent on the exhaustion of conciliatory procedures.[36]

The concommitant conferral of bargaining rights and proscription of strike rights is a major modification of the private sector model of collective bargaining. The right to bargain has long been premised on the parties' "freedom to contact," which is comprised of the employer's right to extend or withhold compensable employment and the employees' right to extend or withhold profit-productive labor. As the Supreme Court has observed in the context of private sector bargaining, "the use of economic pressure by the parties to a labor dispute is not a grudging exception of some policy of completely academic discussion . . . it is part and parcel of the process of collective bargaining."[37] Furthermore, private sector bargaining is seldom regulated by formal procedures or interlaced with compulsory conciliation mechanisms.[38] Rather, it typically involves a test of power and will, virtually unregulated by government.

The denial of teachers' right to strike has been justified on various grounds. At a rhetorical level it is said that "no one has the right to strike the sovereign."[39] But the more substantive opposition to teacher strikes is premised on the belief that organized public employees would have disproportionate political leverage if strikes were permitted. This theory, first articulated by Professors Wellington and Winter in their work, *The Unions and the Cities*,[40] has dominated thinking in public sector bargaining for more than a decade. Central to this "disproportionate power" theory is the contention that neither market nor political restraints will enable local public employers to resist union bargaining demands backed by the threat of strikes.[42] Thus, the strike prohibition is thought necessary to preserve the political and economic integrity of local government.

Notwithstanding statutory prohibitions and public policy appeals, school teachers do strike. Between 1972 and 1980, for example, there were on average more than 145 strikes each school year. Teacher strikes now occur regularly with the commencement of the school year, and teachers lead all other public sector employees in their willingness to engage in job actions. Such strike activity is still considered by many to be an essential element in collective bar-

36. *See* Alaska Stat. § 09.43.030 (1975) (mediation a prerequisite); Hawaii Rev. Stat. § 89-12 (1982) (mediation and fact-finding are prerequisites); Ill. Ann. Stat. ch. 48, ¶ 1712 (Smith-Hurd Supp. 1984) (mediation a prerequisite); Minn. Stat. § 179.64 (1983) (mediation a prerequisite); Mont. Code Ann. § 59-1603 (1983) (no prerequisite); Or. Rev. Stat. § 243.726 (1979) (mediation and fact-finding are prerequisites); 43 Pa. Cons. Stat. §§ 1101.1002, 1101.1003 (1976) (mediation and fact-finding are prerequisites); Vt. Stat. Ann. tit. 21, § 1730 (1978) (mediation and fact-finding are prerequisites); Wis. Stat. § 111.70(4) (1982) (mediation a prerequisite; strike impermissible unless both parties withdraw from binding arbitration).

37. *NLRB v. Insurance Agents' Int'l Union*, 361 U.S. 477, 495 (1960). *See also* Cox, "The Duty to Bargain in Good Faith," 71 *Harv. L. Rev.* 1401, 1409 (1958).

38. *See generally* McCann & Smiley, "The National Labor Relations Act and the Regulation of Public Employee Collective Bargaining," 13 *Harv. J. on Legis.* 479, 510–14 (1976).

39. *See, e.g.*, A. Cresswell & M. Murphy, *supra* note 25, at 363; Hanslowe & Acierno, "The Law and Theory of Strikes by Government Employees," 67 *Cornell L. Rev.* 1055, 1061 (1982).

40. H. Wellington & R. Winter, Jr., *The Unions and the Cities* 24–29 (1971) [hereinafter cited as *The Unions and the Cities*]; *see also* Wellington & Winter, "The Limits of Collective Bargaining in Public Employment," 78 *Yale L.J.* 1107, 1123–25 (1969) [hereinafter cited as "Limits of Collective Bargaining"; Wellington & Winter, "Structuring Collective Bargaining in Public Employment," 79 *Yale L.J.* 805, 807–09 (1970) [hereinafter cited as "Structuring Collective Bargaining"]. In brief form, the Wellington and Winter position is based on the argument that: 1) public services are monopolized by public employees and have no competition from nonunion enterprises; 2) the public will exert excessive political pressure on governmental officials to prevent work stoppages, even at the cost of expensive bargaining concessions; and 3) the costs of settlement are easily disguised in "an already incomprehensible municipal budget or tax structure."

42. *See The Unions and the Cities*, *supra* note 40, at 18–21; "Structuring Collective Bargaining," *supra* note at 40, at 807–08. *See also* W. Garms, J. Gutherie & L. Pierce, *School Finance: The Economics of Public Education* 114 (1978) [hereinafter cited as *School Finance*]; Anderson, "Strikes and Impasses Resolution in Public Employment," 67 *Mich. L. Rev.* 943, 956–60 (1969); *Hanslowe & Acierno*, *supra* note 39, at 1063.

gaining, even though public school teachers are obviously troubled by the prospect of highly-publicized "law-breaking," and school boards by their obligation to invoke statutory sanctions.

As mentioned, most state legislators have attempted to circumvent the strike dilemma with a variety of compulsory, impasse resolution procedures. These procedures have relied on the intervention of third parties—mediators, factfinders, and arbitrators—to reconcile bargaining disputes and to avert strike activity. In theory, management and employees are induced to settle because of the third party's conciliatory power and the public pressure that accumulates behind the intervenor's efforts. In theory, impasse procedures introduce into the bargaining process a degree of moderation and balance otherwise lacking.

The more common impasse resolution procedures have suffered the same fate as statutory strike prohibitions. They are often ineffective in strongly contended bargaining disputes. Thus, more than seventy-five percent of strikes occurring in the period 1972–80 have occurred in states employing conventional, non-binding impasse resolution procedures. Evidence from these states indicates that elaborate conciliatory mechanisms will fail when teachers' unions are determined and school boards unyielding. For it is a characteristic of conventional impasse procedures that they leave intact the school board's freedom to say "no" to teacher demands, without fear of a legal strike reprisal.

There is one impasse procedure that has proven to be overwhelmingly successful in preventing strikes—binding arbitration.[48] Binding arbitration is a relatively recent phenomenon in American labor law, and one that has little precedent in the private sector. It has a long history in other common law countries, however, and is now widely used in non-educational public sector bargaining in the United States. This trend appears to be spreading to educational bargaining, as nineteen states have recognized some form of binding arbitration during the past decade, and seven of these compel binding arbitration to resolve bargaining disputes.[51]

The emergence of binding arbitration in teacher collective bargaining has precipitated a reexamination of procedural values in the labor relations context not unlike that precipitated by the introduction of collective bargaining itself.[52] For in theory binding arbitration is difficult to reconcile with traditions both of educational governance and labor relations.[53] First, arbitration vests ultimate authority in unelected arbitrators, thus undermining a history of local government control of personnel and budgetary matters. Second, arbitration interferes with the process of "free" collective bargaining, which is founded on the parties' power to accept or reject contract proposals. As a result, representatives of local government have begun to reexamine their opposition to a right to strike and many have concluded that, if change is needed, recognition of a teacher's right to strike is preferable to a state-imposed duty to arbitrate. Public employee unions, on the other hand, have begun to rethink their historical insistence on the right to strike. Regardless of the process values supporting unrestricted "power" bar-

48. . . . For summaries of the powerful deterrence to strikes in public sector bargaining generally, *see* B. Downie, *The Behavioral, Economic and Institutional Effects of Compulsory Interest Arbitration* 73–78 (1979); Feuille, "Selected Benefits and Costs of Compulsory Arbitration," 33 *Indus. & Lab. Rel. Rev.* 64, 65 (1979).

51. Binding arbitration is permitted by the following state laws: Hawaii Rev. Stat. §§89-2, 89-11 (1978); Ill. Ann. Stat. ch. 48, ¶ 1712 (Smith-Hurd Supp. 1984) (unless both parties agree to binding arbitration, teachers may strike); Ind. Code § 20-7.5-1-13 (1976); Mont. Code Ann. § 39-31310 (1979); Nev. Rev. Stat. § 288.200 (1981); N.H. Rev. Stat. Ann. § 273-A:12 (1983) (binding on non-economic items only); N.J. Rev. Stat. § 34:13A-7 (1982); N.D. Cent. Code § 15-38.1-13 (1983); Or. Rev. Stat. § 243.712(2) (1983); 43 Penn. Cons. Stat. § 1101.1003 (1976); S.D. Codified Laws Ann. § 3-18-8.1 (1983); Wash. Rev. Code § 41.59.120(5) (1983).

The following state laws employ some form of *compulsory*, binding arbitration: Conn. Gen. Stat. § 10-153 (1979) (compulsory arbitration of all disputed issues); Iowa Code § 20.22 (1977) (compulsory arbitration of all disputed issues); Me. Rev. Stat. Ann. tit. 26, § 965(4) (1974) (compulsory arbitration of all disputed issues, but binding only for non-economic items); Minn. Stat. § 179.69 (1983) (compulsory arbitration of all disputed issues unless one party recognizes the right to strike); Neb. Rev. Stat. § 48.818 (1980) (either party can compel binding arbitration of disputed issues before the Commission of Industrial Relations); R.I. Gen. Laws § 28-9.3-11, 12 (1980) (either party can compel binding arbitration of disputed issues, but only non-economic arbitral decisions are binding); Wis. Stat. § 111.70(4)(cm) (1982) (compulsory arbitration of all disputed issues unless both parties recognize a right to strike).

52. *Compare*, Horton, "Arbitration, Arbitrators, and the Public Interest," 28 *Indus, & Lab. Rel. Rev.* 497 (1975) *with* Krislov, "Arbitration, Arbitrators, and the Public Interest: Comment," 31 *Indus. & Lab. Rel. Rev.* 71 (1977).

53. *See generally* Bernstein, "Alternatives to the Strike in Public Labor Relations," 85 *Harv. L. Rev.* 459 (1971); Gallagher, "The Use of Interest Arbitration in the Public Sector," 33 *Lab. L.J.* 501 (1982); McAvoy, "Binding Arbitration of Contract Terms: A New Approach to the Resolution of Disputes in the Public Sector," 72 *Colum. L. Rev.* 1192 (1972). . . .

gaining, unions are asking whether third-party arbitral resolutions are not preferable to the uncertain, and often disappointing, results of strikes. . . .

A. The Economic Effects of Bargaining

* * *

Collective bargaining laws have done little to alter the dominant role of local school districts in establishing teacher salary levels.[70] One might have expected, therefore, that the economic impact of bargaining would be diluted by its decentralized structure. Quite surprisingly, however, the most prominent early forecasts warned of potentially significant increases in teachers' salaries resulting from local bargaining. Most notably, Professors Wellington and Winter argued in their highly influential work, *The Unions and the Cities*, that local public employees are far less subject to market constraints than private employees, since they tend to monopolize services that lack close substitutes or private competition.[71] Compounding this market failure is the power of unions to exert political pressures on local public employers, and the power of unions to strike in a monopolized field.[72]

The prediction of Wellington and Winter was based primarily on the early bargaining experience of large municipalities like New York City. Since those first "heady" days of public employee unionism, however, bargaining has spread to a variety of municipalities with diverse profiles. It is appropriate, then, to consider whether the past decade's experience with teacher bargaining evidences a strong bargaining effect, or whether bargaining has been assimilated into the pre-existing habits of local school government.

[After reviewing teacher salary studies, the authors conclude that] . . . teacher collective bargaining has produced minimal economic results, which may belie the suggestion that public school employers are unable to counter the bargaining power of unions. In any event, there is good reason to doubt that collective reasoning alone can provide public school teachers with sufficient leverage to restore salaries to a competitive level in the labor market.

* * *

Why has collective bargaining failed to produce the salary inflation that commentators like Wellington and Winter foresaw? One plausible explanation is that most states have denied teachers the right to strike, which Wellington and Winter viewed as a substantial component of public employees' bargaining leverage. Without this leverage, teachers lack full power to exploit their allegedly favorable market

70. . . . Although several states prescribe a minimum salary for teachers, school districts are free to supplement that salary. *See* L. Fischer, D. Schimmel & C. Kelly, *Teachers and the Law* 353–56 (1981).

71. The thesis of Professors Wellington and Winter is summarized by the following excerpt:

> To the extent union power is delimited by market or other forces in the public sector these constraints do not come into play nearly as quickly as in the private.
>
> Market imposed unemployment is an important restraint on unions in the private sector. In the public sector, the trade-off between benefits and employment seems much less important. Government does not generally sell a product the demand for which is closely related to price. There usually are not close substitutes for the products and services provided by government and the demand for them is relatively inelastic. . . . Because much government activity is, and must be, a monopoly product competition, nonunion or otherwise, does not exert a downward pressure on prices and wages. Nor will the existence of a pool of labor ready to work for a wage below union scale attract and create a new, and competitively less expensive, governmental enterprise.

The Unions and the Cities, supra note 40, at 18–19. Professors Wellington and Winter specifically stressed that such problems would result from the unionization of teachers. *Id.* at 30:

> Consider education. . . . [B]ecause the demand for education is relatively inelastic, teachers rarely need fear unemployment as a result of union-induced wage increases, and the threat of an unimportant nonunion rival (competitive private schools) is not to be taken seriously so long as potential consumers of private education must pay taxes to support the public school system.

72. The Wellington and Winter thesis, we should note, gives particular emphasis to the role of the *strike* in providing public employee unions undue bargaining leverage. However, the variables that allegedly work in conjunction with the right to strike—the employees' service monopoly, the ability of local government to conceal budgetary costs, and the employees' propensity to supplement bargaining activity with political activity—can operate independently of strike activity. Thus, the Wellington and Winter thesis has usually not been restricted to a narrow, strike-dependent interpretation in subsequent literature. . . . In any event, the purpose of our discussion is to illustrate that, in public education, the variables identified by Wellington and Winter either do not operate or do not operate with great effect on collective bargaining. Consequently, the imbalance in bargaining power that Wellington and Winter argued would result from granting teachers collective bargaining rights including the right to strike has not developed. . . . For other commentary positing adverse results from public sector bargaining, *see* Anderson, *supra* note 42, at 957–58; Summers, "Public Sector Collective Bargaining Substantially Diminishes Democracy," 1 *Gov't Union Rev.* 1, 5–6 (Winter 1980).

position. Under this view, teacher collective bargaining has been but a stunted version of private sector bargaining and predictably, could not match private sector achievements.

Research on the effects of public employee strikes is surprisingly limited, and thus one can offer only informed speculation as to the importance of the right to strike. Nonetheless, both the available evidence, and the consensus of labor commentators, indicate that the strike leverage of public employees has been considerably overstated. . . .

. . . The consensus of opinion is that: 1) the effects of strike activity are highly inconsistent;[87] 2) public and political resistance to strike pressure has increased dramatically since the early days of collective bargaining; and 3) with increasing frequency, strike action is resorted to as a defensive measure by public employee unions. Furthermore, the political activity of public employee unions in recent years indicates that union leaders no longer regard strikes as a source of substantial bargaining leverage. . . .

Thus, contemporary experience with public employee strikes provides little support for the claim that the strike is a powerful weapon in local government bargaining. Our contention, moreover, is that the political and economic forces at work in educational collective bargaining limit the power of teachers' unions, regardless of whether the right to strike is recognized. A consideration of these forces suggests that the basic market paradigm of commentators like Wellington and Winter was an inapposite description of labor relations in public education, whatever its strengths in describing such relations in other segments of the public sector. In particular, this paradigm failed to account for the evolving characteristics of the teacher labor market, the limited political base of public education, and the virulence of local fiscal conservatism.

A significant component of the theory that teachers' unions have undue bargaining leverage is the presumed monopoly power of public school teachers. As stated by Professors Wellington and Winter:

> [B]ecause the demand for education is relatively inelastic, teachers rarely need fear unemployment as a result of union-induced wage increases, and the threat of an important nonunion rival (competitive private schools) is not to be taken seriously so long as potential consumers of private education must pay taxes to support the public school system.[91]

The monopoly aspect of public school education, however, states but one side of the employment equation. In times of decreasing employment alternatives, public school employers . . . [can provide the only practical employment opportunities for teachers,] thus off-setting (if not overwhelming) the claimed monopoly power of teachers. . . .

An even stronger objection to the monopoly power theory of unionized teachers is suggested by an analysis of the political base of public education. The principal consumers of educational services, exclusive of non-voting pupils, are the parents of those pupils.[99] Current estimates indicate that such consumers comprise less than twenty-five percent of the voting public.[100] Moreover, a growing percentage of this consumer group consists of parents from low income levels, who historically refrain from active participation in voting.[101]

At the same time, non-consumers of public education are required to share its costs, and are permitted to participate in local school funding decisions. Obviously, this segment of the electorate has less to gain from a better-paid teaching staff and less to lose if educational services decline—or are cut off through strike activity. The alleged monopoly power of teachers, accordingly, has little relevance

---

87. *See, e.g.*, L. McDonnell & A. Pascal, [*Organized Teachers in American Schools* 64–65 (1979)] . . .; Kochan, "Dynamics of Dispute Resolution in the Public Sector," in *Public-Sector Bargaining* 150 (1979) . . . .

91. *The Unions and the Cities*, *supra* note 40, at 30.

99. *See* Guthrie, "Emerging Politics of Educational Policy," 3 *Educ. Evaluation and Policy Analysis* 75 (1981); Summers, . . . ["Public Employee Bargaining: A Political Perspective," 83 *Yale L.J.* 1156, 1169 (1974)].

100. *See* Guthrie, *supra* note 99, at 76; *accord* Yudof, "Legalization of Dispute Resolution, Distrust of Authority, and Organizational Theory: Implementing Due Process for Students in the Public Schools," 1981 *Wis. L. Rev.* 891.

101. *See* Yudof, *supra* note 100; *accord* [F. Wirt & M. Kirst, *The Politics of Education: Schools in Conflict* 250 (1982)] . . . ; Kirst & Garms, "The Political Environment of School Finance Policy in the 1980s," in *School Finance Policies and Practices: The 1980s: A Decade of Conflict* 47, 48–49 (J. Guthrie ed. 1980).

to this large segment of the electorate; stated simply, unionized teachers lack practical leverage over most voters and taxpayers.

Professor Summers, in an article that challenges the monolithic view of public employee unions, has observed the importance of the non-consumer's vote when a "special purpose" government like school district is involved. To the extent that non-consumers "vote their pocketbooks," special purpose governments may be at considerable disadvantage in the political process.[103] Studies of school bond referenda confirm that the non-consumers' vote is different from that of the parents of school-aged children. Thus, those who are elderly, those who have no school-aged children, and those who have children in parochial schools are consistently less supportive of public school spending increases.[104]

Therefore, the narrow base of political support for public education suggests that teachers' unions have monopoly power over only a fraction of the public, and that non-consuming taxpayers hold at least a numerical edge in the political process. Another aspect of public school funding which exacerbates the problem is the sheer impact and visibility of the school budget. In their analysis of union political leverage, Professors Wellington and Winter minimized the likelihood of a negative public reaction to a costly wage settlement because "the delayed effect of a particular settlement on an already incomprehensible municipal budget or tax structure is rarely a matter of high visibility. . . ."[105] While this might aptly describe the effect of wage settlements for certain public employee groups, it does not seem characteristic of those for public school teachers.

* * *

B. The Effect of Collective Bargaining On School Governance and Educational Policymaking

In devising public employee bargaining statutes, the states have relied extensively on private sector precedent. One prominent example of this is the frequent adoption of private sector definitions of the scope of the duty to bargain. These definitions typically extend the bargaining duty to all "conditions of employment," subject to the limitation that management need not negotiate matters of "policy" that are central to the direction of the business enterprise.[124] In the field of public employment, these policymaking prerogatives are preserved less for the sake of entrepreneurial freedom than for the maintenance of political control over the provision of governmental services.

Labor critics have continually challenged the equation of the bargaining duty in the public and private sectors.[125] Because of structural differences in the operation of the two sectors, it is alleged, public sector bargaining may result in union domination of the employment enterprise to a degree unknown in private industry. Private sector employers, critics contend, rarely bargain over the nature of the business enterprise or the product produced.[126] And in those areas where bargaining does

---

103. Professor Summers explains this point as follows:

The advantage enjoyed by employees in a single purpose district may be more than offset by the untempered opposition of those taxpayers who find little actual or psychic value for themselves in school expenditures and who therefore count the entire district tax as a loss. If this group is politically dominant, then budget constraints will press parents to oppose higher salaries as an alternative to reducing the number of teachers or failing to replace old equipment.

Summers, *supra* note [99], at 1169–70. . . . Notwithstanding Professor Summer's insight on the unique problems of the school district, his impression was that consumers and non-consumers (or users and non-users as he termed them) had relatively equal political strength. . . . On this point, obviously, we disagree with Professor Summers.

104. *See* H. Hamilton & S. Cohen, *Policy Making by Plebiscite: School Referenda* 181–83 (1974). . . .

105. "Structuring Collective Bargaining," *supra* note 40, at 808.

124. *See, e.g.*, Edwards, "The Emerging Duty to Bargain in the Public Sector," 71 *Mich. L. Rev.* 885, 909 (1973); Sackman, "Defining the Scope of Bargaining in Public Employment," 19 *B.C.L. Rev.* 155, 173–78 (1977); *see generally Fibreboard Paper Products Corp. v. NLRB*, 379 U.S. 203 (1964); *NLRB v. Wooster Div. of Borg-Warner*, 356 U.S. 342 (1958).

125. *See, e.g.*, Summers, *supra* note [99], at 1192–97; "Structuring Collective Bargaining," *supra* note 40, at 865–66.

126. "Structuring Collective Bargaining," *supra* note 40, at 858.

occur, management closely scrutinizes the potential effect of contract proposals by the essential criterion of entrepreneurs—business costs.[127]

By contrast, public sector bargaining is said to generate a more expansive bargaining scope while simultaneously reducing the incentives of public employers to resist union demands. Public employers, it is noted, frequently provide labor-intensive services (like education) which are fundamentally affected by labor policy.[128] Moreover, public employee bargaining often extends to a range of issues that have no direct and ascertainable economic cost. In such situations, the most powerful interest group aligned against employee unions—local taxpayers—will provide little coordinated resistance to union demands.[129]

Thus, under the prevailing theory of public sector bargaining, employee unions are believed to be in a unique position to influence the management and direction of local public services. This concern over undue union influence in local government has special vigor in public education, which is characterized by a continuing struggle between local school government and organized professionals. On one hand, the board of education symbolizes communitarian democracy in its purest form. Board members are neither professional politicians nor professional educators, and they bring to school government a distinctly lay perspective. On the other hand, public school teachers (most of whom are women) suffer from a long history of unilateral school government (run largely by men) that has excluded them from a participatory role in educational policymaking. Thus, since the advent of collective bargaining, union officials have declared their intention to improve teachers' professional status through greater autonomy from school management and greater participation in school policymaking.

Today, there is growing suspicion that organized teachers have prevailed in their struggle with local government and that the schools have suffered as a consequence. . . .

If allegations of an unhealthy union influence in public education have substance, then meaningful labor reform may be a prerequisite to school reform. As we shall contend in the following discussion, however, there is mounting evidence to suggest that the union impact on the schools both has been overstated and misinterpreted. Systematic investigation of unionized school districts reveals that teachers' unions may be relatively less successful in negotiating non-economic items than private sector unions, thus undermining the view that organized teachers have excessive bargaining leverage over local school government in this area. Furthermore, there is increasing reason to think that the formal bargaining achievements of the unions have not initiated significant, systemwide change in the operation of the schools. The paradox of this finding is that the yet-unfulfilled bargaining agenda of the unions may sometimes be in the best interests of public education.

1. A Profile of Collective Bargaining Agreements

Any discussion of teacher bargaining agreements must take account of the transformation in bargaining

---

127. Describing the private sector, Wellington and Winter observe:

> From the employer's point of view, most encroachments on what has been its unilateral power to manage are measured on a single scale: their effect on costs. . . [T]he pressure on the employer, as an enterprise, is to resist any increase in cost and, ultimately, it is hurt no more or less because that cost is extracted through inefficient work rules or high wages. Management resistance to union demands, therefore, will tend to force the union to make trade-offs based on those costs.

Id. at 857.

128. *Id.* at 859.

129. As noted by Wellington and Winter:

> But, where a demand is viewed as involving essentially political costs, trade-offs are more difficult. . . . Interest groups will exert pressure against union demands only when they are directly affected. Otherwise, they will join that large constituency which wants to avoid labor trouble. Trade-offs can occur only when several demands are resisted by roughly the same groups. Thus, budgetary demands can be traded off when they are opposed by taxpayers. But when the identity of the resisting group changes with each demand, political leaders may find it expedient to strike a balance on each issue individually, rather than as a part of a total package, by measuring the political power of each interest group involved against the political power of the constituency pressing for labor peace. Expansion of the subjects of bargaining in the public sector, therefore, may increase the total quantum of union power in the political process.

Id. at 858–59; *accord* Summers, *supra* note [99], at 1182. *But see* Edwards, *supra* note 124, at 932–33 (rejecting any distinction in the bargaining scope for private and public sector employees).

Note also that Professors Wellington and Winter did *not* premise their objection to a broad scope of bargaining on the availability of the strike right. *See, e.g.*, "Structuring Collective Bargaining," *supra* note 40, at 860.

practices that has occurred in recent years. At the outset of teacher collective bargaining, the unions held a decisive organizational advantage through their network of federal, state and local associations. This network could provide both information and negotiating expertise, and could coordinate bargaining strategies among the local unions. Boards of education, by contrast, were independent units of local government whose affiliations were weak and whose labor expertise was minimal. Thus, the early advantage was held by organized teachers, and their initial bargaining success was considerable.

Contemporary bargaining efforts by school boards are characterized by far more expertise, and far less willingness to concede, than in the past. School boards increasingly retain professional labor consultants—usually attorneys—to conduct negotiations.[141] With the assistance of such professionals, management has been more inclined to bargain hard, and to assert claims of management rights.[142] Indeed, school boards now frequently refuse to bargain over issues whose negotiability in the private sector would provoke little challenge.[143]

A profile of teacher bargaining agreements in unionized school districts provides evidence that school government has been far more successful in resisting union demands than earlier predictions would suggest. There is relatively little contract language governing the more formative issues of educational policymaking—issues which one might expect to be prominent in the bargaining agenda of a professional union.[144] It is uncommon to find, for example, contract provisions that determine such matters as the content of the school curriculum, the methods of classroom instruction, the choice of textbooks and teaching materials, the policies for student grading and student discipline, the standards for the hiring of teachers and administrators, and the allocation of the non-salary portions of the school budget.[145] It is doubtlessly true that unions in some school districts have frequently proposed, and occasionally won, contract language governing these items. It is also likely that an appreciable degree of informal consultation occurs between school management and teachers on some of these issues. But the point is that most of the larger issues of school governance continue to be resolved outside the collective bargaining process.

* * *

2. The Principle of Seniority in School Administration

The principle of seniority typically appears in teacher contracts in one of three forms. First, seniority is

141. *See, e.g.*, L. McDonnell & A. Pascal, *supra* note [87], at 41, 48, 51 (1979). . . .

142. *See, e.g.*, *id.* at 41.

143. For example, it is now well-established in the private sector that the scope of bargaining extends to union organizational rights, matters relating to salaries and fringe benefits, employee discipline, employee discharge, work loads and work duties, work hours and scheduling, and time off. *See* J. Weitzman, *The Scope of Bargaining in Public Employment* 7–39 (1975). Dispute over the negotiability of such matters in public education, by contrast, arises with surprising frequency. *See* Disapia, "What's Negotiable in Public Education?" *1 Gov't Union Rev.* 23, 32–51 (1980) (surveying judicial and administrative decisions). . . .

144. The following prediction is illustrative of early expectations concerning the emergence of professional issues in collective bargaining: "We can expect . . . that increasingly teachers will be involved in deciding the content of courses they teach, the textbooks they use, all of the learning activities within the classroom, overall curricular planning, recruiting of new colleagues, and promotion and tenure decisions." Kleingartner, "Collective Bargaining between Salaried Professionals and Public Sector Management," *Pub. Admin. Rev.* 165, 171 (Mar./Apr. 1973). . . .

145. It is difficult to obtain exact data on the prevalence of policy items since most of them seldom appear in systematic contract studies. Our study of teacher collective bargaining agreements in Connecticut reveals the following percentages of policy items:

(a) Teacher participation in curriculum or instructional policy committee—35%;
(b) Teacher participation in textbook selection—20%;
(c) Provision for use of teacher aides—16%;
(d) Student discipline procedure—6%;
(e) Teacher participation in school budgeting decisions—1%;
(f) Teacher participation in hiring decisions—2%; and
(g) Provision for student grading or promotion—4%.

Similar results are reported in the national contract study, L. McDonnell & A. Pascal, *supra* note [87], at 12 (31% of contracts authorize teacher participation in curriculum or instructional policy making, 29% of contracts contain provision for teacher aides, no contracts contain provision for student grading or promotion).

Such matters as student discipline procedures, budgetary control, and curriculum policy are among the examples cited by Professors Wellington and Winter and Professor Summers as unsuitable subjects for collective bargaining. *See* "Structuring Collective Bargaining," *supra* note 40, at 852–55; Summers, *supra* note [99], at 1181–82. Wellington and Winter also referred to class size as an unsuitable subject for bargaining, though Summers believed that the costs trade-off in class size reduction would provide school employers sufficient incentive to bargain vigorously. *Compare* "Structuring Collective Bargaining," *supra* note 40, at 853–54 *with* Summers, *supra* note [99], at 1182.

usually one of the two primary criteria for determining a teacher's compensation, the other is academic attainment. Second, seniority is often an influential, and sometimes a determinative factor, in establishing the order of reductions when the teaching staff must be decreased. Finally, seniority is sometimes a criterion for determining the order in which teachers are to be transferred within a school district. In all three forms, the seniority principle provides a fixed, objective standard by which personnel decisions can be made, but at the same time it reduces the prerogative of school administrators to act in accordance with their best estimate of a teacher's worth and the school system's needs.

The use of a teacher's seniority in determining her compensation is now accepted in the great majority of school districts. This criterion is basic to the "single salary schedule" under which a teacher receives a yearly salary increase corresponding to her years of service and degree status. The only means of progressing in such a system, other than through accumulated service, is to attain a higher academic degree or, better yet, to advance to an administrative position. Such a system stands squarely opposed to now-popular proposals for "merit" pay, which would enable school administrators to reward financially those who are evaluated as superior teachers. By adopting merit-based compensation, it is argued, schools would introduce economic incentives like those present in the private sector, and which are effectively eliminated by the single salary schedule.

Implementation of merit pay schemes promises to be the most contested aspect of contemporary educational reform. Merit pay proposals have already galvanized the support of governmental officials and the resistance of teachers' unions. But the controversy should not obscure the essentially secondary role that collective bargaining has played in determining the structure of teacher compensation. The single salary schedule was introduced into American school systems long before the advent of collective bargaining. Prior to World War II, only twenty percent of the nation's school systems provided compensation bonuses to "superior" teachers. And in 1959, when the first teacher bargaining law was enacted, merit pay plans existed in but six percent of the school districts surveyed in a national sample. Thus, for the most part, collective bargaining agreements formalized a system of compensation that preceded teacher unionism.

The single salary schedule appears to be sustained largely by institutional factors apart from the phenomenon of collective bargaining. Whatever its shortcomings, seniority-based compensation is a pay scheme that is highly acceptable to classroom teachers and is cheaply and easily administered. Past attempts to introduce merit-based schemes, by contrast, have faltered. Interestingly, the most frequently cited explanation for the discontinuance of past merit plans has been the incidence of administrative problems, especially the difficulties encountered in developing fair and accurate evaluation processes. Another major reason for the abandonment of merit plans has been the antipathy of teachers and the breakdown in morale caused by introduction of the plans. It is noteworthy that the phenomenon of collective bargaining has prompted the discontinuance of only eighteen percent of such plans, and that unions have expressly negotiated these plans away in but eight percent of the cases. Furthermore, there appears to have been no less experimentation with merit plans in unionized states than in non-unionized ones.

Therefore, it is important to identify what is, and is not, a product of collective bargaining in the schools, and to understand that the conventions of school administration may have a life independent of collective bargaining. An example of such a convention is the use of seniority to determine the order of staff reductions in the schools. While collective bargaining has no doubt played some role in consolidating the seniority principle in this context, a variety of objective factors independent of bargaining have played no less important roles.

* * *

3. Contractual Regulation of Teachers' Work Practices and the Problem of Productivity

The effort by teachers to bargain over the extent of their work responsibilities is perhaps as controversial as the prevalence of the seniority principle in public education. In recent years, many unions have negotiated express limitations on the length of the teachers' work day and work year, restrictions on the number and size of classes, and either restrictions on or additional compensation for non-instructional duties. Such contractual stipulation of teacher responsibilities represents, at least in form, a major dilution of past administrative powers, which are plenary in the operation of public schools.

The notion that employers should bind themselves to a declared schedule of work responsibilities and compensation is unexceptional in the private sector. In the field of public education, however, such a notion not only alters the traditional prerogatives of school administrators, it arouses suspicions that unionized teachers are negotiating reductions in their own productivity. Whereas teachers are perceived once to have labored the open-ended work day of the true professional, they are now perceived to have negotiated a lighter and shorter work load—and worked to that reduced commitment.

The reports of a reduced work effort among unionized teachers are usually based on informal observations of the schools, and are in this respect reminiscent of perennial complaints about union featherbedding and unproductivity. . . .

* * *

Recent quantitative analysis of the work practices of a national sample of teachers also indicates that unionization does not diminish teachers' productivity. Such analysis discloses, for example, that no significant difference exists in the length of the school day in unionized and non-unionized districts. Specific analysis of teachers' work practices revealed that, while total daily instructional time was somewhat reduced in unionized districts, the amount of time devoted to classroom preparation, administrative duties and parent conferences more than offset the reduction in instructional time. The cumulative effect of unionization, accordingly, was as much to increase productivity as to decrease it, although the research ultimately concluded that the directional shift in marginal productivity was "unclear."

Studies of the union effect on teachers' pupil assignments are similarly inconclusive. Class size research, the most common means of investigating pupil assignments, offers evidence of both decreased and increased pupil loads resulting from collective bargaining. When effects are found, however, they are small, and other research discloses no effect on class size resulting from collective bargaining. . . .

* * *

Whether the current reform literature will support traditional union demands for better working conditions remains to be seen. But the reform literature does give another dimension to the question of teacher productivity. What is good for organized teachers, we have been told, may sometimes be good for education.[202] And in an era of fiscal restraint, organized teachers may provide one of the few checks on the tendency of public school government to economize on the subtle yet important conditions for classroom education.

* * *

"Professional Employees, Collective Bargaining and the Law"

D. Rabban, 15 *Interface* 1, 3–5 (1986). Permission to reprint from the Department for Professional Employees, AFL-CIO.

The reaction to collective bargaining by professional employees seems to fit into three categories. Many maintain that any collective bargaining by professional employees inevitably destroys the autonomy and collegiality that should define professional work. Increasingly, however, professional employees have viewed collective bargaining as a legally enforceable method to preserve or obtain the same prerogatives of professional status that their skeptical colleagues perceive collective bargaining to threaten. A third approach also advocates collective bargaining by professional employees, but seeks to emulate the traditional industrial model. Supporters of this approach claim that those who want to use collective bargaining as a legal support for professional norms, like those who oppose any form of collective bargaining by professional employees, share a romantic view of professionalism that has been rendered obsolete in post-industrial society. According to proponents of applying the industrial model to professsional employment, the professional employees who most need collective bargaining are those who have never had, or who have lost and cannot hope to regain, the idealized image of professional status.

* * *

Provisions in collective bargaining agreements illustrate some of the benefits that can be achieved through the unionization of professional employees. Examples include the participation of musicians in personnel decisions of orchestras, and the guarantees

202. "It becomes apparent that numerous factors can determine the achievement of students in classrooms and that, if achievement is to be used in the productivity equation, there are numerous ways that collective bargaining can influence productivity. In some ways teachers' unions represent a positive force toward improving productivity." A. Cresswell & M. Murphy, *supra* note 25, at 459.

of levels of facilities and staffing obtained from various hospitals by unions of interns and residents. Legal enforcement of collective bargaining agreements has prevented employers from unilaterally abrogating provisions guaranteeing professional standards. . . .

Other legal decisions, however, validate the worst fears of those who oppose unionization as a threat to professional values. Two recent Supreme Court cases highlight this problem. In one, a teachers' union claimed that a provision of state labor law, which required employers to deal exclusively with unions regarding subjects of collective bargaining, forbade dissident school teachers, but not members of the union or the general public, to discuss such a subject during a public meeting of the school board. This claim, though upheld by the state labor board and supreme court, was ultimately rejected by the United States Supreme Court, which concluded that the restriction on the speech of nonunion teachers violated the first amendment.* The Supreme Court also pointed out that "restraining teachers' expressions to the board on matters involving the operation of the schools would seriously impair the board's ability to govern the district." But the labor board and state court decisions demonstrate the dangers to participation in decision-making by professionals posed by the application of traditional principles of labor law.

The 1984 decision by the Supreme Court in *Minnesota State Board for Community Colleges v. Knight*** is an even more dramatic illustration of the threat of unionization to professional values. The Knight case challenged a Minnesota statute requiring the public employer to "meet and confer" with the exclusive representative of its employees over "matters of inherent managerial policy" that are not mandatory subjects of bargaining covered by a separate "meet and negotiate" provision. The union representing the faculty at the Minnesota Community College system designated only union members as faculty participants in the "meet and confer" process. Faculty members in the bargaining unit who chose not to join the union claimed that their exclusion from this process, the only forum for discussing issues of governance in the College system, violated their first amendment rights. Apart from constitutional issues, such a process is inconsistent with fundamental professional norms, which contemplate the right of every faculty member to participate in institutional governance.

The lower federal court held that "when the state compels creation of a representative governance system in higher education and utilizes that forum for ongoing debate and resolution of virtually all issues outside the scope of collective bargaining, it must afford every faculty member a fair opportunity to participate in the selection of governance representatives. The Supreme Court, however, rejected this conclusion. While acknowledging that "there is a strong, if not universal or uniform, tradition of faculty participation in school governance," the majority opinion emphasized that there is no "constitutional right of faculty to participate in policy-making in academic institutions."

The facts of the Knight case indicate the difficulties inherent in applying to collective bargaining by professional employees several traditional labor law concepts: the distinction between mandatory and permissive subjects of bargaining, the principle of exclusive representation, and the problem of company domination. The distinction between mandatory and permissive subjects of bargaining arose as an attempt to define the statutory duty to bargain in good faith. Management and labor must bargain about mandatory subjects—typically defined as wages, hours, and other terms and conditions of employment. Neither party may take unilateral action with respect to a mandatory subject prior to bargaining. Other subjects are permissive, including matters of fundamental managerial policy. Parties are not compelled to bargain about permissive subjects, and may act unilaterally with respect to them.

Because professional employees are generally concerned about the basic policies of the organizations in which they work, they often want to bargain about issues that fall under the permissive category. Indeed, whether to establish structures for professional participation in institutional governance may itself be a permissive subject about which an employer need not bargain. On the other hand, defining issues of professional concern as mandatory subjects may preclude any meaningful involvement by professional employees who do not join the union.†

---

* *City of Madison Joint School District No. 8 v. Wisconsin Employment Relations Commission*, 429 U.S. 167, 97 S.Ct. 421, 50 L.Ed.2d 376 (1976).

** 465 U.S. 271, 104 S.Ct. 1058, 79 L.Ed.2d 299 (1984).

† *See generally* Rabban, "Can American Labor Law Accommodate Collective Bargaining by Professional Employees?" 99 *Yale L.J.* 689 (1990).

The unsuccessful attempts to reconcile traditional principles of labor law with the norms of professional work suggest that many of these principles should be modified or abandoned in the context of professional employment. The principle of exclusive representation and the concept of company domination are uniquely American and are not part of the labor laws of other Western democracies. They derive from the reaction against employer repression of industrial unionism in the years immediately preceding the passage of the NLRA in 1935. Similarly, the distinction between mandatory and permissive subjects of bargaining, by allowing the refusal of an employer even to discuss issues of policy that are typically and understandably of enormous concern to professional employees, does not encourage an appropriate form of collective bargaining by professional employees. Good arguments can be made for not applying other traditional labor law doctrines to collective bargaining by professional employees.

* * *

The emergence of widespread collective bargaining in the public sector during the past two decades, moreover, has prompted the adaptation of many traditional principles of labor law to the special characteristics of public employment. For example, the identification of mandatory or permissive subjects of bargaining is informed by added considerations in the public sector, particularly the view that certain issues of public concern should be determined through the democratic political process rather than through collective bargaining. The differences between professional and industrial employment are in many respects as significant as the differences between public and private employment.

* * *

"Teacher Unions and School Quality: Potential Allies or Inevitable Foes,"

C. Finn, in J. Bunzel, ed., *Challenge to American Schools: The Case for Standards and Values* 99, 106–13, 118–19 (1985). Reprinted by permission.

Teacher unions are here to stay. That much is clear. But it remains to be seen whether they will turn out to be beneficial, harmful, or irrelevant to the quality of education in the nation's public schools in an era when quality matters more to more Americans than at any other time in modern history.

Nearly 90 percent of the 2.1 million public school teachers in the United States today belong to the giant National Education Association (NEA), the fast-growing American Federation of Teachers (AFT), and the handful of independent unions to be found in some communities. Teaching is now one of the most heavily unionized occupations in the society, certainly *the* most unionized white-collar occupation, and there is no reason at all to expect this to change.

Not all teacher union members, however, engage in the central—some would say the defining—activity of trade unionism, namely, collective bargaining. Probably only about three public school teachers in four are employed under the terms of union-negotiated contracts, "meet and confer" arrangements, or "memoranda of understanding."

* * *

In private industry, it would be virtually meaningless to talk of the role of unions that do not bargain collectively. In the public sector, however, salary levels, working conditions, and other terms of employment that hold intense importance for workers are established through the machinery of public policy-making and are thus susceptible to political influence and activity. A public employees' union that does not bargain collectively may nonetheless obtain significant benefits for its members by persuading the governor and legislature (or mayor and town council) to do its bidding. Even the protection of individual workers' rights can be achieved through political action, such as the enactment of tenure laws.

For teachers, union membership—with or without collective bargaining—ordinarily brings an entire additional set of benefits, those historically conferred by participation in a "professional association." For more than a century after its founding in 1857, the NEA (originally the National Teachers' Association) was a professional association for teachers—and, until fairly recently, for other educators such as principals and superintendents. Although the AFT has always styled itself a union, it did not really succeed in acting like one on a large scale until the early 1960s when, first in New York and then in one city after another, it won the right to represent sizable groups of teachers in collective bargaining negotiations that produced contracts. In the ensuing two decades, AFT membership grew tenfold. But throughout its history, the AFT has also provided its members the services and benefits of a professional association.

These take many forms. Some are subtle: a sense of fraternity and fellowship with one's colleagues and peers. Others are mundane but important: inexpensive group insurance policies and similar cushions against misfortune and hard times. Still others are frivolous but attractive: cut-rate tours and excursions, for example. But perhaps the most valuable services are the enhancement of the profession itself and the development of one's own role within it. Thus, much like the bar and medical associations, teacher unions have supplied advanced education (through journals, workshops, institutes, and conventions); codes of ethics and behavior concerning how members of the profession should act and, especially, how they should expect others to act toward them; norms and qualifications for membership in the profession itself (often made binding by incorporation into state licensure requirements); and leadership, representation, and "voice" in the innumerable gatherings, events, and decisions of the larger society that bear on the profession and its work.

Inasmuch as the working conditions, prosperity, and status of any profession are inextricably linked to the (real and perceived) quality of the enterprise in which its members serve, the teachers' unions have generally displayed an interest in the scope, reputation, and efficacy (and, of course, the financing) of public education.

* * *

. . . As unionism spread from one school system to another, a marked change took place in the basic relationship between the teacher and his employer. While indubitably a member of a professional peer group, the individual teacher had traditionally enjoyed—and sometimes been victimized by—a one-to-one relationship with the school system that paid him.

In an exemplary school within a good system, this meant that the teacher was hired, evaluated, and retained according to his ability and performance, that as a respected member of the faculty he participated in decisions about curriculum, standards, and school organization, and that it was thus relatively easy to fuse his interest in a secure job and decent working conditions with the interests he shared with his colleagues in the quality and reputation of the school as a whole.

In a mediocre or bad school, however, the individual teacher could be abused by a capricious or tyrannical principal, his classroom prowess would be irrelevant to the judgments made about him in a highly politicized atmosphere, he might be entirely excluded from important decisions about school content and format, and he would find it impossible to lift his eyes from the harassments of the hour to the overarching goals and performance of the institution.

Thus vulnerable to the circumstances in which he found himself, the lone teacher was also nearly powerless to alter them. Though certain commonalities, such as the uniform salary schedule and the protection of tenure, meant that teachers throughout a system were apt to be treated alike with regard to fundamental bread-and-butter matters, virtually all professional decisions were the prerogative of the school management.

Joining a union was thus a way to bring a semblance of rationality into a world of confusion, to confer stability on an idiosyncratic environment, and to assure teachers some leverage over decisions affecting them, their students, and their schools.

The key was in banding together, and the teachers' strength lay in unity—the customary basis for trade unionism in any occupation or industry. But there was a cost, one well worth paying for teachers in bad situations but more problematic for those in exemplary schools. It lay in submerging the teacher's individuality into the pooled efforts of an organized block of workers, in formalizing many relationships within schools that had previously been informal, and in focusing the attention of the organized teaching force on material issues, yielding the possibility that teachers might find themselves even less involved than before with education policy decisions facing their schools and school systems, less attentive to distinctions of ability and accomplishment among their professional peers, and less able to influence developments outside the four walls of their own classrooms.

In the early years of teacher collective bargaining, according to many studies of the process, most union locals did emphasize bread-and-butter issues, maximizing the material gains for their members and consolidating their own authority as teacher leaders and spokesmen, while school boards did their utmost to retain control over what they deemed "education policy" issues, even as they bargained about salaries, workloads, and working conditions. But as the two sides grew more accustomed to the relationship, as old patterns of "collegial" behavior persisted willy-nilly in the best schools, and as it became clear that one person's notion of a working condition is another's idea of an education policy, more issues began to be thrust into the bargaining process, into the procedures by which contractual provisions are enforced between negotiating sessions, and into consultative arrangements outside the bargaining process.

* * *

As the collective bargaining process matured, as the terms of the new relationships were better understood and their limits explored, it became easier and more common for the union itself to become involved on the teachers' behalf in issues of education policy at the local level, sometimes even to take the lead in proposing improvements to an unimaginative school system. Naturally, the union could exert more muscle in such encounters than could the individual teacher.

* * *

Then came the "educational excellence movement," a phrase increasingly used to identify a decentralized but nationwide effort to infuse American schools with higher standards and enhanced effectiveness.

* * *

The specific proposals that the excellence movement prompted in the several states were numerous and varied. What they had in common was a heavy emphasis on the attainment of higher standards of cognitive skills and knowledge by students, more exacting high school graduation and college entrance requirements, firmer discipline and more homework, greater emphasis on science and the humanities in the curriculum and a corresponding reduction of nonacademic electives and extracurricular activities, better teacher training, higher standards of intellectual aptitude and achievement among entering teachers, various schemes for rewarding "merit" on the part of teachers and for restructuring the teaching "career path" into a "career ladder," restoration of the principal's role to that of "instructional leader," and far greater performance accountability—to be accomplished mostly through testing—for individual students, teachers, entire schools, whole school systems, and even states. In return for such reforms, the excellence movement was willing to commit more money to the schools, and opinion polls indicated widespread public support for this approach: additional resources, even additional taxes, provided that large changes were made in educational policy and sizable gains were demonstrated in pupil achievement. But not another cent for "more of the same."

By and large, the policy thrust of the excellence movement was compatible with the educational priorities of the AFT's Shanker and his national staff, and support for many of its points could be gleaned from policy resolutions passed at AFT conventions over the years. Shanker is also a gifted reader of the political entrails, and he concluded far sooner than most other educators that a rare window of opportunity had opened. He thereupon set about to ensure that his union and the public education enterprise as a whole did not allow it to slam shut.

The NEA, by contrast, was initially blindsided by the excellence movement, which would lead public education in directions almost precisely opposite to those the NEA had been pulling toward. . . .

* * *

The specific policy proposals of the excellence movement were so numerous that it does neither the reformers nor the unions justice to concentrate on a few of them, but it is particularly illuminating to examine one that was guaranteed to give any teachers' union great cause for concern: the notion of differential rewards for individual teachers *according* to their classroom effectiveness. Underlying it, of course, was intense concern over the perceived intellectual weakness of new teachers, the tendency of the best and most experienced teachers to abandon the classroom, and the presence of at least a few "incompetents" within the ranks of the profession.

* * *

All forms of merit pay posed serious problems for teacher unions. All would tend to isolate the individual teacher and compensate him under terms of a series of judgments and agreements that are both unique to him and liable to be changed. Yet the essence of union membership, embodied in a collectively won contract (and in the standard, seniority-based pay scales and tenure laws that antedate and surround the bargaining process), is that teachers are treated by their employers as if they were interchangeable, that individual differences in ability or performance have no bearing on salary or other terms of their employment and that any improvement—or degradation—in status, pay, or working conditions for one will be shared by all.

Public school teaching, to be sure, has never been open to all comers. State certification or licensure is a long-established practice. Nor has the career "path" been completely flat; a teacher can ordinarily get onto a higher salary scale by accumulating additional graduate school credit hours. But while the teacher unions have accommodated themselves to these practices, they have also striven to influence the policies by which exceptions are made, to dominate the procedures by which individual performance judgments are conducted, and to defend individual teachers against any actions that do not hew to those procedures. The union is threatened by any change that would strengthen the hands of state bureaucrats, of lay boards, or of principals and other school "managers" with regard to key determinations about individual reward and progress within the teaching occupation. To oversimplify just a little, the ideal personnel system from the union's standpoint is one that regards teachers as a group rather than as individuals, that treats all members of the occupation alike, and that—when exceptions must be made and judgments about individuals rendered—gives teachers-as-a-group primary responsibility for determinations about teachers-as-individuals.

Acceptance of this last responsibility by AFT and NEA affiliates has actually been rare. Though it is wholly compatible with the practice of "peer evaluation" that is part of the professional tradition, and with the skilled craft guild's practice of training and evaluating newcomers as they progress through the familiar steps from apprentice to journeyman to master craftsman, it clashes with an important tenet of the industrial union: the presumption that any qualitative appraisal of an individual's work is entirely the duty of management. This is, of course, a common presumption among industrial managers as well.

* * *

The unions' responses to the merit pay and master teacher ideas are especially interesting, for here there was no pre-existing policy gap between the AFT and the NEA. And, indeed, there has been no palpable difference in their reactions to the piecework and Christmas bonus versions of this idea. Notwithstanding very strong public support for the general principle of teacher merit pay, notwithstanding myriad commission reports, legislative proposals, and presidential orations lauding that principle, notwithstanding even some evidence from teacher opinion polls that significant numbers of their members themselves endorse the concept, neither union has eased its opposition to schemes that would link an individual teacher's compensation in a particular year to indicators of how much that teacher's students actually learned that year.

* * *

[A]n accumulating body of research about the characteristics of unusually effective schools indicates that those in which children learn the most usually have a "collegial" staff structure and a strong sense of common purpose among teachers, administrators, and other adults in the school. This is often described in such abstract terms as "shared moral order" or "school ethos," but what it really comes down to is that the school's professional staff functions like a team: it has clear objectives, it works together smoothly, its shared goals transcend those of its individual members, and if problems with one or another member of the team arise there is a sense of mutual responsibility for solving them.

Yet the "school team" model of educational staff organization is significantly different from the classic "labor-management" model of workplace organization. That the team approach can be made compatible with unionism is obvious from the fact that some outstanding schools display both characteristics. This is not easy, and it certainly is not automatic. It can be wrecked by a weak, insecure, or authoritarian principal—but it can also be destroyed by local union leadership that is fundamentally hostile to the school administration, that encourages its members to "work to rule" (for many situations during the school day require improvisation and flexibility), or that regards troubled teachers and unsuccessful curricula as management's problems. It can be further impeded by legal, judicial, or contractual constraints—more often encountered thus far in higher education—that bar union members from taking part in collegial decisions that penetrate traditional management domains, or that bar nonunion faculty members from participating in consultative and policy-making forums established through the bargaining process. Indeed, so many factors can prevent or dissipate the team approach that it is little wonder few schools have developed it to a high level of educational success. That it can exist, however, and that it is almost indispensable for school effectiveness, holds immense significance for the future structure of the educational workplace.

NOTES AND QUESTIONS

1. *Teacher Unions and Democratic Accountability*

Are teacher unions good or bad for public education? *See* L. McDonnell and A. Pascal, *Teacher Unions and Educational Reform* (1988). To the extent that such organizations improve working conditions for teachers and make teaching a more attractive occupation, do they not foster excellence in public schools? Or do strong teacher unions interfere with the normal democratic processes through which elected school board members set policy? *See generally* Summers, "Public Employee Bargaining: A Political Perspective," 83 *Yale L. J.* 1156 (1974). Are they too powerful? Do teacher unions have a special access to the political process that other groups lack? *See generally* Summers, "Public Sector Bargaining: Problems of Governmental Decision-Making," 44 *U. Cinn. L. Rev.* 669 (1975). Are they advantaged if the negotiations are conducted behind closed doors? Is it a sufficient answer that school board members are elected and hence may be removed by the voters? Does your answer depend on whether teachers have a right to strike or have won contractual provisions on compulsory arbitration? *See generally* D. Colton and E. Graber, *Teacher Strikes and the Courts* (1982); L. McDonnell and A. Pascal, *Organized Teachers in American Schools* 26 (1979). Why have strikes proven to be less efficacious than many anticipated? *See generally* Burton and Krider, "The Role and Consequences of Strikes by Public Employees," 79 *Yale L. J.* 418 (1970).

Should a distinction be made between bargaining over terms and conditions of employment and bargaining over educational policy? *See generally* "Developments in the Law—Public Employment," 97 *Harv. L. Rev.* 1611, 1682–1700 (1984). Is this distinction the same as the distinction between mandatory and prohibited subjects of bargaining? What are permissive bargaining subjects? How would you treat bargaining over the school curriculum, the length of class sessions, grading, student discipline, class size, use of teacher aides, or textbooks?

There are myriad reported cases grappling with the issue of the scope of collective bargaining for teachers. *See, e.g., Decatur Board of Education v. Illinois Educational Labor Relations Board*, 180 Ill.App.3d 770, 129 Ill. Dec. 693, 536 N.E.2d 743 (1989); *Bay City Education Association v. Bay City Public Schools*, 430 Mich. 370, 422 N.W.2d 504 (1988); *Montgomery County Education Association v. Board of Education of Montgomery County*, 311 Md. 303, 534 A.2d 980 (1987); *Wethersfield Board of Education v. Connecticut State Board of Labor Relations*, 201 Conn. 685, 519 A.2d 41 (1986); *Appeal of Berlin Education Association*, 125 N.H. 779, 485 A.2d 1038 (1984); *West Bend Education Association v. Wisconsin Employment Relations Commission*, 121 Wis.2d 1, 357 N.W.2d 534 (1984); *Foley Education Association v. Independent School District*, 353 N.W.2d 917 (Minn. 1984); *National Education Association—Wichita v. Unified School District No. 259*, 234 Kan. 512, 674 P.2d 478 (1983); *Bethlehem Township Board of Education v. Bethlehem Township Education Association*, 91 N.J. 38, 449 A.2d 1254 (1982).

Is collective bargaining over subjects involving educational policy beneficial so long as the parties do not need to reach agreement? Does collective bargaining simply provide an opportunity for professionals to influence the educational policies of the school? Or does it unduly constrain the discretion of administrators? *See generally* Ubben and Fulmer, "The Relationship of Collective Bargaining to the Decision-Making Power of the Public School Principal," 14 *J. Collective Negs.* 141 (1985).

2. *Professionalism, Community, and Collective Bargaining*

Do teacher unions advance or undermine professionalism? *See* Rabban, "Can American Labor Law Accommodate Collective Bargaining by Professional Employees?" 99 *Yale L. J.* 689 (1990). Are elementary and secondary school teachers professionals? Do they have the autonomy and self-regulatory characteristics normally associated with professional groups, e.g., physicians and lawyers? Is there a "democratic conception of professionalism" that would support the claims of teacher unions? *See* A. Gutmann, *Democratic Education* 80 (1987).

Some commentators urge that effective schools foster an atmosphere of community, a shared sense of purpose, and collegiality among teachers and administrators. In other words, administrators and teachers should view themselves as on the same team. Do you agree? If so, do teacher unions undermine community by emphasizing the distinction between management and employees? By creating a "we–they" mentality? But do not professional teams in baseball and other sports engage in collective bargaining while performing as a team? Or is this not an appropriate analogy?

Does unionization emphasize formal relationships over collegial relationships? Rules over discretion? *See* A. Wise, *Legislated Learning: The Bureaucratization of the American Classroom* 103–06 (1979). Is the goal of collective bargaining to foster uniformity of treatment of teachers, while professionalism emphasizes individualized treatment? What are the dangers in the latter view? In the absence of strong teacher organizations, how can teachers protect themselves from arbitrary administrative decisions? *See generally* Kerchner, "Union-Made Teaching: The Effects of Labor Relations on Teaching Work," 13 *Rev. Research in Educ.* 317 (1986).

Do teacher unions undermine sound educational policies by insisting on seniority rights and resisting many forms of merit pay? *See generally United Teachers of Dade v. Dade County School Board*, 500 So.2d 508 (Fla. 1986).

Do teacher unions undermine the authority of a faculty as a corporate body? If so, what steps can be taken to protect both faculty processes and collective bargaining? What does Professor Rabban suggest?

III. SCHOOLS AND MARKETS

A. Consumer-Voters in the Public Sector: Selecting a School District

The expression of voters' preferences in elections does not exhaust the ways in which citizens can seek to satisfy their preferences for education. A parent can remove his or her child from public school and place the child in a private educational environment, or a parent may seek out a school district that provides the sort of education desired. When citizens move to an affluent school district or one with a heady reputation, or they seek to escape urban schools, they are expressing educational preferences; they are, in a sense, voting with their feet. They leave one community, where apparently a majority does not or cannot agree with their educational preferences, and seek out a community that offers, in their eyes, a superior educational opportunity. Such voters no longer seek to influence political decisions about education within their present district but rather refuse to pay taxes to that district, exit it, and move on to a more compatible school district. *See generally* A. O. Hirschman, *Exit, Voice, and Loyalty* (1970).

In an ideal society, every member would pay an amount (user fee or tax) for an education equaling exactly what it was worth to him or her. The value of the education to the society would be the sum of the indirect benefits to each individual—for example, higher lifetime earnings or preferred life style—and of the direct benefits to all, for example, stimulating conversation and lower crime rates. Parents presumably would make such utilitarian calculations for children too immature to estimate the benefits for themselves. The educational system in that ideal society would allocate fiscal, material, and human resources so expertly that no other combination of information generation and distribution of resources would produce more total benefit among the citizenry.

The achievement of the ideal society is staggering. The prices paid for education by the members would purchase a package of services that, of all other imaginable packages, was best for each member.* It would also be the best imaginable way for society to have spent that portion of its educational resources. What is best for one is best for the many. The sum of all these perfectly efficient transactions by millions of consumers of education would equal the actual production of the most dollar-stretching educational expenditures imaginable for the society. This is true so long as there are not so many packages chosen and available that the society cannot take advantage of economies of scale which would reduce the average minimum cost to a point that would allow for efficient production of the packages. Putting aside

* The text refers to the concept of allocative efficiency in which the *dollar* gains and losses by everyone affected are considered, and for present purposes, allocative efficiency is equated with maximizing utility. If dollars do not adequately describe overall utility—for example, if the dollars were worth more to the poor than to the rich and the policy favored the rich—then an allocatively efficient policy would not necessarily maximize satisfaction.

questions of the influence of inequalities in wealth distribution, the gap between the real world of conflicting interests and the ideal is caused by a lack of information (and perhaps also by an inability to know or calculate benefits). With respect to public services, the means we use to transform our needs into educational outputs are insufficiently sensitive to transmit the necessary information to the producers. Charles Tiebout has described this problem:

> If all consumer-voters could somehow be forced to reveal their true preferences for public goods, then the amount of such goods to be produced and the appropriate benefits tax could be determined. As things now stand, there is no mechanism to force the consumer-voter to state his true preferences; and in fact, the "rational" consumer will understate his preferences and hope to enjoy the goods while avoiding the tax.

Tiebout, "A Pure Theory of Local Expenditures," 64 *J. of Pol. Econ.* 416, 417 (1956).

Economists have long known what conditions are sufficient to achieve the ideal, an ideal in which "each individual . . . would be led by an Invisible Hand to the grand solution of the social maximum position." *Id.* at 422. Those conditions compose the marketplace that has come to be the standard by which to measure real methods of resource allocation. The public sector is often thought to suffer by comparison with the private sector because of its relatively greater distance from those conditions. Tax burdens and education outputs are determined by collective political action through voting and otherwise, and the ideal allocation for each individual and for the collectivity is not achieved. Professor Tiebout, however, suggests in his classic 1956 article that *local* government may represent "a sector where the allocation of public goods (and the reflection of the preferences of the population) need not take a back seat to the private sector." *Id.* at 424.

Tiebout suggests that in choosing where to live, consumers effectively vote with their feet. They pick among communities as they would among products in a private market, looking for the combination of community services—for example, education, police protection, and recreational facilities—that most closely approximates their needs. What variables influence a consumer-voter's decision?

> If he has children, a high level of expenditures on schools may be important. Another person may prefer a community with a municipal golf course. The availability and quality of such facilities and services as beaches, parks, police protection, roads, and parking facilities will enter into the decision-making process. . . . The consumer-voter may be viewed as picking that community which best satisfies his preference for public goods.

Id. at 418. *See also* Inman and Rubinfeld, "The Judicial Pursuit of Local Fiscal Equity," 92 *Harv. L. Rev.* 1662 (1979).

To illustrate the market characteristics of the public sector, Tiebout constructed a marketplace model of local governments that requires certain conditions parallel to those which must prevail in the private marketplace for efficient transactions to take place.

1. Each consumer must know his or her real needs and how to satisfy them best among the competing communities' packages of public goods. If a parent erroneously believes that his or her child would be better off as a musician rather than as an automobile mechanic, the mistaken belief that the child would be better off as a musician creates waste. The parent's tax dollars could have brought more value had they been spent another way, that is, on training the child to be an automobile mechanic. And if the parent chooses to live in School District A rather than School District B because A has a superior music program while B has a superior vocational education program, his or her mistaken preference distorts the market by causing the music program to be overpurchased in relation to the vocational education program.
2. Each consumer is fully mobile and will move to the community where he or she can find the best mesh of community services and needs. There are no significant transaction costs (for example, moving expenses) to relocating. The mobility assumption also screens out distortions caused by factors other than community expenditure patterns. Communities will differ in job opportunities, and some cities will have better and closer shopping centers. Population density, aesthetic appeal, and ambiance may be allocated unequally among communities. But none of these factors will affect the consumer's decision to move in the Tiebout model. Consumers react only to community expenditure patterns and will costlessly move wherever they find the best pack-

age of public services.* Nor does the mobile consumer attempt to persuade the community to change its spending pattern, any more than the community attempts to accommodate itself to the consumer's special needs. The consumer can only stay or leave, and the community notes only whether someone is there.

3. Consumer-voters must have a large number of local communities with differing bundles of public goods from which to choose. This condition ensures that some community will meet each consumer's needs. Ideally, there will be at least one community, even if it has but one citizen, for every consumer preference bundle.** (The bundle is of course limited. It represents the best possible expenditure for the consumer of the dollars he or she is willing or perhaps able to spend on education.) At the state and national level, relatively little opportunity is available to pick and choose among public expenditure patterns. Unless the consumer's preference pattern matches up perfectly with the nation's expenditure pattern, the consumer's preferences are not produced. Under such circumstances, the consumer may seek to influence politically the composition of the national bundle of public services or he or she may move to another nation. *See generally* Hirschman, *supra*. At the state level, American consumer-voters have fifty choices. Local governments, including school districts, provide considerably greater latitude. Morton Grodzins noted in 1966 that the United States contains eighteen thousand general purpose municipalities, three thousand counties, and ninety-two thousand tax-levy governments (including special purpose districts). *See* M. Grodzins, *The American System* 3 (1966). Competition among communities vying for the consumer's presence insures efficient production of services and sensitivity to his or her needs. If the competition is sufficiently intense, the price to the consumer will be the cheapest possible cost to the community for the services provided. This is so because if a community falters, consumers will leave and produce the collapse and dissolution of the government or the subsequent reconstitution of the government, with the succession of new elected officials with a new community expenditure pattern. *But see* P. Schiesl, *The Politics of Efficiency* (1977). An important caveat is that if laws prevent a community from keeping people out or charging user fees, no community may opt for a high price package. This is because the majority and its elected leaders may resist wealth transfers to those who cannot afford the expensive package. This may be reinforced by the inability to control the mobility of capital and labor. *See* P. Peterson, *City Limits* (1981). So too, local districts may be more constrained by fiscal capacity than differences in willingness to tax. *See* chapter 6, *infra*. *See generally* Stein, "Market Maximization of Individual Preferences and Metropolitan Service Responsibility," 25 *Urban Aff. Q.* 86 (1989).

4. Every pattern of community services will have an optimal community size associated with it that represents the point at which neither more nor fewer people could be served without increasing the average cost to those served. To carry the idea to a meticulous extreme, assume that the optimal size of a particular class is twenty students and that the most effective way to teach the materials is to send the whole class to the blackboards. The addition of one student will introduce waste.† If the classroom has five blackboards holding four students each, the teacher must ask the school district either to buy a new blackboard, or she must reduce the effectiveness of her teaching by changing her methods. Buying a new blackboard will be wasteful because the price paid will be for four places at the blackboard, but three places will go unused. Even buying just one small blackboard will be wasteful. The per pupil cost of one large blackboard for four students will be below the price of four small blackboards. Thus the school must pay more for the last child than it did for the first twenty. Waste will also result if class size falls even one student below the optimum. The school district will expend resources that could educate twenty children to educate nineteen, resulting in a higher average cost for each than at the opti-

* This argument is not critical to the Tiebout model. A consumer may consider the community's package of public services and other characteristics in order to reach an overall decision that maximizes satisfaction.

** This argument disregards possible economies of scale.

† This assumes that technological inefficiency may be equated with allocative inefficiency. Considering the other factors that go into a relocation decision, this need not necessarily be the case.

mum. Thus, deviation in either direction from the optimum will create resource misallocation. If four students and one blackboard are added to the class, this may dilute the teacher's ability to supervise the class's work.

5. Community executives will be rational persons who know what the optimal size is for their bundle of services and try to reach or remain there:

> [C]ommunities below the optimum size, through chambers of commerce or other agencies, seek to attract new residents. . . . The case of the city that is too large and tries to get rid of residents is more difficult to imagine. . . . Nevertheless, economic forces are at work to push people out of it. Every resident who moves to the suburbs to find better schools, more parks, and so forth, is reacting, in part, against the pattern the city has to offer. The community which is at the optimum size and tries to remain so is not hard to visualize. . . . [P]roper zoning laws, implicit agreements among realtors, and the like are sufficient to keep the population stable.

6. Finally, the community's production of services and the consumer-voter's consumption of them can have no effects—positive or negative—on any other community and its consumers. This insures that every citizen and his or her community "pay for all the resources their decisions prevent from being used in alternative economically productive ways. . . ." Markovits, "A Basic Structure for Microeconomic Policy Analysis in Our Worst than Second-Best World: A Proposal and Related Critique of the Chicago Approach to the Study of Law and Economics," 1975 *Wis. L. Rev.* 950, 962. If, for example, Centreville builds its high school football stadium in neighboring Jonesville so its own streets will not be clogged by traffic, it is imposing external costs on Jonesville that are not reflected in the price that Centreville residents pay for the privilege of having a stadium. The real value of Centreville's expenditure is the benefit to its citizens minus the harm to the citizens of Jonesville. External benefits can also be conveyed by a community's expenditure pattern, producing a free ride or reduced cost for its neighbors. When outsiders are welcomed at the free park performance of a city-subsidized orchestra, they receive a free ride. When they pay for the ten-dollar ticket at the paid performance, they get a reduced rate because they did not contribute to the subsidy. The real value of the symphony to society is its value to Centreville residents plus its value to the outsiders. As a result the fact that the outsiders' community is at its optimum size does not necessarily mean that its consumer-voters approve of its bundle of services. It may mean that some people in that community want a free ride and would prefer to use services they do not have to pay for. When a service costs less than it is worth, it will be overproduced, and some other services may be underproduced. On the other hand, if the cost to the community producing the service is greater than it is worth, it may be underproduced in relation to other services.

Important consequences flow from understanding how and why the theoretical model works. Most traditional economists believe that the closer we approach each of the optimal conditions, the closer we approach the most allocatively efficient distribution of public resources. Others argue that real-world imperfections can be manipulated instrumentally to offset each other. In some cases, they say, two distortions will be closer to the social maximum position than one distortion. Consider, for example, the Centreville stadium hypothetical example. If Jonesville taxes Centreville at a rate that exactly compensates it for the harm Centreville's stadium imposes, the harm is wiped out. Taxes automatically distort markets. If X is willing to spend only fifty-one cents on a magazine priced at its cost of fifty cents, a tax raising its total cost to him to fifty-five cents keeps it out of his hands or causes a four-cent misallocation. In the stadium example, however, the tax just canceled the harm. Two wrongs make a right. To state the point differently, once both distortions are in place and offsetting each other, the removal of one—thus reducing the total number of distortions—will move us farther from the optimum position.

While the possibility of choosing among school districts, no doubt, creates some increment of consumer choice, the divergencies between the real world and the Tiebout model are numerous. Consider the fact that education is a merit good—that is, a good of such importance that a certain amount of it is allocated to each person regardless of ability to pay and personal preferences. This may reflect a group decision as to what is allocatively efficient or as to what is an equitable allocation of education services. This is the economic meaning of universal and compulsory elementary and secondary education. One notion is that parents, if left to their own devices, may systematically underinvest in education, and this will have adverse consequences for the child and for the entire community. Another is that children from different socioeconomic and other groupings should have an equal education opportunity. For example, a poorly educated child may not grow up to be economically self-sufficient, and there may be increased welfare, public housing, and police protection costs as a result. Equally as fundamental, education is not simply an investment; it is also a consumption good. Education can enrich the individual irrespective of its allocative efficiency. Thus, minimum education services are offered in every community, and this distorts the public sector market model.

The mobility assumption is subject to challenge on any number of grounds. The poor may not be able to afford to move to the community that offers the package of education services they prefer.* The very fact that a district is perceived as offering a superior educational opportunity can itself raise housing prices. There may be a community bias toward the retention of wealthier residents and fears of an in-migration of low-income families. *See* Buchanan, "Principles of Urban Fiscal Structures," 4 *Pub. Choice* 1 (1971). Thus, zoning restrictions and other growth control devices may be used to create barriers to mobility. An urban area may consist of only one countywide or metropolitan school district, thereby denying parents the ability to choose among a variety of district education packages except by moving great distances.

Consider the choice of an education package, for example, as compared to the choice of a retirement community by a senior citizen planning to move to *some* retirement community. First, the senior citizen chooses where to live in the light of his or her preferred package of services. The child's choices must be filtered through the expressed preferences of his or her parents. One decision may be best for the adults, and another for the children. The parents will consider the welfare of the entire family and usually attach great importance to keeping the family together. Even if the child's interests are treated as paramount to those of the family, different children in the same family may have different educational needs. Second, the community developer may go bankrupt unless he or she offers an attractive retirement community package of services at a competitive price. A compulsory education system, financed through compulsory taxes, is not nearly so threatened by such dire consequences if it is not responsive to consumer tastes. Third, the senior citizen is already planning to change communities, whereas the parents still must be persuaded of the desirability of moving. Fourth, and most important, the retirement community will offer nearly the entire package of services that the senior citizen prefers—ambiance, shopping, recreation, restaurants, health care, and so on. The parents must consider many factors beyond the control of the school system: employment opportunities, distance to work, availability of public transportation, minimum housing space requirements for the whole family, and so forth. In other words, there are more components to the choice of a place to live for the working family with school-age children than there are for the retired senior citizen seeking a relatively well-defined retirement environment. The Tiebout model works best if the consumer-voter seeks to maximize his or her satisfaction with respect to a relatively few public and private goods than with respect to a large number. The number of variables may psychologically confuse the consumer and hence render the choice less rational.

Finally, maximizing rational consumer choice with respect to education, a very special public good, presents its own set of problems. If the parents are uneducated, this may mean that they do not know what they or their children need in the way of educational services. This is presumably one of the things one means by describing a person as uneducated. Even if the consumer-voter has a good idea as to his or her educational preferences, the flow of information may not be sufficient to allow rational choice. Accurate information as to the quality of educational services is difficult to come by. Parents could depend on unreliable sources; they may not visit schools; they may not know what to look for if they do visit schools. And unlike goods in the private sector, the cost of the education may not be a reliable guide to its quality. Additional infusions of funds for schools may purchase additional inputs, but once

* This again raises the question of allocative efficiency versus utility. Given the costs of moving, it may not be allocatively efficient to offer the package of services that the poor want. Such a package, however, might maximize overall utility.

a minimum threshold level of expenditure is reached, additional monies may not yield superior outcomes (achievement, self-fulfillment, and so on). *See* chapter 6.

Parents can seek out a school system with a particular racial or socioeconomic student population or a school system that is perceived as providing a physically safe environment, but beyond such factors (which may or may not be determined correctly), parents may not be able to evaluate educational quality because of the lack of knowledge about what constitutes a quality education. The process by which educational inputs are translated into educational outputs remains mysterious. *See* chapters 5 and 6. And this task is further complicated by the fact that parents must not only seek to satisfy the present educational needs of their children but also to project those needs into the future.

The obvious difficulties with respect to exercising consumer choice in education through location decisions have led to efforts to reform public education so that consumers can vote with dollars and not with their feet. The idea is to give all parents the same types of options that the affluent have, with their ability to choose and pay for a private education. The dilemma is how to do this in a world of unequal wealth distribution, a world in which there is widespread commitment to public schooling and equal educational opportunity. In this section, we turn to the various proposals that have been made, their strengths and weaknesses, and to evaluations of the limited experiences with such market proposals.

B. Voucher Plans, Accountability, and Educational Quality

"Politics, Markets, and the Organization of Schools"

J. Chubb & T. Moe, 82 *Amer. Pol. Sci. Rev.* 1065, 1067–70, 1084–85 (1988). Reprinted by permission.

Public schools are controlled by democratic authority and administration. The specifics vary from district to district and state to state, but the basic framework is remarkably uniform throughout the country. The private sector might seem to lack any comparable uniformity. Most private schools are affiliated with a church; some are elite preparatory schools; some are military academies; and there are other types as well. . . . But they all have two important institutional features in common: society does not control them directly through democratic politics, and society does control them—indirectly—through the marketplace. Rather than marvel at diversity, we find it useful to think about schools in terms of these alternative institutions of social control. As a shorthand, we will refer to them as politics and markets.

* * *

Popular myth lauds the role of local citizens and their elected school boards in governing the public schools. But the fact is that the schools are not locally controlled and are not supposed to be. The state and federal governments have legitimate roles to play in financing schools, setting standards, and otherwise imposing their own policies. This means that U.S. citizens everywhere, whether or not they have children in school and whether or not they in the district or even the state, have a legitimate hand in governing each school. . . .

The proper constituency of even a single public school is a huge and heterogeneous one whose interests are variously represented by formally prescribed agents—politicians and administrators—at all levels of government. Parents and students, therefore, are but a small part of the legitimate constituency of "their own" schools. The schools are not meant to be theirs to control and are literally not supposed to provide the kind of education they might want. Public education is shaped by larger social purposes as defined by larger constituencies.

Private schools determine their own goals, standards, and methods. These may reflect the values of owners or patrons, or perhaps a collective such as a diocese. But the market imposes a fundamental constraint. Private schools provide services in exchange for payment, and unless heavily subsidized from the outside, they must please their consumers—students and parents—if they are to prosper. Whatever the constituency of the private school, therefore, it will surely be much smaller and more homogeneous than the democratic constituency of the public school, and students and parents will occupy a much more central position within it.

In the private marketplace, educational choice is founded on what has come to be called, following

Hirschman . . .*, the *exit* option. If parents and students do not like the services they are being provided, they can exit and find another school whose offerings are more congruent with their needs. This process of selection promotes a match between what educational consumers want and what their schools supply. Matching is reinforced by the population effects . . . of selection: schools that fail to satisfy a sufficiently large clientele will be weeded out (or, if subsidized, become an increasing burden).

Selection also forges a strong bond between consumer satisfaction and organization well-being. This gives schools incentives to please their clientele, as well as to set up *voice* mechanisms—committees, associations—that build a capacity for responsiveness into organizational structure. These incentives, too, promote a match—but they are not necessary for success. A school might rigidly adhere to purist doctrine yet succeed because that is what enough consumers happen to want. Either way, the result tends to be the same: a match.

In the public sector, popular control is built around voice. Exit plays a minimal role. The public school is usually a local monopoly, in the sense that all children living in a given area are assigned to a particular school. This does not eliminate choice, since parents can take account of school quality in deciding where to live. But residential decisions involve many factors in addition to education, and once they are made, sunk costs are high. Low or declining quality need not keep parents from moving into an area, and it is even less likely to prompt existing residents to pick up and leave.

It might prompt them to consider a private school. But here they confront a major disincentive: public schools are free, private schools are not. Due to this cost differential, the perceived value of private schools must far outweigh that of public schools if they are to win students. To put it the other way around, public schools, because they are relatively inexpensive, can attract students without seeming to be particularly good at educating them.

Lacking a real exit option, many parents and students will choose a public school despite dissatisfaction with its goals, methods, or personnel. Having done so, they have a right to voice their preferences through the democratic control structure—but everyone else has the same rights, and many are well armed and organized. Voice cannot remedy the mismatch between what parents and students want and what schools provide. Conflict and disharmony are built into the system.

In the private sector, the exit option not only promotes harmony and responsiveness, it also promotes school autonomy. This is true even for schools that are part of a hierarchy, as the Catholic schools are. The reason is that most of the technology and resources needed to please clients are inherently present at the bottom of the hierarchy—in the school—since educational services are based on personal relationships and interactions, on continual feedback, and on the knowledge, skills, and experience of teachers. The school is thus in the best position to know how to enhance its own organizational well-being. Hierarchical control, or any external imposition, tends to be inefficient and counterproductive.

* * *

In the public sector the institutional forces work in the opposite direction. The raison d'être of democratic control is to impose higher-order values on schools and thus limit their autonomy. Exit is an obstacle to control: when the governance structure imposes a policy on parents and students who disagree, exit allows them to avoid compliance by "voting with their feet," thus defeating the purpose of the policy. But public officials do not have to take exit as a given. They can simply pass laws restricting its availability. While private decision makers value autonomy because it helps them cope with problems of exit, public officials eliminate exit in order to facilitate their imposition of higher-order values.

The drive to restrict autonomy is built into the incentive structures of politicians and bureaucrats. Politicians seek political support by responding to various constituency groups, particularly those that are well organized and active. These include teachers' unions and associations of administrators, but also a vast array of groups representing more specialized interests—those of minorities, the handicapped, bilingual education, drivers' education, schools of education, book publishers, and accrediting and testing organizations, among others. These

* A. Hirschman, *Exit, Voice and Loyalty* (1970).

groups typically have financial or occupational stakes in existing educational arrangements, and their policy positions reflect as much. They all want a share of the public's educational resources. They want to influence educational programs. They want to have a say in how the schools are organized and operated. And politicians are only too happy to oblige—this is the path to political popularity. . . .

Bureaucrats play both sides of the governmental fence. Their power rests on the fact that bureaucracy is essential to direct democratic control. The imposition of higher-order values is hardly automatic, particularly given the built-in dissatisfaction of parents and students and the inevitable pressures from teachers and principals for autonomy. Control requires rules and regulations, monitoring, incentive structures, and other means of ensuring that those engaged in the educational process behave as they are supposed to behave. It requires bureaucracy—and bureaucrats.

As public officials they have incentives to expand their budgets, programs, and administrative controls. These are the basics of bureaucratic well-being, and their pursuit is an integral part of the job. But bureaucrats also belong to important interest groups—of administrators, of professionals—that lobby government from the outside (ostensibly) as well. Although traditionally they have portrayed themselves as nonpolitical experts pursuing the greater good, they are in fact a powerful special interest—an interest dedicated to hierarchical control. . . .

The system, in short, is inherently destructive of autonomy. Politicians have the authority to shape the schools through public policy, and, precisely because they have the authority, they are consistently under pressure from interest groups to exercise it. It is in their own best interests to impose choices on the schools. The same is true of bureaucrats, who have occupational and professional stakes in control: a world of autonomous schools would be a world without educational bureaucrats. Thus, while principals and teachers may praise the virtues of autonomy, the "one best system"* is organized against it. Politicians, bureaucrats, and virtually the full spectrum of interest groups tend to see autonomy for what is: a transfer of power and threat to their interests.

* * *

Are private schools also likely to be better than public schools? In an important sense, the answer is *yes*. Parents and students who choose a private school are revealing their judgment of quality: the private school is not only better, it is better by an amount that exceeds the cost differential. Since there is clearly an objective basis for their judgment—they directly experience private education and are free to return to the public sector at any time—we have good reason to believe that private schools are in fact more effective at providing the types of educational services their clients care about.

But are they better at the important things schools ought to be doing? This question cannot be answered without substituting our value judgments for those parents and students. A church school that attracts students on the basis of religious and moral training almost surely outperforms the local public school on this dimension. But this says nothing about their relative effectiveness in transmitting democratic values or an appreciation of cultural diversity. Performance is only desirable if the goals are desirable.

This, of course, is the justification for democratic control. In principle, our institutions are set up to articulate important social goals and to ensure that schools act effectively on them. If private schools do a better job of providing certain services or of pleasing parents and students, this does not mean that society must therefore prefer private to public education. Any evaluation has to depend on a more fundamental judgment about what the schools ought to be doing.

In objective terms the two institutional systems are simply very different, and they give rise to schools that reflect these differences—providing different services in different ways to please different constituencies.

* * *

[Our study] provides the first opportunity to document public-private differences by means of a large, representative sample of schools, and its findings dovetail nicely with major lines of argument in the education literature. If it is true, as Coleman, Hoffer, and Kilgore . . .† and Coleman and Hoffer . . .**

* D. Tyack, *The One Best System* (1974).

† J. Coleman, T. Hoffer, and S. Kilgore, *High School Achievement* (1982).

** J. Coleman and T. Hoffer, *Public and Private Schools* (1987).

have claimed, that private schools outperform public schools on academic grounds, and if the effective schools research is basically correct in the characteristics it tends to associate with effectiveness, then we should find that private schools disproportionately possess these characteristics.

That is just what we find. Private schools have simpler, less constraining environments of administrators, school boards, and parents. They are more autonomous and strongly led. They have clearer goals and stricter requirements, and they put greater stress on academic excellence. Relations between principals and teachers and among teachers themselves are more harmonious, interactive, and focused on teaching. Teachers are more involved in policy decisions, have greater control over their work, and are more satisfied with their jobs.

* * *

Private schools are controlled by society too, but not through politics or bureaucracy. They make their own decisions about policy, organization, and personnel subject to market forces that signal how they can best pursue their own interests. Given their substantial autonomy—and given the incentives for autonomy that are built into the system—it is not surprising to find that principals are stronger leaders; that principals have greater control over hiring and firing; that principals and the teachers they choose have greater respect for, and interaction with, one another; and that teachers—without conflict or formal requirement—are more integrally involved in policy making. These sorts of characteristics are bound up with one another, and they jointly arise from the institutional environment. Different institutions promote different organizational syndromes.

If this is essentially correct, the standard proposals for reforming public schools are misconceived. It is easy to say, for instance, that schools should have greater autonomy or that principals should be stronger leaders. But these sorts of reforms are incompatible with the "one best system" and cannot succeed. Politicians and bureaucrats have little incentive to move forcefully in these directions. Their careers are tied to their own control over the schools, and they are unavoidably responsive to well-organized interests that have stakes in the system's capacity to impose higher-order values on the local schools. Restricting autonomy is what democratic control is all about.

* * *

This does not mean that the public schools must be freed from all democratic governance. But it is instructive that the private schools, which are products of an institutional system that decentralizes power to the producers and immediate consumers of educational services, tend to develop precisely the sorts of organizational characteristics reformers want the public schools to have. Some sort of voucher system, combining broad democratic guidance with a radical decentralization of resources and choice, is at least a reasonable alternative to direct control—one that might transform the public schools into different, more effective organizations, while still leaving them truly public.

* * *

NOTES AND QUESTIONS

1. Privatization

Are the arguments for privatization of public schools more or less compelling than arguments to substitute markets for collective political choices with respect to other types of goods? For example, would they apply equally to hospitals, mail delivery, nursing homes, and retirements plans? Does the polity have more or less of an interest in the public production and consumption of education than in these other services and benefits? *See* chapter 1, *supra*. *See generally* Lott, "An Explanation for Public Provision of Schooling: The Importance of Indoctrination," 33 *J. of Law & Econ.* 199 (1990).

What are the dangers of governing education through market mechanisms? Is such a system consistent with equality of educational opportunity? With instilling democratic attitudes? With the notion of common schooling? Professor Gutmann has argued that "the problem with voucher plans is not that they leave too much room for parental choice but that they leave too little room for democratic deliberation." A. Gutmann, *Democratic Education* 70 (1987). *See also* Lott, *supra* at 201 ("If vouchers were used, the competition for students by teachers would underproduce the indoctrination not individually valued by consumers."). Do you agree? If the state equitably distributes vouchers, which may be used to purchase services from public or private schools, are any or all of these objections overcome? Are Chubb and Moe suggesting that the critical governmental objectives may be achieved through vouchers, while at the same time maximizing parental and student satisfaction? Do you agree? *See generally* M. Manley-Casimir, ed., *Family Choice in Schooling: Issues and Dilemmas* (1982); Rand Corporation, *A Study of Alternatives in American Education* (1978).

2. Institutional Autonomy

Chubb and Moe posit a strong causal link between institutional autonomy and quality of education. They then urge that efforts to render public school more autonomous, to strengthen the discretionary roles of principals and faculty members, are doomed to failure. *But see* Gutmann, *supra* at 70. Why is this? Is it that democratic accountability and institutional and professional autonomy are inherently inconsistent? Do you agree? Is this true of many government enterprises, e.g., public hospitals and sewage plants? Is it feasible to balance discretion and accountability in public schools in ways that achieve the outcomes that Chubb and Moe seek?

Is it true that private schools are not controlled through politics and bureaucracy? What of the extensive regulation of private schools by the state? *See* chapter 1, *supra*. Or is it simply that private schools are less regulated than public schools? Might this situation change if a voucher system were adopted? Under a voucher system, would public schools become more private in character and private schools more public?

"Choice in Public Education"

R. Elmore in W. Boyd and C. Kerchner, eds., *The Politics of Excellence and Choice in Education* 79–86, 93–95 (1988). Reprinted by permission.

Should parents and students be empowered to choose among schools, or among programs within schools? Should educators be empowered to organize and manage schools, to design educational programs, to recruit and select students, and to receive public funds for providing education to those students? These are the two fundamental questions of educational choice.

The first might be called the 'demand side' question. It poses the issue of whether the consumers of education should be given the central role in deciding what kind of education is appropriate for them. The second is the 'supply side' question. It poses the issue of whether the providers of education should be given the autonomy and flexibility to respond to differences in the judgments of consumers about what is appropriate education.

These questions go to the very roots of the finance, organization, and political control of American public education. Education policy in the U.S. is, for the most part, based on the premise that the individual interests of parents, students, and educators should be subordinated to broader public policy objectives. Among these objectives are a broadly educated citizenry, an understanding in the citizenry of the basic principles of democracy, fairness in the distribution of the opportunities and rewards of education, an understanding of and tolerance for others unlike ourselves, and preparation for an economically productive adulthood. These objectives have been expressed in laws, institutions, and processes that set the basic structure and content of American public education.

While there is some variation in the finer details of structure, from state to state, and from community to community, two features cut across all locations and levels. First, the money to pay for education flows from taxpayers to local school boards and to administrators who decide how it will be spent. Consumers do not directly 'purchase' public education, either with their own money or with their share of public revenue. Second, decisions about who attends which school, who teaches in which school, and what is taught in schools are formally lodged with local boards and administrators, operating within a framework of state and federal policy. In other words, finance, attendance, staffing, and curriculum content are locally centralized political and administrative decisions, not private consensual decisions between consumers and providers.

Of course, states have made major inroads into local authority over finance, personnel and content, through tax and revenue equalization, labor relations laws, certification requirements, and content mandates. In this sense, there is a significant degree of state centralization in certain key areas. But at the level of what might be called 'allocation decisions'—that is, deciding who will do what in which setting—local boards and administrators still pay the dominant role. . . .

The organizing principle of this system, then, is local centralization. From the national or state level, education appears to be a highly decentralized enterprise, since most detailed decisions about the conduct of education are delegated to the 15,000 or so local school districts. But from the client's or teacher's point of view, the system appears to be highly centralized and bureaucratic. Decisions about who gets access to what kind of education are determined by centrally administered rules and structures, rather than by the preferences of clients and providers.

To raise the supply side and demand side questions of educational choice, then, is to challenge this basic structure of locally centralized administration and to suggest that if parents, students, and school-level educators were given more choice the system would perform better. The current debate on educational choice is about this proposition.

* * *

Consider the following hypothetical case:

> Ann Orlov is eleven. She and her younger brother Larry live in the city with their parents Harry and Jean. Harry earns $14,000 as a policeman; Jean adds $3000 as a part-time secretary. Ann attends Willis Elementary, the neighborhood public school. She is not unusually bright but has shown a strong interest in art and in the lives and work of artists. She dislikes Willis, in part because so little time is devoted to her special interest. She studies art in a community program on Saturdays, but otherwise—apart from a 45-minute once-a-week art class taught by a specialist—she regards her formal education as a waste of time. She would be delighted to spend her days following the art teacher around, but that is out of the question in view of all the other children to be served. Ann's regular teacher finds it inconsistent both with his own role and with Ann's needs for her to be allowed to sit alone in the back of the classroom all day and draw. The Orlovs have asked the principal at Willis, a sympathetic woman, for aid or advice. Unfortunately she sees no way to help Ann, short of enrollment in another school.
>
> Ann has begged to go to school elsewhere. She would prefer a school that emphasizes art, but would be happy even to be assigned to a teacher whose regular class routine responded to her interests. Her parents want to help, but there are problems. The Orlovs cannot afford Bellwood, the arty but expensive private school that Ann thinks she would like. The modestly priced local Catholic school might serve, but the Orlovs oppose this solution on religious grounds. They might discover a public school in the city with an attractive art program or teacher, one located within reasonable traveling distance; but the school authorities would have to approve Ann's transfer from Willis, and this is not likely. Of course, the Orlovs could move to the attendance area of the other school. They could even move to a different school district. A number of their former neighbors have done so, and some are pleased with the outcome.
>
> For the Orlovs, however, there are limiting conditions. Policemen are supposed to live in the city, so a change of districts for Harry might mean finding a new job. And for many reasons—the park, the neighbors, shopping, the church, the cost of moving—the Orlovs prefer their present neighborhood and would find it painful and expensive to move. Their gravest concern is for Larry, who loves Willis's strong music program, including a boy's chorus in which he solos. Harry and Jean feel any move would be risky. If the student body in the new school is separated into ability groups, they might assign Ann to the wrong program. More important, the Orlovs are worried that, even if the family moves, subsequent shifts in teaching personnel or official policy might leave the whole family even worse off than before.
>
> Armin Schroeder is a young art teacher in the public schools of a blue-collar suburb adjoining the city. He has developed a proposal for a comprehensive elementary curriculum in the symbols and materials of the artist's world. Schroeder has tried to persuade his school authorities to give him an experimental school, but, though sympathetic to experimentation, they are already committed in other directions. In any event, Schroeder's success in his own district would probably be of little help to Ann Orlov; even if there were spaces available, she is not likely to be granted a special transfer outside her district. Schroeder does not have the capital to start such a school on a private basis. Even if he could raise the money, he would probably have to charge more than $1400 a year tuition; he might be able to attract a rich clientele and survive, but he prefers not to run an elitist school. Possibly enough families like the Orlovs would try his school to make it viable—if they could afford it. Most of them could not. The Orlov's savings are insignificant and their responsibilities weighty; family resources are already diminished by $700 paid yearly in various taxes that support education, and the public school is 'free'. Under these circumstances even wealthier people often forego the private alternative they might prefer.

Ann Orlov's case represents what many critics regard as a basic pathology of American public education. 'The state is content to trust the Orlovs with sophisticated decisions regarding food, hours of rest, and other important matters affecting the child', Coons and Sugarman argue. 'Only when it comes to education has the state . . . virtually emasculated the family's options' . . . .[*]

---

[*] J. Coons and S. Sugarman, *Education by Choice: The Case for Family Control* 10 (1978).

The central control exercised by local school systems, Coons and Sugarman continue, is a formula for stagnation, unresponsiveness, and mediocrity. 'Public schools today are rarely permitted to die of unpopularity', they argue. 'Thus, their incentive to innovate is meager, and their capacity to terminate unsuccessful programs is as bad or worse' . . . .**

Furthermore, they argue, the absence of choice and competition works against the very ideals of equal opportunity that the public schools are supposed to embody. 'The poorer the family, the less its ability to furnish home remedies for educational ailments; . . . the more difficult it is to escape an underfinanced or mismanaged public school system by changing residence; and . . . the less its ability to induce the public system to provide the alternative classroom or program it prefers' . . . .***

* * *

The intellectual roots of the current debate on educational choice can be traced from Thomas Paine and Adam Smith in the eighteenth century, through John Stuart Mill in the nineteenth century, to a variety of conservatives, liberals, and radicals in the twentieth century. . . .† In 1962, conservative Milton Friedman‡ . . . proposed a system of publicly financed educational vouchers. In the late 1960s, the idea was picked up by a liberal Democratic administration and elaborated, with financial support from the U.S. Office of Economic Opportunity (OEO), into a proposal for a regulated educational voucher system . . .[1], which was in turn elaborated into a demonstration project in Alum Rock, California . . . .[2] In 1985, the Reagan administration proposed that the federal government's largest education program, Chapter 1 of the Educational Consolidation and Improvement Act, be changed to an individual voucher program for disadvantaged children . . . .[3] And in 1986, the National Governors' Association . . . endorsed greater parental choice in education as one of its main educational priorities.

The common thread in these ideologically divergent views is a profound disillusionment with what David Tyack . . .[4] has called 'the one best system' . . . . This system of locally centralized political and bureaucratic control, Tyack argues, is an outgrowth of the municipal reform movement of the nineteenth century, which tried to substitute enlightened lay leadership and scientific management for political patronage as the organizing principle of public education. The basic structure that grew out of this period—a locally elected lay board of education, a large and functionally specialized central administration, and schools run by principals reporting to the central administration—persists to this day and has a resilience, Tyack argues, that far surpasses its educational effectiveness. Local centralization of administrative functions in public schools, the argument goes, creates a self-interested bureaucracy with strong incentives to maximize its budget, control its clientele and subordinates, and expand its domain of influence, but only very weak incentives to attend to the essential processes of teaching and learning. . . .

Choice in the Existing System

An enlightened public school administrator, confronted with these arguments, would probably reply that they represent a gross caricature of the typical public school system and a complete misunderstanding of the role that parent and student choice play in that system. Many school systems offer a considerable array of choices within and among schools. Parents and students play an active role in the choice of these programs. In fact, our enlightened administrator might continue, community sentiment seems to be running strongly against greater choice and toward clearer, more uniform academic standards for all students, regardless of students' and parents' personal tastes or preferences. The public doesn't always value choice above other possible objectives, the administrator might conclude.

** *Id.* at 154.

*** *Id.* at 26.

† *Id.* at 18–19.

‡ M. Friedman, *Capitalism and Freedom* 85–107 (1962).

1. Center for the Study of Public Policy, *Education Vouchers: A Report on Financing Elementary Education by Grants to Parents* (1970).
2. Rand Corporation, *A Study of Alternatives in American Education* (1978). For an evaluation of the Alum Rock Project, *see* Cohen and Farrar, "Power to the Parents? The Story of Education Vouchers," 48 *The Public Interest* 72 (1977).
3. U.S. Department of Education, *Justice and Excellence: The Case for Choice in Chapter 1* (1985).
4. D. Tyack, *The One Best System: A History of American Urban Education* (1974). *See also* D. Tyack and E. Hansot, *Managers of Virtue: Public School Leadership in America, 1820–1980* (1982).

There is considerable empirical and theoretical support for the enlightened administrator's viewpoint. Consider the array of choices confronting students and parents in the existing system. Some choices, like place of residence and public versus private schooling, are time-consuming, costly to make, and costly to reverse once they are made. These might be called 'lumpy' choices.

Many parents and students, however, make smaller, more manageable educational choices. These require smaller expenditures of money and time, and are easier to reverse. They can have significant consequences for parents, students, and schools. These are somewhat 'smoother' choices. Public school systems frequently offer a range of programs within and among schools, for the academically talented, for the handicapped, for students with specific learning problems, for the artistically, vocationally, or scientifically inclined, and many more. The availability of these options allows parents to exercise educational choice by influencing the assignment of their children to teachers, classes, schools, and special programs within schools or school systems. In some instances—special education, for example—school officials are required by federal and state policy to include parents in choices affecting the assignment of their children.

Some significant proportion of parents actively exploit these opportunities; other parents accept the assignments they are dealt, either because they are unaware that they have choices or because they willingly delegate those choices to others. In some instances, parents and students are 'active choosers', in the sense that they exploit their options; in others, they are 'inactive choosers', in the sense that they defer to the decisions of professionals, they don't acknowledge or understand their options, or they are simply satisfied with what they have. Some parents and students may be consistently more active than others. Some, by virtue of their background or economic circumstances, may be less able to assert their preferences.

The existence of choice, and of active choosers, within public school systems doesn't mean that those systems are necessarily responsive to all clients. The array of choices in a given system, in fact, may be predicated on the assumption that few parents are active choosers. A high proportion of active choosers might disrupt the central determination of attendance, staffing, and content. Indeed, teachers and administrators may intentionally discourage active choice for the majority of their clients to prevent the disruption of central administration.

* * *

The Collective Consequences of Individual Choice

Underlying the argument for increased choice in education is a set of assumptions about the effect of individual choice on the responsiveness and performance of schools. These assumptions might be summarized as follows:

- Parents are more likely to be satisfied with a school they have chosen, and to support their children's learning in such a school.
- Students are more likely to engage in the work of schooling more seriously when they (and their parents) have chosen the kind of school that they find appropriate to their needs.
- Teachers are more likely to enjoy their work and make the commitment necessary to successful teaching when they have chosen the setting in which they work and take an active hand in the construction of their school program.

When parents, students, and educators choose the setting in which education occurs, the argument goes, we should expect better results—in school achievement, attendance, and attainment. The notion of 'community' often figures prominently in these arguments. Enhanced choice, the argument goes, creates communities of shared values that command the loyalty of participants, that set clear expectations, and that are more likely to succeed in accomplishing common goals.

The empirical evidence on these assumptions is suggestive, but hardly definitive. Comparisons of public, private, and Catholic high school achievement seem to show that Catholic schools exceed public schools, controlling for student composition. Furthermore, the Catholic school effects seem greater for minority and low income students. Private schools also show greater achievement than public schools, again controlling for student composition, but the private school advantage is on the order of half as large as the Catholic school advantage. The size of these differences and their statistical and educational significance are matters of considerable debate in the social science community, but the direction of the comparisons is consistent across analyses. . . .*

One important finding of the research on public and non-public schools, which has not been given the same visibility as the public/non-public comparisons, is that 'even the largest estimates of a private school advantage are small relative to the variation in quality among different public schools, among different Catholic schools, and among different non-Catholic private schools. Consequently, in predicting the quality of a student's education, it is less important to know whether the student attended a public school or a private school, than it is to know which school within a particular sector the student attended'. . . .**

A related survey . . . of the attitudes of public and non-public school educators reveals that public school educators perceive more external control over their work, are more likely to stress bureaucratic and public relations aspects of their jobs, and more likely to complain about lacking the essential resources to do their jobs than non-public educators. Non-public educators, on the other hand, are more likely to perceive positive parent and student expectations and are more likely to perceive their schools' goals as clearly communicated than public school educators. Non-public teachers are more likely to perceive their principals as playing a constructive role, and are more likely to know what their colleagues are teaching and to co-ordinate content decisions. Non-public schools are more likely to have school-wide standards on such subjects as homework than public schools. It is important to remember that these results come from a survey of attitudes, rather than practice, and that they conceal wide variation on both the public and non-public sides.

A final piece of evidence comes from the Alum Rock voucher experiment. . . .*** Parents who participated in the voucher experiment expressed a high degree of satisfaction with their schools, although consistently less satisfaction than non-voucher parents. Teachers in voucher schools expressed a high degree of satisfaction with the system at the outset, but their support declined sharply with time. While there is some evidence that voucher programs differed across schools, there is no evidence that they produced differences in student achievement. Geographical proximity, rather than curriculum content, was the major determinant of parental choice.

* * *

So, other things being equal, unrestricted client choice should make all consumers of education better off. But other things are never equal.

If all the significant costs and benefits of education could be represented in the price that consumers were willing to pay, as with toothpaste or breakfast cereal, then there would be no reason, in principle, why consumers shouldn't choose and pay for whatever quantity or type of education they prefer, without any public involvement whatever. But this is not the case for at least three reasons. First, your educational choices have significant effects on my welfare, and *vice versa*. Much of the beneficial effect of schooling derives from association (with other students, with teachers, with communities), rather than from individual consumption. Hence, your decision to leave my school affects my opportunity to learn in ways that are not adequately accounted for in the price of your tuition. Second, we can realize certain collective benefits only if we agree to limit our individual choices, for example, by requiring everyone to have a certain minimum amount of education. These collective benefits include, for example, life in a stable democracy populated by literate voters and the availability of a highly skilled, mobile labor force in the event of a national emergency. Third, we may agree that we value certain things, such as racial equality or access to a decent standard of living for all members of society, because these things are good in themselves, regardless of the material benefits they provide to us. So we may insist that a certain amount of education be provided all members of society to prevent social consequences we regard as bad in and of themselves.

All of these are reasons why we might choose rationally to have the government involved in the provision of education, why government might be empowered to limit individuals' educational choices, and why government involvement in education might promote society's welfare in ways that a purely private market in education might not. . . . Even Mil-

* *See* J. Coleman, T. Hoffer, and S. Kilgore, *High School Achievement: Public, Catholic, and Private Schools Compared* (1982).

** Murname, "A Review Essay: Comparisons of Public and Private Schools: Lessons from the Uproar," 19 *J. of Hum. Res.* 263 (1984).

*** *See* R. Bridge and J. Blackman, *A Study of Alternatives in American Education*, vol. IV (1978).

ton Friedman, who concedes few legitimate governmental constraints on individual choice of any kind, acknowledges the duty of the government 'to require that each child receive a minimum amount of schooling of a specified kind'. . . .

But one cannot parlay a rationale for government *involvement* in education into a rationale for a government *monopoly* over education. For all the reasons argued by the advocates of increased educational choice, a public monopoly would probably increase the problems of responsiveness and performance associated with the current system of limited competition. Perhaps more importantly, some citizens assert a right to choose non-public education for religious or personal reasons that would make a public monopoly impossible to sustain. . . .

* * *

This analysis also underscores why it is important to frame experiments around the problem of choice in both supply-side and demand-side terms. Loosening up choice on the consumer side, through changes in attendance policies, for example, while leaving constraints on the provider side, in the form of limits on staff assignment and content decisions, will result in increasingly diverse client demands being placed on a narrow and rigid structure. Loosening up choice on the producer side, in the form of increased school-level responsibility for staffing content, while leaving constraints on the consumer side, in the form of centralized attendance policies, results in more school-level control, but not necessarily more responsiveness to client demand. Whatever the array of options, reducing central control on one side, without also reducing it on the other, will defeat the purpose of enhanced choice by putting one or the other side at a disadvantage.

Is there any firm evidence upon which to base a judgment that these structural options, or any others we might develop along similar lines, will improve the academic achievement of students? The short answer is no. The evidence, examined earlier, suggests that there is no simple causal relationship between choice, as we have discussed it here, and students' academic performance. Saying there is no direct causal relationship, however, is not the same as saying that there are no grounds for experimentation with choice.

In the absence of such evidence, there are many reasons why it might be useful to experiment deliberately with options of the sort outlined above. First, the limits of local centralization have been clearly established. The centralization of finance, attendance, staffing, and content exact a relatively high cost in administrative overhead, and in the diversion of energy and commitment from the central tasks of teaching and learning. Even the greatest alleged strength of the system—its ability to deliver a relatively standard product to a relatively broad clientele—is undermined, first, by the fact that it is hemorrhaging one-fifth to one-half of its clientele during their adolescent years, and second, that the education of those who remain is, at its best, highly variable in quality, and at its worst, dismal.

A second reason for experimenting is that consumer and producer choice may be values worth recognizing in their own right, regardless of their instrumental relationship to student performance. A basic philosophical premise of democratic thought is that government derives its authority from the people, rather than possessing inherent authority. When nominally democratic institutions like the public schools become bureaucracies with interests of their own, they raise serious questions about their relationship to those they are supposed to serve. Loosening up the structure of schools, providing more influence for citizen-consumers and professional providers, is one way of sending signals to the bureaucracy that its interests are not paramount.

A third rationale for experimenting with new forms of consumer and provider choice is that it may be a way of engaging the creative energy of parents and educators in the solution of serious educational problems, independent of whether choice by itself is a good or effective thing to do. Hierarchies, of the type represented by local centralization, condition clients and providers to look up for solutions, to higher-level administrators and policymakers, rather than inward at themselves or outward toward their peers. Pushing decisions on finance, staffing, attendance, content, and organization out into the schools may result in more attention at that level to the deliberate design of teaching and learning, rather than to the implementation of plans formulated elsewhere.

These arguments in favor of experimentation with policies directed at educational choice, however, should be approached with several cautions. The first and most obvious is that the existing system has proven extraordinarily resilient in the face of attempts to change it. In the Alum Rock voucher experiment, for example, the information educators made available to parents on their educational options was not useful in discerning differences among programs, and there is substantial evidence that the programs themselves did not represent carefully thought out and implemented options. Teachers and administrators fought and defeated proposals to publicize achievement test scores across programs, on the grounds that they did not provide fair comparisons. And teachers and administrators opposed the introduction of a third-party organization to act as an 'impartial' arbiter on questions of information and administration. . . .

The results of other experiments with choice have not been much more encouraging. Teachers and administrators tend to adapt client choice systems to ease their effects on established patterns, rather than adapting their behavior to the new incentives introduced by client choice. Small-scale, within-district experiments create divisions between participants and nonparticipants—parents, teachers, and students alike. These divisions result in charges of inequity that create political problems for school administrators and local board members. Alternative programs tend to lose their distinctiveness and their support among teachers and clients over time. . . .*

A second *caveat* is that recent studies of public secondary schools show that students already are presented with a considerable array of choices among courses and alternative programs within schools, but that the typical student either chooses a program that lacks coherence or defers to a standard program specified by another adult, typically a counselor, which also lacks focus. Only in exceptional instances do highly motivated students choose academically challenging programs. The typical reader accepts this state of affairs as inevitable, though he or she may find it objectionable in principle. . . .* The picture presented by this research is one in which student choice functions to reinforce a mediocre, substandard level of academic content and performance, rather than higher expectations.

On the other hand, there is some evidence that a few public schools are successful at creating environments in which academic learning occurs among students from a variety of backgrounds. These settings are usually described as ones in which educators have clear expectations for academic success, educators provide reinforcement for student achievement, students operate under clear guidelines for behavior and discipline, educators agree on academic objectives, and school leadership supports teachers in instructional and discipline decisions. . . .** Conspicuously absent from this research, however, is any evidence about the influence of parent, student, or teacher choice in those settings on student achievement.

A third caution is that any experiment with educational choice must come to terms with the problem of active versus inactive choosers. There is some evidence that parents differ by race and social class in the amount of information they have about available options and in their preferences for academic content, discipline, and instructional style. . . . One possible consequence of experiments with increased choice for clients and providers is a situation in which nominally neutral mechanisms produce highly segregated school populations. Another possible consequence is one in which active choosers congregate in one set of schools and inactive choosers end up by default in other schools, creating a stratified system which is responsive to the former and ignores the latter. . . .

Finally, there is no guarantee that enhancing client or provider choice will increase the quality of education provided to the average student. Most, if not all, of the power of client choice to improve schooling rests on the ability of clients to make informed choices. High quality information about the content and performance of schools is difficult and costly to get, it must be collected with care, and it must be interpreted with detachment and skepticism after it is collected because it presents a limited pic-

---

* In addition to the works previously cited, *see* M. Metz, *Different by Design: The Context and Character of Three Magnet Schools* (1986); Nault and Uchitelle, "School Choice in the Public Sector: A Case Study of Parental Decision-making," in M. Monley-Casimir, ed., *Family Choice in Schooling: Issues and Dilemmas* (1982).

* *See* A Powell, E. Farrar, and D. Cohen, *The Shopping Mall High School: Winners and Losers in the Educational Marketplace* (1985); E. Boyer, *High School: A Report on Secondary Education in America* (1985); T. Sizer, *Horace's Compromise: The Dilemma of the American High School* (1984).

** *See* S. Lightfoot, *The Good High School* (1983); M. Ruher *et al.*, *Fifteen Thousand Hours: Secondary Schools and Their Effects on Children* (1980); Purkey and Smith, "Effective Schools: A Review," 83 *Elem. Sch. J.* 427 (1983); Rowan *et al.*, "Research on Effective Schools: A Cautionary Note," 12 *Educ. Researcher* 24 (1983).

ture of what schools are about. Supply-side competition introduces strong incentives for providers to present superficial or inaccurate information on effectiveness, to package information to promote their product, and to protect certain types of information that would be useful in making client choices as proprietary. Since providers control the 'technology' of schooling, they have a significant advantage over consumers in the control of useful information. Demand-side competition introduces strong incentives for active choosers to use their market power (money, time, influence, access) to gather and use information that improves their relative position in the market. In other words, one effect of introducing greater choice may simply be to increase competitiveness without increasing quality, because quality is an ambiguous commodity in education.

In summary, the major argument in favor of experiments with increased choice is that they provide a much needed prod to a system that is increasingly bureaucratic in its relations with its clients. The major problems associated with such experiments are either that they will be co-opted by the system they seek to change or that, if they succeed, they will impose the risks of mindless and destructive competitiveness without the benefits of greater attention to quality.

NOTES AND QUESTIONS

1. Market Assumptions

Reconsider the introductory essay, titled "Consumer Voters in the Public Sector: Selecting a School District." on consumer-voters in the public sector. To what extent are the market assumptions of the voucher model unrealistic? What advantages does a voucher plan have over the consumer-voter model in the Tiebout model? Is it that consumer-voters will weigh a myriad of community factors, whereas parents under a voucher plan may choose the best education for their children; that is, the voucher may be spent only on education? Is this an advantage or a disadvantage? Are the transaction costs lower under a voucher plan?

Milton Friedman has asked:

> Private schools are almost all either parochial schools or elite academies. Will the effect of the voucher plan not simply be to subsidize these, while leaving the bulk of the slum dwellers in inferior schools? What reason is there to suppose that alternatives will really arise?

Friedman, "The Voucher Idea," *The New York Times Magazine*, Sept. 23, 1973, at 22, 69.

Friedman suggests that the "absence of alternatives when there is no market does not mean that none would arise when there *is* one." *Id.* at 70. Do you agree? Would those offering high quality educational services move to poor areas or to locations convenient to them?

2. Accountability

Consider this criticism of some voucher plans by Professor Arons:

> In the present scheme of public schooling, formal accountability rests largely upon voter choices made in electing school boards, while informal accountability is a response to pressure groups. The voucher scheme seeks to couple with this individual parental control over a per capita share of finances for schooling. As significant an addition to parental power as this may be, however, it would probably constitute a net loss over the present system if it became a substitute for more direct political control. Imagine a school system composed of a diverse collection of schools run by public authorities, private business corporations, teachers' collectives, parent groups, and community development corporations. The only parental power (other than voting for those who set minimum standards) would rest on consumer choice from among whatever options the schooling "producers" happen to be offering. One can, of course, start his own school, and there is assistance available for doing this, but essentially the choice is limited in the same way as in most consumer markets. The means of production is not controlled by the people who must make do with what is produced, and so it is possible for the producers to manipulate and restrict their offerings for their own purposes. Under such conditions it is probably wishful thinking to say that parents will have more power over the nature of schooling or that the school will need to be more responsive.

Arons, "Equity, Option, and Vouchers," 72 *Teachers Coll. Rec.* 337, 357–58 (1971). How would Professor Elmore respond to this argument? How do you?

3. *Vouchers and Preparation for Democracy*

Do you believe that voucher plans will diminish preparation for democratic citizenship? Consider these remarks by Professor Gutmann:

> To justify public support, the standards to which voucher schools are held must fulfill the public purposes—the "internalities"—of primary education. In keeping with this claim, Coons and Sugarman (unlike Friedman) defend stringent constraints on the admissions processes of voucher schools to ensure that all children—not just white or intellectually talented or well-motivated children—have access to a good education. But are the set of constraints that Coons and Sugarman support sufficient for ensuring that voucher schools satisfy the public purposes of schooling? If a primary purpose of schools is to develop democratic character, then the externalities of education may be more extensive than even a constrained voucher plan admits. The externalities may include, among other things, how children of different intellectual abilities, races, and religions are distributed within classrooms, what subjects are taught and how they are taught, how authority in and over schools is distributed, and so on. The externalities of schooling extend beyond the admissions process, the curriculum, and the authority structure, to encompass almost every aspect of schooling, rendering indefensible the distinction between a publicly mandated "minimum" and parentally chosen standards for voucher schools.
>
> Voucher plans attempt to avoid rather than settle our disagreements over how to develop democratic character through schooling. The attempt succeeds insofar as decisions concerning choice among schools are left to sets of parents, who are more likely to agree with one another than they are with other parents as to what constitutes a good school. The attempt fails insofar as the decisions concerning the constraints to be imposed upon voucher schools must still be collective. The most defensible voucher plans, like Coons and Sugarman's, make room for a set of centrally imposed constraints that reflect our collective interest in primary education. But having admitted the possibility—indeed, the necessity—of imposing a set of collective standards on schools, Coons and Sugarman can no longer rest the case for vouchers on the claim that such plans avoid the need for settling our disagreements over how citizens should be educated.
>
> Minimally constrained voucher plans, like Friedman's, avoid the controversial issue of how schools should educate citizens only at the cost of denying our collective interests in democratic education. Maximally constrained voucher plans, like Coons and Sugarman's, appear to avoid the issue only by shifting our controversies over democratic education from a mixture of local, state, and national politics to a more purely centralized politics. If a voucher plan aims to increase diversity in schooling while providing citizens with more control over how schools educate children, then its effect of relegating collective interests in education to a more centralized politics is counterproductive.

A. Gutmann, *Democratic Education* 68–69 (1987).

What of the danger of government manipulation of political values in traditional public schools?

> As crucial as the family's role may be in learning, what is more important from our perspective is that of all the socializing agents, the family is probably the most difficult to manipulate systematically and directly. This insulation from direct pressure is a consequence of a number of conditions. First, the sheer number of family units presents a communication problem of enormous magnitude. . . .
>
> Even if it were possible to have access to a significant number of families, a successful program of influence would require either extensive monitoring of these many families or separating children from their parents for lengthy periods. . . .
>
> We can thus surmise that where political orientations are largely transmitted through the family, the probability of widespread manipulation is small. . . . No doubt a government with enough resources, patience, and insensitivity to cultural norms regulating appropriate child rearing messages *could* manipulate family political socialization, but there are more efficient methods of manipulation available.
>
> * * *
>
> Usually considered second only to the family in transmitting political orientations is the school. As in the case of the family, it is almost impossible to avoid spending enormous periods of time with this agency of learning. . . . Although the family and school are both of considerable importance, unlike the family the schools provide many more opportunities for systematic manipulation.

R. Weissberg, *Political Learning, Political Choice, and Democratic Citizenship* 144–46 (1974).

Do the advantages of the voucher system in terms of limiting state manipulation of socialization processes outweigh the disadvantages of reducing the government's capacity to instill commonly held democratic values? Do Coons and Sugarman, *supra*, have different concepts of training for democratic citizenship? *See* Kalodner, "Book Review," 67 *Calif. L. Rev.* 1223, 1228 (1978) (Coons and Sugarman want "our citizens trained to be 'autonomous' . . . .

The authors have in mind not the improvement of society but the improvement of the lot of the individual. . . ."). Does a state-mandated minimum in the context of a voucher plan appropriately balance the competing values of community and pluralism?

4. *Vouchers and Equality*

Would voucher plans perpetuate existing inequalities because the poor will choose the wrong types of schools for socioeconomic advancement? Professor Friedman rejects this as mere paternalism:

> Social reformers, and educational reformers in particular, often self-righteously take for granted that the poor have no interest in their children or no competence to choose for them. This, I believe, is a gratuitous insult. The poor have had limited opportunity to choose. But U.S. history has amply demonstrated that given the opportunity, they will often sacrifice greatly, disinterestedly and wisely for their children's welfare.

Friedman, *supra* at 69.

Does Friedman have the better of the argument? Or is it that he regards family choice as more important than equality? *But see* A. Gutmann, *Democratic Education* 65 (1987).

5. *Destruction of Public School Systems*

Would a voucher plan that included all parents and students, private schools as well as public schools, ultimately lead to the demise of public education in the traditional sense? Would this be wise as a matter of policy? Consider these remarks by Professor Coons:

> I cannot share [the] paradoxical view that the brightest hope for the public schools lies in their remaining benign prisons for the lower classes. Most of these schools can survive and prosper—but only if they become a free and open choice for all. The risk they run is real, but it does not lie in the increase of freedom; the enemy they should fear is their reliance upon a captive audience. It can only drive out more of the middle class. The public school will prosper under family choice; indeed, it will prosper *only* under family choice. By respecting the dignity of individuals and families of *all* income classes, this troubled institution will at last come to deserve the title to which it has so long pretended. It will at last be public.

Coons, "Of Family Choice and 'Public' Education," 61 *Phi Delta Kappan* 10, 12–13 (1979).

6. *Vouchers and Religion*

Reread *Committee for Public Education and Religious Liberty v. Nyquist*, 413 U.S. 756, 93 S.Ct. 2955, 37 L.Ed.2d 948 (1973), and the other cases on aid to parochial schools in chapter 1. Would a voucher scheme that would extend to all families and schools, including private religious schools, be constitutional in the light of the First Amendment's prohibition on the "establishment" of religion? *See also Public Funds for Public School of New Jersey v. Byrne*, 590 F.2d 514 (3rd Cir. 1979), *aff'd mem.*, 442 U.S. 907, 99 S.Ct. 2818, 61 L.Ed.2d 273 (1979). *See generally* Sugarman, "Family Choice: The Next Step in the Quest for Equal Educational Opportunity?" 38 *Law & Contemp. Probs.* 513 (1974). Consider these remarks by Professor Sugarman:

> Perhaps we are left, after *Nyquist*, with a sliding scale which depends upon both the nature and specificity of the program itself and the identity of the beneficiaries. Hence, if the government builds structures for voluntary membership associations, it may not build halls of worship for church groups simply because it builds most of its buildings for non-church groups. This is so because the item which the government provides itself is religious. On the other hand, the state would be able to build a hospital for a church group as part of a general program of building hospitals, even though this means that the church could now afford to build a chapel, and even though undeniably religious activities occur in the hospital along with health care. Since hospitals do in the main serve secular functions, and since the program in fact includes a substantial number of beneficiaries which are not religion-associated, further judicial inquiry into whether the state is in fact getting full secular value for money may not be needed to protect the concerns underlying the establishment clause. . . . Viewing the voucher plan scenario under this approach to the "primary effect" test, the argument would be that, while the plan does assist religious schools since the beneficiaries are only in part religious school users, and since schooling is in the main secular, the assistance to religious schools . . . is only incidental.

Sugarman, *supra* at 527–28 (1974).

Do you agree with Professor Sugarman's analysis? Is it easier to disentangle health care from religious activities than secular from nonsecular education? *See generally* Giannella, "Religious Liberty, Nonestablishment, and Doctrinal Development—Part II: The Nonestablishment Principle," 81 *Harv. L. Rev.* 513 (1968). Would it be satisfactory if the amount of the public aid did not exceed the value of the secular education services? *See* Choper, "The Establishment Clause and Aid to Parochial Schools," 56 *Calif. L. Rev.* 260 (1968). Is it possible to create a voucher plan that includes religious schools without advancing religion?

7. *Education Vouchers and Racial Segregation*

a. The Constitutional Question. If a voucher scheme increases racial segregation, either by design or effect, it may be vulnerable to constitutional attack as a denial of equal protection of the laws to black students. The issue has arisen in several southern states that sought to close their public schools and provide vouchers as a means of avoiding judicial mandates to desegregate. In Louisiana, for example, a three-judge district court overturned a statute that would have permitted counties to close their public schools, sell or lease them to others, and then provide "tuition vouchers" that could be cashed in by the "private schools." *Hall v. St. Helena Parish School Board*, 197 F.Supp. 649 (E.D.La. 1961), *aff'd per curiam*, 368 U.S. 515, 82 S.Ct. 529, 7 L.Ed.2d 521 (1962). A subsequent Louisiana statute sought to accomplish the same end. Its rationale was framed in terms of the right of the parent to decide "on the type of education ultimately received by the child. . ."; no mention of race was made in the legislation. The court, noting Louisiana's long history of resistance to desegregation, concluded that "the law was designed to establish and maintain a system of segregated schools" and had the effect of maintaining segregation. *Poindexter v. Louisiana Financial Assistance Commission*, 275 F.Supp. 833 (E.D.La. 1967), *aff'd per curiam*, 88 S.Ct. 693, 19 L.Ed.2d 780 (1968). *See also Coffey v. State Education Finance Commission*, 296 F.Supp. 1389 (S.D.Miss. 1969); *Lee v. Macon County Board*, 267 F.Supp. 458 (M.D.Ala. 1967), *aff'd per curiam, sub nom., Wallace v. United States*, 389 U.S. 571, 389 U.S. 215, 88 S.Ct. 415, 19 L.Ed.2d 422 (1967). The Supreme Court has held unconstitutional Mississippi legislation that provided free textbooks to segregated private schools. *Norwood v. Harrison*, 413 U.S. 455, 93 S.Ct. 2804, 37 L.Ed.2d 723 (1973). *Compare Gilmore v. Montgomery*, 417 U.S. 556, 94 S.Ct. 2416, 41 L.Ed.2d 304 (1974). The complex political and constitutional questions concerning racial discrimination in private education are addressed in chapter 1.

b. The Policy Question. Would a voucher plan increase the racial segregation of students? That answer is likely to turn on such factors as the present level of segregation, the extent to which the racial composition of a school influences parental choice, and the number of parents who prefer integrated schools.

A voucher scheme can be structured to maintain or increase school desegregation: For example, information about the racial composition of the school can be withheld from parents; where a given school has more student applications than places, some or all of its students can be selected by lottery; racial quotas can be fixed; and minority children can be provided with larger grants to make them more attractive to voucher schools. How effective would each of these approaches be?

8. *Implementation of Voucher Plans*

The evidence on the success of early voucher plans is mixed. Why is this? Is it that voucher plans are impractical or that the politics of education inhibits and unduly restricts this form of experimentation? If the latter, does this suggest that any voucher experiment will be tainted?

In the late 1980s, the movement to experiment with school choice plans gained momentum, but this time, in order to overcome objections to subsidizing private schools, the proposals were limited to family choice within the public sector. The following excerpt describes the plan adopted in Minnesota.

"A State Policy Maker's Guide to Public School Choice"

Education Commission of the States, pp. 1–16 (1989). Reprinted with permission of the Ed. Comm. of the States, 707 17th St., Suite 2700, Denver, CO.

At an accelerating pace, state policy makers are considering "public-school choice" as a policy tool to foster school restructuring.

In 1988, Governor Rudy Perpich of Minnesota succeeded in passing legislation that allows students to attend public schools in any district in the state, the governor of New Jersey directed the state commissioner of education to study how greater choice can be offered in the public schools, and the governor of Colorado signed a bill that grants high-school juniors and seniors the option of completing work for their high-school diploma at a public college or university. In all, 20 states are actively involved in deliberations on, or implementation of, some kind of public-school choice plan.

* * *

Now that higher standards are in place, policy makers are looking for additional ways to spur school improvement and student learning. State efforts are beginning to focus on strengthening schools as organizations. To foster educational excellence, a shift from regulation to incentives and mobilization of "institutional capacity" is beginning to occur in many states. Program mandates are being replaced by strategies to empower and to implement effective educational practices in schools.

* * *

Public-school choice reflects several of these themes: more accountability for schools as parents and students vote with their feet, decentralization as more responsibility is given to the school site to make its program attractive to students, competition as schools and sometimes colleges compete for students. But public-school choice, by itself, will not lead to major changes in schools.

For public-school choice to be an effective policy tool, it must be coupled with other school restructuring efforts and provide incentives for schools and districts better to meet national, community and individual educational needs.

Public-school choice gives families the power to choose schools for their children and in so doing creates incentives for schools and districts to attract families and sanctions for failing to retain them. What choice does not do is give schools or districts the capacity to respond to this new challenge. . . .

If the education system is to be capable of meeting the challenge of choice, it is essential that the authority to act to change programs, schedules and quality be given to the people who benefit from the rewards and suffer the consequences of competition. Who are those people? In some cases, the districts; in other cases, the schools.

Interdistrict choice is, on one level, competition among districts. The implication for choice is that districts themselves must have the flexibility to respond to new demands. States with highly regulated systems which seek to promote uniformity in all districts will not gain the benefits of choice unless districts are given the freedom to differentiate themselves.

At another level, interdistrict choice, along with all other forms of choice, is always about competition among schools. Students, after all, attend schools; families are choosing among schools and, most important of all, it is schools, not districts, that policy makers want to improve. If competition is to promote school-based improvement and diversity, then schools themselves must have the authority to make important decisions about the educational program they offer. In short, whether called school-site management or school-based decision making, decentralization of authority is a necessary condition for maximizing the benefits of a changed reward structure.

* * *

A second condition for enhancing the ability of choice to restructure schools is flexibility. Teachers, schools and districts need to be able to respond creatively to the pressures that choice creates. To do so, they need the opportunity to redesign programs, curriculum, instructional approaches and other facets of their school or district.

This flexibility can take the form of new broad guidelines that permit diverse approaches to common goals; waivers available to teachers, schools or districts wanting to try something new; or legislation that encourages teachers and districts to create new schools.

* * *

Public-school choice poses two challenges to traditional systems of accountability which use accreditation to specify the inputs to the educational process and standardized testing to measure the outputs. In the first place, if families are to make informed decisions about schools they will need good information describing the outcomes that they can expect for their children at various schools. In the second place, decentralized schools with the flexibility to create diverse approaches to teaching and learning must be held together not only by common goals, but also by a system of accountability which provides the public with indicators of educational success that go beyond the information provided by family movement and standardized achievement test scores.

* * *

In the view of their supporters, public schools of choice can address these concerns, as well as those linked to school improvement, by providing:

— A mechanism for increasing family autonomy and freedom: families may choose schools for their children that best suit their needs.

— A means for extending choice to those who do not have it because of their race or socioeconomic

status: all families have options within the public-school system.
— A framework for school improvement: the system of rewards and sanctions within which educators operate is restructured.

* * *

Public-school choice is not a single plan. Research has uncovered six different kinds of public-school choice plans, which differ in the way they respond to the community's interest in freedom, equity and school improvement. . . . [T]hese plans differ considerably in the way they address these three public priorities.

— The structures of *interdistrict* choice and *postsecondary options* plans emphasize the rights of families to choose among existing public schools. It is assumed that school improvement will follow from the competition choice creates among schools. To insure that all families have equal access to these choices, the plans require special guidelines regarding transportation, admissions and parent information.
— *Second-chance* plans extend interdistrict choice and postsecondary options to at-risk youth as well as offer them alternatives to traditional schools, thus increasing their range of educational options. In doing so, the plans provide improved learning opportunities for participating students with equity and school-improvement issues a secondary concern.
— The strong suit of *controlled-choice* plans, which require all families to choose the school their child attends, is their overt commitment to equity. To insure that all families have access to schools of acceptable quality, plans must incorporate special provisions for implementing school-based improvement. Because of the priority given to racial balance, parental freedom to choose a school is limited by the requirements of that goal.
— An intradistrict choice plan based on *teacher-initiated schools* views parental freedom as a necessary adjunct of school improvement, but features school restructuring as its centerpiece. Such plans must make special efforts to insure that diverse schools are accessible to and equitably serve all families within a school district.
— *Magnet schools* set school improvement and family choice within a framework that allows some district families to choose from a handful of schools with special resources. Because not all students in a district can attend a magnet school, inequities can be overcome only when all schools in the district are "magnetized."

Minnesota's Open-Enrollment Plan

Students entering kindergarten through grade 12 (including those currently in private schools) may choose to enroll in a public school or program located in a district other than the one in which the pupil lives. While the family may apply for a specific program or school, acceptance into the new district does not guarantee acceptance into a specific school or program.

Beginning with the 1990–91 school year, a student may apply to *any* school district to enroll for the following year. All districts must participate unless their school boards have declared their district closed. In the latter case, resident students may leave to attend another district, but no nonresident students may enroll in the district.

A student may be denied approval to enroll only if the district:

— Has declared itself "closed" to all enrollment-option students
— Lacks space in a grade level, program, or school
— Would fall out of compliance with desegregation guidelines (e.g., Duluth, Minneapolis, St. Paul)

Students may not be excluded because of race or ethnicity, previous academic achievement, athletic or other extracurricular ability, handicapping conditions, lack of proficiency in the English language or previous disciplinary proceedings.

Students enrolled in nonresident districts must reapply every year for admission to that district.

Transportation. The nonresident district will transport students from school-district boundaries to the school. Sometimes resident districts will assist, but usually parents have to provide their own transportation to the border of the new district. The nonresident district may use state funds to reimburse low-income parents for the costs of transportation from the pupil's residence to the border of the nonresident district.

Desegregation. To maintain compliance with a state-approved desegregation plan, a district may establish the number of majority and minority pupils who may transfer into or out of the district, and it may accept or reject applications based on the needs of its desegregation plan.

Parent Information. A participating district is required to provide information about the district, schools, programs, policies and procedures to all interested parties.

Finance. The nonresident district will report to the resident district those students who attend school in that district. The state will then increase the general education and capital expenditures aid for the district of attendance by the per-pupil amount of the home district's state aid.

* * *

What do the Advocates Say?

Parent/Student Involvement. When parents and students are able to choose their school, there is strong evidence to suggest that they become more involved in the school and are more satisfied with the education being provided. It is important to note that when choice is available, even those who do not move are making a choice, so long as they are fully informed about their options.

Increased Educational Choice. Students can benefit from learning opportunities offered in another district but not in their own. For example, they may be able to study an unusual foreign language or to participate in an intensive chemistry program not available in their home district. Elementary students may be able to participate in different pedagogical models, such as open schools, continuous progress, language immersion, etc. When students are placed in programs tailored to their unique needs, their performance improves.

Cooperative Planning. In several instances competition between school districts has been an incentive for contiguous school districts to collaborate on program offerings. This has allowed students to have access to more opportunities than each district could provide on its own. By participating in an educational division of labor, all districts may be able to keep traditional enrollment levels while increasing student learning opportunities.

Flexibility and Convenience. Families can choose schools that suit their needs and convenience. For example, they can select a school near their work place to be closer to their child and after-school care arrangements. California has passed a law allowing this option. Parents can register their child either in the school district in which they live or in the school district in which they work.

In other cases, families who live near school district lines and are actually closer to a school in another district could be allowed to send their children to the nearer school.

* * *

Efficient Utilization of School Facilities. In addition, such collaborative arrangements may be a way to take advantage of underutilized school buildings or available commercial space. This can delay or avoid the necessity of constructing new schools.

Pressure for School Responsiveness. When families have the option to attend school in another district, which removes resources from their home district, a district faces significant pressure to be more accommodating to resident families' needs and concerns. Such accommodation can take the form of offering new programs, of arrangements between districts that allow children to attend schools nearest their home or their parents' work places, or of greater communication between teachers and parents. In general, open enrollment is an incentive for greater flexibility and responsiveness on the part of schools.

* * *

What do the Critics Say?

Increased Educational Inequity. In some interdistrict choice plans, the ability of a family to participate in the plan depends on the adequacy of the information they receive and on the family's ability to provide some of the transportation needed to get to a school in another district. Without extensive parent outreach through diverse methods and in native languages, and without full subsidy of the transportation costs of low-income families, critics fear that not all children will have an equal chance to participate. They are concerned that this might lead to the isolation of poor children within their home districts and the loss of widespread public support for those districts.

Loss of Diversity. Some critics fear that competition between districts will lead them to become more and more like each other and to offer similar rather than diverse educational opportunities. This is cause for concern by those who believe that there is no one best way for all students.

Homogeneity rather than heterogeneity can come about in several ways. First, as families vote with their feet and popular districts are identified, other districts may choose to replicate those programs and to withdraw less popular programs which nonetheless serve some families' needs. Second, as states try to provide families with adequate information about schools, they may be tempted to rely more heavily on standardized tests as a way of providing comparable data. Such "high stakes" tests can directly influence the curriculum and pedagogy of all districts and force them toward a single curriculum and style of teaching. Third, if states think that significant numbers of students will be transferring in and out of districts, they may be tempted to encourage a more uniform curriculum among districts in order to avoid any discontinuity in student learning.

Loss of Resources. Because school financing is universally based on enrollment levels, school districts lose resources whenever families leave. Remaining students can suffer if decreased enrollment translates into smaller budgets, fewer teachers and fewer opportunities.

Financial Base. In some states where districts have unequal amounts of funding per pupil, some of the districts with lower student revenues worry that they will not be able to compete with districts with high revenues. To their way of thinking, competition should not be introduced until all districts have the financial capacity to attract and retain students.

District Consolidation. Small, underfunded districts, in particular, may find themselves losing students to larger districts which are able to offer more comprehensive programs. Under these conditions, interdistrict choice can indirectly lead to school-district consolidation by reallocating students from small to large districts.

Increasing Education Budgets. Interdistrict choice can entice back into the public-school system parents who have placed their children in private schools. While public-school education is a right of all persons, transfers from private to public schools translate into increased state and local expenditures. Without an associated increase in resources, this is money that will be spent on basic educational services to accommodate student transfers from private schools, not on improving programs or raising salaries.

* * *

Ineligibility to Vote in New District. Parents sending children to school in another district do not vote in that district. These parents will have no official voice regarding school-board elections that affect the education their children receive.

Weakened Sense of Community. Family decisions to send children to school in other communities begin to sever the connection between schools and a community's identity. Schools may lose the role they play in some communities as a center of local activities.

Loss of Community Activists. Some of the families who take advantage of choices may be parents who are actively involved in the improvement of schooling. If such families leave a district, the community they leave behind may lose important advocates and constituents for improved public schooling.

* * *

IV. REFORM, REGULATION, AND RESTRUCTURING

Political efforts to bring accountability to public education take many forms, and waves of reform—some might say fads—appear in one era only to disappear in another. From a historical perspective, the most common approach is for state legislatures to regulate, either directly or through state boards of education, the programs and methods of operation of local school districts, seeking to reduce local and professional discretion and thereby to improve the quality of education. These rules vary from state to state, but they often focus on curriculum, tenure, discipline, graduation requirements, class size, attendance, teacher certification, and related subjects. *See generally* D. Kirp and D. Jensen, *School Days, Rule Days* (1986); D. Doyle and T. Hartle, *Excellence in Education: The State Takes Charge* (1985); National Institute of Education, *State Legal Standards for the Provision of Public Education* (1978). These mandates presumably emanate from a sense that hierarchical controls are efficacious in producing reform, that some districts may fall below any reasonable minimum in terms of educational quality, and that statewide decision makers are better equipped in many instances to set educational policy. On the other hand, local districts often retain significant discretion to devise programs and to oversee operations once the state minima have been satisfied.

The recent changes that have occurred in the governing system of education can only be understood against the backdrop of educational research and policy-making. For most of the 1960s the emphasis among researchers and policymakers was on eliminating racial discrimination in education and on examining the relationship between gross educational expenditures and resources (e.g., libraries, class size, foreign language teachers) and student achievement, with particular concern for low income and minority children. Surprisingly, these studies generally did not confirm popular beliefs about the efficacy of money in improving educational performance. *See generally* chapter 5, *infra*. In the 1970s, perhaps in reaction to the earlier studies, the research focus shifted. An "effective schools" literature emerged, seeking to identify the less easily quantifiable characteristics of schools with successful programs, controlling for the socioeconomic status of the students. This literature focused on school leadership, educational climate, fair discipline, teacher training and competency, time spent on learning tasks, homework, and other variables thought to have a significant impact on achievement. *See generally* Yudof, "Educational Policy Research and the New Consensus of the 1980s," *Phi Delta Kappan*, March, 1984, at 456; Purkey and Smith, "Effective Schools: A Review," 83 *Elem. Sch. J.* 427 (1983). It was reinforced in the 1980s by a number of national reports calling for reforms in public education to produce excellence. *See, e.g.*, National Commission on Excellence in Education, *A Nation at Risk* (1983).

Although the literature and many of the suggested reforms of the excellence movement dealt with the educational setting in individual schools and districts, many legislatures responded by enacting more stringent statewide regulations. In addition, the new rules tended to focus less on "inputs," the traditional subject of state regulation, and more on "outputs" or the relationship between school resources and student achievement. This development was in marked contrast to the pessimism of the 1960s with regard to establishing such a nexus. In any event, the result of the new wave of reforms was that the balance of authority between the states and local school districts was altered, with the states taking the more dominant role. Doyle and Finn explain the shift in the following terms:

> With due regard for the handful of jurisdictions that bucked the trend, the general conclusion is . . . clear: We must now begin to regard the states as the senior partners in the financing of public education, rather than as important supplements to predominantly local fiscal structures.
>
> Several reasons may be adduced. Not being bound to the property tax, the states have many more sources of revenue, a significant capacity when school expenditures have soared even as enrollments have dwindled. Categorical state-funded education programs—for the handicapped, the gifted, the non-English speaking, the disadvantaged—have also been enacted by many legislatures. Interest groups—teacher unions, linguistic and ethnic minorities, crusaders for one or another kind of curricular emphasis or special program—have focused their efforts on state capitals and have often been rewarded by the enactment of laws favoring them, by promulgation of regulations benefiting them, and by the appropriation of state funds for programs serving them.
>
> * * *
>
> The past two decades have also witnessed a separate but widespread effort to achieve greater social "equity" through purposeful reform of the financing of American public education, and (at least since the Supreme Court declined, in the *Rodriguez* case, to create a federal constitutional right in this domain) this effort has concentrated on the state capitals.
>
> * * *
>
> Meanwhile, an altogether separate but very powerful wave of education reform has begun to wash over the states. Sometimes dubbed the "excellence" movement, it is a complicated effort to reverse decades of declining test scores, of sagging indicators of teacher competence, of softening pupil performance standards, of proliferating electives in the curriculum, and of mounting numbers of high school "graduates" enter-

ing college or the workforce without having mastered the habits, skills, and knowledge deemed necessary for success.

Unlike earlier waves of education reform, the federal government has had practically nothing to do with this one, save for creating the National Commission on Excellence in Education, whose stern criticisms and stirring rhetoric helped define and legitimize the excellence movement. Although several other of the proliferating national task forces and commissions that have recently appraised and reported on elementary and secondary education did urge Washington to assist with the training of science and math teachers and to mount various other programs, most of the actual reform activity is taking place at the state (and, to a lesser extent, local) level. . . .

These state-level education reforms display two general characteristics. They envision much more statewide homogenization and regulation of public school norms, standards, and procedures. And they include substantially increased education spending by state governments. Many of the reform plans are comprehensive, multipart schemes, ranging from computer literacy to the retraining of school principals, from changes in high school graduation requirements to summer programs for gifted youngsters, from statewide basic skills proficiency tests for sixth graders to mandatory foreign language study for tenth graders. The policy packages differ, but practically all of them include new state-set and state-enforced performance standards for both students and teachers. And while some of these standards are tied to quantitative changes in school inputs and processes, most of them relate to qualitative criteria: can the student—or the teacher—achieve such-and-such a score on such-and-such an examination?

In the past, one has had to look long and hard for serious statewide standards of individual performance. Many states stipulated that high school students had to take three or four "units" of English and a year of American history before they could graduate, but the content of those courses was almost always left to local discretion, as was the appraisal of pupil performance. New York had its "Regents' Examinations," of course, but few states prescribed what or how much a student actually had to learn at any particular stage of his schooling. As for teachers, state "certification" is a long-established procedure, but it has been virtually meaningless. Any graduate of an approved program of teacher education—which generally meant of any teachers' college—was automatically eligible for a license, as was anyone else whose transcript matched a list of course requirements promulgated by the state department of education. New teachers did not have to pass a test of ability or knowledge, nor did they have to demonstrate their classroom prowess to anyone but the university that supervised their practice teaching. Once a teacher had a license, he could ordinarily expect to keep it for life.

At the present time, however, most states are moving rapidly to develop and enforce performance standards for teachers as well as pupils. . . .

* * *

All such reforms narrow the scope of local sovereignty and enlarge the domain of state regulation. Though they do not necessarily alter the formal organization of public education, they leave less to the discretion of local boards and superintendents. They use both carrots and sticks to move the education buggies at a faster average (and more uniform) speed: the carrots of state funding, the sticks of formal regulation and of public opinion aroused by charismatic governors, hounding newspaper editors, and the potential embarrassment resulting from publication of district-by-district and school-by-school scores on state-mandated tests. . . .

* * *

. . . "[L]ocal control of public education" as traditionally conceived is in reality disappearing, even though its facade is nearly everywhere intact. What appears to be happening is that local school systems are evolving in practice into something that they always were in a constitutional sense: subordinate administrative units of a state educational system, with some residual power to modify statewide regulations and procedures in order to ease their implementation within a particular community, and with the residual authority (in most states, though not all) to supplement state spending with locally raised revenues.

Doyle and Finn, "American Schools and the Future of Local Control," *The Public Interest*, Fall, 1984, at 77, 80, 83–85, 90. *See also* F. Wirt and M. Kirst, *The Politics of Education: Schools in Conflict* (1989); W. Firestone, S. Fuhrman, M. Kirst, *The Progress of Reform: An Appraisal of State Education Initiatives* (1989); W. Boyd and C. Kerchner, eds., *The Politics of Excellence and Choice in Education* (1988); T. Timar and D. Kirp, *Managing Educational Excellence* (1988); Doyle and Hartle, *supra;* J. Bunzel, ed., *Challenge to American Schools: The Case for Standards and Values* (1985).

While there appears to be widespread agreement that public schools should be judged on the basis of how well they succeed in educating students, the statewide reforms of the 1980s have given rise to two types of criticisms. First, many commentators and policymakers have challenged the empirical validity of the assumptions and conclusions of the effective schools and excellence movements. Second, the efficacy of top-down, hierarchical rules has been questioned, with many urging that restructuring or even deregulation of education at the district, school, and class levels is required for meaningful reform. The next section focuses on these criticisms and suggestions. That section is followed by a section on the resurgence of legislative efforts to decentralize authority within local school districts and to promote community control of schools. The underlying theme throughout is the relationship among governance structures, law, and educational quality.

A. State Regulation and the Quest for Excellence

"Educational Reform and Institutional Competence"

T. Timar & D. Kirp, 57 *Harv. Educ. Rev.* 308, 309–24, 328 (1987).

Since 1983, more rules and regulations about all aspects of education have been generated by the states than in the previous twenty years. Over 700 statutes affecting some aspect of the teaching profession alone have been enacted nationally over the last two years. The school reform movement has resulted in a whole new body of rules governing the behavior of teachers, students, and administrators. For students, there are rules about participation in sports and other extracurricular activities, about how much and what kind of homework must be done, and about how many times they may miss school before failing their courses. Students are also subject to rules about what kinds of courses they must take, how much time to devote to each subject each day, and what topics each class must cover. For teachers, there are rules regarding placement on career ladders and eligibility for merit pay. For local school trustees, there are rules requiring their participation in training programs. In some states, the law now prescribes how often daily announcements may be made over the school intercom system. There are even rules that permit state officials to place schools deemed unsatisfactory into receivership and to fire school administrators and, presumably, trustees.

Regulation of schooling is not a recent phenomenon. Schools have long been subject to a variety of state controls, such as those specifying teacher tenure and certification, collective bargaining, basic curriculum, and number of days taught. But, historically, such regulations tended to leave a great deal of discretion regarding the governance of schools to local officials. Thus the recent state reforms to promote excellence tend to be highly prescriptive, leaving few areas of school policy untouched.

* * *

The tension between increased state regulation and the need to maintain local flexibility poses a fundamental dilemma in the effort to encourage excellence in the schools. It is a problem rooted in the nature of excellence itself. Excellence cannot be coerced or mandated. Rather, it is a condition to which individuals may aspire. Aspirations to excellence generally arise from subtle and pervasive qualities: a love of learning, a sense of history, a command of analytical skills, an appreciation of humanistic values, and the like. For teachers and adminstrators, excellence means caring about students; being sympathetic to the needs of students with diverse educational and, often, personal problems; demonstrating a commitment to learning. It also includes a host of other attitudes, such as excitement about one's subject matter and a commitment to the domain of the intellect. This commitment entails a dedication to a way of life that is rooted in a historical tradition of cultural enlightment.

Thus, aspirations to excellence cannot be achieved by regulation. Rules simply cannot compel teachers to be more caring toward students or require that administrators be fair. Such regulations would clearly be unenforceable and would probably violate due process norms as well. Consequently, reformers tend to focus on that which can be measured, quantified, and, therefore, enforced. Regulations, such as those concerning the length of the school day, participation in sports, curriculum, and teacher promotion and evaluation, become rough proxies for excellence. The danger is that, as Schrag has noted, it becomes very easy to "systematically confuse rigor with 'basics,' success with test scores, standards with hours spent in the classroom or doing homework. None of that would necessarily be objectionable if it were understood that there is a real difference between kinds of homework, that makework is self-defeating, and that longer classroom exposure to a teacher contemptuous of literature or history or mathematics is worse than no exposure."

* * *

Stripped to its essence, the goal of the current educational reform is to change the behavior of individuals and institutions so that they conform to the goals of the excellence agenda. If one accepts the assumption that those who staff the nation's schools are to blame for the present condition of the nation's educational system, transforming mediocrity into excellence means altering the interaction between student and teacher. If students are inattentive, uninterested, and unmotivated by school, they must be made attentive, interested, and motivated. And if teachers are operating under the well-known institutional ethic of "doing just enough to get by," excellence would demand adoption of a new work ethic consonant with much higher standards. Such a view underestimates the complexity of the problem of educational mediocrity and overestimates the capacity of policymakers to solve it. As psychologists, parole officers, social workers, doctors, and others who work with people eventually discover, behavior is not easily manipulated. Public policymakers have been forced to confront the often unhappy truth that when the successful implementation of policy depends upon changing behavior, failure can often be anticipated.

Altering institutional behavior may prove to be even harder than changing individual behavior. Schools in the United States are highly durable organizations: they have been able to respond to and accommodate almost any change or any demand that has been made of them. School reform movements have occurred about every decade, without altering schools fundamentally. If accommodation is the practiced and well-learned response to demands for change, why should the latest round of reforms prompt a different response?

* * *

. . . The overriding question is whether reform policies yield outcomes consistent with standards of excellence, or instead take on an independent life, disconnected from the policy ends they are intended to serve. Do reforms achieve their intended results by changing individual and institutional behavior, or do reforms simply engender bureaucratization and legalization?

* * *

The literature on effective schools identifies the organizational attributes that make schools effective. The meaning of institutional effectiveness is best captured by the term "ethos," which describes a general condition of life in the schools. Researchers can point to characteristics that are found in effective schools, but they cannot produce a blueprint that shows practitioners how to reproduce those conditions on a large scale.[12]

Excellence is a difficult product for educational policymakers to deliver. High academic standards may require some individuals—students, teachers, parents, administrators—to change their attitudes about schooling. One of the underlying assumptions, for example, is that students can be made to value education intrinsically. An appreciation of education for its own sake, it is thought, can be fostered with some clever policy engineering. Making class periods longer, requiring more school days each year, promoting enrollment in academic courses, creating a curriculum that emphasizes basics, and curtailing students' extracurricular activities are generally thought to be ways of redressing mediocrity.

Many policymakers, however, overlook the fact that students go to school for a variety of reasons. Some are there because they want to go on to college and have careers, others because their friends are there. Still others attend because they like art or shop classes or enjoy extracurricular activities. And then there are those who attend simply because a state law requires them to. For high school students, in particular, school may be competing with other interests—and losing out. . . .

Another dimension of reform, improving the teaching profession, also relies in good measure on strategies to alter entrenched patterns of behavior that lie beyond the bounds of policy manipulation. Incentive-based pay schemes, for example, may have marginal effects, and competency tests may elimi-

12. Larry Cuban, "Transforming the Frog into a Prince: Effective Schools Research, Policy, and Practice at the District Level," 54 *Harvard Educational Review*, 131–32 (1974).

14. Cuban, "Transforming the Frog," pp. 131–32; *see also* Cuban's "School Reform by Remote Control: SB 813 in California," 66 *Phi Delta Kappan*, 213–15 (1984).

nate the bottom 10 percent of teachers—those who cannot read, write, or compute—but those strategies cannot turn "a frog into a prince."[14] Raising the salaries of beginning teachers to $18,000 and raising average annual salaries to $24,000 may encourage highly motivated and intelligent individuals to enter the teaching profession and to stay there. But are higher salaries enough? How well do such salary incentives compete with working conditions in attracting and retaining teachers? Consider the working environment in some urban schools where plaster falls from the ceiling, "street people" and irate parents roam the halls, old *Readers Digests* are the closest and only approximations to textbooks, where there are consistently no toilet paper, towels, or soap in the teachers' restrooms, where midterm exams have to be canceled for lack of paper, and teachers face threats of transfer and layoff throughout the school year.* Those schools that face the most adversity need committed and qualified teachers most, but they are also the least likely to get them. It is doubtful that pay incentives to both currently employed and prospective teachers can outweigh the adverse working conditions in many schools.

* * *

A wide range of behaviors, attitudes, and incentives lies beyond the purview of state policy. The effects of schooling are mitigated by various factors. As education researchers have found, poor children who come from what are euphemistically called "disadvantaged homes"—a sanitized policy term that masks the hardship and poverty of life in the inner city—and who live in slum neighborhoods with all their usual attributes, will find it more difficult to benefit from the current excellence reform efforts than their counterparts who live in affluent suburban environments. Although they may be quite interested in their children's education, many parents with children in inner-city schools often lack the time and resources that more affluent parents possess to devote to their children's educational success. In short, the excellence movement may strike a responsive chord in the parents of inner-city school children but it may prove to be ephemeral as a plan of action. Some schools clearly are more successful than others in teaching poor inner-city children, but it is not easy to create educational policy from a handful of success stories. Government lacks resources to change people's life styles, health habits, and associations. . . .

* * *

A common strategy used by organizations when they cannot meet objectives is simply to substitute objectives they attain. As theorists explain, "Because organizations wish to be regarded as successful, they try to replace objectives whose achievement depends on variables either unknown or outside their control with objectives that can be attained by manipulating the instruments that those groups do control."[30] Rather than changing the conditions that gave rise to reform initially—specific reform policies and strategies themselves are transformed into goals. Policy means become policy ends. They assume a life of their own, independent of the purpose they were intended to serve. Other manifestations of organizational retreat from unattainable objectives include the displacement of external objectives with internal procedures. For example, outputs are often equalized or standardized to ensure that outcomes are measured by organizational effort rather than effect on clients. On the simplest level, this means substituting quantity measures for quality.

Reforms aimed at improving student performance offer a good illustration of shifting objectives to fit goals that organizations can, in fact, achieve. In California, for example, all public school systems are required to submit to the State Department of Education an annual "Performance Report for California Schools: Indicators of Quality." This report is based on various measures of student performance, which are then compared to state "targets." Its intent is to hold districts accountable for student progress toward excellence. According to the document's introduction, the school report will provide evidence of success in meeting the main objectives of school reform: improving the learning atmosphere and improving student performance. The "quality indicators" used to measure excellence focus on the types and numbers of courses taken in high school; student scores on the California Assessment Program (CAP) and the Scholastic Aptitude Test; the number of students taking and passing the Advanced Placement Test; student dropout rates; and the number

* *See* S. Johnson, *Teachers at Work* (1990).

30. Wildavsky, *Speaking Truth to Power*, p. 49; *see also* Robert K. Merton, *Social Theory and Social Structure* (New York: Free Press, 1957)

of weekly homework and writing assignments students complete. Additionally, each district must report the number of minutes devoted to particular subjects in elementary school and the number of minutes students spend in school annually. Even if nothing else happens in California, a lot of paper passes from the over 1,000 districts to the State Department of Education. Some observers have suggested that educators will spend more time reporting various measures of reform than finding ways to make schools more effective.

California's performance indicators represent a happy compromise between state-level policymakers, who need to justify a $3 billion increase in state educational expenditures over three years by demonstrating the success of state reform policies, and local school personnel, who know better than to make promises that they cannot keep. Schools cannot deliver what they do not control. And since they lack control over the most important factors influencing educational outcomes, they focus instead on what they can control. This means numbers. Four years after state reform was enacted, state officials can report that in 1982 high school students spent, on average, 57,728 minutes in school annually, and that by 1986 the average had increased to 64,800. That increase computes to about five or six minutes more per class each day, based on six classes daily, 180 days annually. Other reports indicate how many students take academic courses and how many weekly homework and written assignments they complete. At the present rate of reform, California will soon be awash in numbers.

Numbers are also important, for example, in assessing the success of Tennessee's career-ladder program. According to Tennessee Governor Lamar Alexander, that state's career-ladder program for teachers is a resounding success. But Alexander has only numbers to define success. His conclusion is based upon the fact that state evaluators recommended more than 600 teachers for advancement up the teaching ladder. In all, 40 percent of teachers and administrators who applied for the upper levels of the career ladder completed the requirements "on their first try," and some 400 others "came so close" that most of them would surely complete the requirements. In addition, "thirty-nine thousand teachers and administrators—90 percent of those eligible—earned a step on the Career Ladder in the first year: 15,000 of them took standardized tests, 20,000 of them trained in 40 overtime hours of staff development, and the rest submitted to a state-approved local evaluation. These figures have little significance beyond themselves. The Tennessee program asks us to assume—for there are no data—that those 15,000 teachers who took a standardized test to advance to the first rung of the career ladder are better teachers for having done so. That is the conclusion that Governor Alexander seems to suggest.

Incentive-based pay plans offer another illustration of shifting objectives and criteria to meet goals an organization can achieve. One of the principal difficulties with incentive-based pay plans, however, is that they are theoretically weak, for there is no reliable connection between teacher quality and student achievement. Devising defensible and generally acceptable criteria for meritorious teaching has so far eluded policymakers. Consequently, efforts to impose statewide evaluation criteria for what is only vaguely known promise to be problematic at best. Instead, the focus shifts away from meritorious teaching toward the justification of merit increases.

* * *

Another strategy for shifting from unattainable to attainable objectives is to "metamorphosize" clients. If policy objectives cannot be achieved with one set of clients, another set may fit policy needs better. This strategy has taken various forms in California. While "teaching to the test" is a time-honored tradition in schools, testing for student achievement is a frustrating and vexing enterprise. Students do not always cooperate by attaining the high scores that school officials would like. If students cannot be made to get higher test scores, however, there is nothing to stop schools from testing only those students who show promise of achieving high scores. That is why California's "Cash for CAPs" program, which provides $15 million annually to districts in which scores on the California Assessment Program (CAP) increase for twelfth graders, insists that at least 93 percent of the school's twelfth graders must take the test. This proviso was added only after state officials discovered that some districts were only testing those students most likely to do well.

In the first year of the CAP program, across-the-board scores for seniors increased, but that increase was accompanied by a record drop in numbers of students elibigle to take the test. State officials, however, attributed the high scores to "the movement to reform and excellence." A more convincing explanation for increased test scores—one which may explain the disappearance of 15,000 students—is that schools simply redefined who is a twelfth grader for purposes of testing. Generally, students are assigned to grade level chronologically: a student is classified as a freshman in the first year, a sophomore in the second, and so on. For purposes of testing, however, schools designated as twelfth graders those students who had accumulated sufficient units to graduate in the current year. By redefining students, districts not only decreased the size of the pool from which to draw students, but effectively eliminated those students who had completed three years of school but who had not completed a sufficient number of units to graduate at the end of four years—in all likelihood the school's lowest achievers.

* * *

Policy solutions to complex problems sometimes overshadow the problems they were intended to solve. The very size and complexity of the educational sector, its interdependent relationship with other policy sectors, the multiplicity of motives that animate organizational and individual behavior, and competing incentives and priorities all make it difficult to predict outcomes precisely. Consequently, efforts to ameliorate one problem may create new ones or exacerbate existing ones. The result is that policies often work at cross-purposes to one another.

* * *

Many educators fear that another unintended result of new regulations will be an increase in the dropout rate among students. No one seems to know quite what to do with the large numbers of students who already leave school without graduating. The national dropout rate is about 20 percent. In California, the rate is estimated at close to 30 percent, and is even higher among ethnic minorities. Reducing the dropout rate is an explicit policy goal in a number of states, California among them. Yet no one knows how increasing the number of academically rigorous courses that students must take to graduate will affect the dropout rate.

* * *

The tension between excellence and equity is well illustrated by efforts in states to implement major changes in the standards that govern the teaching profession. State-mandated incentive-based pay schemes such as career-ladder, merit-pay, or master-teacher programs are vulnerable to legal challenge on various grounds. The challenge may focus on the basis for selection: What are the criteria for bonus pay? What are the evaluation standards for receiving additional pay? In Florida, the state affiliates of both the National Education Association and the American Federation of Teachers sued the state's Associate Master Teacher Program as well as the School District Quality Instruction Incentives Program. The merit-pay program paid a $3000-per-year bonus to teachers who qualified. The merit-schools program gave money to those schools in which students excelled on certain tests and on other standards developed under the plan. The suit charged that the merit-pay program cannot be implemented in a nondiscriminatory fashion because of inequities in the law and the way applications were processed by the state department of education. The teachers' lawyers argued that denying special-education teachers, art teachers, teachers of several foreign languages, and counselors an opportunity to qualify as "meritorious" was discriminatory.

* * *

The fact that there is no stable, quantifiable relationship between teacher quality and student achievement, and no legally defensible criterion for meritorious teaching, makes litigation increasingly likely. That is why the objectivity and validity of standards for merit pay are subject to challenge. While Florida requires a teacher to score in the upper quartile of a subject-matter test (or to have a master's degree if no test is available) and to present one classroom observation as a qualifying condition for merit pay, there is no demonstrable connection between those requirements and teaching quality.

* * *

Reforms will fail if they do not prompt schools to forge for themselves an organizational identity. As long as teachers think of themselves as bureaucrats, and if they simply put in their hours with no thought or definition of what it is they are trying to achieve, schools will not change. Teachers who aspire to excellence in themselves and their students regard teaching as their principal activity. The role of police officer or social worker or friend, although part of the job, is secondary to teaching. Schools need an organizational focus; teachers, parents, and administrators must decide on that focus and define it in the daily life of the school. This cannot be done through directives and regulations from state legislatures and centralized bureaucracies. It can only be done in the schools, by school personnel who can create the kinds of organizations that can engender a vision of what education is and ought to be. Since fragmentation is one of the features of schools, it follows that hierarchically imposed regulations, no matter how well intentioned, exacerbate that fragmentation.

* * *

"The Politics of School Restructuring"

T. Timar, 1989 *Politics of Education Association Yearbook* 55, 55–60, 71–72. Reprinted by permission.

A current of the educational reform movement that is attracting increased policy attention is school 're-structuring.' Theodore Sizer's Coalition of Essential Schools and the 'Carnegie Plan', which began as a loose confederation of schools, are moving onto legislative policy agendas. Various states, including Massachusetts, Arkansas, and Washington, as well as school districts such as Dade County, Florida, Rochester, New York, and Santa Fe, New Mexico, have adopted some form of school restructuring as major components of reform. On a national level, the Education Commission of the States, the National Governors' Association, the American Federation of Teachers and the National Education Association are promoting some form of school restructuring among their members. . . .

* * *

Bureaucratic decentralization, which is at the heart of restructuring—whether in the form of school site management, 'choice', or some variation on privatization—swims against a thirty-year current of educational policy reform that relied on centralization and regulation to achieve specific policy goals. Indeed, many state-level school reform strategies adopted since 1983 perpetuate and elaborate the regulatory orientation to school improvement. Teacher and student testing; adoption of state-wide curriculum standards and state-mandated homework, class size, and teacher salary policies are among the most obvious efforts to tighten the reins of local decision makers. Consequently, understanding where the Sizer Coalition and kindred efforts fit into this policy stream is an important issue for school reformers.

* * *

As a school reform strategy, restructuring has its roots in various sources. In large measure, it repudiates central elements in the reform movement of the early 1980s. Without challenging the importance of recent state-initiated reforms, restructuring advocates have reacted to the heavy hand used to effect them. The unprecedented flood of state policies that swept schools in the 1980s aimed at changing them through mandates and regulations. . . .* Critics of these state reform efforts argue that schools as institutions, not students, teachers or curricula must be the target of reform. Tightening curriculum standards, changing teacher certification requirements, or extending the school year, for example, will have negligible effects if schools lack the organizational will and competence to implement them. Furthermore, piecemeal reform policies do not necessarily change the fundamental relationship between teaching and learning. Fundamentally, the critics insist, high quality education is the product of *robust organizational cultures*, not disparate programs. Instead of improving them, state reform strategies relying on regulations and mandates for new programs tended to overwhelm schools with additional baggage or mire them in a regulatory swamp. . . . Historians, like Diane Ravitch, argue that school reform trends and policies of the 1960s and 1970s had—in spite of their social necessity—seriously undermined the institutional competence of schools. . . .**

A further impediment to centralized school reform is the fact that state-level policymakers have a limited repertoire of policy options from which to draw. They can manage macro-policy—funding, teacher certification, textbook adoption, curriculum standards and equity and the like—but have limited control over daily school operations. State policy cannot change what it cannot control. The fact that the most significant locus of educational interaction—student/teacher nexus—is largely embedded

* See T. Timar and D. Kirp, *Managing Educational Excellence* (1988).

** D. Ravitch, *The Troubled Crusade* (1985).

within the interstices of institutional life poses a fundamental dilemma for state-level policy makers.

Criticism of the first wave of state reform drew its power from the Effective Schools literature . . . and from several critical works on the American High School. . . .** These lines of research were largely ignored by policymakers in their initial haste to reform schools. Effective Schools studies underscored the importance of organizational culture and its attendant manifestations. Teacher collegiality, shared decision-making, common goals and clear priorities were essential to forging the disparate experiences and expectations of teachers, administrators, students and parents into coherent organizational cultures. Broader high school studies, e.g., *A Place Called School* . . ., *Horace's Compromise* . . . and *The Shopping Mall High School* . . ., pointed to normative models for school improvement. But they also showed how far short most schools fell of those models. Reality consisted of schools that were characterized by a rampant lack of direction; intellectual incoherence, blandness and sterility; diffuse authority and accountability; and bureaucratic calcification. Even in schools that appeared to work well, a complex set of treaties between teachers and students tend to circumvent intellectual give-and-take and replace genuine efforts to shape the minds and souls of students.

Nationally, various reform reports, including *A Nation Prepared* from the Carnegie Forum on Education and the Economy (1986), *Time for Results* from the National Governors' Association (1986), and *Investing in Our Children* from the Committee for Economic Development (1985), called for fundamental changes in school structure and organization. The Carnegie Forum responded to the perceived need to attract and retain highly qualified individuals to the teaching profession by encouraging schools to develop innovative organization and management systems aimed at giving teachers greater control over their work environment. The Carnegie Forum underscores the need for restructuring by calling for management systems that provide autonomy and discretion at the school site level and encourage innovative organizational strategies to enhance student learning. . . .

. . . While restructuring is a commonly proposed strategy to fix what ails the schools, intentions differ. Kearns' notion of restructuring is anchored in organizational efficiency. The Carnegie Forum and Albert Shanker regard restructuring as the means to empower teachers and thereby improving school effectiveness. Sizer aims to change the fundamental interaction between teacher and child not only in terms of how teaching occurs, but also in terms of what is taught, changing the whole character and mission of the schools. At the heart of Sizer's call for change is the need to examine the cultural norms and ideas that inform school structure. Structural changes are secondary to the ideas that inform them. . . .

The Coalition of Essential Schools is anchored in a set of common principles that aim to reverse the bureaucratic engine responsible for the incoherence and organizational rigidity of public schools. The Coalition's principles focus attention on some common features of schooling: the school's purpose is to help students use their minds well; learning should focus on student mastery of a limited number of skills and areas of knowledge; the academic and social goals of the school should apply to all students; teaching and learning should be personalized; the student is a worker and the teacher is a coach; diplomas should be awarded on the basis of demonstrated competence, not seat time; the school's norms should emphasize trust, decency, and unanxious expectation; faculties should view themselves as generalists, not specialists; and the budget should permit pupil–teacher ratios of no more than 1:80, while allowing staff salaries to become competitive and total school expenditures not to increase by more than 10%. . . .

Other school reformers, like Goodlad, advocate restructuring as a way of improving working conditions for teachers by encouraging greater professional discretion, providing teachers with opportunities to define and administer school policy through school site management—the devolution of greater authority over curriculum, instructional strategies, and resource allocation to the school level. . . .*

One useful conceptual framework for understanding the bureaucratic organization of schools is Aaron

** *See* A. Powell, E. Farrar, and D. Cohen, *The Shopping Mall High School* (1985); J. Goodlad, *A Place Called School* (1984); T. Sizer, *Horace's Compromise* (1984).

* Hawley, "Missing Pieces of the Educational Reform Agenda: Or, Why the First and Second Waves May Miss the Boat," 24 *Educ. Admin. Q.* 416 (1988). *See also* Metz, "Some Missing Elements in the School Reform Movement," 24 *Educ. Admin. Q.* 446 (1988).

Wildavsky and Mary Douglas' . . . models of four cultures.* Within that framework, contemporary schools can be described as hierarchical cultures which are 'strong groups with numerous prescriptions that vary with social roles.' The hierarchical culture of schools is clearly evident by the high degree of role differentiation and specialization within them. The duties and responsibilities of principals, assistant principals, counselors, school psychologists and teachers are functionally differentiated; and teachers, particularly in high schools, rarely have contact with one another outside of their immediate areas or departments. Students, curriculum and instruction are similarly sorted and differentiated according to bureaucratic norms, which define the school's order. Students, teachers and administrators are passive subjects whose professional judgment is often subordinated for the sake of bureaucratic convenience.

Clearly, bureaucratic cultures are organizationally incompatible with schools based on the Coalition principles which subordinate bureaucratic norms to organizational competence. The institutional culture consonant with the goals of the Coalition is Wildavsky's competitive-individualist model. The social ideal of individualistic cultures is described as 'self-regulation'. Such cultures 'favor bidding and bargaining to reduce the need for authority'. The long term effect of such a culture is to build into the organization a dynamic of change—the expectation that the organization will modify itself to respond flexibly to new problems and new demands. For schools, this means that organizational needs are subordinate to the intellectual and spiritual development of students. It is based upon a system of institutional ordering that places its own competence as its highest priority.

By contrast, hierarchical cultures measure themselves by activities and focus on service delivery. Such cultures measure their success quantitatively. For schools, such measures include the number of hours spent in class, the number of credits completed, and the like. Furthermore, considerable organizational energy is spent on the care and feeding of status and role differentiation. Teachers, administrators, counselors, and coaches, for example, spend a good deal of time protecting their turf. Departments within schools similarly guard against encroachment on their areas of expertise.

An organizational metaphor of competitive-individualism is a baseball team. In order to win games and to be competitive against other teams, a team's manager puts together what he believes will be a winning combination of players; and the manager is free to substitute players throughout the game. While players are assigned functional roles, the manager is free to assign players to those roles as situations warrant. He can choose among pitchers, pinch-hitters, utility outfielders, and relief pitchers, as the need arises. During the game, players cover each other's positions as necessary. Playing (and ultimately winning and losing) is a shared responsibility. Everyone has to hit; sometimes the pitcher has to cover first base or home plate. A baseball team exemplifies a dynamic organizational culture which reconfigures itself to be competitive in new situations. Finally, whether a team has a winning or losing season does not depend upon any one player, but the team as a whole. Individual performance is important; but so is a team's 'chemistry'. The manager has much to do with that chemistry. He has to train rookies and keep veterans from becoming burned out.

In contrast to a baseball team, bureaucratic schools resemble factories. As in factories, jobs are differentiated and rigidly defined. Production line workers, supervisors, quality control engineers, and the like have separate duties and responsibilities that are clearly specified. Accountability is based on performance of the specified tasks. The person who puts wheels on cars in an automobile assembly line, for example, is not responsible for the installation of the seats. Once a person becomes a foreman, he no longer works on the production line. Once a teacher becomes a principal, she no longer teaches. The point is not to suggest that schools are strict analogues of baseball teams or factories, but to illustrate the polar extremes of two organizational models. Today's schools are more accustomed to norms that evoke factory rather than baseball images.

Creating an organizational model of competitive-individualism is complicated by the fact that schools must change not only their own micro-cultures, but also district and state policy—the macro-culture in

* A. Wildavsky, "Choosing Preferences by Constructing Institutions: A Cultural Theory of Preference Formation," 81 *Amer. Pol. Sci. Rev.* 3 (1987).

which they are embedded. Schools are parts of complex district bureaucracies. A district's organization, like the school's, is hierarchical, with rigidly assigned roles, responsibilities, and accountability. Personnel and budgetary decisions, two critical elements of organizational autonomy, are generally made at the district level. The start and end of the school day are also decided by the district, especially when bus schedules are a factor. And, with the advent of district-wide collective bargaining, schools must live with contractual provisions entered into by district negotiators.

* * *

There is increasing evidence that schools are products of state and district political cultures. . . . An atomized state policy and political culture will reproduce similar policy cultures at local levels. Hence, the integrated response to restructuring at the school level is unlikely to occur in politically balkanized and programmatically fragmented districts and states. Since a school's political culture is derivative, it cannot create coherence in an environment where there is none.

* * *

Contemporary issues of school governance are further complicated by present patterns of control. The emergence of policy spheres and issue politics over the past 20 years signals new configurations of power and control. The delineation of control along political and jurisdictional lines is incomplete. Competing centers of power have stalemated one another. In urban districts, for example, neither the union nor the board controls schools. Instead, groups compete over issues. Unions generally want to control issues like staff development, merit pay, and career ladders. Administrators want to control finance, resource allocation, and personnel decisions. Other groups control special education issues; yet others bilingual, compensatory education, or gifted and talented. Schools, like the fragmented world of public management in the United States generally, have become more balkanized over the past two decades. While state legislative power has grown, it has also become more widely dispersed. Interest groups, particularly single-interest groups, have proliferated while formal patterns of authority have waned. The 'iron triangles' of educational politics—schools of education, state education departments, and affiliates of the National Education Association—that prevailed until the mid-1960s have given way to more porous systems. Finding the center of control over schools in order to create a more hospitable policy environment for restructuring is like 'nailing Jello to a wall'.

Furthermore, the evidence is not systematic, the state policy trend of the early 1980s toward increased regulation and compliance does not appear to be shifting. States continue to embrace student testing, school accreditation, and teacher certification requirements in efforts to regulate and control schools. . . .

This conclusion does not augur well for states that have the Carnegie model (or some variation of it) to encourage school restructuring or for the Coalition of Essential Schools. As more and more decisions formerly left to local discretion become embodied in state policy, the potential for policy proliferation and fragmentation increases. With few exceptions, states have responded to political pressure by 'giving a little something to everybody'. While such a strategy may have political benefits, it is doubtful whether it can produce good policy. The same factions that contend over policies at the state level have the power to reproduce fractious conflicts at the local level. Consequently, programmatic and procedural responses to restructuring efforts are inevitable.

* * *

Over the past 50 years, the response of schools to external demands has been to multiply programs and regulations. The absence of a broad consensus about the purpose of schooling has created a patchwork of programs to meet various, and often competing, demands. The major threat to restructuring is that it succumbs to that trend. Restructuring must fundamentally alter the way schools do business. That will not happen if it becomes another piece of baggage that schools drag around with them.

* * *

The metaphor of the school as a baseball team evokes an organizational ethos of community of *Gemeinschaft*. It is based on its capacity to achieve unanimity in its goals. Whether its orientation is to produce a winning season or to produce a crop of students who have mastered a set of fundamental skills, its focus of action is organizational competence. Whether restructuring, in its various manifestations, takes root as an effective reform strategy depends on the willingness and capacity of schools to reassess their mission and their strategies for carrying it out. If restructuring is limited to an accumulation of new programs and practices, reform is unlikely. Instead, restructuring will be an exercise in renegotiating existing treaties.

NOTES AND QUESTIONS

1. Identifying the Culprit

What were the causes of the increase in state regulation of public schools in the 1980s? Were the various national reports on the need to achieve excellence in education a part of the problem or of the solution? Do Timar and Doyle and Finn agree on this point? Do they overestimate the impact of research on policy?

Is reliance on hierarchical regulation in education simply another manifestation of the preoccupation of Americans with rules and law? A part of the political culture? Is detailed regulation a sign of public distrust of education professionals? An effort to address a perceived loss of mission and community in public schools? Does regulation make the problem better or worse? *See generally* D. Kirp and D. Jensen, *School Days, Rule Days* (1986); A. Wise, *Legislated Learning* (1979); Yudof, "Legalization of Dispute Resolution, Distrust of Authority, and Organizational Theory: Implementing Due Process for Students in Public Schools," 1981 *Wisc. L. Rev.* 891.

2. Schools as Factories

Do you agree with Timar's observation that schools are modeled on the organization of factories? Is he saying that organizational structures that work well for business enterprises do not work well for public education? *See generally* M. Katz, *Class, Bureaucracy and Schools* (1975); D. Tyack, *The One Best System* (1974); R. Callahan, *Education and the Cult of Efficiency* (1962). Is his point consistent with the premises of the proponents of vouchers? Irrelevant to their premises? What of the criticisms in recent years of American industrial organizations, criticisms that, drawing on the modern economic successes of Japan, suggest that decentralization and cooperation are vital to increase American industrial productivity? Is the factory model itself changing?

3. Bureaucratic Decentralization and Learning Environments

Does bureaucratic decentralization mean the same thing as establishing a community of *Gemeinschaft* in each school? May authority be decentralized, while leaving the learning environment untouched?

What is the empirical basis for the suggestions for reform set forth by those who wish to improve the learning environment? Are their points any more substantiated than those of the proponents of statewide regulation? Are they describing causal relationships or simply describing an ideal educational community? Do their suggestions lend themselves to implementation by government? Or is their point that government cannot legislate learning? Do the critics of regulation return policy-making to the pessimism of the 1960s, the recognition that precious little is known about the relationship between inputs and outputs in the educational process?

4. Competency Testing

For a discussion of the competency testing movement, *see* Catterall, "Standards and School Dropouts: A National Study of Tests Required for High School Graduation," 98 *Amer. J. of Educ.* 1 (1989); Rebell, "Disparity Impact of Teacher Competency on Minorities: Don't Blame the Test-Takers—or the Tests," 4 *Yale Law & Pol. Rev.* 375 (1986); McClung, "Competency Testing Programs: Legal and Educational Issues," 47 *Fordham L. Rev.* 651 (1979); Haney and Madaus, "Making Sense of the Competency Testing Movement," 48 *Harv. Educ. Rev.* 462 (1978).

B. Bureaucratic Decentralization and Community Control

In the late 1960s a movement emerged to attack the bureaucratization of public schooling through structural changes that would foster decentralization and community control. While there were many variations, the basic idea was to subdivide large urban districts into smaller districts, with lay community-based school boards that possessed the authority to make personnel, budgetary, and other decisions. This movement was quite controversial and often resisted by school teachers and administrators. The most famous controversy centered on the experimental community-controlled districts in Brooklyn and

Harlem in New York City funded by the Ford Foundation. The New York schools had been widely criticized for their bureaucratic red tape, inertia, and inefficiency. *See generally* D. Rogers, *110 Livingston Street* (1968). Ultimately the New York City schools were decentralized. *See* F. Wirt and M. Kirst, *Political and Social Foundations of Education* 87–92 (1975); M. Zimet, *Decentralization and School Effectiveness* (1973); M. Fantini, M. Gittell, and R. Magat, *Community Control and the Urban School* (1970); H. Levin, ed., *Community Control of Schools* (1970); M. Berube and M. Gittell, *Confrontation at Ocean Hill-Brownsville* (1969).

For more than fifteen years after the adoption of community control in New York City, little attention was paid to the question by policymakers—albeit some scholars continued to advance such proposals. *See, e.g.*, S. Lightfoot, *Worlds Apart: Relationships Between Families and Schools* (1978); Bell, "Book Review," 92 *Harv. L. Rev.* 1826 (1979); Bell, "Waiting on the Promise of *Brown*," 39 *Law & Contemp. Probs.* 341 (1978). Others voiced concern about the efficacy of community control in rendering school boards and professionals more accountable. *See, e.g.*, Fainstein and Fainstein, "The Future of Community Control," 70 *Am. Pol. Sci. Rev.* 905 (1976); Cohen, "The Price of Community Control," 48 *Commentary* 23 (July 1969). In the late 1980s, however, community control appeared on the agenda in a number of large cities including Los Angeles and Chicago.

"A Case Study of the Recent Chicago School Reform"

K. Wong and S. Rollow, "A Case Study of the Recent Chicago School Reform," (pts. 1 & 2) 34 *Administrator's Notebook* 5, 6 (1990). Reprinted by permission.

[Part I]

Chicago School Reform legislation was signed into law in July, 1988. The preceding two years' citywide effort to mobilize support for educational reform and to craft a legislative package produced a unique set of understandings and a strategy for school improvement. It revised the existing school code by giving parents substantial control over funds and personnel at the school building. The reform also strengthened the oversight authority over the Chicago Public Schools (CPS). Clearly, the Chicago case has important ramifications, both for education here, and for urban education in general.

* * *

The Urban School Improvement Act and the School Finance Authority Act are the legislative background for Chicago's recent school reform. The first was enacted in September, 1985, following an earlier teacher's strike. It was intended as a mechanism for the decentralization of the CPS and to promote increased professionalization of teachers. The second, by contrast, came as a response to the financial bankruptcy of the system which occurred in 1979. Its intent was to create mechanisms that would "assure the financial integrity" of the system. Consequently, one benchmark from which to measure the 1988 efforts toward governance reform are these existing codes. . . .

An Advisory Role for Parents. Parents held largely symbolic powers within the framework of the Urban School Improvement Act. First, at the local school level, they could be members of the Local School Improvement Councils (LSICs) which were authorized to develop a three-year School Improvement Plan (SIP). But according to the way the 1985 legislation was written, LSICs were not at liberty to set the programmatic agenda for their schools. Second, at each of the city's 20 subdistricts, parents were to comprise 70% of the Subdistrict Education Advisory Council membership. These councils were advisory in nature, and there is no evidence to suggest their effectiveness. Indications that they were not a success, however, include the tone of the criticism that was leveled at them in the public forums in 1987, and their restructuring in the recent school reform where they gained substantive powers. Finally, at the top of the system, the membership of the Urban School Improvement Committee intended to "ensure parity" between school personnel on the one hand, and parents and community representatives on the other. Again, this committee was merely advisory to the Board. In the 1988 reform, its functions were taken over by the BOE and the SFA, and the powers of each of these boards were expanded in an effort to assure greater compliance.

* * *

Broadening the Principals' Powers. The 1985 legislation granted additional powers to principals. They assumed primary responsibility for the development and implementation of the SIP. In addition, principals were to be active, regular participants in any staff development planning process. By extending new arenas of powers, these provisions established the principals' authority as instructional leaders.

The "Top of the System". The "top of the system" includes the BOE, the General Superintendent, the Central Administration, and the Chicago Teachers Union. The intent of the Urban School Improvement Act was to shift decision-making away from this level of the CPS and to put it in a position of support to the local schools. This was accomplished by empowering actors at the school level to write and implement school improvement and staff development plans. . . .

The External Oversight Authority. The financially troubled CPS has been monitored by an external oversight authority. The School Finance Authority (SFA) was created in January, 1980 to "assure the financial integrity of the public schools" to the general public and the bonding agencies following the system's financial collapse the previous year. Specifically, the SFA was to "establish procedures, provide powers and impose restrictions . . . to exercise financial control . . . and to furnish financial assistance . . . while leaving principal responsibility for the educational policies of the public schools to the BOE." Thus, the SFA was set up with a singular purpose: to be the guardian of the system's finances, while all educational issues were left to the BOE. Unlike the BOE, the mayor appointed 4 of the 7-member SFA. The Governor appointed three of its members. These appointive powers became a major controversy in the 1988 reform process at the state level.

In the several years prior to the 1988 reform, the CPS was slowly moving toward school restructuring. Limited efforts were made to shift powers from the top of the system to the school building level. The existing school code seemed to have strengthened professional control at school sites, while parents were given largely symbolic representation. To be sure, tenure for principals and teachers remained unchallenged and the central administration's authority seemed secure. The pace of reform, however, was accelerated during 1987 and 1988. To understand such a sweeping restructuring of powers in the CPS in 1988, one needs to look at the politics that shaped the reform process.

* * *

The Education Summit Agreements was the reform proposal that developed from the mobilization process. It was strongly influenced by two visions of school improvement: the populist sentiment for more parental control voiced at the community-wide forums; and the effective schools approach that would pattern schools after efficient business organizations and install a strong principal to manage them. The co-existence of these competing visions in the Summit Agreements seemed rooted in the ways diverse interests were brought into the 2-year mobilization process. While the Summit process was originally designed to forge a school-business partnership, it gradually turned into a mechanism to build a broad community-based coalition for school reform. It was this citywide coalition, which cut across class and racial lines, that helped preserve the key provisions in the reform package during the long legislative sessions.

Formation of Parent Community Council. Immediately following his re-election in 1987, Mayor Harold Washington convened an Education Summit to begin to tackle some of the problems of public education in Chicago. The Summit was conceived in early 1986 as a limited partnership between the Chicago business community and the public high schools. At this early stage, the primary intent was to replicate the "Boston Compact" and motivate high school students to stay in school with the promise of an entry level job in a local business upon graduation. . . .

In the aftermath of a nineteen-day teachers' strike in the fall of 1987, however, the mayor's strategy changed. The strike was the third in six years, the longest Chicago had ever experienced, and perhaps the most futile. Outraged by their settlement, many teachers resigned from the union. The press accused both the BOE and the CTU for their "stranglehold" (*Chicago Tribune*, 1988) on the system, and the gulf between parents and professional educators at the school level had never been wider. Consequently, in an effort to channel frustration and to promote a broad, populist base of support for school reform, in October 1987 Mayor Washington crafted a Parent Community Council (PCC) that became the centerpiece of the Summit. He hand-picked the members of the Council and charged them to sponsor ten parent and community forums throughout the City. From the forum testimony the PCC was to draft a proposal for educational reform that he would sponsor at the Spring legislative session.

Populist Influences. The reform process that the mayor initiated was a democratic one. The ten forums were held during evening hours, and additional hearings were scheduled for school advocacy groups to present their proposals to the Council on weekends. These measures were intended to assure the public and the Council itself that the Summit process was an accessible one for poor and working parents, and that their voices would be well represented in any reform documents drafted by the PCC.

An analysis of the Council membership reveals still another source of populist influence: Of the fifty-four members, only 18.5% were professional educators; 3.7% were clergy; 22% came from business; 5.5% came from unions; 24% were from community organizations; and 20% were CPS parents. These last two groups—parents and representatives of community organizations—represented 44% of the total membership.

The Effective School Approach. A second source of influence was also apparent in the Education Summit process was evident in some of the strategies for reform recommended at the forums. This source, which represents a more professional and technical understanding of school problems and effective approaches to their improvement, has a long history in American education. At the turn of the century, business and factory models were the dominant metaphors, and administrators were trained to manage them effectively. . . .* The legacy of this movement today is "effective schools" run by strong managerial and instructional leaders. . . .** Throughout the reform process, effective schools were championed in the national debate over schools in part because they produce high graduation and attendance rates, high test scores, and few drop outs. These measurable outcomes are compared with that of a successful business, where it is thought that strong management and cost-effective techniques are maximally productive. Targeted to run these effective schools are principals who would receive at least a portion of their training from the corporate sector.

* * *

The populist approach to school restructuring was presented at the neighborhood forums. Virtually every speaker—parents, teachers, principals, and community representatives—blamed the ills of the system on a shortage of money and a governance structure that did not give local actors a decision-making voice. They all recommended that authority be decentralized. Beyond this basic common ground, however, there was much variation. Different complaints and ideas for problem-solving were heard at different forums. For example, at Hispanic forums a preponderance of parents decried the overcrowding in their schools; at black forums the condition of the physical plant and educators' lack of respect and caring for students were two dominant themes; and magnet school parents seemed most vocal about inequalities in funding and educational opportunities provided to students across Chicago and across the state. More specifically, representatives from neighborhoods with different social-economic characteristics looked for different strategies for parental control over school affairs.

. . . One reform strategy was dominant in those forums that included the most racially isolated and poorest school communities, both black and Hispanic. Parents here insisted that they be given a decision-making voice in their local schools. They wanted the right to hire and especially to fire incompetent teachers, and they wanted such teachers removed from the classroom, rather than remediated there. They wanted to share control with the principal over the school's budget and purchasing, and their traditions, language and culture to be respected by school staff and better represented in the school's curriculum.

Parents at these forums, which were held in the city's poorest school attendance areas, launched the most severe criticisms on teachers. They blamed teachers for the recent strike, for locking parents and

* D. Tyack, *The One Best System* (1974).

** R. Edmonds, "Effective Schools for the Urban Poor," 37 *Educ. Leadership* 1 (1979).

students out, and for not adequately teaching their children. Teachers were accused of being insensitive to children's educational, cultural, and emotional needs, and of being in their jobs solely "for the money." Teachers were also accused of strikes and of purposely limiting families' involvement in the schools. Parents demanded that they be given authority to "kick the butts" of these incompetent teachers out of their schools—a sentiment that bordered on mob rule.

Parents in these schools also blamed Central Office administrators for a system that they believed to be a bloated, corrupt, and non-responsive bureaucracy. Finally, they accused downstate politicians for insufficient funding to Chicago's minority schools and blamed their own representatives who consistently refused to raise taxes. Parents often booed when teachers got up to speak at these forums, accusing them of "disrespecting us and our kids . . . of having sick, incompetent minds . . . a fortress mentality . . . freezing us out and limiting us to selling taffy apples."

* * *

. . . Forums also took place at the subdistricts that represented the largest percentage of magnet schools in the system, the largest percentage of middle class and white students in attendance, and the largest number of competing parochial schools in their catchment areas. In contrast to an appeal for direct parental control at the other forums, parents at these community forums asked for a "partnership" among all local school actors—parents, teachers, the principal, (high school) students, and local business and community interests—for virtually all decisions affecting the local school. The proposed partnership would include the determination of instructional programs and their emphases, school and class size, textbook selection, discipline, dress and attendance policies, budgeting, staffing, and purchasing of goods and services. . . .

At these forums, parents did not see teachers as adversaries. Instead, the majority of comments directed toward teachers recommended staff development, recertification, and retraining programs to improve the performance of the instructional staff. . . .

Consensus on Parental Empowerment. The Agreements clearly adopted the populist sentiments as evidenced in the substantive powers given to parents at the school site. The document recommended that the composition of the Local School Body (LSB) include six parents, two community representatives, two teachers and the principal. Each (excluding the principal) was to be elected by his/her own constituency. The single most important power wielded by this parent-dominated board was its right to review—and renew or terminate—the five-year performance contract of the principal, and to select a new administrator from an eligibility list (supplied by the BOE) if the contract was not renewed. The LSB also had advisory powers over text selection (from a centrally approved list), revision of the core curriculum to meet local needs, and the hiring of new school staff. It had approval powers over the principal's annual expenditure plan (from a lump sum budget allocated by the BOE) as well as the School Improvement Plan (SIP). The principal was to be accountable to the LSB for all aspects of the school's educational program.

Parental authority over the SIP also represented a change from existing school code. According to the 1985 legislation, the principal was primarily responsible for the development and the implementation of the SIP. The Agreements, by contrast, state that the LSBs will "delegate the responsibility to develop the SIP to the principal, subject to their approval. The principal [then] implements the plan." . . .

Checking Teachers' Influence. Although tenure for teachers was unchallenged, the Agreements placed new limits on the teachers' collective autonomy at the school site. The existing school code allowed a teachers' committee to develop and implement staff development plans as long as the plans were consistent with the SIP developed by the principal and the advisory parent council. By contrast, the Agreements allow teachers only an "Advisory Committee." In a further diminution of teachers' powers, staff training became subject to the approval of the parent council.

Teacher selection, evaluation, and remediation represent other differences. These issues were traditionally determined by the central administration. The Agreements, by contrast, recommended that powers of selection, remedial procedures, and retention belong to the school principal acting in consultation with the LSB. Here the Agreements seem to be a very direct response to the sentiment expressed by some parents who, at the forums, insisted that incompetent teachers be physically and immediately removed from the classroom and that the school principal have the right to hire and fire teachers.

Finally, there was a change in focus to much more individualistic strategies that were intended to promote leadership among better teachers. These recommendations seem consistent with the effective school approach. The Agreements recommend career ladders, improved salary and benefit packages, and reimbursement and release time for teachers to attend professional conferences. Each of these incentives represent direct payments to individual teachers. . . .

Applying the Effective Model to the Principal's Job. . . . As the "administrative head" of each effective CPS school, principals were recommended to have expanded powers including "legal authority over the entire school, both the building and the staff." This represented a radical departure from past procedures wherein CPS principals were not entrusted with a building key. Further, CPS principals were to direct the development and implementation of an annual reform plan, staff development and incentive plans, and an annual lump sum budget.

Making Principals More Accountable. The Agreements did bow to the populist sentiment expressed at the forums, however, and some of these provisions represent a strange tension with the principal's image as chief executive officer. The most pronounced example is the principals' five-year performance contract that strips them of seniority rights and tenure. This idea did not come out of the effective schools literature. Instead, it was similar to the provision in the Agreements that teachers' selection and evaluation be determined at the school level. Both reforms acknowledge the populist sentiment that was so forcefully expressed at the PCC forums; a response to parents who argued that educators should be removed if they are "disrespectful . . . incompetent . . . and don't care about us and our kids." Arguing that the performance contract is, in effect, an elimination of their "property right," the Chicago Principals Association was the sole organization that refused to endorse the Summit Agreements.

* * *

[Part II]

While the mobilization phase set the tone and the direction for Chicago School reform, it was the formal legislative phase that defined the specific strategies that were adopted. If the former seemed to have brought in the previously underrepresented, then the latter was dominated by key institutional actors. When the reform proposals moved into the legislative arena, the process was marked by leadership conflict between Democrats and Republicans, extensive use of formal rules and institutional procedures by key lawmakers and the governor, and organized efforts by major lobbying groups to influence specific reform provisions. These political conflicts within the institutional context set the tone for the drafting of Senate Bill 1839, a Democratic sponsored bill that was passed without Republican support, and then SB 1840, a legislative compromise that resulted from the Governor's amendatory veto of SB 1839. . . .

Dominance of Institutional Actors in SB 1839. Senate hearings on school reform in Spring 1988 marked the beginning of the formal legislative phase. Prominent individuals and interest groups were featured during these hearings. For example, State Superintendent of Education Ted Sanders proposed strong state monitoring over the CPS, including a "receivership" if the district failed to implement reform. The AFL-CIO, Illinois Federation of Teachers, and Chicago Teachers Union wanted to preserve the seniority clause in hiring practices at the school level. The Black Legislative Caucus was particularly concerned about a shift in oversight powers from the mayor's office to the governor. And finally, the Education Summit, the coalition of parent and community groups initially mobilized by the late mayor, came up with its own draft legislation that the acting mayor sponsored in Springfield.

These were diverse proposals, and all of them were channeled through the legislative process. Shortly after the Senate hearings, the chair of the Senate Education Committee and other key legislators brought the interest groups into a closed door session. By early May, the Education Committee drafted SB 1839 under the direction of its chair and other Democrats. This bill was subsequently sponsored by the majority of the committee as their legislative vehicle for school reform.

* * *

. . . The Republicans . . . disagreed with the Democratic bill on a number of key issues. They wanted to reduce the powers of the district's central administration, to give parents more opportunity for school choice, to allow principals more discretion, and to break the teachers' union by granting "mini-contracts" between local schools and their teachers. The bill was subsequently passed by 68 to 37 in the Democratic-controlled House on July 2, 1988. Only four House Republicans supported the bill.

Controversy over the Governor's Amendatory Veto. Given the Republicans' strong opposition, it came as no surprise that the Republican governor exercised his amendatory veto on SB 1839. Thompson was opposed to two key provisions. First, he wanted to expand his oversight influence. Toward this end, he proposed a power sharing plan whereby he would name three of the six members of an oversight authority, the mayor would name three, and, together they would select a chair. This amendment was unacceptable to the Black Legislative Caucus. As the chair put it: "We're not going to give the governor the right to run the Chicago Public Schools. It is important that Chicagoans run Chicago schools". . . . Second, according to Thompson's amendments, principals would be authorized to hire teachers without regard for seniority. This provision was successfully defended against by a coalition of union lobbyists. . . .

The Democratic Proposal: Senate Bill 1839. Perhaps the most remarkable feature of SB 1839 is the degree to which it adheres to and then operationalizes the key recommendations of the Education Summit Agreements. On the one hand, the consistency is unexpected because the Agreements developed from and were authored by a parent dominated populist mobilization for reform, whereas the formal legislative process that produced SB 1839 was controlled by politicians (including those outside of Chicago) and organized lobbying groups. This outcome is that much more impressive, given the prolonged and often secretive political maneuvering that punctuated the formal legislative phase as described previously. On the other hand, the policy consensus produced from the mobilization phase clearly guided the legislative decisions on parental empowerment and professional accountability. Issues regarding broader governance at the top of the system, however, were left to the legislators to decide.

Because SB 1839 so closely maps onto the earlier Agreements, an exhaustive review of its provisions is not necessary. Rather, we will once again consider the way the legislation allocates powers among all of the key actors at different levels of CPS decision-making. Differences between the Agreements and SB 1839 will be highlighted.

Parents' Powers Legitimized. SB 1839 maintained all of the responsibilities and powers that were recommended for parents in the Agreements. These include authority over the principal's performance contract (although it is shortened from five to three years), the hiring of new staff, the approval of the annual expenditure plan and the school improvement plan, and advisory powers over school policies and programs that affect students and instruction. One power that parents lose is their ability to approve the "structure and organization of the Teachers Advisory Committee." This committee became an independent and elected faculty organization.

* * *

The relatively low priority given to teachers' professional development is one of the areas where SB 1839 differed markedly from the Agreements' recommendations. Whereas the Agreements made professionalization a major and urgent focus of the reform agenda, SB 1839 did practically nothing to insure that teachers at all CPS schools would have these opportunities. Further, SB 1839 was relatively silent on the issue of creating staff incentive plans, organizing teacher training centers, and other mechanisms toward teacher professionalization as outlined in the Agreements. It stated merely that the Illinois State Board of Education (ISBE) "is directed to consult with institutions of higher education and to study and recommend to the General Assembly ways to improve teacher training."

Making Instructional Leadership Accountable to Parents. Principals' authority remains consistent between the Agreements and SB 1839. Principals were subject to a three-year (instead of a five-year) performance contract controlled by the local parent council. Likewise, SB 1839 endorsed the recommendation that principals assume instructional leadership, a sentiment that seemed pervasive throughout the parent forum testimony. For example, in SB 1839 principals were responsible for all educational aspects of the school—the development and implementation of the school improvement plan, the annual expenditure plan, new hiring, the physical plant—and they were encouraged to consult with the LSC regarding these issues. Principals were to work collaboratively with their staff and parents regarding the refinement of discipline and attendance policies, as well as the school's curricula and instructional program to meet local needs.

Defining Reform Responsibilities for the Top of the System. SB 1839 is noteworthy primarily for the measures it took with regard to the highest levels of CPS management: the Board of Education (BOE), general superintendent, and central administration. The Agreements recommended that the top of the system work in collaboration with schools to support their efforts at school improvement, and that decision-making and spending be directed to this level as much as possible. SB 1839 operationalized all these recommendations.

First, SB 1839 directed the BOE to maintain many of its responsibilities toward the development and implementation of system-wide policies and procedures: for example, student testing and assessment programs; staff certification and evaluation, research and evaluation; system-wide curricular goals and objectives. However, the BOE would no longer have exclusive control over these policies and their implementation. Rather, the basic intent of SB 1839 was to create a system whereby the BOE took responsibility for developing system-wide policy guidelines—for example, it developed a standard core curriculum for all schools—but decision-makers at the school level would have authority to revise and tailor that curricula to meet local needs. Consequently, this dialogue between the top and bottom of the system became a policy in itself: a new structure of decision-making, the primary intent of which was to set up standards of performance that would be equitable toward the whole system, and would operate in a context responsive to local needs. Additional examples include the provision for the BOE to develop standard performance contracts for principals and subdistrict superintendents which could be revised by their Councils, as well as the articulation of system-wide attendance and discipline policies that were intended to respond to all students fairly and yet could be modified at the school level to better meet the needs of specific students. Thus, the BOE maintained many of its traditional obligations for centralized policy-making and planning, but actors at different levels of the system were authorized to revise and otherwise inform these plans.

Strengthening the Oversight on Reform Implementation. SB 1839 made CPS more accountable to external oversight. With regard to financial oversight, SB 1839 maintained the School Finance Authority (SFA) as the financial watch-dog of the system. It directed the SFA to conduct a management study to recommend a minimum administrative structure for the CPS. This provision had much more weight to it than the suggestion of the Agreements that the general superintendent "develop strategies to streamline the central administration, and prioritize and direct resources to the classroom level." Further, there was to be an immediate administrative spending cap placed on the central office, and any personnel reductions should come from the ranks of administrators.

With regard to oversight of the BOE on the implementation of school reform, the Agreements recommended that the mayor's office, the General Assembly, and the Education Summit work together to create an "entity" that would "monitor and ensure the implementation of school reform." SB 1839 carried through on this recommendation, creating a School Reform Authority (SRA) with powers to approve, facilitate and monitor the BOE's annual system-wide reform plan. It could reject and replace or amend that plan. The SRA could also request union waivers to facilitate reform, and it could modify BOE policies toward this same objective. Finally, it could suspend or terminate the contract of any BOE employee who would block reform.

A Compromise: SB 1840. As discussed earlier, SB 1839 was never signed into law by the governor. Rather, Thompson submitted an amended bill to the legislature when it met in the Fall of 1988, and haggling over Chicago school reform took up most of the legislative session. SB 1840 received the same level of intense media attention, public debate and scrutiny, and closed-door bargaining that had characterized the drafting of SB 1839. And the result—SB 1840—was again unanticipated. Most insiders to the process—members of the Parent Community Council (PCC), the Summit staff, the mayor's chief lobbyist, parents who lobbied downstate—expected the reform bill to die in the House. Perhaps even more surprising than its passage was the fact that SB 1840 differed from the previous draft in only a few key areas and these referred mainly to oversight at the top of the system. The distribution of powers across the system and among actors at other levels of the system remained virtually intact. Consequently, rather than reviewing the roles and responsibilities of different actors, we will invoke a different organization by summarizing and providing some analysis of significant changes between SB 1839 and SB 1840.

Granting Substantive Powers at the School Level. The authority and responsibilities of the LSC did not change. Principals' performance contracts were extended to four years, and there would be a lottery in June 1989 to determine which half of the principals were up for CPS contract renewal the following year.

Supernumerary teachers were granted some relief in the new legislation. They were to be given priority ranking on the eligibility lists that were distributed to principals who had open positions at their schools. Further, in spite of lump sum budgeting, supernumeraries were guaranteed a continuation of their full benefits and salary by the BOE if they were hired to replace a teacher who was being paid at a lower level. Finally, if they were not hired by a school principal, they were still guaranteed a job in the system with full pay and benefits.

* * *

With the adoption of SB 1840, the CPS now confronts the challenge of reform implementation. The reform legislation has already had its impact. The mobilization process produced a broad-based coalition that is committed to school improvement. This coalition has survived a difficult political process and it is likely to continue as reforms are implemented. Moreover, for the first time in Chicago school history, parents have substantial control over crucial school resources. There is now a real opportunity for parents to influence policies that will affect their children. Given this new role, parental involvement is likely to increase. The election of local school councils in October, 1989 provided the first real test for Chicago school reform and marked the beginning of a new era in Chicago schools.

V. PRIVATE REMEDIES: EDUCATION MALPRACTICE SUIT

Thus far the focus has been on changes in governmental structures, professionalism, empowerment of local communities, electoral reforms, the introduction of market mechanisms, state regulation, and other legal and political approaches to defining and producing more accountability in public education. Some commentators have suggested, however, that school districts should be directly accountable to students for the educational harms that they inflict on them. *See, e.g.*, Ratner, "A New Legal Duty for Urban Public Schools: Effective Education in Basic Skills," 63 *Tex. L. Rev.* 777 (1985); Loscalzo, "Liability for Malpractice in Education," 14 *J. of Law & Educ.* 595 (1985); Elson, "A Common Law Remedy for the Educational Harms Caused by Incompetent or Careless Teaching," 73 *Nw. U. L. Rev.* 641 (1978); Note, "Educational Malpractice: Can the Judiciary Remedy the Growing Problem of Functional Illiteracy?" 13 *Suffolk U. L. Rev.* 27 (1979). *But see* Yudof, "Effective Schools and Federal and State Constitutions: A Variety of Opinions," 63 *Tex. L. Rev.* 865 (1985); Comment, "Educational Malpractice," 64 *U. Det. L. Rev.* 717 (1987). Just as lawyers and physicians, in appropriate circumstances, may be held liable under common law tort principles for professional incompetence, so too, they argue, educators should be held to professional standards. *See* Foster, "Educational Malpractice: A Tort for the Untaught?" 19 *U. B. C. L. Rev.* 161 (1985). The theory is that the prospect of large monetary recoveries constitutes a form of accountability, deterring negligent educational practices and the retention of incompetent teachers and compensating the victims for their losses. *See* Note, "Educational Malpractice," 124 *U. Pa. L. Rev.* 755 (1976). *See generally* Foster, *supra*.

The courts have not been hospitable to education malpractice claims. The first and most publicized educational malpractice suit was *Peter W. v. San Francisco Unified School District, infra*.

Peter W. v. San Francisco Unified School District

60 Cal.App.3d 814, 131 Cal.Rptr. 854 (1976).

Rattigan, Associate Justice.

The novel—and troublesome—question on this appeal is whether a person who claims to have been inadequately educated, while a student in a public school system, may state a cause of action in tort against the public authorities who operate and administer the system. We hold that he may not.

* * *

On plaintiff's appeal, which is from the judgment, the question is whether a cause of action is stated against defendants in any of the complaint's seven counts. . . .

The first count, which is the prototype of the others (each of which incorporates all of its allegations by reference), sounds in negligence. Its opening allegations may be summarized, and quoted in part, as follows:

> Defendant district is "a unified school district . . . existing under the laws of the State of California" and functioning under the direction of its governing board and superintendent of schools. Plaintiff is an 18-year-old male who was recently graduated from a high school operated by the district. He had theretofore been enrolled in its schools, and had attended them, for a period of twelve years. Allegations explicitly charging negligence next appear as follows:
>
> "XI. Defendant school district, its agents and employees, negligently and carelessly failed to provide plaintiff with adequate instruction, guidance, counseling and/or supervision in basic academic skills such as reading and writing, although said school district had the authority, responsibility and ability . . . [to do so] . . . . Defendant school district, its agents and employees, negligently failed to use reasonable care in the discharge of its duties to provide plaintiff with adequate instruction . . . in basic academic skills and failed to exercise that degree of professional skill required of an ordinary prudent educator under the same circumstances [,] as exemplified, but not limited to [,] the following acts:"

In five enumerated subsections which follow in the same paragraph ("XI."), plaintiff alleges that the school district and its agents and employees, "negligently and carelessly" in each instance, (1) failed to apprehend his reading disabilities, (2) assigned him to classes in which he could not read "the books and other materials," (3) allowed him "to pass and advance from a course or grade level" with knowledge that he had not achieved either its completion or the skills "necessary for him to succeed or benefit from subsequent courses," (4) assigned him to classes in which the instructors were unqualified or which were not "geared" to his reading level, and (5) permitted him to graduate from high school although he was "unable to read above the eighth grade level, as required by Education Code section 8573, . . . thereby depriving him of additional instruction in reading and other academic skills."

The first count continues with allegations of proximate cause and injury: "XII. . . . [A]s a direct and proximate result of the negligent acts and omissions by the defendant school district, its agents and employees, plaintiff graduated from high school with a reading ability of only the fifth grade [*sic*]. As a further proximate result . . . [thereof] . . ., plaintiff has suffered a loss of earning capacity by his limited ability to read and write and is unqualified for any employment other than . . . labor which requires little or no ability to read or write. . . ."

In the closing paragraphs of the first count, plaintiff alleges general damages based upon his "permanent disability and inability to gain meaningful employment"; special damages incurred as the cost of compensatory tutoring allegedly required by reason of the "negligence, acts and omissions of defendants"; that he had presented to the school district an appropriate and timely claim for such damages; and that the claim had been rejected in its entirety.

* * *

A public entity may be held vicariously liable for the conduct of its employee, under Government Code section 815.2, subdivision (a)* . . . only if it established that the employee would be personally liable for the conduct upon some "acceptable theory of liability." . . .

According to the familiar California formula, the allegations requisite to a cause of action for negligence are (1) facts showing a duty of care in the defendant, (2) negligence constituting a breach of the duty, and (3) injury to the plaintiff as a proximate result. . . . The present parties do not debate the adequacy of plaintiff's first count with respect to the elements of negligence, proximate cause, and injury; they focus exclusively upon the issue (which we find dispositive, as will appear) of whether it alleges facts sufficient to show that defendants owed him a "duty of care."

* "815.2. (a) A public entity is liable for injury proximately caused by an act or omission of an employee of the public entity within the scope of his employment if the act or omission would, apart from this section, have given rise to a cause of action against that employee or his personal representative."

The facts which it shows in this respect—or not—appear in its allegations that he had been a student undergoing academic instruction in the public school system operated and administered by defendants. He argues that these facts alone show the requisite "duty of care" upon three judicially recognized theories, for which he cites authorities, pertaining to the public schools.

According to the first theory, "[a]ssumption of the function of instruction of students imposes the duty to exercise reasonable care in its discharge." (Summarizing this and the other two theories advanced by plaintiff, we quote the pertinent captions of his opening brief.) The decisions he cites for his first theory have no application here; in each, the question was whether a public employee's discharge of a function, the performance of which he had "assumed" in the exercise of his discretion, was reached by statutes which granted him immunity from tort liability for the results of his discretionary actions.

Plaintiff's second theory is that "[t]here is a special relationship between students and teachers which supports [the teachers'] duty to exercise reasonable care." He cites for this theory a wide-ranged array of decisions which enforced or addressed various "rights," "opportunities," or privileges of public school students (particularly in equal protection contexts), but none of which involved the question whether the school authorities owed them a "duty of care" in the process of their academic education. (*See, e.g., Lau v. Nichols* (1973) 414 U.S. 563, 564–68 . . .; *Ward v. Flood* (1874) 48 Cal. 36, 50–51; *Serrano v. Priest* (1971) 5 Cal.3d 584, 606–07, 96 Cal.Rptr. 601, 487 P.2d 1241; *Governing Board v. Metcalf* (1974) 36 Cal.App.3d 546, 550, 111 Cal.Rptr. 724.) The third theory is that the "[d]uty of teachers to exercise reasonable care in instruction and supervision of students is recognized in California." The decisions cited here are inapplicable because they establish only that public school authorities have a duty to exercise reasonable care for the *physical safety* of students under their supervision. (*See, e.g., Dailey v. Los Angeles Unified Sch. Dist.* (1970) 2 Cal.3d 741, 745–47, 87 Cal.Rptr. 376, 470 P.2d 360.)

For want of relevant authority in each instance, plaintiff's allegations of his enrollment and attendance at defendants' schools do not plead the requisite "duty of care," relative to his academic instruction, upon any of the three theories he invokes. Of course, no reasonable observer would be heard to say that these facts did not impose upon defendants a "duty of care" within any common meaning of the term; given the commanding importance of public education in society, we state a truism in remarking that the public authorities who are dutybound to educate are also bound to do it with "care." But the truism does not answer the present inquiry, in which "duty of care" is not a term of common parlance; it is instead a legalistic concept of "duty" which will sustain liability for negligence in its breach, and it must be analyzed in that light.

* * *

["Duty of care" is] . . . an essential factor in any assessment of liability for negligence. . . . [W]hether a defendant owes the requisite "duty of care," in a given factual situation, presents a question of law which is to be determined by the courts alone. . . . [J]udicial recognition of such duty in the defendant, with the consequence of his liability in negligence for its breach . . . [may be] dictated or precluded by considerations of public policy. . . .[3]

* * *

On occasions when the Supreme Court [of California] has opened or sanctioned new areas of tort liability, it has noted that the wrongs and injuries involved were both comprehensible and assessable within the existing judicial framework. . . . This is simply not true of wrongful conduct and injuries allegedly involved in educational malfeasance. Unlike the activity of the highway or the marketplace, classroom methodology affords no readily acceptable standards of care, or cause, or injury. The science of pedagogy itself is fraught with different and conflicting theories of how or what a child should be taught, and any layman might—and commonly does—have his own emphatic views on the subject. The "injury" claimed here is plaintiff's inability to read and write. Substantial professional authority

3. "Protection" of the plaintiff is the initial element in the Restatement formula defining the requisites of a cause of action for negligence. The formula's essentials include negligence, causation, and injury (the "invasion of an interest" of the plaintiff) but, unlike the California formula, the first element is not a "duty of care" in the defendant: it is the condition that the "*interest invaded is protected.*" (Res.2d Torts, § 281 [emphasis added].).

attests that the achievement of literacy in the schools, or its failure, are influenced by a host of factors which affect the pupil subjectively, from outside the formal teaching process, and beyond the control of its ministers. They may be physical, neurological, emotional, cultural, environmental; they may be present but not perceived, recognized but not identified.*

We find in this situation no conceivable "workability of a rule of care" against which defendants' alleged conduct may be measured . . ., no reasonable "degree of certainty that . . . plaintiff suffered injury" within the meaning of the law of negligence . . ., and no such perceptible "connection between the defendant's conduct and the injury suffered," as alleged, which would establish a causal link between them within the same meaning. . . .

These recognized policy considerations alone negate an actionable "duty of care" in persons and agencies who administer the academic phases of the public educational process. Others, which are even more important in practical terms, command the same result. Few of our institutions, if any, have aroused the controversies, or incurred the public dissatisfaction, which have attended the operation of the public schools during the last few decades. Rightly or wrongly, but widely, they are charged with outright failure in the achievement of their educational objectives; according to some critics, they bear responsibility for many of the social and moral problems of our society at large. Their public plight in these respects is attested in the daily media, in bitter governing board elections, in wholesale rejections of school bond proposals, and in survey upon survey. To hold them to an actionable "duty of care" in the discharge of their academic functions, would expose them to the tort claims—real or imagined—of disaffected students and parents in countless numbers. They are already beset by social and financial problems which have gone to major litigation, but for which no permanent solution has yet appeared. (*See, e.g., Crawford v. Board of Education* (1976) 17 Cal.3d 280, 130 Cal.Rptr. 724, 551 P.2d 28; *Serrano v. Priest, supra,* 5 Cal.3d 584, 96 Cal.Rptr. 601, 487 P.2d 1241.) The ultimate consequences, in terms of public time and money, would burden them—and society—beyond calculation.

* * *

In each of his last five counts . . . plaintiff repleads all the allegations of the first one. He further alleges, in each, that he had incurred "the damages alleged herein" "as a direct and proximate result" of a specified violation, by one or more of the defendants and as to him, of a respectively described "duty" (or "mandatory duty") allegedly imposed upon them by an express provision of law.[5] The theory of each count is that it states a cause of action for breach of a "mandatory duty" under Government Code section 815.6.[6]

If it be assumed that each of these counts effectively pleads the district's failure to have exercised "reasonable diligence to discharge the duty" respectively alleged, as mentioned in the statute . . . none states a cause of action. This is because the statute imposes liability for failure to discharge only such "mandatory duty" as is "imposed by an enactment that is designed to protect against the risk of a particular kind of injury." . . . The various "enactments" cited in these counts (*see* fn. 5 *ante*) are not so "designed." We have already seen that the failure of educational achievement may not be characterized as an "injury" within the meaning of tort law. It further appears that the several "enactments" have been conceived as provisions directed to the attainment of optimum educational results, but not as

* *See generally* chapter 6.

5. The third count thus refers to the district's and the governing board's having violated their "mandatory duty," allegedly imposed upon them by Education Code section 10759 and Title V of the California Administrative Code, "of keeping the parents and natural guardians of minor school children advised as to their accurate educational progress and achievements." The fourth count alleges a violation, by the district, of its "duty of instructing plaintiff, and other students, in the basic skills of reading and writing" as imposed "under the Constitution and laws of the State of California." The fifth count refers to the district's having graduated plaintiff from high school as a violation of a "mandatory duty not to graduate students from high school without demonstration of proficiency in basic skills" as allegedly imposed by Education Code section 8573 et seq. The sixth count speaks to a violation, by the governing board, of its "mandatory duty" to inspect and evaluate the district's educational program pursuant to Education Code sections 1053 and 8002; the seventh, to the district's violation of its "mandatory duty," allegedly imposed by Education Code section 8505, "to design the course of instruction offered in the public schools to meet the needs of the pupils for which the course of study is prescribed."

6. "815.6. Where a public entity is under a mandatory duty imposed by an enactment that is designed to protect against the risk of a particular kind of injury, the public entity is liable for an injury of that kind proximately caused by its failure to discharge the duty unless the public entity establishes that it exercised reasonable diligence to discharge the duty."

safeguards against "injury" of any kind: i.e., as administrative but not protective. Their violation accordingly imposes no liability under Government Code section 815.6.

Plaintiff's second count requires separate treatment because the theory of liability invoked in it is materially different from those reflected in the others. After incorporating into it all the allegations of the first count, he further alleges as follows:

"Defendant school district, its agents and employees, falsely and fraudulently represented to plaintiff's mother and natural guardian that plaintiff was performing at or near grade level in basic academic skills such as reading and writing. . . ." The representations were false. The charged defendants knew that they were false, or had no basis for believing them to be true." As a direct and proximate result of the intentional or negligent misrepresentation made . . ., plaintiff suffered the damages set forth herein."

For the public policy reasons heretofore stated with respect to plaintiff's first count, we hold that this one states no cause of action for *negligence* in the form of the "misrepresentation" alleged. The possibility of its stating a cause of action for *intentional* misrepresentation, to which it expressly refers in the alternative, is assisted by judicial limitations placed upon the scope of the governmental immunity which is granted, as to liability for "misrepresentation," by Government Code section 818.8. . . .

The second count nevertheless does not state a cause of action, for intentional misrepresentation, because it alleges no facts showing the requisite element of *reliance* upon the "misrepresentation" it asserts. . . .

The judgment of dismissal is affirmed.

Caldecott, P.J., and Christian, J., concur.

NOTES AND QUESTIONS

1. Duty of Care, Negligence, and Causation

Why did the *Peter W.* court rest its decision on the duty of care component of a negligence action? If there is no duty of care as a matter of law, does this not preclude future successful claims where negligence, cause, and injury may be factually demonstrated? Would an ad hoc case-by-case approach be better? *See* Foster, "Educational Malpractice: A Tort for the Untaught,?" 19 *U. B. C. L. Rev.* 161, 191, 237 (1985). Is the duty of care concept simply broad-based judicial policy-making in disguise? That is, is not the court simply determining who should bear the losses occasioned by a teacher's or a school district's alleged negligence? *See* Note, "Educational Malpractice: Can the Judiciary Remedy the Growing Problem of Functional Illiteracy,?" 13 *Suffolk U. L. Rev.* 27, 33–37 (1979) (hereinafter "Functional Illiteracy"). *See* Note, "Educational Malpractice," 124 *Pa. L. Rev.* 755, 760–66 (1976) (hereinafter "Educational Malpractice"). Did the court reach the right result on the duty of care? One commentator contends that *Peter W.* is wrongly decided, that the court made no serious and substantial effort at analysis of the duty. Foster, *supra* at 191.

Notwithstanding the court's analysis, is the real problem one of tying some negligent behaviors to the specific harms suffered by students who are functionally illiterate? *See* Foster *supra* at 234–41. Consider Professor Sugarman's analysis of the negligence doctrine:

> Instead of making paint manufacturers automatically liable when children get sick from eating [lead] paint, we might adopt a narrower rule and make them liable *only* if the cost of flavoring [the paint so as to make it bad tasting to children] is cheaper than the cost of the damage claims. According to this rule, manufacturers will be liable only when they choose the less economically efficient course of action. This narrower rule defines being "negligent"—failing to take a cost-effective precaution. Therefore, the availability of damage claims to victims under the negligence rule acts primarily as an incentive to assure that victims challenge inefficiency. Under negligence, victims who are injured in cases when the safety precaution proposed to the defendant is not cost effective are not compensated. . . . We may translate these alternate bases for liability into the context of suits against schools. Assume that there are some children for whom there are no cost-effective measures available to make them learners; I will call them "inevitable nonlearners." If schools are only liable when they are negligent, that is, when they could have done something cost effective to prevent nonlearning, lawsuits will be unsuccessful as long as the schools act efficiently. . . . Before we assume that liability . . . will reduce the incidence of nonlearning, we must determine whether the schools can introduce cost-effective methods of learning which they are not now using.

Sugarman, "Accountability Through the Courts," 82 *Sch. Rev.* 233, 251–52 (1974). *But see* Foster, *supra*.

To deter teacher and school official negligence, must there be a reasonable, cost-effective means of producing the desired educational outcome? If the student is an "inevitable nonlearner," if present knowledge about how to produce an educational outcome is insufficient, if education is the responsibility of many persons over many years, then in what sense would liability for education malpractice deter negligent teaching? *See generally* Sugarman, *supra* at 246. What if the plaintiff could show that there were students in other school districts, with similar characteristics, who have been successfully taught? *See* Ratner, "A New Legal Duty for Urban Public Schools: Effective Education in Basic Skills," 63 *Tex. L. Rev.* 777, 800 (1985). Are there established professional standards for nonnegligent teaching? *See* Foster, *supra* at 217–28; R. Strickland, J. Phillips, and W. Phillips, *Avoiding Teacher Malpractice* 64 (1976); Sugarman, *supra* at 235; Elson, "A Common Law Remedy for the Educational Harms Caused by Incompetent or Careless Teaching," 73 *Nw. L. Rev.* 641 (1978); "Functional Illiteracy" at 39–40. In this regard, Baratz and Hartle have criticized the suggestion that educational and medical malpractice are analogous:

> The analogy to medical malpractice might appear unavoidable. However, the connection with medicine is tenuous, at best. . . .
>
> *First*, a medical "illness" can usually be defined with some precision; consensus can be achieved regarding what constitutes a broken arm or a cancerous tumor. This is not the case, however, when educators are asked to define functional illiteracy.
>
> *Second*, medical malpractice suits hold doctors accountable to "accepted practice." Generally, there are established practices for remedying particular conditions. But in education, few such standard practices or procedures are available.
>
> *Third*, in medicine the treatment is usually administered by a single individual within a fixed, usually short, period of time. In education, many persons with varying degrees of authority participate in a fragmented process, and are responsible in varying degrees for the success or failure of a child's education.
>
> *Fourth*, the patient is usually passive in medical treatment, and the doctor generally bears sole responsibility for the results. Education, on the other hand, is an interactive process—the child is expected to participate and indicate when he is experiencing difficulties, and the parents are expected to participate, too.

Baratz and Hartle, " 'Malpractice' in the Schools," *The Progressive*, June 1977, at 33, 34. *See generally* chapter 6. *Compare* Elson, *supra;* Sugarman, *supra* at 250.

While Baratz and Hartle may have overstated the state of medical knowledge, at least in some types of medical malpractice suits (*see* "Functional Illiteracy" at 40), do they not make an almost irresistable case that the nature of education is such that education malpractice suits are generally not appropriate under negligence theories? *But see* Ratner, *supra;* Elson, *supra;* Martinez, "Educational Malpractice: California School District Held Not Liable for Negligence in Instruction in Academic Subjects," 22 *Inequality in Education* 132 (1977); "Functional Illiteracy" at 46–48. *See generally* Abel, "Can a Student Sue the Schools for Educational Malpractice,?" 44 *Harv. Educ. Rev.* 416 (1974); Comment, "Educational Negligence: A Student's Cause of Action for Incompetent Academic Instruction," 58 *N. C. L. Rev.* 561 (1980). Is it responsive to argue that we may justifiably suspect incompetence when a child of normal intelligence has not gained basic skills? *See* Ratner, *supra;* Sugarman, *supra* at 250. Would it be responsive to argue that other children with similar IQs perform better in similar schools in similar communities with similar programs? *See* Ratner, *supra;* "Educational Malpractice" at 791. If so, would this be a form of strict liability, i.e., liability without proof of negligence? *But see* Ratner, *supra* at 857–59.

2. *Statutorily Defined Standards of Care*

What standard of care did the court embrace? Is it appropriate to adopt a "reasonable man" standard? *See* Foster, *supra* at 207 (not appropriate). What of a "prudent parent standard?" *See Foster, supra* at 209–17; Hoyano, "The 'Prudent Parent': The Elusive Standard of Care," 18 *U.B.C. L. Rev.* 1 (1984). A professional standard based on custom and practice in the teaching profession? *See* Foster, *supra* at 220; Elson, *supra* at 713.

It is common enough for courts to conclude that there is a duty of care and negligent behavior when a person violates some state law and the law was intended to avoid the very type of injury that is the subject of the civil litigation. *See Restatement (Second) of Torts* § 288 (1965). An example would be when a motorist fails to stop his vehicle at a stop sign, in violation of local or state statutes defining traffic offenses, and runs his vehicle into another automobile—thereby inflicting injury to person and property. Is the *Peter W.* court correct in holding that the California statutes dealing with course of study, examination, graduation requirements, and so on do not provide a basis for a finding of a duty of care? Is this a matter of legislative intent, or is it a question of discerning whether the risks addressed by the statutes are the same as the types of injuries allegedly suffered by *Peter W.*? *See* "Educational Malpractice" at 779–81. Is the difficulty that the statutes are largely hortatory or that they define inputs and do not define duties with respect to outcomes?

In a state that has adopted a minimum competency education approach and defined minimum standards for grade promotion and high school graduation, should these standards be used to define the duty of care in education malpractice suits? *See* "Functional Illiteracy" at 43–45. Does it make sense to deny promotions and degrees while preserving a cause of action for damages for education malpractice? Would it make more sense to require the state to provide remedial instruction rather than damages? Would this eliminate the speculativeness of damages in cases such as *Peter W.* while avoiding "ruinous expense" to the school district, teachers, or administrators? *See* "Educational Malpractice" at 758.

3. *Nature of the Injury*

In *Peter W.*, the plaintiff sought "money damages for mental distress, pain, and suffering arising from his 'teacher-caused' reading deficiency." "Educational Malpractice" at 760. In the absence of physical injury or an intentional as opposed to negligent tort, should such injuries provide the basis for a damage recovery?

> Although courts have recently recognized the intentional infliction of mental distress as a basis for tort recovery, courts generally have not permitted a recovery for negligently inflicted mental distress without accompanying physical injury. The demand in *Doe* seems to go far beyond any recovery allowed by courts in negligence suits, but it might be made more realistically in an intentional tort action. Even in the latter case, however, difficulties of proof may make success . . . highly unlikely. . . .

Id. See also Wilson v. Continental Insurance Companies, 67 Wis.2d 310, 274 N.W.2d 679 (1979); *Pierce v. Board of Education*, 44 Ill.App.3d 324, 3 Ill.Dec. 67, 358 N.E.2d 67 (1976), *rev'd* 69 Ill.2d 89, 12 Ill.Dec. 731, 370 N.E.2d 535 (1977). *But see* Foster, *supra* at 230–31.

Is this another reason to deny recovery in education malpractice cases? Does this analysis satisfactorily distinguish cases in which educators and education institutions have been held liable for the negligent infliction of physical injuries, for example, mishaps in the gym class or chemistry laboratory? *See generally* H.C. Hudgins and R.S. Vacca, *Law and Education*, ch. 4 (1979).

4. *Strict Liability*

Would a standard of strict liability be preferable to one of negligence in educational malpractice suits? That is, schools and school personnel would be held responsible for educational deprivations suffered by their students irrespective of their negligence or lack of it. This would result in the losses being shifted to educators and school systems even if there were no cost-effective means of preventing or limiting the injury. Is this an adequate response to the problem of avoiding judicial case-by-case determinations of fault and causation? Does it resolve the problem of many actors over many years contributing to the injury? Does it avoid the difficulty of parental and student "contributory negligence"?

What are the policy implications of strict liability? Would it open school districts to tremendous liability, leading either to increased taxes or to reduced educational offerings? Is it wise to socialize the costs (spread the risk) of educational injuries in this fashion? Should legislatures rather than courts decide the liability-without-fault question, "just as the liability-without-fault rules regarding industrial accidents were the product of workmen's compensation laws"? *See* Sugarman, *supra* at 241. Would strict liability amount to a state education insurance program or welfare in a different garb?

5. *Preventive Education*

Consider education malpractice suits from the perspective of the individual teacher or school administrator:

> The situation in the teaching profession was summed up quite well by Senator Birch Bayh when he said the primary concern in many American schools "is no longer education but, preservation."
>
> Said one teacher, commenting on the idea of educational malpractice suits, "You know, it is rather like somebody trying to sue a clergyman because a member of the family didn't go to heaven, even though he went to church, listened to the sermons and put money in the collection plate."

Newell, "Teacher Malpractice," 83 *Case and Comment* 3, 10 (1978).

If a primary concern is self-preservation and risk aversion, might not educational malpractice suits have an impact on teachers and schools even if recoveries are rare or nonexistent? In what ways might a teacher change his or her behavior? Would he or she be more likely to keep copious records, to treat the "chart" rather than the "patient," to attribute failure to the student or parents or to resist pressures for social promotion? *Cf.* Yudof, "Procedural Fairness and Substantive Justice: Due Process, Bureaucracy, and the Public Schools," in J. Newitt, ed., *Future Trends in Education Policy* 109 (1979); Kirp, "Proceduralism and Bureaucracy: Due Process in the School Setting," 28 *Stan. L. Rev.* 841 (1976); Yudof, "Liability for Constitutional Torts and the Risk-Averse Public School Official," 49 *S. Cal. L. Rev.* 1322 (1976).

In this regard, what is the significance of the fact that in many states the school districts might not be liable for negligent torts under notions of sovereign immunity? *See generally* Hudgins and Vacca, *supra* at 73–90. Or that only individual teachers and administrators may be sued or that teachers and administrators may be indemnified by the state or have professional liability insurance (assuming it is available)? That state and local governments may provide a free legal defense to individual educators acting in their official capacities in all or more civil contexts? *See generally* "Functional Illiteracy" at 60–61; Yudof, *supra*. Does this diminish the likely favorable or adverse consequences of successful or unsuccessful education malpractice suits?

6. *Misrepresentation*

Do you agree with the *Peter W.* court that there is no evidence that the plaintiff relied on representations that he was progressing normally in his reading development? What of lost opportunities to secure remedial assistance? What of the possibility of changing over to a private school? What sort of proof of reliance would persuade the court, or is it really saying that there is no duty on the part of school officials to portray accurately the progress of a student? What are the policy arguments for and against such a no-duty rule? Consider these remarks by Professor Sugarman:

> A jury might well agree with Peter that the school made some serious mistakes and could have taken not-too-expensive action to help him read. Some of the school's errors were in communication: (1) through conferences and misleading report cards, Peter and his family were told that he was making progress when he really was not; (2) he was counseled into courses that were too difficult for him rather than being informed about and counseled toward available remedial programs. Other complaints suggested by Peter Doe's story deal with procedural problems: either the school has inadequate procedures to identify students needing remedial help, or, assuming the school used proven diagnostic procedures, those procedures failed to diagnose that Peter needed remedial help. While the financial burden of making these procedural changes may be greater than improving the lines of communication, a jury will probably not consider them overly costly.

Sugarman, *supra* at 244. *See also* Comment, "Educational Malpractice," 64 *U. Det. L. Rev.* 717, 725 (1987).

Does Professor Sugarman's analysis suggest that the *Peter W.* court feared that juries would be sympathetic to misrepresentation claims? Are the standards for misrepresentation better defined than are the standards for educational negligence? Can school authorities adjust their conduct so as to avoid misrepresenting a student's progress? Is the problem one of showing "intentional" misrepresentation? What should the remedy be in a case of proven intentional misrepresentation?

Should school districts be required to disclose information about how teachers are assigned and how children are grouped into classes or tracks? *See* Sugarman and Friedman, "School Sorting and Disclosure: Disclosure to Families as a School Reform Strategy—Part II: Policy and Legal Analysis," 17 *J. of Law & Educ.* 147 (1988).

7. *Other Education Malpractice Suits*

In *Donohue v. Copiague Union Free School District*, 47 N.Y.2d 440, 418 N.Y.S.2d 375, 391 N.E.2d 1352 (1979), the New York Court of Appeals (the highest court in New York) reached a result in an education malpractice suit that was essentially similar to that reached in *Peter W.* The court, however, admitted that education malpractice suits might well fit within traditional negligence notions, including the duty of care, citing Elson, *supra* at 693–744. It opined, however, that such claims should not be entertained as a matter of public policy:

> To entertain a cause of action for "educational malpractice" would require the courts not merely to make

judgments as to the validity of broad educational policies . . . but, more importantly, to sit in review of the day-to-day implementation of these policies. . . . [This] . . . would constitute blatant interference with the responsibility for the administration of the public school system lodged by Constitution and statute in school administrative agencies.

418 N.Y.S.2d at 378, 391 N.E.2d at 1354. *See also Torres v. Little Flower Children's Services*, 64 N.Y.2d 119, 485 N.Y.S.2d 15, 474 N.E.2d 223 (1984); *D.S.W. v. Fairbanks North Star Borough School Dist.*, 628 P.2d 554 (Alaska 1981).

Is this essentially the same reasoning the *Peter W.* court adopted in analyzing the duty of care? Is it a recognition that courts are relatively poor monitors for accountability purposes? *But see* Elson, *supra.* In this respect, how, if at all, does education malpractice differ from school segregation (chapter 5) or restraints on student liberties (chapter 2)? Is the court's confidence in the accountability functions of administrative agencies well placed?

For results similar to *Peter W.* and *Donohue, see Trustees of Columbia University v. Jacobsen*, 53 N.J.Super. 574, 148 A.2d 63 (App.Div.), *aff'd* 31 N.J. 221, 156 A.2d 251, *cert. denied*, 363 U.S. 808, 80 S.Ct. 1243, 4 L.Ed.2d 1150 (1960); *McNeil v. Board of Education*, No. L-17297 (Super.Ct.Law Div. N.J., 1978).

In *Hoffman v. Board of Education*, 64 A.D.2d 369, 410 N.Y.S.2d 99 (S.Ct., App.Div., 1978), a New York appellate court upheld a substantial judgment against a school district, reducing a $750,000 jury verdict to $500,000. In that case, plaintiff had been placed in classes for children with retarded mental development for eleven years, based upon a certified psychologist's determination that the plaintiff had an IQ of 74 (75 was the cutoff point for assignment to such classes). Thirteen years later, it was determined that plaintiff was not retarded. No effort had been made to ascertain the "social history" of the plaintiff, the mother was not informed that plaintiff was classified as retarded by only one IQ point, and plaintiff's intelligence was never retested despite high scores on a "reading readiness" examination. Plaintiff apparently suffered from some "severe speech problem," which may have had an impact on his IQ score. A neurologist and psychiatrist testified at trial that

[P]laintiff has a marked stutter, that his articulation was not clear and that he had difficulty in making himself understood. On neurological testing he found him to be normal in all respects and he ruled out any brain damage. . . . His opinion was that plaintiff was not mentally retarded, but that he had a "defective self-image and feelings of inadequacy." This was because plaintiff had been placed in a class of mentally retarded children and "this result[ed] in an alteration in his concept of himself, particularly because he is intelligent enough to appreciate the position in which he is placed." . . . He testified the plaintiff was still trainable and that he could be helped with special education and psycho-therapeutic support, but even that could not "correct all the damage of ten years or more of deprivation educationally and characterization as a mentally retarded person."

Id. at 105.

Given these facts, is the *Hoffman* case distinguishable from *Donohue* and *Peter W.*? *See also In re Peter H.*, 66 Misc.2d 1097, 323 N.Y.S.2d 302 (Fam.Ct. 1971) (defendant school district ordered to pay one year tuition for a private education). On appeal in the *Hoffman* case, the New York Court of Appeals reversed the lower court, relying on its reasoning in *Donohue.* 49 N.Y.2d 121, 424 N.Y.S.2d 376, 400 N.E.2d 317 (1979). *See also Brosnan v. Livonia Public Schools*, 123 Mich. App. 377, 333 N.W.2d 288 (1983); *Tubell v. Dade County Public Schools*, 419 So.2d 388 (Fla. App. 1982).

8. Contract Actions

A number of courts have been willing to entertain contract actions brought by students against private schools, alleging that the private school did not live up to its contractual obligations contained in catalogs or other documents. *See, e.g., Russell v. Salve Regina College*, 890 F.2d 484 (1st Cir. 1989); *Warren v. Drake University*, 886 F.2d 200 (8th Cir. 1989); *Doherty v. Southern College of Optometry*, 862 F.2d 570 (6th Cir. 1988); *Dr. Franklin Perkins School v. Freeman*, 741 F.2d 1503 (7th Cir. 1984); *Corso v. Creighton University*, 731 F.2d 529 (8th Cir. 1984); *VanLoock v. Curran*, 489 So.2d 525 (Ala. 1986); *King v. American Academy of Dramatic Arts*, 102 Misc.2d 1111, 425 N.Y.S.2d 505 (1980); *Basch v. George Washington University*, 370 A.2d 1364 (D.C. Ct.App., 1977) (language of bulletin expressed an expectancy and not an enforceable promise); *Behrend v. State*, 55 Ohio App.2d 135, 379 N.E.2d 617 (1977) (plaintiffs stated a cause of action under an implied contract). *See generally* "Functional Illiteracy" at 30–31; Sernas, "Students

Filing 'Consumer' Suits," 11 *Chronicle of Higher Education*, Nov. 24, 1975, at 1; Comment, "Consumer Protection and Higher Education: Student Suits Against Schools," 37 *Ohio St. L.J.* 608 (1976); "Educational Malpractice" at 785–86.

Given the analysis of educational malpractice suits, should contract claims against private education institutions be entertained? Should they be entertained against public institutions? What would constitute proof of a contractual undertaking? How would a contract recovery differ in theory or effect from a recovery based upon misrepresentation? *See generally* Ray, "Toward Contractual Rights for College Students," 10 *J. of Law & Educ.* 163 (1981).

Can a private educational institution alter the terms of the "contract" at will, for example, by changing graduation requirements? *See Mahavongsanan v. Hall*, 529 F.2d 448 (5th Cir. 1976); *Slaughter v. Brigham Young University*, 514 F.2d 622 (10th Cir. 1975).

Can education malpractice be premised on an implied or express contract or estoppel theory? *See* Jerry, "Recovery in Tort in Educational Malpractice: Problems of Theory and Policy," 29 *Kan. L. Rev.* 195 (1981); "Educational Malpractice" at 784–89.

Professor Dodd has urged that contract theories are conceptually and legally inappropriate to define the relationship between students and schools:

> There is little in the student-university relationship, particularly as it has been viewed by the courts, that reflects principles and policies that are associated with theories of contract. To the limited extent that the law of contract now in strained use and tort theory are readily separable, and they are not, contracts center around promises. Contract liability is imposed by the law for the protection of a single, limited interest, that of having the promises of others performed. Indeed, many would further limit that definition to include primarily promises in the "commercial realm." Further, "[c]ontract obligations are created to enforce promises which are manifestations not only of a present intention to do or not to do something, but also of a commitment to the future. They are, therefore, obligations based on the manifested intention of the parties to a bargaining transaction. This article has delineated the lack of a true bargaining and promise orientation in the student-university context, and hence, the intrinsically non-contractual nature of that relationship. Indeed, the myriad of individual student problems that can arise in a university situation would defy an attempt to embody in fair, written terms all of the "promises" inherent in such a situation.
>
> The student-university relationship instead seems to fall more naturally into the realm of tort analysis. Tort liability generally is "based upon the relations of persons with others; and those relations may arise generally, with large groups or classes of persons, or singly, with an individual. The wrongs or injuries described in this article flow from the relationship between student and university. Although this relationship is created by a contract of sorts, through the payment of tuition, its survival extends beyond notions of contract. At least historically, too, one of the closest analogues to the student-university relationship has been the familial relationship. Perhaps that similarity helped to prevent the development of tort theory in education cases; the recognition of intra-familial tort liability is relatively recent.

Dodd, "The Non-Contractual Nature of the Student-University Contractual Relationship," 33 *Kan. L. Rev.* 701, 730–31 (1985). Do you agree with her conclusions?

9. *Intentional Infliction of Emotional Distress*

May a student who is suspended or expelled from a private educational institution recover for intentional infliction of emotional distress? *See Russell v. Salve Regina College*, 890 F.2d 484 (1st Cir. 1989) (college's conduct in asking overweight nursing student to withdraw may be unprofessional but not sufficiently outrageous to constitute a tort), *cert. granted*, 111 S.Ct. 33, 112 L.Ed.2d 10 (1991).

FIVE

Equal Educational Opportunity and Race

I. INTRODUCTION

This chapter and the two chapters that follow focus on what educational opportunities the individual student is entitled to receive from the state. These entitlements are embodied in federal and state constitutions and laws, and they function as constraints on the ways in which public schools operate. Typically they are defined and vindicated through the judicial process. Demands upon public schools can be affirmative, asserting an entitlement to a minimum educational opportunity, equal access to the schooling process, or a specified educational outcome; or they may be framed negatively, asserting a right to be free of race, sex, or class discrimination in the operation of the public schools.

This chapter deals with the fully matured and litigated definition of equal educational opportunity: the rights of students to be free of racial discrimination. The chapter is organized primarily along historical lines. The complex issues presented by segregation in both the North and the South, the scope of unlawful racial segregation, the Civil Rights Act of 1964, and the controversy over racial-balance remedies can be understood best against the backdrop of historical changes in social attitudes and governmental policy. In addition, the materials examine the ethical and policy implications of racial discrimination. Why is state-created segregation unconstitutional? What is the impact of segregation on the educational achievement of students? What ethical, social, and economic costs attach to the alternative means of undoing racial segregation in the schools? Is the goal desegregation or racially integrated schools? How are such concepts defined and implemented?

Finally, this chapter raises sensitive issues of federalism and democracy. It examines the relationship among the federal courts, Congress, and the president in the context of school desegregation, as well as the relationship among the federal courts, the U.S. Department of Education, and local school districts. More importantly, it seeks to assess the role of the judiciary in carrying out what now appears to have been a social revolution of mammoth proportions. Other groups have sought, either through litigation or legislation, to use the approach taken by racial minorities defining equal educational opportunity. Thus this chapter provides the necessary background for understanding the developments described in chapters 6 and 7.

II. THE JUDICIAL RESPONSE TO SCHOOL SEGREGATION: THE *BROWN* DECISION

A. *Brown I:* Legal and Policy Implications

Brown v. Board of Education
347 U.S. 483, 74 S.Ct. 686, 98 L.Ed. 873 (1954).

Mr. Chief Justice Warren delivered the opinion of the Court.

These cases come to us from the states of Kansas, South Carolina, Virginia, and Delaware. They are premised on different facts and different local conditions, but a common legal question justifies their consideration together in this consolidated opinion.[1]

In each of the cases, minors of the Negro race, through their legal representatives, seek the aid of the courts in obtaining admission to the public schools of their community on a nonsegregated basis. In each instance, they have been denied admission to schools attended by white children under laws requiring or permitting segregation according to race. This segregation was alleged to deprive the plaintiffs of the equal protection of the laws under the Fourteenth Amendment. In each of the cases other than the Delaware case, a three-judge federal district court denied relief to the plaintiffs on the so-called "separate but equal doctrine" announced by this court in *Plessy v. Ferguson*, 163 U.S. 537. Under that doctrine, equality of treatment is accorded when the races are provided substantially equal facilities, even though these facilities be separate. In the Delaware case, the Supreme Court of Delaware adhered to that doctrine, but ordered that the plaintiffs be admitted to the white schools because of their superiority to the Negro schools.

The plaintiffs contend that segregated public schools are not "equal" and cannot be made "equal," and that hence they are deprived of the equal protection of the laws. Because of the obvious importance of the question presented, the Court took jurisdiction. Argument was heard in the 1952 Term, and reargument was heard this term on certain questions propounded by the Court.

Reargument was largely devoted to the circumstances surrounding the adoption of the Fourteenth Amendment in 1868. It covered exhaustively consideration of the Amendment in Congress, ratification by the states, then existing practices in racial segregation, and the views of proponents and opponents of the Amendment. This discussion and our own investigation convince us that, although these sources cast some light, it is not enough to resolve the problem with which we are faced. At best, they

---

1. In the Kansas case, *Brown v. Board of Education*, the plaintiffs are Negro children of elementary school age residing in Topeka. They brought this action in the United States District Court for the District of Kansas to enjoin enforcement of a Kansas statute which permits, but does not require, cities of more than 15,000 population to maintain separate school facilities for Negro and white students. Kan. Gen. Stat. § 72-1724 (1949). Pursuant to that authority, the Topeka Board of Education elected to establish segregated elementary schools. Other public schools in the community, however, are operated on a nonsegregated basis. The three-judge District Court convened under 28 U.S.C. §§ 2281 and 2284, found that segregation in public education has a detrimental effect upon Negro children, but denied relief on the ground that the Negro and white schools were substantially equal with respect to buildings, transportation, curricula, and educational qualifications of teachers. 93 F.Supp. 797. The case is here on direct appeal under 28 U.S.C. § 1253.

In the South Carolina case, *Briggs v. Elliott*, the plaintiffs are Negro children of both elementary and high school age residing in Clarendon County. They brought this action in the United States District Court for the Eastern District of South Carolina to enjoin enforcement of provisions in the state constitution and statutory code which require the segregation of Negroes and whites in public schools. S.C. Const. Art. XI, § 7; S.C. Code § 5377 (1942). The three-judge District Court, . . . denied the requested relief. The court found that Negro schools were inferior to the white schools and ordered the defendants to begin immediately to equalize the facilities. But the court sustained the validity of the contested provisions and denied the plaintiffs admission to the white schools during the equalization program. 98 F.Supp. 529. This Court vacated the District Court's judgment and remanded the case for the purpose of obtaining the court's views on a report filed by the defendants concerning the progress made in the equalization program. 342 U.S. 350. On remand, the District Court found that substantial equality had been achieved except for buildings and that the defendants were proceeding to rectify this inequality as well. 103 F.Supp. 920. The case is again here on direct appeal under 28 U.S.C. 1253. . . .

In the Virginia case, *Davis v. County School Board*, the plaintiffs are Negro children of high school age residing in Prince Edward County. They brought this action in the United States District Court for the Eastern District of Virginia to enjoin enforcement of provisions in the state constitution and statutory code which require the segregation of Negroes and whites in public schools. Va. Const. § 140, Va. Code § 22-221 (1950). The three-judge District court, . . . denied the requested relief. The court found the Negro school inferior in physical plant, curricula, and transportation, and ordered the defendants forthwith to provide substantially equal curricula and transportation and to "proceed with all reasonable diligence and dispatch to remove" the inequality in physical plant. But, as in the South Carolina case, the court sustained the validity of the contested provisions and denied the plaintiffs admission to the white schools during the equalization program. 103 F.Supp. 337. The case is here on direct appeal under 28 U.S.C. § 1253.

In the Delaware case, *Gebhart v. Belton*, the plaintiffs are Negro children of both elementary and high school age residing in New Castle County. They brought this action in the Delaware Court of Chancery to enjoin enforcement of provisions in the state constitution and statutory code which require the segregation of Negroes and whites in public schools. Del. Const., Art. X, § 2; Del. Rev. Code § 2631 (1935). The Chancellor gave judgment for the plaintiffs and ordered their immediate admission to schools previously attended only by white children, on the ground that the Negro schools were inferior with respect to teacher training, pupil-teacher ratio, extracurricular activities, physical plant, and time and distance involved in travel. 87 A.2d 862. The Chancellor also found that segregation itself results in inferior education for Negro children . . ., but did not rest his decision on that ground. *Id.*, at 865. The Chancellor's decree was affirmed by the Supreme Court of Delaware, which intimated, however, that the defendants might be able to obtain a modification of the decree after equalization of the Negro and white schools had been accomplished. 91 A.2d 137, 152. The defendants, contending only that the Delaware courts had erred in ordering the immediate admission of the Negro plaintiffs to the white schools, applied to this court for certiorari. The writ was granted, 344 U.S. 891. The plaintiffs, who were successful below, did not submit a cross-petition.

are inconclusive. The most avid proponents of the post-War Amendments undoubtedly intended them to remove all legal distinctions among "all persons born or naturalized in the United States." Their opponents, just as certainly, were antagonistic to both the letter and the spirit of the Amendments and wished them to have the most limited effect. What others in Congress and the state legislatures had in mind cannot be determined with any degree of certainty.

An additional reason for the inconclusive nature of the Amendment's history, with respect to segregated schools, is the status of public education at that time. In the South, the movement toward free common schools, supported by general taxation, had not yet taken hold. Education of white children was largely in the hands of private groups. Education of Negroes was almost nonexistent, and practically all of the race were illiterate. In fact, any education of Negroes was forbidden by law in some states. Today, in contrast, many Negroes have achieved outstanding success in the arts and sciences as well as in the business and professional worlds. It is true that public school education at the time of the Amendment had advanced further in the North, but the effect of the Amendment on Northern States was generally ignored in the congressional debates. Even in the North, the conditions of public education did not approximate those existing today. The curriculum was usually rudimentary; ungraded schools were common in rural areas; the school term was but three months a year in many states; and compulsory school attendance was virtually unknown. As a consequence, it is not surprising that there should be so little in the history of the Fourteenth Amendment relating to its intended effect on public education.

In the first cases in this court construing the Fourteenth Amendment, decided shortly after its adoption, the court interpreted it as proscribing all state-imposed discriminations against the Negro race. The doctrine of "separate but equal" did not make its appearance in this court until 1896 in the case of *Plessy v. Ferguson, supra*, involving not education but transportation.[6] American courts have since labored with the doctrine for over half a century. In this Court, there have been six cases involving the "separate but equal" doctrine in the field of public education. In *Cumming v. County Board of Education*, 175 U.S. 528, and *Gong Lum v. Rice*, 275 U.S. 78, the validity of the doctrine itself was not challenged. In more recent cases, all on the graduate school level, inequality was found in that specific benefits enjoyed by white students were denied to Negro students of the same educational qualifications. *Missouri ex rel. Gaines v. Canada*, 305 U.S. 337; *Sipuel v. Oklahoma*, 332 U.S. 631; *Sweatt v. Painter*, 339 U.S. 629; *McLaurin v. Oklahoma State Regents*, 339 U.S. 637. In none of these cases was it necessary to re-examine the doctrine to grant relief to the Negro plaintiff. And in *Sweatt v. Painter, supra*, the Court expressly reserved decision on the question whether *Plessy v. Ferguson* should be held inapplicable to public education.

In the instant cases, that question is directly presented. Here, unlike *Sweatt v. Painter*, there are findings below that the Negro and white schools involved have been equalized, or are being equalized, with respect to buildings, curricula, qualifications and salaries of teachers, and other "tangible" factors. Our decision, therefore, cannot turn on merely a comparison of these tangible factors in the Negro and white schools involved in each of the cases. We must look instead to the effect of segregation itself on public education.

In approaching this problem, we cannot turn the clock back to 1868 when the Amendment was adopted, or even to 1896 when *Plessy v. Ferguson* was written. We must consider public education in the light of its full development and its present place in American life throughout the Nation. Only in this way can it be determined if segregation in public schools deprives these plaintiffs of the equal protection of the laws.

Today, education is perhaps the most important function of state and local governments. Compulsory school attendance laws and the great expenditures for education both demonstrate our recognition of the importance of education to our democratic society. It is required in the performance of our most basic public responsibilities, even service in the armed

6. The doctrine apparently originated in *Roberts v. City of Boston*, [5 Cush. 198,] 59 Mass. 198, 206 (1850), upholding school segregation against attack as being violative of a state constitutional guarantee of equality. Segregation in Boston public schools was eliminated in 1855. Mass. Acts 1855, c. 256. But elsewhere in the North segregation in public education has persisted in some communities until recent years. It is apparent that such segregation has long been a nationwide problem, not merely one of sectional concern.

forces. It is the very foundation of good citizenship. Today it is a principal instrument in awakening the child to cultural values, in preparing him for later professional training, and in helping him to adjust normally to his environment. In these days, it is doubtful that any child may reasonably be expected to succeed in life if he is denied the opportunity of an education. Such an opportunity, where the state has undertaken to provide it, is a right which must be made available to all on equal terms.

We come then to the question presented: Does segregation of children in public schools solely on the basis of race, even though the physical facilities and other "tangible" factors may be equal, deprive the children of the minority group of equal educational opportunities? We believe that it does.

In *Sweatt v. Painter, supra*, in finding that a segregated law school for Negroes could not provide them equal educational opportunities, this Court relied in large part on "those qualities which are incapable of objective measurement but which make for greatness in a law school." In *McLaurin v. Oklahoma State Regents, supra*, the Court, in requiring that a Negro admitted to a white graduate school be treated like all other students, again resorted to intangible considerations: ". . . his ability to study, to engage in discussions and exchange views with other students, and, in general, to learn his profession." Such considerations apply with added force to children in grade and high schools. To separate them from others of similar age and qualifications solely because of their race generates a feeling of inferiority as to their status in the community that may affect their hearts and minds in a way unlikely ever to be undone. The effect of this separation on their educational opportunities was well stated by a finding in the Kansas case by a court which nevertheless felt compelled to rule against the Negro plaintiffs:

> Segregation of white and colored children in public schools has a detrimental effect upon the colored children. The impact is greater when it has the sanction of the law; for the policy of separating the races is usually interpreted as denoting the inferiority of the Negro group. A sense of inferiority affects the motivation of a child to learn. Segregation with the sanction of law, therefore, has a tendency to retard the educational and mental development of Negro children and to deprive them of some of the benefits they would receive in a racial[ly] integrated school system.

Whatever may have been the extent of psychological knowledge at the time of *Plessy v. Ferguson*, this finding is amply supported by modern authority.[11] Any language in *Plessy v. Ferguson* contrary to this finding is rejected.

We conclude that in the field of public education the doctrine of "separate but equal" has no place. Separated educational facilities are inherently unequal. Therefore we hold that the plaintiffs and others similarly situated for whom the actions have been brought are, by reason of the segregation complained of, deprived of the equal protection of the laws guaranteed by the Fourteenth Amendment. This disposition makes unnecessary any discussion whether such segregation also violates the Due Process Clause of the Fourteenth Amendment.

Because these are class actions, because of the wide applicability of this decision, and because of the great variety of local conditions, the formulation of decrees in these cases presents problems of considerable complexity. On reargument, the consideration of appropriate relief was necessarily subordinated to the primary question—the constitutionality of segregation in public education. We have now announced that such segregation is a denial of the equal protection of the laws. In order that we may have the full assistance of the parties in formulating decrees, the cases will be restored to the docket, and the parties are requested to present further argument on Questions 4 and 5 previously propounded by the Court for the reargument this term.[13] The Attorney General of the United States is again invited to participate. The Attorneys General of the states re-

11. K. B. Clark, *Effect of Prejudice and Discrimination on Personality Development* (Mid-century White House Conference on Children and Youth, 1950); Witmer and Kotinsky, *Personality in the Making*, c. 6 (1952); Deutscher and Chein, "The Psychological Effects of Enforced Segregation: A Survey of Social Science Opinion," 26 *J. Psychol.* 259 (1948); Chein, "What Are the Psychological Effects of Segregation under Conditions of Equal Facilities?" 3 *Int. J. Opinion and Attitude Res.* 229 (1949); Brameld, "Educational Costs," in *Discrimination and National Welfare*, 44–48 (MacIver ed. 1949); Frazier, *The Negro in the United States*, 674–81 (1949). And see generally Myrdal, *An American Dilemma* (1944).

13. "4. Assuming it is decided that segregation in public schools violates the Fourteenth Amendment

"(a) would a decree necessarily follow providing that, within the limits set by normal geographic school districting, Negro children should forthwith be admitted to schools of their choice, or

quiring or permitting segregation in public education will also be permitted to appear as *amici curiae* upon request to do so. . . .

It is so ordered.

NOTES AND QUESTIONS

1. **Brown I** *and the "Separate But Equal" Doctrine*

Brown I must be understood in light of the court's prior decision in *Plessy v. Ferguson*, 163 U.S. 537, 16 S.Ct. 1138, 41 L.Ed. 256 (1896), which established that "separate but equal" accommodations do not violate the Fourteenth Amendment. In *Plessy*, the Court upheld a Louisiana statute that provided that "all railway companies . . . shall provide equal but separate accommodations for the white, and colored races. . . ." The Court wrote:

> The object of the [fourteenth] amendment was undoubtedly to enforce the absolute equality of the two races before the law, but in the nature of things it could not have been intended to abolish distinctions based upon color, or to enforce social, as distinguished from political equality, or a commingling of the two races upon terms unsatisfactory to either. Laws permitting, and even requiring, their separation in places where they are liable to be brought into contact do not necessarily imply the inferiority of either race to the other, and have been generally, if not universally, recognized as within the competency of the state legislatures in the exercise of their police power. The most common instance of this is connected with the establishment of separate schools for white and colored children, which has been held to be a valid exercise of the legislative power even by courts of States where the political rights of the colored race have been longest and most earnestly enforced.

Plessy, 163 U.S. at 544, 16 S.Ct. at 1140. Justice Harlan, in dissent, stated:

> Our Constitution is color-blind, and neither knows nor tolerates classes among citizens. In respect of civil rights, all citizens are equal before the law. . . . The law regards man as man, and takes no account of his surroundings or of his color when his civil rights as guaranteed by the supreme law of the land are involved. It is, therefore, to be regretted that this high tribunal, the final expositor of the fundamental law of the land, has reached the conclusion that it is competent for a state to regulate the enjoyment by citizens of their civil rights solely upon the basis of race. . . . *Id.* at 560, 16 S.Ct. 1146.

The *Plessy* standard subsequently was extended to public schooling. In *Gong Lum v. Rice*, 275 U.S. 78, 85–86, 48 S.Ct. 91, 93, 72 L.Ed. 172 (1927), the Supreme Court, almost without analysis, treated the separate but equal rule as an orthodox constitutional principle applicable to public education. *See also Cumming v. Richmond County Board of Education*, 175 U.S. 528, 20 S.Ct. 197, 44 L.Ed. 262 (1899).

Did *Brown* explicitly repudiate *Plessy* when it held that "in the field of public education the doctrine of separate but equal has no place"? *See generally* Kauper, "Segregation in Public Education: The Decline of *Plessy v. Ferguson*," 53 *Mich. L. Rev*. 1137 (1954); McKay, "Segregation and Public Recreation," 40 *Va. L. Rev*. 697 (1954). Or is it more accurate to say that *Brown* was decided within the ambit of the *Plessy* rule but that the Court simply found that in the context of public education, "separate educational facilities are inherently unequal?" Why did the Court choose not to overrule *Plessy* directly?

Professor Hutchinson observes:

> Warren made his opinion acceptable to Reed, and perhaps also to Clark, by appearing to do no more than rest the decision on prior precedents and at least superficially analogous language from those precedents. The elements producing unanimity in *Brown* included not only the refinement of the issues over time, but also the appeal to a slowly growing body of case law that, by its very existence, rebutted the claim by the states . . . that history was on the side of segregation.

"(b) may this Court, in the exercise of its equity powers, permit an effective gradual adjustment to be brought about from existing segregated systems to a system not based on color distinctions?

"5. On the assumption on which questions 4(a) and (b) are based, and assuming further that this Court will exercise its equity powers to the end described in question 4(b),

"(a) should this Court formulate detailed decrees in these cases;

"(b) if so, what specific issues should the decrees reach;

"(c) should this Court appoint a special master to hear evidence with a view to recommending specific terms for such decrees;

"(d) should this Court remand to the courts of first instance with directions to frame decrees in these cases, and if so what general directions should the decrees of this Court include and what procedures should the courts of first instance follow in arriving at the specific terms of more detailed decrees?"

Hutchinson, *infra* at 43–44. *Plessy* was subsequently overruled in *Gayle v. Browder*, 352 U.S. 903, 77 S.Ct. 145, 1 L.Ed.2d 114 (1956) (per curiam), a case concerned with segregated seating on buses.

2. *Legal Developments from* Plessy *to* Brown

The National Association for the Advancement of Colored People (NAACP) initiated its attack on *Plessy* in *Missouri ex rel. Gaines v. Canada*, 305 U.S. 337, 59 S.Ct. 232, 83 L.Ed. 208 (1938). Gaines, a black law school applicant, was obliged by Missouri to attend a law school outside the state because Missouri had not yet established a separate law school for blacks. Missouri would have defrayed Gaines' out-of-state tuition fees. The Court held that the "separate but equal doctrine" required Missouri to provide its black citizens with an educational opportunity equal to that of its white citizens and that the availability of services in adjacent states did not meet this obligation. This was the first time the court "provided content to the 'equal' branch of the 'separate but equal' doctrine." Hutchinson, "Unanimity and Desegregation: Decisionmaking in the Supreme Court, 1948–1958," 68 *Geo.L.J.* 1, 5 (1979).

Three more education cases were litigated before the Supreme Court by the NAACP: *Sipuel v. Board of Regents of the University of Oklahoma*, 332 U.S. 631, 68 S.Ct. 299, 92 L.Ed. 247 (1948), *Sweatt v. Painter*, 339 U.S. 629, 70 S.Ct. 848, 94 L.Ed. 1114 (1950), both of which concerned law school admissions, and *McLaurin v. Oklahoma State Regents*, 339 U.S. 637, 70 S.Ct. 851, 94 L.Ed. 1149 (1950), which applied to graduate programs other than law.

The opinion in *Sweatt* recognized the need to compare both the tangible factors of Texas's separate law schools, and the intangible factors such as prestige, faculty reputation, and experience of the administration as integral parts of the equality determination. "Moreover," said the Court,

> the law school, the proving ground for legal learning and practice, cannot be effective in isolation from the individuals and institutions with which the law interacts. Few students and no one who has practiced law would choose to study in an academic vacuum, removed from the interplay of ideas and the exchange of views with which the law is concerned. The law school to which Texas is willing to admit petitioner excludes from its student body members of the racial groups which number 85% of the population of the State and include most of the lawyers, witnesses, jurors, judges and other officials with whom petitioner will inevitably be dealing when he becomes a member of the Texas Bar.

Sweatt, 339 U.S. at 634, 70 S.Ct. at 850.

Two features of this historical sketch stand out: the Supreme Court increasingly recognized that interaction with others was part of the learning process itself rather than merely a social by-product; and the NAACP strategy obliged the Court to focus on the "equal" provision of the *Plessy* rule, compelling it to determine whether separateness might carry with it subtle and unquantifiable inequalities. *See generally* Hutchinson, *supra;* Ransmeier, "The Fourteenth Amendment and the 'Separate But Equal' Doctrine," 50 *Mich.L.Rev.* 203 (1951); Roche, "Education, Segregation and the Supreme Court—A Political Analysis," 99 *U.Pa.L.Rev.* 949 (1951). The next logical step was to extend such reasoning to the primary and secondary schools. *See* R. Kluger, *Simple Justice* (1975), for an excellent and very readable account of the NAACP's strategy in these pre-*Brown* cases and the planning that led to the Supreme Court's decision in *Brown*.

3. *Debate About the "Original Meaning" of the Fourteenth Amendment*

One of the fundamental debates in *Brown* concerned the intended scope of the Fourteenth Amendment. A number of justices had been greatly troubled by a perceived lack of legislative or judicial history to support a holding that school segregation was unconstitutional. *See* R. Kluger, *Simple Justice* 590–609 (1975); Hutchinson, "Unanimity and Desegregation: Decision-making in the Supreme Court, 1948–1958," 68 *Geo. L.J.* 1, 40 (1979). The NAACP attorneys representing the plaintiffs contended that congressional debates from the era in which the amendment was enacted demonstrate that it was designed to operate "as a prohibition against the imposition of any racial classification in respect to civil rights." Counsel for the southern school districts argued that such a reading misread and distorted the words and history of the amendment. In their eyes, the abolitionist movement's sole target had been slavery, and banning slavery does not reach the question of mixed or segregated schools.

The Court concluded that the legislative history is ambiguous on the issue raised by the parties. Does the language of the amendment, and its presence in conjunction with the Thirteenth Amendment, favor either side of this debate? How important should legislative history be in constitutional interpretation and application? *See generally* Brest, "The Misconceived Quest for the Original Understanding," 60 *B.U.L. Rev.* 204 (1980); Bickel, "The Original Understanding and the Segregation Decision," 69 *Harv.L.Rev.* 1 (1955); Frank and Munro, "The Original Understanding of 'Equal Protection of the Laws'," 1972 *Wash. U. L. Q.* 421. *But see* R. Berger, *Government by Judiciary* (1977).

4. Brown I: *A Case About Education or a Case About Race?*

a. Education. Is *Brown* most appropriately described as a case about education? In other words, is the central thrust of *Brown* the idea that all children must be afforded equal educational opportunities and that segregated schooling is antithetical to that policy, just as inferior textbooks or teachers might be? Certainly, the encomium to education in the *Brown* opinion gives support to this view. Does treating *Brown* as a case primarily concerned with educational equality imply that all school segregation—adventitious as well as deliberate—is constitutionally defective? Does it imply that the Court is treating the student peer group as an educational resource? *See generally* Cohen, "Defining Racial Equality in Education," 16 *U.C.L.A. L. Rev.* 255 (1969). Should the focus of relief be "on obtaining real educational effectiveness which may entail the improvement of presently desegregated schools as well as the creation or preservation of model black schools"? Bell, "*Brown v. Board of Education* and the Interest-Convergence Dilemma," 93 *Harv. L. Rev.* 518, 532 (1980).

Bolling v. Sharpe, 347 U.S. 497, 74 S.Ct. 693, 98 L.Ed. 884 (1954), the companion case to *Brown,* applied that decision to the District of Columbia (not a "state" under the Fourteenth Amendment). The Court stated that "The Fifth Amendment [does] not contain an equal protection clause. . . . But, as this Court has recognized, discrimination may be so unjustifiable as to be violative of [Fifth Amendment] due process. Classifications based solely upon race must be scrutinized with particular care, since they are contrary to our traditions and hence constitutionally suspect." 347 U.S. at 499, 74 S.Ct. at 694. But in Chief Justice Warren's original proposed opinion for the Court, he took a very different tack:

> This Court has applied similar reasoning to analogous situations in the field of education, the very subject now before us. Thus children and parents are deprived of the liberty protected by the Due Process Clause when the children are prohibited from pursuing certain courses, or from attending private schools and foreign-language schools. Such prohibitions were found to be unreasonable, and unrelated to any legitimate governmental objective. Just as a government may not impose arbitrary restrictions on the parent's right to educate his child, the government must not impose arbitrary restraints on access to the education which the government itself provides.

"Memorandum on the *District of Columbia Case* from the Chief Justice to the Conference" (May 7, 1954), *reprinted in* Hutchinson, *supra* at 93–94 App.

In effect, Warren proposed that education be treated as a "fundamental" interest under the Fifth Amendment's due process clause, and the first sentence of the quoted excerpt specifically was grounded in *Meyer v. Nebraska, Bartels v. Iowa, Pierce v. Society of Sisters,* and *Farrington v. Tokushige. Id. See* chapter 1. In response to objections by Justice Frankfurter and perhaps other Justices, Warren abandoned the "fundamental" interest approach. "With a flick of the wrist he changed *Bolling v. Sharpe* from an education case into a race case, and the equal protection component of the fifth amendment was born." Hutchinson, *supra* at 46. The birth has not been well received by some. *See, e.g.,* Linde, "Judges, Critics, and the Realist Tradition," 82 *Yale L.J.* 227, 233–34 (1972).

b. Race. Is *Brown* more aptly described as a case primarily concerned with racial constraints and freedom of association? If so, does the holding in *Brown* become applicable to any situation in which racial segregation occurs, provided, of course, that the requisite governmental involvement can be demonstrated? Historic judicial hostility to state-imposed racial classification and the numerous per curiam extensions of *Brown* striking down racial separation in noneducation areas suggest that race may have been the critical factor. *See, e.g., Watson v. Memphis,* 373 U.S. 526, 83 S.Ct. 1314, 10 L.Ed.2d 529 (1963); *New Orleans City Park Improvement Ass'n v. Detiege,* 358 U.S. 54, 79 S.Ct. 99, 3 L.Ed.2d 46 (1958) (per curiam).

c. Race and Education. Is *Brown* best treated as both an education and a race case; that is, one that posits a relationship between unconstrained racial association, equality of educational resources, and equality of opportunity, with the benefits of equality seen as following from school desegregation?

d. Unanimity. Why is *Brown* so difficult to interpret? Professor Hutchinson posits that the quest for unanimity ultimately led to obfuscation:

> [U]nanimity both masked the uncertainty within the Court over how to police *Brown* and contained what otherwise could have erupted into severe and debilitating division over the precise meaning of the revolutionary decision. . . . Indeed, the Court's continuing desire to be united outweighed its responsibility to be persuasive on enough occasions that it has been recently asked if, on balance, unanimity was worth the price. The question, which is now compelling in hindsight, is anachronistic: to the judges faced with *Brown* and its aftermath, the costs of disunity were much too high to accept.

Hutchinson, *supra* at 87.

Why was unanimity thought to be so important?

5. *Ethical Principles and Social Science Evidence*

a. Quality of Social Science Evidence in Brown. The social science evidence that *Brown* relied on to assess the effects of segregation has been attacked on methodological and interpretive grounds. *See, e.g.*, Cahn, "Jurisprudence," 30 *N.Y.U. L. Rev.* 150 (1955); Garfinkel, "Social Science Evidence and the School Desegregation Cases," 21 *J. Pol.* 37 (1959); Van Den Haag, "Social Science Testimony in the Desegregation Cases—A Reply to Professor Kenneth Clark," 6 *Vill. L. Rev.* 69 (1960). In this regard, consider the following excerpts from the social scientists' amicus brief in *Brown*, which illustrates the type of empirical data before the Supreme Court:

> [T]he opinion stated by a large majority (90 percent) of social scientists who replied to a questionnaire concerning the probable effects of enforced segregation under conditions of equal facilities [is] . . . that, regardless of the facilities which are provided, enforced segregation is psychologically detrimental to the members of the segregated group [here, the blacks].
>
> * * *
>
> The available scientific evidence indicates that much, perhaps all, of the observable differences among various racial and national groups may be adequately explained in terms of environmental differences.
>
> * * *
>
> Comprehensive reviews of . . . instances [of desegregation] clearly establish the fact that desegregation has been carried out successfully in a variety of situations although outbreaks of violence had been commonly predicted.

Is this survey really evidence at all? *See* Arkes, "The Problem of Kenneth Clark," 58 *Commentary* 37 (1974). Dr. Kenneth B. Clark, one of the moving forces behind the introduction of empirical data in the *Brown* case, has commented: "By providing such evidence, the social scientists made it possible to avoid the need to obtain proof of individual damage and to avoid assessment of the equality of facilities in each individual school situation. The assumption of inequality could now be made wherever segregation existed." Clark, "The Social Scientists, the Brown Decision, and Contemporary Confusion," in L. Friedman, ed., *Argument* xxxvii (1969). Might the appellants have submitted empirical evidence of greater probative force without resorting to a school-by-school survey of each district involved in the litigation? Do you agree with Clark's conclusion? Should the lawyers for appellants in *Brown* be faulted for relying on such inconclusive data? *See* Greenberg, "Social Scientists Take the Stand," 54 *Mich. L. Rev.* 953 (1956).

If the school districts had submitted evidence indicating that segregated schooling has little effect on variations in school performance and that differences in family background or home environment were critical, *see, e.g.*, J. Coleman *et al.*, *Equal Educational Opportunity* (1966) (The Coleman Report), or differences in heredity, *see* Jensen, "How Much Can We Boost IQ and Scholastic Achievement," 39 *Harv. Ed. Rev.* 1 (1969), what weight should the trial court or the Supreme Court have given such evidence in determining the nature and scope of the constitutional right? *See generally* B. Levin and W. Hawley, eds., "School Desegregation: Lessons of the First Twenty-Five Years," 42 *Law & Contemp. Probs.* 1 (1978) (pt. 1). What if the evidence indicated that following desegregation the achievement levels of black students remained unchanged or declined? *See, e.g.*, H. Gerard and N. Miller, *School Desegregation: A Long-Term Study* (1975). What if the evidence showed that racial attitudes worsened rather than improved after desegregation? *See, e.g.*, Armor, "The Evidence on Busing," 28 *Pub. Interest* 90 (1972). *See*, respectively, Crain and Mahard, "Desegregation and Black Achievement: A Review of the Research," 42 *Law & Contemp. Probs.* 17 (1978) (pt. 2), and Epps, "The Impact of School Desegregation on the Self-Evaluation and Achievement Orientation of Minority Children," *id.* at 57, for contrasting evidence.

Would long-term versus short-term effects be more relevant? *See* Braddock, Crain, and McPartland, "A Long-Term View of School Desegregation: Some Recent Studies of Graduates as Adults," 66 *Phi Delta Kappan* 259 (1984).

Did the decision in *Plessy*, which rejected the argument that segregation might be stigmatizing or otherwise injurious, invite reliance on psychological and sociological data by the Court and appellants in *Brown? See* R. Kluger, *Simple Justice* 705–7 (1975); J. Peltason, 58 *Lonely Men* 49 (1961). Might this reliance be explained by the necessity of giving a controversial decision an aura of legitimacy by demonstrating that it was consistent with both a constitutional and empirical calculus? *See* Cohen and Weiss, "Social Science and Social Policy: Schools and Race," in R. Rist and R. Anson, eds., *Education, Social Science, and the Judicial Process* 72, 79 (1977).

b. The Controversy. To what extent does the *Brown* opinion rest upon the social science evidence cited in footnote 11 rather than upon principles of law? Legal scholars have addressed both the significance of the social science evidence to the result and the propriety of the Court's reliance on social science research to justify the desegregation decisions. Professor Frank Goodman, for example, has observed that "Constitutional scholars, whatever their views as to the correctness of the decision, have been reluctant to believe that the Court relied to any great extent on the 'modern authorities' cited in its opinion." Goodman, "De Facto School Segregation: A Constitutional and Empirical Analysis," 60 *Calif. L. Rev*. 275, 279 (1972). *See also*, Black, "The Lawfulness of the Segregation Decisions," 69 *Yale L.J.* 421 (1960); Cahn, "Jurisprudence," 30 *N.Y.U. L. Rev*. 150 (1955); Heyman, "The Chief Justice, Racial Segregation, and the Friendly Critics," 49 *Calif. L. Rev*. 104 (1961); Yudof, "School Desegregation: Legal Realism, Reasoned Elaboration, and Social Science Research in the Supreme Court," 42 *Law & Contemp. Probs*. 57 (1978) (pt. 2).

For additional insight into the significance of the evidence of footnote 11 to some members of the Court, *see* Justice Jackson's memorandum of February 15, 1954, on the school desegregation decision, quoted in part in R. Kluger, *Simple Justice* at 689 (1975). For the views of Chief Justice Warren and several other members of the Court, *see* Kluger, *supra* at 705–07.

B. *Brown II*: The Scope of Relief

Brown v. Board of Education

349 U.S. 294, 75 S.Ct. 753, 99 L.Ed. 1083 (1955).

Mr. Chief Justice Warren delivered the opinion of the Court.

These cases were decided on May 17, 1954. The opinions of that date, declaring the fundamental principle that racial discrimination in public education is unconstitutional, are incorporated herein by reference. All provisions of federal, state, or local law requiring or permitting such discrimination must yield to this principle. There remains for consideration the manner in which relief is to be accorded.

Because these cases arose under different local conditions and their disposition will involve a variety of local problems, we requested further argument on the question of relief. . . .

These presentations were informative and helpful to the Court in its consideration of the complexities arising from the transition to a system of public education freed of racial discrimination. The presentations also demonstrated that substantial steps to eliminate racial discrimination in public schools have already been taken, not only in some of the communities in which these cases arose, but in some of the states appearing as *amici curiae*, and in other states as well. Substantial progress has been made in the District of Columbia and in the communities in Kansas and Delaware involved in this litigation. The defendants in the cases coming to us from South Carolina and Virginia are awaiting the decision of this Court concerning relief.

Full implementation of these constitutional principles may require solution of varied local school problems. School authorities have the primary responsibility for elucidating, assessing, and solving these problems; courts will have to consider whether the action of school authorities constitutes good faith implementation of the governing constitutional principles. Because of their proximity to local conditions and the possible need for further hearings, the courts which originally heard these cases can best perform this judicial appraisal. Accordingly, we believe it appropriate to remand the cases to those courts.

In fashioning and effectuating the decrees, the courts will be guided by equitable principles. Traditionally, equity has been characterized by a practical flexibility in shaping its remedies and by a facility for adjusting and reconciling public and private needs. These cases call for the exercise of these traditional attributes of equity power. At stake is the personal interest of the plaintiffs in admission to public schools as soon as practicable on a nondiscriminatory basis. To effectuate this interest may call for elimination of a variety of obstacles in making the transition to school systems operated in accordance with the constitutional principles set forth in our May 17, 1954, decision. Courts of equity may properly take into account the public interest in the elimination of such obstacles in a systematic and effective manner. But it should go without saying that the vitality of these constitutional principles cannot be allowed to yield simply because of disagreement with them.

While giving weight to these public and private considerations, the courts will require that the defendants make a prompt and reasonable start toward full compliance with our May 17, 1954, ruling. Once such a start has been made, the courts may find that additional time is necessary to carry out the ruling in an effective manner. The burden rests upon the defendants to establish that such time is necessary in the public interest and is consistent with good faith compliance at the earliest practicable date. To that end, the courts may consider problems related to administration, arising from the physical condition of the school plant, the school transportation system, personnel, revision of school districts and attendance areas into compact units to achieve a system of determining admission to the public schools on a nonracial basis, and revision of local laws and regulations which may be necessary in solving the foregoing problems. They will also consider the adequacy of any plans the defendants may propose to meet these problems and to effectuate a transition to a racially nondiscriminatory school system. During this period of transition, the courts will retain jurisdiction of these cases.

The judgments below, except that in the Delaware case, are accordingly reversed and the cases are remanded to the District Courts to take such proceedings and enter such orders and decrees consistent with this opinion as are necessary and proper to admit to public schools on a racially nondiscriminatory basis with all deliberate speed the parties to these cases. The judgment in the Delaware case—ordering the immediate admission of the plaintiffs to schools previously attended only by white children—is affirmed on the basis of the principles stated in our May 17, 1954, opinion, but the case is remanded to the Supreme Court of Delaware for such further proceedings as that court may deem necessary in light of this opinion.

It is so ordered.

NOTES AND QUESTIONS

1. *"All Deliberate Speed": An Unusual Remedy?* The "all deliberate speed" standard describes an unspecified remedy that would take effect in an undefined interval of time. That standard differs from the typically precise formulations of relief that usually require immediate implementation. As Professor Bickel points out:

> In the vast majority of cases—barring those that are dismissed outright as not suitable for adjudication—the normal and expected judgment of the court is a crisp and specific writing which tells one of the parties exactly what he must do, such as pay a judgment, deliver certain real estate, cease from doing something, or, indeed, go to jail. The equivalent in these cases would have been a decree ordering the named children, and perhaps, since these were class actions, all children in the five school districts affected who were similarly situated, to be admitted forthwith to the white schools of their choice.

A. Bickel, *The Least Dangerous Branch* 247 (1962). *See also* McKay, " 'With All Deliberate Speed'—A Study of School Desegregation," 31 *N.Y.U. L. Rev.* 991 (1956).

Does the Court's approach minimize the legal significance of the injury suffered by the actual plaintiffs who initiated *Brown I?* Did the Court, in characterizing *Brown* as a test case of broad dimensions, submerge the claims of the individual plaintiffs into the hypothesized claims of all African Americans—with the consequence that an eventual remedy ("with all deliberate speed") for all blacks would ultimately benefit the particular parties who had brought the suit? *See* Hartman, "The Right to Equal Educational Opportunities as a Personal and Present Right," 9 *Wayne L. Rev.* 424 (1963); Lusky, "The Stereotype: Hard Core of Racism," 13 *Buff. L. Rev.* 450, 458 (1964). *See generally* Fiss, "Groups and the Equal Protection Clause," 5 *J. Philosophy & Pub. Aff.* 107 (1976). In this sense, is "all deliberate speed" analogous to "prospective overruling"?

Typically a prospective decree is one that overrules a prior decision but does not apply the new rule to the case before it, leaving the parties without relief. *See* Comment, "Prospective Overruling and Retroactive Application in the Federal Courts," 71 *Yale L.J.* 907 (1962). Does the "all deliberate speed" standard spring from practical problems in implementation rather than from considerations of more abstract principles of justice? *See* E. Warren, *The Memoirs of Earl Warren* 288–89 (1977). *See generally* Yudof, "Implementation Theories and Desegregation Realities," 32 *Ala. L. Rev.* 441 (1981).

If a more straightforward and forceful standard, as urged by the NAACP, had been embraced by the Court's decree, would actual desegregation have occurred more quickly? Justice Black once stated that the "deliberate speed" formula "delayed the process of outlawing segregation" and that "the Court should have forced its judgment on the counties it affected that minute." "Justice Black and the Bill of Rights," 9 *Sw. U. L. Rev.* 937, 941 (1977) (transcript of interview with Justice Black). *See also* Carter, "The Warren Court and Desegregation," 67 *Mich. L. Rev.* 237 (1968). Might such a decree have engendered even more hostile resistance than that which greeted the "all deliberate speed" mandate?

2. Brown II *and the Lower Federal Courts*

Because the Court placed responsibility for school desegregation in the hands of federal district courts and local school boards, delay in the implementation of *Brown* was inevitable. *See generally* H. Rodgers and C. Bullock, *Law and Social Change*, ch. 4 (1972); G. Orfield, *The Reconstruction of Southern Education* 15–18 (1969). The Court had not developed adequate guidelines for school desegregation, and thus much time was to be wasted in lower courts converting nebulous doctrine into understandable and administrable constitutional law. *See* Carter, "Equal Educational Opportunities for Negroes—Abstraction or Reality," 1968 *U. Ill. L.F.* 160, 177–80.

III. THE PROGRESS OF SCHOOL DESEGREGATION: 1954–1968

A. Southern Resistance

From 1955 until *Cooper v. Aaron*, 358 U.S. 1, 78 S.Ct. 1401, 3 L.Ed.2d 5 (1958), the Supreme Court failed to grant "plenary consideration to any case involving racial segregation in education." Hutchinson, "Unanimity and Desegregation: Decision-making in the Supreme Court, 1948–1958," 68 *Geo. L.J.* 1 (1979). The Court's policy was apparently to dispose summarily of race cases by per curiam orders in order "to maximize the effect of *Brown* and to minimize controversy and resistance." Hutchinson, *supra* at 61. *See also* S. Wasby, A. D'Amato, and R. Metrailer, *Desegregation from* Brown *to* Alexander (1977); Bickel and Wellington, "Legislative Purpose and the Judicial Process: The Lincoln Mills Case," 71 *Harv. L. Rev.* 1, 3–4 (1957).

From 1954 until 1964, progress in the desegregation of southern school districts was miniscule. In 1964, in seven of the eleven states, only 2.14 percent of black students attended desegregated schools. H. Horowitz and K. Karst, *Law, Lawyers, and Social Change* 239 (1969). As Professors Horowitz and Karst have noted, in the decade after *Brown* "the desegregation of southern school districts was not characterized by speed, deliberate or otherwise. . . . The fact is that most of the putative beneficiaries of the legal principle declared in *Brown* [were] frustrated in the vindication of their rights." *Id.* at 239–40 (1969).

The modes of southern resistance were varied. On March 12, 1956, ninety-six congressmen from the South issued a manifesto in which they promised to use "all lawful means" to maintain segregation and "commended those states which have declared the intention to resist." Popular opposition to school desegregation, supported by political leaders playing on the race issue, often resulted in massive resistance to the enforcement of *Brown*. *See Bush v. Orleans Parish School Board*, 187 F.Supp. 42 (S.D. La. 1960), *aff'd*, 365 U.S. 569, 81 S.Ct. 754, 5 L.Ed.2d 806. The myriad new pupil assignment laws, "interposition" plans, and other ingenious schemes demonstrated the truth of the popular saying, "as long as we can legislate, we can segregate." *See generally* Meador, "The Constitution and the Assignment of Pupils to Public Schools," 45 *Va. L. Rev.* 517 (1959); Bickel, "The Decade of School Desegregation: Progress and Prospects," 64 *Colum. L. Rev.* 193 (1964); B. Muse, *Ten Years of Prelude: The Story of Integration Since the Supreme Court's 1954 Decision* (1964).

The most important of these devices was the pupil assignment law, which purported to assign pupils to schools on the basis of considerations and characteristics other than race. In practice such laws perpetuated one-race schools. On one occasion, the Supreme Court affirmed a three-judge court decision upholding a pupil placement act. *Shuttlesworth v. Birmingham Board of Education*, 358 U.S. 101, 79 S.Ct. 221, 3 L.Ed.2d 145 (1958). *See* Johnson, "School Desegregation Problems in the South: An Historical Perspective," 54 *Minn. L. Rev.* 1157 (1970). A popular variation of pupil assignment laws was the "minority to majority transfer" arrangement. After formally desegregating, a Southern school district would grant to any students who constituted a racial minority in their new school the option of transferring back to their old school in which their race was a majority. In *Goss v. Board of Education*, 373 U.S. 683, 83 S.Ct. 1405, 10 L.Ed.2d 632 (1963), the Supreme Court struck down such plans as in violation of *Brown*: "Here the right of transfer, which operates solely on the basis of a racial classification, is a one-way ticket leading to but one destination, *i.e.*, the majority race of the transferee and continued segregation." 373 U.S. at 687, 83 S.Ct. at 1408.

B. Measuring the Impact of *Brown*

In the light of the early history of noncompliance, some commentators questioned whether *Brown* was wisely decided. Although empirical proof of the proposition is lacking and likely to remain so, the symbolic consequences of *Brown*, transcending the immediate difficulties in securing compliance, contributed significantly to the creation of a political and social environment in which progress toward racial justice became possible. *See, e.g.*, W. Murphy and J. Tanenhaus, *The Study of Public Law* 38 (1972); Frantz, "Is the First Amendment Law?—A Reply to Professor Mendelson," in L. Levy, ed., *Judicial Review and the Supreme Court* 161 (1967). The costs of *Brown* in terms of social dislocation, controversy, delay, and judicial energy were great. Yet there has been significant progress toward achieving racial equality since *Brown*. *See generally* G. Orfield, *Must We Bus?* (1978); C.V. Woodward, *The Strange Career of Jim Crow* (3d ed. 1974); H. Commager, ed., *The Struggle for Racial Equality* (1967). This progress has manifested itself not only in the integration of the public schools, but also in voting, employment, public accommodations, and housing.

Too often judges and lawyers ignore a fundamental truth that is obvious to laypeople and politicians: Regardless of the formal rules of constitutional adjudication, a judicial declaration that a state law is constitutional is likely to enshrine it as the recommended solution of a difficult question of public policy. *Plessy v. Ferguson* serves as a constant reminder of this proposition. Although certainly not a golden age of race relations, the early post-Reconstruction years saw a clumsy search for accommodation between the "old heritage of slavery and the new and insecure heritage of legal equality." It was a time of experimentation and testing in which blacks found a place in society they had never before enjoyed. Yet as the twentieth century approached, the trend reversed, heralded by widespread adoption of Jim Crow legislation and the Supreme Court's refusal to uphold the civil rights of blacks. *See* Woodward, *supra* at 67–109.

In *Plessy v. Ferguson*, the Supreme Court legitimated the abandonment of black rights, placing the judicial seal of approval on a racial ostracism that reached all phases of life. The Court not only created a doctrinal justification for racist policies, but also symbolically affirmed the Social Darwinists' theory that whites were superior to blacks. This judicial *coup de grace* certainly accounts, at least in part, for the lack of progress toward racial justice in the decades after *Plessy*. A reaffirmation of *Plessy* in *Brown* might well have portended a similar blow to racial equality and the civil rights movement—not only in the courts, but also in the legislatures, the voting booths, the universities, and the job and housing markets.

The judicial declaration that discrimination by race in pupil assignment was unconstitutional undoubtedly helped to mold public opinion and prod the legislative and executive branches of government into action. Certainly federal governmental hopes for racial justice preceded the *Brown* decision. Under the "separate but equal doctrine," the Supreme Court had struck down a number of racially discriminatory practices in the late post-*Plessy* period, and in 1948 President Truman had courageously declared: "We shall not . . . finally achieve the ideals for which this nation was founded so long as any American suffers discrimination as a result of his race, or religion, or color, or the land of origin of his forefathers." Numerous private groups, including the NAACP, worked forcefully for the protection of Negro rights, and the political consciousness of blacks rose dramatically. The combination of private and public movement toward racial justice might well have enabled the Supreme Court to do in 1954 what it was apparently incapable of doing in 1896. But cause and effect merge; whatever the forces that brought *Brown* into being, those forces were strengthened by the decision itself. In the early years after *Brown*, reform proposals that would have allowed the Attorney General to sue local school boards that engaged in segregation were seriously considered. Proposals for federal aid to education that would have strengthened the dual school system were defeated. Nondiscrimination clauses were inserted by the U.S. Department of Health, Education, and Welfare in contracts with colleges participating in National Defense Education Act programs. Federal funds were denied to local school districts that forced children living on military bases to attend segregated schools.

Perhaps the most immediate result of *Brown* was to arouse black organizations and their white liberal allies: "*Brown* . . . awakened a new consciousness of group identity among blacks and a fresh awareness of the possibilities of removing the discrepancy between their supposed and actual rights." W. Murphy and J. Tanenhaus, *The Study of Public Law* 38 (1972). This awakening probably led to the confrontations between civil rights groups and southern political leadership. The impact of those confrontations on American public opinion and on the federal leadership was profound, leading to the 1964 Civil Rights Act, the greatest blow to southern resistance to desegregation. G. Orfield, *The Reconstruction of Southern Education* 2–3, 33–46 (1969).

C. The Administrative-Judicial Era

During the post-*Brown II* period, the Supreme Court appeared reluctant to intervene, letting the standards by which desegregation litigation was to be decided evolve in the lower courts. Ambiguity in *Brown I* and *II*, the Court's post-*Brown II* silence, and the reluctance of lower federal courts and school boards contributed to the delay in implementing *Brown*. However, the failure of the Congress and the president to support the Court was also significant. *See* G. Orfield, *The Reconstruction of Southern Education* 15–22 (1969); J. Vander Zanden, *Race Relations in Transition* 88–94 (1966). The awesome political ramifications of *Brown* required the active assistance of the other branches of government, but this support did not materialize in the early post-*Brown* years.

Significant progress toward desegregation in the South came only with what has been characterized as the "administrative-judicial era" (H. Rodgers and C. Bullock, *Law and Social Change* 18 (1972)), which began with passage of the Civil Rights Act of 1964, 42 U.S.C.A. §§ 2000c, d (1970). *See generally* G. Orfield, *The Reconstruction of Southern Education* (1969). This legislation empowered the Department of Health, Education, and Welfare to withhold federal funds from school districts that discriminated against blacks and gave the Attorney General authority to file desegregation suits on the complaint of private citizens. 42 U.S.C.A. §§ 2000c-6, d-1 (1970). *See generally* Note, "The Courts, HEW, and Southern School Desegregation," 77 *Yale L.J.* 321, 356–64 (1967). Under the Civil Rights Act of 1964, HEW promulgated guidelines requiring school districts to make a good faith start toward desegregation. U.S. Office of Education, HEW, *General Statement of Policies under Title VI of the Civil Rights Act of 1964 Respecting Desegregation of Elementary and Secondary Schools* (1965), *reprinted in Price v. Denison Independent School District Board of Education*, 348 F.2d 1010, 1015 (5th Cir. 1965). *See also* U.S. Office of Education, HEW, *Revised Statement of Policies for School Desegregation Plans under Title VI of the Civil Rights Act of 1964*, 45 C.F.R. § 181 (1967). The relationship between the HEW guidelines and developing constitutional standards has been explored by Professor Read, "Judicial Evolution of the Law of School Integration Since *Brown v. Board of Education*," 39 *Law & Contemp. Probs.* 7, 20–26 (1975). *See also* L. Graglia, *Disaster by Decree* (1976).

Judge Wisdom once noted that "a national effort, bringing together Congress, the executive, and the judiciary may be able to make meaningful the right of Negro children to equal educational opportunities. *The courts acting alone have failed.*" *United States v. Jefferson County Board of Education*, 372 F.2d 836, 847 (5th Cir. 1966) (emphasis added), *aff'd*, 380 F.2d 385, *cert. denied*, 389 U.S. 840, 88 S.Ct. 67, 19 L.Ed.2d 103. Is this an assessment of the relative competency of the courts? Does it imply that the Congress, the executive branch, and the courts *will* succeed where the courts alone have failed? *See* Comment, "The Courts, HEW, and Southern School Desegregation," 77 *Yale L.J.* 321,

339–56 (1967). How significant is the symbolic effect of all three branches of government joining forces to ensure school desegregation?

IV. DESEGREGATION: EVOLUTION OF A CONSTITUTIONAL STANDARD

A. Introduction

One of the persistent and complex themes in the school desegregation cases is what standard should be used to determine whether the constitution has been violated; that is, when has a violation of the equal protection clause occurred, giving rise to the duty of the school board to desegregate? *See generally* J. H. Wilkinson, *Serving Justice* 133–34 (1974). *See also* T. van Geel, "Racial Discrimination from Little Rock to Harvard," 49 *Cin.L.Rev.* 49 (1980); Sedler, "The Constitution and School Desegregation: An Inquiry into the Nature of the Substantive Right," 68 *Ky.L.J.* 879 (1979–80). Is the constitutional violation the use of a racial classification, the constitutional wrong being the school board's deliberate exclusion of black students from white schools, or is the constitutional wrong the maintenance of racially identifiable schools? If the latter is the violation, is it still a violation if the racially identifiable schools arose not as a result of deliberate and intentionally discriminatory policies adopted by the school authorities but rather as a result of racially neutral policies superimposed on existing demographic segregation? *See, e.g.*, W. Stephan and J. Feagin, eds., *School Desegregation: Past, Present, and Future* 69–131 (1980); Goodman, "De Facto School Segregation: A Constitutional and Empirical Analysis," 60 *Calif.L.Rev.* 275 (1972).

The other persistent issue is concerned with remedy: that is, once it has been determined that the equal protection clause has been violated, what is the scope of the remedy that should be imposed on school boards by the courts? Is a policy of race-neutral student assignment a sufficient remedy? These two issues—violation and remedy—obviously overlap. The nature and scope of the remedy might vary according to the conception of the violation. Commentators have long argued over whether active integration or merely passive nondiscrimination is the appropriate remedy, and the view that is taken depends partly on what one conceives is the scope of the constitutional violation. *See, e.g.*, Dworkin, "Social Sciences and Constitutional Rights—The Consequences of Uncertainty," in R. Rist and R. Anson, eds., *Education, Social Science, and the Judicial Process* 20 (1977); Graglia, "From Prohibiting Segregation to Requiring Integration: Developments in the Law of Race and the Schools Since *Brown*," in Stephan and Feagin, *supra* at 69; Brest, "The Supreme Court, 1975 Term—Foreword: In Defense of the Antidiscrimination Principle," 90 *Harv.L.Rev.* 1 (1976); Kanner, "From Denver to Dayton: The Development of a Theory of Equal Protection Remedies," 72 *Nw.U.L.Rev.* 382 (1977); Wolf, "Northern School Desegregation and Residential Choice," 1977 *Sup.Ct.Rev.* 63. The differing positions are discussed in Yudof, "School Desegregation: Legal Realism, Reasoned Elaboration, and Social Science Research in the Supreme Court," 42 *Law & Contemp. Probs.* 57 (1978) (pt. 2).

B. *Green*: Divining the Constitutional Violation from the Court's Remedial Requirements?

Green v. County School Board arose in a rural district in Virginia that had maintained a dual school system by law. The New Kent County school district had made no attempts to desegregate its schools until 1965 when it adopted a freedom-of-choice plan. *Green* has a historic place in the evolution of constitutional standards, and it triggered a major change in the nature and pace of desegregation in the South.

Green v. County School Board

391 U.S. 430, 88 S.Ct. 1689, 20 L.Ed.2d 716 (1968).

Mr. Justice Brennan delivered the opinion of the Court.

The question for decision is whether, under all the circumstances here, respondent School Board's adoption of a "freedom-of-choice" plan which allows a pupil to choose his own public school constitutes adequate compliance with the Board's responsibility "to achieve a system of determining admission to the public schools on a nonracial basis. . . ." *Brown v. Board of Education*, 349 U.S. 294, 300–01 (*Brown II*).

Petitioners brought this action in March 1965 seeking injunctive relief against respondent's continued maintenance of an alleged racially segregated school system. New Kent County is a rural county in Eastern Virginia. About one-half of its population of some 4,500 are Negroes. There is no residential segregation in the county; persons of both races reside throughout. The school system has only two schools, the New Kent school on the east side of the county and the George W. Watkins school on the west side. In a memorandum filed May 17, 1966, the District Court found that the "school system serves approximately 1,300 pupils, of which 740 are Negro and 550 are White. The School Board operates one white combined elementary and high school [New Kent], and one Negro combined elementary and high school [George W. Watkins]. There are no attendance zones. Each school serves the entire county." The record indicates that twenty-one school buses—eleven serving the Watkins school and ten serving the New Kent school—travel overlapping routes throughout the county to transport pupils to and from the two schools.

The segregated system was initially established and maintained under the compulsion of Virginia constitutional and statutory provisions mandating racial segregation in public education, Va. Const. Art. IX, § 140 (1902); Va. Code § 22-221 (1950). These provisions were held to violate the Federal Constitution in *Davis v. County School Board of Prince Edward County*, decided with *Brown v. Board of Education*, 347 U.S. 483, 487 (*Brown I*). The respondent School Board continued the segregated operation of the system after the *Brown* decisions, presumably on the authority of several statutes enacted by Virginia in resistance to those decisions. Some of these statutes were held to be unconstitutional on their face or as applied. One statute, the Pupil Placement Act, Va. Code § 22-232.1 *et seq.* (1964), not repealed until 1966, divested local boards of authority to assign children to particular schools and placed that authority in a State Pupil Placement Board. Under that Act children were each year automatically reassigned to the school previously attended unless upon their application the State Board assigned them to another school; students seeking enrollment for the first time were also assigned at the discretion of the State Board. To September 1964, no Negro pupil had applied for admission to the New Kent school under this statute and no white pupil had applied for admission to the Watkins school.

The School Board initially sought dismissal of this suit on the ground that petitioners had failed to apply to the State Board for assignment to New Kent school. However on August 2, 1965, five months after the suit was brought, respondent School Board, in order to remain eligible for federal financial aid, adopted a "freedom-of-choice" plan for desegregating the schools. Under that plan, each pupil, except those entering the first and eighth grades, may annually choose between the New Kent and Watkins schools and pupils not making a choice are assigned to the school previously attended; first- and eighth-grade pupils must affirmatively choose a school. After the plan was filed the District Court denied petitioners' prayer for an injunction and granted respondent leave to submit an amendment to the plan with respect to employment and assignment of teachers and staff on a racially nondiscriminatory basis. The amendment was duly filed and on June 28, 1966, the District Court approved the "freedom-of-choice" plan as so amended. The Court of Appeals for the Fourth Circuit, *en banc*, 382 F.2d 338, affirmed the District Court's approval of the "freedom-of-choice" provisions of the plan. . . . We granted certiorari, 389 U.S. 1003.

The pattern of separate "white" and "Negro" schools in the New Kent County school system established under compulsion of state laws is precisely the pattern of segregation to which *Brown I* and *Brown II* were particularly addressed, and which *Brown I* declared unconstitutionally denied Negro school children equal protection of the laws. Racial identification of the system's schools was complete, extending not just to the composition of student bodies at the two schools but to every facet of school operations—faculty, staff, transportation, extracurricular activities and facilities. In short, the State, acting through the local school board and school officials, organized and operated a dual system, part "white" and part "Negro."

It was such dual systems that fourteen years ago *Brown I* held unconstitutional and a year later *Brown II* held must be abolished; school boards operating such school systems were *required* by *Brown II* "to effectuate a transition to a racially nondiscriminatory school system." 349 U.S. at 301. It is of course true that for the time immediately after *Brown II* the concern was with making an initial break in a long-established pattern of excluding Negro children from schools attended by white children. The principal focus was on obtaining for those Negro children courageous enough to break with tradition a place in the "white" schools. *See, e.g.*, *Cooper v. Aaron*, 358 U.S. 1. Under *Brown II* that immediate goal was only the first step, however. The transition to a unitary, nonracial system of public education was and is the ultimate end to be brought about; it was because of the "complexities arising from the transition to a system of public education freed of racial discrimination" that we provided for "all deliberate speed" in the implementation of the principles of *Brown I*, 349 U.S. at 299–301.

It is against this background that 13 years after *Brown II* commanded the abolition of dual systems we must measure the effectiveness of respondent School Board's "freedom-of-choice" plan to achieve that end. The School Board contends that it has fully discharged its obligation by adopting a plan by which every student, regardless of race, may "freely" choose the school he will attend. The Board attempts to cast the issue in its broadest form by arguing that its "freedom-of-choice" plan may be faulted only by reading the Fourteenth Amendment as universally requiring "compulsory integration," a reading it insists the wording of the Amendment will not support. But that argument ignores the thrust of *Brown II*. In the light of the command of that case, what is involved here is the question whether the Board has achieved the "racially nondiscriminatory school system" *Brown II* held must be effectuated in order to remedy the established unconstitutional deficiencies of its segregated system. In the context of the state-imposed segregated pattern of long standing, the fact that in 1965 the Board opened the doors of the former "white" school to Negro children and of the "negro" school to white children merely begins, not ends, our inquiry whether the Board has taken steps adequate to abolish its dual, segregated system. *Brown II* was a call for the dismantling of well-entrenched dual systems tempered by an awareness that complex and multifaceted problems would arise which would require time and flexibility for a successful resolution. School boards such as the respondent then operating state-compelled dual systems were nevertheless clearly charged with the affirmative duty to take whatever steps might be necessary to convert to a unitary system in which racial discrimination would be eliminated root and branch. *See Cooper v. Aaron, supra*, at 7; *Bradley v. School Board*, 382 U.S. 103; *cf. Watson v. City of Memphis*, 373 U.S. 526. The constitutional rights of Negro school children articulated in *Brown I* permit no less than this; and it was to this end that *Brown II* commanded school boards to bend their efforts.

In determining whether respondent School Board met that command by adopting its "freedom-of-choice" plan, it is relevant that this first step did not come until some eleven years after *Brown I* was decided and ten years after *Brown II* directed the making of a "prompt and reasonable start." This deliberate perpetuation of the unconstitutional dual system can only have compounded the harm of such a system. Such delays are no longer tolerable, for "the governing constitutional principles no longer bear the imprint of newly enunciated doctrine." . . . The burden on a school board today is to come forward with a plan that promises realistically to work, and promises realistically to work *now*.

. . . It is incumbent upon the school board to establish that its proposed plan promises meaningful and immediate progress toward disestablishing state-imposed segregation. It is incumbent upon the district court to weigh that claim in light of the facts at hand and in light of any alternatives which may be shown as feasible and more promising in their effectiveness. Where the court finds the board to be acting in good faith and the proposed plan to have real prospects for dismantling the state-imposed dual system "at the earliest practicable date," then the plan may be said to provide effective relief. Of course, the availability to the board of other more promising courses of action may indicate a lack of good faith; and at least it places a heavy burden upon the board to explain its preference for an apparently less effective method. Moreover, whatever plan is adopted will require evaluation in practice, and the court should retain jurisdiction until it is clear that state-imposed segregation has been completely removed. *See . . . Raney v. Board of Education. . . .*

We do not hold that "freedom of choice" can have no place in such a plan. We do not hold that a "freedom-of-choice" plan might of itself be unconstitutional, although that argument has been urged upon us. Rather, all we decide today is that in desegregating a dual system a plan utilizing "freedom of choice" is not an end in itself. As Judge Sobeloff has put it,

> "Freedom of choice" is not a sacred talisman; it is only a means to a constitutionally required end—the abolition of the system of segregation and its effects. If the means prove effective, it is acceptable, but if it fails to undo segregation, other means must be used to achieve this end. The school officials have the continuing duty to take whatever action may be necessary to create a "unitary, nonracial system." *Bowman v. County School Board*, 382 F.2d 326, 333 (4th Cir. 1967) (concurring opinion).

Accord, *Kemp v. Beasley*, 389 F.2d 178 (8th Cir. 1968); *United States v. Jefferson County Board of Education, supra*. Although the general experience under "freedom of choice" to date has been such as to indicate its ineffectiveness as a tool of desegregation,[5] there may well be instances in which it can serve as an effective device. Where it offers real promise of aiding a desegregation program to effectuate conversion of a state-imposed dual system to a unitary, nonracial system there might be no objection to allowing such a device to prove itself in operation. On the other hand, if there are reasonably available other ways, such for illustration as zoning, promising speedier and more effective conversion to a unitary, nonracial school system, "freedom of choice" must be held unacceptable.

The New Kent School Board's "freedom-of-choice" plan cannot be accepted as a sufficient step to "effectuate a transition" to a unitary system. In three years of operation not a single white child has chosen to attend Watkins school and although 115 Negro children enrolled in New Kent school in 1967 (up from 35 in 1965 and 111 in 1966) 85 percent of the Negro children in the system still attend the all-Negro Watkins school. In other words, the school system remains a dual system. Rather than further the dismantling of the dual system, the plan has operated simply to burden children and their parents with a responsibility which *Brown II* placed squarely on the School Board. The Board must be required to formulate a new plan and, in light of other courses which appear open to the Board, such as zoning, fashion steps which promise realistically to convert promptly to a system without a "white" school and a "Negro" school, but just schools.

The judgment of the Court of Appeals is vacated insofar as it affirmed the District Court and the case is remanded to the District Court for further proceedings consistent with this opinion.

It is so ordered.

NOTES AND QUESTIONS

1. Green *and* Brown

Is *Green* concerned with determining when the Constitution has been violated or with what the appropriate remedy is once a constitutional violation has been established? To what extent has the Court made clear what the violation is? In the first line of the *Green* opinion, Justice Brennan states that the question for decision is whether the school board has complied with *Brown v. Board of Education* by "determining admission to the public schools on a nonracial basis." If this is the issue, how can the result in the case be defended? Did the defendants assign students according to their race? Were the assignments not made on the basis of racially neutral choices made by black and white parents?

Justice Brennan attempts to deal with these problems by contending that although the initial concern after *Brown II* was the assignment of African American youngsters to white schools from which they were excluded solely because of their race, that was only a first step toward the ultimate goal: the "transition to a unitary, nonracial system of public education." What is a unitary school system?

a. Racial Classification Ethic and Remedies. If prohibition of racial classifications underlies the desegregation cases and if the constitutional wrong identified in those cases is the exclusion of blacks from white schools, isn't the logical remedy the admission of black students to the schools from which they were excluded because of their race? *See* Bickel,

---

5. The views of the United States Commission on Civil Rights, which we neither adopt nor refuse to adopt, are as follows:

"Freedom-of-choice plans, which have tended to perpetuate racially identifiable schools in the Southern and border States, require affirmative action by both Negro and white parents and pupils before such disestablishment can be achieved. There are a number of factors which have prevented such affirmative action by substantial numbers of parents and pupils of both races:

"(a) Fear of retaliation and hostility from the white community continue to deter many Negro families from choosing formerly all-white schools;

"(b) During the past school year [1966–67], as in the previous year, in some areas of the South, Negro families with children attending previously all-white schools under free choice plans were targets of violence, threats of violence and economic reprisal by white persons and Negro children were subjected to harassment by white classmates notwithstanding conscientious efforts by many teachers and principals to prevent such misconduct.

"(c) During the past school year, in some areas of the South public officials improperly influenced Negro families to keep their children in Negro schools and excluded Negro children attending formerly all-white schools from official functions;

"(d) Poverty deters many Negro families in the South from choosing formerly all-white schools. Some Negro parents are embarrassed to permit their children to attend such schools without suitable clothing. In some districts special fees are assessed for courses which are available only in the white schools;

"(e) Improvements in facilities and equipment . . . have been instituted in all-Negro schools in some districts in a manner that tends to discourage Negroes from selecting white schools." *Southern School Desegregation, 1966–1967*, 88 (1967). *See id.*, at 45–69; *Survey of School Desegregation in the Southern and Border States, 1965–1966*, 30–44, 51–52 (U.S. Comm'n on Civil Rights 1966).

"The Decade of School Desegregation: Progress and Prospects," 64 *Colum.L.Rev.* 193, 212 (1964). Yet in *Green* the Court emphasized the abolition of racially identifiable schools. Can that be done other than by integrating black and white students throughout the system? Of what significance is the Court's comment that the school board relied on children and their parents to dismantle the dual system rather than undertaking the responsibility itself?

b. The "Bad Faith" Argument. Proponents of the racial neutrality principle have attempted to explain the integration remedy by focusing on the bad faith of many school boards in implementing *Brown*. In *Green*, for example, the school board had not taken any steps to eliminate segregation until 1965, eleven years after *Brown I*. According to this theory, the duty to integrate "might be justified as a prophylactic, a way of making certain that a school board's policy of racial segregation has in fact been discarded." Goodman, "De Facto Segregation: A Constitutional and Empirical Analysis," 60 *Calif.L.Rev.* 275, 293 (1972). If only racial classifications are forbidden, and a school board has abandoned its policy of making such classifications, of what relevance is its good or bad faith?

Does the harm to blacks in *Green* lie in the self-evident proposition that the school board took race into account in adopting its freedom-of-choice plan? Does this justify the "arbitrary" remedy of integration? *See* Simon, "Racially Prejudiced Governmental Actions: A Motivation Theory of the Constitutional Ban Against Racial Discrimination," 15 *San Diego L.Rev.* 1041, 1122–27 (1978); Yudof, "School Desegregation: Legal Realism, Reasoned Elaboration, and Social Science Research in the Supreme Court," 42 *Law & Contemp. Probs.* 57, 58 (1978) (pt. 2). What remedy would you propose? *See, e.g., Crawford v. Board of Education*, 17 Cal. 3d 280, 305–06, 130 Cal. Rptr. 724, 741, 551 P.2d 28, 45 (1976), *aff'd*, 458 U.S. 527, 102 S.Ct. 3211, 73 L.Ed.2d 948.

c. Elimination of Discriminatory Effects of Past Segregation. Another explanation of the integration remedy in *Green* is that integration is necessary to eliminate the discriminatory effects of past practices. *See Hearings on School Busing Before Subcomm. No. 5 of the House Comm. on the Judiciary*, 92d Cong., 2d. Sess., ser. 32, pt. 3, at 1631–32 (1972) (statement of Professor Wright); Cox, "The Role of Congress in Constitutional Determinations," 40 *U. Cin.L.Rev.* 199, 258 (1971). Integration is not a substantive entitlement; rather it stands as a remedy to cure past instances of racial discrimination in the public schools. What is the relationship between the past discrimination in *Green* and the unacceptability of the freedom-of-choice plan? Can it be persuasively argued that the prior dual school system has influenced the current assignment choices of black and white parents?

Was *Green* premised on the view that the choices of blacks were dictated by economic and physical threats made against them? Why did the Court include footnote 5? Might the difficulties of the case-by-case search for coercion have led the Court to adopt a per se rule against freedom-of-choice plans? Is there any language in the opinion to support this position?

Might *Green* rest on the principle that any form of segregation is particularly injurious in previously de jure school districts because the past discrimination could have "helped to shape the attitudes of the community, both black and white, toward Negroes and Negro schools"? Goodman, "De Facto Segregation: A Constitutional and Empirical Analysis," 60 *Calif.L.Rev.* 275, 295 (1972). Is this approach realistic? Is the stigma of assignment to an all-black school limited to previously *de jure* systems? Will integration necessarily change these perceptions?

2. A Plan That "Promises Realistically to Work Now"

The Supreme Court did not further define what it meant when it said a plan had to "work" and what "effects" had to be undone and how, nor what it meant by a "unitary system." The Court did, however, make clear what it meant by "now" in *Alexander v. Holmes County Board of Education*, 396 U.S. 19, 90 S.Ct. 29, 24 L.Ed.2d 19 (1969) and *Carter v. West Feliciana Parish School Board*, 396 U.S. 290, 90 S.Ct. 608, 24 L.Ed.2d 530 (1970), in which it held that a few months' delay in desegregation to avoid disruption during the school year was impermissible and peremptorily ordered *immediate* desegregation. It was these decisions, even more than *Green*, that moved the South from minimal desegregation to significant levels of integration.

C. Establishing the Constitutional Violation in the South: *Swann* and the Connection Between Past *De Jure* Conduct and Present Segregative Effects

Swann v. Charlotte-Mecklenburg Board of Education, 402 U.S. 1, 91 S.Ct. 1267, 28 L.Ed.2d 554 (1971), raises questions about the extent to which past constitutional violations have causal connections to present segregation, thus creating a continuing violation that must be overcome. *Swann* arose in a state "having a long history of maintaining two sets of schools in a single school system deliberately operated to carry out a governmental policy to separate pupils in schools solely on the basis of race. That was what *Brown v. Board of Education* was all about." But the school board argued that the present segregated pattern of school attendance was not due to deliberate assignment by race on the part of school officials but rather to the nature of residential patterns. If there is a "continuing violation" that has not yet been overcome, what may a district court compel the school district to do?

Swann v. Charlotte-Mecklenburg Board of Education

402 U.S. 1, 91 S.Ct. 1267, 28 L.Ed.2d 554 (1971).

Chief Justice Burger delivered the opinion of the Court:

We granted certiorari in this case to review important issues as to the duties of school authorities and the scope of powers of federal courts under this Court's mandates to eliminate racially separate public schools established and maintained by state action. . . .

This case and those argued with it arose in States having a long history of maintaining two sets of schools in a single school system deliberately operated to carry out a governmental policy to separate pupils in schools solely on the basis of race. That was what *Brown v. Board of Education* was all about. These cases present us with the problem of defining in more precise terms than heretofore the scope of the duty of school authorities and district courts in implementing *Brown I* and the mandate to eliminate dual systems and establish unitary systems at once. Meanwhile district courts and courts of appeals have struggled in hundreds of cases with a multitude and variety of problems under this Court's general directive. Understandably, in an area of evolving remedies, those courts had to improvise and experiment without detailed or specific guidelines. This Court, in *Brown I*, appropriately dealt with the large constitutional principles; other federal courts had to grapple with the flinty, intractable realities of day-to-day implementation of those constitutional commands. Their efforts, of necessity, embraced a process of "trial and error," and our effort to formulate guidelines must take into account their experience. . . .

I

The Charlotte-Mecklenburg school system, the 43rd largest in the Nation, encompasses the city of Charlotte and surrounding Mecklenburg County, North Carolina. The area is large—550 square miles—spanning roughly 22 miles east-west and 36 miles north-south. During the 1968–69 school year the system served more than 84,000 pupils in 107 schools. Approximately 71% of the pupils were found to be white and 29% Negro. As of June 1969 there were approximately 24,000 Negro students in the system, of whom 21,000 attended schools within the city of Charlotte. Two-thirds of those 21,000—approximately 14,000 Negro students—attended twenty-one schools which were either totally Negro or more than 99% Negro.

This situation came about under a desegregation plan approved by the District Court at the commencement of the present litigation in 1965, 243 F.Supp. 667 (W.D.N.C.), *aff'd*, 369 F.2d 29 (4th Cir. 1966), based upon geographic zoning with a free-transfer provision. The present proceedings were initiated in September 1968 by petitioner Swann's motion for further relief based on *Green v. County School Board*, 391 U.S. 430 (1968), and its companion cases. All parties now agree that in 1969 the system fell short of achieving the unitary school system that those cases require. . . .

In April 1969 the District Court ordered the school board to come forward with a plan for both faculty and student desegregation. . . . [I]n February 1970, the District Court was presented with two alternative pupil assignment plans—the finalized "board plan" and the "Finger plan." . . .

The Board Plan

. . . The [board] plan . . . provided racially mixed faculties and administrative staffs, and modified its free-transfer plan into an optional majority-to-minority transfer system.

The board plan proposed substantial assignment of Negroes to nine of the system's 10 high schools, producing 17% to 36% Negro population in each. The projected Negro attendance at the tenth school, Independence, was 2%.

As for junior high schools, the board plan rezoned the 21 school areas so that in 20 the Negro attendance would range from 0% to 38%. The other school, located in the heart of the Negro residential area, was left with an enrollment of 90% Negro.

The board plan with respect to elementary schools relied entirely upon gerrymandering of geographic zones. More than half of the Negro elementary pupils were left in nine schools that were 86% to 100% Negro; approximately half of the white elementary pupils were assigned to schools 86% to 100% white.

The Finger Plan

The plan submitted by the court-appointed expert, Dr. Finger, adopted the school board zoning plan for senior high schools with one modification: it required that an additional 300 Negro students be transported from the Negro residential area of the city to the nearly all-white Independence High School.

The Finger plan for the junior high schools employed much of the rezoning plan of the board, combined with the creation of nine "satellite" zones. Under the satellite plan, inner-city Negro students were assigned by attendance zones to nine outlying predominately white junior high schools, thereby substantially desegregating every junior high school in the system.

The Finger plan departed from the board plan chiefly in its handling of the system's 76 elementary schools. Rather than relying solely upon geographic zoning, Dr. Finger proposed use of zoning, pairing, and grouping techniques, with the result that student bodies throughout the system would range from 9% to 38% Negro. . . .

On February 5, 1970, the District Court adopted the board plan, as modified by Dr. Finger, for the junior and senior high schools, 311 F.Supp. 265. The court rejected the board elementary school plan and adopted the Finger plan as presented. . . .

On appeal the Court of Appeals affirmed the District Court's order as to faculty desegregation and the secondary school plans, but vacated the order respecting elementary schools. While agreeing that the District Court properly disapproved the board plan concerning these schools, the Court of Appeals feared that the pairing and grouping of elementary schools would place an unreasonable burden on the board and the system's pupils. The case was remanded to the District Court for reconsideration and submission of further plans. . . .

II

Nearly 17 years ago this Court held, in explicit terms, that state-imposed segregation by race in public schools denies equal protection of the laws. At no time has the Court deviated in the slightest degree from that holding or its constitutional underpinnings. None of the parties before us challenges the Court's decision [in *Brown I* and *II*].

Over the 16 years since *Brown II*, many difficulties were encountered in implementation of the basic constitutional requirement that the State not discriminate between public school children on the basis of their race. Nothing in our national experience prior to 1955 prepared anyone for dealing with changes and adjustments of the magnitude and complexity encountered since then. Deliberate resistance of some to the Court's mandates has impeded the good-faith efforts of others to bring school systems into compliance. The detail and nature of these dilatory tactics have been noted frequently by this Court and other courts.

By the time the Court considered *Green v. County School Board*, 391 U.S. 430, in 1968, very little progress had been made in many areas where dual school systems had historically been maintained by operation of state laws. In *Green*, the Court was confronted with a record of a freedom-of-choice program that the District Court had found to operate in fact to preserve a dual system more than a decade after *Brown II*. While acknowledging that a freedom-of-choice concept could be a valid remedial measure in some circumstances, its failure to be effective in *Green* required that: "The burden on a school board today is to come forward with a plan that promises realistically to work . . . *now* . . . until it is clear that state-imposed segregation has been completely removed." *Green, supra,* at 439.

This was plain language, yet the 1969 Term of Court brought fresh evidence of the dilatory tactics of many school authorities. *Alexander v. Holmes County Board of Education,* 396 U.S. 19, restated the basic obligation asserted in *Griffin v. School Board,* 377 U.S. 218, 234 (1964), and *Green, supra,* that the remedy must be implemented *forthwith.*

The problems encountered by the district courts and courts of appeals make plain that we should now try to amplify guidelines, however incomplete and imperfect, for the assistance of school authorities and courts. The failure of local authorities to meet their constitutional obligations aggravated the massive problem of converting from the state-enforced discrimination of racially separate school systems. This process has been rendered more difficult by changes since 1954 in the structure and patterns of communities, the growth of student population, movement of families, and other changes, some of which had marked impact on school planning, sometimes neutralizing or negating remedial action before it was fully implemented. Rural areas accustomed for half a century to the consolidated school systems implemented by bus transportation could make adjustments more readily than metropolitan areas with dense and shifting population, numerous schools, congested and complex traffic patterns.

III

The objective today remains to eliminate from the public schools all vestiges of state-imposed segregation. Segregation was the evil struck down by *Brown I* as contrary to the equal protection guarantees of the Constitution. That was the violation sought to be corrected by the remedial measures of *Brown II.* That was the basis for the holding in *Green* that school authorities are "clearly charged with the affirmative duty to take whatever steps might be necessary to convert to a unitary system in which racial discrimination would be eliminated root and branch." . . .

If school authorities fail in their affirmative obligations under these holdings, judicial authority may be invoked. Once a right and a violation have been shown, the scope of a district court's equitable powers to remedy past wrongs is broad, for breadth and flexibility are inherent in equitable remedies.

* * *

In seeking to define even in broad and general terms how far this remedial power extends it is important to remember that judicial powers may be exercised only on the basis of a constitutional violation. Remedial judicial authority does not put judges automatically in the shoes of school authorities whose powers are plenary. Judicial authority enters only when local authority defaults.

School authorities are traditionally charged with broad power to formulate and implement educational policy and might well conclude, for example, that in order to prepare students to live in a pluralistic society each school should have a prescribed ratio of Negro to white students reflecting the proportion for the district as a whole. To do this as an educational policy is within the broad discretionary powers of school authorities; absent a finding of a constitutional violation, however, that would not be within the authority of a federal court. As with any equity case, the nature of the violation determines the scope of the remedy. In default by the school authorities of their obligation to proffer acceptable remedies, a district court has broad power to fashion a remedy that will assure a unitary school system.

The school authorities argue that the equity powers of federal district courts have been limited by Title IV of the Civil Rights Act of 1964, 42 U.S.C. § 2000c [*et seq.*] The language and the history of Title IV show that it was enacted not to limit but to define the role of the Federal Government in the implementation of the *Brown I* decision. . . . [T]he provisions of Title IV of the Civil Rights Act of 1964 [do not demonstrate] an intention to restrict [official] powers or withdraw from courts their historic equitable remedial powers. The legislative history of Title IV indicates that Congress was concerned that the Act might be read as creating a right of action under the Fourteenth Amendment in the situation of so-called "de facto segregation," where racial imbalance exists in the schools but with no showing that this was brought about by discriminatory action of state authorities. In short, there is nothing in the Act that provides us material assistance in answering the question of remedy for state-imposed segregation in violation of *Brown I.* The basis of our decision must be the prohibition of the Fourteenth Amendment that no State shall "deny to any person within its jurisdiction the equal protection of the laws."

IV

* * *

We turn now to the problem of defining with more particularity the responsibilities of school authorities in desegregating a state-enforced dual school system in light of the Equal Protection Clause. . . .

In *Green*, we pointed out that existing policy and practice with regard to faculty, staff, transportation, extracurricular activities, and facilities were among the most important indicia of a segregated system. 391 U.S. at 435. Independent of student assignment, where it is possible to identify a "white school" or a "Negro school" simply by reference to the racial composition of teachers and staff, the quality of school buildings and equipment, or the organization of sports activities, a *prima facie* case of violation of substantive constitutional rights under the Equal Protection Clause is shown.

When a system has been dual in these respects, the first remedial responsibility of school authorities is to eliminate invidious racial distinctions. With respect to such matters as transportation, supporting personnel, and extracurricular activities, no more than this may be necessary. Similar corrective action must be taken with regard to the maintenance of buildings and the distribution of equipment. In these areas, normal administrative practice should produce schools of like quality, facilities, and staffs. Something more must be said, however, as to faculty assignment and new school construction.

In the companion *Davis* case [402 U.S. 33], the Mobile school board has argued that the Constitution requires that teachers be assigned on a "colorblind" basis. It also argues that the Constitution prohibits district courts from using their equity power to order assignment of teachers to achieve a particular degree of faculty desegregation. We reject that contention.

In *United States v. Montgomery County Board of Education*, 395 U.S. 225 (1969), the District Court set as a goal a plan of faculty assignment in each school with a ratio of white to Negro faculty members substantially the same throughout the system. This order was predicated on the District Court finding that:

> The evidence does not reflect any real administrative problems involved in immediately desegregating the substitute teachers, the student teachers, the night school faculties, and in the evolvement of a really legally adequate program for the substantial desegregation of the faculties of all schools in the system commencing with the school year 1968–69.

Quoted at 395 U.S., at 232.

The District Court in *Montgomery* then proceeded to set an initial ratio for the whole system of at least two Negro teachers out of each 12 in any given school. The Court of Appeals modified the order by eliminating what it regarded as "fixed mathematical" ratios of faculty and substituted an initial requirement of "*substantially or approximately*" a five-to-one ratio. With respect to the future, the Court of Appeals held that the numerical ratio should be eliminated and that compliance should not be tested solely by the achievement of specified proportions. *Id.*, at 234.

We reversed the Court of Appeals and restored the District Court's order in its entirety, holding that the order of the District Judge

> "was adopted in the spirit of this Court's opinion in *Green* . . . in that his plan 'promises realistically to work, and promises realistically to work *now*.' The modifications ordered by the panel of the Court of Appeals, while of course not intended to do so, would, we think, take from the order some of its capacity to expedite, by means of specific commands, the day when a completely unified, unitary, nondiscriminatory school system becomes a reality instead of a hope. . . . We also believe that under all the circumstances of this case we follow the original plan outlined in *Brown II* . . . by accepting the more specific and expeditious order of [District] Judge Johnson. . . ."

395 U.S. at 235–236.

The principles of *Montgomery* have been properly followed by the District Court and the Court of Appeals in this case.

The construction of new schools and the closing of old ones are two of the most important functions of local school authorities and also two of the most complex. They must decide questions of location and capacity in light of population growth, finances, land values, site availability, through an almost endless list of factors to be considered. The result of this will be a decision which, when combined with one technique or another of student assignment, will determine the racial composition of the student body in each school in the system. Over the long run, the consequences of the choices will be far reaching. People gravitate toward school facilities, just as schools are located in response to the needs of people. The location of schools may thus influence the patterns of residential development of a metropolitan area and have important impact on composition of inner-city neighborhoods.

In the past, choices in this respect have been used as a potent weapon for creating or maintaining a state-segregated school system. In addition to the classic pattern of building schools specifically intended for Negro or white students, school authorities have sometimes, since *Brown*, closed schools which appeared likely to become racially mixed through changes in neighborhood residential patterns. This was sometimes accompanied by building new schools in the areas of white suburban expansion farthest from Negro population centers in order to maintain the separation of the races with a minimum departure from the formal principles of "neighborhood zoning." Such a policy does more than simply influence the short-run composition of the student body of a new school. It may well promote segregated residential patterns which, when combined with "neighborhood zoning," further lock the school system into the mold of separation of the races. . . .

In ascertaining the existence of legally imposed school segregation, the existence of a pattern of school construction and abandonment is thus a factor of great weight. In devising remedies where legally imposed segregation has been established, it is the responsibility of local authorities and district courts to see to it that future school construction and abandonment are not used and do not serve to perpetuate or reestablish the dual system. When necessary, district courts should retain jurisdiction to assure that these responsibilities are carried out. *Cf. United States v. Board of Public Instruction*, 395 F.2d 66 (5th Cir. 1968); *Brewer v. School Board*, 397 F.2d 37 (4th Cir. 1968).

V

The central issue in this case is that of student assignment, and there are essentially four problem areas:

(1) to what extent racial balance or racial quotas may be used as an implement in a remedial order to correct a previously segregated system;
(2) whether every all-Negro and all-white school must be eliminated as an indispensable part of a remedial process of desegregation;
(3) what the limits are, if any, on the rearrangement of school districts and attendance zones, as a remedial measure; and
(4) what the limits are, if any, on the use of transportation facilities to correct state-enforced racial school segregation.

(1) **Racial Balances or Racial Quotas** . . . . We are concerned in these cases with the elimination of the discrimination inherent in the dual school systems, not with myriad factors of human existence which can cause discrimination in a multitude of ways on racial, religious, or ethnic grounds. . . . We do not reach in this case the question whether a showing that school segregation is a consequence of other types of state action, without any discriminatory action by the school authorities, is a constitutional violation requiring remedial action by a school desegregation decree. This case does not present that question and we therefore do not decide it.

Our objective in dealing with the issues presented by these cases is to see that school authorities exclude no pupil of a racial minority from any school, directly or indirectly, on account of race; it does not and cannot embrace all the problems of racial prejudice, even when those problems contribute to disproportionate racial concentrations in some schools.

In this case it is urged that the District Court has imposed a racial balance requirement of 71% to 29% on individual schools. The fact that no such objective was actually achieved—and would appear to be impossible—tends to blunt that claim, yet in the opinion and order of the District Court of December 1, 1969, we find that court directing

> that efforts should be made to reach a 71–29 ratio in the various schools so that there will be no basis for contending that one school is racially different from the others. . . . [t]hat no school [should] be operated with an all-black or predominantly black student body, [and] [t]hat pupils of all grades [should] be assigned in such a way that as nearly as practicable the various schools at various grade levels have about the same proportion of black and white students.

The District Judge went on to acknowledge that variation "from that norm may be unavoidable." This contains intimations that the "norm" is a fixed mathematical racial balance reflecting the pupil constituency of the system. If we were to read the holding of the District Court to require, as a matter of substantive constitutional right, any particular degree of racial balance or mixing, that approach would be disapproved and we would be obliged to reverse. The constitutional command to desegregate schools does not mean that every school in every community must always reflect the racial composition of the school system as a whole.

As the voluminous record in this case shows, the predicate for the District Court's use of 71% to 29% ratio was twofold: first, its express finding, approved by the Court of Appeals and not challenged here, that a dual school system had been maintained by the school authorities at least until 1969; second, its finding, also approved by the Court of Appeals, that the school board had totally defaulted in its acknowledged duty to come forward with an acceptable plan of its own. . . .

We see therefore that the use made of the mathematical ratios was no more than a starting point in the process of shaping a remedy, rather than an inflexible requirement. From that starting point the District Court proceeded to frame a decree that was within its discretionary powers, as an equitable remedy for the particular circumstances. As we said in *Green*, a school authority's remedial plan or a district court's remedial decree is to be judged by its effectiveness. Awareness of the racial composition of the whole school system is likely to be a useful starting point in shaping a remedy to correct past constitutional violations. In sum, the very limited use made of mathematical ratios was within the equitable remedial discretion of the District Court.

(2) One-Race Schools. The record in this case reveals the familiar phenomenon that in metropolitan areas minority groups are often found concentrated in one part of the city. In some circumstances certain schools may remain all or largely of one race until new schools can be provided or neighborhood patterns change. Schools all or predominantly of one race in a district of mixed population will require close scrutiny to determine that school assignments are not part of state-enforced segregation.

In light of the above, it should be clear that the existence of some small number of one-race, or virtually one-race, schools within a district is not in and of itself the mark of a system that still practices segregation by law. The district judge or school authorities should make every effort to achieve the greatest possible degree of actual desegregation and will thus necessarily be concerned with the elimination of one-race schools. No *per se* rule can adequately embrace all the difficulties of reconciling the competing interests involved; but in a system with a history of segregation the need for remedial criteria of sufficient specificity to assure a school authority's compliance with its constitutional duty warrants a presumption against schools that are substantially disproportionate in their racial composition. Where the school authority's proposed plan for conversion from a dual to a unitary system contemplates the continued existence of some schools that are all or predominately of one race, they have the burden of showing that such school assignments are genuinely nondiscriminatory. The court should scrutinize such schools, and the burden upon the school authorities will be to satisfy the court that their racial composition is not the result of present or past discriminatory action on their part. . . .

(3) Remedial Altering of Attendance Zones. The maps submitted in these cases graphically demonstrate that one of the principal tools employed by school planners and by courts to break up the dual school system has been a frank—and sometimes drastic—gerrymandering of school districts and attendance zones. An additional step was pairing, "clustering," or "grouping" of schools with attendance assignments made deliberately to accomplish the transfer of Negro students out of formerly segregated Negro schools and transfer of white students to formerly all-Negro schools. More often than not, these zones are neither compact or contiguous; indeed they may be on opposite ends of the city. As an interim corrective measure, this cannot be said to be beyond the broad remedial powers of a court.

Absent a constitutional violation there would be no basis for judicially ordering assignments of students on a racial basis. All things being equal, with no history of discrimination, it might well be desirable to assign pupils to schools nearest their homes. But all things are not equal in a system that has been deliberately constructed and maintained to enforce racial segregation. The remedy for such segregation may be administratively awkward, inconvenient, and even bizarre in some situations and may impose burdens on some; but all awkwardness and inconvenience cannot be avoided in the interim period when remedial adjustments are being made to eliminate the dual school systems.

No fixed or even substantially fixed guidelines can be established as to how far a court can go, but it must be recognized that there are limits. The objective is to dismantle the dual school system. "Racially neutral" assignment plans proposed by school authorities to a district court may be inadequate; such plans may fail to counteract the continuing effects of past school segregation resulting from discriminatory location of school sites or distortion of school size in order to achieve or maintain an artificial racial separation. When school authorities present a district court with a "loaded game board," affirmative action in the form of remedial altering of attendance zones is proper to achieve truly nondiscriminatory assignments. In short, an assignment plan is not acceptable simply because it appears to be neutral.

In this area, we must of necessity rely to a large extent, as this court has for more than 16 years, on the informed judgment of the district courts in the first instance and on courts of appeals.

We hold that the pairing and grouping of noncontiguous school zones is a permissible tool and such action is to be considered in light of the objectives sought. . . .

(4) Transportation of Students. The scope of permissible transportation of students as an implement of a remedial decree has never been defined by this Court and by the very nature of the problem it cannot be defined with precision. No rigid guidelines as to student transportation can be given for application to the infinite variety of problems presented in thousands of situations. Bus transportation has been an integral part of the public education system for years, and was perhaps the single most important factor in the transition from the one-room schoolhouse to the consolidated school. Eighteen million of the nation's public school children, approximately 39%, were transported to their schools by bus in 1969–70 in all parts of the country.

The importance of bus transportation as a normal and accepted tool of educational policy is readily discernible in this and the companion case, *Davis, supra*. The Charlotte school authorities did not purport to assign students on the basis of geographically drawn zones until 1965 and then they allowed almost unlimited transfer privileges. The District Court's conclusion that assignments of children to the school nearest their home serving their grade would not produce an effective dismantling of the dual system is supported by the record.

Thus the remedial techniques used in the District Court's order were within that court's power to provide equitable relief; implementation of the decree is well within the capacity of the school authority.

The decree provided that the buses used to implement the plan would operate on direct routes. Students would be picked up at schools near their homes and transported to the schools they were to attend. The trips for elementary school pupils average about seven miles and the District Court found that they would take "not over 35 minutes at the most." This system compares favorably with the transportation plan previously operated in Charlotte under which each day 23,600 students on all grade levels were transported an average of 15 miles one way for an average trip requiring over an hour. In these circumstances, we find no basis for holding that the local school authorities may not be required to employ bus transportation as one tool of school desegregation. Desegregation plans cannot be limited to the walk-in school.

An objection to transportation of students may have validity when the time or distance of travel is so great as to either risk the health of the children or significantly impinge on the educational process. District courts must weigh the soundness of any transportation plan in light of what is said in subdivisions (1), (2), and (3) above. It hardly needs stating that the limits on time of travel will vary with many factors, but probably with none more than the age of the students. The reconciliation of competing values in a desegregation case is, of course, a difficult task with many sensitive facets but fundamentally no more so than remedial measures courts of equity have traditionally employed.

VI

The Court of Appeals, searching for a term to define the equitable remedial power of the district courts, used the term "reasonableness." In *Green, supra*, this Court used the term "feasible" and by implication, "workable," "effective," and "realistic" in the mandate to develop "a plan that promises realistically to work, and . . . to work *now*." On the facts of this case, we are unable to conclude that the order to the District Court is not reasonable, feasible and workable. However, in seeking to define the scope of remedial power or the limits on remedial power of courts in an area as sensitive as we deal with here, words are poor instruments to convey the sense of basic fairness inherent in equity. Substance, not semantics, must govern, and we have sought to suggest the nature of limitations without frustrating the appropriate scope of equity.

At some point, these school authorities and others like them should have achieved full compliance with this Court's decision in *Brown I*. The systems would then be "unitary" in the sense required by our decisions in *Green* and *Alexander*.

It does not follow that the communities served by such systems will remain demographically stable, for in a growing, mobile society, few will do so. Neither school authorities nor district courts are constitutionally required to make year-by-year adjustments of the racial composition of student bodies once the affirmative duty to desegregate has been accomplished and racial discrimination through official action is eliminated from the system. This does not mean that federal courts are without power to deal with future problems; but in the absence of a showing that either the school authorities or some other agency of the State has deliberately attempted to fix or alter demographic patterns to affect the racial composition of the schools, further intervention by a district court should not be necessary.

For the reasons herein set forth, the judgment of the Court of Appeals is affirmed as to those parts in which it affirmed the judgment of the District Court. The order of the District Court, dated August 7, 1970, is also affirmed.

It is so ordered.

NOTES AND QUESTIONS

1. Per se Violation or Rebuttable Presumption?

Does the Court suggest that there is a causal connection between the school district's past discriminatory actions and the present pattern of segregated schools? Does this mean that in a system formerly segregated by law, plaintiffs can invoke a presumption that the current segregated patterns are "vestiges" of past state-imposed segregation? What must defendants show to rebut this presumption? Are southern school districts, unlike some northern districts, under a duty to racially balance all schools regardless of the degree to which the current segregated pattern could arise from fortuitous residential segregation rather than deliberate state policy? *See* Fiss, "The Charlotte-Mecklenburg Case—Its Significance for Northern School Desegregation," 38 *U. Chi. L.Rev.* 697, 704–05 (1971). Is the presumed causal relationship empirically defensible? *Compare* Farley, "Residential Segregation and Its Implications for School Integration," 39 *Law & Contemp. Probs.* 164 (1975), *with* Wolf, "Northern School Desegregation and Residential Choice," 1977 *Supr.Ct.Rev.* 63.

2. Relevance of the Length of Time Between Past Segregative Acts and Present Segregation

At what point in time might the relationship between a system's past segregative acts and present segregation have become so attenuated as to be incapable of supporting a finding of *de jure* segregation warranting judicial intervention?

In *Keyes v. School District No. 1*, 413 U.S. 189, 210, 93 S.Ct. 2686, 2698, 37 L.Ed.2d 548 (1973), the first major Northern desegregation case, the Court stated "if the actions of school authorities were to any degree motivated by segregative intent and the segregation resulting from these actions continues to exist, the fact of remoteness in time certainly does not make those actions any less 'intentional'." Does this statement mean that a district which was previously *de jure* segregated must first have racially balanced all of its schools before it can argue that resegregation is the result of changing residential patterns? If so, then in the absence of the implementation of a complete racial balance remedy, is not the presumption that the segregated pattern is still a "vestige" of previous state-imposed segregation an irrebuttable presumption? What does this suggest with regard to the question of a "continuing" violation and attributing "intent" to a school board in 1979 for actions taken by a school board in 1954, which had an entirely different membership?

If a school board complies with a court order to desegregate, but resegregation occurs almost immediately, might a district court order further desegregation? In *Pasadena City Board of Education v. Spangler*, 427 U.S. 424, 96 S.Ct. 2697, 49 L.Ed.2d 599 (1976), the Court ruled that it may not. It held that a district court could not require pupil reassignments to maintain a racial balance some four or five years after the original decree was implemented unless the original decree had been violated or further deliberate segregative practices had occurred. Is *Spangler* consistent with *Green*? Does *Spangler* permit a form of freedom-of-choice plan wherein parents can "vote with their feet" once the formality of a unitary system is implemented?

3. Swann *and the Discretion of District Courts*

Once plaintiffs have established that a constitutional violation exists, the district court must formulate a decree that will provide a remedy for the constitutional wrong. The *Brown II* Court, in remanding the cases consolidated in *Brown I* to the federal district courts in which they originated, told the lower courts that they were to be guided by traditional principles of equity in fashioning remedial decrees. "Traditionally, equity has been characterized by a practical flexibility in shaping its remedies and by a facility for adjusting and reconciling public and private needs." *Brown v. Board of Education*, 349 U.S. 294, 300, 75 S.Ct. 753, 756, 99 L.Ed.2d 1083 (1955).

While *Swann* alone might be read as merely upholding the broad discretionary powers of an equity court, the Supreme Court's decision in a companion case, *Davis v. Board of School Commissioners*, 402 U.S. 33, 91 S.Ct. 1289, 28 L.Ed.2d 577 (1971), casts doubt on this interpretation. Chief Justice Burger, who wrote the *Davis* opinion on behalf of a unanimous Court, saw the fundamental issue in *Davis* as the failure of the court of appeals to consider the possible use of busing and split zoning in its desegregation order for Mobile. Apparently, that court had "felt constrained to treat the eastern part of metropolitan Mobile in isolation from the rest of the school system." 402 U.S. at 38, 91 S.Ct. at 1292. Citing *Swann*, Burger pointed out that

> "neighborhood school zoning," whether based directly on home-to-school distance or on "unified geographic zones," is not the only constitutionally permissible remedy; nor is it *per se* adequate to meet the remedial responsibilities of local boards. Having once found a violation, the district judge or school authorities should make every effort to achieve the greatest possible degree of actual desegregation, taking into account the practicalities of the situation. A district court may and should consider the use of all available techniques including restructuring of attendance zones and both contiguous and noncontiguous attendance zones. . . . The measure of any desegregation plan is its effectiveness.

402 U.S. at 37, 91 S.Ct. at 1291.

Is Chief Justice Burger's reference to the "effectiveness" standard consistent with his assertion that busing is a remedy that the lower courts have the discretionary power to order? Consider these remarks by Professor Powe:

> The . . . language [of *Davis*] is ambiguous. What is meant by "inadequate consideration" of busing and split zoning? Who gave the "inadequate consideration"? The Court observed that a "district court may and should consider the use of all available techniques" of desegregation. Yet that was just what Judge Thomas [the district court judge] did. . . . His order . . . was explicit; since the Supreme Court had not mandated racial balance, he was not going to order busing across [an interstate highway]. . . .
>
> The Supreme Court in effect underscored the following language first used in the *Green* trilogy: "The measure of any desegregation plan is its effectiveness." District judges may well have large discretion in choosing a remedy, as *Swann* suggests, but it is a one-way discretion and must be used to facilitate integration. . . . Judge Thomas erred not by failing to consider busing, but by rejecting it. . . .

Powe, "The Road to *Swann*: Mobile County Crawls to the Bus," 51 *Tex.L.Rev.* 505, 523–25 (1973). To what extent is it relevant that interstate highways were sometimes located with the intent to separate black and white neighborhoods? Can a busing order perpetuate segregative effects of decisions by non-school officials?

4. Swann: *Permissible Remedial Techniques and Their Limits*

a. Racial Quotas. In *Green v. County School Board*, the Court struck down a freedom-of-choice plan as ineffective because only 15 percent of the black students attended a previously all-white school and none of the whites attended the black school. Thus the Court began to focus on the percentage of the races in each school. With *Swann*, the Supreme Court turned its attention to *how* the unitary system required by *Green* was to be achieved in the context of a large urban school district.

Swann recognizes the appropriateness of racial quotas as a "starting point" for judicial analysis. But what weight should this "starting point" be given? If the measure of a desegregation plan is its effectiveness, may quotas be used to calculate that effectiveness? How do you distinguish racial quotas in this context from those adopted by institutions of higher learning for special admissions programs? *See Johnson v. Board of Education*, 604 F.2d 504, 518 (7th Cir. 1979) (consideration of quotas designed to overcome *de facto* segregation), *vacated and re-*

manded, 449 U.S. 915, 101 S.Ct. 339, 66 L.Ed.2d 162 (distinguishing *Regents of University of California v. Bakke*, 438 U.S. 265, 98 S.Ct. 2733, 57 L.Ed.2d 750 (1978)).

b. One-Race Schools. While not requiring the elimination of all one-race schools, the *Swann* opinion places the burden of demonstrating that they are "genuinely nondiscriminatory" on the school board. *Davis* suggests that the burden is a heavy one. Under what circumstances would one-race schools be permissible? Would *Swann* permit the existence of an all-black school if the community sought such a school to heighten ethnic solidarity and to remedy deficiencies in basic developmental skills? *See* Comment, "Alternative Schools for Minority Students: The Constitution, The Civil Rights Act and the Berkeley Experiment," 61 *Calif.L.Rev.* 858 (1973).

c. Limits on the Use of Busing. Although the Supreme Court explicitly approved intradistrict transportation ("busing") to achieve a unitary school system, it noted that there were limits to the use of that remedy. Busing, according to the Court, may be used where "feasible," but its use is limited by regard for times and distances that would "either risk the health of the children or significantly impinge on the educational process." How long a bus ride would this be? Should the maximum permissible length of time or the distance traveled vary according to the age of the child? What kind of evidence should a court consider to determine whether the educational process will be impinged upon or if a child's health will be impaired? By what standards should a court determine that convenience, health, and other costs of busing do or do not outweigh the advantages of a particular remedy? Lacking more detailed guidance from the Supreme Court, lower courts have taken varied approaches to these questions. *See* Levin, "School Desegregation Remedies and the Role of Social Science Research," 42 *Law & Contemp. Probs.* 1 (1978) (pt. 2).

V. DESEGREGATION: AN EMERGING NATIONAL STANDARD

A. Introduction

Racial segregation in the public schools is not a phenomenon limited to the South. In 1967, the United States Commission on Civil Rights found that in fifteen major northern cities, roughly three in four African American students attended majority black schools. In nine of the fifteen cities, more than half of the African American students attended 90 to 100 percent black schools. United States Commission on Civil Rights, *Racial Isolation in the Public Schools* (1967). In 1970, the Department of Health, Education, and Welfare reported that 57.6 percent of all black students in thirty-two northern and western states attended 80 to 100 percent minority schools. Dimond, "School Segregation in the North: There Is But One Constitution," 7 *Harv.C.R.—C.L. L.Rev.* 1 (1972). One study showed that in 1976 nearly one third of all minority students in six northern industrial states (Illinois, Indiana, Michigan, New York, Ohio, and Pennsylvania) were attending segregated schools. Institute for Southern Studies, *Just Schools* (1979). *See also* G. Orfield, *Must We Bus?* (1978).

The causes of northern racial segregation are complex, interrelated, and often debated. In some school districts in the North, purposeful segregation of the southern variety was apparent:

> [I]n some places in the North . . . laws and policies explicitly authorized segregation by race. State statutes authorizing separate but equal public schools were on the books in Indiana until 1959, in New Mexico and Wyoming until 1954, and in New York until 1938. Other northern states authorized such segregation after the Civil War and did not repeal their authorizing statutes until early in the twentieth century.

United States Commission on Civil Rights, *Racial Isolation in the Public Schools* (1967). *See also Beckett v. School Board*, 308 F.Supp. 1274, 1311–15 (E.D. Va. 1969), *rev'd*, 434 F.2d 408 (4th Cir.), *cert. denied*, 399 U.S. 929, 90 S.Ct. 2247, 26 L.Ed.2d 796.

The division of many metropolitan areas into a large number of school districts, each serving distinct racial and socioeconomic groups, has contributed to the phenomenon. Demographic trends (with African Americans concentrated in inner cities and whites divided between inner cities and suburbs), disparities in personal income between the races, segregation in housing (sometimes encouraged by federal, state, and local policies), and the availability of nearly all-white private schools have reinforced racial segregation resulting from school district organization and neighborhood school assignment policies. *See also* K. Tauber, *Negroes in Cities* (1965); Wolf, "Northern School Desegregation and Residential Choice," 1977 *Sup. Ct. Rev.* 63.

Early constitutional attacks on school desegregation in the North met with varied judicial responses. *Compare Bell v. School City of Gary*, 324 F.2d 209 (7th Cir. 1963), *cert. denied*, 377 U.S. 924, 84 S.Ct. 1223, 12 L.Ed.2d 216 (1964) and *Deal v. Cincinnati Board of Education*, 369 F.2d 55 (6th Cir. 1966), *cert. denied*, 389 U.S. 847, 88 S.Ct. 39, 19 L.Ed.2d 114 (1965) *with Kelly v. Guinn*, 456 F.2d 100 (9th Cir. 1972), *cert. denied*, 413 U.S. 919, 93 S.Ct. 3048, 37 L.Ed.2d 1041 and *Johnson v. San Francisco Unified School District*, 339 F.Supp. 1315 (N.D.Cal.1971), *vacated and remanded*, 500 F.2d 349 (9th Cir. 1974).

In *Bell v. School City of Gary*, the plaintiffs argued that segregation, whatever its cause, is inherently harmful and therefore unconstitutional. They did not attempt to prove specific harm. Is this argument constitutionally sound under *Brown*? Is a black child who finds himself or herself in a segregated school likely to care whether the racial isolation is purposeful or not? *See* A. Bickel, *The Supreme Court and the Idea of Progress* 119 (1970).

The *Bell* decision sharply distinguished fortuitous or de facto segregation and de jure segregation that was a result of deliberate board policies. In *Kelly*, on the other hand, the Court ruled that northern school segregation violates the Fourteenth Amendment, but it did not do so by repudiating the *de jure/de facto* distinction; rather, it expanded the scope of de jure segregation.

B. Northern School Desegregation and the Supreme Court

Keyes v. School District No. 1

413 U.S. 189, 93 S.Ct. 2686, 37 L.Ed.2d 548 (1973), *rehearing denied*, 414 U.S. 883, 94 S.Ct. 27, 38 L.Ed.2d 131.

Mr. Justice Brennan delivered the opinion of the Court.

This school desegregation case concerns the Denver, Colorado, school system. That system has never been operated under a constitutional or statutory provision that mandated or permitted racial segregation in public education. Rather, the gravamen of this action, brought in June 1969 in the District Court for the District of Colorado by parents of Denver school children, is that respondent School Board alone, by use of various techniques such as the manipulation of student attendance zones, schoolsite selection and a neighborhood school policy, created or maintained racially or ethnically (or both racially and ethnically) segregated schools throughout the school district, entitling petitioners to a decree directing desegregation of the entire school district.

The boundaries of the school district are coterminus with the boundaries of the city and county of Denver. There were in 1969, 119 schools with 96,580 pupils in the school system. In early 1969, the respondent School Board adopted three resolutions, Resolutions 1520, 1524, and 1531, designed to desegregate the schools in the Park Hill area in the northeast portion of the city. Following an election which produced a Board majority opposed to the resolutions, the resolutions were rescinded and replaced with a voluntary student transfer program. Petitioners then filed this action, requesting an injunction against the rescission of the resolutions and an order directing that the respondent School Board desegregate and afford equal educational opportunity "for the School District as a whole." The District Court found that by the construction of a new, relatively small elementary school, Barrett, in the middle of the Negro community west of Park Hill, by the gerrymandering of student attendance zones, by the use of so-called "optional zones," and by the excessive use of mobile classroom units, among other things, the respondent School Board had engaged over almost a decade after 1960 in an unconstitutional policy of deliberate racial segregation with respect to the Park Hill schools. The court therefore ordered the Board to desegregate those schools through the implementation of the three rescinded resolutions. 303 F. Supp. 279 and 289 (1969).

Segregation in Denver schools is not limited, however, to the schools in the Park Hill area, and not satisfied with their success in obtaining relief for Park Hill, petitioners pressed their prayer that the District Court order desegregation of all segregated schools in the city of Denver, particularly the heavily segregated schools in the core city area. But that court concluded that its finding of a purposeful and systematic program of racial segregation affecting thousands of students in the Park Hill area did not, in itself, impose on the School Board an affirmative duty to eliminate segregation throughout the school district. Instead, the court fractionated the district and held that petitioners must make a fresh showing of *de jure* segregation in each area of the city for which they seek relief. Moreover, the District Court held that its finding of intentional segregation in Park Hill was not in any sense material to the question of segregative intent in other areas of the city. Under this restrictive approach, the District Court concluded that petitioners' evidence of intentionally discriminatory School Board action in areas of the district other than Park Hill was insufficient to "dictate the conclusion that this is *de jure* segregation which calls for an all-out effort to desegregate. It is more like *de facto* segregation, with respect to which the rule is that the court cannot order desegregation in order to provide a better balance." 313 F. Supp. 61, 73 (1970).

Nevertheless, the District Court went on to hold that the proofs established that the segregated core city schools were educationally inferior to the predominantly "white" or "Anglo" schools in other parts of the district—that is, "separate facilities . . . unequal in the quality of education provided." *Id.*, at 83. Thus, the court held that, under the doctrine of *Plessy v. Ferguson*, 163 U.S. 537 (1896), respondent School Board constitutionally "must at a minimum . . . offer an equal educational opportunity," . . . and, therefore, although all-out desegregation "could not be decreed, . . . the only feasible and constitutionally acceptable program—the only program which furnishes anything approaching substantial equality—is a system of desegregation and integration which provides compensatory education in an integrated environment." 313 F. Supp. 90, 96 (1970). The District Court then formulated a varied remedial plan to that end which was incorporated in the Final Decree.

Respondent School Board appealed, and petitioners cross-appealed, to the Court of Appeals for the Tenth Circuit. That court sustained the District Court's finding that the Board had engaged in an unconstitutional policy of deliberate racial segregation with respect to the Park Hill schools and affirmed the Final Decree in that respect. As to the core city schools, however, the Court of Appeals reversed the legal determination of the District Court that those schools were maintained in violation of the Fourteenth Amendment because of the unequal educational opportunity afforded, and therefore set aside so much of the Final Decree as required desegregation and educational improvement programs for those schools. 445 F.2d at 990. . . .

II

In our view, the only other question that requires our decision at this time is . . . whether the District Court and the Court of Appeals applied an incorrect legal standard in addressing petitioners' contention that respondent School Board engaged in an unconstitutional policy of deliberate segregation in the core city schools. Our conclusion is that those courts did not apply the correct standard in addressing that contention.

Petitioners apparently concede for the purposes of this case that in the case of a school system like Denver's, where no statutory dual system has ever existed, plaintiffs must prove not only that segregated schooling exists but also that it was brought about or maintained by intentional state action. Petitioners proved that for almost a decade after 1960 respondent School Board had engaged in an unconstitutional policy of deliberate racial segregation in the Park Hill schools. Indeed, the District Court found that "[b]etween 1960 and 1969 the Board's policies with respect to these northeast Denver schools show an undeviating purpose to isolate Negro students" in segregated schools "while preserving the Anglo character of [other] schools." 303 F. Supp. at 294. This finding did not relate to an insubstantial or trivial fragment of the school system. On the contrary, respondent School Board was found guilty of following a deliberate segregation policy at schools attended, in 1969, by 37.69 percent of Denver's total Negro school population, including one-fourth of the Negro elementary pupils, over two-thirds of the Negro junior high pupils, and over two-fifths of the Negro high school pupils. In addition, there was uncontroverted evidence that teachers and staff had for years been assigned on a minority teacher to minority school basis throughout the school system. Respondent argues, however, that a finding of state-imposed segregation as to a substantial portion of the school system can be viewed in isolation from the rest of the district, and that even if state-imposed segregation does exist in a substantial part of the Denver school system, it does not follow that the District Court could predicate on that fact a finding that the entire school system is a dual system. We do not agree. We have never suggested that plaintiffs in school desegregation cases must bear the burden of proving the elements of *de jure* segregation as to each and every school or each and every student within the school system. Rather, we have held that where plaintiffs prove that a current condition of segregated schooling exists within a school district where a dual system was compelled or authorized by statute at the time of our decision in *Brown v. Board of Education*, 347 U.S. 483 (1954) (*Brown I*), the State automatically assumes an affirmative duty "to effectuate a transition to a racially nondiscriminatory school system," *Brown v. Board of Education*, 349 U.S. 294, 301 (1955) (*Brown II*), see also *Green v. County School Board*, 391 U.S. 430, 437–38 (1968), that is, to eliminate from the public schools within their school system "all vestiges of state-imposed segregation." *Swann v. Charlotte-Mecklenburg Board of Education*, 402 U.S. 1, 15 (1971).[11]

This is not a case, however, where a statutory dual system has ever existed. Nevertheless, where plaintiffs prove that the school authorities have carried out a systematic program of segregation affecting a substantial portion of the students, schools, teachers and facilities within the school system, it is only common sense to conclude that there exists a predicate for a finding of the existence of a dual school system. Several considerations support this conclusion. First, it is obvious that a practice of concentrating Negroes in certain schools by structuring attendance zones or designating "feeder" schools on the basis of race has the reciprocal effect of keeping other nearby schools predominantly white.[12] Similarly, the practice of building a school—such as the Barrett Elementary School in this case—to a certain size and in a certain location, "with conscious knowledge that it would be a segregated school," 303 F.Supp. at 285, has a substantial reciprocal effect on the racial composition of other nearby schools. So also, the use of mobile classrooms, the drafting of student transfer policies, the transportation of students, and the assignment of faculty and staff, on racially identifiable bases, have the clear effect of earmarking schools according to their racial composition, and this, in turn, together with the elements of student assignment, and school construction, may have a profound reciprocal effect on the racial composition of residential neighborhoods within a metropolitan area, thereby causing further racial concentration within the schools. We recognized this in *Swann*. . . .

In short, common sense dictates the conclusion that racially inspired school board actions have an impact beyond the particular schools that are the subjects of those actions. This is not to say, of course, that there can never be a case in which the geographical structure of or the natural boundaries within a school district may have the effect of dividing the district into separate, identifiable and unrelated units. Such a determination is essentially a question of fact to be resolved by the trial court in the first instance, but such cases must be rare. In the absence of such a determination, proof of state-imposed segregation in a substantial portion of the district will suffice to support a finding by the trial court of the existence of a dual system. . . .

III

Although petitioners had already proved the existence of intentional school segregation in the Park Hill schools, this crucial finding was totally ignored when attention turned to the core city schools. Plainly, a finding of intentional segregation as to a portion of a school system is not devoid of probative value in assessing the school authorities' intent with respect to other parts of the same school system. On the contrary, where, as here, the case involves one

11. Our Brother Rehnquist argues in dissent that *Brown v. Board of Education* did not impose an "affirmative duty to integrate" the schools of a dual school system but was only a "prohibition against discrimination" "in the sense that the assignment to a child of a particular school is not made to depend on his race. . . ."

That is the interpretation of *Brown* expressed 18 years ago by a three-judge court in *Briggs v. Elliott*, 132 F.Supp. 776, 777 (1955): "The Constitution, in other words, does not require integration. It merely forbids discrimination." But *Green v. County School Board*, 391 U.S. 430, 438 (1968), rejected that interpretation insofar as *Green* expressly held that "School boards . . . operating state-compelled dual systems were nevertheless clearly charged [by *Brown II*] with the affirmative duty to take whatever steps might be necessary to convert to a unitary system in which racial discrimination would be eliminated root and branch." *Green* remains the governing principle, *Alexander v. Holmes County Board of Education*, 396 U.S. 19 (1969); *Swann v. Charlotte-Mecklenburg Board of Education*, 402 U.S. I, 15 (1971). See also *Kelley v. Metropolitan County Board of Education*, 317 F. Supp. 980, 984 (1970).

12. . . . Judge Wisdom has recently stated: "Infection at one school infects all schools. To take the most simple example, in a two-school system, all blacks at one school means all or almost all whites at the other." *United States v. Texas Education Agency*, 467 F.2d 848, 888 (5th Cir. 1972).

school board, a finding of intentional segregation on its part in one portion of a school system is highly relevant to the issue of the board's intent with respect to other segregated schools in the system. This is merely an application of the well-settled evidentiary principle that "the prior doing of other similar acts, whether clearly a part of a scheme or not, is useful as reducing the possibility that the act in question was done with innocent intent." 2 J. Wigmore, *Evidence* 200 (3d ed. 1940). . . .

Applying these principles in the special context of school desegregation cases, we hold that a finding of intentionally segregative school board actions in a meaningful portion of a school system, as in this case, creates a presumption that other segregated schooling within the system is not adventitious. It establishes, in other words, a prima facie case of unlawful segregative design on the part of school authorities, and shifts to those authorities the burden of proving that other segregated schools within the system are not also the result of intentionally segregative actions. This is true even if it is determined that different areas of the school district should be viewed independently of each other because, even in that situation, there is high probability that where school authorities have effectuated an intentionally segregative policy in a meaningful portion of the school system, similar impermissible considerations have motivated their actions in other areas of the system. We emphasize that the differentiating factor between *de jure* segregation and so-called *de facto* segregation to which we referred in *Swann* is *purpose* or *intent* to segregate. Where school authorities have been found to have practiced purposeful segregation in part of a school system, they may be expected to oppose system-wide desegregation, as did the respondents in this case, on the ground that their purposefully segregative actions were isolated and individual events, thus leaving plaintiffs with the burden of proving otherwise. But at that point where an intentionally segregative policy is practiced in a meaningful or significant segment of a school system, as in this case, the school authorities cannot be heard to argue that plaintiffs have proved only "isolated and individual" unlawfully segregative actions. In that circumstance, it is both fair and reasonable to require that the school authorities bear the burden of showing that their actions as to other segregated schools within the system were not also motivated by segregative intent.

This burden-shifting principle is not new or novel. There are no hard-and-fast standards governing the allocation of the burden of proof in every situation. The issue, rather, "is merely a question of policy and fairness based on experience in the different situations." 9 J. Wigmore, *Evidence* § 2486, at 275 (3d ed. 1940). In the context of racial segregation in public education, the courts, including this court, have recognized a variety of situations in which "fairness" and "policy" require state authorities to bear the burden of explaining actions or conditions which appear to be racially motivated. Thus, in *Swann*, 402 U.S. at 18, we observed that in a system with a "history of segregation," "where it is possible to identify a 'white school' or a 'Negro school' simply by reference to the racial composition of teachers and staff, the quality of school buildings and equipment, or the organization of sport activities, a *prima facie* case of violation of substantive constitutional rights under the Equal Protection Clause is shown." Again, in a school system with a history of segregation, the discharge of a disproportionately large number of Negro teachers incident to desegregation "thrust[s] upon the School Board the burden of justifying its conduct by clear and convincing evidence." *Chambers v. Hendersonville City Board of Education*, 364 F.2d 189, 192 (4th Cir. 1966) (*en banc*). . . .

Nor is this burden-shifting principle limited to former statutory dual systems. See, *e.g.*, *Davis v. School District of the City of Pontiac*, 309 F.Supp. 734, 743–44 (E.D.Mich. 1970), *aff'd*, 443 F.2d 573 (6th Cir. 1971); *United States v. School District No. 151*, 301 F.Supp. 201, 228 (N.D.Ill. 1969), *modified on other grounds*, 432 F.2d 1147 (7th Cir. 1970). . . .

In discharging that burden, it is not enough, of course, that the school authorities rely upon some allegedly logical, racially neutral explanation for their actions. Their burden is to adduce proof sufficient to support a finding that segregative intent was not among the factors that motivated their actions. The courts below attributed much significance to the fact that many of the Board's actions in the core city area antedated our decision in *Brown*. We reject any suggestion that remoteness in time has any relevance to the issue of intent. If the actions of school authorities were to any degree motivated by segregative intent and the segregation resulting from those actions continues to exist, the fact of remoteness in time certainly does not make those actions any less "intentional."

This is not to say, however, that the prima facie case may not be met by evidence supporting a finding that a lesser degree of segregated schooling in the core city area would not have resulted even if the Board had not acted as it did. In *Swann*, we suggested that at some point in time the relationship between past segregative acts and present segregation may become so attenuated as to be incapable of supporting a finding of *de jure* segregation warranting judicial intervention. 402 U.S., at 31–32. See also *Hobson v. Hansen*, 269 F.Supp. 401, 495 (D.C. 1967), *aff'd sub nom., Smuck v. Hobson*, 132 U.S. App.D.C. 372, 408 F.2d 175 (1969). We made it clear, however, that a connection between past segregative acts and present segregation may be present even when not apparent and that close examination is required before concluding that the connection does not exist. Intentional school segregation in the past may have been a factor in creating a natural environment for the growth of further segregation. Thus, if respondent School Board cannot disprove segregative intent, it can rebut the prima facie case only by showing that its past segregative acts did not create or contribute to the current segregated condition of the core city schools.

The respondent School board invoked at trial its "neighborhood school policy" as explaining racial and ethnic concentrations within the core city schools, arguing that since the core city area population had long been Negro and Hispano, the concentrations were necessarily the result of residential patterns and not of purposefully segregative policies. We have no occasion to consider in this case whether a "neighborhood school policy" of itself will justify racial or ethnic concentrations in the absence of a finding that school authorities have committed acts constituting *de jure* segregation. It is enough that we hold that the mere assertion of such a policy is not dispositive where, as in this case, the school authorities have been found to have practiced *de jure* segregation in a meaningful portion of the school system by techniques that indicate that the "neighborhood school" concept has not been maintained free of manipulation. . . .

The judgment of the Court of Appeals is modified to vacate instead of reverse the parts of the Final Decree that concern the core city schools, and the case is remanded to the District Court for further proceedings consistent with this opinion.

It is so ordered.

Mr. Chief Justice Burger concurs in the result.

Mr. Justice White took no part in the decision of this case.

Mr. Justice Douglas.

While I join the opinion of the Court, I agree with my Brother Powell that there is, for the purposes of the Equal Protection Clause of the Fourteenth Amendment as applied to the school cases, no difference between *de facto* and *de jure* segregation. The school board is a state agency and the lines that it draws, the locations it selects for school sites, the allocation it makes of students, the budgets it prepares are state action for Fourteenth Amendment purposes. . . . If a "neighborhood" or "geographical" unit has been created along racial lines by reason of the play of restrictive covenants that restrict certain areas to "the elite," leaving the "undesirables" to move elsewhere, there is state action in the constitutional sense because the force of law is placed behind those covenants.

There is state action in the constitutional sense when public funds are dispersed by urban development agencies to build racial ghettoes. . . .

When a state forces, aids, or abets, or helps create a racial "neighborhood," it is a travesty of justice to treat that neighborhood as sacrosanct in the sense that its creation is free from the taint of state action.

The Constitution and Bill of Rights have described the design of a pluralistic society. The individual has the right to seek such companions as he desires. But a State is barred from creating by one device or another ghettoes that determine the school one is compelled to attend.

Mr. Justice Powell concurring in part and dissenting in part.

I concur in the remand of this case for further proceedings in the District Court, but on grounds that differ from those relied upon by the Court.

This is the first school desegregation case to reach this Court which involves a major city outside the South. It comes from Denver, Colorado, a city and a State which have not operated public schools under constitutional or statutory provisions which mandated or permitted racial segregation. . . .

The situation in Denver is generally comparable to that in other large cities across the country in which there is a substantial minority population and where desegregation has not been ordered by the federal courts. There is segregation in the schools of many of these cities fully as pervasive as that in southern cities prior to the desegregation decrees of the past decade and a half. The focus of the school desegregation problem has now shifted from the South to the country as a whole. Unwilling and footdragging as the process was in most places, substantial progress toward achieving integration has been made in Southern States. No comparable progress has been made in many nonsouthern cities with large minority populations primarily because of the *de facto/de jure* distinction nurtured by the courts and accepted complacently by many of the same voices which denounced the evils of segregated schools in the South. But if our national concern is for those who attend such schools, rather than for perpetuating a legalism rooted in history rather than present reality, we must recognize that the evil of operating separate schools is no less in Denver than in Atlanta.

I

In my view we should abandon a distinction which long since has outlived its time, and formulate constitutional principles of national rather than merely regional application. When *Brown v. Board of Education*, 347 U.S. 483 (1954) (*Brown I*), was decided, the distinction between *de jure* and *de facto* segregation was consistent with the limited constitutional rationale of that case. The situation confronting the Court, largely confined to the Southern States, was officially imposed racial segregation in the schools extending back for many years and usually embodied in constitutional and statutory provisions.

The great contribution of *Brown I* was its holding in unmistakable terms that the Fourteenth Amendment forbids state-compelled or authorized segregation of public schools. 347 U.S. at 488, 493–95. Although some of the language was more expansive, the holding in *Brown I* was essentially negative: It was impermissible under the Constitution for the States, or their instrumentalities, to force children to attend segregated schools. The forbidden action was *de jure*, and the opinion in *Brown I* was construed—for some years and by many courts—as requiring only state neutrality, allowing "freedom of choice" as to schools to be attended so long as the State itself assured that the choice was genuinely free of official restraints.

But the doctrine of *Brown I*, as amplified by *Brown II*, 349 U.S. 294 (1955), did not retain its original meaning. In a series of decisions extending from 1954 to 1971 the concept of state neutrality was transformed into the present constitutional doctrine requiring affirmative state action to desegregate school systems. The keystone case was *Green v. County School Board*, 391 U.S. 430, 437–438 (1968), where school boards were declared to have "the affirmative duty to take whatever steps might be necessary to convert to a unitary system in which racial discrimination would be eliminated root and branch." The school system before the Court in *Green* was operating in a rural and sparsely settled county where there were no concentrations of white and black populations, no neighborhood school system (there were only two schools in the county), and none of the problems of an urbanized school district. The Court properly identified the freedom-of-choice program there as a subterfuge, and the language in *Green* imposing an affirmative duty to convert to a unitary system was appropriate on the facts before the Court. There was, however, reason to question to what extent this duty would apply in the vastly different factual setting of a large city with extensive areas of residential segregation, presenting problems and calling for solutions quite different from those in the rural setting of New Kent County, Virginia.

But the doubt as to whether the affirmative duty concept would flower into a new constitutional principle of general application was laid to rest by *Swann v. Charlotte-Mecklenburg Board of Education*, 402 U.S. 1 (1971), in which the duty articulated in *Green* was applied to the urban school system of metropolitan Charlotte, North Carolina. . . .

Whereas *Brown I* rightly decreed the elimination of state-imposed segregation in that particular section of the country where it did exist, *Swann* imposed obligations on southern school districts to eliminate conditions which are not regionally unique but are similar both in origin and effect to conditions in the rest of the country. As the remedial obligations of *Swann* extend far beyond the elimination of the outgrowths of the state-imposed segregation outlawed in *Brown*, the rationale of *Swann* points inevitably towards a uniform, constitutional approach to our national problem of school segregation.

II

The Court's decision today, while adhering to the *de jure/de facto* distinction, will require the application of the *Green/Swann* doctrine of "affirmative duty" to the Denver School Board despite the absence of any history of state-mandated school segregation. The only evidence of a constitutional violation was found in various decisions of the School

Board. I concur in the Court's position that the public school authorities are the responsible agency of the state, and that if the affirmative duty doctrine is sound constitutional law for Charlotte, it is equally so for Denver. I would not, however, perpetuate the *de jure/de facto* distinction nor would I leave to petitioners the initial tortuous effort of identifying "segregative acts" and deducing "segregative intent." I would hold, quite simply, that where segregated public schools exist within a school district to a substantial degree, there is a *prima facie* case that the duly constituted public authorities (I will usually refer to them collectively as the "school board") are sufficiently responsible to impose upon them a nationally applicable burden to demonstrate they nevertheless are operating a genuinely integrated school system.

A

The principal reason for abandonment of the *de jure/de facto* distinction is that, in view of the evolution of the holding in *Brown I* into the affirmative duty doctrine, the distinction no longer can be justified on a principled basis. In decreeing remedial requirements for the Charlotte/Mecklenburg school district, *Swann* dealt with a metropolitan, urbanized area in which the basic causes of segregation were generally similar to those in all sections of the country, and also largely irrelevant to the existence of historic, state-imposed segregation at the time of the *Brown* decision. Further, the extension of the affirmative duty concept to include compulsory student transportation went well beyond the mere remedying of that portion of school segregation for which former state segregation laws were ever responsible. Moreover, as the Court's opinion today abundantly demonstrates, the facts deemed necessary to establish *de jure* discrimination present problems of subjective intent which the courts cannot fairly resolve. . . .

. . . .In the evolutionary process since 1954, decisions of this Court have added a significant gloss to [*Brown*]. Although nowhere expressly articulated in these terms, I would now define it as the right, derived from the Equal Protection Clause, to expect that once the State has assumed responsibility for education, local school boards will operate *integrated school systems* within their respective districts. This means that school authorities, consistent with the generally accepted educational goal of attaining quality education for all pupils, must make and implement their customary decisions with a view toward enhancing integrated school opportunities.

The term "integrated school system" presupposes, of course, a total absence of any laws, regulations or policies supportive of the type of "legalized" segregation condemned in *Brown*. A system would be integrated in accord with constitutional standards if the responsible authorities had taken appropriate steps to (i) integrate faculties and administration; (ii) scrupulously assure equality of facilities, instruction and curricula opportunities throughout the district; (iii) utilize their authority to draw attendance zones to promote integration; and (iv) locate new schools, close old ones, and determine the size and grade categories with this same objective in mind. Where school authorities decide to undertake the transportation of students, this also must be with integrative opportunities in mind.

The foregoing prescription is not intended to be either definitive or all-inclusive, but rather an indication of the contour characteristics of an *integrated school system* in which all citizens and pupils may justifiably be confident that racial discrimination is neither practiced nor tolerated. An integrated school system does not mean—and indeed could not mean in view of the residential patterns of most of our major metropolitan areas—that *every school* must in fact be an integrated unit. A school which happens to be all or predominantly white or all or predominantly black is not a "segregated" school in an unconstitutional sense if the system itself is a genuinely integrated one.

Having school boards operate an integrated school system provides the best assurance of meeting the constitutional requirement that racial discrimination, subtle or otherwise, will find no place in the decisions of public school officials. Courts judging past school board actions with a view to their *general integrative effect* will be best able to assure an absence of such discrimination while avoiding the murky, subjective judgments inherent in the Court's search for "segregative intent." Any test resting on so nebulous and elusive an element as a school board's segregative "intent" provides inadequate assurance that minority children will not be shortchanged in the decisions of those entrusted with the nondiscriminatory operation of our public schools.

Public schools are creatures of the State, and whether the segregation is state-created or state-assisted or merely state-perpetuated should be irrelevant to constitutional principle. The school board exercises pervasive and continuing responsibility over the long-range planning as well as the daily operations of the public school system. It sets policies on attendance zones, faculty employment and assignments, school construction, closings and consolidations, and myriad other matters. School board decisions obviously are not the sole cause of segregated school conditions. But if, after such detailed and complete public supervision, substantial school segregation still persists, the presumption is strong that the school board, by its acts or omissions, is in some part responsible. Where state action and supervision are so pervasive and where, after years of such action, segregated schools continue to exist within the district to a substantial degree, this Court is justified in finding a prima facie case of constitutional violation. The burden then must fall on the school board to demonstrate it is operating an "integrated school system." . . .

The Court today does move for the first time toward breaking down past sectional disparities, but it clings tenuously to its distinction. It searches for *de jure* action in what the Denver School Board has done or failed to do, and even here the Court does not rely upon the results or effects of the Board's conduct but feels compelled to find segregative intent. . . . I can discern no basis in law or logic for holding that the motivation of school board action is irrelevant in Virginia and controlling in Colorado. . . . The net result of the Court's language, however, is the application of an *effect* test to the actions of southern school districts and an *intent* test to those in other sections, at least until an initial *de jure* finding for those districts can be made. Rather than straining to perpetuate any such dual standard, we should hold forthrightly that significant segregated school conditions in whatever section of the country are a prima facie violation of constitutional rights.

B

There is thus no reason as a matter of constitutional principle to adhere to the *de jure/de facto* distinction in school desegregation cases. In addition, there are reasons of policy and prudent judicial administration which point strongly toward the adoption of a uniform national rule. The litigation heretofore centered in the South already is surfacing in other regions. The decision of the Court today, emphasizing as it does the elusive element of segregative intent, will invite numerous desegregation suits in which there can be little hope of uniformity of result. . . .

This Court has recognized repeatedly that it is "extremely difficult for a court to ascertain the motivation, or collection of different motivations, that lie behind a legislative enactment." *Palmer v. Thompson*, 403 U.S. 214, 224 (1971); *McGinnis v. Royster*, 410 U.S. 263, 276–77 (1973); *United States v. O'Brien*, 391 U.S. 367, 381 (1968). Whatever difficulties exist with regard to a single statute will be compounded in a judicial review of years of administration of a large and complex school system.[16] Every act of a school board and school administration, and indeed every failure to act where affirmative action is indicated, must now be subject to scrutiny. . . .

Mr. Justice Rehnquist, dissenting.

. . . . Underlying the Court's entire opinion is its apparent thesis that a district judge is at least permitted to find that if a single attendance zone between two individual schools in the large metropolitan district is found by him to have been "gerrymandered," the school district is guilty of operating a "dual" school system, and is apparently a candidate for what is in practice a federal receivership. Not only the language of the Court in the opinion, but its reliance on the case of *Green v. County School Board*, 391 U.S. 430, 437–38 (1968), indicates that such would be the case. It would there-

16. As one commentator has expressed it:

"If the courts are indeed prepared to inquire into motive, thorny questions will arise even if one assumes that racial motivation is capable of being proven at trial. What of the case in which one or more members of a school board, but less than a majority, are found to have acted on racial grounds? What if it appears that the school board's action was prompted by a mixture of motives, including constitutionally innocent ones that alone would have prompted the board to act? What if the members of the school board were not themselves racially inspired but wished to please their constituents, many of whom they knew to be so? If such cases are classified as unconstitutional de jure segregation, there is little point in preserving the de jure/de facto distinction at all. And it may well be that the difference between any of these situations and one in which racial motivation is altogether lacking is too insignificant, from the standpoint of both the moral culpability of the state officials and the impact upon the children involved, to support a difference in constitutional treatment." Goodman, "*De Facto* Segregation: A Constitutional and Empirical Analysis," 60 *Calif.L.Rev.* 275, 284–85 (1972).

fore presumably be open to the District Court to require, *inter alia*, that pupils be transported great distances throughout the district to and from schools whose attendance zones have not been gerrymandered. Yet unless the Equal Protection Clause of the Fourteenth Amendment now be held to embody a principle of "taint," found in some primitive legal systems but discarded centuries ago in ours, such a result can only be described as the product of judicial fiat.

Green . . . represented a marked extension of the principles of *Brown v. Board of Education*. . . . The drastic extension of *Brown* which *Green* represented was barely, if at all, explicated in the latter opinion. To require that a genuinely "dual" system be disestablished, in the sense that the assignment of a child to a particular school is not made to depend on his race, is one thing. To require that school boards affirmatively undertake to achieve racial mixing in schools where such mixing is not achieved in sufficient degree by neutrally drawn boundary lines is quite obviously something else.

The Court's own language in *Green* makes it unmistakably clear that this significant extension of *Brown's* prohibition against discrimination, and the conversion of that prohibition into an affirmative duty to integrate, was made in the context of a school system which had for a number of years rigidly excluded Negroes from attending the same schools as were attended by whites. Whatever may be the soundness of that decision in the context of a genuinely "dual" school system, where segregation of the races had once been mandated by law, I can see no constitutional justification for it in a situation such as that which the record shows to have obtained in Denver. . . .

NOTES AND QUESTIONS

1. The De Jure/De Facto *Distinction*

The Court retains the distinction between *de facto* segregation, which is unintentional, and *de jure* segregation, which is purposeful or intentional.

a. What Is Intentional Segregation? Why did the Court quote from the district court's opinion, saying that often a school location and size decision is made "with conscious knowledge that the result would be a segregated school . . ."? Is "conscious knowledge" the same as "discriminatory intent"? *See generally* Brest, "The Supreme Court, 1975 Term–Foreword: In Defense of the Antidiscrimination Principle," 90 *Harv. L. Rev.* 1 (1976). What of the Court's reference to student transfer, student transportation, and faculty assignment policies that have the "effect" of creating a dual school system? Is the meaning of the reference changed by the notation that these decisions were made on "racially identifiable bases"? What evidence does the Court cite for this proposition?

b. Proving Intentional Segregation. How should a court determine whether school segregation was racially motivated? Suppose some members of the board of education admitted that they voted to close a school to avoid integration, but others joined in the vote for unrelated reasons. Is it enough that any single member of a decision-making body was improperly motivated? What if a board member was influenced only in part by racial considerations? What impact will the *Keyes* decision have on the willingness of board members to reveal their motivations? Will courts imply motive from the segregatory decisions themselves? If so, what is left of the *de facto/de jure* distinction?

Is the Court, in reality, addressing itself to "institutional" intent or prejudice? How may it be proven? *See* Note, "Reading the Mind of the School Board: Segregative Intent and the De Facto/De Jure Distinction," 86 *Yale L.J.* 317 (1976). Is the relevant question whether the board would have acted as it did "but for" racial prejudice? *See* Simon, "Racially Prejudiced Governmental Actions: A Motivation Theory of the Constitutional Ban Against Racial Discrimination," 15 *San Diego L. Rev.* 1041, 1059 (1978). Suppose a decision (for example, maintenance of neighborhood attendance zones) is influenced by racial prejudice, but there is substantial reason to believe that the same decision would have been made even in the absence of a concern for race?

c. Proving Intentional Segregation in Keyes. What proof did the plaintiffs offer in *Keyes* to demonstrate unlawful intent to segregate? Are there any references in the Court's opinion to specific racial pronouncements by board members? Does the decision to build a small elementary school in the middle of the black community necessarily indicate a discriminatory intent? If parents in some areas were given a choice of more than one school, and black parents chose predominantly black schools and white parents chose predominantly white schools, is this proof that school authorities had adopted the policy with the purpose of fostering segregation? Does the "excessive" use of mobile classrooms reveal segregatory intent?

d. Relevance of Intention to Discriminate. Why is intentional segregation unconstitutional while other forms of segregation are not? If segregation is stigmatizing, harmful, or otherwise undesirable as a matter of public policy, how do the good or bad motivations of governmental decision makers alter the equation? Is Justice Powell correct when he asserts: "Public schools are creatures of the state, and whether the segregation is state-created or state-assisted or merely state-perpetuated should be irrelevant to constitutional principle"?

e. Burden of Proof. In the Court's view, which party must prove intentional segregation? Does the burden shift once some intentional discrimination has been proven?

f. De Jure *Segregation: North and South.* Justice Powell stated in *Keyes* that he could discern "no basis in law or logic for holding that the motivation of school board action is irrelevant in Virginia and controlling in Colorado." Is this a fair statement of the majority's position? Is not the enactment of compulsory segregation laws in the South the clearest example of an intention to discriminate? Is intention to discriminate simply more difficult to prove in the North?

2. *What Is a Segregated School?*

Is a school segregated when it has more than 70 to 75 percent blacks? Is it segregated when the ratio of blacks to whites is greater than the ratio in the entire student population of the school district? If desegregation is premised on the denial of equal educational opportunity to blacks, should the courts determine at what point the school becomes sufficiently segregated to injure black students? Is there an underlying assumption "that whites are better [educational] resources than blacks"? Dimond, "School Segregation in the North: There Is But One Constitution," 7 *Harv. C.R.–C.L. Rev.* 1, 16 (1972).

3. *Relationship Between Racially Motivated Acts and Obligation to Desegregate*

a. Past Discrimination and Present Segregation. The Court notes that "if the actions of school authorities were to any degree motivated by segregative intent and the segregation resulting from those actions continues to exist, the fact of remoteness does not make those actions any less 'intentional.' " How close must the relationship be between the past segregatory acts and the present segregation? What does it mean to say that past school segregation policies "may have been a factor in creating a natural environment for the growth of further segregation"? Does the Court's emphasis on broadly construing the causal relationship between past segregatory acts and present school segregation, combined with the shifting of the burden of persuasion to the defendants, preordain the results in northern desegregation cases? Has the Court, without being explicit, adopted Justice Powell's view that there is an affirmative obligation to integrate the public schools whether or not the segregation is de jure?

b. De Jure *Segregation in Part of the System.*

The issue: The Court frames the issue narrowly: When substantial segregation exists in part of a school system, is the entire system a dual school system that must be wholly desegregated? The district court had ordered the desegregation of schools outside Park Hill on the theory that a segregated school, irrespective of racial motivation or state action, deprived minority children of an equal educational opportunity. Could the Court have passed on the district court's determination without deciding whether de facto segregation was constitutional? *See* Goodman, "*De Facto* Segregation: A Constitutional and Empirical Analysis," 60 *Calif. L. Rev* 275, 276 n.6 (1972). Could it have done so without reviewing the social science evidence of the effect of segregation on achievement?

Resolving the issue: The Court treats the issue of substantial segregation in a part of the system as relevant in two ways to a system-wide determination of de jure segregation. First, the Court notes that *de jure* segregation in part of the system may determine the racial composition of other neighborhoods within a metropolitan area, thereby causing the segregation of schools outside the tainted area of the city. This is particularly true since the decision to maintain segregated schools in one area necessarily limits the possibilities for integration in other areas. The Court admits that sometimes this will not be the case but intimates that such occasions are rare. Second, the Court holds that intentional segregation in a portion of a school system creates a presumption that segregation elsewhere in the system is racially motivated, shifting the burden of proof to the defendants.

Result: Can the Court's treatment of less than system-wide discrimination be accurately described as a sort of "Catch 22"? If substantial racially motivated segregation is found, lower courts will usually find that the entire system has been tainted. If the school district does convince the court that the *de jure* practices are isolated episodes, there is still a presumption that any other segregation in the system is racially motivated. Consider also the burden of proof borne by the district. It must prove that "segregative intent was not among the factors that motivated their actions." Does the Court's elaboration of evidentiary rules largely obliterate the *de facto/de jure* distinction?

4. "The Essential Element of De Jure Segregation" Further Defined: Washington v. Davis *and* Arlington Heights

In *Washington v. Davis*, 426 U.S. 229, 96 S.Ct. 2040, 48 L.Ed.2d 597 (1976), two rejected black applicants for the Washington, D.C., police force challenged the department's use of a standardized test designed to screen out unqualified applicants. They argued that the test disqualified a disproportionate number of minority applicants in violation of the Equal Protection Clause of the Fourteenth Amendment. The Court of Appeals held that the evidence of discriminatory impact was sufficient to shift the burden of proving the test's efficacy and racial neutrality to defendants. The Supreme Court reversed, holding that "[d]isproportionate impact is not irrelevant, but it is not the sole touchstone of an invidious racial discrimination forbidden by the Constitution." 426 U.S. at 242, 96 S.Ct. at 2084.

Village of Arlington Heights v. Metropolitan Housing Development Corporation, 429 U.S. 252, 97 S.Ct. 555, 50 L.Ed.2d 450 (1977), involved a challenge by a nonprofit developer to the refusal of housing authorities to rezone land for the building of racially integrated low and moderate income housing, arguing that the refusal was racially discriminatory. The Supreme Court, citing *Washington v. Davis* and *Keyes*, said that proof of racially discriminatory purpose is necessary. The Court noted that determining whether "invidious discriminatory purpose" was a motivating factor would include an examination of both circumstantial and direct evidence of intent to discriminate. While a racially disproportionate impact of the official action "may provide an important starting point . . . , impact alone is not the determinative." The Court suggested that the historical background of the official action, the specific sequence of events leading up to the official action, departures from the normal procedural sequence, and the legislative or administrative history "might afford evidence that improper purposes are playing a role." Thus, as applied to school desegregation cases, *Washington v. Davis* and *Arlington Heights* suggest that mere racial imbalance would not be enough to trigger a presumption of discriminatory intent; there must be some independent evidence of that intent.

a. Intent: A Subjective or Objective Standard? Because *Keyes*, *Washington v. Davis*, and *Arlington Heights* make intention the linchpin of the constitutional violation, proof of discriminatory intention has become a crucial factor in desegregation cases. With the increase in northern desegregation cases, the difficulty of proving intent has also increased as there is often no prior history of discriminatory legislation. Different approaches have evolved:

(1) Subjective Intent. Some lower courts have held that intent must be proven directly by recourse to the minutes of school board meetings or by other direct evidence that racial factors entered the challenged decision. *See, e.g., Johnson v. San Francisco Unified School District*, 500 F.2d 349 (9th Cir. 1974); *Soria v. Oxnard School District*, 488 F.2d 579, 585, 588 (9th Cir. 1973), *cert. denied*, 416 U.S. 951, 94 S.Ct. 1961, 40 L.Ed.2d 301 (1974); *Husbands v. Pennsylvania*, 395 F. Supp. 1107 (E.D. Pa. 1975).

(2) The Objective Standard. Without direct evidence of intent, some courts have inferred segregative intent from school board actions that have the foreseeable effect of fostering segregation. *See Oliver v. Kalamazoo Board of Education*, 368 F. Supp. 143, 161 (W.D. Mich. 1973), *aff'd*, 508 F.2d 178, 181–82 (6th Cir. 1974), *cert. denied*, 421 U.S. 963, 95 S.Ct. 1950, 44 L.Ed.2d 449 (1975).

(3) A Middle Standard. The Second Circuit has refused to apply a purely objective test of intent but does not require full proof of a subjective intent either. In *Arthur v. Nyquist*, 573 F.2d 134, 142 n.15 (2d Cir. 1978), *cert denied*, 439 U.S. 860, 99 S.Ct. 179, 58 L.Ed.2d 169, the court explained the problem with an objective standard:

> Since most racial imbalance, once established, is foreseeable, any policy which permits such imbalance to continue would, on a strictly objective theory, amount

> to *de jure* segregation. We believe that such a theory sweeps more broadly than necessary, collapsing the distinction between *de jure* and *de facto* segregation.

573 F.2d 134, 142 n. 15.

The Second Circuit therefore suggested that foreseeability be coupled with an examination of alternative courses of action and other factors. *See also Armstrong v. O'Connell*, 451 F. Supp. 817 (E.D. Wis. 1978).

Is the Second Circuit's criticism of the "objective standard" merited? How else is subjective intent proven other than by the introduction of "objective" evidence from which inferences of a subjective state of mind could reasonably be drawn? Does the alternative formula say anything more than that when nonracial explanations of decisions are implausible, inferences of racial prejudice will be drawn?

b. Reconciling Washington v. Davis, Arlington Heights, *and* Keyes. Following the *Washington v. Davis* and the *Arlington Heights* decisions, the Supreme Court remanded a number of cases, which explicitly relied on the objective "foreseeability" test of intention, with instructions that the lower courts reconsider their findings of intent in light of these decisions. *School District of Omaha v. United States*, 433 U.S. 667, 97 S.Ct. 2905, 53 L.Ed.2d 1039 (1977); *Brennan v. Armstrong*, 433 U.S. 672, 97 S.Ct. 2907, 53 L.Ed.2d 1044 (1977); *Austin Independent School District v. United States*, 429 U.S. 990, 97 S.Ct. 519, 50 L.Ed.2d 603 (1976); *Board of School Commissioners of Indianapolis v. Buckley*, 429 U.S. 1068, 97 S.Ct. 802, 50 L.Ed.2d 786 (1977).

These somewhat cryptic signals to the lower courts were expanded upon but not clarified by *Dayton Board of Education v. Brinkman*, 433 U.S. 406, 97 S.Ct. 2766, 53 L.Ed.2d 851 (1977). In an unpublished opinion, the district court found three constitutional violations in the Dayton school system: (1) racially imbalanced schools; (2) the use of optional attendance zones which, in some instances, would allow white high school students to transfer out of what would have been integrated schools; and (3) the rescission by the school board of resolutions adopted but not yet implemented by the previous school board to provide for voluntary desegregation of these schools. It did not, however, mandate a district-wide racial balance remedy. On appeal, a district-wide desegregation plan was ordered. *Brinkman v. Gilligan*, 503 F.2d 684, 693–97 (6th Cir. 1974). This decision was vacated by a unanimous Supreme Court, and the case was remanded for new findings and conclusions about violations in light of *Washington v. Davis* and *Arlington Heights*. Read narrowly, the Court only addressed itself to the failure of the appellate court to reverse the district court's findings of facts before mandating a district-wide remedy. But the opinion of Justice Rehnquist, for the Court, did not stop with this admonition:

> Judged most favorably to the petitioners, then, the District Court's findings of constitutional violations did not, under our cases, suffice to justify the remedy imposed. . . . We realize, of course, that the task of factfinding in a case such as this is a good deal more difficult than is typically the case in a more orthodox lawsuit. Findings as to the motivations of multimembered public bodies are of necessity difficult, cf. *Village of Arlington Heights v. Metropolitan Housing Development Corp.*, . . . and the question of whether demographic changes resulting in racial concentration occurred from purely neutral public actions or were instead the intended result of actions which appeared neutral on their face but were in fact invidiously discriminatory is not an easy one to resolve. . . .
>
> [T]he Court of Appeals simply had no warrant in our cases for imposing the systemwide remedy which it apparently did. . . . It is clear from the findings of the District Court that Dayton is a racially mixed community, and that many of its schools are predominantly white or predominantly black. This fact without more, of course, does not offend the Constitution.

433 U.S. at 414, 417, 97 S.Ct. at 2772, 2774.

Is Justice Rehnquist repudiating *Keyes*?

c. School Board Liability for Intentionally Discriminatory Actions by Other Governmental Agencies. Should school boards be liable for correcting segregation that is the result of intentionally discriminatory action of other governmental agencies? *Swann* expressly reserved that issue for future decision. 402 U.S. at 23. *See also Delaware State Board of Education v. Evans*, 446 U.S. 923, 100 S.Ct. 1862, 64 L.Ed.2d 278 (1980) (Justice Rehnquist, dissenting). Several lower court cases, however, have focused on the actions of other governmental agencies that might have contributed to residential segregation in order to find that the pattern of segregated schooling resulting from neighborhood assignment plans constitutes *de jure* segregation. *See United States v. Board of School Commissioners*, 573 F.2d 400 (7th Cir. 1978), *cert. denied*, 439 U.S. 824, 99 S.Ct. 93, 58 L.Ed.2d 116; *Evans v. Buchanan*, 393 F.Supp. 428 (D. Del.

1975), *cert. denied sub nom.*, *Delaware State Board of Education v. Evans*, 446 U.S. 923, 100 S.Ct. 1862, 64 L.Ed.2d 278; *Bradley v. Milliken*, 338 F.Supp. 582, 587 (E.D. Mich. 1971), *rev'd on other grounds*, 418 U.S. 717, 94 S.Ct. 3112, 41 L.Ed.2d 1069. Cases repudiating school board liability for nonboard actions include *Higgins v. Board of Education*, 508 F.2d 779, 788–89 (6th Cir. 1974) and *Alvarado v. El Paso Independent School District*, 426 F.Supp. 575, 595 (W.D. Tex. 1976), *aff'd*, 593 F.2d 577 (5th Cir. 1979).

Why should school boards be responsible for the constitutional violations of other governmental agencies? *See* Feagin, "School Desegregation: A Political-Economic Perspective," in *School Desegregation*, W. Stephan and J. Feagin, eds., 25 (1980). Should these other agencies at least be parties to the school desegregation suit? *See Hart v. Community School Board*, 383 F.Supp. 699 (E.D. N.Y. 1974), *aff'd*, 512 F.2d 37 (2d Cir. 1975), in which the school board impleaded city, state, and federal housing and urban development agencies on the theory that they had fostered residential segregation which resulted in school segregation.

In *Hart v. Community School Board of Brooklyn*, *supra*, the district court, although agreeing that some acts of the housing authority exacerbated the segregated condition of the school, held the intentional acts and omissions of the school board were the real cause of the segregation. The court, however, retained jurisdiction over the third party defendants for remedial purposes. On appeal, the court recommended that all nonliable parties be dismissed. 512 F.2d 37 (2d Cir. 1975). In *Bell v. Board of Education, Akron Public Schools*, 683 F.2d 963 (6th Cir. 1982), the plaintiffs argued that the school board was liable for intentionally segregative actions of other governmental agencies that caused residential segregation, which, together with geographic attendance zoning as the primary method of school assignment, produced racially segregated schools. The plaintiffs argued that the obligation to remedy the constitutional violation fell on the school authorities as they were the only parties that could remedy the school segregation. The court declined to hold the school board "otherwise innocent of segregative intent" liable for "discriminatory conduct of the FHA in making housing loans and local housing authorities in the construction and rental of public housing." 683 F.2d at 968. *See* Levin & Moise, "School Desegregation Litigation in the Seventies and the Use of Social Science Evidence: An Annotated Guide," 39 *Law & Contemp. Prob.* 50 (1975).

In *United States v. Yonkers Board of Education*, the city, its public housing agency, and the school board were sued and the court found all defendants liable. While the court suggested the evidence justified holding both the city and the school board liable independently for intentional segregative acts, it concluded that the most important factors indicated a joint effort to create and maintain a racially segregated school system. 624 F.Supp. 1276 (S.D.N.Y. 1985), *aff'd*, 837 F.2d 1181 (2d Cir.). Thus both the school board and the city were ordered to remedy the segregation in the schools. Among other remedies, the city was required to build two hundred units of public housing and develop a plan for additional subsidized housing units in other parts of the city. 635 F.Supp. 1577 (S.D.N.Y. 1986).

5. The Supreme Court and Northern School Desegregation Revisited: Columbus II *and* Dayton II

Some of the questions raised in the preceding pages, such as the relationship between past segregative acts and present school segregation, the standard for proving discriminatory intent, and the basis for finding a system-wide violation, resurfaced in *Columbus II* and *Dayton II*.

The Columbus, Ohio, school system was highly segregated at the time *Columbus Board of Education v. Penick*, 443 U.S. 449, 99 S.Ct. 2941, 61 L.Ed.2d 666 (1979) (*Columbus II*), was decided by the Supreme Court. The board contended, however, that the segregated school system was not operated as such with any racially discriminatory purpose and that whatever unconstitutional conduct might have occurred in the past had had no system-wide segregative impact.

a. De Jure *Segregation in 1954*. Recall that *Keyes* involved a system that was found to have intentionally been segregated even though it had never operated under a statutory or constitutional provision mandating or permitting segregation. Moreover, once deliberate segregation was found to exist in part of the school system, the question was whether that would make the entire system a dual school system. These issues were a part of *Columbus II* as well. Justice White's opinion dealt with these issues as follows:

> First, although at least since 1888 there had been no statutory requirement or authorization to operate segregated schools, the District Court found that in

1954, when *Brown I* was decided, the Columbus Board was not operating a racially neutral, unitary school system, but was conducting "an enclave of separate, black schools on the near east side of Columbus," and that "[t]he then-existing racial separation was the direct result of cognitive acts or omissions of those school board members and administrators who had originally intentionally caused and later perpetuated the racial isolation. . . ." . . . Such separateness could not "be said to have been the result of racially neutral official acts.". . .

* * *

The Board insists that, since segregated schooling was not commanded by state law and since not all schools were wholly black or wholly white in 1954, the District Court was not warranted in finding a dual system. But the District Court found that the "Columbus Public Schools were *officially* segregated by race in 1954," . . .; and in any event, there is no reason to question the finding that as the "direct result of cognitive acts or omissions" the Board maintained "an enclave of separate, black schools on the near east side of Columbus." . . . Proof of purposeful and effective maintenance of a body of separate black schools in a substantial part of the system itself is prima facie proof of a dual school system and supports a finding to this effect absent sufficient contrary proof by the Board, which was not forthcoming in this case. *Keyes, supra*, at 203.

Columbus II, 443 U.S. at 455–58, 99 S.Ct. at 2945–47.

b. Remoteness in Time Between Past Segregatory Acts and the Present Segregation. As in *Keyes*, the Court in *Columbus II* had to determine the relationship between past segregatory acts and present segregation and whether plaintiffs or defendants bore the burden of demonstrating the relationship. Justice White noted that since the decision in *Brown II*, the Columbus school board was under "a continuous constitutional obligation to disestablish its dual school system." Both lower courts had found that the board had failed to discharge its duty. Justice White explained that:

. . . each instance of a failure or refusal to fulfill this affirmative duty continues the violation of the Fourteenth Amendment. *Dayton I*, 433 U.S. at 413–14; *Wright v. Council of City of Emporia*, 407 U.S. 451, 460 (1972); *United States v. Scotland Neck Board of Education*, 407 U.S. 484 (1972) (creation of a new school district in a city that had operated a dual school system but was not yet the subject of court-ordered desegregation.)

* * *

In determining whether a dual school system has been disestablished, *Swann* also mandates that matters aside from student assignments must be considered. . . . Further, *Swann* stated that in devising remedies for legally imposed segregation the responsibility of the local authorities and district courts is to ensure that future school construction and abandonment are not used and do not serve to perpetuate or reestablish the dual school system. *Id.*, at 20–21. As for student assignments, the Court said:

No *per se* rule can adequately embrace all the difficulties of reconciling the competing interests involved; but in a system with a history of segregation the need for remedial criteria of sufficient specificity to assure a school authority's compliance with its constitutional duty warrants a presumption against schools that are substantially disproportionate in their racial composition. Where the school authority's proposed plan for conversion from a dual to a unitary system contemplates the continued existence of some schools that are all or predominantly of one race, they have the burden of showing that such school assignments are genuinely nondiscriminatory. *Id.*, at 26.

The Board's continuing "affirmative duty to disestablish the dual school system" is therefore beyond question, . . . and it has pointed to nothing in the record persuading us that at the time of trial the dual school system and its effects had been disestablished. The Board does not appear to challenge the finding of the District court that at the time of trial most blacks were still going to black schools and most whites to white schools. Whatever the Board's current purpose with respect to racially separate education might be, it knowingly continued its failure to eliminate the consequences of its past intentionally segregative policies. The board "never actively set out to dismantle this dual system." . . .

Id. at 459–61, 99 S.Ct. at 2947–48.

The nature of the "continuing violation" is further elaborated in the companion case of *Dayton Board of Education v. Brinkman*, 443 U.S. 526, 535, 99 S.Ct. 2971, 2977, 61 L.Ed.2d 720 (1979) (*Dayton II*).

Part of the affirmative duty imposed by our cases . . . is the obligation not to take any action that would impede the process of disestablishing the dual system and its effects. . . . The Dayton Board, however, had engaged in many post-*Brown* actions that had the effect of increasing or perpetuating segregation. . . . [T]he measure of the post-*Brown* conduct of a school board under an unsatisfied duty to liquidate a dual system is the effectiveness, not the purpose, of the actions in

> decreasing or increasing the segregation caused by the dual system. . . . As was clearly established in *Keyes* and *Swann*, the Board had to do more than abandon its prior discriminatory purpose. . . . The Board has had an affirmative responsibility to see that pupil assignment policies and school construction and abandonment practices "are not used and do not serve to perpetuate or re-establish the dual school system," *Columbus* [443 U.S.], at 460, and the Board has a 'heavy burden' of showing that actions that increased or continued the effects of the dual system serve important and legitimate ends . . . .

Dayton II, 443 U.S. at 537–38, 99 S.Ct. at 2978–80.

In his dissenting opinion in *Dayton II*, Justice Rehnquist argues that the majority's "affirmative duty" requirement makes a determination of the school board's segregative intent after 1954 irrelevant. Does the majority's decision mean that unless the school board at some period between 1954 and the present had racially balanced all of the schools in the system, it would continue to be liable for segregated schools regardless of whether there was a demonstrated relationship between the segregative acts taken prior to 1954 and present segregation? *See Adams v. United States*, 620 F.2d 1277 (8th Cir. 1980), *cert. denied*, 449 U.S. 826, 101 S.Ct. 88, 66 L.Ed.2d 29. Who has misread *Swann*, *Keyes*, and *Dayton I*—the majority or the dissenters?

c. Subjective or Objective Standard of Intent. Although the Court seemed to indicate that the failure "effectively to eliminate the continuing consequences of its intentional systemwide segregation in 1954" was enough to compel a system-wide remedy, it also noted that the district court had found that

> . . . in the intervening years there had been a series of Board actions and practices that could not "reasonably be explained without reference to racial concerns," . . . and that "intentionally aggravated, rather than alleviated," racial separation in the schools. . . . These matters included the general practice of assigning black teachers only to those schools with substantial black student populations, a practice that was terminated only in 1974 as the result of a conciliation agreement with the Ohio Civil Rights Commission; the intentionally segregative use of optional attendance zones, discontiguous attendance areas, and boundary changes; and the selection of sites for new school construction that had the foreseeable and anticipated effect of maintaining the racial separation of the schools. The court generally noted that "[s]ince the 1954 *Brown* decision, the Columbus defendants or their predecessors were adequately put on notice of the fact that action was required to correct and to prevent the increase in" segregation, yet failed to heed their duty to alleviate racial separation in the schools. . . .
>
> * * *
>
> . . . [The District Court recognized that under prior Supreme Court] cases disparate impact and foreseeable consequences, without more do not establish a constitutional violation. . . . Nevertheless, the District Court correctly noted that actions having foreseeable and anticipated disparate impact are relevant evidence to prove the ultimate fact, forbidden purpose. Those cases do not forbid "the foreseeable effects standard from being utilized as one of the several kinds of proofs from which an inference of segregative intent may be properly drawn." . . . Adherence to a particular policy or practice, "with full knowledge of the predictable effects of such adherence upon racial imbalance in a school system is one factor among many others which may be considered by a court in determining whether an inference of segregative intent should be drawn." The District Court thus stayed well within the requirements of *Washington v. Davis* and *Arlington Heights. See Personnel Administrator of Massachusetts v. Feeney*, 442 U.S. 256, 279 n.25, 99 S.Ct. 2282, 2296 n.25, 60 L.Ed.2d 870 (1979).

Columbus II, 443 U.S. at 461–64, 99 S.Ct. at 2948–50.

d. Proof of Intentional Segregative Action. Has the majority in *Columbus II* modified the standard for determining racially discriminatory intent or purpose as articulated in *Arlington Heights*? Does the "affirmative duty" standard hold school boards liable for the foreseeable consequences of every action taken by school officials and also for the failure to take action? *See Personnel Administrator v. Feeney*, 442 U.S. 256, 99 S.Ct. 2282, 60 L.Ed.2d 870 (1979), which rejected the tort-law standard of intent—that one intends the reasonably foreseeable results of one's conduct—as applied to claims of discrimination.

e. To Which School Board Can Racial Motivation Be Attributed? Even if there is clear and convincing proof that the Dayton and Columbus school boards of twenty-five years ago took racially motivated actions that resulted in a dual school system in 1954, does it matter that the members of today's school boards might not act out of similar motivations? Is the "Board" a single, continuous entity over time? *See generally* Note, "Reading the Mind of the School Board: Segregative Intent and the De Facto/De Jure Distinction," 86 *Yale L.J.* 317 (1976).

Is it likely that the existence of racially imbalanced schools in most major urban areas is caused primarily by the unconstitutional conduct of school officials, regardless of when that conduct occurred? According to Mr. Justice Powell, racially imbalanced schools result "primarily from familiar segregated housing patterns, which—in turn—are caused by social, economic, and demographic forces for which no school board is responsible." *Columbus II*, 443 U.S. at 480, 99 S.Ct. at 2952 (Powell, J., dissenting). *See also Austin Independent School District v. United States*, 429 U.S. 990, 994, 97 S.Ct. 517, 519, 50 L.Ed.2d 603 (1976) (Powell, J., concurring). Thus, for Mr. Justice Powell, system-wide remedies "lack any principled basis when the absence of integration in all schools cannot reasonably be attributed to discriminatory conduct." *Columbus II*, 443 U.S. at 482, 99 S.Ct. at 2952.

f. The Dissenting Opinion in Columbus II. Justice Rehnquist (joined by Justice Powell) dissented from the majority's positions in *Columbus II* on the remoteness in time between past segregatory acts and present segregation, on who has the burden of demonstrating the relationship between past segregatory acts and present segregation, and on the standard for determining intentional segregation:

> . . . As a matter of history, case law, or logic, there is nothing to support the novel proposition that the primary inquiry in school desegregation cases involving systems without a history of statutorily mandated racial assignment is what happened in those systems before 1954. As a matter of history, 1954 makes no more sense as a benchmark—indeed it makes *less* sense—than 1968, 1971 or 1973. Perhaps the latter year has the most to commend it, if one insists on a benchmark, because in *Keyes* this Court first confronted the problem of school segregation in the context of systems without a history of statutorily mandated segregation of the races.
>
> . . . It is sophistry to suggest that a school board in Columbus in 1954 could have read *Brown* and gleaned from it a constitutional duty "to diffuse black students throughout the system" or take whatever other action the Court today thinks it should have taken. . . .
>
> * * *
>
> Causality plays a central role in *Keyes* as it does in all equal protection analysis. The *Keyes* Court held that before the burden of production shifts to the school board, the plaintiffs must prove "that the school authorities have carried out a systematic program of segregation *affecting a substantial portion of the students, schools, teachers and facilities within the school system.*" 413 U.S., at 201 (emphasis added). The Court recognized that a trial court might find "that a lesser degree of segregated schooling . . . would not have resulted even if the Board had not acted as it did," and "that at some point in time the relationship between past segregative acts and present segregation may become so attenuated as to be incapable of supporting a finding of *de jure* segregation warranting judicial intervention." *Id.*, at 211. . . . The relevance of past acts of the school board was to depend on whether "segregation resulting from those actions continues to exist." . . . That inquiry is not central under the approach approved by the Court today. Henceforth, the question is apparently whether pre-1954 acts contributed in some unspecified manner to segregated conditions that existed in 1954. If the answer is yes, then the only question is whether the school board has exploited all integrative opportunities that presented themselves in the subsequent 25 years. If not, a systemwide remedy is in order, despite the plaintiff's failure to demonstrate a link between those past acts and current racial imbalance.
>
> * * *
>
> . . . [The finding of a "dual" school system in 1954] was predicated on the presence of four predominantly black elementary schools and one predominantly black junior high school on the "near east side of Columbus," a then and now black residential area. The Columbus School Board at that time employed, as it does now, a neighborhood school policy. The specific Board actions that the District Court cited were racial assignment of teachers and gerrymandering along part of the border between two school districts. The Court concludes that these violations involved a substantial part of the Columbus school system in 1954, and invokes *Keyes* for the proposition that the finding of a dual school system follows "absent sufficient contrary proof by the Board, which was not forthcoming in this case." . . .
>
> There are two major difficulties with this use of *Keyes*. First, without any explanation the Court for the first time applies it to define the character of a school system remote in time—here 25 or more years ago—without any examination of the justifications for the *Keyes* burden-shifting principles when those principles are used in this fashion. Their use is a matter of " 'policy and fairness,' " 413 U.S., at 209 (quoting Wigmore), and I think the *Keyes* "presumption" scores poorly on both counts when focused on a period beyond memory and often beyond records. . . .
>
> My second concern about the Court's use of the *Keyes* presumption may render my first concern academic. For . . . the Court today endorses views re-

garding the neighborhood school policy and racially identifiable neighborhoods that essentially makes the *Keyes* presumption irrebuttable.

* * *

It is most unfortunate that the Court chooses not to speak clearly today. *Dayton I* and *Keyes* are not overruled, yet their essential messages are ignored. The Court does not intimate that it has fathomed the full implications of the analysis it has sanctioned—an approach that would certainly make school desegregation litigation a "loaded game board," *Swann*, 402 U.S., at 28, but one at which a school board could never win. A school system's only hope of avoiding a judicial receivership would be a voluntary dismantling of its neighborhood school program. If that is the Court's intent today, it had indeed accepted the role of Judge Learned Hand's feared "Platonic Guardians" and intellectual integrity—if not the Constitution or the interests of our beleaguered urban school systems and their students of all races—would be better served by discarding the pretextual distinction between *de facto* and *de jure* segregation. Whether the Court's result be reached by the approach of Pilate or Plato, I cannot subscribe to it.

443 U.S. at 501–02, 505–10, 525, 99 S.Ct. at 2958–59, 2960–63, 2971 (Rehnquist, J. and Powell, J., dissenting).

C. Constitutionality of State Limits on Voluntary Actions by School Boards to Eliminate *De Facto* Segregation

Washington v. Seattle School District No. 1

458 U.S. 457, 102 S.Ct. 3187, 73 L.Ed.2d 896 (1982).

Justice Blackmun delivered the opinion of the Court.

* * *

Seattle School District No. 1 (District), which is largely coterminous with the city of Seattle, Wash., is charged by state law with administering 112 schools and educating approximately 54,000 public school students. About 37% of these children are of Negro, Asian, American Indian, or Hispanic ancestry. Because segregated housing patterns in Seattle have created racially imbalanced schools, the District historically has taken steps to alleviate the isolation of minority students; since 1963, it has permitted students to transfer from their neighborhood schools to help cure the District's racial imbalance.

Despite these efforts, the District in 1977 came under increasing pressure to accelerate its program of desegregation. In response, the District's Board of Directors (School Board) enacted a resolution defining "racial imbalance" as "the situation that exists when the combined minority student enrollment in a school exceeds the districtwide combined average by 20 percentage points, provided that the single minority enrollment . . . of no school will exceed 50 percent of the student body." 473 F.Supp. 996, 1006 (W.D. Wash. 1979). The District resolved to eliminate all such imbalance from the Seattle public schools by the beginning of the 1979–1980 academic year.

. . . The District . . . concluded that mandatory reassignment of students was necessary if racial isolation in its schools was to be eliminated. Accordingly, in March 1978, the School Board enacted the so-called "Seattle Plan" for desegregation. The plan, which makes extensive use of busing and mandatory reassignments, desegregates elementary schools by "pairing" and "triading" predominately minority with predominately white attendance areas, and by basing student assignments on attendance zones rather than on race. . . . The District represents that the plan results in the reassignment of roughly equal numbers of white and minority students, and allows most students to spend roughly half of their academic careers attending a school near their homes. . . .

The desegregation program, implemented in the 1978–1979 academic year, apparently was effective: the District Court found that the Seattle Plan "has substantially reduced the number of racially imbalanced schools in the district and has substantially reduced the percentage of minority students in those schools which remain racially imbalanced." 473 F.Supp., at 1007.

* * *

In late 1977, shortly before the Seattle Plan was formally adopted by the District, a number of Seattle residents who opposed the desegregation strategies being discussed by the School Board formed an organization called the Citizens for Voluntary Integration Committee (CiVIC). . . . CiVIC drafted a statewide initiative designed to terminate the use of mandatory busing for purposes of racial integration. This proposal, known as Initiative 350, provided that "no school board . . . shall directly or indirectly require any student to attend a school other than the school which is geographically nearest or next nearest the student's place of residence . . . and which offers the course of study pursued by such student. . . ." *See* Wash.Rev. Code § 28A.26.010 (1981). The initiative then set out, however, a number of broad exceptions to this requirement: a student may be assigned beyond his neighborhood school if he "requires special education, care, or guidance," or if "there are health or safety hazards, either natural or man made, or physical barriers or obstacles . . . between the student's place of residence and the nearest or next nearest school," or if "the school nearest or next nearest to his place of residence is unfit or inadequate because of overcrowding, unsafe conditions or lack of physical facilities." *See ibid.* Initiative 350 also specifically proscribed use of seven enumerated methods of "indirec[t]" student assignment—among them the redefinition of attendance zones, the pairing of schools, and the use of "feeder" schools—that are a part of the Seattle Plan. *See* § 28A.26.030. The initiative envisioned busing for racial purposes in only one circumstance: it did not purport to "prevent any court of competent jurisdiction from adjudicating constitutional issues relating to the public schools." *See* § 28A.26.060.

* * *

On November 8, 1978, two months after the Seattle Plan went into effect, Initiative 350 passed by a substantial margin, drawing almost 66% of the vote statewide. The initiative failed to attract majority support in two state legislative districts, both in Seattle. In the city as a whole, however, the initiative passed with some 61% of the vote. Within the month, the District, together with the Tacoma and Pasco school districts, initiated this suit against the State in United States District Court for the Western District of Washington, challenging the constitutionality of Initiative 350 under the Equal Protection Clause of the Fourteenth Amendment. The United States and several community organizations intervened in support of the District; CiVIC intervened on behalf of the defendants.

* * *

The District Court then held Initiative 350 unconstitutional, for three independent reasons. The court first concluded that the initiative established an impermissible racial classification, in violation of *Hunter v. Erickson*, 393 U.S. 385 . . . (1969), and *Lee v. Nyquist*, 318 F.Supp. 710 (W.D.N.Y. 1970) (three-judge court), *summarily aff'd*, 402 U.S. 935 . . . (1971), "because it permits busing for non-racial reasons but forbids it for racial reasons." 473 F.Supp., at 1012. The court next held Initiative 350 invalid because "a racially discriminatory purpose was one of the factors which motivated the conception and adoption of the initiative." *Id.*, at 1013. . . .

* * *

We believe that the Court of Appeals properly focused on *Hunter* and *Lee*, for we find the principle of those cases dispositive of the issue here. In our view, Initiative 350 must fall because it does "not attemp[t] to allocate governmental power on the basis of any general principle." *Hunter v. Erickson*, 393 U.S., at 395, 89 S.Ct., at 563 (Harlan, J., concurring). Instead, it uses the racial nature of an issue to define the governmental decision-making structure, and thus imposes substantial and unique burdens on racial minorities.

* * *

Noting that Initiative 350 nowhere mentions "race" or "integration," appellants suggest that the legislation has no racial overtones; they maintain that *Hunter* is inapposite because the initiative simply permits busing for certain enumerated purposes while neutrally forbidding it for all other reasons. We find it difficult to believe that appellants' analysis is seriously advanced, however, for despite its facial neutrality there is little doubt that the initiative was effectively drawn for racial purposes. Neither the initiative's sponsors, nor the District Court, nor the Court of Appeals had any difficulty perceiving the racial nature of the issue settled by Initiative 350. . . .

* * *

We are . . . satisfied that the practical effect of Initiative 350 is to work a reallocation of power of the kind condemned in *Hunter*. The initiative removes the authority to address a racial problem—and only a racial problem—from the existing decision-making body, in such a way as to burden minority interests. Those favoring the elimination of *de facto* school segregation now must seek relief from the state legislature, or from the statewide electorate. Yet authority over all other student assignment decisions, as well as over most other areas of educational policy, remains vested in the local school board. Indeed, by specifically exempting from Initiative 350's proscriptions most non-racial reasons for assigning students away from their neighborhood schools, the initiative expressly requires those championing school integration to surmount a considerably higher hurdle than persons seeking comparable legislative action. . . .

* * *

. . . The issue here, after all, is not whether Washington has the authority to intervene in the affairs of local school boards; it is, rather, whether the State has exercised that authority in a manner consistent with the Equal Protection Clause. . . .

At the outset, it is irrelevant that the State might have vested all decision-making authority in itself, so long as the political structure it in fact erected imposes comparative burdens on minority interests; that much is settled by *Hunter* and by *Lee*. And until the passage of Initiative 350, Washington law in fact had established the local school board, rather than the State, as the entity charged with making decisions of the type at issue here. Like all 50 States, . . . Washington of course is ultimately responsible for providing education within its borders. . . . But Washington has chosen to meet its educational responsibilities primarily through "state and local officials, boards, and committees," § 28A.02.020, and the responsibility to devise and tailor educational programs to suit local needs has emphatically been vested in the local school boards.

* * *

Given this statutory structure, we have little difficulty concluding that Initiative 350 worked a major reordering of the State's educational decision-making process. Before adoption of the initiative, the power to determine what programs would most appropriately fill a school district's educational needs—including programs involving student assignment and desegregation—was firmly committed to the local board's discretion. The question whether to provide an integrated learning environment rather than a system of neighborhood schools surely involved a decision of that sort. . . . After passage of Initiative 350, authority over all but one of those areas remained in the hands of the local board. By placing power over desegregative busing at the state level, then, Initiative 350 plainly "differentiates between the treatment of problems involving racial matters and that afforded other problems in the same area." *Lee v. Nyquist*, 318 F.Supp., at 718. . . .

* * *

To be sure, "the simple repeal or modification of desegregation or anti-discrimination laws, without more, never has been viewed as embodying a presumptively invalid racial classification." *Crawford v. Los Angeles Board of Education*, 458 U.S. 527, 539, ... *See Dayton Board of Education v. Brinkman*, 443 U.S. 526, 531 n.5 . . . (1979). . . .

Initiative 350, however, works something more than the "mere repeal" of a desegregation law by the political entity that created it. It burdens all future attempts to integrate Washington schools in districts throughout the State, by lodging decision-making authority over the question at a new and remote level of government. . . .

Accordingly, the judgment of the Court of Appeals is

Affirmed.

Justice Powell, with whom The Chief Justice, Justice Rehnquist, and Justice O'Connor join, dissenting.

The people of the State of Washington, by a two to one vote, have adopted a neighborhood school policy. The policy is binding on local school districts but in no way affects the authority of state or federal courts to order school transportation to remedy violations of the Fourteenth Amendment. Nor does the policy affect the power of local school districts to establish voluntary transfer programs for racial integration or for any other purpose.

In the absence of a constitutional violation, no decision of this Court compels a school district to adopt or maintain a mandatory busing program for racial integration. Accordingly, the Court does not hold that the adoption of a neighborhood school policy by *local* school districts would be unconstitutional. Rather, it holds that the adoption of such a policy at the *State* level—rather than at the local level—violates the Equal Protection Clause of the Fourteenth Amendment.

I dissent from the Court's unprecedented intrusion into the structure of a state government. The School Districts in this case were under no Federal Constitutional obligation to adopt mandatory busing programs. The State of Washington, the governmental body ultimately responsible for the provision of public education, has determined that certain mandatory busing programs are detrimental to the education of its children. . . .

* * *

The principles that should guide us in reviewing the constitutionality of Initiative 350 are well established. To begin with, we have never held, or even intimated, that absent a federal constitutional violation, a State *must* choose to treat persons differently on the basis of race. In the absence of a federal constitutional violation requiring race-specific remedies, a policy of strict racial neutrality by a State would violate no federal constitutional principle. . . .

In particular, a neighborhood school policy and a decision *not* to assign students on the basis of their race, does not offend the Fourteenth Amendment. The Court has never held that there is an affirmative duty to integrate the schools in the absence of a finding of unconstitutional segregation. . . . Indeed, even where desegregation is ordered because of a constitutional violation, the Court has never held that racial balance itself is a constitutional requirement. . . . And even where there have been segregated schools, once desegregation has been accomplished no further constitutional duty exists upon school boards or States to maintain integration. See *Pasadena City Board of Education v. Spangler*, 427 U.S. 424 . . . (1976).

Moreover, it is a well-established principle that the States have "extraordinarily wide latitude . . . in creating various types of political subdivisions and conferring authority upon them." *Holt Civic Club v. Tuscaloosa*, 439 U.S. 60, 71 . . . (1978). The Constitution does not dictate to the States a particular division of authority between legislature and judiciary or between state and local governing bodies. It does not define institutions of local government.

* * *

Application of these settled principles demonstrates the serious error of today's decision—an error that cuts deeply into the heretofore unquestioned right of a State to structure the decision-making authority of its government. In this case, by Initiative 350, the State has adopted a policy of racial neutrality in student assignments. The policy in no way interferes with the power of State or Federal Courts to remedy constitutional violations. And if such a policy had been adopted by any of the school districts in this litigation there could have been no question that the policy was constitutional.

The issue here arises only because the Seattle School District—in the absence of a then established State policy—chose to adopt race specific school assignments with extensive busing. It is not questioned that the District itself, at any time thereafter, could have changed its mind and cancelled its integration program without violating the Federal Constitution. Yet this Court holds that neither the legislature nor the people of the State of Washington could alter what the District had decided.

The Court argues that the people of Washington by Initiative 350 created a racial classification, and yet must agree that identical action by the Seattle School District itself would have created no such classification. This is not an easy argument to answer because it seems to make no sense. School boards are the creation of supreme State authority, whether in a State Constitution or by legislative enactment. Until today's decision no one would have questioned the authority of a State to abolish school boards altogether, or to require that they conform to any lawful State policy. And in the State of Washington, a neighborhood school policy would have been lawful.

Under today's decision this heretofore undoubted supreme authority of a State's electorate is to be curtailed whenever a school board—or indeed any other state board or local instrumentality—adopts a race specific program that arguably benefits racial minorities. Once such a program is adopted, *only* the local or subordinate entity that approved it will have authority to change it. The Court offers no authority or relevant explanation for this extraordinary subordination of the ultimate sovereign power of a State to act with respect to racial matters by subordinate bodies. It is a strange notion—alien to our system—that local governmental bodies can forever preempt the ability of a State—the sovereign power—to address a matter of compelling concern to the State. The Constitution of the United States does not require such a bizarre result.

* * *

NOTES AND QUESTIONS

1. Education as a State Function

The states have plenary power with regard to education, although most states have delegated considerable educational policy-making authority to local school districts. In doing so, however, states have "not surrendered their prerogatives, but have merely determined the machinery by which the state function shall be performed." E. Bolmeier, *The School in the Legal Structure* 63 (1968). Thus in most states the local school district is merely a subordinate arm of the state agency. The state legislature at any time can consolidate, merge, or eliminate school districts at will, without the consent of the districts. The powers of local boards may be changed at any time. Why then does the majority in *Seattle* hold that the state, through its voters, cannot decide that a neighborhood school assignment policy is the most appropriate educational policy and require local districts to carry out that policy?

2. Crawford *and Restrictions on Court-Ordered Busing*

Crawford v. Board of Education of Los Angeles, 458 U.S. 527, 102 S.Ct. 3211, 73 L.Ed.2d 948 (1982), was decided the same day as *Seattle. Crawford* involved a state constitutional amendment approved by California voters in a referendum that prevented state courts from using mandatory pupil reassignment and busing except where there was a violation of the Equal Protection Clause of the Fourteenth Amendment to the U.S. Constitution and where federal courts would be permitted to impose such a remedy. In other words, the amendment prevents the state courts from using busing to remedy state-created rights, a remedial technique previously upheld by the California courts where there was a finding of racial imbalance, regardless of its cause. *Jackson v. Pasadena City School District*, 59 Cal.2d 876, 31 Cal.Rptr. 606, 382 P.2d 878 (1963) (en banc). The Court upheld the California amendment. How can the Seattle and Los Angeles cases be distinguished? Why is the action of the California voters treated differently from that of the Washington voters?

D. Racial Segregation and School District Boundaries: *Milliken v. Bradley*

Milliken v. Bradley

418 U.S. 717, 94 S.Ct. 3112, 41 L.Ed.2d 1069 (1974).

Mr. Chief Justice Burger delivered the opinion of the Court.

We granted certiorari in these consolidated cases to determine whether a federal court may impose a multidistrict, areawide remedy to a single-district *de jure* segregation problem absent any finding that the other included school districts have failed to operate unitary school systems within their districts, absent any claim or finding that the boundary lines of any affected school district were established with the purpose of fostering racial segregation in public schools, absent any finding that the included districts committed acts which effected segregation within the other districts, and absent a meaningful opportunity for the included neighboring school districts to present evidence or be heard on the propriety of a multidistrict remedy or on the question of constitutional violations by those neighboring districts.

I

The action was commenced in August 1970 by the respondents . . . on behalf of . . . "all school children in the City of Detroit, Michigan, and all Detroit resident parents who have children of school age." The named defendants in the District Court included the Governor of Michigan, the Attorney General, the State Board of Education, the State Superintendent of Public Instruction, the Board of Education of the city of Detroit, its members, and the city's former superintendent of schools. . . .

The trial of the issue of segregation in the Detroit school system began on April 6, 1971, and continued through July 22, 1971, consuming some 41 trial days. On September 27, 1971, the District Court issued its findings and conclusions on the issue of segregation, finding that "Governmental actions and inaction at all levels, federal, state and local, have combined, with those of private organizations, such as loaning institutions and real estate associations and brokerage firms, to establish and to maintain the pattern of residential segregation throughout the Detroit metropolitan area." 338 F.Supp. 582, 587 (E.D. Mich.1971). While still addressing a Detroit-only violation, the District Court reasoned:

> While it would be unfair to charge the present defendants with what other governmental officers or agencies have done, it can be said that the actions or the failure to act by the responsible school authorities, both city and state, were linked to that of these other governmental units. When we speak of governmental action we should not view the different agencies as a collection of unrelated units. Perhaps the most that can be said is that all of them, including the school authorities, are, in part, responsible for the segregated condition which exists. And we note that just as there is an interaction between residential patterns and the racial composition of the schools, so there is a cor-

responding effect on the residential pattern by the racial composition of the schools.

Ibid.

[The Court then discussed the findings of the District Court with regard to intentional segregative actions taken by the Detroit Board of Education. The District Court's ultimate finding that the Detroit school district was de jure segregated by actions of Detroit officials was not questioned by the Supreme Court, 418 U.S. at 738 n. 18, and the Court assumed, *arguendo,* that the state was also responsible for the segregated schools within Detroit. 418 U.S. at 748. *See also Milliken v. Bradley (Milliken II),* 433 U.S. 267–70 n.1 (1977).]

. . . Accordingly, the District Court proceeded to order the Detroit Board of Education to submit desegregation plans limited to the segregation problems found to be existing within the city of Detroit. At the same time, however, the state defendants were directed to submit desegregation plans encompassing the three-county metropolitan area[10] despite the fact that the 85 outlying school districts of these three counties were not parties to the action and despite the fact that there had been no claim that these outlying districts had committed constitutional violations. . . .

. . . [The] District Court issued its findings and conclusions on the three Detroit-only plans submitted by the city Board and the respondents. It found that the best of the three plans "would make the Detroit school system more identifiably Black . . . thereby increasing the flight of Whites from the city and the system." . . . From this the court concluded that the plan "would not accomplish desegregation . . . within the corporate geographical limits of the city." . . . Accordingly, the District Court held that it "must look beyond the limits of the Detroit school district for a solution to the problem," and that "[s]chool district lines are simply matters of political convenience and may not be used to deny constitutional rights." . . .

. . . Thereafter, on June 14, 1972, the District Court issued its ruling on the "desegregation area" and related findings and conclusions. The court acknowledged at the outset that it had "taken no proofs with respect to the establishment of the boundaries of the 86 public school districts in the counties [in the Detroit area], nor on the issue of whether, with the exclusion of the city of Detroit school district, such school districts have committed acts of de jure segregation." Nevertheless, the court designated 53 of the 85 suburban school districts plus Detroit as the "desegregation area" and appointed a panel to prepare and submit "an effective desegregation plan" for the Detroit schools that would encompass the entire desegregation area. The plan was to be based on 15 clusters, each containing part of the Detroit system and two or more suburban districts, and was to "achieve the greatest degree of actual desegregation to the end that, upon implementation, no school, grade or classroom [would be] substantially disproportionate to the overall pupil racial composition."

. . . The Court of Appeals held, first, that the record supported the District Court's findings and conclusions on the constitutional violations committed by the Detroit Board, . . . and by the state defendants. . . . It stated that the acts of racial discrimination shown in the record are "causally related to the substantial amount of segregation found in the Detroit school system," . . . and that "the District Court was therefore authorized and required to take effective measures to desegregate the Detroit Public School System." . . .

The Court of Appeals also agreed with the District Court that "any less comprehensive a solution than a metropolitan area plan would result in an all black school system immediately surrounded by practically all white suburban school systems, with an overwhelmingly white majority population in the total metropolitan area."

. . . The court went on to state that it could "not see how such segregation can be any less harmful to the minority students than if the same result were accomplished within one school district." . . .

Accordingly, the Court of Appeals concluded that "the only feasible desegregation plan involves the crossing of the boundary lines between the Detroit

10. These counties cover 1,952 square miles, Michigan Statistical Abstract (9th ed. 1972), and the area is approximately the size of the State of Delaware (2,057 square miles). . . . The populations of Wayne, Oakland, and Macomb Counties were 2,666,751; 907,871; and 625,309, respectively, in 1970. Detroit, the State's largest city, is located in Wayne County.

In the 1970–1971 school year, there were 2,157,449 children enrolled in school districts in Michigan. There are 86 independent, legally distinct school districts within the tri-county area, having a total enrollment of approximately 1,000,000 children. In 1970, the Detroit Board of Education operated 319 schools with approximately 276,000 students.

School District and adjacent or nearby school districts for the limited purpose of providing an effective desegregation plan." . . . It reasoned that such a plan would be appropriate because of the State's violations, and could be implemented because of the State's authority to control local school districts. . . . An interdistrict remedy was thus held to be "within the equity powers of the District Court." . . .

II

* * *

Viewing the record as a whole, it seems clear that the District Court and the Court of Appeals shifted the primary focus from a Detroit remedy to the metropolitan area only because of their conclusion that total desegregation of Detroit would not produce the racial balance which they perceived as desirable. Both courts proceeded on an assumption that the Detroit schools could not be truly desegregated—in their view of what constituted desegregation—unless the racial composition of the student body of each school substantially reflected the racial composition of the population of the metropolitan area as a whole. . . .

Here the District Court's approach to what constituted "actual desegregation" raises the fundamental question, not presented in *Swann*, as to the circumstances in which a federal court may order desegregation relief that embraces more than a single school district. The court's analytical starting point was its conclusion that school district lines are no more than arbitrary lines on a map drawn "for political convenience." Boundary lines may be bridged where there has been a constitutional violation calling for interdistrict relief, but the notion that school district lines may be casually ignored or treated as a mere administrative convenience is contrary to the history of public education in our country. No single tradition in public education is more deeply rooted than local control over the operation of schools; local autonomy has long been thought essential both to the maintenance of community concern and support for public schools and to quality of the educational process. See *Wright v. Council of the City of Emporia*, 407 U.S., at 469. Thus, in *San Antonio School District v. Rodriguez*, 411 U.S. 1, 50 (1973), we observed that local control over the educational process affords citizens an opportunity to participate in decisionmaking, permits the structuring of school programs to fit local needs, and encourages "experimentation, innovation, and a healthy competition for educational excellence."

The Michigan educational structure involved in this case, in common with most States, provides for a large measure of local control, and a review of the scope and character of these local powers indicates the extent to which the interdistrict remedy approved by the two courts could disrupt and alter the structure of public education in Michigan. The metropolitan remedy would require, in effect, consolidation of 54 independent school districts historically administered as separate units into a vast new super school district. . . . Entirely apart from the logistical and other serious problems attending large-scale transportation of students, the consolidation would give rise to an array of other problems in financing and operating this new school system. Some of the more obvious questions would be: What would be the status and authority of the present popularly elected school boards? Would the children of Detroit be within the jurisdiction and operating control of a school board elected by the parents and residents of other districts? What board or boards would levy taxes for school operations in these 54 districts constituting the consolidated metropolitan area? What provisions could be made for assuring substantial equality in tax levies among the 54 districts, if this were deemed requisite? What provisions would be made for financing? Would the validity of long-term bonds be jeopardized unless approved by all of the component districts as well as the State? What body would determine that portion of the curricula now left to the discretion of local school boards? Who would establish attendance zones, purchase school equipment, locate and construct new schools, and indeed attend to all the myriad day-to-day decisions that are necessary to school operations affecting potentially more than three-quarters of a million pupils? . . .

It may be suggested that all of these vital operational problems are yet to be resolved by the District Court, and that this is the purpose of the Court of Appeals' proposed remand. But it is obvious from the scope of the interdistrict remedy itself that absent a complete restructuring of the laws of Michigan relating to school districts the District Court will become first, a *de facto* "legislative authority" to resolve these complex questions, and then the "school superintendent" for the entire area. This is a task which few, if any, judges are qualified to perform and one which would deprive the people of control of schools through their elected representatives.

Of course, no state law is above the Constitution. School district lines and the present laws with respect to local control, are not sacrosanct and if they conflict with the Fourteenth Amendment federal courts have a duty to prescribe appropriate remedies. . . . But our prior holdings have been confined to violations and remedies within a single school district. We therefore turn to address, for the first time, the validity of a remedy mandating cross-district or interdistrict consolidation to remedy a condition of segregation found to exist in only one district.

The controlling principle consistently expounded in our holdings is that the scope of the remedy is determined by the nature and extent of the constitutional violation. *Swann*, 402 U.S., at 16. Before the boundaries of separate and autonomous school districts may be set aside by consolidating the separate units for remedial purposes or by imposing a cross-district remedy, it must first be shown that there has been a constitutional violation within one district that produces a significant segregative effect in another district. Specifically, it must be shown that racially discriminatory acts of the state or local school districts, or of a single school district have been a substantial cause of interdistrict segregation. Thus an interdistrict remedy might be in order where the racially discriminatory acts of one or more school districts caused racial segregation in an adjacent district, or where district lines have been deliberately drawn on the basis of race. . . .

The record before us, voluminous as it is, contains evidence of *de jure* segregated conditions only in the Detroit schools; indeed, that was the theory on which the litigation was initially based and on which the District Court took evidence. . . . With no showing of significant violation by the 53 outlying school districts and no evidence of any interdistrict violation or effect, the court went beyond the original theory of the case as framed by the pleadings and mandated a metropolitan area remedy. To approve the remedy ordered by the court would impose on the outlying districts, not shown to have committed any constitutional violation, a wholly impermissible remedy based on a standard not hinted at in *Brown I* and *II* or any holding of this Court.

In dissent, Mr. Justice White and Mr. Justice Marshall undertake to demonstrate that agencies having statewide authority participated in maintaining the dual school system found to exist in Detroit. They are apparently of the view that once such participation is shown, the District Court should have a relatively free hand to reconstruct school districts outside of Detroit in fashioning relief. Our assumption, *arguendo*, . . . that state agencies did participate in the maintenance of the Detroit system, should make it clear that it is not on this point that we part company. The difference between us arises instead from established doctrine laid down by our cases. . . .

. . . [T]he remedy [in desegregation cases] is necessarily designed, as all remedies are, to restore the victims of discriminatory conduct to the position they would have occupied in the absence of such conduct. Disparate treatment of white and Negro students occurred within the Detroit school system, and not elsewhere, and on this record the remedy must be limited to that system. . . .

The constitutional right of the Negro respondents residing in Detroit is to attend a unitary school system in that district. Unless petitioners drew the district lines in a discriminatory fashion, or arranged for white students residing in the Detroit District to attend schools in Oakland and Macomb Counties, they were under no constitutional duty to make provisions for Negro students to do so. The view of the dissenters, that the existence of a dual system in *Detroit* can be made the basis for a decree requiring cross-district transportation of pupils, cannot be supported on the grounds that it represents merely the devising of a suitably flexible remedy for the violation of rights already established by our prior decisions. It can be supported only by drastic expansion of the constitutional right itself, an expansion without any support in either constitutional principle or precedent.

III

We recognize that the six-volume record presently under consideration contains language and some specific incidental findings thought by the District Court to afford a basis for interdistrict relief. However, these comparatively isolated findings and brief comments concern only one possible interdistrict violation and are found in the context of a proceeding that, as the District Court conceded, included no proof of segregation practiced by any of the 85 suburban school districts surrounding Detroit. The Court of Appeals, for example, relied on five factors which, it held, amounted to unconstitutional state action with respect to the violations found in the Detroit system:

(1) It held the State derivatively responsible for the Detroit Board's violations on the theory that actions of Detroit as a political subdivision of the State were attributable to the State. Accepting, *arguendo,* the correctness of this finding of state responsibility for the segregated conditions within the city of Detroit, it does not follow that an interdistrict remedy is constitutionally justified or required. With a single exception, discussed later, there has been no showing that either the State or any of the 85 outlying districts engaged in activity that had a cross-district effect. The boundaries of the Detroit School District, which are coterminous with the boundaries of the city of Detroit, were established over a century ago by neutral legislation when the city was incorporated; there is no evidence in the record, nor is there any suggestion by the respondents, that either the original boundaries of the Detroit School District, or any other school district in Michigan, were established for the purpose of creating, maintaining, or perpetuating segregation of races. There is no claim and there is no evidence hinting that petitioner outlying school districts and their predecessors, or the 30-odd other school districts in the tricounty area—but outside the District Court's "desegregation area"—have ever maintained or operated anything but unitary school systems. . . . Where the schools of only one district have been affected, there is no constitutional power in the courts to decree relief balancing the racial composition of that district's schools with those of the surrounding districts.

(2) There was evidence introduced at trial that, during the late 1950's, Carver School District, a predominantly Negro suburban district, contracted to have Negro high school students sent to a predominantly Negro school in Detroit. At the time, Carver was an independent school district that had no high school because, according to the trial evidence, "Carver District . . . did not have a place for adequate high school facilities." 484 F.2d, at 231. Accordingly, arrangements were made with Northern High School in the abutting Detroit School District so that the Carver high school students could obtain a secondary school education. . . .

According to the Court of Appeals, the arrangement during the late 1950's which allowed Carver students to be educated within the Detroit District was dependent upon the "tacit or express" approval of the State Board of Education and was the result of the refusal of the white suburban districts to accept the Carver students. Although there is nothing in the record supporting the Court of Appeals' supposition that suburban white schools refused to accept the Carver students, it appears that this situation, whether with or without the State's consent, may have had a segregative effect on the school populations of the two districts involved. However, since "the nature of the violation determines the scope of the remedy," *Swann,* 402 U.S., at 16, this isolated instance affecting two of the school districts would not justify the broad metropolitanwide remedy contemplated by the District Court and approved by the Court of Appeals, particularly since it embraced potentially 52 districts having no responsibility for the arrangement and involved 503,000 pupils in addition to Detroit's 276,000 students.

(3) The Court of Appeals cited the enactment of state legislation (Act 48) which had the effect of rescinding Detroit's voluntary desegregation plan (the April 7 Plan). That plan, however, affected only 12 of 21 Detroit high schools and had no causal connection with the distribution of pupils by race between Detroit and the other school districts within the tri-county area.

(4) The court relied on the State's authority to supervise schoolsite selection and to approve building construction as a basis for holding the State responsible for the segregative results of the school construction program in Detroit. Specifically, the Court of Appeals asserted that during the period between 1949 and 1962 the State Board of Education exercised general authority as overseer of site acquisitions by local boards for new school construction, and suggested that this state-approved school construction "fostered segregation throughout the Detroit Metropolitan area." 484 F.2d, at 241. This brief comment, however, is not supported by the evidence taken at trial since that evidence was specifically limited to proof that schoolsite acquisition and school construction within the city of Detroit produced *de jure* segregation *within* the city itself. . . .

(5) The Court of Appeals also relied upon the District Court's finding:

> This and other financial limitations, such as those on bonding and the working of the state aid formula whereby suburban districts were able to make far larger per pupil expenditures despite less tax effort, have created and perpetuated systematic educational inequalities.

Id., at 239.

However, neither the Court of Appeals nor the District Court offered any indication in the record or in their opinions as to how, if at all, the availability of state-financed aid for some Michigan students outside Detroit, but not for those within Detroit, might have affected the racial character of any of the State's school districts. . . .

Reversed and remanded.

Mr. Justice Stewart, concurring.

* * *

The [lower] courts were in error for the simple reason that the remedy they thought necessary was not commensurate with the constitutional violation found. Within a single school district whose officials have been shown to have engaged in unconstitutional racial segregation, a remedial decree that affects every individual school may be dictated by "common sense," see *Keyes v. School District No. 1, Denver, Colorado*, 413 U.S. 189, 203, and indeed may provide the only effective means to eliminate segregation "root and branch," *Green v. County School Board of New Kent County*, 391 U.S. 430, 438, and to "effectuate a transition to a racially nondiscriminatory school system." *Brown v. Board of Education*, 349 U.S. 294, 301. See *Keyes, supra*, at 198–205. But in this case the Court of Appeals approved the concept of a remedial decree that would go beyond the boundaries of the district where the constitutional violation was found, and include schools and schoolchildren in many other school districts that have presumptively been administered in complete accord with the Constitution.

* * *

This is not to say, however, that an interdistrict remedy of the sort approved by the Court of Appeals would not be proper, or even necessary, in other factual situations. Were it to be shown, for example, that state officials had contributed to the separation of the races by drawing or redrawing school district lines, see *Haney v. County Board of Education of Sevier County*, 429 F.2d 364; cf. *Wright v. Council of the City of Emporia*, 407 U.S. 451; *United States v. Scotland Neck Board of Education*, 407 U.S. 484; by transfer of school units between districts, *United States v. Texas*, 321 F.Supp. 1043, aff'd, 447 F.2d 441; *Turner v. Warren County Board of Education*, 313 F.Supp. 380; or by purposeful, racially discriminatory use of state housing or zoning laws, then a decree calling for transfer of pupils across district lines or for restructuring of district lines might well be appropriate.

In this case, however, no such interdistrict violation was shown. Indeed, no evidence at all concerning the administration of schools outside the city of Detroit was presented other than the fact that these schools contained a higher proportion of white pupils than did the schools within the city. Since the mere fact of different racial compositions in contiguous districts does not itself imply or constitute a violation of the Equal Protection Clause in the absence of a showing that such disparity was imposed, fostered, or encouraged by the State or its political subdivisions, it follows that no interdistrict violation was shown in this case.[2] The formulation of an interdistrict remedy was thus simply not responsive to the factual record before the District Court and was an abuse of that court's equitable powers.

* * *

[The dissenting opinion of Mr. Justice Douglas is omitted.]

Mr. Justice White, with whom Mr. Justice Douglas, Mr. Justice Brennan, and Mr. Justice Marshall join, dissenting.

2. My Brother Marshall seems to ignore this fundamental fact when he states, . . . that "the most essential finding [made by the District Court] was that Negro children in Detroit had been confined by intentional acts of segregation to a growing core of Negro schools surrounded by a receding ring of white schools." This conclusion is simply not substantiated by the record presented in this case. The record here does support the claim made by the respondents that white and Negro students within Detroit who otherwise would have attended school together were separated by acts of the State or its subdivision. However, segregative acts within the city alone cannot be presumed to have produced—and no factual showing was made that they did produce—an increase in the number of Negro students *in the city as a whole*. It is this essential fact of a predominantly Negro school population in Detroit—caused by unknown and perhaps unknowable factors such as in-migration, birth rates, economic changes, or cumulative acts of private racial fears—that accounts for the "growing core of Negro schools," a "core" that has grown to include virtually the entire city. The Constitution simply does not allow federal courts to attempt to change that situation unless and until it is shown that the State, or its political subdivisions, have contributed to cause the situation to exist. No record has been made in this case showing that the racial composition of the Detroit school population or that residential patterns within Detroit and in the surrounding areas were in any significant measure caused by governmental activity, and it follows that the situation over which my dissenting Brothers express concern cannot serve as the predicate for the remedy adopted by the District Court and approved by the Court of Appeals.

* * *

Regretfully, and for several reasons, I can join neither the Court's judgment nor its opinion. The core of my disagreement is that deliberate acts of segregation and their consequences will go unremedied, not because a remedy would be infeasible or unreasonable in terms of the usual criteria governing school desegregation cases, but because an effective remedy would cause what the Court considers to be undue administrative inconvenience to the State. The result is that the State of Michigan, the entity at which the Fourteenth Amendment is directed, has successfully insulated itself from its duty to provide effective desegregation remedies by vesting sufficient power over its public schools in its local school districts. If this is the case in Michigan, it will be the case in most States.

. . . [The] proposed intracity remedies were beset with practical problems. None of the plans limited to the school district was satisfactory to the District Court. The most promising proposal, submitted by respondents, who were the plaintiffs in the District Court, would "leave many of its schools 75 to 90 percent Black." 484 F.2d 215, 244 (CA6 1973). Transportation on a "vast scale" would be required; 900 buses would have to be purchased for the transportation of pupils who are not now bused. *Id.*, at 243. The District Court also found that the plan "would change a school system which is now Black and White to one that would be perceived as Black, thereby increasing the flight of Whites from the city and the system, thereby increasing the Black student population." *Id.*, at 244. For the District Court, "[t]he conclusion, under the evidence in this case, is inescapable that relief of segregation in the public schools of the City of Detroit cannot be accomplished within the corporate geographical limits of the city." *Ibid.*

The District Court therefore considered extending its remedy to the suburbs. After hearings, it concluded that a much more effective desegregation plan could be implemented if the suburban districts were included. In proceeding to design its plan on the basis that student bus rides to and from school should not exceed 40 minutes each way as a general matter, the court's express finding was that "[f]or all the reasons stated heretofore—including time, distance, and transportation factors—desegregation within the area described is physically easier and more practicable and feasible, than desegregation efforts limited to the corporate geographic limits of the city of Detroit." 345 F.Supp. 914, 930 (E.D. Mich. 1972).

The Court of Appeals agreed with the District Court that the remedy must extend beyond the city limits of Detroit. . . .

This Court now reverses the Court of Appeals. It does not question the District Court's findings that *any* feasible Detroit-only plan would leave many schools 75 to 90 percent black and that the district would become progressively more black as whites left the city. Neither does the Court suggest that including the suburbs in a desegregation plan would be impractical or infeasible because of educational considerations, because of the number of children requiring transportation, or because of the length of their rides. Indeed, the Court leaves unchallenged the District Court's conclusion that a plan including the suburbs would be physically easier and more practical and feasible than a Detroit-only plan. Whereas the most promising Detroit-only plan, for example, would have entailed the purchase of 900 buses, the metropolitan plan would involve the acquisition of no more than 350 new vehicles.

Despite the fact that a metropolitan remedy, if the findings of the District Court accepted by the Court of Appeals are to be credited, would more effectively desegregate the Detroit schools, would prevent resegregation, and would be easier and more feasible from many standpoints, the Court fashions out of whole cloth an arbitrary rule that remedies for constitutional violations occurring in a single Michigan school district must stop at the school district line. Apparently, no matter how much less burdensome or more effective and efficient in many respects, such as transportation, the metropolitan plan might be, the school district line may not be crossed. Otherwise, it seems, there would be too much disruption of the Michigan scheme for managing its educational system, too much confusion, and too much administrative burden.

* * *

. . . Obviously, whatever difficulties there might be, they are surmountable; for the Court itself concedes that, had there been sufficient evidence of an interdistrict violation, the District Court could have fashioned a single remedy for the districts implicated rather than a different remedy for each district in which the violation had occurred or had an impact.

I am even more mystified as to how the Court can ignore the legal reality that the constitutional violations, even if occurring locally, were committed by governmental entities for which the State is responsible and that it is the State that must respond to the command of the Fourteenth Amendment. An interdistrict remedy for the infringements that occurred in this case is well within the confines and powers of the State, which is the governmental entity ultimately responsible for desegregating its schools. The Michigan Supreme Court has observed that "[t]he school district is a State agency," *Attorney General ex rel. Kies v. Lowrey*, 131 Mich. 639, 644, 92 N. W. 289, 290 (1902), and that " '[e]ducation in Michigan belongs to the State. It is no part of the local self-government inherent in the township or municipality, except so far as the legislature may choose to make it such. The Constitution has turned the whole subject over to the legislature. . . .' " *Attorney General ex rel. Zacharias v. Detroit Board of Education*, 154 Mich. 584, 590, 118 N. W. 606, 609 (1908).

* * *

Until today, the permissible contours of the equitable authority of the district courts to remedy the unlawful establishment of a dual school system have been extensive, adaptable, and fully responsive to the ultimate goal of achieving "the greatest possible degree of actual desegregation." There are indeed limitations on the equity powers of the federal judiciary, but until now the Court has not accepted the proposition that effective enforcement of the Fourteenth Amendment could be limited by political or administrative boundary lines demarcated by the very State responsible for the constitutional violation and for the disestablishment of the dual system. Until now the Court has instead looked to practical considerations in effectuating a desegregation decree such as excessive distance, transportation time, and hazards to the safety of the schoolchildren involved in a proposed plan. . . .

Finally, I remain wholly unpersuaded by the Court's assertion that "the remedy is necessarily designed, as all remedies are, to restore the victims of discriminatory conduct to the position they would have occupied in the absence of such conduct." . . . In the first place, under this premise the Court's judgment is itself infirm; for had the Detroit school system not followed an official policy of segregation throughout the 1950's and 1960's, Negroes and whites would have been going to school together. There would have been no, or at least not as many, recognizable Negro schools and no, or at least not many, white schools, but "just schools," and neither Negroes nor whites would have suffered from the effects of segregated education, with all its shortcomings. . . . Confining the remedy to the boundaries of the Detroit district is quite unrelated either to the goal of achieving maximum desegregation or to those intensely practical considerations, such as the extent and expense of transportation, that have imposed limits on remedies in cases such as this. The Court's remedy, in the end, is essentially arbitrary and will leave serious violations of the Constitution substantially unremedied.

* * *

Mr. Justice Marshall, with whom Mr. Justice Douglas, Mr. Justice Brennan, and Mr. Justice White join, dissenting.

In *Brown v. Board of Education*, 347 U.S. 483 (1954), this Court held that segregation of children in public schools on the basis of race deprives minority group children of equal educational opportunities and therefore denies them the equal protection of the laws under the Fourteenth Amendment. . . .

After 20 years of small, often difficult steps toward that great end, the Court today takes a giant step backwards. Notwithstanding a record showing widespread and pervasive racial segregation in the educational system provided by the State of Michigan for children in Detroit, this Court holds that the District Court was powerless to require the State to remedy its constitutional violation in any meaningful fashion. Ironically purporting to base its result on the principle that the scope of the remedy in a desegregation case should be determined by the nature and the extent of the constitutional violation, the Court's answer is to provide no remedy at all for the violation proved in this case, thereby guaranteeing that Negro children in Detroit will receive the same separate and inherently unequal education in the future as they have been unconstitutionally afforded in the past.

* * *

II

. . . [T]he District Court's decision to expand its desegregation decree beyond the geographical limits of the city of Detroit rested in large part on its conclusions (A) that the State of Michigan was ultimately responsible for curing the condition of segregation within the Detroit city schools, and (B) that a Detroit-only remedy would not accomplish this task. In my view, both of these conclusions are well supported by the facts of this case and by this Court's precedents.

A

To begin with, the record amply supports the District Court's findings that the State of Michigan, through state officers and state agencies, had engaged in purposeful acts which created or aggravated segregation in the Detroit schools. The State Board of Education, for example, prior to 1962, exercised its authority to supervise local schoolsite selection in a manner which contributed to segregation. 484 F.2d 215, 238 (CA6 1973). Furthermore, the State's continuing authority, after 1962 to approve school building construction plans had intertwined the State with site-selection decisions of the Detroit Board of Education which had the purpose and effect of maintaining segregation.

The State had also stood in the way of past efforts to desegregate the Detroit city schools. In 1970, for example, the Detroit School Board had begun implementation of its own desegregation plan for its high schools, despite considerable public and official resistance. The State Legislature intervened by enacting Act 48 of the Public Acts of 1970, specifically prohibiting implementation of the desegregation plan and thereby continuing the growing segregation of the Detroit school system. Adequate desegregation of the Detroit system was also hampered by discriminatory restrictions placed by the State on the use of transportation within Detroit. . . .

Also significant was the State's involvement during the 1950's in the transportation of Negro high school students from the Carver School District past a closer white high school in the Oak Park District to a more distant Negro high school in the Detroit system. . . .

Aside from the acts of purposeful segregation committed by the State Legislature and the State Board of Education, the District Court also concluded that the State was responsible for the many intentional acts of segregation committed by the Detroit Board of Education, an agency of the State. The majority is only willing to accept this finding *arguendo*. . . I have no doubt, however, as to its validity under the Fourteenth Amendment.

* * *

Under Michigan law a "school district is an agency of the State government." *School District of the City of Lansing v. State Board of Education*, 367 Mich. 591, 600, 116 N.W.2d 866, 870 (1962). It is "a legal division of territory, created by the State for educational purposes, to which the State has granted such powers as are deemed necessary to permit the district to function as a State agency." *Detroit Board of Education v. Superintendent of Public Instruction*, 319 Mich. 436, 450, 29 N.W.2d 902, 908 (1947). Racial discrimination by the school district, an agency of the State, is therefore racial discrimination by the State itself, forbidden by the Fourteenth Amendment. . . .

* * *

Vesting responsibility with the State of Michigan for Detroit's segregated schools is particularly appropriate as Michigan, unlike some other States, operates a single statewide system of education rather than several separate and independent local school systems. The majority's emphasis on local governmental control and local autonomy of school districts in Michigan will come as a surprise to those with any familiarity with that State's system of education. School districts are not separate and distinct sovereign entities under Michigan law, but rather are " 'auxiliaries of the State,' " subject to its "absolute power." *Attorney General of Michigan ex rel. Kies v. Lowrey*, 199 U.S. 233, 240 (1905). The courts of the State have repeatedly emphasized that education in Michigan is not a local governmental concern, but a state function.

* * *

The State's control over education is reflected in the fact that, contrary to the Court's implication, there is little or no relationship between school districts and local political units. To take the 85 outlying local school districts in the Detroit metropolitan area as examples, 17 districts lie in two counties, two in three counties. One district serves five municipalities; other suburban municipalities are fragmented into as many as six school districts. Nor is there any apparent state policy with regard to the size of school districts, as they now range from 2,000 to 285,000 students.

Centralized state control manifests itself in practice as well as in theory. The State controls the financing of education in several ways. The legislature contributes a substantial portion of most school districts' operating budgets with funds appropriated from the State's General Fund revenues raised through statewide taxation. The State's power over the purse can be and is in fact used to enforce the State's powers over local districts. In addition, although local districts obtain funds through local property taxation, the State has assumed the responsibility to ensure equalized property valuations throughout the State. The State also establishes standards for teacher certification and teacher tenure; determines part of the required curriculum; sets the minimum school term; approves bus routes, equipment, and drivers; approves textbooks; and establishes procedures for student discipline. The State Superintendent of Public Instruction and the State Board of Education have the power to remove local school board members from office for neglect of their duties.

Most significantly for present purposes, the State has wide-ranging powers to consolidate and merge school districts, even without the consent of the districts themselves or of the local citizenry. See, *e.g.*, *Attorney General ex rel. Kies v. Lowrey*, 131 Mich. 639, 92 N.W. 289 (1902), aff'd, 199 U.S. 233 (1905). Indeed, recent years have witnessed an accelerated program of school district consolidations, mergers, and annexations, many of which were state imposed. . . .

Whatever may be the history of public education in other parts of our Nation, it simply flies in the face of reality to say, as does the majority, that in Michigan, "[n]o single tradition in public education is more deeply rooted than local control over the operation of schools. . . ."

* * *

Under a Detroit-only decree, Detroit's schools will clearly remain racially identifiable in comparison with neighboring schools in the metropolitan community. Schools with 65% and more Negro students will stand in sharp and obvious contrast to schools in neighboring districts with less than 2% Negro enrollment. Negro students will continue to perceive their schools as segregated educational facilities and this perception will only be increased when whites react to a Detroit-only decree by fleeing to the suburbs to avoid integration. School district lines, however innocently drawn, will surely be perceived as fences to separate the races when, under a Detroit-only decree, white parents withdraw their children from the Detroit city schools and move to the suburbs in order to continue them in all-white schools. The message of this action will not escape the Negro children in the city of Detroit. See *Wright*, 407 U.S., at 466. It will be of scant significance to Negro children who have for years been confined by *de jure* acts of segregation to a growing core of all-Negro schools surrounded by a ring of all-white schools that the new dividing line between the races is the school district boundary.

Nor can it be said that the State is free from any responsibility for the disparity between the racial makeup of Detroit and its surrounding suburbs. The State's creation, through *de jure* acts of segregation, of a growing core of all-Negro schools inevitably acted as a magnet to attract Negroes to the areas served by such schools and to deter them from settling either in other areas of the city or in the suburbs. By the same token, the growing core of all-Negro schools inevitably helped drive whites to other areas of the city or to the suburbs. . . .

. . . The rippling effects on residential patterns caused by purposeful acts of segregation do not automatically subside at the school district border. With rare exceptions, these effects naturally spread through all the residential neighborhoods within a metropolitan area. . . .

The State must also bear part of the blame for the white flight to the suburbs which would be forthcoming from a Detroit-only decree and would render such a remedy ineffective. Having created a system where whites and Negroes were intentionally kept apart so that they could not become accustomed to learning together, the State is responsible for the fact that many whites will react to the dismantling of that segregated system by attempting to flee to the suburbs. Indeed, by limiting the District Court to a Detroit-only remedy and allowing that flight to the suburbs to succeed, the Court today allows the State to profit from its own wrong and to perpetuate for years to come the separation of the races it achieved in the past by purposeful state action.

The majority asserts, however, that involvement of outlying districts would do violence to the accepted principle that "the nature of the violation determines the scope of the remedy." *Swann*, *supra*, at 16. . . . Not only is the majority's attempt to find in this single phrase the answer to the complex and difficult questions presented in this case hopelessly simplistic, but more important, the Court reads these words in a manner which perverts their obvious meaning. The nature of a violation determines the scope of the remedy simply because the function of any remedy is to cure the violation to which it is addressed. In school segregation cases . . . a remedy which effectively cures the violation is what is required. . . . To read this principle as banning a district court from imposing the only effective remedy for past segregation . . . is, in my view, to turn a simple commonsense rule into a cruel and meaningless paradox. Ironically, by ruling out an inter-district remedy, the only relief which promises to cure segregation in the Detroit public schools, the majority flouts the very principle on which it purports to rely.

Nor should it be of any significance that the suburban school districts were not shown to have themselves taken any direct action to promote segregation of the races. Given the State's broad powers over local school districts, it was well within the State's powers to require those districts surrounding the Detroit school district to participate in a metropolitan remedy. The State's duty should be no different here than in cases where it is shown that certain of a State's voting districts are malapportioned in violation of the Fourteenth Amendment. See *Reynolds v. Sims*, 377 U.S. 533 (1964). Overrepresented electoral districts are required to participate in reapportionment although their only "participation" in the violation was to do nothing about it. Similarly, electoral districts which themselves meet representation standards must frequently be redrawn as part of a remedy for other over- and under-inclusive districts. No finding of fault on the part of each electoral district and no finding of a discriminatory effect on each district is a prerequisite to its involvement in the constitutionally required remedy. By the same logic, no finding of fault on the part of the suburban school districts in this case and no finding of a discriminatory effect on each district should be a prerequisite to their involvement in the constitutionally required remedy.

* * *

NOTES AND QUESTIONS

1. **Milliken I:** ***Of Wrongs and Remedies***

Milliken was the first case in which a majority of the Supreme Court overturned a lower court order that had sought to bring about greater integration. Indeed, it marked the first time in more than thirty-five years that the Court had rejected the position of the NAACP on desegregation in a written opinion. The decision was greeted with widespread criticism among scholars to the effect that the Court was turning back on its previous decisions. *See, e.g.*, Lawrence, "Segregation 'Misunderstood': The *Milliken* Decision Revisited," 12 *U.S.F.L. Rev.* 15 (1977); Taylor, "The Supreme Court and Urban Reality: A Tactical Analysis of *Milliken v. Bradley*," 21 *Wayne L. Rev.* 751 (1975). *But see* L. Graglia, *Disaster by Decree* (1976); Wolf, "Northern Desegregation and Residential Choice," 1977 *Sup. Ct. Rev.* 63.

Was the Supreme Court's decision inconsistent with its earlier cases? In *Keyes*, the Court said that *de jure* segregation in a substantial or meaningful portion of a school district triggered the presumption that the segregation in the remaining part of the school district was also *de jure*, thus requiring a system-wide racial balance remedy unless the defendants can rebut the presumption. Why then should not a finding of de jure segregation in the central city, attributable in part to the actions of the state, trigger a presumption of a reciprocal segregative effect in the suburbs? Is the connection between constitutional wrong and proposed remedy any more speculative in *Milliken* than in *Swann* or *Keyes*? Did the majority chastise the lower courts for doing precisely what it had presaged in its decisions in those cases? *See* Yudof, "School Desegregation: Legal Realism, Reasoned Elaboration, and Social Science Research in the Supreme Court," 42 *Law & Contemp. Prob.* 57, 93–97 (1978) (pt. 2).

2. The Role of "White Flight" in Determining the Extent of the Remedy

Was the approach taken by the district court in *Milliken* a response to white flight? Much of the testimony before the district judge stressed that a "city-only" remedy would result in the rapid departure of most of the remaining whites, leaving behind a nearly all-black school district. Does the majority's decision in *Milliken* ensure that there will be white flight by indicating that the suburbs will be a "safe haven" for those who otherwise would be caught up in a desegregation decree? Is it constitutionally appropriate for federal courts to seek to prevent such demographic shifts? *See Pasadena City Board of Education v. Spangler*, 427 U.S. 424, 96 S.Ct. 2697, 49 L.Ed.2d 599 (1976); *Spencer v. Kugler*, 404 U.S.

1027, 92 S.Ct. 707, 30 L.Ed.2d 723 (1972). *But see Delaware State Board of Education v. Evans,* 446 U.S. 923, 100 S.Ct. 1862, 64 L.Ed.2d 278 (1980).

To what extent may a court take white flight into account in devising a school desegregation remedy? The fear of white flight to the suburbs (or private schools) has been used by some courts to limit a system-wide remedy. Mr. Justice Powell, in his dissenting opinion in *Columbus II*, argued against a remedy requiring school boards to racially balance every school because "parents, unlike school officials, are not bound by these decrees and may frustrate them through the simple expedient of withdrawing their children from a public school system in which they have lost confidence." 433 U.S. at 484. *See also Estes v. Metropolitan Branches of Dallas NAACP*, 444 U.S. 437, 100 S.Ct. 716, 62 L.Ed.2d 626 (1980) (Powell, J., with whom Stewart and Rehnquist, J.J., join, dissenting). Justice Powell attributes this white flight not to "a racist response to integration *per se*" but to "a natural reaction to the displacement of professional and local control that occurs when courts go into the business of restructuring and operating school systems." *Columbus II*, 443 U.S. at 485. What are the reasons for the exodus of white students from the central city schools? Consider this summary of the evidence by Professor David Armor:

> First, the *fact* that white loss is associated with desegregation in some instances is not in dispute. Second, it is a conditional relationship: it occurs under some conditions but not others. Third, the effect is seen most clearly in the year that desegregation takes place. . . .
>
> First, the effect appears to depend upon a substantial proportion of Black (or minority) students, perhaps on the order of 20–25%. Second, the effect appears strongest for central-city districts surrounded by accessible white suburbs (e.g. Boston) and weakest for large metropolitan school districts surrounded by minimally developed rural areas (e.g., Charlotte, North Carolina). Finally, the effect appears strongest when there is a significant shift in the racial balance of schools, and primarily when white reassignment is involved in the shift.

Armor, "White Flight and the Future of School Desegregation," in W. Stephan and J. Feagin, eds., *School Desegregation* 187, 196–97 (1980).

Might some white families seek to escape from central cities for reasons other than those given by Powell, for example, lower taxes, better housing, less crime, or superior municipal services? *See* Farley, "Racial Integration in the Public Schools, 1967–1972: Assessing the Effects of Governmental Policies," 8 *Soc. Focus* 3 (1975). Consider also to what extent white flight is really a reflection of the more rapidly declining birth rates among whites.

If a judge believes that a system-wide desegregation remedy will result in white flight and the resegregation of the entire school district, what is the judge to do? Does it make sense to order a "fruit-basket turnover [of the school population] through busing to create [uniform racial balance] throughout the system" if it was clear that within a few months' time the school district population would be all-minority as a result of white flight? *See Calhoun v. Cook*, 332 F.Supp. 804, 806, 808 (N.D. Ga. 1971), *vacated in part and remanded*, 451 F.2d 583 (5th Cir.). On the other hand, what did the Court in *Brown II* mean when it said that "the vitality of these constitutional principles cannot be allowed to yield simply because of disagreement with them?" *See* Gewirtz, "Remedies and Resistance," 92 *Yale L.J.* 585, 632–43 (1983).

3. Milliken I: *A Case about Desegregation or Federalism?*

Chief Justice Burger, in discussing the reasons that a metropolitan remedy was impermissible in *Milliken*, noted that the consolidation of fifty-four independent school districts would not only create logistical and administrative problems, but would also alter the status of the presently *popularly elected* school boards and would necessitate turning the district court into a legislature to resolve such complex issues as the financing of the new units, the drawing of attendance zones, and the construction of new schools. The court would then have to function as a school superintendent in order to make the day-to-day operational decisions. If the "condition that offends the Constitution" is limited to the boundaries of the Detroit school district, then such major dislocations of the separate and autonomous suburban school districts were unwarranted. *But see Delaware State Board of Education v. Evans*, 446 U.S. 923, 100 S.Ct. 1862, 64 L.Ed.2d 278 (1980).

4. *Local Control of Schools*

Are there considerations that might militate against an interdistrict remedy even if intentional segregative acts occurred on an interdistrict basis? What weight should the concern for preserving "local control" be given in the desegregation context? *See* Shane,

"School Desegregation Remedies and the Fair Governance of Schools," 132 *U.Pa.L.Rev.* 1041, 1097–1104 (1984). In several cases prior to the statement in *Milliken* that "no single tradition in public education is more deeply rooted than local control over the operation of schools . . .," the Supreme Court has suggested that local autonomy in public education is a very substantial interest. *See San Antonio Independent School District v. Rodriguez*, 411 U.S. 1, 49–50, 93 S.Ct. 1278, 1304–05, 36 L.Ed.2d 16 (1973); *Wright v. Council of the City of Emporia*, 407 U.S. 451, 469, 92 S.Ct. 2196, 2206, 33 L.Ed.2d 51 (1972). The Sixth Circuit, however, had devoted nearly four pages of its opinion to a review of the evidence of state control over education in Michigan, noting that "under the Constitution and laws of Michigan . . . the public school system is a State function and that local school districts are instrumentalities of the State created for administrative convenience." 484 F.2d 215, 246 (6th Cir. 1973). *See* Gewirtz, "Remedies and Resistance," 92 *Yale L.J.* 585, 647–49 (1983).

5. When Are Interdistrict Remedies Permissible?

After *Milliken*, what must plaintiffs be able to demonstrate in order to obtain a metropolitan remedy? *See Little Rock School District v. Pulaski County Special School District No. 1*, 778 F.2d 404 (8th Cir. 1985), *cert denied*, 476 U.S. 1186, 106 S.Ct. 2926, 91 L.Ed.2d 554 (1986); *Newburg Area Council v. Board of Education*, 510 F.2d 1358 (6th Cir. 1974), *cert. denied*, 429 U.S. 1074, 97 S.Ct. 812, 50 L.Ed.2d 792 (1977); *United States v. Board of School Commissioners*, 456 F.Supp. 183 (S.D. Ind. 1978), *vacated and remanded*, 429 U.S. 1068, 97 S.Ct. 800, 50 L.Ed.2d 786 (1977); *Evans v. Buchanan*, 393 F.Supp. 428 (D. Del. 1975), *aff'd mem.*, 423 U.S. 963, 96 S.Ct. 381, 46 L.Ed.2d 293. *See also Delaware State Board of Education v. Evans*, 446 U.S. 923, 100 S.Ct. 1862, 64 L.Ed.2d 278 (1980).

In *Liddell v. Missouri*, 731 F.2d 1294 (8th cir. 1984), *cert denied*, 469 U.S. 816, 105 S.Ct. 82, 83 L.Ed.2d 30, the Court of Appeals approved a settlement agreement that called for an interdistrict remedy despite the fact that there was no finding of an interdistrict violation. The agreement included a provision that required the state to fund the voluntary transfer of students between the city and sixteen suburban school districts. The court indicated that because the state had been found to be a "primary constitutional wrongdoer," it could be required to take "those actions which will further the desegregation of the city schools even if the actions required will occur outside the boundaries of the city school district." *Liddell v. Board of Education*, 677 F.2d 626, 630 (8th Cir. 1982), *cert. denied*, 459 U.S. 877, 103 S.Ct. 172, 74 L.Ed.2d 142. Under the settlement agreement, the largest voluntary school transfer program in the country developed, with 12,000 children attending schools outside of their designated districts each day. The sixteen suburban districts agreed to accept the voluntary transfer of black city students (and white suburban students were to be attracted to city schools with special programs) out of fear that if the case went to trial, the suburban districts might be found to have contributed to the constitutional violation and be merged into a single metropolitan district. The court distinguished *Milliken I* on the ground that, considering the "breadth, gravity and duration of the state's violation," it was appropriate for the district court to mandate an equally comprehensive remedy. 731 F.2d at 1308. Moreover, the court noted that the remedy does not "threaten the autonomy of local school districts" because they are neither coerced nor reorganized and "retain the rights and powers accorded them by state and federal laws." *Id.*

See also Jenkins by Agye v. Missouri, 807 F.2d 657 (8th Cir. 1986). *See* Gewirtz, "Choice In Transition: School Desegregation and the Corrective Ideal," 86 *Colum L.Rev.* 728, 779–82 (1986).

6. Court-Ordered Remedies Other than Pupil Reassignment: Milliken II

"School Desegregation Remedies and the Role of Social Science Research"

B. Levin, 42 *Law & Contemp. Probs.* 1, 30–33 (1978). Reprinted with permission.

In *Milliken II*,[185] the Supreme Court was faced with the question of whether it was within the scope of a district court's remedial powers to require compensatory education programs, in-service training programs for teachers, and guidance and counseling programs as part of the desegregation plan. The in-

185. *Milliken v. Bradley*, 433 U.S. 267, 97 S.Ct. 2749, 53 L.Ed.2d 745 (1977).

clusion of these and similar educational components was challenged on the ground that such remedies exceeded the scope of the constitutional violation.[187] Since the constitutional violation was racially discriminatory pupil assignments, it was argued, the desegregation plan must be limited to reassignment of the pupils.

The district court had heard extensive testimony from both academic experts and school officials on each of the four major components. With regard to the first component, remedial reading, the court declared that "[t]here is no educational component more directly associated with the process of desegregation than reading." The remedial reading program was to redress the lower reading ability of black students compared to that of white students. Inservice training for teachers was also supported by substantial testimony, primarily from state and local school officials. The third component related to testing. There was evidence that prior testing had been racially and culturally biased, and thus the court ordered bias-free testing programs to be instituted. The fourth component on which there was extensive testimony with regard to its importance in the desegregation process was a counseling and guidance program.[194]

* * *

The Supreme Court's decision in *Milliken II* held that since the purpose of a remedy was to restore the victims of discriminatory conduct to the position they would have occupied in the absence of discrimination, a desegregation plan might have to include programs to undo the inequalities caused by a dual system. The Court concluded that the compensatory programs and other educational components mandated by the district court were "aptly tailored to remedy the consequences of the constitutional violation."

> Children who have been . . . educationally and culturally set apart from the larger community will inevitably acquire habits of speech, conduct, and attitudes reflecting their cultural isolation. They are likely to acquire speech habits, for example, which vary from the environment in which they must ultimately function and compete, if they are to enter and be a part of that community. This is not peculiar to race; in this setting, it can affect any children who, as a group, are isolated by force of law from the mainstream. . . .
>
> Pupil assignment alone does not automatically remedy the impact of previous, unlawful educational isolation; the consequences linger and can be dealt with only by independent measures. In short, speech habits acquired in a segregated system do not vanish simply by moving the child to a desegregated school. The root condition shown by this record must be treated directly by special training at the hands of teachers prepared for that task.

a. The Standard for Ancillary Relief. Under what circumstances may a court prescribe the educational programming to be provided by the school system? How can the courts decide which programs will cure the "condition that offends the Constitution" and will restore the victims of discrimination to the position they would have occupied in the absence of discrimination? *Milliken v. Bradley*, 433 U.S. 267, 282, 97 S.Ct. 2749, 2758, 53 L.Ed.2d 745 (1977). How is it possible to determine what that position is? What role might expert testimony play? *See Jenkins v. Missouri*, 639 F.Supp. 19, 24 (W.D. Mo. 1985); *Berry v. School District of Benton Harbor*, 515 F.Supp. 344, 369 (W.D. Mich. 1981).

b. The Role of District Courts. Does the standard articulated in *Milliken II* require district courts to substitute themselves for school officials and determine *which* compensatory reading program is most likely to restore the victim to the position he or she would have occupied except for the unconstitutional

---

187. It should be noted that it was not the Detroit city school board, in *Milliken II*, that challenged the remedial programs ordered by the district court. These programs were under attack from the state defendants. The trial court had ordered the state to pay half the cost of the programs, a sum estimated at $5.8 million. Brief of Petitioners at 13. The state argued that (1) the district court had no authority to order the ancillary relief, but was restricted to ordering pupil reassignment, *id.* at 21, and (2) even if the special relief was needed, the state could not be compelled to pay for it under the eleventh amendment. Brief of Petitioners at 34. The Court denied both claims. 433 U.S. at 288, 290, 97 S.Ct. at 2761, 2762.

194. . . . Charles Wells, Assistant Superintendent of the Detroit Public Schools, testified that the counseling and guidance component was needed: "Because we feel that this counseling support is necessary to relate educationally to the adjustments required in desegregation." Brief of Respondent, *supra*, Appendix at 51. Mr. Wells also testified that a revised counseling and guidance component was needed to eradicate previous counseling practices that stereotyped black children. Brief of Respondent at 26 & Appendix at 52.

Professor Ashworth described the need for a guidance and counseling program to eliminate the effects of past segregation:

> [W]hat we are saying is that in order to correct the inequalities for the students and right the wrongs of students that the person has to be retrained and that program has to be revamped . . . students have been counseled in or out of certain programs based on their race. If this had not been so the Aero Mechanics would not be 84 percent white in a school system that is more than 70 percent black.

Brief of Respondent, *supra*, at 26 & Appendix at 34.

conduct? *See* Justice Powell's comment that the district court had "virtually assumed the role of school superintendent and school board." *Milliken v. Bradley*, 433 U.S. 267, 297, 97 S.Ct. 2749, 2765, 53 L.Ed.2d 745 (1977) (Powell, J., concurring in the judgment). How significant is it that local school officials joined plaintiffs in *Milliken II* in pressing for the remedial programs? What are the financial implications of such court-ordered programming?

c. *Compensatory Programs as a Substitute for Pupil Reassignment Remedies*. In the light of the facts that Detroit had a minority student population that exceeded 80 percent, and that the Court had earlier struck down a metropolitan desegregation plan, does *Milliken II* suggest that a remedy involving remedial education programming may be substituted for a remedy that involves busing? *Cf. Calhoun v. Cook*, 522 F.2d 717 (5th Cir. 1975), *rehearing denied*, 525 F.2d 1203. *But see Bradley v. Milliken*, 620 F.2d 1143 (6th Cir. 1980); *Jenkins v. Missouri*, 639 F.Supp. 19 (W.D. Mo. 1985). Or are compensatory programs only ancillary to the desegregation of a school system?

7. *The Role of Social Science Evidence in Determining the Extent of the Remedy*

In *Brown v. Board of Education*, the Court referred to segregation as generating "a feeling of inferiority [among blacks] as to their status in the community that may affect their hearts and minds in a way unlikely ever to be undone." And it quoted with favor the finding of the lower court that "segregation with the sanction of law . . . has a tendency to [retard] the educational and mental development of Negro children. . . ." And in the now-famous footnote 11, the Court cited what it called modern authority on the effects of segregation on black children. These references have given support to a sociological interpretation of the desegregation cases. Among the arguments that have been made are that segregated schools harm African American children in a number of ways: There is a "lessening of motivation, alienation of the child from the educational institution, distortion of personal relationships, and various forms of antisocial behavior." Fiss, "Racial Imbalance in the Public Schools: The Constitutional Concepts," 78 *Harv.L.Rev.* 564, 569 (1965).

It has also been argued that segregated schools are academically inferior and thus African American children who attend such schools are impaired in their ability to compete in society. *Id.* at 570. *See generally Hart v. Community School Board*, 383 F.Supp. 699, 739 (E.D.N.Y.1974); N. St. John, *School Desegregation: Outcomes for Children* (1975). The converse argument is that integrated schools will lessen the achievement gap between black and white students and, ultimately, the gap in educational and economic attainment between white and black adults. *See, e.g.*, Crain and Mahard, "School Racial Composition and Black College Attendance and Achievement Test Performance," 51 *Soc. of Educ.* 81 (1978). Further, the hope is that desegregation of the schools will improve relations between the races. *See generally* National Opinion Research Center, *Southern Schools: An Evaluation of the Effects of the Emergency School Assistance Program and of School Desegregation* (1973).

Extensive debates among social scientists have centered on the impact of mandatory desegregation, particularly through the use of busing, on minority achievement, aspirations, self-concept, college attendance, and on race relations. The classic debate on the effects of busing on minorities is that between David Armor in "The Evidence on Busing," 28 *Pub. Interest* 90 (1972) and Thomas Pettigrew and his colleagues in Pettigrew, Useem, Normand, and Smith, "Busing: A Review of the 'Evidence'," 30 *Pub. Interest* 88 (1973), and Armor's response to Pettigrew, et al. This debate is summarized by Krol, "Desegregation and Academic Achievement," in D. Bartz and M. Maehr, *Advances in Motivation and Achievement*, Vol. 1 (1984), at 81–82, as follows:

> . . . In his original articles and in his reply to Pettigrew et al. . . ., Armor seriously questioned the effectiveness of busing and other strategies as techniques for improving minority achievement. He presented evidence that busing in six different locations had not had a positive effect on minority student performance. Much of Armor's review of the literature concentrated on a comparison of the academic gains of bused and non-bused siblings. Armor concluded that there were not significant differences in academic gains between the bused group and the non-bused brothers and sisters.
>
> Armor's conclusion was quickly challenged by Pettigrew et al. . . . Pettigrew contended that Armor's review of the literature was incomplete, biased, misleading, and that it lacked a thorough analysis of the studies selected. He singled out a study conducted by Armor . . . in Boston as being unrepresentative and inadequately discussed and noted that a great deal of the evidence used by Armor to make his point came from the study. Pettigrew then went on to present a list of eight studies which had not been reviewed by

> Armor that were purported to support the success of various desegregation programs. Pettigrew limited his discussion and analysis to these eight studies even though he had chastised Armor for performing an incomplete and inadequate review of the literature. . . .
>
> Armor replied to Pettigrew's reply by accusing Pettigrew, et al. . . . of applying a "double double standard" to the research literature. He said the first double standard related to the burden of proof . . . :
>
> > To initiate the action one can use any type of social science data whether or not it directly tests the policy in question and regardless of its technical accuracy. But once the integration policy is in full force, it cannot be questioned unless one can *conclusively prove* that school integration *cannot* have an effect on educational benefits.
>
> The second double standard related to the appropriateness of scientific evidence in arguing the question of busing: "One willingly applies social science findings to public policy if they are in accordance with one's values but declares them irrelevant if they contradict one's values." . . . In addition to these accusations, Armor responded to Pettigrew's criticism of the . . . [Boston] research and pointed out that many of the studies cited by Pettigrew were biased and inadequate.

a. Controversy over Evidence. It may well be that many of the issues discussed in the Armor–Pettigrew debate cannot be definitively answered unless a carefully controlled social experiment is undertaken. Such experimentation is rare in education, largely because parents resist the coercion (and possible educational injury) that experimentation implies.

The debate has continued. *See, e.g.*, N. St. John, *School Desegregation Outcomes for Children* (1975); Coleman, "New Incentives for Desegregation," 7 *Human Rights* 10 (1978); Crain and Mahard, "Desegregation and Black Achievement: A Review of the Research," 42 *Law & Contemp. Probs.* 17 (1978) (pt. 1); Epps, "The Impact of School Desegregation on the Self-Evaluation and Achievement Orientation of Minority Children," *Id.* at 57; McConahay, "The Effects of School Desegregation Upon Students' Racial Attitudes and Behavior: A Critical Review of the Literature and a Prolegomenon to Future Research," *Id.* at 77. *See Columbus Board of Education v. Penick*, 443 U.S. 449, 485 n.5, 99 S.Ct. 2941, 2952, n. 5, 61 L.Ed.2d 666 (1977) (Powell, J., dissenting).

Some critics argue for more policy relevant research on desegregated schools. Instead of simply documenting achievement outcomes, researchers should investigate factors that lead to more effective desegregated schools. The question should not be whether desegregation works, but rather under what conditions it operates most effectively. For a summary of some components of effective desegregation, *see* Henderson, von Euler, and Schneider, "Remedies for Segregation: Some Lessons From Research," 3 *Educ. Evaluation and Pol'y Analysis* 4 (1981) at 67.

b. The Burden of Proving Harm. In the light of the controversy over the effects of desegregation, where should the legal burden of proof of injury rest? Is it necessary for black litigants to prove that integration favorably affects academic performance, racial attitudes, or psychological well-being before a court may order integration? Is it fair to cast this burden on school officials, thereby mandating integration unless school officials can prove that integration is harmful or has no positive effects? Should the constitutionality of segregation turn, wholly or in part, on allocations of burdens of proof?

c. Social Science Evidence and Constitutional Decisions. What weight should the courts attach to social science studies of the effects of desegregation? *See generally* Yudof, "School Desegregation: Legal Realism, Reasoned Elaboration, and Social Science Research in the Supreme Court," 42 *Law & Contemp. Probs.* 57 (1978). Are Pettigrew and his colleagues correct in asserting that: "The courts' interpretation of the Fourteenth Amendment of the United States Constitution, and not social scientists' opinions about black responses, ultimately governs the racial desegregation of the public schools and court-ordered transportation which may be needed to achieve it"?

In view of the fact that there is considerable disagreement among social scientists as to the research findings and the conclusions to be drawn from those findings, is the adversary process the appropriate way of dealing with controversial social science issues? *See* P. Ellsworth and J. Getman, *Law and the Social Sciences* (1986), at 620–21, describing some of the difficulties of using social science evidence at the appellate level:

> How is the court to choose in an argument involving the adequacy of the data base, the significance of regression co-efficients, and the choice of appropriate control analyses? In a situation like this, one party may, in fact, have the stronger arguments, but the court can only conclude . . . that experts disagree. But disagree-

ment among experts should not be grounds for disregarding the empirical issues entirely. Instances of complete unanimity among the social science community are extremely rare, and it would be unfortunate if the Court were to insist on a standard of absolute agreement before accepting social science data. . . .

Ellsworth and Getman discuss the problem of the "battle of the experts" at the trial court level as follows:

> . . . [T]here is no reason to believe that the skill of effective courtroom testimony is highly correlated with the skill of scientific expertise, and there is every reason to believe that a trial attorney, if forced to choose, will prefer the better witness to the better scientist. Even an excellent scientist is likely to be less than perfectly coherent, and perhaps less than perfectly honest, on the witness stand. Unable to anticipate questions, to prepare answers in advance, or to offer full explanations; threatened by contemptuous attacks with no opportunity for rebuttal; restricted by a good cross-examiner to yes and no answers—the scientists are not apt to appear at their best. A facile dogmatism may sound better—and read better in the record—than a more hesitant and more accurate response. The mode of presentation and the kinds of questions asked are often so foreign to the professional experience of most research scientists that it is difficult to believe that the answers given in this context could possibly be the best account of the research or that the interchange could provide a valid test for deciding what is scientifically true and what is not.

Id. at 623.

Courts rarely rely on social science research in determining whether segregation is unconstitutional, and when they have done so, they have been preemptorily reversed. *See Stell v. Savannah-Chatham County Board of Education*, 220 F.Supp. 667 (S.D. Ga. 1963), *rev'd*, 333 F.2d 55 (5th Cir.), *cert. denied*, 379 U.S. 933, 85 S.Ct. 332, 13 L.Ed.2d 344. *See also Evers v. Jackson Municipal Separate School District*, 232 F.Supp. 241 (S.D. Miss. 1964), *aff'd*, 357 F.2d 653 (5th Cir.), *cert. denied*, 384 U.S. 961, 86, S.Ct. 1586, 16 L.Ed.2d 673. Courts have continued, however, to refer to social science research with regard to questions concerning the nature and extent of the remedies to be applied. *See* Levin, "School Desegregation Remedies and the Role of Social Science Research," 42 *Law & Contemp. Probs.* 1 (1978) (pt. 2). Professor Levin examines the extent to which courts rely on social science evidence in deciding on the ages of the children to be bused and the distances, whether magnet schools can be used, whether the potential for white flight mandates a lesser remedy, and whether compensatory educational programs may be included in a desegregation decree.

d. Other Studies of the Effects of Desegregation. The social science literature on the effects of desegregation is immense. For the interested reader, the following books and articles afford a useful starting place: Coleman, et al., *Equality of Educational Opportunity* (1966); B. Levin and W. Hawley, *The Courts, Social Science, and School Desegregation* (1975); F. Mosteller and P. Moynihan, *On Equality of Educational Opportunity* (1970); R. O'Reilly, *Racial and Social Class Isolation in the Schools* (1970); N. St. John, *School Desegregation Outcomes for Children* (1975); Clark, "Desegregation: An Appraisal of the Evidence," 9 *J. Social Issues* 2 (1953); Crain, "School Integration and Occupational Achievement of Negroes," 75 *Am. J. Soc.* 593 (1971); Frary and Goolsby, "Achievement of Integrated and Segregated Negroes and White First Graders in a Southern City," 8 *Integrated Educ.* 48 (1970); Katz, "Review of Evidence Relating to Effects of Desegregation on the Intellectual Performance of Negroes," 19 *Am. Psych.* 381 (1964); Katz, "The Socialization of Academic Motivation in Minority Group Children," in D. Levine, ed., *Nebraska Symposium on Motivation* (1967); Kiesling, "The Value to Society of Integrated Education and Compensatory Education," 61 *Geo. L.J.* 857 (1973); Symposium, "School Desegregation: Lessons of the First Twenty-five Years," 42 *Law & Contemp. Probs.* (B. Levin and W. Hawley, eds., 1978); Braddock, Crain, and McPartland, "A Long-Term View of Desegregation: Some Recent Studies of Graduates as Adults," 66 *Phi Delta Kappan*, 259 (1984).

E. Desegregation in Multi-Ethnic Districts

Although most of the case law in the school desegregation area was the result of lawsuits brought by African Americans, the benefits of the equal protection clause have been sought by other minorities, the largest group being Latinos. Should Latinos be treated as an identifiable class for purposes of determining whether a school or school system is segregated? *See Cisneros v. Corpus Christi Independent School District*, 467 F.2d 142 (5th Cir. 1972), *cert. denied*, 413 U.S. 920, 93 S.Ct. 3053, 37 L.Ed.2d 1041; *United States v. Texas Educ. Agency*, 467

F.2d 848 (5th Cir. 1972), *vacated sub nom. Austin Independent School District v. United States*, 429 U.S. 990, 97 S.Ct. 517, 50 L.Ed.2d 603.

The Supreme Court in *Keyes* dealt with this issue as follows:

> [A] word must be said about the district court's method of defining a "segregated" school. Denver is a triethnic, as distinguished from a biracial, community. The overall racial and ethnic composition of the Denver public schools is 66% Anglo, 14% Negro and 20% Hispano. The District Court, in assessing the question of *de jure* segregation in the core city schools, preliminarily resolved that Negroes and Hispanos should not be placed in the same category to establish the segregated character of a school. 313 F.Supp. at 69. Later, in determining the schools that were likely to produce an inferior educational opportunity, the court concluded that a school would be considered inferior only if it had "a concentration of either Negro or Hispano students in the general area of 70 to 75%." 313 F.Supp. at 77. We intimate no opinion whether the District Court's 70 to 75% requirement was correct. The District Court used those figures to signify educationally inferior schools, and there is no suggestion in the record that those same figures were or would be used to define a "segregated" school in the *de jure* context. What is or is not a segregated school will necessarily depend on the facts of each particular case. In addition to the racial and ethnic composition of a school's student body, other factors such as the racial and ethnic composition of faculty and staff and the community and administration attitudes toward the school must be taken into consideration. . . .
>
> We conclude, however, that the District Court erred in separating Negroes and Hispanos for purposes of defining a "segregated" school. We have held that Hispanos constitute an identifiable class for purposes of the Fourteenth Amendment. *Hernandez v. Texas*, 347 U.S. 475 (1954). . . . [T]here is . . . much evidence that in the Southwest Hispanos and Negroes have a great many things in common. The United States Commission on Civil Rights has recently published two reports on Hispano education in the Southwest. Focusing on students in the states of Arizona, California, Colorado, New Mexico, and Texas, the Commission concluded that Hispanos suffer from the same educational inequities as Negroes and American Indians. In fact, the District Court itself recognized that "one of the things which the Hispano has in common with the Negro is economic and cultural deprivation and discrimination." 313 F.Supp. at 69. This is agreement that, though of different origins, Negroes and Hispanos in Denver suffer identical discrimination in treatment when compared with the treatment afforded Anglo students. In that circumstance, we think petitioners are entitled to have schools with a combined predominance of Negroes and Hispanos included in the category of "segregated" schools.

Keyes v. School District No. 1, 413 U.S. 189, 195–98, 93 S.Ct. 2686, 2690–92, 37 L.Ed.2d 548 (1973).

NOTES AND QUESTIONS

1. Which Minorities Constitute an Identifiable Class?

The *Keyes* Court notes that Hispanics in the Southwest have suffered "economic and cultural deprivation and discrimination" identical to that of blacks. If this is the necessary and sufficient test, would *all* Spanish-speaking students fit into that category, for example, the Puerto Ricans or Colombians in New York? Does *Keyes* indicate that *Brown* should be extended to other minorities—such as Asian students?

Is the finding that Latinos (or other minorities) have suffered "educational inequities" sufficient, or must there be evidence of intentional segregative action? *See Zamora v. New Braunfels Independent School District*, 519 F.2d 1084 (5th Cir. 1975); *United States v. Texas Education Agency*, 467 F.2d 848 (5th Cir. 1972).

2. Multi-ethnic Remedies

Do *Keyes* and *Swann*, read together, mean that schools must be ethnically as well as racially balanced? Many advocates of bilingual education for Latinos have opposed the dispersal of Latino students on the ground that the bilingual programs will be jeopardized. May a court order pupil reassignment for African American and white students to end racially segregated schools at the same time that Latino students are permitted to remain in ethnically isolated schools or classrooms in order to permit bilingual–bicultural instruction? *See Tasby v. Estes*, 412 F. Supp. 1192 (N.D. Tex. 1976), *remanded on other grounds, aff'd in part*, 572 F.2d 1010 (5th Cir. 1978); *Keyes v. School District No. 1*, 380 F. Supp. 673, 692 (D. Colo. 1974), *rev'd on this point*, 521 F.2d 465, 480 (10th Cir. 1972), *cert. denied*, 423 U.S. 1066, 96 S.Ct. 806, 46 L.Ed.2d 657 (1976). The district court in the Boston school desegregation case ordered the assignment of Hispanic students before the assignment of black and white students in order to prevent their dispersal. *Morgan v. Kerrigan*, 401 F.Supp.

216, 242, 252 (D. Mass. 1975), *aff'd*, 530 F.2d 401 (1st Cir.), *cert. denied*, 426 U.S. 935, 96 S.Ct. 2648, 49 L.Ed.2d 386 (1976). *See* Roos, "Bilingual Education: The Hispanic Response to Unequal Educational Opportunity," 42 *Law & Contemp. Probs.* 111, 136–37 (1978) (pt. 2), for a description of the court's order.

Latinos, who in many cases have not entered a school desegregation case until the remedy phase, have at times successfully argued for a bilingual component in a remedial plan. *See, e.g., United States v. Texas Education Agency*, 342 F. Supp. 24 (E.D. Tex. 1971), *rev'd on other grounds*, 467 F.2d 848 (5th Cir. (1972)). *But see Keyes v. School District No. 1*, 521 F.2d 465 (10th Cir. 1975), *cert. denied*, 432 U.S. 1066, 96 S.Ct. 806, 46 L.Ed.2d 657 (1976). Might *Milliken II* provide a constitutional basis for this argument? *Bradley v. Milliken*, 402 F. Supp. 1096, 1118 (E.D. Mich. 1975), *aff'd in part, rev'd on other grounds*, 540 F.2d 229 (6th Cir. (1976)), *aff'd*, 443 U.S. 267, 97 S.Ct. 2749, 53 L.Ed.2d 745 (1977). Is there a plausible causal relationship between segregation and limited English-speaking ability?

F. Who Pays for Equal Educational Opportunity: State Responsibility

A number of courts, relying on *Milliken II*, have ordered the state or other governmental units to share the costs of implementing and maintaining desegregation and compensatory education programs with the local school board. *See Jenkins v. Missouri*, 807 F.2d 657, 683 (8th Cir. 1986) (en banc), *aff'd in part and remanded*, ___ U.S. ___, 110 S.Ct. 1651 (1990); *Liddell v. State of Missouri*, 731 F.2d 1294 (8th Cir. 1984); *Little Rock School District v. Pulaski County Special School District No. 1*, 778 F.2d 404 (8th Cir. 1985); *Reed v. Rhodes*, 662 F.2d 1219 (6th Cir. 1981), *cert. denied*, 455 U.S. 1018, 102 S.Ct. 1713, 72 L.Ed.2d 135 (1982); *Brinkman v. Gilligan*, 610 F.Supp. 1288 (S.D. Ohio 1985); *Arthur v. Nyquist*, 547 F.Supp. 468 (W.D.N.Y. 1982). In each case, the State has been found liable to some degree for the segregation. *See Kelley v. Board of Education of Nashville and Davidson County*, 836 F.2d 986 (6th Cir. 1987); and *United States v. Texas Education Agency*, 790 F.2d 1262 (5th Cir. 1986), both holding that the state did not have to share in the costs as there was no finding that the state was liable for the segregation. Generally, state funding is ordered only when it is necessary to the continuance of a program that materially aids desegregation and not for programs that merely improve the educational quality of the school district. *See Arthur v. Nyquist, supra*. However, the state may not force a school district to pay for desegregation out of general education funds. *Id.*

After a district court found that the Kansas City, Missouri School District (KCMSD) and the state of Missouri had operated an unconstitutionally segregated school system, the court ordered a detailed desegregation remedy and allocated the cost of the remedy between the state and the city school district.

The *Milliken II*-type remedy provided for improvements in the quality of the curriculum, tutoring programs, child development programs, magnet schools, including a 25 acre farm and 25 acre wild land area for science study, and extensive (and expensive) capital improvements. Missouri v. Jenkins, ___ U.S. ___, 110 S.Ct. 1651 (1990). However, Missouri's constitution and state laws placed limits on the local property tax rate that a district can levy, thus preventing KCMSD from raising the revenues necessary to fund its share of the desegregation remedy. The district court ordered KCMSD to impose a property tax levy that would be sufficient to raise the necessary funds. The Supreme Court held that in the circumstances of this case, the tax increase ordered by the district court violated principles of federal/state comity. However, Justice White, writing for the majority, did not completely rule out the imposition of a tax rate increase by a federal court, but noted that "before taking such a drastic step the district court was obliged to assure itself that no permissible alternative would have accomplished the required task." *Id.* at 1663. The Court found that in this case, there was an alternative route the district court could have followed that would have been less intrusive: "it could have authorized or required KCMSD to levy property taxes at a rate adequate to fund the desegregation remedy and could have enjoined the operation of state laws that would have prevented KCMSD from exercising this power." *Id.* The majority distinguished the court's imposing its own tax increase on the school district from the court's ordering the school district to levy a tax increase, as follows:

> Authorizing and directing local government institutions to devise and implement remedies not only protects the function of those institutions but, to the extent possible, also places the responsibility for solutions to

> the problems of segregation upon those who have themselves created the problems. . . . Whatever the merits of this argument [that an order to increase taxes violates Article III of the Constitution] when applied to the district court's own order increasing taxes, a point we have not reached . . . , a court order directing a local government body to levy its own taxes is plainly a judicial act within the power of the federal court. . . .

Id. at 1663, 1666. The majority stated that federal judicial power can go further and set aside state-imposed limitations on local taxing authority "where there is reason based in the Constitution for not observing the statutory limitation." *Id.* at 1666.

> Here the KCMSD may be ordered to levy taxes despite the statutory limitations on its authority in order to compel the discharge of an obligation imposed on KCMSD by the Fourteenth Amendment. To hold otherwise would fail to take account of the obligations of local governments, under the Supremacy Clause, to fulfill the requirements that the Constitution imposes on them. . . . Even though a particular remedy may not be required in every case to vindicate constitutional guarantees, where (as here) it has been found that a particular remedy is required, the State cannot hinder the process by preventing a local government from implementing that remedy.

Id. at 1666.

VI. ESTABLISHING UNITARY STATUS AND ITS LEGAL SIGNIFICANCE

A. Determining When a Formerly Dual School System Has Achieved Unitary Status

---

Jacksonville Branch, NAACP v. Duval County School Board

883 F.2d 945 (11th Cir. 1989).

Vance, Circuit Judge.

This action was filed in April, 1985 by the Jacksonville branch of the NAACP ("NAACP") on behalf of all black schoolchildren in Duval County, Florida. The complaint alleged that defendant, the Duval County School Board ("Board"), had acted since 1975 to increase racial segregation in its public schools. The district court consolidated this action with *Mims v. Duval County School Bd.*, a case which culminated in 1971 with the issuance of a permanent injunction requiring the Board to integrate the school system. *See Mims v. Duval County School Bd.*, 329 F.Supp. 123 (M.D.Fla.), *aff'd*, 447 F.2d 1330 (5th Cir. 1971). After a trial on the merits, the district court found that the Duval County school system has achieved unitary status within the meaning of *Swann v. Charlotte-Mecklenburg Bd. of Educ.*, 402 U.S. 1, 91 S.Ct. 1267, 28 L.Ed.2d 554 (1971), and *Green v. County School Bd.*, 391 U.S. 430, 88 S.Ct. 1689, 20 L.Ed.2d 716 (1968), and therefore dissolved the injunction. For the reasons stated below, we reverse.

I. Background

Legal efforts to dismantle Duval County's segregated school system began in 1960, when a lawsuit was filed seeking to compel the school board to comply with the mandate of *Brown v. Board of Educ.*, 349 U.S. 294, 75 S.Ct. 753, 99 L.Ed. 1083 (1955) ("*Brown II*"), to effectuate an immediate transition to a racially nondiscriminatory system. . . .

* * *

Since 1971, the school system has been subject to the permanent injunction set forth in former District Judge Tjoflat's memorandum opinion published at 329 F.Supp. 123 ("*Mims* order"). . . .

II. Facts

The Duval County school district is geographically the largest school district in the United States. Approximately 101,000 children, 65% of whom were white and 35% of whom were black, attended its more than 140 schools in 1984. The black student population has increased by 7% since the 1971 *Mims* order.

* * *

III. Discussion

The district court found that the Duval County school system has achieved unitary status and accordingly dissolved the injunction under which the school district had been operating since 1969. Appellant urges that we reverse this finding on the ground that the school district has not successfully eliminated the effects of the past system of state-imposed segregation. The critical question thus is under what circumstances judicial supervision must be terminated because the school district has achieved unitary status. The Supreme Court has not addressed this question. In several decisions, however, the Court describes the substantive goals that school desegregation remedies should achieve to redress fully the harms resulting from the prior system of state-imposed segregation. Our analysis of these cases and our review of the record in this case convinces us that the Duval County School Board has not sufficiently eliminated the vestiges of its previously discriminatory system to entitle it to a declaration of unitary status.

In *Brown v. Board of Educ.*, 347 U.S. 483, 74 S.Ct. 686, 98 L.Ed. 873 (1954) (*"Brown I"*), the Supreme Court held that the maintenance of separate school systems for black and white students violates the equal protection clause of the Fourteenth Amendment and that school districts must operate one school system for all students. *Id.* at 495, 74 S.Ct. at 692; *see also Brown II*, 349 U.S. at 300–01, 75 S.Ct. at 756–57 (instructing school authorities how to comply with commands of *Brown I.*) In subsequent decisions, the Court explained that the ultimate obligation of school districts was to effect a "transition to a unitary, nonracial system of public education. . . ." *Green v. County School Bd.*, 391 U.S. 430, 436, 88 S.Ct. 1689–1693, 20 L.Ed.2d 716 (1968); *see also Alexander v. Holmes County Bd. of Educ.*, 396 U.S. 19, 20, 90 S.Ct. 29, 29–30, 24 L.Ed.2d 19 (1969). After a school system has successfully eliminated all vestiges of state-imposed segregation, *see Swann v. Charlotte-Mecklenburg Bd. of Educ.*, 402 U.S. at 15, 91 S.Ct. at 1275–76, it attains unitary status[2] and court supervision is no longer warranted. *Swann*, 402 U.S. at 31–32, 91 S.Ct. at 1283–84.

The Court in *Green* confirmed that school districts operating segregated school systems were "charged with the affirmative duty to take whatever steps might be necessary to convert to a unitary school system in which racial discrimination would be eliminated root and branch." 391 U.S. at 437–38, 88 S.Ct. at 1694. *Swann* reiterated that the goal was to "eliminate from the public schools all vestiges of state-imposed segregation." 402 U.S. at 15, 91 S.Ct. at 1275–76. The Court pointed to the ability to identify the "race" of a school based upon the racial composition of its teachers and staff and the quality of its facilities and extracurricular activities as an indication of continued segregation. Because school authorities exercise extensive control over faculty and staff assignments and the allocation of resources, racial disproportionality in these areas is difficult to explain as other than the product of the prior state-imposed system of segregation:

> Independent of student assignment, where it is possible to identify a "white school" or a "Negro school" simply by reference to the racial composition of teachers and staff, the quality of school buildings and equipment, or the organization of sports activities, a *prima facie* case of violation of substantive constitutional rights under the Equal Protection Clause is shown.

Id. at 18, 91 S.Ct. at 1277. The existence of schools whose student bodies are composed almost entirely of one race constitutes less compelling evidence of continued segregation:

> [T]he existence of some small number of one-race, or virtually one-race, schools within a district is not in and of itself the mark of a system that still practices segregation by law. . . . [B]ut in a system with a history of segregation the need for remedial criteria of sufficient specificity to assure a school authority's compliance with its constitutional duty warrants a presumption against schools that are substantially disproportionate in their racial composition.

Id. at 26, 91 S.Ct. at 1281.

Once a prima facie case of continued segregation in a previously dual school system is established, the burden is upon the school authorities to show that such continued segregation is not the result of present or past discriminatory actions. *Id.* "In discharging that burden, it is not enough, of course, that the school authorities rely upon some allegedly logical, racially neutral explanation for their actions. Their burden is to adduce proof sufficient to support a finding that segregative intent was not *among* the factors that motivated their actions." *Keyes v. School*

2. There has been some confusion in the lower courts surrounding the definition of "unitary." In *Georgia State Conference of Branches of NAACP v. Georgia*, 775 F.2d 1403, 1413 n. 12 (11th Cir.1985), we distinguished a unitary school system from a system that has achieved unitary status. A unitary system, we explained, is one which has not operated segregated schools for a period of several years. A system that has achieved unitary status is "one which is not only unitary but has eliminated the vestiges of its prior discrimination and has been adjudicated as such through the proper judicial procedures." *Id.* We retain this definitional distinction for purposes of this opinion. *Cf. United States v. Lawrence County School Dist.*, 799 F.2d 1031, 1037 (5th Cir.1986) (reconciling inconsistent uses of term "unitary").

Dist., 413 U.S. 189, 210, 93 S.Ct. 2686, 2698, 37 L.Ed.2d 548 (1973) (emphasis added). The remoteness in time of the school authorities' intentionally discriminatory actions is irrelevant. In *Keyes*, the Court explained that

> If the actions of school authorities were to any degree motivated by segregative intent and the segregation resulting from those actions continues to exist, the fact of remoteness in time certainly does not make those actions any less "intentional."
>
> . . . Intentional school segregation in the past may have been a factor in creating a natural environment for the growth of further segregation. Thus, . . . [the school board] can rebut the prima facie case only by showing that its past segregative acts did not create or contribute to the current segregated condition of [the schools].

Id. at 201–11, 93 S.Ct. at 2698–99. Proof that school authorities presently intend to maintain a segregated school system therefore is not required. "[T]he measure of the post-*Brown I* conduct of a school board under an unsatisfied duty to liquidate a dual system is the effectiveness, not the purpose, of the actions in decreasing or increasing the segregation caused by the dual system." *Dayton Bd. of Educ. v. Brinkman*, 443 U.S. 526, 538, 99 S.Ct. 2971, 2979, 61 L.Ed.2d 720 (1979).

These cases make clear that no previously segregated school system can be declared to have achieved unitary status as long as there is continued segregation, as demonstrated by racial identification in faculty and staff assignments, extracurricular activities and facilities, *see Swann*, 402 U.S. at 18, 91 S.Ct. at 1277; *Green*, 391 U.S. at 435, 88 S.Ct. at 1692–93, and to a lesser extent, student assignments, *see Swann*, 402 U.S. at 26, 91 S.Ct. at 1281. Where it is possible to distinguish "black schools" from "white schools" on the basis of racial disproportionality in these highly visible areas, it is clear that the original desegregation plan has failed to achieve its objectives. A declaration of unitary status is also inappropriate when the evidence shows that the school authorities have not consistently acted in good faith to implement the objectives of the plan. *See Green*, 391 U.S. at 439, 88 S.Ct. at 1694–95 ("availability to the board of other more [desegregative] courses of action may indicate a lack of good faith [placing] a heavy burden upon the board to explain its preference for an apparently less effective method.").

The district court's determination that the Duval County school system has achieved unitary status is clearly erroneous.[3] The evidence showed that the larger schools in the system had administrative staffs composed exclusively of members of one race. The race of the staff in these schools almost without exception matched the predominant race of the student body. In the area of faculty assignments, the evidence showed that the Board has never complied with the 1969 injunction requiring teachers to be assigned according to a 70% to 30% white-to-black ratio at each school. Approximately thirty schools have varied consistently by more than 10% from the target ratio since 1972. Disproportionately black faculties were found at schools with predominantly black students. The same was true for department chairpersons and coaches.

The Board offers several explanations for these deviations from the *Mims* order. Mr. Herb Sang, the Duval County school superintendent, testified that the reasons for the overrepresentation of black administrators at predominantly black schools were that promotions were usually made within the schools and that consideration was given to administrators' preference in location when making assignments. As to the Board's failure to comply with the seventy to thirty ratio with respect to faculty assignments, appellee's witnesses testified that principals have the final authority to approve or disapprove any transfer. Teachers' preference in location was also cited as an explanation.

These "allegedly logical, racially neutral explanation[s]," *see Keyes*, 413 U.S. at 210, 93 S.Ct. at 2698, do not suffice to discharge the Board's burden of demonstrating that these disparities were not the result of the prior segregated system. The Board was required to show that "its past segregative acts did not create or contribute to the current segregated condition" of the schools. *Id.* at 211, 93 S.Ct. at 2699. Instead, the Board's evidence merely refuted the inference that the Board was presently engaging in intentionally discriminatory practices. This evi-

3. A declaration that a school has achieved unitary status is a finding of fact subject to review under the clearly erroneous standard. *United States .v. Texas Educ. Agency*, 647 F.2d 504, 506 (5th Cir. Unit A 1981), *cert. denied*, 454 U.S. 1143, 102 S.Ct. 1002, 71 L.Ed.2d 295 (1982); *accord Riddick v. School Bd.*, 784 F.2d 521, 533 (4th Cir.1986).

dence does not defeat the presumption that the current imbalances are causally related to prior segregation. *See Brown v. Board of Educ.*, No. 87–1668, slip op. at 20 (10th Cir. June 2, 1989) (burden of rebutting presumption that current disparities are causally related to prior segregation rests on defendants) (citing *School Bd. v. Baliles*, 829 F.2d 1308, 1311 (4th Cir. 1987)).

The evidence also revealed a failure to comply with the *Mims* order in the area of student assignments. Segregation in the district as a whole has increased since 1972. In that year, eight schools had majority black populations; in 1985, twenty-seven schools fell into that category. Appellant asserts that the district's use of portable classrooms and leasing of additional classroom space were partially responsible for this increased segregation. It is unnecessary for us to make a determination as to the actual effect of these practices, however, in light of the board's concession that no studies were conducted to assess their potential impact on the system's racial imbalances. The Board's failure to consider the objective of desegregation in its efforts to alleviate overcrowding violates its affirmative duty to desegregate. *Pitts v. Freeman*, 755 F.2d 1423, 1427 (11th Cir. 1985).

* * *

In short, we hold that the Duval County School Board's consistent failure to comply with the provisions of the *Mims* injunction and order, as well as its actions and omissions in the areas of faculty and staff assignment, have perpetuated the effects of the prior system of segregation. The district court's determination that the school district has achieved the objectives of the injunction and order therefore was clearly erroneous. Accordingly, we reverse the finding of the district court that the Duval County school system has achieved unitary status, vacate its order dissolving the *Mims* injunction and remand for further proceedings consistent with this opinion.

NOTES AND QUESTIONS

1. Essential Factors in Proving Unitary Status

A second Eleventh Circuit panel in 1989 held that in order to achieve unitary status, a school system formerly declared segregated must achieve desegregation for a period of at least three years, as measured simultaneously by all six *Green* factors (student assignment, faculty, staff, transportation, extracurricular activities, and facilities). *Pitts v. Freeman*, 887 F.2d 1438, 1445–46 (11th Cir. 1989) (citing *Green v. County School Bd.*, 391 U.S. 430, 435, 88 S.Ct. 1689, 1692, 20 L.Ed.2d 716 (1968)). The First Circuit, however, has concluded that a school system's failure to achieve unitariness in some of the *Green* factors does not preclude a finding of unitariness in others and that remedies should be limited to the factors not yet found to be unitary. *Morgan v. Nucci*, 831 F.2d 313, 318 (1st Cir. 1987).

2. The Relevance of Intent

The *Duval County* court suggests that once a school board is under an "affirmative duty to desegregate," 883 F.2d at 953, there is no need to prove "that school authorities presently intend to maintain a segregated school system" in order to prevent a finding of unitariness. *Id.* at 951. Is intent therefore irrelevant in this context? If "continued segregation" in the absence of present intent to segregate prevents a finding of unitariness, why does the *Duval County* court speak of the evidentiary burden school authorities face "to show that such continued segregation is not the result of present or past discriminatory actions"? *Id.* How would school authorities discharge that burden?

B. The Legal Significance of Achieving Unitary Status

Board of Education of Oklahoma City Public Schools v. Dowell

——— U.S. ———, 111 S.Ct. 630, 112 L.Ed.2d 715 (1991).

Rehnquist, Chief Justice.

Petitioner Board of Education of Oklahoma City sought dissolution of a decree entered by the District Court imposing a school desegregation plan. The District Court granted relief over the objection of respondents Robert L. Dowell, et al., black students and their parents. The Court of Appeals for the Tenth Circuit reversed, holding that the Board would be entitled to such relief only upon " 'nothing less than a clear showing of grievous wrong evoked by new and unforeseen conditions . . . .' " 890 F.2d 1483, 1490 (1989) (citation omitted). We hold that the Court of Appeals' test is more stringent than is required either by our cases dealing with injunctions or by the Equal Protection Clause of the Fourteenth Amendment.

I

This school desegregation litigation began almost 30 years ago. In 1961, respondents, black students and their parents, sued petitioners, the Board of Education of Oklahoma City (Board), to end *de jure* segregation in the public schools. In 1963, the District Court found that Oklahoma City had intentionally segregated both schools and housing in the past, and that Oklahoma City was operating a "dual" school system—one that was intentionally segregated by race. *Dowell v. School Board of Oklahoma City Public Schools*, 219 F.Supp. 427 (WD Okla.). In 1965, the District Court found that the School Board's attempt to desegregate by using neighborhood zoning failed to remedy past segregation because residential segregation resulted in one-race schools. *Dowell v. School Board of Oklahoma City Public Schools*, 244 F.Supp. 971, 975 (WD Okla.). Residential segregation had once been state imposed, and it lingered due to discrimination by some realtors and financial institutions. *Ibid.* The District Court found that school segregation had caused some housing segregation. *Id.*, at 976–77. In 1972, finding that previous efforts had not been successful at eliminating state imposed segregation, the District Court ordered the Board to adopt the "Finger Plan," *Dowell v. Board of Education of Oklahoma City Public Schools*, 338 F.Supp. 1256, *aff'd* 465 F.2d 1012 (CA10), *cert. denied*, 409 U.S. 1041 (1972), under which kindergarteners would be assigned to neighborhood schools unless their parents opted otherwise; children in grades 1–4 would attend formerly all white schools, and thus black children would be bused to those schools; children in grade five would attend formerly all black schools, and thus white children would be bused to those schools; students in the upper grades would be bused to various areas in order to maintain integrated schools; and in integrated neighborhoods there would be stand-alone schools for all grades.

In 1977, after complying with the desegregation decree for five years, the Board made a "Motion to Close Case." The District Court held in its "Order Terminating Case":

> The Court has concluded that [the Finger Plan] worked and that substantial compliance with the constitutional requirements has been achieved. The School Board, under the oversight of the Court, has operated the Plan properly, and the Court does not foresee that the termination of its jurisdiction will result in the dismantlement of the Plan or any affirmative action by the defendant to undermine the unitary system so slowly and painfully accomplished over the 16 years during which the cause has been pending before this court. . . .

This unpublished order was not appealed.

In 1984, the School Board faced demographic changes that led to greater burdens on young black children. As more and more neighborhoods became integrated, more stand-alone schools were established, and young black students had to be bused further from their inner-city homes to outlying white areas. In an effort to alleviate this burden and to increase parental involvement, the Board adopted the Student Reassignment Plan (SRP), which relied on neighborhood assignments for students in grades K–4 beginning in the 1985–1986 school year. Busing continued for students in grades 5–12. . . .

In 1985, respondents filed a "Motion to Reopen the Case," contending that the School District had not achieved "unitary" status and that the SRP was a return to segregation. Under the SRP, 11 of 64 elementary schools would be greater than 90% black, 22 would be greater than 90% white plus other minorities, and 31 would be racially mixed. The District Court refused to reopen the case, holding that its 1977 finding of unitariness was *res judicata* as to those who were then parties to the action, and that the district remained unitary. *Dowell v. Board of Education of Oklahoma City Public Schools*, 606 F.Supp. 1548 (WD Okla. 1985). . . . Because unitariness had been achieved, the District Court concluded that court-ordered desegregation must end.

The Court of Appeals for the Tenth Circuit reversed, *Dowell v. Board of Education of Oklahoma City Public Schools*, 795 F.2d 1516, *cert. denied*, 479 U.S. 938 (1986). It held that, while the 1977 order finding the district unitary was binding on the parties, nothing in that order indicated that the 1972 injunction itself was terminated. The court reasoned that the finding that the system was unitary merely ended the District Court's active supervision of the case, and because the school district was still subject to the desegregation decree, respondents could challenge the SRP. The case was remanded to determine whether the decree should be lifted or modified.

On remand, the District Court found that demographic changes made the Finger Plan unworkable, that the Board had done nothing for 25 years to promote residential segregation, and that the school district had bused students for more than a decade in good-faith compliance with the court's orders. 677 F.Supp. 1503 (WD Okla. 1987). The District Court found that present residential segregation was the result of private decisionmaking and economics, and that it was too attenuated to be a vestige of former school segregation. It also found that the district had maintained its unitary status, and that the neighborhood assignment plan was not designed with discriminatory intent. The court concluded that the previous injunctive decree should be vacated and the school district returned to local control.

The Court of Appeals again reversed, 890 F.2d 1483 (CA10 1989). . . . Relying on *United States v. Swift & Co.*, 286 U.S. 106 (1932), it held that a desegregation decree remains in effect until a school district can show "grievous wrong evoked by new and unforseen conditions," 286 U.S., at 119, and "dramatic changes in conditions unforseen at the time of the decree that . . . impose extreme and unexpectedly oppressive hardships on the obligor." 890 F.2d, at 1490 (quoting T. Jost, "From *Swift* to *Stotts* and Beyond: Modification of Injunctions in the Federal Courts," 64 *Tex.L.Rev.* 1101, 1110 (1986)). Given that a number of schools would return to being primarily one-race schools under the SRP, circumstances in Oklahoma City had not changed enough to justify modification of the decree. The Court of Appeals held that, despite the unitary finding, the Board had the " 'affirmative duty . . . not to take any action that would impede the process of disestablishing the dual system and its effect.' " 890 F.2d, at 1504 (quoting *Dayton Bd. of Education v. Brinkman*, 443 U.S. 526, 538 (1979)).

We granted the Board's petition for certiorari, 494 U.S. ____, 110 S.Ct. 1521, 108 L.Ed.2d 761 (1990), to resolve a conflict between the standard laid down by the Court of Appeals in this case and that laid down in *Spangler v. Pasadena City Board of Education*, 611 F.2d 1239 (CA9 1979), and *Riddick v. School Bd. of City of Norfolk*, 784 F.2d 521 (CA4 1986). We now reverse the Court of Appeals.

II

* * *

The lower courts have been inconsistent in their use of the term "unitary." Some have used it to identify a school district that has completely remedied all vestiges of past discrimination. *See, e.g., United States v. Overton*, 834 F.2d 1171, 1175 (CA5 1987); *Riddick v. School Bd. of City of Norfolk, supra*, at 533–534; *Vaughns v. Board of Education of Prince George's Cty.*, 758 F.2d 983, 988 (CA4 1985). Under that interpretation of the word, a unitary school district is one that has met the mandate of *Brown v. Board of Education*, 349 U.S. 294 (1955), and *Green v. New Kent County School Board*, 391 U.S. 430 (1968). Other courts, however, have used "unitary" to describe any school district that has currently desegregated student assignments, whether or not that status is solely the result of a court-imposed desegregation plan. *See, e.g.*, 890 F.2d, at 14. In other words, such a school district could be called unitary and nevertheless still contain vestiges of past discrimination. That there is such confusion is evident in *Georgia State Conference of Branches of NAACP v. Georgia*, 775 F.2d 1403 (CA11 1985), where the Court of Appeals drew a distinction between a "unitary school district" and a district that has achieved "unitary status." The court explained that a school district that has not operated segregated schools as proscribed by *Green v. New Kent County School Board, supra*, and *Swann v. Charlotte-Mecklenburg Bd. of Education*, 402 U.S. 1 (1971), "for a period of several years" is unitary, but that a school district cannot be said to have achieved "unitary status" unless it "has eliminated the vestiges of its prior discrimination and has been adjudicated as such through the proper judicial procedures." *Georgia State* Conference, supra, at 1413, n. 12.

. . . The constitutional command of the Fourteenth Amendment is that "no State shall . . . deny to any person . . . the equal protection of the laws." Courts have used the terms "dual" to denote a school system which has engaged in intentional segregation of students by race, and "unitary" to describe a school system which has been brought into compliance with the command of the Constitution. We are not sure how useful it is to define these terms more precisely, or to create subclasses within them. . . . The District Court's 1977 order is unclear with respect to what it meant by unitary and the necessary result of that finding. . . . In *Pasadena City Bd. of Education v. Spangler*, 427 U.S. 424 (1976), we held that a school board is entitled to a rather precise statement of its obligations under a desegregation decree. If such a decree is to be terminated or dissolved, respondents as well as the school board are entitled to a like statement from the court.

III

The Court of Appeals relied upon language from this Court's decision in *United States v. Swift and Co., supra*, for the proposition that a desegregation decree could not be lifted or modified absent a showing of "grievous wrong evoked by new and unforeseen conditions." *Id.*, at 119. It also held that "compliance alone cannot become the basis for modifying or dissolving an injunction," 890 F.2d, at 1491, relying on *United States v. W. T. Grant Co.*, 345 U.S. 629, 633 (1953). We hold that its reliance was mistaken.

* * *

United States v. United Shoe Machinery Corp., 391 U.S. 244 (1968), explained that the language used in *Swift* must be read in the context of the continuing danger of unlawful restraints on trade which the Court had found still existed. *Id.*, at 248. "*Swift* teaches . . . a decree may be changed upon an appropriate showing, and it holds that it may not be changed . . . if the purposes of the litigation as incorporated in the decree . . . have not been fully achieved." *Ibid.* (emphasis is deleted). In the present case, a finding by the District Court that the Oklahoma City School District was being operated in compliance with the commands of the Equal Protection Clause of the Fourteenth Amendment, and that it was unlikely that the school board would return to its former ways, would be a finding that the purposes of the desegregation litigation had been fully achieved. No additional showing of "grievous wrong evoked by new and unforeseen conditions" is required of the school board.

In *Milliken v. Bradley (Milliken II)*, 433 U.S. 267 (1977), we said:

> [F]ederal-court decrees must directly address and relate to the constitutional violation itself. Because of this inherent limitation upon federal judicial authority, federal-court decrees exceed appropriate limits if they are aimed at eliminating a condition that does not violate the Constitution or does not flow from such a violation. . . .

Id., at 282.

From the very first, federal supervision of local school systems was intended as a temporary measure to remedy past discrimination. *Brown* considered the "complexities arising from the *transition* to a system of public education freed of racial discrimination" in holding that the implementation of desegregation was to proceed "with all deliberate speed." 349 U.S., at 299–301 (emphasis added). *Green* also spoke of the "*transition* to a unitary, nonracial system of public education." 391 U.S., at 436 (emphasis added).

Considerations based on the allocation of powers within our federal system, we think, support our view that quoted language from *Swift* does not provide the proper standard to apply to injunctions entered in school desegregation cases. Such decrees, unlike the one in *Swift*, are not intended to operate in perpetuity. Local control over the education of children allows citizens to participate in decision-making, and allows innovation so that school programs can fit local needs. *Milliken v. Bradley (Milliken I)*, 418 U.S. 717, 742 (1974); *San Antonio Independent School District v. Rodriguez*, 411 U.S. 1, 50 (1973). The legal justification for displacement of local authority by an injunctive decree in a school desegregation case is a violation of the constitution by the local authorities. Dissolving a desegregation decree after the local authorities have operated in compliance with it for a reasonable period of time properly recognizes that "necessary concern for the important values of local control of public school systems dictates that a federal court's regulatory control of such systems not extend beyond the time required to remedy the effects of past intentional discrimination. *See Milliken v. Bradley [Milliken II]*, 433 U.S. at 280–82." *Spangler v. Pasadena City Bd. of Education*, 611 F.2d, at 1245, n. 5 (Kennedy, J., concurring).

* * *

A district court need not accept at face value the profession of a school board which has intentionally discriminated that it will cease to do so in the future. But in deciding whether to modify or dissolve a desegregation decree, a school board's compliance with previous court orders is obviously relevant. In this case the original finding of *de jure* segregation was entered in 1961, the injunctive decree from which the Board seeks relief was entered in 1972, and the Board complied with the decree in good faith until 1985. Not only do the personnel of school boards change over time, but the same passage of time enables the District Court to observe the good faith of the school board in complying with the decree. The test espoused by the Court of Appeals would condemn a school district, once governed by a board which intentionally discriminated, to judicial tutelage for the indefinite future. Neither the principles governing the entry and dissolution of injunctive decrees, nor the commands of the Equal Protection Clause of the Fourteenth Amendment, require any such Draconian result.

Petitioners urge that we reinstate the decision of the District Court terminating the injunction, but we think that the preferable course is to remand the case to that court so that it may decide, in accordance with this opinion, whether the Board made a sufficient showing of constitutional compliance as of 1985, when the SRP was adopted, to allow the injunction to be dissolved. The District Court should address itself to whether the Board had complied in good faith with the desegregation decree since it was entered, and whether the vestiges of past discrimination had been eliminated to the extent practicable.

In considering whether the vestiges of *de jure* segregation had been eliminated as far as practicable, the District Court should look not only at student assignments, but "to every facet of school operations—faculty, staff, transportation, extra-curricular activities and facilities." *Green*, 391 U.S., at 435. *See also*, *Swann*, 402 U.S., at 18 ("Existing policy and practice with regard to faculty, staff, transportation, extra-curricular activities, and facilities" are "among the most important indicia of a segregated system").

After the District Court decides whether the Board was entitled to have the decree terminated, it should proceed to decide respondent's challenge to the SRP. A school district which has been released from an injunction imposing a desegregation plan no longer requires court authorization for the promulgation of policies and rules regulating matters such as assignment of students and the like, but it of course remains subject to the mandate of the Equal Protection Clause of the Fourteenth Amendment. If the Board was entitled to have the decree terminated as of 1985, the District Court should then evaluate the Board's decision to implement the SRP under appropriate equal protection principles. *See Washington v. Davis*, 426 U.S. 229 (1976); *Arlington Heights v. Metropolitan Housing Development Corp.*, 429 U.S. 252 (1977).

The judgment of the Court of Appeals is reversed, and the case is remanded to the District Court for further proceedings consistent with this opinion.

It is so ordered.

Justice Souter took no part in the consideration or decision of this case.

Justice Marshall, with whom Justice Blackmun and Justice Stevens join, dissenting.

Oklahoma gained statehood in 1907. For the next 65 years, the Oklahoma City School Board maintained segregated schools—initially relying on laws requiring dual school systems; thereafter, by exploiting residential segregation that had been created by legally enforced restrictive covenants. In 1972—18 years after this Court first found segregated schools unconstitutional—a federal court finally interrupted this cycle, enjoining the Oklahoma City School Board to implement a specific plan for achieving actual desegregation of its schools.

The practical question now before us is whether, 13 years after that injunction was imposed, the same School Board should have been allowed to return many of its elementary schools to their former one-race status. The majority today suggests that 13 years of desegregation was enough. The court remands the case for further evaluation of whether the purposes of the injunctive decree were achieved sufficient to justify the decree's dissolution. However, the inquiry it commends to the District Court fails to recognize explicitly the threatened reemergence of one-race schools as a relevant "vestige" of de jure segregation.

In my view, the standard for dissolution of a school desegregation decree must reflect the central aim of our school desegregation precedents. In *Brown v. Board of Education*, 347 U.S. 483 (1954) (*Brown I*), a unanimous Court declared that racially "separate educational facilities are inherently unequal." *Id.*, at 495. This holding rested on the Court's recognition that state-sponsored segregation conveys a message of "inferiority as to the status [of Afro-American school children] in the community that may affect their hearts and minds in a way unlikely ever to be undone." *Id.*, at 494. Remedying this evil and preventing its recurrence were the motivations animating our requirement that formerly de jure segregated school districts take all feasible steps to eliminate racially identifiable schools. *See Green v. New Kent County School Bd.*, 391 U.S. 430, 442 (1968); *Swann v. Charlotte-Mecklenburg Bd. of Education*, 402 U.S. 1, 25–26 (1971).

I believe a desegregation decree cannot be lifted so long as conditions likely to inflict the stigmatic injury condemned in *Brown I* persist and there remain feasible methods of eliminating such conditions. Because the record here shows, and the Court of Appeals found, that feasible steps could be taken to avoid one-race schools, it is clear that the purposes of the decree have not yet been achieved and the Court of Appeals' reinstatement of the decree should be affirmed. I therefore dissent.

I

In order to assess the full consequence of lifting the decree at issue in this case, it is necessary to explore more fully than does the majority the history of racial segregation in the Oklahoma City schools. This history reveals nearly unflagging resistance by the Board to judicial efforts to dismantle the City's dual education system.

* * *

. . . [B]y 1972, 11 years after the plaintiffs had filed suit and 18 years after our decision in *Brown I*, the School Board continued to resist integration and in some respects the Board had worsened the situation. Four years after this Court's admonition to formerly *de jure* segregated school districts to come forward with realistic plans for *immediate* relief, *see Green v. New Kent County School Bd.*, 391 U.S. 430, 439 (1968), the Board still had offered no meaningful plan of its own. Instead, "[i]t rationalize[d] its intransigence on the constitutionally unsound basis that public opinion [was] opposed to any further desegregation." *Dowell v. Board of Education of Oklahoma City Public Schools*, 338 F.Supp. 1256, 1270 (WD Okla.), *aff'd*, 465 F.2d 1012 (CA10), *cert. denied*, 409 U.S. 1041 (1972). The District Court concluded: "This litigation has been frustratingly interminable, not because of insuperable difficulties of implementation of the commands of the Supreme Court . . . and the Constitution . . . but because of the unpardonable recalcitrance of the . . . Board." 338 F.Supp., at 1271. Consequently, the District Court ordered the Board to implement the only available plan that exhibited the promise of achieving actual desegregation— the "Finger Plan" offered by the plaintiffs. *Id.*, at 1269.

In 1975, after a mere three years of operating under the Finger Plan, the Board filed a "Motion to Close Case," arguing that it had " 'eliminated all vestiges of state imposed racial discrimination in its school system.' " *Dowell v. Board of Education of Oklahoma City Public Schools*, 606 F.Supp. 1548, 1551 (WD Okla. 1985) (quoting motion), *rev'd*, 795 F.2d 1516 (CA10), *cert. denied*, 479 U.S. 938 (1986). In 1977, the District Court granted the Board's motion and issued an "Order Terminating Case." The court concluded that the Board had "operated the [Finger] Plan properly" and stated that it did not "foresee that the termination of . . . jurisdiction will result in the dismantlement of the [Finger] Plan or any affirmative action by the defendant to undermine the unitary system." App. 174–175. The order ended the District Court's active supervision of the school district but did not dissolve the injunctive decree. The plaintiffs did not appeal this order.

The Board continued to operate under the Finger Plan until 1985, when it implemented the Student Reassignment Plan (SRP). The SRP superimposed attendance zones over some residentially segregated areas. As a result, considerable racial imbalance reemerged in 33 of 64 elementary schools in the Oklahoma City system with student bodies either greater than 90 percent Afro-American or greater than 90 percent non-Afro-American. *Dowell*, 606 F.Supp., at 1553. More specifically, 11 of the schools ranged from 96.9 percent to 99.7 percent Afro-American, and approximately 44 percent of all-Afro-American children in grades K–4 were assigned to these virtually all-Afro-American schools. *See* 890 F.2d 1483, 1510, n. 4. (CA10 1989) (Baldock, J., dissenting). . . .

In response to the SRP, the plaintiffs moved to reopen the case. Ultimately, the District Court dissolved the desegregation decree, finding that the school district had been "unitary" since 1977 and that the racial imbalances under the SRP were the consequence of residential segregation arising from "personal preferences." 677 F.Supp., at 1512. . . .

II

I agree with the majority that the proper standard for determining whether a school desegregation decree should be dissolved is whether the purposes of the desegregation litigation, as incorporated in the decree, have been fully achieved. . . . I strongly disagree with the majority, however, on what must be shown to demonstrate that a decree's purposes have been fully realized. In my view, a standard for dissolution of a desegregation decree must take into account the unique harm associated with a system of racially identifiable schools and must expressly demand the elimination of such schools.

A

Our pointed focus in *Brown I* upon the stigmatic injury caused by segregated schools explains our unflagging insistence that formerly *de jure* segregated school districts extinguish all vestiges of school segregation. The concept of stigma also gives us guidance as to what conditions must be eliminated before a decree can be deemed to have served its purpose.

* * *

Concern with stigmatic injury also explains the Court's requirement that a formerly *de jure* segregated school district provide its victims with "make whole" relief. In *Milliken v. Bradley*, 418 U.S. 717 (1974) *(Milliken I)*, the court concluded that a school desegregation decree must "restore the victims of discriminatory conduct to the position they would have occupied in the absence of such conduct." *Id.*, at 746. In order to achieve such "make whole" relief, school systems must redress any *effects* traceable to former *de jure* segregation. See *Milliken v. Bradley*, 433 U.S. 267, 281–288 (1977) *(Milliken II)* (upholding remedial education programs and other measures to redress the substandard communication skills of Afro-American students formerly placed in segregated schools). The remedial education upheld in *Milliken II* was needed to help prevent the stamp of inferiority placed upon Afro-American children from becoming a self-perpetuating phenomenon. *See id.*, at 287.

Similarly, avoiding reemergence of the harm condemned in *Brown I* accounts for the Court's insistence on remedies that insure lasting integration of formerly segregated systems. . . . This focus on "achieving and *preserving* an integrated school system," *Keyes v. School Dist. No. 1, Denver, Colo.*, 413 U.S. 189, 251, n. 31 (1973) (Powell, J., concurring in part and dissenting in part) (emphasis added), stems from the recognition that the reemergence of racial separation in such schools may revive the message of racial inferiority implicit in the former policy of state-enforced segregation.

Just as it is central to the standard for evaluating the formation of a desegregation decree, so should the stigmatic injury associated with segregated schools be central to the standard for dissolving a decree. The Court has indicated that "the ultimate end to be brought about" by a desegregation remedy is "a unitary, nonracial system of public education." *Green, supra*, at 436. We have suggested that this aim is realized once school officials have "eliminate[d] from the public schools *all* vestiges of state-imposed segregation," *Swann, supra*, at 15 (emphasis added), whether they inhere in the school's "faculty, staff, transportation, extracurricular activities and facilities," *Green, supra*, at 435, or even in "the community and administration['s] attitudes toward [a] school," *Keyes, supra*, at 196. Although the Court has never explicitly defined what constitutes a "vestige" of state-enforced segregation, the function that this concept has performed in our jurisprudence suggests that it extends to any condition that is likely to convey the message of inferiority implicit in a policy of segregation. So long as such conditions persist, the purposes of the decree cannot be deemed to have been achieved.

B

* * *

By focusing heavily on present and future compliance with the Equal Protection Clause, the majority's standard ignores how the stigmatic harm identified in *Brown I* can persist even after the State ceases actively to enforce segregation. . . . In sum, our school-desegregation jurisprudence establishes that the *effects* of past discrimination remain chargeable to the school district regardless of its lack of continued enforcement of segregation, and the remedial decree is required until those effects have been finally eliminated.

III

Applying the standard I have outlined, I would affirm the Court of Appeals' decision ordering the District Court to restore the desegregation decree. For it is clear on this record that removal of the decree will result in a significant number of racially identifiable schools that could be eliminated.

. . . Against the background of former state-sponsorship of one-race schools, the persistence of racially identifiable schools perpetuates the message of racial inferiority associated with segregation. Therefore, such schools must be eliminated whenever feasible.

* * *

The majority equivocates on the effect to be given to the reemergence of racially identifiable schools.

It instructs the District Court to consider whether those " 'most important indicia of a segregated system' " have been eliminated, reciting the facets of segregated school operations identified in *Green*— " 'faculty, staff, transportation, extra-curricular activities and facilities.' " . . . And, by rendering "*res nova*" the issue whether *residential* segregation in Oklahoma City is a vestige of former *school* segregation, . . . the majority accepts at least as a theoretical possibility that vestiges may exist beyond those identified in *Green*. Nonetheless, the majority hints that the District Court could ignore the effect of residential segregation in perpetuating racially identifiable schools if the court finds residential segregation to be "the result of private decisionmaking and economics." . . .

This equivocation is completely unsatisfying. First, it is well established that school segregation "may have a profound reciprocal effect on the racial composition of residential neighborhoods." *Keyes*, 413 U.S., at 202; *see also Columbus Bd. of Education*, 443 U.S., at 465, n. 13 (acknowledging the evidence "that school segregation is a contributing cause of housing segregation"). The record in this case amply demonstrates this form of complicity in residential segregation on the part of the Board. The District Court found as early as 1965 that the Board's use of neighborhood schools "served to . . . extend areas of all Negro housing, destroying in the process already integrated neighborhoods and thereby increasing the number of segregated schools." 244 F.Supp., at 977. It was because of the School Board's responsibility for residential segregation that the District Court refused to permit the Board to superimpose a neighborhood plan over the racially isolated northeast quadrant. *See id.*, at 976–977.

Second, there is no basis for the majority's apparent suggestion that the result should be different if residential segregation is now perpetuated by "private decisionmaking." The District Court's conclusion that the racial identity of the northeast quadrant now subsists because of "personal preferences," 677 F.Supp., at 1512, pays insufficient attention to the roles of the State, local officials, and the Board in creating what are now self-perpetuating patterns of residential segregation. Even more important, it fails to account for the *unique* role of the School Board in creating "all-Negro" schools clouded by the stigma of segregation—schools to which white parents would not opt to send their children. That such negative "personal preferences" exist should not absolve a school district that played a role in creating such "preferences" from its obligation to desegregate the schools to the maximum extent possible.

I also reject the majority's suggestion that the length of federal judicial supervision is a valid factor in assessing a dissolution. The majority is correct that the Court has never contemplated perpetual judicial oversight of former *de jure* segregated school districts. Our jurisprudence requires, however, that the job of school desegregation be fully completed and maintained so that the stigmatic harm identified in *Brown I* will not recur upon lifting the decree. Any doubt on the issue whether the School Board has fulfilled its remedial obligations should be resolved in favor of the Afro-American children affected by this litigation.

* * *

We should keep in mind that the court's active supervision of the desegregation process ceased in 1977. Retaining the decree does not require a return to active supervision. It may be that a modification of the decree which will improve its effectiveness and give the school district more flexibility in minimizing busing is appropriate in this case. But retaining the decree seems a slight burden on the school district compared with the risk of not delivering a full remedy to the Afro-American children in the school system.

IV

Consistent with the mandate of *Brown I*, our cases have imposed on school districts an unconditional duty to eliminate *any* condition that perpetuates the message of racial inferiority inherent in the policy of state-sponsored segregation. The racial identifiability of a district's schools is such a condition. Whether this "vestige" of state-sponsored segregation will persist cannot simply be ignored at the point where a district court is contemplating the dissolution of a desegregation decree. In a district with a history of state-sponsored school segregation, racial separation, in my view, *remains* inherently unequal.

I dissent.

NOTES AND QUESTIONS

1. When Does the District Court's Jurisdiction Cease?

After *Dowell*, does the determination of unitariness by a district court mean that its jurisdiction thereby ceases? Does the *Dowell* majority indicate what the standard by which unitariness is to be determined should be? To what extent is the lapse of a number of years during which the school board has complied with a school desegregation decree sufficient to permit the court to end its jurisdiction? What is a "reasonable period of time" for the school board to have acted in compliance with a desegregation decree?

Has the *Dowell* Court provided adequate guidelines to enable district courts to determine whether the vestiges of past discrimination have been eliminated "to the extent practicable"? May the school board return to a neighborhood school assignment plan once it shows that it has complied with the decree for a period of years *and* has completely eliminated segregation in its *schools*, even though the schools will resegregate because of segregated housing patterns? Or does the Supreme Court decision require that district courts first determine whether segregated housing patterns are themselves "vestiges" of de jure school segregation? If the latter, how does a district court determine whether, and how much, of the housing segregation is the result of past school desegregation rather than the result of "private decision making and economics"?

2. The Burden of Proof

In challenging subsequent school board actions that may lead to resegregation, must the plaintiff prove discriminatory intent or is a showing of segregative effects sufficient? The circuits are also split on this issue. The Tenth Circuit concluded that a school board that has established unitariness but that has not convinced the district court to dissolve an injunction "bears a 'heavy burden' to show that its implementation of [new programs] does not 'serve to perpetuate or re-establish the dual school system.' " *Dowell*, 890 F.2d at 1493 (quoting *Dayton Board of Education v. Brinkman*, 443 U.S. 526, 538, 99 S.Ct. 2971, 2979, 61 L.Ed.2d 720 (1979)). Those challenging board actions may bear an initial burden to show that the original decree has been violated, but the burden then shifts "to defendants to produce evidence of changed circumstances or oppressive hardship." *Id.* The Fourth Circuit, however, concluded that a finding of unitariness not only requires the termination of jurisdiction but also shifts the burden to plaintiffs to prove that later actions by the board are motivated by discriminatory intent. *Riddick*, 784 F.2d at 534. Similarly, the Fifth Circuit reasoned that a finding of unitariness means that only intentional discrimination constitutes a new constitutional violation and that a challenged school board should no longer bear the "burden of proving that its decisions are free of segregative purpose." *Overton*, 834 F.2d at 1171.

Where does the Supreme Court decision leave the burden of proof? The dissenting opinion in *Dowell* notes that:

> The majority does not discuss the burden of proof under its test for dissolution of a school desegregation decree. However, every presumption we have established in our school desegregation cases has been against the school district found to have engaged in *de jure* segregation. *See Dayton Bd. of Education v. Brinkman*, 443 U.S. 526, 537 (1979) (conduct resulting in increased segregation was presumed to be caused by past intentional discrimination where dual system was never affirmatively remedied); *Keyes v. School Dist. No. 1, Denver, Colo.*, 413 U.S. 189, 208 (1973) (proof of state-imposed segregation in a substantial portion of a school district will support a prima facie finding of a system-wide violation, thereby shifting the burden to school authorities to show that current segregation is not caused by past intentional discrimination); *Swann v. Charlotte-Mecklenburg Bd. of Education*, 402 U.S. 1, 26 (1971) (establishing a presumption against racially identifiable schools once past state discrimination has been shown, thereby shifting the burden to the school district to show that current segregation was not caused by past intentional discrimination). Moreover, in addition to the "affirmative duty" placed upon school districts to eliminate vestiges of their past discrimination, *Green*, 391 U.S., at 437–438, school districts initially have the burden of coming forward with desegregation plans and establishing that such plans promise to be effective. *Id.*, at 439. And, while operating under a decree, a school board has a "heavy burden" to justify use of less effective or resegregative methods. *Ibid. Accord, Dayton, supra*, at 538; *Wright*

> *v. Council of City of Emporia*, 407 U.S. 451, 467 (1972).
>
> Given the original obligation placed on formerly *de jure* segregated school districts to provide an effective remedy that will eliminate all vestiges of its segregated past, a school district seeking dissolution of an injunctive decree should also bear the burden of proving that this obligation has been fulfilled. *Cf. Keyes, supra*, at 211, n. 17 (noting that the plaintiffs should not bear the burden of proving "non-attenuation").

Dowell, —U.S. at —, 111 S.Ct. at 647, n. 10.

Does a finding of unitariness necessarily mean that all discriminatory intent has been eliminated? *See* Note, "Allocating the Burden of Proof After a Finding of Unitariness in School Desegregation Litigation," 100 *Harv.L.Rev.* 653, 667 (1987). Does the Tenth Circuit court's position in *Dowell, supra*, make it difficult for school districts recently declared unitary to respond to "white flight" without risking being found in violation of the old injunction? On the other hand, is the position taken by the *Riddick* and *Overton* courts likely to lead to the acceptance of "white flight" as a legitimate reason for allowing school boards to reduce busing? In *Riddick*, the school board adopted a "neighborhood school" assignment plan in place of the plan that had been adopted by the court in 1971 that used pairing and clustering and required busing across town. The plan had eliminated all of Norfolk's one-race schools. In 1975, the district court declared the Norfolk system unitary. The new plan led to 10 schools becoming all-black and 14 schools majority white. The school system argued the plan was necessary because white flight caused by busing meant that the Norfolk schools were faced with imminent resegregation. *See* Note, "The Unitary Finding and the Threat of School Resegregation: *Riddick v. School Board*," 65 *N.C.L. Rev.* 631, 637 (1987). Does this invite "widespread evasion of achievable desegregation" by a school board with a proven history of segregative intent? *See* Note, "Allocating the Burden of Proof After a Finding of Unitariness in School Desegregation Litigation," 100 *Harv.L.Rev.* 653, 664 (1987).

3. *The Current Status of Desegregation*

The vast majority of large urban school districts are now predominantly minority—whether due to white flight as a result of court-ordered desegregation, middle class flight due to crime or deteriorating municipal services, demographic changes, economic changes, segregative housing practices, or a combination of these or other reasons. Recent studies measuring changes in segregation between 1967–1986 in large urban districts show that for African Americans, the pattern of desegregation appears to be related to court orders, the initial racial composition of the district, and demographic changes. The study finds that African Americans enrolled in school systems with metropolitan-wide desegregation orders have remained very much more integrated since the court-ordered desegregation plans were imposed in the early 1970s than other school systems. Latinos in central cities, on the other hand, have become much more segregated since the 1960s. Finally, the study shows that Asians in urban school districts have become a significant and very rapidly growing part of the school population. The study found that whites who move out of large urban school districts are replaced not by blacks but by a mixture of blacks, Hispanics, and Asians, many of whom are isolated from each other. The study also noted that only 3.3 percent of white students now attend schools in central city school districts. G. Orfield and F. Monfort, *Racial Change and Desegregation In Large School Districts* (1988). *See also* F. Welch and A. Light, *New Evidence on School Desegregation* (1987). Another study confirms that the percentage of blacks nationwide attending all-black or majority black schools dropped from 64 percent in 1968 to 33.2 percent in 1980, with virtually no change since then. G. Orfield, F. Monfort, and M. Aaron, *Status of School Desegregation 1968–1986* (1989).

VII. SCHOOL DESEGREGATION: THE ROLE OF THE POLITICAL BRANCHES

A. Federal Legislation Prohibiting Discrimination on the Basis of Race

The passage of the Civil Rights Act of 1964, 42 U.S.C.A. § 2000c,d (1970), shifted the burden of litigation from minority litigants to the federal government. This legislation empowered the Department of Health, Education, and Welfare (now the Department of Education) to withhold federal funds from school districts that continued to discriminate against blacks and gave the Attorney General authority to file desegregation suits on the complaint of private citizens. 42 U.S.C.A. §§ 2000c-6, d-1 (1970). *See generally* Note, "The Courts, HEW, and Southern School Desegregation," 77 *Yale L.J.* 321,

356–64 (1967). Under the Civil Rights Act of 1964, HEW promulgated guidelines requiring school districts to make a good faith start toward desegregation. U.S. Office of Education, HEW, "General Statement of Policies under Title VI of the Civil Rights Act of 1964 Respecting Desegregation of Elementary and Secondary Schools (1965)," *reprinted in Price v. Denison Independent School District*, 348 F.2d 1010, 1015 (5th Cir. 1965). *See also* U.S. Office of Education, HEW, "Revised Statement of Policies for School Desegregation Plans under Title VI of the Civil Rights Act of 1964," 45 C.F.R. § 181 (1967).

Title IV

42 U.S.C. § 2000c (1970).

§ 2000c-6. Civil actions by the attorney general. . . .

(a) Whenever the attorney general receives a complaint in writing—

(1) signed by a parent or group of parents to the effect that his or their minor children, as members of a class of persons similarly situated, are being deprived by a school board of the equal protection of the laws, or

(2) signed by an individual, or his parent, to the effect that he has been denied admission to or not permitted to continue in attendance at a public college by reason of race, color, religion, or national origin, and the attorney general believes the complaint is meritorious and certifies that the signer or signers of such complaint are unable in his judgment, to initiate and maintain appropriate legal proceedings for relief and that the institution of an action will materially further the orderly achievement of desegregation in public education, the attorney general is authorized, after giving notice of such complaint to the appropriate school board or college authority and after certifying that he is satisfied that such board or authority has had a reasonable time to adjust the conditions alleged in such complaint, to institute for or in the name of the United States a civil action in any appropriate district court of the United States against such parties and for such relief as may be appropriate, and such court shall have and shall exercise jurisdiction of proceedings instituted pursuant to this section, provided that nothing herein shall empower any official or court of the United States to issue any order seeking to achieve a racial balance in any school by requiring the transportation of pupils or students from one school to another or one school district to another in order to achieve such racial balance, or otherwise enlarge the existing power of the court to insure compliance with constitutional standards. The attorney general may implead as defendants such additional parties as are or become necessary to the grant of effective relief hereunder. . . .

(b) The attorney general may deem a person or persons unable to initiate and maintain appropriate legal proceedings within the meaning of subsection (a) of this section when such person or persons are unable, either directly or through other interested persons or organizations, to bear the expense of the litigation or to obtain effective legal representation; or whenever he is satisfied that the institution of such litigation would jeopardize the personal safety, employment, or economic standing of such person or persons, their families, or their property. . . .

§ 2000c-8. Personal suits for relief against discrimination in public education

Nothing in this subchapter shall affect adversely the right of any person to sue for or obtain relief in any court against discrimination in public education.

Pub. L. 88–352, Title IV, § 409, July 2, 1964, 78 Stat. 249.

§ 2000c-9. Classification and assignment

Nothing in this subschapter shall prohibit classification and assignment for reasons other than race, color, religion, or national origin.

Pub. L. 88–352, Title IV, § 410, July 2, 1964, 78 Stat. 249.

Title VI

42 U.S.C. § 2000d (1970).

§ 2000d. Prohibition against exclusion from participation in, denial of benefits of, and discrimination under federally assisted programs on ground of race, color, or national origin.

No person in the United States shall, on the ground of race, color, or national origin, be excluded from participation in, be denied the benefits of, or be subjected to discrimination under any program or activity receiving federal financial assistance.

Pub. L. 88–352, Title VI, § 601, July 2, 1964, 78 Stat. 252.

§ 2000d-1. Federal authority and financial assistance to programs or activities by way of grant, loan, or contract other than contract of insurance or guaranty. . . rules and regulations; approval by president; compliance with requirements; reports to congressional committees; effective date of administrative action.

Each federal department and agency which is empowered to extend federal financial assistance to any program or activity, by way of grant, loan, or contract other than a contract of insurance or guaranty, is authorized and directed to effectuate the provisions of section 2000d of this title with respect to such program or activity by issuing rules, regulations, or orders of general applicability which shall be consistent with achievement of the objectives of the statute authorizing the financial assistance in connection with which the action is taken. No such rule, regulation, or order shall become effective unless and until approved by the president. Compliance with any requirement adopted pursuant to this section may be effected (1) by the termination of or refusal to grant or to continue assistance under such program or activity to any recipient as to whom there has been an express finding on the record, after opportunity for hearing, of a failure to comply with such requirement, but such termination or refusal shall be limited to the particular political entity, or part thereof, or other recipient as to whom such a finding has been made and, shall be limited in its effect to the particular program, or part thereof, in which such noncompliance has been so found, or (2) by any other means authorized by law: *Provided, however*, that no such action shall be taken until the department or agency concerned has advised the appropriate person or persons of the failure to comply with the requirement and has determined that compliance cannot be secured by voluntary means. In the case of any action terminating, or refusing to grant or continue, assistance because of failure to comply with a requirement imposed pursuant to this section, the head of the federal department or agency shall file with the committees of the House and Senate having legislative jurisdiction over the program or activity involved a full written report of the circumstances and the grounds for such action. No such action shall become effective until thirty days have elapsed after the filing of such report.

Pub. L. 88–352, Title VI, § 602, July 2, 1964, 78 Stat. 252.

* * *

§ 2000d-6. Policy of United States as to application of nondiscrimination provisions in schools of local educational agencies—Declaration of uniform policy [1972 Supp.].

(a) It is the policy of the United States that guidelines and criteria established pursuant to Title VI of the Civil Rights Act of 1964 and section 182 of the Elementary and Secondary Education Amendments of 1966 dealing with conditions of segregation by race, whether *de jure* or *de facto*, in the schools of the local educational agencies of any state shall be applied uniformly in all regions of the United States whatever the origin or cause of such segregation.

(b) Such uniformity refers to one policy applied uniformly to *de jure* segregation wherever found and such other policy as may be provided pursuant to law applied uniformly to *de facto* segregation wherever found.

(c) Nothing in this section shall be construed to diminish the obligation of responsible officials to enforce or comply with such guidelines and criteria in order to eliminate discrimination in federally assisted programs and activities as required by Title VI of the Civil Rights Act of 1964.

(d) It is the sense of the Congress that the Department of Justice and the Department of Health, Education, and Welfare should request such additional funds as may be necessary to apply the policy set forth in this section throughout the United States.

Pub. L. 91–230, § 2, April 13, 1970, 84 Stat. 121.

NOTES AND QUESTIONS

1. Section 2000c-6 of Title IV

a. Purpose and Significance. What is the purpose of § 2000c-6, which authorizes civil rights actions by the Attorney General? Is it to reduce the financial burdens imposed on individuals and civil rights groups, or is it to place the power and prestige of the federal government behind the desegregation movement? Is the Attorney General likely to be more successful than private litigants in particular litigations? If so, for what reasons—greater resources, greater judicial sympathy?

b. Relationship to Private Litigants. What role does § 2000c-6 envision for private litigants? *See also* § 2000c-8. Would it permit both private parties and the Attorney General to participate in the same litigation, even if the Attorney General and the private parties disagree on the theory of the suit or the appropriateness of a particular remedy? What difficulties might this pose for courts? Should the Attorney General be permitted to intervene in private suits? *See* 42 U.S.C. § 2000h-2 (1970).

c. Complaint Procedures. What is the difference between paragraphs (a)(1) and (a)(2) of § 2000c-6 with respect to complaint procedures? Does (a)(1) apply to all denials of equal protection, whether or not segregation is involved? If so, how does the complaint procedure embodied in this section differ from that in (a)(2), which explicitly applies to denials of admissions based on race? Under both sections, the Attorney General must determine whether a complaint is "meritorious" before he or she acts.

d. Enforcement of Brown. What impact might § 2000c-6 have on the course of desegregation in the South? If the issue is one of securing compliance with court decrees, overcoming the recalcitrance of federal district courts, and resolving the ambiguity of Supreme Court decisions, how would the addition of the United States as a party resolve any of these difficulties?

e. Racial Balance. How should the language in § 2000c-6, stating that "nothing herein shall empower any official or court . . . to issue any order seeking to achieve a racial balance in any school," be construed? *Compare United States v. Jefferson County Board of Education*, 372 F.2d 836 (5th Cir. 1966), *aff'd*, 380 F.2d 385 (1967) (*en banc*), *cert denied*, 389 U.S. 840, 88 S.Ct. 77, 19 L.Ed.2d 104, *with* L. Graglia, *Disaster by Decree* 46–52, 58–66 (1976). Would the limitation, if construed to prohibit racial balance remedies where de jure segregation had occurred, be constitutional? Would it be a limit only on the Department of Justice or would it also extend to private litigants in desegregation suits?

2. Section 2000d of Title VI

Does section 2000d restate the principle embodied in *Brown I* and *II*? What is the difference between discrimination and the denial of benefits? Why did Congress limit governmental review under this section to programs receiving federal assistance?

3. Section 2000d-1

a. Administration of § 2000d-1. The process of identifying a violation of § 2000d is left to existing federal agencies, but their regulations must be approved by the president. Why might Congress have adopted this approach?

b. Fund Cutoffs. Why did Congress limit the fund cutoff for noncompliance with §2000d "to the particular program, or part thereof, in which such noncompliance has been so found. . ."? *See Board of Public Instruction v. Finch*, 414 F.2d 1068 (5th Cir. 1969).

While funding cutoffs have been rare, the threat of such cutoffs has been thought to be the strongest weapon against local officials in the effort to desegregate public schools. *See generally*, G. Orfield, *The Reconstruction of Southern Education*, 252–58 (1969). *Compare* Badger and Browning, "Title I and Comparability: Recent Developments," 7 *Clearinghouse Rev.* 263 (1973); *Natonabah v. Board of Education*, 355 F.Supp. 716 (D.N.M. 1973). Would this be true in all districts? Suppose a district were composed largely of black students, most of whom qualified for assistance to disadvantaged children under Title I of the Elementary and Secondary Education Act, 20 U.S.C.A. § 241a-m (1970). Who would be the greater loser as a result of a fund cutoff? Does this particular weapon run the risk of dividing private litigants and the federal government, with the former opposing a fund cutoff and the latter advocating it?

c. Alternatives to Fund Cutoffs. In addition to allowing the administering agency to achieve compliance by terminating or refusing aid to recipients who refuse to comply with desegregation requirements, Title VI also empowers the agency to proceed "by any other means authorized by law." This represents an effort to provide an alternative to the severe step of denying federal aid. One such alternative, which would entail reliance on the courts, is suggested by the standard paragraph in the form all recipients must sign which states that the appropriate assurance of compliance "is given in consideration of and for the purpose of obtaining any and all federal grants, loans, contracts, property, discounts or other federal financial assistance. . . . The applicant recognizes and agrees that such federal financial assistance will be extended in reliance on the representations and agreements made in the assurance and that the United States or the state agency . . . jointly or severally shall have the right to seek enforcement of this assurance."

HEW included this wording with the specific intent of making assurances enforceable in a court action asking for specific performance. Does this approach seem preferable to cutoffs?

4. Enforcement of the Civil Rights Act

The primary responsibility for enforcing Title VI of the Civil Rights Act was given to the Office of Education within the Department of Health, Education, and Welfare. Historically, the United States Office of Education had been a powerless agency without any policymaking functions whose sole responsibility was to collect educational statistics and publish reports. The impotency of the Office of Education derived from traditional American adherence to localism in educational matters, the office's small staff, and its total dependence on local and state education officials. Orfield, *supra* at 9. Needless to say, the Office of Education, even under the able leadership of Francis Keppel, was not prepared for the monumental task that confronted it after the enactment of the Civil Rights Act of 1964. Vast institutional and staffing changes were required. Chaos in the early months of the "administrative-judicial era" was not uncommon, but despite these problems, substantial progress was made in desegregating southern schools. *See* Orfield, *id.* at 147–50. *See generally* B. Radin, *Implementation, Change, and the Federal Bureaucracy* (1977).

Subsequently, the Office for Civil Rights (OCR) was moved out of the Office of Education directly to the Office of the Secretary of HEW. OCR investigates complaints of discrimination filed by individuals and groups, and it conducts OCR-initiated compliance reviews of selected institutions triggered by its analysis of statistical reports. When school districts or universities are found to have violated Title VI, they are given an opportunity to achieve compliance voluntarily. If, after negotiations, voluntary compliance is not obtained, OCR initiates an administrative hearing or refers the matter to the Department of Justice for initiation of court proceedings. If OCR prevails in the administrative hearing, the Secretary of HEW may terminate federal funds. The termination order can then be appealed to the appropriate U.S. Circuit Court of Appeals.

Under the Department of Education Organization Act, Pub. L. No. 96–88, 93 Stat. 669 (1979), the position of OCR director has been elevated to the level of an assistant secretary, appointed by the president, with authority not previously accorded that position.

The current regulations state that school systems receiving federal funds may not:

> (i) Deny an individual any service, financial aid, or other benefit provided under the program;
>
> (ii) Provide any service, financial aid, or other benefit to an individual which is different, or is provided in a different manner, from that provided to others under the program;
>
> (iii) Subject an individual to segregation or separate treatment in any matter related to his receipt of any service, financial aid, or other benefit under the program;
>
> (iv) Restrict an individual in any way in the enjoyment of any advantage or privilege enjoyed by others receiving any service, financial aid, or other benefit under the program;
>
> (v) Treat an individual differently from others in determining whether he satisfies any admission, enrollment, quota, eligibility, membership or other requirement or condition which individuals must meet in order to be provided any service, financial aid, or other benefit provided under the program;
>
> (vi) Deny an individual an opportunity to participate in the program through the provision of services or otherwise or afford him an opportunity to do so which is different from that afforded others under the program (including the opportunity to participate in the program as an employee but only to the extent set forth in paragraph (c) of this section);
>
> (vii) Deny a person the opportunity to participate as a member of a planning or advisory body which is an integral part of the program.

The regulations further provide that:

> (2) A recipient, in determining the types of services, financial aid, or other benefits, or facilities which will be provided under any such program, or the class of individuals to whom, or the situations in which, such services, financial aid, other benefits, or facilities will be provided under any such program, or the class of individuals to be afforded an opportunity to participate in any such program, may not directly or through contractual or other arrangements, utilize criteria or methods of administration which have the effect of subjecting individuals to discrimination because of their race, color, or national origin, or have the effect of defeating or substantially impairing accomplishment of the objectives of the program as respect individuals of a particular race, color, or national origin.
>
> * * *
>
> (6)(ii) Even in the absence of such prior discrimination, a recipient in administering a program may take affirmative action to overcome the effects of conditions which resulted in limiting participation by persons of a particular race, color, or national origin.

34 C.F.R. § 80.3. This section also includes provisions that apply to faculty and staff.

5. Intent versus Effect Standard for Title VI

Title VI, 42 U.S.C.A. § 2000d, prohibits discrimination on the basis of race, color, or national origin in federally aided programs. The regulations implementing this requirement provide that: "A recipient

. . . may not . . . utilize criteria or methods of administration which have the *effect* of subjecting individuals to discrimination because of their race, color, or national origin. . . ." 34 C.F.R. § 80.3(2). (Emphasis added.)

In *Lau v. Nichols*, 414 U.S. 563, 94 S.Ct. 786, 39 L.Ed.2d 1 (1974) (discussed in chapter 7), the Supreme Court held that a school system's failure to provide English language instruction to Chinese-speaking students denied them a meaningful opportunity to participate in the educational program offered by the school district and thus was a violation of Title VI. The Court, specifically citing the HEW guidelines, declared that "[d]iscrimination is barred which has the *effect* even though no purposeful design is present." *Id.* at 568, 94 S.Ct. at 789. Subsequently, in *Regents of the University of California v. Bakke*, 438 U.S. 265, 98 S.Ct. 2733, 57 L.Ed.2d 750 (1978), five members of the Supreme Court took the position that the standard for a Title VI violation ought to be the same as the standard for an equal protection clause violation. Four of these five justices suggested that the *Lau* "effects-only" standard was in serious doubt. 438 U.S. at 352 (Brennan, White, Marshall, and Blackmun, J.J., concurring and dissenting). The four remaining justices refused to consider whether the statute and the Constitution required similar or different standards.

In *Guardians Association v. Civil Service Commission*, 463 U.S. 582, 103 S.Ct. 322, 77 L.Ed.2d 866 (1983), which also cast some doubt on *Lau v. Nichols*, the Supreme Court confronted the question of "whether the private plaintiffs in this case need to prove discriminatory intent to establish a violation of Title VI of the Civil Rights Act of 1964, 42 U.S.C. § 2000d, *et seq.*, and administrative implementing regulations promulgated thereunder." The case involved "a challenge by black and Hispanic police officers . . . to several written examinations administered by New York City between 1968 and 1970 that were used to make entry-level appointments to the city's police department . . . through October 1974." Appointments were made in the order of test scores, and plaintiff black and Hispanic officers were hired later than otherwise similarly situated whites. When police officers were laid off in 1975 in accordance with a "last-hired, first-fired," policy, the result was that minority officers were disproportionately affected by the layoffs.

The Court split badly in the case, with the judgment of the Court announced by Justice White in an opinion joined only by Justice Rehnquist (except for Part II). Five justices (White and dissenters Stevens, Brennan, Blackmun, and Marshall) held that the "Court of Appeals erred in requiring proof of discriminatory intent," though they reached this conclusion by a variety of routes. "A different majority, however, would not allow compensatory relief in the absence of proof of discriminatory intent." Two justices would never grant private relief under Title VI and one justice would deny *all* relief unless discriminatory intent were proven.

6. "Under Any Program or Activity"

Title VI, Section 2000d, provides that no person may "be excluded from participation in, be denied the benefits of, or be subjected to discrimination under *any program or activity* receiving federal financial assistance." (Emphasis added.) Section 2000d-1 provides that compliance with any of the regulations implementing Title VI may be affected by a cutoff of funds "under such program or activity . . . but . . . shall be limited in its effect to the particular program or part thereof, in which such noncompliance has been so found." What might "program or activity" mean? Should the Department of Education and the courts interpret the language broadly or narrowly? Up until 1984, the Department construed Title VI and Title IX, which parallels Title VI in the area of sex discrimination, broadly. Thus, for example, the Department and courts had considered athletics sponsored by educational institutions to be an integral part of the educational program or activity provided by the institution and therefore covered by Title VI and Title IX, if the school system received federal assistance under various federal programs, even though athletics received no direct federal funds. In 1984, however, in a case involving Title IX, the Supreme Court construed "program or activity" narrowly. In *Grove City College v. Bell*, 465 U.S. 555, 104 S.Ct. 1211, 79 L.Ed.2d 516 (1984), Justice White, writing for the majority, determined that Grove City College, which accepted no direct federal assistance but enrolled students who received Federal Basic Educational Opportunity Grants (BEOGs), is subject to Title IX of the Educational Amendments, and having so determined, found it necessary to identify the "education program or activity" at the college that was "receiving federal financial assistance." The majority concluded as follows:

> An analysis of Title IX's language and legislative history led us to conclude . . . that "an agency's authority under Title IX both to promulgate regulations

and to terminate funds is subject to the program-specific limitations of §§ 901 and 902." Although the legislative history contains isolated suggestions that entire institutions are subject to the nondiscrimination provision whenever one of their programs receives federal assistance, we cannot accept the Court of Appeals' conclusion that in the circumstances present here Grove City itself is a "program or activity" that may be regulated in its entirety. . . .

To the extent that the Court of Appeals' holding that BEOG's received by Grove City's students constitute aid to the entire institution rests on the possibility that federal funds received by one program or activity free up the College's own resources for use elsewhere, the Court of Appeals' reasoning is doubly flawed. First, there is no evidence that the federal aid received by Grove City's students results in the diversion of funds from the College's own financial aid program to other areas within the institution. Second, and more important, the Court of Appeals' assumption that Title IX applies to programs receiving a larger share of a school's own limited resources as a result of federal assistance earmarked for use elsewhere within the institution is inconsistent with the program-specific nature of the statute. Most federal educational assistance has economic ripple effects throughout the aided institution, and it would be difficult, if not impossible, to determine which programs or activities derive such indirect benefits. Under the Court of Appeals' theory, an entire school would be subject to Title IX merely because one of its students received a small BEOG or because one of its departments received an earmarked federal grant. This result cannot be squared with Congress' intent.

The Court of Appeals' analogy between student financial aid received by an educational institution and nonearmarked direct grants provides a more plausible justification for its holding, but it too is faulty. Student financial aid programs, we believe, are *sui generis*. In neither purpose nor effect can BEOG's be fairly characterized as unrestricted grants that institutions may use for whatever purpose they desire. The BEOG program was designed, not merely to increase the total resources available to educational institutions, but to enable them to offer their services to students who had previously been unable to afford higher education. It is true, of course, that substantial portions of the BEOGs received by Grove City's students ultimately find their way into the College's general operating budget and are used to provide a variety of services to the students through whom the funds pass. However, we have found no persuasive evidence suggesting that Congress intended that the Department's regulatory authority follow federally aided students from classroom to classroom, building to building, or activity to activity.

* * *

We conclude that the receipt of BEOG's by some of Grove City's students does not trigger institutionwide coverage under Title IX. In purpose and effect, BEOGs represent federal financial assistance to the College's own financial aid program, and it is that program that may properly be regulated under Title IX.

* * *

Dissenting from this part of the opinion, Justice Brennan, writing for himself and Justice Marshall, looked to the history of Title VI to argue that the majority's narrow definition of "program or activity" was incorrect.

. . . [T]he Court completely disregards the broad remedial purposes of Title IX that consistently have controlled our prior interpretations of this civil rights statute. Moreover, a careful examination of the statute's legislative history, the accepted meaning of similar statutory language in Title VI, and the post-enactment history of Title IX will demonstrate that the Court's narrow definition of "program or activity" is directly contrary to congressional intent.

"Title IX was patterned after Title VI of the Civil rights Act of 1964." *Cannon*, 441 U.S., at 694, 99 S.Ct., at 1956. Except for the substitution of the word "sex" in Title IX to replace the words "race, color, or national origin" in Title VI, and for the limitation of Title IX to "education" programs or activities, the two statutes use identical language to describe their scope. The interpretation of this critical language as it already existed under Title VI is therefore crucial to an understanding of congressional intent in 1972 when Title IX was enacted using the same language.

The voluminous legislative history of Title VI is not easy to comprehend, especially when one considers the emotionally and politically charged atmosphere operating at the time of its enactment. . . . For every instance in which a legislator equated the word "program" with a particular grant statute, there is an example of a legislator defining "program or activity" more broadly.

. . . [B]y including the programatic language in Title VI, Congress sought to allay fears on the part of many legislators that one isolated violation of the statute's antidiscrimination provisions would result in the wholesale termination of federal funds. In particular, "Congress was primarily concerned with two facets of the termination power: the possibility that noncompliance in a single school district might lead to termination of funds to the entire state; and the possibility that discrimination in the education program might result in the termination of federal assistance to unrelated federally financed programs, such as highways." . . .

But even accepting that there is some uncertainty concerning the 1964 understanding of "program or activity," . . . there were two principal indicators of the accepted interpretation of the program-specific language in Title VI that were available to Members of Congress in 1972 when Title IX was enacted—the existing administrative regulations promulgated under Title VI, and the available judicial decisions that had already interpreted those provisions.

The Title VI regulations first issued by the Department of Health, Education, and Welfare during the 1960s, and remaining in effect during 1972, could not have been clearer in the way they applied to educational institutions. *See generally* 45 C.F.R. pt. 80 (1972). For example, § 80.4(d) explained the assurances required from, among others, institutions of higher education that received federal financial assistance:

> (d) *Assurances from institutions.*
>
> (1) In the case of any application for Federal financial assistance to an institution of higher education (including assistance for construction, for research, for a special training project, for a student loan program, or for any other purpose), the assurance required by this section shall extend to admission practices *and to all other practices relating to the treatment of students.*
>
> (2) The assurance required with respect to an institution of higher education, . . . insofar as the assurance relates to the institution's practices with respect to admission or other treatment of individuals as students, . . . or to the opportunity to participate in the provision of services or other benefits to such individuals, *shall be applicable to the entire institution unless the applicant establishes, to the satisfaction of the responsible Department official, that the institution's practices in designated parts or programs of the institution will in no way affect its practices in the program of the institution for which Federal financial assistance is sought, or the beneficiaries of or participants in such program.* . . .

Nor were there any outstanding court decisions in 1972 that would have led Congress to believe that Title VI was much narrower in scope. . . .

. . . [I]n *Board of Public Instruction v. Finch,* 414 F.2d 1068 (CA5 1969), the court spoke more directly to the program-specific limitation in Title VI. Although the court refused "to assume . . . that defects in one part of a school system automatically infect the whole," . . . and rejected the definition of the term "program" offered by the Department, . . . the court also noted that "the purpose of the Title VI cutoff is best effectuated by separate consideration of the use or intended use of federal funds under each grant statute." . . . In particular, although "there will . . . be cases from time to time where a particular program, within a state, within a county, within a district, even within a school . . ., is effectively insulated from otherwise unlawful activities," termination of federal funds is proper if "they are administered in a discriminatory manner, or if they support a program which is infected by a discriminatory environment." . . . To this end, the court remanded the case to the Department for specific findings on the relationship, if any, between the three types of federal grants received by the school system (federal aid for the education of children from low-income families, for supplementary education centers, and for adult education) and the system's discriminatory practices.

In short, the judicial interpretations of Title VI existing in 1972 were either in agreement with the expansive reach of the Department's regulations, . . . or sanctioned a broad-based termination of federal aid if the funded programs were affected by discriminatory practices. . . .

If any doubt remains about the congressional intent underlying the program-specific language included in Title IX, it is removed by the unique postenactment history of the statute. . . .

Regulations promulgated by the Department to implement Title IX, . . . included an interpretation of program specificity consistent with the view of Title VI and with the congressional intent behind Title IX outlined above. . . . Introductory remarks explained the basis for the agency's decision:

> [T]itle IX will be consistent with the interpretation of similar language contained in Title VI of the Civil Rights Act of 1964. . . . Therefore, an education program or activity or part thereof operated by a recipient of Federal financial assistance administered by the Department will be subject to the requirements of this regulation if it receives or benefits from such assistance. This interpretation is consistent with the only case specifically ruling on the language contained in Title VI, which holds that Federal funds may be terminated under Title VI upon a finding that they "[are] infected by a discriminatory environment."

40 Fed.Reg., at 24128 (quoting *Finch,* 414 F.2d, at 1078–79).

Thus, the agency charged with the statute's implementation initially interpreted the program-specific language of Title IX in a manner consistent with the view of Congress' intent outlined above—to allow for application of the statute to an entire institution if the institution is comprised of education programs or activities that receive or benefit from federal moneys.

* * *

Under the Court's holding, . . . Grove City College is prohibited from discriminating on the basis of sex in its own "financial aid program," but is free to discriminate in other "programs or activities" operated by the institution. . . .

The absurdity of the Court's decision is further demonstrated by examining its practical effect. According to the Court, the "financial aid program" at Grove City College may not discriminate on the basis of sex because it is covered by Title IX, but the College is not prohibited from discriminating in its admissions, its athletic programs, or even its various academic departments. The Court thus sanctions practices that Congress clearly could not have intended: for example, after today's decision, Grove City College would be free to segregate male and female students in classes run by its mathematics department. This would be so even though the affected students are attending the College with the financial assistance provided by federal funds. If anything about Title IX were ever certain, it is that discriminatory practices like the one just described were meant to be prohibited by the statute.

* * *

465 U.S. at 582–602, 104 S.Ct. at 1225–36.

What is the likely effect of *Grove City College* on the application of Title VI to a school district which discriminates in its athletics program by having separate African American and white teams and which receives no federal funds, although the school system as a whole receives federal assistance under various federal statutes? Could the Office for Civil Rights proceed against a school district's ability-grouping system that was found to discriminate against African American students if the district receives federal funds for the handicapped under the Education for All Handicapped Children Act, funds for the disadvantaged under Chapter One of the Elementary and Secondary Education Act, and Vocational Education Act funds?

Following pronouncements by the Reagan administration that Title VI would be interpreted in the same way as Title IX had been in the *Grove City* decision, a bipartisan coalition brought about the adoption of the Civil Rights Restoration Act which defines "program or activity" to mean "a college, university" or "a local educational agency," "any part of which is extended federal financial assistance."

SEC. 2. The Congress finds that—

(1) certain aspects of recent decisions and opinions of the Supreme Court have unduly narrowed or cast doubt upon the broad application of Title IX of the Education Amendments of 1972, section 504 of the Rehabilitation Act of 1973, the Age Discrimination Act of 1975, and Title VI of the Civil Rights Act of 1964; and

(2) legislative action is necessary to restore the prior consistent and long-standing executive branch interpretation and broad, institution-wide application of those laws as previously administered.

SEC. 6. Title VI of the Civil Rights Act of 1964 is amended by adding at the end the following new section:

"SEC. 606. For the purposes of this title, the term 'program or activity' and the term 'program' mean all of the operations of—

"(1)(A) a department, agency, special purpose district, or other instrumentality of a State or of a local government; or

"(B) the entity of such State or local government that distributes such assistance and each such department or agency (and each other State or local government entity) to which the assistance is extended, in the case of assistance to a State or local government;

"(2)(A) a college, university, or other postsecondary institution, or a public system of higher education; or

"(B) a local educational agency (as defined in section 198(a)(10) of the Elementary and Secondary Education Act of 1965), system of vocational education, or other school system; . . .

42 U.S.C. § 2000d (1988).

B. Congressional Reactions to Federal Enforcement

In 1972, following the Supreme Court's decision in *Swann*, at least fifty-nine constitutional amendments addressed to school desegregation and busing were proposed in Congress. *See Hearings on School Busing Before Subcomm. No. 5 of the House Comm. on the Judiciary*, 92d Cong., 2d Sess., Ser. 32, pt. 3, at xii–xiii (1972). Congress, rejecting an administration proposal that would have effectively banned busing for integration below the seventh grade, enacted a busing moratorium as part of the Education Amendments of 1972:

Title VIII—General Provisions Relating to the Assignment or Transportation of Students

Prohibition Against Assignment or Transportation of Students to Overcome Racial Imbalance

Section 801. No provision of this act shall be construed to require the assignment or transportation of students or teachers in order to overcome racial imbalance.

Prohibition Against Use of Appropriated Funds for Busing

Section 802(a). No funds appropriated for the purpose of carrying out any applicable program may be used for the transportation of students or teachers (or for the purchase of equipment for such transportation) in order to overcome racial imbalance in any school or school system, or for the transportation of students or teachers (or for the purchase of equipment for such transportation) in order to carry out a plan of racial desegregation of any school or school system, except on the express written voluntary request of appropriate local school officials. No such funds shall be made available for transportation when the time or distance of travel is so great as to risk the health of the children or significantly impinge on the educational process of such children, or where the educational opportunities available at the school to which it is proposed that any such student be transported will be substantially inferior to those opportunities offered at the school to which such student would otherwise be assigned under a nondiscriminatory system of school assignments based on geographic zones established without discrimination on account of race, religion, color, or national origin.

(b) No officer, agent, or employee of the Department of Health, Education, and Welfare (including the Office of Education), the Department of Justice, or any other federal agency shall, by rule, regulation, order, guideline, or otherwise (1) urge, persuade, induce, or require any local education agency, or any private non-profit agency, institution, or organization to use any funds derived from any state or local sources for any purpose, unless constitutionally required, for which federal funds appropriated to carry out any applicable program may not be used, as provided in this section, or (2) condition the receipt of federal funds under any federal program upon any action by any state or local public officer or employee which would be prohibited by clause (1) on the part of a federal officer or employee. . . .

NOTES AND QUESTIONS

1. Statutory Interpretation

In light of the *Swann* decision, was the 1972 busing moratorium law intended to prevent the integration of public schools in previously *de jure* school systems? In fact, the Supreme Court viewed the busing moratorium law as limited to de facto segregation, rendering it consistent with *Swann*. *See Drummond v. Acree*, 409 U.S. 1228, 93 S.Ct. 18, 34 L.Ed.2d 33 (1972).

2. The Equal Educational Opportunities Act of 1974

Congress again limited busing in the Equal Educational Opportunities Act of 1974, 20 U.S.C.A. §§ 1701 *et seq.* (the Esch Amendment). Section 1713 establishes a priority for remedies: the assignment to neighborhood schools, taking into account school capacity and natural barriers; the assignment to neighborhood schools but considering school capacity only; the transfer of students from schools where their racial group is a majority to schools where their group is a minority; the creation or revision of attendance zones with minimum transportation; the building of new schools or the closing of old ones; the creation of magnet schools; and finally, "any other plan." Section 1755 then provides that "notwithstanding any other provision of law, . . . no court of the United States shall order the implementation of any plan to remedy a finding of de jure segregation which involves the transportation of students, unless the court first finds that all alternative remedies are inadequate." Moreover, when busing is ordered, no student may be bused beyond the school next closest to his or her home, unless the courts determine that more extensive busing is needed to ensure the protection of constitutional rights. 20 U.S.C.A. §§ 1714 and 1718.

If the courts interpreted these restrictions on the use of busing as a limitation on the power of federal courts to remedy unconstitutional segregation, would these laws be constitutional? In other words, to what extent can Congress define the scope of the Equal Protection Clause by limiting the range of judicial remedies? *See generally* Cox, "The Role of Congress in Constitutional Determinations," 40 *U. Cin.L.Rev.* 199, 253, 257–61 (1971); Cox, "The Supreme Court, 1965 Term, Foreword: Constitutional Adjudication and the Promotion of Human Rights," 80 *Harv.L.Rev.* 91 (1966); *Hearings on School Busing Before Subcomm. No. 5 of the House Committee on the Judiciary*, 92d Cong., 2d Sess., Ser. 32, pt. 3, at 1631–32 (1972) (statement of Professor Wright).

The First Circuit Court of Appeals construed the 1974 amendments in the following manner:

> By explicitly leaving the district court the power to determine the adequacy of remedies, the Act neces-

> sarily does not restrict the breadth of discretion of that court to determine what scope of remedy is judicially required. Thus the Act manifests a purpose not to limit judicial power but to guide and channel its exercise.

Morgan v. Kerrigan, 530 F.2d 401, 412 (1st Cir. 1976), *cert. denied*, 426 U.S. 935, 96 S.Ct. 2648, 49 L.Ed.2d 386. *See also Brinkman v. Gilligan*, 518 F.2d 853, 856 (6th Cir. 1975), *cert. denied*, 423 U.S. 1000, 96 S.Ct. 433, 46 L.Ed.2d 376.

3. Restrictions on the Agency

An amendment to the Labor-HEW appropriations bill for fiscal 1976 (the Byrd Amendment) prohibited HEW (now the Department of Education) from using funds, either directly or indirectly, to force a school district to transport a student beyond the school nearest his or her home for reasons of race. Appropriations acts in subsequent years also carried this restriction. In 1977, the Eagelton-Biden Amendment, modifying the Byrd Amendment, prohibited the use of federal funds by HEW to require busing to implement desegregation plans that involve the pairing or clustering of schools or other methods of reorganizing the grade structure of schools.

Has Congress acted unconstitutionally by restricting the agency's ability to require busing remedies? In a case challenging these amendments, the Court of Appeals for the District of Columbia Circuit held that since HEW could still encourage school districts found to be in noncompliance with Title VI to adopt a voluntary busing plan and could refer cases to the Justice Department to initiate court action, the amendments were not unconstitutional on their face. *Brown v. Califano*, 627 F.2d 1221 (D.C. Cir. 1980).

C. Efforts to Compel Administrative Enforcement

After the election of President Nixon, significant changes were made in the federal role in civil rights enforcement. In *Alexander v. Holmes County Board of Education*, 396 U.S. 19, 90 S.Ct. 29, 24 L.Ed.2d 19 (1969), the Supreme Court rejected the administration's request for a one-year delay of school integration in southern school districts and ordered the immediate integration of previously de jure school districts. That case marked the first split between the government and the NAACP since they joined forces in supporting the passage of the Civil Rights Act. Subsequently, a joint HEW and Department of Justice statement on school desegregation was made public. While noteworthy for its lack of clarity, it was widely interpreted as signifying a slowdown in the integration process. H. Rogers and C. Bullock, *Law and Social Change* 89–90 (1972). *See generally* G. Orfield, *Must We Bus?* (1978).

President Nixon's opposition to school busing was further evidenced in the administration of Title VI of the Civil Rights Act of 1964 by HEW. Civil rights groups charged that the Nixon administration had relaxed its standards with respect to school desegregation by refusing to threaten or employ the ultimate sanction of a cutoff of federal funds in noncomplying districts. Suit was filed against the Secretary of Health, Education, and Welfare, and, in an extraordinary decision, the United States Court of Appeals for the District of Columbia ordered HEW to take "appropriate action to end segregation in public educational institutions receiving federal funds." *Adams v. Richardson*, 480 F.2d 1159 (D.C. Cir. 1973). In that case, the court affirmed an order requiring HEW to commence enforcement proceedings against school districts found to be in violation of Title VI and the Supreme Court's ruling in *Swann v. Charlotte-Mecklenburg Board of Education*, 402 U.S. 1, 91 S.Ct. 1267, 28 L.Ed.2d 554 (1971), request explanations of disproportionate racial distributions from school districts, and monitor all school districts under court desegregation orders. The court found that:

> HEW is actively supplying segregated institutions with federal funds, contrary to the expressed purposes of Congress. It is one thing to say the Justice Department lacks the resources necessary to locate and prosecute every civil rights violator; it is quite another to say HEW may affirmatively continue to channel federal funds to defaulting schools. The anomaly of this latter assertion fully supports the conclusion that Congress's clear statement of an affirmative enforcement duty should not be discounted.
>
> Appellants attempt to avoid the force of this argument by saying that, although enforcement is required, the means of enforcement is a matter of absolute agency discretion, and that they have chosen to seek voluntary compliance in most cases. This position is untenable in light of the plain language of the statute. . . .
>
> Although the Act does not provide a specific limit to the time period within which voluntary compliance may be sought, it is clear that a request for voluntary compliance, if not followed by responsive action on the part of the institution within a reasonable time,

> does not relieve the agency of the responsibility to enforce Title VI by one of the two alternative means contemplated by the statute. A consistent failure to do so is a dereliction of duty reviewable in the courts. . . .

In a subsequent case, HEW was found to have "over-relied" on "voluntary negotiations over protracted time periods" and demonstrated its reluctance to bring enforcement proceedings to bear in southern school districts with substantial segregation. *Adams v. Weinberger*, 391 F.Supp. 269 (D.D.C. 1975). In *Brown v. Weinberger*, 417 F.Supp. 1215 (D.D.C. 1976), a suit brought on behalf of public school students in thirty-three northern and western states, the court held that HEW had failed to fulfill its duties under Title VI. In *Adams v. Califano*, 430 F.Supp. 118 (D.D.C. 1977), HEW was found to be in violation of Title VI in continuing to provide federal aid to public institutions of higher education in six southern states that had failed to desegregate. Additional classes of plaintiffs as well as other statutory civil rights guarantees were included in the litigation. *Adams v. Mathews*, 536 F.2d 417 (D.C. Cir. 1976). In 1977, a consent order was entered into that established time frames governing the processing of complaints and a schedule for compliance reviews under Title VI, Title IX, and Section 504 of the Rehabilitation Act. In 1982, the Department of Education, then under a new administration, moved to vacate the 1977 order.

Women's Equity Action League v. Cavazos

906 F.2d 742 (D.C. Cir. 1990).

R. Ginsburg, Circuit Judge.

[The circuit court had requested briefing and argument on whether, in light of certain post-1973 decisions, "plaintiffs may maintain a broad-gauged right of action directly against the federal government officers charged with monitoring and enforcing funding recipients' compliance with discrimination proscriptions."]

We revisit in this opinion a case involving discrimination in federally-funded educational enterprises. The case originated in the district court twenty years ago and has grown ever larger in the two decades since its initiation. Eventually, the action cast the district court as nationwide overseer or pacer of procedures government agencies use to enforce civil rights prescriptions controlling educational institutions that receive federal funds. In a prior opinion, we held that plaintiffs had standing to sue, i.e., that they satisfied the threshold constitutional (article III) requirement to maintain the litigation. *Women's Equity Action League v. Cavazos*, 879 F.2d 880 (D.C. Cir. 1989).

We now conclude, however, that Congress has not explicitly or implicitly authorized the grand scale action plaintiffs delineate. We are impelled to reach this terminal point by pathmarking decisions made during the pendency of this litigation, most critically, *Cannon v. University of Chicago*, 441 U.S. 677 (1979), and *Council of and for the Blind v. Regan*, 709 F.2d 1521 (D.C. Cir. 1983) (en banc).

I. The History of the Controversy

This litigation began in 1970 when black students attending racially segregated public schools in seventeen states complained of the delinquency of the Department of Health, Education, and Welfare (HEW) in enforcing Title VI of the Civil Rights Act of 1964, 42 U.S.C. § 2000d. Over the past two decades, the once contained action expanded to colossal proportions: the litigation came to encompass enforcement by units of the Department of Education and the Department of Labor of four civil rights measures as they pertain to the education systems of all fifty states—Title VI, forbidding discrimination on account of race or national origin in any federally-assisted program; Title IX of the Education Amendments of 1972, 20 U.S.C. §§ 1681–86, prohibiting discrimination on the basis of sex or visual impairment in educational institutions receiving federal funds; Executive Order 11246, . . . proscribing discrimination by government contractors; and Section 504 of the Rehabilitation Act of 1972, 29 U.S.C. § 794, barring federal fund recipients from discriminating against the handicapped.

As the litigation swelled in scope, it shifted in focus. Plaintiffs at first demanded relief from executive defiance of congressional commands, in the form of a deliberate policy of nonenforcement. At the end of 1987, however, the district court observed: "[P]laintiffs [no longer] claim that defendants have abrogated their statutory responsibilities, but rather that, in carrying them out, they do not always process complaints, conduct investigations, issue letters of findings, or conduct compliance reviews as promptly or expeditiously as plaintiffs would like."

See *Adams v. Bennett*, 675 F.Supp. 668, 680 (D.D.C. 1987).

The government had argued in *Adams v. Richardson* that plaintiffs possessed no right of action under the Administrative Procedure Act (APA), . . . because enforcement of Tile VI was committed to agency discretion by law. Rejecting that argument, we pointed to plaintiffs' allegation that HEW had "consciously and expressly adopted a general policy which is in effect an abdiction of its statutory duty." 480 F.2d at 1162.[2] Under the statute, this court held, a federal agency lacks discretion to desist when its request to a state or school district for voluntary compliance is not met by responsive action within a reasonable time. *Id.* at 1163. *Adams v. Richardson* did not treat the question whether an APA action might be precluded by reason of the availability of another adequate remedy. See 5 U.S.C. § 704 (subjecting to judicial review "final agency action for which there is no other adequate remedy in a court"); *Council of and for the Blind v. Regan*, 709 F.2d 1521, 1531–33 (D.C. Cir. 1983) (en banc).

. . . Plaintiffs identify four purported sources of their claims for relief—the civil rights statutes themselves; the APA . . .; the Mandamus Act; and the United States Constitution. We conclude that none of these asserted sources authorizes the continuing, across-the-board federal court superintendence of executive enforcement plaintiffs seek. We therefore affirm the district court's dismissal of this action and pretermit the other issues briefed and argued.

II. Pivotal Doctrinal Developments

The expansion of this litigation coincided with doctrinal shifts that curtailed the availability of suits directly against federal enforcement authorities for tardigrade administration of antidiscrimination prescriptions. With respect to implied private remedies under the antidiscrimination laws, *Cannon v. University of Chicago* was the bellwether decision.

Cannon confirmed an implied private remedy under Titles VI and IX against federal fund recipients who engage in proscribed discrimination. Simultaneously, however, *Cannon* pointed the lower courts away from the implication of discrete, broad-gauged rights of action against federal enforcement agencies. The message of *Cannon* was that no private right of action should be inferred from federal legislation absent a showing of approbation from the lawmaking branch. Moreover, *Cannon's* examination of the legislative history of Title VI suggested that Congress wished to ward off suits against the government of the very kind plaintiffs now press.

Just as *Cannon* cautioned against generous judicial recognition of implied rights of action from federal regulatory measures, so *Council of and for the Blind* controlled recourse to the APA. . . . *Council of and for the Blind* thus confirmed that "if other remedies are adequate, federal courts will not oversee the overseer." . . . With these doctrinal developments in mind, we turn to plaintiffs' claims to a right of action against federal funding agencies.

III. Implied Rights of Action

It bears emphasis that this litigation, as now contoured, is in no part situation specific. Plaintiffs do not challenge the federal funding agency defendants for supporting any particular institution or program. Instead, they seek across-the-board continuing federal court supervision of the process by which the agencies ensure compliance with the antidiscrimination mandates. As *Cannon* made clear, to hold that an enactment provides an implied right of action of the sort plaintiffs plead, the court must be satisfied that the enactor intended to create such a right. . . . [W]e discern no legislative intent to authorize the grand scale, long term rights of action plaintiffs claim here.

Plaintiffs rely . . . on *Brown v. Califano*, 627 F.2d 1221, 1233 n. 73 (D.C. Cir. 1980), which suggested in dictum that "a private individual could challenge in court HEW's continued funding of a noncomplying district." We do not gainsay that suggestion. Authorization to sue the federal government in a situation-specific suit for improperly funding a particular entity or enterprise, however, is not equivalent to a permit to demand across-the-board judicial supervision of continuing federal agency enforcement. . . .

2. The government does "not ask this panel to reconsider that holding," . . . and we do not do so. We conclude instead that plaintiffs no longer have any claim under the APA because, for the injuries they continue to assert, they have another adequate remedy. . . .

In addition to emphasizing legislative intent as the touchstone for judicial recognition of implied rights of action, *Cannon* indicated, through its examination of the legislative history of Tile VI, that Congress did not countenance the type of action plaintiffs have mounted. The Court observed that, as ultimately enacted, Title VI represented "a compromise aimed at protecting individual rights without subjecting the Government to suits." . . .

The *Cannon* opinion contrasts two private remedies: 1) suit against a discriminatory fund recipient to terminate the offending discrimination; and 2) suit against the government to terminate federal funding. . . . The Court found strong support in legislative history for the former, but resistance on the part of lawmakers toward the latter. . . . Plaintiffs maintain, however, that they seek no termination of funding. Instead, plaintiffs say, they sue only to assure that federal agencies do the job Congress entrusted to them by promptly processing complaints and compliance reviews. The distinction plaintiffs press is infirm on two counts. First, the schedule set out in the consent decree leads in the end to fund termination if voluntary compliance is not achieved. Second, an overarching, broad-gauged suit against the federal monitors that bypasses the discriminatory recipients is inconsistent with a legislative compromise "conducive to implication of a private remedy against a [particular] discriminatory recipient," but not "to implication of a private remedy [directly and broadly] against the Government." . . .

* * *

IV. Right of Action Under the Administrative Procedure Act

In *Council of and for the Blind*, . . . we judged a statutory remedy specifically against the discriminating entity "adequate," and therefore preclusive of a default remedy under the APA. . . .

Plaintiffs urge, however, that individual actions against discriminators cannot redress the systematic lags and lapses by federal monitors about which they complain. . . . Suits directly against the discriminating entities may be arduous, and less effective in providing systematic relief, than continuing judicial oversight of federal government enforcement. But under our precedent, situation-specific litigation affords an adequate, even if imperfect, remedy. So far as we can tell, the suit targeting specific discriminatory acts of fund recipients is the only court remedy Congress has authorized for private parties, situated as plaintiffs currently are.

* * *

[Discussion of actions under Mandamus Act and Constitution is omitted.]

Conclusion

In sum, instructed by currently controlling precedent, we hold that the generalized action plaintiffs pursue against federal executive agencies lacks the requisite green light from the legislative branch. We do not suggest that such an action could not be authorized. See *Women's Equity Action League v. Cavazos* (holding that plaintiffs possess article III standing). The courts, however, may not on their own initiative create the claim for relief. That authority resides in Congress. For the reasons stated, the district court's dismissal of plaintiffs' complaints is

Affirmed.

NOTES AND QUESTIONS

1. Private Suits/Public Agencies

Should private parties be permitted to file lawsuits to compel an administrative agency to comply with its own guidelines and regulations? If HEW or its successor agency is reluctant to seek fund cutoffs, what impact would *Adams v. Richardson* and subsequent cases be likely to have on its policies? Can a court order an administrative agency to be diligent and to act in good faith in administering a law? To what effect? Does this case raise a separation of powers issue?

2. Impact of* Adams v. Richardson *on other Statutory Guarantees

The Office for Civil Rights of the Department of Health, Education, and Welfare claimed that the district court's order to enforce Title VI within certain time frames meant that there would be no resources available to review Title IX and Section 504 complaints. Can a court determine what resources should be allocated to the enforcement of each statute?

3. The Consent Agreement Settling Adams

In the December, 1977 consent agreement, the plaintiffs in *Adams v. Richardson* (involving school districts in seventeen southern states), *Brown v. Weinberger* (involving school districts in thirty-three northern and western states), and *Women's Equity Action League* (seeking resources for the enforcement of Title IX) agreed to drop their cases in exchange for the agency's promise to eliminate the backlog of three thousand complaints by September 30, 1979, and to double the staff by immediately hiring 898 new personnel. The consent agreement also established timetables for civil rights complaints for all fifty states for all three civil rights statutes—Title VI, Title IX, and Section 504.

By 1981, the backlog of complaints in the Department of Education had increased in size. What recourse would plaintiffs have? If the Department responds that it was unable to hire additional staff because the Office of Management and Budget disapproved, or Congress refused to appropriate the funds, what action can the court take?

4. Basis of Decision

Has the court's opinion in *Women's Equity Action League v. Cavazos* eviscerated the holding in *Adams v. Richardson?* Is it that plaintiffs are raising different allegations or that, while plaintiffs once had a cause of action, intervening decisions made it clear that the court was incorrect in initially finding that plaintiffs had a cause of action against the agency?

VIII. "SECOND GENERATION" PROBLEMS

A. Introduction

School systems can remain segregated even after a court-ordered school desegregation plan has been implemented. Through practices such as ability grouping and the use of exclusionary disciplinary measures, minority children may continue to be isolated from white children. These practices can bring about resegregation among schools, within a school, or even within a classroom. One difficulty is determining whether these practices are intentionally used to segregate or whether they are educationally motivated and racially neutral but have the effect of segregating students. If the latter is the case, do such practices still violate the Fourteenth Amendment? *See Washington v. Davis*, 426 U.S. 229, 96 S.Ct. 2040, 48 L.Ed.2d 597 (1976); *Village of Arlington Heights v. Metropolitan Housing Corporation*, 429 U.S. 252, 97 S.Ct. 555, 50 L.Ed.2d 450 (1977). Do they violate Title VI of the Civil Rights Act of 1964? (*See* discussion *supra* at 552–53).

Many of the legal and policy problems raised in this section clearly extend beyond the question of racial discrimination, particularly with regard to student classification practices, but since most of the litigation has focused on the effects of these practices on minority students, these issues will be dealt with here. Similar questions are raised in chapter 7, particularly with respect to the mentally and physically handicapped.

B. Student Classification Practices

Until recently, the focus for both policymakers and lawyers was primarily on educational issues at the national, state, or district level rather than on what happens within the schools. While courts have struggled to define equality of educational opportunity and to demarcate the liberties that students retain while attending public school, they generally have been unwilling to review pedagogical judgments, such as the classification or sorting of students—that is, differentiations made among students, ostensibly based solely on intellectual performance or potential.

Ability grouping (or tracking) and assignment to special classes for handicapped children as well as the devices that facilitate classification—testing, grading, and counseling—have been heavily criticized. Among the chief criticisms leveled at present classification practices are: (1) that they misidentify or misclassify significant numbers of students; (2) that they are racially discriminatory; and (3) that they deny some students an equal educational opportunity.

Perhaps more than almost any other issue, student classification presses at the limits of judicial competence to affect educational policy. The minuteness of many within-school and within-class decisions makes it difficult to conceive of them as posing legally manageable problems. Such decisions are complex, interrelated, and numerous. For that reason, a court that undertook routinely to review them might well find itself acting as schoolmaster in an uncomfortably literal sense. Furthermore, these practices, are at the heart of the school official's claim to professional competence; any challenge could be perceived as a threat to that competence and for that reason strenuously resisted. Whether such resistance is indeed proper—whether, for some or all of the questions considered in this section, judicial involvement is inappropriate—is a critical and unresolved issue.

1. The Nature and Purpose of Classification.

"Schools as Sorters: The Constitutional and Policy Implications of Student Classification"

D. Kirp, 121 *U.Pa.L.Rev.* 705, 710–17 (1973). Reprinted with permission.

Public schools regularly sort students in a variety of ways. [*See* survey data reported in W. Findley and M. Bryan, *Ability Grouping: 1970* (1971).] They test them when they first arrive at school and at regular intervals thereafter in order to identify aptitude—*i.e.*, capacity to learn. Although such capacity may not in fact be measured, and may indeed be unsusceptible to measurement, what is important for descriptive purposes is the fact that schools act on the assumption that tests can measure aptitude.

From primary school until graduation, most schools group (or track) students on the basis of estimated intellectual ability, both within classrooms—the brighter "tigers" separated from the less intelligent "clowns"—and in separate classes. In primary school grouping, the pace of instruction, but typically not its content, is varied. Grouping decisions may be made for each school subject—the cleverest in arithmetic may be dullards at spelling—or a given group may stay intact for the entire curriculum. During the school year, students are graded. Those grades, combined with aptitude and achievement test results and teacher recommendations, determine whether a child is promoted to the next grade level and into which ability group he is placed.

In secondary school, variations among educational "tracks" reflect both interest and ability. There, for the first time in his educational career, the student may be offered choices. As the process actually works, however, grammar school success usually means college track or academic high school assignment while mediocre grade school performance leads frequently to placement in a general (noncollege preparatory), business, or vocational program. It is counselors, and not students, who frequently make these decisions, by matching school offerings to their own estimates of each student's ability and potential. [*See* A. Cicourel and J. Kitsuse, *The Educational Decision Makers* (1963).] That classification determines both the nature of the secondary school education—Shakespeare, shorthand or machine shop—and the gross choices—college or job—available after the twelfth grade.

Students whom the school cannot classify in this manner are treated as "special" or "exceptional" children.* . . .

* * *

1. Historical Development of Classification. While, as one testing manual contends, "the original [classification] was when God . . . looked at everything he made and saw that it was *very good*" [W. Mehrens and I. Lehmann, *Standardized Tests in Education*, 3 (1969)], only during the past sixty years have schools devoted considerable effort to classifying and sorting students. The prototypal common school, energetically promoted by Horace Mann and Henry Barnard, was designed to provide a common educational experience for all comers—all, that is, who could afford to stay in school for an extended period of time. . . .

The arrival of significant numbers of immigrants from Eastern and Southern Europe late in the nineteenth century obliged school officials to provide instruction for children who spoke no English and had little, if any, previous schooling. It made no sense to place these students in regular classes; they needed assistance of a kind that schools had not previously been asked to provide. Urban school systems created "opportunity classes," special programs designed to overcome the students' initial difficulties and to prepare them for regular schoolwork.

Other societal factors served to promote the need for differentiation among students. The insistence that schools be "businesslike" and efficient was increasingly heard, and American educators began to adopt the modern business corporation's complex organizational structure as their model. [*See* R. Cal-

* "Special education" refers to classes for students with particular and acute learning disabilities. The disability may be defined in terms of test scores, physical impediments (i.e., classes for the blind, deaf and dumb, or perceptually handicapped), or psychological disturbance (i.e., classes for the emotionally disturbed). . . .

lahan, *Education and the Cult of Efficiency* (1962); G. Counts, *The Social Composition of Boards of Education: A Study in the Social Control of Public Education* (1927).] Further, the increasingly complex American economy and society demanded a differentiation of skills that a common education simply couldn't provide. . . .

The advent of standardized aptitude testing early in the twentieth century provided a useful means of identifying and placing those students. [*See generally* R. Herrnstein, *I.Q. in the Meritocracy* (1973).] . . . Intelligence tests were increasingly used by American educators because they accorded with the educator's demand for categorization and efficiency. Tests offered scientific justification for the differentiated curriculum, enabling it to function with some rationality. . . .

2. *Current School Needs* . . . Grouping, special education assignment, and exclusion have significant and similar school purposes. They: (1) provide mechanisms for differentiating among students; (2) offer rewards and sanctions for school performance; (3) ease the tasks of teachers and administrators by restricting somewhat the range of ability among students in a given classroom; and (4) purportedly improve student achievement.

Interestingly, the first two purposes—sorting and rewarding-punishing—are seldom mentioned by school officials. The sorting function is self-evident: where previously there existed just students, classification permits the parceling out of students among different educational programs. That certain of these classifications reward and others punish is apparent from investigations of the effects of grouping on students' self-perception [*See* J. Barker Lunn, *Streaming in the Primary School* (1970); W. Borg, *Ability Grouping in the Public Schools* (1966) (originally appeared in 34 *J. Experimental Educ.*, Winter 1965, at 1); Mann, "What Does Ability Grouping Do to the Self-Concept?" 36 *Childhood Educ.* 356 (1960); *cf.* M. Goldberg, A. H. Passow, and J. Justman, *The Effects of Ability Grouping* (1966).] The reward-punishment facet of classification represents one aspect of the school's stress on intellectual competition, with praise accompanying only performance that the school or teacher defines as successful.

The third and fourth purposes—easing the tasks of teachers and administrators, and improving the education of students—are more commonly advanced. These purposes—one emphasizing benefits to teachers and administrators, the other emphasizing benefits to students—permit school officials to view classification as an unmixed blessing. There is little recognition that classification may have decidedly limited educational benefits for schoolchildren and that certain sorting practices may even do educational injury. The belief that classification helps everyone is significant for two reasons. It partially explains the popularity that grouping enjoys among teachers: only 18.4 percent of teachers surveyed by the National Education Association preferred to teach nongrouped classes. [Research Division, National Education Association, *Teachers' Opinion Poll: Ability Grouping*, 57 *N.E.A.J.* 53 (1968).] It also underscores the problems that reformers—whether pedagogues or lawyers—unhappy with present classification practices are likely to encounter in seeking to restructure them. . . .

2. Racial Discrimination and Ability Grouping. Few schools, if any, sort students explicitly on the basis of race. Classification in large systems is routinely handled by a school official who knows nothing about a given student except his or her academic record. The grounds on which school administrators defend sorting—its alleged benefits to both students and teachers—reveal no apparent racial motivation.

Yet school sorting does have significant racial consequences. It tends to concentrate minority children in less-advanced school programs. The proportion of minority students assigned to special programs for the educable mentally retarded and placed in slow learners' classes and nonacademic high school programs is typically two or three times greater than their proportion of the school-age population. Racial disproportionality does not, however, characterize programs for students with readily identifiable handicaps, such as classes for the trainable mentally retarded or blind, for example.

The policy implications of racial overrepresentation in less-advanced school programs are difficult to assess. If African American students are proportionately in greater need of special educational services, then there appears to be nothing illegitimate in providing those services, even if some degree of racial isolation becomes inevitable. Educators instituting these programs would be responding to the assertion often made by African American spokespersons that the regular curriculum is not geared to the educational needs and experiences of the African

American community. But if the mechanisms of classification are racially biased, if the special programs do not meet the special needs of African American children, or if the classification scheme is a disguised effort to segregate the races, racial overrepresentation in less-advanced programs could give rise to legitimate policy concerns. Legal challenges to classification schemes that allegedly discriminate on the basis of race have arisen from two situations: (1) efforts by formerly dual school systems to adopt new classification schemes; and (2) use of particular classifications—notably, special classes for the mildly (or educable) mentally retarded—in districts that lack a history of de jure segregation.

Lemon v. Bossier Parish School Board

444 F.2d 1400 (5th Cir. 1971).

Before Gewin, Goldberg, and Dyer, Circuit Judges.

Per Curiam:

This is an appeal from an order of the district court approving a school board plan for the operation of the public schools in Plain Dealing, Louisiana. The plan in question provides that students in grades 4–12 will be assigned to one of two schools in the system on the basis of scores made on the California Achievement Test. Plaintiffs appeal, contesting the validity of the board's plan.

We think it obvious that the plan approved by the district court, insofar as it provides for the assignment of students on the basis of achievement test scores, is not in compliance with previous orders of this court in school desegregation cases. In *Singleton v. Jackson Municipal Separate School District*, 419 F.2d 1211 (5th Cir. 1969), *rev'd in part on other grounds*, 396 U.S. 290, this court sitting en banc said: "This suit seeks to desegregate two school districts, Marshall County and Holly Springs, Mississippi. The district court approved plans which would assign students to schools on the basis of achievement test scores. We pretermit a discussion of the validity per se of a plan based on testing except to hold that testing cannot be employed in any event until unitary school systems have been established." 419 F.2d at 1219.

Since *Singleton* we have repeatedly rejected testing as a basis for student assignments, *United States v. Sunflower County School District*, 430 F.2d 839 (5th Cir. 1970); *United States v. Tunica County School District*, 421 F.2d 1236 (5th Cir. 1970), and we see no occasion to depart from this rule in the present case. The Plain Dealing School System has been a unitary system for only one semester. This is insufficient to even raise the issue of the validity of testing itself. In *Singleton* we made it clear that regardless of the innate validity of testing, it could not be used until a school district had been established as a unitary system. We think at a minimum this means that the district in question must have for several years operated as a unitary system. . . .

Vacated and remanded with direction.

NOTES AND QUESTIONS

1. Basis of Decision

What is the constitutional basis for the *Lemon* decision? If the court is simply asserting that a formerly dual school system has an obligation to remedy all vestiges of de jure segregation, why is an ability-grouping plan necessarily inconsistent with that objective? *See also Reed v. Rhodes*, 455 F.Supp. 569 (N.D. Ohio 1978); *Moses v. Washington Parish School Board*, 330 F.Supp. 1340 (E.D.La. 1971), *aff'd*, 456 F.2d 1285 (5th Cir. 1972) (per curiam), *cert. denied*, 409 U.S. 1013, 93 S.Ct. 431, 34 L.Ed.2d 307. Is the court suggesting that the prior discrimination might cause or perpetuate lower black achievement and thus, despite its neutral gloss, assignment according to ability is discriminatory? *See McNeal v. Tate County School District*, 508 F.2d 1017 (5th Cir. 1975).

Is the court assuming that black students will predominate in the lower track, whites in the upper track? If so, why is that of constitutional concern? Is the court suggesting that the motive for adopting ability grouping is racial prejudice? In this regard, would the district's past grouping practices be relevant? *See* Simon, "Racially Prejudiced Governmental Actions: A Motivation Theory of the Constitutional Ban Against Racial Discrimination," 15 *San Diego L. Rev.* 1041 (1978). What if the lower tracks offered well-designed and implemented remedial programs? *Cf. Copeland v. School Bd.*, 464 F.2d 932 (4th Cir. 1972). *See generally* Shea, "An Educational Perspective of the Legality of Intelligence Testing and Ability Grouping," 6 *J. of Law & Educ.* 137 (1977).

Is the use of testing as a basis for student assignments in a district that has not operated as a unitary system for more than a few years *per se* invalid? If not, how might defendant school officials demonstrate that the assignment scheme is legitimate? Several cases have implied that school officials would have to show that the assignment scheme is not based on the present result of past segregation, and that the assignment scheme will remedy past segregation through better educational opportunities. *See, e.g., Georgia State Conference of Branches of NAACP v. Georgia*, 775 F.2d 1403 (11th Cir. 1985); *United States v. Gadsden County School District*, 572 F.2d 1049 (5th Cir. 1978); *Montgomery v. Starkville Municipal Separate School District*, 665 F.Supp. 487 (N.D. Mass. 1987); *Bond v. Keck*, 616 F.Supp. 581 (D.C. Mo. 1985).

2. *Testing*

The *Lemon* court views the constitutionality of "testing *per se*" as a "complex and troubling question." What might be legally troubling about testing: the use of tests, the reliability of tests identifying student ability, the likelihood that test use will yield racial overrepresentation in less-advanced school programs, the competency of courts to pass on such educational issues? *See Moses v. Washington Parish School Board*, 330 F.Supp. 1340 (E.D. La. 1971).

3. *Intraschool Grouping and Unitary School Systems*

Would the result in the *Lemon* case have changed if defendants had proposed grouping within schools rather than between them? *See Moses v. Washington Parish School Board, supra*. Should there be any difference in legal standards between intraschool and interschool grouping?

In *Morales v. Shannon*, 516 F.2d 411 (5th Cir. 1975), *cert. denied*, 423 U.S. 1034, 96 S.Ct. 566, 46 L.Ed.2d 408, the Fifth Circuit found that the concentration of Mexican-American students in the lower tracks of the junior and senior high schools of Uvalde, Texas, was the result of test scores, grades, and teacher recommendations. The court was led to conclude:

> Given that ability groupings are not unconstitutional per se, the statistical results of the groupings here are not so abnormal or unusual in any instance as to justify an inference of discrimination. The record shows no more than the use of a non-discriminatory teaching practice or technique, a matter which is reserved to educators under our system of government.

516 F.2d at 414.

Are *Morales* and *Lemon* distinguishable?

C. Ability Grouping and Equal Educational Opportunities

The basic premise of school classification is that treating children who have identifiably different needs differently will increase the educational opportunities available to all. That premise has been questioned by critics who assert that particular classifications diminish, rather than enhance, educational opportunity.

Alleged diminution of educational opportunity may rest on three quite different grounds: (1) students assigned to certain programs receive fewer tangible resources than students assigned to other programs; (2) certain programs, because of their structural rigidity or inefficacy, restrict the educational potential of students assigned to them; and (3) certain programs unnecessarily stigmatize students.

Outside the racial discrimination context, no court has assessed whether particular classifications deny equal educational opportunity. *Hobson v. Hansen*, the most famous of the classification cases, focuses primarily on the race and class discrimination that tracking assertedly fosters. *See generally* Bersoff, "Regarding Psychologists Testily: Legal Regulation of Psychological Assessment in the Public Schools," 39 *Md. L. Rev.* 27, 44–58 (1979). Yet *Hobson* raises questions broader than race and class discrimination; it suggests that other nonracial aspects of classification might be the subject of constitutional challenge.

Hobson v. Hansen

269 F.Supp. 401 (D.D.C. 1967), *aff'd sub. nom. Smuck v. Hobson*, 408 F.2d 175 (D.C. Cir. 1969) (en banc).

Judge Wright:

* * *

IV. THE TRACK SYSTEM

The District of Columbia school system employs a form of ability grouping commonly known as the track system, by which students at the elementary and secondary level are placed in tracks or curriculum levels according to the school's assessment of each student's ability to learn. . . . As the evidence in this case makes painfully clear, ability grouping as presently practiced in the District of Columbia school system is a denial of equal educational opportunity to the poor and a majority of the Negroes attending school in the nation's capital, a denial that contravenes not only the guarantees of the Fifth Amendment but also the fundamental premise of the track system itself. What follows, then, is a discussion of that evidence—an examination of the track system: in theory and in reality. . . .

Purpose and Philosophy. Dr. Hansen [Superintendent of Schools] believes that the comprehensive high school (and the school system generally) must be systematically organized and structured to provide differing levels of education for students with widely differing levels of academic ability. This is the purpose of the track system. In expressing the track system's philosophy Dr. Hansen has said, "Every pupil in the school system must have the maximum opportunity for self-development and this can best be brought about by adjusting curriculum offerings to different levels of need and ability as the pupil moves through the stages of education and growth in our schools." . . .

Student Types. Within the student body Dr. Hansen sees generally four types of students: the intellectually gifted, the above-average, the average, and the retarded. He assumes that each of these types of students has a maximum level of academic capability and, most importantly, that that level of ability can be accurately ascertained. The duty of the school is to identify these students and provide a curriculum commensurate with their respective abilities. Dr. Hansen contends that the traditional school curriculum—including the usual two-level method of ability grouping—does a disservice to those at either end of the ability spectrum.

The gifted student is not challenged, so that he becomes bored, lazy, and perhaps performs far below his academic potential; his intellectual talents are a wasted resource. The remedy lies in discovering the gifted student, placing him with others of his own kind, thereby stimulating him through this select association as well as a rigorous, demanding curriculum to develop his intellectual talent. Indeed, "the academically capable student should be required as a public necessity to take the academically challenging honors curriculum."

On the other hand, continues Dr. Hansen, the retarded or "stupid" student typically has been forced to struggle through a curriculum he cannot possibly master and only imperfectly comprehends. Typically he is slow to learn and soon falls behind in class; he repeatedly fails, sometimes repeating a grade again and again; he becomes isolated, frustrated, depressed, and—if he does not drop out before graduation—graduates with a virtually useless education. Here the remedy is seen as separating out the retarded student, directing him into a special curriculum geared to his limited abilities and designed to give him a useful "basic" education—one which makes no pretense of equalling traditionally taught curricula.

In short, Hansen views the traditional school curriculum as doing too little for some students and expecting too much of others. As for the latter type, whom Dr. Hansen characterizes as "the blue-collar student," going to school—a "white-collar occupation"—can be an artificial experience. "Twelve years of white-collar experience is unrealistic preparation for the young man or woman who will suddenly make the change into work clothes for jobs in kitchens, stockrooms, street maintenance or building construction. . . ."

Tracking. In order to tailor the educational process to the level appropriate to each student, Dr. Hansen adopted the track system. Each track is intended to be a separate and self-contained curriculum, with the educational content ranging from the very basic to the very advanced according to the track level. In the elementary and junior high schools three levels are used: Basic or Special Academic (retarded students), General (average and above-average), and Honors (gifted). In the senior high school a fourth level is added: the Regular Track, a college-preparatory track intended to accommodate the above-average student.

The significant feature of the track system in this regard is its emphasis on the ability of the student. A student's course of instruction depends upon what the school system decides he is capable of handling. . . .

Flexibility. Dr. Hansen, while assuming that some students can be educated to their maximum potential in one of the four curricula, also anticipates that not all students will neatly or permanently fit into a track. Thus a second important assumption underlying the track system is that tracking will be a flexible process. Flexibility encompasses two things:

First, although a student today may demonstrate an ability level which calls, for example, for placement in the General Track, a constant and continuing effort must be made to assure that he is at his true ability level. This calls for instruction directed toward correcting any remediable educational problems which account for the student's present poor performance; and it calls for close analysis and counseling to determine whether these remediable deficiencies exist and when they have been sufficiently corrected. When the latter is determined, the student is to be upgraded to the next higher track. Second, even though a student may not be in a position to make an across-the-board move from one track to another, his ability level may be such that he needs to take courses in two track levels on a subject-by-subject basis. This process, known as cross-tracking, is critical: it is the mechanism the system relies upon to assure that students whose ability levels vary according to particular subjects are not thwarted in developing their strong areas because their weak areas result in their being placed in a lower curriculum level. It also serves as a way of selectively raising the intensity of instruction on a subject-matter basis as a part of the process of gradually upgrading a student.

Fundamental Assumptions. . . .

The express assumptions of this approach are three: *First*, a child's maximum educational potential can and will be accurately ascertained. *Second*, tracking will enhance the prospects for correcting a child's remediable educational deficiencies. *Third*, tracking must be flexible so as to provide an individually tailored education for students who cannot be pigeonholed in a single curriculum. . . .

[The court discusses differences in purpose, criteria for admission, and curriculum among the four tracks. It then analyzes the overrepresentation of poor and minority students in lower tracks.]

. . . Flexibility in Pupil Programming.

The importance of flexibility to the proper operation of the track system has been adverted to earlier in this opinion. . . .

* * *

[However] flexibility in pupil programming in the District of Columbia school system is an unkept promise.

1. Movement Between Tracks: Upgrading. [A]t least 85% of those assigned to the special academic track—and it appears that something over 90% is more typical—remain at the lowest achievement level. Although it cannot be said that an assignment to the Special Academic Track inevitably is permanent, neither can it be said that the chances of progressing into a more challenging curriculum are very high.

Plaintiffs have charged that this lack of movement is attributable to a complex of causes: the simplified curriculum, coupled with the absence of variety in the students' levels of ability, does not stimulate the Special Academic student; remedial training is inadequate; Special Academic teachers are not formally trained for special educational problems; teachers underestimate the potential of their students and therefore undereducate them. None of these reasons can be either isolated or proved with absolute certainty. Nonetheless, there is substantial evidence . . . that the cause of limited upgrading in the Special Academic Track lies more with faults to be found in the system than with the innate disabilities of the students. And certainly the results . . . do not support the thesis that tracking is flexible. . . .

. . . [T]he pattern observed with respect to upgrading from the Special Academic Track is repeated in all track levels. Movement between tracks borders on the nonexistent. . . .

* * *

Viewed as a whole, the evidence of overall movement between tracks conclusively demonstrates the defendants' failure to translate into practice one of the most critical tenets of the track system: "Pupil placement in a curriculum must never be static or unchangeable. Otherwise, the four-track system will degenerate into a four-rut system." The tragedy has occurred.

2. Movement Between Tracks: Cross-Tracking. . . . In practice cross-tracking of the sort described is confined to the senior high level, there being structural reasons why elementary and junior high pupils do not really "cross-track." And . . . even at the senior high school level cross-tracking proves to be the exception, not the rule. . . .

* * *

Defendants have not explained why so few students in the three lower curricula (Special Academic, General, and Regular) do any cross-tracking. However, there is substantial evidence, some of it already discussed in relation to upgrading, pointing to several reasons.

The first is that students are being denied permission to cross-track—or discouraged from seeking that permission—on the assumption that they cannot handle a more difficult assignment. . . .

Another reason, related to the first, is . . . that many students do not obtain effective, individual counseling on programs, counseling that is obviously necessary if a student is to be directed to a curricular program fitted to his needs and abilities. . . . Absent this close attention, the student will remain locked into his assigned curriculum, unless the student or his parents are disposed to question the merits of that continued assignment.

A third reason for limited cross-tracking, . . . is the inability to qualify for the more advanced courses either for lack of the prerequisite fundamental courses or because of continuing academic deficiencies. . . . A fourth reason . . . is the substantial possibility that some school principals, or their staffs, take a very restrictive view of cross-tracking. . . .

Causes of Discrimination and the Collapse of Track Theory. . . .

Here the focus will be on the major institutional shortcomings that not only thrust the disadvantaged student into the lower tracks but tend to keep him there once placed. The first area of concern is the lack of kindergartens and Honors programs in certain [predominantly black] schools; the second relates to remedial and compensatory programs for the disadvantaged and educationally handicapped student; and the third, and most important, involves the whole of the placement and testing process by which the school system decides who gets what kind of education. . . .

[The court finds that disadvantaged students have less access to kindergarten programs (which, the court asserts, may be "indispensable to their success in the whole of their academic career") and to honors track instruction.]

. . . ***Remedial and Compensatory Education.*** One purpose of the track system is to facilitate remedial education for students who are temporarily handicapped in basic academic skills. In addition, the school system has recognized that it must provide a substantial number of its students with special compensatory education programs for there to be any real hope of their becoming qualified for the more advanced tracks. There is substantial evidence, however, that neither the remedial nor the compensatory education programs presently in existence are adequate; rather the disadvantaged student consigned to the lower track tends simply to get the lesser education, not the push to a higher level of achievement.

Remedial Programs: Curricular

Special Academic Track. . . .

* * *

Defendants have made it quite clear that a child placed in a Special Academic class will receive a slower-paced, simplified course of instruction.

General Track. . . . [T]here is no evidence of a systematized remedial program being included within the General curriculum itself. Instead, as with the Special Academic Track, the prevailing philosophy is to teach children at existing ability levels; those that indicate potential for a more advanced curriculum must be approved for cross-tracking or upgrading. . . . And again, as with the Special Academic Track, evidence of such intertrack movement shows relatively few moving up. . . . What has not been made clear, however, is how a student given a steady diet of simplified materials can keep up, let alone catch up, with children his own age who are proceeding in a higher curriculum at a faster pace and with a more complex subject-matter content. While much has been made of the "enriched" Honors curriculum . . . nothing has been said to indicate that the slower learner—who almost certainly is in some degree slow due to a disadvantaged background—is also given an enriched curriculum to stimulate him to higher achievement. . . .

. . . Special Remedial and Compensatory Education Programs.

It is because of the high proportion of disadvantaged children in the District school system that it is imperative that special programs outside the regular school curriculum be adopted so that the disadvantaged child has a real opportunity to achieve at his maximum level of ability. . . .

* * *

. . . It is true that the schools alone cannot compensate for all the handicaps that are characteristic of the disadvantaged child; but it is the schools that must—as defendants admit—lead the attack on the verbal handicaps which are the major barrier to academic achievement. . . .

The track system adds to that obligation, however, because tracking translates ability into educational opportunity. When a student is placed in a lower track, in a very real sense his future is being decided for him; the kind of education he gets there shapes his future progress not only in school but in society in general. Certainly, when the school system undertakes this responsibility it incurs the obligation of living up to its promise to the student that placement in a lower track will not simply be a shunting off from the mainstream of education, but rather will be an effective mechanism for bringing the student up to his true potential. Yet in the District the limited scope of remedial and compensatory programs, the miniscule number of students upgraded, and the relatively few students cross-tracking make inescapable the conclusion that existing programs do not fulfill that promise. . . .

[The court examines what it terms "the most important single aspect of the track system . . . the process by which the school system goes about sorting students into the different tracks. This importance stems from the fact that the fundamental premise of the sorting process is the keystone of the whole track system: that school personnel can with reasonable accuracy ascertain the maximum potential of each student and fix the content and pace of his education accordingly." 269 F.Supp. at 473–4. The court concludes that aptitude tests are the primary basis for sorting; that "there is substantial evidence that defendants presently lack the techniques and the facilities for ascertaining the innate learning abilities of a majority of District schoolchildren . . . [and that] lacking these techniques and facilities, defendants cannot justify the placement and retention of these children in lower tracks on the supposition that they could do no better, given the opportunity to do so." 269 F.Supp. at 488.]

* * *

The Self-Fulfilling Prophecy. The real tragedy of misjudgments about the disadvantaged student's abilities is, as described earlier, the likelihood that the student will act out that judgment and confirm it by achieving only at the expected level. Indeed, it may be even worse than that, for there is strong evidence that performance in fact *declines*. . . . and while the tragedy of misjudgments can occur even under the best of circumstances, there is reason to believe the track system compounds the risk.

First, the fundamental commitment of the track system is to educate *ability*, not just the student. By assuming the responsibility of deciding who gets what kind of educational opportunity, the school system places a dear price on teacher misjudgments. Thus, when a misjudgment does occur, the result will be institutionally to shunt the student into a curriculum paced to his presumed abilities, where he is likely to progress only at the speed at which he is taught.[146] A sixth-grade student nourished on third-grade instruction is apt to finish the year with a third-grade education; yet the haunting question: could he have done better?

Another aspect of . . . the track system is its tendency to reinforce the psychological impact of being adjudged of low ability. By consigning students to specifically designated curricula, the track system makes highly visible the student's status within the school structure. To the unlearned, tracks can become pejorative labels, symptomatic of which is the recent abandonment of the suggestive "Basic" for the more euphemistic "Special Academic" as the nomenclature of the lowest track. And even if a student may be unaware of labels, he cannot ignore the physical fact of being separated from his fellow students.

None of this is to suggest either that a student should be sheltered from the truth about his academic deficiencies or that instruction cannot take account of varying levels of ability. It is to say that a system that presumes to tell a student what his ability is and what he can successfully learn incurs an obligation to take account of the psychological damage that can come from such an encounter between the student and the school; and to be certain that it is in a position to decide whether the student's deficiencies are true, or only apparent. The District of Columbia school system has not shown that it is in such a position.

146. . . . [A]nother risk of reinforcing a child's present disabilities [is] the lack of contact with students having a command of standard English. The homogeneous class, by grouping students similarly handicapped, removes a source of stimulation available in a mixed ability setting.

Opinion of Law

* * *

The sum result of . . . [t]he infirmities [of the track system], when tested by the principles of equal protection and due process, is to deprive the poor and a majority of the Negro students in the District of Columbia of their constitutional right to equal educational opportunities.

At the outset it should be made clear that what is at issue here is not whether defendants are entitled to provide different kinds of students with different kinds of education. Although the equal protection clause is, of course, concerned with classifications which result in disparity of treatment, not all classifications resulting in disparity are unconstitutional. If classification is reasonably related to the purposes of the governmental activity involved and is rationally carried out, the fact that persons are thereby treated differently does not necessarily offend.

Ability grouping is by definition a classification intended to discriminate among students, the basis of that discrimination being a student's capacity to learn. Different kinds of educational opportunities are thus made available to students of differing abilities. Whatever may be said of the concept of ability grouping in general, it has been assumed here that such grouping can be reasonably related to the purposes of public education. Plaintiffs have eschewed taking any position to the contrary. Rather the substance of plaintiffs' complaint is that in practice, if not by design, the track system—as administered in the District of Columbia public schools—has become a system of discrimination founded on socioeconomic and racial status rather than ability, resulting in the undereducation of many District students. . . .

* * *

Remedy

* * *

As to the remedy with respect to the track system, the track system simply must be abolished. In practice, if not in concept, it discriminates against the disadvantaged child, particularly the Negro. Designed in 1955 as a means of protecting the school system against the ill effects of integrating with white children the Negro victims of *de jure* separate but unequal education, it has survived to stigmatize the disadvantaged child of whatever race relegated to its lower tracks—from which tracks the possibility of switching upward, because of the absence of compensatory education, is remote.

Even in concept the track system is undemocratic and discriminatory. Its creator admits it is designed to prepare some children for white-collar, and other children for blue-collar, jobs. Considering the tests used to determine which children should receive the blue-collar special, and which the white, the danger of children completing their education wearing the wrong collar is far too great for this democracy to tolerate. Moreover, any system of ability grouping which, through failure to include and implement the concept of compensatory education for the disadvantaged child or otherwise, fails in fact to bring the great majority of children into the mainstream of public education denies the children excluded equal educational opportunity and thus encounters the constitutional bar. . . .

* * *

Decree

* * *

It is further ordered, adjudged and decreed that the defendants be, and they are hereby, permanently enjoined from operating the track system in the District of Columbia public schools. . . .

NOTES AND QUESTIONS

1. Scope of the Decision

Hobson declares that the tracking system "simply must be abolished." What is the basis for that conclusion? Is it the fact that black and poor students are assigned in disproportionate numbers to the lowest tracks? *See Johnson v. San Francisco Unified School District*, 339 F.Supp. 1315 (N.D.Cal. 1971), *vacated and remanded*, 500 F.2d 349 (9th Cir. 1974). *But see Berkelman v. San Francisco Unified School District*, 501 F.2d 1264 (9th Cir. 1974) (assignment to college preparatory high school based on previous academic achievement is constitutional). Is the decision based on the inadequacy of aptitude tests as a means of assigning these students to tracks? Does the inadequacy lie in the failure to measure innate ability for all students or only for poor and black students? *See* Bersoff, "Regarding Psychologists Testily: Legal Regulation of Psychological Assessment in the Public Schools," 39 *Md. L. Rev.* 27, 51–58 (1979); Shea, "An Educational Perspective of the Legality of Intelligence Testing and Ability Grouping," 6 *J. of Law & Educ.* 137, 147–48 (1977). Is the inflexibility of the classification system or the inadequacy of education provided for lower-track students the basis for the decision? *See Berkelman v. San Francisco Unified School District, supra.* Should a distinction be drawn between tracking in the elementary grades and tracking in the high schools? *See* Orfield, "How to Make Desegregation Work: The Adaptation of Schools to Their Newly-Integrated Student Bodies," 39 *Law & Contemp. Probs.* 314, 326–27 (1975).

If *Hobson* is not primarily a race case, then what is the constitutional warrant for the decision—that education is a "fundamental" constitutional interest, or that (even unintentional) classifications by socioeconomic status are suspect? *But see San Antonio Independent School District v. Rodriguez*, chapter 6.

The *Hobson* decision was affirmed on appeal. *Smuck v. Hobson*, 408 F.2d 175 (D.C. Cir. 1969) (en banc). The court held:

> The district court's decree must be taken to refer to the "track system" as it existed at the time of the decree . . . [Neither] the school board nor Superintendent Hansen were satisfied with the track system as it was or desired a freeze in its features. . . .
>
> Therefore, the provision of the decree below directing abolition of the track system will not be modified. We conclude that this directive does not limit the discretion of the school board with full recognition of the need to permit the school board latitude in fashioning and effectuating the remedies for the ills of the District school system. . . . The simple decree enjoining the "track system" does not interpose any realistic barrier to flexible school administration by a school board genuinely committed to attainment of more quality and equality of educational opportunity.

408 F.2d at 189–90.

Does the appellate court's interpretation undercut the force of Judge Wright's conclusion? Does it allow the school district to implement a different type of track system? *Compare id. with Spangler v. Pasadena City Board of Education*, 311 F.Supp. 501, 504 (C.D. Cal. 1970), *aff'd*, 427 F.2d 1352 (9th Cir.), *cert. denied*, 402 U.S. 943, 91 S.Ct. 1607, 29 L.Ed.2d 111 (1971)(intraschool grouping of students violates equal protection clause but, given "delicate educational nature of decisions," only reexamination of grouping policies is required). Or is the appellate decision consistent with Judge Wright's statement that: "What is at issue here is not whether defendants are entitled to provide different kinds of students with different kinds of education. . . . [I]t has been assumed here that [ability] grouping can be reasonably related to the purposes of public education [and thus be found constitutionally valid]." *See* Shea, *supra* at 153–54; Orfield, *supra* at 324–28.

2. *Rigidity of the System*

Hobson notes that the assignments of relatively few students are changed. This phenomenon is not unique to Washington. One study of urban school systems found that fewer than 10 percent of all students assigned to special education classes ever returned to the regular program. Gallagher, "The Special Education Contract for Mildly Handicapped Children," 38 *J. Exceptional Children* 527, 529 (1972). The court of appeals opinion in *Hobson* observes: "In some cases statistics are ineluctably ambiguous in their import—the fact that only a small percentage of pupils are reassigned may indicate either general adequacy of initial assignments or inadequacy of review." *Smuck v. Hobson*, 408 F.2d 175, 187 (D.C. Cir. 1969). Does any of the evidence reviewed by the trial court suggest which of these hypotheses might in fact be correct? Might the small percentage simply reflect the accuracy of the school district's assignments—that most students belong where they are originally placed?

One recent study showed that 63 percent of all teachers in the United States find tracking useful, and it is clear that the practice is deeply ingrained. It is found in almost all secondary schools and in most elementary schools. *Academic Tracking*, Report of the NEA Subcommittee on Academic Tracking (1990). This study concluded that, as practiced in most schools, academic tracking does more harm than good. The way tracking operates in most schools is that the students are segregated all or most of the day based on general achievement or behavior rather than on skill in a particular subject. In addition, the groupings are rigid and likely to create racially identifiable classes. At some point, virtually all students are ability grouped, with minority students (African

Americans, Latinos, Native Americans) disproportionately placed in low ability and special education classes. In most cases, students are in these tracks for their entire school careers. Another major finding in the study was that minority students are significantly under-represented in what are called "gate keeper classes"—courses such as eighth grade algebra or ninth grade geometry—which are prerequisites to higher level courses. The report noted that often these "gatekeeper classes" are not even offered in low socioeconomic status schools. Without these foundation courses, students are prevented from pursuing careers in certain fields such as science or engineering.

A study by the Rand Corporation found that disproportionately high numbers of African American and Latino students are assigned to low-ability mathematics and science classes, while very few minorities gain access to high-ability classes. In addition, the study found that low ability classes are taught by less qualified teachers and receive fewer resources, including science laboratories and equipment. Even in elementary schools, 65 percent of math and science classes are tracked and the tracking is strongly correlated with race, although tracking in these earlier years is less based on an academic record than in high school. The report determined that high-ability students in the least advantaged and predominantly minority schools may actually have fewer opportunities and less qualified teachers than low-ability students in schools that are more than 90 percent white. The report concludes that although tracking is "commonly viewed as a neutral, educationally sound response to wide ranges of student aptitude and achievement . . . such groupings are easily and commonly confounded with race and social class. Moreover, the differences in opportunities they provide actually limit instruction rather than fine-tune it." J. Oakes, *Multiplying Inequalities: The Effects of Race, Social Class, and Tracking on Opportunities to Learn Mathematics and Science* (Rand Corp. 1990). "Because schools judge so many low-income and minority students to have low ability, many of these students suffer from being in classrooms that offer less, even if their schools, as a whole, do not." *Id.* at x-xi. The implications the study draws from the findings are that "although schools may *think* that they ration good teaching to those students who can most profit from it, *we find no empirical evidence to justify unequal access to valued science and mathematics curriculum, instruction, and teachers.*" (Emphasis in original.) *Id.* at xi.

3. Educational Outcomes: Social Science Evidence

Hobson notes that classification can affect student achievement: "A sixth-grade student nourished on third-grade instruction is apt to finish the year with a third-grade education; yet the haunting question: could he have done better?" There have been numerous studies of the educational efficacy of ability grouping and special education. These studies attempt to answer a question slightly different from the one posed in *Hobson:* Is a given student likely to learn more in an ability-grouped system than he would in a heterogeneously grouped system? In general the evidence suggests that grouping is most efficacious for children with profound problems (below 25 IQ, autistic) and least efficacious for children in the normal range of intelligence. *See generally* Kirp, "Schools as Sorters: The Constitutional and Policy Implications of Student Classification," 121 *U. Pa. L. Rev.* 905 (1973).

One recent study undertook a comprehensive review of the research published on ability grouping of elementary school students dating back to 1932. This study examines the effects of between- and within-class ability grouping on achievement. The study found as follows: Assigning students to self-contained classes according to ability does not enhance student achievement; the research is unclear on the achievement outcomes of schemes in which students remain in heterogenous classes most of the day, but are regrouped by ability within grade levels for reading and/or mathematics; research on within-class ability grouping, although limited to mathematics and upper elementary schools, supports the use of within-class grouping if the number of groups is kept small—achievement effects were found to be slightly larger for low than for higher average achievers. R. Slavin, *Ability Grouping and Student Achievement in Elementary Schools: A Best-Evidence Synthesis* (1986). Another recent study reviewing the research literature on ability grouped class assignments led to the conclusion that ability grouping in self-contained classes does not increase either achievement or self-esteem of students of any ability level, and negatively affects low ability students. Dawson, "Beyond Ability Grouping: A Review of the Effectiveness of Ability Grouping and its Alternatives," 16 *School Psychology Review* 348 (1987).

A study that summarizes the findings of over fifty research studies on ability grouping of *secondary* school students found that grouping had a very small, positive overall effect on student achievement, with the effect being strongest for high ability students in special honors classes. Those research studies which included students of all ability levels showed virtually no difference in achievement between grouping arrangements for students of high, middle, or low ability. No difference was found on student self-concept or attitude toward school, although students in grouped classes did have somewhat more positive attitudes toward the subject they were studying than ungrouped students. Kulik and Kulik, "Effects of Ability Grouping on Secondary School Students: A Meta-Analysis of Evaluation Findings," 19 *Am. Educ. Res. J.* 415 (1982). *But see* Marsh, "Self-Concept, Social Comparison, and Ability Grouping: A Reply to Kulik and Kulik," 21 *Am. Educ. Res. J.* 799 (1984) (suggesting that ability grouping may have a negative effect on academic self-concept).

An increasing number of education experts argue that the practice of grouping by ability is psychologically damaging to children and of little or no value educationally. *See, e.g.*, J. Oakes, *Keeping Track, How Schools Structure Inequality* (Rand Corp. 1985). Others argue that the problem is not tracking but how it is used. A recent study, based on research in seven school districts in California, outlines the sorting process, examining how students are assigned at all grade levels to schools, teachers, and courses, and how initial assignments are changed, if they are. The authors argue that disclosure to parents of how the school district's sorting process works is important, and they weigh the cost and benefits of disclosure. Friedman & Sugarman, "School Sorting and Disclosure: Disclosure to Families as a School Reform Strategy, Part I: Existing Practices and the Social Interests in School Information Disclosure," 17 *Jour. Law & Educ.* 53 (1988). The authors subsequently argue the possibility of relying on the Fourteenth Amendment Due Process Clause as a doctrinal basis for compelling disclosure, at least "where the sorting decisions are readily subject to discretionary abuse or neglect and where the consequences of the wrong decision are potentially severe." Sugarman & Friedman, "School Sorting and Disclosure: Disclosure to Families as a School Reform Strategy, Part II: Policy and Legal Analysis," 17 *Jour. Law & Educ.* 147, 200 (1988).

4. Stigma

Hobson notes the stigma that attaches to placement in a slow track or special education class. "By consigning students to specifically designated curricula, the track system makes the student's status highly visible within the school structure. To the unlearned, tracks can become pejorative labels, symptomatic of which is the recent abandonment of the suggestive 'Basic' for the more euphemistic 'Special Academic' as the nomenclature of the lowest track."

The following excerpt describes in greater detail the process of stigmatization:

> Many of the classifications that schools impose on students are stigmatizing. However well-motivated the decision or complex the factual bases leading to a particular classification, the classification lends itself to simplified labels. . . .
>
> These adverse school classifications [e.g., placement in slow learner tracks or special education classes] reduce both the individual's sense of self-worth and his value in the eyes of others. For many children, this process is particularly painful because it is novel. It represents the first formal revelation of differentness. The school's inclination to cope with a particular learning or social problem by isolating those who share that problem reinforces the child's sense of stigma. . . .
>
> The stigmatized child, who "tends to hold the same beliefs about identity that [others] do," comes to learn, through contact with the school, that he has in effect been devalued by both the school and the society. [*See* L. A. Dexter, *The Tyranny of Schooling* (1964).]
>
> Children perceive all too well what the school's label means. Jane Mercer observes that those assigned to special education classes "were ashamed to be seen entering the MR room because they were often teased by other children about being MR . . . [and] dreaded receiving mail that might bear compromising identification." . . .
>
> Students assigned to the general or slow learner track described similar feelings: "General teachers make kids feel dumb. Their attitude is, 'Well, nobody's been able to do anything with you, and I can't do better.' " [Harvard Center for Law and Education, "Putting the Child in Its Place," 41 (1971).]
>
> Differences among school children clearly exist, and it would be folly to ignore them: to treat everyone in exactly the same fashion typically benefits no one. Yet even with that qualification, the consequentiality of the school's classification is an awesome fact with which the child must cope. Its psychological ramifications extend beyond the child; they reach his family, and those with whom the child has contact. . . .

> The stigma is further exacerbated, at least in part, by the school's curriculum. The curriculum offered to the "slow" or "special" child is less demanding than that provided for "normal" children; even if the child assigned to the special class does creditable work, he falls further behind the school norm. The initial assignment becomes a self-fulfilling prophesy; the child's belief in his inferiority is reinforced by the knowledge that he is increasingly unable to return to the regular school program. In addition, because his classmates and teachers make fewer demands on him (for by definition less can be expected of the handicapped than the normal), he comes to accept their judgment of acceptable progress as his own. . . .
>
> Slow track assignment makes college entrance nearly impossible and may discourage employers from offering jobs; assignment to a special education program forecloses vocational options. . . . While many children labeled retarded by the school do come to lead normal lives, the stigma persists. . . .

D. Kirp, "Schools as Sorters: The Constitutional and Policy Implications of Student Classification," 121 *U. Pa. L. Rev.* 705, 733–37 (1973).

Stigma is not a phenomenon that admits of ready empirical confirmation. While some studies of student self-perception suggest that students in less advanced school programs typically refer to themselves as "dumb" or "lazy," other students reach inconclusive or inconsistent results. A summary of this research suggests that "the impact of ability grouping on the affective development of children is to build (inflate?) the egos of the high groups and reduce the self-esteem of average and low groups in the total student population." W. Findley and M. Bryan, *Ability Grouping: 1970*, 40 (1971). *See also* Mann, "What Does Ability Grouping Do to the Self-Concept?" 36 *Childhood Educ.* 356 (1960); Borg and Pepich, "Grouping of Slow Learning High School Pupils," 41 *J. Secondary Educ.* 231 (1966); Jones, "Labels and Stigma in Special Education," 38 *J. Exceptional Children* 553 (1972). Few of these studies attempt to relate stigma to student achievement.

What is the legal significance of governmentally imposed stigma? Is the problem one of appropriate process before labeling takes place: *See Paul v. Davis* and the discussion of procedural due process in chapter 3.

5. *Equal Educational Opportunity*

Does the discussion of student achievement and stigma suggest that classification does in fact deny some students—those placed in slower tracks and special classes for the mildly handicapped—equal educational opportunity? In the absence of racial discrimination, what is the constitutional basis for such a claim? *See San Antonio Independent School District v. Rodriguez*, 411 U.S. 1, 93 S.Ct. 1278, 36 L.Ed.2d 16 (1973). Is a constitutional challenge to particular school classifications on the ground that they do not benefit (and might in fact harm students) just another way of stating that particular programs do not meet the educational needs of children assigned to them? These and related questions are considered in chapter 6. Is is constitutionally relevant that the needs argument requires the creation of additional classifications with special school programs for each, while the no-benefit argument would probably restrict the number of permissible classifications?

6. *Racially Specific Harm*

Assignment to a less-advanced program might give rise to a claimed denial of equal educational opportunity, premised on the assertion that such placement secures no educational benefit—and may even cause injury. But assuming that the motivation for placement is not discriminatory, what does the fact of racial overrepresentation add to the constitutional argument? Are minority students more likely to be harmed by such placement than their white peers are?

Fragmentary evidence suggests a positive answer. Although few studies have examined the racially specific harm of sorting, one reanalysis of the Coleman Report did attempt to assess the impact of intraschool segregation on the verbal achievement of black students. It concluded that while *school* integration does not benefit blacks, *classroom* integration does improve black students' test scores. Since proportionately more whites than blacks are assigned to higher tracks, advanced track placement does influence student success. But the differences in verbal achievement between black students in mostly white classes and those in mostly black classes cannot simply be explained by selection processes that operate within the school. Classroom segregation itself causes harm for black students in fast as well as slow classes; classroom desegregation has racially specific benefits. *See* McPartland, "The Relative Influences of school and of Classroom Desegregation in the Academic Achievement of Ninth Grade Negro Students," 25 *J. Social Issues* 93 (1969). *Compare* Zito and Bardon, "Achievement Motivation among Negro Adolescents in Regular and Special Education Programs," 74 *Am. J. Mental Deficiency* 20 (1969).

The United States Civil Rights Commission's reexamination of the Coleman data noted a subtler (and difficult to document) effect of intraschool segregation: Black students in nominally integrated schools, "accorded separate treatment, with others of their race, in a way which is obvious to them as they travel through their classes, felt inferior and stigmatized." 2 *United States Commission on Civil Rights, Racial Isolation in the Public Schools* 86–87 (1967). The harm caused by interschool segregation appeared to the Commission far less substantial than the harm caused by intraschool segregation; while interschool segregation resulted from the relatively impersonal criterion of neighborhood residence, intraschool segregation was clearly caused by personal and pejorative judgments of ability. *See also* Jones, Erickson, and Crowell, "Increasing the Gap between Whites and Blacks: Tracking as a Contributory Source," 4 *Educ. & Urban Soc'y* 339 (1972).

7. *Race and Intelligence*

Some researchers have sought to explain minority overrepresentation in less-advanced programs on the ground that blacks are genetically inferior to whites. That viewpoint is seldom asserted publicly by school officials, but may in fact be the rationale for some classification practices.

a. Empirical Evidence: Pro and Con. Since the publication of Professor Arthur Jensen's article, "How Much Can We Boost IQ and Scholastic Achievement?" in the Winter 1969 issue of the *Harvard Education Review*, a controversy has raged over the degree to which intelligence is genetically determined. *See generally* R. Canero, *Intelligence: Genetic and Environmental Influences* (1971). The focus of the debate is whether inherited elements of intelligence are responsible for the substantially lower IQ scores of lower social class groups (including most blacks) and whether these differences provide pedagogical justification for elaborate classification schemes in the public schools. Not surprisingly, the debate has often been more acrimonious than scholarly. *See generally* R. J. Herrnstein, *I.Q. in the Meritocracy*, 3–59 (1973). One famous study by Cyril Burt, concluding that IQ heritability is roughly .80, is now widely thought to rely on falsified data. *See* M. Weinberg, *Minority Students: A Research Appraisal* 47 (1977), discussing Burt, "Inheritance of General Intelligence," 27 *Am. Psych.* 175 (1972).

Professor Jensen asserts that IQ tests, while measuring more than innate ability, for example, acquisition of information, reflect a general ability that underlies surface skills. *See also* H. J. Eysenck, *The Inequality of Man* 55–56 (1975). This quality, commonly referred to as *g*, Jensen asserts, is largely inherited. *See* A. Jensen, *Bias in Mental Testing* (1980). Since IQ highly correlates with social class and race, he concludes that these IQ differences between populations reflect real genetic variation between social strata. This is true for Jensen even after steps are taken to eliminate cultural bias in testing. Thus, Jensen argues, much of the disparity in IQ scores between blacks and whites must be attributed to inherited differences in intelligence. *See also* Herrnstein, *supra*. In a more recent article, Jensen states that because intelligence is "more biological than psychological or behavioral in nature, educational interventions may have a relatively small effect on IQ or scholastic achievement. Jensen, "Compensatory Education and the Theory of Intelligence," 66 *Phi Delta Kappan* 554, 558 (1985).

Critics of Professors Jensen and Herrnstein do not deny that an individual's intelligence is highly influenced by his genetic background. As both Jensen and Herrnstein make clear, the overwhelming evidence supports this assumption. Nor do the critics deny the undeniable: that the IQ test scores of children from low socioeconomic backgrounds, including most blacks, are substantially lower than those of middle-class white children. Rather the critics challenge the interpretation of the evidence, which asserts that the differences in IQ scores between racial and socioeconomic groups are largely genetic and not environmental in origin. *See, e.g.*, Green, "In Defense of Measurement," 33 *Am. Psych.* 664 (1978). The critics frequently contend that tests, "rather than reflecting cultural inferiority, are indicative of the educational—not genetic—deficiencies of minority children and . . . perhaps the inadequacy of public schools in their present state." Bersoff, "Regarding Psychologists Testily: Legal Regulation of Psychological Assessment in the Public Schools," 39 *Md. L. Rev.* 27, 52–53 (1979).

Cole and Bruner argue that standard intelligence tests, adapted to use in schools, are effective for certain well-established organizational purposes and are fairly effective measures of the performance of certain subcultural groups, particularly the white upper-middle class. It is questionable, in their view, whether they give accurate indications of the abilities of poor and minority children because the demands of their lives are so different from those of middle-class children. These children score poorly on IQ tests because they have not developed many of the skills demanded by schools and tests. Cole and Bruner, "Cultural Differences and Inferences about Psychological Processes," 57 *Am. Psych.* 10, 874 (1971).

Theories about intelligence are changing. Many researchers now view intelligence more as a collection of developed rather than innate abilities. The emphasis is shifting from selection or classification to collecting information that will improve understanding of the way individual students learn. Curtis and Glaser, in an article tracing the history of ideas about intelligence, describe the change in emphasis:

> Educators' disaffection with intelligence tests has been an outgrowth of the shift in emphasis in education from selection of those who will profit most from schooling to ensuring that each individual will profit the most from his or her schooling. Tests that predict scholastic achievement are of relatively little use in planning for improved instruction or understanding learning problems. . . .

Curtis and Glaser, "Changing Conceptions of Intelligence," in *Review of Research in Education* 111, 133 (D. Berliner ed. 1981).

b. Constitutional Implications. How might courts employ data suggesting that the inherited intelligence of blacks is less than that of whites in deciding a case in which a classificatory scheme is attacked because of the overrepresentation of blacks in less-advanced educational programs? Is the evidence clear enough to permit any such conclusions to be drawn from it? Might a court decide that the racial isolation attributable to classification decisions is unconstitutional notwithstanding the lower test scores of blacks—whether those scores are genetically or environmentally determined? *Cf.* Reschly, "Nonbiased Assessment," in G. Phye and D. Reschly, eds., *School Psychology: Perspectives and Issues* (1979); Hunter and Schmidt, "Critical Analysis of the Statistical and Ethical Implications of Various Definitions of Test Bias," 83 *Psych. Bull.* 1053 (1976).

D. Misclassification and Test Bias

Any sorting decision—for example, assignment to an advanced track or to a class for the mildly retarded—is typically based both on certain nominally objective criteria, such as aptitude tests, and on more subtle judgments of ability and potential, such as teacher evaluations.

Misclassification can mean several quite different things. It may denote the misapplication of approved criteria. If the criteria are objective, the issue may be relatively simple to resolve, but if the criteria are judgmental, resolution becomes more difficult.

Misclassification might also denote disputes over the criteria themselves. For example, those who assert that IQ tests are incapable of measuring intellectual potential contend that those tests should not be used to assign students to tracks. One study of 378 educable mentally retarded students from thirty-six school districts in the Philadelphia area notes such misclassification. The researchers tested mildly handicapped students with a battery of tests, rather than the single IQ test typically used by school systems; they found the diagnosis for 25 percent of the youngsters to be clearly erroneous, while, for an additional 43 percent, the diagnosis was questionable. Garrison and Hammill, "Who Are the Retarded?" 38 *J. Exceptional Children* 13 (1971). The judgment of system-made error is premised on the assumption that the researchers' multiple criteria are better classifying instruments than using a single criterion.

In *Hobson v. Hansen*, 269 F.Supp. 401, 490 (D.D.C. 1967), the district court noted an instance of this type of misclassification:

> In 1965 Dr. Hansen announced a change in official policy: thenceforth, no student was to be assigned to the Special Academic Track without first being evaluated by a clinical psychologist and, if necessary, undergoing an individual test of ability. In September of that year 1,272 students, either already in the Special Academic Track or about to be enrolled in it on the recommendations of their teachers and principals, were reevaluated by the psychologists under the new order. As a result of this reevaluation approximately 820, almost two-thirds, were discovered to have been improperly judged as requiring assignment to the Special Academic curriculum. . . .

Does either type of misclassification pose issues of constitutional dimension? Would a parent have a constitutional right to have his child reclassified: (1) on the basis that the school had incorrectly scored the aptitude test which was administered; (2) on the basis that the retesting of the child by an independent psychologist yielded a score considerably higher than that recorded by the school; or (3) on the basis that the aptitude test did not in fact measure the child's aptitude because it was not administered in the child's primary language? *See, e.g., Guadalupe Organization, Inc. v. Tempe School District No.* 3, Civ. No. 71-435 (D. Ariz., filed August 9, 1971) (settled by consent decree, Jan. 24, 1972); *Covarrubias v. San Diego Unified School District*, Civ. No. 70-394-S (S.D. Cal., filed Feb. 1971) (settled by consent decree, July 31, 1972); *Diana v. State Board of Education*, C.A. No. C-70-37 R.F.P. (N.D. Cal., filed Jan., 1970) (settled by stipulation of the parties, Feb. 3, 1970).

Aptitude or IQ tests are the primary basis for determining in which educational program a given student should be placed. But are IQ tests in fact appropriate classifying instruments? *See generally* J. Salvia and J. Ysseldyke, *Assessment in Special and Remedial Education* (1978); Cronbach, "Five Decades of Public Controversy Over Mental Testing," 30 *Am. Psych.* 1 (1975). Do IQ tests predict educational success? Do they accurately measure ability? Do they distinguish between students in need of different types of education? As Judge Irving Goldberg has noted, "[a] sorting device would be invalid to the extent that it does not measure aptitude for a group of students . . . the basis for separation is simply irrational." *Allen v. City of Mobile*, 466 F.2d 122, 127 (5th Cir. 1972) (Goldberg, J., dissenting), *cert. denied*, 412 U.S. 909, 93 S.Ct. 2292; 36 L.Ed.2d 975 (1973). *See generally* Bersoff, "Regarding Psychologists Testily: Legal Regulation of Psychological Assessment in the Public Schools," 39 *Md. L. Rev.* 27 (1979); Shea, "An Educational Perspective of the Legality of Intelligence Testing and Ability Grouping," 6 *J. of Law & Educ.* 137 (1977); Note, "The Legal Implications of Cultural Bias in the Intelligence Testing of Disadvantaged School Children." 61 *Geo. L. Rev.* 1027 (1973).

While the predictive power of IQ tests is far from perfect, might the IQ test be better able to estimate future academic performance than school grades or teacher recommendations—the other plausible criteria for school classifications which may be limited in their utility by their subjectivity and the likelihood that teacher biases and prejudices will be reflected in the results? *See* Sowell, "Race and Intelligence," in *Black Education: Myths and Tragedies* (1972):

> It is easy enough to criticize IQ, college entrance examinations, and other such tests and to show that they need much improvement. But the practical question at any given point in time is, what are the alternatives? Other selection devices and criteria have ranged from ineffective to disastrous. Moreover, it is precisely the black students who need IQ tests most of all, for it is precisely with black students that alternative methods of spotting intellectual ability have failed. Dr. Martin Jenkins, who has conducted more studies of high-IQ black children than anyone else, has commented on how frequently even children with IQ's of 150 have not been spotted as outstanding by their teachers.

Critics have asserted that IQ tests have many shortcomings:

1. Their questions are ambiguous, a trap for the overly thoughtful who rightly recognize that more than one answer may be correct.
2. They treat intelligence (or more accurately, school intelligence) in aggregate terms, failing to recognize that a given student is likely to be competent at some things but not at others, and that combining those strengths and weaknesses into a single score necessarily misdescribes and oversimplifies the notion of intelligence.
3. They fail to measure "adaptive behavior," the capacity to survive in society, and place too high a premium on school intelligence.
4. The tests do not indicate why a given student did poorly in a particular subject. That a child scores in the fortieth percentile in mathematics aptitude, for example, does not tell the teacher what he did not understand or why he did not understand it. It provides no basis for educational intervention to improve performance.
5. The intelligence tests treat a highly mutable phenomenon—aptitude—as a given with which the school can work. They identify intelligence as static and not dynamic, and fail to account for the uneven growth patterns of individual children.

See R. Canero, ed., *Intelligence: Genetic and Environmental Influences* (1971); B. Hoffman, *The Tyranny of Testing* (1962); C. Senna, ed., *The Fallacy of I.Q.* (1973); E. Sharp, *The I.Q. Cult* (1972); J. Franseth and R. Koury, *Survey of Research Grouping as Related to Pupil Learning* (United States Office of Education, HEW) (1966); Heber, "A Manual of Terminology and Classification in Mental Retardation," *Am. J. Mental Deficiency* (monograph Supp. 1961); Stodolsky and Lesser, "Learning Patterns in the Disadvantaged," 37 *Harv.Educ.Rev.* 540 (1967).

Many of the asserted shortcomings of IQ tests relate more to the use made of test results than to the basic construction of the test instrument. Often school officials and teachers view test scores punitively rather than remedially: they are used to label students as "smart" or "dumb" or to distinguish "college material" from future blue-collar workers. In that sense, IQ test results become self-fulfilling prophecies.

Criticism of aptitude tests as a basis for student classification acquires particular force when these tests lead to the overrepresentation of minorities in classes for the educable mentally retarded (EMR) or other low-ability groupings. *See, e.g.*, Bersoff, *supra*; Bernal, "A Response to 'Educational Uses of Tests with Disadvantaged Subjects,' " 30 *Am. Psych.* 93 (1975); Cleary, Humphreys, Kendrick, and Wesman, "Educational Uses of Tests with Disadvantaged Students," 30 *Am. Psych.* 15 (1975); Jackson, "On the Report of the Ad Hoc Committee on Educational Uses of Tests with Disadvantaged Students: Another Psychological View from the Association of Black Psychologists," 30 *Am. Psych.* 88 (1975). Aptitude tests and their use by schools are condemned on several grounds: (1) aptitude tests reward white and middle-class values and skills, especially the ability to speak standard English, and thus penalize minority children because of their backgrounds; (2) the impersonal environment in which aptitude tests are given depresses the scores of minority students, who become anxious or apathetic in such situations; (3) aptitude tests, standardized (or "normed") for white, middle-class children, cannot determine the intelligence of minority children whose backgrounds differ notably from those of the normed population. *See Hobson v. Hansen*, 269 F.Supp. 401, 473–88 (D.D.C. 1967), *aff'd sub nom., Smuck v. Hobson*, 408 F.2d 175 (D.C. Cir. 1969). *See generally* Note, "Test Validation in the Schools," 58 Tex.L.Rev. 1123 (1980).

Larry P. v. Riles

793 F.2d 969 (9th Cir. 1984).

Poole, Circuit Judge:

The State Superintendent of Public Instruction appeals a decision holding that IQ tests used by the California school system to place children into special classes for the educable mentally retarded (E.M.R.) violated federal statutes and the equal protection clauses of the United States and California Constitutions. The district court enjoined the use of non-validated IQ tests, and ordered the state to develop plans to eliminate the disproportionate enrollment of black children in E.M.R. classes. We affirm on the statutory grounds and reverse on the federal and state constitutional issues.

* * *

The district court permanently enjoined the defendants from utilizing any standardized IQ test for the identification of black E.M.R. children or their placement into E.M.R. classes, without securing prior approval of the court. *Id.* at 989. The court ordered the defendants to direct each school district to re-evaluate every black child currently identified as an E.M.R. pupil without using standardized intelligence tests.

Further, the defendants were "ordered to monitor and eliminate disproportionate placement of black children in California's E.M.R. classes." . . .

II. Facts

* * *

In the mid-60's California created programs for several categories of students with educational problems. The "educable mentally retarded" (E.M.R.) program was for schoolchildren of retarded intellectual development who are considered incapable of being educated through the regular educational program, but who could benefit from special educational facilities to make them economically useful and socially adjusted. The "trainable mentally retarded" (T.M.R.) category was for children with more severe retardation than educable mentally retarded. Cal.Educ.Code § 56515 (West 1978) (repealed 1980). . . .

The E.M.R. classes are for children who are considered "*incapable* of learning in the regular classes," and the E.M.R. curriculum "is not designed to help students learn the skills necessary to return to the regular instructional program." *Id.* at 941 (emphasis in original). The E.M.R. classes are designed only to teach social adjustment and economic usefulness. *Id.*

"The [E.M.R.] classes are conceived of as 'dead-end classes,' " and a misplacement in E.M.R. causes a stigma and irreparable injury to the student. *Id.* at 941-42.

. . . [B]lack children have been significantly overrepresented in E.M.R. classes. For example, in

1968–69, black children were about 9% of the state school population, yet accounted for 27% of the E.M.R. population. *Id.* at 938.

"These apparent overenrollments could not be the result of chance. For example, there is less than a one in a million chance that the overenrollment of black children and the underenrollment of non-black children in the E.M.R. classes in 1976–77 would have resulted under a colorblind system." *Id.* at 944. To explain this overenrollment, the defendants proffered a theory that there is a higher incidence of mental retardation among the black population. The district court found that this theory fails to account for the problem, because even "if it is assumed that black children have a 50 percent greater incidence of this type of mental retardation, there is still less than a one in 100,000 chance that the enrollment could be so skewed towards black children. . . . [Further,] the disproportionate E.M.R. enrollment of black children is not duplicated in the classes for the so-called 'trainable mentally retarded' children." . . .

. . . In 1969 "the [State] Department [of Education (SDE)] proposed and the State Board of Education adopted, an addition to the California Administrative Code requiring that approved IQ tests be used as part of the E.M.R. placement process." *Larry P.*, 495 F.Supp. at 946. The district court found that the SDE moved extremely quickly and unsystematically to select those IQ tests for the mandatory list. The district court further found that the person who oversaw this selection was not an expert in IQ testing, and that the SDE did not expressly consider or investigate the problems concerning the disproportionate enrollment of minorities or the cultural bias of IQ tests despite its awareness of these problems. In addition, the SDE contacted no independent testing experts regarding the compilation of the list, and ignored requests from field personnel to take more time to select tests.

* * *

The district court found that the requirement of parental consent for E.M.R. placement does not overcome any deficiencies caused by bias in the placement process, because "that consent is rarely withheld, particularly by minorities, since the mystique of teacher authority and IQ scores tends to overwhelm parents." *Id.* at 950 n. 51.

Since the moratorium on IQ testing in 1975, the total percentage of black children in E.M.R. classes has not changed substantially. The district court, however, examined the data concerning *new* E.M.R. placements, which were made without IQ tests, and found that uncontradicted expert testimony showed that the four percent drop in the placement of black children into E.M.R. classes is not likely to have occurred by chance. *Id.* at 951–52.

On the average, black children score fifteen points, or one standard deviation, below white children on standardized intelligence tests. Thus, utilizing the premoratorium criteria used by California for E.M.R. placement, "approximately two percent of the total population fall below the two standard deviation cutoff, while about 15 percent of black children fall below that level." *Id.* at 954.

The court found that "the tests were never designed to eliminate cultural biases against black children; it was assumed in effect that black children were less 'intelligent' than whites. . . . The tests were standardized and developed on an all-white population, and naturally their scientific validity is questionable for culturally different groups." *Id.* at 956–57. Since the 1920's it has been generally known that black persons perform less well than white persons on the standardized intelligence tests. IQ tests had been standardized so that they yielded no bias because of sex. For example, when sample tests yielded different scores for boys and girls, the testing experts assumed such differences were unacceptable and modified the tests so that the curve in the standardization sample for boys and girls was identical. No such modifications on racial grounds has ever been tried by the testing companies. The district court noted that "the experts have from the beginning been willing to tolerate or even encourage tests that portray minorities, especially blacks, as intellectually inferior." *Id.* at 955.

The district court analyzed and rejected the defendants' arguments advanced at trial that would explain the test score differences, which theorized that the lower scores for blacks were the result of actual, relevant differences between black and white children. The first argument is the genetic argument, which states that natural selection has resulted in black persons having a "gene pool" with lower intelligence than whites. The district court found the assumptions underlying the genetic argument highly suspect, and in any event that the defendants "were unwilling to admit any reliance on [this theory] for policy-making purposes." *Id.*

The second theory is the socioeconomic argument, which theorizes that because of blacks' lower socioeconomic status, they are at a greater risk for all kinds of diseases due to malnutrition and poor medical attention. The district court found that the facts did not support this theory, since it did not explain why more severe mental retardation, *e.g.* that consistent with placement into classes for the trainable mentally retarded children, does not occur in greater proportions among blacks and poorer sections of the population. *Id.* at 956.

The district court found that the appellants failed to show that the IQ tests were validated for blacks with respect to the characteristics consistent with E.M.R. status and placement in E.M.R. classes, *i.e.*, that the defendants failed to establish that the IQ tests were accurate predictors that black elementary schoolchildren who scored less than 70 were indeed mentally retarded. *Id.* at 971–73.

The district court found that alternatives to IQ testing for E.M.R. placement have been in effect since the state moratorium on IQ testing in 1975. These procedures, in which schools take more time and care with their assessments for E.M.R. classification and rely more on observational data, are less discriminatory than under the IQ-centered standard. *Id.* at 973–74.

The district court found that defendants were guilty of intentional discrimination in the use of the IQ tests for E.M.R. placement. The court based this determination on the facts that the historical background of the IQ tests shows cultural bias; the adoption of the mandatory IQ testing requirement in 1969 was riddled with procedural and substantive irregularities, in which no outside sources were consulted by the State Board and the question of bias was never considered, even though the officials were well aware of the bias and disproportionate placement problems caused by the IQ tests (this problem having been addressed in a legislative resolution); the defendants' "complete failure to ascertain or attempt to ascertain the validity of the tests for minority children;" and the failure of the state to investigate and act on legal requirements to report significant variances in racial and ethnic composition in E.M.R. classes. *Id.* at 980–82. The court noted that "the SDE's actions revealed a complacent acceptance of those disproportions, and that complacency was evidently built on easy but unsubstantiated assumptions about the incidence of retardation or at least low intelligence among black children." *Id.* at 983.

* * *

VI. Rehabilitation Act

* * *

In summary, the Education For All Handicapped Children Act specifically requires that tests and evaluation procedures be free of racial and cultural bias. Both the EAHCA and the Rehabilitation Act require that the tests used for evaluation be validated for the specific purpose for which they are used, and that placement not be based upon a single criterion but on a variety of sources. . . .

Appellant argues that the IQ tests were validated for the specific purposes for which they are used. Appellant analogizes to Title VII cases, notably *Washington v. Davis*, 426 U.S. 229, 96 S.Ct. 2040, 48 L.Ed.2d 597 (1976), for the proposition that tests that are valid predictors of future performance can be utilized even if they have a discriminatory impact. There are two problems with appellant's proposition. First, the employment context is quite different from the educational situation. As the district court stated, "[i]f tests can predict that a person is going to be a poor employee, the employer can legitimately deny that person a job, but if tests suggest that a young child is probably going to be a poor student, the school cannot on that basis alone deny that child the opportunity to improve and develop the academic skills necessary to success in our society." *Larry P.*, 495 F.Supp. at 969. Assigning a student to an E.M.R. class denies that child the opportunity to develop the necessary academic skills, since E.M.R. classes do not teach academic subjects and are essentially a dead-end academic track. Second, and more important, the question for predictive validity in schools is not whether the standardized intelligence tests predict future school performance generally, as appellant argues, but whether the tests predict specifically that black elementary schoolchildren (as opposed to white elementary schoolchildren) who score at or below 70 on the IQ tests are mentally retarded and incapable of learning the regular school curriculum. In this case, the appellant would have to have shown that the tests are a proven tool to determine which students have characteristics consistent with E.M.R. status and placement in E.M.R. classes, *i.e.*, "whose mental capabilities make it impossible for them to profit from the regular educational programs" even with remedial instruction. The regulations place the burden of showing such validation on the defendants.

The district court found that defendants failed to show that the tests were validated for placing black students with scores of 70 or less in E.M.R. classes. The district court noted that very few studies had examined the difference of IQ predictability for black as compared to white populations, and that those studies which had examined this problem found the tests much less valid for blacks than for whites. Further, the district court found that, even assuming the tests were validated for placement of white schoolchildren in E.M.R. classes, such validation for blacks had been generally assumed but not established. For example, the tests had been adjusted to eliminate differences in the average scores between the sexes, but such adjustment was never made to adjust the scores to be equal for black and white children. *Id.* at 971. The court found that the reason for this was a basic assumption of a lower level of intelligence in blacks than in whites. The fact that early test developers indeed made this assumption is borne out by the literature and testimony at trial. *See id.* at 954–60. In addition, no studies have been made, either by the defendants or the testing companies, to investigate the reasons for the one standard deviation difference in test scores between the races or to determine whether test redesign could eliminate any bias. *Id.* at 971. There was expert testimony that a much larger percentage of black than white children had been misplaced in E.M.R. classes. Based on the evidence in the record, the district court finding that the appellant had not established validation of the test is not clearly erroneous.

The district court also found that the appellant did not utilize the variety of information required by statute and regulation to make E.M.R. placements, but relied primarily on the IQ test. This finding also is not clearly erroneous. Testimony showed that school records lacked sufficient evidence of educational history, adaptive behavior, social and cultural background or health history for these factors to have been utilized in placement. *See* IV, *supra*.

* * *

VII. Title VI

Title VI of the Civil Rights Act of 1964, 42 U.S.C. § 2000d, provides that:

> No person in the United States shall, on the ground of race, color, or national origin, be excluded from participation in, be denied the benefits of, or be subjected to discrimination under any program or activity receiving federal financial assistance.

Regulations issued under this statutory mandate require that recipients of federal funding may not

> utilize criteria or methods of administration which have the effect of subjecting individuals to discrimination because of their race, color, or national origin, or have the effect of defeating or substantially impairing accomplishment of the objectives of the program as respect individuals of a particular race, color, or national origin.

34 C.F.R. § 100.3(b)(2), originally adopted as 45 C.F.R. § 80.3(b)(2).

In *Guardians Association v. Civil Service Commission of City of New York*, 463 U.S. 582, 103 S.Ct. 3221, 77 L.Ed.2d 866 (1983), a majority of the Court held that a violation of Title VI required proof of discriminatory intent.[7] A different majority held, however, that proof of discriminatory effect suffices to establish liability when the suit is brought to enforce regulations issued pursuant to the statute rather than the statute itself.

The appellees relied on the regulations issued pursuant to Title VI. *Larry P.*, 495 F.Supp. at 965.

7. The Court previously held that no discriminatory intent must be proved to show a violation of the statute. *Lau v. Nichols*, 414 U.S. 563, 568, 94 S.Ct. 786, 789, 39 L.Ed.2d 1 (1974). This circuit has expressly followed *Lau*. *Guadalupe Organization v. Tempe Elementary School*, 587 F.2d 1022, 1029 (9th Cir.1978); *De La Cruz. v. Tormey*, 582 F.2d 45, 61, n. 16 (9th Cir.1978), *cert. denied*, 441 U.S. 965, 99 S.Ct. 2416, 60 L.Ed.2d 1072 (1979). The district court applied *Lau* while recognizing that subsequent dicta in Supreme Court opinions questioned that conclusion. *E.g.*, *Board of Education of New York v. Harris*, 444 U.S. 130, 159–60, 100 S.Ct. 363, 379–40, 62 L.Ed.2d 275 (1979) (dissenting opinion of Stewart, Powell, and Rehnquist); *Regents of the University of California v. Bakke*, 438 U.S. 265, 284–87, 98 S.Ct. 2733, 2745–46, 57 L.Ed.2d 750 (1978). Nevertheless, even after *Bakke*, the Supreme Court reaffirmed an "effects" standard. *Fullilove v. Klutznick*, 448 U.S. 448, 479–80, 100 S.Ct. 2758, 2775–76, 65 L.Ed.2d 902 (1980). Despite these conflicting signals, a majority of Justices now agree that discriminatory intent is required. *Guardians Association*, 103 S.Ct. at 3236-37 (Powell, J. and Burger, C.J.): 103 S.Ct. at 3237 (Rehnquist, J., concurring in the judgment); 103 S.Ct. at 3237–38 (O'Connor, J., concurring); 103 S.Ct. at 3253 (Stevens, J., dissenting and joined by Brennan and Blackmun, J.J.).

The lower court held that the placement mechanisms for E.M.R. classes operated with a discriminatory effect in violation of the regulations and HEW's "interpretative guidelines". *Id.* In light of appellees' reliance on the regulations, we find it appropriate to apply a discriminatory effect analysis.

A prima facie case is demonstrated by showing that the tests have a discriminatory impact on black schoolchildren. *Board of Education of New York v. Harris*, 444 U.S. 130, 151, 100 S.Ct. 363, 375, 62 L.Ed.2d 275 (1979). Once a plaintiff has established a prima facie case, the burden then shifts to the defendant to demonstrate that the requirement which caused the disproportionate impact was required by educational necessity.

Appellees clearly demonstrated the discriminatory impact of the challenged tests. It is undisputed that black children as a whole scored ten points lower than white children on the tests, and that the percentage of black children in E.M.R. classes was much higher than for whites. As discussed previously, these test scores were used to place black schoolchildren in E.M.R. classes and to remove them from the regular educational program. The burden therefore shifted to the defendants to demonstrate that the IQ tests which resulted in the disproportionate placement of black children were required by educational necessity.

Appellant argues first that E.M.R. classes are a benefit for, rather than adverse discrimination against, black children, implying that appellees did not even establish a prima facie case. However, the district court found that improper placement in E.M.R. classes has a definite adverse effect, in that E.M.R. classes are dead-end classes which de-emphasize academic skills and stigmatize children improperly placed in them. *Larry P.*, 495 F.Supp. at 941–42. Even appellant's witnesses testified that it would be extremely improper for a non-mentally retarded child to be placed in an E.M.R. classroom. Though the E.M.R. class might be a benefit for those students who are educable mentally retarded, it is clearly damaging to a non-retarded student to be placed in those classes. The district court's finding is not clearly erroneous, and thus appellees established a prima facie case of a Title VI violation based upon discriminatory effect.

Appellant next argues that even if the impact is adverse, it is not caused by discriminatory criteria (the IQ tests), but by other nondiscriminatory factors: (1) placement is based on a variety of information and evaluation tools that are non-discriminatory, and not solely on the IQ tests; (2) the tests are validated for black schoolchildren, and therefore accurately reflect mental retardation in black children; and (3) blacks have a higher percentage of mental retardation than whites.

Appellant's first two arguments have been discussed in VI, *supra*, and are unavailing. Appellant's third argument is that the disproportionate number of black children in E.M.R. classes is based on a higher incidence of mental retardation in blacks than in whites that is due to poor nutrition and poor medical care brought on by the lower socioeconomic status of blacks. This argument also fails. Appellees showed, and the district court made a finding, that "the overrepresentation of black children in E.M.R. classes cannot be explained away solely on the grounds of the generally lower socio-economic status of black children and their parents." *Id.* at 956. The district court specifically found the testimony of appellant's experts in support of this argument failed to explain why more severe mental retardation does not occur in greater proportions among the poorer sections of the population. In addition, there was testimony from other experts that poor nutrition or medical care during early life does not affect later performance on IQ scores, unless it is a severe malnutrition of a type that is rare in this country. This finding of the district court has not been shown to be clearly erroneous.

* * *

VIII. Equal Protection Violation

* * *

We cannot, however, sustain the finding of a violation by Superintendent Riles of the equal protection clause of the fourteenth amendment on the theory that the pervasiveness of discriminatory effect can, without more, be equated with the discriminatory intent required by *Washington v. Davis*. Accordingly, we reject these facts of the trial court and reverse the conclusions that the Superintendent was guilty of intentional discrimination under the fourteenth amendment.

* * *

X. Remedy

The district court, in addition to enjoining the use of nonvalidated intelligence tests and requiring reevaluation of every current black E.M.R. pupil, ordered the defendants to require every school district that had a racial disproportion in E.M.R. classes to devise a three-year remedial plan, and to bring to the court's attention any disparities that persist at the end of this period. *Larry P.*, 495 F.Supp. at 989–90.

* * *

Appellant . . . contends that the court's order to eliminate the disproportionate enrollment requires an impermissible quota. The district court's order, though, does not impose any quota on future E.M.R. placements. Even with respect to eliminating *present* disproportionate enrollment, the district court allowed an error leeway of one standard deviation. Further, the district court does not require that students properly placed in an E.M.R. class be removed. The court only required that any disproportion in excess of one standard deviation after three years be brought to the court's attention. If the school district can show, utilizing properly validated procedures complying with applicable statutes, that the black students in the E.M.R. classes properly belong there, there would be no need to eliminate the remaining disproportion. Since there are no fixed numerical requirements, the district court's order is not an impermissible quota. *See Regents of the University of California v. Bakke*, 438 U.S. 265, 98 S.Ct. 2733, 57 L.Ed.2d 750 (1978).

* * *

Enright, District Judge, dissenting in part and concurring in part:

* * *

I. Federal Statutory Claims

* * *

In the instant case, the appellees have shown only that a higher percentage of blacks were placed in the E.M.R. classes. As I interpret those cases applying a discriminatory effects analysis, the appellees should have been required to show that a disproportionate number of minority students were *improperly placed* by virtue of their IQ test scores.

Proper placement in the E.M.R. classes is a benefit, not a stigmatic dead-end assignment. As discussed in the majority opinion, these classes were established to assist students incapable of satisfactory achievement in the regular school curriculum. The program was thought to be extremely helpful to enrollees in that it permitted those individuals to acquire skills within their capabilities that in turn would permit them to have useful and productive lives and thus reach their full potential. It is, and always has been, a completely voluntary program, requiring two fully informed parental consents, one for permission to initially test and one to place a child in such a program. Placement in the program requires testing, evaluation and observation by trained personnel, as well as the objective measure of IQ testing procedures. Once enrolled, parents had the option *at any time* to withdraw their child from the program.

Yet, solely because of the disproportionate number of black children within the E.M.R. program, the district court struck down the heretofore accepted IQ tests and required the composition of the class to mirror the racial percentages of the school district. That holding ignores the beneficial aspect of proper placement and misstates the appellees' burden of proof. Before the tests in question can be labeled as discriminatory, there must be a showing that they produced improper placement into the E.M.R. program. No such showing was made. The only arguable finding of specific misplacement is the conclusory observation of the district court that

> while we see no reason to enter into the cases of the named plaintiffs, we can observe that the only relevant evidence on their cases indicated that they were not retarded.

* * *

That analysis assumes that the statistical disparity in the composition of the classes is caused by improper placement of black children. Upon that unsubstantiated premise rests the district court's finding that the appellees made an initial showing of discriminatory impact. The burden then shifted to the defendants to justify the use of IQ tests in the E.M.R. placement process, despite the fact that none of the named appellees were shown to have been improperly placed in the classes. In so doing, the district court and the majority invert the allocation of proof on the critical issue presented in the case; namely, did the appellants' testing procedures place black children in the E.M.R. program who did not belong there.

Though regrettable, it is not surprising the district court neglected to ascertain the validity of the specific E.M.R. placements. It would seem difficult, if not impossible, to identify an individual as a proper candidate for the E.M.R. program without employing some form of standardized IQ testing. Faced with the unenviable task of pinpointing educably retarded children on the basis of subjective data independent of the challenged IQ tests, the district court elected to base its conclusions on the supposition detailed above. Yet, the school districts are left in the same difficult position of proving that certain black students belong in the E.M.R. program in those districts where statistical disparity remains.

It is clear that the causes of racially disparate placement are complex, as well as controversial. Experts in the area have disagreed in the past and continue to disagree. The particular methodology chosen and the understandable failure to account for the universe of potential explanatory variables opens every purported finding to criticism. The record in this case shows that widely recognized IQ tests employed by defendants have long been hailed for their ability to correct the exact abuse complained of in this case—misevaluations and misplacement. Educators recognize that subjective evaluation, uncorroborated by objective criteria, carries enormous potential for abuse and misplacement based on the personal or cultural values of the evaluator. Here we strike the only objective criteria.

* * *

NOTES AND QUESTIONS

1. Cultural Bias

How does the *Larry P.* court deal with the question of cultural bias in IQ testing given the evidence that IQ tests are no worse predictors for minorities than for whites? Does the existence of differential scores between blacks and whites prove cultural bias? Is the problem that blacks in EMR classes (as well as whites) receive an inadequate education and that the tests are unacceptable because they are used to reach the judgment that a class of children cannot profit from regular classes? *See* Note, "Test Validation in the Schools," 58 *Tex.L.Rev*. 1123, 1139, 1151–53 (1980).

In *Parents in Action on Special Education v. Hannon*, 506 F.Supp. 831 (N.D. Ill. 1980), the court was confronted with the same issue as in *Larry P.* but reached a different result. After a thorough examination of the Wechsler Intelligence Scale for Children (WISC), the WISC Revised (WISC-R), and the Stanford-Binet, the tests used to help determine educable mentally handicapped (EMH) status in the Chicago school system, the court concluded that these tests, when used in conjunction with other criteria that are statutorily mandated for determining EMH status, do not discriminate against African American children. *Id.* at 883. Although the court found several questions on these tests were culturally biased, it concluded that the possibility of theses questions causing an improper EMH placement was "practically nonexistent." *Id.* at 876. The court relied on the fact that these tests required that a child had to have a certain number of consecutive misses on the test, which becomes increasingly more difficult, before the child's educational status is determined. Thus, even if a child missed a question because it was culturally biased, this would not prejudice the child as he or she would have to miss several more questions in a row before a determination of the child's IQ is made. *Id.* at 875. The court also pointed out that most of the racially biased questions occur at a level of difficulty that is beyond the level which EMH students could reach. *Id.* at 875-76. Finally, and most important, the court emphasized the fact that there is an extensive assessment process involved in making the determination of EMH status that goes far beyond reliance on these tests. *Id.* at 879-80.

What evidence shows that IQ tests are culturally biased? Would minority students perform better on so-called culture-free tests? So far, efforts to create culture-free tests have been unavailing. *See, e.g.*, Reschly, "Nonbiased Assessment," in G. Phye and D. Reschly, eds., *School Psychology: Perspectives and Issues* 215 (1979); Ebel, "The Social Consequences of Educational Testing," in A. Anastasi, ed., *Testing Problems in Perspective* 18 (1966); Chase and Pugh, "Social Class and Performance on an Intelligence Test," 8 *J. Educ. Measurement* 197 (1971). What is a culture-free test? For example, would the language in which the test is given be considered part of the cultural bias? Should IQ tests be administered in one's primary language? Would this include minority dialects? *Cf. Martin Luther King Jr. Elementary School Children v. Michigan Board of Education*, 451 F.Supp. 1324 (E.D. Mich. 1978). Does the definition of cultural bias depend upon the purposes to which the test results will be put? That is, is an English language test appropriate for placement in a remedial English class but not appropriate for classification as a retarded student?

Whatever the shortcomings of aptitude tests, do they not merely confirm that nonmiddle-class and minority children do poorly in schools as presently organized? If tests are culturally biased, are school curricula and employer expectations also biased? *See* Comment, "Ability Grouping in Public Schools: A Threat to Equal Protection?," 1 *Conn. L.Rev.* 150, 161 (1968). Does this suggest that using a culturally neutral (or culturally relevant) test for minority students might well be an academic exercise unless such tests were accompanied by drastic alterations in schooling and hiring practices? *See* Green, "In Defense of Measurement," 33 *Am. Psych.* 664, 669 (1978).

2. Larry P. *and* Hobson

In the *Hobson* case, Judge Wright made the following comment:

> When standard aptitude tests are given to low income Negro children, or disadvantaged children, . . . the tests are less precise and less accurate—so much so that tests scores become practically meaningless. Because of the impoverished circumstances that characterize the disadvantaged child, it is virtually impossible to tell whether the test score reflects lack of ability—or simply lack of opportunity. Moreover, the probability that test scores of the Negro child or the disadvantaged child will be depressed because of somewhat unique psychological influences further compounds the risk of inaccuracy.

269 F.Supp. at 485.

Is this consistent with the position taken in *Larry P.*? Is it fair to say that *Larry P.* questions the efficacy of using IQ tests to make EMR placements for all students, whereas *Hobson* focused only on their alleged inadequacies for minority students? If so, why then is *Larry P.* a race case? Is it that the harm of IQ tests is greater for minority students?

Professor Bersoff has questioned the assumption that IQ tests are less accurate for blacks than for others. Bersoff, "Regarding Psychologists Testily: Legal Regulation of Psychological Assessments in the Public Schools," 39 *Md. L.Rev.* 27, 52, 56 (1979). *See* Cleary, Humphreys, Kendrick, and Wesman, "Educational Uses of Tests with Disadvantaged Students," 30 *Am. Psych.* 15, 24 (1975). Is this another way of saying that the education system and not the tests is the "villain"? Professor Bersoff adds:

> [F]rom the psychometric point of view the [*Hobson*] court's gravest error was its insistence that grouping can only be based on tests that measure innate ability. No psychologist who has written on the subject believes that tests measure hereditary endowment solely.

Bersoff *supra*, at 51, citing, *inter alia*, A. Jensen, *Bias in Mental Testing* (1980).

In the *Hobson* case, Judge Wright notes that the standard aptitude tests are less accurate in the case of low-income black children "because of the impoverished circumstances that characterize the disadvantaged child." In *Larry P.*, the school district had argued that "because of blacks' lower socioeconomic status, they are at a greater risk for all kinds of diseases due to malnutrition and poor medical attention." On what basis did the court dismiss this argument? The *Hannon* court concluded, however, that the socioeconomic argument was a valid one. The court found that the lack of cognitive stimulation, which is essential for intellectual development, is often associated with economic poverty in the home. Thus, the fact that blacks score lower on the tests used to determine educable mentally handicapped status than whites is a result of their lower economic status. *Hannon*, *supra*, at 877–88. Even though both *Larry P.* and *Hannon* label the argument as one based on socioeconomic status, is the theory explaining the discrepancies in test scores between whites and blacks in *Hannon* the same as that put forward in *Larry P.*? Assuming the *Hannon* court was correct that the discrepancy in test scores is due to lack of intellectual stimulation because of poverty, does it follow that these children belong in classes for the educable mentally retarded?

For a useful analysis and discussion of the disproportionate assignment of minority students to special education classes, the placement procedures used, and the effects of such placements, see K. Heller, W. Holtzman & S. Messick, *Placing Children in Special Education: A Strategy for Equity* (1982).

> [T]he main purpose of assessment in education is to improve instruction and learning. Children are or should be assessed in order to identify strengths and weaknesses that necessitate specific forms of remediation or educational practice. . . .
>
> . . . A concern with disproportion per se dictates a focus on bias in assessment instruments and a search for instruments that will reduce disproportion. A concern with instructional utility leads to a search for assessment procedures and instruments that will aid in selecting or designing effective programs for all children. We believe that better assessment and a closer link between assessment and instruction will in fact reduce disproportion, because minority children have been the victims of poor instruction. We also believe the problem should be attacked at its roots, which lie

in the presumption that learning problems must imply deficiencies in the child and in consequent inattention to the role of education itself in creating and ameliorating these problems.

This viewpoint has led us to urge a greater emphasis on systematic intervention *before* a child is referred for individual assessment. When poor instruction has been ruled out as a cause of learning failure, it becomes appropriate to look for problems within the child or in the child's environment outside the school, again with an eye toward problems that can be corrected; this is the purpose of individual assessment.

Id. at 72. The authors also pose the following question:

> Rather than inquiring about the causes of disproportion and how to remedy the problem of disproportion in special education and in EMR classes in particular, a different and more constructive perspective is to ask: Under what circumstances does disproportion constitute a problem? While remedies to disproportion per se are based on an assumption that the disproportions in themselves constitute an inequity, the educational and social conditions under which such an assumption is true should be examined explicitly. Three aspects of the regular and special education programs and placement procedures are most salient in this regard: Disproportion is a problem (1) if children are invalidly placed in programs for mentally retarded students; (2) if they are unduly exposed to the likelihood of such placement by virtue of having received poor-quality regular instruction; or (3) if the quality and academic relevance of the special instruction programs block students' educational progress, including decreasing the likelihood of their return to the regular classroom.

Id. at 17–18.

E. Segregation, Disproportional Racial Impact, and Competency Tests

1. Introduction. I.Q. tests are not the only tests to have been challenged in the courts. In the last decade many states and school districts have required students to pass a test, often referred to as a competency or minimum competency test, before they can be promoted to the next grade or graduated from high school. Competency tests are supposed to test essential skills and competencies. The rationale is that using these tests will improve education by ending "social promotion" of incompetent students, and raise the level of educational achievement. *See generally*, Haney and Madaus, "Making Sense of the Competency Testing Movement," 48 *Harv.L.Rev.* 462 (1978). Haney and Madaus describe some of the problems with minimum-competency-based testing programs:

> Discussions often proceed as if competencies or skills can be easily identified. Efforts have been made to use experts or "objective analysis" to determine those skills needed by adults to "function" or to "survive" in society. These efforts have resulted in very detailed specifications of competencies and life skills. But brief reflection suggests that the meaning of minimum functioning in society is very hard to pin down. . . .
>
> Since some "life skills"—for example, filling out tax forms or looking something up in the yellow pages—are not directly taught in many schools, it might be unfair, and perhaps even illegal, to deny someone a high school diploma for lack of proficiency skills not taught in school. A fundamental issue in the competency-testing movement, then, is whether to assess competencies that will be needed later in life or restrict testing to the more traditional school skills, on the assumption that they have some relationship to success beyond school.
>
> The latter approach seems to have been the one adopted by most states planning minimum-competency testing. . . . Such schemes give attention mainly to skills in reading, writing, and arithmetic. . . .
>
> . . . Agreement on what desirable areas of competence might be . . . may be considerably easier to establish than the cut-off point for minimum competency. . . . "[E]very attempt to derive a criterion score [for example, to define minimum competency] is either blatantly arbitrary or derives from a set of arbitrary premises.". . . [E]laborate statistical techniques cannot do away with the subjectivity involved in setting cut-off scores.
>
> In practice, the setting of minimum scores seems to be the result of compromise between judgments of what minimums seem plausible to expect and judgments about what proportions of failure seem politically tolerable. . . .
>
> . . . *Time* magazine ran an article on the Florida [minimum competency test] results under the headline, "Florida flunks," with the subtitle "A Scandal for Schools." The Florida results revealed differing failure rates on the mathematics and communication tests. Eight percent failed the latter, while 36 percent failed the former. As a result, the state of Florida allocated $10 million for remedial instruction in arithmetic. The inference . . . was that achievement in mathematics was lower than in communication skills. However, . . . an alternative explanation [was offered] for the differing failure rates—namely, that the math items on average were more difficult than items on the language examination.
>
> The problems of test development and its cost have led some states and localities simply to adopt com-

> mercially available tests of reading and mathematics as their initial competence assessment devices. In Florida, for example, items from the Adult Performance Level Test and others developed by ETS have been used . . . , a practice that raises issues of curricular [tests should measure topics actually covered in the curriculum] and instructional [topics in the curriculum have actually been taught to the students tested] validity. Imposition of readily available tests can very easily come to determine skills taught, rather than having desired skills guide the selection of appropriate assessment techniques.

Haney and Madaus, *supra*, at 462–72. *See also* McClung, "Competency Testing Programs: Legal and Educational Issues," 47 *Fordham L.Rev.* 651 (1979).

A majority of states have now mandated some form of competency testing. As of 1984, at least nineteen of them required the tests for high school graduation. Anderson and Pipho, "State Mandated Testing and the Fate of Local Control," 66 *Phi Delta Kappan* 3, 210–11 (1984).

2. ***Debra P. v. Turlington*: Disproportionate Impact on Minorities.** Under the Florida Educational Accountability Act of 1976, the legislature had established three standards for graduation from Florida public high school: (1) completion of a specified minimum number of credits as determined by the local school board; (2) mastery of certain basic skills; and (3) satisfactory performance on a functional literacy test as determined by the Florida State Board of Education. The legislature later amended the Act to require passage of a functional literacy test in order to receive a regular high school diploma. Those who failed the test but who had completed the requisite minimum hours of study would receive only a certificate of completion. Each school district was placed under an obligation to develop a remedial program for those unable to meet the Act's standards.

The state administered a State Student Assessment Test (SSAT) in 1977, 1978, and 1979, and the results consistently demonstrated a disparate failure rate between blacks and whites. The first time the test was administered, 25% of the white students and 78% of the black students failed. While the passing rates improved when students retook the test, even after the third administration ten times more black students failed the test than white students. Florida had operated a dual school system from 1885 to 1967, and substantial racial isolation existed in the period 1967–1971. With the commencement of the school year 1971–1972, physical desegregation of schools in Florida was formally accomplished. According to a federal court in Florida, there were numerous difficulties encountered by black students during the 1971–1979 period:

> Although children of all races suffered in the initial years of integration, black children suffered to a greater degree. The most significant burden which accompanied black children into the integrated schools was the existence of years of inferior education. . . . Other problems presented to black children were disparate busing schedules, lingering racial stereotypes, disproportionate terminations of black principals and administrators, and a high incidence of suspensions. . . . Additionally, the state during part of this period did not offer the leadership or the funding to mount a wide-scale attack on the educational deficits created during segregation. Remediation with specifically delineated objectives and programs did not commence until 1977.

Debra P. v. Turlington, 474 F.Supp. 244, 252 (M.D. Fla.1979), *aff'd in part*, 644 F.2d 397 (5th Cir. 1981).

NOTES AND QUESTIONS

*1. **Relationship Between Past** De Jure **Segregation and Present Minority Failure Rates***

Is the Florida competency testing scheme unconstitutional as applied to African American students? Consider the district court's holding:

> In the Court's opinion, punishing the victims of past discrimination for deficits created by an inferior educational environment neither constitutes a remedy nor creates better educational opportunities. When students regardless of race are permitted to commence and pursue their education in a unitary school system without the taint of the dual school system, then a graduation requirement based on a neutral test will be permitted. The Court must conclude that utilization of the SSAT II in the present context . . . is a violation of the equal protection clause of the Fourteenth Amendment, ...

Debra P. v. Turlington, 474 F.Supp. at 257.

Does it follow from the proposition that black students are not responsible for their high rate of failure on the competency test in Florida that the test is unconstitutional or that there is no substantial state interest in determining competencies, irrespective of the reasons for failure?

Is the district court persuasive that there is a cause-and-effect relationship between past de jure segregation practices in Florida and present black failure rates on the State Student Assessment Test? The court of appeals, in affirming the lower court's decision, states that the defendants had "failed to demonstrate either that the disproportionate failure of blacks was not due to the present effects of past intentional segregation or, that, as presently used, the diploma sanction was necessary to remedy those effects." *Debra P. v. Turlington*, 644 F.2d 397, 407 (5th Cir. 1981), *on remand*, 564 F.Supp. 177 (M.D. Fla. 1983), *aff'd*, 730 F.2d 1405 (11th Cir. 1984). Under what circumstances might a state that has previously engaged in racial discrimination successfully carry its burden of proof?

At what point in time would it become constitutional for Florida to impose competency tests on its black students? In *Debra P.* the state was required to wait until students who had attended dual school systems had graduated before the new testing requirement could take effect. *Debra P.*, 730 F.2d at 1414. This was done so that residual effects of early inferior schooling could not be a factor in the way blacks scored on the test. The court also found that the testing requirement may actually help to compensate for past inequities, since it sets standards that will help to motivate both students and staff. *Id.* at 1416. *See also Johnson v. Sikes*, 540 F.Supp. 761 (S.D. Ga. 1982), holding that plaintiffs prevailed on their claim that the competency test required for graduation discriminated on the basis of race, and ordered defendants not to impose the diploma sanction until the class of 1983, since that would be the first group of graduating students who began their education after the abolition of the segregated school system. The court also held that the school district could reinstate the diploma sanction only if it could show that the increased educational opportunities of the test outweighed any lingering causal connection between the past discriminatory tracking system and the imposition of the diploma sanction. The circuit court dismissed the appeal on procedural grounds. 730 F.2d 644 (11th Cir. 1984).

See Love v. Turlington, 733 F.2d 1562 (11th Cir. 1984), in which an 11th grade aptitude test that more blacks than whites failed was upheld because the test was designed only to target students who needed remedial work, and was not used as a basis for granting or denying a diploma. *See also* Bester v. Tuscaloosa City Board of Education, 722 F.2d 1514 (11th Cir. 1984).

2. *Feasibility of Competency-Based Education*

Is competency-based education not feasible? How else might a legislature approach the problem of social promotions and undeserved degrees? Is there no consensus about the competencies that should be achieved? If the tests are limited to a few widely accepted skills and competencies, if a reasonable effort is made to teach those skills in schools, and if the tests are geared to insuring minimal ability to function as a citizen, taxpayer, employee, and so on, should the fact that the scheme is far from perfect be troubling?

3. *Educational Failure*

Can a test truly separate the competent from the incompetent? Are students just above a passing score likely to be very different in ability from those just below the cutoff? Is the argument over whether competencies can be measured, or is it over who shall measure and how such competencies will be measured? If a student fails a course, is not promoted, or drops out of high school, is this not a "competency" decision made by teachers? Those who argue against competency-based education (with its companion testing instruments) presumably believe that teachers are thought to be better able to make such judgments. What evidence is there to support this proposition? Or is it that, in such a sensitive area, policymakers should prefer decentralized decision making, eschewing standardized written tests as the sole measures of competence? Might teacher-created examinations suffer from the same flaws as standardized tests (lack of instructional verification, cultural bias)? Might teachers sometimes be less objective?

Are critics of minimum competency testing implicitly suggesting that children should not fail, that they are stigmatized by failure? Or is it that critics believe that competency tests create failures that would not otherwise exist? Do competency tests and traditional classroom tests attempt to measure the same thing?

4. Constitutionality of the Test for Any Group

If a competency test is unconstitutional as applied to blacks who receive an inferior educational experience, does it follow that the tests are unconstitutional for any group that receives an inferior education? Consider the alternative holding of the court of appeals in *Debra P.*:

> . . . It is clear that in establishing a system of free public education and in making school attendance mandatory, the state has created an expectation in the students. From the students' point of view, the expectation is that if a student attends school during those required years, and indeed more, and if he takes and passes the required courses, he will receive a diploma. This is a property interest as that term is used constitutionally. *See Goss v. Lopez*, 419 U.S. 565, 579 . . . (1975). . . .
>
> Based upon this implied property right, we find that the trial court was correct in holding that the implementation schedule for the test violated due process of law. In its finding, the court quoted from the report of the state's own task force:
>
> > "The problems created by the abrupt schedule for implementing the Functional Literacy Test were the most severe for the members of Florida high school graduation class of 1979. At the eleventh hour and with virtually no warning, these students were told that the requirements for graduation had been changed. They were suddenly required to pass a test constructed under the pressure of time and covering content that was presumed to be elementary but that their schools may or may not have taught them recently, well, or perhaps at all."
>
> The due process violation potentially goes deeper than deprivation of property rights without adequate notice. When it encroaches upon concepts of justice lying at the basis of our civil and political institutions, the state is obligated to avoid action which is arbitrary and capricious, does not achieve or even frustrates a legitimate state interest, or is fundamentally unfair. *See St. Ann v. Palisi*, 495 F.2d 423, 425 n.5 (5th Cir. 1974). We believe that the state administered a test that was, at least on the record before us, fundamentally unfair in that it *may* have covered matters not taught in the schools of the state.

644 F.2d 397, 403–404 (5th Cir. 1981).

Do the Florida tests, under the circumstances outlined by the court, violate procedural or substantive due process? *Compare Wells v. Banks*, 153 Ga.App. 581, 266 S.E.2d 270 (App. 1980), rejecting plaintiffs' due process claim as adequate notice had been provided by the school district that passing achievement tests in reading and math would be required for graduation. Are the tests "fundamentally unfair" in some constitutional sense? Why may not a state condition a diploma or license on knowledge of matters "not taught in the schools of the state"? *See* Note, "Testing the Test: the Due Process Implications of Minimum Competency Testing," 59 *N.Y.U. L.Rev.* 577 (1984).

Would language minorities (for example, Latinos) who are not given the competency tests in their primary language have a constitutional claim similar to that of blacks in *Debra P.*?

5. Rights and Duties Created by Competency-Based Requirements

Might the existence of state-mandated minimum competency tests that purport to test essential skills and competencies that students should have learned at various stages in their school career establish a duty on the part of the state to provide remedial education adequate to enable students to pass these tests? *See* Liebman, "Implementing *Brown* in the 90's: Political Reconstruction, Liberal Recollection, and Litigatively Enforced Legislative Reform," 76 *Va. L. Rev.* 349 (1990), in which Professor Liebman argues that competency-based or educational performance standards mandated by the state could establish a judicially enforceable right to a minimally adequate education. *Cf. Peter W. v. San Francisco Unified School District*, 60 Cal. App.3d 814, 131 Cal. Rptr. 854 (1976).

SIX

Equal Educational Opportunity and School Finance

I. INTRODUCTION

The denial of equal educational opportunity is, as shown in the previous chapter, one doctrinal source for objection to discrimination based on race. But for policymakers and courts, the concept has other meanings and uses as well. Historically, educational opportunity has been defined primarily in resource (or input) terms; its elements included a universally available and free education, a common curriculum, and equality of resources—teachers, texts, and the like—within a given school district. *See* Coleman, "The Concept of Equality of Educational Opportunity," 38 *Harv. Educ. Rev.* 7 (1968). But there are variations in per pupil expenditures and educational services on at least three levels. As a result of differences among states in taxable wealth and taxing capacity, *interstate* disparities in per pupil expenditures are significant. In 1988, Connecticut was one of the highest spending states ($6,230 per pupil) and Mississippi was one of the lowest spending states ($2,548). Thus the gap in per pupil expenditures between the two states amounted to $3,682. As a recent report has noted, however, the disparity between the poorest district in one state and one of the highest spending districts in another state are orders of higher magnitude.

> For example, in the lowest-spending district in Mississippi, the Pontotoc County School system, per pupil spending in 1986–87 was only $1,324. This paltry sum should be viewed not just against the expenditure of $4,018 per child in Claiborne County, the highest-spending district in Mississippi, but against the $11,752 and $10,544 per student expended by Shoreham-Wading River and Great Neck, respectively, two of the wealthiest districts in the state of New York. It cannot seriously be argued that the nine to ten thousand dollar-per-child difference between the poorest Mississippi schools and the wealthy Long Island schools is accounted for in cost-of-living differences alone. And it seems highly unlikely that this disparity, amounting to well over $200,000 for each class of 25 children, has no impact on the quality of education provided by these school systems.

Taylor and Piché, "A Report on Shortchanging Children: The Impact of Fiscal Inequity on the Education of Students at Risk," prepared for the House Committee on Education and Labor, 19–20 (December 1990). Taylor and Piché also note that "states with the lowest per pupil expenditures are generally also the states with the greatest concentrations of economically disadvantaged students." *Id.* at 19. Thus, Connecticut ranks second lowest in the percentage of children under eighteen in poverty in 1985 (11.8 percent), while Mississippi ranks highest (34.3 percent). *Id.* at 73, Table 2.

Intrastate or *interdistrict* variations refer to differences in per pupil expenditures among districts within a single state. In many states, the level of spending in one district within a state is often three or four times that of another district within the state. There are extremes where the differences are as great as twenty to one or more.

Intradistrict variations refer to the level of spending per pupil within a single urban school district, which may be considerably higher in schools serving children from middle-class backgrounds than the amount spent per child in schools with a predominantly poor and minority student body. While interstate and intradistrict inequality remain extremely important issues, starting in the late 1960s and early 1970s, the attention of the courts and state legislatures has been drawn to the question of inequalities in educational opportunity between school districts. Fiscal pressures on school districts, taxpayer revolts against the rising cost of education, and a rising concern with equity on the part of school-finance scholars, legal experts, citizens' groups, foundations, various other reform-minded organizations, and even governmental officials combined to bring into being the school finance reform movement of the 1970s. *See* Fuhrman, *State Education Policies: The Case of School Finance Reform* (Education Commission of the States, December 1979).

The scope of the reform movement is as impressive as the variety of its participants. Stephen Carroll found that, between 1972 and 1979, at least twenty-two states had modified their educational finance systems. Some of these states responded to political pressures; others responded to judicial decisions and orders. Carroll, *The Search for Equality in School Finance: Summary and Conclusions* (2420-NIE, The Rand Corporation, March 1979). In 1980, roughly thirty states were or had been involved in litigation over their systems of school finance.

As the reform movement progressed the principles, theories, and economic analyses evolved and became increasingly sophisticated and complex. This chapter presents the story of this reform, beginning with an introduction that sets the stage for the judicial opinions and other materials to follow. Section II considers interdistrict inequalities in expenditures per pupil, and it presents cases and materials in roughly chronological order. Section III turns to the issue of intradistrict inequalities in educational expenditures, an issue that has received considerably less judicial and scholarly attention.

II. DESCRIBING AND ASSESSING THE HISTORICAL SYSTEM

A. Property Taxes and Inequalities in Expenditures

Although education is primarily a state responsibility, and local school districts are administrative units of the state, with the sole exception of Hawaii (which is fully state-funded), the financing of public schools is a joint enterprise of the state and its local school districts. Historically, in most states the local property tax was the major source of education revenues. In the late 1970s, the local contribution was close to 60 percent nationwide, and the state share was 40 percent. By the following decade, the state share was approximately 54 percent, and the local share of the nonfederal educational dollar was 46 percent. However, more recent data indicate that there has been some slippage, with reliance on the local property tax rising.

These national averages conceal tremendous variation among the states. In 1984–85, the state contribution for the State of New Hampshire was 7 percent, with 93 percent coming from the local property tax, while in California, the state contribution was 90.6 percent, and the local contribution 9.4 percent.

The first step in raising revenue from a property tax is to assess the value of the property to be taxed. Assessment of property poses an extremely difficult problem for technical reasons—it is often difficult to establish the market value of such different kinds of property as residences, farmland, factories, utilities, golf courses—and for political reasons; that is, there is often great pressure to hold down assessments, particularly assessments on residential relative to commercial property. Once the total assessed value of property within a district is determined, the local government (school board) must adopt its budget. The projected expenditures of the government unit minus its income from other sources is the amount to be raised by local property taxes. This amount divided by the assessed valuation of the property within the jurisdiction of the government gives the tax rate to be applied to the property. This tax rate is usually expressed in mills (one-tenth of one cent or one-thousandth of a dollar). To compare the ability of school districts to raise revenues, a standardized unit, obtained by dividing the total value of the district's assessed property by the number of pupils in the district, is used. Since the tax rate is the unit used to determine the district's "willingness" or "effort" to support its schools, a combined measure of ability and effort is derived by multiplying the district's tax rate by its assessed valuation per pupil. This figure is the amount of local revenue per pupil. For a more detailed discussion of property taxes, *see* W. I. Garms, J. W. Guthrie, and L. C. Pierce, *School Finance* 132–39 (1978).

Inequalities in revenues per pupil among school districts within a state are primarily the result of differences among districts in per pupil taxable property base. The differences often are three or four to one. However, in 1968–69 in California the difference between the district with the lowest property value and the district with the highest assessed value per pupil was $50,885 in Beverly Hills to $3,706 in Baldwin Park. *Serrano v. Priest*, 5 Cal. 3d 584, 600 n. 15, 96 Cal. Rptr. 601, 612 n. 15, 487 P.2d 1241, 1252 n. 15 (1971). Disparities in per pupil property wealth in some states have only increased since then. In 1985–86, the wealthiest district in Texas had $14 million in property wealth per pupil, while the poorest district in Texas had $20,000 in per pupil property wealth. *Kirby v. Edgewood Indep. School Dist.*, 761 S.W.2d 859, 867–68 (Tex. Ct. App. 1988) (Gammage J., dissenting), *rev'd*, 777 S.W.2d 391 (Tex. 1989).

While interdistrict disparities are principally attributable to disparities in property wealth per pupil, they are also attributable to differences in tax rates and inequitable property assessment practices. Because of the differences in the capacity of school districts to raise revenues and the difficulty that some school districts with very limited property tax bases had in raising sufficient funds for even a minimal program, states historically have provided funds to school districts to supplement the locally raised revenues. State aid has taken a variety of forms:

The flat grant program. Many states provided a basic or "flat grant"—funds distributed on the basis of equal dollars per pupil to each school district, regardless of whether the district was property-rich or property-poor. For a period, a number of states financed education solely through flat grants distributed to school districts on top of the revenues generated from the local property tax base. Today, no state relies solely on flat grants as a means of distributing state funds for education. Connecticut was the last state to do so. Its financing system was successfully challenged in *Horton v. Meskill*, 31 Conn. Supp. 377, 332 A.2d 113 (1974), *aff'd*, 172 Conn. 615, 376 A.2d 359 (1977), and Connecticut adopted a different plan. The flat grant program assumes that a specific basic or minimum level of education should be guaranteed to every student. The state distributes this minimum level of dollars per pupil to every school district; any additional amount spent on education is a matter for the individual school district to decide, but it is not subsidized by the state. The difficulty is that the flat grant is not based on any particular level of education that the dollar buys, nor does it take into account pupils with special, more costly, needs, or differences in the cost of providing the same educational services in rural, urban, and suburban school districts.

The foundation program. Under this approach, the state guarantees to every district a certain minimum level of revenue per pupil, provided the district makes a minimum effort of its own by imposing a stipulated minimum property tax rate. The amount that the district will pay is computed in accordance with this legislatively determined tax rate, and the state provides the difference between the amount contributed from local revenues at that tax rate and the state-guaranteed minimum. Thus, a district with a low property base will raise only limited revenue at the specified tax rate, and the state will make up the difference. A property-rich district may raise more than the state-guaranteed minimum at the specified tax rate and thus will receive no "equalization aid" from the state.

The difficulty with the foundation program is similar to that with the flat grant program, that is, that any relation between the state-guaranteed foundation and what is necessary for a minimally adequate education is, in most cases, fortuitous, and will not take into account differences among the needs of pupils or the cost of delivering comparable educational services.

Percentage equalizing. Under this approach, the state does not provide any specific dollar amount that it has determined is the minimum necessary for a basic education but instead assists the district, depending upon its "ability" (property tax base per pupil), to determine the amount of education the district itself thinks is appropriate. Thus, the district determines the size of its budget—how much it wants to spend for education—and the state provides a percentage of that budget. The percentage that the state provides is based on the district's "aid ratio," which is based on the assessed value per pupil of the district and the assessed value per pupil of the state as a whole. An explanation of the formula is provided by Garms, et al., *supra*, at 913:

> [The] aid ratio is defined by means of a formula usually written in the form
>
> $$\left(1 - f\frac{y_i}{\bar{y}}\right)$$
>
> where y_i is the assessed valuation per pupil of the district, $\bar{y}$ is the assessed valuation per student of the state as a whole, and f is a scaling factor that is usually set somewhere between 0 and 1.
>
> For example, if assessed valuation per pupil of the district were $10,000 and that of the state $40,000, and the scaling factor were .5, the aid ratio for the district would be
>
> $$\left(1 - .5 \times \frac{10{,}000}{40{,}000}\right) = .875$$
>
> This means that the state would provide 87.5 percent of the budget of the district, with the district expected to raise the remaining 12.5 percent from local taxes. . . .
>
> If the district had instead had an assessed valuation per pupil of $40,000, the aid ratio remaining at .5, the state would have provided 50 percent of the budget. . . . When a district's assessed valuation per pupil becomes twice that of the state, the aid ratio becomes zero. . . .

Each of these formulas, even the flat grant, can be demonstrated to have an equalizing effect; that is, it reduces the differences among districts in the amount of money spent per pupil and in the capacity to raise money. But the equalizing effect is often not strong, even when these formulas are not encumbered by special provisions added for political reasons. Typically, however, legislatures have added "save harmless" provisions to their formulas that, for example, guarantee districts the same amount of aid they received the prior year even though a straight application of the formula would indicate a lowering of state aid for that district in the coming year. In short, the formulas in practice have the effect of maintaining the disparities among districts in the amount of money spent per pupil.

B. Defining Equal Educational Opportunity

There are a number of ways in which equal educational opportunity can be defined. One is *equal access to education*, which assumes that, in the area of school finance, every child must have the same minimum level of school services, reflected by the state's guaranteeing a minimum education expenditure level. The flat grant and foundation programs are based on this assumption, which permits localities to add their own resources to the state's guaranteed minimum. The result, however, is wide variations in expenditures per pupil that reflect disparities in the quality and level of school services provided students. "All other things being equal, it is hard to imagine that students from poorly funded school districts with large classes, inadequately prepared teachers, and limited course offerings have the same opportunity to learn as their more fortunate counterparts in districts spending two or three times the state average." Garms, et al., *supra* at 22.

A second definition is *equal educational treatment*. This definition is based on the fact that different student populations have different needs, and the nature and level of school services provided to those students should vary according to need. Categorical funds, which are funds directed to certain target pupil populations, are often the approach taken. Federal funds, in particular, often are based on this definition of equality of educational opportunity. For example, handicapped students or students whose native language is not English may need additional resources to bring them to the same "starting line" as other students. Thus, equal treatment for all pupils would require *unequal* resources.

Yet a third definition is *equality of educational outcomes*. The concern here is that the measure of equality should be equal student achievement, at least in terms of certain basic skills.

When, as a moral, policy, or constitutional matter, should one conclude that inequalities among districts in the amount of money spent per pupil are wrong or impermissible? A variety of standards for assessing whether a school financing system provides students with an equal educational opportunity is available. Some of these standards measure equal educational opportunity in terms of "inputs," that is, dollars per pupil or the educational resources those dollars purchase (books per pupil, square feet per pupil, or number of pupils per qualified teacher).

Inputs are to be distinguished from the "outcomes" of the educational process, such as reading achievement, attitudes, motivation, and so forth.

Input standards can be negative, the generalized formulation of such a standard being as follows: The pattern of distribution of inputs (whether it be expenditures per pupil, books per pupil, pupil-teacher ratios) within a state must not be a function of (be determined by, caused by, correlated with) _____. The blank could be filled in with such phrases as: the per-pupil property wealth of the school district in which the students reside; the median family income of the district in which the students reside; the "taste" for education of the voters in the district in which the students reside; the wealth of the pupils' own families; and the race, religion, or ethnic origin of the pupil. It is important to note that the negative-input standard does not require equality in the allocation of resources; it only demands that if there are inequalities, they must not be caused by or determined by a particular variable that is deemed a morally irrelevant basis for allocating resources.

There are also negative-outcome standards. Such a standard could state that academic achievement must not be a function of the social-class background of the students. This standard implies that to the extent students from lower socioeconomic backgrounds have lower achievement levels than other students, extra efforts must be made by schools to change this pattern. The correlation between social-class background and school achievement must be broken; that is, it should no longer be possible to state with any degree of certainty that because a given student is black and from a poor family he or she will do less well on standardized achievement tests than the national average. Stated differently, school achievement must be the result of individual talent only. Coleman, "The Concept of Equality of Educational Opportunity," 38 *Harv. Educ. Rev.* 7 (1968).

There are also positive-input and positive-outcome standards. An example of a positive-input standard is one that requires resources to be allocated among pupils within the state on the basis of complete equality. A variation of this standard is one that requires equal resources for a basic education, permitting local leeway for an "enriched" program. *See Seattle School Dist. No. 1 v. Washington*, 90 Wash. 2d 476, 585 P.2d 71 (1978). Another positive-input standard is one specifying that variations in the allocation of resources may not exceed certain limits, for example, the variation in expenditures per pupil may not exceed one hundred dollars. *See Serrano v. Priest*, Civ. No. 938, 254 (Los Angeles Co. Super. Ct., Cal., April 10, 1974).

Full-fledged positive-outcome standards are perhaps the most appealing but also the most demanding standards. These directly address what most people are concerned about—educational outcomes. They are truly *educational* standards, whereas the negative-input standard is concerned simply with general fairness or equity. But outcome standards, while appealing, are hard to attain given the present state of knowledge as to what it is that promotes learning. These problems aside, examples of positive-output standards include the following: All children of normal or above normal ability shall learn to read at a seventh-grade reading level as measured by a standardized test; or all normal children shall at least achieve functional literacy. A different kind of positive-output standard might require that every child be equipped "for his role as a citizen, and as a competitor in the labor market." *Robinson v. Cahill*, 62 N.J. 473, 515, 303 A.2d 273, 295 (1973).

Standards that speak in terms of pupil needs are hard to classify—they speak in terms of inputs, but the level of educational resources each pupil or type of pupil requires has to be related to outcomes. For example, a student with a learning disability might require more educational resources to achieve a certain reading level than a nonhandicapped child. An educationally or economically disadvantaged student might require some form of compensatory education to enable him or her to achieve at grade level. The ultimate standard of this kind requires that each student be given the resources necessary to develop his or her talents to their fullest.

There is yet a different category of standards that is related to neither input nor output but can be most properly described as one of taxpayer equity. For example, one such standard requires equal tax incidence according to the ability to pay. Application of this standard usually results in the imposition of a progressive or proportional tax system. Another standard is that equal effort (equal tax rates) produce an equal yield. In the case of school districts, this means freeing the tie between "capacity"—the district's per pupil property value—and "effort"—the district's tax rate. This standard is a variation of the negative-input standard that requires that the amount of money spent per child shall not be a function of property wealth per pupil other than that of the state as a whole. *See Serrano v. Priest*, (*Serrano I*), *contra Robinson v. Cahill*, 62 N.J. 473, 502–3, 303 A.2d 273, 288 (1973).

Choosing among these and other similar standards is no easy task. The input standards are simple to use and administer but might be educationally irrelevant. Moreover, does it make a difference in the educational opportunity a child is afforded if the amount of money spent by the public school on his or her education is not a function of the property wealth of the school district but continues to be a function of the taste of the district's voters for education? The outcome standards are more truly "educational" standards, but they may be difficult to achieve for a variety of political, economic, and scientific reasons. *See generally* Yudof, "Equal Educational Opportunity and the Courts," 51 *Tex. L. Rev.* 411 (1973).

Finally, on what basis can the judiciary impose some of these standards? The judiciary may not have the constitutional warrant, the institutional capacity, or the political support to impose a particular standard. *See* Kurland, "Equal Educational Opportunity: The Limits of Constitutional Jurisprudence Undefined," 35 *U. Chi. L. Rev.* 583 (1968).

C. Expenditures and Achievement

A concern with equity and fairness as a simple matter of justice is one thing, but as a practical matter, does it make an educational difference to pupils if their school district spends less money on them than another district spends on on its pupils? The relationship between resources and outcomes is problematic.

In 1964, pursuant to §402 of the 1964 Civil Rights Act, the U.S. Office of Education undertook a "survey . . . concerning the lack of availability of equal educational opportunities. . . ." It was the second largest social science research project in history; background and achievement test data for some 570,000 pupils, and information concerning some 60,000 teachers and 4,000 school facilities was gathered by a group headed up by sociologist James S. Coleman.

The conclusions of *Equality of Educational Opportunity Survey* (1966) (usually referred to and hereafter cited as the *Coleman Report*) are surprising on several counts. First, the differences in resources available to minority and white students are small, and while on balance the differences favor the whites, that is not always the case. This pattern seems to hold true in the South—still largely segregated at the time of the report—as well as elsewhere in the nation. Some notable differences between minority and white schools do, however, emerge: Minority schools have less academic and accelerated instruction, were less likely to be accredited, and the teachers of minorities had lower verbal test scores than the teachers of whites. And regional differences in resource availability persist: Southern schools are generally less well endowed than schools elsewhere. Professors Mosteller and Moynihan, commenting on these data, observe: "In 1966 the nation had come much closer to achieving [the] classical notion of equality of educational opportunity [equality of resources] than most of us realized then or realize now." Mosteller and Moynihan, "A Pathbreaking Report," in *On Equality of Educational Opportunity* 3, 11–12 (1972).

Second, and even more interesting, the *Coleman Report* analyzed "the relation of variation in school facilities to variation in levels of academic achievement. It reported *so little relation as to make it almost possible to say there was none.*" *Coleman Report* at 15 (emphasis added). School expenditures, exposure to schooling, facilities (rooms per teacher, laboratories, and the like), access to libraries or textbooks, class size, teacher background and training—none of these input measures had much effect on student outcomes. Pupil-teacher ratio showed so little relationship to achievement that it was dropped from the final analysis. District per-pupil instructional expenditure for grades six, nine, and twelve accounted for a mere .09 percent of the "variance" in educational achievement of black students in the North, and .29 percent for white northerners.

What do these findings mean? The popular but incorrect reading of the *Coleman Report* is that schools "don't make a difference." As Professors Mosteller and Moynihan rightly note: "This is absurd. Schools make a very great difference to children. Children don't think up algebra on their own. . . . But given that schools have reached their present levels of quality, the observed variation in schools were reported by EEOR to have little affect upon school achievement." Mosteller and Moynihan, *supra* at 21.

Certain resources do affect school achievement. The student's home background (including region, degree of urbanization, socioeconomic status, and ethnic group) was found to be the primary determinant of school success; that variable, however, is largely unreachable by any school policy. Student achievement also varied with the social class of other students in the school: Children of low socioeconomic status appeared to benefit significantly from exposure to more affluent and more highly motivated peers. But the general picture that emerged from the *Coleman Report* was clear and discouraging. "[S]chools receive children who already differ widely in their levels of educational achievement. The schools thereafter do not close the gaps between students aggregated into ethnic/racial groups. Things end much as they begin." Mosteller and Moynihan, *id.*

Scholars criticized the *Coleman Report* on methodological grounds: It was suggested that the way in which input-outcome relationships were calculated was structured to minimize the importance of school factors; that the sample was not properly done; that there were too many nonresponses and too many districts that refused to cooperate with the survey. The most detailed criticism concluded:

> We have attempted to show that both the measurement of school resources and the control of social background of the student were inadequate, and that the statistical techniques used were inappropriate. By no means do we wish to suggest that the actual relations are the opposite of what the report concludes or that further research will not substantiate some of the report's findings; but until better evidence is found, we will have to remain agnostic about which relationships prevail.

Bowles and Levin, "The Determinants of Scholastic Achievement—An Appraisal of Some Recent Evidence," 3 *J. Human Resources* 3, 23 (1968).

The *Coleman Report* data were reanalyzed over a four-year period by a group of Harvard social scientists. Christopher Jencks, who examined resource-outcome relationships for northern urban schools, noted:

> (1) Eliminating all school-to-school differences in mean achievement would only reduce the overall inequality of sixth-grade academic outcomes by 16 to 22 percent in the urban North. [In other words, 78 to 84 percent of the differences lie within, not among, schools.]
>
> (2) Only a handful of the school policies and resources measured in the EEOS were appreciably related to the racial and socioeconomic backgrounds of urban sixth graders. [In other words, there is little correspondence between school resources and student characteristics, thus making it impossible to disentangle the effects of the two types of factors.]
>
> (3) Differences in achievement among students from the same socioeconomic and racial background were not related to most of the school characteristics measured in the EEOS. This was especially true of reading and math achievement. Where achievement was associated with a school characteristic, the nature and direction of causality were almost always in doubt. [Some resources, such as library books, appear to be associated with *lower* achievement.]
>
> (4) Ninety percent of the variation in northern urban elementary schools' mean verbal achievement, 85 percent of the variation in their mean math achievement, and 80 percent of the variation in their mean reading achievement were accounted for by region, racial composition, and socioeconomic composition. An additional 2 or 3 percent could probably be accounted for by variations in initial ability.

Jencks, "The Coleman Report and the Conventional Wisdom," in F. Mosteller and D. Moynihan, eds., *On Equality of Educational Opportunity* 69, 104–05 (1972).

Professor Eric Hanushek has summarized the results that have accumulated from 112 studies (other than the *Coleman Report*) on the effects of schools and teachers on the performance of students. These studies examined the relationship between such school inputs as expenditures per pupil, pupil-teacher ratios, educational level of the teachers, teachers' years of experience, teacher salaries, and facilities with such outcome variables as student achievement on standardized reading tests. Professor Hanushek found that the vast majority of these studies found no statistically significant relationship between these inputs and any of the measured student outcomes.

Professor Hanushek concludes that there is little reason to believe that any of the purchased inputs have a consistent impact in the expected (and desired) direction. His policy conclusion is that, insofar as finance reform is aimed at helping students rather than taxpayers, we should pay less attention to school finance reform and more attention to introducing greater flexibility in the hiring, pay, and promotion of teachers. Hanushek, "Throwing Money at Schools," 1 *J. Am. Pub. Pol. & Mgt.* 19 (1981).

Several studies, however, have indicated that some school factors—such as class size and teacher experience—are significant. *See* Summers and Wolfe, "Do Schools Make a Difference?" 67 *Am. Econ.*

Rev. 639 (1977); M. Rutter, B. Maugham, P. Mortimer, and J. Ouston, *Fifteen Thousand Hours: Secondary Schools and Their Effects on Children* (1979). Still more recent studies that are micro- rather than macro-analyses, analyzing resource allocation *within* classrooms, show very different results. MacPhail-Wilcox and King, "Resource Allocation Studies: Implications for School Improvement and School Finance Research," 11 *Jour. Educ. Finance* 416 (1986). MacPhail-Wilcox and King note that

> Given the standardization of educational curricula, administrative practices, and certification regulations since the turn of the century and the limitations inherent in large scale analyses, it is not surprising that micro-analytical studies linking student performance to teacher traits, processes, and behaviors yield statistically stronger relations than do macro-analytic studies. The latter largely ignore the fact that teachers, indeed students themselves, can vary students' access to and consumption of resources in the classroom. . . .
>
> Generally, researchers working at the classroom level conclude that curriculum content, pedagogical strategy, learning materials, time allocated for and engaged in learning, teacher use of time, and climate explain significant variation in student outcomes. Homework practices, teacher expectations, role definitions, sense of efficacy, provision of "wait time" for student response, amount of criticism and praise, and time allocated for instructional monitoring and feedback on performance are other important sources of explanation.
>
> * * *
>
> These findings seem to reflect important linkages between teacher behaviors and student achievement. . . .
>
> This emerging research also suggests that teachers alter teaching practices and instructional conditions depending upon such student characteristics as socioeconomic status, gender, race and age. Low socioeconomic students are less frequently instructed in a small group, individualized, or tutored settings than are high socioeconomic students.

Id. at 426–27.

A review of the recent literature on school effectiveness finds that it attempts to challenge the assumption that differences among schools have little effect on student academic achievement.

> The quest to discover how to increase the academic achievement of students from all walks of life has not been overwhelmingly successful. Many factors shown to have a dramatic influence on student learning—family background and related variables . . .—are not easy to manipulate, at least not in the short run. Other variables that can be measured and, in theory, changed relatively easily, usually by spending money, have been found to bear little relationship to achievement: decreasing class size, raising teacher salaries, buying more library books, changing the reading series, constructing new school buildings, or adding compensatory education programs. . . .
>
> In contrast, the new literature on the determinants of achievement is concerned with variables relating to (1) how schools and school districts are structured and make decisions; (2) the process of change in schools and school districts; and (3) how classrooms and schools can be changed to increase the time spent on productive instruction. Although these variables are less susceptible to mechanical changes in policy, they are alterable . . .—generally with difficulty, but often for little money. Variables that influence achievement can be found at all levels of local schooling—the classroom, the school, and the district. Examples at each level include increasing classroom "academic learning time" . . . , creating a school atmosphere conducive to learning . . . , and district allowance of school-site management. . . .
>
> It is one thing to demand that all schools be effective; it is an entirely different matter to assume, without further research, that what has positive effects in one setting will invariably have the same effects in another. There is also a dearth of longitudinal studies. It is not clear that the reading scores of a third-grade class in an effective school will look the same when that class is in the sixth or eighth grade. Similarly, though a few studies control for random variations by examining schoolwide achievement scores for several years prior to the beginning of the study, it is again not clear that a designated effective school will remain so in the future—or was in the past. Any cutoff line is arbitrary, but it seems reasonable and prudent to expect an effective school to have been so historically and to remain effective before raising the banner of success over its doors.
>
> * * *
>
> . . . The history of education reform demonstrates that, no matter how well-planned, systematic interventions in schools are not always successful in form or outcome. . . . In fact, current theories of school organization suggest that there are structural and procedural characteristics of schools that mitigate against this sort of top-down change. . . .
>
> . . . We believe that the most important organization-structure variables are the following:
>
> 1. School-site management: A number of studies indicate that the leadership and staff of a school need considerable autonomy in determining the exact means

by which they address the problem of increasing academic performance. . . .

2. Instructional leadership: Though we are suspicious of the "great principal" theory, it seems clear that leadership is necessary to initiate and maintain the improvement process. . . . The principal is uniquely positioned to fill this role, and certainly his or her support is essential very early on. . . . Nevertheless, groups of teachers or other administrators can provide leadership.

3. Staff stability: Once a school experiences success, keeping the staff together seems to maintain, and promote further, success. . . . Frequent transfers are destructive and likely to retard, if not prevent, the growth of a coherent and ongoing school personality.

4. Curriculum articulation and organization: At the secondary school level, a planned, purposeful program of courses seems to be academically more beneficial than an approach that offers many electives and few requirements. . . .

5. Schoolwide staff development: Essential change involves altering people's attitudes and behaviors as well as providing them with new skills and techniques. In order to influence an entire school, the staff development should be schoolwide rather than specific to individual teachers and should be closely related to the instructional program of the school. . . .

6. Parental involvement and support: Though the evidence is more mixed here, it is reasonable to assume that parents need to be informed of school goals and student responsibilities, especially with regard to homework. . . . Our feeling is that parent involvement is not sufficient, but that obtaining parental support is likely to influence student achievement positively.

7. Schoolwide recognition of academic success: A school's culture is partially reflected in its ceremonies, its symbols, and the accomplishments it chooses to recognize officially. Schools that make a point of publicly honoring academic achievement and stressing its importance through the appropriate use of symbols, ceremonies, and the like encourage students to adopt similar norms and values. . . .

8. Maximized learning time: If schools choose to emphasize academics, then a greater portion of the school day would be devoted to academic subjects . . . , students would spend more time during class periods in active learning activities . . . , and class periods would be free from interruptions by the loudspeaker, messages from the counseling office, or disruptions from the hall or yard outside. . . .

9. District support: Fundamental change, building-level management, staff stability, and so on all depend on support from the district office. Few, if any, of the variables found to be significant are likely to be realized without district support. . . .

Purkey and Smith, "Effective Schools: A Review," 83 *The Elementary School Journal* 427 (1983).

NOTES AND QUESTIONS

1. Fiscal Equalization and the Quality of Education

Do these contradictory studies suggest that approaches to school finance reform that emphasize fiscal equalization or inputs to schooling are not likely to have any impact on the quality of education? Do they suggest a different remedy for inequities in resources than equalizing inputs? How might a remedy be devised to affect outcomes? Do courts have the ability to address these issues or can they only address problems in the process that have led to inequities in funding, rather than channel new funds into areas that will make a difference?

2. Non-School Factors that Affect Achievement

A Boston study has demonstrated a clear link between an improvement in pupils' academic performance and their participation in the Federal School Breakfast Program. Low income, mostly minority elementary students, who had been receiving breakfast at school showed an average test score increase of 48.4 points from the year before, while the scores of students not eating school breakfast rose 40.9 points on a 600-point scale. "U.S. School Breakfast Program Lifts Test Scores," *New York Times*, June 22, 1988 at B6. Does this suggest that factors outside of school, rather than unequal distribution of in-school resources, affect academic achievement? Or that additional resources should be provided to certain target student populations that would help to bring them up to the same "starting line"? Regardless of whether it is good social or educational policy, is there a constitutional basis for requiring such targeted resources?

III. INTERDISTRICT INEQUALITIES

A. Introduction

As the materials in the previous section emphasize, there exists in all states (except perhaps Hawaii which constitutes a single school district) a wide range of per-pupil expenditures among local school districts. Whether this difference constitutes a "problem" depends upon the standard one chooses for assessing the system. One of the first efforts to define the problem and seek a solution through the courts is represented by the decision in *McInnis v. Shapiro*, 293 F.Supp. 327 (N.D. Ill. 1968), *aff'd sub nom., McInnis v. Ogilvie*, 394 U.S. 322, 89 S.Ct. 1197, 22 L.Ed.2d 308 (1969). The data in the case showed that per-pupil expenditures among school districts varied between $480 and $1000 despite some effort on the part of the state through its state aid formula to equalize differences. The plaintiffs in the case argued that these differences were unconstitutional but seemed to suggest different and conflicting reasons for this conclusion. On the one hand, the plaintiffs argued that only a financing scheme that apportioned funds according to the needs of the students would satisfy the Fourteenth Amendment. However, they also suggested that a system that allocated funds on the basis of flat dollar equality or assured that equal tax rates yielded equal dollars would be constitutionally permissible. The district court did not dwell on this confusion but denied relief on a variety of grounds: a lack of judicially manageable standards, the rationality of the system insofar as it promoted local control, the fact that the allocation of public revenues was a basic policy decision more appropriately handled by a legislature than a court, and the fact that the Constitution did not require allocation either on the basis of need or on the basis of equal dollars per pupil.

Although the *McInnis* case was a setback to those seeking to reform educational finance, it did not signal the end of attempts to use the courts for that purpose. The reform effort was set in motion again with the publication of two books: A. Wise, *Rich Schools, Poor Schools: The Promise of Equal Educational Opportunity* (1968) and J. Coons, W. Clune, and S. Sugarman, *Private Wealth and Public Education* (1970). Of these, the latter was destined to become the moving force behind two of the most notable school finance cases, *Serrano v. Priest, infra*, and *San Antonio Independent School District v. Rodriguez, infra*.

Coons and his colleagues argued that Supreme Court precedent could be read to support the following proposition: The quality of public education may not be a function of wealth other than the total wealth of the state. Coons, Clune, and Sugarman, *supra* at 304. They called this proposition the *principle of fiscal neutrality*, in that it is designed to sever the correlation between local district property wealth per pupil and the amount of money spent per pupil. Fully implemented, the proposition would achieve the result that equal tax rates produced equal yields. It would not require that districts choose the same tax rates, however, thus preserving local control over how much money was to be raised locally. Inequalities in expenditures could persist under this standard, but they would not be caused by inequalities in property wealth per pupil. An important assumption was that the principle of fiscal neutrality would achieve not just taxpayer equity but also educational equity, because equal fiscal capacity—it was hoped and predicted—would mean that educational offerings would be equalized among districts. As just noted, however, the equalization of educational offerings is not a necessary result of the application of the fiscal neutrality principle.

Coons, Clune and Sugarman fastened on the principle of fiscal neutrality for a number of legal, tactical, and policy reasons. First, they believed that the Supreme Court's own precedents seemed to be moving toward the notion that government may not discriminate on the basis of wealth. For example, in *Griffin v. Illinois*, 351 U.S. 12, 76 S.Ct. 585, 100 L.Ed. 891 (1956), and *Douglas v. California*, 372 U.S. 353, 83 S.Ct. 814, 9 L.Ed.2d 811 (1963), the Supreme Court ordered that a state must provide indigent criminal defendants appealing their convictions with a free trial transcript and a lawyer, respectively. These cases, it was argued, established the proposition that the "poor" constituted a "suspect" class entitled to special judicial protection and that governmental differences in treatment between rich and poor could only be sustained under the Fourteenth Amendment's equal protection clause if the government had a compelling interest and the differences in treatment were necessary to the achievement of that interest. It was thus an easy step to say that it was discrimination on the basis of wealth when the amount of money spent on a child (the quality of a child's education) differed depending upon the property wealth of the district in which the child resided. This was discrimination on the basis of school district wealth, equally as obnoxious as the discrimination on the basis of personal wealth that occurred in the cases of *Griffin* and *Douglas*.

Second, it was argued that education was a "fundamental interest," as that term was understood by the Supreme Court in the context of the equal protection clause; hence, since the finance system affected a fundamental interest, the courts had to examine the system in light of the strict scrutiny standard of review. Coons and his colleagues contended that the finance system could not survive strict scrutiny; that is, it did not serve a compelling state interest, and that even if local control were a compelling interest, the existing system was not "necessary" to the achievement of local control. Other finance systems (discussed below) would serve the interest of local control and yet not make the quality of a child's education a function of local district wealth.

Third, Coons and his coauthors also believed that the fiscal neutrality principle would be acceptable to the courts because it was judicially manageable and did not involve the courts in usurping the prerogative of the state legislatures to design their own system of school finance. The principle could be complied with in a number of different ways, and the choice among these ways was to be left to the legislature. A description of some of the options follows.

NOTES AND QUESTIONS

1. Legislative Options

a. Alternative Revenue Sources. What are alternatives to the local property tax as sources of revenue? An increase in state taxes, particularly the sales or income taxes, or the imposition of a statewide property tax for education, would offer more flexibility in raising funds for education than a local property tax because they would not be subject to annual local voter approval. Statewide taxes would also break the connection between per-pupil spending and local district wealth. If either the state sales tax or the state income tax were used alone as the substitute revenue producer for revenues raised from local property taxes, the impact on taxpayers in many states would be significant. One study showed that California would have had to increase its state sales tax by 5 cents on the dollar to replace revenues generated by all local school property taxes; using the state income tax to replace revenues generated by all local school property taxes would have necessitated an increase of 125 percent. B. Levin, M. Cohen, T. Muller, and W. Scanlon, *Paying for Public Schools: Issues of School Finance in California* 31 (1972). Thus, use of either the state sales tax or the state income tax as the sole substitute for revenues raised by the local property tax may not be politically feasible. The use of a statewide property tax, however, also creates problems. A statewide property tax that would generate the same amount of revenue produced by the local property tax in a state would mean that large cities in particular would have a heavy tax burden. Generally, in major urban areas there are comparatively low property taxes for education but high property taxes for other public services. Increasing the property tax might hasten the deterioration of some cities. A statewide property tax would also mean substantial increases in the tax rates of rural areas. Levin, "Alternatives to the Present System of School Finance: Their Problems and Prospects," 61 Georgetown L.J. 879, 911–12 (1973).

b. Alternative Methods of Distributing Resources. Alternative distribution criteria can be grouped into several categories: (1) full state funding alternatives with state aid distribution formulas that require no local contribution on the part of districts; (2) partial state funding alternatives with state aid distribution formulas that permit some local contribution and therefore allow the local school district to retain some measure of fiscal autonomy; (3) redrawing the district boundaries to ensure districts of approximately equal wealth, thus giving each district equal fiscal capacity but allowing individual district choice as to the amount to be raised for education; (4) full state funding with the state providing funds directly to the individual school rather than to the school district; and (5) some variety of family voucher system under which funds are provided by the government to parents to be used for their child's education at any public or private school in which the parent elects to enroll his or her child.

(1) *Full state funding.* Revenues raised through a statewide property tax or some other state tax could be distributed (a) on an equal per-pupil basis to school districts, (b) according to some measure of educational need developed by the state, or (c) according to a formula taking account of the varying costs—based on such factors as cost-of-living differentials—of providing schooling within a given district. The major argument against these approaches has been the anticipated loss of local control by eliminating district wealth as a factor in the level of education spending, and thus eliminating district choice as to the level of expenditures desired.

(2) *Partial state funding.* Under partial state funding alternatives, local property tax revenues remain a factor in school expenditures. State aid is

distributed according to formulas that compensate for differences among districts in local property values. The distribution of state aid is based on local ability to pay, with the highest level of state aid going to poorer districts and state aid per pupil declining as district wealth increases. This method is intended to ensure that districts of the same fiscal capacity receive the same percentage of state aid, but it does not necessarily bring about the equalization of expenditures, since these plans, in theory, place no restriction on the amount of local revenues that can be raised and obtained for use by the district.

To equalize expenditures, a partial state funding plan must impose ceilings on local expenditures, or wealthy districts will still have an advantage in raising additional revenues. One approach that has been suggested is "district power equalizing," (DPE) in which a district's expenditure level is a function only of its taxing effort and not its property wealth. Under district power equalization formulas, local expenditure levels are based on the local tax rate chosen by the district. If local property values are too low to produce the revenues called for under the state's guaranteed expenditure level for the specific tax rate selected, the state would supply the difference. This sometimes is called a guaranteed yield plan. If, on the other hand, local wealth was so high that the tax levy produced *more* than the state guarantee, the state would "recapture" the surplus. The following tables on page 603 demonstrate, in very simplistic fashion, how power equalization would work.

It is clear that "devising a remedy that will redress the inequalities resulting from present methods of school finance will be more complex than simply redistributing revenues or transferring taxing responsibility from one level of government to another." *Id.* at 923.

2. *"Minimum Protection" Theory*

Professor Frank Michelman of Harvard suggested an alternative approach to that which measures educational opportunity by comparison. Michelman, "Foreword: On Protecting the Poor Through the Fourteenth Amendment," 83 *Harv.L.Rev.* 7 (1969). His focus was not on equality of educational offerings, but on a basic level of education that would be constitutionally protected. In effect, he read the equal protection clause as a "minimum protection" clause, and argued that the government is constitutionally required to provide an adequate level of basic needs and services, or what he terms "welfare rights." His belief that inequalities in educational offerings trigger minimum protection concerns arises from his view that educational inequality and educational deprivation are so closely intertwined, especially in a competitive situation such as a market-oriented society, that "the minimum is significantly a function of the maximum and to that extent calls for equalization." *Id.* at 58. Stated baldly, it is small comfort to an athlete to get coaching once a week when his or her competitor gets coaching six days a week and is therefore able to win the race. In this competitive situation, one day a week is not minimally adequate, even though it might be minimally adequate for purposes of maintaining good health.

From this perspective, Professor Michelman examines the adequacy of the principle of fiscal neutrality and DPE. He concludes that DPE is in effect morally bankrupt because it substitutes place/wealth-determined inequalities for simple place-determined inequalities—hardly much of an advance from the perspective of the child. At the extreme, DPE would even seem to permit a district to discontinue its effort altogether, with the result that access to education for those children would depend on their ability to pay the tuition fees of private schools. Hence DPE seems to permit "serious *wealth*-determined inequalities among children in *the same* district." *Id.* at 54. In the less extreme case, a low-effort district could simply decide to let families who wish to do so purchase music and athletic instruction privately rather than offer it through the schools. Hence, in this way DPE also creates wealth-determined inequalities in access to "extracurricular" activities. Professor Michelman concludes that he fails to understand why interdistrict wealth-determined inequalities are invidious to advocates of fiscal neutrality but the sort of intradistrict inequalities just described are not.

Professor Michelman notes that the demands of minimum protection can, in principle, be satisfied by a foundation system that ensures each district an acceptable minimum level of resources but allows each district to add on to these levels from its own unequalized tax base. This add-on is allowable "as long as the competitive-inequality gap does not grow too large." *Id.* at 57. For a discussion of the difficulty in defining the level of education or other basic needs or services that would be constitutionally required under Professor Michelman's "minimum protection" theory, *see* Levin, "Education as a Constitutional Entitlement: A Proposed Judicial Stan-

TABLE 1

	District Property Value Per Pupil	*District Tax Rate*	*Actual Property Tax Collections Per Pupil*	*Net Gain Or Loss*	*Guaranteed By State*
District A	$40,000	1.10%	$440	+$110	$550
District B	$60,000	1.10%	$660	−$110	$550

TABLE 2

	District Property Value Per Pupil	*District Tax Rate*	*Actual Property Tax Collections Per Pupil*	*Net Gain Or Loss*	*Guaranteed By State*
District A	$40,000	1.65%	$660	+$165	$825
District B	$60,000	1.10%	$660	−$110	$550

Under the example in Table 1, the state has guaranteed an expenditure level of $550 per pupil for every district taxing at a rate of 1.10 percent. This approach, in effect, treats every district as if it had a property base of $50,000 per pupil. District A can only raise $440 at this tax rate, so the state gives it an additional $110 per pupil. District B, however, raises $660 per pupil at this tax rate, so it must give $110 per pupil to the state treasury. Table 2 indicates what happens if District A should tax itself at a higher rate. If District B chooses to continue to tax itself at 1.10 percent, it cannot spend more than $550 per pupil. Should District B also decide to increase its tax rate to 1.65 percent, however, it will be able to spend $825 per pupil even though at that tax rate it would raise $990 per pupil. This scheme means that in order to spend $825 per pupil, District B must give up $165 to the state for every pupil in its school system.

Levin, "Alternatives to the Present System of School Finance, Their Problems and Prospects," 61 *Georgetown L. J.* 879, 919–920 (1973).

dard for Determining How Much Is Enough," 1979 *Wash. U.L.Q.* 703, 707–08.

B. Fiscal Neutrality in the Courts

Serrano v. Priest

5 Cal. 3d 584, 96 Cal.Rptr. 601, 487 P.2d 1241 (1971).

Sullivan, Justice:

[Plaintiffs' complaint set forth basically two causes of action. First, plaintiff children alleged that the California system of finance relied heavily on local property taxes which caused substantial disparities among the school districts in the amount of money spent per pupil and that this arrangement violated the equal protection clauses of the U.S. and California constitutions because it constituted discrimination on the basis of wealth. Second, plaintiff taxpayers alleged that, as a direct result of the finance scheme, they were required to pay a higher tax rate than taxpayers in other school districts in order to obtain for their children the same or lesser educational opportunities afforded children in those other districts. Defendants demurred, asserting that none of the claims stated facts sufficient to constitute a cause of action. The trial court sustained the demurrers and dismissed the complaints, and the plaintiffs appealed.

After reviewing the procedural history of the case, the court examined the California public school financing system, assuming the facts as alleged by the plaintiffs to be correct for purposes of ruling on the legal sufficiency of the complaint. The court noted that the plaintiffs alleged that the existing system relied heavily on local property taxation which resulted in differences in the amount of money spent per pupil among the districts, differences which state aid did not equalize. State aid was provided in the form of both a flat grant and in the form of "equalization aid" distributed in inverse proportion to the wealth of the districts. Additional "supplemental aid" was available to subsidize particular poor school districts that were willing to make an extra local tax effort. Nevertheless great disparities remained; for example, Baldwin Park spent $577.49 per pupil in 1968–69, Pasadena, $840.19, and Beverly Hills, $1,231.72.]

Having disposed of these preliminary matters, we take up the chief contention underlying plaintiffs' complaint, namely that the California public school financing scheme violates the equal protection clause of the Fourteenth Amendment to the United States Constitution.[11]

As recent decisions of this court have pointed out, the United States Supreme Court has employed a two-level test for measuring legislative classifications against the equal protection clause. "In the area of economic regulation, the high court has exercised restraint, investing legislation with a presumption of constitutionality and requiring merely that distinctions drawn by a challenged statute bear some rational relationship to a conceivable legitimate state purpose. [Citations.]

> On the other hand, in cases involving 'suspect classifications' or touching on 'fundamental interests,' [fns. omitted] the court has adopted an attitude of active and critical analysis, subjecting the classification to strict scrutiny. [Citations.] Under the strict standard applied in such cases, the state bears the burden of establishing not only that it has a *compelling* interest which justifies the law but that the distinctions drawn by the law are *necessary* to further its purpose.

(*Westbrook v. Mihaly* (1970) 2 Cal.3d 765, 784–785, 87 Cal.Rptr. 839, 852, 471 P.2d 487, 500, *vacated on other grounds* (1971) 403 U.S. 915, 91 S.Ct. 2224, 29 L.Ed.2d 692; *In re Antazo* (1970) 3 Cal.3d 100, 110–111, 89 Cal.Rptr. 255, 473 P.2d 999; *see Purdy & Fitzpatrick v. State of California* (1969) 71 Cal.2d 566, 578–579, 79 Cal.Rptr. 77, 456 P.2d 645.)

* * *

Plaintiffs contend that the school financing system classifies on the basis of wealth. We find this proposition irrefutable. As we have already discussed, over half of all educational revenue is raised locally by levying taxes on real property in the individual school districts. Above the foundation program minimum ($355 per elementary student and $488 per high school student), the wealth of a school district, as measured by its assessed valuation, is the major determinant of educational expenditures. Although the amount of money raised locally is also a function of the rate at which the residents of a district are willing to tax themselves, as a practical matter districts with small tax bases simply cannot levy taxes at a rate sufficient to produce the revenue that more affluent districts reap with minimal tax efforts. For example, Baldwin Park citizens, who paid a school tax of $5.48 per $100 of assessed valuation in 1968–1969, were able to spend less than half as much on education as Beverly Hills residents, who were taxed only $2.38 per $100. (Cal. Dept. of Ed., op. cit. *supra*, Table III-16, p. 43.)

* * *

More basically, however, we reject defendants' underlying thesis that classification by wealth is constitutional so long as the wealth is that of the district, not the individual. We think that discrimination on the basis of district wealth is equally invalid. The commercial and industrial property which augments a district's tax base is distributed unevenly throughout the state. To allot more educational dollars to the children of one district than to those of another merely because of the fortuitous presence of such property is to make the quality of a child's education dependent upon the location of private commercial and industrial establishments. Surely, this is to rely on the most irrelevant of factors as the basis for educational financing. . . .

* * *

But plaintiffs' equal protection attack on the fiscal system has an additional dimension. They assert that the system not only draws lines on the basis of wealth but that it "touches upon," indeed has a direct and significant impact upon, a "fundamental interest," namely education. It is urged that these two grounds,

11. The complaint also alleges that the financing system violates article I, sections 11 and 21, of the California Constitution. Section 11 provides: "All laws of a general nature shall have a uniform operation." Section 21 states: "No special privileges or immunities shall ever be granted which may not be altered, revoked, or repealed by the Legislature; nor shall any citizen, or class of citizens, be granted privileges or immunities which, upon the same terms, shall not be granted to all citizens." We have construed these provisions as "substantially the equivalent" of the equal protection clause of the Fourteenth Amendment to the federal Constitution. (*Dept. of Mental Hygiene v. Kirchner* (1965) 62 Cal.2d 586, 588, 43 Cal.Rptr. 329, 400 P.2d 321.) Consequently, our analysis of plaintiffs' federal equal protection contention is also applicable to their claim under these state constitutional provisions.

particularly in combination, establish a demonstrable denial of equal protection of the laws. To this phase of the argument we now turn our attention.

Until the present time wealth classifications have been invalidated only in conjunction with a limited number of fundamental interests—rights of defendants in criminal cases *(Griffin; Douglas; Williams; Tate; Antazo)* and voting rights (*Harper; Cipriano v. City of Houma* (1969) 395 U.S. 701, 89 S.Ct. 1987, 23 L.Ed.2d 647; *Kramer v. Union School District* (1969) 395 U.S. 621, 89 S.Ct. 1886, 23 L.Ed.2d 583; *cf. McDonald v. Board of Elections*). Plaintiffs' contention—that education is a fundamental interest which may not be conditioned on wealth—is not supported by any direct authority.

We, therefore, begin by examining the indispensable role which education plays in the modern industrial state. This role, we believe, has two significant aspects: first, education is a major determinant of an individual's chances for economic and social success in our competitive society; second, education is a unique influence on a child's development as a citizen and his participation in political and community life. "[T]he pivotal position of education to success in American society and its essential role in opening up to the individual the central experiences of our culture lend it an importance that is undeniable." (Note, "Developments in the Law–Equal Protections" (1969) 82 *Harv.L.Rev.* 1065, 1129.) Thus, education is the lifeline of both the individual and society.

* * *

We are convinced that the distinctive and priceless function of education in our society warrants, indeed compels, our treating it as a "fundamental interest."

First, education is essential in maintaining what several commentators have termed "free enterprise democracy"—that is, preserving an individual's opportunity to compete successfully in the economic marketplace, despite a disadvantaged background. Accordingly, the public schools of this state are the bright hope for entry of the poor and oppressed into the mainstream of American society.

Second, education is universally relevant. "Not every person finds it necessary to call upon the fire department or even the police in an entire lifetime. Relatively few are on welfare. Every person, however, benefits from education . . . ." [Fn. omitted.] (Coons, Clune & Sugarman, *supra*, 57 *Cal.L.Rev.* at p. 388.)

Third, public education continues over a lengthy period of life—between 10 and 13 years. Few other government services have such sustained, intensive contact with the recipient.

Fourth, education is unmatched in the extent to which it molds the personality of the youth of society. While police and fire protection, garbage collection and street lights are essentially neutral in their effect on the individual psyche, public education actively attempts to shape a child's personal development in a manner chosen not by the child or his parents but by the state. (Coons, Clune & Sugarman, *supra*, 57 *Cal.L.Rev.* at p. 389.) "[T]he influence of the school is not confined to how well it can teach the disadvantaged child; it also has a significant role to play in shaping the student's emotional and psychological make-up." (*Hobson v. Hansen, supra*, 269 F.Supp. 401, 483.)

Finally, education is so important that the state has made it compulsory—not only in the requirement of attendance but also by assignment to a particular district and school. Although a child of wealthy parents has the opportunity to attend a private school, this freedom is seldom available to the indigent. In this context, it has been suggested that "a child of the poor assigned willy-nilly to an inferior state school takes on the complexion of a prisoner, complete with a minimum sentence of 12 years." (Coons, Clune & Sugarman, *supra*, 57 *Cal.L.Rev.* at p. 388.)

We now reach the final step in the application of the "strict scrutiny" equal protection standard—the determination of whether the California school financing system, as presently structured, is necessary to achieve a compelling state interest.

The state interest which defendants advance in support of the current fiscal scheme is California's policy "to strengthen and encourage local responsibility for control of public education." (Ed.Code, §17300.) We treat separately the two possible aspects of this goal: first, the granting to local districts of effective decision-making power over the administration of their schools; and second, the promotion of local fiscal control over the amount of money to be spent on education.

The individual district may well be in the best position to decide whom to hire, how to schedule its educational offerings, and a host of other matters which are either of significant local impact or of such a detailed nature as to require decentralized determination. But even assuming arguendo that local administrative control may be a compelling state interest, the present financial system cannot be considered necessary to further this interest. No matter how the state decides to finance its system of public education, it can still leave this decision-making power in the hands of local districts.

The other asserted policy interest is that of allowing a local district to choose how much it wishes to spend on the education of its children. Defendants argue: "[I]f one district raises a lesser amount per pupil than another district, this is a matter of choice and preference of the individual district and reflects the individual desire for lower taxes rather than an expanded educational program, or may reflect a greater interest within that district in such other services that are supported by local property taxes as, for example, police and fire protection or hospital services."

We need not decide whether such decentralized financial decision-making is a compelling state interest, since under the present financing system, such fiscal freewill is a cruel illusion for the poor school districts. We cannot agree that Baldwin Park residents care less about education than those in Beverly Hills solely because Baldwin Park spends less than $600 per child while Beverly Hills spends over $1,200. As defendants themselves recognize, perhaps the most accurate reflection of a community's commitment to education is the rate at which its citizens are willing to tax themselves to support their schools. Yet by that standard, Baldwin park should be deemed far more devoted to learning than Beverly Hills, for Baldwin Park citizens levied a school tax of well over $5 per $100 of assessed valuation, while residents of Beverly Hills paid only slightly more than $2.

In summary, so long as the assessed valuation within a district's boundaries is a major determinant of how much it can spend for its schools, only a district with a large tax base will be truly able to decide how much it really cares about education. The poor district cannot freely choose to tax itself into an excellence which its tax rolls cannot provide. Far from being necessary to promote local fiscal choice, the present financing system actually deprives the less wealthy districts of that option. . . .

* * *

The judgment is reversed and the cause remanded to the trial court with directions to overrule the demurrers and to allow defendants a reasonable time within which to answer.

Wright, C. J., and Peters, Tobriner, Mosk and Burke, JJ., concur. McComb, Justice (dissenting) [omitted].

NOTES AND QUESTIONS

*1. **Reaction to*** **Serrano**

Serrano articulated the principle that the quality of a child's education cannot be a function of the wealth of his or her parents and neighbors. This was translated into a principle of fiscal neutrality that stated that the level of expenditures per pupil may not be a function of wealth, other than the wealth of the state as a whole. This principle was argued to federal and state courts around the country. Within eighteen months of the *Serrano* decision, 53 suits were filed in 38 states challenging those states' systems of financing education.

*2. **California Legislature's Initial Response to*** **Serrano**

After the California Supreme Court's decision in *Serrano I*, the California legislature passed an act (SB 90) that altered, in some important respects, the educational finance system of California. While primarily intended to provide property tax relief, SB 90 did attempt to respond to the constitutional challenge of *Serrano I*. Most significantly, the law placed a ceiling on how quickly districts increase their revenues. High-spending districts were limited to a smaller increase than low-spending districts. Thus, over time, low-spending districts could catch up with high-spending districts, assuming the high-spending districts did not exercise their prerogative under SB 90 to vote a tax override that would lift the ceiling on expenditure increases. A recent study shows that this assumption was not a valid one. Voters approved approximately 40 percent of 580 referenda to override the ceiling on expenditure increases. Fischel, "Did Serrano Cause Proposition 13?" 42 *National Tax J.* 465 (1989).

San Antonio Independent School District v. Rodriguez

411 U.S. 1, 93 S.Ct. 1278, 36 L.Ed.2d 16 (1973).

[Shortly after the decision in *Serrano*, a three-judge federal district court adopted the approach taken by the *Serrano* court and ordered the state to bring the system of financing education into compliance with the principle of fiscal neutrality. *Rodriguez v. San Antonio Independent School District*, 337 F.Supp. 280 (W.D. Tex. 1971). The State of Texas appealed to the Supreme Court.]

Mr. Justice Powell delivered the opinion of the Court.

This suit attacking the Texas system of financing public education was initiated by Mexican-American parents whose children attended the elementary and secondary schools in the Edgewood Independent School District, an urban school district in San Antonio, Texas. They brought a class action on behalf of school children throughout the State who are members of minority groups or who are poor and reside in school districts having a low property tax base. Named as defendants were the State Board of Education, the Commissioner of Education, the State Attorney General, and the Bexar County (San Antonio) Board of Trustees. The complaint was filed in the summer of 1968 and a three-judge court was impaneled in January 1969. In December 1971 the panel rendered its judgment in a *per curiam* opinion holding the Texas school finance system unconstitutional under the Equal Protection Clause of the Fourteenth Amendment. The State appealed, and we noted probable jurisdiction to consider the far-reaching constitutional questions presented. . . . For the reasons stated in this opinion we reverse the decision of the District Court. . . .

[The Court summarizes the early evolution of Texas' school financing scheme. It notes the failure of earlier schemes to take into account wealth disparities among school districts.]

Recognizing the need for increased state funding to help offset disparities in local spending and to meet Texas' changing educational requirements, the state legislature in the late 1940's undertook a thorough evaluation of public education with an eye toward major reform. In 1947, an 18 member committee, composed of educators and legislators, was appointed to explore alternative systems in other States and to propose a funding scheme that would guarantee a minimum or basic educational offering to each child and that would help overcome interdistrict disparities in taxable resources. The Committee's efforts led to the passage of the Gilmer-Aiken bills, named for the Committee's cochairmen, establishing the Texas Minimum Foundation School Program. Today this Program accounts for approximately half of the total educational expenditures in Texas. . . .

The design of [the new] complex system was twofold. First, it was an attempt to assure that the Foundation Program would have an equalizing influence on expenditure levels between school districts by placing the heaviest burden on the school districts most capable of paying. Second, the Program's architects sought to establish a Local Fund Assignment that would force every school district to contribute to the education of its children but that would not by itself exhaust any district's resources. . . .

The school district in which appellees reside, the Edgewood Independent School District, has been compared throughout this litigation with the Alamo Heights Independent School District. This comparison between the least and most affluent districts in the San Antonio area serves to illustrate the manner in which the dual system of finance operates and to indicate the extent to which substantial disparities exist despite the state's impressive progress in recent years. Edgewood is one of seven public school districts in the metropolitan area. Approximately 22,000 students are enrolled in its 25 elementary and secondary schools. The district is situated in the core-city sector of San Antonio in a residential neighborhood that has little commercial or industrial property. The residents are predominately of Mexican-American descent: approximately 90% of the student population is Mexican-American and over 6% is Negro.

The average assessed property value per pupil is \$5,960—the lowest in the metropolitan area—and the median family income (\$4,686) is also the lowest. At an equalized tax rate of \$1.05 per \$100 of assessed property—the highest in the metropolitan area—the district contributed \$26 to the education of each child for the 1967–1968 school year above its Local Fund Assignment for the Minimum Foundation Program. The Foundation Program contributed \$222 per pupil for a state-local total of \$248. Federal funds added another \$108 for a total of \$356 per pupil.

Alamo Heights is the most affluent school district in San Antonio. Its six schools, housing approximately 5,000 students, are situated in a residential community quite unlike the Edgewood District. The school population is predominantly "Anglo," having only 18% Mexican-Americans and less than 1% Negroes. The assessed property value per pupil exceeds \$49,000 and the median family income is \$8,001.

In 1967–68 the local tax rate of $.85 per $100 of valuation yielded $333 per pupil over and above its contribution to the Foundation Program. Coupled with the $225 provided from that Program, the district was able to supply $558 per student. Supplemented by a $36 per-pupil grant from federal sources, Alamo Heights spent $594 per pupil. . . .

Although the 1967–1968 school year figures provide the only complete statistical breakdown for each category of aid, more recent partial statistics indicate that the previously noted trend of increasing state aid has been significant. For the 1970–1971 school year, the Foundation School Program allotment for Edgewood was $356 per pupil, a 62% increase over the 1967–1968 school year. Indeed, state aid alone in 1970–1971 equaled Edgewood's entire 1967–1968 school budget from local, state, and federal sources. Alamo Heights enjoyed a similar increase under the Foundation Program, netting $491 per pupil in 1970–71. . . .[35]

Despite these recent increases, substantial interdistrict disparities in school expenditures found by the District Court to prevail in San Antonio and in varying degrees throughout the State still exist. And it was these disparities, largely attributable to differences in the amounts of money collected through local property taxation, that led the District Court to conclude that Texas' dual system of public school financing violated the Equal Protection Clause. . . .

. . . We must decide, first, whether the Texas system of financing public education operates to the disadvantage of some suspect class or impinges upon a fundamental right explicitly or implicitly protected by the Constitution, thereby requiring strict judicial scrutiny. If so, the judgment of the District Court should be affirmed. If not, the Texas scheme must still be examined to determine whether it rationally furthers some legitimate, articulated state purpose and therefore does not constitute an invidious discrimination in violation of the Equal Protection Clause of the Fourteenth Amendment.

II

The District Court's opinion does not reflect the novelty and complexity of the constitutional questions posed by appellees' challenge to Texas' system of school financing. In concluding that strict judicial scrutiny was required, that court relied on decisions dealing with the rights of indigents to equal treatment in the criminal trial and appellate processes,[45] and on cases disapproving wealth restrictions on the right to vote.[46] Those cases, the District Court concluded, established wealth as a suspect classification. Finding that the local property tax system discriminated on the basis of wealth, it regarded those precedents as controlling. It then reasoned, based on decisions of this Court affirming the undeniable importance of education, that there is a fundamental right to education and that, absent some compelling state justification, the Texas system could not stand.

We are unable to agree that this case, which in significant aspects is *sui generis*, may be so neatly fitted into the conventional mosaic of constitutional analysis under the Equal Protection Clause. Indeed, for the several reasons that follow, we find neither the suspect classification nor the fundamental interest analysis persuasive.

A

The wealth discrimination discovered by the District Court in this case, and by several other courts that have recently struck down school financing laws in other States,[48] is quite unlike any of the forms of wealth discrimination heretofore reviewed by this Court. . . .

The case comes to us with no definitive description of the classifying facts or delineation of the disfavored class. . . . The Texas system of school financing might be regarded as discriminating (1) against "poor" persons whose incomes fall below

35. Although the Foundation Program has made significantly greater contributions to both school districts over the last several years, it is apparent that Alamo Heights has enjoyed a larger gain. The sizable difference between the Alamo Heights and Edgewood grants is due to the emphasis in the State's allocation formula on the guaranteed minimum salaries for teachers. Higher salaries are guaranteed to teachers having more years of experience and possessing more advanced degrees. Therefore, Alamo Heights, which has a greater percentage of experienced personnel with advanced degrees, receives more state support. In this regard the Texas Program is not unlike that presently in existence in a number of other States. . . .

45. *E.g., Griffin v. Illinois*, 351 U.S. 12 (1956); *Douglas v. California*, 372 U.S. 353 (1963).

46. *Harper v. Virginia Bd. of Elections*, 383 U.S. 663 (1966); *McDonald v. Board of Election*.

48. *Serrano v. Priest*, 5 Cal.3d 584, 487 P.2d 1241 (1971); *Van Dusartz v. Hatfield*, 334 F.Supp. 870 (Minn. 1971); *Robinson v. Cahill*, 118 N.J. Super. 223, 287 A.2d 187 (1972); *Milliken v. Green*, 389 Mich. 1, 203 N.W.2d 457 (1972), rehearing granted, Jan. 1973.

some identifiable level of poverty or who might be characterized as functionally "indigent," or (2) against those who are relatively poorer than others, or (3) against all those who, irrespective of their personal incomes, happen to reside in relatively poorer school districts. Our task must be to ascertain whether, in fact, the Texas system has been shown to discriminate on any of these possible bases and, if so, whether the resulting classification may be regarded as suspect.

The precedents of this Court provide the proper starting point. The individuals or groups of individuals who constituted the class discriminated against in our prior cases shared two distinguishing characteristics: because of their impecunity they were completely unable to pay for some desired benefit, and as a consequence, they sustained an absolute deprivation of a meaningful opportunity to enjoy that benefit. In *Griffin v. Illinois*, 351 U.S. 12 (1956), and its progeny, the Court invalidated state laws that prevented an indigent criminal defendant from acquiring a transcript, or an adequate substitute for a transcript, for use at several stages of the trial and appeal process. The payment requirements in each case were found to occasion *de facto* discrimination against those who, because of their indigency, were totally unable to pay for transcripts. . . .

Williams v. Illinois, 399 U.S. 235 (1970), and *Tate v. Short*, 401 U.S. 395 (1971), struck down criminal penalties that subjected indigents to incarceration simply because of their inability to pay a fine. Again, the disadvantaged class was composed only of persons who were totally unable to pay the demanded sum. Those cases do not touch on the question whether equal protection is denied to persons with relatively less money on whom designated fines impose heavier burdens. . . .

Finally, in *Bullock v. Carter*, 405 U.S. 134 (1972), the Court invalidated the Texas filing fee requirement for primary elections. Both of the relevant classifying facts found in the previous cases were present there. The size of the fee, often running into the thousands of dollars and, in at least one case, as high as $8,900, effectively barred all potential candidates who were unable to pay the required fee. . . .

Only appellees' first possible basis for describing the class disadvantaged by the Texas school finance system—discrimination against a class of definably "poor" persons—might arguably meet the criteria established in these prior cases. Even a cursory examination, however, demonstrates that neither of the two distinguishing characteristics of wealth classifications can be found here. First, in support of their charge that the system discriminates against the "poor," appellees have made no effort to demonstrate that it operates to the peculiar disadvantage of any class fairly definable as indigent, or as composed of persons whose incomes are beneath any designated poverty level. Indeed, there is reason to believe that the poorest families are not necessarily clustered in the poorest property districts. A recent and exhaustive study of school districts in Connecticut concluded that "it is clearly incorrect . . . to contend that the 'poor' live in 'poor' districts. . . . Thus, the major factual assumption of *Serrano*—that the educational financing system discriminates against the 'poor'—is simply false in Connecticut."[53] Defining "poor" families as those below the Bureau of the Census "poverty level," the Connecticut study found, not surprisingly, that the poor were clustered around commercial and industrial areas—those same areas that provide the most attractive sources of property tax income for school districts. . . .

Second, neither appellees nor the District Court addressed the fact that, unlike each of the foregoing cases, lack of personal resources has not occasioned an absolute deprivation of the desired benefit. The argument here is not that the children in districts having relatively low assessable property values are receiving no public education; rather, it is that they are receiving a poorer quality education than that available to children in districts having more assessable wealth. Apart from the unsettled and disputed question whether the quality of education may be determined by the amount of money expended for it, a sufficient answer to appellees' argument is that at least where wealth is involved the Equal Protection Clause does not require absolute equality or precisely equal advantages. . . .[57]

For these two reasons—the absence of any evidence that the financing system discriminates against

53. Note, "A Statistical Analysis of the School Finance Decisions: On Winning Battles and Losing Wars," 81 *Yale L.J.* 1303, 1328–29 (1972).

57. *E.g., Bullock v. Carter*, 405 U.S. 134, 137, 149 (1972); *Mayer v. Chicago*, 404 U.S. 189, 194 (1971); *Draper v. Washington*, 372 U.S. 487, 495–96 (1963); *Douglas v. California*, 372 U.S. 353, 357 (1963).

any definable category of "poor" people or that it results in the absolute deprivation of education—the disadvantaged class is not susceptible of identification in traditional terms.[60]

As suggested above, appellees and the District Court may have embraced a second or third approach, the second of which might be characterized as a theory of relative or comparative discrimination based on family income. Appellees sought to prove that a direct correlation exists between the wealth of families within each district and the expenditures therein for education. That is, along a continuum, the poorer the family the lower the dollar amount of education received by the family's children. . . .

[A] survey of approximately 10% of the school districts in Texas . . . [shows] only that the wealthiest few districts in the sample have the highest median family incomes and spend the most on education, and that the several poorest districts have the lowest family incomes and devote the least amount of money to education. For the remainder of the districts—96 districts composing almost 90% of the sample—the correlation is inverted, *i.e.*, the districts that spend next to the most money on education are populated by families having next to the lowest median family incomes while the districts spending the least have the highest median family incomes. It is evident that, even if the conceptual questions are answered favorably to appellees, no factual basis exists upon which to found a claim of comparative wealth discrimination.

This brings us, then, to the third way in which the classification scheme might be defined—*district* wealth discrimination. Since the only correlation indicated by the evidence is between district property wealth and expenditures, it may be argued that discrimination might be found without regard to the individual income characteristics of district residents. . . .

However described, it is clear that appellees' suit asks this Court to extend its most exacting scrutiny to review a system that allegedly discriminates against a large, diverse, and amorphous class, unified only by the common factor of residence in districts that happen to have less taxable wealth than other districts. The system of alleged discrimination at the class it defines have none of the traditional indicia of suspectness: the class is not saddled with such disabilities, or subjected to such a history of purposeful unequal treatment, or relegated to such a position of political powerlessness as to command extraordinary protection from the majoritarian political process.

We thus conclude that the Texas system does not operate to the peculiar disadvantage of any suspect class. But in recognition of the fact that this Court has never heretofore held that wealth discrimination alone provides an adequate basis for invoking strict scrutiny, appellees have not relied solely on this contention. They also assert that the State's system impermissibly interferes with the exercise of a "fundamental" right and that accordingly the prior decisions of this Court require the application of the strict standard of judicial review. . . .

B

In *Brown v. Board of Education*, 347 U.S. 483 (1954), a unanimous Court recognized that "education is perhaps the most important function of state and local governments. . . ." This theme, expressing an abiding respect for the vital role of education in a free society, may be found in numerous opinions of Justices of this Court writing both before and after *Brown* was decided. . . .

Nothing this Court holds today in any way detracts from our historic dedication to public education. We are in complete agreement with the conclusion of the three-judge panel below that "the grave significance of education both to the individual and to our society" cannot be doubted. But the importance of a service performed by the State does not determine whether it must be regarded as fundamental for purposes of examination under the Equal Protection Clause. . . . [The Court discusses *Shapiro v. Thompson*, 394 U.S. 618 (1969), which struck

60. An educational financing system might be hypothesized, however, in which the analogy to the wealth discrimination cases would be considerably closer. If elementary and secondary education were made available by the State only to those able to pay a tuition assessed against each pupil, there would be a clearly defined class of "poor" people—definable in terms of their inability to pay the prescribed sum—who would be absolutely precluded from receiving an education. That case would present a far more compelling set of circumstances for judicial assistance than the case before us today. After all, Texas has undertaken to do a good deal more than provide an education to those who can afford it. It has provided what it considers to be an adequate base education for all children and has attempted, though imperfectly, to ameliorate by state funding and by the local assessment program the disparities in local tax resources.

down welfare residence requirements as an infringement on the constitutionally guaranteed "right to interstate travel." It distinguishes *Lindsey v. Normet*, 405 U.S. 56 (1972), which rejected a constitutional challenge to procedural limitations on tenants in suits brought by landlords, and *Dandridge v. Williams*, 397 U.S. 471 (1970), which rejected a constitutional challenge to Maryland's setting a welfare ceiling for families, as cases involving no explicitly constitutionally guaranteed right.]

The lesson of these cases in addressing the question now before the Court is plain. It is not the province of this Court to create substantive constitutional rights in the name of guaranteeing equal protection of the laws. Thus the key to discovering whether education is "fundamental" is not to be found in comparisons of the relative societal significance of education as opposed to subsistence or housing. Nor is it to be found by weighing whether education is as important as the right to travel. Rather, the answer lies in assessing whether there is a right to education explicitly or implicitly guaranteed by the Constitution. . . .

Education, of course, is not among the rights afforded explicit protection under our Federal Constitution. Nor do we find any basis for saying it is implicitly so protected. As we have said, the undisputed importance of education will not alone cause this Court to depart from the usual standard for reviewing a State's social and economic legislation. It is appellees' contention, however, that education is distinguishable from other services and benefits provided by the State because it bears a peculiarly close relationship to other rights and liberties accorded protection under the Constitution. Specifically, they insist that education is itself a fundamental personal right because it is essential to the effective exercise of First Amendment freedoms and to intelligent utilization of the right to vote. In asserting a nexus between speech and education, appellees urge that the right to speak is meaningless unless the speaker is capable of articulating his thoughts intelligently and persuasively. The "marketplace of ideas" is an empty forum for those lacking basic communicative tools. Likewise, they argue that the corollary right to receive information becomes little more than a hollow privilege when the recipient has not been taught to read, assimilate, and utilize available knowledge.

A similar line of reasoning is pursued with respect to the right to vote. Exercise of the franchise, it is contended, cannot be divorced from the educational foundation of the voter. The electoral process, if reality is to conform to the democratic ideal, depends on an informed electorate: a voter cannot cast his ballot intelligently unless his reading skills and thought processes have been adequately developed.

We need not dispute any of these propositions. The Court has long afforded zealous protection against unjustifiable governmental interference with the individual's rights to speak and to vote. Yet we have never presumed to possess either the ability or the authority to guarantee to the citizenry the most *effective* speech or the most *informed* electoral choice. That these may be desirable goals of a system of freedom of expression and of a representative form of government is not to be doubted. These are indeed goals to be pursued by a people whose thoughts and beliefs are freed from governmental interference. But they are not values to be implemented by judicial intrusion into otherwise legitimate state activities.

Even if it were conceded that some identifiable quantum of education is a constitutionally protected prerequisite to the meaningful exercise of either right, we have no indication that the present levels of educational expenditure in Texas provide an education that falls short . . . [N]o charge fairly could be made that the system fails to provide each child with an opportunity to acquire the basic minimal skills necessary for the enjoyment of the rights of speech and of full participation in the political process.

Furthermore, the logical limitations on appellees' nexus theory are difficult to perceive. How, for instance, is education to be distinguished from the significant personal interests in the basics of decent food and shelter? Empirical examination might well buttress an assumption that the ill-fed, ill-clothed, and ill-housed are among the most ineffective participants in the political process and that they derive the least enjoyment from the benefits of the First Amendment. If so, appellees' thesis would cast serious doubt on the authority of *Dandridge v. Williams* . . . and *Lindsey v. Normet*. . . .

C

We need not rest our decision, however, solely on the inappropriateness of the strict scrutiny test. A century of Supreme Court adjudication under the Equal Protection Clause affirmatively supports the application of the traditional standard of review, which requires only that the State's system be shown to bear some rational relationship to legitimate state purposes. This case represents far more than a challenge to the manner in which Texas provides for the education of its children. We have here nothing less than a direct attack on the way in which Texas has chosen to raise and disburse state and local tax revenues. We are asked to condemn the State's judgment in conferring on political subdivisions the power to tax local property to supply revenues for local interests. In so doing, appellees would have the Court intrude in an area in which it has traditionally deferred to state legislatures. . . .

[T]he Justices of this Court lack both the expertise and the familiarity with local problems so necessary to the making of wise decisions with respect to the raising and disposition of public revenues. Yet we are urged to direct the States either to alter drastically the present system or to throw out the property tax altogether in favor of some other form of taxation. No scheme of taxation, whether the tax is imposed on property, income, or purchases of goods and services, has yet been devised which is free of all discriminatory impact. In such a complex arena in which no perfect alternatives exist, the Court does well not to impose too rigorous a standard of scrutiny lest all local fiscal schemes become subjects of criticism under the Equal Protection Clause.[85]

In addition to matters of fiscal policy, this case also involves the most persistent and difficult questions of educational policy, another area in which this Court's lack of specialized knowledge and experience counsels against premature interference with the informed judgments made at the state and local levels. . . . On even the most basic questions in this area the scholars and educational experts are divided. Indeed, one of the major sources of controversy concerns the extent to which there is a demonstrable correlation between educational expenditures and the quality of education[86]—an assumed correlation underlying virtually every legal conclusion drawn by the District Court in this case. Related to the questioned relationship between cost and quality is the equally unsettled controversy as to the proper goals of a system of public education. . . . In such circumstances the judiciary is well advised to refrain from imposing on the States inflexible constitutional restraints that could circumscribe or handicap the continued research and experimentation so vital to finding even partial solutions to educational problems and to keeping abreast of ever changing conditions.

It must be remembered also that every claim arising under the Equal Protection Clause has implications for the relationship between national and state power under our federal system. . . . [I]t would be difficult to imagine a case having a greater potential impact on our federal system than the one now before us, in which we are urged to abrogate systems of financing public education presently in existence in virtually every State.

The foregoing considerations buttress our conclusion that Texas' system of public school finance is an inappropriate candidate for strict judicial scrutiny. These same considerations are relevant to the determination whether that system, with its conceded imperfections, nevertheless bears some rational relationship to a legitimate state purpose. It is to this question that we next turn our attention. . . .

The Texas system of school finance . . . , [w]hile assuring a basic education for every child in the State, . . . permits and encourages a large measure

85. Those who urge that the present system be invalidated offer little guidance as to what type of school financing should replace it. The most likely result of rejection of the existing system would be statewide financing of all public education with funds derived from taxation of property or from the adoption or expansion of sales and income taxes. See Simon, ["The School Finance Decisions: Collective Bargaining and Future Finance Systems," 82 *Yale L.J.* 409, 439–40 (1973).] The authors of ***Private Wealth and Public Education**, supra*, n13, at 201–242, suggest an alternative scheme, known as "district power equalizing." In simplest terms, the State would guarantee that at any particular rate of property taxation the district would receive a stated number of dollars regardless of the district's tax base. To finance the subsidies to "poorer" districts, funds would be taken away from the "wealthier" districts that, because of their higher property values, collect more than the stated amount at any given rate. This is not the place to weigh the arguments for and against "district power equalizing," beyond noting that commentators are in disagreement as to whether it is feasible, how it would work, and indeed whether it would violate the equal protection theory underlying appellees' case. President's Commission on School Finance, *Schools, People & Money* 32–33 (1972); Bateman and Brown, "Some Reflections on *Serrano v. Priest*," 49 *J. Urban L.* 701, 706–8 (1972); Brest, Book Review, 23 *Stan. L.Rev.* 591, 594–96 (1971); Goldstein, *supra*, [n.68], at 542–43; Wise, "School Finance Equalization Lawsuits: A Model Legislative Response," 2 *Yale Rev. L. & Soc. Action* 123, 125 (1971); Silard and White, "Intrastate Inequalities in Public Education: The Case for Judicial Relief Under the Equal Protection Clause," 1970 *Wis.L.Rev.* 7, 29–30.

86. The quality-cost controversy has received considerable attention. Among the notable authorities on both sides are the following: C. Jencks, *Inequality* (1972); C. Silberman, *Crisis in the Classroom* (1970); Office of Education, *Equality of Educational Opportunity* (1966) (The Coleman Report); *On Equality of Educational Opportunity* (Moynihan and Mosteller eds., 1972); J. Guthrie, G. Kleindorfer, H. Levin, and R. Stout, *Schools and Inequality* (1971); President's Comm'n on School Finance, *supra*, n85; Swanson, "The Cost-Quality Relationship, in The Challenge of Change in School Finance," *10th Nat'l Educational Ass'n Conf. on School Finance* 151 (1967).

of participation in and control of each district's schools at the local level. . . .

The persistence of attachment to government at the lowest level where education is concerned reflects the depth of commitment of its supporters. In part, local control means, as Professor Coleman suggests, the freedom to devote more money to the education of one's children. Equally important, however, is the opportunity it offers for participation in the decision-making process that determines how those local tax dollars will be spent. . . .

Appellees do not question the propriety of Texas' dedication to local control of education. To the contrary, they attack the school financing system precisely because, in their view, it does not provide the same level of local control and fiscal flexibility in all districts. Appellees suggest that local control could be preserved and promoted under other financing systems that resulted in more equality in educational expenditures. While it is no doubt true that reliance on local property taxation for school revenues provides less freedom of choice with respect to expenditures for some districts than for others,[107] the existence of "some inequality" in the manner in which the State's rationale is achieved is not alone a sufficient basis for striking down the entire system. . . . The people of Texas may be justified in believing that other systems of school financing, which place more of the financial responsibility in the hands of the State, will result in a comparable lessening of desired local autonomy. That is, they may believe that along with increased control of the purse strings at the state level will go increased control over local policies.[109]

Appellees further urge that the Texas system is unconstitutionally arbitrary because it allows the availability of local taxable resources to turn on "happen-stance." They see no justification for a system that allows, as they contend, the quality of education to fluctuate on the basis of the fortuitous positioning of the boundary lines of political subdivisions and the location of valuable commercial and industrial property. But any scheme of local taxation—indeed the very existence of identifiable local governmental units—requires the establishment of jurisdictional boundaries that are inevitably arbitrary. . . .

Moreover, if local taxation for local expenditures were an unconstitutional method of providing for education then it might be an equally impermissible means of providing other necessary services customarily financed largely from local property taxes, including local police and fire protection, public health and hospitals and public utility facilities of various kinds. We perceive no justification for such a severe denigration of local property taxation and control as would follow from appellees' contentions. . . .

In sum, to the extent that the Texas system of school financing results in unequal expenditures between children who happen to reside in different districts, we cannot say that such disparities are the product of a system that is so irrational as to be invidiously discriminatory. Texas has acknowledged its shortcomings and has persistently endeavored—not without some success—to ameliorate the differences in levels of expenditures without sacrificing the benefits of local participation. The Texas plan is not the result of hurried, ill-conceived legislation. It certainly is not the product of purposeful discrimination against any group or class. . . .

IV

The complexity of these [school finance] problems is demonstrated by the lack of consensus with respect to whether it may be said with any assurance that

107. Mr. Justice White suggests in his dissent that the Texas system violates the Equal Protection Clause because the means it has selected to effectuate its interest in local autonomy fail to guarantee complete freedom of choice to every district. He places special emphasis on the statutory provision that establishes a maximum rate of $1.50 per $100 valuation at which a local school district may tax for school maintenance. Tex. Educ. Code §20.04(d) (1972). The maintenance rate in Edgewood when this case was litigated in the District Court was $.55 per $100, barely one-third of the allowable rate. [The tax rate of $1.05 per $100, see *supra* at 658, is the equalized rate for maintenance and for the retirement of bonds.] Appellees do not claim that the ceiling presently bars desired tax increases in Edgewood or in any other Texas district. Therefore, the constitutionality of that statutory provision is not before us and must await litigation in a case in which it is properly presented. Cf. *Hargrave v. Kirk*, 313 F.Supp. 944 (M.D. Fla. 1970), *vacated*, 401 U.S. 476 (1971).

109. This theme—that greater state control over funding will lead to greater state power with respect to local educational programs and policies—is a recurrent one in the literature on financing public education. Professor Simon, in his thoughtful analysis of the political ramifications of this case, states that one of the most likely consequences of the District Court's decision would be an increase in the centralization of school finance and an increase in the extent of collective bargaining by teacher unions at the state level. He suggests that the subjects for bargaining may include many "nonsalary" items, such as teaching loads, class size, curricular and program choices, questions of student discipline, and selection of administrative personnel—matters traditionally decided heretofore at the local level. Simon, ["The School Finance Decisions: Collective Bargaining and Future Systems," 82 *Yale L.J.* 409, 434–36 (1973)]. . . .

the poor, the racial minorities, or the children in overburdened core-city school districts would be benefitted by abrogation of traditional modes of financing education. Unless there is to be a substantial increase in state expenditures on education across the board—an event the likelihood of which is open to considerable question—these groups stand to realize gains in terms of increased per-pupil expenditures only if they reside in districts that presently spend at relatively low levels, *i.e.*, in those districts that would benefit from the redistribution of existing resources. Yet recent studies have indicated that the poorest families are not invariably clustered in the most impecunious school districts. Nor does it now appear that there is anymore than a random chance that racial minorities are concentrated in property-poor districts. Additionally, several research projects have concluded that any financing alternative designed to achieve a greater equality of expenditures is likely to lead to higher taxation and lower educational expenditures in the major urban centers, a result that would exacerbate rather than ameliorate existing conditions in those areas.

These practical considerations, of course, play no role in the adjudication of the constitutional issues presented here. But they serve to highlight the wisdom of the traditional limitations on this Court's function. . . . We hardly need add that this Court's action today is not to be viewed as placing its judicial imprimatur on the status quo. The need is apparent for reform in tax systems which may well have relied too long and too heavily on the local property tax. And certainly innovative thinking as to public education, its methods and its funding, is necessary to assure both a higher level of quality and greater uniformity of opportunity. These matters merit the continued attention of the scholars who already have contributed much by their challenges. But the ultimate solutions must come from the lawmakers and from the democratic pressures of those who elect them.

Reversed.

Mr. Justice Stewart, concurring.

The method of financing public schools in Texas, as in almost every other State, has resulted in a system of public education that can fairly be described as chaotic and unjust. It does not follow, however, and I cannot find, that this system violates the Constitution of the United States. I join the opinion and judgment of the Court because I am convinced that any other course would mark an extraordinary departure from principled adjudication under the Equal Protection Clause of the Fourteenth Amendment. . . .

Mr. Justice White, with whom Mr. Justice Douglas and Mr. Justice Brennan join, dissenting. . . .

I cannot disagree with the proposition that local control and local decision making play an important part in our democratic system of government. *Cf. James v. Valtierra*, 402 U.S. 137 (1971). Much may be left to local option, and this case would be quite different if it were true that the Texas system, while insuring minimum educational expenditures in every district through state funding, extended a meaningful option to all local districts to increase their per-pupil expenditures and so to improve their children's education to the extent that increased funding would achieve that goal. The system would then arguably provide a rational and sensible method of achieving the stated aim of preserving an area for local initiative and decision.

The difficulty with the Texas system, however, is that it provides a meaningful option to Alamo Heights and like school districts but almost none to Edgewood and those other districts with a low per-pupil real estate tax base. In these latter districts, no matter how desirous parents are of supporting their schools with greater revenues, it is impossible to do so through the use of the real estate property tax. In these districts the Texas system utterly fails to extend a realistic choice to parents, because the property tax, which is the only revenue-raising mechanism extended to school districts, is practically and legally unavailable. . . .

. . . If the State aims at maximizing local initiative and local choice, by permitting school districts to resort to the real property tax if they choose to do so, it utterly fails in achieving its purpose in districts with property tax bases so low that there is little if any opportunity for interested parents, rich or poor, to augment school district revenues. Requiring the State to establish only that unequal treatment is in furtherance of a permissible goal, without also requiring the State to show that the means chosen to effectuate that goal are rationally related to its achievement, makes equal protection analysis no more than an empty gesture. In my view, the parents and children, in Edgewood, and in like districts, suffer from an invidious discrimination violative of the Equal Protection Clause. . . .

There is no difficulty in identifying the class that is subject to the alleged discrimination and that is entitled to the benefits of the Equal Protection Clause. I need go no farther than the parents and children in the Edgewood district, who are plaintiffs here and who assert that they are entitled to the same choice as Alamo Heights to augment local expenditures for schools but are denied that choice by state law. This group constitutes a class sufficiently definite to invoke the protection of the Constitution . . . [I]n the present case we would blink reality to ignore the fact that school districts, and students in the end, are differentially affected by the Texas school financing scheme with respect to their capability to supplement the Minimum Foundation School Program. At the very least, the law discriminates against those children and their parents who live in districts where the per-pupil tax base is sufficiently low to make impossible the provision of comparable school revenues by resort to the real property tax which is the only device the State extends for this purpose.

Mr. Justice Marshall, with whom Mr. Justice Douglas concurs, dissenting.

The Court today decides, in effect, that a State may constitutionally vary the quality of education which it offers its children in accordance with the amount of taxable wealth located in the school districts within which they reside. The majority's decision represents an abrupt departure from the mainstream of recent state and federal court decisions concerning the unconstitutionality of state educational financing schemes dependent upon taxable local wealth. More unfortunately, though, the majority's holding can only be seen as a retreat from our historic commitment to equality of educational opportunity and as unsupportable acquiescence in a system which deprives children in their earliest years of the chance to reach their full potential as citizens. The Court does this despite the absence of any substantial justification for a scheme which arbitrarily channels educational resources in accordance with the fortuity of the amount of taxable wealth within each district. . . .

[Justice Marshall reviews the workings of the Texas school finance scheme. He notes that: "The necessary effect of the Texas local property tax is . . . to favor property rich districts and to disfavor property poor ones." That disparity, he adds: "cannot be dismissed as the result of lack of local effort—that is, lower tax rates—by property poor districts. To the contrary, the data presented below indicate that the poorest districts tend to have the highest tax rates and the richest districts tend to have the lowest tax rates." Justice Marshall then turns to other sources of school revenues. Federal funds, which pay for some 10 percent of the total cost of public education in Texas, do not "ameliorate significantly the widely varying consequences for Texas school districts and children of the local property tax element of the state financing scheme." And state funds, which pay half of Texas' education bill tend "to subsidize the rich at the expense of the poor." The allocation criteria enable property rich districts to claim a larger share of educational costs than property poor districts; the economic index upon which state aid is calculated includes factors which are not "predictive of a district's ability to raise revenues through local property taxes."]

I

The Court acknowledges that "substantial interdistrict disparities in school expenditures" exist in Texas . . . and that these disparities are "largely attributable to differences in the amounts of money collected through local property taxation". . . . But instead of closely examining the seriousness of these disparities and the invidiousness of the Texas financing scheme, the Court undertakes an elaborate exploration of the efforts Texas has purportedly made to close the gaps between its districts in terms of levels of district wealth and resulting educational funding. Yet, however praiseworthy Texas' equalizing efforts, the issue in this case is not whether Texas is doing its best to ameliorate the worst features of a discriminatory scheme, but rather whether the scheme itself is in fact unconstitutionally discriminatory in the face of the Fourteenth Amendment's guarantee of equal protection of the laws. When the Texas financing scheme is taken as a whole, I do not think it can be doubted that it produces a discriminatory impact on substantial numbers of the school-age children of the State of Texas. . . .

B

The appellants do not deny the disparities in educational funding caused by variations in taxable district property wealth. They do contend, however, that whatever the differences in per-pupil spending among Texas districts, there are no discriminatory consequences for the children of disadvantaged districts. . . .

In my view, though, even an unadorned restatement of this contention is sufficient to reveal its absurdity. Authorities concerned with educational quality no doubt disagree as to the significance of variations in per-pupil spending. . . . We sit, however, not to resolve disputes over educational theory but to enforce our Constitution. It is an inescapable fact that if one district has more funds available per pupil than another district, the former will have greater choice in educational planning than will the latter. In this regard, I believe the question of discrimination in educational quality must be deemed to be an objective one that looks to what the State provides its children, not to what the children are able to do with what they receive. . . .

Hence, even before this Court recognized its duty to tear down the barriers of state-enforced racial segregation in public education, it acknowledged that inequality in the educational facilities provided to students may be discriminatory state action as contemplated by the Equal Protection Clause. As a basis for striking down state enforced segregation of a law school, the Court in *Sweatt v. Painter*, 339 U.S. 629, 633–34 (1950), stated:

> [W]e cannot find substantial equality in the educational opportunities offered white and Negro law students by the State. In terms of number of the faculty, variety of courses and opportunity for specialization, size of the student body, scope of the library, availability of law review and similar activities, the [white only] Law School is superior. . . . It is difficult to believe that one who had a free choice between these law schools would consider the question close.

See also McLaurin v. Oklahoma State Regents for Higher Education, 339 U.S. 637 (1950). Likewise it is difficult to believe that if the children of Texas had a free choice, they would choose to be educated in districts with fewer resources, and hence with more-antiquated plants, less-experienced teachers, and a less-diversified curriculum. In fact, if financing variations are so insignificant to educational quality, it is difficult to understand why a number of our country's wealthiest school districts, which have no legal obligation to argue in support of the constitutionality of the Texas legislation, have nevertheless zealously pursued its cause before this Court. . . .

At the very least, in view of the substantial interdistrict disparities in funding and in resulting educational inputs shown by appellees to exist under the Texas financing scheme, the burden of proving that these disparities do not in fact affect the quality of children's education must fall upon the appellants. *Cf. Hobson v. Hansen*, 327 F.Supp. 844, 860–61 (D.D.C. 1971). Yet appellants made no effort in the District Court to demonstrate that educational quality is not affected by variations in funding and in resulting inputs. . . .

Nor can I accept the appellants' apparent suggestion that the Texas Minimum Foundation School Program effectively eradicates any discriminatory effects otherwise resulting from the local property tax element of the Texas financing scheme. Appellants assert that, despite its imperfections, the Program "does guarantee an adequate education to every child." The majority, in considering the constitutionality of the Texas financing scheme, seems to find substantial merit in this contention. . . . But I fail to understand how the constitutional problems inherent in the financing scheme are eased by the Foundation Program. . . .

The suggestion may be that the state aid received via the Foundation Program sufficiently improves the position of property poor districts *vis-à-vis* property rich districts—in terms of educational funds—to eliminate any claim of interdistrict discrimination in available educational resources which might otherwise exist if educational funding were dependent solely upon local property taxation. . . . But as has already been seen, we are hardly presented here with some *de minimis* claim of discrimination resulting from the play necessary in any functioning system; to the contrary, it is clear that the Foundation Program utterly fails to ameliorate the seriously discriminatory effects of the local property tax.

Alternatively, the appellants and the majority may believe that the Equal Protection Clause cannot be offended by substantially unequal state treatment of persons who are similarly situated so long as the State provides everyone with some unspecified amount of education which evidently is "enough." The basis for such a novel view is far from clear. . . . The Equal Protection Clause is not addressed to the minimal sufficiency but rather to the unjustifiable inequalities of state action. It mandates nothing less than that "all persons similarly circumstanced shall be treated alike." *F. S. Royster Guano Co. v. Virginia*, 253 U.S. 412, 415 (1920).

Even if the Equal Protection Clause encompassed some theory of constitutional adequacy, discrimination in the provision of educational opportunity would certainly seem to be a poor candidate for its application. Neither the majority nor appellants inform us how judicially manageable standards are to be derived for determining how much education is "enough" to excuse constitutional discrimination. One would think that the majority would heed its own fervent affirmation of judicial self-restraint before undertaking the complex task of determining at large what level of education is constitutionally sufficient. . . .

C

Despite the evident discriminatory effect of the Texas financing scheme, both the appellants and the majority raise substantial questions concerning the precise character of the disadvantaged class in this case. . . .

[W]hile on its face the Texas scheme may merely discriminate between local districts, the impact of that discrimination falls directly upon the children whose educational opportunity is dependent upon where they happen to live. Consequently, the District Court correctly concluded that the Texas financing scheme discriminates, from a constitutional perspective, between school children on the basis of the amount of taxable property located within their local districts. . . .

A number of theories of discrimination have, to be sure, been considered in the course of this litigation. Thus, the District Court found that in Texas the poor and minority group members tend to live in property poor districts, suggesting discrimination on the basis of both personal wealth and race. . . . Although I have serious doubts as to the correctness of the Court's analysis in rejecting the data submitted below,[56] I have no need to join issue on these factual disputes.

I believe it is sufficient that the overarching form of discrimination in this case is between the school children of Texas on the basis of the taxable property wealth of the districts in which they happen to live. To understand both the precise nature of this discrimination and the parameters of the disadvantaged class it is sufficient to consider the constitutional principle which appellees contend is controlling in the context of educational financing. In their complaint appellees asserted that the Constitution does not permit local district wealth to be determinative of educational opportunity. This is simply another way of saying, as the District Court concluded, that consistent with the guarantee of equal protection of the laws, "the quality of public education may not be a function of wealth, other than the wealth of the state as a whole." . . . Under such a principle, the children of a district are excessively advantaged if that district has more taxable property per pupil than the average amount of taxable property per pupil considering the State as a whole. By contrast, the children of a district are disadvantaged if that

---

56. The Court rejects the District Court's finding of a correlation between poor people and poor districts with the assertion that "there is reason to believe that the poorest families are not necessarily clustered in the poorest property districts" in Texas. . . . In support of its conclusion the Court offers absolutely no data—which it cannot on this record—concerning the distribution of poor people in Texas to refute the data introduced below by appellees; it relies instead on a recent law review note concerned solely with the State of Connecticut, Note, "A Statistical Analysis of the School Finance Decisions: On Winning Battles and Losing Wars," 81 *Yale L.J.* 1303 (1972). Common sense suggests that the basis for drawing a demographic conclusion with respect to a geographically large, urban-rural, industrial-agricultural State such as Texas from a geographically small, densely populated, highly industrialized State such as Connecticut is doubtful at best.

Furthermore, the article upon which the Court relies to discredit the statistical procedures employed by Professor Berke to establish the correlation between poor people and poor districts based its criticism primarily on the fact that only 4 of the 110 districts studied were in the lowest of the five categories, which were determined by relative taxable property per pupil, and most districts clustered in the middle three groups. See Goldstein, "Interdistrict Inequalities in School Financing: A Critical Analysis of *Serrano v. Priest* and Its Progeny," 120 *U. Pa. L.Rev.* 504, 524 n 67 (1972). But the Court fails to note that the four poorest districts in the sample had over 50,000 students which constituted 10% of the students in the entire sample. It appears, moreover, that even when the richest and the poorest categories are enlarged to include in each category 20% of the students in the sample, the correlation between district and individual wealth holds true.

Finally, it cannot be ignored that the data introduced by appellees went unchallenged in the District Court. The majority's willingness to permit appellants to litigate the correctness of those data for the first time before this tribunal—where effective response by appellees is impossible—is both unfair and judicially unsound.

district has less taxable property per pupil than the state average. . . . Whether this discrimination, against the school children of property poor districts, inherent in the Texas financing scheme is violative of the Equal Protection Clause is the question to which we must now turn.

II

* * *

A

To begin, I must once more voice my disagreement with the Court's rigidified approach to equal protection analysis. *See Dandridge v. Williams*, 397 U.S. 471, 519–21 (1970) (dissenting opinion); *Richardson v. Belcher*, 404 U.S. 78, 90 (1971) (dissenting opinion). The Court apparently seeks to establish today that equal protection cases fall into one of two neat categories which dictate the appropriate standard of review—strict scrutiny or mere rationality. But this Court's decisions in the field of equal protection defy such easy categorization. A principled reading of what this Court has done reveals that it has applied a spectrum of standards in reviewing discrimination allegedly violative of the Equal Protection Clause. This spectrum clearly comprehends variations in the degree of care with which the Court will scrutinize particular classifications, depending, I believe, on the constitutional and societal importance of the interest adversely affected and the recognized invidiousness of the basis upon which the particular classification is drawn. . . .

I therefore cannot accept the majority's labored efforts to demonstrate that fundamental interests, which call for strict scrutiny of the challenged classification, encompass only established rights which we are somehow bound to recognize from the text of the Constitution itself. To be sure, some interests which the Court has deemed to be fundamental for purposes of equal protection analysis are themselves constitutionally protected rights. . . .

[But] I would like to know where the Constitution guarantees the right to procreate, *Skinner v. Oklahoma*, 316 U.S. 535, 541 (1942), or the right to vote in state elections, *e.g.*, *Reynolds v. Sims*, 377 U.S. 533 (1964), or the right to an appeal from a criminal conviction, *e.g.*, *Griffin v. Illinois*, 351 U.S. 12 (1956). These are instances in which, due to the importance of the interests at stake, the Court has displayed a strong concern with the existence of discriminatory state treatment. But the Court has never said or indicated that these are interests which independently enjoy full-blown constitutional protection. . . .

The majority is, of course, correct when it suggests that the process of determining which interests are fundamental is a difficult one. But I do not think the problem is insurmountable. And I certainly do not accept the view that the process need necessarily degenerate into an unprincipled, subjective "picking-and-choosing" between various interests or that it must involve this court in creating "substantive constitutional rights in the name of guaranteeing equal protection of the laws." . . . Although not all fundamental interests are constitutionally guaranteed, the determination of which interests are fundamental should be firmly rooted in the text of the Constitution. The task in every case should be to determine the extent to which constitutionally guaranteed rights are dependent on interests not mentioned in the Constitution. As the nexus between the specific constitutional guarantee and the nonconstitutional interest draws closer, the nonconstitutional interest becomes more fundamental and the degree of judicial scrutiny applied when the interest is infringed on a discriminatory basis must be adjusted accordingly. . . .

[Justice Marshall next discusses several cases which, while assertedly testing the constitutionality of legislation against the traditional equal protection "rationality" standard, in fact reject the "two tier" review approach. In *Eisenstadt v. Baird*, 405 U.S. 438 (1972), the Court struck down a Massachusetts statute which denied unmarried persons access to contraceptive devices on the same basis as married persons. ". . . [A]lthough there were conceivable state interests intended to be advanced by the state—*e.g.*, deterrence of premarital sexual activity; regulation of the dissemination of potentially dangerous articles—the Court was not prepared to accept these interests on their face, but instead proceeded to test their substantiality by independent analysis." A similar standard of review was applied in *James v. Strange*, 407 U.S. 128 (1972), which held unconstitutional a state statute providing for recoupment from indigent convicts of legal defense fees paid by the state, and in *Reed v. Reed*, 404 U.S. 71 (1971), which struck down a statute which gave men preference over women when persons of equal entitlement apply for assignment as administrator of a particular estate. To Justice Marshall, "*James* and *Reed* can only be understood as instances in which the particularly invidious character of the classification caused the Court to pause and scrutinize with more than traditional care the rationality of state discrimination." And, notes Justice Marshall, *Weber v. Aetna Cas. & Sur. Co.*, 406 U.S. 164 (1972), which held unconstitutional a portion of a state workman's compensation statute that relegated unacknowledged illegitimate children of the deceased to a lesser status with respect to benefits than that enjoyed by legitimate children of the deceased, is the clearest recent example of the "Court's sensitivity to the invidiousness of the basis for discrimination. . . ."]

In summary, it seems to me inescapably clear that this Court has consistently adjusted the care with which it will review state discrimination in light of the constitutional significance of the interests affected and the invidiousness of the particular classification. . . . The majority suggests, however, that a variable standard of review would give this Court the appearance of a "superlegislature." . . . I cannot agree. Such an approach seems to me a part of the guarantees of our Constitution and of the historic experiences with oppression of and discrimination against discrete, powerless minorities which underlie that document. In truth, the Court itself will be open to the criticism raised by the majority so long as it continues on its present course of effectively selecting in private which cases will be afforded special consideration without acknowledging the true basis of its action.

. . . Opinions such as those in *Reed* and *James* seem drawn more as efforts to shield rather than to reveal the true basis of the Court's decisions. Such obfuscated action may be appropriate to a political body such as a legislature, but it is not appropriate to this Court. Open debate of the bases for the Court's action is essential to the rationality and consistency of our decision-making process. Only in this way can we avoid the label of legislature and ensure the integrity of the judicial process.

Nevertheless, the majority today attempts to force this case into the same category for purposes of equal protection analysis as decisions involving discrimination affecting commercial interests. By so doing, the majority singles this case out for analytic treatment at odds with what seems to me to be the clear trend of recent decisions in this Court, and thereby ignores the constitutional importance of the interest at stake and the invidiousness of the particular classification, factors that call for far more than the lenient scrutiny of the Texas financing scheme which the majority pursues. . . .

B

. . . [T]he fundamental importance of education is amply indicated by the prior decisions of this Court, by the unique status accorded public education by our society, and by the close relationship between education and some of our most basic constitutional values.

The special concern of this Court with the educational process of our country is a matter of common knowledge. [citing *Brown v. Board of Educ.*, 347 U.S. 483, 493 (1954): "Today, education is perhaps the most important function of state and local governments"; *Wisconsin v. Yoder*, 406 U.S. 205, 213 (1972): "Providing public schools ranks at the very apex of the function of a State."] . . .

Education directly affects the ability of a child to exercise his First Amendment interest both as a source and as a receiver of information and ideas, whatever interests he may pursue in life. . . .

Of particular importance is the relationship between education and the political process. . . . Education serves the essential function of instilling in our young an understanding of and appreciation for the principles and operation of our governmental processes. Education may instill the interest and provide the tools necessary for political discourse and debate. Indeed, it has frequently been suggested that education is the dominant factor affecting political consciousness and participation. . . .[72] But of most immediate and direct concern must be the dem-

72. That education is the dominant factor in influencing political participation and awareness is sufficient, I believe, to dispose of the Court's suggestion that, in all events, there is no indication that Texas is not providing all of its children with a sufficient education to enjoy the right of free speech and to participate fully in the political process. . . . There is, in short, no limit on the amount of free speech or political participation that the Constitution guarantees. Moreover, it should be obvious that the political process, like most other aspects of social intercourse, is to some degree competitive. It is thus of little benefit to an individual from a property poor district to have "enough" education if those around him have more than "enough."

onstrated effect of education on the exercise of the franchise by the electorate. The right to vote in federal elections is conferred by Art. I, §2, and the Seventeenth Amendment of the Constitution, and access to the state franchise has been afforded special protection because it is "preservative of other basic civil and political rights," *Reynolds v. Sims*, 377 U.S. 533, 562 (1964). Data from the Presidential Election of 1968 clearly demonstrates a direct relationship between participation in the electoral process and level of educational attainment; and, as this Court recognized in *Gaston County v. United States*, 395 U.S. 285, 296 (1969), the quality of education offered may influence a child's decision to "enter or remain in school." It is this very sort of intimate relationship between a particular personal interest and specific constitutional guarantees that has heretofore caused the Court to attach special significance, for purposes of equal protection analysis, to individual interests such as procreation and the exercise of the state franchise.[74]

While ultimately disputing little of this, the majority seeks refuge in the fact that the Court has "never presumed to possess either the ability or the authority to guarantee to the citizenry the most *effective* speech or the most *informed* electoral choice." . . . This serves only to blur what is in fact at stake. With due respect, the issue is neither provision of the most *effective* speech nor of the most *informed* vote. Appellees do not now seek the best education Texas might provide. . . . The issue is . . . one of discrimination that affects the quality of the education which Texas has chosen to provide its children; and, the precise question here is what importance should attach to education for purposes of equal protection analysis of that discrimination. . . . The factors just considered, including the relationship between education and the social and political interests enshrined within the Constitution, compel us to recognize the fundamentality of education and to scrutinize with appropriate care the bases for state discrimination affecting equality of educational opportunity in Texas' school districts—a conclusion which is only strengthened when we consider the character of the classification in this case.

C

. . . This Court has frequently recognized that discrimination on the basis of wealth may create a classification of a suspect character and thereby call for exacting judicial scrutiny. . . . The majority, however, considers any wealth classification in this case to lack certain essential characteristics which it contends are common to the instances of wealth discrimination that this Court has heretofore recognized. We are told that in every prior case involving a wealth classification, the members of the disadvantaged class have "shared two distinguishing characteristics: because of their impecunity they were completely unable to pay for some desired benefit, and as a consequence, they sustained an absolute deprivation of a meaningful opportunity to enjoy that benefit." . . . I cannot agree.

In *Harper*, the Court struck down as violative of the Equal Protection Clause an annual Virginia poll tax of $1.50, payment of which by persons over the age of 21 was a prerequisite to voting in Virginia elections. In part, the Court relied on the fact that the poll tax interfered with a fundamental interest—the exercise of the state franchise. In addition, though, the Court emphasized that "[l]ines drawn on the basis of wealth or property . . . are traditionally disfavored." 383 U.S. at 668. Under the first part of the theory announced by the majority the disadvantaged class in *Harper*, in terms of a wealth analysis, should have consisted only of those too poor to afford the $1.50 necessary to vote. But the *Harper* Court did not see it that way. In its view, the Equal Protection Clause "bars a system which excludes [from the franchise] those unable to pay a fee to vote or who *fail to pay*." . . . So far as the Court was con-

74. I believe that the close nexus between education and our established constitutional values with respect to freedom of speech and participation in the political process makes this a different case from our prior decisions concerning discrimination affecting public welfare, see, *e.g.*, *Dandridge v. Williams*, 397 U.S. 471 (1970), or housing, see, *e.g.*, *Lindsey v. Normet*, 405 U.S. 56 (1972). There can be no question that, as the majority suggests, constitutional rights may be less meaningful for someone without enough to eat or without decent housing. . . . But the crucial difference lies in the closeness of the relationship. Whatever the severity of the impact of insufficient food or inadequate housing on a person's life, they have never been considered to bear the same direct and immediate relationship to constitutional concerns for free speech and for our political processes as education has long been recognized to bear. Perhaps, the best evidence of this fact is the unique status which has been accorded public education as the single public service nearly unanimously guaranteed in the constitution of our States. . . . Education, in terms of constitutional values, is much more analogous in my judgment, to the right to vote in state elections than to public welfare or public housing. . . .

cerned, the "degree of the discrimination [was] irrelevant." . . . Thus, the Court struck down the poll tax *in toto;* it did not order merely that those too poor to pay the tax be exempted; complete impecunity clearly was not determinative of the limits of the disadvantaged class, nor was it essential to make an equal protection claim.

Similarly, *Griffin* and *Douglas* refute the majority's contention that we have in the past required an absolute deprivation before subjecting wealth classifications to strict scrutiny. The Court characterizes *Griffin* as a case concerned simply with the denial of a transcript or an adequate substitute therefore, and *Douglas* was involving the denial of counsel. But in both cases the question was in fact whether "a State that [grants] *appellate review* can do so in a way that discriminates against some convicted defendants on account of their poverty." *Griffin v. Illinois*, [351 U.S.] at 18. . . . In that regard, the Court concluded that inability to purchase a transcript denies "the poor an adequate *appellate review* accorded to all who have money enough to pay the costs in advance," . . . and that "the type of an *appeal* a person is afforded . . . hinges upon whether or not he can pay for the assistance of counsel," *Douglas v. California*, [372 U.S.] at 355–56. . . . The right of appeal itself was not absolutely denied to those too poor to pay; but because of the cost of a transcript and of counsel, the appeal was a substantially less meaningful right for the poor than for the rich. It was on these terms that the Court found a denial of equal protection, and those terms clearly encompassed degrees of discrimination on the basis of wealth which do not amount to outright denial of the affected right or interest.[77]

This is not to say that the form of wealth classification in this case does not differ significantly from those recognized in the previous decisions of this Court. Our prior cases have dealt essentially with discrimination on the basis of personal wealth. Here, by contrast, the children of the disadvantaged Texas school districts are being discriminated against not necessarily because of their personal wealth, or the wealth of their families, but because of the taxable property wealth of the residents of the district in which they happen to live. The appropriate question, then, is whether the same degree of judicial solicitude and scrutiny that has previously been afforded wealth classifications is warranted here. . . .

. . . [D]iscrimination on the basis of group wealth in this case likewise calls for careful judicial scrutiny. First, it must be recognized that while local district wealth may serve other interests, it bears no relationship whatsoever to the interest of Texas school children in the educational opportunity afforded them by the State of Texas. Given the importance of that interest, we must be particularly sensitive to the invidious characteristics of any form of discrimination that is not clearly intended to serve it, as opposed to some other distinct state interest. Discrimination on the basis of group wealth may not, to be sure, reflect the social stigma frequently attached to personal poverty. Nevertheless, insofar as group wealth discrimination involves wealth over which the disadvantaged individual has no significant control, it represents in fact a more serious basis of discrimination than does personal wealth. For such discrimination is no reflection of the individual's characteristics or his abilities. . . .

The disability of the disadvantaged class in this case extends as well into the political processes upon which we ordinarily rely as adequate for the protection and promotion of all interests. Here legislative reallocation of the State's property wealth must be sought in the face of inevitable opposition from significantly advantaged districts that have a strong vested interest in the preservation of the status quo, a problem not completely dissimilar to that faced by underrepresented districts prior to the Court's intervention in the process of reapportionment, *see Baker v. Carr*, 369 U.S. 186, 191–92 (1962).

Nor can we ignore the extent to which, in contrast to our prior decisions, the State is responsible for the wealth discrimination in this instance. . . . The means for financing public education in Texas are selected and specified by the State. It is the State that has created local school districts, and tied educational funding to the local property tax and thereby to local district wealth. . . . In short, this case, in contrast to the Court's previous wealth discrimina-

77. Even if I put aside the Court's misreading of *Griffin* and *Douglas*, the Court fails to offer any reasoned constitutional basis for restricting cases involving wealth discrimination to instances in which there is an absolute deprivation of the interest affected. As I have already discussed, . . . the Equal Protection Clause guarantees equality of treatment of those persons who are similarly situated; it does not merely bar some form of excessive discrimination between such persons.

tion decisions, can only be seen as "unusual in the extent to which governmental action *is* the cause of the wealth classifications."

D

The only justification offered by appellants to sustain the discrimination in educational opportunity caused by the Texas financing scheme is local educational control. . . .

. . . I do not question that local control of public education, as an abstract matter, constitutes a very substantial state interest. [*Citing Wright v. Council of Emporia*, 407 U.S. 451 (1972).] The State's interest in local educational control—which certainly includes questions of educational funding—has deep roots in the inherent benefits of community support for public education. Consequently, true state dedication to local control would present, I think, a substantial justification to weigh against simply interdistrict variations in the treatment of a State's school children. But I need not now decide how I might ultimately strike the balance were we confronted with a situation where the State's sincere concern for local control inevitably produced educational inequality. For on this record, it is apparent that the State's purported concern with local control is offered primarily as an excuse rather than as a justification for interdistrict inequality.

In Texas, statewide laws regulate in fact the most minute details of local public education. For example, the State prescribes required courses. All textbooks must be submitted for state approval, and only approved textbooks may be used. The State has established the qualifications necessary for teaching in Texas public schools and the procedures for obtaining certification. The State has even legislated on the length of the school day.

Moreover even if we accept Texas' general dedication to local control in educational matters, it is difficult to find any evidence of such dedication with respect to fiscal matters. It ignores reality to suggest . . . that the local property tax element of the Texas financing scheme reflects a conscious legislative effort to provide school districts with local fiscal control. If Texas had a system truly dedicated to local fiscal control one would expect the quality of the educational opportunity provided in each district to vary with the decision of the voters in that district as to the level of sacrifice they wish to make for public education. In fact, the Texas scheme produces precisely the opposite result. Local school districts cannot choose to have the best education in the State by imposing the highest tax rate. Instead, the quality of the educational opportunity offered by any particular district is largely determined by the amount of taxable property located in the district—a factor over which local voters can exercise no control. . . .

. . . If, for the sake of local education control, this Court is to sustain interdistrict discrimination in the educational opportunity afforded Texas school children, it should require that the State present something more than the mere sham now before us.

III

In conclusion, it is essential to recognize that an end to the wide variations in taxable district property wealth inherent in the Texas financing scheme would entail none of the untoward consequences suggested by the Court or by the appellants.

First, affirmance of the District Court's decisions would hardly sound the death knell for local control of education. It would mean neither centralized decision-making nor federal court intervention in the operation of public schools. Clearly, this suit has nothing to do with local decision making with respect to educational policy or even educational spending. It involves only a narrow aspect of local control—namely, local control over the raising of educational funds. In fact, in striking down interdistrict disparities in taxable local wealth, the District Court took the course which is most likely to make true local control over educational decision-making a reality for *all* Texas school districts.

Nor does the District Court's decision even necessarily eliminate local control of educational funding. The District Court struck down nothing more than the continued interdistrict wealth discrimination inherent in the present property tax. Both centralized and decentralized plans for educational funding not involving such interdistrict discrimination have been put forward.[98] The choice among these or other alternatives would remain with the State, not with the federal courts. . . .

Still, we are told that this case requires us "to condemn the State's judgment in conferring on political subdivisions the power to tax local property to supply revenues for local interests." . . . Yet no one in the course of this entire litigation has ever questioned the constitutionality of the local property tax as a device for raising educational funds. The District Court's decision, at most, restricts the power of the State to make educational funding dependent exclusively upon local property taxation so long as there exists interdistrict disparities in taxable property wealth. But it hardly eliminates the local property tax as a source of educational funding or as a means of providing local fiscal control.

The Court seeks solace for its action today in the possibility of legislative reform. The Court's suggestions of legislative redress and experimentation will doubtless be of great comfort to the school children of Texas' disadvantaged districts, but considering the vested interests of wealthy school districts in the preservation of the status quo, they are worth little more. The possibility of legislative action is, in all events, no answer to this Court's duty under the Constitution to eliminate unjustified state discrimination. . . .

I would therefore affirm the judgment of the District Court.

[Justice Brennan's dissenting opinion is omitted.]

[Appendices are omitted.]

NOTES AND QUESTIONS

1. Poverty as a Suspect Classification

The majority opinion first wrestles with whether the so-called "new equal protection" test is to be used. This test requires the state to demonstrate that its differential treatment is justified because it serves a compelling state interest that cannot be satisfied by some less onerous alternative; that is, the means chosen is necessary to the achievement of a compelling end. The use of this test is triggered when the state has either afforded inferior treatment to a "suspect class" or has detrimentally affected a "fundamental interest." Justice Powell turns first to the question of whether the state system of finance afforded inferior treatment of a suspect class. How was it argued that a suspect class was involved in this case? In discussing the concept of a suspect class in terms of poor persons, the majority concludes that in its earlier poverty discrimination cases, the disadvantaged class "shared two distinguishing characteristics: because of their impecunity they were completely unable to pay for some desired benefit, and as a consequence, they sustained an absolute deprivation of a meaningful opportunity to enjoy that benefit." Is the Court correctly construing its prior poverty cases? Should *complete* inability to pay and *absolute* deprivation be the only basis for judicial concern? Were the criminal defendants who could not afford a trial transcript or a lawyer absolutely deprived of an opportunity to appeal their cases? Might the standard of judicial review of asserted discrimination against the poor vary with (1) the nature of the burden placed on them by the state of their poverty and (2) the nature of the state's justification for imposing that burden? *See* Brest, Book Review, 23 *Stan.L.Rev.* 591 (1971).

The data convinced the majority that equating a suspect class with relative poverty was not sustained by the facts in the case. See footnote 56 of Justice Marshall's opinion. Is it important that despite the overall trend, the bulk of the districts fall in the middle range where the relationship of family in-

---

98. Centralized educational financing is, to be sure, one alternative. . . . Central financing would leave in local hands the entire gamut of local educational policy making—teachers, curriculum, school sites, the whole process of allocating resources among alternative educational objectives.

A second possibility is the much discussed theory of district power equalization put forth by Professors Coons, Clune, and Sugarman in their seminal work, *Private Wealth and Public Education* 201–42 (1970). Such a scheme would truly reflect a dedication to local fiscal control. Under their system, each school district would receive a fixed amount of revenue per pupil for any particular level of tax effort regardless of the level of local property tax base. Appellants criticize this scheme on the rather extraordinary ground that it would encourage poorer districts to overtax themselves in order to obtain substantial revenues for education. But under the present discriminatory scheme, it is the poor districts that are already taxing themselves at the highest rates, yet are receiving the lowest returns.

District wealth reapportionment is yet another alternative which would accomplish directly essentially what district power equalization would seek to do artificially. . . .

A fourth possibility would be to remove commercial, industrial, and mineral property from local tax rolls, to tax this property on a statewide basis, and to return the resulting revenues to the local districts in a fashion that would compensate for remaining variations in the local tax bases.

None of these particular alternatives are necessarily constitutionally compelled; rather, they indicate the breadth of choice which would remain to the State if the present inter-district disparities were eliminated.

come to expenditures is reversed? Should the Court have rested so heavily on this point given the possibility that in other states the inverse relationship of family income to expenditures is likely to be stronger? *See* Grubb and Michelson, "Public School Finance in a Post-*Serrano* World," 8 *Harv.C.R.–C.L.L.Rev.* 550 (1973). Was it relevant to the decision in this case that there might be a strong negative relationship between family income and expenditures per pupil in other states? What does this tell us about the role of the Court as policymaker? Could the decision in this case have been written to leave open the possibility of federal challenges in other states based on the association of family income and school expenditures? Should the Court, as a matter of constitutional law, recognize the existence of wealth discrimination when there is a negative correlation between family wealth and school expenditures? How strong as a constitutional matter must the correlation be to warrant the finding of wealth discrimination? Would this approach open the door to challenges to the financing of all local government, and if so, should the Court open this possibility? *Cf. Hawkins v. Town of Shaw*, 437 F.2d 1286 (5th Cir. 1971), *aff'd on rehearing*, 461 F.2d 1171 (5th Cir. 1972) (*en banc*).

The Court dismisses the third wealth discrimination argument on the ground that its own precedents should not be read to permit defining wealth discrimination as concerned with discrimination against residents of poor districts. Does the majority adequately answer the argument of Justice Marshall in his dissent? Why does the majority want to limit its special protection to those groups that have the "traditional indicia of suspectness"? Is the real issue dividing Justice Powell and Justice Marshall the proper role of the federal courts in our system of government? *See* Levin, "The Courts, Congress, and Educational Adequacy: The Equal Protection Predicament," 39 *Md.L.Rev.* 187, 198–202 (1979), for a discussion of the criticisms of the *Rodriguez* majority's treatment of the suspect class issue. *See also* Coons, "Recent Trends in Science Fiction: *Serrano* Among the People of Number," 6 *J. of Law and Educ.* 23 (1977).

2. *Education as a Fundamental Interest*

Justices Powell and Marshall both concede the importance of education as a basic social good. Yet the majority declines to treat education as a "fundamental" interest whose unequal provision requires "strict judicial scrutiny." The Court equates fundamental interests with rights "explicitly or implicitly guaranteed in the Constitution." Is that standard consistent with prior opinions? What might an implicit constitutional guarantee be? Is Justice Marshall's nexus approach preferable? Does it provide any stopping place for continued expansion of judicial power?

Plaintiffs sought to limit the use of the principle of fiscal neutrality to education by arguing that its relationship to constitutionally guaranteed rights was unique among state-supported goods. The majority, however, was not persuaded: "Empirical examination might well buttress an assumption that the ill-fed, ill-clothed, and ill-housed are among the most ineffective participants in the political process and that they derive the least enjoyment from the benefits of the First Amendment." Is education constitutionally distinguishable from other public goods? If fiscal neutrality were to apply to education, why should it not also apply to other public services? How can fiscal neutrality be limited?

3. *Minimally Adequate Education*

In two places in the opinion the majority makes the point that the appellees did not allege nor prove that they were denied a minimally adequate education. Thus the majority seems to have adopted Professor Michelman's minimum protection argument. Yet consider the following passage from the Brief of the Appellees to the Supreme Court:

> To be sure complete denial of all educational opportunity is more compelling than a relative denial. But in view of the magnitude of the differences in the capacity of state-created school districts in Texas to raise education dollars, and in light of the vast disparities in educational expenditures between districts, plaintiffs have surely been injured in a comparable way. A complete denial of all educational opportunity is not necessary to demonstrate an unconstitutional deprivation.

Brief of Appellees at 38.

Professor Michelman claims that "the minimum is significantly a function of the maximum and to that extent calls for equalization." He then adds that gross disparities in educational expenditures are "sufficient to raise a strong suspicion that lack of money is resulting in severe educational deprivation."

Michelman, "The Supreme Court, 1968 Term—Foreword: On Protecting the Poor Through the Fourteenth Amendment," 83 *Harv.L.Rev.* 7, 58 (1969). Did the majority misapply Professor Michelman's approach?

Justice Marshall strongly resists the minimum protection argument. Is Justice Marshall convincing when he argues that the Constitution does not embrace the minimal protection theory and that this approach provides no judicially manageable standards?

4. *Money and Quality*

Justice Powell's opinion notes the "considerable dispute among educators" about the relationship between school resources and outcomes. Is the Court suggesting that existing inequalities are invulnerable to constitutional attack unless such a relationship is established? Does this viewpoint adequately deal with Justice Marshall's argument that inequalities in what is actually delivered to students by way of services is what counts?

Who should have the burden of proof in the money-quality debate? Consider the following argument: (1) The state should not be allowed to deny that money determines quality since the whole system of educational finance in every state is predicated on the proposition that money does make a difference. (2) Hence, the burden of proof should be on the state to prove that spending above a certain minimum is wasteful. (3) If it is doubtful that spending above a minimum is less efficacious, it is unfair that only children of rich districts are insured against the unknown. (4) The social science dispute on this point is based on educational quality measured only in terms of reading scores—a measure much too narrow since it excludes such effects of money as whether or not a child learns to play the violin or swim.

The *Rodriguez* decision raises the problem of the use of social science data by the courts. When should the courts rely on common sense—on what everybody "knows"—and when should they defer to social science? Here, for example, common sense suggests that money can and does make a difference as to what services and programs are available to children, yet Justice Powell cites social science research to support the notion that we know little about the effects of money. When should a court defer to social science "not for its wisdom but for its very ignorance"? *See* Coons, "Recent Trends in Science Fiction: *Serrano* Among the People of Number," 6 *J. of Law & Educ.* 23, 31 (1977).

5. *The Rational Basis Standard*

The majority finds that since the finance system neither discriminates on the basis of a suspect class nor touches on a fundamental interest, the scheme must be assessed in terms of the rational basis standard of review. Does the Court make a case for the idea that the existing system is rationally related to the purpose of promoting local control? Does Justice Powell adequately answer the dissents of Justices White and Marshall? Could not the state promote local control even more effectively if it adopted the district power equalizing concept? Does local autonomy require local control of the funding of public education? Is local control consistent with the fact that education is a state-delegated function? *See* Briffault, "Our Localism: Part I—The Structure of Local Government Law," 90 *Colum.L.Rev.* 1 (1990). What about the intermediate test of equal protection articulated in *Craig v. Boren*, 429 U.S. 190, 97 S.Ct. 451, 50 L.Ed.2d 397 (1976)—that a classification be substantially related to an important governmental interest? *See also Orr v. Orr*, 440 U.S. 268, 99 S.Ct. 1102, 59 L.Ed.2d 306 (1979). A version of the intermediate scrutiny standard, the "sliding scale" test, has been applied in one school finance case. *Board of Education, Levittown v. Nyquist*, 94 Misc.2d 466, 408 N.Y.S.2d 606 (1978).

6. *The Role of the Supreme Court*

At numerous places in the *Rodriguez* opinion, Justice Powell reflects on problems faced by a court in dealing with public school financing. He expresses concern for maintaining the federal system, for not shifting too much power to the judicial branch of the central government. How strong a consideration is this factor? Why does it play a role in this case but not in *Brown v. Board of Education* discussed in chapter 5? When should a concern for maintaining the federal system enter into the calculus of deciding a case?

7. *Post-*Rodriguez *Challenges*

Does the majority opinion suggest any basis for challenging school finance systems under the Equal Protection Clause? What minimal level of education might be a fundamental right? What, short of absolute deprivation of education, might trigger closer scrutiny?

The Supreme Court's opinion in *Rodriguez* distinguishes interdistrict financing inequities from a state "financing system [that] occasioned an absolute denial of educational opportunities to any of its children." The Court also notes that a tuition assessment plan that "absolutely precluded [poor children] from receiving an education . . . would present a far more compelling set of circumstances for judicial assistance than the case before us today."

Those statements raise a constitutional question: Under what circumstances, if any, is exclusion of a class of children from the public schools— or, more broadly, from publicly supported educational services—constitutionally justifiable?

Plyler v. Doe

457 U.S. 202, 1025 S.Ct. 2382, 72 L.Ed.2d 786 (1982).

Justice Brennan delivered the opinion of the Court.

The question presented by these cases is whether, consistent with the Equal Protection Clause of the Fourteenth Amendment, Texas may deny to undocumented school-age children the free public education that it provides to children who are citizens of the United States or legally admitted aliens.

I

Since the late nineteenth century, the United States has restricted immigration into this country. Unsanctioned entry into the United States is a crime, 8 U.S.C. § 1325, and those who have entered unlawfully are subject to deportation, 8 U.S.C. §§ 1251–1252. But despite the existence of these legal restrictions, a substantial number of persons have succeeded in unlawfully entering the United States, and now live within various States, including the State of Texas.

In May 1975, the Texas legislature revised its education laws to withhold from local school districts any state funds for the education of children who were not "legally admitted" into the United States. The 1975 revision also authorized local school districts to deny enrollment in their public schools to children not "legally admitted" to the country. Tex.Educ.Code Ann. § 21.031 (Vernon Cum. Supp. 1981). These cases involve constitutional challenges to those provisions.

No. 80–1538
Plyler v. Doe

This is a class action, filed in the United States District Court for the Eastern District of Texas in September 1977, on behalf of certain school-age children of Mexican origin residing in Smith County, Texas, who could not establish that they had been legally admitted into the United States. The action complained of the exclusion of plaintiff children from the public schools of the Tyler Independent School District. The Superintendent and members of the Board of Trustees of the School District were named as defendants; the State of Texas intervened as a party-defendant. . . .

* * *

The District Court held that illegal aliens were entitled to the protection of the Equal Protection Clause of the Fourteenth Amendment, and that § 21.031 violated that Clause. Suggesting that "the state's exclusion of undocumented children from its public schools . . . may well be the type of invidiously motivated state action for which the suspect classification doctrine was designed," the court held that it was unnecessary to decide whether the statute would survive a "strict scrutiny" analysis because, in any event, the discrimination embodied in the statute was not supported by a rational basis [458 F.Supp. 569, 585]. . . . The District Court also concluded that the Texas statute violated the Supremacy Clause.[5] *Id.*, at 590–592.

The Court of Appeals for the Fifth Circuit upheld the District Court's injunction. 628 F.2d 448 (1980). The Court of Appeals held that the District Court had erred in finding the Texas statute preempted by federal law.[6] With respect to equal protection, however, the Court of Appeals affirmed in all essential

5. The court found § 21.031 inconsistent with the scheme of national regulation under the Immigration and Nationality Act, and with federal laws pertaining to funding and discrimination in education. The court distinguished *DeCanas v. Bica*, 424 U.S. 351 . . . (1976), by emphasizing that the state bar on employment of illegal aliens involved in that case mirrored precisely the federal policy, of protecting the domestic labor market, underlying the immigration laws. The court discerned no express federal policy to bar illegal immigrants from education, 458 F.Supp., at 590–592.

6. The Court of Appeals noted that *DeCanas v. Bica, supra*, had not foreclosed all state regulation with respect to illegal aliens, and found no express or implied congressional policy favoring the education of illegal aliens. The court therefore concluded that there was no preemptive conflict between state and federal law. 628 F.2d, at 451–454.

respects the analysis of the District Court, *id.*, at 454–458, concluding that § 21.031 was "constitutionally infirm regardless of whether it was tested using the mere rational basis standard or some more stringent test," *id.*, at 458. We noted probable jurisdiction. . . .

No. 80–1934
In Re: Alien Children Litigation

During 1978 and 1979, suits challenging the constitutionality of § 21.031 and various local practices undertaken on the authority of that provision were filed in the United States District Courts for the Southern, Western, and Northern Districts of Texas. Each suit named the State of Texas and the Texas Education Agency as defendants, along with local officials. In November 1979, the Judicial Panel on Multidistrict Litigation, on motion of the State, consolidated the claims against the State officials into a single action to be heard in the District Court for the Southern District of Texas. A hearing was conducted in February and March 1980. In July 1980, the court entered an opinion and order holding that § 21.031 violated the Equal Protection Clause of the Fourteenth Amendment. 501 F.Supp. 544.[7] . . . While appeal of the District Court's decision was pending, the Court of Appeals rendered its decision in No. 81–1538. Apparently on the strength of that opinion, the Court of Appeals, on February 23, 1981, summarily affirmed the decision of the Southern District. We noted probable jurisdiction, . . . and consolidated this case with No. 81–1538 for briefing and argument.[8]

II

The Fourteenth Amendment provides that "No State shall . . . deprive any person of life, liberty, or property, without due process of law; nor deny to *any person within its jurisdiction* the equal protection of the laws." Appellants argue at the outset that undocumented aliens, because of their immigration status, are not "persons within the jurisdiction" of the State of Texas, and that they therefore have no right to the equal protection of Texas law. We reject this argument. Whatever his status under the immigration laws, an alien is surely a "person" in any ordinary sense of that term. Aliens, even aliens whose presence in this country is unlawful, have long been recognized as "persons" guaranteed due process of law by the Fifth and Fourteenth Amendments. *Shaughnessy v. Mezei*, 345 U.S. 206, 212 . . . (1953); *Wong Wing v. United States*, 163 U.S. 228, 238 . . . (1896); *Yick Wo v. Hopkins*, 118 U.S. 356, 369 . . . (1886). Indeed, we have clearly held that the Fifth Amendment protects aliens whose presence in this country is unlawful from invidious discrimination by the Federal Government.[9] *Mathews v. Diaz*, 426 U.S. 67, 77 . . . (1976).

Appellants seek to distinguish our prior cases, emphasizing that the Equal Protection Clause directs a State to afford its protection to persons *within its jurisdiction* while the Due Process Clauses of the Fifth and Fourteenth Amendments contain no such assertedly limiting phrase. In appellants' view, persons who have entered the United States illegally are not "within the jurisdiction" of a State even if they are present within a State's boundaries and subject to its laws. Neither our cases nor the logic of the Fourteenth Amendment supports that constricting construction of the phrase "within its jurisdiction." We have never suggested that the class of persons who might avail themselves of the equal protection guarantee is less than coextensive with that entitled to due process. To the contrary, we have recognized that both provisions were fashioned to protect an identical class of persons, and to reach every exercise of State authority.

> The Fourteenth Amendment to the Constitution is not confined to the protection of citizens. It says: "Nor shall any state deprive any person of life, liberty or property without due process of law; nor deny to any person within its jurisdiction the equal protection of the laws." *These provisions are universal in their application, to all persons within the territorial jurisdiction*, without regard to any differences of race, color, or of nationality; and the protection of the laws is a pledge of the protection of equal laws.

Yick Wo, *supra*, 118 U.S., at 369 . . . (emphasis added).

---

7. The court concluded that § 21.031 was not preempted by federal laws or international agreements. 501 F.Supp. 544, 584–596.

8. Appellees in both cases continue to press the argument that § 21.031 is preempted by federal law and policy. In light of our disposition of the Fourteenth Amendment issue, we have no occasion to reach this claim.

9. It would be incongruous to hold that the United States, to which the Constitution assigns a broad authority over both naturalization and foreign affairs, is barred from invidious discrimination with respect to unlawful aliens, while exempting the States from a similar limitation. . . .

In concluding that "all persons within the territory of the United States," including aliens unlawfully present, may invoke the Fifth and Sixth Amendment to challenge actions of the Federal Government, we reasoned from the understanding that the Fourteenth Amendment was designed to afford its protection to all within the boundaries of a State. . . .

There is simply no support for appellants' suggestion that "due process" is somehow of greater stature than "equal protection" and therefore available to a larger class of persons. To the contrary, each aspect of the Fourteenth Amendment reflects an elementary limitation on state power. To permit a State to employ the phrase "within its jurisdiction" in order to identify subclasses of persons whom it would define as beyond its jurisdiction, thereby relieving itself of the obligation to assure that its laws are designed and applied equally to those persons, would undermine the principal purpose for which the Equal Protection Clause was incorporated in the Fourteenth Amendment. The Equal Protection Clause was intended to work nothing less than the abolition of all caste- and invidious class-based legislation. That objective is fundamentally at odds with the power the State asserts here to classify persons subject to its laws as nonetheless excepted from its protection.

* * *

Our conclusion that the illegal aliens who are plaintiffs in these cases may claim the benefit of the Fourteenth Amendment's guarantee of equal protection only begins the inquiry. The more difficult question is whether the Equal Protection Clause has been violated by the refusal of the State of Texas to reimburse local school boards for the education of children who cannot demonstrate that their presence within the United States is lawful, or by the imposition by those school boards of the burden of tuition on those children. It is to this question that we now turn.

III

* * *

. . . The Equal Protection Clause was intended as a restriction on state legislative action inconsistent with elemental constitutional premises. Thus we have treated as presumptively invidious those classifications that disadvantage a "suspect class," or that impinge upon the exercise of a "fundamental right." With respect to such classifications, it is appropriate to enforce the mandate of equal protection by requiring the State to demonstrate that its classification has been precisely tailored to serve a compelling governmental interest. . . .

A

Sheer incapability or lax enforcement of the laws barring entry into this country, coupled with the failure to establish an effective bar to the employment of undocumented aliens, has resulted in the creation of a substantial "shadow population" of illegal migrants—numbering in the millions—within our borders.[17] This situation raises the specter of a permanent caste of undocumented resident aliens, encouraged by some to remain here as a source of cheap labor, but nevertheless denied the benefits that our society makes available to citizens and lawful residents. The existence of such an underclass presents most difficult problems for a Nation that prides itself on adherence to principles of equality under law.[19]

The children who are plaintiffs in these cases are special members of this underclass. Persuasive arguments support the view that a State may withhold its beneficence from those whose very presence within

17. The Attorney General recently estimated the number of illegal aliens within the United States at between 3 and 6 million. In presenting to both the Senate and House of Representatives several presidential proposals for reform of the immigration laws—including one to "legalize" many of the illegal entrants currently residing in the United States by creating for them a special status under the immigration laws—the Attorney General noted that this subclass is largely composed of persons with a permanent attachment to the nation, and that they are unlikely to be displaced from our territory. . . .

19. We reject the claim that "illegal aliens" are a "suspect class." No case in which we have attempted to define a suspect class . . . has addressed the status of persons unlawfully in our country. Unlike most of the classifications that we have recognized as suspect, entry into this class, by virtue of entry into this country, is the product of voluntary action. Indeed, entry into the class is itself a crime. In addition, it could hardly be suggested that undocumented status is a "constitutional irrelevancy." With respect to the actions of the federal government, alienage classifications may be intimately related to the conduct of foreign policy, to the federal prerogative to control access to the United States, and to the plenary federal power to determine who has sufficiently manifested his allegiance to become a citizen of the Nation. No State may independently exercise a like power. But if the Federal Government has by uniform rule prescribed what it believes to be appropriate standards for the treatment of an alien subclass, the States may, of course, follow the federal direction. See *DeCanas v. Bica*, 424 U.S. 351 . . . (1976).

the United States is the product of their own unlawful conduct. These arguments do not apply with the same force to classifications imposing disabilities on the minor *children* of such illegal entrants. At the least, those who elect to enter our territory by stealth and in violation of our law should be prepared to bear the consequences, including, but not limited to, deportation. But the children of those illegal entrants are not comparably situated. Their "parents have the ability to conform their conduct to societal norms," and presumably the ability to remove themselves from the State's jurisdiction; but the children who are plaintiffs in these cases "can affect neither their parents' conduct nor their own status." *Trimble v. Gordon*, 430 U.S. 762, 770 (1977). Even if the State found it expedient to control the conduct of adults by acting against their children, legislation directing the onus of a parent's misconduct against his children does not comport with fundamental conceptions of justice. "[V]isiting . . . condemnation on the head of an infant is illogical and unjust. Moreover, imposing disabilities on the . . . child is contrary to the basic concept of our system that legal burdens should bear some relationship to individual responsibility or wrongdoing. Obviously, no child is responsible for his birth and penalizing the . . . child is an ineffectual—as well as unjust—way of deterring the parent." *Weber v. Aetna Casualty & Surety Co.*, 406 U.S. 164, 175 . . . (1972) (footnote omitted).

Of course, undocumented status is not irrelevant to any proper legislative goal. Nor is undocumented status an absolutely immutable characteristic since it is the product of conscious, indeed unlawful, action. But § 21.031 is directed against children, and imposes its discriminatory burden on the basis of a legal characteristic over which children can have little control. It is thus difficult to conceive of a rational justification for penalizing these children for their presence within the United States. Yet that appears to be precisely the effect of § 21.031.

Public education is not a "right" granted to individuals by the Constitution. *San Antonio School District [v. Rodriguez*, 411 U.S. 1, 35 (1973)]. . . . But neither is it merely some governmental "benefit" indistinguishable from other forms of social welfare legislation. Both the importance of education in maintaining our basic institutions, and the lasting impact of its deprivation on the life of the child, mark the distinction. The "American people have always regarded education and the acquisition of knowledge as matters of supreme importance." *Meyer v. Nebraska*, 262 U.S. 390, 400, . . . (1923). . . .

. . . [E]ducation has a fundamental role in maintaining the fabric of our society. We cannot ignore the significant social costs borne by our Nation when select groups are denied the means to absorb the values and skills upon which our social order rests.

In addition to the pivotal role of education in sustaining our political and cultural heritage, denial of education to some isolated group of children poses an affront to one of the goals of the Equal Protection Clause: the abolition of governmental barriers presenting unreasonable obstacles to advancement on the basis of individual merit. Paradoxically, by depriving the children of any disfavored group of an education, we foreclose the means by which that group might raise the level of esteem in which it is held by the majority. But more directly, "education prepares individuals to be self-reliant and self-sufficient participants in society." *Wisconsin v. Yoder, supra*, 406 U.S. at 221. . . . Illiteracy is an enduring disability. The inability to read and write will handicap the individual deprived of a basic education each and every day of his life. The inestimable toll of that deprivation on the social, economic, intellectual, and psychological well-being of the individual, and the obstacle it poses to individual achievement, makes it most difficult to reconcile the cost or the principle of a status-based denial of basic education with the framework of equality embodied in the Equal Protection Clause. . . .

B

These well-settled principles allow us to determine the proper level of deference to be afforded § 21.031. Undocumented aliens cannot be treated as a suspect class because their presence in this country in violation of federal law is not a "constitutional irrelevancy." Nor is education a fundamental right; a State need not justify by compelling necessity every variation in the manner in which education is provided to its population. *See San Antonio School Dist. v. Rodriguez*, 411 U.S. 1, 28–39 . . . (1973). But more is involved in this case than the abstract question whether § 21.031 discriminates against a suspect class, or whether education is a fundamental right. Section 21.031 imposes a lifetime hardship on a discrete class of children not accountable for their disabling status. The stigma of illiteracy will mark them for the rest of their lives. By denying these children a basic education, we deny them the ability to live within the structure of our civic institutions, and foreclose any realistic possibility that they will contribute in even the smallest way to the progress of our Nation. In determining the rationality of § 21.031, we may appropriately take into account its costs to the Nation and to the innocent children who are its victims. In light of these countervailing costs, the discrimination contained in § 21.031 can hardly be considered rational unless it furthers some substantial goal of the State.

IV

It is the State's principal argument, and apparently the view of the dissenting Justices, that the undocumented status of these children *vel non* establishes a sufficient rational basis for denying them benefits that a State might choose to afford other residents. The State notes that while other aliens are admitted "on an equality of legal privileges with all citizens under nondiscriminatory laws," *Takahashi v. Fish & Game Comm'n*, 334 U.S. 410, 420 . . . (1948), the asserted right of these children to an education can claim no implicit congressional imprimatur. Indeed, on the State's view, Congress' apparent disapproval of the presence of these children within the United States, and the evasion of the federal regulatory program that is the mark of undocumented status, provides authority for its decision to impose upon them special disabilities. Faced with an equal protection challenge respecting the treatment of aliens, we agree that the courts must be attentive to congressional policy; the exercise of congressional power might well affect the State's prerogatives to afford differential treatment to a particular class of aliens. But we are unable to find in the congressional immigration scheme any statement of policy that might weigh significantly in arriving at an equal protection balance concerning the State's authority to deprive these children of an education.

The Constitution grants Congress the power to "establish a uniform Rule of Naturalization." Art. I., § 8. Drawing upon this power, upon its plenary authority with respect to foreign relations and international commerce, and upon the inherent power of a sovereign to close its borders, Congress has developed a complex scheme governing admission to and status within our borders. . . .

As we recognized in *DeCanas v. Bica*, 424 U.S. 351 . . . (1976), the States do have some authority to act with respect to illegal aliens, at least where such action mirrors federal objectives and furthers a legitimate state goal. In *DeCanas*, the State's program reflected Congress' intention to bar from employment all aliens except those possessing a grant of permission to work in this country. 424 U.S., at 361. . . . In contrast, there is no indication that the disability imposed by § 21.031 corresponds to any identifiable congressional policy. The State does not claim that the conservation of state educational resources was ever a congressional concern in restricting immigration. More importantly, the classification reflected in § 21.031 does not operate harmoniously within the federal program.

To be sure, like all persons who have entered the United States unlawfully, these children are subject to deportation. 8 U.S.C. §§ 1251–1252. But there is no assurance that a child subject to deportation will ever be deported. An illegal entrant might be granted federal permission to continue to reside in this country, or even to become a citizen. *See, e.g.*, 8 U.S.C. §§ 1252, 1253(h), 1254. In light of the discretionary federal power to grant relief from deportation, a State cannot realistically determine that any particular undocumented child will in fact be deported until after deportation proceedings have been completed. It would of course be most difficult for the State to justify a denial of education to a child enjoying an inchoate federal permission to remain.

We are reluctant to impute to Congress the intention to withhold from these children, for so long as they are present in this country through no fault of their own, access to a basic education. In other contexts, undocumented status, coupled with some articulable federal policy, might enhance State authority with respect to the treatment of undocumented aliens. But in the area of special constitutional sensitivity presented by this case, and in the absence of any contrary indication fairly discernible in the present legislative record, we perceive no national policy that supports the State in denying these children an elementary education. The State may borrow the federal classification. But to justify its use as a criterion for its own discriminatory policy, the State must demonstrate that the classification is reasonably adapted to "*the purposes for which the state desires to use it*." *Oyama v. California*, 332

U.S. 633, 664–665 . . . (1948) (Murphy, J., concurring) (emphasis added). We therefore turn to the state objectives that are said to support § 21.031.

V

Appellants argue that the classification at issue furthers an interest in the "preservation of the state's limited resources for the education of its lawful residents." . . . Of course, a concern for the preservation of resources standing alone can hardly justify the classification used in allocating those resources. . . . The State must do more than justify its classification with a concise expression of an intention to discriminate. *Examining Board v. Flores de Otero*, 426 U.S. 572, 605 . . . (1976). Apart from the asserted state prerogative to act against undocumented children solely on the basis of their undocumented status—an asserted prerogative that carries only minimal force in the circumstances of this case—we discern three colorable state interests that might support § 21.031.

First, appellants appear to suggest that the State may seek to protect the State from an influx of illegal immigrants. While a State might have an interest in mitigating the potentially harsh economic effects of sudden shifts in population, § 21.031 hardly offers an effective method of dealing with an urgent demographic or economic problem. There is no evidence in the record suggesting that illegal entrants impose any significant burden on the State's economy. To the contrary, the available evidence suggests that illegal aliens underutilize public services, while contributing their labor to the local economy and tax money to the State fisc. 458 F.Supp., at 578; 501 F.Supp., at 570–571. The dominant incentive for illegal entry into the State of Texas is the availability of employment; few if any illegal immigrants come to this country, or presumably to the State of Texas, in order to avail themselves of a free education. Thus, even making the doubtful assumption that the net impact of illegal aliens on the economy of the State is negative, we think it clear that "[c]harging tuition to undocumented children constitutes a ludicrously ineffectual attempt to stem the tide of illegal immigration," at least when compared with the alternative of prohibiting the employment of illegal aliens. . . .

Second, while it is apparent that a state may "not . . . reduce expenditures for education by barring [some arbitrarily chosen class of] children from its schools," *Shapiro v. Thompson*, 394 U.S. 618, 633 . . . (1969), appellants suggest that undocumented children are appropriately singled out for exclusion because of the special burdens they impose on the State's ability to provide high quality public education. But the record in no way supports the claim that exclusion of undocumented children is likely to improve the overall quality of education in the State.[25] . . . Of course, even if improvement in the quality of education were a likely result of barring some *number* of children from the schools of the State, the State must support its selection of *this* group as the appropriate target for exclusion. In terms of educational cost and need, however, undocumented children are "basically indistinguishable" from legally resident alien children. . . .

Finally, appellants suggest that undocumented children are appropriately singled out because their unlawful presence within the United States renders them less likely than other children to remain within the boundaries of the State, and to put their education to productive social or political use within the State. Even assuming that such an interest is legitimate, it is an interest that is most difficult to quantify. The State has no assurance that any child, citizen or not, will employ the education provided by the State within the confines of the State's borders. In any event, the record is clear that many of the undocumented children disabled by this classification will remain in this country indefinitely, and that some will become lawful residents or citizens of the United States. . . .

VI

If the State is to deny a discrete group of innocent children the free public education that it offers to other children residing within its borders, that denial must be justified by a showing that it furthers some

25. Nor does the record support the claim that the educational resources of the State are so direly limited that some form of "educational *triage*" may be deemed a reasonable (assuming that it were a permissible) response to the State's problems. 501 F.Supp., at 579–581.

substantial state interest. No such showing was made here. Accordingly, the judgment of the Court of Appeals in each of these cases is

Affirmed.

Justice Marshall, concurring.

While I join the Court opinion, I do so without in any way retreating from my opinion in *San Antonio School District v. Rodriguez*, 411 U.S. 1, 70–133. . . . (Marshall, J., dissenting). I continue to believe that an individual's interest in education is fundamental, and that this view is amply supported "by the unique status accorded public education by our society, and by the close relationship between education and some of our most basic constitutional values." *Id.*, at 111. . . . Furthermore, I believe that the facts of these cases demonstrate the wisdom of rejecting a rigidified approach to equal protection analysis, and of employing an approach that allows for varying levels of scrutiny depending upon "the constitutional and societal importance of the interest adversely affected and the recognized invidiousness of the basis upon which the particular classification is drawn." *Id.*, at 99. . . .

Justice Blackmun, concurring.

I join the opinion and judgment of the Court.

Like Justice Powell, I believe that the children involved in this litigation "should not be left on the streets uneducated." . . . I write separately, however, because in my view the nature of the interest at stake is crucial to the proper resolution of this case.

* * *

I joined Justice Powell's opinion for the Court in *Rodriguez*, and I continue to believe that it provides the appropriate model for resolving most equal protection disputes. . . .

With all this said, however, I believe the Court's experience has demonstrated that the *Rodriguez* formulation does not settle every issue of "fundamental rights" arising under the Equal Protection Clause. Only a pedant would insist that there are *no* meaningful distinctions among the multitude of social and political interests regulated by the States, and *Rodriguez* does not stand for quite so absolute a proposition. To the contrary, *Rodriguez* implicitly acknowledged that certain interests, though not constitutionally guaranteed, must be accorded a special place in equal protection analysis. . . .

* * *

In my view, when the State provides an education to some and denies it to others, it immediately and inevitably creates class distinctions of a type fundamentally inconsistent with those purposes, mentioned above, of the Equal Protection Clause. Children denied an education are placed at a permanent and insurmountable competitive disadvantage, for an uneducated child is denied even the opportunity to achieve. And when those children are members of an identifiable group, that group—through the State's action—will have been converted into a discrete underclass. Other benefits provided by the State, such as housing and public assistance, are of course important; to an individual in immediate need, they may be more desirable than the right to be educated. But classifications involving the complete denial of education are in a sense unique, for they strike at the heart of equal protection values by involving the State in the creation of permanent class distinctions. *Cf. Rodriguez*, 411 U.S., at 115, n. 74 . . . (Marshall, J., dissenting). In a sense, then, denial of an education is the analogue of denial of the right to vote: the former relegates the individual to second-class social status; the latter places him at a permanent political disadvantage.

This conclusion is fully consistent with *Rodriguez*. The Court there reserved judgment on the constitutionality of a state system that "occasioned an absolute denial of educational opportunities to any of its children," noting that "no charge fairly could be made that the system [at issue in *Rodriguez*] fails to provide each child with an opportunity to acquire . . . basic minimal skills." 411 U.S., at 37. . . . Here, however, the State has undertaken to provide an education to most of the children residing within its borders. And, in contrast to the situation in *Rodriguez*, it does not take an advanced degree to predict the effects of a complete denial of education upon those children targeted by the State's classification. In such circumstances, the voting decisions suggest that the State must offer something more than a rational basis for its classification.

* * *

Because I believe that the Court's carefully worded analysis recognizes the importance of the equal protection and preemption interests I consider crucial, I join its opinion as well as its judgment.

Justice Powell, concurring.

I join the opinion of the Court, and write separately to emphasize the unique character of the case before us.

The classification in question severely disadvantages children who are the victims of a combination of circumstances. Access from Mexico into this country, across our 2,000 mile border, is readily available and virtually uncontrollable. Illegal aliens are attracted by our employment opportunities, and perhaps by other benefits as well. This is a problem of serious national proportions, as the Attorney General recently has recognized. *See ante*, at 2395, n. 17. It therefore is certain that illegal aliens will continue to enter the United States and, as the record makes clear, an unknown percentage of them will remain here. I agree with the Court that their children should not be left on the streets uneducated.

Although the analogy is not perfect, our holding today does find support in decisions of this Court with respect to the status of illegitimates. In *Weber v. Aetna Casualty & Surety Co.*, 406 U.S. 164, 175 . . . (1972) we said: "visiting . . . condemnation on the head of an infant" for the misdeeds of the parents is illogical, unjust, and "contrary to the basic concept of our system that legal burdens should bear some relationship to individual responsibility or wrongdoing."

In this case, the State of Texas effectively denies to the school-age children of illegal aliens the opportunity to attend the free public schools that the State makes available to all residents. They are excluded only because of a status resulting from the violation by parents or guardians of our immigration laws and the fact that they remain in our country unlawfully. The respondent children are innocent in this respect. They can "affect neither their parent's conduct nor their own status." *Trimble v. Gordon*, 430 U.S. 762, 770 . . . (1977).

Our review in a case such as this is properly heightened. *See id.*, at 767. . . . *Cf. Craig v. Boren*, 429 U.S. 190 . . . (1976). The classification at issue deprives a group of children of the opportunity for education afforded all other children simply because they have been assigned a legal status due to a violation of law by their parents. These children thus have been singled out for a lifelong penalty and stigma. A legislative classification that threatens the creation of an underclass of future citizens and residents cannot be reconciled with one of the fundamental purposes of the Fourteenth Amendment. In these unique circumstances, the Court properly may require that the State's interests be substantial and that the means bear a "fair and substantial relation" to these interests.[3] . . .

In my view, the State's denial of education to these children bears no substantial relation to any substantial state interest. Both of the district courts found that an uncertain but significant percentage of illegal alien children will remain in Texas as residents and many eventually will become citizens. The discussion by the Court, *ante*, at Part V, of the State's purported interests demonstrates that they are poorly served by the educational exclusion. Indeed, the interests relied upon by the State would seem to be insubstantial in view of the consequences to the State itself of wholly uneducated persons living indefinitely within its borders. By contrast, access to the public schools is made available to the children of lawful residents without regard to the temporary nature of their residency in the particular Texas school district. The Court of Appeals and the District Courts that addressed this case concluded that the classification could not satisfy even the bare requirements of rationality. One need not go so far to conclude that the exclusion of appellee's class of children from state-provided education is a type of punitive discrimination based on status that is impermissible under the Equal Protection Clause.

In reaching this conclusion, I am not unmindful of what must be the exasperation of responsible citizens and government authorities in Texas and other states similarly situated. Their responsibility, if any, for the influx of aliens is slight compared to that imposed by the Constitution on the federal government. . . . But it hardly can be argued rationally that anyone benefits from the creation within our

3. The Chief Justice argues in his dissenting opinion that this heightened standard of review is inconsistent with the Court's decision in *San Antonio School District v. Rodriguez*, 411 U.S. 1 . . . (1973). But in *Rodriguez* no group of children was singled out by the State and then penalized because of their parent's status. Rather, funding for education varied across the State because of the tradition of local control. Nor, in that case, was any group of children totally deprived of all education as in this case. If the resident children of illegal aliens were denied welfare assistance, made available by government to all other children who qualify, this also—in my opinion—would be an impermissible penalizing of children because of their parents' status.

borders of a subclass of illiterate persons many of whom will remain in the State, adding to the problems and costs of both State and National Governments attendant upon unemployment, welfare, and crime.

Chief Justice Burger, with whom Justice White, Justice Rehnquist, and Justice O'Connor join, dissenting.

Were it our business to set the Nation's social policy, I would agree without hesitation that it is senseless for an enlightened society to deprive any children—including illegal aliens—of an elementary education. I fully agree that it would be folly—and wrong—to tolerate creation of a segment of society made up of illiterate persons, many having a limited or no command of our language.[1] However, the Constitution does not constitute us as "Platonic Guardians" nor does it vest in this Court the authority to strike down laws because they do not meet our standards of desirable social policy, "wisdom," or "common sense." . . .

. . . The failure of enforcement of the immigration laws over more than a decade and the inherent difficulty and expense of sealing our vast borders have combined to create a grave socio-economic dilemma. It is a dilemma that has not yet even been fully assessed, let alone addressed. However, it is not the function of the judiciary to provide "effective leadership" simply because the political branches of government fail to do so.

* * *

I

* * *

. . . [B]y patching together bits and pieces of what might be termed quasi-suspect-class and quasi-fundamental-rights analysis, the Court spins out a theory custom-tailored to the facts of these cases.

In the end, we are told little more than that the level of scrutiny employed to strike down the Texas law applies only when illegal alien children are deprived of a public education. . . . If ever a court was guilty of an unabashedly result-oriented approach, this case is a prime example.

* * *

The Court first suggests that these illegal alien children, although not a suspect class, are entitled to special solicitude under the Equal Protection Clause because they lack "control" over or "responsibility" for their unlawful entry into this country. . . . Similarly, the Court appears to take the position that § 21.031 is presumptively "irrational" because it has the effect of imposing "penalties" on "innocent" children. . . . However, the Equal Protection Clause does not preclude legislators from classifying among persons on the basis of factors and characteristics over which individuals may be said to lack "control." Indeed, in some circumstances persons generally, and children in particular, may have little control over or responsibility for such things as their ill-health, need for public assistance, or place of residence. Yet a state legislature is not barred from considering, for example, relevant differences between the mentally healthy and the mentally ill, or between the residents of different counties,[5] simply because these may be factors unrelated to individual choice or to any "wrongdoing." . . .

The Court does not presume to suggest that appellees' purported lack of culpability for their illegal status prevents them from being deported or otherwise "penalized" under federal law. Yet would deportation be any less a "penalty" than denial of privileges provided to legal residents? Illegality of presence in the United States does not—and need not—depend on some amorphous concept of "guilt" or "innocence" concerning an alien's entry. Similarly, a State's use of federal immigration status as a basis for legislative classification is not necessarily rendered suspect for its failure to take such factors into account.

The Court's analogy to cases involving discrimination against illegitimate children . . . is grossly misleading. The State has not thrust any disabilities

1. It does not follow, however, that a State should bear the costs of educating children whose illegal presence in this country results from the default of the political branches of the federal government. A State has no power to prevent unlawful immigration, and no power to deport illegal aliens; those powers are reserved exclusively to Congress and the Executive. . . .

5. Appellees "lack control" over their illegal residence in this country in the same sense as lawfully resident children lack control over the school district in which their parents reside. Yet in *San Antonio School District v. Rodriguez*, 411 U.S. 1 . . . (1973), we declined to review under "heightened scrutiny" a claim that a State discriminated against residents of less wealthy school districts in its provision of educational benefits. There was no suggestion in that case that a child's "lack of responsibility" for his residence in a particular school district had any relevance to the proper standard of review of his claims. The result was that children lawfully here but residing in different counties received different treatment.

upon appellees due to their "status of birth." *Cf. Weber v. Aetna Casualty & Surety Co.*, 406 U.S. 164, 176, 92 S.Ct. 1400, 1407, 31 L.Ed.2d 768 (1972). Rather, appellees' status is predicated upon the circumstances of their concededly illegal presence in this country, and is a direct result of Congress' obviously valid exercise of its "broad constitutional powers" in the field of immigration and naturalization. U.S. Const., Art. I, § 8, cl. 4; *see Takahashi v. Fish & Game Commission*, 334 U.S. 410, 419, 68 S.Ct. 1138, 1142, 92 L.Ed. 1478 (1948). This Court has recognized that in allocating governmental benefits to a given class of aliens, one "may take into account the character of the relationship between the alien and this country." *Mathews v. Diaz*, 426 U.S. 67, 80, 96 S.Ct. 1883, 1891, 48 L.Ed.2d 478 (1976). When that "relationship" is a federally prohibited one, there can, of course, be no presumption that a State has a constitutional duty to include illegal aliens among the recipients of its governmental benefits.

* * *

The second strand of the Court's analysis rests on the premise that, although public education is not a constitutionally guaranteed right, "neither is it merely some governmental 'benefit' indistinguishable from other forms of social welfare legislation." . . .

The importance of education is beyond dispute. Yet we have held repeatedly that the importance of a governmental service does not elevate it to the status of a "fundamental right" for purposes of equal protection analysis. *San Antonio School District v. Rodriguez*, 411 U.S. 1, 30–31 . . . (1973); *Lindsey v. Normet*, 405 U.S. 56, 73–74 . . . (1972). In *San Antonio School District, supra*, Justice Powell, speaking for the Court, expressly rejected the proposition that state laws dealing with public education are subject to special scrutiny under the Equal Protection Clause. Moreover, the Court points to no meaningful way to distinguish between education and other governmental benefits in this context. Is the Court suggesting that education is more "fundamental" than food, shelter, or medical care?

* * *

Once it is conceded—as the Court does—that illegal aliens are not a suspect class, and that education is not a fundamental right, our inquiry should focus on and be limited to whether the legislative classification at issue bears a rational relationship to a legitimate state purpose. . . .

The State contends primarily that § 21.031 serves to prevent undue depletion of its limited revenues available for education, and to preserve the fiscal integrity of the State's school financing system against an ever-increasing flood of illegal aliens—aliens over whose entry or continued presence it has no control. Of course such fiscal concerns alone could not justify discrimination against a suspect class or an arbitrary and irrational denial of benefits to a particular group of persons. Yet I assume no member of this Court would argue that prudent conservation of finite state revenues is *per se* an illegitimate goal. Indeed, the numerous classifications this Court has sustained in social welfare legislation were invariably related to the limited amount of revenues available to spend on any given program or set of programs. *See e.g., Jefferson v. Hackney*, 406 U.S. 535, 549–551 . . . (1972); *Dandridge v. Williams*, 397 U.S. 471 . . . (1970). The significant question here is whether the requirement of tuition from illegal aliens who attend the public schools—as well as from residents of other States, for example—is a rational and reasonable means of furthering the State's legitimate fiscal ends.[10]

Without laboring what will undoubtedly seem obvious to many, it simply is not "irrational" for a State to conclude that it does not have the same responsibility to provide benefits for persons whose very presence in the State and this country is illegal as it does to provide for persons lawfully present. By

10. The Texas law might also be justified as a means of deterring unlawful immigration. While regulation of immigration is an exclusively federal function, a State may take steps, consistent with federal immigration policy, to protect its economy and ability to provide governmental services from the "deleterious effects" of a massive influx of illegal immigrants. . . . The Court maintains that denying illegal aliens a free public education is an "ineffectual" means of deterring unlawful immigration, at least when compared to a prohibition against the employment of illegal aliens. . . . Perhaps that is correct, but it is not dispositive: the Equal Protection Clause does not mandate that a State choose either the most effective and all-encompassing means of addressing a problem or none at all. . . . Texas might rationally conclude that more significant "demographic or economic problems" . . . are engendered by the illegal entry into the State of entire families of aliens for indefinite periods than by the periodic sojourns of single adults who intend to leave the State after short-term or seasonal employment. It blinks reality to maintain that the availability of governmental services such as education plays no role in an alien family's decision to enter, or remain in, this country; certainly, the availability of a free bilingual public education might well influence an alien to bring his children rather than travel alone for better job opportunities.

definition, illegal aliens have no right whatever to be here, and the State may reasonably, and constitutionally, elect not to provide them with governmental services at the expense of those who are lawfully in the State.

* * *

The Court maintains—as if this were the issue—that "barring undocumented children from local schools would not necessarily improve the quality of education provided in those schools." . . . However, the legitimacy of barring illegal aliens from programs such as medicare or medicaid does not depend on a showing that the barrier would "improve the quality" of medical care given to persons lawfully entitled to participate in such programs. Modern education, like medical care, is enormously expensive, and there can be no doubt that very large added costs will fall on the State or its local school districts as a result of the inclusion of illegal aliens in the tuition-free public schools. The State may, in its discretion, use any savings resulting from its tuition requirement to "improve the quality of education" in the public school system, or to enhance the funds available for other social programs, or to reduce the tax burden placed on its residents; each of these ends is "legitimate." The State need not show, as the Court implies, that the incremental cost of educating illegal aliens will send it into bankruptcy, or have a "grave impact on the quality of education" . . . ; that is not dispositive under a "rational basis" scrutiny. . . .

Denying a free education to illegal alien children is not a choice I would make were I a legislator. Apart from compassionate considerations, the long-range costs of excluding any children from the public schools may well outweigh the costs of educating them. But that is not the issue; the fact that there are sound *policy* arguments against the Texas legislature's choice does not render that choice an unconstitutional one.

II

The Constitution does not provide a cure for every social ill, nor does it vest judges with a mandate to try to remedy every social problem. . . .

Congress, "vested by the Constitution with the responsibility of protecting our borders and legislating with respect to aliens," . . . bears primary responsibility for addressing the problems occasioned by the millions of illegal aliens flooding across our southern border. Similarly, it is for Congress, and not this Court, to assess the "social costs borne by our Nation when select groups are denied the means to absorb the values and skills upon which our social order rests." . . .

The solution to this seemingly intractable problem is to defer to the political processes, unpalatable as they may be to some.

NOTES AND QUESTIONS

1. Standard of Review

What is the standard of review employed by the majority? How does the Court define the class that is discriminated against? On what basis does the Court determine that the classification is not suspect inasmuch as the classification imposes disabilities on those who cannot affect their own status? Is the problem that by singling out illegal aliens as a way of holding down educational costs, the school district established a classification that was both underinclusive and overinclusive? Could the school district achieve its objective without judicial interference by a more careful delineation of the class of difficult-to-educate students it wants to exclude?

How does the Court define the interest or right that is being infringed? Why is the policy adopted by the state to preserve limited resources for its lawful (and taxpaying) residents not an important state goal? Why is it not an important state goal to discourage immigration into the state?

Has the Court adopted Justice Marshall's sliding scale of equal protection? *San Antonio Independent School District v. Rodriguez, supra.*, at 618–19. Has the Court moved to a variable standard of review?

2. Absolute Versus Relative Deprivation

The Supreme Court's opinion in *Rodriguez* distinguishes interdistrict financing inequities from a state "financing system [that] occasioned an absolute denial of educational opportunities to any of its children." The Court also notes that a tuition assessment plan that "absolutely precluded [poor children] from receiving an education . . . would present a far more compelling set of circumstances for judicial assistance than the case before us today." *supra.*, at 610, n. 60. In *Plyler*, the illegal alien (or undocumented) children were absolutely barred from a tuition-free education, since Texas law permits school districts to charge tuition or to exclude illegal aliens altogether. Would it have made a difference in the outcome of the case if the illegal alien children involved were given free education through grade eight, and then excluded from the public schools or charged tuition? Could the state, in order to save resources for its lawful residents, bar undocumented alien students from such extracurricular activities as band and sports?

3. Other Excluded Classes

Are Educable Mentally Retarded (EMR) or Trainable Mentally Retarded (TMR) children similar in constitutional status to the illegal aliens in *Plyler*, or would the state be able to justify denying mentally retarded children a publicly supported education? What about students excluded for disciplinary or other reasons?

4. Functional Exclusion

When one group of students is excluded from attendance in the public schools, it is clear the government has meted out different treatment to two different groups of students, often for reasons that do not pass judicial scrutiny. Are these total exclusion cases analogous to situations in which all students are provided the *same* educational service but some students are less able to take advantage of the program than others? Can students claim that the school program provided to all students is so unsuitable for them that, as a group, they are effectively excluded from obtaining an adequate education; that is, that they are "functionally excluded?"

This problem was raised in *Lau v. Nichols*, 483 F.2d 791 (9th Cir. 1973), *rev'd.*, 414 U.S. 563, 94 S.Ct. 786, 39 L.Ed.2d 1 (1974). Petitioners were among 2,856 non-English-speaking Chinese pupils in the San Francisco schools who sought an injunction requiring the school district to provide them with special instruction in English. They did not challenge the use of English as the medium of instruction nor did they challenge the requirement that mastery of English was a prerequisite for graduation from a public high school. But, plaintiffs argued, imposing these requirements without providing them with special instruction so they could learn English violated the Equal Protection Clause of the Fourteenth Amendment and Title VI of the Civil Rights Act of 1964, 42 U.S.C. Ann. 1 § 2000d (1974). Petitioners' Civil Rights Act claim ultimately prevailed in the Supreme Court; see chapter 7. This note concentrates on the constitutional arguments raised by petitioners, but not addressed by the Supreme Court.

Plaintiffs argued that the policy of the state and school district to use English as the basic language of instruction without providing special assistance in English to non-English-speaking students denied these students a public education just as effectively as if they had been barred from the school. Indeed, they asserted this policy created two classes of pupils: those who obtained access to a public education in their mother tongue and those who were effectively denied any public education at all. This latter group of students were said to constitute a "suspect class," insofar as the apparently neutral policy of offering the same program to all children regardless of language background actually excluded a specific and identifiable national and racial-ethnic group from effective participation in the schools. The discrimination was based on a characteristic intimately connected with their nationality, their language. Since this case involved both an absolute denial of public education and the use of a suspect classification, plaintiffs argued, the court should apply the strict scrutiny standard of review. Were such a standard utilized, plaintiffs contended, San Francisco could not provide compelling justification for its policy of exclusion. Neither the absence of a mandate to teach English to non-English-speaking children nor insufficient funds could constitute a rational justification, much less a compelling interest.

The court of appeals, in ruling for the school district, accepted the school district's basic argument that there was no basis for requiring affirmative action to remedy disabilities for which the state cannot be held accountable. In the words of the court:

> Every student brings to the starting line of his educational career different advantages and disadvantages caused in part by social, economic and cultural background, created and continued completely apart from any contribution by the school system. That some of these may be impediments which can be overcome does not amount to a "denial" by the Board of educational opportunities within the meaning of the Fourteenth Amendment should the Board fail to give them special attention, this even though they are characteristic of a particular ethnic group. Before the Board may be found to constitutionally deny special remedial attention to such deficiencies there must first be found a constitutional duty to provide them (sic).

483 F.2d at 797–98.

Is the plight of the *Lau* plaintiffs the same, similar to, or different from that of the illegal alien children who are actually excluded from school in *Plyler v. Doe*? Are the *Lau* plaintiffs absolutely deprived of educational services or educational opportunity, a meaningful educational opportunity, or an opportunity as potentially useful as that provided other students? *Compare Board of Education v. Rowley*, 458 U.S. 176, 102 S.Ct. 3034, 73 L.Ed.2d 690 (1982), chapter 7 *infra*.

For certain children, notably the profoundly retarded (those with IQ scores below 30), "education" could mean learning to use the bathroom and tie one's shoes. Is that the sort of education that publicly supported instruction should provide? If not, on whom should the burden of providing such instruction fall? If the cost of providing a "suitable" education to a handicapped child is five times the cost of providing other students with an education, must the district reduce its expenditures for other students to provide this student a "suitable" education? *See Mills v. Board of Education*, 348 F.Supp. 866 (D.D.C. 1972); *Pennsylvania Ass'n for Retarded Children (PARC) v. Commonwealth*, 334 F.Supp. 1257 (E.D. Pa. 1971), 343 F.Supp. 279 (E.D. Pa. 1972).

5. When Might Education Be a Fundamental Right?

Has the Supreme Court left open the possibility that it may some day recognize access to a minimally adequate public education as a fundamental right? *See Papasan v. Allain*, 478 U.S. 265, 283, 106 S.Ct. 2932, 2943, 92 L.Ed.2d 209 (1986), in which Justice White described *Rodriguez* as not foreclosing the possibility "that some identifiable quantum of education is a constitutionally protected prerequisite to the meaningful exercise of either the right to speak or the right to vote." Justice White continued:

> As *Rodriguez* and *Plyler* indicate, this Court has not yet definitively settled the questions whether a minimally adequate education is a fundamental right and whether a statute alleged to discriminatorily infringe that right should be accorded heightened equal protection review. . . .
>
> This case is therefore very different from *Rodriguez*,
> w[illegible] differential financing available to school
> [illegible] traceable to school district funds available
> [illegible]al estate taxation, not to a state decision
> [illegible] resources unequally among school dis-
> [illegible]nality of the disparity in *Rodriguez*, therefore, which rested on the fact that funding disparities based on differing local wealth were a necessary adjunct of allowing meaningful local control over school funding, does not settle the constitutionality of disparities alleged in this case. . . .

Id. at 285–90, 106 S.Ct. at 2944–46.

What are the boundaries that define the extent to which the federal Equal Protection Clause addresses disparities in the provision of education, and to what extent will differential treatment rise to the level of unconstitutionality in light of *Plyler* and *Papasan* as read against *Rodriguez*? *See also Kadrmas v. Dickinson Public Schools*, 487 U.S. 450, 108 S.Ct. 2481, 101 L.Ed.2d 399 (1988), *infra*, where the dissenting opinion emphasized that ". . . the Court therefore does not address the question whether a state constitutionally could deny a child access to a minimally adequate education. In prior cases, this Court explicitly has left open the question whether such a deprivation of access would violate a fundamental constitutional right. That question remains open today." *Id.* 487 U.S. at 466 n.1, 108 S.Ct. at 2491 n.1. What situation might lead the Court to find that education is a fundamental right? What might the Court mean by a minimally adequate education? What is needed "to provide each child with an opportunity to acquire the basic minimum skills necessary for the enjoyment of the rights of speech and of full participation in the political process"? 411 U.S. at 38, 93 S.Ct. at 1299. How could plaintiffs, in light of the conflicting studies, relate the level of resources to such outcomes as the ability to fully participate in the political process? What factors relating resource disparity to classifications other than district wealth might also trigger heightened scrutiny?

C. State Equal Protection Clause Litigation

Rodriguez appeared to have eliminated the *federal* Equal Protection Clause as a basis for holding California's financing system unconstitutional. When *Serrano* was remanded for trial, the trial judge noted that *Serrano I* had relied on the state's equivalent of the Equal Protection Clause as well as on the Fourteenth Amendment, and thus held that education was a fundamental right under the *state* constitution, requiring the state to show a compelling interest in order to permit this right to be conditioned on district wealth. This was affirmed by the California Supreme Court in *Serrano II*. 18 Cal. 3d 728, 135 Cal.Rptr. 345, 557 P.2d 929 (1976). The state supreme court noted that although California's equal protection provisions are "substantially the equivalent of" the Equal Protection Clause of the Fourteenth Amendment to the United States Constitution, they "are possessed of an independent vitality which, in a given case, may demand an analysis different from that which would obtain if only the federal standards were applicable." *Id.* at 764, 135 Cal.Rptr. at 366, 557 P.2d at 950. The court also pointed out that while considerations of federalism may have been one basis for the Supreme Court's decision in *Rodriguez*, "[t]he constraints of federalism, so necessary to the proper functioning of our unique system of national government, are not applicable to this Court in its determination of whether our own state's public school financing system runs afoul of state constitutional provisions." *Id.* at 766–67, 135 Cal. Rptr. at 368, 557 P.2d at 952. Thus, *Serrano* became purely a state constitutional decision.

SB 90, which had been enacted by the California legislature following *Serrano I*, was reviewed by the trial judge, who found that California's system of financing education still did not meet the fiscal neutrality principle adopted by the California Supreme Court in *Serrano I* inasmuch as SB 90 failed to reduce expenditure disparities in any meaningful way. Thus, the court found the plaintiffs had proven their allegation of the existence of wealth-determined disparities in expenditures, and this was affirmed. 18 Cal. 3d 728, 135 Cal.Rptr. 345, 557 P.2d 929 (1976).

In deciding whether these disparities affected the quality of the education provided, Judge Jefferson rejected an outcome measure of quality and instead adopted an input measure. Using this measure, he found that the higher-spending districts were able to purchase services, programs, materials, and equipment that low-spending districts could not. The major factual premises of the plaintiff's case having been established, the judge then proceeded to the remedy. Most significantly, the court ordered that whatever the financial scheme adopted by the state legislature, it must reduce per pupil expenditure disparities to less than one hundred dollars per pupil and reduce variations in tax rates to nonsubstantial variations, and that this must be accomplished within six years.

NOTES AND QUESTIONS

1. Legislative Response to Serrano II

In September 1977, the California legislature responded to *Serrano II* by the adoption of yet another amendment to its school finance system, AB 65. This was an intricate bill that significantly increased the foundation level, continued the flat grant, and imposed a revenue limit with voter override, but power equalized the tax override the districts could vote. This bill took the state a step closer to meeting the fiscal neutrality standard, but it still left large expenditure differences correlated with property wealth in place. *See* A. Frentz and R. Marshall, Jr., *AB 65: California's Reply to Serrano* (1978). Then, in 1978, California voters adopted Proposition 13, an amendment to the California Constitution. The proposition provided four things: (1) No property should be taxed at more than 1 percent of 1975 fair market value; (2) municipalities may impose "special taxes" by a two-thirds vote of the electors; (3) assessments may not grow more than 2 percent annually from their 1975–76 levels, to which they were rolled back, except for property sold after 1975–76; and (4) no increase in state taxes may be enacted without a two-thirds vote of each legislature. Provision one rolled back property taxes in California and in effect imposed a statewide local property tax of 1 percent. Most districts in the state were unable to support their educational programs on the basis of this 1 percent property tax, requiring the state to bail them out by using \$2.2 billion of the \$3 billion state surplus to make up the difference. Proposition 13 turned California toward full state funding. Thus, differences in spending among school districts are now most importantly determined by how state aid is distributed—a very different source of inequalities than was the target of *Serrano I* and *II*.

2. Serrano III

The legislature subsequently adopted AB 8 which was designed over time to bring the high-spending and low-spending districts together by imposing strict revenue limits on high-spending districts and providing state aid to low-spending districts. However, the failure to achieve this by the court's 1980 deadline resulted in the plaintiffs returning to court to seek an order requiring compliance with *Serrano II*.

In *Serrano v. Priest*, 200 Cal.App.3d 897, 226 Cal.Rptr. 584 (1986) *(Serrano III)*, the appellate court affirmed the decision of the trial judge, who found that the state had complied with the "*Serrano* mandate" by overcoming disparities in educational spending to the point that "remaining differences in spending are not significant, either mathematically or educationally." *Id.* at 620. Although *Serrano II* had said that spending differences had to be reduced to no greater than one hundred dollars, the *Serrano III* court rejected rigid reliance on the hundred dollar figure, although it also held that the state had met that standard once the hundred dollar figure was adjusted for inflation. "Thus, in 1982–83, 93.2% of the state's ADA [were] in districts within a hundred dollar band adjusted for inflation. The comparable figure for 1974 was 56%." *Id.* at 614. The court further held that remaining disparities were "justified by legitimate state interests." *Id.* at 616. These interests included "the need for an orderly transition from the old wealth-related system to the new state-funded system," *id.*, and cost differences due to climate and other factors. *Id.* at 617. Although the new funding system had largely succeeded in "level[ing] up low revenue limit districts, high revenue districts had suffered by the combined impact of the equalization formulas, declining enrollment, and inflation." *Id.* at 618. Such "leveling down" had had especially great impact on districts with high proportions of poor and minority students and "further leveling down would produce far more harm than good." *Id.* at 621.

3. *The Fiscal Neutrality Principle*

Is the principle of fiscal neutrality concerned with the level of educational expenditures for children, or is it primarily a principle of taxpayer equity with little apparent concern for the educational program children receive? Is the principle of fiscal neutrality a proper response to a finding that education is a fundamental interest? Is it plausible to assume that equalizing fiscal capacity to raise money will result in greater equality in the provision of education services?

Is the trial court's remedy, affirmed by the California Supreme Court in *Serrano II*, consistent with the principle of fiscal neutrality? Does it logically follow from the principle of fiscal neutrality that expenditures per pupil may not vary among districts by more than one hundred dollars? Does the principle require that tax rates be equal? Would district power equalizing be acceptable?

If the principle of fiscal neutrality is primarily directed toward achieving taxpayer equity, is it even an adequate notion of taxpayer equity? Is not the real problem from the taxpayer's perspective the proportion of one's income that must be paid out for schooling? As a matter of taxpayer equity, should not the aim of reformers be to move away from the property tax to a proportional or progressive tax system? *See* Goldstein, "Interdistrict Inequalities in School Financing: A Critical Analysis of *Serrano v. Priest* and its Progeny," 120 *U.Pa.L.Rev.* 504 (1972). What differences does it make to the individual taxpayer that equal tax rates produce an equal yield if the tax system itself is regressive?

Current economic theory and evidence suggest that variations in tax rates and public services across communities may cause property values to vary. Thus, tax rates and services could determine property wealth more than property wealth determines tax rates and expenditures. A useful nontechnical summary of this "capitalization" literature is to be found in Wendling, *Expenditures and Tax Capitalization: Its Relation to School Finance and Tax Reform* (Report No. F79–11, Education Commission of the States, December 1979).

One possible implication of this body of research is that the system of financing education is already "wealth neutral." That is, the real cost of purchasing educational services might be the same in all districts. The real cost is the tax bill plus the cost of housing. There is some evidence indicating that for the individual living in a district filled with highly valued industrial property which increases per pupil property wealth and reduces the tax liability, the cost of housing will be higher because of the lower tax liability. The individual residing in a purely residential district, however, will have a higher tax liability but lower housing costs for a comparable house since the higher tax liability on those houses dampens demand. The total (housing cost plus tax liability) works out to be the same for both. *Id.* at 25–26.

In these circumstances, judicial imposition of the fiscal neutrality principle coupled with legislative adoption of a district power equalizing formula could result in a number of unanticipated consequences. Depending on the district power equalizing formula (with or without recapture provisions), the real cost of schooling in the property-poor district could increase (DPE would, in effect, drive up the cost of housing), decreasing in the property-rich district for individuals who buy or sell a house after DPE has been implemented. Similarly, if full state funding were adopted, other equally surprising results could occur, for example, windfall gains and losses in property values. It has been argued that *Serrano* may have helped generate support for the passage of Proposition 13 among well-to-do voters who previously had supported high property taxes because the locally controlled taxes were tied to additional revenue for local schools. But since under *Serrano* local voters could no longer "buy" good local schools without supporting public education in poorer communities, the voters may prefer a system in which local property taxes are significantly reduced. Fischel, "Did *Serrano* Cause Proposition 13?" 42 *Nat'l Tax J.* 465, 467 (1989). Fischel argues another unanticipated consequence of the application of the fiscal neutrality principle in *Serrano*. He argues that California's support for education expenditures dropped in relation to other states following *Serrano*. "The decline in school spending, which was underway before Proposition 13, has paralleled a drop in measures of scholastic achievement. . . . The combination of *Serrano* and Prop 13 seems to have cut meat along with the fat. . . ." *Id.* He also contends that the increased equality in spending for education per pupil has not been reflected in decreased disparity of achievement among rich and poor districts. "Coupled with the apparent decline of statewide achievement . . . , *Serrano* looks like a victory of the appearance of equality over substance." *Id.* at 472.

In light of the complexities involved in implementing fiscal neutrality, is it a principle the courts should adopt as a matter of constitutional law?

The principle of fiscal neutrality also permits expenditure variations to be a function of the voters' taste for education in each of the various school districts of the state. Should the quality of a child's education be a function of the stinginess of the residents in a particular school district? Should the quality of a child's education be only a function of the desires of the state legislature? Or should it be a function of the desires and wealth of a child's family or only a function of the desires of the family and not of its wealth? *See* Coons and Sugarman, "Family Choice in Education: A Model State System for Vouchers," 59 *Calif.L.Rev.* 321 (1971). Is it, however, fair to leave a child at the mercy of the educational tastes of his or her parents? The problem is now brought full circle: Who should determine the quality of a child's education?

The principle of fiscal neutrality has met with a mixed reception in other state courts. Only a few courts have held their state systems of financing education unconstitutional along the lines of *Serrano II*, finding that those systems violated their state equal protection clauses. *See, e.g., Washakie County School District No. 1 v. Herschler*, 606 P.2d 310 (Wyo. 1980); *Horton v. Meskill*, 172 Conn. 615, 376 A.2d 359 (1977). In these states, the courts ruled that wealth was a suspect class and that education was a fundamental right.

States in which the courts specifically concluded that wealth was *not* a suspect classification include Colorado, *Lujan v. Colorado State Board of Education*, 649 P.2d 1005 (Colo. 1982); Maryland, *Hornbeck v. Somerset County Board of Education*, 295 Md. 597, 458 A.2d 758 (1983); and Oklahoma, *Fair School Finance Council Inc. v. State of Oklahoma*, 746 P.2d 1135 (Okl. 1987). *See also Shofstall v. Hollins*, 110 Ariz. 88, 515 P.2d 590 (1973), *Thompson v. Engelking*, 96 Idaho 793, 537 P.2d 635 (1976), *Northshore School District No. 417 v. Kinnear*, 84 Wash. 2d 685, 530 P.2d 178 (1974), finding that under the state equal protection clause, education was not a fundamental right. Since education is explicitly mentioned in every state constitution, what might the reasoning be for finding that it is *not* fundamental?

4. District Power Equalizing

a. Backlash Litigation: Attacks on DPE Formulas. A number of states have included a DPE formula in their newly reformed school finance systems. Under a "pure" district power equalizing formula, the state "recaptures" revenues raised in excess of the predetermined spending level and distributes the excess (together with additional state funds, if necessary) to poorer school districts where, because of low property values, the selected tax rates cannot generate sufficient revenues to meet the predetermined per-pupil expenditure levels. Where the DPE formula has included a "recapture" provision, it has come under legal attack, as described in Levin, "Current Trends in School Finance Reform Litigation: A Commentary," 1977 *Duke L.J.* 1099.

b. Effects of DPE on Other Local Governmental Services. If only educational services are power equalized, what are the likely effects for other local governmental services? Will local government now spend more money on education than on police and fire services, for example? Will property-poor local governments attempt to shift some of their functions to the school budget? What will property-rich local governments do—attempt to shift functions out of the school budget to those budgets not subject to district power equalizing? Might rich families, living in districts subject to a DPE scheme that uses recapture, vote for reduced spending in their districts or move from those property-rich districts into property-poor districts and use private schools? *See* C. Benson, *The Economics of Public Education* 363–65 (3d ed. 1978). Should a court consider these questions when deciding whether to impose the principle of fiscal neutrality?

D. A Different Approach in New Jersey: Guaranteeing "Thorough and Efficient" Education

The plaintiffs in *Rodriguez* and *Serrano* pursued their rights under the equal protection clauses of the U.S. Constitution and California State Constitution. In February 1970, a complaint was filed in a New Jersey court that contained the same equal protection prayer for relief lodged in *Rodriguez* and *Serrano.* It also advanced an argument "that the New Jersey constitution's 'thorough and efficient' education clause required the state to afford each child 'at least such instruction as is necessary to fit it for the ordinary duties of citizenship' and 'to provide the minimum education to all children . . . so that they may be able to read, write and function in a political environment.' " Tractenberg, "*Robinson v. Cahill:* The 'Thorough and Efficient' Clause," 38 *Law & Contemp. Probs.* 312, 315 (1974). With the filing of this complaint, a new line of litigation based on the education clauses of state constitutions began.

The trial court in *Robinson v. Cahill* concluded that the system of school finance in New Jersey violated the federal and state equal protection rights of taxpayers and students of poor districts and that the low level of funding of the existing finance law did not ensure all students of the "thorough and efficient system of free public schools" guaranteed by the state constitution. *Robinson v. Cahill,* 118 N.J. Super. 223, 287 A.2d 187 (1972). The state obtained a stay of the court's order and appealed.

Robinson v. Cahill

62 N.J. 473, 303 A.2d 273 (1973).

The opinion of the Court was delivered by Weintraub, CJ.

[The opinion begins by describing the New Jersey education finance system, similar in pertinent respects to the Texas legislation reviewed in the *Rodriguez* decision.]

The question whether the equal protection demand of our State Constitution is offended remains for us to decide. Conceivably a State Constitution could be more demanding. For one thing, there is absent the principle of federalism which cautions against too expansive a view of a federal constitutional limitation upon the power and opportunity of the several States to cope with their own problems in the light of their own circumstances. . . .

We hesitate to turn this case upon the State equal protection clause. The reason is that the equal protection clause may be unmanageable if it is called upon to supply categorical answers in the vast area of human needs, choosing those which must be met and a single basis upon which the State must act. The difficulties become apparent in the argument in the case at hand. [The court rejects constitutional arguments premised either on wealth being a suspect classification, or education meriting treatment as a fundamental interest.]

The remaining question is whether certain provisions of our State Constitution . . . [are violated by the current system of financing public education in New Jersey].

The provisions relating to public education were added to the Constitution of 1844 by amendments adopted in 1875. Art. IV, §7, ¶6, was amended by adding this sentence: "The legislature shall provide for the maintenance and support of a thorough and efficient system of free public schools for the instruction of all the children in this State between the ages of five and eighteen years." This provision is now Art. VIII, §4, ¶1, of the 1947 Constitution. The other amendment in 1875 added Art. IV, §7, ¶11, which prohibits "private, local or special laws" in "enumerated cases," among which appears: "Providing for the management and support of free public schools." The quoted provision is item (7) in Art. IV, §7, ¶9, of the 1947 Constitution, with the word "control" substituted for the word "support." . . .

* * *

It seems clear that the 1875 amendment has not been understood to prohibit the State's use of local government with local tax responsibility in the discharge of the constitutional mandate. . . .

. . . [I]t cannot be said the 1875 amendments were intended to ensure statewide equality among taxpayers. But we do not doubt that an equal educational opportunity for children was precisely in mind. The mandate that there be maintained and supported "a thorough and efficient system of free public schools for the instruction of all the children in the State between the ages of five and eighteen years" can have no other import. Whether the State acts directly or imposes the role upon local government, the end product must be what the Constitution commands. A system of instruction in any district of the state which is not thorough and efficient falls short of the constitutional command. Whatever the reason for the violation, the obligation is the State's to rectify it. If local government fails, the state government must compel it to act, and if the local government cannot carry the burden, the State must itself meet its continuing obligation. . . .

. . . Today, a system of public education which did not offer high school education would hardly be thorough and efficient. The Constitution's guarantee must be understood to embrace that educational opportunity which is needed in the contemporary setting to equip a child for his role as a citizen and as a competitor in the labor market.

We are brought then to the question whether the State has fulfilled its obligation to afford all pupils that level of instructional opportunity which is comprehended by a thorough and efficient system of education for students between the ages of five and eighteen. . . .

The trial court found the constitutional demand had not been met and did so on the basis of discrepancies in dollar input per pupil. We agree. We deal with the problem in those terms because dollar input is plainly relevant and because we have been shown no other viable criterion for measuring compliance with the constitutional mandate. The constitutional mandate could not be said to be satisfied unless we were to suppose the unlikely proposition that the lowest level of dollar performance happens to coincide with the constitutional mandate and that all efforts beyond the lowest level are attributable to local decisions to do more than the State was obliged to do.

Surely the existing statutory system is not visibly geared to the mandate that there be "a thorough and efficient system of free public schools for the instruction of all the children in this state between the ages of five and eighteen years." Indeed the State has never spelled out the content of the educational opportunity the Constitution requires. Without some such prescription, it is even more difficult to understand how the tax burden can be left to local initiative with any hope that statewide equality of educational opportunity will emerge. . . .

On its face the [1970] statutory scheme has no apparent relation to the mandate for equal educational opportunity. . . .

We have outlined the formula of the 1970 act to show . . . it is not demonstrably designed to guarantee that local effort plus the State aid will yield to all the pupils in the State that level of educational opportunity which the 1875 amendment mandates. We see no basis for a finding that the 1970 Act, even if fully funded, would satisfy the constitutional obligation of the State. . . .

[I]f the State chooses to assign its obligation under the 1875 amendment to local government, the State must do so by a plan which will fulfill the State's continuing obligation. To that end the State must define in some discernible way the educational obligation and must *compel* the local school districts to raise the money necessary to provide that opportunity. The State has never spelled out the content of the constitutionally mandated educational opportunity. Nor has the State *required* the school districts to raise moneys needed to achieve that unstated standard. Nor is the State aid program designed to compensate for local failures to reach that level. It must be evident that our present scheme is a patchy product reflecting provincial contests rather than a plan sensitive only to the constitutional mandate. . . .

Upon the record before us, it may be doubted that the thorough and efficient system of schools required by the 1875 amendment can realistically be met by reliance upon local taxation. The discordant correlations between the educational needs of the school districts and their respective tax bases suggest any such effort would likely fail. . . .

Although we have dealt with the constitutional problem in terms of dollar input per pupil, we should not be understood to mean that the State may not recognize differences in area costs, or a need for additional dollar input to equip classes of disadvantaged children for the educational opportunity. Nor do we say that if the State assumes the cost of providing the constitutionally mandated education, it may not authorize local government to go further and to tax to that further end, provided that such authorization does not become a device for diluting the State's mandated responsibility.

The present system being unconstitutional, we come to the subject of remedies. We agree with the trial court that relief must be prospective. The judiciary cannot unravel the fiscal skein. Obligations incurred must not be impaired. And since government must go on, and some period of time will be needed to establish another statutory system, obligations hereafter incurred pursuant to existing statutes will be valid in accordance with the terms of the statutes. . . .

Subject to the modifications expressed in this opinion and the matters reserved in the preceding paragraph, the judgment of the trial court is affirmed.

NOTES AND QUESTIONS

1. The Standard of Robinson I

Robinson I concludes that Art. IV, §7 was not intended to provide taxpayer equity but to protect children. From this perspective, the court finds that New Jersey's financing scheme is not a "thorough and efficient" system because it does not provide for equal educational opportunity for children. Does "efficient" mean equitable? Does "thorough"? What is the court's conception of equal educational opportunity? Is it an input or output theory of equal educational opportunity? Does the court require equal expenditures per pupil, no wealth discrimination, minimal adequacy? What does the court mean when it says that "The consitutional mandate could not be said to be satisfied unless we were to suppose the unlikely proposition that the lowest level of dollar performance happens to coincide with the constitutional mandate and that all efforts beyond the lowest level are attributable to local decisions to do more than the state was obliged to do"? Might it be argued that the court in *Robinson I* has no standard of its own but is merely troubled by the state's creation of a system of finance without itself first spelling out "the content of the educational opportunity the constitution requires"? Is the court asking the legislature to develop its own definition of what the constitution requires and then redesign the state system to meet that standard? Or does the court have its own notion of what the state constitution requires? Considering *Robinson I* alone, what is it that the legislature must do to comply with the state's constitution? How does the court's approach differ from that in *Serrano*?

2. **Robinson II** ***through*** **Robinson VII**

One month after *Robinson I*, the New Jersey Supreme Court took up the issue of the remedial timetable and held that it would not disturb the existing statutory scheme unless the legislature failed to enact, by December 31, 1974, legislation compatible with *Robinson I. Robinson II*, 63 N.J. 196, 306 A.2d 65 (1973). In November 1973, the state chose a new governor whose task it became to develop proposed legislation in response to *Robinson I* and *II*. The case forced the governor to consider new criteria for governing local educational programs, a new system of state aid, and a new way of raising sufficient money to pay for the new state aid system. He made his proposals for change to the legislature on May 15, 1974, but the legislature was unable to reach agreement, particularly on a new tax plan. Thus the court's December 31, 1974, deadline came and went. The court therefore ordered oral argument to be held on the relief to be granted for the coming school year, commencing July 1, 1975. *Robinson III*, 67 N.J. 35, 335 A.2d 6 (1975). In May of that year *Robinson IV* was issued. In order to give the legislature yet more time to work on the complex problem that the court had handed it, the court limited its remedy to the 1976–77 school year. The provisional remedy ordered redistribution of two kinds of existing state aid in such a way as to benefit property-poor school districts. *Robinson IV*, 67 N.J. 333, 339 A.2d 193 (1975). The state legislature finally adopted a new system of school finance on September 29, 1975.

The 1975 Act contained the following provisions: It established a goal that the public schools prepare all students, regardless of social class, so that they could function politically, economically, and socially in a democratic society; the creation of an elaborate monitoring system involving the use of state-administered standardized tests of basic skill areas; the formulation of plans by local districts for achieving the legislatively mandated goal noted above; a delegation of power to the state commissioner to rectify local defects in providing an adequate education, including forcing an increase in the amount of the local budget; and a modified system for allocating state aid. The modified plan still provided minimum aid on a per pupil basis, limited annual budget increases, and took steps to equalize per-pupil tax resources by establishing a guaranteed property valuation per pupil. The court, on January 30, 1976, said that if the system were fully funded, the new law would be constitutional despite the fact that its basic financial provisions were similar to those in the law struck down in *Robinson I*. The court gave the legislature until April 6, 1976, to fund the law. *Robinson* V, 69 N.J. 449, 355 A.2d 129 (1976). But the legislature deadlocked on a new tax bill, the law went unfunded, and *Robinson* was back in the court. On May 13, 1976, its patience having run out, the court enjoined every public officer—state, county, or municipal—from expending any funds for the support of the public school system. New Jersey schools were shut down by court order. *Robinson VI*, 70 N.J. 155, 358 A.2d 457 (1976). The immediate effect of the shutdown was to shift sufficient votes in the state senate to enable the passage of New Jersey's first state income tax on July 9, 1976. That same day the court dissolved its order closing the schools. *Robinson VII*, 70 N.J. 464, 360 A.2d 400 (1976).

3. Robinson *and the Policymaking Process*

In a detailed historical account of the litigation of the *Robinson* case, Professor Richard Lehne concludes that *Robinson* had few positive effects and a number of negative ones. He believes that *Robinson* did shift somewhat the allocation of state aid within the state to the benefit of property-poor districts but to the disadvantage of districts with large numbers of poor families—districts that had benefited from the old formula replaced by the 1975 Act. R. Lehne, *The Quest for Justice* 173 (1978). Lehne sees *Robinson* as an agenda-setting case—a case that forced the other branches of government to move an issue already in the public realm higher on their political agenda. It was not a decision-making case in which the court itself settled an issue.

Is it a proper use of judicial power merely to set an agenda rather than decide specific issues? Do *Robinson I* through *Robinson VII* represent a better approach than *Serrano I* and *II* or *Rodriguez? See* Kirp, "Law, Politics, and Equal Educational Opportunity," 47 *Harv.Educ.Rev.* 117 (1977).

4. State Education Clause Litigation

Following *Robinson I*, school finance reformers sought success by relying on such state education clauses as the obligation to maintain and support "a thorough and efficient system of free public schools." In addition to New Jersey, seven other states mandate "a thorough and efficient" system of free public schools: Maryland, Minnesota, Ohio, Pennsylvania, South Dakota, West Virginia, and Wyoming. Another seven states use *either* "thorough" *or* "efficient": Arkansas, Colorado, Delaware, Idaho, Illinois, Kentucky, and Texas. Others use "general" or "uniform," and some use a combination, such as mandating the state to establish and maintain "a general, uniform and thorough system of public, free schools." *See, e.g.*, Idaho Const. art. IX, §1.

Despite the *Robinson v. Cahill* decision, school finance reform litigation based on state education clauses moved slowly and fitfully. Indeed, more states found their systems did *not* violate the state equal protection clause than did in the decade or so following *Robinson*. Recently, however, there have been significant reversals. In the late 1980s, a number of state supreme courts sought to compel their legislatures to remedy disparities between rich and poor districts based on the state education clause. In a nineteen-month period between 1988 and 1990, four state high courts struck down their school finance systems—Kentucky, New Jersey, Montana, and Texas.

a. Kentucky. In 1989, the Supreme Court of Kentucky found that

> Kentucky's system of common schools is underfunded and inadequate; is fraught with inequalities and inequities throughout the 177 local school districts; is ranked nationally in the lower 20–25 percent in virtually every category that is used to evaluate educational performance; and is not uniform among the districts in educational opportunities.

Rose v. The Council for Better Education, Inc., 790 S.W.2d 186 (Ky. 1989). Why would the court compare the academic outcomes on standardized tests produced by the Kentucky school system as a whole to national averages, rather than focusing solely on inequalities in inputs and outputs among districts within the state?

The court defined the state constitutional mandate to provide an "efficient system of common schools throughout the state," Ky. Const. §183, as one that

> must have as its goal to provide each and every child with at least the seven following capacities: (i) sufficient oral and written communication skills to enable students to function in a complex and rapidly changing civilization; (ii) sufficient knowledge of economic, social, and political systems to enable the student to make informed choices; (iii) sufficient understanding of governmental processes to enable the student to understand the issues that affect his or her community, state, and nation; (iv) sufficient self-knowledge and knowledge of his or her mental and physical wellness; (v) sufficient grounding in the arts to enable each student to appreciate his or her cultural and historical heritage; (vi) sufficient training or preparation for advanced training in either academic or vocational fields so as to enable each child to choose and pursue life work intelligently; and (vii) sufficient levels of academic or vocational skills to enable public school students to compete favorably with their counterparts in surrounding states, in academics or in the job market.

Id. at 212. What expertise does the court have to enable it to determine the seven basic skills an "efficient" educational system must produce? Is not this decision one for the legislature to make?

The Kentucky state supreme court declared that the system of common schools "must be adequately funded to achieve its goals" and that every child "must be given the same opportunity and access to an adequate education. This obligation cannot be shifted to local counties and local school districts." *Id.* The court said local taxes may, however, be used "to supplement the uniform, equal educational effort that the General Assembly must provide." *Id.*

The court did not stop at striking down the state's system of financing but in an unprecedented action declared the state's entire public school system unconstitutional.

> This decision applies to the statutes creating, implementing and financing the *system* and to all regulations, etc., pertaining thereto. This decision covers the creation of local school districts, school boards, and the Kentucky Department of Education to the Minimum Foundation Program and Power Equalization Program. It covers school construction and maintenance, teacher certification—the whole gamut of the common school system in Kentucky.
>
> * * *
>
> . . . Section 183 places an absolute duty on the General Assembly to re-create, re-establish a new system of common schools in the Commonwealth.

Id. at 215.

In holding that an efficient educational system is one that has as its goal the development of seven specific skills, and ordering the General Assembly to recreate the educational system, did the Kentucky court take an approach preferable to the "agenda setting" approach of *Robinson*, or did it make a policy decision that more properly should be made by the legislature?

b. Texas.

(1) *Edgewood I.* The Texas Supreme Court, in *Edgewood Independent School District v. Kirby*, 777 S.W.2d 391 (Tex. 1989), found its state system of financing education to be in violation of the constitutional mandate that requires an efficient system of public schools. The court noted that over 50 percent of the total cost of education is provided by the local school districts from the local property tax, and that the disparity in taxable property wealth per student between the wealthiest district and poorest district amounted to a 700 to 1 ratio. The average property wealth in the one hundred wealthiest districts was more than twenty times that of the average property wealth in the one hundred poorest districts. The court gave as an illustration two school districts within the same county: Edgewood Independent School District has $38,854 in property wealth per student while Alamo Heights Independent School District has $570,109 in property wealth per student. Ironically, these are the same two school districts that figured in *Rodriguez*.

The *Edgewood* court noted that the state's foundation program is supposed to ensure that each school district has sufficient funds to provide its students with at least a basic education, but the program "does not cover even the cost of meeting the state-mandated minimum requirements." *Id.* at 392. Because of disparities in district property wealth, the court found that variations in spending per pupil ranged from $2,112 to $19,333 and noted that, in general, the lower expenditures in the property-poor districts were not the result of lack of tax effort.

> Generally, the property-rich districts can tax low and spend high while the property-poor districts must tax high merely to spend low. . . . The one hundred poorest districts had an average tax rate of 74.5 cents and spent an average of $2,978 per student. The one hundred wealthiest districts had an average tax rate of 47 cents and spent an average of $7,233 per student. . . . [Thus] property-poor districts are trapped in a cycle of poverty from which there is no opportunity to free themselves. Because of their inadequate tax base, they must tax at significantly higher rates in order to meet minimum requirements for accreditation; yet their educational programs are typically inferior.

Id. at 393.

The court also found that the amount of money spent per student was significantly related to the educational opportunity available to that student.

> High-wealth districts are able to provide for their students broader educational experiences including more extensive curricula, more up-to-date technological equipment, better libraries and library personnel, teacher aides, counseling services, lower student–teacher ratios, better facilities, parental involvement programs, and drop-out prevention programs. They are also better able to attract and retain experienced teachers and administrators.

Id.

The court relied on the requirement in the Texas Constitution that the Legislature "establish and make suitable provision for the support and maintenance of an efficient system of public free schools." *Id.* The court concluded that the inequalities in per-pupil expenditures produced by the present system were "directly contrary to the constitutional vision of efficiency." *Id.* at 396.

> Efficiency . . . does not allow concentration of resources in property-rich school districts that are taxing low when property-poor districts that are taxing high cannot generate sufficient revenues to meet even minimum standards. There must be a direct and close correlation between a district's tax effort and the educational resources available to it; in other words, districts must have substantially equal access to similar revenues per pupil at similar levels of tax effort.

Id. at 397. The court did note that the state could recognize differences in area costs or costs associated with providing educational opportunities for special pupil populations. The court also indicated that local school districts could supplement "an efficient system established by the legislature; however, any local enrichment must derive solely from local tax effort." *Id.* at 398.

Has the Texas Supreme Court mandated a district power equalizing system of school finance? What courses of action are left to the legislature in providing an efficient system?

(2) Edgewood II—A More Stringent Standard? Following the decision in *Edgewood I*, the state legislature enacted Senate Bill 1. In *Edgewood II*, 804 S.W.2d 491 (Tex. 1991), the state supreme court found that the school finance system of the State of Texas was still unconstitutional. The court noted that Senate Bill 1 maintains the foundation program that was viewed as inadequate in *Edgewood I*.

> Each district that taxes itself at or above a minimum level is guaranteed a certain base level of funding. . . . The second tier . . . is designed to equalize the ability of school districts to raise revenue to supplement their basic allotment. At this tier, all districts receive a guaranteed revenue per weighted student for each cent of local effort above the tier 1 minimum level. The state funds the difference between the guaranteed revenue and the amount each cent of local tax effort generates. If a district is so wealthy that each cent of tax effort generates more than the guaranteed revenue per weighted student, it receives no tier 2 revenue from the state.

Id. at 495.

The state argued that as more funds are shifted to lower wealth districts, there would be substantial equity among those districts educating 95 percent of the students in the state. The court noted, however, that by limiting the Senate Bill 1 funding formula to districts in which 95 percent of the students attend school, "the 170,000 students in the wealthiest districts are still supported by local revenues drawn from the same tax base as the 1 million students in the poorest districts:"

> The fundamental flaw of Senate Bill 1 lies not in any particular provisions but in its overall failure to restructure the system. Most property owners must bear a heavier tax burden to provide a less expensive education for students in their districts, while property owners in a few districts bear a much lighter burden

> to provide more funds for their students. Thus, Senate Bill 1 fails to provide "a direct and close correlation between a district's tax effort and the educational resources available to it." 777 S.W.2d at 397.

Id. at 496.

The court then suggested that the legislature consider consolidation of school districts or tax base consolidation as possible ways of achieving an "efficient" system. Has the court stepped into the role of the legislature when it proposes that the legislature consider these remedies? Is the court, by holding that the state must include all school districts, requiring the legislature to "recapture" funds that the wealthiest districts can raise through local property taxes in order to subsidize other districts? Does *Edgewood II* require either consolidation of school districts so that property values per pupil are equal or district power equalizing with complete recapture, or might other financing alternatives satisfy the *Edgewood II* court?

The state had argued that the annual cost of equalizing *all* districts to the revenue levels that the richest districts can now attain would be approximately four times the annual cost of operating the entire state government. *Id.* at 495–96. Does the court suggest that the state constitution compels that the wealthiest 5 percent of districts be included in the equalization formulas, regardless of cost?

(3) Edgewood III—A Retreat? The plaintiffs filed a motion for rehearing on the specific question of whether a 1931 precedent would prevent recapture and redistribution of local property taxes for purposes of equalization. *Edgewood III*, 804 S.W.2d 499 (Tex. February 25, 1991). The court held that funds raised in one school district could not be redistributed to other school districts under the specific wording of the state's education clause. In addition, the court decided that the plaintiffs' motion raised the question whether the legislature may authorize school districts to determine whether unequalized local enrichment is permissible. The court found that "because the constitution does permit such enrichment, without equalization, local taxes cannot be considered 'state taxes subject to state-wide recapture.' " *Id.* The court went on to comment, beyond what the plaintiffs were seeking in their motion for rehearing, that the school financing system is unconstitutional "not because *any* unequalized local supplementation is employed, but because the State relies so heavily on unequalized local funding in attempting to discharge its duty to 'make suitable provision for the support and maintenance of an efficient system of public free schools.' " *Id.* at 500. Although the first two decisions had been unanimous, there were four justices who dissented from the opinion on motion for rehearing in *Edgewood III*, arguing that the court had exceeded its jurisdiction under the motion for rehearing and was backing off of its bolder position in *Edgewood II* because of political pressure.

Has the court's opinion in *Edgewood III*, by barring recapture and permitting unequalized local enrichment, weakened its rulings in *Edgewood I* and *Edgewood II*? Was *Edgewood II* wrongly decided? Does *Edgewood III* return to the standard of *Edgewood I*? Note that in *Edgewood I*, the court had stated that local school districts would not be "precluded from supplementing an efficient system established by the legislature; however any local enrichment must derive solely from local tax effort." *Id.* at 398. In a footnote in *Edgewood II*, the court noted that "the question of local enrichment continues to be controlled by this court's opinion in *Edgewood I*." *Id.* at 495, n. 11.

c. The significance of the 1989 cases. In the same year that the Kentucky and Texas supreme courts found their state's systems of financing education unconstitutional, the Montana supreme court did the same. *Helena Elementary School District No. 1 v. State*, 236 Mont. 44, 769 P.2d 684 (1989). The Texas, Kentucky, and Montana decisions were the first since the 1970s to rely exclusively on their state constitutions' educational clauses. The only two decisions prior to these cases to do so were *Robinson v. Cahill*, 62 N.J. 473, 303 A.2d 273 (1973), and *Seattle School District No. 1 v. State*, 90 Wash. 2d 476, 585 P.2d 71 (1978). *See* Thro, "The Third Wave: The Impact of the Montana, Kentucky, and Texas Decisions on the Future of Public School Finance Reform Litigation," 19 *Jour. Law & Educ.* 219 (1990).

Whether these cases presage a new wave of school finance litigation remains to be seen. Litigation is pending in about ten states. For a good summary of both the state equal protection clause and the state education clause litigation, *see* Thro, "To Render Them Safe: The Analysis of State Constitutional Provisions in Public School Finance Reform Litigation," 75 *Va.L.Rev.* 1639 (1989).

E. Educational Needs, Outcomes, Municipal Overburden, and Cost Differentials

Abbott v. Burke

119 N.J. 287, 575 A.2d 359 (1990).

[In 1981, a suit was brought on behalf of school children from Camden, East Orange, Jersey City, and Irvington. In that suit, it was contended that the Public School Education Act of 1975, upheld (if the legislature fully funded the law) in *Robinson* V, 69 N.J. 449, 355 A.2d 129 (1976), violated the state constitution's thorough and efficient clause.]

Wilentz, J.

We again face the question of the constitutionality of our school system. We are asked in this case to rule that the Public School Education Act of 1975 . . . violates our Constitution's thorough and efficient clause. We find that under the present system the evidence compels but one conclusion: the poorer the district and the greater its need, the less the money available, and the worse the education. That system is neither thorough nor efficient. We hold the Act unconstitutional as applied to poorer urban school districts. Education has failed there, for both the students and the State. We hold that the Act must be amended to assure funding of education in poorer urban districts at the level of property-rich districts; that such funding cannot be allowed to depend on the ability of local school districts to tax; that such funding must be guaranteed and mandated by the State; and that the level of funding must also be adequate to provide for the special educational needs of these poorer urban districts in order to redress their extreme disadvantages.

* * *

On this record we find a constitutional deficiency only in the poorer urban districts, and our remedy is limited to those districts. We leave unaffected the disparity in substantive education and funding found in other districts throughout the state, although that disparity too may some day become a matter of constitutional dimension. . . .

* * *

I. Description of the Issue

Predictably flowing from our decision in *Robinson v. Cahill*, 69 N.J. 449 (1976) (*Robinson* V), the issue now before us is whether the Act, declared facially constitutional, is constitutional as applied. . . .

* * *

II. The Constitutional Provision

* * *

The initial construction of the thorough and efficient clause was permeated by the concept of equality. . . . [In *Robinson I*, we noted] that "we do not doubt that an equal educational opportunity for children was precisely in mind." *Id.*at 513.

What that equality meant, while not precisely defined, was indicated in several ways. First, in deciding that the statute then in place was unconstitutional as not affording a thorough and efficient education, we relied solely on the disparity of funding, i.e., on the fact that the dollars spent on education per pupil varied from one district to another. . . . Rather than on equality, our decision was based on the proposition that the Constitution required a certain level of education, that which equates with thorough and efficient; it is that level that all must attain; that is the only equality required by the Constitution. Embedded in our observation that if the lowest level of expenditures per pupil constituted a thorough and efficient education, then the constitutional mandate would be met was the clear implication that no matter how many districts were spending well beyond that level, the system would be constitutional. Second, we noted that the State, while assigning the obligation to local government to afford a thorough and efficient education, had never defined "in some discernible way the educational obligation," "the content of the constitutionally mandated educational opportunity"; it was "an unstated standard." *Id.* at 519. Again, the clear import is not of a constitutional mandate governing expenditures per pupil, equal or otherwise, but a requirement of a specific substantive level of education. Equality of expenditures per pupil could not have been constitutionally mandated when we recognized the right of districts to spend more to address students' special needs (the "need for additional dollar input to equip classes of disadvantaged children for the educational opportunity") and disclaimed any intent to deprive the State of the power to "authorize local government to go further" than "the constitutionally mandated education" and "to tax to that further end." *Id.* at 520. Our only condition was that such excess "not become a device for diluting the State's mandated responsibility." *Ibid.*

. . . [O]ur holding in *Robinson I* was clear and formed the basis for our holding in *Robinson* V: a thorough and efficient education requires a certain level of educational opportunity, a minimum level, that will equip the student to become "a citizen and . . . a competitor in the labor market." *Robinson I*. . . .

* * *

The change of focus from the dollar disparity in *Robinson I* to substantive educational content in *Robinson* V is clear; it was the main theme underlying the Court's determination that the Act was constitutional. Noting at the outset that for the first time we had before us a statute that defined the constitutional obligation, provided for its implementation through both state and local administration, required that implementation to be monitored, directed the State to compel compliance where that monitoring revealed deficiencies, and provided a funding mechanism to achieve the constitutional goal, we observed that the state's school-aid provisions "must be considered not in comparative isolation, but as part of the whole proposal formulated by the Legislature." *Robinson* V. . . . Although the opinion sketched the State-aid formula, it dwelt in considerable detail on the new approach to a thorough and efficient education: its definition, its involvement of both the State and district in fleshing out the details, standards, and elements against which thorough and efficient was to be measured, its requirements of reporting and monitoring, the whole range of remedies available to the Commissioner and the Board for corrective action to force districts to upgrade their educational offerings when monitoring revealed deficiencies, and the non-delegable duty of the State to do so. . . . The only question about financing was not whether it provided equal dollars per pupil—indeed, we noted that "there may be and probably are legitimate differences between and among districts and students" . . . , but whether it was sufficient to support the entire system and its goal of achieving a thorough and efficient education throughout the state.

* * *

Most telling of our view of the constitutional mandate was that, while noting that the funding mechanism would equalize only about 64% of the districts if fully funded . . . , we nevertheless observed that the Act eliminated "gross disparities in per pupil expenditures and tax resources." . . . [W]hether the Act would be found to be constitutional after its funding and implementation would depend on a test of it "as applied in the future to any individual school district at any particular time. . . ."

* * *

. . . [T]he requirement of a thorough and efficient education to provide "that educational opportunity which is needed in the contemporary setting to equip a child for his role as a citizen and as a competitor in the labor market," *Robinson I* . . . meant that poorer disadvantaged students must be given a chance to be able to compete with relatively advantaged students. The Act and its system of education have failed in that respect, and it is that failure that we address in this case.

* * *

IV. Facts and Conclusions

* * *

A. The Funding Scheme

* * *

The Act gives poorer districts—poor in terms of property valuation per pupil—taxing power to raise more money for school purposes than what a school district with the average property valuation and no equalization aid could raise. Putting aside for the moment the impact of "municipal overburden" (a condition in many poorer districts where the cost of local government—police, firefighters, other municipal employees, road maintenance, garbage collection, etc.—is so high that the municipality and the school district are reluctant to increase taxes for any purpose, including education), equalization aid attempts to obliterate the enormous disparity between rich and poor for school tax purposes; it creates, instead of rich and poor districts, two different classes: those districts with a guaranteed tax base—almost two-thirds of the districts in the state—and those with a tax base in excess of the guaranteed tax base of $233,100, running from $223,667 to $7.8 million and clustering at $300,000 (1984–85 figures). . . .

* * *

B. Educational Funding Disparities

. . . [T]he funding and spending disparities referred to in *Robinson I* are worse now than they were before adoption of the Act. . . . Prior to the Act, in 1971–72, the spread between the lowest and highest spending districts was $700 per pupil to $1,500 per pupil a difference of $800. *Robinson V* . . . . This difference of $800 per pupil reflects the range between the absolute highest spending districts and the absolute lowest. . . . In 1975–76, the year immediately prior to the Act, districts at the fifth percentile spent $1,076, while districts at the ninety-fifth spent $1,974, a difference of $898. For a few years after the Act was funded, the disparity diminished, but thereafter it generally increased to the point where in 1984–85 districts at the fifth percentile spent $2,687, while districts at the ninety-fifth percentile spent $4,755, a disparity of $2,068 per pupil. The disparity in expenditures is significant even when adjusted for inflation—in 1975-dollars, the disparity grew from $898 per pupil in 1975–76 to $1,135 per pupil in 1984–85.

The impact of this disparity, solely in dollar terms, is that on the average, in 1984–85, a group of richer districts with 189,484 students spend 40% more per pupil than a group of poorer districts with 355,612 students; one provides an education worth $4,029 per pupil, the other $2,861. . . .

That disadvantage in expenditures per pupil is clearly related to all of the other aspects of poverty that define poorer urban districts and their youth. Although the statistical relationships are the subject of considerable dispute, we conclude that generally they show that the poorer the district—measured by equalized valuation per pupil, or by other indicators of poverty—the less the per pupil expenditure; the poorer and more urban the district, the heavier its municipal property tax, the greater the school tax burden; whatever the measure of disadvantage, need, and poverty—the greater it is, the less there is to spend.

* * *

For most districts, plaintiffs have failed to prove substantively that a thorough and efficient education does not exist. . . . Given the State's attempt to achieve thorough and efficient education, we doubt that any showing of expenditure disparity in the absence of some independent evidence of substantive failure would warrant a conclusion that a thorough and efficient education does not exist. But expenditure disparity does play a role, an important one, in our conclusion that the constitutional level has not been achieved in the poorer urban districts. This disparity has multiple relevance: to the extent educational quality is deemed related to dollar expenditures, it tends to prove inadequate quality of education in the poorer districts, unless we were to assume that the substantial differential in expenditures is attributable to an education in the richer districts far beyond anything that thorough and efficient demands; it indicates even more strongly the probability that the poorer districts' students will be unable to compete in the society entered by the richer districts' students; and by its consistency over the years, it suggests that the system as it now operates is unable to correct this.

* * *

. . . [W]e do not believe a thorough and efficient education in the poorer urban districts "can realistically be met" by reliance on the system now in place. While local taxation no longer has the same impact, it is still significant. More than that, however, we believe that because of the complex factors leading to a failure of thorough and efficient in the poorer urban districts, including disparity of expenditures, we are no more likely ever to achieve thorough and efficient than we believed we could by relying on local taxation in *Robinson I*. Combined with these disparities of wealth and expenditure are the much more serious disparities of educational need, students in the poorer urban districts dramatically disadvantaged compared to their peers in the affluent suburbs. These intractable differences of wealth and need between the poorer and the richer, and the "discordant correlations" within a poorer district between its students' educational needs and its ability to spend, are more than the present funding system can overcome. The failure has gone on too long; the factors are ingrained; the remedy must be systemic. The present scheme cannot cure it.

* * *

. . . [T]he State may be correct in its contention that measured against the entire spectrum of districts in the state, the disparities and their relationships are not sufficient to condemn the system, because they exist significantly only when the extremes are compared. That gives little comfort to those students confined to the poorest districts, and they number in the hundreds of thousands (in 1984–85 there were 280,081 resident students in the twenty-nine poorer urban districts, about 25% of the entire public school population). Their deprivation is real, of constitutional magnitude, and not blunted in the least by the State's statistical analysis.

C. Substantive Educational Opportunity: The Administration of the Act by the Commissioner and the Board

* * *

. . . While we know of expenditure disparity, we have no reason to believe the actual funding level in most districts is below that needed to achieve a thorough and efficient education. . . . Under those circumstances our State Constitution does not require that this entire system be scrapped and replaced by another at enormous expense based solely on expenditure disparities. We do not imply anything about the importance of such disparities when considered as a matter of policy. . . .

. . . Before this Court voids the statute, overrules the Board and the Commissioner, and orders the Legislature to provide a new system, the constitutional failure must be clear. As to most districts of the state, it is not. But as to some—the poorer urban districts—it is glaringly clear.

1. Municipal Overburden. "Municipal overburden" is the excessive tax levy some municipalities must impose to meet governmental needs other than education. It is a common characteristic in poorer urban districts, a product of their relatively low property values against which the local tax is assessed and their high level of governmental need. The governmental need includes the entire range of goods and services made available to citizens: police and fire protection, road maintenance, social services, water, sewer, garbage disposal, and similar services. Although the condition is not precisely defined, it is usually thought of as a tax rate well above the average.

The underlying causes of municipal overburden are many and complex. Its consequences in this case, however, are clear and simple. The poorer urban school districts, sharing the same tax base with the municipality, suffer from severe municipal overburden; they are extremely reluctant to increase taxes for school purposes. Not only is their local tax levy well above average, so is their school tax rate. The oppressiveness of the tax burden on their citizens by itself would be sufficient to give them pause before raising taxes. Additionally, the rates in some cases are so high that further taxation may actually decrease tax revenues by diminishing total property values, either directly because of the tax-value relationship, or indirectly by causing business and industry to relocate to another municipality.

Plaintiffs argue that municipal overburden restricts these poorer urban districts' ability to raise more money through increased school taxes to achieve a thorough and efficient education. . . .

The Commissioner's position is that municipal overburden is irrelevant to the constitutional issue. He maintains that the school board is obliged as a matter of statutory and constitutional duty to raise as much money as is needed for a thorough and efficient education no matter what the tax consequences, no matter how much the tax increase, no matter how high the present tax, and no matter how high the present local municipal tax. If tax inequity exists, that may be a concern for the Legislature but it must not be for the school district. . . .

We respectfully disagree. The social and economic pressures on municipalities, school districts, public officials, and citizens of these disaster areas—many poorer urban districts—are so severe that tax increases in any substantial amount are almost unthinkable. . . .

* * *

. . . Our conclusion concerning municipal overburden is that it effectively prevents districts from raising substantially more money for education. It is a factual conclusion. . . . That factual finding is one of the bases for our conclusion that the funding mechanism of the Act will never achieve a thorough and efficient education because it relies so heavily on a local property base already over-taxed to exhaustion.

D. The Quality of Education in the Poorer Urban Districts

The primary basis for our decision is the constitutional failure of education in poorer urban districts. . . . Our conclusion that the constitutional mandate has not been satisfied is based both on the absolute level of education in those districts and the comparison with education in affluent suburban districts.

* * *

. . . [T]he level of education offered to students in some of the poorer urban districts is tragically inadequate. Many opportunities offered to students in richer suburban districts are denied to them. For instance, exposure to computers is necessary to acquire skills to compete in the workplace. In South Orange/Maplewood school district, kindergartners are introduced to computers; children learn word processing in elementary school; middle school students are offered beginning computer programming; and high school students are offered advanced courses in several programming languages or project-oriented independent studies. Each South Orange/ Maplewood school has a computer lab.

By contrast, many poorer urban districts cannot offer such variety of computer science courses. While Princeton has one computer per eight children, East Orange has one computer per forty-three children, and Camden has one computer per fifty-eight children. Camden can offer formal computer instruction to only 3.4% of its students. . . .

Science education is deficient in some poorer urban districts. Princeton has seven laboratories in its high school, each with built-in equipment. South Brunswick elementary and middle schools stress hands-on, investigative science programs. However, many poorer urban districts offer science classes in labs built in the 1920's and 1930's, where sinks do not work, equipment such as microscopes is not available, supplies for chemistry or biology classes are insufficient, and hands-on investigative techniques cannot be taught. In Jersey City and Irvington, middle school science classes are taught without provision for laboratory experience. . . .

The disparity in foreign-language programs is dramatic. Montclair's students begin instruction in French or Spanish at the pre-school level. In Princeton's middle school, fifth grade students must take a half-year of French and a half-year of Spanish. Most sixth graders continue with one of these languages. Many begin a second language in the ninth grade, where four-year programs in German, Italian, Russian, and Latin are offered. French and Spanish are offered on two tracks, one for students who began instruction in middle school and the other for those who begin in the ninth grade. Advanced placement courses are available. In contrast, many of the poorer urban schools do not offer upper level foreign language courses, and only begin instruction in high school. . . .

Music programs are vastly superior in some richer suburban districts. South Brunswick offers music classes starting in kindergarten; Montclair begins with preschoolers. Millburn and South Brunswick offer their middle school students a music curriculum that includes courses such as guitar, electronic-piano laboratory, and music composition on synthesizers. Princeton offers several performing groups, including bands, choruses, and small ensembles. However, Camden and Paterson do not offer a music course until the fourth grade; only introductory level music courses are offered in high school. In 1981, Camden eliminated all its elementary school music teachers and provided "helpers" to assist in teaching music. Many poorer urban school districts have inadequate space for instrumental music lessons, bands, and choruses. . . .

Art programs in some poorer urban districts suffer compared to programs in richer suburban districts. In Montclair, the art program begins at the preschool level; there is an art teacher in every elementary school; every school has at least one art room; and the district has purchased a variety of art equipment, such as a kiln for ceramic artwork. In contrast, art programs in some poorer urban districts are sparse. There are no art classrooms in East Orange elementary schools, and art teachers, who must travel from class to class, are limited in the forms of art they can teach. . . .

In South Brunswick school district, the industrial-arts program includes an automotive shop, a woodworking shop, a metal shop, a graphics shop, and a greenhouse for a horticultural course. The vocational education program has a computer drafting laboratory and a graphics laboratory with a darkroom. In Camden, state-of-the-art equipment is not purchased; the old equipment in the classrooms is not maintained or repaired. There have even been problems heating the industrial-arts wing of the school.

Physical education programs in some poorer urban districts are deficient. While many richer suburban school districts have flourishing gymnastics, swimming, basketball, baseball, soccer, lacrosse, field hockey, tennis, and golf teams, with fields, courts, pools, lockers, showers, and gymnasiums, some poorer urban districts cannot offer students such activities. In East Orange High School there are no such sports facilities; the track team practices in the second floor hallway. . . .

Many of these poorer urban districts are burdened with teaching basic skills to an overwhelming number of students. They are essentially "basic skills districts." In 1985, 53% of Camden's children received remedial education; in East Orange, 41%; in Irvington, 30%. By contrast, only 4% of the students in Millburn school district received remedial education.

* * *

Thorough and efficient means more than teaching the skills needed to compete in the labor market, as critically important as that may be. It means being able to fulfill one's role as a citizen, a role that encompasses far more than merely registering to vote. It means the ability to participate fully in society, in the life of one's community, the ability to appreciate music, art, and literature, and the ability to share all of that with friends. As plaintiffs point out in so many ways, and tellingly, if these courses are not integral to a thorough and efficient education, why do the richer districts invariably offer them? . . .

The State contends that the education currently offered in these poorer urban districts is tailored to the students' present need, that these students simply cannot now benefit from the kind of vastly superior course offerings found in the richer districts. . . . The State's conclusion is that basic skills are what they need first, intensive training in basic skills. We note, however, that these poorer districts offer curricula denuded not only of advanced academic courses but of virtually every subject that ties a child, particularly a child with academic problems, to school—of art, music, drama, athletics, even, to a very substantial degree, of science and social studies. . . .

. . . [C]onstitutionally, these districts should not be limited to such choices. However desperately a child may need remediation in basic skills, he or she also needs at least a modicum of variety and a chance to excel.

Equally, if not more important, the State's argument ignores the substantial number of children in these districts, from the average to the gifted, who can benefit from more advanced academic offerings. Since little else is available in these districts, they too are limited to basic skills.

The level of substantive education is proven by plaintiffs through other indicators. Plaintiffs have selected what are sometimes regarded as strong indicators of educational quality, and have measured them among districts. Teacher ratios (the number of teachers per 1,000 pupils), the average experience of instructional staff, their average level of education . . . .

As to each one of these indicators, the poorer urban districts suffer by comparison to the rich. Indeed, although the incremental showing is far from dramatic, teacher ratios, experience, and education consistently improve as the districts' property wealth, per pupil expenditure, socioeconomic status or other similar factor improves. . . .

* * *

In summary, although the evidence of substantive educational level is insufficient to prove systemic lack of thorough and efficient, it is more than sufficient to prove the constitutional deficiency in a limited number of districts. . . . Disparity exists . . . between education in these poorer urban districts and that in the affluent suburban districts; it is severe and forms an independent basis for our finding of a lack of a thorough and efficient education in these poorer urban districts—these students simply cannot possibly enter the same market or the same society as their peers educated in wealthier districts.

E. The Quality of Students' Needs in the Poorer Urban Districts

This record shows that the educational needs of students in poorer urban districts vastly exceed those of others, especially those from richer districts. The difference is monumental, no matter how it is measured. Those needs go beyond educational needs, they include food, clothing and shelter, and extend to lack of close family and community ties and support, and lack of helpful role models. They include the needs that arise from a life led in an environment of violence, poverty, and despair. Urban youth are often isolated from the mainstream of society. Education forms only a small part of their home life, sometimes no part of their school life, and the dropout is almost the norm. There are exceptions, fortunately, but substantial numbers of urban students fit this pattern. The goal is to motivate them, to wipe out their disadvantages as much as a school district can, and to give them an educational opportunity that will enable them to use their innate ability.

* * *

The dropout rate in these poorer urban districts is further testimony both to their failure and to the students' needs. The "unofficial" dropout rate (1984–85) for some urban high schools can be as high as 47%. A district cannot deliver a thorough and efficient education to a dropout. For a multitude of tragic reasons, these students lack the most basic requirement for achieving a thorough and efficient education—the will to learn. That characteristic is assumed, accepted, a given, in richer suburban districts.

* * *

Obviously, we are no more able to identify what these disadvantaged students need in concrete educational terms than are the experts. What they don't need is more disadvantage, in the form of a school district that does not even approach the funding level that supports advantaged students. They need more, and the law entitles them to more.

* * *

Alternative education programs for students identified as potential dropouts are suggested as necessary to motivate a substantial number of students in poorer urban districts. Several richer suburban districts provide individualized tutoring and vocational education to students in need of alternative education. However, in Jersey City, several alternative education programs were eliminated, and only a program for students in legal trouble is provided. . . .

* * *

In *Robinson I* we observed that the State may "recognize . . . a need for additional dollar input to equip classes of disadvantaged [students] for the educational opportunity." . . .

It is clear to us that in order to achieve the constitutional standard for the student from these poorer urban districts—the ability to function in that society entered by their relatively advantaged peers—the totality of the district's educational offering must contain elements over and above those found in the affluent suburban district. If the educational fare of the seriously disadvantaged student is the same as the "regular education" given to the advantaged student, those serious disadvantages will not be addressed, and students in the poorer urban districts will simply not be able to compete. A thorough and efficient education requires such level of education as will enable all students to function as citizens and workers in the same society, and that necessarily means that in poorer urban districts something more must be added to the regular education in order to achieve the command of the Constitution. . . .

. . . We realize that perhaps nothing short of substantial social and economic change affecting housing, employment, child care, taxation, welfare will make the difference for these students; and that this kind of change is far beyond the power or responsibility of school districts. We have concluded, however, that even if not a cure, money will help, and that these students are constitutionally entitled to that help.

If the claim is that additional funding will not enable the poorer urban districts to satisfy the thorough and efficient test, the constitutional answer is that they are entitled to pass or fail with at least the same amount of money as their competitors.

If the claim is that these students simply cannot make it, the constitutional answer is, give them a chance. The Constitution does not tell them that since more money will not help, we will give them less; that because their needs cannot be fully met, they will not be met at all. It does not tell them they will get the minimum because that is all they can benefit from. Like other states, we undoubtedly have some "uneducable" students, but in New Jersey there is no such thing as an uneducable district, not under our Constitution.

All of the money that supports education is public money, local money no less than state money. It is authorized and controlled, in terms of source, amount, distribution, and use, by the State. The students of Newark and Trenton are no less citizens than their friends in Millburn and Princeton. They are entitled to be treated equally, to begin at the same starting line. Today the disadvantaged are doubly mistreated: first, by the accident of their environment and, second, by the disadvantage added by an inadequate education. The State has compounded the wrong and must right it.

F. Impact of the Level of Funding on the Quality of Education

The State's claim that the statistical evidence fails to prove a significant relationship between education expenditures and property wealth is joined with a more fundamental objection: money is not a critical factor in the quality of education in the first place. The position is not quite that extreme, of course—obviously, a certain minimum amount is needed to operate an effective school system, as the Commissioner notes. But beyond that minimum amount, not clearly defined in the record, the difference, the excess, is characterized as an unreliable indicator of the quality of education, and what the money buys—better staff ratios, more experienced teachers, equipment, more varied course offerings—is not determinative either. The conclusion is that since all districts in the state have much more than whatever the minimum amount may be, the excess and the differences in the excess, are irrelevant to the quality of education.

* * *

We deal here with questions of educational theory debated over the years, and now debated by experts of the very highest order. These issues have come to the fore not just in this case but throughout the nation, with states struggling as we are here in New Jersey to find an answer to urban problems, especially urban education. . . . The only thing universally agreed on is that those schools are failing. After that, controversy abounds. Our observation, simplistic perhaps, that "money is only one of a number of elements [involved in education]," *Robinson* V . . . still represents most of what one can profitably glean from this controversy for the purposes of this litigation. More concretely, while we are unable to conclude from this record that the State is clearly wrong, we would not strip all notions of equal and adequate funding from the constitutional obligation unless we were convinced that the State was clearly right.

The results of all of this research . . . shows beyond doubt that money alone has not worked. . . . But it does not show that money makes no difference. What it strongly suggests is that money can be used more effectively than it is being used today. The inconclusiveness of the research is conceded, at least to the extent of admitting that although money is not the main determinant of the quality of education no one is quite convinced what is, nor totally confident about what works. . . .

* * *

V. Findings

* * *

We find that in order to provide a thorough and efficient education in these poorer urban districts, the State must assure that their educational expenditures per pupil are substantially equivalent to those of the more affluent suburban districts, and that, in addition, their special disadvantages must be addressed.

* * *

VI. Remedy

* * *

Whatever the legislative remedy, . . . it must assure that these poorer urban districts have a budget per pupil that is approximately equal to the average of the richer suburban districts, whatever that average may be, and be sufficient to address their special needs.

* * *

We have not attempted to address disparity of spending as such. To the extent that the State allows the richer suburban districts to continue to increase that disparity, it will, by our remedy, be required to increase the funding of the poorer urban districts. We limit our remedy at this point to increasing funding where we find a deficiency. We do not require equalized funding statewide. We are satisfied, however, that whatever degree of statewide equality the Legislature may wish to achieve, or may find it feasible to achieve, it cannot constitutionally do so for these poorer urban districts simply by raising the guaranteed tax base under the present formula. These districts, even assuming the most generous GTB increase, will not be willing or able to fund what is required for a thorough and efficient education. Their need to conserve their tax dollars, their need not to increase their total tax rate, will inevitably persuade them not to spend more but to tax less.

* * *

NOTES AND QUESTIONS

1. *The* Abbott v. Burke *Decision*

Is the court's decision in *Abbott v. Burke* a much stronger mandate for equal educational opportunity than what was required in *Robinson I*? Note that while the court did not mandate any controls on local spending by affluent districts, the court did specify that to the extent that high property-wealth districts increased their spending, the state must "increase the funding of the poorer urban districts." *Id.* at 410. Is the *Abbott* court applying a positive outcomes standard? Is the court requiring the state to ensure—or make its best efforts to do so—that all students are able to compete for the same kind of jobs? Must everyone be a computer programmer or brain surgeon? In light of what is presently known about the resource-outcome relationship, is an outcomes standard implementable? Professor Jencks has concluded that educational inequality is of marginal importance in predicting who will or will not be successful in the race for life's rewards. C. Jencks et al., *Inequality* (1972).

2. Board of Education, Levittown v. Nyquist

In 1974, twenty-seven low-property-wealth suburban school districts filed a *Serrano*-type complaint in a New York court. Subsequently, the four major cities of the state—New York, Rochester, Buffalo, and Syracuse—sought and were granted permission to intervene in the action despite the fact that their interests were at odds with the original plaintiffs. The urban intervenors raised arguments directed toward protecting their special interests as cities with their peculiar problems—interests not necessarily given cognizance by the principle of fiscal neutrality.

The arguments of the city school districts to indicate that special financial burdens borne by the cities placed them in a position comparable to that of property-poor districts included:

> (1) demands on municipal budgets (from which local funds for education are secured) for non-education needs peculiar to cities ("municipal overburden"), (2) diminished purchasing power of the municipal education dollar, (3) significantly greater student absenteeism (with a resulting adverse effect both because of added operational costs and because State aid is largely allocated on the basis of average daily attendance), and (4) larger concentrations in cities of pupils with special educational needs, all four of which may be comprehended within the term "metropolitan overburden." These factors are said to result in greatly disparate educational opportunities available to children in the cities' public schools when compared to the offerings of some of the school districts not located within cities.
>
> . . . The intervenors argue that although they are not disadvantaged in their ability to raise gross revenue from local sources, in consequence of the economic factors of metropolitan overburden the net effective economic ability of the city districts falls well below that of non-city districts . . . .

Board of Education, Levittown v. Nyquist, 57 N.Y.2d 27, 36, 453 N.Y.S.2d 643, 646, 439 N.E.2d 359, (1982).

The *Levittown* court rejected the claim of intervenors that they were denied equal protection under the state constitution. The court noted that with respect to the intervenors' argument "that metropolitan overburden is an unequalizing force which must be remedied by compensating increases in State aid to city school districts, a response is . . . that the cited inequalities existing in cities are the product of demographic, economic, and political factors intrinsic to the cities themselves, and cannot be attributed to legislative action or inaction." *Id.* at 41. The court noted that although education must then compete for municipal dollars with other forms of public service for which non-municipal school districts are not responsible, the disbursement of funds from the property tax and other sources of revenue "are decisions to be made by municipal governmental bodies." *Id.* at 42.

The claim that the system violated the education article of the New York State Constitution, which merely requires that the "Legislature shall provide for the maintenance and support of a system of free common schools, wherein all the children of this state may be educated," art. XI, §1, was also rejected. The court interpreted the constitutional provision as mandating the legislature to provide a system of free schools in the state, and that as long as a sound basic education is provided to all students, the constitutional requirement is met. "Because decisions as to how public funds will be allocated among the several services for which by constitutional imperative the Legislature is required to make provision are matters peculiarly appropriate for formulation by the Legislative body . . . , we would be reluctant to override those decisions by mandating an even higher priority for education in the absence, possibly, of gross and glaring inadequacy—something not shown to exist in consequence of the present school financing system." *Id.* at 48–49.

Was the *Levittown* court correct in determining that the constitutional mandate was only for a minimum and not an equal education? Are there differences in the education clauses between the New Jersey and the New York constitutions that explain the differing results in the two cases? Is education just one of a number of municipal services competing for funds so that it is up to the municipalities to decide how to allocate funds among the services once the basic education is provided? What *is* that basic or minimum level of education? Does the *Levittown* court focus primarily on overburden in terms of noneducational services that cities must provide from the property tax? What about other kinds of "overburden"?

3. Municipal Overburden

The "fiscal neutrality" or wealth-free standard, devised in response to a system in which low property values correlated with low per-pupil expenditures, failed to recognize the peculiar fiscal problems of central city schools. The argument is that these problems stem not from low property values but from the higher noneducational public services that central cities must support out of the property tax, such as police and fire protection or health and welfare services. The comparatively high percentage of the property tax allocated for those non-education services acts as a constraint on the tax rate levied for education. Most suburban and rural school districts are not so heavily burdened by these noneducational expenses, permitting most of their property tax revenues to be allocated to the schools.

In providing state aid to equalize the varying capabilities of the state's school districts to finance public education, must a state system of financing take into account the noneducational services that cities must provide from property tax revenues? If the purpose of the fiscal neutrality principle is to equalize fiscal capacity, why would not the extent to which property tax revenues must be used to support *other* public services affect the capacity of the district to raise funds for education? Professor Coons and his colleagues, however, argue that the principle of fiscal neutrality is aimed at the fact that existing systems of finance are "designed to create differences in school quality; it may not and does not follow that there is a constitutional objection to . . . every act of the state with a similar effect. An area may be 'city poor' . . . and the condition may affect school spending, but the cause of this relative poverty is by definition outside the system of public finance." J. Coons, W. Clune, and S. Sugarman, *Private Wealth and Public Education* 311 (1970). To what extent does the *Abbott* court take into account municipal overburden? Can the different approaches of *Levittown* and *Abbott* concerning municipal overburden be attributed to the fact that in New Jersey urban school districts have both low property values and high "municipal overburden" while in New York the four largest cities have high property values, although substantial property tax revenues are still needed for other governmental services?

4. Education Overburden

Both the *Levittown* city intervenors and the *Abbott* plaintiffs argued that they have a higher proportion than other types of districts of those students who require greater than average educational resources—such as the handicapped, the educationally disadvantaged, and students with limited English-language skills. These translate into such "education overburdens" as impaired learning readiness; impaired mental, emotional, and physical health; mental retardation and other learning disabilities; and English-language difficulties. Because of inadequate resources, programs to address these "overburdens" cannot be adequately provided.

Would either the state education clause or the state equal protection clause constitutionally compel states to recognize the needs of such students? Is this an argument that expenditures must be on the basis of pupils' *educational needs* without regard to the fiscal capacity of local school districts? If so, are there judicially manageable standards for determining how much is needed? Who is to determine what a student's needs are? If a budding Picasso demands the services of a highly talented art teacher to develop his or her artistic potential, must the court, legislature, and school district agree that this is what the school needs? Even if it were possible for a court to determine the issue of need, how can the court decide if a particular program is in fact suited to whatever the need is? Does that mean that the program must guarantee that a particular skill or level of understanding will be achieved? Does this suggest a needs standard is really an outcomes standard in disguise? Or does a needs standard only require that the program be reasonably designed to address the student's needs in light of existing educational knowledge? How does the *Abbott* court treat these issues?

5. *Cost Differentials*

In distributing aid to the larger cities, should the state formula take into account "cost differentials," that is, the fact that higher prices or wage rates mean that urban districts have to spend more per pupil than rural or suburban school districts to provide a comparable educational program? This price-wage differential reflects area "labor market" differences and the fact that cities generally have a higher proportion of professional staff with advanced degrees and years of experience. Site acquisition costs and the costs per square foot of constructing school facilities are also substantially higher in cities than in suburban and rural areas, as are the costs of plant maintenance and security. *See generally* B. Levin, T. Muller, and C. Sandoval, *The High Cost of Education in Cities* (1973).

Is a system of finance that fails to take these cost differentials into account unconstitutionally discriminatory? This issue was confronted in *Seattle School District No. 1 v. State,* 90 Wash.2d 476, 585 P.2d 71 (1978). The trial court implicitly accepted a "cost differentials" principle that would take into account the wage-price differences central cities often have to pay to provide the same educational offering that the typical student receives in a suburban or rural school district. *See* Levin, "Current Trends in School Finance Reform Litigation: A Commentary," 1977 *Duke L.J.* 1099, 1115–16, for a discussion of the three possible methods for determining the "basic education" that the state constitutionally is required to provide, each of which would take into account cost differences.

6. *The Complexity of School Finance Reform*

The area of school finance reform has become increasingly complex—courts have gone from a simple "fiscal neutrality" theory to a variety of legal theories. In addition, there has been litigation on the special needs of cities, or of certain target pupil populations. Does this suggest that there are no judicially manageable standards in this area? How much education is "enough" to justify, in a constitutional sense, inequalities among school districts within a state in educational offerings? Are there judicially manageable standards for determining "enough"?

IV. INTRADISTRICT INEQUALITIES

A. Introduction

Most reform efforts have been directed toward reforming interdistrict differences in the distribution of educational resources per pupil, rather than toward intradistrict or even intraschool inequalities in the distribution of resources. Yet in a number of urban school districts, the level of spending per pupil is often considerably higher in those schools serving children from middle class backgrounds than in schools where the student body is predominantly poor and minority. As noted in the preceding section, the principal source of inequalities in interdistrict per-pupil expenditures is the heavy reliance on the local property tax to fund education and the underlying inequalities in revenues generated by the use of this tax. These inequalities are due to differences among districts in property values per pupil, differences in tax rates, and inequitable property assessment practices. These factors, of course, cannot explain intradistrict differences in expenditures per pupil. Moreover, arguments regarding the value of local control, which prevailed in *San Antonio School District v. Rodriguez,* have no relevance when one is concerned with how a school board distributes resources among the buildings within a school system or how the principal distributes resources within his or her school.

B. Inequality in Washington, D.C.

Hobson v. Hansen
327 F.Supp. 844 (D.D.C. 1971).

J. Skelly Wright, Circuit Judge.

[In *Hobson v. Hansen,* 269 F.Supp. 401 (D.D.C. 1967), *aff'd en banc sub nom., Smuck v. Hobson,* 408 F.2d 175 (D.C. Cir. 1969), the court considered three related constitutional problems: the segregation of students in the District of Columbia school system; the tracking system by which students were assigned to different educational programs on the basis of tested aptitude*; and inequities in the distribution of resources within the District. This last issue is of concern here.

The court sought to determine (1) whether the distribution of educational resources favored white over black students, and (2) if so, whether such discrimination was legally justifiable. A host of inputs were considered: the age, physical condition, and educational adequacy of school buildings; library books and facilities; school congestion; such factors assertedly relevant to assessing faculty quality as teacher experience, faculty education, and reliance on temporary (noncertified) teachers; textbooks and supplies, curricula and special programs; and per-pupil expenditures. In each area, the court identified inequities which favored white students. Predominantly black schools, for example, were filled to 115 percent of capacity, while predominantly white schools had 23 percent of their space unfilled; teachers at white schools were better educated, more experienced, and were more typically certified than their counterparts at black schools. Financial disparities were notable, with the median per-pupil expenditure for schools with 85 to 100 percent black students being $292 and the median per-pupil expenditure for schools with 0 to 15 percent black students being $392.

Having found these various inequalities to be in violation of the equal protection clause, the court ordered the school board to "transport volunteering Negro students from the city's overcrowded elementary schools into the partly vacant white schools west of the Park." With regard to teacher inequalities, the court noted that it would "defer formulation of specific provisions for faculty equalization at least until the dust surrounding this fall's 'substantial' teacher integration settles."

In 1970, the plaintiffs moved for further relief, with the court noting that it had assumed that as a result of compliance with other items of the 1967 decree, including abolition of the track system and optional attendance zones, and integration of school faculties, overall resource distribution would be equalized, and thus the court did not need a specific remedy for the inequality in per-pupil expenditures. Plaintiffs, however, sought further relief "in view of the fact that the spread in total expenditures per pupil at various district elementary schools had increased by over 100% since 1964."]

After a year of discovery and argument by memoranda, the record now before the court indicates that a striking differential in per-pupil expenditures for teachers' salaries and benefits exists between schools east and west of the Park. . . . The area west of the Park, where despite voluntary busing the public school population is today 74 percent white, is decidedly favored over the rest of the city where the school population is 98 percent black, and is especially favored over Anacostia, one of the most poor and black sections of the city. . . .

[The court noted that the differences between west of the Park elementary schools and Anacostia elementary schools in fiscal 1971 in pupil-teacher ratios was 18.1/1 compared to 22.6/1, or 24.9 percent smaller, while the differences in teacher expenditures per pupil were $696 in west of the Park elementary schools and $478 in Anacostia elementary schools, or 40 percent greater in the schools west of the Park.]

* * *

[T]he court has considered and rejected defendants' argument that the observed wide discrepancies in teacher expenditures per pupil favoring schools west of the Park are random and do not favor any particular racial group or economic class of children. The court has also rejected defendants' position that, even if an objective pattern of discrimination exists, it does so solely or primarily for technological reasons (*i.e.*, economics of scale) which are beyond defendants' control and which cannot be remedied by a court order. Now the court comes to defendants' ultimate defense: that even if a pattern of unequal expenditures does exist, and even if the differential expenditures per pupil are within defendants' control, the resulting real resource differentials are nonetheless inconsequential as they relate to equal educational opportunity.

Teacher expenditure per pupil is a sum, of course, which reflects both the size of the class in which a given student finds himself and the salary paid his teacher. With regard to the average teacher salary component of teacher expenditures per pupil, defendants take the position that the different salaries

*The portion of the 1967 *Hobson* opinion concerning student classification appears in ch. 5.

paid teachers are primarily rewards for experience, and that experience has not been shown to have a significant correlation with a teacher's productivity measured by student achievement tests. The short response to this position is that defendants are seeking to reopen and relitigate an issue which has already been decided in the 1967 *Hobson* opinion.

It is almost an affront to common sense to say, as do defendants, that a pattern of spending so discriminatory on its face as the one which exists in the District reflects no discrimination in "educational opportunity." To overcome the heavy burden against them, defendants lean in part on an argument by their expert, Dave O'Neill, that only teacher experience of six years and less has educational consequence. But even if this assumption, which O'Neill admits is really an "intuitive hunch," were true, the west of the Park school is still favored in that it has a higher percentage of teachers with six years or more experience than schools in the rest of the city. Moreover, as the court reads them, the rather inconclusive educational studies tell us only that teachers seem to be *over*compensated for experience relative to their productivity. That is, researchers consistently find some relationship between experience and achievement, though not so great as is traditionally paid for. In the absence of more conclusive studies, large differentials such as exist in the District of Columbia cannot be condoned.

Moreover, the Board cannot be allowed in one breath to justify budget requests to the Congress and to the District of Columbia City Council by stressing the connection between longevity and quality teaching, and then in the next breath to disavow any such connection before the court. Speaking before the City Council on the subject of teacher salary legislation, the chairman of the school board said:

> The Board recognizes that to achieve quality education in the District of Columbia public schools it is imperative that students must be housed in educational facilities conducive to learning and be taught by a highly motivated and well-trained teaching staff. It believes that in order to accomplish this objective, it must begin to offer a salary schedule attractive enough to retain its experienced master teachers. . . .

Under these circumstances, where teacher experience has not been proved to be unrelated to educational opportunity, where the administration itself has chosen to reward experience, and where a pattern of racial and socioeconomic discrimination in expenditures continues in the District, the law requires either that experienced teachers be distributed uniformly among the schools in the system or that some offsetting benefit be given to those schools which are denied their fair complement of experienced teachers.[22]

22. At the same time they argue that the longevity component of teachers' salaries is unrelated to the effectiveness of their performance—an argument which I reject for the reasons outlined above—defendants seek to justify the current spending pattern and to prove themselves innocent of discriminatory intent by giving several alternative reasons why a policy which rewards longevity might be employed. In this regard, defendants seek first to "explain" the presence of the most experienced and most educated teachers in the schools west of the park as being merely "historical. . . ."

[D]efendants [also] maintain that there are at least three sound theoretical economic reasons why length of service might be compensated in excess of its associated productivity increases. According to defendants:

"(1) Turnover costs supply a rationale for an age-earnings profile that starts with earnings below productivity and, as experience accumulates, begins to pay wages in excess of productivity. . . .

"(2) The market for teachers services has a supply side as well as a demand side. Union pressures are another possible explanation for salary patterns. If more experienced teachers control the union, they will use negotiations to get high salaries for themselves relative to new teachers. . . .

"(3) A third reason why the relative pay of experienced teachers may be higher than their relative productivity has to do with costs which are the same for all teachers, regardless of experience. Examples of such costs are hiring costs and the cost of providing a classroom for the teacher. . . .

Any worry that shifts in teaching personnel necessitated by an equalization order "would breach the contract which has been effected with the Washington Teachers Union" (Benjamin Henley, Acting Superintendent of Schools, Supplemental Affidavit of August 12, 1970) is quickly allayed by reference to the contract itself which provides that "the fundamental transfer policy shall take into consideration the following factors: . . . legal requirements as ordered by the courts or Congress. . . ." The other alternative reasons offered by defendants for rewarding experience without regard to productivity smack of *post hoc* rationalization, are extremely speculative, and are essentially makeweights. Without pursuing them in detail in this opinion, the court rejects them. . . .

[In its 1967 *Hobson* opinion which set] a *minimum* standard, the court did not wish to preclude the school administration from focusing, if it saw fit, on equality of output, in terms of giving each student an equal opportunity to attain his own unique potential, rather than on equality of inputs. But the minimum required was that there be an equality of inputs in terms of objective resources. Under injunction to refrain from further discrimination, defendants have failed to comply with this "minimum." The court having found that an unequal distribution of the most experienced and highly paid teachers in favor of the predominantly white west of the Park area *does* favor this area as well in educational opportunity, no excuse for this continuing racial discrimination short of a "compelling state interest" is worthy of this court's attention at this late date in the history of the case.

Defendants have also alleged that the observed variations in pupil-teacher ratios—the second and larger component of the widely disparate teacher expenditures per pupil—are of no consequence in terms of educational performance or opportunity. Without here going into this contention exhaustively, the court rejects it for much the same reasons as those given in the discussion of the value of teacher experience. The outside studies referred to in the Michelson and O'Neill reports [reports submitted by expert witnesses for plaintiffs and defendants, respectively] are themselves inconclusive. There are so many other variables to be controlled in a study of the relationship between teacher-pupil ratio and educational product that the indefiniteness of the studies made to date is not the least bit surprising. . . .

In the end the court finds itself most persuaded, once again, by defendants own words, uttered before the lawyerly rationalization process began in earnest. . . . [I]n the program justification for the 1972 fiscal budget we read that "class size is one of the most important factors in maximizing education achievement." . . . Thus do defendants put themselves in the awkward position of asking to be applauded for their expensive efforts to reduce class sizes generally and of requesting funds for further reduction of class sizes under the rationale of productivity, while inconsistently maintaining for purposes of this litigation that no discrimination results when class sizes remain significantly smaller in west of the Park schools as compared with those in the rest of the city.

Plaintiffs' *prima facie* case of discrimination in the provision of educational opportunity, based upon the pattern of unequal expenditures which favors the schools west of the Park, is strongly buttressed by further evidence in the record concerning the results of citywide sixth grade reading achievement tests. The record shows that the west of the Park elementary schools produced an average reading achievement test score that was significantly higher—indeed 2.4 grades higher—than the average for the rest of the city. Obviously, these results tend to corroborate the presumption created by the pattern of expenditures that the city provides a better educational opportunity to its richer, white students. . . .

These achievement test results suggest that not only are the children in schools east of the Park being denied an educational opportunity equal to those west of the Park, but also they in fact are not being as well educated. Thus these test scores reflect the result of the discrimination against the east of the Park children in per-pupil expenditure. The burden of establishing that these test results reflect something other than the proven discriminatory distribution of educational opportunity falls upon defendants. And once again defendants have failed to meet their burden.

* * *

Four years after this court's first *Hobson* opinion, defendants have by their own admission failed to equalize the access of all students to dollar resources for teachers' salaries and benefits. Although defendants have argued strenuously that there is no proven connection between the showing that black students have unequal access to dollars and the crucial constitutional showing that black students are denied equal educational opportunity, the court has found otherwise. . . .

The court finds further that defendants have failed to offer the legal justification or compelling state interest necessary to overcome the presumptive invalidity of awarding benefits which affect the fundamental interests of and results in discrimination against a racial minority. . . .

Whatever may be the differences in constitutional concern between purely *de facto* and purely *de jure* segregation, it is too late for defendants to suggest that discrimination of constitutional dimension does not arise where a school board has knowingly favored in an unjustified and substantial way predominantly white schools over predominantly black schools. Since 1967, following the rationale of *Hobson*, several of the circuits have rejected the rational relationship test in finding a violation of the equal protection clause where the state has acted affirmatively and where the direct *effect* of the challenged state action was inescapably discriminatory to the enjoyment of an important right by a racial minority. . . .

. . . For reasons already discussed, the court finds that plaintiffs' initially requested relief requiring equalization of total expenditures per pupil across the system would sweep too broadly and would require the school administration to equalize some inputs which have little or nothing to do with educational opportunity. But upon careful consideration, the court does find that the equalization order approach is a good one, provided it is focused upon expenditures per pupil for teachers' salaries and benefits, so as to cover only inputs which do have a direct bearing on the quality of a child's education.

Having found continuing substantial discrimination, the court cannot agree with defendants' expert that an equalization order would amount to "much ado about nothing." Defendants stress that implementation of the proposed order would result merely in an increase of $3.39 per black child across the city. . . . Defendants' figure of $3.39 per child masks the fact that some individual black schools are shockingly far below the citywide average expenditure per pupil level. Thus, to take one of many possible examples, if teacher expenditures per pupil in fiscal 1971 at the Draper School (actually $362) had been at the citywide average ($497), they would have increased by $135 per pupil. The increase in total teacher expenditures would then have been approximately $147,000. Under salary scales currently in effect, this would have permitted the addition of perhaps fifteen new teachers at Draper. This addition would have reduced the pupil-teacher ratio from the present 25 to 1 to 18 to 1. Even defendants' expert seems to concede that such a reduction has a beneficial effect on school outcomes when measured by achievement test scores.

* * *

Wherefore it is ordered, adjudged and decreed that

1. On and after October 1, 1971, per-pupil expenditures for all teachers' salaries and benefits from the regular District of Columbia budget (excluding . . . all funds not from the regular congressional appropriation) in any single elementary school (*not* "administrative unit") shall not deviate by more than 5 percent from the mean per-pupil expenditure for all teachers' salaries and benefits at all elementary schools in the District of Columbia school system as that mean is defined in this paragraph. The 5 percent limit may be exceeded only for adequate justification on an individual school basis shown to this court in advance. "Adequate justification" shall include provision of compensatory education for educationally deprived pupils at certain schools or provision of special educational services for the mentally retarded or physically handicapped at certain schools or for other "exceptional" students. It shall also include a showing that variance above or below the 5 percent limit is accounted for *solely* on the basis of economics or diseconomics for scale. For purposes of this order, the "mean" shall be computed *after* excluding from the computation total expenditures for all teachers' salaries and benefits and total average daily membership at all schools for which permission to exceed the 5 percent limitation because of compensatory education or education of "exceptional" students is sought and granted. . . .

NOTES AND QUESTIONS

1. Politics of Educational Budget Making

The allocation of the education budget is the most crucial issue to confront the school board. The budget is prepared by the superintendent and his or her staff and presented to the board; it is a document that reflects internal bureaucratic bargaining. Teachers and noncertificated service personnel present their demands—either through union representatives or informally—to the superintendent before formal submission. When the budget is presented, the administrative staff "has in mind a definite dollar amount, or percentage figure, which they believe the board will accept." James, Kelly, and Garms, "The School Budget Process in Large Cities," *in* M. Kirst, ed., *The Politics of Education* 74, 82 (1970). In large cities, the power of the school bureaucracy over the budget is countered to some extent by various interest groups—unions, taxpayers' groups, and the like—who rely on their own professional research staffs to prepare "counterbudgets." As a consequence, the school board typically finds itself balancing a variety of conflicting pressures: middle-class parents seeking better (and more costly) educational programs; school personnel seeking more money for higher salaries and better working conditions; and taxpayers' groups anxious to keep costs and taxes as low as possible.

While specifics may vary, the bargaining that characterizes education budget making is a general organizational phenomenon. *See* A. Wildavsky, *The Politics of the Budgetary Process* (1964). Two effects of the process are worth noting: (1) The give and take that characterizes decisions over dollars makes dramatic change unlikely from one year to the next, for budgetary increases or cutbacks are likely to arouse strong political opposition; (2) individuals and groups who are both outside the system and unable to wield considerable political pressure are in essence shut out of the budgetary bargaining. The historic powerlessness of these groups—notably poor and minority communities—has meant that their educational needs, translated into budget terms, are considered last, although that political pattern has changed noticeably in recent years.

Does this discussion suggest a possible explanation for the black–white resource disparities noted in both *Hobson* opinions? Does it indicate what difficulties might beset the implementation of the second *Hobson* decision?

2. Hobson I

Why did the *Hobson* court choose to examine some but not all inputs in assessing whether blacks receive fewer educational resources than do whites? Is the court tacitly assuming that these inputs affect educational outcomes, that they are perceived as important by the black community, or that taken together, they constitute the bulk of the district's school budget? Should the court distinguish between such factors as age of school buildings and teacher experience? If so, on what constitutional basis? Can any of the disparities in resources examined in *Hobson* be justified on demographic or other nondiscriminatory grounds? Would assignment of teachers by seniority constitute such a ground?

After discussing "the range of inequities" in resources provided to black and white students, the court ignores all of them except teacher inequalities. Had the court chosen to equalize distribution of each of the factors discussed in the opinion, how would it have gone about the task?

The court's examination of resource inequities is predicated on the presence of segregation. Does that fact suggest that *Plessy v. Ferguson*'s insistence on equality remains good law? Does the court's analysis apply only in situations where minority students receive fewer resources than do whites? Would the decision be the same if the district were 100 percent white? Would it if it were 100 percent black? Would it be the same if resources were randomly distributed, adversely affecting no definable group but accomplishing no educationally defensible end? Is the latter situation representative of what the court terms "the arbitrary quality of thoughtlessness"?

Donald L. Horowitz, in a book devoted to examining the role of courts in the formation of social policy, devotes a chapter to the litigation in *Hobson*. D. Horowitz, *The Courts and Social Policy* (1977). He concludes that an anticipated effect of *Hobson I*—equalization of per-pupil expenditures—did not in fact result for a number of reasons. Expenditure equalization as a by-product of the decree to relieve overcrowding east of the park and to achieve faculty integration did not occur because relatively few pupils were bused and because the attempt to integrate faculties did not involve any special effort to redistribute highly paid teachers. *Id.* at 117.

3. Hobson II: *The Court's Analysis*

(a) The *Hobson II* opinion focuses exclusively on black–white inequities in teacher expenditure. Horowitz explains this focus as partially the result of the tactics of plaintiff's counsel. Of all the inputs that could have been focused upon, for example, equalization of test scores of teachers' verbal abilities, equalization of years of experience, and so forth, Horowitz writes that in the end it was decided to focus on per-pupil expenditures as a whole because they were identified in *Hobson I* and because it was an objective measure that could be judicially enforced. Horowitz, *supra* at 121–22. The court itself on its own initiative further narrowed the issue to the equalization of inequities in expenditures for teachers. The question then becomes why. Is the court suggesting that money spent on teachers is somehow "most important"? Does educational research support this contention? Is the court's attention focused on teachers' salaries and benefits (as opposed to salaries for librarians and counselors, books, and so on) because these are the biggest items in the school budget? Horowitz reports that counsel for the school district did not object. Why do you suppose there was no objection?

(b) Once disparities in teacher salaries and pupil-staff ratios between "white" and "black" schools were demonstrated, the court placed the burden on the school district either to rebut the inference of discrimination or to offer "compelling" justification for the disparities. Given the state of knowledge about the effectiveness of various school inputs, does the placement of the burden decide the outcome? If so, is the approach constitutionally justifiable? Are there policy reasons that support the standard of review adopted by the court? *See* Hornby and Holmes, "Equalization of Resources within School Districts," 58 *Va.L.Rev.* 1119, 1143–55 (1972).

(c) The *Hobson II* court never heard the oral testimony of witnesses. Instead, an exchange of memoranda—drafted in part by social scientists representing the parties—assessed the plausibility of the school district's justifications for salary inequalities.

While the court makes ample use of this material (*see*, for example, footnotes 21 and 22), it criticizes both parties' presentations:

> The reports by the experts—one noted economist plus assistants for each side—are less helpful than they might have been for the simple reason that they do not begin from a common data base, disagree over crucial statistical assumptions, and reach different conclusions. . . . [T]he studies by both experts are tainted by a vice well known in the statistical trade—data shopping and scanning to reach a preconceived result; and the court has had to reject parts of both reports as unreliable because biased. . . . [T]he court has been forced back to its own common sense approach to a problem which, though admittedly complex, has certainly been made more obscure than was necessary. The conclusion I reach is based upon burden of proof, and upon straightforward moral and constitutional arithmetic.

327 F.Supp. at 859.

Precisely what does "straightforward moral and constitutional arithmetic" mean? Are the factual issues in *Hobson*—determining, for example, whether teacher experience improves classroom effectiveness—best resolved by adversary presentation? Would the court have been better served had it appointed its own expert? How might such an expert have resolved the methodological disputes that continue to divide economists? Do these issues bear at all on the discussion of social science evidence in the context of racial discrimination (*see* chapter 5)? For further discussion of the *Hobson* economists' debate, *see* Michelson, "For the Plaintiffs—Equal Resource Allocation," 7 *J. Human Resources* 283 (1972); O'Neil, Gray, and Horowitz, "For the Defendants—Educational Equality and Expenditure Equalization Orders," 7 *J. Human Resources* 307 (1972).

(d) In their legal memoranda to the court, plaintiffs focused on the fact that poor students had fewer teacher-dollars spent on them than did middle-class students. The *Hobson* opinion, however, adheres to the racial discrimination issue, even though over 95 percent of the Washington, D.C., student population was black at the time of the litigation. Is the court suggesting that discrimination against the poor does not raise constitutional questions analogous to those presented by discrimination against minorities? *See Dandridge v. Williams*, 397 U.S. 471, 90 S.Ct. 1153, 25 L.Ed.2d 491 (1970) (per-household ceilings on welfare grants); *James v. Valtierra*, 402 U.S. 137, 91 S.Ct. 1331, 28 L.Ed.2d 678 (1971) (referendum requirement for low-cost housing construction); *San Antonio Independent School District v. Rodriguez*, 411 U.S. 1, 93 S.Ct. 1278, 36 L.Ed.2d 16 (1973). Has the court misdescribed the facts of the case in order to reach what it regards as a desirable policy outcome, or in order to avoid appellate reversal?

4. Hobson II: *Remedy and Aftermath*

(a) The *Hobson* remedy requires expenditure equalization within 5 percent of mean expenditure. If, for example, the district spends an average of $600 per student on teachers' salaries, expenditures between $570 and $630 require no justification. What is the practical justification for this limited flexibility?

The court permits expenditure deviations greater than 5 percent with "adequate justification." Is justification limited to instances where additional help is provided on a "catch-up" basis to slow or handicapped students? Could a program for the gifted be justified to the court? Is the court converting into constitutional doctrine what philosopher John Rawls has termed "the difference principle": "All social primary goods—liberty and opportunity, income and wealth, and the bases of self-respect—are to be distributed equally unless an unequal distribution of any or all of these goods is to the advantage of the least favored." J. Rawls, A *Theory of Justice* 303 (1971).

(b) Recall that in analyzing patterns of discrimination, *Hobson* focuses on black–white disparities. Is the appropriate cure for such discrimination equalization of expenditures for black and white students? How does the court justify a remedy which also bars expenditure inequalities among schools attended exclusively by black (or white) students?

(c) The court in *McInnis v. Shapiro*, 293 F.Supp. 327, 335 (N.D. Ill. 1968), characterized an equal dollars standard as "rigid," and rejected the approach: "Expenditures are not . . . the exclusive yardstick of a child's educational needs." *See also* Kurland, "Equal Educational Opportunity: The Limits of Constitutional Jurisprudence Undefined," 35 *U.Chi. L.Rev.* 583 (1968). Is the *Hobson II* remedy subject to the same criticism? Are the differences between *Hobson* and *McInnis* analytically reconcilable?

Is it easier—as a matter of either law or policy—for a court to remedy disparities within a given school district than to remedy interdistrict disparities? Consider the following comment, contrasting the two issues:

> Since partition of the municipal budget has already occurred, the court [assessing intradistrict inequalities] need not consider the entire budgetary process. . . . Moreover, action by the court will not entail substantial interference with the political process. Most intradistrict allocation decisions are administrative in character and therefore somewhat isolated from electoral control. Finally, the protection of students from excessive discrimination would seem to be a function for which the courts have peculiar institutional competence.

Schoettle, "The Equal Protection Clause in Public Education," 71 *Colum.L.Rev.* 1355, 1412 (1971).

(d) The Washington, D.C., school system was sharply divided over *Hobson*. The school board president, Anita F. Allen, noted: "I am very much disappointed—and astounded—that the judge expects us to move teachers wholesale. I think people, both black and white, will question the wisdom of moving teachers because they are either too old or too young for a particular school building." Yet ten days later, the board of education voted eight to one not to appeal the ruling. "Wholesale" teacher transfer is indeed one way of complying with the equalization order; are there fiscally feasible alternatives?

(e) Donald Horowitz notes that during the course of *Hobson II*, the equalization issue got progressively narrower so

> that what began as an effort to equalize all resources ended in a decree equalizing only per-pupil expenditures on teachers' salaries. . . . As soon as the decree was issued, a similar process of narrowing the options for implementing it was set in motion. . . . The result of the forces that operated was to dictate implementation of the decree by one method only—transferring teachers—and later almost entirely by transferring special-subject or resource teachers.

D. Horowitz, *The Courts and Social Policy* 146 (1977).

This tactic was hit upon as the only available alternative after rejecting the idea of moving students (by mandatory busing) and deciding to move as few teachers as possible. The most easily moved teachers were the special subject teachers because of union rules, less resistance from principals, and the ease of finding funds to compensate losses in special programs. *Id.* at 148–49. The result of the school's policy of transferring special subject teachers was to break the significant negative correlation between school size and the ratio of resource teachers to pupils: now resource teachers were distributed more equitably. The additional effect was to change the ratio from 1:200 to 1:500 between 1971 and 1974 in schools attended predominantly by disadvantaged pupils. Thus, the implementation of *Hobson II* had the perverse effect of hurting the schools of the disadvantaged. *Id.* at 152–53. The apparent reason for this perverse result was that in order to maintain compliance with *Hobson II* as enrollments dropped in many schools, the district shifted away resource teachers.

5. Hobson II *and* Rodriguez: Washington v. Davis

Hobson I and *II* were decided prior to *San Antonio Independent School District v. Rodriguez*, which is a relevant precedent since *Hobson II* was based on the U.S. Constitution. Are *Hobson I* and *Hobson II* still good law after *Rodriguez?* After the Supreme Court's decision in *Washington v. Davis*, discussed in chapter 5?

In *Brown v. Board of Education, Chicago*, 386 F.Supp. 110 (N.D. Ill. 1974), inequalities in the distribution of resources within the city of Chicago were challenged on wealth and race discrimination grounds. As to the wealth discrimination claim, the court concluded that *Rodriguez* required the plaintiffs to establish—in order to trigger the use of strict scrutiny—that a group of poor persons whose incomes fell below some identifiable level of poverty were absolutely deprived of a minimally adequate education. Since the plaintiffs had failed to establish these two points, inequalities in per-pupil staffing expenditures had to be assessed in light of the rational basis standard of review pursuant to which the court concluded the existing inequalities were justifiable. ". . . [A]dministrative convenience, sudden unexpected demographic changes, and response to the special educational need of certain neighborhoods serve as sufficient justification for the Board's policies." 386 F.Supp. at 123.

As for the racial discrimination claim, the court concluded that the plaintiff's data were sufficient to establish a *prima facie* case of discrimination, but, in this pre-*Washington v. Davis* decision, the court did not use a standard that required the plaintiff to prove intent or motive. Despite the finding of racial discrimination, the court did not issue an injunction since the school board had convinced the court that it had undertaken a series of programs to correct the funding disparities between black and white schools.

Brown is the only intradistrict disparity decision since *Rodriguez*. Why are so few intradistrict disparity suits brought while interdistrict disparity decisions continue to be handed down with some frequency?

V. THE RIGHT TO A "FREE" PUBLIC EDUCATION

A. Introduction

Almost every state constitution has an express provision guaranteeing a free public education although, as noted earlier in this chapter, the specific constitutional language varies among the states. Moreover, education is compulsory up to a certain age in every state. (See chapter 1). What does it mean to have a right to a free public education? Can school districts charge tuition, or fees for textbooks, supplies and materials, particular courses, lab equipment, towels and lockers, transcripts, etc.? What about transportation fees for children who are compelled to attend school but who are too far from any school to be able to get there on their own? Are these user fees permissible under the "free" public education mandated by state constitutions? Even if such fees are not part of the constitutionally mandated free public education, is it a violation of the Equal Protection Clause if indigent children are unable to participate either wholly or less beneficially because of inability to pay the fees? This section will explore some of these issues, which raise questions not only concerning what is a "free" education, but also what is integral to that education that must be provided free of charge, and whether the state can make education compulsory without providing equality of access to that education.

B. The School Fees Cases

The issue of school fees has been addressed by state courts for over a century. *See Irvin v. Gregory*, 86 Ga. 605, 13 S.E. 120 (1891) (incidental fees of $5 to $10 per year were unconstitutional if children could be excluded from attending public school if *unwilling* as well as unable to pay the fee). The majority of older cases invalidated tuition fees, relying on the state constitutional provisions providing for free schools. *See, e.g., Special School District v. Bangs*, 144 Ark. 34, 221 S.W. 1060 (1920); *State ex rel. Roberts v. Wilson*, 221 Mo.App. 9, 297 S.W. 419 (1927); *Batty v. Board of Education*, 67 N.D. 6, 269 N.W. 49 (1936). *Cf. Plyler v. Doe*, 457 U.S. 202, 102 S.Ct. 2382, 72 L.Ed.2d 786 (1982).

More recent cases fall into two categories: textbook fees or fees for particular materials, courses, and activities.

Textbook fees. More than half the recent cases challenging textbook fees have been unsuccessful. *See, e.g., Marshall v. School District No. 3, Morgan Co.*, 191 Colo. 451, 553 P.2d 784 (1976); *Carpio v. Tucson High School District*, 111 Ariz. 127, 524 P.2d 948 (1974), *cert. den.*, 420 U.S. 982, 95 S.Ct. 1412, 43 L.Ed.2d 664 (1975). But, with the exception of Arizona, *see Carpio, supra*, all of the states where textbook fees were upheld had some procedure for providing texts free of charge to children of indigent parents. In *Carpio*, however, the Arizona Supreme Court held that the failure of the state to provide free textbooks to high school children had a rational basis. "It is within the Legislature's discretion to say what the limits of a free education should be beyond the minimum set forth in the Arizona Constitution." 111 Ariz. at 130, 513 P.2d at 951.

In a substantial number of cases, however, textbook fees have been invalidated. *See, e.g., Paulson v. Minidoka County School District*, 93 Idaho 469, 463 P.2d 935 (1970) (books are necessary and therefore must be free); *Bond v. Public Schools of Ann Arbor School District*, 383 Mich. 693, 178 N.W.2d 484 (1970) (books must be free either under the "necessary element of any school's activity" or the "integral fundamental part of the elementary and secondary education" test); *Cardiff v. Bismarck Public School District*, 263 N.W.2d 105 (N.D. 1978) (constitutional provision mandating "free public schools" does not mean merely "free from tuition" but also includes textbooks).

Fees for materials, courses, and activities. These cases fall into three categories: (1) "reasonable" fees are upheld, even for required courses; (2) fees for required courses or necessary items are barred, but fees for supplemental or extracurricular courses or activities are upheld; and (3) even fees for extracurricular activities violate the free public education guarantee of the state constitution. Many of these cases, at least those in the latter two categories, turn on whether the particular course or activity is deemed part of the "education" that is guaranteed or is supplemental. Other cases turn on what is meant by "free" education.

In many of the cases that upheld instructional and course fees for required as well as elective courses, the courts ruled that the constitutional mandate to provide "free public schools" meant "without tuition," which is satisfied as long as public funds are used to provide the school building and staff salaries necessary for a basic system of public education. *See, e.g., Sneed v. Greensboro City Board of Education*, 299 N.C. 609, 264 S.E.2d 106 (1980).

Those cases that struck down fees for required courses or "necessary" items, but permitted the charging of fees for supplemental courses or extracurricular activities, viewed the constitutional requirement of free public schools as including "necessary" elements of a school's activity, *Paulson v. Minidoka County School District*, 93 Idaho 469, 463 P.2d 935 (1970), or even including any fees in connection with courses for which academic credit is given, *Concerned Parents v. Caruthersville School District*, 548 S.W.2d 554 (Mo. 1977). Some courts state that no fees may be charged for any course or activity reasonably related to the academic and educational goals of a particular system. Thus, a New Jersey court has held that driver's education is an essential part of the constitutionally mandated "thorough and efficient" education but that "behind-wheel training" was not essential and therefore could be subject to a fee. *Parsippany-Troy Hills Education Association v. Board of Education*, 188 N.J. Super. 161, 457 A.2d 15 (1983).

Those courts that have struck down fees for extracurricular activities have extended the guarantee of free schooling to cover even interscholastic athletics when thought to be an integral part of the total education process. *Bond v. Public Schools of Ann Arbor School District*, 383 Mich. 693, 178 N.W.2d 484 (1970).

The policy arguments on both sides of the issue have been stated as follows:

> The use of fees relieves the burden on taxpayers and allows the school to purchase and uniformly provide items so all students have the proper type of material at the time it is needed. Fees allow schools to offer specialized activities to those who are interested when they might not feel justified in expenditures for a small number of students. Fees may give individual parents a sense of responsibility by providing certain incidental needs for their children rather than depending upon the community.
>
> But fees cause a hardship, especially on poorer families. They are a problem for teachers, sponsors, and school secretaries to collect and handle. They result in less participation in activities.

Note, "Student Fees in Public School: New Statutory Authority, 16 *Washburn L.J.* 439, 440 n. 8 (1977).

C. The Supreme Court and Access to a Minimal Level of Education Revisited

In *San Antonio Independent School District v. Rodriguez*, 411 U.S. 1, 93 S.Ct. 1278, 36 L.Ed.2d 16 (1973), the majority indicated that some minimal level of adequate education might be required under the Fourteenth Amendment. *Id.* at 36–37. *See* Levin, "The Courts, Congress, and Educational Adequacy: The Equal Protection Predicament," 39 *Md.L.Rev.* 187 (1979). *Plyler v. Doe*, 457 U.S. 202, 102 S.Ct. 2382, 72 L.Ed.2d 786 (1982), gave a heightened equal protection scrutiny to the "important" interest in education when the class denied access to an education by being singled out for tuition charges was comprised of undocumented alien children. For children who live too far from their school to get there on their own, should the failure to provide transportation or the charging of user fees for transportation, effectively denying access to education for those unwilling or unable to pay the fee, be similarly treated?

Kadrmas v. Dickinson Public Schools

487 U.S. 450, 108 S.Ct. 2481, 101 L.Ed.2d 399 (1988).

O'Connor, J.

[Under North Dakota law, the school board of any school district that had not been reorganized could charge a fee for bus service. Reorganized school districts, however, may not permit a charge for bus transportation, so that in those districts, all students who ride the bus do so for free. Of the 310 school districts in North Dakota, only eight—primarily the larger school districts—had not reorganized. The Dickinson School District was one of those eight. Thus, only those eight districts are permitted to charge a fee for busing.

Sarita Kadrmas lived with her family about sixteen miles from the elementary school she attended. The Kadrmas family is at or near "the officially defined poverty level." Unable to pay the fee, as well as their other bills, the family refused to sign a contract obligating them to pay the user fee for school bus service—$97—for the 1985 school year. Since the school bus no longer picked up Sarita, the family arranged to transport her to school privately. The North Dakota Supreme Court concluded that the fees authorized by statute are "rationally related to the legitimate governmental objective of allocating limited resources and that the statute does not discriminate on the basis of wealth so as to violate federal or state equal protection rights." 402 N.W.2d 897, 903 (N.D. 1987).]

* * *

Unless a statute provokes "strict judicial scrutiny" because it interferes with a "fundamental right" or discriminates against a "suspect class," it will ordinarily survive an equal protection attack so long as the challenged classification is rationally related to a legitimate governmental purpose. See, *e.g.*, *San Antonio School Dist. v. Rodriguez*, 411 U.S. 1, 16–17, 93 S.Ct. 1278, 1287–1288, 36 L.Ed.2d 16 (1973); *Plyler v. Doe*, 457 U.S. 202, 216–217, . . . (1982). . . . Appellants contend that Dickinson's user fee for bus service unconstitutionally deprives those who cannot afford to pay it of "minimum access to education." . . . Sarita Kadrmas, however, continued to attend school during the time that she was denied access to the school bus. Appellants must therefore mean to argue that the busing fee unconstitutionally places a greater obstacle to education in the path of the poor than it does in the path of wealthier families. Alternatively, appellants may mean to suggest that the Equal Protection Clause affirmatively requires government to provide free transportation to school, at least for some class of students that would include Sarita Kadrmas. Under either interpretation of appellants' position, we are evidently being urged to apply a form of strict or "heightened" scrutiny to the North Dakota statute. Doing so would require us to extend the requirements of the Equal Protection Clause beyond the limits recognized in our cases, a step we decline to take.

We have previously rejected the suggestion that statutes having different effects on the wealthy and the poor should on that account alone be subjected to strict equal protection scrutiny. . . . Nor have we accepted the proposition that education is a "fundamental right," like equality of the franchise, which should trigger strict scrutiny when government interferes with an individual's access to it. . . .

Relying primarily on *Plyler v. Doe*, *supra*, however, appellants suggest that North Dakota's 1979 statute should be subjected to "heightened" scrutiny. This standard of review, which is less demanding than "strict scrutiny" but more demanding than the standard rational relation test, has generally been applied only in cases that involved discriminatory classifications based on sex or illegitimacy. . . . In *Plyler*, which did not fit this pattern, the State of Texas had denied to the children of illegal aliens the free public education that it made available to other residents. Applying a heightened level of equal protection scrutiny, the Court concluded that the State had failed to show that its classification advanced a substantial state interest. 457 U.S., at 217–218, and n. 16, 224, 230, 102 S.Ct., at 2395, and n. 16, 2398, 2401–02. We have not extended this holding beyond the "unique circumstances," *id.*, at 239, 102 S.Ct., at 2406 (Powell, J., concurring), that provoked its "unique confluence of theories and rationales," *id.*, at 243, 102 S.Ct., at 2408–09 (Burger, C. J., dissenting). Nor do we think that the case before us today is governed by the holding in *Plyler*. Unlike the children in that case, Sarita Kadrmas has not been penalized by the government for illegal conduct by her parents. . . . On the contrary, Sarita was denied access to the school bus only because her parents would not agree to pay the same user fee charged to all other families that took advantage of the service. Nor do we see any reason to suppose that this user fee will "promot[e] the creation and perpetuation of a sub-class of illiterates within our boundaries, surely adding to the problems and costs of unemployment, welfare, and crime." *Id.*, at 230, . . . The case before us does not resemble *Plyler*, and we decline to extend the rationale of that decision to cover this case.

Appellants contend, finally, that whatever label is placed on the standard of review, this case is analogous to decisions in which we have held that government may not withhold certain especially important services from those who are unable to pay for them. . . .

[Cases such as *Griffin v. Illinois*, 351 U.S. 12 (1956) (right to appellate review of a criminal conviction conditioned on the purchase of a trial transcript) are distinguishable from the one before us today, as] each involved a rule that barred indigent litigants from using the judicial process in circumstances where they had no alternative to that process. Decisions invalidating such rules are inapposite here.

In contrast to the "utter exclusiveness of court access and court remedy," *United States v. Kras*, 409 U.S. 434, 445, 93 S.Ct. 631, 638, 34 L.Ed.2d 626 (1973), North Dakota does not maintain a legal or a practical monopoly on the means of transporting children to school. Thus, unlike the complaining parties in all the cases cited by appellants, the Kadrmas family could and did find a private alternative to the public school bus service for which Dickinson charged a fee. That alternative was more expensive, to be sure, and we have no reason to doubt that genuine hardships were endured by the Kadrmas family when Sarita was denied access to the bus. Such facts, however, do not imply that the Equal Protection Clause has been violated. . . .

Applying the appropriate test—under which a statute is upheld if it bears a rational relation to a legitimate government objective—we think it is quite clear that a State's decision to allow local school boards the option of charging patrons a user fee for bus service is constitutionally permissible. The Constitution does not require that such service be provided at all, and it is difficult to imagine why choosing to offer the service should entail a constitutional obligation to offer it for free. No one denies that encouraging local school districts to provide school bus service is a legitimate state purpose or that such encouragement would be undermined by a rule requiring that general revenues be used to subsidize an optional service that will benefit a minority of the district's families. It is manifestly rational for the State to refrain from undermining its legitimate objective with such a rule.

* * *

In sum, the statute challenged in this case discriminates against no suspect class and interferes with no fundamental right. Appellants have failed to carry the heavy burden of demonstrating that the statute is arbitrary and irrational. The Supreme Court of North Dakota correctly concluded that the statute does not violate the Equal Protection Clause of the Fourteenth Amendment, and its judgment is

Affirmed.

Justice Marshall, with whom Justice Brennan joins, dissenting.

In *San Antonio Independent School Dist. v. Rodriguez*, 411 U.S. 1, 93 S.Ct. 1278, 36 L.Ed.2d 16 (1973), I wrote that the Court's holding was a "retreat from our historic commitment to equality of educational opportunity and [an] unsupportable acquiescence in a system which deprives children in their earliest years of the chance to reach their full potential." *Id.*, at 71, 93 S.Ct., at 1316 (Marshall, J., dissenting). Today, the Court continues the retreat from the promise of equal educational opportunity by holding that a school district's refusal to allow an indigent child who lives 16 miles from the nearest school to use a schoolbus service without paying a fee does not violate the Fourteenth Amendment's Equal Protection Clause. Because I do not believe that this Court should sanction discrimination against the poor with respect to "perhaps the most important function of state and local governments," *Brown v. Board of Education*, 347 U.S. 483, 493, 74 S.Ct. 686, 691, 98 L.Ed. 873 (1954), I dissent.

The Court's opinion suggests that this case does not concern state action that discriminates against the poor with regard to the provision of a basic education. The Court notes that the particular governmental action challenged in this case involves the provision of transportation, rather than the provision of educational services. See *ante*, at 2488. Moreover, the Court stresses that the denial of transportation to Sarita Kadrmas did not in fact prevent her from receiving an education; notwithstanding the denial of bus service, Sarita's family ensured that she attended school each day. See *ante*, at 2487, 2488.[1] . . . This case involves state action that places a special burden on poor families in their pursuit of education. Children living far from school can receive a public education only if they have access to transportation; as the state court noted in this case, "a child must reach the schoolhouse door as a prerequisite to receiving the educational opportunity offered therein." 402 N.W.2d 897, 901 (N.D. 1987). Indeed, for children in Sarita's position, imposing a fee for transportation is no different in practical effect from imposing a fee directly for education. Moreover, the fee involved in this case discriminated against Sarita's family because it necessarily fell more heavily upon the poor than upon wealthier members

1. The Court therefore does not address the question whether a State constitutionally could deny a child access to a minimally adequate education. In prior cases, this Court explicitly has left open the question whether such a deprivation of access would violate a fundamental constitutional right. See *Papasan v. Allain*, 478 U.S. 265, 289, 106 S.Ct. 2932, 2946, 92 L.Ed.2d 209 (1986); *San Antonio Independent School Dist. v. Rodriguez*, 411 U.S. 1, 25, n. 60, 36–37, 93 S.Ct. 1278, 1292, n. 60, 1298–99, 36 L.Ed.2d 16 (1973). That question remains open today.

of the community. . . . This case therefore presents the question whether a State may discriminate against the poor in providing access to education. I regard this question as one of great urgency.

* * *

The North Dakota statute discriminates on the basis of economic status. This Court has determined that classifications based on wealth are not automatically suspect. See, *e.g.*, *Maher v. Roe*, 432 U.S. 464, 470–471, 97 S.Ct. 2376, 2980–81, 53 L.Ed.2d 484 (1977). Such classifications, however, have a measure of special constitutional significance. . . . The Court has proved most likely to take such action when the laws in question interfered with the access of the poor to the political and judicial processes. One source of these decisions, in my view, is a deep distrust of policies that specially burden the access of disadvantaged persons to the governmental institutions and processes that offer members of our society an opportunity to improve their status and better their lives. The intent of the Fourteenth Amendment was to abolish caste legislation. See *Plyler v. Doe*, 457 U.S. 202, 213, 102 S.Ct. 2382, 2392, 72 L.Ed.2d 786 (1982). When state action has the predictable tendency to entrap the poor and create a permanent underclass, that intent is frustrated. See *id.*, at 234, 102 S.Ct., at 2403 (Blackmun, J., concurring). Thus, to the extent that a law places discriminatory barriers between indigents and the basic tools and opportunities that might enable them to rise, exacting scrutiny should be applied.

The statute at issue here burdens a poor person's interest in an education. The extraordinary nature of this interest cannot be denied. . . . A statute that erects special obstacles to education in the path of the poor naturally tends to consign such persons to their current disadvantaged status. By denying equal opportunity to exactly those who need it most, the law not only militates against the ability of each poor child to advance herself, but also increases the likelihood of the creation of a discrete and permanent underclass. Such a statute is difficult to reconcile with the framework of equality embodied in the Equal Protection Clause.

This Court's decision in *Plyler v. Doe*, *supra*, supports these propositions. The Court in *Plyler* upheld the right of the children of illegal aliens to receive the free public education that the State of Texas made available to other residents. The Court in that case engaged in some discussion of alienage, a classification not relevant here. The decision, however, did not rest upon this basis. Rather, the Court made clear that the infirmity of the Texas law stemmed from its differential treatment of a discrete and disadvantaged group of children with respect to the provision of education. The Court stated that education is not "merely some governmental 'benefit' indistinguishable from other forms of social welfare legislation." 457 U.S., at 221, 102 S.Ct., at 2396. The Court further commented that the state law "poses an affront to one of the goals of the Equal Protection Clause: the abolition of governmental barriers presenting unreasonable obstacles to advancement on the basis of individual merit." *Id.*, at 221–222, 102 S.Ct., at 2397. Finally, the Court called attention to the tendency of the Texas law to create a distinct underclass of impoverished illiterates who would be unable to participate in and contribute to society. See *id.*, at 222–224, 102 S.Ct., at 2397–98. The *Plyler* Court's reasoning is fully applicable here. As in *Plyler*, the State in this case has acted to burden the educational opportunities of a disadvantaged group of children, who need an education to become full participants in society.

The State's rationale for this policy is based entirely on fiscal considerations. The State has allowed Dickinson and certain other school districts to charge a nonwaivable flat fee for bus service so that these districts may recoup part of the costs of the service. The money that Dickinson collects from applying the busing fee to indigent families, however, represents a minuscule proportion of the costs of the bus service. As the Court notes, *ante*, at 2485, all of the fees collected by Dickinson amount to only 11% of the cost of providing the bus service, and the fees collected from poor families represent a small fraction of the total fees. Exempting indigent families from the busing fee therefore would not require Dickinson to make any significant adjustments in either the operation or the funding of the bus service. Indeed, as the Court states, most school districts in the State provide full bus service without charging any fees at all. See *ante*, at 2490. The state interest involved in this case is therefore insubstantial; it does not begin to justify the discrimination challenged here.

* * *

. . . For the poor, education is often the only route by which to become full participants in our society. In allowing a State to burden the access of poor persons to an education, the Court denies equal opportunity and discourages hope. I do not believe the Equal Protection Clause countenances such a result. I therefore dissent.

[Dissenting opinion by Stevens, J., in which Blackmun, J. joined, omitted]

NOTES AND QUESTIONS

1. The Kadrmas *Decision*

The Supreme Court in *Plyler v. Doe* stated that although "public education is not a 'right' granted to individuals by the constitution . . . neither is it merely some governmental 'benefit' indistinguishable from other forms of social welfare legislation." 457 U.S. 202, 221, 102 S.Ct. 2382, 2396, 72 L.Ed.2d 786 (1982). In that case, the Court applied a heightened level of scrutiny, because education is an important, albeit not fundamental, interest. Are not indigent children who cannot pay for transportation to school deprived of minimum access to education just as much as were the undocumented alien children in *Plyler*? Is *Kadrmas* about the right to free transportation as part of the obligation to provide free public schooling—that is, is getting *to* the school an integral part of the education the state is mandated to provide for free? Or is this case an equal access to education case—that is, a case involving discrimination on the basis of wealth? Would the result have been different if Sarita Kadrmas had not had alternate means of transportation and thus had been denied access to an education because of inability to pay the busing fee? Or is it that the Court interpreted that the interest was in busing rather than in education and thus not sufficiently important to trigger heightened judicial review? What if a school district required students to buy their own pencils and some children were too poor to do so?

Are the injured plaintiffs in *Plyler*—children of undocumented aliens who are not responsible for their status—a class deserving of greater protection than indigent children? But are children of indigent parents any more responsible for their status than the undocumented alien children in *Plyler*, or illegitimate children, to whom the heightened level of scrutiny has also been applied? *See, e.g.*, *Trimble v. Gordon*, 430 U.S. 762, 97 S.Ct. 1459, 52 L.Ed.2d 31 (1977). In the cases involving illegitimate children, the identification of a burdened class alone, without the presence of an important interest, has been sufficient to trigger heightened scrutiny.

The Court determined that the rational basis test was the appropriate test. Is conditioning access to a basic public education on the payment of user fees a rational nondiscriminatory means of conserving resources? Does it make the user fee more or less rational that schooling is compulsory and the parents of Sarita, if they did not find alternative means of transportation to get her to the school, could have been prosecuted for violating the compulsory school law?

Education has been held to be a fundamental right under the North Dakota state constitution. *In the Interest of G.H.*, 218 N.W.2d 441 (N.D. 1974). Should that have produced a different result in the North Dakota state supreme court under a state equal protection clause analysis?

2. **Plyler *after* Kadrmas**

Following *Kadrmas*, has *Plyler* been limited to the "unique circumstances" of that case? Under the North Dakota statute, the Kadrmas family could have requested that the school board waive the fee, so that there was an opportunity for indigents to be bused to school without having to pay. *See* Biegel, "Reassessing the Applicability of Fundamental Rights Analysis: the Fourteenth Amendment and the Shaping of Educational Policy after *Kadrmas v. Dickinson Public Schools*," 74 *Corn.L.Rev.* 1078 (1989), arguing that the Court should have applied the intermediate level of scrutiny in *Kadrmas*, and that with a stronger case, the Supreme Court may yet apply *Plyler* and recognize "the existence of intermediate judicial review in an education context." *Id.* at 1099.

SEVEN

Equal Educational Opportunity and Excellence: The Evolving Federal Role

I. THE FEDERAL ROLE IN EDUCATIONAL POLICYMAKING

A. Introduction

During the past quarter century, education law has undergone three noteworthy transformations: legalization, centralization (with accompanying regulation), and, most recently, a degree of decentralization (with some accompanying deregulation). Much of this book has been devoted to an examination of the first transformation, the increased involvement of the federal judiciary in matters historically considered policy issues that have traditionally been the domain of politicians and educators, not judges; matters that had been viewed as discretionary, not implicating legal rights. As a result of this transformation, a rather barren field, which had concerned itself with such matters as the liability of school districts for accidents to students, has been made over into a new area of law, which touches on virtually all questions of educational policy significance to educational policy. During this first transformation, which extends roughly from *Brown* to *Rodriguez*, educational policymaking was constitutionalized.

If the first transformation involves the constitutionalization of educational policy in realms as diverse as the distribution of resources and the treatment of student discipline, the second involves an increased reliance on political processes, culminating in the elaboration of statutorily based rights. Beginning with the passage of the 1964 Civil Rights Act, the legislative and executive branches of the federal government assumed a more activist role in defining and legislating educational rights. Aggrieved groups, that in the recent past had gone to court, obtained through legislation much of—and in some instances more than—what they sought through litigation. The claims of racial minorities and women, as well as those of the handicapped, the limited-English-proficient, Native Americans, migrants, and the educationally disadvantaged, have to some extent been honored by the federal government. The creation, in 1979, of a Department of Education was meant at the time to signal a more aggressive federal role. Courts have played a part in this process, but it is a secondary part that involves delineating and enforcing rights created by the other branches of government.

This federal activism on behalf of the disadvantaged was substantially slowed with the 1980 election of Ronald Reagan. *See* Meyer, "Social Programs and Social Policy," J. Palmer, ed., *Perspectives on the Reagan Years* 88 (1986). President Reagan broke with every president since Truman by proposing to decentralize education and reduce federal involvement. *See* T. Bell, *The Thirteenth Man: A Reagan Cabinet Memoir* (1988); Pincus, "From Equity to Excellence: The Rebirth of Educational Conservatism," *Social Policy* 50 (Winter 1984); Verstegen and Clark, "The Diminution in Federal Expenditures for Education During the Reagan Administration," 70 *Phi Delta Kappan* 134 (Oct. 1988); Birman &

Ginsburg, "The Federal Role in Elementary and Secondary Education: New Directions and Continuing Concerns," 14 *Urban Lawyer* 471 (Summer 1982).

Numbers tell part of the story. Between 1980 and 1988, federal outlays for the Department of Education decreased as a percentage of the gross national product from .6 percent to .4 percent; funding for the department as a percentage of the federal budget declined from 2.5 percent to 1.8 percent. And the federal share of all primary and secondary educational expenditures dropped from 8.7 percent to 6.2 percent.

Key equal opportunity programs for the handicapped, the limited English-proficient, and the educationally disadvantaged remained intact. They escaped the 1981 consolidation of forty-three separate programs—among them, the grants under the Emergency School Aid Act for problems of desegregation—into a single block grant. But these programs suffered cuts, ranging from 6 percent to 54 percent, between 1980 and 1988. The block grant, which was meant to support state and local school improvement efforts, was cut 76 percent. And these budget levels were substantially higher than the budgets proposed by President Reagan.

This pattern of federal withdrawal from redistributive education policy may change again. During the 1989 educational summit, President George Bush acknowledged something his predecessor would never have accepted: that the federal government has a key—if unspecified—role in financing educational programs that help poor children, minorities, and the handicapped. It remains to be seen whether this signals a renascence of interest in the idea of equal educational opportunity as federal policy, whether dollars will accompany general commitments, and how the equal opportunity principle will be administered.

Equal opportunity was the critical principle during the expansionist era, with Washington attending to the claims of various disadvantaged groups. Court decisions afforded new legitimacy to particular equity-based concerns that were then pressed in Congress (and state legislatures) and thus provided an impetus for an essentially political solution. This dynamic interaction did not cease with legislative assumption of responsibility. These statutes require judicial interpretation; courts are called upon to interpret administrative regulations and assess the fit between regulation and statute. *See generally* D. Kirp and D. Jensen, eds., *School Days, Rule Days: The Legalization and Regulation of American Education* (1986).

But the substantive focus of educational policy has shifted since 1980, with excellence replacing equal opportunity as the dominant concern. *See* chapter 4. The concluding section of the chapter addresses this issue. For the present, what merits mention is that excellence, unlike equal opportunity, is a concept inherently resistant to legalization. It does not readily translate into rights, but instead reflects a "morality of aspiration." *See* L. Fuller, *The Morality of Law* (1962).

These shifts—from court to legislature (and, sometimes, back again)—necessarily imply new roles for lawyers and educators. Lawyers cannot be content with simply pursuing legal grievances in the courts: The classes they represent might be better served by legislation or administrative orders than by a court decision. Further, the issues lawyers are asked to address require more than technical legal competence. Law has also to become part of educators' policy-shaping calculus, because law affects what they do. This implies the use of law in preventive fashion to forestall entanglements with the courts or administrative agencies. It also implies using the law creatively, as an instrument of sound policy. These considerations make the extent of the federal role especially relevant to both lawyers and educators.

This chapter looks at the *life cycle* of an equity claim, from its *initiation*, through its incorporation into legislatively guaranteed *entitlement*, to its *implementation*. It also considers the legal dimensions of the educational excellence agenda. With respect to most of the issues addressed in this casebook—the free speech rights of students, the equitable distribution of resources within school districts, the evenhanded treatment of blacks and whites—lawmakers announce rights but cannot guarantee their implementation. This is true whether the lawmaker is a court, a legislature, or an administrative agency. The extent to which rights are implemented depends on myriad factors, among them the nature of the right, the sources of support and opposition, the normative commitment of lawmakers and implementors, and the sanctions for nonimplementation.

Lawyers have routinely presumed that the law operates in conformity with what the lawmakers say it is. This positivist view of the law in action is empirically wrong. "Illegal" behavior occurs in education as elsewhere. To the extent that lawyers have turned their attention to this reality, they have assumed that the social order should be brought into line with the legal edict by maximizing compliance with the law. Yet compliance may not be achievable, given the complexity of implementation. Further, it can be argued that compliance is not always desirable because it introduces undue rigidities; better, it is said, to look at the degree of sensible change in policy and practice attributable to the legal initiative. Such a perspective is foreign to the lawyer, who might well respond that good policy is for the lawmaker, not the implementor, to determine. These tensions—between law as conceived and law as implemented and between compliance and policy change—are noted throughout this chapter.

For further general reading on these issues, *see* Kirp and Jensen, *supra;* Kirp, "Law, Politics, and Equal Educational Opportunity: The Limits of Judicial Involvement," 47 *Harv. Educ. Rev.* 117 (1977) (on legislative-judicial interplay); Chayes, "The Role of the Judge in Public Law Litigation," 89 *Harv. L. Rev.* 1281 (1976) (taking a positive view of the new judicial role); D. Horowitz, *The Courts and Social Policy* (1977) (criticizing this new role); E. Bardach, *The Implementation Game* (1977) (discussing implementation issues, particularly in the legislative context); Cohen, "Policy and Organization: The Impact of State and Federal Educational Policy on School Governance," 52 *Harv. Educ. Rev.* 474 (1982); T. Becker and M. Feeley, eds., *The Impact of Supreme Court Decisions* 2d ed. (1973) (a look at compliance with judicial decisions).

B. From Constitutional to Statutory Entitlement: An Illustrative Example

Lau v. Nichols

414 U.S. 563, 94 S.Ct. 786, 39 L.Ed.2d 1 (1974).

Mr. Justice Douglas delivered the opinion of the Court.

* * *

This class suit brought by non-English speaking Chinese students[1] against officials responsible for the operation of the San Francisco Unified School District seeks relief against the unequal educational opportunities which are alleged to violate the Fourteenth Amendment. No specific remedy is urged upon us. Teaching English to the students of Chinese ancestry who do not speak the language is one choice. Giving instructions to this group in Chinese is another. There may be others. Petitioner asks only that the Board of Education be directed to apply its expertise to the problem and rectify the situation.

The District Court denied relief. The Court of Appeals affirmed, holding that there was no violation of the Equal Protection Clause of the Fourteenth Amendment nor of § 601 of the Civil Rights Act of 1964, which excludes from participation in federal financial assistance, recipients of aid which discriminate against racial groups. . . .

The Court of Appeals reasoned that "every student brings to the starting line of his educational career different advantages and disadvantages caused in part by social, economic and cultural background, created and continued completely apart from any contribution by the school system." 483 F.2d, at 797. Yet in our view the case may not be so easily decided. . . .

We do not reach the Equal Protection Clause argument which has been advanced but rely solely on § 601 of the Civil Rights Act of 1964, 42 U.S.C. § 2000d, to reverse the Court of Appeals.

That section bans discrimination based "on the ground of race, color, or national origin," in "any program or activity receiving Federal financial assistance." The school district involved in this litigation receives large amounts of federal financial assistance. HEW, which has authority to promulgate regulations prohibiting discrimination in federally assisted school systems, 42 U.S.C. § 2000d, in 1968 issued one guideline that "school systems are responsible for assuring that students of a particular race, color, or national origin are not denied the opportunity to obtain the education generally obtained by other students in the system." 33 CFR

1. A report adopted by the Human Rights Commission of San Francisco and submitted to the Court by respondent after oral argument shows that, as of April 1973, there were 3,457 Chinese students in the school system who spoke little or no English. The document further showed 2,136 students enrolled in Chinese special instruction classes, but at least 429 of the enrollees were not Chinese but were included for ethnic balance. Thus, as of April 1973, no more than 1,707 of the 3,457 Chinese students needing special English instruction were receiving it.

§ 4955. In 1970 HEW made the guidelines more specific, requiring school districts that were federally funded "to rectify the language deficiency in order to open" the instruction to students who had "linguistic deficiencies," 35 Fed. Reg. 11595.

By § 602 of the Act HEW is authorized to issue rules, regulations, and orders to make sure that recipients of federal aid under its jurisdiction conduct any federally financed projects consistently with § 601. HEW's regulations specify, 45 CFR § 80.3(b)(1), that the recipients may not:

> "Provide any service, financial aid, or other benefit to an individual which is different, or is provided in a different manner, from that provided to others under the program;
>
> * * *
>
> "Restrict an individual in any way in the enjoyment of any advantage or privilege enjoyed by others receiving any service, financial aid, or other benefit under the program;"
>
> Discrimination among students on account of race or national origin that is prohibited includes "discrimination in the availability or use of any academic . . . or other facilities of the grantee or other recipient."

Discrimination is barred which has that *effect* even though no purposeful design is present: a recipient "may not . . . utilize criteria or methods of administration which have the effect of subjecting individuals to discrimination" or has "the effect of defeating or substantially impairing accomplishment of the objectives of the program as respects individuals of a particular race, color, or national origin." *Id.*, 80.3(b)(2).

It seems obvious that the Chinese-speaking minority receives less benefits than the English-speaking majority from respondents' school system which denies them a meaningful opportunity to participate in the educational program—all earmarks of the discrimination banned by the Regulations. In 1970 HEW issued clarifying guidelines (35 Fed. Reg. 11595) which include the following:

"Where inability to speak and understand the English language excludes national origin-minority group children from effective participation in the educational program offered by a school district, the district must take affirmative steps to rectify the language deficiency in order to open its instructional program to these students." . . .

Respondent school district contractually agreed to "comply with title VI of the Civil Rights Act of 1964 . . . and all requirements imposed by or pursuant to the Regulations" of HEW (45 CFR Pt. 80) which are "issued pursuant to that title . . ." and also immediately to "take any measures necessary to effectuate this agreement." The Federal Government has power to fix the terms on which its money allotments to the States shall be disbursed. . . .

We accordingly reverse the judgment of the Court of Appeals and remand the case for the fashioning of appropriate relief.

Reversed. . . .

Mr. Justice Blackmun, with whom the Chief Justice joins, concurring in the result. . . .

. . . I stress the fact that the children with whom we are concerned here number about 1800. This is a very substantial group that is being deprived of any meaningful schooling because they cannot understand the language of the classroom. We may only guess as to why they have had no exposure to English in their preschool years. Earlier generations of American ethnic groups have overcome the language barrier by earnest parental endeavor or by the hard fact of being pushed out of the family or community nest and into the realities of broader experience.

I merely wish to make plain that when, in another case, we are concerned with a very few youngsters, or with just a single child who speaks only German or Polish or Spanish or any language other than English, I would not regard today's decision, or the separate concurrence, as conclusive upon the issue whether the statute and the guideline require the funded school district to provide special instruction. For me, numbers are at the heart of this case and my concurrence is to be understood accordingly.

NOTES AND QUESTIONS

1. The Constitutional and Statutory Issues

Recall that the Court of Appeals decided *Lau* on Fourteenth Amendment grounds. Moreover, both parties stressed constitutional, not statutory, issues in their arguments before the Supreme Court. Why did the Court choose to decide the case on statutory grounds? What are the relevant doctrinal differences between the basis for a Title VI suit, on the one hand, and an Equal Protection Clause-based suit on the other? Recall in this context the discussion in chapter 5 of the need to prove "intentional" discrimination under Title VI and the Fourteenth Amendment. *See Regents of the University of California v. Bakke,* 438 U.S. 265 (1978). Of what doctrinal or practical moment are these distinctions? *Compare Board of Education of the City School District of the City of New York v. Califano,* 584 F.2d 576 (2d Cir. 1978), *aff'd,* 444 U.S. 130, 100 S.Ct. 363, 62 L.Ed.2d 275 (1979). (The Emergency School Aid Act authorizes HEW to withhold funds from a school district whose faculty assignment policies have a disparate racial impact without a showing that the policies are intentionally discriminatory according to the constitutional standard.)

Title VI bans, in pertinent part, discrimination based on "national origin." In what sense is the claim of the *Lau* plaintiffs based on national origin rather than linguistic disability (which is not specifically covered by the Act)? Is it relevant, in appraising the Court's reliance on Title VI, that in basing the decision on Title VI the Court is upholding the standards of a coordinate branch of government rather than acting on its own? Is it relevant that Title VI is subject to congressional revision?

2. Lau v. Nichols: *Scope of the Decision*

Discrimination is what Title VI bans. "Affirmative steps" are what the HEW guidelines require. How do the guidelines square with the statute? Does nondiscrimination require affirmative action in this context? If so, why? What is the defendant school district required to do after *Lau?* Would a "total immersion in English" program satisfy the Court? How much deference should be accorded to HEW-approved remedies—more than if the case had been decided on constitutional grounds?

3. Lau *and Numbers: Justice Blackmun's Concurrence*

Justice Blackmun finds significance in the relatively large size of the plaintiff class: "For me, numbers are at the heart of this case." Is this a shorthand reference to economies of scale in offering bilingual programs? Should the size of the class determine whether that class has rights under Title VI of the Civil Rights Act? In this respect, does Title VI differ from the Equal Protection Clause, which speaks of depriving a "person" of rights?

4. *The Rights of the Non-English-Speaking*

Part V of this chapter elaborates on the claims asserted by the non-English-speaking.

C. The Emergence of a Significant Federal Educational Presence

"ESEA: The Office of Education Administers a Law"

Stephen K. Bailey and Edith Mosher, *ESEA: The Office of Education Administers a Law* (Syracuse: Syracuse University Press, 1968) pp 1–36. By permission of the publisher.

I. The Historical Setting

In America, government interest in education dates back at least to the "old deluder Satan" law in the colony of Massachusetts in 1642. Intermittently at first, but with increasing consistency in the nineteenth and twentieth centuries, public education came to be considered a matter of government interest and concern. However, for most of American history, the view prevailed that education was primarily a function of local authority and control—even though both State governments and the Federal government had a substantial impact upon the course and direction of American educational development. Until the twentieth century, the Federal government's main impact was through land grants for educational purposes. The influence of State governments came to be felt increasingly during the nineteenth century in the standardization of minimal educational requirements and services. The fact remains, however, that up to the end of World War II, local educational programs were financed and determined in large part by local school systems.

* * *

In the scant period of 13 years (1954–1967), however, a sea change has occurred. The Federal government's interest in stimulating change and improving quality in public education at the precollegiate level has been increasingly visible in four fields: (1) desegregation; (2) education related to defense and to vocations; (3) aid to research; and (4) education of the economically and culturally disadvantaged, and of the handicapped. Federal activity—judicial, legislative, and executive—in these four areas has unquestionably affected the traditional, decentralized autonomies of American education. This is especially true when one adds the fact that Federal aid to parochial school children was an important corollary, even a precondition, of many of these new Federal thrusts, and that Supreme Court decisions on the place of religion in the schools had widespread impact. Quality and equality of opportunity in education have become matters of national concern. All levels of government, and a variety of branches and agencies at each level, are now deeply involved in a complex and uneasy partnership whose collective aims are transforming educational priorities and methods. Education, like so many other governmental services, has now become involved in a "marble cake," not a "layer cake," of federalism.

* * *

The New Educational Demands

The postwar years in the United States were marked by a series of demands upon the educational system that were unprecedented in scope and magnitude. Any one of the new demands would have produced disquiet and concern. Together they constituted an explosive admixture.

The Postwar Explosion in the Learning Force. An unanticipated increase in the birth rate, and an equally unanticipated growth in school attendance through high school and beyond, placed unprecedented strains on the staff and facilities of American education.

* * *

How were these additional students to be housed? Who would teach them? Who would pay for the facilities and staff needed to serve them? If no other educational demands had existed in the postwar years, the sheer volume of responsibility for teaching millions of additional children would by itself have produced extraordinary claims upon the educational system.

The Knowledge Explosion. Concomitant to the school population explosion was an intellectual and technological explosion. The postwar rate of technological invention and economic growth; breakthroughs in electronic communications, and in the speed and ease of publishing and disseminating information; the heightened mobility of people and ideas; the intractability and unprecedented responsibilities of the cold war; the vast outpouring of research findings in the social and behavioral sciences; and the rising expectations of the dispossessed at home and abroad—all combined to challenge the adequacy of the American educational system. How could it produce the skills needed to understand, and ultimately manage, these new forces? . . .

Other scholars and intellectual brokers brought other points of view to America's educational problems. Economists . . . began to point out that education was a nation's most important investment in sustaining and promoting a viable economy in a highly technological culture. . . .

This vast increase in concern and analysis led reformers to wonder whether anything short of substantial Federal infusions of money could move the educational system off its traditional dead center. Were pupils being educated well enough and fast enough to adapt to a world in massive flux? Could new knowledge be controlled by a new wisdom?

The notion that demands for substantial help from the Federal treasury might well be feasible grew as the fiscal performance of the Federal tax system showed increasing resiliency—especially in the early 1960's. . .

Segregation. A major catalyst to the educational ferment of the 1950's and early 1960's, and a source of new demands on the educational system, was the Supreme Court's historic decision of 1954 on school segregation. . . .

In terms of the dynamics of national educational policy, *Brown v. Board of Education* . . . made visible the condition of Negro education in America and thereby highlighted the social and economic costs and consequences of prejudice, cultural deprivation, and poverty. These costs and consequences were being felt increasingly outside of the American South. During the 1950's, approximately a quarter of a million Negroes a year moved from rural southern farms to northern and western industrial cities. By and large miserably educated, they found themselves relegated to welfare rolls, forced by prejudice and income to live in segregated slum housing, and unrelated to existing job markets. Negro children constituted the largest percentage of "drop-outs" from the schools. Too frequently their unutilized energies and their frustrations led to delinquency and crime. Altogether, Negroes constituted the most intractable element in hard-core poverty across the land.

Although the impact of the Negro migration was uneven, hundreds of school districts—particularly in large cities—found themselves facing the postwar years with an influx of pupils from a tragic subculture largely unrelated to the middle-class orientation of urban education. The educational demands prompted by this in-migration were insistent and almost cruelly complex, especially since it was accompanied by a flight of middle-class whites to the suburbs.

Poverty and Cultural Deprivation. Closely tied to the segregation issue was the question of the relationship of education to the nation's economic health. By the early 1960's, two issues had become particularly prominent. First, although over-all national productivity had been steadily increasing since the end of World War II, marked disparities in income and in employment opportunities persisted. Large pockets of unemployment and poverty remained, especially in the large cities and in dispersed rural slums. These disparities came to be viewed not only as a deterrent to regional prosperity and a violation of the individual's right to the dignity of gainful employment, but as a blot on America's international reputation as a humane democracy.

The second issue related particularly to young people. Although their numbers were increasing in proportion to the total population, they accounted for a disproportionately high percentage of the unemployed. As noted earlier, problems such as school drop-outs and juvenile delinquency were all parts of the same picture. It was becoming more obvious that ignorance, unemployment, and dependency were interrelated and self-perpetuating. High incidence of unemployment and dependency invariably correlated with low educational achievement. Traditional educational programs appeared to be both unable to hold such young people for a sufficient training period, and unable to train effectively those who did stay aboard.

During the mid-50's, the superintendents and board members of the country's largest cities formed a Great Cities Program for School Improvement to study the special problems of urban areas. One of their basic concerns was the needs of educationally disadvantaged children, especially Negroes. It was becoming obvious that conventional educational designs were inadequate to meet the learning problems of the culturally deprived, and it seemed that desegregation alone was not the answer. . . .

Parochial Schools. . . . [A]fter the war, inflation, the explosion in the learning force (which affected parochial schools quite as much as public schools), and a shortage of teaching staff placed an enormous financial burden upon parochial schools. Increasingly, church fathers went to public sources to find funds for supplementary services like transportation and school health. The justification was that such services were for the benefit of the child and did not support religious instruction. The Supreme Court upheld this position in *Everson v. Board of Education*. . . .

* * *

Two other Supreme Court cases on the church-state issue followed in 1948 and 1952. In *McCollum v. Board of Education*, the Court ruled that children released 30 minutes a week for religious instruction could not receive such instruction in public school facilities. Four years later, in *Zorach v. Clauson*, the Court ruled that "released-time" was permissible if religious instruction took place on private property.

These court decisions were both the cause and effect of increased parochial school demands upon public resources in the post-war years. The demands were often subtle and indirect, but they were persistent and politically powerful. And the fact that many States had strict constitutional prohibitions against direct or indirect aid to parochial schools gave a special impetus to asserting church claims upon Federal largess.

Limited and Inadequate Resources

This congeries of new demands fell upon an educational system woefully shy of institutional, human, and fiscal resources. Some of these inadequacies were long-standing, but some at least were traceable to World War II and its aftermaths, and to the Great Depression which preceded it.

Deferred Investment and Postwar Inflation. A major war inevitably produces massive shifts in any society's allocation of resources. The war machine is a great maw that consumes enormous quantities of human and physical goods and services. The effects of World War II upon the American school system were manifold but one of its most profound effects was to defer capital outlays for schools. This deferment came on top of ten years of depression during which time capital outlay for public elementary and secondary schools had dropped from $370 million in 1929–30 to only $258 million in 1939–40. By the late 1940's, America's school plant was by and large old, dilapidated, and overcrowded. . . .

Heroic measures were taken by State and local governments and local school districts to adjust tax levies and tax assessment policies to help close the inflation gap. . . . But the demands for new buildings, equipment, staff, and services continued to outrun revenues. As local school districts and their property-tax payers came to feel the fiscal pinch, both local and professional educational interests pressured State governments to increase both general and categorical aid to education. But States were also suffering from fiscal rigidities and inadequacies and were forced increasingly to turn toward the Federal government. . . .

Traditionalism and Educational Balkanization. It is conceivable that the American educational system could have weathered the fiscal storms and the winds of change of the postwar period without undue strain, if its own ship had been in order. But it was not. Conservative in outlook and fragmented in structure, the American school system had developed an entrenched neglect of efforts to improve educational productivity. It was both too ponderous and too Balkanized to be regenerative.

Local Autonomy.

* * *

The historic Balkanization of the American school system into tens of thousands of districts—most of them of a patently inefficient size—was unlikely to produce talents and economies of a scale relevant to the educational demands of the postwar years. Little scope was afforded for innovative activities, and almost none for project-planning aimed at external sources of aid. . . .

At the State level, not more than a half dozen State educational agencies had either the resources, the leadership, or the quality of staff needed to give spirited direction to grass roots educational improvement for meeting the extraordinary demands of the postwar years.

Fiscal Disparities. The scatteration of local school districts had for generations produced glaring financial, and consequently educational, inequities. As long as schools were almost entirely supported from a local property tax base, the quality of education tended to vary in direct proportion to the availability of local tax revenues. . . .

. . . In the postwar years, the persistence of a large degree of disparity in local economic resources, educational requirements, and tax effort, was another indication of the gap which existed between new educational demands on the one hand and the capacity of the educational system to respond effectively and equitably to them.

* * *

The Old United States Office of Education. Even if the stars had been propitious during the postwar years for a dramatic response of the Federal government to the new educational demands, there would have been a serious question about the administrative capacity of the U.S. Office of Education to adjust imaginatively and effectively to its vast new educational responsibilities. USOE had lived most of its life since 1867 as a stepchild of other Federal departments and agencies—notably the Department of the Interior and HEW's forerunner, the Federal Security Agency—dominated by noneducational concerns. Until the late 1950's, limited largely to the collection and dissemination of educational statistics, and to technical consultancies, the Office was almost entirely service-oriented rather than operations-oriented. . . . It had few friends apart from the National Education Association, the American Association of School Administrators and the Council of Chief State School Officers, whose Washington staffs and whose constituencies found the statistical and advisory services of USOE of direct value. There was at least some validity to the widely held assumption that USOE was, in fact, the "kept" Federal agent of these major private educational associations.

Over the decades, Congress had virtually ignored USOE—occasionally criticizing it for "meddling" if it showed initiative; for ineptitude if it did not. Financially it was starved; administratively it was victimized. . . .

. . . [T]he total appropriation for the United States Office of Education did not reach the $1 million mark until the 1930's, and even then three quarters of this amount was specifically awarded for educating Eskimos in Alaska. Even when vast new responsibilities were added to the work of the Office in the 1950's, and its visibility was increased by the word *Education* appearing in the title of its new departmental home (HEW, 1953), it received inadequate authorizations and appropriations for staff and for effective program management. . . .

* * *

Expediential Responses

The irresistible force of new educational demands was not exactly stopped by the immovable object of limited and inadequate resources—for the latter turned out not to be totally immovable. But the irresistible force was enormously slowed, and in the two decades following World War II the gap between need and response was, if anything, widened. . . .

At the national level, a few developments occurred incrementally in the late 1940's, notably the GI Bill and the creation of the National Science Foundation (hereafter NSF). Although addressed largely to the needs of higher education, these provided spin-offs for elementary and secondary education in terms of teacher training and/or support for curricular revisions—especially in the sciences. And NSF was a harbinger of later Federal programs addressed directly to the support of educational research.

A Federal program was passed in 1950, solidifying World War II legislation that was passed to provide financial aid to school districts impacted by Federal defense plants and other Federal establishments. These plants and establishments were tax exempt, yet they inevitably involved a substantial increase in the local labor force and in the need for schools for the children of federally sponsored workers. . . . Following the dramatic orbiting of Sputnik by the Russians in the fall of 1957, Congress, with presidential backing, passed the National Defense Education Act (NDEA) of 1958. The Act provided for substantial Federal support to secondary-school and higher-education programs to increase the quantity and quality of scientists, engineers, and foreign-language specialists throughout the American educational system. It established fellowships and supported curricula-revision aimed at a major transformation of defense-related aspects of the American educational system. It also provided for student loans, guidance counseling, grants for audio-visual aid and for various additional types of technical assistance. Although NDEA was later criticized for warping the educational curriculum away from the humanities and the social studies, it was nonetheless an important harbinger of the kinds of Federal support for American education that blossomed in the mid-1960's. It was categorical aid; it affected both secondary and higher education; it was substantial in the volume of funding; some of its titles included religious affiliated institutions among NDEA's beneficiaries; and it proclaimed that education was a matter of national concern. But it was still a far cry from general Federal aid for the nation's elementary and secondary schools. And even within its own limited domain, the Act tended to strengthen superior and wealthier secondary schools that had the staff, the equipment, the matching funds, and the students to profit from marginal infusions of Federal money for science, mathematics, and foreign languages. Poorer schools in the countryside and in the urban ghettos were left largely untouched. Like the renewals of impacted area legislation, extensions of NDEA went forward with almost no effect upon the substantive concerns of those seeking some answer to education's general need for massive Federal support.

* * *

Political Inventiveness and Legislative Forerunners

In the field of Federal school aid, the half-decade 1960–64 was filled with political inventiveness and some major breakthroughs in cognate legislative areas; but it was a period of massive frustration in regard to the central target issue.

* * *

The Kennedy Education Bill of 1961. The struggle peaked early. In what the President called "probably the most important piece of domestic legislation of the year," he asked in early 1961 for grants of $2.3 billion over three years to be used by the States primarily for construction of public elementary and high school classrooms and for boosting public teachers' salaries; and an even greater amount over a five-year period for higher education facilities, and for construction loans and student scholarships to both public and private colleges. . . .

But under the Kennedy proposal, aid to private elementary and secondary schools was barred, and the Catholic hierarchy issued a pronouncement that unless the public school bill included private school loans, it should be defeated.

It did not, and it was.

* * *

To the observant, victory could be discerned in the very ashes of defeat. These new ideas and directions that emerged over a four year period can be classified as follows: (1) the shift toward program aid; (2) attempts to improve the quality of education; (3) emphasis on "educationally disadvantaged" children.

Increasingly Categorical Limits on Federal Grants. From 1961 on, there was a gradual shift in Congress from aid proposals for teachers' salaries and school construction under general State administration, to proposals with a specific program emphasis under federally set standards.

* * *

Cognate Developments

While these various shifts in forces [support from teachers' organizations for targeted, not just general aid; efforts to resolve the church-state issue] were occurring in the field of school aid, other domestic legislation was being developed and passed in the areas of civil rights and poverty, and precedents were being set for liberalizing Federal aid to church-related institutions. These cognate developments were important antecedents to the emergence of the Elementary and Secondary Education Act of 1965.

Civil Rights.

* * *

. . . By outlawing discrimination in all federally-aided programs, the Civil Rights Act of 1964 added full presidential and congressional authority to the Supreme Court's school desegregation mandate of 1954. . . . Hopefully, the mobilization of the legal, fiscal, and administrative resources of the Federal government under the 1964 Act would be more effective and quicker than litigation alone. The Attorney General was given authority to intervene in school desegregation suits or to initiate such suits. And a threat of withdrawal of funds from States with discriminatory practices was a powerful weapon—a weapon that became even more powerful as Federal aid to education increased.

One of the most important aspects of the Civil Rights Act of 1964 was the fact that . . . the race issue was removed from the political calculus of those supporting or attacking increased Federal aid to education. . . . [T]he passage of ESEA in 1965 was testament to the fact that the civil rights issue vis-a-vis education had been at least temporarily blunted by the previous passage of the Civil Rights Act of 1964.

Poverty Legislation.

* * *

. . . [The] Economic Opportunity Act of 1964 (hereafter EOA) created a number of programs such as the Job Corps, the Neighborhood Youth Corps, and Adult Basic Education. Some of these programs were logical extensions of past Federal experiments. Conceptually, however, the Act leapt beyond the goals of vocational education. Its overriding purpose was to mobilize "the human and financial resources of the Nation to combat poverty by opening to everyone opportunity for education and training and opportunity to work."

The Economic Opportunity Act presaged the Elementary and Secondary Education Act of 1965 in at least two respects: its stress upon the importance of variety and innovation; and its acknowledgement of the special needs of educationally disadvantaged children. And, of course, both acts reflected in turn the influence of scholarly evidence that the handicaps of poverty are translated into educational disadvantage at a very early age, and that those who come to adulthood without adequate schooling will have at best a future of uncertain, unskilled employment and low income. It should also be noted that "the church-state settlement" in Title II of the Economic Opportunity Act provided a strategic precedent for ESEA.

Church-State Relations. The judicial tight-rope walking that marked church-state relations in the post-war years was accompanied by legislative actions and pressure-group détentes that had the effect of liberalizing traditional concepts of appropriate public assistance to church-related institutions. The

GI Bill, the National Defense Education Act, the National Science Foundation Act, college housing loans, the National School Lunch Act, and the Hill-Burton Hospital Construction Act all involved Federal assistance to sectarian institutions. And an increasing number of people came to argue that the very fact of tax exemption for religious property, including parochial schools, was a tacit acceptance of the notion that certain kinds of public assistance for parochial schools, had in fact been accepted for generations as within the legitimate sanctions of the Constitution. Furthermore, in the postwar years, a number of State legislatures and local school systems had authorized the practice of "shared-time"—allowing parochial school children to attend public school classes during certain hours on certain days each week. . . . More than any other single issue, the church-state controversy precluded the formation of a workable coalition to pass the Kennedy general-aid-to-education bills in 1961 and 1963.

From the ashes of these two defeats there emerged two realities which were to have important effects upon the future of Federal aid: first, a new grasp of political realities on the part of both Catholic and professional public educational associations, and a recognition that intransigencies on both sides had in fact denied children the benefit of extensive Federal resources for education; and second, the realization on the part of key policy makers in Washington that if substantial Federal aid to elementary and secondary education were to emerge, compromises . . . would have to be reached. . . .

* * *

Overview

These were the forces and developments that led to the passage of the Elementary and Secondary Education Act of 1965. Explosive postwar demands; inadequate institutional, human, and financial resources at all levels of government; a series of expediential, if sometimes heroic, responses; and political inventions born of frustration—all of these had combined to set the stage for a new legislative breakthrough. But the breakthrough would be a far cry from the general aid bills, for school construction and teachers' salaries for public schools only, that had dominated the congressional educational agenda during the postwar years.

D. On Implementing Equal Educational Opportunity Entitlements: From Policy as Formulated to Policy in Operation

"Millions of Title I dollars misspent," "bilingual programs scored as ineffective," "procedural tangles produce snafus in aid to the handicapped": in the realm of educational policy, such stories are commonplace. They call our attention to the fact that something is not working in the policy realm; they identify disparities between the law as adopted (whether by court or legislature) and the law as it in fact operates.

While each of the situations noted above describes a problem of implementation, the problems differ importantly. The Title I story seems, on the surface, to involve a failure of a government agency to comply with the law; the failure with respect to bilingualism concerns the results achieved even when a legal mandate has been adhered to; the handicapped story speaks of displaced priorities, with proceduralism assuming a life of its own. Each of these implementation problems calls for policy attention. Each also poses issues that are legally relevant.

The excerpt that follows addresses issues of policy implementation, noting pitfalls in the process and suggesting structural ways of avoiding or compensating for those pitfalls. Treat it both as a "case"—to be appraised in its specific terms, much like a legal case—and as an illustration of a generic issue.

"Complexity and Control: What Legislators and Administrators Can Do About Implementation"

R. Elmore, L. S. Shulman and G. Sykes, eds., *Handbook of Teaching and Policy* 342–69 (1983). Reprinted by permission.

The major theme of the paper is that the complexity of implementation requires a substantial rethinking of legislative and administrative control. The traditional devices that legislators have relied upon to control policy implementation—more specific legislation, tighter regulations and procedures, centralized authority, and closer monitoring of compliance—probably have the opposite effect that they are intended to have. Rather than increasing control, they increase complexity. And as complexity increases, control itself is threatened. The central task of this paper is to develop alternatives to the traditional techniques of legislative and administrative control.

When we speak of government agencies or programs being "out of control," we generally mean that they are aimless, unresponsive to policymakers and clients, sluggish, uncoordinated, or self-serving. Control, then, consists of bringing administrative actions into line with the expectations of policymakers and citizens. But this general notion of control conceals two very different meanings: One meaning is the *control that superiors exercise over subordinates* and the other is the *control that individuals exercise over their own actions.* In the first instance we're talking about *hierarchical control*—authority, supervision, regulation, coercion—and in the second we're talking about *delegated control*—individual responsibility, initiative, and discretion. A bit of common sense tells us that both kinds of control are required for successful implementation. Hierarchical control is the means by which policymakers (legislators and high-level administrators) affect the actions of subordinates (mid-level managers and service deliverers). But the administrative structure would soon collapse if individuals didn't exercise some degree of responsibility, initiative and control over their own actions. Imagine a group of policymakers presiding over a bureaucracy in which no one acted unless they were explicitly told to do something. The success of policymakers depends, to a very large degree, on the skill and initiative of policy implementors.

Hierarchical control and delegated control have very different effects on administrative complexity. The former leads toward greater complexity, the latter toward less. The more a government invests in hierarchical control, the more effort it devotes to writing regulations, specifying procedures, monitoring performance, and enforcing compliance. The more a government invests in delegated control, the more it relies on individual judgment as a substitute for complex administrative procedure, but the less assurance it has of strict compliance. The crucial trade-off for policymakers, then, is between more complexity with greater hierarchical control and less complexity with greater delegated control. . . .

Regulatory and Programmatic Views of Implementation

Let's begin with a fairly common implementation problem that surfaces in a legislative hearing. We break in in the middle of an exchange between a legislative committee chairman and the head (Commissioner) of a large executive agency. The Chairman has been reviewing a number of programs in the Commissioner's agency and he comes to one that has been the subject of some criticism—we'll call it the 320(d) program. The person who is directly responsible for administering the 320(d) program—we'll call him the Director—doesn't participate in this exchange, but we'll hear from him later.

Chairman:

As you're probably aware, Commissioner, we've heard testimony from a number of people that funds from the 320(d) program are being misspent by local agencies—they're being used to fund questionable activities and they're not effectively reaching the target population. What is your estimate of the situation?

Commissioner:

I am as concerned as you are about these criticisms of the program. I've spoken at length with the program's Director and I've asked for a complete review. You must understand our problem here, though, Mr. Chairman. We're dealing with independent units of local government and they have ideas of their own about how to spend program funds. The 320(d) program gives local agencies a fair amount of discretion in the use of funds. We've written the regulations so as to spell out the purposes and activities that we have determined are consistent with legislative intent. But the law says that each agency is to construct its own program consistent with its own local needs.

Chairman:

Well what's the difficulty then? Why are we getting complaints? Do we need to amend the legislation to give your agency more control over local decisions? Do you need to rewrite the regulations? Or do you just need to tighten up your enforcement of existing regulations?

Commissioner:

We're not absolutely certain ourselves what the solution is, but I expect the Director's review to produce some recommendations that will help us decide what to do. I don't think I'm incorrect in saying, am I, that the intent of the legislation is not to pre-empt local decisions but to encourage local agencies to develop their own programs?

Chairman:

I think that is a correct statement of the intent. But it's also true, is it not, that when we find evidence that the program is not reaching the target population we ought to do something about it?

Commissioner:

Yes. If we find that agencies are not complying with the regulations and the intent of the law, we will act on those cases. And if we find that we need additional authority, we will ask for legislative amendments. Is that satisfactory?

Chairman:

Fair enough. We'll expect to hear from you in the near future.

Commissioner:

As soon as the Director completes his review.

This exchange illustrates most of the factors that define an implementation problem: The program has somehow missed its mark; the evidence that most troubles the Chairman is that local agencies are not serving the people the legislature intended them to serve. Is there something that can be done, either to the legislation or the administration of the program, to remedy this problem? For his part, the Commissioner is carefully trying to establish two basic points with the Chairman: The first is that the responsibility for operating the 320(d) program is lodged with the Director; it's the Director's responsibility to determine whether the program is missing its mark and to develop a solution if he finds that the problem actually exists. The second point is that the operation of the program depends, in a very basic sense, on local agencies taking responsibility for the program at the delivery level; if local agencies fail, the program fails.

Notice how the complexity develops. The Chairman and the Commissioner are sitting at the top of a very tall pyramid trying to diagnose a problem that is occurring at the bottom. Between the top and the bottom are at least two layers of administrative machinery—the Director's office and a large number of local agencies. The complexity of the problem is a function of both the distance from the top to the bottom—the number of levels—and the number of actors at each level. The farther down the pyramid we go, the larger the number of transactions that are necessary to get anything done. It is for this reason that delegated control is so important. The Chairman and Commissioner can't pretend to manage the Director's program, nor can the Director pretend to manage the wide variety of programs at the local level. Policy—legislation, regulations, guidelines, and informal agreements—is what holds the levels together, but delegated control is what makes the policy work at any given level.

Notice also that the Chairman and the Commissioner seem to have agreed already on the solution to the problem—tighter regulation and more hierarchical control. Imagine the following scenario: The Director conducts his study and finds that, indeed, there are examples of questionable local decisions. The Chairman, the Commissioner, and the Director agree that no new legislative authority is required, but that the Director needs to tighten up his monitoring of local spending. In operational terms this means that the Director's staff will spend a larger proportion of their time questioning local administrators about their program decisions. It also means that the regulations and guidelines which define legitimate local expenditures will become more complex and detailed, requiring more attention to compliance. As questions of compliance increase, the Director's staff and local administrators will focus a larger proportion of their conversations with each other on interpretation of the rules.

The element that is missing in this scenario is any direct concern for *whether the program is actually working*. After all the rules and regulations are complied with, do we actually know that the program's beneficiaries are better off? Does compliance assure success?

The Chairman and the Commissioner, without really intending to, have taken a *regulatory view* of implementation. They have, for the sake of simplifying their problem, chosen to equate success with tighter hierarchical control and greater compliance. The problem with this view is that, while we can demonstrate that greater hierarchical control produces greater compliance, we cannot assure that greater compliance produces better results. In fact, we could argue that in some instances there is a negative relationship between compliance and better results because results used for regulation cannot be used for service delivery. Regulation constitutes a diversion of resources from substance to surveillance.

There is an alternative to the regulatory view which I will call the *programmatic view*. This view focuses on delegated control instead of hierarchical control and it defines the important issue not as compliance but as the *capacity to deliver a service*. In order to decide whether tighter regulation will solve their problem, the Chairman and the Commissioner must first decide whether they're interested in compliance as an end in itself or whether they're interested in compliance as a means of improving the performance of the 320(d) program.

In some instances it makes sense to view compliance as the primary goal. Certain types of policies are primarily regulatory in intent—school desegregation, affirmative action, auto emission standards, pure food and drug laws, occupational safety and health standards. These policies exist to regulate private choices in accordance with public standards of equity and safety. Other policies, however, are not primarily regulatory in intent. Housing, education, social service, and health policies, for example, exist primarily to deliver services rather than to regulate private choices. In these policies, compliance is secondary to *improving and supporting the capacity of public organizations to deliver services*. The quality of public services depends heavily on delegated control; the choices that go into constructing an effective health care delivery program or an education program are too complex to be entirely structured by a uniform set of regulations. In fact, the quality of service and the capacity of the program to respond to human needs are often hindered rather than helped by hierarchical control. . . .

For most legislators and administrators, implementation means writing and enforcing regulations. My aim is to demonstrate that the solution of implementation problems requires a broader, programmatic view. How would the exchange between the Chairman and the Commissioner be different if they took a programmatic, rather than a regulatory, view of the problem?

The most obvious difference would be that the discussion would focus much more on service delivery than on regulation. So in order to proceed we will need some more information about the 320(d) program. Let's assume the following: The 320(d) program grew out of concern by the state legislature over declining test scores in reading and math achievement. After hearing testimony from a number of experts on testing, basic skills, and teaching, the Education Committee settled upon a strategy. Local school districts would be asked to survey their student populations, using whatever instruments they felt were appropriate, and to develop a plan for improving performance in reading and math. The state would offer supplementary grants to local districts, through the Department of Education, for the purpose of assessing student needs, developing basic skill programs, and implementing them. In order to qualify for support, a local district would be required to submit a plan describing how it would identify students needing help and what services it would provide to those students. The State Department of Education would review the plans to assure their consistency with the law and provide assistance to local districts requesting help in starting programs. In an effort to hold local districts accountable, the law required the "renewal of grants to local districts shall be conditioned on demonstrated progress in achieving the objectives of the local plan," and gave the State Commissioner of Education the authority to establish criteria for determining whether local districts were making adequate progress.

Imagine one year later. Virtually every school system in the state is participating in the 320(d) program and the State Department of Education has established an office, headed by the Director, to administer the program. In a routine legislative oversight hearing, involving a general review of the Department's programs, the Education Committee hears testimony from parent representatives and an advocacy group representing disadvantaged children that local education agencies are "abusing" the 320(d) program by using it to support their general education program, rather than focusing the funds on children with serious problems in reading and math. Local school system representatives counter this criticism by arguing that local plans have been reviewed by the State Department of Education and found consistent with the law. The Chairman of the Education Committee asks the Commissioner of Education to present the Department's case.

The following exchange is a replay of the first one which shows how the Chairman and Commissioner might attack the problem in a programmatic rather than a regulatory way:

Chairman:

As you're probably aware, Commissioner, we've heard testimony from United Parents for Education and the Children's Advocacy Group alleging that 320(d) funds are not reaching children with the greatest need for help in reading and math. Can you confirm or deny these reports? And can you explain why this appears to be happening?

Commissioner:

I've asked the Director of the 320(d) program to investigate this problem, Mr. Chairman, and I've spoken with him at some length prior to this hearing. I've also asked him to conduct a study and report back to me as soon as possible. At this point, we have several alternative explanations, and we're not sure which of them is correct.

One explanation might be that local administrators are simply not paying adequate attention to the way they use 320(d) funds. If this is true, our program staff simply has not been vigilant enough in monitoring compliance with program regulations.

But I would stress that this is only one possible explanation.

Another one might be that some dispersion of funds is unavoidable if reasonably sound educational practice is followed. For example, the only way to assure that the funds are targeted exclusively on children with serious basic skill problems is to isolate those children completely from the regular school program for all or part of the school day. But many teachers and school administrators would argue that we shouldn't isolate these children from the regular school program. This is a matter of professional judgment and there's no real agreement on which is the best strategy. We know for sure, though, that if kids with basic skill problems are left in regular classrooms there will at least be the appearance of diluting program funds.

Still another explanation might be that there aren't any clear-cut standards for what constitutes a basic skill deficit. Each school system has a different set of standards for deciding who needs help. Some systems concentrate on the fewest kids with the greatest needs. Some try to help everyone who falls below the national norm on a reading or math test. And some try to help those kids who are most likely to improve, which means less attention for the kids with the toughest problems. Again, these are professional judgments for which there aren't necessarily any correct answers.

So when you look at the program as a whole you see a lot of variation in how local systems approach the problem of basic skills. Some of the variation may be due to poor administration and some may be due to equally legitimate differences of approach.

Chairman:

If I hear you correctly, then, you're saying that the basic issue is how much local autonomy we're willing to permit in the program. Is that correct?

Commissioner:

That's correct.

Chairman:

But if we allow local school systems complete freedom to decide who needs help, aren't we bound to see abuses and sloppy administration?

Commissioner:

I'd like to think that our Department can distinguish poor administration from legitimate professional judgments by local schoolpeople. And I think the way to make that distinction is to look at the local program and ask administrators why they've chosen to design it one way or another.

Chairman:

Would it help to have clearer standards in the law about what kind of children should be served by the program?

Commissioner:

It might. But I think we also ought to allow for the possibility that clearer standards might hurt the program. Right now we've got a lot of interesting and promising local programs going, largely as a result of the autonomy we've given local districts. I wouldn't like to see us restrict that diversity because of some standard we've established. Also, it's not clear to me that we know enough to say exactly who should be served by the program. I'm more comfortable giving that decision mainly to the people who are closest to the problem.

Chairman:

You seem to be telling me that there's nothing we can do to respond to criticisms coming from parents and other people who are also very close to the problem. With all due respect, I'm not sure I can accept that.

Commissioner:

I'd like to be able to respond to those criticisms too, Mr. Chairman, but I want to respond in a way that preserves the quality of the program at the local level, rather than in a way that imposes our standards on local districts. Also, I'd like to be able to respond in a way that puts the Department in the role of providing useful guidance and information to local districts rather than just policing them.

Chairman:

Let's agree, though, that we've got to do something to respond to these criticisms and do it fairly quickly. We'll expect to hear from you in the near future.

Commissioner:

As soon as the Director completes his review.

What distinguishes this exchange from the previous one is its concern with program operations rather than regulation, with delegated control rather than hierarchical control. The Chairman is no less insistent on the seriousness of the problem; in fact, his questions are sharper because they focus more specifically on program operations. Furthermore, the Chairman has not sacrificed his central concern—constituent complaints. The Chairman cannot be expected to care as much about administrative problems as the Commissioner. His major concern is political issues that arise in the implementation process. An important constituency has raised a question about the Department's implementation strategy. The Chairman wants a satisfactory answer from the Commissioner because his political survival—as a legislator and committee chairman—depends largely on his ability to respond effectively to constituent claims. The Chairman's approach to questioning the Commissioner demonstrates that legislators can take an aggressive programmatic stance on implementation issues without departing from their role as adjudicators of conflicting political interests.

The Commissioner has managed to give a relatively complete account of the administrative problems raised by the 320(d) program without suggesting that they are susceptible to a simple regulatory solution. He has also managed to communicate that his Department's interest in the program involves more than just policing compliance; he wants to support and guide the development of effective local programs, which is a much more demanding (and incidentally more interesting) task. The Commissioner is concerned about the stakes involved in the trade-off between hierarchical and delegated control. He understands that the more effort the Department invests in enforcing compliance, the less resources it will be able to focus on program substance. He also understands that variation in the way local districts respond to the legislation can be an advantage as well as a disadvantage; he sees it as a source of ideas for improving the program rather than as a threat to his authority. . . .

Coping with Variations in Implementation

We've left the Chairman, the Commissioner, and the Director with a difficult problem, though: how to distinguish legitimate variations in the way local districts implement the 320(d) program from outright failures of implementation. . . . Whether we regard variability as good or bad depends on the standard we use. If we take a strictly regulatory view, our standard of success is compliance and all variability is suspect because it suggests non-compliance. But if we take a programmatic view, our standard of success is the capacity of program participants to produce desired effects. . . .

We are tempted to say that the more implementors agree with the intent of a policy, the less variability we would expect in the way a policy is implemented. In fact, research on implementation suggests otherwise. We have already described one circumstance under which we would expect wide variations in the implementation of a policy even when implementors agree on the intent—where there are legitimate professional differences on the most effective way to address a problem at the operating level. There are at least five additional circumstances under which we would expect variability in the presence of agreement:

1. *Incompatibility with Other Commitments.* Implementors typically have multiple responsibilities. No matter how much they agree with the intent of a policy, they may have other responsibilities that conflict with or divert attention from it. . . .
2. *Variation in Sense of Urgency.* People cannot be expected to share the same sense of urgency in implementing a policy, even if they agree on its intent. The ability of individuals and organizations to focus on a policy depends on the immediacy of other problems competing for their attention. . . .
3. *Existing Policies that Slow or Deflect Implementation.* Policies are implemented in the context of other policies, and their mutual effects produce variations in implementation. . . .
4. *Disagreements over the Assignment of Organizational Responsibilities.* Over time, administrative agencies develop stable relationships with each other. A new policy often disrupts these relationships. . . .
5. *Lack of Resources.* One of the touchiest issues of federally and state-mandated policies is the resources they bring with them. Regardless of how well-funded a new program is, it exacts some cost from implementing agencies. The availability of local resources to supplement outside resources varies widely from setting to setting. . . .

Some proportion of variability in implementation can, however, be explained by disagreement and ambiguity over the aims of policy. . . . It is possible to categorize the variety of ways that disagreements with policy are expressed in the implementation process.

1. *Diversion of Resources.* When the implementation of a policy requires the transfer of money from one agency to another, a certain proportion of the funds will be used to support existing or new activities that have no direct relationship to the purposes of the policy. New funds are sometimes used to increase administrative staff and reduce workloads, to mollify important constituency groups, or to free up existing funds for other purposes. . . .
2. *Deflection of Goals.* As implementation progresses, policies attract the attention of constituencies with their own objectives and their own visions of what a good program should be. These groups view success or failure of the policy in terms of their own objectives rather than those of the legislature or the administrative agency. As a consequence, program activities become directed at goals that have little or no relationship to what leg-

islators and high-level administrators consider to be the central objective of the program. . . .

3. *Outright Resistance.* In the final analysis, policies may require implementors to do things that they oppose and are able to resist. In some instances, opposition takes the form of tokenism or passive resistance . . . in some instances, opposition takes the form of active resistance. School systems may simply refuse to participate or test the department's mettle by openly refusing to implement certain requirements.

All of these actions, can, to a degree, be countered with tighter regulation. Administrators can prescribe more detailed rules for expenditure of funds, they can require that certain organizational features be part of every local project, and they can devote additional time to direct surveillance and to actions designed to demonstrate their willingness to enforce compliance. All of these devices are part of the administrative machinery of virtually every service delivery program. But each of these devices has a tangible cost associated with it.

Each additional increment of regulation brings an increment of administrative complexity—an additional step in the grant application process, another person responsible for monitoring compliance, a more elaborate system of checks and sign-offs, etc. There are practical limits on the amount of administrative complexity a program can bear and still focus on its capacity to deliver tangible benefits. At some point the investment in regulatory machinery becomes greater than the investment in service delivery, and at that point the emphasis shifts from producing an effect to maintaining a complex surveillance and enforcement system. . . .

If the Director of the 320(d) program is smart, he will design his program review around the issue of local program capacity rather than around the issue of compliance. If he focuses on compliance, he risks increasing the complexity of his task. If he focuses on local capacity, he looks for opportunities to increase delegated control and hence to reduce the complexity of his task. But he also has to attend to the Chairman's concern—whether the program is reaching its target group. One solution to this problem is to design the review around the question, "What variations in local projects seem to enhance their capacity to reach their target group effectively and which seem to undermine their capacity?" That question does two things: It accepts local variability as a fact, and it relates variability to success. Hence, the Director has effectively said that *he will use variability of implementation as a device for improving the program.*

Let's suppose now that the Director has completed his review. Being alert to the distinction between capacity and compliance, he has designed the review around a series of questions that relate 320(d) funds to evidence of change in local practice and to locally generated information on student outcomes. With the assistance of an outside contractor, the Director has sampled 60 local districts out of the roughly 200 in the state receiving 320(d) funds. The major findings of the review are as follows:

1. *Use of teacher-generated curriculum materials seems to be associated with greater change in teaching practice.* Where teachers have worked together compiling and adapting curriculum materials, rather than simply using standard materials, there is evidence that 320(d) funds have had greater influence on their classroom practice.

2. *First-year test results at the local level indicate that evidence of improvement in basic skills is positively related to the amount of time teachers report they spend on focused instructional activity in reading and math.* A rough count of the time teachers report they spend on basic skill instruction is positively related to differences in classroom performance on standardized achievement tests.

3. *In 12 of the 60 local districts more than 30 percent of 320(d) funds were used for activities that could not be related directly to instruction.* A review of local project budgets showed that most local districts spent between 15 and 25 percent of their 320(d) funds on activities not directly related to classroom instruction; in 12 of the 60, however, this proportion was 30 percent or greater.

4. *Ten of the 60 local districts followed the practice of removing students from regular classrooms for basic skill instruction; 40 of the 60 made some form of individualized instruction available; and 10 made all basic skill instruction available only through group instruction in the regular classroom.* No systematic relation*ship could be found between these grouping practices and student outcomes on standardized achievement tests.*

5. *Five of the 60 local districts were unable to provide an explicit statement of how students were selected for basic skill instruction; 30 of the 60 indicated that their criteria of selection were based primarily on teachers' evaluations; and the remaining 25 relied primarily on standardized tests.*

Allowing for the tentativity of results like these, we can begin to piece together a crude picture of how much variability there is in local practice and the degree to which variability represents intentional noncompliance or local adaptation. One might want to look more closely, for example, at the 12 districts that spent more than 30 percent of their 320(d) funds on non-instructional activities and at the five districts that could not explain their selection procedures. Simple indicators like these can be used to sort out serious compliance problems. But the other evidence indicates considerable diversity in local practice that can be used to focus on more-or-less successful variations. Findings (1) and (5), for example, indicate a heavy reliance on teacher judgments in the selection of children and curriculum materials. One might want to take a closer look at how teachers exercise this judgment, with an eye to informing other teachers of apparently successful practices. Findings (2) and (4) give some hints about practices that local administrators can affect—instructional time and grouping practices—and their relationship to student success. In short, the review speaks both to issues of compliance and capacity and it does at least a crude justice to local variability.

Now the important question is how the Director, the Commissioner and the Chairman can address these issues in a constructive way. The following exchange takes place after the Director's review is completed:

Chairman:

I've looked at your review of the 320(d) program and I have a number of questions to ask you. Perhaps the best place to start is to ask whether your review has given you any clearer idea of how many local districts have just plain failed to do anything useful for children with basic skill problems.

Director:

Let me begin by saying that I think there are few, if any, districts that have failed to do anything useful. But our review has led us to focus more sharply on those districts that seem to be having the greatest difficulty getting programs underway. We found that five of the 60 districts we surveyed were unable to state how they selected students for attention; these districts are out of compliance with the law and regulations, which say very clearly that recipients of 320(d) funds must state their selection criteria. So we intend to take a close look at the remaining districts in the state to discover how many of them have the same problem. When we've identified this group of districts, we'll focus a portion of our staff time on working with them to assure that their programs meet minimum standards of compliance.

Chairman:

That sounds reasonable. What about districts that meet the minimum requirements but still aren't teaching kids reading and math? Is there anything you can do about that?

Director:

I think there are a couple of ways to get at that problem. One way is to take a closer look at how 320(d) funds are being used by local districts. Our finding, for example, that about one-fifth of the districts we surveyed use more than 30 percent of the funds for non-instructional purposes suggests that we've got some kind of problem getting the resources to the kids. We may need some new legislative authority. If we do, we'll ask for it.

Another way of getting at the problem is to look for particularly outstanding programs or practices and find some way of communicating these to the districts that need them. We've started to get a handle on that with our findings about teacher-developed materials, instructional time, and grouping practices. But it's become clear to us that we need to know a lot more about local programs before we start publicizing ways of improving local practices. That's why I'd like to focus most of our effort on identifying and understanding successful programs, rather than enforcing compliance with the regulations. It just seems to me that the payoff is potentially greater when you try to understand what makes programs work.

Chairman:

If you're prepared to demonstrate to me that you've got the compliance issue under control, I agree that it makes sense to work on identifying successful programs. I guess I'm not clear where all this leads, though. When we understand a few things about successful programs, what do we do next? Do we write them into the law?

Commissioner:

I have great difficulties with the idea of requiring all local districts to do things that we find are associated with success in a few settings. In the first place, we can never be sure about the conditions that make for local success; they're probably much more complicated than our data tell us they are. Second, it seems to me we have to think about the effect of mandating practice on local initiative. How much inventive ability are we losing when we tell people how to do their jobs? As a policy matter, then, I would argue that it's good to have information available on successful practices, but we shouldn't be in the business of telling people how to use it.

Director:

I agree with the Commissioner. The last thing I want to do as an administrator is to tell teachers how to teach reading and math. That seems to me to defeat the purpose of having a solid group of professionals in the classrooms. What we can do, though, is increase the level of information on successful practices and increase the opportunities for exchange of that information. It seems to me that we are uniquely well situated to do that.

Chairman:

I'm generally pleased with the responsiveness of the review and with your comments about how you intend to proceed. I still have questions about this issue of how to improve local practice, but they're better saved until you have more information. Can we agree to get together again and focus primarily on that issue?

Commissioner:

I certainly would welcome the opportunity.

Director:

As would I.

Notice how the ground has shifted from the first two exchanges. The central issue of the first two exchanges—why aren't 320(d) funds getting to the kids who need them most?—has now been broken down into three more precise questions: How are districts selecting children for participation in the program? How are districts allocating 320(d) funds between instructional and non-instructional costs? And how do local instructional practices relate to the benefits children gain from the program? The Chairman, the Director, and the Commissioner understand the difference between regulatory and programmatic issues and have used this distinction to isolate problems that can be solved with compliance from those that have more complex programmatic solutions. Furthermore, they have . . . begun to distinguish instances where hierarchical control is appropriate from those where delegated control is appropriate. . . .

The Power of the Bottom Over the Top

Up to this point we've defined the implementation problem exclusively from the point of view of policymakers and high-level administrators. We've been concerned with the ability of people at the top of the pyramid to understand and control the actions of people at the bottom. Let's shift positions now and try to see the problem from the point of view of those at the bottom.

In a very basic sense, the most important actors in the 320(d) programs are individual teachers and students. An enduring fact of all service delivery programs—education, health care, social services, manpower, and so forth—is that they depend heavily on the quality of the interaction between service-giver and client. If we isolate the factors that have the greatest effect on the quality of this interaction, we quickly discover that very few, if any, of them are subject to direct administrative control. . . . Much of the success of the service in education depends on the sensitivity of the teacher to the individual attributes of students and on the teacher's ability to maintain a well-organized, task-oriented classroom. The role of administrators in the instructional process is necessarily marginal. Teachers work almost exclusively in self-contained classrooms, exercising a high degree of discretion in the management of classroom activities. . . .

. . . All of the things that administrators do are at least one step removed from the critical face-to-face transaction between teacher and student.

Think for a moment about the individual teacher's role in the 320(d) program. Word comes to the teacher from a variety of sources—state and local school administration, parents, newspapers, et cetera—that something needs to be done to improve reading and math skills. The teacher searches his or her experience for clues to the accuracy of this assessment and forms a positive or negative attitude toward the assessment. Then the district formulates a program in response to the 320(d) legislation and guidelines; maybe teachers are involved in formulating the program, maybe not. For the teacher, the net effect of the program will be judged by whether it enhances or obstructs the instructional process in the classroom. . . .

Teachers receive a variety of signals about what to do in the classroom. In addition to the signals they receive from the 320(d) program about reading and math skills, they also hear about their responsibility for teaching democratic values, discipline, the free enterprise system, health and nutrition, career choice, and the history of western civilization, to mention a few. It is the teacher's responsibility to turn these signals into a well-organized strategy of instruction that responds to the range of skills and abilities he or she finds among students in the classroom. In short, *teachers will make most of the important discretionary choices in the implementation of the 320(d) program.*

If school district administrators are smart, they will recognize this fact and *design their implementation strategy around maximizing the individual teacher's control of the instructional process.* But in order to do this they, like the Chairman, Commissioner, and Director, must recognize the difference between compliance and capacity. . . . [T]he essential problem for local school administrators is how to direct teachers' attention to the basic skills problem and then provide the resources to respond to the problem in a way that acknowledges teacher control. . . .

Let's back away from the specifics of the 320(d) program for a moment and think about the general features of the system we've been describing. The system is *bottom-heavy* and *loosely coupled*. It is bottom heavy because the closer we get to the bottom of the pyramid, the closer we get to the factors that have the greatest effect on the program's success or failure. It is loosely coupled because the ability of one level to control the behavior of another is weak and largely negative. This characterization is true, in varying degrees, of all the relationships we've examined thus far: the Chairman's ability to control the Commissioner, the Commissioner's ability to control the Director, the Director's ability to control local school administrators, and the local school administrators' ability to control teachers. The skillful use of delegated control is central to making implementation work in bottom-heavy, loosely coupled systems. *When it becomes necessary to rely mainly on hierarchical control, regulation, and compliance* to get the job done, *the game is essentially lost.* Moving from delegated control to hierarchical control means moving from reliance on existing capacity, ingenuity, and judgment to reliance on rules, surveillance, and enforcement procedures. Regulation increases complexity and invites subversion; it diverts attention from accomplishing the task to understanding and manipulating rules.

Two criticisms are commonly levelled at bottom-heavy, loosely coupled systems: they are inefficient and they protect incompetence. Inefficiency, the critics argue, stems from redundancy. Too many people making autonomous choices, with no rational division of labor, results in overlap, duplication, and a general confusion of functions. In the 320(d) program, the critics would argue that it is absurd to think of each teacher essentially inventing his or her own reading and math curriculum; the inefficiencies would be enormous. It would be much more sensible to develop a few model curricula from the best available sources and train teachers how to use them. Likewise, the critics argue, not everyone can be trusted to exercise autonomy in the correct way; lack of central control allows pockets of incompetence to develop and remain essentially immune from discovery. Some teachers and administrators are simply incapable of performing adequately without close supervision. To the extent that bottom-heavy, loosely coupled systems protect the inept, they reinforce inefficiency. These criticisms point to simple, straightforward solutions: We should "streamline" administrative structures, eliminating overlap and duplication, tightening coordination and control. We should hold people accountable for the results they produce, stating clear performance standards and regularly evaluating them.

Proposals of this type stem from a set of assumptions about the operation of complex administrative structures that do not stand up in the face of accumulating evidence. First, take the notion that redundant systems are inefficient and streamlined systems are efficient. Do we say that a commercial aircraft with a triple-redundant landing gear system is inefficient? Of course not. Redundancy is a powerfully efficient device for increasing the reliability and safety of the aircraft. Would we say that a house wired in series is more efficient than one wired in parallel? Series wiring uses rougly half the amount of wiring material, but the result is that each connection is wholly dependent on the preceeding one for its electrical current. In contrast, parallel wiring allows each connection to function independently of others. Thus, redundancy dramatically increases the reliability of an electrical system at a relatively modest additional cost. To say that redundant systems are inefficient is not only superficial but largely false.

Tightly coupled, highly centralized administrative structures are like houses wired in series; there is so little rudundancy that the failure of one unit means the collapse of the whole system. If the organization's task is relatively simple, say brick-making, the system's failure is of little consequence and can be remedied easily. But if the task is complex, like the implementation of the 320(d) program, the absence of redundancy can be disastrous; a small failure anywhere in the system can disrupt a long, interdependent line of relationships, creating confusion and disorder. Bottom-heavy, loosely coupled systems are difficult to administer, but they are extraordinarily rich and robust because they are redundant. *The more complex the task, the more important redundancy is to the efficient accomplishment of the task.*

Furthermore, *most of the redundancies that we observe in the implementation of policy are the result of deliberate political choices.* The division of authority between federal, state, and local government is highly redundant; these relations are characterized by enormous overlap of functions, continual dispute over the proper boundaries of authority, and a high level of ambiguity over who is responsible for what function. The complexity of these relations makes implementation difficult, but a more streamlined, rationalized system would not necessarily be more effective. Existing jurisdictional boundaries, in effect, protect us against too heavy a reliance on the competence or incompetence of any single level of government. The political genius of federalism, then, stems from its skillful reliance on redundancy.

Returning to the 320(d) program example, the redundancy of delegated control can be seen as a sort of "fail-safe" device. The more responsibility is devolved toward the bottom of the system, the greater the number of people who will be actively involved in searching for a solution to the reading and math problem, and the higher the likelihood that more effective programs will be designed and implemented at the local level. The more responsibility is centralized, the more people will rely on direction from above, and the fewer people will be actively engaged in searching for solutions to the problem. Moreover, hierarchical control puts the responsibility for finding solutions to the reading and math problem in the hands of those who are least likely to discover them—administrators. Alert administrators understand that delegated control and redundancy are an important form of insurance against organizational failure.

But what about the argument that bottom-heavy, loosely coupled systems protect the incompetent? There is no question that errors are more visible in tightly-coupled, centralized systems. What could be more visible than one individual or one unit of an organization bringing the entire system to a grinding halt? The more redundant the system, the more difficult it is to find ineffective parts because the parts are less visible. But suppose our purpose was not to ferret out and penalize incompetence as much as it was to improve the overall performance of the system. If we define our purpose this way, redundancy becomes a powerful asset rather than a liability. . . .

Where does this leave the Chairman, the Commissioner and the Director? It seemingly leaves them in a very difficult position. . . .

. . . What we have done is to pare away the easy, superficial solutions to implementation problems and focus on the more difficult, challenging ones. Legislators and high-level administrators have a significant role in these solutions, but that role requires them to adopt a somewhat different view of the process than they conventionally hold. . . .

People at the top of the system tend to think of themselves as initiators of the implementation process; for them implementation consists of a series of actions emanating from the top and reaching to the bottom. Suppose, for purposes of discussion, we simply reverse this logic.

. . . Instead of beginning at the top of the system with a new policy and reasoning through a series of actions required to implement it, begin at the bottom of the system, with the most concrete set of actions, and reason backward to the policy. In the case of the 320(d) program, the reasoning process might look something like this:

1. *What is the problem?* Poor performance by children on standardized measures of reading and math skill.
2. *Where do we attack the problem?* In the classroom.
3. *What has to happen in the classroom to improve reading and math performance?* Teachers: more instructional time on reading and math, better instructional skills, materials closely related to the teacher's strategy and style of instruction, access to other teachers confronted with the same problem. Students: motivation to master the content, reward for learning.
4. *What can the local school system do to increase the likelihood that these things will happen in the classroom?* Remove conflicting instructional requirements, provide access to training for teachers, provide resources (released time, extra compensation, production of materials, etc.) for teachers to develop reading and math instruction, identify students with the greatest need, communicate program to parents.
5. *What can the state education department do to increase the likelihood that these things will happen in local districts?* Remove conflicting policy requirements (with legislative concurrence), transfer information on unusually successful practices from one setting to an-

other, assure fiscal responsibility of local districts receiving state support for basic skill programs.

6. *What can the legislature do to increase the likelihood that the state education department and local school districts will successfully address the basic skills problem?* Remove conflicting policy requirements, authorize and appropiate funds, establish rules of fiscal responsibility, establish basic elements of program design: classroom as the basic delivery unit, local district support for teacher-produced curriculum, state support for transfer of unusually successful practices.

This is a very crude version of mapping backwards, but it . . . forces an analytic structure on discussions of implementation: Begin with a definition of the problem, define the delivery-level unit with the greatest effect on the problem, describe what needs to happen in that unit to solve the problem, then describe for each successive level above that unit what needs to be done to support activity at the delivery level. . . .

Control has a new meaning if we take this point of view. The ability of one level of the system to control the behavior of the next is no longer the central issue. Instead, we're thinking of *where to locate the maximum amount of delegated control, how to get resources into the hands of those who exercise it*, and *what forms of organization enhance the likelihood of success at the delivery level*. Control exercised in this way minimizes investment in surveillance and maximizes investment in the capacity to exercise discretionary choices that directly affect quality of service. In this sense, delegated control is more efficent than hierarchical control. . . .

How would all this look in practice? Suppose we've gone through a full authorization cycle of the 320(d) program and it's now time for the legislature to consider whether the program should be renewed and what changes should be made if it is renewed. The Commissioner and the Director have prepared a package of legislative amendments for which they would like the Chairman's endorsement. These amendments include authority for:

—the state department of education to make grants to groups of teachers for curriculum development;
—teachers to contract, independently of the school system, for in-service training with state support;
—local school districts to contract with other school systems for the transfer of exemplary practices; and
—the state department to identify and disseminate information on exemplary practices.

In addition, the Commissioner and Director have prepared some administrative regulations that do not require new legislative authority. They have forwarded the regulations to the Chairman for review and comment. They include:

—a limit of 20 percent on 320(d) funds that can be used by local districts for activities not directly related to classroom instruction (instructional activities are defined as materials, teacher training, and released time for training); and
—a requirement that local districts make available for public comment criteria for selection of children for special instruction using 320(d) funds.

The following exchange explores the rationale for these amendments and regulations.

Chairman:

I've reviewed your proposed changes for the 320(d) program and I have a number of questions to ask you. The best place to start, I think, is with the basic question of how you expect these proposals to affect the performance of the individual student in the classroom. Commissioner?

Commissioner:

The 320(d) program rises or falls on the quality of instruction in classrooms. We're not certain, and we probably never will be, what creates a productive level of interaction between teacher and student. It's not so important that we know, but it's very important that teachers know. So the Department has deliberately settled on a strategy of putting resources where they are most likely to affect quality of instruction—this means putting them largely in the hands of teachers. We expect that by focusing teachers' attention on the problem of instruction in reading and math, and by increasing interaction among teachers on this subject, we will enhance their ability to respond to individual students with reading and math problems. We don't expect to generate a few "big solutions" to these problems, but we do expect to increase the level of attention focused on the problems at the classroom level.

Chairman:

Director?

Director:

You'll recall that our interim review of the program showed a positive relationship between teacher involvement in curriculum-building and changes in classroom practice. We intend to test whether this relationship holds over the long run. In order to test it, we've got to increase the level of activity at the classroom level and create more opportunities for teachers to interact on curriculum matters. We're betting that this will have a payoff for students with reading and math problems.

Chairman:

We've heard testimony from a number of people who don't share your view. Yesterday we heard from the Council of Local School Administrators. Their representative said that the proposals "make the job of districtwide coordination of reading and math instruction more difficult" and that they "constitute a direct intervention by the state in local school affairs." We also heard from a local superintendent who said that the proposals are "a direct attempt to undermine the chain of command in school district administration." Don't these people have a point? Aren't you short-circuiting a lot of administrative relationships by increasing the control of teachers over program resources?

Director:

I think it's important to put our recommendations in the context of the whole program. The school system is still the administering agency for the 320(d) program at the local level. Local school systems are responsible for selecting and assigning teachers and for designing the local program. We've taken extra care to give local districts maximum flexibility in administering program funds. We haven't required them to select or assign students who receive 320(d) benefits in a certain way; we've simply said they should publicize their criteria for selection. We've only resorted to explicit regulations where we have found that local practices sometimes keep funds from reaching teachers and students. Our proposal to limit non-instructional expenditures to 20 percent is designed to limit the amount of money local districts can use to support administrators who have no direct instructional role. For districts who have taken the task of improving classroom instruction seriously, this requirement poses no particular difficulty.

We view the proposals for support of teacher-initiated curriculum development and training not as an intervention in local district decisions but as a direct investment in activity that is likely to improve the quality of instruction. All we've done is to assure that some fraction of program funds is available for problem-solving and information-sharing at the delivery level, where the need is greatest. If increasing teachers' access to practical information threatens districtwide coordination or supervisory relationships, then it seems to me the district has a problem that goes beyond the 320(d) program. We don't expect teacher-initiated projects to cause problems in districts that have a strong commitment to the support of classroom instruction.

Chairman:

Don't the proposals create a lot of overlap and confusion at the local level, though? If everything works as planned, there will probably be district-sponsored training of teachers, training initiated by teachers themselves, and training that results from cross-district exchanges of information about successful practices. Isn't there a more efficient way of getting at the problem?

Director:

If you mean, "Is there a simpler way to deliver training?" I think the answer is yes. We could locate all the responsibility for training in one place—with the state or with local districts. But this would restrict the number of possibilities for exchanging information and locate responsibility in the hands of people who don't necessarily understand the problems at the classroom level.

We think the payoff is likely to be greater if we increase the frequency of contact among those closest to the problem, providing them with a lot of options for access to information. If we increase the likelihood of successful classroom programs, then the strategy isn't necessarily inefficient.

Commissioner:

As a matter of policy, I'm uncomfortable with the idea of locating sole responsibility for training in the hands of any single authority. It doesn't seem to me a good way to increase the inventive ability that is applied to a problem. I'm more interested in ways of capitalizing on diversity rather than controlling it.

Chairman:

The committee has also heard testimony from the Children's Advocacy Group that is somewhat critical of your proposals. They've said, "The Department stops short of using its full regulatory authority to assure that the neediest children get the greatest access to 320(d) funds." Your proposals don't seem to speak to this issue, do they, Commissioner?

Commissioner:

We're faced with a fairly difficult choice here, Mr. Chairman. As I see it, we've got to decide whether to define the Department's role primarily in regulatory terms or primarily in terms of enhancing local capacity. I've said a number of times that I prefer the latter. But issues like the one raised by the Children's Advocacy Group make my position difficult to argue. We've thought a great deal about whether we want to use the Department's regulatory power to require local districts to select students for the 320(d) program in a certain way. We've decided that we're not in favor of it for two reasons. First, we think our resources are better used in activities that affect the quality of local programs rather than in those that assure local compliance with state guidelines. Second, we don't feel confident deciding how students should be selected, and we're more comfortable leaving that decision in the hands of local districts. So we've settled on a fairly straightforward requirement that districts should publicize their selection criteria. That at least gives local groups a chance to influence the local district's decision.

Chairman:

Thank you. We'll look carefully at your proposals.

This exchange demonstrates the essential logic of mapping backwards. The Chairman's first concern is the effect of Department proposals at the delivery level. Then he backs through the system, using previous testimony of school administrators and advocacy groups, to consider the administrative consequences of the Department's proposals at the local and state level. The Chairman's logic means that the discussion will center on delivery-level problems rather than the competing claims of rival bureaucracies. The Chairman may well reject the Department's proposals on essentially political grounds; it is, after all, his responsibility to weigh competing political claims. But by virtue of the logic of his questioning he is sensitive to the delivery-level effects of political choices.

For their part, the Commissioner and the Director have made a number of strategic choices in assembling their package of proposals. They've decided to bet that shifting resources toward the delivery level and increasing interaction among teachers at that level, even when it results in redundancy and overlap, will increase the likelihood that the program will affect students. They've decided to minimize the Department's regulatory role and to focus regulatory attention only on those matters in which it is relatively easy to determine compliance. The 20 percent requirement can be enforced simply by checking local applications for funds against expenditure reports filed by local districts. On the touchy issue of how students should be selected for attention, they have decided to rely on local politics.

The strategy is far from foolproof. There is no guarantee that teachers will capitalize on the availability of funds for training and curriculum-building. Local districts will, no doubt, invent ingenious ways of asserting control over teacher-initiated projects. Where districts are given wide latitude by the Department, there will be failures as well as successes. And the Department's ability to initiate exchange relationships between weak districts and strong ones will depend on its cleverness and diplomacy. But despite the obvious problems of the strategy, its major strength lies in the fact that it is predicated on the principle of increasing capacity at the delivery level. If the strategy fails to do that, then it needs to be revised.

Conclusion

Complexity can work both for and against successful implementation. When complexity results from hierarchical control, within organizations and across levels of government, it diverts resources from problem-solving and focuses them on surveillance and compliance, it increases the number of steps required to translate a policy into action, and it contrains the inventive capacity of delivery-level personnel. In this sense, hierarchical control *reduces* the likelihood that policies will result in delivery-level effects. But delegated control allows policymakers to capitalize on complexity at the delivery level, using it as a source of ideas for *increasing* the capacity to deliver services. Out of delivery-level complexity grows variability in the way implementors respond to policy. Variability, far from being a threat to successful implementation, produces valuable information about more and less successful practices. If some mechanism exists for capitalizing on variability at the delivery level, then complexity operates to raise the level of knowledge required for successful implementation. Out of this basic understanding of complexity and control come a few prescriptions for how legislators and administrators can deal effectively with implementation problems:

Distinguish between compliance and capacity. There is a critical difference between the ability or willingness of implementors to comply with rules and their capacity to successfully deliver a service. Implementation depends more on capacity than it does on compliance. A large part of the skill required to solve implementation problems depends on the ability of policymakers to determine where compliance is required and where success depends on enhancing delegated control.

Distinguish between implementation variations that result from a failure to comply with basic regulations and those that result from differences in capacity. The two sources of variation require completely different responses. Variability, in and of itself, does not prove either the success or failure of implementation. The portion of variability that results from a failure to comply with basic regulations can be addressed with surveillance and enforcement. But variability that results from differences among implementors in their ability to define and solve delivery problems is a major resource in improving delivery-level performance. If policymakers view all variability as suspect, they not only increase the complexity of their regulatory task, they also eliminate the main source of ideas for successful implementation.

Regulate only those activities for which it is possible to specify a clear standard of performance and which constitute minimum prior conditions for successful implementation. If a certain proportion of a local project's budget is not spent on activities directly related to the delivery of services, one can say that some defensible minimum condition for successful implementation has not been met. The vaguer the standard of performance, the more effort is required to enforce the standard, and the less resources will be targeted at the delivery level. Standards which go beyond minimum conditions of successful implementation effectively put decision-making responsibility in the hands of people with limited knowledge of delivery-level problems.

Focus resources as close as possible to the point of delivery. Policies designed to improve the delivery of services depend heavily on discretionary choices at the delivery level. In order to have maximum effect, resources have to flow primarily to those points in the delivery system where they are most likely to affect discretionary choices. The further away from the point of delivery, the less the likelihood that resources will affect the capacity to deliver, and the greater the complexity of the administrative mechanism required to move resources. The practical effect of this strategy is to increase the complexity of interaction among those closest to the delivery level and decrease the complexity of mechanisms designed to control their behavior from above.

Evaluate policy alternatives by mapping backwards from the point of delivery to the point where policy decisions are made. If delivery-level performance is the basic determinant of successful implementation, then consideration of policies ought to start with their delivery-level effect. Begin with a statement of the problem to which the policy is addressed, define the delivery-level unit with the greatest effect on the problem, describe what needs to happen in that unit to solve the problem, and then describe for each successive level above that unit what needs to be done to support activity at the delivery level.

NOTES AND QUESTIONS

1. Who Implements?

Elmore focuses on the implementation of a statute that affects the structure and operation of a complex organization. *See also* Elmore, "Backward Mapping: Implementation Research and Policy Decisions," 94 *Pol. Sci. Q.* 601 (1979–80); Weick, "Administering Education in Loosely Coupled Schools," 63 *Phi Delta Kappan* 673 (1982). What of a court decision—a desegregation decision or a decision upholding students' due process rights—that has similarly profound organizational effects? Does such a decision raise similar implementation issues? *See generally* Yudof, "Legalization of Dispute Resolution, Distrust of Authority, and Organizational Theory: Implementing Due Process for Students in the Public Schools," 1981 *Wisc. L. Rev.* 891. Is it appropriate for the court, in framing its remedy, to attend to the kinds of concerns noted by Elmore? What might such a remedy-framing process look like? *See* Diver, "The Judge as Political Power-Broker: Superintending Structural Change in Public Institutions," 65 *Va. L. Rev.* 43 (1979).

2. Implementation and Statutory Drafting

In the legislative context, can the prospects for effective implementation be improved in the drafting process? Is implementation largely a technical problem that can be addressed by clearer and tighter drafting, or is it largely a political and ideological problem? Would redrafting of the legislation underlying the 320(d) program significantly affect implementation of the program?

3. Is Full Implementation Ever Possible?

In "The Conditions of Effective Implementation: A Guide to Accomplishing Policy Objectives," 5 *Policy Analysis* 481 (1979), Paul Sabatier and Daniel Mazmanian argue that a statute or appellate court decision can be implemented successfully if (1) the statute incorporates a sound technical theory, that is, a theory that predicts that a given set of resources will produce a given set of outcomes; (2) the statute contains unambiguous policy directives and coherently structures the implementation process; (3) the leaders of the implementing agencies are skillful and committed to the statute's objectives; (4) the program is actively supported by organized interest groups; and (5) the relative priority of statutory objectives is not significantly undermined by changing socioeconomic conditions.

Consider these preconditions in the light of what you know about the field of education. How likely is it that they will be satisfied? What does this suggest about the nature of the implementation process in education? Compare Chubb, "Why the Current Wave of School Reform Will Fail," 90 *The Public Interest* 28 (Winter 1988); Cohen, "Policy and Organization: The Impact of State and Federal Education Policy on School Governance," 52 *Harv. Educ. Rev.* 474 (1982).

4. The Regulatory versus the Programmatic View of Implementation

Do you share Elmore's view that regulation—tighter hierarchical control and compliance with legal mandate—is, in some instances, inimical to effective implementation of a policy change? If so, how does one determine when programmatic "capacity-building" rather than regulatory efforts are appropriate? Who should make this determination: the draftsman of the legislation, the program administrator, or those who actually carry out the program's mandate? *See generally* D. Kirp and T. Timar, *Managing Educational Excellence* (1988).

5. The 320(d) Program

How do you evaluate the way in which the problems identified with the 320(d) program were resolved in the excerpt? From the perspective of a policymaker, do they make good sense? From a lawyer's perspective, does the lack of an enforceable—or even coherent—standard against which to measure compliance with a statute afford reason for concern? Is there a danger that "compliance" may come to mean whatever those in the field choose to do? Does adding another layer of government complicate the issue?

6. Implementation and Equal Opportunity

The 320(d) program is, of course, an invention; programs to aid the educationally disadvantaged, the limited-English-proficient, and the handicapped are not. In reviewing the process by which each of those federal initiatives has been implemented, consider Elmore's approach.

II. CHAPTER 1, EDUCATION CONSOLIDATION AND IMPROVEMENT ACT OF 1981 (ECIR): EQUITY AND THE "EDUCATIONALLY DISADVANTAGED"

The educationally disadvantaged—students primarily from poor families who perform far below grade level in school—were the first major beneficiaries of the new federal largess in education. The benefits program for this group was developed as an integral part of President Lyndon Johnson's War on Poverty. More has been spent on the educationally disadvantaged than on any other group discussed in this chapter. Funding since the program began has totaled more than $40 billion. By looking at Chapter 1, one can trace the course of federal involvement in a particular domain through its several stages: policy inception, program adoption, early implementation failures, and subsequent program modifications.

From the outset, this program exhibited the difficulties as well as the potential of federal involvement in education. Its very purpose was uncertain: Was the act designed primarily to provide special educational services for the educationally disadvantaged, or was it to benefit school systems, using the number of educationally deprived merely as the basis for funding? The implementation strains identified in the Elmore essay are present (indeed, Elmore's fictitious program borrows a great deal from the Chapter 1 implementation literature). Present also are the variety of compliance devices—maximizing local discretion, compliance through litigation, administrative accountability, encouraging the politicization of the program through parental involvement—designed to secure one or another objective.

The size and scope of the program, as well as its detailed requirements, made it a prime target for the Reagan administration, which hoped to eliminate the program entirely, giving local districts authority to spend all federal education funds as they wished. Though that effort was resisted by Congress, Chapter 1 contains fewer mandates to the states than the predecessor Title I legislation; it is a halfway house on the road to the "new federalism."

A. Chapter 1: Scope of the Act

The "educationally deprived" are the designated beneficiaries of Chapter 1, as they were of Title I.

How does one structure a program that assures that this group is especially benefitted, that (as advocates put it) educational systems discriminate in favor of the educationally disadvantaged? A quarter of a century ago, when Title I was adopted, one school of thought stressed the compensatory nature of the program: Title I would "compensate" for the deficits of the child's background. Another approach treated Title I as "remedial," providing aid to make up for what the schools had failed to give these children. Because so little was—and is—known about what educational programs make the most sense for this population, it seemed appropriate to provide substantial flexibility in program design, allowing school districts (which presumably know most about the particular needs of their students) the dominant say in program design. How can these two goals—flexibility and assurances of special benefit—be achieved? What mix of federal, state, and local involvement is most likely to produce the outcome? To that question, Title I and Chapter 1 offer somewhat different answers.

Chapter 1 is a complex piece of legislation. It requires that moneys expended under the act be used to expand and improve the educational programs for educationally deprived children residing in school attendance areas having high concentrations of children from low-income families. Special programs must be designed to meet the special educational needs of this group of children.

The following excerpt elaborates on these requirements as fixed in the current law and identifies some of the ways in which the legislation has been modified.

"Report on Changes Under Chapter 1 of the Education Consolidation and Improvement Act"

Prepared for the Subcommittee on Elementary, Secondary, and Vocational Education of the Committee on Education and Labor of the U.S. House of Representatives (1985).

Federal compensatory education programs arose from Congress's perception that states and local school districts were not doing enough to meet the special needs of the educationally deprived child. Many local school boards did not recognize the nature of the problem, and the ones that did, rarely invested the large amount of local resources needed to operate adequate compensatory programs. . . . Local politics also reduced the likelihood of an adequate local solution to the problem: typically the majority of the educationally deprived came from socioeconomic groups with low political influence, and school boards were vulnerable to pressures from more affluent parents for lower taxes and greater services for their children.

Economic factors also helped to cause underfunding of compensatory education at the local level. High concentrations of educationally deprived children were often found in districts with the least taxable local wealth. Consequently, districts with the greatest need for compensatory programs were frequently the least able to fund those programs. Moreover, many of the benefits of education spilled beyond the boundaries of the state and local jurisdictions that had to bear the full cost of educating the students in their care. This increased the tendency of these jurisdictions to spend less on compensatory education than was in the national interest.

For their part, states funded few special programs for educationally deprived children. State aid to low-income districts had failed to give those districts enough resources to cope with the problem, and states did not compel districts to use the resources at their disposal to provide adequate services for children who were educationally deprived. In addition, the highest concentrations of educationally deprived students were generally found in the lowest-income states, particularly in the South, with the lowest overall per-pupil educational spending and the least state support for programs of compensatory education.

In response to this situation, in 1965 Congress enacted Title I of the Elementary and Secondary Education Act. Title I's Declaration of Policy described the law's purpose:

> In recognition of the special educational needs of children of low-income families and the impact that concentrations of low-income families have on the ability of local educational agencies to support adequate educational programs, the Congress hereby declares it to be the policy of the United States to provide financial assistance (as set forth in this title) to local educational agencies serving areas with concentrations of children from low-income families to expand and improve their educational programs by various means (including preschool programs) which contribute particularly to meeting the special educational needs of educationally deprived children.

Title I established a three-tier division of responsibility among the federal government, states, and local school districts. School districts ("local educational agencies", or LEAs) were responsible for the actual details of designing and operating programs for educationally deprived children. State educational agencies (SEAs) approved school districts' applications for Title I funds and supervised those districts to ensure that the program served the targeted students. The federal government, through the U.S. Office of Education, allocated Title I funds to states, made certain that states enforced the law's provisions, and provided regulations and interpretations of those provisions. The purpose of federal enforcement was to ensure that federal funds would be used in every state to serve the children that Congress intended the program to serve. Without a framework of federal enforcement, some states might fail to enforce the law's provisions, and the purpose of the program would be defeated. . . .

Chapter 1 retains many basic provisions of Title I. Chapter 1's Declaration of Policy recognized the continuity of purpose between Title I and Chapter 1:

> to continue to provide financial assistance to meet the special needs of educationally deprived children, on the basis of entitlements calculated under Title I of the Elementary and Secondary Act of 1965. . . . Further, the Congress recognizes the special educational needs of children of low-income families, and that concentrations of such children in local educational agencies adversely affect their ability to provide educational programs that will meet the needs of such children. . . .

Under Chapter 1 as under Title I, the federal government provides grants to states based on a formula that takes into account state per-pupil expenditures and the number of low-income children in each county in the state. States, in turn, distribute the money to school districts based on counts of low-income children derived from census or National School Lunch Program data. Districts can only operate Chapter 1 programs in "eligible" schools. This means, with certain exceptions spelled out in the 1983 Technical Amendments to Chapter 1, schools with a higher-than-district-average number or percentage of low-income children.

As under Title I, Chapter 1-funded services in eligible schools must be targeted on the specific children with the greatest level of educational deprivation. To be eligible to receive Chapter 1 funds, school districts must identify these children, determine in which grades and subject areas Chapter 1 services are most needed, and develop programs to help educationally deprived children catch up with their peers. Unless certain restrictive conditions hold, Chapter 1-funded services cannot be offered to the general student population, but only to those children identified as educationally deprived. Children in the program have to receive more intensive educational services than children not in the program, and federal dollars can pay only for the incremental cost of the additional services. Schools and children participating in the program have to receive their fair share of state and local educational dollars, except that (unlike under Title I) districts may allocate all of their state and local compensatory education dollars to non-Chapter 1 schools. School districts must make arrangements to serve private school children who would have been eligible for Chapter 1 services had they attended public school.

Like Title I, Chapter 1 requires districts to evaluate the effectiveness of their federally-funded compensatory programs by a set of methods that includes objective tests of the students' achievement in basic skills. Districts must examine whether these gains are sustained over time, and must use the evaluation results to make necessary changes in the design of the program.

The enactment of the Education Consolidation and Improvement Act was the result of a drive by Congressional Republicans to reduce the regulatory role of the U.S. Department of Education (ED), shifting to the states much of the responsibility for making decisions about how the law should be interpreted and enforced. . . .

ECIA removed most of the language in Title I spelling out the authority and responsibilities of states, the federal government, and local school districts, and limited the U.S. Department of Education's authority to write regulations. The result has not been the elimination of federal enforcement entirely, which Congress had no intention of doing. Federal supervision and enforcement remains in the form of audits conducted by the Department of Education's Office of the Inspector General (IG), IG supervision of audits conducted under the Single Audit Act, and federal program reviews of states to ensure that state monitoring, enforcement, and technical assistance are adequate. . . .

* * *

The increase in state responsibilities was accompanied by reduced funding for state Chapter 1 offices to carry out those responsibilities. . . . The justification for reducing the state administrative allocation was that Chapter 1's simpler requirements ought to be less expensive to administer, freeing a higher portion of a reduced appropriation for direct services to children. This argument overlooked the possibility that the states' administrative role might change, with states taking on a more active role in providing technical assistance to help LEAs improve the effectiveness of their programs.

Chapter 1 also eliminated the Title I requirement for Parent Advisory Councils (PACs) in districts and individual school buildings, and substituted a requirement that Chapter 1 programs be "designed and implemented in consultation with parents and teachers." . . .

* * *

Chapter 1 also relaxed certain Title I requirements, such as the requirement that districts maintain the same level of state and local spending from year to year and that districts spend a proportionate share of state and local compensatory education money in schools served by Chapter 1 funds. . . .

In addition to modifying the law, Congress reduced spending on Chapter 1 programs. . . .

The number of children served by Title I/Chapter 1 declined by about 640,000 between the 1979–80 and 1982–83 school years. . . .

School districts responded to reductions in funding by reducing real spending per pupil to make the existing Chapter 1 dollars stretch farther. . . .

The changes made by the Education Consolidation and Improvement Act reflected three criticisms by Congressional Republicans of Title I: that the law and its accompanying regulations had become too complex, that the federal regulatory role in defining acceptable practices under Title I had become too large, and that specific Title I requirements imposed too much of a paperwork and "red tape" burden on states and local school districts. . . .

Much confusion in the early implementation of Title I grew out of the fact that in the eyes of those in Congress who passed the legislation, Title I actually had two purposes. One was to provide financial assistance to *school districts* suffering from the adverse "impact that concentrations of low-income families have on (their) ability . . . to support adequate educational programs." . . .

The second purpose of Title I was to provide aid directly to educationally deprived *children* by funding programs to meet their "special educational needs." . . .

If Title I aid was to meet the special educational needs of educationally deprived children, however, the program could not simply be one of general aid to school districts. That was the view of regulators in the U.S. Office of Education (USOE) when they set out to interpret the Congressional intent behind the legislation. . . .

Many school districts, on the other hand, treated Title I as general aid. They reasoned that anything which helped them to strengthen their overall educational program would also help meet the needs of the educationally deprived. . . .

This situation began to change after 1969, largely as a result of an influential report by Ruby Martin and Phyllis McClure, two researchers for the Washington Research Project of the NAACP Legal Defense and Educational Fund. Using data gathered by federal auditors, Martin and McClure documented the use of Title I funds for general aid, and the use of those funds in the South to pay educational expenses for black students that were provided for white students out of local resources. . . .

In the Education Amendments of 1969, Congress prohibited the use of Title I funds to supplant local expenditures, and required that districts not discriminate against Title I schools in their allocation of state and local funds. . . .

Pressure from Congress for greater federal enforcement of Title I's provisions led to major changes in the administration of the program. In 1970 USOE began regular monitoring of SEAs, pressuring them to enforce the law. At the same time, the agency began pressuring SEAs to return money that federal auditors had found districts had misspent. During the 1970's, states tightened up their enforcement of Title I's requirements. . . .

As Title I matured, the law and regulations became more complex, as is frequently the case with legislation that is amended numerous times to take into account situations that the program's originators did not foresee. This complexity became a focus of criticism of the program by some conservatives in Congress. . . .

The critics' argument was that although heavy regulation may have been necessary in the early days of the program to assure that Title I funds were appropriately targeted and that parents were involved in the program, the regulations had become too detailed and burdensome and had outlived much of their usefulness.

The proponents of preserving the requirements in Title I argued, on the other hand, that the program was working well precisely because of the federal regulatory structure that had been established; that there was still political pressure on many districts to use federal funds for general aid or local tax relief; and that without backing from the federal government, some States might not act to prevent school districts from giving in to those pressures. These proponents argued further that many districts would avoid involving parents unless the law mandated specific forms of parent involvement; and that loosening the regulatory requirements on districts would "send the wrong message"—that Congress no longer cared whether schools used all of the Title I funds to help educationally deprived children. . . .

* * *

Chapter 1 retains Title I's three-tier division of responsibility between the federal government, states, and local school districts. LEAs continue to design and operate Chapter 1 programs, and bear the primary responsibility for ensuring that these programs effectively serve the needs of educationally deprived children. States approve LEA applications for Chapter 1 funds, and by implication, must ascertain whether districts are following the practices described in their applications. The U.S. Department of Education disburses Chapter 1 funds, issues regulations "which are deemed necessary to reasonably insure that there is compliance with the specific requirements and assurances required by (the statute)," and withholds funds from states, as needed to enforce compliance with the law.

Title I clearly spelled out the division of labor between the federal government, states, and local school districts, and left no doubt that the federal government was the ultimate "standard-setter" for what was and was not in compliance with the law. ECIA's sponsors sought to reduce the U.S. Department of Education's rulemaking powers, by including language in the statute limiting ED's authority to write regulations. By implication, states acquired an increased responsibility for defining the limits of acceptable practice.

However, two problems accompanied this transfer of responsibility to the states. In its desire to simplify, Congress omitted nearly all of Title I's provisions defining specific state powers and responsibilities. This left unclear what some of those powers and responsibilities were. Second, the law reduced federal rulemaking authority but preserved federal enforcement powers through the audit process. The inevitable result is that a certain amount of "rulemaking" is likely to occur through the audit process, as local and federal auditors take exception to practices for which no clear guidelines exist. . . .

The Department of Education allocates Chapter 1 money to states (and through states, to LEAs) according to the same formula used under Title I. This formula takes into account average state per-pupil school expenditures, the state's number of children from families below the poverty level, and the number of children in households with higher than poverty-level incomes currently on the state's AFDC rolls. . . .

Chapter 1 created uncertainty about the extent of the Department of Education's power and responsibilities. Although ECIA gives the Department authority "to issue regulations . . . which are deemed necessary to reasonably insure that there is compliance with the specific requirements and assurances required by this chapter," the law also states that "In all other matters relating to the details of planning, developing, implementing, and evaluating programs and projects . . . the Secretary shall not issue regulations." The law here seems to tell the Department, "make necessary regulations but not unnecessary ones," but there is little guidance on what types of regulations are necessary. The Department's response to this ambiguous statutory language has been to issue regulations which do little more than paraphrase the statute. . . .

* * *

Federal audits are conducted by the Office of the Inspector General, a division in the Department of Education separate from the Division of Compensatory Education that administers Chapter 1. . . .

The frequency of IG audits since the passage of Chapter 1 has remained approximately the same as in the 1970s under Title I. . . .

States continue to occupy a wide range of positions along a continuum from a "strong state leadership" stance to a "local control" orientation. At one end of this continuum is a "strong leader" state that reports that the change from Title I to Chapter 1 has made little difference in its state, as the SEA makes the rules for LEAs anyway. A number of states fall at the other end of the continuum, relying on the federal government to define what is and is not required. . . .

Nearly all states report shifting or attempting to shift emphasis from monitoring to ensure compliance with the law, to offering more technical assistance to LEAs to improve the quality of their Chapter 1 projects. In most cases, this change of emphasis results from states' belief that monitoring has become easier and more routine over time, and they can afford to devote more time to working with LEAs to make certain the program actually makes a difference. . . .

* * *

According to state Chapter 1 directors, the methods districts use to select schools and children to receive Chapter 1 services have changed little from those used under Title I. . . .

Title I's rules on school and child eligibility were intended to ensure that districts concentrate aid on the children in greatest need, instead of spreading limited federal dollars among so many students that those dollars could not make a difference. Accordingly, Title I restricted the schools that its services could be offered in, and required LEAs to develop a systematic method of determining which students would participate in Title I-funded programs. . . .

With certain exceptions described in the law, a district could operate Title I programs only in schools with a higher-than-district-average number or percentage of low-income children. If funds were inadequate to offer programs in all the eligible schools, the LEA had to select schools for service in the order they were ranked. . . .

Once a district had determined which schools were eligible for services, the LEA had to decide in how many schools to operate Title I programs. Here the district had two conflicting considerations. On the one hand, a district attempting to serve too many schools might spread its limited Title I resources too thin and not offer a program "of sufficient size, scope, and quality to give reasonable promise of substantial progress toward meeting the special educational needs of the children being served" as the law required. On the other hand, leaving eligible schools unserved also meant failing to serve children in need of the program. . . .

Chapter 1 incorporates word-for-word Title I's requirements that LEAs serve private school children living in attendance areas served by the district's Chapter 1 program.

* * *

Chapter 1 school and student selection provisions require that aid be targeted to children with the greatest educational need, in schools with the highest concentrations of low-income or educationally deprived children. This targeting grew out of Congress's intent that the money be used entirely to address the special needs of a particular population of students.

However, this intent would not be met if school districts spent Chapter 1 money on other groups of children or used the money for general tax relief, or failed to provide educationally deprived children with their fair share of state and local services. Realization of this led, under Title I, to the enactment of five fiscal requirements:

> —*Maintenance of Effort.* An LEA could receive Title I aid in a given year only if the district's state- and locally-funded educational expenditures had not declined in the preceding year.
> —*Prohibition of General Aid.* Title I funds had to be spent exclusively to meet the special educational needs of educationally deprived children, and could not be spread around to meet the school's general instructional or noninstructional expenses.
> —*Supplement-Not-Supplant.* A district could not use Title I money to pay for services that would have been provided with state and local funds had Title I funding not been available.
> —*Excess Costs.* Districts had to provide more intensive services to Title I students than non-Title I students were receiving, and Title I funds could be used to pay only for the incremental cost of the additional services.
> —*Comparability.* Districts could not discriminate against or among Title I-funded schools in the provision of state and local resources. State and local spending per pupil had to be roughly "comparable" among all schools in a district.

Chapter 1 repealed the excess cost requirement, and relaxed the maintenance of effort, supplement-not-supplant, and comparability requirements in significant ways. . . .

Chapter 1 modified Title I's maintenance-of-effort provision. Chapter 1 allows LEAs to reduce their level of state and local expenditure in a given year by 10 percent (measured on an aggregate or per-pupil basis, whichever is most favorable to the LEA) without being out of compliance with maintenance of effort. . . .

* * *

Title I's early regulations stated that money intended to "meet the special educational needs of educationally deprived children" should be spent entirely for that purpose, and not be used to meet the district's general expenses. . . .

Two provisions enacted by Congress in the 1978 Education Amendments gave LEAs more flexibility to use Title I funds to benefit non-Title I students under certain circumstances. One allowed LEAs, in schools with a more than 75 percent low-income student body, to use Title I funds for schoolwide projects benefiting all the students in the school. In order to use this provision, a district had to match the Title I funds with state and local funds, in proportion to the percentage of non-educationally deprived students in the school.

A second provision enabled LEAs to permit a limited number of non-Title I children to participate in the Title I project if it was impractical to exclude them, and if the inclusion of those children would not increase program costs or decrease the availability or effectiveness of services to Title-I-eligible children.

Chapter 1, as enacted in 1981, prohibited the use of federal compensatory funds for general aid but dropped both of the Title I provisions that gave districts more flexibility. In 1983 the Technical Amendments restored the provision allowing schoolwide projects. . . .

Congress's intent to aid educationally deprived children would not be met if LEAs used Chapter 1 money to replace state and local funds that would otherwise have been spent on those children, and shifted the state and local money to other schools or children or back to local taxpayers. To the extent that such a shift occurred, the federal dollars would in effect be going to the groups to whom the funds were shifted, rather than to the students that Congress intended to help. . . .

Congress retained the supplement-not-supplant requirement in Chapter 1. . . . A significant change . . . occurred in the case of state and local compensatory education (SCE) funds. In the mid-1970s several states and LEAs had sought to use these funds as a complement to Title I, using Title I funds to serve children in Title I schools and SCE funds to serve educationally deprived children in non-Title I schools. This practice clearly violated the supplement-not-supplant rule, as the introduction of federal compensatory education money into Title I schools displaced state and local compensatory funds from those schools. . . .

Under ECIA, as clarified by the Technical Amendments, the supplement-not-supplant requirement no longer applies to SCE programs. . . . Consequently, states or districts are free to concentrate all of these funds in non-Chapter 1 schools if they so desire. However, ED does not regard state compensatory education services as exempt from the supplement-not-supplant requirement if those services are mandated by state law. . . .

In the mid-1960s, segregated school systems in the South spent a much smaller amount of state and local resources, per pupil, in their black schools than in their white schools. When Title I was enacted, many of these school systems used the Title I funds to make up some of the difference. . . .

Consequently, beginning in 1968 the Title I regulations prohibited discrimination against Title I schools in the provision of state and local educational services. . . .

In April, 1970, Congress amended the statute to require that:

> State and local funds will be used in the district of such [local educational] agency to provide services in project areas which, taken as a whole, are at least comparable to services being provided in areas in such district which are not receiving funds under this title . . . each local educational agency receiving funds shall report on or before July 1, 1971, and on or before July 1 of each year thereafter with respect to its compliance with this clause.

The requirement that LEAs equalize per-pupil expenditures between schools was controversial because school districts had traditionally placed their most inexperienced teachers in schools in the lowest-income neighborhoods, and allowed more experienced teachers to transfer to schools in more affluent areas. Thus, equalizing per-pupil expenditures would have compelled districts to transfer large numbers of experienced teachers into schools in low-income areas. . . .

* * *

By the late 1970s . . . a district had to show that the ratio of state- and locally-funded instructional staff to students, and its per-pupil state and local expenditures on instructional salaries, were no more than five percent less in each Title I school than the average of the non-Title I schools. . . .

* * *

Of all the fiscal provisions, comparability underwent the greatest change under Chapter 1. Chapter 1 . . . stated that a school district could satisfy the comparability requirement by providing an assurance in its application that the district has "a districtwide salary schedule; a policy to ensure equivalence among schools in teachers, administrators, and auxiliary personnel; and a policy to ensure equivalence among schools in the provision of curriculum materials and instructional supplies." . . .

When Title I, ESEA was enacted in 1965, one of its provisions, inserted on the insistence of Senator Robert Kennedy, was that "effective procedures, including provision for appropriate objective measurements of educational achievement, will be adopted for evaluating at least annually the effectiveness of the programs in meeting the special educational needs of educationally deprived children. . ." .

By the late 1970s, the Title I evaluation provisions had been modified to assign responsibility as follows:

> —LEAs collected and analyzed evaluation data at least once every three years, and were required to use the evaluation results to improve their Title I projects. . . .
> —States evaluated their state-operated programs in a similar fashion. . . .
> —USOE developed acceptable evaluation models and a common format for states to use in reporting evaluation results.

* * *

The advantages of a common nationwide reporting system were that the system facilitated cross-district and cross-state comparisons, and made it possible to aggregate LEAs' and states' data into national data which could then be used to make statements about the effectiveness of the program.

Title I also incorporated language, later dropped by Chapter 1, instructing LEAs and USOE to disseminate information about effective programs and practices. The availability of a common evaluation and reporting system made it easier to make the comparisons needed to determine what the most effective programs and practices were.

Chapter 1 preserved the ESEA requirement that LEAs evaluate their Title I programs to determine their effectiveness, but deleted the requirement that districts use one of the three evaluation models adopted by the Department of Education. . . .

The general impression one gets from talking to directors is of an evaluation process little changed from that under Title I. The critical evaluation issue, as it was under Title I, is how districts can use the results of these evaluations to improve their programs. . . .

The greatest change between Title I and Chapter 1 was the change in the parent participation requirements. Parent involvement had originally been introduced into Title I in part because of the belief, shared by many Title I activists and USOE, that parents would serve as a watchdog to keep the schools responsive to their children's educational needs. Parents, in this view, would help enforce the law's targeting requirements by calling attention to any violations.

However, as the original supporters of Title I parent involvement realized and a growing body of educational research suggests, parent involvement is also important for a different reason: improving the effectiveness of Chapter 1 programs. By involving parents in working with teachers and reinforcing and promoting Chapter 1 learning objectives in the home, schools can have an impact on student achievement. The positive effect that parent-teacher co-operation has on children's learning is one of the consistent findings of educational research, so much so that one of the less favorable recent assessments of the effectiveness of compensatory education concludes that:

> The studies we surveyed reveal that there is no input, no approach, no program characteristic that is repeatedly found to be relatively or absolutely effective—*with the possible exception of parent involvement*. . . .

Throughout the history of ESEA and ECIA, Congress has attempted to strike a balance between being prescriptive enough to guarantee that desired levels of parent involvement occur, but not so prescriptive as to deny districts the flexibility needed to design a parent involvement program suitable to local conditions. . . .

Under Title I, Congress had moved steadily towards the "more prescriptive" side. . . . USOE in 1971 issued a regulation requiring each LEA to establish a district-wide Parent Advisory Council.

The Education Amendments of 1974 required districts and individual buildings with more than 40 Title I students or one full-time Title I teacher to have elected Parent Advisory Councils (PACs). The amendments enacted in 1978 . . . added requirements about the size and composition of PACs in buildings or districts with more than 75 Title I students. . . .

Chapter 1 represented a major swing toward less prescriptive parent involvement requirements. The law repealed all parent council requirements, mandating only that Chapter 1 programs "be implemented in consultation with parents and teachers of [Chapter 1] children." . . .

* * *

NOTES AND QUESTIONS

1. *Chapter 1 and Federalism*

Does the allocation of authority among federal, state, and local government agencies, as set forth in the excerpt above, match the competencies of each level of government? *See* chapter 4. Do the changes worked by Chapter 1 make things better or worse?

2. *Program Beneficiaries*

If Chapter 1 is supposed to benefit the educationally deprived, why are funds initially allocated on the basis of poverty levels rather than educational deprivation? How could an educational deprivation allocation formula be constructed? Would it be sensible, for instance, to rely on the results of a nationwide academic achievement test in allocating Chapter 1 funds?

Should districts with proportionately few poor or educationally deprived youngsters qualify for Chapter 1 funds, or should funds be concentrated in districts with high proportions of such students?

3. *Chapter 1 and Fund Allocation*

The various fund allocation provisions are designed to assure that funds be used to meet the special—not the ordinary—educational needs of educationally deprived children; that is, they are designed to prevent districts from using Chapter 1 as general aid. On the face of the provisions, do they accomplish this objective? Are they likely to generate undesirable side effects—for example, excess paperwork or reluctance on the part of school districts to adopt programs that cannot easily be defended as "special" (for example, programs that do not remove children from the regular classroom)? How would Elmore (section A, *supra)* appraise the fund allocation provisions?

4. *How Clear Is the Legal Framework?*

A report published by the Rand Corporation notes that "decision-making relationships are left unclear" by the Chapter 1 legislation "and compliance standards are uncertain." That ambiguity, the report notes, has left state and local administrators uncertain of what new autonomy they now enjoy. L. Darling-Hammond and E. Marks, *The New Federalism in Education: State Responses to the 1981 Education Consolidation and Improvement Act* (1983).

B. Implementing Chapter 1

How has compliance with the Title I/Chapter 1 mandate been monitored? And, beyond compliance, how have the broader aims of the legislation—to aid the educationally disadvantaged—been promoted?

Within three years of the passage of Title I, reports of noncompliance—produced by both the Office of Education and by outside investigators—were commonplace. *See* Washington Research Project of the Southern Center for Studies in Public Policy and the NAACP Legal Defense and Educational Fund, *Title I of ESEA: Is It Helping Poor Children?* (1969). Community groups as well as their attorneys pressed for educational programs consistent with the legal mandate and responsive to parent-perceived needs. Litigation was one strategy adopted with this end in view. *See* Yudof, "Title I and Empowerment: A Litigation Strategy," 5 *Inequality in Educ.* 11–12 (1970).

Nicholson v. Pittenger

364 F.Supp. 669 (E.D.Pa. 1973).

Joseph S. Lord, III, Chief Judge.

The gist of plaintiffs' complaint is that defendants have approved Title I applications for Philadelphia without first making certain determinations required by statute, and that these applications violated various statutory restrictions governing the use of Title I funds. These determinations and violations fall within four categories: (1) comparability; (2) supplanting; (3) concentration; and (4) evaluation. Plaintiffs seek a declaration of these violations by defendants and an injunction prohibiting defendants from approving future Title I applications from Philadelphia which contain these violations.

Plaintiffs allege that defendants . . . approv[e] Title I applications for Philadelphia which do not provide comparable educational services in schools receiving Title I funds and in schools not receiving Title I funds. . . .

We, of course, would not want, in any way, to curtail the flow of federal funds to the already financially beleaguered Philadelphia school system. However, the past applications from Philadelphia clearly have not satisfied the requirements of comparability.

During the 1970–1971 school year, 102 elementary, junior, and senior high schools in Philadelphia which were receiving Title I funds had comparability violations. . . . These 102 schools amount to 53% of the schools receiving Title I funds in Philadelphia. During the 1971–1972 school year, 138 elementary, junior, and senior high schools had comparability violations. . . . Despite these comparability violations, defendants approved the 1971–1972 and 1972–1973 Title I applications for Philadelphia. . . .

* * *

[W]e will enjoin defendants from approving any Title I applications for the School District of Philadelphia, beginning with the 1973–1974 school year, unless those applications either show Philadelphia's compliance with the requirements of comparability . . . or contain an adequate assurance that such comparability will be achieved and maintained during the periods for which the applications are submitted.

Plaintiffs allege that defendants approv[e] Title I applications which use Title I funds to supplant services provided in schools not receiving Title I funds. . . .

[D]efendants have not required the School District of Philadelphia to submit the information necessary to make a determination as to the existence or absence of supplanting. For example, defendants have not required Philadelphia to submit lists of educational programs provided in non-Title I schools, nor have defendants required Philadelphia to submit lists of employees and job descriptions of employees who work in non-Title I schools. Therefore, defendants have no way to determine whether or not Title I programs in Title I schools are similar to non-Title I programs in non-Title I schools, or whether or not non-Title I employees perform the same jobs as Title I employees.

In fact, plaintiffs offered substantial evidence of and we find as a fact that there has been supplanting in Title I financed art, music, and reading programs in Title I schools, which are also provided without Title I funds in non-Title I schools. Similarly, art teachers, teaching aids, music teachers, and reading teachers paid with Title I funds perform the same functions as their counterparts in non-Title I schools, who are paid with State and local funds.

Therefore, we will enjoin defendants from approving any Title I applications for the School District of Philadelphia, beginning with the 1973–1974 school year, unless defendants make adequate determinations as to the absence of supplanting violations.

Plaintiffs allege that defendants approv[e] Title I applications from the School District of Philadelphia which do not indicate that Title I programs will be concentrated in those schools with the highest concentrations of eligible students. . . . [D]efendants have not required Philadelphia to submit information from which it could be determined whether or not a program financed with Title I funds is of sufficient size, scope, and quality to meet the special educational needs of educationally deprived children. Moreover, defendants have established no criteria to determine whether or not there has been adequate concentration in terms of actual Title I expenditures per child. Defendants have no information from which to determine for Philadelphia the concentration of Title I funds either in terms of Title I dollars per Title I school or per Title I students.

In fact, rather than concentrating its Title I funds on a limited number of educationally deprived children, the School District of Philadelphia includes 96% of the eligible children in its Title I programs. . . . During the 1972–1973 school year, the ratio of State and local funds to Title I funds for each participating Title I child in the School District of Philadelphia was $928 to $174, or 5.5 to 1. For 1971–1972, the ratio was $820 to $172, or 4.8 to 1.

Therefore, we shall enjoin defendants from approving any Title I applications for the School District of Philadelphia, beginning with the 1973–1974 school year, unless defendants obtain information from which it can be determined whether or not programs to be financed with Title I funds are of sufficient size, scope, and quality to meet the special educational needs of educationally deprived children, and unless Title I funds are concentrated on a limited number of projects and applied to a limited number of educationally deprived children, in a manner consistent with the statute and regulations above.

Finally, plaintiffs allege that defendants . . . approv[e] Title I applications which fund documented ineffective programs and which do not have adequate evaluative procedures nor adequate information relating to the educational achievement of students. . . .

. . . [D]efendants have not required, as a condition to approving a Title I application, information which would enable a determination of how extensive any specific educational deficiency may be throughout the school district. Defendants also have no criteria to determine whether or not the local educational agency's Title I programs offer a reasonable promise of substantial progress. Moreover, defendants have approved Title I applications which do not state on a program-by-program basis the degree of change expected by the end of the school year.

Plaintiffs list 6 Title I programs in Philadelphia that contain no description of the methods or procedures to be used to evaluate them; 17 programs for which the description of methods and procedures to be used to evaluate them do not have sufficient detail to enable defendants to appraise their potential effectiveness; 21 programs where the evaluation methods and procedures of the School District of Philadelphia fail, in whole or in part, to address program objectives; 6 programs that do not have clearly stated objectives; 12 programs which have received previous evaluations indicating the failure of the programs to achieve some or all of their objectives in one of the preceding years; and 12 programs where evaluations focused on questions related not to whether objectives were met, but to how programs were managed.

Therefore, we . . . shall order defendants to develop adequate evaluation methods and procedures for Title I projects. . . .

NOTES AND QUESTIONS

1. **Nicholson v. Pittenger:** ***Scope of the Decision***

What precisely does the court order? Is the order likely to bring Philadelphia in compliance with the law? What further compliance problems do you anticipate? What further judicial orders, if any, would be appropriate?

2. The Inefficacy of Private Litigation

Surprisingly little private litigation has been brought to enforce Title I or Chapter 1. Some thirty cases have been filed, and most of those were settled. Generally, as in *Nicholson*, courts accepted plaintiffs' claims but provided only limited relief. *See, e.g., Alexander v. Califano*, 432 F.Supp. 1182 (N.D. Cal. 1977); *Natonabah v. Board of Education*, 355 F.Supp. 716 (D.N.M. 1973); *Community School Board, District 3 v. Board of Education*, 66 Misc.2d 739, 321 N.Y.S.2d 949 (Sup.Ct. 1971). Do those results speak to the limitations of securing reform through litigation?

3. Parent Participation

Participation and litigation were viewed as complementary means to the same end: the creation of a political base, at the local level, responsive to the concerns of the eligible community, able to act as a countervailing power to state officials and local education. Indeed, one of the objectives of litigation was to secure effective parent participation. *See* Breezer, "Title I Parent Advisory Councils: To What Extent Must They Be Involved?" 7 *J. Law and Educ.* 15 (1978).

Through Parent Advisory Councils (PACs), parents were given formal responsibilities for program management. Under Title I, parents were entitled to select the PAC; a majority of its members were parents of children to be served by Title I projects; representatives of children attending schools that were eligible for, but not receiving, Title I funds, were included on the PAC. The PAC was entitled to information relating to legal requirements of Title I and to any state or federal audit reports. Parents generally were entitled to "participate in the establishment of [Title I] programs, and . . . to make recommendations with respect to the instructional goals of the program. . . ."

Congress eliminated the PAC requirement in the 1981 legislation. This is perhaps the biggest change in the law, and the issue remains controversial. Those who oppose a federal PAC mandate argue that a uniform requirement fails to distinguish significant differences between urban and rural districts; that states and school districts should choose their own form of parent involvement, not have one imposed on them; and that, historically, PACs promoted political activity that had little to do with educating children. Those who would reinstate PACs argue that, in the 1970s, they were effective instruments of parental involvement, and that eliminating them has simply led districts to diminish the role of parents (half the states report significantly less organized parental involvement). *See* Plunkett, "From Title I to Chapter 1: The Evolution of Compensatory Education," 66 *Phi Delta Kappan* 533 (April 1985). They also urge that limiting parental involvement affects the education of Chapter 1 children (*see* A. Henderson, ed., *Parent Participation-Student Achievement: The Evidence Grows, An Annotated Bibliography* (1981)) and that political mobilization of parents is a good, not a bad, thing—that it invites more democratic decision-making on the local level and, nationally, encourages organized political resistance to cuts in Chapter 1 funding. Would you reinstate the requirement?

4. Federal Monitoring and Enforcement Activities

With varying degrees of vigilance, the federal government has sought to enforce Title I and Chapter 1 mandates and, more ambitiously, to prod districts into strengthening the quality of their educational programs. Lawsuits to recover misspent funds have been the chief compliance-promoting instrument.

Bennett v. Kentucky Department of Education

470 U.S. 656, 105 S.Ct. 1544, 84 L.Ed.2d 590 (1985).

Justice O'Connor delivered the opinion of the Court.

This case . . . concerns an effort by the Federal Government to recover Title I funds that were allegedly misused by a State. . . . [T]he dispute is whether the Secretary correctly demanded repayment based on a determination that Kentucky violated requirements that Title I funds be used to supplement, and not to supplant, state and local expenditures for education.

* * *

In order to assure that federal funds would be used to support additional services that would not otherwise be available, the Title I program from the outset prohibited the use of federal grants merely to replace state and local expenditures.

* * *

In 1976, federal auditors found that Kentucky had approved Title I programs for fiscal year 1974 that violated the prohibitions on supplanting. . . . The disputed programs involved "readiness classes" offered by 50 local education agencies for educationally disadvantaged children in place of regular first- and second-grade classes. . . . Participating students received their entire academic instruction in the readiness classes, and a substantial number of the students were expected to be promoted to the next higher grade level the following year.

. . . Title I funds were used to pay all the instructional salaries and a portion of the administrative support costs for the readiness classes. . . . Students in these classes did receive locally funded "enrichment services," *i.e.*, art, physical education, music, and library, that were available to students enrolled in regular classes. . . . It is not disputed, however, that Title I funds defrayed substantially all the costs of educating students in the readiness classes. . . . The auditors concluded that supplanting of state and local expenditures had occurred for children in readiness classes who were promoted to the next higher regular grade. . . . Based on this finding, the auditors estimated that $704,237 in Title I funds had been misused, and the Department issued a final determination letter demanding repayment.

* * *

In reviewing the final order demanding repayment, the Court of Appeals acknowledged that the Secretary's interpretation of the supplanting prohibition was reasonable and would govern subsequent grants. . . . Nonetheless, the court concluded that Kentucky was not liable for misusing Title I funds during fiscal year 1974. The Court of Appeals viewed the issue to be "the fairness of imposing sanctions upon the Commonwealth of Kentucky for its 'failure to substantially comply' with the requirements [of Title I]." . . . The statute and regulations concerning supplanting, the court maintained, were not "unambiguous." . . . Moreover, Congress specifically gave state and local officials discretion to develop particular programs to be supported by Title I funds. . . . In these circumstances, the Court of Appeals concluded that it would be unfair to assess a penalty against Kentucky where there was no evidence of bad faith and the disputed programs complied with a reasonable interpretation of the law. . . .

* * *

We note initially that the Court of Appeals erred in characterizing the issue to be the fairness of imposing sanctions against the State for its failure to comply substantially with the requirements of Title I. Although recovery of misused Title I funds clearly is intended to promote compliance with the requirements of the grant program, a demand for repayment is more in the nature of an effort to collect upon a debt than a penal sanction. . . . The state gave certain assurances as a condition for receiving the federal funds, and if those assurances were not complied with, the Federal Government is entitled to recover amounts spent contrary to the terms of the grant agreement. . . .

* * *

Nor do we think that the absence of bad faith absolves a State from liability if funds were in fact spent contrary to the terms of the grant agreement. In *Bell v. New Jersey* [461 U.S. 773 (1983)] we explained that where a State obtains grants by providing assurances that the funds will be used on programs that comply with Title I, the State has no right to retain funds that are in fact misused. . . . Our discussion in no way suggested that the "misuse" of Title I funds depended on any subjective intent attributable to grant recipients.

* * *

In reviewing a determination by the Secretary that a State has misused Title I funds, a court should consider whether the findings are supported by substantial evidence and reflect an application of the proper legal standards. . . . The disagreement in this case concerns whether the Secretary properly determined that the readiness programs approved by Kentucky violated assurances that Title I funds would be used to supplement state and local expenditures. The Government argues that a reviewing court should simply defer to the Secretary's interpretation of the requirements of Title I so long as it is reasonable. Without disputing the reasonableness of the interpretation advanced by the Secretary, Kentucky contends that because the grant program was in the nature of a contract, any ambiguities with respect to the obligations of the State must be resolved against the party who drafted the agreement, *i.e.*, the Federal Government. Thus, the parties dispute the fundamental nature of the obligations assumed under Title I: the Government suggests that the State guaranteed that the use of the funds would satisfy whatever interpretation of the program requirements the Secretary might reasonably adopt; the State argues that liability for the misuse of funds results only if grants were spent in violation of an unambiguous requirement.

The contentions of the parties can be properly evaluated only against the background of the actual operation of Title I. The grant program provided federal aid for compensatory education for disadvantaged children, but expressly left the selection and development of particular projects to local control. State education agencies approved program applications and monitored compliance by local school districts, obtained funds from the Federal Government, and subsequently channeled the money back to the local level. Thus, the States essentially served as conduits for what became a massive flow of federal funds.

Although Congress in 1965 articulated the general goals of Title I, the statute and the initial regulations did not precisely outline the permissible means for implementing those goals. Uncertainty in this regard was compounded by the fact that during the first years following the passage of Title I, the Office of Education did not vigorously enforce the requirements of the program. . . . In 1970, Congress acknowledged that funds had been misused because of weaknesses in administration, and directed the Office of Education to strengthen its monitoring of the program requirements. . . . Management of Title I by the Office of Education improved during the 1970's, but problems in clarifying the program requirements remained. . . . Congress in 1974 directed the NIE to conduct a comprehensive three-year study of federal compensatory education programs, including Title I. . . .

The NIE study was the primary impetus for the Education Amendments of 1978. In considering those Amendments, Congress noted evidence that the Office of Education was "implementing administrative requirements in a manner which is neither clear nor consistent, and that this inconsistency is confusing States and local education agencies about their obligations." . . . This confusion, Congress observed, resulted in part from the diffuse legal framework for Title I. In addition to the statutory provisions and the regulations, the Office of Education sent program guides to state education agencies explaining the requirements and their application to particular situations. . . .

Congress accepted the NIE's conclusion that many of the questions concerning the requirements of Title I would be resolved if the various materials prepared by the Office of Education were "assembled, summarized, and interrelated." . . . The NIE study and the extensive review of Title I's administration by Congress indicate that the requirements of the program, while not always clear, evolved and became more specific over time and were explained in materials beyond the statute and its implementing regulations.

Although we agree with the State that Title I grant agreements had a contractual aspect, the program cannot be viewed in the same manner as a bilateral contract governing a discrete transaction. . . . The Federal Government established general guidelines for the allocation and use of funds, and the States agreed to follow those guidelines in approving and monitoring specific projects developed and operated at the local level. Given the structure of the grant program, the Federal Government simply could not prospectively resolve every possible ambiguity concerning particular applications of the requirements of Title I. . . . Moreover, the fact that Title I was an ongoing, cooperative program meant that grant recipients had an opportunity to seek clarification of the program requirements. Accordingly, we do not believe that ambiguities in the requirements should invariably be resolved against the Federal Government as the drafter of the grant agreement.

* * *

We agree with the Secretary that the readiness classes approved by Kentucky clearly violated existing statutory and regulatory provisions that prohibited supplanting. It is undisputed that Title I funds were used to pay substantially all the costs for the basic education of students in the readiness classes. Absent these classes funded by Title I, the participating students would have received instruction in regular classes supported by state and local funds. Both the statutory provision and the implementing regulations expressly required that Title I funds not be used to supplant state and local funds for the *pupils* participating in Title I programs. . . .

Based on the language of the statute and the regulation, we cannot agree that there was an ambiguity whether the supplanting prohibition would be satisfied if state and local funding was maintained at the level of the school district, school, or grade. Separate statutory provisions required that state and local spending not be reduced at the level of school districts . . . or individual schools. . . . Although funding was maintained at the level of particular grades, because Title I students were placed in separate classes supported by federal funds, the consequence was to increase per-pupil state and local expenditures for students who remained in regular first- and second-grade classes. No plausible reading of the statute or regulations suggests that this result comports with the prohibitions on supplanting. . . .

NOTES AND QUESTIONS

1. Audits and Litigation

States have regularly—and often unsuccessfully—challenged demands for reimbursement of misspent federal education funds. California in particular has been at loggerheads with the Department of Education. *See, e.g., State of California, Department of Education v. Bennett*, 849 F.2d 1227 (9th Cir. 1988) (disallowing conference expenses but allowing recovery for the cost of field trips which included non-Chapter 1 as well as Chapter 1 pupils); *State of California, Department of Education v. Bennett*, 843 F.2d 333 (9th Cir. 1988) (upholding disallowance of expenditures for graduate training of migrant student counselors). *See also Virginia Department of Education v. Secretary of Education*, 806 F.2d 78 (4th Cir. 1986); *State of Indiana, Department of Public Instruction v. Bell*, 728 F.2d 938 (7th Cir. 1984).

2. The Impact of Audits

What effects do audits—with their potential for requiring repayment and the greater likelihood of official embarrassment—have on the management of Chapter 1 programs? Donald Burns, who participated in a massive federal evaluation of Title I, reached the following conclusions on this question:

> [M]any local district officials have interpreted the rules in the most conservative and restrictive way. . . . As a consequence, creativity and imagination in program planning have suffered. . . . Another consequence is the increasing role that lawyers and accountants are playing in program decisions. . . . [These professionals]—not teachers and principals—are being asked to render final judgment on program plans, because they are the ones who will be responsible for contesting any negative findings from federal auditors.

Burns, "A Case Study of Federal Involvement in Education," 33 *Proceedings of the Academy of Political Science* 87 (1978). *Compare* McLaughlin, Shields, and Rezasbek, "State and Local Response to Chapter 1 of the Education Consolidation and

Improvement Act, 1981," *National Institute of Education*, Grant No. OB-NIE-G-83-0003 (1986).

3. *Strengthening Chapter 1*

Imagine that you are a staff member working for the Education and Labor Committee of the House of Representatives, which is once again considering revisions in Chapter 1. Four proposals are on the table: (1) do nothing; (2) convert Chapter 1 into a block grant to the states, allowing them to spend the funds on education as they think best (an idea proposed by President Reagan in 1981); (3) concentrate Chapter 1 on the poorest schools in the poorest neighborhoods; require the principals, teachers and parents to work together to create an effective school; then hold those principals and teachers accountable for the results, with rewards for the successful and penalties for those not making progress (*see* Savage, "Why Chapter 1 Hasn't Made Much Difference," 69 *Phi Delta Kappan* 581 (April 1987); Peterson, Rebe, and Wong, "The Evolution of the Compensatory Education Program," unpub. paper, prepared for the Conference on Alternative Strategies in Chapter 1, Department of Education, 1986); and (4) turn Chapter 1 into a voucher program, with each eligible child receiving several hundred dollars worth of instructional help from either a public or participating private school (an idea advanced by both the Reagan and Bush administrations; recall the discussion of educational vouchers in chapter 4, *supra*).

Which alternative would you choose and why? *Compare* Jennings, "Working in Mysterious Ways: The Federal Government and Education," 70 *Phi Delta Kappan* 62 (Sept. 1988), which describes the Hawkins–Stafford School Improvement Amendments of 1988, the most recent tinkering with Chapter 1.

III. THE HANDICAPPED: FROM "INCAPABLE OF BENEFITING" FROM AN EDUCATION TO THE RIGHT TO AN "APPROPRIATE" EDUCATION

A. Introduction

Although programs for the handicapped have been urged since the mid-nineteenth century, the education received by handicapped children was historically viewed as a matter of discretionary governmental largess. That situation has changed dramatically. Judicial decisions in the early 1970s asserted that handicapped children enjoyed constitutional entitlements to an "appropriate" education, the meaning of which would vary with the nature of the handicap, and to procedural protections against arbitrary treatment. These constitutional entitlements, never passed upon by the Supreme Court, have been given a federal statutory basis, as Congress—through Section 504 of the Rehabilitation Act and the Education for All Handicapped Children Act (EAHCA)—has specified a broad set of rights, both substantive and procedural in nature, for the handicapped. Subsequent court decisions have elaborated on the meaning of those statutorily based rights and have reassessed constitutionally rooted claims.

As part of its effort to reduce Washington's role in education, the Reagan administration sought to repeal EAHCA, consolidating it, along with other categorical programs, in a block grant that states could spend as they wished. That proposal was rejected by Congress.

This section traces the early constitutionalization of the rights of the handicapped through the development of federal legislation and its subsequent interpretation in the courts. It examines the interplay between substantive and procedural entitlements, focusing specifically on the feasibility of giving meaning to "appropriate" education through due process hearings. As one might expect from the earlier treatment of implementation issues, changes in policy of this magnitude are not effortlessly achieved. Court decisions and legislation do not, by themselves, guarantee differences in educational practice. These issues are also explored.

The following excerpt briefly describes the education that was typically provided to the handicapped as recently as 1970 and the criticisms it provoked.

"Legal Reform of Special Education: Empirical Studies and Procedural Proposals"

D. Kirp, W. Buss, and P. Kuriloff, Reprinted from *California Law Review*, Vol. 62, pp. 40, 41–45.

Education of the Handicapped

Handicapped, or "exceptional" or "special" children form an extraordinarily diverse group, estimated to include between 8.7 and 35 percent of the entire student population.[2] From the viewpoint of the general educator, all that the handicapped have in common is that they differ from normal students. Some have problems so severe that their need for special educational attention is self-evident; they literally cannot survive without almost constant assistance.[3] The learning deficiency of most exceptional children, however, is slight and hard to detect.[4] Children who systematically write letters backwards, write in mirror fashion, or seem not to read some letters are common phenomena in lower elementary grades. In many cases, children who have physical disabilities which might interfere with learning cannot be distinguished by school officials from their supposedly normal classmates. Children with slight loss of hearing or sight can often compensate for their difficulty and thus go undetected until a systematic screening program is introduced, as can children with psycholinguistic learning disabilities. Typically, state law denies the most severely handicapped youngsters any right to publicly supported schooling. For the rest, a bewildering variety of special categories distinguishing both type of handicap (*e.g.*, between blindness and retardation) and severity of handicap (*e.g.*, between educable and trainable retardates) have been adopted.

A. Criticisms and Suggested Reforms of Classification Schemes

1. The Severely Handicapped. Most severely handicapped children are classified as ineducable and are denied access to publicly supported instruction. But this practice is inconsistent with the research findings that all children are educable, that is, able through instruction to move from relative dependence to relative independence. Many of these children—estimated to number between 450,000 and 4,000,000—spend their entire lives in state-run institutions, which, while providing minimal care, lack the resources to undertake any training in self-help. Private schools licensed by the states do train children with specific handicaps. But because these schools are self-supporting, they generally enroll only children from well-to-do homes. While a few states have sought to alleviate this fiscal inequity by providing vouchers for handicapped youngsters, the burden of caring for the severely handicapped falls most heavily upon the poor, the group least able to sacrifice the time and energy needed to ensure adequate educational help.

Even when public schools provide some instruction for the severely handicapped, they do not do enough. Autistic children, for example, require costly, highly structured, professionally staffed programs. Placing autistic children in any other type of program is viewed as the functional equivalent of excluding them from school.

These criticisms of the education of severely handicapped children view the public schools as doing nothing, or too little, for this group. The suggested remedy is to create additional special programs or make available additional resources for existing programs for hard-to-educate children. The criticisms provoked by the schools' treatment of the mildly handicapped, however, are quite different.

2. The Mildly Handicapped. Special programs for the mildly handicapped have been faulted for a host of reasons: they misclassify students, enroll a disproportionate share of minority children, appear educationally inefficacious, and too readily become permanent assignments.

a. Misclassification. "Misclassification," as the critics use that term, means two quite different phenomena. First, it may denote the misapplication of agreed-upon criteria. When, for example, the school violates state law by assigning a student with a 100 I.Q., to a class for the mildly retarded, misclassification is evident. . . .

Misclassification also may denote a dispute over how data are gathered so that established criteria can be applied. Even if a school consistently distinguishes between handicapped and normal students on the basis of a particular test, the test itself may be inadequate or susceptible to multiple interpretations. Many documented instances of misclassification are of this variety. In Washington, D.C., for example, the school system concluded that up

2. N.Y. *State Comm'n, Report on the Quality, Cost and Financing of Elementary and Secondary Educ.* 9B.2 (1972). The spread in the figures is almost wholly accounted for by disparities in estimating the percentage of brain-injured and learning-disabled children.

3. *See generally* Kirk, "Research in Education," in *Mental Retardation* 57 (H. Stevens & R. Heber eds. 1964).

4. *See* E. Rubin, C. Simson & M. Betwee, *Emotionally Handicapped Children and the Elementary School* 3132, 3134 (1966). *See also* Dunn, "Special Education for the Mildly Retarded: Is Much of It Justifiable?" in *Problems and Issues in the Education of Exceptional Children* 382 (R. Jones ed. 1971).

to two-thirds of its mildly handicapped students were in fact normal. This reversal in judgment resulted from the substitution of individually administered I.Q. tests for group aptitude tests.[10] . . .

*b. **Differential Vulnerability.*** That certain types of students are particularly vulnerable to special classification makes the critics uneasy. Not all children are even considered for special programs, and those who are do not represent a random sample of the student population. Students who make life difficult for the regular classroom teacher are most apt to have their normal status questioned: more boys than girls[12] and more aggressive than quiescent students are identified as possibly handicapped. White students typically must display both intellectual and behavioral quirks to be considered for special classification, while intellectual difficulties alone are sufficient to render black or Mexican-American students suspect.[13] Non-white students are overrepresented in programs for the mildly handicapped by as much as 250 percent relative to their proportion of the school-age population,[14] a fact which evokes considerable political concern. Overrepresentation diminishes the possibility of school integration, may diminish the educational opportunities of minority students, and calls into question the legitimacy of the entire system of special education classification. Differential vulnerability may lead the school both to ignore the special needs of students who do not disrupt the classroom and to underestimate the educational potential of minority students.

*c. **Efficacy.*** The efficacy of programs for the mildly handicapped frequently has been questioned. Studies comparing the performance of matched groups of students in regular and special programs generally conclude that, despite the additional resources in special programs, special classes generally have either no effect or a slightly adverse effect on both the motivation and achievement of students assigned to them. Furthermore, these programs may impose a stigma of "differentness" without securing offsetting benefits.

*d. **Permanent Placement.*** Special program assignment for the mildly handicapped is supposed to be temporary, enabling the student ultimately to return to the regular class. In fact, special placements often prove to be permanent assignments: one survey of urban school systems found that fewer than ten percent of the students identified as mildly handicapped ever returned to regular classes. Regular review of special class placement coupled with a commitment to return students to regular programs as soon as possible, might well resolve this problem.

B. The Constitution and Education for the Handicapped

Mills v. Board of Education

348 F.Supp. 866 (D.D.C. 1972).

Waddy, District Judge.

This is a civil action brought on behalf of seven children of school age by their next friends in which they seek a declaration of rights and to enjoin the defendants from excluding them from the District of Columbia Public Schools and/or denying them publicly supported education and to compel the defendants to provide them with immediate and adequate education and educational facilities in the public schools or alternative placement at public expense. They also seek additional and ancillary relief to effectuate the primary relief. They allege that although they can profit from an education either in regular classrooms with supportive services or in special classes adopted to their needs, they have been labeled as behavioral problems, mentally retarded, emotionally disturbed or hyperactive, and denied admission to the public schools or excluded therefrom after admission, with no provision for alternative educational placement or periodical review. . . .

The Problem

The genesis of this case is found (1) in the failure of the District of Columbia to provide publicly supported education and training to plaintiffs and other "exceptional" children, members of their class, and

10. *Hobson v. Hansen,* 269 F.Supp. 401, 490–91 (D.D.C. 1967), *appeal dismissed,* 393 U.S. 801, 89 S.Ct. 40, 21 L.Ed.2d 85 (1968), *aff'd en banc sub nom. Smuck v. Hobson,* 408 F.2d 175, 187 (D.C. Cir. 1969).

12. *See* N. Frazier & M. Sadker, *Sexism in School and Society* 86–94 (1973).

13. *See* J. Mercer, *Labeling the Mentally Retarded* 67–82 (1973); *cf.* Jensen, "A Theory of Primary and Secondary Familial Mental Retardation," in 4 *Int'l. Rev. of Research in Mental Retardation* 33 (N. Ellis ed. 1970).

14. *See* Kirp, "Schools as Sorters: The Constitutional and Policy Implications of Student Classification," 121 *U. Pa. L. Rev.* 705, 759–62 (1973).

(2) the excluding, suspending, expelling, reassigning and transferring of "exceptional" children from regular public school classes without affording them due process of law.

The problem of providing special education for "exceptional" children (mentally retarded, emotionally disturbed, physically handicapped, hyperactive and other children with behavioral problems) is one of major proportions in the District of Columbia. The precise number of such children cannot be stated because the District has continuously failed to comply with § 31-208 of the District of Columbia Code which requires a census of all children aged 3 to 18 in the District to be taken. Plaintiffs estimate that there are "22,000 retarded, emotionally disturbed, blind, deaf, and speech or learning disabled children, and perhaps as many as 18,000 of these children are not being furnished with programs of specialized education." According to data prepared by the Board of Education, Division of Planning, Research and Evaluation, the District of Columbia provides publicly supported special education programs of various descriptions to at least 3,880 school age children. However, in a 1971 report to the Department of Health, Education and Welfare, the District of Columbia Public Schools admitted that an estimated 12,340 handicapped children were not to be served in the 1971–72 school year.

Each of the minor plaintiffs in this case qualifies as an "exceptional" child. . . .

Although all of the named minor plaintiffs are identified as Negroes the class they represent is not limited by their race. They sue on behalf of and represent all other District of Columbia residents of school age who are eligible for a free public education and who have been, or may be, excluded from such education or otherwise deprived by defendants of access to publicly supported education.

* * *

Plaintiffs Are Entitled to Relief

Plaintiffs' entitlement to relief in this case is clear. The applicable statutes and regulations and the Constitution of the United States require it.

Statutes and Regulations

Section 31-201 of the District of Columbia Code requires that:

> Every parent, guardian, or other person residing . . . in the District of Columbia who has custody or control of a child between the ages of seven and sixteen years shall cause said child to be regularly instructed in a public school or in a private or parochial school or instructed privately during the period of each year in which the public schools of the District of Columbia are in session. . . .

Under § 31-203, a child may be "excused" from attendance only when ". . . upon examination ordered by . . . [the Board of Education], [the child] is found to be unable mentally or physically to profit from attendance at school: Provided, however, that if such examination shows that such child may benefit from specialized instruction adapted to his needs, he shall attend upon such instruction."

Failure of a parent to comply with § 31-201 constitutes a criminal offense. DC Code § 31-207. The Court need not belabor the fact that requiring parents to see that their children attend school under pain of criminal penalties presupposes that an educational opportunity will be made available to the children. The Board of Education is required to make such opportunity available. . . .

The Constitution—Equal Protection and Due Process

* * *

In *Hobson v. Hansen*, 269 F.Supp. 401 (D.C. Cir. 1967), Circuit Judge J. Skelly Wright . . . stated that "the Court has found the due process clause of the Fourteenth Amendment elastic enough to embrace not only the First and Fourth Amendments, but the self-incrimination clause of the Fifth, the speedy trial, confrontation and assistance of counsel clauses of the Sixth and the cruel and unusual clause of the Eighth." (269 F.Supp. 401, 493, citations omitted.) Judge Wright concluded "from these considerations the court draws the conclusion that the doctrine of equal educational opportunity—the equal protection clause in its application to public school education—is in its full sweep a component of due process binding on the District under the due process clause of the Fifth Amendment."

In *Hobson v. Hansen*, *supra*, Judge Wright found that denying poor public school children educational opportunities equal to that available to more affluent public school children was violative of the Due Process Clause of the Fifth Amendment. *A fortiori*, the defendants' conduct here, denying plaintiffs and their class not just an equal publicly supported education but all publicly supported education while providing such education to other children, is violative of the Due Process Clause.

* * *

The Defense

The Answer of the defendants to the Complaint contains the following:

> These defendants say that it is impossible to afford plaintiffs the relief they request unless:
> (a) The Congress of the United States appropriates millions of dollars to improve special education services in the District of Columbia; or
> (b) These defendants divert millions of dollars from funds already specifically appropriated for other educational services in order to improve special educational services. These defendants suggest that to do so would violate an Act of Congress and would be inequitable to children outside the alleged plaintiff class.

This Court is not persuaded by that contention.

The defendants are required by the Constitution of the United States, the District of Columbia Code, and their own regulations to provide a publicly-supported education for these "exceptional" children. Their failure to fulfill this clear duty to include and retain these children in the public school system, or otherwise provide them with publicly-supported education, and their failure to afford them due process hearing and periodical review, cannot be excused by the claim that there are insufficient funds. In *Goldberg v. Kelly*, 397 U.S. 254 (1969) the Supreme Court, in a case that involved the right of a welfare recipient to a hearing before termination of his benefits, held that Constitutional rights must be afforded citizens despite the greater expense involved. The Court stated . . . that "the State's interest that his [welfare recipient] payments not be erroneously terminated, clearly outweighs the State's competing concern to prevent any increase in its fiscal and administrative burdens." Similarly the District of Columbia's interest in educating the excluded children clearly must outweigh its interest in preserving its financial resources. If sufficient funds are not available to finance all of the services and programs that are needed and desirable in the system, then the available funds must be expended equitably in such a manner that no child is entirely excluded from a publicly supported education consistent with his needs and ability to benefit therefrom. The inadequacies of the District of Columbia Public School System, whether occasioned by insufficient funding or administrative inefficiency, certainly cannot be permitted to bear more heavily on the "exceptional" or handicapped child than on the normal child.

Implementation of Judgment

* * *

Inasmuch as the Board of Education has presented for adoption by the Court a proposed "Order and Decree" embodying its present plans for the identification of "exceptional" children and providing for their publicly supported education, including a time table, and further requiring the Board to formulate and file with the Court a more comprehensive plan, the Court will not now appoint a special master as was requested by plaintiffs. . . .

Judgment and Decree. . .

[I]t is hereby ordered, adjudged and decreed that summary judgment in favor of plaintiffs and against defendants be, and hereby is, granted, and judgment is entered in this action as follows:

1. That no child eligible for a publicly supported education in the District of Columbia public schools shall be excluded from a regular public school assignment by a Rule, policy, or practice of the Board of Education of the District of Columbia or its agents unless such child is provided (a) adequate alternative educational services suited to the child's needs, which may include special education or tuition grants, and (b) a constitutionally adequate prior hearing and periodic review of the child's status, progress, and the adequacy of any educational alternative. . . .

3. The District of Columbia shall provide to each child of school age a free and suitable publicly-supported education regardless of the degree of the child's mental, physical or emotional disability or impairment. Furthermore, defendants shall not exclude any child resident in the District of Columbia from such publicly-supported education on the basis of a claim of insufficient resources. . . .

5. Defendants shall provide each identified member of plaintiff class with a publicly-supported education suited to his needs within thirty days of the entry of this order.

* * *

9.a. Defendants shall utilize public or private agencies to evaluate the educational needs of all identified "exceptional" children and, within twenty days of the entry of this order, shall file with the Clerk of this Court their proposal for each individual placement in a suitable educational program, including the provision of compensatory educational services where required. . . .

10.a. Within forty-five days of the entry of this order, defendants shall file with the Clerk of the Court, with copy to plaintiffs' counsel, a comprehensive plan which provides for the identification, notification, assessment, and placement of class members. Such plan shall state the nature and extent of efforts which defendants have undertaken or propose to undertake to

(1) describe the curriculum, educational objectives, teacher qualifications, and ancillary services for the publicly supported educational programs to be provided to class members; and

(2) formulate general plans of compensatory education suitable to class members in order to overcome the present effects of prior educational deprivations. . . .

11. The defendants shall make an interim report to this Court on their performance within forty-five days of the entry of this order. Such report shall show:

(1) The adequacy of Defendants' implementation of plans to identify, locate, evaluate and give notice to all members of the class.

(2) The number of class members who have been placed, and the nature of their placements.

(3) The number of contested hearings before the Hearing Officers, if any, and the findings and determinations resulting therefrom.

12. Within forty-five days of the entry of this order, defendants shall file with this Court a report showing the expunction from or correction of all official records of any plaintiff with regard to past expulsions, suspensions, or exclusions effected in violation of [plaintiff's] procedural rights . . . together with a plan for procedures pursuant to which parents, guardians, or their counsel may attach to such students' records any clarifying or explanatory information which the parent, guardian or counsel may deem appropriate. . . .

13. Hearing Procedures.

a. Each member of the plaintiff class is to be provided with a publicly supported educational program suited to his needs, within the context of a presumption that among the alternative programs of education, placement in a regular public school class with appropriate ancillary services is preferable to placement in a special school class.

b. Before placing a member of the class in such a program, defendants shall notify his parent or guardian of the proposed educational placement, the reasons therefore, and the right to a hearing before a Hearing Officer if there is an objection to the placement proposed. Any such hearing shall be held in accordance with the provision of Paragraph 13.e., below.

c. Hereinafter, children who are residents of the District of Columbia and are thought by any of the defendants, or by officials, parents or guardians, to be in need of a program of special education, shall neither be placed in, transferred from or to, nor denied placement in such a program unless defendants shall have first notified their parents or guardians of such proposed placement, transfer or denial, the reasons therefore, and of the right to a hearing before a Hearing Officer if there is an objection to the placement, transfer or denial of placement. Any such hearings shall be held in accordance with the provisions of Paragraph 13.e., below. . . .

e. Whenever defendants take action regarding a child's placement, denial of placement, or transfer, as described in Paragraphs 13.b. or 13.c., above, the following procedures shall be followed.

(1) Notice required hereinbefore shall be given in writing by registered mail to the parent or guardian of the child.

(2) Such notice shall:

(a) describe the proposed action in detail;

(b) clearly state the specific and complete reasons for the proposed action, including the specification of any tests or reports upon which such action is proposed;

(c) describe any alternative educational opportunities available on a permanent or temporary basis;

(d) inform the parent or guardian of the right to object to the proposed action at a hearing before the Hearing Officer;

(e) inform the parent or guardian that the child is eligible to receive, at no charge, the services of a federally or locally funded diagnostic center for an independent medical, psychological and educational evaluation and shall specify the name, address and telephone number of an appropriate local diagnostic center;

(f) inform the parent or guardian of the right to be represented at the hearing by legal counsel; to examine the child's school records before the hearing, including any tests or reports upon which the proposed action may be based, to present evidence, including expert medical, psychological and educational testimony; and, to confront and cross-examine any school official, employee, or agent of the school district or public department who may have evidence upon which the proposed action was based.

(3) The hearing shall be at a time and place reasonably convenient to such parent or guardian.

(4) The hearing shall be scheduled not sooner than twenty (20) days waivable by parent or child, nor later than forty-five (45) days after receipt of a request from the parent or guardian.

(5) The hearing shall be a closed hearing unless the parent or guardian requests an open hearing.

(6) The child shall have the right to a representative of his own choosing, including legal counsel. If a child is unable, through financial inability, to retain counsel, defendants shall advise child's parents or guardians of available voluntary legal assistance including the Neighborhood Legal Services Organization, the Legal Aid Society, the Young Lawyers Section of the D. C. Bar Association, or from some other organization.

NOTES AND QUESTIONS

1. Pennsylvania Association for Retarded Children (PARC) v. Commonwealth

A consent order in *PARC*, 334 F.Supp. 1257 (E.D. Pa. 1971), 343 F.Supp. 279 (E.D. Pa. 1972), issued prior to *Mills*, required Pennsylvania to provide a "free, public program of education and training appropriate to the child's capacity, within the context of a presumption that, among the alternative programs of education and training required by statute to be available, placement in a regular public school class is preferable to placement in a special public school class [that is, a class for "handicapped" children] and placement in a special public school class is preferable to placement in any other type of program of education and training." 334 F.Supp. at 1260. The basis for that requirement was the stipulation that "Having undertaken to provide a free public education to all of its children, including its exceptional children, the Commonwealth of Pennsylvania may not deny any mentally retarded child access to a free public program of education and training." 334 F.Supp. at 1259. Although it is a consent order, *PARC* is generally regarded as the first "right to education" case concerning the handicapped.

2. Mills v. Board of Education: *Substantive Entitlement*

The class of plaintiffs in *Mills* is considerably broader than in *PARC*. It includes not only retarded children but all children excluded from publicly supported instruction. By holding such exclusions unconstitutional, does *Mills* suggest that all children have a right to attend public schools or a right to publicly supported instruction? Would the outcome in *Mills* differ if a school district sought to cut off all public funds for schooling (recall the discussion of "minimum protection" in chapter 6)?

In *Mills* one fairly typical plaintiff, Janice King, is described by the court as "brain-damaged and retarded, with right hemiplegia." 348 F.Supp. at 870. Suppose the cost of providing her a "suitable" education is five times the cost of providing the "normal" student an education. Assuming that no additional money is forthcoming from nonlocal sources, must the district reduce its expenditures for other students in order to provide King a "suitable" education? How would a court respond to the argument that such reductions deny "suitable" instruction to nonhandicapped students?

PARC and *Mills* assert that all children are capable of benefiting from education. What does this mean? For certain children, notably the profoundly retarded (those with IQ scores below 30), "education" may mean learning to use the bathroom and tie one's shoes. Is that the sort of education that publicly supported instruction should provide? If not, on whom should the burden of providing such instruction fall?

Concerning the scope of *Mills* and *PARC*, *see* Kirp, "Schools as Sorters: The Constitutional and Policy Implications of Student Classification," 121 *Pa. L. Rev.* 705 (1973); Haggerty and Sacks, "Education of the Handicapped: Towards a Definition of an Appropriate Education," 50 *Temple L.Q.* 961, 967–75 (1977); Krass, "The Right to Public Education for Handicapped Children: A Primer for the New Advocate," 1976 *Ill. L. Forum* 1016, 1044–47.

3. Mills, PARC, *and* Rodriguez

How can *Mills* and *PARC*, which speak of an entitlement to a "suitable" or "appropriate" education, be reconciled with the federal school finance cases? *See* chapter 6.

Is there a difference between satisfying a student's needs—the standard rejected in the *McInnis* case—and providing a "suitable" education? If so, does the difference somehow inhere in the nature of the plaintiff classes—if so, how?

What bearing does the holding of *San Antonio Independent School District v. Rodriguez*, 411 U.S. 1, 93 S.Ct. 1278, 36 L.Ed.2d 16 (1973), that education is not a constitutionally fundamental right, have on *Mills* and *PARC* (*see* chapter 6)? If the school officials made regular classroom instruction available to the litigants, would that satisfy the constitutional standard set forth in *Rodriguez?* Does the requirement of "appropriate" instruction go further than the "minimum education" to which *Rodriguez, in dictum*, makes mention? Is it constitutionally relevant that *Rodriguez* addresses school financing, while *PARC* and *Mills* focus on access to educational services? Does the critical difference between these cases rest in the fact that "educational handicap" deserves to be treated as a suspect classification? (In that context, recall the *Rodriguez* criteria for determining what constitutes a suspect class: "a class . . . saddled with such disabilities, or subjected to such a history of purposeful unequal treatment, or relegated to such a position of political powerlessness as to command extraordinary protection from the majoritarian political process." 411 U.S. at 28.) *Compare Fialkowski v. Shapp*, 405 F.Supp. 946 (E.D.Pa. 1975) and *Interest of G.H.*, 218 N.W.2d 441 (N.D. 1974) *with New York State Association for Retarded Children, Inc. v. Rockefeller*, 357 F.Supp. 752 (E.D.N.Y. 1973) and *Cuyahoga County Association for Retarded Children and Adults v. Essex*, 411 F.Supp. 46 (N.D. Ohio 1976). *See generally* Gartner and Lipsky, "Beyond Special Education: Toward a Quality System for All Students," 57 *Harv. Educ. Rev.* 367 (1987).

4. Mills v. Board of Education: *The Procedural Entitlement*

Traditionally, procedural protection under the due process clause of the Fourteenth Amendment is provided to assure that official action is not arbitrary but rather consistent with general guidelines for ensuring fairness in governmental decisions. As Professor Fuller has noted:

> [A]djudication must take place within the framework of accepted or imposed standards of decision before the litigant's participation in the decision can be meaningful. If the litigant has no idea on what basis the tribunal will decide the case, his . . . opportunity to present proofs and arguments becomes useless. . . . [T]here must be an extralegal community, existent or in the process of coming into existence, from which principles of decision may be derived.

Fuller, "Adjudication and the Rule of Law," *1960 Proceedings of the American Society of International Law*, 1, 5–7.

Does *Mills* provide the parents of handicapped children with such "standards of decision"? Just how is the hearing officer to determine whether a proposed education is "suitable"? What is the nexus between procedural protection and substantive rights in *Mills?* What purpose is served by such procedural safeguards as an independent hearing officer, access to records, the right to an independent evaluation? Should similar procedures be used in disputes over grading? How do these procedures differ from those that courts have required in student discipline cases? Should they differ? *See* chapter 3.

5. Impact of Procedural Safeguards

Sociologist Michael Young notes: "Castes or classes are universal, and the measure of harmony that prevails within a society is everywhere dependent upon the degree to which stratification is sanctioned by its code of morality." M. Young, *The Rise of the Meritocracy* 152 (1961). Does proceduralization in fact render differential treatment of the handicapped more legitimate? If so, is this a good or bad consequence?

C. The Federal Statutory Framework

The judicial successes in *Mills* and *PARC* spawned substantial popular and scholarly attention and similar lawsuits in more than thirty states. This campaign was designed to demonstrate that the handicapped have a constitutional entitlement to an appropriate education; it was also meant to persuade a broader public that the handicapped deserved to be more equitably treated. In the Rehabilitation Act (Section 504), 29 U.S.C.A. §§ 1401–1461, Congress attended to their claims. That legislation codifies *Mills* and *PARC* in several respects; it is also substantially more detailed in its specification of rights than the prior case law. *See generally* L. Rothstein, *Rights of Physically Handicapped Persons* (1984).

1. The Rehabilitation Act (Section 504).

Southeastern Community College v. Davis

442 U.S. 397, 99 S.Ct. 2361, 60 L.Ed.2d 980 (1979).

Mr. Justice Powell delivered the opinion of the Court.

This case presents a matter of first impression for this Court: Whether § 504 of the Rehabilitation Act of 1973, which prohibits discrimination against an "otherwise qualified handicapped individual" in federally funded programs "solely by reason of his handicap," forbids professional schools from imposing physical qualifications for admission to their clinical training programs.

I

Respondent, who suffers from a serious hearing disability, seeks to be trained as a registered nurse. During the 1973–1974 academic year she was enrolled in the College Parallel program of Southeastern Community College, a state institution that receives federal funds. Respondent hoped to progress to Southeastern's Associate Degree Nursing program, completion of which would make her eligible for state certification as a registered nurse. In the course of her application to the nursing program, she was interviewed by a member of the nursing faculty. It became apparent that respondent had difficulty understanding questions asked, and on inquiry she acknowledged a history of hearing problems and dependence on a hearing aid. She was advised to consult an audiologist.

On the basis of an examination at Duke University Medical Center, respondent was diagnosed as having a "bilateral, sensori-neural hearing loss." . . . A change in her hearing aid was recommended, as a result of which it was expected that she would be able to detect sounds "almost as well as a person would who has normal hearing," . . . But this improvement would not mean that she could discriminate among sounds sufficiently to understand normal spoken speech. Her lipreading skills would remain necessary for effective communication. . . .

Southeastern next consulted Mary McRee, Executive Director of the North Carolina Board of Nursing. On the basis of the audiologist's report, McRee recommended that respondent not be admitted to the nursing program. In McRee's view, respondent's hearing disability made it unsafe for her to practice as a nurse. In addition, it would be impossible for respondent to participate safely in the normal clinical training program, and those modifications that would be necessary to enable safe participation would prevent her from realizing the benefits of the program. . . .

After respondent was notified that she was not qualified for nursing study because of her hearing disability, she requested reconsideration of the decision. The entire nursing staff of Southeastern was assembled, and McRee again was consulted. . . . [T]he staff voted to deny respondent admission.

Respondent then filed suit in the United States District Court for the Eastern District of North Carolina, alleging . . . a violation of § 504 of the Rehabilitation Act of 1973. . . .

II

. . . Section 504 by its terms does not compel educational institutions to disregard the disabilities of handicapped individuals or to make substantial modifications in their programs to allow disabled persons to participate. Instead, it requires only that an "otherwise qualified handicapped individual" not be excluded from participation in a federally funded program "solely by reason of his handicap," indicating only that mere possession of a handicap is not a permissible ground for assuming an inability to function in a particular context.[6]

The court below, however, believed that the "otherwise qualified" persons protected by § 504 in-

6. The Act defines "handicapped individual" as follows:

"The term 'handicapped individual' means any individual who (A) has a physical or mental disability which for such individual constitutes or results in a substantial handicap to employment and (B) can reasonably be expected to benefit in terms of employability from vocational rehabilitation services provided pursuant to subchapters I and III of this chapter. For the purposes of subchapters IV and V of this chapter, such term means any person who (A) has a physical or mental impairment which substantially limits one or more of such person's major life activities, (B) has a record of such an impairment, or (C) is regarded as having such an impairment." [Section 7] of the Rehabilitation Act of 1973, 87 Stat. 359 as amended, 88 Stat. 1619, 89 Stat. 2, 29 U.S.C.A. § 706(5). . . .

clude those who would be able to meet the requirements of a particular program in every respect except as to limitations imposed by their handicap. . . . Taken literally, this holding would prevent an institution from taking into account any limitation resulting from the handicap, however disabling. It assumes, in effect, that a person need not meet legitimate physical requirements in order to be "otherwise qualified." We think the understanding of the District Court is closer to the plain meaning of the statutory language. An otherwise qualified person is one who is able to meet all of a program's requirements in spite of his handicap.

The regulations promulgated by the Department of HEW to interpret § 504 reinforce, rather than contradict, this conclusion. According to these regulations, a "[q]ualified handicapped person" is, "[w]ith respect to postsecondary and vocational education services, a handicapped person who meets the academic and technical standards requisite to admission or participation in the [school's] education program or activity. . . ." 45 CFR § 84.3(k)(3) (1978). An explanatory note states:

> "The term 'technical standards' refers to *all* nonacademic admissions criteria that are essential to participation in the program in question." 45 CFR pt. 84, App. A, p. 405 (1978) (emphasis supplied).

A further note emphasizes that legitimate physical qualifications may be essential to participation in particular programs.[7] We think it clear, therefore, that HEW interprets the "other" qualifications which a handicapped person may be required to meet as including necessary physical qualifications.

III

The remaining question is whether the physical qualifications Southeastern demanded of respondent might not be necessary for participation in its nursing program. It is not open to dispute that, as Southeastern's Associate Degree Nursing program currently is constituted, the ability to understand speech without reliance on lipreading is necessary for patient safety during the clinical phase of the program. As the District Court found, this ability also is indispensable for many of the functions that a registered nurse performs.

Respondent contends nevertheless that § 504, properly interpreted, compels Southeastern to undertake affirmative action that would dispense with the need for effective oral communication. First, it is suggested that respondent can be given individual supervision by faculty members whenever she attends patients directly. Moreover, certain required courses might be dispensed with altogether for respondent. It is not necessary, she argues, that Southeastern train her to undertake all the tasks a registered nurse is licensed to perform. Rather, it is sufficient to make § 504 applicable if respondent might be able to perform satisfactorily some of the duties of a registered nurse or to hold some of the positions available to a registered nurse.

Respondent finds support for this argument in portions of the HEW regulations discussed above. In particular, a provision applicable to postsecondary educational programs requires covered institutions to make "modifications" in their programs to accommodate handicapped persons, and to provide "auxiliary aids" such as sign-language interpreters. Respondent argues that this regulation imposes an obligation to ensure full participation in covered programs by handicapped individuals and, in particular, requires Southeastern to make the kind of adjustments that would be necessary to permit her safe participation in the nursing program.

We note first that on the present record it appears unlikely respondent could benefit from any affirmative action that the regulation reasonably could be interpreted as requiring. Section 84.44(d)(2), for example, explicitly excludes "devices or services of a

---

This definition comports with our understanding of § 504. A person who has a record of, or is regarded as having, an impairment may at present have no actual incapacity at all. Such a person would be exactly the kind of individual who could be "otherwise qualified" to participate in covered programs. And a person who suffers from a limiting physical or mental impairment still may possess other abilities that permit him to meet the requirements of various programs. Thus, it is clear that Congress included among the class of "handicapped" persons covered by § 504 a range of individuals who could be "otherwise qualified." See S. Rep. No. 93–1297, pp. 38–39 (1974).

7. The note states:

"Paragraph (k) of § 84.3 defines the term 'qualified handicapped person.' Throughout the regulation, this term is used instead of the statutory term 'otherwise qualified handicapped person.' The Department believes that the omission of the word 'otherwise' is necessary in order to comport with the intent of the statute because, read literally, 'otherwise' qualified handicapped persons include persons who are qualified except for their handicap, rather than in spite of their handicap. Under such a literal reading, a blind person possessing all the qualifications for driving a bus except sight could be said to be 'otherwise qualified' for the job of driving. Clearly, such a result was not intended by Congress. In all other respects, the terms 'qualified' and 'otherwise qualified' are intended to be interchangeable." 45 CFR pt. 84, App. A, p. 405.

personal nature" from the kinds of auxiliary aids a school must provide a handicapped individual. Yet the only evidence in the record indicates that nothing less than close, individual attention by a nursing instructor would be sufficient to ensure patient safety if respondent took part in the clinical phase of the nursing program. . . . Furthermore, it also is reasonably clear that § 84.44(a) does not encompass the kind of curricular changes that would be necessary to accommodate respondent in the nursing program. In light of respondent's inability to function in clinical courses without close supervision, Southeastern, with prudence, could allow her to take only academic classes. Whatever benefits respondent might realize from such a course of study, she would not receive even a rough equivalent of the training a nursing program normally gives. Such a fundamental alteration in the nature of a program is far more than the "modification" the regulation requires.

Moreover, an interpretation of the regulations that required the extensive modifications necessary to include respondent in the nursing program would raise grave doubts about their validity. If these regulations were to require substantial adjustments in existing programs beyond those necessary to eliminate discrimination against otherwise qualified individuals, they would do more than clarify the meaning of § 504. Instead, they would constitute an unauthorized extension of the obligations imposed by that statute.

The language and structure of the Rehabilitation Act of 1973 reflect a recognition by Congress of the distinction between the evenhanded treatment of qualified handicapped persons and affirmative efforts to overcome the disabilities caused by handicaps. Section 501(b), governing the employment of handicapped individuals by the Federal Government, requires each federal agency to submit "an affirmative action program plan for the hiring, placement, and advancement of handicapped individuals. . . ." These plans "shall include a description of the extent to which and methods whereby the special needs of handicapped employees are being met." Similarly, § 503(a), governing hiring by federal contractors, requires employers to "take affirmative action to employ and advance in employment qualified handicapped individuals. . . ." The President is required to promulgate regulations to enforce this section.

Under § 501(c) of the Act, by contrast, state agencies such as Southeastern are only "encourage[d] . . . to adopt . . . such policies and procedures." Section 504 does not refer at all to affirmative action, and except as it applies to federal employers it does not provide for implementation by administrative action. A comparison of these provisions demonstrates that Congress understood accommodation of the needs of handicapped individuals may require affirmative action and knew how to provide for it in those instances where it wished to do so. . . . [E]ven if HEW has attempted to create such an obligation itself, it lacks the authority to do so.

IV

We do not suggest that the line between a lawful refusal to extend affirmative action and illegal discrimination against handicapped persons always will be clear. It is possible to envision situations where an insistence on continuing past requirements and practices might arbitrarily deprive genuinely qualified handicapped persons of the opportunity to participate in a covered program. Technological advances can be expected to enhance opportunities to rehabilitate the handicapped or otherwise to qualify them for some useful employment. Such advances also may enable attainment of these goals without imposing undue financial and administrative burdens upon a State. Thus, situations may arise where a refusal to modify an existing program might become unreasonable and discriminatory. Identification of those instances where a refusal to accommodate the needs of a disabled person amounts to discrimination against the handicapped continues to be an important responsibility of HEW.

In this case, however, it is clear that Southeastern's unwillingness to make major adjustments in its nursing program does not constitute such discrimination. The uncontroverted testimony of several members of Southeastern's staff and faculty established that the purpose of its program was to train persons who could serve the nursing profession in all customary ways. . . . This type of purpose, far from reflecting any animus against handicapped individuals, is shared by many if not most of the institutions that train persons to render professional service. It is undisputed that respondent could not participate in Southeastern's nursing program unless the standards were substantially lowered. Section

504 imposes no requirement upon an educational institution to lower or to effect substantial modifications of standards to accommodate a handicapped person.[12]

One may admire respondent's desire and determination to overcome her handicap, and there well may be various other types of service for which she can qualify. In this case, however, we hold that there was no violation of § 504 when Southeastern concluded that respondent did not qualify for admission to its program. Nothing in the language or history of § 504 reflects an intention to limit the freedom of an educational institution to require reasonable physical qualifications for admission to a clinical training program. Nor has there been any showing in this case that any action short of a substantial change in Southeastern's program would render unreasonable the qualifications it imposed.

V

Accordingly, we reverse the judgment of the court below, and remand for proceedings consistent with this opinion.

So ordered.

NOTES AND QUESTIONS

1. Rehabilitation Act, Section 504: Scope of the Act

Section 504 is the analog for the handicapped of the 1964 Civil Rights Act. *See generally* L. Rothstein, *Rights of Physically Handicapped Persons* 22–23 (1984). Like that Act, it guarantees nondiscrimination "solely by reason of . . . handicap." How do the guarantees of due process bear on the entitlement to nondiscrimination? What about the entitlement to an "appropriate education"?

45 C.F.R. § 84.34(b)(1)(i) defines an "appropriate education," which the school district must provide, as one "designed to meet individual education needs of handicapped persons as adequately as the needs of nonhandicapped persons. . . ." What does this provision mean? Must all handicapped children perform as well as the nonhandicapped? Must they show the same academic progress? May the school district satisfy the requirement by treating the handicapped and the nonhandicapped in the same fashion, or does "adequacy" require that the handicapped receive something more? *See* Rothstein, *supra* at 22–23. Does adequacy turn on the treatment of nonhandicapped children in a particular school district? For example, would a wealthy district be expected to do more for its handicapped pupils than a poor district? How does *Davis* affect your reading of this regulation?

Is discrimination the appropriate framework for analyzing the claims of the handicapped? Consider Rebell, "Structural Discrimination and the Rights of the Disabled," 74 *Georgetown L.J.* 1435, 1437–41 (1986):

> . . . [D]espite the history and continuing vestiges of invidious discrimination against the handicapped, their situation clearly is not the same as that of victims of racial discrimination. The very notion of "disability" or "handicap" implies inherent limitations which, in many situations, do justify differential treatment of a disabled person. In addition, some of the "stereotyping" that results in the exclusion of disabled persons from jobs or activities they could adequately perform stems from . . . a well-intentioned, though often misplaced, concern that certain activities would be detrimental to the particular disabled person. . . . [I]n contrast with the brutal history of racism in America, the treatment of the disabled has reflected a complex mixture of stereotyping and sympathy, apprehension and accommodation.
>
> Legal attempts to deal with problems of discrimination against the disabled are complicated by two other distinguishing features. First is the difficulty of defining precisely who are "the handicapped". . . .
>
> The second distinguishing feature is that "handicapping" conditions are, to a large extent, relative and socially defined characteristics, not absolute criteria. . . .
>
> To date, no principled legal standard geared to the conceptual differences between race discrimination and discrimination against the disabled has been articulated by the courts. . . . The lack of coherent doctrine in this area allows for virtually unbridled judicial discretion. . . .

---

12. . . . Southeastern's program, structured to train persons who will be able to perform all normal roles of a registered nurse, represents a legitimate academic policy, and is accepted by the State. In effect, it seeks to ensure that no graduate will pose a danger to the public in any professional role in which he or she might be cast. Even if the licensing requirements of North Carolina or some other State are less demanding, nothing in the Act requires an educational institution to lower its standards.

See also Yudof, "Education for the Handicapped: *Rowley* in Perspective," 92 *Amer. J. Educ.* 163 (1984).

2. Southeastern Community College v. Davis: *Scope of the Decision*

Is the Court correct in interpreting "otherwise qualified" as "one who is able to meet all of a program's requirements in spite of his handicap" and not as including "those who would be able to meet the requirements of a particular program in every respect except as to limitations imposed by their handicap"? What are the practical consequences of this reading of the Act?

The Court distinguishes between "affirmative action" and "discrimination," suggesting that under the Act a government agency is not obliged to do more than afford "evenhanded treatment." What does this distinction mean? Could a school, for example, refuse to install the ramp that an "otherwise qualified" individual requires to gain access to the building and on that basis deny him or her admission to the school (assuming no other legislation speaks explicitly to this issue)? Would the Court require some but not "extensive modifications" in a program in order to accommodate the handicapped? *See* Rothstein, *supra* at 83. What financial and administrative burdens are permissibly imposed? What of other burdens that the handicapped assertedly impose? Could a professor who conducts his or her classes as platonic dialogues refuse to admit a mute student on the ground that such a student could not fully participate in, and hence was not qualified for, the course? What if an applicant to a professional school has a mental disorder? Can the application be denied if he or she is emotionally unstable? *See* Rothstein, *supra* at 83.

Does the *Davis* court suggest that discrimination, as developed in the racial context, is an appropriate framework to apply in the context of disability? Is there an alternative judicially cognizable framework?

3. *Subsequent Developments in Section 504*

In *Alexander v. Choate*, 469 U.S. 287, 105 S.Ct. 712, 83 L.Ed.2d 661 (1985), the Supreme Court unanimously approved a decision by the State of Tennessee to reduce inpatient hospital days to each eligible recipient, a change that had a disproportionate detrimental impact on handicapped patients. The justices did not insist on a showing that the rule was motivated by discriminatory animus to warrant § 504 review. But they rejected a claimed entitlement to equal results, holding that so long as the handicapped were given equal access to the benefit at issue, and so long as the access was "meaningful," further judicial inquiry was not justified. As in *Davis*, the alternative seemed too open-ended to the justices, but *Alexander* adopts a more expansive interpretation of § 504. It builds on the *Davis* discussion of exceptions to the absence of an affirmative action requirement to conclude: "while a . . . [recipient of federal funds] need not be required to make 'fundamental' or 'substantial' modifications to accommodate the handicapped, it may be required to make 'reasonable' ones." 469 U.S. at 300, 105 S.Ct. at 719.

4. *Primary and Secondary Schools: The Implications of Section 504*

Under § 504, how should the following cases be decided:

a. A handicapped student demands full tuition reimbursement for private instruction; the state provides only partial tuition support and concedes that no "appropriate" public instruction is provided. Is it relevant that the handicapped student is indigent? *See Burlington School Committee v. Department of Education*, 471 U.S. 359, 105 S.Ct. 1996, 85 L.Ed.2d 385 (1985); *Doe v. Brookline School Committee*, 722 F.2d 910 (1st Cir. 1983); *Kruse v. Campbell*, 431 F.Supp. 180 (E.D.Va. 1977), *vacated and remanded*, 434 U.S. 808, 98 S.Ct. 38, 54 L.Ed.2d 65 (1977); Rothstein, *supra* at 46–47. The question of whether damage recoveries are available to private plaintiffs under Section 504 has divided federal courts. *See* Rothstein *supra*.

b. A student with vision in only one eye seeks to participate in contact sports, with the attendant risk of injury to the functioning eye. *See Kampmeier v. Nyquist*, 553 F.2d 296 (2d Cir. 1977); Rothstein, *supra* at 92–93.

c. A student under psychiatric care is moved from his parents' to his grandparents' home because of "deep hostilities." He now seeks to play football for his newly adopted school. State regulations, passed to eliminate recruiting of athletes by high school coaches, bar unmarried students not living with their natural parents or guardians from playing interscholastic athletics for one year. *See Doe v. Marshall*, 459 F.Supp. 1190 (S.D.Tex. 1978).

d. Black students allege that the educable mentally retarded program is racially discriminatory because there are disproportionate numbers of blacks in those classes and because of allegations of misclassification. *See Georgia State Conference of*

Branches of NAACP v. State of Georgia, 775 F.2d 1403 (11th Cir. 1985). *See generally* Rothstein, *supra* at ch. 3; Wegner, "Educational Rights of Handicapped Children: Three Federal Statutes and an Evolving Jurisprudence: Part I—The Statutory Maze," 17 *J. of Law and Educ.* 387 (1988).

2. The Education for All Handicapped Children Act (EAHCA). The Education for All Handicapped Children Act (EAHCA), enacted in 1975, codifies *Mills* and *PARC*, and moves well beyond those cases in the rights it affords to handicapped children. The legislation (sometimes referred to by its bill number, Public Law 94–142) combines a civil rights and an entitlement approach. *See* Yudof, "Education for the Handicapped: *Rowley* in Perspective," 92 *Amer. J. of Educ.* 163 (1984). It both outlaws discrimination and guarantees educational services. "Full educational opportunity" and a "free appropriate public education" are the substantive standards; it also requires an "individualized educational program" (IEP), a plan for "specifically designed instruction to meet the unique needs of handicapped children." The legislation states a preference for mainstreaming, requiring the placement of handicapped children in regular classrooms "to make the maximum extent appropriate." Section 1412(5). Parental participation is part of the panoply of rights, with parents guaranteed notice of any changes in the educational placement of their child and an opportunity to contest changes through a due process hearing, an administrative appeal, and the right to sue in state or federal district court. *See generally* L. Rothstein, *Rights of Physically Handicapped Persons* § 2.12 *et seq.* (1984). By the beginning of 1990, more than one hundred such EAHCA suits had been brought. *See generally* Tucker, "Section 504 of the Rehabilitation Act After Ten Years of Enforcement: The Past and Future," 1989 *U. Ill. L. Rev.* 845.

a. The Substantive Entitlement.

Board of Education v. Rowley

458 U.S. 176, 102 S.Ct. 3034, 73 L.Ed.2d 690 (1982).

Justice Rehnquist delivered the opinion of the Court.

This case arose in connection with the education of Amy Rowley, a deaf student at the Furnace Woods School in the Hendrick Hudson Central School District, Peekskill, New York. Amy has minimal residual hearing and is an excellent lipreader. During the year before she began attending Furnace Woods, a meeting between her parents and school administrators resulted in a decision to place her in a regular kindergarten class in order to determine what supplemental services would be necessary to her education. Several members of the school administration prepared for Amy's arrival by attending a course in sign-language interpretation, and a teletype machine was installed in the principal's office to facilitate communication with her parents who are also deaf. At the end of the trial period it was determined that Amy should remain in the kindergarten class, but that she should be provided with an FM hearing aid which would amplify words spoken into a wireless receiver by the teacher or fellow students during certain classroom activities. Amy successfully completed her kindergarten year.

As required by the Act, an IEP [individual educational plan] was prepared for Amy during the fall of her first-grade year. The IEP provided that Amy should be educated in a regular classroom at Furnace Woods, should continue to use the FM hearing aid, and should receive instruction from a tutor for the deaf for one hour each day and from a speech therapist for three hours each week. The Rowleys agreed with the IEP but insisted that Amy also be provided a qualified sign-language interpreter in all of her academic classes. Such an interpreter had been placed in Amy's kindergarten class for a two-week experimental period, but the interpreter had reported that Amy did not need his services at that time. The school administrators likewise concluded that Amy did not need such an interpreter in her first-grade classroom. They reached this conclusion after consulting the school district's Committee on the Handicapped, which had received expert evidence from Amy's parents on the importance of a sign-language interpreter, received testimony from Amy's teacher and other persons familiar with her academic and social progress, and visited a class for the deaf.

When their request for an interpreter was denied, the Rowleys demanded and received a hearing before an independent examiner. After receiving evidence from both sides, the examiner agreed with the administrators' determination that an interpreter was not necessary because "Amy was achieving educationally, academically, and socially" without such assistance. . . .

The District Court found that Amy "is a remarkably well-adjusted child" who interacts and communicates well with her classmates and has "developed an extraordinary rapport" with her teachers. It also found that "she performs better than the average child in her class and is advancing easily from grade to grade," but "that she understands considerably less of what goes on in class than she would if she were not deaf" and thus "is not learning as much, or performing as well academically, as she would without her handicap." This disparity between Amy's achievement and her potential led the court to decide that she was not receiving a "free appropriate public education," which the court defined as "an opportunity to achieve [her] full potential commensurate with the opportunity provided to other children." According to the District Court, such a standard "requires that the potential of the handicapped child be measured and compared to his or her performance, and that the remaining differential or 'shortfall' be compared to the shortfall experienced by nonhandicapped children."

* * *

A divided panel of the United States Court of Appeals for the Second Circuit affirmed. . . .

This is the first case in which this Court has been called upon to interpret any provision of the [Education for All Handicapped Children] Act.

. . . The Act does expressly define "free appropriate public education":

> The term "free appropriate public education" means *special education* and *related services* which (A) have been provided at public expense, under public supervision and direction, and without charge, (B) meet the standards of the State educational agency, (C) include an appropriate preschool, elementary, or secondary school education in the State involved, and (D) are provided in conformity with the individualized education program. . . .

* * *

According to the definitions contained in the Act, a "free appropriate public education" consists of educational instruction specially designed to meet the unique needs of the handicapped child, supported by such services as are necessary to permit the child "to benefit" from the instruction. Almost as a checklist for adequacy under the Act, the definition also requires that such instruction and services be provided at public expense and under public supervision, meet the State's educational standards, approximate the grade levels used in the State's regular education, and comport with the child's IEP. Thus, if personalized instruction is being provided with sufficient supportive services to permit the child to benefit from the instruction, and the other items on the definitional checklist are satisfied, the child is receiving a "free appropriate public education" as defined by the Act.

* * *

Noticeably absent from the language of the statute is any substantive standard prescribing the level of education to be accorded handicapped children. Certainly the language of the statute contains no requirement like the one imposed by the lower courts—that States maximize the potential of handicapped children "commensurate with the opportunity provided to other children."

. . . By passing the Act, Congress sought primarily to make public education available to handicapped children. But in seeking to provide such access to public education, Congress did not impose upon the States any greater substantive educational standard than would be necessary to make such access meaningful. Indeed, Congress expressly "recognize[d] that in many instances the process of providing special education and related services to handicapped children is not guaranteed to produce any particular outcome." . . .

Thus, the intent of the Act was more to open the door of public education to handicapped children on appropriate terms than to guarantee any particular level of education once inside.

* * *

That the Act imposes no clear obligation upon recipient States beyond the requirement that handicapped children receive some form of specialized education is perhaps best demonstrated by the fact that Congress, in explaining the need for the Act, equated an "appropriate education" to the receipt of some specialized educational services. The Senate Report states: "[T]he most recent statistics provided by the Bureau of Education for the Handicapped estimate that of the more than 8 million children . . . with handicapping conditions requiring special education and related services, only 3.9 million such children are receiving an appropriate education." . . .

It is evident from the legislative history that the characterization of handicapped children as "served" referred to children who were receiving some form of specialized educational services from the States, and that the characterization of children as "unserved" referred to those who were receiving no specialized educational services. . . .

Respondents contend that "the goal of the Act is to provide each handicapped child with an equal educational opportunity." . . . We think, however, that the requirement that a State provide specialized educational services to handicapped children generates no additional requirement that the services so provided be sufficient to maximize each child's potential "commensurate with the opportunity provided other children." . . .

The educational opportunities provided by our public school systems undoubtedly differ from student to student, depending upon a myriad of factors that might affect a particular student's ability to assimilate information presented in the classroom. The requirement that States provide "equal" educational opportunities would thus seem to present an entirely unworkable standard requiring impossible measurements and comparisons. Similarly, furnishing handicapped children with only such services as are available to nonhandicapped children would in all probability fall short of the statutory requirement of "free appropriate public education"; to require, on the other hand, the furnishing of every special service necessary to maximize each handicapped child's potential is, we think, further than Congress intended to go. Thus to speak in terms of "equal" services in one instance gives less than what is required by the Act and in another instance more. The theme of the Act is "free appropriate public education," a phrase which is too complex to be captured by the word "equal" whether one is speaking of opportunities or services.

The District Court and the Court of Appeals thus erred when they held that the Act requires New York to maximize the potential of each handicapped child commensurate with the opportunity provided nonhandicapped children. Desirable though that goal might be, it is not the standard that Congress imposed upon States which receive funding under the Act. Rather, Congress sought primarily to identify and evaluate handicapped children, and to provide them with access to a free public education.

* * *

Implicit in the congressional purpose of providing access to a "free appropriate public education" is the requirement that the education to which access is provided be sufficient to confer some educational benefit upon the handicapped child. . . .

The determination of when handicapped children are receiving sufficient educational benefits to satisfy the requirements of the Act presents a more difficult problem. The Act requires participating States to educate a wide spectrum of handicapped children, from the marginally hearing-impaired to the profoundly retarded and palsied. It is clear that the benefits obtainable by children at one end of the spectrum will differ dramatically from those obtainable by children at the other end, with infinite variations in between. One child may have little difficulty competing successfully in an academic setting with nonhandicapped children while another child may encounter great difficulty in acquiring even the most basic of self-maintenance skills. We do not attempt today to establish any one test for determining the adequacy of educational benefits conferred upon all children covered by the Act. Because in this case we are presented with a handicapped child who is receiving substantial specialized instruction and related services, and who is performing above average in the regular classrooms of a public school system, we confine our analysis to that situation.

The Act requires participating States to educate handicapped children with nonhandicapped children whenever possible. When that "mainstreaming" preference of the Act has been met and a child is being educated in the regular classrooms of a public school system, the system itself monitors the educational progress of the child. Regular examinations are administered, grades are awarded, and yearly advancement to higher grade levels is permitted for those children who attain an adequate knowledge of the course material. The grading and advancement system thus constitutes an important factor in determining educational benefit. Children who graduate from our public school systems are considered by our society to have been "educated" at least to the grade level they have completed, and access to an "education" for handicapped children is precisely what Congress sought to provide in the Act.

* * *

When the language of the Act and its legislative history are considered together, the requirements imposed by Congress become tolerably clear. Insofar as a State is required to provide a handicapped child with a "free appropriate public education," we hold that it satisfies this requirement by providing personalized instruction with sufficient support services to permit the child to benefit educationally from that instruction. Such instruction and services must be provided at public expense, must meet the State's educational standards, must approximate the grade levels used in the State's regular education, and must comport with the child's IEP. In addition, the IEP, and therefore the personalized instruction, should be formulated in accordance with the requirements of the Act and, if the child is being educated in the regular classrooms of the public education system, should be reasonably calculated to enable the child to achieve passing marks and advance from grade to grade. . . .

When the elaborate and highly specific procedural safeguards contrasted with the general and somewhat imprecise substantive admonitions contained in the Act, we think that the importance Congress attached to these procedural safeguards cannot be gainsaid. It seems to us no exaggeration to say that Congress placed every bit as much emphasis upon compliance with procedures giving parents and guardians a large measure of participation at every stage of the administrative process . . . as it did upon the measurement of the resulting IEP against a substantive standard. We think that the Congressional emphasis upon full participation of concerned parties throughout the development of the IEP, as well as the requirements that state and local plans be submitted to the Commissioner for approval, demonstrate the legislative conviction that adequate compliance with the procedures prescribed would in most cases assure much if not all of what Congress wished in the way of substantive content in an IEP.

Thus the provision that a reviewing court base its decision on the "preponderance of the evidence" is by no means an invitation to the courts to substitute their own notions of sound educational policy for those of the school authorities which they review. . . .

A court's inquiry in suits . . . is twofold. First, has the State complied with the procedures set forth in the Act? And second, is the individualized educational program developed through the Act's procedures reasonably calculated to enable the child to receive educational benefits? If these requirements are met, the State has complied with the obligations imposed by Congress and the courts can require no more.

In assuring that the requirements of the Act have been met, courts must be careful to avoid imposing their view of preferable educational methods upon the States. The primary responsibility for formulating the education to be accorded a handicapped child, and for choosing the educational method most suitable to the child's needs, was left by the Act to state and local educational agencies in cooperation with the parents or guardian of the child.

* * *

Applying these principles to the facts of this case, we conclude that the Court of Appeals erred in affirming the decision of the District Court. Neither the District Court nor the Court of Appeals found that petitioners had failed to comply with the procedures of the Act, and the findings of neither court would support a conclusion that Amy's educational program failed to comply with the substantive requirements of the Act. On the contrary, the District Court found that the "evidence firmly establishes that Amy is receiving an 'adequate' education, since she performs better than the average child in her class and is advancing easily from grade to grade." In light of this finding, and of the fact that Amy was receiving personalized instruction and related services calculated by the Furnace Woods school administrators to meet her educational needs, the lower courts should not have concluded that the Act requires the provision of a sign-language interpreter. Accordingly, the decision of the Court of Appeals is reversed and the case is remanded for further proceedings consistent with this opinion.

* * *

Justice White, with whom Justice Brennan and Justice Marshall join, dissenting.

In order to reach its result in this case, the majority opinion contradicts itself, the language of the statute, and the legislative history. Both the majority's standard for a "free appropriate education" and its standard for judicial review disregard congressional intent.

The majority first turns its attention to the meaning of a "free appropriate public education." The Act provides:

> The term "free appropriate public education" means special education and related services which (A) have been provided at public expense, under public supervision and direction, and without charge, (B) meet the standards of the State educational agency, (C) include

> an appropriate preschool, elementary, or secondary school education in the State involved, and (D) are provided in conformity with the individualized education program required. . . .

The majority reads this statutory language as establishing a congressional intent limited to bringing "previously excluded handicapped children into the public education systems of the States and requiring the States to adopt *procedures* which would result in individualized consideration of and instruction for each child." . . . In its attempt to constrict the definition of "appropriate" and the thrust of the Act, the majority opinion states, "Noticeably absent from the language of the statute is any substantive standard prescribing the level of education to be accorded handicapped children. Certainly the language of the statute contains no requirement like the one imposed by the lower courts—that States maximize the potential of handicapped children commensurate with the opportunity provided to other children." . . .

* * *

The majority opinion announces a different substantive standard, that "Congress did not impose upon the States any greater substantive standard than would be necessary to make such access meaningful." While "meaningful" is no more enlightening than "appropriate," the Court purports to clarify itself. Because Amy was provided with *some* specialized instruction from which she obtained *some* benefit and because she passed from grade to grade, she was receiving a meaningful and therefore appropriate education.[2]

This falls far short of what the Act intended. The Act details as specifically as possible the kind of specialized education each handicapped child must receive. It would apparently satisfy the Court's standard of "access to specialized instruction and related services which are individually designed to provide educational benefit to the handicapped child," for a deaf child such as Amy to be given a teacher with a loud voice, for she would benefit from that service. The Act requires more. It defines "special education" to mean "specifically designed instruction, at no cost to parents or guardians, to *meet the unique needs* of a handicapped child. . . ." § 1401(16) (emphasis added). Providing a teacher with a loud voice would not meet Amy's needs and would not satisfy the Act. The basic floor of opportunity is instead, as the courts below recognized, intended to eliminate the effects of the handicap, at least to the extent that the child will be given an equal opportunity to learn if that is reasonably possible. Amy Rowley, without a sign language interpreter, comprehends less than half of what is said in the classroom—less than half of what normal children comprehend. This is hardly an equal opportunity to learn, even if Amy makes passing grades.

* * *

I agree that the language of the Act does not contain a substantive standard beyond requiring that the education offered must be "appropriate." However, if there are limits not evident from the face of the statute on what may be considered an "appropriate education," they must be found in the purpose of the statute or its legislative history. The Act itself announces it will provide a "*full* educational opportunity to all handicapped children" (emphasis added). This goal is repeated throughout the legislative history . . . in statements too frequent to be "passing references and isolated phrases. Indeed, at times the purpose of the Act was described as tailoring each handicapped child's educational plan to enable the child "to achieve his or her maximum potential."

* * *

The Court's discussion of the standard for judicial review is as flawed as its discussion of a "free ap-

2. As further support for its conclusions, the majority opinion turns to *Pennsylvania Association for Retarded Children v. Commonwealth of Pennsylvania (PARC)*, 334 F.Supp. 1257 (1971), 343 F.Supp. 279 (E.D.Pa. 1972) and *Mills v. Board of Education of the District of Columbia*, 348 F.Supp. 866 (D.D.C. 1972). That these decisions served as an impetus for the Act does not, however, establish them as the limits of the majority quotes from *Mills* . . . sets a standard not of *some* education, but of educational opportunity equal to that of non-handicapped children.

Indeed, *Mills*, relying on decisions since called into question by this Court's opinion in *San Antonio School District v. Rodriguez*, 411 U.S. 1, 93 S.Ct. 1278, 36 L.Ed.2d 16 (1973), states,

> "In *Hobson v. Hansen* [269 F.Supp. 401 (D.D.C.).] Judge Wright found that denying poor public school children educational opportunity equal to that available to more affluent public school children was violative of the Due Process Clause of the Fifth Amendment. A *fortiori*, the defendants' conduct here, denying plaintiffs and their class not just an equal publicly supported education but all publicly supported education while providing such education to other children, is violative of the Due Process Clause." 348 F.Supp., at 875.

Whatever the effect of *Rodriguez* on the validity of this reasoning, the statement exposes the majority's mischaracterization of the opinion and thus of the assumptions of the legislature that passed the act.

propriate public education." According to the Court, a court can ask only whether the State has "complied with the procedures set forth in the Act" and whether the individualized education program is "reasonably calculated to enable the child to receive educational benefit." Both the language of the Act and the legislative history, however, demonstrate that Congress intended the courts to conduct a far more searching inquiry.

* * *

The legislative history shows that judicial review is not limited to procedural matters and that the state educational agencies are given first, but not final, responsibility for the content of a handicapped child's education. The Conference Committee directs courts to make an "independent decision." The deliberate change in the review provision is an unusually clear indication that Congress intended courts to undertake substantive review instead of relying on the conclusions of the state agency.

* * *

Thus, the Court's limitations on judicial review have no support in either the language of the Act or the legislative history. Congress did not envision that inquiry would end if a showing is made that the child is receiving passing marks and is advancing from grade to grade. Instead, it intended to permit a full and searching inquiry into any aspect of a handicapped child's education. The Court's standard, for example, would not permit a challenge to part of the IEP; the legislative history demonstrates beyond doubt that Congress intended such challenges to be possible, even if the plan as developed is reasonably calculated to give the child some benefits.

* * *

NOTES AND QUESTIONS

1. **Board of Education v. Rowley:** ***Scope of the Decision***

a. The Substantive Standard

In *Rowley*, the first Supreme Court appraisal of the EAHCA, the justices attempt to give meaning to its vaguely worded core mandate: the right to a "free appropriate public education." " '[F]ree appropriate public education' [is] a phrase too complex to be captured by the word 'equal,' " says Justice Rehnquist. Do you agree? *See generally* L. Rothstein, *Rights of Physically Handicapped Persons* § 2.17 (1984).

Is the standard the majority embraces—the "educational benefit" standard—consistent with congressional intent? Does it provide useful guidance to administrators or judges, or does it invite purely *ad hoc* decisions? How different is it from the "commensurate opportunity" standard proposed by the lower court and adopted by most circuits before *Rowley? See, e.g., Springdale School Dist. No. 50 v. Grace*, 656 F.2d 300 (8th Cir. 1981); *Battle v. Commonwealth of Pennsylvania*, 629 F.2d 269 (3d Cir. 1980). How different is it from "minimal access," on the one side; "full potential," on the other? In *Grace*, the appeals court reconsidered its decision—keeping a deaf child in a regular class with a certified specialist rather than sending her on to a special school for the deaf—after *Rowley*, but found no reason to alter either its conclusion or its reasoning. Does this suggest a defiant lower court—or a Supreme Court distinction without a difference? *See* Gallegos, "Beyond *Board of Education v. Rowley*," 97 *Amer. J. Educ.* 258 (1989).

Among the commentaries on *Rowley*'s "appropriateness" standard, *see* Broadwell and Walden, " 'Free Appropriate Public Education' After *Rowley*: An Analysis of Recent Court Decisions," 17 *J. of Law and Educ.* 35 (1988); Gallegos, *supra;* Wegner, "Variations on a Theme—The Concept of Equal Educational Opportunity and Programming Decisions Under the Education for All Handicapped Children Act of 1975," 48 *Law and Contemp. Probs.* 169 (1985); Hill, "Legal Conflicts in Special Education: How Competing Paradigms in the Education for All Handicapped Children Act Create Litigation," 64 *U. Detroit L. Rev.* 129 (1986); Myers and Jenson, "The Meaning of 'Appropriate' Educational Programming Under the Education for All Handicapped Children Act," 1984 *So. Ill. U. L. Rev.* 401; Yudof, "Education for the Handicapped: *Rowley* in Perspective," 92 *Amer. J. Educ.* 163 (1984).

Is educational benefit a useful standard when applied, not to an obviously bright, hearing-impaired child like Amy Rowley, but to severely mentally retarded or emotionally disturbed children who often cannot function in the regular classroom? *See* Rebell, "Structural Discrimination and the Rights of the Disabled," 74 *Georgetown L. J.* 1435, 1475 (1986): "[I]n many cases the educational benefits standard becomes almost synonymous with the maximum benefits standard: a school district might need to expend virtually unlimited resources if it is required to teach severely handicapped and profoundly retarded children certain minimal self-help skills." *See also* Yudof, *supra*.

In applying *Rowley*, may a court take into account the resources of a school district, making comparisons with existing levels of service for the nonhandicapped? *See* Bartlett, "The Role of Cost in Educational Decisionmaking for the Handicapped Child," 48 *Law and Contemp. Probs.* 7 (1985). *But see* Rothstein, *supra* at 36.

b. The Procedural Standard

In language reminiscent of the majority opinion in *Rodriguez v. San Antonio Independent School District*, chapter 6 *supra*, the *Rowley* court stresses that "courts lack the specialized knowledge and experience necessary to resolve persistent and difficult questions of educational policy." For that reason, the justices emphasize procedural regularity over substantive standards. *See also Doe by and through Doe v. Defendant I*, 898 F.2d 1186 (6th Cir. 1990). Is that an appropriate allocation of authority based on institutional competence? Will lower courts abide that allocation? *See* Gallegos, *supra*.

2. *Applying the* Rowley *Standard*

How should the following issues be resolved?

a. The school district proposes regular classroom placement while the parents argue for a private school placement. *See Manuel R. v. Ambach*, 635 F.Supp. 791 (E.D.N.Y. 1986).

Does it matter that state and local officials disagree about which program is appropriate? *See Karl v. Board of Education*, 736 F.2d 873 (2d Cir. 1984). May a court rely on additional evidence of appropriateness, not considered by school administrators, in determining appropriate placement? *See Russell by and through Russell v. Jefferson School District*, 609 F.Supp. 605 (N.D.Cal. 1985). How relevant is a child's failing school performance in a court's evaluation of appropriate placement? *See Adams v. Hansen*, 632 F.Supp. 858 (N.D.Cal. 1985).

How relevant is it that a child, though able to cope in school, presents major behavior problems at home? So long as some educational benefit is secured, is the *Rowley* standard satisfied? *Compare Doe v. Anrig*, 692 F.2d 800, 808 (1st Cir. 1982) ("forcing [a handicapped child] into an unreceptive, perhaps hostile, home environment after an entire lifetime of residential placement, would adversely affect his educational development") *and McKenzie v. Smith*, 771 F.2d 1527, 1533 (D.C.Cir. 1985) (" 'potentially explosive emotional situation' ") *with Ahern v. Keene*, 593 F.Supp. 902, 906, 907 (D.Del. 1984) (at home, the child "talked loudly to herself and to imaginary friends, withdrew into a fantasy world . . . wandered away from home, talked to strangers, occasionally related in a bizarre and inappropriate manner" but at school the child's emotional problems did not " 'present a problem in the classroom' and did not interfere with her learning").

If the state establishes a higher standard for the education of the handicapped than the *Rowley* standard—for instance, a "best achieve success" standard or "maximum possible development" standard—how does this affect the court's reviewing role? *See Geis v. Board of Education*, 774 F.2d 575 (3d Cir. 1985); *David D. v. Dartmouth School Committee*, 775 F.2d 411 (1st Cir. 1985).

b. The school recommends institutional placement, but the parent insists on a less restrictive educational environment consistent with the "mainstreaming" philosophy of the statute. Is mainstreaming just a policy choice? One factor for the court to consider? Is it a preliminary requirement that must be met before deciding whether the requisite benefit is being provided? *See* A.W. *by and through* W.W. *v. Northwest R-1 School District*, 813 F.2d 158 (8th Cir. 1987), *cert. denied*, 489 U.S. 847, 108 S.Ct. 144, 98 L.Ed.2d 100 (1987); *Mark A. v. Grant Wood Area Education Agency*, 795 F.2d 52 (8th Cir. 1986), *cert. denied*, 480 U.S. 836, 107 S.Ct. 1579, 94 L.Ed.2d 769 (1987); *Springdale School District No. 50 v. Grace*, 693 F.2d 41 (8th Cir. 1981), *cert. denied*, 461 U.S. 927, 103 S.Ct. 2086, 77 L.Ed.2d 298 (1983); *Roncker v. Walter*, 700 F.2d 1058, 1062 (6th Cir. 1983), *cert. denied*, 464 U.S. 864, 104 S.Ct. 196, 78 L.Ed.2d 171 (1983) ("In [*Rowley*], the dispute is simply one of [pedagogy]. . . . In the present case, the question . . . involves a determination of whether the school district has satisfied the Act's requirement that handicapped children be educated alongside nonhandicapped children to the maximum extent appropriate. . . . Since Congress has decided that mainstreaming is appropriate, the states must accept that decision if they desire federal funds"). *See* Gallegos, *supra* at 278–81.

Does it matter that the dispute concerns not a single child but a state policy of placing all severely handicapped children in special, separate schools? *See St. Louis Developmental Disability Treatment*

Center Parents' Ass'n v. Mallory, 767 F.2d 518 (8th Cir. 1985).

c. Parents claim that, without summer school, their handicapped children will regress and so lose skills acquired during the school year. *See Yaris v. Special Sch. Dist.*, 728 F.2d 1055 (8th Cir. 1984); *Alamo Heights v. Independent School Dist. Board of Education*, 790 F.2d 1153 (5th Cir. 1986). *See generally* Gallegos, *supra* at 281–82.

Does it matter that prohibition of summer school is a statewide policy, not an individual determination about educational benefit? *See Crawford v. Pittman*, 708 F.2d 1028 (5th Cir. 1983).

d. A handicapped child seeks more than twelve years of publicly supported education. *See Helms v. Independent Sch. Dist. No.* 3, 750 F.2d 1208 (9th Cir. 1984).

e. Timothy W., a multiply handicapped and profoundly mentally retarded child, suffers from complex developmental disabilities, spastic quadriplegia, cerebral palsy, seizure disorder, and cortical blindness. The boy's pediatrician, noting that the youngster responds to sounds, recommends that the district institute a regime emphasizing physical therapy and stimulation; another developmental pediatrician reports that the child has no educational potential. The district proposes to offer no education on the grounds that Timothy is incapable of benefiting from one. *Timothy W. v. Rochester, N.H. School Dist.*, 875 F.2d 954 (1st Cir. 1989), *cert. denied sub nom. Rochester, N.H. School Dist. v. Timothy W.*, ___ U.S. ___, 110 S.Ct. 519, 107 L.Ed.2d 520, 58 U.S.L.W. 3351 (1989).

f. District A believes "learning disabilities" are best dealt with by involving the student in regular class activities, with the teacher providing supplementary help when possible. The parents of a District A child who has been diagnosed as "learning disabled" believe that only a special class can adequately deal with their child's problems. District B has developed an elaborate set of special programs to deal with the problems of the learning disabled. The parents of a child whom officials in the district have assigned to such a program disagree, preferring that their child receive the benefits of schooling with nonhandicapped children. Both parents challenge the district's recommendation. How should the matter be resolved?

The issue is complicated by several policy-relevant facts. Evidence concerning the efficacy of special programs for the learning disabled is inconclusive. So too is evidence concerning the stigmatizing effects of such programs. Some argue that special assignment carries a stigma, while others assert that it is more stigmatizing to be labeled as a dummy or crazy in the regular class. Teachers in regular classes are generally untrained to handle handicapped children; they claim that to assign such children to their classes (at least without abundant extra help) makes teaching and learning impossible. Advocates of mainstreaming, by contrast, often decry classes for the mildly handicapped as dumping grounds for students the district has given up on. Nonhandicapped students are also affected by the presence of handicapped children: To the extent that they come to see that "handicapped" does not mean strange or bad, that is all to the good. To the extent that handicapped children absorb disproportionate amounts of the teacher's time, their presence may not be a benefit. How are these facts to be weighted?

3. *"Related Services" and the EAHCA*

All the services for handicapped children discussed to this point—summer school, tutoring and the like—are educational in nature. What is the standard to be applied when school authorities refuse to provide services that relate to the health of a handicapped student? *See* Gallegos, *supra* at 282.

In *Irving Independent School District v. Tatro*, 466 U.S. 923, 104 S.Ct. 1703, 80 L.Ed.2d 176 (1984), the Supreme Court took up the issue. Eight-year-old Amber Tatro was born with spina bifida. To maintain her health, she required clean intermittent catheterization services. But the school district refused to provide catheterization, arguing that this was a "medical service" which, under the Act, need not be offered.

In upholding Amber's claim, the Supreme Court purports to apply the *Rowley* standard. "[O]nly those services necessary to aid a handicapped child to benefit from special education must be provided, regardless [of] how easily a school nurse or lay person could furnish them." But "without having services available during the school day, Amber cannot attend school and thereby 'benefit from special education.' " The Court rejects the argument that three hours of schooling, with no catheterization provided, offers some educational benefit (rather as hearing half the words spoken in a classroom, according to the justices in *Rowley*, offers some benefit). *See also T.G. v. Board of Education*, 788 F.2d 420 (3d Cir. 1984). And it reads the "medical services" exception narrowly, to exclude only services that a doctor, rather than a nurse or lay person, must provide.

Just how different are *Tatro* and *Rowley? See* Gallegos, *supra* at 271. Both children needed specialized personnel to benefit from the school program. Is the difference that Tatro sought help under the related services section while the Rowleys relied on the free appropriate public education section of the Act? If so, is this a sensible distinction to draw?

4. Process and Substance Entwined: The Fiscal Responsibility Question

In *Burlington School Committee v. Massachusetts Department of Education*, 471 U.S. 359, 105 S.Ct. 1996, 85 L.Ed.2d 385 (1985), the Supreme Court addressed one of the most common disputes arising under the EAHCA: whether parents who send their handicapped child to private school can obtain reimbursement from the responsible public agency. The justices did not pass on the appropriateness, under the Act, of the private placement but only on the scope of the reviewing court's authority once the court finds such placement to be appropriate:

> . . . In a case where a court determines that a private placement desired by the parents was proper under the Act and that an IEP calling for placement in a public school was inappropriate, it seems clear beyond cavil that "appropriate" relief would include a prospective injunction directing the school officials to develop and implement at public expense an IEP placing the child in a private school.
>
> If the administrative and judicial review under the Act could be completed in a matter of weeks, rather than years, it would be difficult to imagine a case in which such prospective injunctive relief would not be sufficient. As this case so vividly demonstrates, however, the review process is ponderous. A final judicial decision on the merits of an IEP will in most instances come a year or more after the school term covered by that IEP has passed. In the meantime, the parents who disagree with the proposed IEP are faced with a choice: go along with the IEP to the detriment of their child if it turns out to be inappropriate or pay for what they consider to be the appropriate placement. If they choose the latter course, which conscientious parents who have adequate means and who are reasonably confident of their assessment normally would, it would be an empty victory to have a court tell them several years later that they were right but that these expenditures could not in a proper case be reimbursed by the school officials. If that were the case, the child's right to a *free* appropriate public education, the parents' right to participate fully in developing a proper IEP, and all of the procedural safeguards would be less than complete. Because Congress undoubtedly did not intend this result, we are confident that by empowering the court to grant "appropriate" relief Congress meant to include retroactive reimbursement to parents as an available remedy in a proper case.
>
> In this Court, the Town repeatedly characterizes reimbursement as "damages," but that simply is not the case. Reimbursement merely requires the Town to belatedly pay expenses that it should have paid all along and would have borne in the first instance had it developed a proper IEP. Such a *post-hoc* determination of financial responsibility was contemplated in the legislative history:
>
> > "If a parent contends that he or she has been forced, at that parent's own expense, to seek private schooling for the child because an appropriate program does not exist within the local educational agency responsible for the child's education and the local educational agency disagrees, that disagreement and *the question of who remains financially responsible* is a matter to which the due process procedures established under [the predecessor to § 1415] appl[y]."
> >
> > . . .
>
> See 34 CFR § 300.403(b) (1984) (disagreements and question of financial responsibility subject to the due process procedures).
>
> Regardless of the availability of reimbursement as a form of relief in a proper case, the Town maintains that the [parents of the handicapped child] have waived any right they otherwise might have to reimbursement because they violated § 1415(e)(3), which provides:
>
> > "During the pendency of any proceedings conducted pursuant to [§ 1415], unless the State or local educational agency and the parents or guardian otherwise agree, the child shall remain in the then current educational placement of such child. . . ."
>
> We do not agree with the Town that a parental violation of § 1415(e)(3) constitutes a waiver of reimbursement. The provision says nothing about financial responsibility, waiver, or parental right to reimbursement at the conclusion of judicial proceedings. Moreover, if the provision is interpreted to cut off parental rights to reimbursement, the principal purpose of the Act will in many cases be defeated in the same way as if reimbursement were never available. As in this case, parents will often notice a child's learning difficulties while the child is in a regular public school program. If the school officials disagree with the need for special

education or the adequacy of the public school's program to meet the child's needs, it is unlikely they will agree to an interim private school placement while the review process runs its course. Thus, under the Town's reading of § 1415(e)(3), the parents are forced to leave the child in what may turn out to be an inappropriate educational placement or to obtain the appropriate placement only by sacrificing any claim for reimbursement. The Act was intended to give handicapped children both an appropriate education and a free one; it should not be interpreted to defeat one or the other of those objectives. We think at least one purpose of § 1415(e)(3) was to prevent school officials from removing a child from the regular public school classroom over the parents' objection pending completion of the review proceedings.

This is not to say that § 1415(e)(3) has no effect on parents. While we doubt that this provision would authorize a court to order parents to leave their child in a particular placement, we think it operates in such a way that parents who unilaterally change their child's placement during the pendency of review proceedings, without the consent of state or local school officials, do so at their own financial risk. If the courts ultimately determine that the IEP proposed by the school officials was appropriate, the parents would be barred from obtaining reimbursement for any interim period in which their child's placement violated § 1415(e)(3).

b. The Procedural Entitlement. The EAHCA is weak on substance, strong on procedure. It "guarantees procedures whereby parents may challenge the appropriateness of their child's educational program, but provides only the most general guidelines for resolving the substantive questions such challenges may present." Note, "Enforcing the Right to an 'Appropriate' Education: The Education for All Handicapped Children Act of 1975," 92 *Harv. L. Rev.* 1103 (1979). Both in evaluation procedures and in due process hearings, which may be requested in instances of disagreement between parents and school officials, the EAHCA seeks to protect against discrimination. *See Doe v. Defendant I*, 898 F.2d 1186 (6th Cir. 1990).

The EAHCA does not specifically speak to the authority of school officials to discipline handicapped students. But the extensive procedural protections built into the Act, primarily intended as safeguards against reclassification of handicapped children for pedagogical reasons, have been read to create procedural rights in disciplinary situations. *See generally* Comment, "The Legal Limits of School Discipline for Children with Handicaps," 69 *Ore. L. Rev.* 117 (1990).

Honig v. Doe

484 U.S. 305, 108 S.Ct. 592, 98 L.Ed.2d 686 (1988).

Justice Brennan delivered the opinion of the Court.

As a condition of federal financial assistance, the Education of the Handicapped Act requires States to ensure a "free appropriate public education" for all disabled children within their jurisdictions. In aid of this goal, the Act establishes a comprehensive system of procedural safeguards designed to ensure parental participation in decisions concerning the education of their disabled children and to provide administrative and judicial review of any decisions with which those parents disagree. Among these safeguards is the so-called "stay-put" provision, which directs that a disabled child "shall remain in [his or her] then current educational placement" pending completion of any review proceedings, unless the parents and state or local educational agencies otherwise agree. 20 U.S.C. § 1415(e)(3). Today we must decide whether, in the face of this statutory proscription, state or local school authorities may nevertheless unilaterally exclude disabled children from the classroom for dangerous or disruptive conduct growing out of their disabilities. . . .

I

In the Education of the Handicapped Act . . . Congress sought "to assure that all handicapped children have available to them . . . a free appropriate public education which emphasizes special education and related services designed to meet their unique needs, [and] to assure that the rights of handicapped children and their parents or guardians are protected." § 1400(c). . . .

* * *

. . . In responding to these problems, Congress did not content itself with passage of a simple funding statute. Rather, the EHA confers upon disabled students an enforceable substantive right to public education in participating States, see *Board of Education of Hendrick Hudson Central School Dist. v. Rowley*, 458 U.S. 176, 102 S.Ct. 3034, 73 L.Ed.2d

690 (1982),[1] and conditions federal financial assistance upon a State's compliance with the substantive and procedural goals of the Act. Accordingly, States seeking to qualify for federal funds must develop policies assuring all disabled children the "right to a free appropriate public education," and must file with the Secretary of Education formal plans mapping out in detail the programs, procedures and timetables under which they will effectuate these policies. 20 U.S.C. §§ 1412(1), 1413(a). Such plans must assure that, "to the maximum extent appropriate," States will "mainstream" disabled children. . . .

The primary vehicle for implementing these congressional goals is the "individualized educational program" (IEP), which the EHA mandates for each disabled child. Prepared at meetings between a representative of the local school district, the child's teacher, the parents or guardians, and, whenever appropriate, the disabled child, the IEP sets out the child's present educational performance, establishes annual and short-term objectives for improvements in that performance, and describes the specially designed instruction and services that will enable the child to meet those objectives. § 1401(19). The IEP must be reviewed and, where necessary, revised at least once a year in order to ensure that local agencies tailor the statutorily required "free appropriate public education" to each child's unique needs. § 1414(a)(5).

Envisioning the IEP as the centerpiece of the statute's education delivery system for disabled children, and aware that schools had all too often denied such children appropriate educations without in any way consulting their parents, Congress repeatedly emphasized throughout the Act the importance and indeed the necessity of parental participation in both the development of the IEP and any subsequent assessments of its effectiveness. See §§ 1400(c), 1401(19), 1412(7), 1415(b)(1)(A), (C), (D), (E), and 1415(b)(2). Accordingly, the Act establishes various procedural safeguards that guarantee parents both an opportunity for meaningful input into all decisions affecting their child's education and the right to seek review of any decisions they think inappropriate. These safeguards include the right to examine all relevant records pertaining to the identification, evaluation, and educational placement of their child; prior written notice whenever the responsible educational agency proposes (or refuses) to change the child's placement or program; an opportunity to present complaints concerning any aspect of the local agency's provision of a free appropriate public education; and an opportunity for "an impartial due process hearing" with respect to any such complaints. § 1415(b)(1), (2).

At the conclusion of any such hearing, both the parents and the local educational agency may seek further administrative review and, where that proves unsatisfactory, may file a civil action in any state or federal court. § 1415(c), (e)(2). In addition to reviewing the administrative record, courts are empowered to take additional evidence at the request of either party and to "grant such relief as [they] determine[ ] is appropriate." § 1415(e)(2). The "stay-put" provision at issue in this case governs the placement of a child while these often lengthy review procedures run their course. It directs that:

> "During the pendency of any proceedings conducted pursuant to [§ 1415], unless the State or local educational agency and the parents or guardian otherwise agree, the child shall remain in the then current educational placement of such child. . . ." § 1415(e)(3).

The present dispute grows out of the efforts of certain officials of the San Francisco Unified School District (SFUSD) to expel two emotionally disturbed children from school indefinitely for violent and disruptive conduct related to their disabilities. In November 1980, respondent John Doe assaulted another student at the Louise Lombard School, a developmental center for disabled children. Doe's April

1. Congress' earlier efforts to ensure that disabled students received adequate public education, had failed in part because the measures it adopted were largely hortatory. In the 1966 amendments to the Elementary and Secondary Education Act of 1965, Congress established a grant program "for the purpose of assisting the States in the initiation, expansion, and improvement of programs and projects . . . for the education of handicapped children." Pub.L. 89–750, § 161, 80 Stat. 1204. It repealed that program four years later and replaced it with the original version of the Education of the Handicapped Act, Pub.L., 91–230, 84 Stat. 175, Part B of which contained a similar grant program. Neither statute, however, provided specific guidance as to how States were to use the funds, nor did they condition the availability of the grants on compliance with any procedural or substantive safeguards. In amending the EHA to its present form, Congress rejected its earlier policy of "merely establish[ing] an unenforceable goal requiring all children to be in school." 121 Cong.Rec. 37417 (1975) (remarks of Sen. Schweiker). Today, all 50 states and the District of Columbia receive funding assistance under the EHA. U.S. Dept. of Education, Ninth Annual Report to Congress on Implementation of Education of the Handicapped Act (1987).

1980 IEP identified him as a socially and physically awkward 17 year old who experienced considerable difficulty controlling his impulses and anger. . . .

On November 6, 1980, Doe responded to the taunts of a fellow student in precisely the explosive manner anticipated by his IEP: he choked the student with sufficient force to leave abrasions on the child's neck, and kicked out a school window while being escorted to the principal's office afterwards. . . . Doe admitted his misconduct and the school subsequently suspended him for five days. Thereafter, his principal referred the matter to the SFUSD Student Placement Committee (SPC or Committee) with the recommendation that Doe be expelled. On the day the suspension was to end, the SPC notified Doe's mother that it was proposing to exclude her child permanently from SFUSD and was therefore extending his suspension until such time as the expulsion proceedings were completed. The Committee further advised her that she was entitled to attend the November 25 hearing at which it planned to discuss the proposed expulsion.

After unsuccessfully protesting these actions by letter, Doe brought this suit against a host of local school officials and the state superintendent of public education. Alleging that the suspension and proposed expulsion violated the EHA, he sought a temporary restraining order cancelling the SPC hearing and requiring school officials to convene an IEP meeting. The District Judge granted the requested injunctive relief and further ordered defendants to provide home tutoring for Doe on an interim basis; shortly thereafter, she issued a preliminary injunction directing defendants to return Doe to his then current educational placement at Louise Lombard School pending completion of the IEP review process. Doe re-entered school on December 15, 5½ weeks, and 24 school days, after his initial suspension.

Respondent Jack Smith was identified as an emotionally disturbed child by the time he entered the second grade in 1976. School records prepared that year indicated that he was unable "to control verbal or physical outburst[s]" and exhibited a "[s]evere disturbance in relationships with peers and adults." . . . Further evaluations subsequently revealed that he had been physically and emotionally abused as an infant and young child and that, despite above average intelligence, he experienced academic and social difficulties as a result of extreme hyperactivity and low self-esteem. . . .

Based on these evaluations, SFUSD placed Smith in a learning center for emotionally disturbed children. His grandparents, however, believed that his needs would be better served in the public school setting and, in September 1979, the school district acceded to their requests and enrolled him at A.P. Giannini Middle School. His February 1980 IEP recommended placement in a Learning Disability Group, . . . [and] noted that Smith was easily distracted, impulsive, and anxious; it therefore proposed a half-day schedule and suggested that the placement be undertaken on a trial basis.

At the beginning of the next school year, Smith was assigned to a full-day program; almost immediately thereafter he began misbehaving. School officials met twice with his grandparents in October 1980 to discuss returning him to a half-day program; although the grandparents agreed to the reduction, they apparently were never apprised of their right to challenge the decision through EHA procedures. The school officials also warned them that if the child continued his disruptive behavior—which included stealing, extorting money from fellow students, and making sexual comments to female classmates—they would seek to expel him. On November 14, they made good on this threat, suspending Smith for five days after he made further lewd comments. His principal referred the matter to the SPC, which recommended exclusion from SFUSD. As it did in John Doe's case, the Committee scheduled a hearing and extended the suspension indefinitely pending a final disposition in the matter. On November 28, Smith's counsel protested these actions on grounds essentially identical to those raised by Doe, and the SPC agreed to cancel the hearing and to return Smith to a half-day program at A.P. Giannini or to provide home tutoring. Smith's grandparents chose the latter option and the school began home instruction on December 10; on January 6, 1981, an IEP team convened to discuss alternative placements.

After learning of Doe's action, Smith sought and obtained leave to intervene in the suit. . . .

* * *

II

At the outset, we address the suggestion, raised for the first time during oral argument, that this case is moot. Under Article III of the Constitution this

Court may only adjudicate actual, ongoing controversies. . . .

In the present case, we have jurisdiction if there is a reasonable likelihood that respondents will again suffer the deprivation of EHA-mandated rights that gave rise to this suit. We believe that, at least with respect to respondent Smith, such a possibility does in fact exist and that the case therefore remains justiciable.

Respondent John Doe is now 24 years old and, accordingly, is no longer entitled to the protections and benefits of the EHA, which limits eligibility to disabled children between the ages of three and 21. See 20 U.S.C. § 1412(2)(B). . . .

Respondent Jack Smith, however, is currently 20 and has not yet completed high school. Although at present he is not faced with any proposed expulsion or suspension proceedings, and indeed no longer even resides within the SFUSD, he remains a resident of California and is entitled to a "free appropriate public education" within that State. His claims under the EHA, therefore, are not moot if the conduct he originally complained of is " 'capable of repetition, yet evading review.' " *Murphy v. Hunt*, 455 U.S. 478, 482, 102 S.Ct. 1181, 1183, 71 L.Ed.2d 353 (1982). Given Smith's continued eligibility for educational services under the EHA, the nature of his disability, and petitioner's insistence that all local school districts retain residual authority to exclude disabled children for dangerous conduct, we have little difficulty concluding that there is a "reasonable expectation," . . . that Smith would once again be subjected to a unilateral "change in placement" for conduct growing out of his disabilities were it not for the state-wide injunctive relief issued below. . . .

* * *

III

The language of § 1415(e)(3) is unequivocal. It states plainly that during the pendency of any proceedings initiated under the Act, unless the state or local educational agency and the parents or guardian of a disabled child otherwise agree, "the child *shall* remain in the then current educational placement." § 1415(e)(3) (emphasis added). Faced with this clear directive, petitioner asks us to read a "dangerousness" exception into the stay-put provision on the basis of either of two essentially inconsistent assumptions: first, that Congress thought the residual authority of school officials to exclude dangerous students from the classroom too obvious for comment; or second, that Congress inadvertently failed to provide such authority and this Court must therefore remedy the oversight. Because we cannot accept either premise, we decline petitioner's invitation to re-write the statute.

Petitioner's arguments proceed, he suggests, from a simple, common-sense proposition: Congress could not have intended the stay-put provision to be read literally, for such a construction leads to the clearly unintended, and untenable, result that school districts must return violent or dangerous students to school while the often lengthy EHA proceedings run their course. We think it clear, however, that Congress very much meant to strip schools of the *unilateral* authority they had traditionally employed to exclude disabled students, particularly emotionally disturbed students, from school. In so doing, Congress did not leave school administrators powerless to deal with dangerous students; it did, however, deny school officials their former right to "self-help," and directed that in the future the removal of disabled students could be accomplished only with the permission of the parents or, as a last resort, the courts.

. . . Congress passed the EHA after finding that school systems across the country had excluded one out of every eight disabled children from classes. In drafting the law, Congress was largely guided by the recent decisions in *Mills v. Board of Education of District of Columbia*, 348 F.Supp. 866 (1972), and *PARC*, 343 F.Supp. 279 (1972), both of which involved the exclusion of hard-to-handle disabled students. *Mills* in particular demonstrated the extent to which schools used disciplinary measures to bar children from the classroom. There, school officials had labeled four of the seven minor plaintiffs "behavioral problems," and had excluded them from classes without providing any alternative education to them or any notice to their parents. . . . After finding that this practice was not limited to the named plaintiffs but affected in one way or another an estimated class of 12,000 to 18,000 disabled students, . . . [*Mills*, 348 F.Supp.] at 868–869, 875, the District Court enjoined future exclusions, suspensions, or expulsions "on grounds of discipline." . . .

Congress attacked such exclusionary practices in a variety of ways. It required participating States to educate *all* disabled children, regardless of the severity of their disabilities, 20 U.S.C. § 1412(2)(C), and included within the definition of "handicapped" those children with serious emotional disturbances. § 1401(1). It further provided for meaningful parental participation in all aspects of a child's educational placement, and barred schools, through the stay-put provision, from changing that placement over the parent's objection until all review proceedings were completed. Recognizing that those proceedings might prove long and tedious, the Act's drafters did not intend § 1415(e)(3) to operate inflexibly, see 121 Cong.Rec. 37412 (1975) (remarks of Sen. Stafford), and they therefore allowed for interim placements where parents and school officials are able to agree on one. Conspicuously absent from § 1415(e)(3), however, is any emergency exception for dangerous students. This absence is all the more telling in light of the injunctive decree issued in *PARC*, which permitted school officials unilaterally to remove students in " 'extraordinary circumstances.' " . . . 343 F.Supp., at 301. Given the lack of any similar exception in *Mills*, and the close attention Congress devoted to these "landmark" decisions . . . we can only conclude that the omission was intentional; we are therefore not at liberty to engraft onto the statute an exception Congress chose not to create.

. . . Our conclusion that § 1415(e)(3) means what it says does not leave educators hamstrung. The Department of Education has observed that, "[w]hile the [child's] placement may not be changed [during any complaint proceeding], this does not preclude the agency from using its normal procedures for dealing with children who are endangering themselves or others." Comment following 34 CFR § 300.513 (1987). Such procedures may include the use of study carrels, timeouts, detention, or the restriction of privileges. More drastically, where a student poses an immediate threat to the safety of others, officials may temporarily suspend him or her for up to 10 school days.[8] This authority, which respondent in no way disputes, not only ensures that school administrators can protect the safety of others by promptly removing the most dangerous of students, it also provides a "cooling down" period during which officials can initiate IEP review and seek to persuade the child's parents to agree to an interim placement. And in those cases in which the parents of a truly dangerous child adamantly refuse to permit any change in placement, the 10-day respite gives school officials an opportunity to invoke the aid of the courts under § 1415(e)(2), which empowers courts to grant any appropriate relief.

. . . Petitioner contends, however, that the availability of judicial relief is more illusory than real, because a party seeking review under § 1415(e)(2) must exhaust time-consuming administrative remedies, and because under the Court of Appeals' construction of § 1415(e)(3), courts are as bound by the stay-put provision's "automatic injunction," 793 F.2d, at 1486, as are schools. It is true that judicial review is normally not available under § 1415(e)(2) until all administrative proceedings are completed, but as we have previously noted, parents may by-pass the administrative process where exhaustion would be futile or inadequate. . . . While many of the EHA's procedural safeguards protect the rights of parents and children, schools can and do seek redress through the administrative review process, and we have no reason to believe that Congress meant to require schools alone to exhaust in all cases, no matter how exigent the circumstances. The burden in such cases, of course, rests with the school to demonstrate the futility or inadequacy of administrative review, but nothing in § 1415(e)(2) suggests that schools are completely barred from attempting to make such a showing. Nor do we think that § 1415(e)(3) operates to limit the equitable powers of district courts such

8. The Department of Education has adopted the position first espoused in 1980 by its Office of Civil Rights that a suspension of up to 10 school days does not amount to a "change in placement" prohibited by § 1415(e)(3). U.S. Dept. of Education, Office of Special Education Programs, Policy Letter (Feb. 26, 1987). Ed. for Handicapped L. Rep. 211:437 (1987). The EHA nowhere defines the phrase "change in placement," nor does the statute's structure or legislative history provide any guidance as to how the term applies to fixed suspensions. Given this ambiguity, we defer to the construction adopted by the agency charged with monitoring and enforcing the statute. See *INS v. Cardoza-Fonseca*, 480 U.S. 421, 428, 107 S.Ct. 1207, 1211, 94 L.Ed.2d 434 (1987). Moreover, the agency's position comports fully with the purposes of the statute: Congress sought to prevent schools from permanently and unilaterally excluding disabled children by means of indefinite suspensions and expulsions; the power to impose fixed suspensions of short duration does not carry the potential for total exclusion that Congress found so objectionable. Indeed, despite its broad injunction, the District Court in *Mills v. Board of Education of District of Columbia*, 348 F.Supp. 866 (DC 1972), recognized that school officials could suspend disabled children on a short-term, temporary basis. See *id*, at 880. *Cf. Goss v. Lopez*, 419 U.S. 565, 574–576, 95 S.Ct. 729, 736–737, 42 L.Ed.2d 725 (1975) (suspension of 10 school days or more works a sufficient deprivation of property and liberty interests to trigger the protections of the Due Process Clause). Because we believe the agency correctly determined that a suspension in excess of 10 days does constitute a prohibited "change in placement," we conclude that the Court of Appeals erred to the extent it approved suspensions of 20 and 30 days' duration.

that they cannot, in appropriate cases, temporarily enjoin a dangerous disabled child from attending school. As the EHA's legislative history makes clear, one of the evils Congress sought to remedy was the unilateral exclusion of disabled children by *schools*, not courts. . . .

In short, then, we believe that school officials are entitled to seek injunctive relief under § 1415(e)(2) in appropriate cases. In any such action, § 1415(e)(3) effectively creates a presumption in favor of the child's current educational placement which school officials can overcome only by showing that maintaining the child in his or her current placement is substantially likely to result in injury either to himself or herself, or to others. In the present case, we are satisfied that the District Court, in enjoining the state and local defendants from indefinitely suspending respondent or otherwise unilaterally altering his then current placement, properly balanced respondent's interest in receiving a free appropriate public education in accordance with the procedures and requirements of the EHA against the interests of the state and local school officials in maintaining a safe learning environment for all their students. . . . [The opinions of Justice Rehnquist, concurring, and Justice Scalia, dissenting, on the mootness issue are deleted.]

NOTES AND QUESTIONS

1. Honig v. Doe: *Scope of the Decision*

In holding that a dangerous handicapped student may not be expelled from school, does the Court fairly read the procedural requirements of EAHCA?

How does the standard of the act differ from the constitutional due process protections that, under *Goss v. Lopez*, chapter 3, *supra*, all students enjoy? Is that difference in treatment appropriate? Does it suggest that the handicapped are less responsible individuals? More in need of protection?

After the Court's holding that a handicapped student's assignment can be changed only with the permission of the parents or the court, how can a school system maintain order? *See* Comment, "The Legal Limits of School Discipline for Children with Handicaps," 69 *Ore. L. Rev.* 117, 128 (1990). Are in-school punishments—detention and restricted privileges or short term suspension in the case of immediate danger—permitted? *See Hayes through Hayes v. Unified School District* No. 377, 669 F.Supp. 1519 (D.Kan. 1987). Are such "cooling down" approaches sufficient to meet the threat of a student like Doe, who choked a fellow student hard enough to leave bruises, then kicked out a school window? May a school impose a series of ten-day suspensions on such a student?

Should it matter that the student's misconduct is directly related to his or her disability—as in *Honig*, where the student was emotionally disturbed? Or is it always possible to establish some tie between misconduct and handicap? *See, e.g., School Board of Prince William County, Va. v. Malone*, 762 F.2d 1210 (4th Cir. 1985); *Kaelin v. Grubbs*, 682 F.2d 595 (6th Cir. 1982).

2. Other Due Process Issues

a. Budgets. A state, acting for budgetary reasons, closes a day-treatment facility for emotionally handicapped students; the students are transferred to a program that is not comparable. They assert that this is a change of placement, requiring a prior hearing. How should a court respond? *See Tilton by Richardson v. Jefferson County Bd. of Educ.*, 705 F.2d 800 (6th Cir. 1983); *Concerned Parents v. New York City Board of Education*, 629 F.2d 751 (2d Cir. 1980); *Brookline School Committee v. Golden*, 628 F.Supp. 113 (D.Mass. 1986).

b. Transcripts. Are handicapped students entitled to free written transcripts of their administrative hearings under a provision of the EAHCA that assures parties "the right to a written or electronic verbatim record"? *See Edward B. v. Paul*, 814 F.2d 52 (1st Cir. 1987).

c. Whose Rights? May a child's mother agree to the child's withdrawal from school, or does the right to an education under the EAHCA belong to the child, not the mother? *See Jackson v. Franklin County School Board*, 806 F.2d 623 (5th Cir. 1986).

d. Impartial Panels. May officers and employees of local school boards constitute the administrative appeal panel under the EAHCA or are they too closely aligned with the state to be impartial? *See Mayson by Mayson v. Teague*, 749 F.2d 652 (11th Cir. 1984).

e. Evaluation. The EAHCA proscribes racial or cultural bias in evaluation procedures, requires administration of tests in the child's native language, and assures that no single procedure be the basis for placement.

How is the thoroughness of evaluation procedures to be determined? Are cost considerations relevant here? 45 C.F.R. § 121a.503(b) provides that "a parent has the right to an independent educational evaluation at public expense if the parent disagrees with an evaluation obtained by the public agency. However, the public agency may initiate a hearing . . . to show that its evaluation is appropriate. If the final decision is that the evaluation is appropriate, the parent still has the right to an independent educational evaluation, but not at public expense." What does this provision mean? May the district demand a hearing prior to authorizing an independent evaluation? If so, on what basis does the hearing officer determine whether the evaluation is "appropriate"? How can parents effectively challenge that appraisal unless their child has been independently evaluated?

Racial bias in testing procedures typically refers to treatment of racial or ethnic groups, not individuals. See the discussion of this issue in chapter 5, *supra*. Moreover, the expense of data gathering effectively limits such claims to class suits. *See Griggs v. Duke Power Company*, 401 U.S. 424, 91 U.S. 849, 28 L.Ed.2d 158 (1971). Does the act create any effective mechanism for testing assertions of group bias? *Cf. Georgia State Conf. of Branches of NAACP v. State of Georgia*, 775 F.2d 1403 (11th Cir. 1985) (challenge to assignment of disproportionate number of black children to special education classes, based partly on Section 504 of the Rehabilitation Act).

Minimum competency tests pose a different type of evaluation problem. During the 1980s, several states adopted such tests as a prerequisite for graduation. Are handicapped students entitled to additional time to prepare for the test? Does denying them diplomas for failing the test deprive them of a free appropriate public education? *See Brookhart v. Illinois State Board of Educ.*, 697 F.2d 179 (7th Cir. 1983).

D. AIDS and the Federal Statutory Framework: A Case Study

Martinez v. School Board of Hillsborough County, Florida

861 F.2d 1502 (11th Cir. 1988).

Vance, Circuit Judge:

This case involves the appropriate educational placement of a mentally retarded child infected with the human immunodeficiency virus, the virus that causes Acquired Immunodeficiency Syndrome (AIDS). Appellant, Eliana Martinez, is seven years old and has an I.Q. of 41. This classifies her as a trainably mentally handicapped child. Eliana was born prematurely and received thirty-nine blood transfusions in the first four months of life. In April 1985 Eliana was diagnosed as suffering from AIDS Related Complex. She now is in the late stages of AIDS but her condition has been stabilized for several months. The court below found that Eliana is not toilet trained and suffers from thrush, a disease that can produce blood in the saliva. Eliana sucks her thumb and forefinger frequently, resulting in saliva on her fingers.

In the summer of 1986, Mrs. Martinez attempted to enroll Eliana in the special classroom for trainably mentally handicapped ("TMH") children in the public school system of Hillsborough County, Florida. Based on the recommendation of an interdisciplinary review team, the Hillsborough County School Board decided that the appropriate educational placement for Eliana was homebound instruction. Mrs. Martinez requested an administrative hearing, pursuant to the Education of the Handicapped Act. . . . On August 25, 1987, a hearing officer of the Florida Division of Administrative Hearings upheld the school board's decision. Having exhausted the administrative remedies prescribed under the EHA, Mrs. Martinez brought this action on behalf of Eliana challenging the hearing officer's determination. . . .

* * *

The district court heard extensive expert testimony on the risk of transmission. It found that there was a "remote theoretical possibility" of transmission of the AIDS virus through tears, saliva and urine. It held that the most appropriate educational placement for Eliana is as follows: Eliana will be taught in a separate room to be constructed in the TMH classroom with a large glass window and sound system to allow Eliana to see and hear the students in the main classroom. A full-time aide will remain in the room with Eliana and attempt to toilet train her and teach her not to mouth her fingers. Another child can enter the room only if a waiver is obtained from the child's parents absolving the school board from liability. Eliana can be taught in the main classroom when she becomes toilet trained and no longer places her fingers in her mouth. At that time, a full-time aide will ensure that an appropriate distance between Eliana and other children is maintained. The school nurse will be available for consultation if questions arise as to the advisability of Eliana being in the classroom on a certain day. 692 F.Supp. 1293.

Mrs. Martinez appealed the trial court's decision. We vacate and remand for further proceedings consistent with this opinion.

Two overlapping federal statutes establish the framework for determining appropriate educational placement for handicapped children—the Education of the Handicapped Act (the "EHA"), and section 504 of the Rehabilitation Act of 1973 ("section 504"). . . .

When the EHA and section 504 are read together, a complementary set of standards emerges to determine the appropriate educational setting for a handicapped child. . . . Under the EHA, the trial court must first determine if the state has complied with the procedures prescribed under that statute. . . . These procedures include the requirement that

> to the maximum extent appropriate, handicapped children . . . are [to be] educated with children who are not handicapped. . . .

See Department of Educ. v. Katherine D., 727 F.2d 809 (9th Cir. 1983). . . . Second, the court must determine whether the educational program developed by the state was "reasonably calculated to enable the child to receive educational benefits." . . .

Section 504 of the Rehabilitation Act more broadly provides:

> No otherwise qualified handicapped individual . . . shall, solely by reason of his handicap, be excluded from the participation in, be denied the benefits of, or be subjected to discrimination under any program or activity receiving Federal financial assistance or under any program or activity conducted by any Executive agency or by the United States Postal Service.

29 U.S.C. § 794 (1982). In considering whether an exclusion is prohibited by section 504, a trial judge must first determine whether the individual is "otherwise qualified." When a person is handicapped with a contagious disease this task requires the judge to conduct an individualized inquiry and to make appropriate findings of fact, "based on reasonable medical judgments . . . about (a) the nature of the risk (how the disease is transmitted), (b) the duration of the risk (how long is the carrier infectious), (c) the severity of the risk (what is the potential harm to third parties) and (d) the probabilities the disease will be transmitted and will cause varying degrees of harm." *School Bd. v. Arline*, 480 U.S. 273 (1987). As a second step the court must evaluate whether reasonable accommodations would make the handicapped individual otherwise qualified.

When a child with an infectious disease seeks relief under both the EHA and section 504 of the Rehabilitation Act, the relationship between these two statutory frameworks is particularly intricate. The trial judge must first determine the most appropriate educational placement for the handicapped child under EHA procedures. Next, the court must determine whether the child is otherwise qualified within the meaning of section 504 to be educated in this setting, despite the communicable disease. . . . If not, the court must consider whether reasonable accommodations could reduce the risk of transmission so as to make the child otherwise qualified to be educated in that setting. In considering accommodations that would make the child "otherwise qualified," the court must bear in mind the requirement that to the maximum extent appropriate, the child is to be educated in the least restrictive environment. . . .

As the parties agreed, the appropriate educational placement for Eliana under the EHA would be the regular TMH classroom if she did not suffer from AIDS. This presented the question whether the exclusion of Eliana from that setting is unlawful under section 504. In conducting this inquiry, the trial court had to determine whether Eliana was otherwise qualified to be educated in the regular TMH classroom. The trial court found a "remote theoretical possibility" of transmission with respect to tears, saliva and urine. This does not rise to the "significant" risk level that is required for Eliana to be excluded from the regular TMH classroom. . . . The court below made no findings with respect to the overall risk of transmission from all bodily substances, including blood in the saliva, to which other children might be exposed in the TMH classroom. Accordingly, we remand with directions that the trial court make findings as to the overall risk of transmission so that it can determine whether Eliana is otherwise qualified to attend classes in the TMH classroom.

If the risk of transmission supports a finding that Eliana is not "otherwise qualified" to attend classes with the other children in the TMH classroom, the court must consider whether reasonable accommodations would make her so. . . . The court must be guided by the requirement that, to the maximum extent appropriate, these accommodations place the child in the least restrictive environment that would make the child otherwise qualified. Additionally, the court must consider the financial burden the accommodation would impose on the institution. *See Southeastern Community College v. Davis*, 442 U.S. 397, 412 . . . (1979) (accommodation not reasonable if it imposes "undue financial and administrative burdens").

* * *

Central to the administrative framework under the EHA is the requirement that relief be tailored to the particular needs of each child. Accordingly, a trial court must base its remedial decision on evidence of the probable effect of a proposed accommodation on the child. The record below contains no findings with respect to the effect on Eliana of isolating her with an aide in a separate room in the TMH classroom. On remand, the court must hear evidence concerning the effect of any accommodation that would be reasonable based upon the risk of transmission. This evidence must, at the minimum, relate to the effect of the proposed remedy on her psychological and educational development. . . .

* * *

NOTES AND QUESTIONS

1. *The Interplay Between EAHCA and Section 504*

In *Smith v. Robinson*, 468 U.S. 992, 104 S.Ct. 3457, 82 L.Ed.2d 746 (1984), the Supreme Court held that Congress intended the Education for All Handicapped Children Act to be the exclusive avenue for raising legal claims about the provision of "free appropriate public education" for handicapped children. The decision meant such claims could not be brought under Section 504 of the Rehabilitation Act of 1973 or under 42 USC § 1983, the statute most commonly relied on for raising constitutional claims.

The 1986 Handicapped Children's Protection Act reversed *Smith* and reestablished the rights of handicapped students under these statutes. *See* Gallegos, "Beyond *Board of Education v. Rowley*: Educational Benefit for the Handicapped," 97 *Amer. J. Educ.* 258, 270 (1989). For children with AIDS, this is a crucial entitlement.

2. *AIDS as a Handicap*

The recently enacted Americans with Disabilities Act of 1990 defined "disability" in such a way as to include AIDS. But in 1986, in a case before the Supreme Court, the Justice Department argued that fear of contagion—even avowedly irrational fear—justified discrimination against those with AIDs. Under considerable political pressure, however, the Department reversed itself in 1988, and, in *School Board v. Arline*, 480 U.S. 273, 107 S.Ct. 1123, 94 L.Ed.2d 307 (1987), the Court held that the possibility of such irrational fears and the resulting stigmatization, was a primary reason for applying the protection of the Rehabilitation Act to those with contagious diseases.

Although the justices in *Arline* explicitly declined to apply their rationale to AIDS, lower courts have treated children with AIDS as handicapped within the meaning of Section 504. The courts have not treated them as handicapped within the definition of EAHCA, unless, as in *Martinez*, their illness or some other condition limits their ability to learn and thus creates a need for special education. In all cases except the *Martinez* district court case, courts have ordered their admission to the classroom. *See, e.g., Doe v. Dolton Elementary School District No. 148*, 694 F.Supp. 440 (N.D.Ill. 1988); *Doe by Doe v. Belleville Public School District No. 118*, 672 F.Supp. 342 (S.D.Ill. 1987); *Ray v. School District of DeSoto County*, 666 F.Supp. 1525 (M.D.Fla. 1987); *Thomas v. Atascadero Unified School Dist.*, 662 F.Supp. 376 (C.D.Cal. 1986); *Robertson by Robertson v. Granite City Community Unit School District No. 9*, 684 F.Supp. 1002 (S.D.Ill. 1988). *Compare Kohl by Kohl v. Woodhaven Learning Center*, 865 F.2d 930 (8th Cir. 1989) (exclusion of student with contagious hepatitis B challenged under Section 504). *See generally*, Note, "AIDS in the Classroom: A New Perspective on Educating School-Age Children Inflicted with HIV," 9 *Rev. of Lit.* 149 (1990); Note, "Public Schools and Public Health: Exclusion of Children with AIDS," 5 *J. of Law and Politics* 605 (1989); Note, "Undoing a Lesson of Fear in the Classroom: The Legal Recourse of AIDS-Linked Children," 135 *U. Pa. L. Rev.* 193 (1986); Note, "Protecting Children with AIDS against Arbitrary Exclusion from School," 74 *Calif. L. Rev.* 1373 (1986).

3. Martinez: *Scope of the Decision*

Does the court correctly weave together the relevant statutory requirements in fixing the standard for review? How is the trial court to proceed in ascertaining the precise risk of transmission that Eliana poses? How much risk is significant? A one in a million possibility? One in a hundred thousand? One in a thousand? In defining significance, what is the appropriate standard of comparison? The risk of a health hazard from exposure to asbestos in schools? The risk of death from a school bus accident?

In balancing the interests, how are administrative burdens to be weighed? Are these burdens simply costs? Do they include community reaction (which in this case was substantial and hostile to the admission of Eliana)? How is the stigmatizing effect of isolation on Eliana to be evaluated? What is the place of medical testimony in this calculus? Epidemiological evidence? Is an "individualized" inquiry a reliable method of determining truth—or a mask for judicial predilection on a vexing issue?

4. *The Social and Political Context*

More than technical questions of statutory interpretation are involved here. In the realm of rights for school children, few issues since desegregation have aroused such controversy as the matter of whether to admit children with AIDS to school.

Across the country, the specter of AIDS in the schools sometimes has stirred panic. It has prompted heated school board meetings, student boycotts, and lawsuits. It has made the national news, turning a teenager named Ryan White—kept out of school in Kokomo, Indiana, and ultimately forced from his town—into a spokesman for tolerance. It has made the Ray family, whose home was torched when they sent their three hemophiliac sons to school, a focus of national concern. Eliana Martinez, too, drew widespread attention as the "girl behind the screen."

The particulars of the disease partly explain this reaction. AIDS is routinely deadly, and it can lie dormant in the body for as long as a decade. Moreover, it has primarily affected gays and intravenous drug users. While children are often described as "innocent victims," the taint that their disease carries may fuel demands for their exclusion from school.

Since the early days of the epidemic, the scientific establishment has opposed such calls for exclusion. The Centers for Disease Control has consistently urged that, in general, children with AIDS pose no real risk to their classmates. Only in rare instances—cases like Eliana Martinez's, for instance, where a child cannot control his or her bodily functions—is individual review thought to be appropriate. *See* "Education and Foster Care of Children Infected with Human T-Lymphotropic Virus Type III/Lymphadenopathy-Associated Virus," 34 *Morbidity & Mortality Weekly Report* 517 (1985). But science and popular perceptions do not always agree.

"Learning by Heart: AIDS and Schoolchildren in America's Communities"

At 11:25 A.M. on the morning of September 8, 1986, the nineteen kindergartners in Classroom Six at the Santa Rosa Road Elementary School in Atascadero, California, were settling down for story time. It was the fifth day of the new term. Lori Parker, the young kindergarten teacher, and her aide, Pat Broker, were moving around the room. They coaxed the children into putting away their Unifix cubes and Cuisenaire rods and sitting, mouse quiet, in a semicircle to hear what was happening in *The Napping House*.

Two of the youngsters, Ryan Thomas and a classmate, were whispering and giggling to each other—or so the most widely accepted version of the story goes. Ryan, a wide-eyed munchkin of a child, was a blur of energy. His usual playmate, Justin Smyres, sat a few feet away, feeling abandoned. Justin is big for his age, more than a head taller than Ryan, often insecure about his ability to make friends and able to get his way by the sheer force of his size.

Angry at being left out, Justin elbowed Ryan in the head then grabbed Ryan's hair and yanked him down, forcing Ryan's face into his lap. Ryan struggled vainly to get up. Then he bit Justin, who yelped, drawing Pat Broker's attention, and Justin turned Ryan loose.

Such incidents happen thousands of times each year in schoolrooms across America. They are perfectly commonplace—except when the boy who bites happens to have AIDS. That bite, and the Atascadero school district's quick suspension of mercy, became the AIDS story for the fall of 1986.

Eight previous months of meticulous planning—hours and hours of meetings aimed at finding a rational solution to the highly charged question of whether a young child with AIDS should be allowed in school—went by the board. It was as if Atascadero's worst nightmare had come true. A carefully crafted arrangement, which enabled Ryan to enroll in a small class of kindergartners whose parents had agreed to the placement, was abandoned overnight. The whole controversy was taken out of the community and dumped in the lap of a federal court judge. . . .

No case of AIDS being transmitted through a bite has been documented, and all the credible medical evidence says that the odds against this happening are extremely high. But that evidence is known only to specialists who read the medical journals. To most parents, the bite of a child with AIDS is an awesomely fearful event which, even if unintended, seems to pile risk upon risk. To allow an AIDS-stricken child who bites into the same school as one's own youngster can appear to stretch compassion beyond its breaking point.

* * *

During the past few years, Atascadero has grown quickly and haphazardly. When the state highway was widened, it bisected the community, turning it into what one resident described as "seven exits off a freeway." Some 20,000 people live in Atascadero, twice the population of a decade ago, many in garden apartments and characterless tract-style homes slapped up to meet the demand.

Newcomers are typically refugees from southern California who come to escape the problems of the city. Many of them retired couples, they fled from multiracial urban life in favor of a town that is nearly all white, hoping to leave behind drugs and street people, pornography and homosexuals and all the rest. Such innocence is only a dream, though, for marijuana fields—and the other temptations of the outside world—are close by. In 1986, after a drug bust at the high school, the school board got so worried about drug dealing that it authorized a baby-faced cop to go underground. Two years earlier, state investigators were everywhere, looking into stories that a porn ring centered in nearby Bakersfield was mutilating young children in snuff films and burying their bodies. Nothing ever came of the investigation—except scared parents.

Aside from a concern to keep spending down, which has made the local homeowners' association a potent political force, residents are not much interested in participating in Atascadero's civic life. Indeed, not until 1979, more than half a century after the notion was first talked about, did Atascadero become a town by voting for incorporation, and a sizeable minority of the citizenry would be just as happy if the county still ran things.

Traditionally, the same civic apathy applied to the public schools. In size, the Atascadero Unified School District is the biggest in California, almost as big as Rhode Island. But size did not translate into quality; parents cared more about boosting the Future Farmers of America, or about getting *Catcher in the Rye* and *Of Mice and Men* off the library shelves, than about academics. They put very little money into the educational program, and the neglect showed. Teachers set low expectations for their students, of whom only a handful went off to college. Equipment in the science labs and vocational classrooms was ancient. In athletics, the Atascadero Greyhounds were always the doormat. "Why can't we be as good as San Luis Obispo?" teachers would lament.

Academic standards have been raised considerably since 1977, when Anthony Avina became superintendent. Students now perform in the top twenty-five percent, statewide, on academic achievement tests. Even the athletic teams are in better repute—the Greyhounds regularly win the league football championship—and the district has found state money to spruce up its schools. . . .

But many of the old ways endure. Emil LaSalle, a rancher elected to the board in 1983, won his seat on a pledge to reintroduce the Future Farmers of America into the school curriculum. A sizeable group feels that too much emphasis is currently being placed on academics, that the schools are becoming too college-prep oriented. And Atascadero's schools have had no sex education, because fundamentalist ministers, who carry considerable weight in the town, insist that teaching about sex promotes promiscuity and homosexuality.

Although San Luis Obispo County, which includes both Atascadero and San Luis Obispo, had already recorded seventeen AIDS cases by late 1985, AIDS itself was just the subject of scabrous jokes before the tumult over four-year-old Ryan Thomas. Soon enough, the townspeople got an education in AIDS; and until the bite, that education served them decently well.

In November 1985, Tony Avina had received a startling piece of news from Allan Gathright, a *San Jose Mercury News* reporter: the following September, a four-year-old child with AIDS would be enrolling in kindergarten. The minute that the reporter, who had been tipped off by a county health worker, left Avina's office, the superintendent dashed off a memo alerting his key staff people.

* * *

Until 1983, when several new members were elected to the Atascadero board, Avina "ran the school district as his own show," recalls Carl Brown, a New England transplant who teaches English at Cal Poly–San Luis Obispo and is one of the reform-minded board members. But with Brown, as well as Roy King, self-styled "retired zoologist loudmouth potmaker and intellectual," and Emil LaSalle, farmer and prideful curmudgeon, joining the seven-member board, Avina had to tread warily.

Avina was initially inclined to keep Ryan Thomas out of school. "He didn't start with the liberal high ground," notes George Rowland, the San Luis Obispo County Public Health Director, who became the school district's medical authority on AIDS. For his part, Avina points out that "this is an issue that could have blown Atascadero apart." A few months earlier, when Roy King urged the superintendent to "look at AIDS" and how it might become a problem for the school system, Avina replied: "I wouldn't touch it with a ten foot pole." "Back then," Avina recalls, "nobody wanted to talk about AIDS. It was too closely linked to homosexuality."

Robin and Judy Thomas, Ryan's parents, who first approached Avina shortly after the reporter's visit, wanted a quick decision about their son. In a letter to the superintendent, Dr. Joseph Church, the Los Angeles pediatric AIDS specialist who had diagnosed Ryan's condition, wrote: "I strongly urge that [Ryan] be allowed to attend regular school." But Avina saw things from a different vantage point. He had a conservative community to worry about—a community that, as board member Roy King noted, "may not be culturally ready to accept the fact that a gay disease, 'God's punishment,' is here." "I knew there would be outrage," says Avina, and to contain the outrage he appointed an AIDS advisory committee.

The committee was expected to acquaint itself with the latest medical evidence on AIDS in developing a school systemwide policy. It was February 1986, just half a year after AIDS had become an issue in Kokomo and Queens, and few people in the bucolic community of Atascadero knew much about the scientific findings on AIDS. Even more important, Avina believed, the process of talking things through was meant "to ventilate, to make people feel okay with the final decision."

This was the only way Atascadero could come to terms with AIDS, the superintendent thought. "We need plenty of public input," he told the Thomases. But medical expert Rowland concluded that Avina had acted "as much out of cowardice as anything else . . . he wanted to jump in front of the bandwagon." And to Robin and Judy Thomas, forming a committee looked like a classic bureaucrat's ploy for stalling.

It was a "y'all come committee," as Avina described it, and dozens of people did show up for meeting after meeting. There was the superintendent, making an appearance not to offer his opinion but to tell people his ambition: that "everyone is going to win." There was Roy King, who turned himself into an AIDS expert. "I made damn sure people knew that there are gays in the schools right now . . . I wanted the gay community protected."

Many of the parents who came were aghast at the idea of Ryan's attending school. "We're not big fanatics," declared Kathy Wentzel, mother of an elementary school child. "We don't say 'We're scared of AIDS, period.' We've done a lot of studying ourselves. And the doctors in our town believe an AIDS child should not be in school." Robin Thomas was there, too, carrying his son Ryan on his shoulders, a visible reminder that they were not debating an abstract issue but deciding how a boy with a fatal virus in his bloodstream would live out his life.

Avina recalls the meetings as "establishing a climate of respect for one another's opinions." But AIDS touches on so many deep-rooted feelings of dread that passions can drive out managed courtesies, and in Atascadero things sometimes got visceral. "One of the mothers stuck her kid in my face and screamed, 'Why do you want to kill my child?,' " Robin Thomas remembers. The Thomases received obscene calls and hate mail, and they weren't the only ones to be harassed. Kathy Wentzel answered her phone one day and heard a man demand, in a muffled voice, that "you bitches stay out of the Thomas situation or else."

Gradually, though, both sides gave ground. The Thomases agreed to certain precautions, like a separate locked toilet for Ryan, which while medically unnecessary did ease some people's fears. Many parents were reassured by George Rowland, who had shaped San Luis Obispo County's AIDS policy and was on hand to explain how AIDS is transmitted. Those who stuck to what Rowland described as a "line 'em up and shoot 'em philosophy" muttered about pulling their children out of school, but they never commanded much popular support.

Rowland embraced the message that leading AIDS researcher Dr. Merle Sande had delivered to his fellow doctors in a just-published *New England Journal of Medicine* editorial: it was indeed "time to take a more influential and active role in quelling this hysteria over the casual transmission of AIDS." . . . The quiet-spoken public health official was able to neutralize many of the fears that Atascaderans brought with them to the meetings. Some of their questions had been asked before, in Kokomo and in Swansea. But this case posed a new dimension: Ryan Thomas was nearly ten years younger than Ryan White or Mark Hoyle; for children so young, the Centers for Disease Control guidelines urged caution. And to those who saw Ryan Thomas at the placement committee sessions, often asleep in his father's arms, he seemed immature even for his age. Parents wondered whether he could be counted on to understand the gravity of his disease and to act responsibly. "How about blisters popping on the monkey bars?" they asked. "What about sweat or saliva in the sandbox?" And at every meeting, parents worried about biting.

"I didn't give them guarantees—there are no guarantees—but I did let them know how extremely unlikely it was that anyone could catch AIDS in school," says Rowland. "Would you send your child to school with Ryan?" Rowland was asked. "Absolutely," he replied. Over a period of months, Rowland persuaded a popular local pediatrician, Dr. James Tedford, to endorse Ryan's enrollment, and Tedford's conversion helped to change the minds of others.

The committee sought the help of the California State Department of Education. But the state's education and health departments were preoccupied with fussing over who had responsibility for AIDS and schools. "The district felt isolated," says Avina. "It was as if the state were saying, 'Let's step back and watch what happens.' " The guidelines the committee finally drafted were more restrictive than the policy recommended by the CDC. They applied not only to children with AIDS but also to their siblings—which plainly violated California law—a provision prompted by lingering fear that AIDS could be transmitted casually. The guidelines also created a placement committee, whose concerns any AIDS-afflicted child wanting to attend school would have to satisfy. And, uniquely among school districts, they gave parents a veto over whether their children would remain in the same classroom as a youngster with AIDS.

At a school board meeting held in the modernistic high school media center on April 13, 1986, nearly one hundred parents debated the new rules. Though the rules mentioned no specific cases, Ryan Thomas was on everyone's mind. Almost all the parents who spoke out that night wanted the boy kept at home. "You"—the school district—"are subjecting my children to the possibility of slow ultimate death," David Marazza insisted, and the liability-minded father demanded that Atascadero take out a $10 million surety bond for each of his children. Avina tried playing peacemaker—"Nobody's wrong, everybody's right: this is too complex an issue," he said—but the vociferousness of the opposition scared the school board into putting off its decision. Two weeks later, though, with the opposition "all exploded out," in board member Roy King's words, the board gave the policy its unanimous assent.

During the mid-May kindergarten "roundup" at the Santa Rosa Road School, which Ryan would be attending if the placement committee approved, nineteen parents signed permission slips saying that it was fine to place Ryan in the same class as their children.

"I'm proud to announce that this is an academic kindergarten," Principal Chuck Wilbur said at the roundup, and that emphasis on rigor has made the Santa Rosa Road School the most highly regarded in Atascadero. Real estate ads make a point of noting when a home is located in "the SRR attendance zone." Although the school has enough low-income pupils to qualify for federal aid, its achievement scores are the highest in the district, and its "back to basics" education philosophy appeals to many parents. "Santa Rosa Road was the best school in the district for AIDS to happen in," says Superintendent Avina. "The chemistry is great between parents and teachers."

When Principal Wilbur, an emigré from Los Angeles, realized that Ryan would likely be enrolling in Santa Rosa Road, he began assiduously to deliver an education on AIDS to everyone associated with the school. Presentations were directed at teachers and janitors. . . . The school's PTA put on two meetings, inviting doctors to explain the facts about AIDS, and while the PTA's parent leaders had strong views of their own, they were constrained to remain neutral. . . .

Students also were instructed on AIDS; afterwards, when the sixth-grade teacher took a poll, the majority voted that Ryan belonged in school. Yet on the playground that spring, the free-floating anxieties of the young found voice. There was talk about "the homosexuals in Africa," surely a garbled translation of their parents' dinner conversation, and the ultimate invective became "I hope you get AIDS."

Just before school was to begin in September 1986, the placement committee that was to recommend whether Ryan Thomas would attend kindergarten met for two hours with the family. It was hard going.

Almost no one in the room except the Thomases was enthusiastic about Ryan's starting school. In an assessment of Ryan's readiness for kindergarten, conducted during the summer by Kris McDermott, a retired school principal, Ryan had not performed well. The boy was "very young in what he can do," McDermott reported to the committee. "He has very few skills." Leslie Sherwin, a parent on the committee, told the Thomases that Ryan might be best off in a "Mommy and Me" class, while Greg Howe, co-president of the Santa Rosa PTA, renewed his concerns about biting. Christene Owre, a school nurse, was troubled about how Ryan would deal with stress. "It's not just Ryan that's at risk of getting sick, it's other children," pediatrician Jim Tedford reminded the group. And Roger Grass, a lawyer who represented the Atascadero schools, noted that four-year-olds were not legally required to attend school. "Use your best judgment," Grass urged the other members of the committee.

The committee ultimately gave its reluctant approval to Ryan's attending kindergarten. Although committee members would have preferred that the youngster spend a year in preschool, the Thomases had already pursued that possibility, only to be told that their son was too old. The idea that Ryan stay home for a year of maturing was not an unusual suggestion—each of Superintendent Avina's own children had done so—but the Thomases rejected it out of hand. They disputed McDermott's evaluation of their son's abilities. What he needed most, they felt, was the companionship of other children.

The first day of school had already been held, with Ryan at home, when the school board convened to make its final determination. This was no discussion about rules but the real thing, and seventy parents came, almost all of them bent on keeping Ryan out. . . .

The school board unanimously sided with its placement committee. As the committee's chairwoman, school psychologist Michelle Andre, told the board, "There is no medical reason that Ryan Thomas cannot attend school." Although two families did remove their children from Santa Rosa Road, the controversy seemed to be at an end. Avina congratulated the community for its "humaneness"—an earned pat on the back, since Atascadero had accomplished what Swansea had done. . . .

* * *

During the months preceding the opening of school, a four-by-eight-foot sign stood in front of the Thomases' bungalow: "Stop AIDS Discrimination," the sign read, "Help Get Ryan in School," a visible symbol of the battle being waged. Ryan's battle had really begun when he was born, two months premature and weighing just four pounds. The infant had to be flown several hundred miles north to Oakland for blood transfusions to keep him alive; but as the family learned early in 1985, the blood had carried the AIDS virus. "I didn't know anything about AIDS," says Ryan's father Robin, "except that it was a homosexual-type disease and that everyone died who had it."

During the first few years of his life, Ryan was constantly in and out of the hospital with painful ear infections and bouts of pneumonia. In the spring of 1985, just after the AIDS diagnosis, Ryan's temperature zoomed to 105. . . .

Ryan Thomas made it through the bout with pneumocystis pneumonia and began receiving the twice-monthly two-hour transfusions of gamma globulin that are standard treatment for young AIDS patients. . . .

* * *

The Thomases were determined that their son should lead a normal life, and that meant going to school. They knew it wouldn't be easy. "People who were friends for fifteen years stopped talking to us right after we told them about Ryan," Robin Thomas recalls. Robin says he was fired by the home-insulation firm he worked for, after his boss informed him that "city officials" had complained that he was "making too much noise" about his son's right to attend school. . . .

* * *

Although employees at the local Denny's restaurant raised over $1,100 for Ryan during the 1985 Christmas season, the Thomases felt cut off, able to trust only their family and the reporters, including Allan Gathright from the *Mercury-News*, who attached themselves to their cause. "The Thomases had so much of a 'make my day' attitude," says Jennifer Bacon, whose daughter was in Ryan's kindergarten class, "that sometimes they couldn't see the people who wanted to help them." They identified with the Whites in Kokomo, cheering when Ryan White won his court case in April 1986 and encouraged when Charles Vaughan, Jr., one of the Whites' lawyers, volunteered to assist them in Atascadero.

Fighting for a cause is nothing new for Robin Thomas. As an Atascadero High School student in the early 1970s, recently arrived from Los Angeles, he showed up with shoulder-length hair. School officials ordered him to get it cut. Robin refused—"I wanted the right to decide for myself," he says, recalling the incident—and was suspended. It was the principle, not the coiffure, that mattered. To prove his point, Robin went to his graduation, wife and infant son Richard by his side, sporting a crew cut. Getting Ryan into school came to feel like the same kind of issue.

During the winter and spring of 1986, the Thomases' distrust was fueled by what they regarded as the animosity of their neighbors and the conniving of the school system. "When are you going to get off your duffs and do something?" an angry Robin Thomas demanded of the school board early in 1986, before the advisory committee had even held its first meeting. . . .

The Thomases were understandably impatient—maybe too impatient—for their child. Everything that went wrong became part of a conspiracy against them. They felt uneasy about Avina, unconvinced that the superintendent cared about their son's welfare. They were angry when the placement committee held off meeting until the last possible moment in September, angry too at what they considered the insults of the parents who had spoken out against Ryan's admission. "Don't take it personally," those parents kept saying, but to the Thomases it was *all* personal.

The TV cameras, which had appeared at the May roundup, were back to capture the first few days in Classroom Six of the Santa Rosa Road Elementary School. This time they recorded Judy Thomas making sandwiches for her son and Ryan walking into his new classroom holding his brother Robert's hand. . . .

"Ryan blended well with everyone," said his teacher, Lori Parker. . . .

Once the term began, though, things seemed to be fine. All the precautions were in place, with pencils and crayons for individual students and a teacher's aide to escort Ryan to his own locked bathroom stall. "The kids treat Ryan like a prince," Parker said, and other teachers helped out too. " 'Keep up the good work,' they'd say, and 'Come into my classroom and escape from the media.' "

Some parents were upset about what they regarded as the Thomases' publicity-mongering. "They linger on TV," said PTA co-president Gerrie Dahlen. "They're using Ryan to get the recognition they never had before." And Judy Thomas confessed to a moment of sadness at Ryan's leaving home. "I'm missing one very important part of my life right now," she said, since the boy she called her "little shadow" was not by her side. But Robin Thomas was exultant. It was worth all the fighting, he declared, "just to see Ryan today with the other kids."

Then came the bite.

To the parents of the children involved, the episode wasn't a big deal. Ryan had only defended himself. "I bit him because I couldn't get up," he told his parents, who learned about the incident from a note safety-pinned to his pants. Besides, his bite hadn't even broken the skin; Justin Smyres had been wearing jeans. "Maybe some illiterate people believe you can get AIDS from a bite," said Mike Smyres, Justin's father, who blamed his own son for going after Ryan in a fit of jealousy, "but I know there's only two ways you can get AIDS, and that's through blood or sex—period."

Superintendent Avina took the bite far more seriously. Lon Allen, editor of the *News*, received a call from Avina that night, and the superintendent was distraught. "Ryan bit a child today; it just makes me sick." The superintendent quickly reached a decision: Ryan had to go. . . .

That night, a contingent of top-level administrators, including Avina, Avina's top aide Paul Anderson, and Principal Chuck Wilbur, visited the Smyres house to inspect the bite personally. All those high-powered eyes saw what the teacher's aide had reported—no broken skin, just a little redness. Nonetheless, Ryan was immediately suspended from school, and the placement committee was reconvened.

Ryan's story, which until then had attracted mostly local attention, instantly went national. "Reporters were coming out of the woodwork," Robin Thomas recalls. "There were calls from as far away as New York and Toronto. Sometimes it seemed like we were watching a movie."

Now it was The Bite, an incident abstracted from its particular facts. . . .

On September 15, the school board voted unanimously to insist on a psychological determination of whether Ryan was likely to act out again. Reluctantly, Robin Thomas went along. The report by the board-appointed psychologist described Ryan as "lovable . . . an attractive" child who "does not appear to be angry or prone to excessive impulsivity," but went on to note that, under extraordinary pressure, Ryan might possibly lash out. This evaluation could be said to describe any child, but it unnerved the placement committee, which wondered whether a single bite foreshadowed a pattern of biting. If so, that would be grounds for excluding anyone, not just Ryan.

Committee members were equally frightened by a letter from two German doctors, published that week in the British medical journal *Lancet* and widely publicized in the popular press, which purported to describe the first instance of a child transmitting AIDS by biting. Public Health Director Rowland wasn't convinced by the letter—"speculation, not a scientific study," he labeled it—for he knew the research findings on AIDS and saliva. These studies indicated that the virus had been isolated in the saliva of several AIDS patients but not in most other similar specimens. Moreover, the amounts were minute, so saliva was an extremely unlikely route of transmission—as one San Francisco researcher said, it would take several gallons of AIDS-infected saliva, poured directly into the bloodstream, to expose an individual to AIDS.

Rowland estimated the probability of AIDS being transmitted by biting at one in one hundred thousand, and, on the basis of the psychological report on Ryan, estimated the odds that the boy would bite again, this time breaking the skin, at one in ten. Rowland's calculations made for odds of a million to one against Ryan Thomas spreading his disease through a bite. Research on biting, unknown to Rowland, confirmed the extreme unlikelihood of spreading AIDS this way. . . .

Rowland proposed that the risk of transmission through biting be explained to the parents of Ryan's classmates—who, after all, had volunteered to enroll their children in Classroom Six—and that the choice be left up to them. But the placement committee rejected that idea, and urged instead that Ryan be barred from school until the following fall. "While people talked about rights," said committee chair Michelle Andre, "we focused on the needs of everyone."

Five days later, on October 6, the school board took up the matter in a public meeting. By this time, ACLU lawyers were representing the Thomases, and they had requested a two week postponement before the board made its decision. "We wanted to stay out of court," says the Southern California ACLU's legal director, Paul Hoffman. "We thought we could put together a powerful argument that would convince the board to let Ryan back in."

But Superintendent Avina, caught up in the antagonisms of the hour, sensed a trap. He dismissed the ACLU's suggestion as nothing more than a way for the ACLU to buy time so that it could prepare its lawsuit. . . .

* * *

Every school board member except one voted to keep Ryan home—but only until January 1987, when enrollment would again be up for review. The lone dissenting vote on the school board came from Emil LaSalle, who feared a possible lawsuit.

* * *

. . . In a matter of days, the ACLU filed suit against the Atascadero schools in federal district court, demanding the immediate reinstatement of Ryan Thomas.

* * *

The ACLU's job was compounded by the legal difficulty of the Thomases' case. It is one thing to believe that Atascadero had panicked into overreacting, something altogether different to persuade a federal court judge that a boy with AIDS was entitled to the protections of the 1973 federal Rehabilitation Act—a question never before decided in federal court. Moreover, the school district could plausibly rely on the CDC guidelines, which suggested a more "restrictive" setting for children who "display behavior such as biting." That's why Atascadero's lawyer, Roger Grass, had boasted to the placement committee that the Thomases "didn't have a prayer."

Shortly before the hearing, Paul Hoffman at the ACLU received a call from School Legal Service, a Bakersfield firm that handles the legal business of numerous southern California school districts including Atascadero. "We've got news that will make the ACLU want to back off the Thomas case right away."

The "news" came from the report of a nurse to whom Judy Thomas had confided in July. Ryan had bitten another child, the nurse reported. He had also shaved off his eyebrows and tried setting a plant on fire with a lighter. Hoffman checked out the story with the Thomases and emerged unimpressed. It turned out that, a year earlier, Ryan had been bitten hard by a little girl. She claimed that Ryan bit her back, but she had no teeth marks. The other incidents were equally inconsequential. At age two, after watching his father shave, Ryan had taken a razor to his eyebrows. The same year, he learned to use a lighter when his grandmother taught him to light her cigarettes. When Judy found him practicing on a rubber plant, a talking-to from an Atascadero fireman ended the pyrotechnics. These were "ordinary childhood problems," as Judy Thomas said, nothing to make—or dismiss—a federal case over.

* * *

Frank Fekete, the School Legal Service lawyer who argued Atascadero's case, stressed how "reasonable" the school district had been, how it had bent over backwards to do what was best for both the family and the community. Fekete also talked about the supposedly shocking revelations, eyebrow-shaving and the like, contained in the nurse's report. "We have a child here who has set fires, cut electrical cords," he declared. This was no ordinary pupil, Fekete added, citing the guidelines of the American Academy of Pediatrics, but one who posed a "greater risk." The Thomases were holding back, he contended, keeping Ryan's problems a secret.

That claim stirred ACLU lawyer Paul Hoffman to passionate retort. Arms waving, voice rising, the attorney demolished the claim that Ryan was a disturbed youngster. He mocked the notion that Atascadero had been reasonable: on the contrary, he insisted, "The district simply won't listen, [not even to] their own public health officer." No other Atascadero child had been put through such hoops just to be admitted to school, Hoffman reminded the court—all because of a risk no greater than "a jet engine falling from the sky."

Comparing AIDS to a jet engine's descent from the heavens was a flashy way of making an argument that, by the fall of 1986, was indeed substantiated by research on how AIDS was transmitted. All research showed the same thing: AIDS was spread only by blood or sperm. Six separate studies of 234 relatives (but not sexual partners) of persons with AIDS had been conducted, and not a single instance of household transmission of the virus had been found. A several-year study of hemophiliac children living in a French boarding school, youngsters particularly likely to bleed and inclined to roughhouse with one another, reached the same conclusion.

One report that Hoffman relied on directly addressed transmission through biting. Thirty health care workers had been bitten and scratched by a brain-damaged hemophiliac with AIDS. Despite the fact that some of the lesions were severe enough to produce scars, not one of the workers carried the AIDS virus.

There was, to be sure, the *Lancet* letter of September 20, concerning the alleged transmission of AIDS from an infected sibling to his older brother through a bite. That report had understandably frightened the Atascadero placement committee, but it was not good science. Hoffman solicited a declaration from Dr. Edward Gomperts, director of the hemophilia Comprehensive Care Center at Los Angeles' Children's Hospital, who pointed out that the mother who reported the bite was not sure she had seen teeth imprints. Moreover, she had no recollection of bleeding or a break in the skin, the only remotely plausible way, said Gomperts, that a bite could spread the disease.

All this evidence, ACLU attorney Hoffman argued, rendered out of date the CDC's fifteen-month-old guidelines, with their cautions about children who display biting behavior. Such cautions were also directed to children who bite regularly, children pediatricians describe as biters, and Ryan did not fit that description. (On this point, the CDC's Dr. Martha Rogers, who helped draft the guidelines, agrees. "If we thought AIDS could be transmitted in a minor bite," Rogers says, "we wouldn't have put [preschoolers] in school at all because kids that age sometimes do bite.")

* * *

Judge Stotler asked few questions during the hour-long argument and, immediately after, read a brief prepared opinion. The school board found itself in a "difficult position," the judge acknowledged, but "there is no evidence that Ryan Thomas poses a significant risk of harm to his kindergarten class-mates or teachers." Ryan could return to school immediately. . . .

* * *

. . . No appeal was filed.

That was the end of the legal story—but not the end of Ryan Thomas's troubles. All along, the Thomases had said they were fighting not for their son's readmission but for the right to decide what was best for him. The day after Thanksgiving vacation, Ryan returned to school. He was nervous, Judy Thomas told reporters, and at the end of the school day, the boy who had earlier relished attention was too shy to talk.

The youngster who, during the first days of school, was described by Lori Parker as the class darling, was now insisting that he "hated" school; he wanted his mother or one of his brothers constantly in class with him. "He felt like he was under so much pressure, like everybody was watching him and waiting for him to do something wrong," said Robin Thomas.

On December 4, 1986, Judy Thomas took her "little shadow" out of school. She blamed the school district for willing Ryan to fail. She also blamed herself. "We've been so uptight. Ryan has probably picked up on that."

Happily, young children change their minds. After staying home for a week, Ryan decided to try school one more time when his parents assured him he would be free to call it quits again if life in Classroom Six proved too stressful. The boy has since remained in school, though on some days he refuses to attend, and he has stayed healthy, too. Judy Thomas was hoping that Ryan could at last be "just like the other kids." Meanwhile, though, parents of some of the other youngsters in Classroom Six were reporting that their children were being ostracized, that the stigma of AIDS had spread to them. . . .

* * *

As Ryan enrolled in first grade in September 1987, camera crews from the local TV station were again present. Otherwise, though, both the family and the town have stayed out of the limelight. "There are times I didn't know if we could make it," recalls Robin Thomas. But then he adds, with a show of bravery: "I'd do it again, though. They're not going to tell me where Ryan can and can't go."

The Thomases remain very much on the fringe of life in Atascadero. Like Jeanne White in Kokomo, they are accused of using their child's fatal disease as a way of making themselves rich. Even Jennifer Bacon and Kay Wells, parents who sympathized with their plight, have sometimes been puzzled by their behavior. "You can't just make a freak show out of a kid, dragging him from reporter to reporter," says Bacon. And Wells notes that "Robin can give the impression that he's more interested in having won the case than in his son. And he hasn't always done the most expedient or politic thing." But Wells sees the other side of this story too. "I couldn't handle myself at all times with aplomb. When you see the tears, you get a feel for the struggle those people have gone through."

The hostility in the community has occasionally bubbled to the surface. In February 1987, four men drove into the driveway to the Thomases' front yard and tried to entice Ryan into their car with promises of candy and a trip to Disneyland. Police refused to investigate what Robin Thomas believes was an attempted kidnapping.

That episode made the family anxious to move away from Atascadero, to start over as the Whites did when they left Kokomo. The Thomases had hoped that their son's story, like Ryan White's, would be made into a TV movie. If that happened, they planned on using the money to move to Los Angeles—anonymous, laissez faire Los Angeles. But the TV movie did not materialize, and the possibility of a new beginning has receded into the realm of daydreams. . . .

When the story of young Ryan Thomas is just a dim recollection, when outsiders no longer associate Atascadero with the fateful bite, this town—very much like Kokomo—is likely once again to think about AIDS, not as an epidemic that for the foreseeable future can only grow worse, but as a freak occurrence. "After the court rules, the situation isn't going to go away," ACLU attorney Hoffman had warned during the court hearing, but to Superintendent Tony Avina, the decision really meant that the Atascadero Unified School District could return to the business of worrying about the education of its other 4,499 students.

It is in towns like Atascadero, where passions seldom run high, that you might anticipate a relatively conflict-free resolution of the AIDS crisis. Here, after all, were decently educated people who watch the evening news and read the national newsweeklies, and who in 1986 could grasp as well as any layman the fact that AIDS is not easily spread. Here townspeople had been given a chance to voice their concerns and to draft a policy that the school system adopted. By the fall of 1986, when Ryan was admitted to school, a peaceful resolution seemed at hand.

The bite, of course, undid everything—the bite and Superintendent Avina's reaction. If Ryan Thomas had been a thirteen-year-old who could control his emotions and his behavior, not an impulsive kindergartner who bit another child at a moment of stress, the process of decision-making constructed by the superintendent would have worked. But parents' fears were reawakened by the bite. Here was a child, they said aloud, who posed a special menace, and here was a family of transients, they said sotto voce, that was more interested in publicity than in the needs of their dying son.

Tony Avina's reaction to the bite only reinforced those fears. A more meticulous administrator confronted with the same news would have avoided a rush to judgment. He would have learned quickly about the differences between an incidental bite and habitual biting, and about the tenuous relationship between biting and AIDS—even as Sam Hannon in Lorraine had set out to learn about AIDS and homosexual behavior. A good leader would have used that knowledge, as Jack McCarthy did in Swansea, to keep the peace—to invite a full deliberation that could bring all the facts to light. . . .

The judicial decision delivered a civics lesson, to anyone who chose to listen. It was a reminder to Atascaderans that they were not free to decide things entirely as they pleased, that the concept of rights—codified in the federal Rehabilitation Act, ultimately deriving from the underlying constitutional right of any person in this society to fair treatment—defined the outer bounds of their discretion. Judge Stotler's reasoned judgment echoed an observation that Alexis de Tocqueville had made about America a century and a half earlier—when civil discourse breaks down, the concept of rights, interpreted by a judge, ultimately defines the terms of membership in a community. It is the rights embedded in a national covenant that make it so hard for communities to banish the feared and disliked, whether they are Nazis in Skokie, Illinois, or blacks in Forsythe County, Georgia, or street people or homosexuals or children with AIDS.

Such lessons are better learned in public conversations that allow ideas and values some room for play. Public talk can become a way of sorting out the reality of people's fears and the tolerability of risks, as well as a way of understanding the wounds that building walls can inflict on those who construct the barriers. But without a leader to point out those values, the conversations in Atascadero in the weeks after the bite were fed by fear. In such circumstances, it is better that the idea of rights acquire meaning in a distant courthouse than not at all. . . .

* * *

This theme of a gay plot to set the AIDS agenda was repeated by an Atascadero contingent that ventured more directly into politics. The group did not endorse political extremist Lyndon LaRouche's state ballot initiative on AIDS—which contemplated quarantining people with the AIDS virus—because, as Santa Rosa Road parent Kathy Wentzel said, "This meant taking on powerful homosexuals." However, Wentzel and several others flew to Sacramento to meet with their state assemblyman, Republican Eric Seastrand. They urged Seastrand to introduce a bill requiring that school districts be notified whenever a child with AIDS was enrolled—California's privacy laws protect the confidentiality of that information—and advanced the same proposal at the statewide PTA convention. But their idea went nowhere. It was homosexuals, they surmised, who were undermining such measures.

These frustrated Atascaderans saw themselves as rebuked by the court and shut out of the political discourse. Now they were reaching for a scapegoat: the "powerful" homosexuals. It was irrelevant that this attribution of power had little basis in fact, that California's AIDS policy was primarily being shaped, not by influential homosexuals, but by a conservative Republican governor with little inclination to court gay voters. What counted was the perception of these citizens of Atascadero that their lives were being manipulated by malevolent outside forces. Homosexuals were assigned a role like that given such historically despised groups as the Jews. The message of the judicial ruling in *Thomas v. Atas-*

cadero Unified School District—that, in the end, the school board and the superintendent had acted without evidence, had succumbed to the fears of the community—went ignored, as Atascadero's leaders were quick to redescribe history. . . . "If it wasn't for the bite, this town would be lauded for the way it handled the issue," says Tony Avina. But what the superintendent cannot see is the impact of his own behavior on the unfolding of the Ryan Thomas story, his politically charged reaction to the biting incident and the strong feelings his reaction invited.

"There was no crisis," declared an editorial in the *Atascadero News*, the local weekly that determinedly puts a pleasant face on things. Among Atascaderans themselves, the general sentiment is that nothing much had happened, that the pace of community growth remained a far bigger issue than AIDS would ever be, that the Ryan Thomas story had been blown out of all proportion, sensationalized by that familiar enemy, the reporters who grabbed what they wanted and ran.

In Atascadero, the reluctance to teach schoolchildren about the dangers of AIDS persists. AIDS is regarded as part of sex education, which remains a touchy subject the superintendent is unwilling to pursue. "They still think it's Happy Valley," says County Medical Director George Rowland. "They still believe it can't happen here."

E. Implementing the Right to an "Appropriate" Education

The utility of a rights-centered approach is problematic not just with respect to AIDS; similar questions need to be asked about handicapped children generally.

The changes in educational practice with respect to handicapped children worked by federal statute and court decisions are truly massive. Substantial numbers of children previously denied any schooling are to be brought into the system; an appropriate education is to be provided for all handicapped young people; efforts are to be made to integrate handicapped and normal children to the greatest extent possible; procedural protections and safeguards concerning incorrect or biased evaluations hedge a process previously left to professional discretion.

Imagine yourself a lawyer, educator, or policymaker charged with implementation responsibilities in this domain. What problems are you likely to confront?

"The Allure of Legalization Reconsidered: The Case of Special Education"

D. Neal and D. Kirp in *School Days, Rule Days: The Legalization and Regulation of Education*, D. Kirp, D. Jensen, eds. (1986).

The evolutionary nature of legalization in special education policy (through PARC, Mills, and EAHCA) precluded any detailed consideration of the appropriateness of a legalized model in the education setting, at least in the policy formulation stage. Now that some of the major abuses that led to the court decisions and ultimately the legislation have been corrected, questions are being raised about the appropriateness of legalization in the education setting.

This reappraisal poses serious issues of policy. Does it make sense to impose on education a policy mold which does not place much faith in the professional discretion of the service provider? The implications of this shift are not lost on educators who may understandably resent the implicit loss of confidence. More generally, does legalization fit the needs and demands of schools—or of children? The imposition of legalization onto ongoing complex organizations, such as schools, also creates particular problems. Studies of the implementation history speak less of the promise of legalization and more of its pathology: compliance with the letter rather than the spirit of the law; preparation of standard form IEPs, resentment that handicapped children have gained a priority that does or may gain them more than their fair share of the education dollar; and defensive strategies, such as the tape recording of IEP meetings, to protect the interests of the school district and teachers.

Yet the story is more complex than this. While implementation studies view the due process procedures as a separate and severable part of the federal legislation, these procedures are an integral part of a legislative scheme which adopts a legalized policy style. The appropriateness of this policy style must be judged with reference to the place of special education in the school system, not by focusing only on the due process hearings ignoring this overall context. To be sure, the benefits to special education flowing from the federal presence—more money, more initiatives, and the like—must be offset by the costs of the due process hearings. Yet the question is whether these gains could have been achieved without the legalized policy style of PL 94-142.

A radical reorientation of priorities in special education was needed in the American context and those who shaped PL 94-142 judged that legalization was the only way to bring it about. That view has much to recommend it. In certain situations shock treatment is called for to convince service deliverers in an ongoing institution that established patterns and values must be changed. Legalization was not the first but the last in a series of approaches taken by educators of the handicapped. Years of campaigning had not convinced the education community of the justice of the claims made on behalf of the handicapped.

Legalization was a plausible approach. While law may not be the only way to reorder priorities or legitimate claims—the availability of a great deal of new money for special education or the operation of a competitive market, for example, might have brought about the same result—law and legal sanctions offered a surer and more direct means of institutionalizing the values promoted by the proponents of change. The embodiment of values in law and the possibility of sanctions offer powerful reference points to those implementing a reform, serving as a rallying point for claims on the system and a powerful mechanism for responding to arguments from competing value positions. The law also provides a frame in which values can be translated into services and new values and services can emerge, for it requires the adjustment of power positions of the various groups with a system. Proponents of the new values gain power in the institution and can introduce still further changes on behalf of their interests.

In short, legalization is neither so cost-free as its proponents suggested nor so defective as subsequent analyses contend. In what follows we explore the effects of legalization by examining the implementation of PL 94-142 and the due process mechanisms in particular.

* * *

The studies of the implementation of the due process aspects of PL 94-142 are the best available indicators of the effects of legalization but they need to be evaluated with caution. For one thing, they report a fairly short experience of the legislation and necessarily do not deal with the possibility that implementation improves over time. For another, they are flawed in a variety of ways. The research typically relies on small, non-random samples of individuals involved in the hearings. While valid as a guide to the experience of those who undertake a hearing, these cases focus on the deficiencies of the process. They do not speak to the appropriateness of the due process procedures generally, or to the level of satisfaction in general of parents of handicapped children with the new law. This research approach shortchanges the systemic effect of the procedural reforms. Moreover, since the studies only report the cost-legislation experience, the ill-effects attributed to the due process procedures may simply be old problems transferred from other forms or made more visible by the existence of the hearings.

* * *

The notification and procedures required to draw up the IEP and hold the meeting are generally in place. After some early hearings where schools failed to comply with notice deadlines, and the like, the mechanics of the IEP procedures seem to be operating.

The qualitative picture is not as clear. Two types of IEP meetings have been identified: a legalistic form in which half the time is devoted to narrow procedural requirements, and a child-oriented form, faithful to the spirit of the law. IEP sessions in which the parents are overwhelmed with professional jargon and other strategies used by schools to minimize the portion of their resources devoted to meetings have been reported in two states. There are also hearsay accounts of IEPs prepared in advance where the parent is pressured to sign on the dotted line, but little evidence to indicate how widespread this practice is.

Reactions of the IEP process are mixed. Parents generally seem satisfied, even enthusiastic, about the development of the IEP, but in the districts characterized as legalistic, one third of the parents describe the meetings as formalistic. Teachers generally regard the IEP as useful but reports differ as to whether there is a high degree of actual use of the IEP as an instructional tool or such use is the exception rather than the rule. Even this more pessimistic accounting acknowledges that the IEP has the force of law and serves as new found leverage both within the school and the district and provides a basis for a due process hearing.

* * *

The total number of due process hearings held pursuant to the Education for All Handicapped Children Act is not known. Scattered reports suggest wide variations from state to state. In California, 278 hearings were held in 1978–79, the first year of uniform state regulations, and one-third of these were held in two school districts. That number represents just 0.08 percent of California's special education population. A nationwide study of twenty-two sites found half had experienced hearings; seven had only one hearing. Massachusetts had 350 hearings between 1974 and 1979.

As with litigation generally, it is difficult to say whether those figures represent a large percentage of hearings relative to the number of people who had grievances. Data from other comparable contexts—welfare, for instance—suggest that hearings are highly unusual phenomena in relation to the number of people or even the number of complaints in a given area. Right to education hearings are not atypical in this regard.

The impact of hearings, however, cannot be measured simply in terms of the number of hearings held. The prospect of a hearing and estimations of its likely outcome shape the behavior of participants, both in the formulation of their basic relationships and in the way they handle their disputes. The shadow of the law extends well beyond the formally affected parties.

* * *

Middle class parents bring the majority of hearings—the proportion of middle class users was as high as 82 percent in one study—leading one commentator to observe that (d)ue process and appeal procedures are used to advantage by the well-to-do and almost not at all by the poor.

The middle class are usually best able to press their claims. Factors similar to those identified in other contexts seem to be at work in relation to reliance on hearings in the special education context. People in ongoing relationships are unlikely to resort to legal sanctions. Parents who know that their children will have to deal with the local school district personnel for twelve years are understandably reluctant to resort to legal action, with the anxieties that such undertakings generate, in all but the most serious cases. The opportunities for reprisal even after an outcome favorable to the parents, and the difficulties of enforcing such a decision in the face of an intransigent school district pose too great a risk.

Middle and upper class parents do not face such high odds, for they have an exit strategy. Their complaints typically assert the inability of the local school district to provide appropriate education and claim reimbursement for tuition in private schools. If this proves unsuccessful, these parents can pay for the private schooling themselves. Lower class parents do not have this option, when they are involved in hearings at all, it is most often to resist changes proposed by the school, rather than to initiate change. The ongoing nature of their relationship with the school system means that circumspection is probably in the best interests of these parents. This pattern points up an important limitation on the capacity of due process to bring about change in professionally-run bureaucracies. It also raises questions about the wisdom of placing primary reliance on due process to effect policy change.

Adversariness and legalism seem to characterize the conduct of hearings, rather than adopting an informal negotiating format, the due process hearings tend to provide a forum for culmination of long-term bad relations between the school and the parents involved. Involving lawyers aggravates the situation, rendering proceedings more legalistic. Emphasis on compliance with procedural matters such as notices, signatures, and time deadlines offers an easy substitute for harder substantive questions, such as the meaning to be given to the word "appropriate" in the phrase "free, appropriate, public education" in a given case. This legalistic pattern seems particularly evident in the earlier stages of implementation. As schools have learned to comply with the forms of the law opportunities for evasion have diminished, and there is some evidence of reduced formalism as in reliance on pre-hearing hearings and negotiations among the participants.

Parents generally reported both considerable expense and psychological cost in the hearing process. They often felt themselves blamed either for being bad parents or for being troublemakers.

School districts regarded the hearings as expensive, time-consuming and a threat to their professional judgment and skill. The private school placements which parents often sought are enormously costly and also carry an implied criticism of the public school program. Directors of special education programs often regarded parents seeking these placements as "ripping off" the school system, depriving other children of the benefits that would otherwise accrue to the public school program. They complained about inconsistency in interpreting the appropriateness criterion from one hearing to the next and difficulties in accounting to the school board for expensive new services endorsed in hearings. Special education administrators see themselves as caught in a cross-fire between parents and hearings officers who charge them with denying entitlements and school boards who blame them for failing to hold the line on expensive new services.

Some school districts which have experienced a number of hearings have developed an array of defensive strategies. There are reports of districts tape-recording IEP meetings, retaining lawyers, tightening up on procedures and interpreting education and related services narrowly; all ways of sticking to the letter of the law. Other districts negotiated extra services with parents who promised not to pursue a hearing or threatened to demand a hearing in order to coerce parents into accepting an IEP.

While a few participants in due process hearings regarded them as positive experiences, allowing some sort of catharsis and a forum in which an independent party could suggest a solution, most held a negative view. In many instances, hearings have become an additional weapon with which the disputants can bludgeon one another. Parents see themselves as pursuing the best interests of their child while the school district is anxious to preserve limited resources.

* * *

The negative effects of the due process hearings should not be exaggerated. Even though they impose a high economic and psychological cost on all involved, their incidence is concentrated on relatively few school districts. Furthermore, these are districts where parents have a long history of dissatisfaction with the school system. The hearings provide an arena in which old conflicts are played out, and sometimes escalated. In view of this the assertion that the introduction of due process procedures has caused relations between schools and parents to deteriorate must be treated with extreme caution.

* * *

The implementation studies discussed in the previous section assess the appropriateness of legalization in special education without either attending to the wider context of the education system or proposing plausible alternative means of rectifying the indisputable abuses of the past. To focus exclusively on the due process procedures in isolation and to identify the undesirable effects associated with them misses the broader institutional changes associated with the legislation, of which the due process procedures form an integral component.

Passage of PL 94-142 has had an enormous effect on special education. More than 230,000 children were identified and provided with education within the first two years after passage of the law and the rate of increase is steady.

There has been an enormous increase in special education expenditure which has produced not only cash benefits, but also augmented the prestige and attractiveness of special education as a field of endeavor. The formal procedures mandated by the Education for All Handicapped Children Act are in place and many new programs are being developed in school districts.

Much of this change might have been achieved without reliance on such a legalized policy style. Implicit in the criticisms of due process procedures is the suggestion that the policy-makers were wrong in believing that the legalized model was essential to achieve their purposes, and that legalization is inappropriate in the context of education. Even if we remain skeptical about the causal links between the due process hearings and the effect attributed to them by the studies canvassed in the previous section, there is reason enough to raise concerns about the appropriateness of the due process procedures in the school setting. . . .

* * *

Leaving substantive determinations to due process hearings had both the virtues and the vices of legalization. It contemplates principled arguments about the amount and type of services due to a given child. This may be preferable to such alternatives as centralized bureaucratic decision-making, with its attendant problems of distance and rigid categorizations or professional judgments which are often paternalistic and give undue weight to the needs of the professionals at the expense of the handicapped student. The legalized model also creates problems. Handicapped children are accorded formal rights not made available to other children in the education system. There is for instance, a tendency for rights to know no dollar limitations. Yet the reality that school administrators face is that they have limited budgets and must make difficult decisions about the just distribution of those funds among competing sectors of the school system.

Ambiguity surrounding the word "appropriate" also produces tension between schools and parents. School officials complain about parents looting the public treasury to obtain private school placements and express frustration that they feel unable to put these sorts of arguments to the hearings officers. This limitation may be attributable to the tendency of due process hearings to individualize problems but it is not a necessary interpretation of the legislation. Acting on this perception, school administrators are resorting to indirect means of protecting funds, adopting defensive or delaying tactics, and attempting to translate arguments based on the needs of the school system in general into arguments about a particular child. For their part, parents' expectations may have been raised to unrealistic levels by the law. Their concern is likely to reside exclusively with their child, in their eyes the word "appropriate" may have come to mean whatever is appropriate regardless of the cost. This would explain parental frustration with school districts, and their perception concerning the lack of candor in the school officials with whom they deal.

While this dispute over the relevance of costs is party attributable to the fact that entitlements of handicapped children, but not those of nonhandicapped children, are clearly spelled out, it is also partly a function of the adjudicative process itself. The hearing mechanism is, in its ideal form, a case-by-case process: it formally assumes that two parties are disputing in a contextual vacuum. That fiction alone is enough to give rise to considerable frustrations. Moreover, different hearing officers will render different decisions on similar cases. There is no consistent interpretation of "appropriate" and there does not appear to be much communication among hearing officers about their decisions. While this may change as precedents develop, several factors—the variegated nature of appropriateness, the fact that hearings officers lack either the legal or educational expertise to render consistent judgments, and the variability of schools and handicapping conditions—make consistency unlikely. . . .

The broadest concerns relate to the effects of legalization of special education on the school as a bureaucratic/professional organization. Schools face serious problems of coordination, confronting acutely complex questions of distributive justice among different elements of their program, of management *vis-a-vis* their own professional staff, and of accountability to the community, especially to the parents of currently enrolled students. The meaning of a good education is controversial, and limited in any case by funding realities. Potential lines of conflict run in every direction: between school board and teachers, teacher and principal, teacher and student, and teacher and parents.

The effect of legalization on special education entails a radical reorientation of this complex network. It empowers what was previously an out group: the handicapped must now be included in policy decisions. No one in the school system can maintain that handicapped children should be excluded from school, at least not publicly. The force of the state and the moral authority of the law is available to the handicapped.

Legalization has also improved the status of the special education professional. In an era of shrinking education budgets, special education has received an infusion of new money. It has become an attractive area for new teachers and a way for existing teachers to earn additional salary and avoid retrenchment. Special education teachers are assuming places in school administrations which, hitherto, they had not held, and this too will affect the organizational goals of schools and strengthen the perceived legitimacy of the claims of the handicapped.

The pathologies of legalization must also be owned. There is some evidence that the values promoted by the legislation are provoking resistance from the education community.

Despite increased funding there are too few resources to treat all handicapped children individually. By distinguishing the handicapped children from the regular school network and granting them rights not enjoyed by other school children, the law potentially distorts the allocation of resources. This potential is aggravated by the legal model which treats the parties to a dispute as discrete from the system in which they are located.

Finally, legalization betrays a mistrust of schools. It may inhibit the discretion of professionals whose judgment should be exercised creatively on behalf of the child. In the past that distrust may have been deserved. But legalization can be a blunt instrument, undermining healthy as well as malevolent exercise of discretion. Special education teachers now find themselves as "defendants" in due process hearings. This represents a marked change from their self-perception, prior to passage of PL 94–142, as lone advocates for the handicapped child. From the viewpoint of the handicapped it would be disastrous to alienate this group, particularly in view of their role as primary service providers and their new status in the school hierarchy. Encouraging mediation and negotiation, rather than due process hearings, should diminish this danger. . . . In this way, parents and teachers could be reunited in the task of providing the best education, within budget constraints, for handicapped children.

Finally, the utility of the due process hearing as a compliance device is dubious. Individualization, lack of coordination and the settlement of strategic cases to avoid hearings suggest systemic problems which may be missed by the individualized nature of the hearings. Hearings alone are ill-suited for the task of precipitating systemic review and reform. Agency-wide review, litigation, and political change remain key parts of appraising and modifying any program.

Only in the context of those wider considerations may the appropriateness of legalization be assessed. Legalization jolted the education system into according handicapped children a fair share of the education pie. As the system comes to accept the presence of handicapped children and recognizes the legitimacy of their claims and, as special education teachers acquire new status in school hierarchies, there are sound reasons to diminish reliance on some aspects of the legalized structure of special education. . . .

* * *

NOTES AND QUESTIONS

1. Legalization as a Policy Strategy

a. *Appraising the Evidence.* A survey of five diverse school districts finds considerable variation in response, depending on the capacity of the district (its wealth and willingness to respond) and the participation of parents. Singer and Butler, "The Education for All Handicapped Children Act: Schools as Agents of Social Reform," 57 *Harv. Educ. Rev.* 125 (1987).

b. *Rights as Trumps.* The EAHCA provides benefits to the handicapped that are not afforded to other groups: guarantees of an appropriate education, procedural safeguards, and protection against sanctions. Is it appropriate to treat the claim of the handicapped to an education as a civil right?

Consider the position of the Heritage Foundation, which criticizes the federal legislation for resting "on the questionable assumption that the responsibility for disabled individuals is primarily society's as a civil right," and argues that "public schools should not be required to educate those children who cannot, without damaging the main purposes of public education, function in a normal classroom setting." Heritage Foundation, "The Crisis: Washington Shares the Blame," *The Heritage Foundation Backgrounder* 1, 12 (1984).

What are the consequences of assigning rights to some but not all children—in terms of equity? political clout? formal claims on resources? *Compare* Kirp, "Professionalization as a Policy Choice: British Special Education in Comparative Perspective," 44 *World Politics* 137 (1982), *reprinted in* J. Chambers and W. Hartman, eds., *Special Education Policies: Their History, Implementation and Finance* (1983).

c. *Changing the Law.* Imagine that you are a staffer on the House Education Subcommittee, which once again is considering the policy approach taken by EAHCA. Does the Kirp and Neel analysis suggest any changes in its structure that would make sense? For instance, would it be possible—and desirable—to rely less on formal procedures and more on professional judgment? *See generally* Pittenger & Kuriloff, "Educating the Handicapped: Reforming a Radical Law," 66 *Public Interest* 72 (Winter 1982); Benveniste, "Implementation and Intervention Strategies: The Case of PL 94–142," in D. Kirp and D. Jensen, eds., *School Days, Rule Days: The Legalization and Regulation of Education* 146 (1986).

2. Beyond Special Education

Even as classical discrimination is a framework not easily applied to the claims of the handicapped (see the discussion, *supra*, and Rebell, "Structural Discrimination and the Rights of the Disabled," 74 *Georgetown L. J.* 1435 (1986), it may be that special treatment, of the sort provided by PL 94–142, works against the interests of this group. Or so Alan Gartner and Dorothy Kerzner Lipsky argue in "Beyond Special Education: Toward a Quality System for All Students," 57 *Harv. Educ. Rev.* 367 (1987):

> [I]n special education . . . the child and family are considered impaired, instruction is disability-focused,

professional personnel are often trained and certified to work with specific disabilities, and attention to societal issues is often considered too political and not the business of educational institutions. The assumptions underlying such beliefs can be tersely summarized: "(1) Disability is a condition that individuals have; (2) disabled/typical is a useful and objective distinction; and (3) special education is a rationally conceived and coordinated system of services that help children labeled disabled. . . . This view of students labeled as handicapped, however, adversely affects expectations regarding their academic achievement. It causes them to be separated from other students; to be exposed to a watered-down curriculum; to be excused from standards and tests routinely applied to other students; to be allowed grades that they have not earned; and, in some states, to be permitted special diplomas.

The rationale given for such watered-down expectations is that they are in the best interest of the child. Professionals often suggest that a child be placed in an environment where he or she will be "safe . . . because he would never be asked to do things there 'we know he cannot do.' "

Not only do "small expectations" excuse students from academic performance; they have also led state education departments, school systems, and the courts to excuse them from the social and behavioral expectations and standards set for other students. The medical or clinical model that undergirds special education inextricably leads to the belief that persons with a handicap, especially the severely disabled, are not capable of making choices or decisions. . . . Having denied individuals with disabilities autonomy and decision-making authority—in effect denying them the respect given to people whom society respects—we then excuse their behavior, ascribing it to the disability. . . .

An alternative way to serve students with mild and moderate handicaps is to integrate them into general education programs at the building level.

* * *

While clearly an improvement over the present special education practice, this broad proposal nonetheless continues a dual system approach for a smaller (more severely impaired) population. As described a decade ago, such students will continue to be faced with consequences of negative attitudes and lowered expectations, with teachers making comparisons between them "in relation to degrees of handicap rather than comparing [their] skill levels to the criteria of nonhandicapped skill performance." . . .

How then does one shape an educational system to include students with disabilities, one which is both consonant with and builds toward an inclusive society? Clearly, it is not done by taking students from the general education setting and labeling them as "deficient," nor is it done, as in special education, by focusing on the setting in which instruction takes place. Rather, research indicates that we must focus on the features of instruction that can produce improved learning for students.

An important step toward a restructured unitary system is expressed in a concept called "Rights without Labels": namely, the provision of needed services for students without the deleterious consequences of classification and labeling.

Regardless of the conceptual undergirding or the organizational arrangements of education for students with handicapping conditions, special education practice needs substantial improvement. In maintaining a separate special education system, however, no matter how refined or improved, education will continue to operate based on a set of organizational and individual assumptions that disabled and nondisabled youngsters require two distinct sets of services, which in turn require distinct funding, service delivery, and organization. While PL 94–142 requires educational services for students with handicapping conditions, it does not require a special education system.

There is an alternative to separate systems: a merged or unitary system. The conception of a unitary system requires a "paradigm shift," a fundamental change in the way we think about differences among people, in the ways we choose to organize schools for their education, and in how we view the purpose of that education. It rejects the bimodal division of handicapped and nonhandicapped students, and recognizes that individuals vary—that single-characteristic definitions fail to capture the complexity of people. Moreover, it rejects the belief, common to all human services work that incorporates a medical or deviancy model, that the problem lies in the individual and the resolution lies in one or another treatment modality. The unitary system, in contrast, requires adaptations in society and in education, not solely in the individual. . . .

In the United States, there is a body of "adaptive education" approaches and specific educational practice attuned to individual differences that have been shown to be effective for students with handicapping conditions. Asserting the legal duty to provide effective schooling, lawyers at the Public Interest Law Center of Philadelphia put it succinctly: "Play school is out. Schooling is a profession. The law requires that practice in the schools measure up to the art of what has been demonstrated by the professional to be possible. What is done must be calculated to be effective." . . .

The ultimate rationale for quality education of students in an integrated setting is based not only on law or pedagogy, but also on values. What kinds of people are we? What kind of society do we wish to develop?

> What values do we honor? The current failure to provide a quality education to all students and the perpetuation of segregated settings expresses one set of answers to these questions. To change the outcome, we need to develop another set of values. . . .

Does the integrationist approach advanced by Gartner and Lipsky make educational sense? Do schools have the capacity—the willingness—to make the "paradigm shift" that is demanded? How might this approach be implemented? Should advocates for the handicapped fear that, under the guise of offering special treatment in a common setting, school administrators would provide little for their clientele?

The authors suggest that such integration is not just a claim rooted in pedagogy or values but also based on law—that truly common schooling is tantamount to effective education, and that such education is a legal right. Nearly two decades after *PARC* and *Mills*, does this suggestion portend a second wave of constitutional claims for the handicapped? Would you urge such a legal strategy?

IV. WOMEN: EQUAL OPPORTUNITY AND CHOICE

While American public schools are for the most part coeducational institutions, differences in the treatment of male and female students have long been commonplace. Some differences such as the exclusion of women from school sports teams are obvious. Others are more subtle—textbooks that define male and female roles differently and teachers who treat boys and girls differently.

During the 1970s, gender-based differentiation in education, like gender-based differentiation generally, became the subject of litigation. Differentiation in the treatment of married or pregnant students, gender-specific curricular restrictions, and sex-differentiated rules for athletic participation have each been said to deny equal opportunity to women; the permissibility of "separate but equal" educational opportunity afforded single-sex schools and programs has also been questioned.

Many of these issues were addressed by Congress in Title IX of the 1972 Education Amendments. Since the passage of that act, the nonjudicial branches have become primary definers and enforcers of equal educational opportunity with respect to gender. Yet, as one might anticipate, the implementation effort has hardly been unproblematic. Particularly in the realm of athletics, opposition has been substantial and enforcement consequently vacillating. Title IX also leaves unresolved (or, from the viewpoint of the advocate, it unsatisfactorily resolves) many of the central educational policy issues concerning gender and schooling: Sexism in texts, for instance, goes deliberately unaddressed in the federal law. Even after the passage of Title IX, these issues have been raised in constitutional litigation.

A. The Search for a Constitutional Standard

Sex-distinguishing legislation has been historically pervasive. Numerous state and federal laws treat women and men differently with respect to social conduct, familial responsibility, obligations of citizenship (for example, service in the armed forces), access to jobs and public accommodations, labor regulations, and criminal sentencing. *See* L. Kanowitz, *Women and the Law: The Unfinished Revolution* (1969). This body of legislation was premised either on the presumed need to protect women or on assumed essential gender-specific differences in ability. *See* Note, "Sex Discrimination and Equal Protection: Do We Need a Constitutional Amendment?" 84 *Harv. L. Rev.* 1499, 1500 (1971).

Historically, judicial review of challenges to such sex distinctions was characterized "by two prominent features: a vague but strong substantive belief in women's separate place, and an extraordinary methodological casualness in reviewing state legislation based on such stereotypical views of women." Brown, Emerson, Falk, and Freedman, "The Equal Rights Amendment: A Constitutional Basis for Equal Rights for Women," 80 *Yale L.J.* 871, 876 (1971). In *Goesaert v. Cleary*, 335 U.S. 464, 69 S.Ct. 198, 93 L.Ed. 163 (1948), for example, the Supreme Court upheld a Michigan statute that barred a woman from being licensed as a bartender unless she was "the wife or daughter of the male owner of a licensed liquor establishment." The *Goesaert* Court, finding that the subject "need not detain us long," applied the "reasonable classification" test and virtually ignored the obvious effect of the statute—monopolization of the bartending profession for men. In *Hoyt v. Florida*, 368 U.S. 57, 82 S.Ct. 159, 7 L.Ed.2d 118 (1961) (overruled in *Taylor v. Louisiana*, 419 U.S. 522, 95 S.Ct. 692, 42 L.Ed.2d 690 [1975]), the Court adopted the same approach in upholding legislation that excluded women from jury service unless they voluntarily applied. "We cannot say that it is constitutionally impermissible for a state, acting in pursuit of the general welfare, to conclude that a woman should be relieved from the civic duty of jury service unless she herself determines that such service is consistent with her own special responsibilities." 368 U.S. at 62, 82 S.Ct. at 162.

Beginning with its decision in *Reed v. Reed*, 404 U.S. 71, 92 S.Ct. 251, 30 L.Ed.2d 225 (1971), the Supreme Court looked more carefully at claims of gender discrimination. In *Reed*, the Court purported to apply the traditional equal protection test, concluding that a state probate code provision which gave preference to men as administrators of the estates of those dying intestate served no rational purpose. But the Court tacitly rejected the state's assertion that "men are as a rule more conversant with business affairs than . . . women," and in doing so actually applied a standard of review less deferential to the state than mere rationality. *See generally* Note, "Legislative Purpose, Rationality, and Equal Protection," 82 *Yale L.J.* 123, 150–51 (1972). In *Frontiero v. Richardson*, 411 U.S. 677, 93 S.Ct. 1764, 36 L.Ed.2d 583 (1973), a plurality of the Court was willing to equate gender with race for purposes of equal protection, defining both as constitutionally suspect classifications that require a "compelling" state justification. But the other four justices who concurred in the result would not go so far, and all of the justices have subsequently retreated from this position.

The standard that the Court presently applies in most gender cases was first announced in *Craig v. Boren*, 429 U.S. 190, 97 S.Ct. 451, 50 L.Ed.2d 397 (1976), in which the Court struck down an Oklahoma statute prohibiting the sale of 3.2 percent beer to males but not to females between the ages of eighteen and twenty-one: "Classifications by gender must serve *important* governmental objectives and must be *substantially* related to achievement of those objectives." 429 U.S. at 197, 97 S.Ct. at 456 (emphasis added). This standard is far more demanding than the conventional equal protection standard but less rigorous than that applied in the race cases. Its use has generally but not universally resulted in judicial rejection of legislation differentiating on the basis of sex. *Compare Califano v. Goldfarb*, 430 U.S. 199, 97 S.Ct. 1021, 51 L.Ed.2d 270 (1977), *with Califano v. Webster*, 430 U.S. 313, 97 S.Ct. 1192, 51 L.Ed.2d 360 (1977). "Important" and "substantial" are, of course, judicial terms of art, that acquire meaning from a series of decisions over time. Other standards have, from time to time, contended for attention. *See, e.g., Rostker v. Goldberg*, 453 U.S. 57, 101 S.Ct. 2646, 69 L.Ed.2d 478 (1981) and *Michael M. v. Superior Court of Sonoma County*, 450 U.S. 464, 101 S.Ct. 1200, 67 L.Ed.2d 437 (1981) (are men and women "similarly situated" with respect to the aim of the law?); *Mississippi University for Women v. Hogan*, 458 U.S. 718, 102 S.Ct. 3331, 73 L.Ed.2d 1090 (1982) (an "exceedingly persuasive justification" for sex-based distinctions required). *See* Williams, "The Equality Crisis: Some Reflections on Culture, Courts and Feminism," 7 *Women's Rights Law Reporter* 175 (1982).

The Supreme Court's opinions leave several central issues open. Although the Court in *Boren* speaks of classifications based on gender and thus suggests that laws disadvantaging women or men are equally problematic, the extent to which women can be provided with special benefits, either to offset or compensate for past sex-based discrimination, remains unclear. *See Johnson v. Transportation Agency*, 480 U.S. 616, 107 S.Ct. 1442, 94 L.Ed.2d 615 (1987); *Califano v. Webster*, 430 U.S. 313, 97 S.Ct. 1192, 51 L.Ed.2d 360 (1977); *Schlesinger v. Ballard*, 419 U.S. 498, 95 S.Ct. 572, 42 L.Ed.2d 610 (1975); *Kahn v. Shevin*, 416 U.S. 351, 94 S.Ct. 1734, 40 L.Ed.2d 189 (1974). Although this issue poses concerns comparable to affirmative action on behalf of racial minorities, the Court has not seriously tried to reconcile its positions in the two spheres.

The cases also fail to clarify how ostensibly gender-neutral actions that markedly disadvantage one sex—either because they are based on a sex-specific trait such as childbearing or because they provide special treatment to a predominantly single-sex group—are to be decided. *See Personnel Administrator of Massachusetts v. Feeney*, 442 U.S. 256, 99 S.Ct. 2282, 60 L.Ed.2d 870 (1979); Kirp and Robyn, "Pregnancy, Justice, and the Justices," 57 *Tex. L. Rev.* 947 (1979).

The analogy between race and sex deserves some attention. Even though the analogy is not fully embraced in *Boren*, that opinion indicates that sex-based classifications are offensive nonetheless. Consider the plurality opinion in *Frontiero*, which argues that the two should be legally indistinguishable:

> There can be no doubt that our nation has had a long and unfortunate history of sex discrimination. Traditionally, such discrimination was rationalized by an attitude of "romantic paternalism" which, in practical effect, put women not on a pedestal, but in a cage. . . .
>
> As a result of notions such as these, our statute books gradually became laden with gross, stereotypical dis-

tinctions between the sexes and, indeed, throughout much of the nineteenth century the position of women in our society was, in many respects, comparable to that of blacks under the pre-Civil War slave codes. Neither slaves nor women could hold office, serve on juries, or bring suit in their own names, and married women traditionally were denied the legal capacity to hold or convey property or to serve as legal guardians of their own children. . . . And although blacks were guaranteed the right to vote in 1870, women were denied even that right—which is itself "preservative of other basic civil and political rights"—until adoption [of] the Nineteenth Amendment half a century later.

It is true, of course, that the position of women in America has improved markedly in recent decades. Nevertheless, it can hardly be doubted that, in part because of the high visibility of the sex characteristic, women still face pervasive, although at times more subtle, discrimination in our educational institutions, on the job market and, perhaps most conspicuously, in the political arena. . . .

Moreover, since sex, like race and national origin, is an immutable characteristic determined solely by the accident of birth, the imposition of special disabilities upon the members of a particular sex because of their sex would seem to violate "the basic concept of our system that legal burdens should bear some relationship to individual responsibility. . . ." *Weber v. Aetna Casualty and Surety Co.*, 406 U.S. 164, 175, 92 S.Ct. 1400, 1406, 31 L.Ed.2d 768 (1972). And what differentiates sex from such nonsuspect statuses as intelligence or physical disability, and aligns it with the recognized suspect criteria, is that the sex characteristic frequently bears no relation to ability to perform or contribute to society. As a result, statutory distinctions between the sexes often have the effect of invidiously relegating the entire class of females to inferior legal status without regard to the actual capabilities of its individual members.

We might also note that, over the past decade, Congress has itself manifested an increasing sensitivity to sex-based classifications. In Title VII of the Civil Rights Act of 1964, for example, Congress expressly declared that no employer, labor union, or other organization subject to the provisions of the act shall discriminate against any individual on the basis of "race, color, religion, *sex*, or national origin." Similarly, the Equal Pay Act of 1963 provides that no employer covered by the act "shall discriminate . . . between employees on the basis of *sex*." And § 1 of the Equal Rights Amendment, passed by Congress on March 22, 1972, and submitted to the legislatures of the states for ratification, declares that "equality of rights under the law shall not be denied or abridged by the United States or by any state on account of sex." Thus, Congress has itself concluded that classifications based upon sex are inherently invidious, and this conclusion of a coequal branch of government is not without significance to the question presently under consideration. . . .

411 U.S. 677, 684–88 (1973).

How persuasive is this reasoning? Consider the following observations in Rossi, "Sex Equality: The Beginning of Ideology," 29 *Humanist* 3, 4–5 (1969):

> . . . [T]here are also fundamental differences between sex as a category of social inequality and the categories of race, religion, or ethnicity. . . .
>
> In the case of race, religion, and ethnicity, we are literally dealing with minority groups in the American population, whether Mexican, Indian, Jewish, Catholic, or black. This is not the case for sex, since women are actually a numerical majority in the population.
>
> While the potential is present for numerical strength to press for the removal of inequalities, this is counterbalanced by other ways in which women are prevented from effectively utilizing their numerical strength. . . . [Because] women are for the most part *evenly distributed throughout the population* [, they] can exert political pressure in segmental roles as consumers, workers, New Yorkers, or the aged; but not as a cohesive political group based on sex solidarity.
>
> Age and sex are the earliest social categories an individual learns. The differentiation between mother and father, or parent and child, is learned at a tender, formative stage of life; and consequently, we carry into adulthood a set of age and sex-role expectations that are extremely resistant to change.
>
> As a result of early sex-role socialization, there is bound to be a lag between political and economic emancipation of women and the inner adjustment to equality of both men and women. Even in radical political movements, women have often had to caucus and fight for their acceptance as equal peers to men. Without such efforts on their own behalf, women are as likely to be "girl Friday" assistants in a radical movement espousing class and racial equality as they are in a business corporation, a labor union, or a conservative political party. . . .
>
> Racial, ethnic, and religious conflict can reach an acute stage of political strife in the movement for equality, without affecting the solidarity of the families of blacks, whites, Jews, or Gentiles. Such strife may, in fact, increase the solidarity of these family units. A "we versus them" dichotomy does not cut into family units in the case of race, religion, or ethnicity as it does in the case of sex. Since women typically live in greater intimacy with men than they do with other women, there is potential conflict within family units when women press hard for sex equality. Their demands are on predominantly male legislators and em-

> ployers in the public domain—husbands and fathers in the private sector. A married black woman can affiliate with an activist civil rights group with no implicit threat to her marriage. For a married woman to affiliate with an activist women's rights group might very well trigger tension in her marriage. . . . A large proportion of married women [who] have not combated sex discrimination . . . fear conflict with men, or benefit in terms of a comfortable high status in exchange for economic dependence upon their husbands. There are many more women in the middle class who benefit from sex inequality than there are blacks in the middle class who benefit from racial inequality.

Do Professor Rossi's observations suggest that sex and race discrimination should be treated as constitutionally different phenomena or that they are politically different phenomena? How should the Court have resolved this question—and with what implications for educational policy and law? *See also* D. Kirp, M. Yudof and M. Franks, *Gender Justice* (1986); B. Barber, *Liberating Feminism* (1976); Wasserstrom, "Racism, Sexism, and Preferential Treatment: An Approach to the Topics," 24 *U.C.L.A. L.Rev.* 581 (1977). *See generally* J. Ely, *Democracy and Distrust: A Theory of Judicial Review* 166–69 (1980).

B. The Legislative Framework: Title IX of the Education Amendments of 1972

While the 1964 Civil Rights Act proscribes some types of discrimination on the basis of sex, that provision has not been directly applied to the schools. During the 1970 Congressional hearings, Daisy Shaw, the Director of Educational and Vocational Guidance for the New York Schools, urged that some federal action be taken: "A special commission or task force [should] be appointed . . . looking into the educational practices starting with Headstart and kindergarten to see what practices we engage in that brainwash girls from an early age to see themselves in a subservient role. . . ." Representative Edith Green was skeptical: "I don't think [Congress] would be receptive. I think the majority of our colleagues see that as the woman's role and why have a commission to study it. I suspect, from public opinion polls, that that sentiment is shared by the American people." *Hearings on Sec. 805 of H.R. 16098 Before the Special Subcomm. on Education of the Comm. on Education and Labor*, 91st Cong., 2d Sess., (June 17, 1970). *See generally* H. Graham, *The Civil Rights Era: Origins and Development of National Policy* 393–420 (1990).

Title IX—Prohibition of Sex Discrimination
Sex Discrimination Prohibited

20 U.S.C. §§ 1681–86 (1972 Education Amendments).

Sec. 901. (a) No person in the United States shall, on the basis of sex, be excluded from participation in, be denied the benefits of, or be subjected to discrimination under any education program or activity receiving federal financial assistance, except that:

(1) in regard to admissions to educational institutions, this section shall apply only to institutions of vocational education, professional education, and graduate higher education, and to public institutions of undergraduate higher education;

(2) in regard to admissions of educational institutions, this section shall not apply (A) for one year from the date of enactment of this act, nor for six years after such date in the case of an educational institution which has begun the process of changing from being an institution which admits only students of one sex to being an institution which admits students of both sexes, but only if it is carrying out a plan for such a change which is approved by the commissioner of education or (B) for seven years from the date an educational institution begins the process of changing from being an institution which admits only students of only one sex to being an institution which admits students of both sexes, but only if it is carrying out a plan for such a change which is approved by the commissioner of education, whichever is the later;

(3) this section shall not apply to an educational institution which is controlled by a religious organization if the application of this subsection would not be consistent with the religious tenets of such organization;

(4) this section shall not apply to an educational institution whose primary purpose is the training of individuals for the military services of the United States, or the merchant marine; and

(5) in regard to admissions this section shall not apply to any public institution of undergraduate higher education which is an institution that traditionally

and continually from its establishment has had a policy of admitting only students of one sex.

(b) Nothing contained in subsection (a) of this section shall be interpreted to require any educational institution to grant preferential or disparate treatment to the members of one sex on account of an imbalance which may exist with respect to the total number or percentage of persons of that sex participating in or receiving the benefits of any federally supported program or activity, in comparison with the total number or percentage of persons of that sex in any community, state, section, or other area: *Provided*, That this subsection shall not be construed to prevent the consideration in any hearing or proceeding under this title of statistical evidence tending to show that such an imbalance exists with respect to the participation in, or receipt of the benefits of, any such program or activity by the members of one sex.

(c) For purposes of this title an educational institution means any public or private preschool, elementary, or secondary school, or any institution of vocational, professional, or higher education, except that in the case of an educational institution composed of more than one school, college, or department which are administratively separate units, such term means each such school, college, or department.

Federal Administrative Enforcement

Sec. 902. Each federal department and agency which is empowered to extend federal financial assistance to any education program or activity, by way of grant, loan, or contract other than a contract of insurance or guaranty, is authorized and directed to effectuate the provisions of section 901 with respect to such program or activity by issuing rules, regulations, or orders of general applicability which shall be consistent with achievement of the objectives of the statute authorizing the financial assistance in connection with which the action is taken. No such rule, regulation, or order shall become effective unless and until approved by the president. Compliance with any requirement adopted pursuant to this section may be effected (1) by the termination of or refusal to grant or to continue assistance under such program or activity to any recipient as to whom there has been an express finding on the record, after opportunity for hearing, of a failure to comply with such requirement, but such termination or refusal shall be limited to the particular political entity, or part therof, or other recipient as to whom such a finding has been made, and shall be limited in its effect to the particular program, or part thereof, in which such noncompliance has been so found, or (2) by any other means authorized by law: *Provided, however*, That no such action shall be taken until the department or agency concerned has advised the appropriate person or persons of the failure to comply with the requirement and has determined that compliance cannot be secured by voluntary means. In the case of any action terminating, or refusing to grant or continue, assistance because of failure to comply with a requirement imposed pursuant to this section, the head of the federal department or agency shall file with the committees of the House and Senate having legislative jurisdiction over the program or activity involved a full written report of the circumstances and the grounds for such action. No such action shall become effective until thirty days have elapsed after the filing of such report. . . .

Interpretation with Respect to Living Facilities

Sec. 907. Notwithstanding anything to the contrary contained in this title, nothing contained herein shall be construed to prohibit any educational institution receiving funds under this act, from maintaining separate living facilities for the different sexes.

"Nondiscrimination on the Basis of Sex in Education Programs and Activities, Receiving or Benefiting from Federal Financial Assistance"

Department of Education Regulations, 34 C.F.R. § 106.1–106.71.

Subpart C—Discrimination on the Basis of Sex in Admission and Recruitment Prohibited

§ 106.21 Admission

(a) *General*. No person shall, on the basis of sex, be denied admission, or be subjected to discrimination in admission, by any recipient to which this subpart applies, except as provided in §§ 106.16 and 106.17.

(b) *Specific prohibitions.* (1) In determining whether a person satisfies any policy or criterion for admission, or in making any offer of admission, a recipient to which this Subpart applies shall not:

(i) Give preference to one person over another on the basis of sex, by ranking applicants separately on such basis, or otherwise;

(ii) Apply numerical limitations upon the number or proportion of persons of either sex who may be admitted; or

(iii) Otherwise treat one individual differently from another on the basis of sex.

(2) A recipient shall not administer or operate any test or other criterion for admission which has a disproportionately adverse effect on persons on the basis of sex unless the use of such test or criterion is shown to predict validly success in the education program or activity in question and alternative tests or criteria which do not have such a disproportionately adverse effect are shown to be unavailable.

(c) *Prohibitions relating to marital or parental status.* In determining whether a person satisfies any policy or criterion for admission, or in making any offer of admission, a recipient to which this subpart applies:

(1) Shall not apply any rule concerning the actual or potential parental, family, or marital status of a student or applicant which treats persons differently on the basis of sex;

(2) Shall not discriminate against or exclude any person on the basis of pregnancy, childbirth, termination of pregnancy, or recovery therefrom, or establish or follow any rule or practice which so discriminates or excludes;

(3) Shall treat disabilities related to pregnancy, childbirth, termination of pregnancy, or recovery therefrom in the same manner and under the same policies as any other temporary disability or physical condition; and

(4) Shall not make pre-admission inquiry as to the marital status of an applicant for admission, including whether such applicant is "Miss" or "Mrs." A recipient may make preadmission inquiry as to the sex of an applicant for admission, but only if such inquiry is made equally of such applicants of both sexes and if the results of such inquiry are not used in connection with discrimination prohibited by this part.

§ 106.22 Preference in admission

A recipient to which this subpart applies shall not give preference to applicants for admission, on the basis of attendance at any educational institution or other school or entity which admits as students or predominantly members of one sex, if the giving of such preference has the effect of discriminating on the basis of sex in violation of this subpart.

Subpart D—Discrimination on the Basis of Sex in Education Programs and Activities Prohibited

§ 106.31 Education programs and activities

(a) *General.* Except as provided elsewhere in this part, no person shall, on the basis of sex, be excluded from participation in, be denied the benefits of, or be subjected to discrimination under any academic, extracurricular, research, occupational training, or other education program or activity operated by a recipient which receives or benefits from Federal financial assistance. This subpart does not apply to actions of a recipient in connection with admission of its students to an education program or activity of (1) a recipient to which Subpart C does not apply, or (2) an entity, not a recipient, to which Subpart C would not apply if the entity were a recipient.

(b) *Specific prohibitions.* Except as provided in this subpart, in providing any aid, benefit, or service to a student, a recipient shall not, on the basis of sex:

(1) Treat one person differently from another in determining whether such person satisfies any requirement or condition for the provision of such aid, benefit, or service;

(2) Provide different aid, benefits, or services or provide aid, benefits, or services in a different manner;

(3) Deny any person any such aid, benefit, or service;

(4) Subject any person to separate or different rules of behavior, sanctions, or other treatment;

(5) Apply any rule concerning the domicile or residence of a student or applicant, including eligibility for instate fees and tuition;

(6) Aid or perpetuate discrimination against any person by providing significant assistance to any agency, organization, or person which discriminates

on the basis of sex in providing any aid, benefit or service to students or employees;

(7) Otherwise limit any person in the enjoyment of any right, privilege, advantage or opportunity.

. . . This subpart does not apply to actions of a recipient in connection with admission of its students to an education program or activity of (1) a recipient to which Subpart C does not apply, or (2) an entity, not a recipient, to which Subpart C would not apply if the entity were a recipient.

§ 106.34 Access to course offerings

A recipient shall not provide any course or otherwise carry out any of its education program or activity separately on the basis of sex, or require or refuse participation therein by any of its students on such basis, including health, physical education, industrial, business, vocational, technical, home economics, music, and adult education courses.

(a) With respect to classes and activities in physical education at the elementary school level, the recipient shall comply fully with this section as expeditiously as possible but in no event later than one year from the effective date of this regulation. With respect to physical education classes and activities at the secondary and post-secondary levels, the recipient shall comply fully with this section as expeditiously as possible but in no event later than three years from the effective date of this regulation.

(b) This section does not prohibit grouping of students in physical education classes and activities by ability as assessed by objective standards of individual performance developed and applied without regard to sex.

(c) This section does not prohibit separation of students by sex within physical education classes or activities during participation in wrestling, boxing, rugby, ice hockey, football, basketball and other sports the purpose or major activity of which involves bodily contact.

(d) Where use of a single standard of measuring skill or progress in a physical education class has an adverse effect on members of one sex, the recipient shall use appropriate standards which do not have such effect.

(e) Portions of classes in elementary and secondary schools which deal exclusively with human sexuality may be conducted in separate sessions for boys and girls.

(f) Recipients may make requirements based on vocal range or quality which may result in a chorus or choruses of one or predominantly one sex.

§ 106.35 Access to schools operated by L.E.A.s

A recipient which is a local educational agency shall not, on the basis of sex, exclude any person from admission to:

(a) Any institution of vocational education operated by such recipient; or

(b) Any other school or educational unit operated by such recipient, unless such recipient otherwise makes available to such person, pursuant to the same policies and criteria of admission, courses, services, and facilities comparable to each course, service and facility offered in or through such schools.

§ 106.36 Counseling and use of appraisal and counseling materials

(a) *Counseling*. A recipient shall not discriminate against any person on the basis of sex in the counseling or guidance of students or applicants for admission.

(b) *Use of appraisal and counseling materials*. A recipient which uses testing or other materials for appraising or counseling students shall not use different materials for students on the basis of their sex or use materials which permit or require different treatment of students on such basis unless such different materials cover the same occupations and interest areas and the use of such different materials is shown to be essential to eliminate sex bias. Recipients shall develop and use internal procedures for ensuring that such materials do not discriminate on the basis of sex. Where the use of a counseling test or other instrument results in a substantially disproportionate number of members of one sex in any particular course of study or classification, the recipient shall take such action as is necessary to assure itself that such disproportion is not the result of discrimination in the instrument or its application.

(c) *Disproportion in classes*. Where a recipient finds that a particular class contains a substantially disproportionate number of individuals of one sex, the recipient shall take such action as is necessary to assure itself that such disproportion is not the result of discrimination on the basis of sex in counseling or appraisal materials or by counselors.

§ 106.40 Marital or parental status

(a) *Status generally.* A recipient shall not apply any rule concerning a student's actual or potential parental, family, or marital status which treats students differently on the basis of sex.

(b) *Pregnancy and related conditions.* (1) A recipient shall not discriminate against any student, or exclude any student from its education program or activity, including any class or extracurricular activity, on the basis of such student's pregnancy, childbirth, false pregnancy, termination of pregnancy or recovery therefrom, unless the student requests voluntarily to participate in a separate portion of the program or activity of the recipient.

(2) A recipient may require such a student to obtain the certification of a physician that the student is physically and emotionally able to continue participation in the normal education program or activity so long as such a certification is required of all students for other physical or emotional conditions requiring the attention of a physician.

(3) A recipient which operates a portion of its education program or activity separately for pregnant students, admittance to which is completely voluntary on the part of the student as provided in paragraph (b)(1) of this section shall ensure that the instructional program in the separate program is comparable to that offered to non-pregnant students.

(4) A recipient shall treat pregnancy, childbirth, false pregnancy, termination of pregnancy and recovery therefrom in the same manner and under the same policies as any other temporary disability with respect to any medical or hospital benefit, service, plan or policy which such recipient administers, operates, offers or participates in with respect to students admitted to the recipient's educational program or activity.

(5) In the case of a recipient which does not maintain a leave policy for its students, or in the case of a student who does not otherwise qualify for leave under such a policy, a recipient shall treat pregnancy, childbirth, false pregnancy, termination of pregnancy and recovery therefrom as a justification for a leave of absence for so long a period of time as is deemed medically necessary by the student's physician, at the conclusion of which the student shall be reinstated to the status which she held when the leave began.

§ 106.41 Athletics

(a) *General.* No person shall, on the basis of sex, be excluded from participation in, be denied the benefits of, be treated differently from another person or otherwise be discriminated against in any interscholastic, intercollegiate, club or intramural athletics offered by recipient, and no recipient shall provide any such athletics separately on such basis.

(b) *Separate teams.* Notwithstanding the requirements of paragraph (a) of this section, a recipient may operate or sponsor separate teams for members of each sex where selection for such teams is based upon competitive skill or the activity involved is a contact sport. However, where a recipient operates or sponsors a team in a particular sport for members of one sex but operates or sponsors no such team for members of the other sex, and athletic opportunities for members of that sex have previously been limited, members of the excluded sex must be allowed to try out for the team offered unless the sport involved is a contact sport. For the purposes of this part, contact sports include boxing, wrestling, rubgy, ice hockey, football, basketball and other sports the purpose or major activity of which involves bodily contact.

(c) *Equal opportunity.* A recipient which operates or sponsors interscholastic, intercollegiate, club or intramural athletics shall provide equal athletic opportunity for members of both sexes. In determining whether equal opportunities are available the Director will consider, among other factors:

(1) Whether the selection of sports and levels of competition effectively accommodate the interests and abilities of members of both sexes;

(2) The provision of equipment and supplies;

(3) Scheduling of games and practice time;

(4) Travel and per diem allowance;

(5) Opportunity to receive coaching and academic tutoring;

(6) Assignment and compensation of coaches and tutors;

(7) Provision of locker rooms, practice and competitive facilities;

(8) Provision of medical and training facilities and services;

(9) Provision of housing and dining facilities and services;

(10) Publicity.

Unequal aggregate expenditures for members of each sex or unequal expenditures for male and female teams if a recipient operates or sponsors separate teams will not constitute noncompliance with this section, but the Director may consider the failure to provide necessary funds for teams for one sex in assessing equality of opportunity for members of each sex.

* * *

§ 106.42 Textbooks and curricular material

Nothing in this regulation shall be interpreted as requiring or prohibiting or abridging in any way the use of particular textbooks or curricular materials.

NOTES AND QUESTIONS

1. Scope of Coverage

How does the congressional understanding of sex discrimination in Title IX differ from its treatment of racial discrimination in Title VI (*see* chapter 5, *supra*)? Note each of the practices deemed *not* to constitute sex discrimination or otherwise excluded from the scope of the legislation and regulations paying particular attention to the treatment of athletes. Do these, taken together, constitute a coherent governmental policy with respect to sex discrimination?

The language of § 901(a) of the legislation, barring exclusion, denial of benefits, or discrimination on the basis of sex, mirrors the language of the 1964 Civil Rights Act (42 U.S.C. § 1983). Does this suggest that—with the exceptions enumerated in §§ 901(1)–(5) and 907—Congress views race and sex discrimination as similar, or do the exceptions indicate a very different perception?

2. Textbooks and Curriculum

The regulations exclude textbook or curricular content from the scope of administrative purview (34 C.F.R. § 106.42). That exclusion was premised on a concern that federal intervention in such matters would "thrust the Department into the role of Federal censor" and possibly violate the First Amendment (40 Fed. Reg. 24135). Do you find this a plausible contention? Is federal nonintervention a sound policy determination? How does the existence of textbook review and adoption procedures at the state and local levels or the existence of state statutes mandating curricula that positively demonstrate the achievements of women, for example, Iowa Code Ann. § 257.25 (1974) and Mich. Comp. Laws Ann. § 340.3612 (Supp. 1975), affect your response?

3. Title IX and Sexual Harassment

Sexual harassment, both of students and school and university employees, has been much in the news. Is harassment tantamount to discrimination under Title IX? In *Alexander v. Yale University*, 631 F.2d 178 (2d Cir. 1980), the court concluded that it was, while dismissing the since-graduated students' complaint as moot. Should a general atmosphere in which sexual harassment is assertedly condoned be sufficient to establish a violation of the law, or must actual denial of educational benefits by the university be shown?

C. Denial or Restriction of Educational Opportunity

In several areas, women have either been excluded from or provided with less of a given educational opportunity than men. Pregnant women, but not their impregnators, have been barred from high school. Certain courses, such as shop and vocational education, were historically open only to males. Athletic competition has been restricted to male students. Admission criteria for selective academic high schools have been set higher for women than for men. Each of these practices presents the following questions:

1. How might a school district justify a policy restricting the educational opportunities of women? Would such justifications pass judicial muster?

2. Assuming that the school's policy does discriminate against female students, what remedy is legally appropriate (or mandated)? For example, if females have historically been excluded from athletic teams, would the school district meet its legal obligation by opening these teams to them on a freedom-of-choice basis? Should significant deviations from the school's male/female ratio in shop classes be treated as indicating sex-based discrimination? Does the response depend on whether the claim is based on Title IX or the equal protection clause?

3. In each case, a "separate-but-equal" remedy is theoretically plausible. These diverse situations should provoke consideration of when, if at all, such a solution might be valid in the sex discrimination context.

1. Pregnancy and Marriage. At least until the early 1970s, most school districts excluded pregnant students from regular classes at some time during their pregnancy, Knowles, "High School, Marriage and the Fourteenth Amendment," 11 *J. Fam. L.* 711, 732 (1972), a practice that may have contributed to the "feminization" of poverty. *See* Fox-Genovese, "Women's Rights, Affirmative Action and the Myth of Individualism," 54 *Geo. Wash. L. Rev.* 338 (1986). In *Perry v. Grenada Municipal Separate School District*, 300 F.Supp. 748 (N.D. Miss. 1969), however, the court enjoined the school district from excluding unwed mothers from its schools. But the opinion suggests that under some circumstances a school might bar a pregnant student because of the corrupting effect she might have on other students.

The Title IX regulations specifically prohibit discrimination on the basis of pregnancy. If, however, the school maintains a separate program for mothers and expectant mothers, the student may ask to participate in that program. Participation must be entirely voluntary, and the program's instructional component must be comparable to what is generally offered by the school.

Many school districts historically restricted the educational opportunities available to married students. The exclusion of married students, premised on a desire to deter teenage marriage or to protect innocent teenagers from the company of young marrieds, has generally been overturned on nonconstitutional grounds. In *McLeod v. State ex rel. Colmer*, 154 Miss. 468, 475, 122 So. 737, 738 (1929), for example, the Mississippi Supreme Court noted: "Marriage is a domestic relation highly favored by the law. When the relation is entered into with correct motives, the effect on the husband and wife is refining and elevating, rather than demoralizing. Pupils associating in school with a child occupying such a relation, it seems, would be benefited instead of harmed." *See also Anderson v. Canyon Independent School District*, 412 S.W.2d 387 (Tex. Civ. App. 1967), *Alvin Independent School District v. Cooper*, 404 S.W.2d 76 (Tex. Civ. App. 1966).

School districts have more frequently barred married students from participating in extracurricular activities. The rationales for such rules include discouraging early marriage, preventing fraternization that might cause undue interest in sex among unmarrieds, freeing the individual student's time for marital responsibilities, and keeping schools free of jealousy between spouses. While in the past courts have upheld such practices, *see Kissick v. Garland Independent School District*, 330 S.W.2d 708 (Tex. Civ. App. 1959), more recent decisions have struck down these rules, either as denials of equal protection, as impermissible invasions of students' rights to privacy, or as an infringement on the "fundamental right of marriage." *Moran v. School District No. 7, Yellowstone County*, 350 F.Supp. 1180 (D. Mont. 1972), for example, recognized that the right to attend school includes the right to participate in extracurricular activities. The court found a violation of the equal protection clause in that the board discriminated against married students without showing it to be a reasonable action within statutory authority for a legitimate purpose. *Indiana High School Athletic Association v. Raike*, 164 Ind.App. 169, 329 N.E.2d 66 (1975), held that rules barring married students from interscholastic competition do not bear a fair and substantial relation to the objective of promoting wholesomeness in competition.

The Title IX regulations bar discrimination against married students in classes or extracurricular activities. *See* 34 C.F.R. § 106.40(a).

2. Curriculum.

a. Exclusion. In many school districts, women were traditionally barred from taking shop or vocational courses. The reasons for this exclusion have rarely been articulated but appear to have included tradition, the asserted inappropriateness of such courses for females, and concern that the allegedly less-coordinated female student might be more injury-prone than her male counterpart. Several intrepid young women successfully challenged such practices. In each instance the case was settled before judicial decision. *See* Martinez, "Sexism in Public Education: Litigation Issues," 18 *Inequality in Education* 5 (1974); Note, "Teaching Woman Her Place: The Role of Public Education in the Development of Sex Roles," 24 *Hastings L.J.* 1191 (1973). One student who litigated her way into a metal shop class subsequently won the outstanding student award for metalwork. West, "Women's Liberation, or Exploding the Fairy Princess Myth," *Scholastic Teacher* 6 (Nov. 1971).

In these cases, is the student's claim stronger because she is a female? Might a male who is denied admission to a home economics course persuade a court to overturn that determination on constitutional grounds? Is the fact that wood shop is closely linked to a female student's career plans legally relevant? Or does exclusion from any course—whatever its relative importance to the student or class of students—demand searching judicial review if it is sex-based? What justification, if any, should satisfy a court?

How does Title IX deal with exclusion from particular courses on grounds of sex? Does the nature of the course matter? *See* 34 C.F.R. § 106.34.

Vocational testing and counseling can also channel students into careers regarded as conventionally appropriate for their sex. The test instruments may vary according to sex, or counselors may offer different advice to male and female students. *See, e.g.*, Ahrons, "Counselors' Perceptions of Career Images of Women," 8 *J. Voc. Behav.* 197 (1976); Donahue and Costar, "Counselor Discrimination Against Young Women in Career Selection," 24 *J. Counseling Psych.* 481 (1977); Lesser, "Are We Still Sexist? A Recent Study of Counselor Attitudes," 24 *Sch. Counselor* 85 (1976). How does Title IX respond to this set of issues?

Even if elective courses are made available to both sexes, a disproportionate number of one sex may opt to enroll in a particular course. Suppose that five years after a high school abandons sex-separate courses, 90 percent of the students in shop classes are male, and 95 percent of the students enrolled in home economics classes are female. Would it change your view if the disproportion occurred in science and math? *See* Tobias and Weisbrod, "Anxiety and Mathematics: An Update," 50 *Harv. Educ. Rev.* 63 (1980). Does that situation pose problems, either under the equal protection clause or Title IX? Should the school be required to achieve "sex balance"? Merge the two courses? How, if at all, does the situation differ from that presented by *Green v. New Kent County Board of Education*, where under a freedom-of-choice plan adopted to remedy racial segregation, one school remained all black, the other largely white? *See* chapter 5.

Under Title IX, schools can establish separate male and female choruses and can provide separate sex education instruction. What is the rationale for these exceptions to the norm of nondifferentiation? Is it proper to treat such differences as nondiscriminatory?

b. Differential Treatment. In other and more subtle ways, schools treat boys and girls differently. As Nancy Frazier and Myra Sadker point out, in *Sexism in School and Society* (1973), both sexes may be victimized by this differentiation. Boys get more negative attention, in a domain widely regarded as a feminine environment. Boys earn lower grades than girls with comparable IQs, and are more likely to drop out. For their part, girls are rewarded for those stereotypical traits—neatness, conformity, docility—that serve them badly outside of school. At least until recently, school textbooks served to reinforce sex role differences, minimizing the contributions of women. Are these issues amenable to policy resolution—through mandated changes in textbooks, for example? Are the harms legally cognizable? *See* Comment, "Sex Discrimination: The Textbook Case," 62 *Calif. L. Rev.* 1312 (1974). In these instances is it discrimination—or impingement on students' liberty interests—that is objectionable?

3. Scholarships and School Admission Standards.

Sharif by Salahuddin v. New York State Education Department

709 F.Supp. 345 (S.D.N.Y. 1989).

Walker, District Judge:

This case raises the important questions of whether New York State denies female students an equal opportunity to receive prestigious state merit college scholarships by its sole reliance upon the Scholastic Aptitude Test ("SAT") to determine eligibility. To the Court's knowledge, this is the first case where female students are seeking to use the federal civil rights statute prohibiting sex discrimination in federally-funded educational programs to challenge a state's reliance on standardized tests. This case also presents a legal issue of first impressions: whether discrimination under Title IX can be established by proof of disparate impact without proof of intent to discriminate.

After careful consideration, this Court finds that defendants are discriminating against female plaintiffs and their putative class in violation of Title IX and the equal protection clause of the U.S. Constitution. For the reasons set forth below, this Court enjoins the State Education Department and its Commissioner from awarding the merit scholarships at issue solely on the basis of the SAT.

* * *

New York State, in one of the most expensive merit scholarship programs in the country, each year makes 26,000 academic achievement awards to New York's high school graduates.

In 1974, . . . the legislature restructured its awards, creating two types of awards: first, "general awards" which provide substantial monetary assistance, and second, "academic performance awards" which recognize achievement. Classifying Regents Scholarships as "academic performance awards," the legislature reduced the awards to a stipend of $250, and increased the number of awards to 25,000 to be allocated by county of residence.

* * *

In the "general awards" category, the legislature created a Tuition Assistance Program ("TAP") to fund college students based upon financial need. The legislature made TAP awards available to all students enrolled in approved programs and are given to those who demonstrate the ability to complete such program's courses, and who satisfy financial need requirements established by the Commissioner of Education. . . .

* * *

In 1977, the legislature directed that the scholarships be awarded on the basis of "nationally established competitive examinations. . . . [T]he SED [State Education Department] chose the SAT, the test taken by the greatest number of students." [T]he entire SAT is labeled an "aptitude" test, and the SAT's only purpose is to test two subjects—Math and English.

In response to allegations that the SED's practice of relying solely upon the SAT in awarding Regents and Empire State Scholarships discriminated against females who consistently scored below males. The legislature altered the criteria for scholarship eligibility—on a one-year, experimental basis—to require the SED Commissioner to base awards on a formula which at least includes a measure of high school performance, and which may include nationally established examinations.

* * *

Despite comparability difficulties, the SED chose to use GPAs [grade point averages] as the best available measure of high school achievement. In awarding the Regents and Empire Scholarships for the 1988 graduates, the SED gave equal weight to students' SAT scores and GPAs, as the measure of high school performance.

* * *

In 1988, under the procedure using a combination of grades and SATs weighted equally women received substantially more Regents and Empire Scholarships than in all prior years in which the SAT had been the sole criterion. In both 1987 and 1988, young women comprised approximately 54 percent of the applicant pool for the scholarship, yet the results in 1988 when grades and SATs were used were markedly different. The results are summarized as follows:

	Winners of Empire State Scholarships of Excellence		**Winners of Regents College Scholarships**	
	Males	*Females*	*Males*	*Females*
1988	62	38	51	49
1987	72	28	57	43

When GPAs were used in 1988, the mean GPAs were: 85 for females and 84.4 for males.

* * *

In September, 1989, the SED determined that it would award Regents and Empire Scholarships to 1989 high school graduates on the basis of SAT scores alone. It is the SED's sole reliance on SAT scores for 1989 graduates that plaintiffs complain denies them equal protection under the fourteenth amendment to the U.S. Constitution and violates Title IX of the Education Amendments of 1972.

* * *

The Educational Testing Service ("ETS") developed the SAT in order to predict academic performance in college. . . . It is undisputed, however, that the SAT predicts the success of students differently for males and females. In other words, while the SAT will predict college success as well for males within the universe of males as for females within the universe of females, when predictions are within the combined universe of males and females, the SAT *underpredicts* academic performance of females in their freshman year of college, and *overpredicts* such academic performance for males. The SAT has never been validated as a measure of past high school performance.

Both the ETS and the College Board, which administers the SAT, specifically advise against exclusive reliance upon the SAT, even for the purpose for which the SAT has been validated—predicting future college performance. Instead, ETS researchers recommend that college admissions counselors use a combination of high school grades and test scores because this combination provides the highest median combination with freshman grades.

* * *

Both the Empire and Regents Scholarships are intended to reward past academic achievement of high school students, and to encourage those students who have demonstrated such achievement to pursue their education in New York State. . . . It is undisputed, however, that the SAT was developed and validated to serve a different purpose—*predicting* performance *in college.*

. . . [I]t is the SED's current position that the SAT provides a good measure of high school performance because it "measures skills and knowledge primarily developed in school." . . .

* * *

Plaintiffs invoke the protections provided by Title IX, which prohibits sex discrimination in federally-funded educational programs. Plaintiffs do not claim that defendants have intentionally discriminated against them based on their sex. Rather, they claim that defendants' practice of sole reliance upon SAT scores to award prestigious state scholarships disparately impacts female students. To this Court's knowledge, this is the first disparate impact case challenging educational testing practices under Title IX.

Neither the Supreme Court nor any court in the Second Circuit has determined whether intent must be shown in Title IX cases. This Court, however, is not without substantial guidance. Recognizing that "Title IX was patterned after Title VI of the Civil Rights Act of 1964," *Grove City College v. Bell*, 465 U.S. 555, 566, . . . (1984) courts examining Title IX questions have looked to the substantial body of law developed under Title VI, 42 U.S.C. § 2000d, which prohibits race discrimination in federally-funded programs, and Title VII, 42 U.S.C. § 2000e, which prohibits discrimination in employment. *See, e.g., Mabry v. State Board of Community Colleges and Occupational Education*, 813 F.2d 311, 317 (10th Cir.), *cert. denied*, 484 U.S. 849, 108 S.Ct. 148, 98 L.Ed.2d 104 (1987); *Haffer v. Temple University*, 678 F.Supp. 517, 539 (E.D.Pa. 1987).

In *Guardians Association v. Civil Service Commission*, 463 U.S. 582 . . . (1983), the Supreme Court held that a violation of Title VI itself requires proof of discriminatory intent. However, a majority also agreed that proof of discriminatory effect suffices to establish liability when a suit is brought to enforce the regulations promulgated under Title VI, rather than statute itself. *See also Alexander v. Choots*, 469 U.S. 287, 293–294, 105 S.Ct. 712, 716, 83 L.Ed.2d 661 (1985); *Latinos Unidos de Chelsea v. Secretary of Housing*, 799 F.2d 774, 785 n. 20 (1st Cir. 1986).

Plaintiffs' amended complaint explicitly alleges both violations of Title IX and its implementing regulations. This Court finds no persuasive reason not to apply Title VI's substantive standards to the present Title IX suit. . . .

The Title IX implementing regulations, like the regulations promulgated under Title VI, to which Title IX is frequently compared, are consistent with the interpretation of the comprehensive reach of the statute. Several Title IX regulations specifically prohibit facially neutral policies. For example, the provision governing admissions procedures, 34 C.F.R. § 106.21(b)(2), prohibits a recipient from

> administer[ing] or operat[ing] any test or other criteria for admission which has a disproportionately adverse effect on persons on the basis of sex unless the use of such test or criterion is shown to predict validly success in the education program or activity in question and alternative tests or criteria which do not have such a

disproportionate adverse effect are shown to be unavailable.

See also 34 C.F.R. §§ 106.22, 106.23(b), 106.34(d), 106.37(b), 106.52, and 106.53(b).

Based upon a reading of the Title IX regulations, as well as the decisions that apply them, the Court finds that Title IX regulations, like the Title VI regulations at issue in *Guardians*, prohibit testing practices with a discriminatory *effect* on one sex. Consequently, plaintiffs need not prove intentional discrimination. . . .

In educational testing cases, courts have required defendants to show an "educational necessity." For example, the Eleventh Circuit, in *Georgia State Conf. of Branches of NAACP v. State of Georgia*, 775 F.2d 1403 (11th Cir. 1985), held that defendants had a burden of proving that their practices in question bore "a manifest demonstrable relationship to classroom education." *Id.* at 1413. *See also Board of Education v. Harris*, 444 U.S. 130, 151 . . . (1979) ("educational necessity" analogous to "business necessity").

Applying the Title VII formulations to this Title IX case as modified to take into account "educational necessity," this Court finds that plaintiffs have demonstrated a likelihood of success on the merits. Plaintiffs have met their burden of establishing a *prima facie* case through persuasive statistical evidence and credible expert testimony that the composition of scholarship winners tilted decidedly toward males and could not have occurred by a random distribution.

Plaintiffs, moreover, have established that the probability, absent discriminatory causes, that women would consistently score 60 points less on the SAT than men is nearly zero. . . . [T]his court finds that plaintiffs have demonstrated that the State's practice of sole reliance upon the SAT disparately impacts young women.

Thus, to prevail, defendants must show a manifest relationship between use of the SAT and recognition and award of academic achievement in high school. The Court finds that defendants have failed to show even a reasonable relationship between their practice and their conceded purpose. The SAT was not designed to measure achievement in high school and was never validated for that purpose. Instead, in arguing that the SAT somehow measures high school performances, defendants rely upon anecdotal evidence that the SAT partially tracks what is generally learned in high school Math and English courses. This argument is meritless.

Plaintiffs have offered substantial evidence that the SATs do not mirror high school Math and English classes.

Moreover, even if SATs provided a partial measurement of what is learned in high school Math and English, these two courses constitute only 2 percent of a high school student's studies.

Plaintiffs have offered an alternative to sole reliance upon the SAT: a combination of GPAs and SATs. The SED's use of this alternative in 1988 sharply reduced the disparate impact against females caused by the use of the SAT alone. A significantly greater number of female students received scholarships in 1988 than in each prior year in which the SED relied solely upon the SAT. Defendants concede that females had a greater opportunity to receive scholarships under the combination system. Defendants also concede that grades are the best measure of high school achievement within the walls of a single school. Instead, they argue that since there is a disparity among schools and their grading systems it is both unfair and impossible to use grades as part of the scholarship eligibility determination. Defendants plan instead to develop a statewide achievement test. While this Court does not dispute the apparent advantages of a statewide achievement test—if indeed a valid test can be developed—it does not agree that pending the implication of such a test, use of grades would be either unfair or infeasible.

While a combination system—using both GPAs and SATs—is not a perfect alternative, it is the best alternative presently available.

* * *

The SED cannot justify its discriminatory practice because any alternative would be more difficult to administer. All states giving merit scholarships awards, with the exception of New York and Massachusetts, use GPAs, without concern for either administrative difficulties, grade inflation or the comparability of grades. . . .

[P]laintiffs also have established a likelihood that they will succeed on their equal protection claim. The classification of scholarship applicants solely on the basis of SAT scores violates the equal protection clause of the Fourteenth Amendment because this method is not rationally related to the state's goal of rewarding students who have demonstrated academic achievement.

Under the lowest standard of equal protection review—the "rational relationship standard"—"[t]he State may not rely on a classification whose relationship to an asserted goal is so attenuated as to render the distinction arbitrary or irrational." *City of Cleburne v. Cleburne Living Center*, 473 U.S. 432, 446, . . . (1985). Although considerable deference is given to the decisions of legislators and state administrators under the rational basis test, the test "is not a toothless one." *Baccus v. Karger*, 692 F.Supp. 290, 298 (S.D.N.Y. 1988) (invalidating New York bar rule that required applicants for bar admission to have commenced the study of law after their 18th birthday). . . .

For the reasons stated above, the SED's use of the SAT as a proxy for high school achievement is too unrelated to the legislative purpose of awarding academic achievement in high school to survive even the most minimal scrutiny. The evidence is clear that females score significantly below males on the SAT while they perform equally or slightly better than males in high school. Therefore, the SED's use of the SAT as the sole criterion for awarding Regents and Empire Scholarships discriminates against females and, since such a practice is not rationally related to the legislative purpose, it unconstitutionally denies young women equal protection of the laws and must be enjoined on that ground as well.

* * *

Defendants' practice of relying solely upon SAT scores in awarding Regents and Empire Scholarships deprives young women of the opportunity to compete equally for these prestigious scholarships in violation of both Title IX and the Constitution's equal protection clause. Defendants are hereby ordered to discontinue such discriminatory practices and, instead, to award Regents and Empire Scholarships in a manner that more accurately measures students' high school achievement. For the present year, the best available alternative is a combination of grades and SATs. The SAT component is justified, not as a measure of achievement, but to weight the GPA component. The Court, however, does not limit the SED's discretion to develop other alternatives in the future, including a statewide achievement test.

NOTES AND QUESTIONS

1. Disparate Impact

Is the court in *Sharif* correct in allowing, under Title IX, a showing of disparate impact—that is, a showing that women fare less well than men—rather than requiring evidence that discrimination is the motivating factor behind the use of the test? Had plaintiffs been required to show discriminatory intent, could they have prevailed? How does your appraisal of this question bear on the treatment of the same issue in the context of race, as discussed in chapter 5?

2. Grades and Scholarships

Most states, as the *Sharif* opinion notes, rely partly on students' grades in awarding state scholarships. But would reliance on grades be preferable to using the SAT scores, as New York State does? Are grades a reliable indicia of school performance? Are they comparable across subjects? Across schools? What if one sex had higher grades, on average, than the other? Would the development of a state exam be a preferable alternative?

3. Admission

May an academically selective high school set different admission standards for male and female applicants? Does the fact that the academic high school for boys has a larger capacity for students than the academic high school for girls provide a justification? *See Bray v. Lee*, 337 F.Supp. 934 (D.Mass. 1972). Suppose a district chose to admit equal numbers of young men and women to maintain "a balanced community representation of the population." *See Berkeleman v. San Francisco Unified School District*, 501 F.2d 1264 (9th Cir. 1974). What if a balance could be achieved only by setting a higher standard for one sex? How does Title IX affect differential admissions? Which of the following factors are relevant: the level of the institution, the historical practices of the institution, or the rationale proferred? *See* 20 U.S.C.A. § 1681(a)(1).

4. Athletics

Force v. Pierce City R-VI School District

570 F.Supp. 1020 (W.D. Mo. 1983).

Ross T. Roberts, District Judge.

Nichole Force, a thirteen year old female student enrolled in the eighth grade at the Pierce City, Missouri, Junior High School, seeks an injunction which would allow her to compete for a place on the school's eighth grade football team. Her claims are relatively simple and straightforward: that defendants' refusal to accord her that opportunity is based—and based solely—upon the fact that she is a female rather than a male, and that a sex-based determination of that sort violates her right to the equal protection of the laws under the Fourteenth Amendment, and in turn 42 U.S.C. § 1983.

* * *

Sometime during the spring of 1982, Nichole Force mentioned to her mother that she was greatly looking forward, that coming fall, to trying out for the seventh grade football team. Since Nichole had already been involved to a considerable extent in athletics (swimming, diving, organized softball, organized basketball and elementary school football), and since she had grown up with two brothers who excelled at football and who encouraged and helped her in her own athletic endeavors, her mother was perhaps less startled than some mothers might have been. Family debate ensued, nonetheless. After an apparently frank and thorough discussion on the matter, Mrs. Force decided to approach the school authorities to see what might be done.

Mrs. Force spoke first with the boys' athletics coach for the school. He stated that so long as the school administration approved, he would let Nichole participate. Mrs. Force then sought out the appropriate school administrative officials. They advised her that the matter would have to be presented to the Board for its decision.

* * *

. . . [T]he Board voted unanimously to deny the request. According to Mrs. Force, defendant [Superintendent] John Williams explained the decision to her by stating that while "they all agreed" Nichole would be a good football player and would have no problems playing, if she were permitted to play the same allowance would have to be made for all other girls as well.

* * *

The record makes clear, and I find, that defendants' refusal to grant plaintiff's request is the product of a gender-based classification. Stated simply, only males are permitted to compete for a place on the Pierce City Junior High School eighth grade football team. Since Nichole is a female, that opportunity is denied to her.

The principles which must govern in this situation are summarized in . . . the Supreme Court's recent decision in *Mississippi University for Women v. Hogan*, 458 U.S. 718, 102 S.Ct. 3331, 73 L.Ed.2d 1090 (1982). . . .

> Because the challenged policy expressly discriminates among applicants on the basis of gender, it is subject to scrutiny under the Equal Protection Clause of the Fourteenth Amendment. 404 U.S. 71, 75. . . . Our decisions also establish that the party seeking to uphold a statute that classifies individuals on the basis of their gender must carry the burden of showing an "exceedingly persuasive justification" for the classification. . . .
>
> The burden is met only by showing at least that the classification serves "important governmental objectives and that the discriminatory means employed" are "substantially related to the achievement of those objectives." . . .
>
> Although the test for determining the validity of a gender based classification is straightforward, it must be applied free of fixed notions concerning the roles and abilities of males and females. Care must be taken in ascertaining whether . . . the objective itself reflects archaic and steretypic notions. Thus if the . . . objective is to exclude or "protect" members of one gender because they are presumed to suffer from an inherent handicap or to be innately inferior, the objective itself is illegitimate. . . .
>
> If the State's objective is legitimate and important, we next determine whether the requisite direct, substantial relationship between objective and means is present. The purpose of requiring that close relationship is to assure that the validity of the classification is determined through reasoned analysis rather than through the mechanical application of traditional, often inaccurate, assumptions about the proper roles of men and women. The need for the requirement is amply revealed by reference to the broad range of statutes already invalidated by this Court, statutes that relied upon the simplistic, outdated assumption that gender could be used as a "proxy for other, more germane bases of classification," . . . to establish a link between objective and classification.

Defendants do not quarrel with the fact that the present case must be governed by these principles; indeed they candidly acknowledge that fact. They argue, rather, that in the circumstances shown here a gender-based classification fully satisfies those principles. To that end, they identify four "important governmental objectives" which are said to be at stake: (a) maximization of equal athletic educational opportunities for all students, regardless of gender; (b) maintenance of athletic educational programs which are as safe for participants as possible; (c) compliance with Title IX of the Educational Amendments of 1972 and the regulations thereunder; and (d) compliance with the constitution and by-laws of MSHSAA [Missouri State High School Athletic Association]. . . .

Defendants' suggestion with respect to the necessity of compliance with Title IX can, I think, be dealt with in relatively short order. There is in fact nothing whatsoever in Title IX, or in its implementing regulations (34 C.F.R. § 106.41(b)), which would mandate the action defendants have taken here.[3] To the contrary, Title IX's regulations leave each school free to choose whether co-educational participation in a contact sport will be permitted. *Yellow Springs Exempted Village School District Board of Education v. Ohio High School Athletic Association*, 647 F.2d 651, 655–56 (6th Cir. 1981). Allowing Nichole Force to compete with males for a place on the Pierce City Junior High School eighth grade football team would no more violate those regulations than would refusing her that opportunity. Title IX simply takes a neutral stand on the subject.

Nor in my judgment can defendants' point regarding compliance with MSHSAA rules withstand scrutiny. A school can hardly validate an otherwise unconstitutional act (assuming for the moment that there is one here) by noting that it has agreed with other schools to commit that act. . . .

. . . Defendants' first two points, however, have more meat to their bones, and are deserving of more detailed treatment. Each will be examined separately below.

* * *

One might wonder, at first blush, how denying all females the right to participate in a sport—which is the case here, since Pierce City eighth grade girls are not allowed to compete for a place on the only football team which might be available to them—will result in maximizing the participation of both sexes in athletics. And the short answer is that it probably does not. Defendants' argument in this regard, however, is sufficiently sophisticated to merit more than first blush treatment.

That argument proceeds on three interrelated theories. Defendants suggest, first, that males (as a class) will outperform females (as a class) in most athletic endeavors, given male size, speed and greater ratio of lean body mass. That being so, the argument proceeds, the best way in which to encourage and maximize female participation in athletics is by providing separate male and female teams, where males compete only against males and females only against females, since otherwise males will dominate the competition and ultimately discourage female participation. Pursuant to this idea, defendants have established separate interscholastic athletic programs for the two sexes in the Pierce City secondary schools, with the fall season sport being football for males and volleyball for females. But if (second) Nichole Force is permitted to compete for a place on the football team, then other girls must be accorded the same privilege, and boys must be allowed to compete for positions on the volleyball team. When (third) that happens, the girls will lose their best athletes, the boys will come to dominate volleyball, and overall female participation will ultimately wither.

Based upon the expert testimony presented in this case I am willing to accept the proposition that the average male, even at age 13, will to some extent outperform the average female of that age in most athletic events, although the matter may be open to some dispute.[6] And I note, without being called upon to decide the issue, that a number of courts

3. 34 C.F.R. § 106.41(b) reads as follows:

"(b) *Separate teams.* Notwithstanding the requirements of paragraph (a) of this section, a recipient may operate or sponsor separate teams for members of each sex where selection for such teams is based upon competitive skill or the activity involved is a contact sport. However, where a recipient operates or sponsors a team in a particular sport for members of one sex but operates or sponsors no such team for members of the other sex, and athletic opportunities for members of that sex have previously been limited, members of the excluded sex must be allowed to try-out for the team offered unless the sport involved is a contact sport. For the purposes of this part, contact sports include boxing, wrestling, rugby, ice hockey, football, basketball and other sports the purpose or major activity of which involves bodily contact."

6. The various studies and statistics relied upon by both defendants' expert, Dr. Harold Falls (a professor in Health, Physical Education and Biology at Southwest Missouri State College and the Director of the Human Performance Laboratory there), and plaintiff's expert, Dr. N. Peggy Burke (Chairman of the Department of Physical Education at the University of Iowa), suggest that at age 13 the average female tends to be slightly taller and heavier than the average male of that age, although there is a wide range of variance amongst all the members in both sexes. It would appear, on the other hand, that the average boy at that age has a very slightly higher ratio of lean body mass (muscle and bone mass) to fat mass, and a somewhat higher ratio of lean body mass to heighth, has heavier bones, may have somewhat more speed and upper body strength, and has somewhat better motor coordination.

have held that the establishment of separate male/female teams in a sport is a constitutionally permissible way of dealing with the problem of potential male athletic dominance. *See Ritacco v. Norwin School District*, 361 F.Supp. 930 (W.D.Pa. 1973); *Bucha v. Illinois High School Association*, 351 F.Supp. 69 (N.D.Ill. 1972); *Ruman v. Eskew*, 168 Ind.App. 428, 343 N.E.2d 806 (1976), and *cf. O'Connor v. Board of Education of School District No. 23*, 645 F.2d 578, 581 (7th Cir.), *cert. den.* 454 U.S. 1084, 102 S.Ct. 641, 70 L.Ed.2d 619 (1981); *on remand* 545 F.Supp. 376 (1981); *Hoover v. Meiklejohn*, 430 F.Supp. 164, 170 (D.Colo. 1977); *Gilpin v. Kansas State Activities Ass'n., Inc.*, 377 F.Supp. 1233, 1243 (D.Kan. 1973); *Attorney General v. Massachusetts Interscholastic Athletic Association, Inc.*, 378 Mass. 342, 393 N.E.2d 284, 296 (1979). Beyond these two points, however, I am unable to accept defendants' argument.

The principal difficulty with the remaining portions of that argument, it seems to me, is that the various hypotheses used to bind it together are just that—hypotheses, and nothing more. There is, for example, no factual indication that the girls' eighth grade volleyball team will be blighted by the defection of its best players to the football field, if Nichole Force is allowed to play football. To the contrary, defendants' own testimony is that Nichole Force is the first and only girl, at any grade level, who has ever made a request to play football. And for that matter, if defendants are correct in their position that females are unable to compete successfully with males in athletics, particularly in contact sports, it is to be expected that such defections would be short-lived in any event, and that the situation would prove to be self-regulating. *See Fortin v. Darlington Little League*, 514 F.2d 344, 350 (1st Cir. 1975).

Nor is there any factual indication that eighth grade boys at Pierce City Junior High School are waiting eagerly for volleyball to be desegregated. Again to the contrary, there is no indication that any boy has ever expressed a desire to play on the volleyball team. Indeed, there may be something of a false premise involved in the idea that volleyball in the Pierce City R-VI School District is in fact segregated, since nothing in the MSHSAA rules would prevent boys from competing with girls on a volleyball team, and since defendants themselves have never articulated any such rule.[7] Instead, it would seem, the question has simply never arisen. And in any event, it is by no means clear that the District would be constitutionally required to permit boys to participate in girls' volleyball, even if girls were allowed to participate in football. *See Clark v. Arizona Interscholastic Association*, 695 F.2d 1126, 1131–32 (9th Cir. 1982); *Petrie v. Illinois High School Association*, 75 Ill.App.3d 980, 31 Ill.Dec. 653, 394 N.E.2d 855 (1979) (both holding, on a theory similar to that utilized in *Regents of the University of California v. Bakke*, 438 U.S. 265, 98 S.Ct. 2733, 57 L.Ed.2d 750 (1978), that the governmental interest in redressing past discrimination against women in athletics is sufficient to justify a regulation which excludes boys from participating on girls' teams, even though girls are allowed to compete on boys' teams).[8]

Finally, even if by some chance defendants' worst case scenario should be realized, there might still be no need for the general breakdown which defendants postulate. For example, if a sufficient number of girls wish to play football, one obvious solution

---

Some of these characteristics, particularly lean body mass ratios, relate to achievement of sexual maturity (which in girls averages between the 12th and 13th years), since girls begin to develop more fat mass at sexual maturity. But in any event there is some overlap with respect to these characteristics as between males and females at age 13, although the extent of that overlap was disputed by Dr. Falls and Dr. Burke. After age 13 these differences begin to widen appreciably as between the "average" boy and the "average" girl, and by the time the later teens are reached the "average" male has not only greatly widened the gap in terms of lean body mass ratio, but has also considerably surpassed the "average" female in terms of heighth and total body weight.

All of the above physiological factors are said to have a bearing on one's physical ability to compete in a sport. There are, obviously, other factors involved as well, including conditioning, desire and intelligence. And according to Dr. Burke, the statistics may also be skewed to some extent by the fact that conditioning can have a bearing on lean body mass ratios, and the fact that females have in the past been less physically active than males, by virtue of the roles society has assigned them, although there are no studies to support this.

7. In fact, according to one construction which has been given the regulations under Title IX, the School District might already be *required* to let boys participate on the volleyball team, regardless whether girls play football. *See Gomes v. Rhode Island Interscholastic League*, 469 F.Supp. 659 (D.R.I. 1979), *vacated as moot*, 604 F.2d 733 (1st Cir. 1979). *Contra, Mularadelis v. Haldane Central School Board*, 74 App.Div.2d 248, 427 N.Y.S.2d 458 (1980).

8. *But see Gomes v. Rhode Island Interscholastic League, supra* n. 7, and *Attorney General v. Massachusetts Interscholastic Athletic Association, supra* (both holding that such "reverse" disparate treatment is impermissible).

would be to organize a girls' football team; or if so many boys wish to play volleyball that they would dominate the girls' competition in that sport, to form a boy's volleyball team. . . . Such solutions would of course presumably involve added expense to the District, but there is no evidence on how troublesome that factor might be, and I cannot decide this case by adding speculation on that subject to an already lengthy list of other speculative items.

* * *

. . . There is, however, a further point implicit in defendants' argument on this subject which should be addressed before passing on: the apparent assumption that if, in the interest of maximizing equal athletic opportunities, it is constitutionally permissible to establish separate male and female teams in a given sport and to exclude each sex from the other's team . . . then it is equally permissible, in that same interest, to designate separate male and female sports and to exclude each sex from participation in the other's sport. That is a proposition I am unwilling to accept, at least as a general matter. . . .

Each sport has its own relatively unique blend of requirements in terms of skills and necessary physical attributes, and each person, male or female, will for a variety of reasons probably find one or another sport more enjoyable and rewarding than others. In point of fact, volleyball is *not* football; and baseball is *not* hockey; and swimming is *not* tennis. Accordingly, if the idea is to "maximize educational athletic opportunities for all students, regardless of gender," it makes no sense, absent some substantial reason, to deny all persons of one sex the opportunity to test their skills at a particular sport. Of course there may be certain exceptional instances in which there is a "substantial reason" for such an exclusion, as for example where peculiar safety and equipment requirements demand it, *see Lafler v. Athletic Board of Control*, 536 F.Supp. 104 (W.D.Mich. 1982) (boxing), or perhaps where excluding males is necessary to redress past inequality and to foster female participation.

* * *

I [do not] . . . question the fact that the "maintenance of athletic educational programs which are as safe for participants as possible" is an "important governmental objective." Indeed, that would seem obvious. Again, however, the facts of this case do not demonstrate a sufficiently "substantial" relationship between that objective and a blanket rule which prohibits all eighth grade females from competing for a place on the Pierce City Junior High School eighth grade football team.

There is no evidence, or even any suggestion, that Nichole Force herself could not safely participate in that football program. And while I do find, from the expert testimony presented, that a "typical" (i.e., average) 13 year old female would in fact, to some degree, have a higher potential for injury in mixed-sex football than would a "typical" (i.e., average) 13 year old male, this does not in my judgment greatly assist the defendants' argument.[12] The problem, of course, is that not all 13 year old females are "typical," any more than all 13 years old males are "typical." Indeed, as defendants' own expert candidly admitted, some 13 year old females could safely play eighth grade football in mixed sex competition, and some 13 year old males could not. And yet I note that the Pierce City R-VI School District permits *any* male to compete in football, regardless of his size, speed, body type, lean body mass, fat body mass, bone structure, "Q" angle measurement or any other factor which might have a bearing on his potential for injury.

In short, the "safety" factor which defendants would utilize to prevent any female from playing eighth grade football—including those who could play safely—is not applied to males at all, even to those who could not play safely. . . .

It is of course true, as defendants point out, that the Supreme Court has recognized that governmental bodies are free to take into account *actual* differences between the sexes, including physical ones, with the result that a statute or policy which employs a gender based classification will be upheld where that classification merely reflects the fact that the sexes are not "similarly situated" in certain circum-

12. There are apparently no studies which have compared the incidence of injuries as between males and females playing football, or any other contact sport at age 13, either on segregated teams or co-educational teams. The potential for injury, however, at least in contact sports, is said to be related to the physical characteristics mentioned in footnote 5, particularly lean body mass ratios. If that is so, to that extent perhaps the "average" boy at age 13 will have somewhat less potential for injury in football than the "average" girl at age 13. In addition, girls who have reached sexual maturity (on the average between 12 and 13 years, although in some instances much later) begin to develop a wider hip structure, and the angle between the hip and the knee (called the "Q angle") increases, with resulting potential for increased knee injury. How significant that increased "Q angle" is, and just what its real potential for increased knee injury in football might be, was a subject disputed by Dr. Falls and Dr. Burke.

stances. *See Michael M. v. Superior Court of Sonoma County*, 450 U.S. 464, 469, 101 S.Ct. 1200, 1204, 67 L.Ed.2d 437 (1981) (noting, in reference to a statutory rape law which penalized males only, that "only women may become pregnant," *id.* at 471, 101 S.Ct. at 1205). I do not, however, read such observations to be an endorsement of the use of broad generalizations which—while perhaps empirically supported *as generalizations*—do not hold true for all members of a sex. In fact the Supreme Court has rather consistently rejected that idea, . . . since a gender based classification which results from ascribing a particular trait or quality to one sex, when not all share that trait or quality, is not only inherently unfair but generally tends only to perpetuate "stereotypic notions" regarding the proper roles of men and women.

This is not to say that reliance upon a factually established generalization concerning a particular male or female trait might never be appropriate. But there must obviously be a substantial justification . . . for using such an imprecise and potentially mischievous tool for these purposes; and the only justification which might even arguably be applied in such circumstances would be that of "administrative ease" to the governmental body. That, in turn, is an argument, which has never fared well at the hands of the Supreme Court, . . . and I reject it here for the simple reason that it is sophistry to suggest a concern with the "administrative burden" of weeding out physically unfit 13 year old females in connection with a football program when there is no concern at all with weeding out physically unfit 13 year old males involved in the same program. In fact, I think, it might be rather difficult to sustain a requirement that females competing for a place on a particular athletic team be subjected to a fitness screening program, when males competing for a place on the same team are subjected to none at all.

I conclude, accordingly, that there is an insufficient relationship between defendants' announced goal of "safety" and a rule which automatically excludes all eighth grade females from competing with eighth grade males for a place on a football team. That holding, I note, is consistent with the result reached by virtually every other court which has considered this same sort of "safety" argument in connection with male/female competition in contact sports. . . .[14]

* * *

Nichole Force obviously has no legal entitlement to a starting position on the Pierce City Junior High School eighth grade football team, since the extent to which she plays must be governed solely by her abilities, as judged by those who coach her. But she seeks no such entitlement here.

Instead she seeks simply a chance, like her male counterparts, to display those abilities. She asks, in short, only the right to try.

I do not suggest there is any such thing as a constitutional "right to try." But the idea that one should be allowed to try—to succeed or to fail as one's abilities and fortunes may dictate, but in the process at least to profit by those things which are learned in the trying—is a concept deeply engrained in our way of thinking; and it should indeed require a "substantial" justification to deny that privilege to someone simply because she is a female rather than a male. I find no such justification here.[16] . . .

NOTES AND QUESTIONS

1. The Constitutional Standard

In cases alleging discrimination in athletic programs, courts have applied a variety of constitutional standards. Moreover, each standard—the "middle tier" scrutiny test of *Boren*, the beefed up "rationality" test of *Reed v. Reed*, the "exceedingly persuasive justification" standard of *Hogan*—is applied in diverse ways. Does the *Force* court apply the prevailing standard correctly? Is it too flexible to be a "standard" at all?

---

14. I do not consider the holding in *Lafler v. Athletic Board of Control, supra*, to be inconsistent with the reasoning expressed here and in those cases cited above. As the court there noted, the necessity that plaintiff (a female) wear a protective chest covering would violate Amateur Boxing Federation rules, and I gather would give her something of an unfair advantage in any event. The court expressly noted the difference between the case before it and cases involving football, soccer and baseball. . . .

16. For those interested, or merely curious, there would appear to be five other reported cases, involving football in whole or in part, which reach the same result reached here: *Leffel v. Wisconsin Interscholastic Athletic Ass'n, supra* (all sports); *Clinton v. Nagy, supra* (football); *Attorney General v. Massachusetts Interscholastic Athletic Association, Inc., supra* (all sports); *Darrin v. Gold, supra* (football); and *Commonwealth v. Pennsylvania Interscholastic Association, supra* (all sports). I find no cases involving football which reach a contrary result.

2. *The Availability of Separate Programs for Women*

The *Force* court suggests that a separate women's football team would be a satisfactory solution. Do you agree? Would the casual observer, noting the existence of a girls' and boys' tennis team, assume that the two were of equal caliber? What of the able female athlete who—if not for the separation—could successfully compete for a place on the all-boys team? If she is not "stigmatized," are her opportunities nevertheless limited on the basis of her sex?

What if separate but different programs are provided for women athletes? In some states, women's basketball teams consist of six players, impose half-court restrictions, and permit only forwards to shoot. Suppose female athletes allege that the restrictions on shooting and dribbling limit their possibilities of being awarded a college basketball scholarship. How should such challenges be resolved? *See Dodson v. Arkansas Activities Association*, 468 F.Supp. 394 (E.D.Ark. 1979); *Jones v. Oklahoma Secondary School Activities Association*, 453 F.Supp. 150 (W.D. Okl. 1977).

3. *Contact Versus Noncontact Sports*

The *Force* court considers the argument that female athletes are more likely to suffer injury. Is it a failure of proof or a failure of argument that persuades the court? Other courts, upholding the right of women to participate in noncontact sports, have distinguished those sports from their rougher cousins. *See, e.g., Magill v. Avonworth Baseball Conference*, 364 F.Supp. 1212 (W.D.Pa. 1973), *aff'd on other grounds*, 516 F.2d 1328 (3d Cir. 1975). Is the distinction a valid one? To what sports should it be applied—soccer, baseball, wrestling? Is it physical violence or the possibility of physical intimacy that really is at issue in these cases?

4. *Discrimination Against Male Athletes?*

May a school field only a female volleyball team, thereby denying a male volleyball enthusiast the chance to compete? Is it relevant that volleyball has been introduced to the school in order to foster female interest in sports or that some females might not compete on a team if males were also eligible? *See Gomes v. Rhode Island Interscholastic League*, 469 F.Supp. 659 (D.R.I. 1979). May a school permit females to try out for the men's team while barring males from trying out for the women's team in order to preserve the emergent female sports program? *See Attorney General v. Massachusetts Interscholastic Athletic Association, Inc.*, 378 Mass. 342, 393 N.E.2d 284 (1979).

5. *Athletics and Media*

May schools and universities keep female reporters out of the locker rooms in male-only sports such as football and baseball? *Cf. Ludtke v. Kuhn*, 461 F.Supp. 86 (S.D.N.Y. 1978).

6. *Title IX and Athletics*

As the *Force* opinion notes, Title IX leaves schools free to determine whether to allow co-educational participation in contact sports. 34 C.F.R. § 106.41(b). Could the relative weakness of the statutory standard stem from the political controversy that underlies the issue of female participation in school-sponsored athletics?

At the college level, funding women's athletics has proved to be a continuing concern. The decision in *NCAA v. Board of Regents of Oklahoma*, 468 U.S. 85, 104 S.Ct. 2948, 82 L.Ed.2d 70 (1984), voiding the National Collegiate Athletic Association's control of television contracts, has reduced available revenues at some schools. *See* "Big TV Revenues Now Tougher to Get, Most College Football Powers Discover," *Chronicle of Higher Education*, Jan. 9, 1985, at 37. But the nation's 105 major universities have committed themselves to sponsor at least seven women's and eight men's sports programs.

Does it violate Title IX to have separate athletic directors for men's and women's athletics?

7. *Further Reading*

The issues raised in *Force* are canvassed in K. Tokarz, *Women, Sports and the Law: A Comprehensive Research Guide to Sex Discrimination in Sports* (1966); Wong and Ensor, "Sex Discrimination in Athletics: A Review of Two Decades of Accomplishments and Defeats," 21 *Gonzaga L. Rev.* 345 (1985–86); Tokarz, "Separate But Unequal Educational Sports Programs: The Need for a New Theory of Equality," 1 *Berkeley Women's L. J.* 1 (1985); Note, "Sex Discrimination in High School Athletics: An Examination of Applicable Legal Doctrines," 66 *Minn. L. Rev.* 1185 (1985); Note, "Where the Boys Are: Can 'Separate' Be Equal in Sports?" 58 *U.S.C. L. Rev.* 1425 (1985).

8. *The Equal Rights Amendment and Equal Opportunities in Athletics*

Would passage of the Equal Rights Amendment to the United States have affected the outcome of any of these cases? Decisions reached under state equal rights amendments suggest an answer. A rule barring girls from competing against boys in any athletic contest was struck down in one state, *Commonwealth by Packel v. Pennsylvania Interscholastic Athletic Association*, 18 Pa. Cmwlth. Ct. 45, 334 A.2d 839 (1975), as was a rule denying young women the opportunity to compete in interscholastic high school football. *Darrin v. Gould*, 85 Wash.2d 859, 540 P.2d 882 (1975) (en banc). In *Darrin*, the Washington Supreme Court held that the state would need to demonstrate a compelling justification for following the athletic association rule. Since males as well as females are prone to football injury, fear of injury would not suffice as a reason. *See* Comment, "*Blair v. Washington State University*: Making State ERA's a Potent Remedy for Sex Discrimination in Athletics," 14 *J. of Coll. & Univ. Law* 575 (1988).

9. *Implementing Equal Opportunity with Respect to Athletics*

No issue arising under Title IX has aroused so much interest, and so much controversy, as athletic opportunities. Observed former Health, Education and Welfare Department Secretary Caspar Weinberger, "I had not realized until the comment period [on HEW's proposed Title IX regulations] that athletics is the single most important thing in the United States." N.Y. *Times*, June 27, 1975, § 1 at 16.

Sports programs for women expanded substantially after the passage of Title IX. During the period from 1971 to 1978, for example, the number of female participants in organized high school sports increased from 294,000 to 2,038,000—an increase of over 600 percent. In contrast, between fall 1971 and fall 1977, the enrollment of females in high school decreased from approximately 7,600,000 to approximately 7,150,000—a decrease of over 5 percent.

The growth in athletic participation by high school women has been reflected on the campuses of the nation's colleges and universities. During the period from 1971 to 1976 the enrollment of women in the nation's institutions of higher education rose 52 percent, from 3,400,000 to 5,201,000. During this same period, the number of women participants in sports increased from 16,386 to 25,541, or 55 percent. In intercollegiate sports, women's participation increased 102 percent, from 31,852 to 64,375. These developments reflect the growing interest of women in competitive athletics, as well as the efforts of colleges and universities to accommodate those interests. 44 Fed. Reg. 71419 (1979).

These changes did not occur painlessly. Equalization of athletic opportunities at the collegiate level has been of special concern. The Title IX regulations promulgated in 1975 note ten factors—among them the selection of sports, the provision of equipment and supplies, coaching and tutoring opportunities, and practice and competitive facilities—relevant in determining whether equality exists. Just how these factors would be weighted remained unclear. Three years later, HEW undertook to draft a "Policy Interpretation" of the regulation. A December 1978 draft proposed that compliance be established by a showing that "average per capita" expenditures for male and female athletes were substantially equal in the area of "readily financially measurable" benefits and opportunities and that benefits and opportunities in areas not financially measurable "were comparable." Universities, faced with the specter of "equalizing" expenditures on big-time football and women's field hockey, reacted sharply. Confronted with over seven hundred comments on the proposal, HEW modified its stance, abandoning financial equality measures in favor of a "governing principle . . . that male and female athletes should receive equivalent treatment, benefits, and opportunities." 44 Fed. Reg. 71414 (1979).

D. Single-Sex Educational Institutions

The previous section speaks generally to situations in which one sex receives demonstrably less of a particular educational offering. The questions raised by such situations concern not the fact of differentness, but the adequacy of the justification for an apparent inequity. The permissibility of maintaining single-sex institutions poses a different sort of issue.

Mississippi University for Women v. Hogan

458 U.S. 718, 102 S.Ct. 3331, 73 L.Ed.2d 1090 (1982).

Justice O'Connor delivered the opinion of the Court.

This case presents the narrow issue of whether a state statute that excludes males from enrolling in a state-supported professional nursing school violates the Equal Protection Clause of the Fourteenth Amendment.

I

The facts are not in dispute. In 1884, the Mississippi legislature created the Mississippi Industrial Institute and College for the Education of White Girls of the State of Mississippi, now the oldest state-supported all-female college in the United States. 1884 Miss.Gen.Laws, Ch. XXX, § 6. The school, known today as Mississippi University for Women (MUW), has from its inception limited its enrollment to women.[1]

In 1971, MUW established a School of Nursing, initially offering a two-year associate degree. Three years later, the school instituted a four-year baccalaureate program in nursing and today also offers a graduate program. The School of Nursing has its own faculty and administrative officers and establishes its own criteria for admission.

Respondent, Joe Hogan, is a registered nurse but does not hold a baccalaureate degree in nursing. Since 1974, he has worked as a nursing supervisor in a medical center in Columbus, the city in which MUW is located. In 1979, Hogan applied for admission to the MUW School of Nursing's baccalaureate program. Although he was otherwise qualified, he was denied admission to the School of Nursing solely because of his sex. School officials informed him that he could audit the courses in which he was interested, but could not enroll for credit. . . .

Hogan filed an action in the United States District Court for the Northern District of Mississippi, claiming the single-sex admissions policy of MUW's School of Nursing violated the Equal Protection Clause of the Fourteenth Amendment. Hogan sought injunctive and declaratory relief, as well as compensatory damages.

Following a hearing, the District Court denied preliminary injunctive relief. . . . The court concluded that maintenance of MUW as a single-sex school bears a rational relationship to the state's legitimate interest "of providing the greatest practical range of educational opportunities for its female student population." . . . Furthermore, the court stated, the admissions policy is not arbitrary because providing single-sex schools is consistent with a respected, though by no means universally accepted, educational theory that single-sex education affords unique benefits to students. . . . Stating that the case presented no issue of fact, the court informed Hogan that it would enter summary judgment dismissing his claim unless he tendered a factual issue. When Hogan offered no further evidence, the District Court entered summary judgment in favor of the State. . . .

The Court of Appeals for the Fifth Circuit reversed, holding that, because the admissions policy discriminates on the basis of gender, the District Court improperly used a "rational relationship" test to judge the constitutionality of the policy. 646 F.2d 1116, 1118. Instead, the Court of Appeals stated, the proper test is whether the State has carried the heavier burden of showing that the gender-based classification is substantially related to an important governmental objective. . . .

On rehearing, the State contended that Congress, in enacting § 901(a)(5) of Title IX of the Education Amendments of 1972, Pub.L. 92–318, 86 Stat. 373, 20 U.S.C. § 1681 *et seq.*, expressly had authorized MUW to continue its single-sex admissions policy by exempting public undergraduate institutions that traditionally have used single-sex admissions policies from the gender discrimination prohibition of Title IX.[5] Through that provision, the State argued, Con-

1. . . . Mississippi maintains no other single-sex public university or college. Thus, we are not faced with the question of whether States can provide "separate but equal" undergraduate institutions for males and females. *Cf. Vorchhemmer v. School District of Philadelphia*, 532 F.2d 880 (CA3 1975), aff'd by an equally divided court, 430 U.S. 703 (1977) . . .

5. Section 901(a) of Title IX, Education Amendments of 1972, Pub. L. 92–318, 86 Stat. 373, 20 U.S.C. § 1681(a)(§ 1681), provides in part:

"(a) No person in the United States shall, on the basis of sex, be excluded from participation in, be denied the benefits of, or be subjected to discrimination under any education program or activity receiving Federal financial assistance, except that:

"(1) in regard to admissions to educational institutions, this section shall apply only to institutions of vocational education, professional education, and graduate higher education, and to public institutions of undergraduate higher education;

* * *

"(5) in regard to admissions this section shall not apply to any public institution of undergraduate higher education which is an institution that traditionally and continually from its establishment has had a policy of admitting only students of one sex. . . ."

gress limited the reach of the Fourteenth Amendment by exercising its power under § 5 of the Amendment.[6] The Court of Appeals rejected the argument, holding that § 5 of the Fourteenth Amendment does not grant Congress power to authorize States to maintain practices otherwise violative of the Amendment. 653 F.2d 223.

We granted certiorari, . . . and now affirm the judgment of the Court of Appeals.[7]

II

We begin our analysis aided by several firmly established principles. Because the challenged policy expressly discriminates among applicants on the basis of gender, it is subject to scrutiny under the Equal Protection Clause of the Fourteenth Amendment. *Reed v. Reed*, 404 U.S. 71, 75 . . . (1971). That this statute discriminates against males rather than against females does not exempt it from scrutiny or reduce the standard of review.[8] *Caban v. Mohammed*, 441 U.S. 380, 394 . . . (1979); *Orr v. Orr*, 440 U.S. 268, 279 . . . (1979). Our decisions also establish that the party seeking to uphold a statute that classifies individuals on the basis of their gender must carry the burden of showing an "exceedingly persuasive justification" for the classification. *Kirchberg v. Feenstra*, 450 U.S. 455, 461 . . . (1981); *Personnel Administrator of Massachusetts v. Feeney*, 442 U.S. 256, 273 . . . (1979). The burden is met only by showing at least that the classification serves "important governmental objectives and that the discriminatory means employed" are "substantially related to the achievement of those objectives." . . .[9]

Although the test for determining the validity of a gender-based classification is straightforward, it must be applied free of fixed notions concerning the roles and abilities of males and females. Care must be taken in ascertaining whether the statutory objective itself reflects archaic and stereotypic notions. Thus, if the statutory objective is to exclude or "protect" members of one gender because they are presumed to suffer from an inherent handicap or to be innately inferior, the objective itself is illegitimate. *See Frontiero v. Richardson*, 411 U.S. 677, 684, 685 . . . (1973) (plurality opinion).[10]

If the State's objective is legitimate and important, we next determine whether the requisite direct, substantial relationship between objective and means is present. The purpose of requiring that close relationship is to assure that the validity of a classifi-

6. Section 5 of the Fourteenth Amendment provides:

"The Congress shall have power to enforce, by appropriate legislation, the provisions of this article."

7. Although some statements in the Court of Appeals' decision refer to all schools within MUW, see 646 F.2d, at 1119, the factual underpinning of Hogan's claim for relief involved only his exclusion from the nursing program. Complaint ¶ 8–10, and the Court of Appeals' holding applies only to Hogan's individual claim for relief. 646 F.2d, at 1119–20. . . . [W]e decline to address the question of whether MUW's admissions policy, as applied to males seeking admission to schools other than the School of Nursing, violates the Fourteenth Amendment.

8. Without question, MUW's admissions policy worked to Hogan's disadvantage. Although Hogan could have attended classes and received credit in one of Mississippi's state-supported coeducational nursing programs, none of which was located in Columbus, he could attend only by driving a considerable distance from his home. . . . A similarly situated female would not have been required to choose between foregoing credit and bearing that inconvenience. Moreover, since many students enrolled in the School of Nursing hold full-time jobs. . . . Hogan's female colleagues had available an opportunity, not open to Hogan, to obtain credit for additional training. The policy of denying males the right to obtain credit towards a baccalaureate degree thus imposed upon Hogan "a burden he would not bear were he female." *Orr v. Orr*, 440 U.S. 268, 273 . . . (1979).

9. In his dissenting opinion, Justice Powell argues that a less rigorous test should apply because Hogan does not advance a "serious equal protection claim. . . ." Justice Blackmun, without proposing an alternative test, labels the test applicable to gender-based discrimination as "rigid" and productive of "needless conformity." . . . Our past decisions establish, however, that when a classification expressly discriminates on the basis of gender, the analysis and level of scrutiny applied to determine the validity of the classification do not vary simply because the objective appears acceptable to individual members of the Court. While the validity and importance of the objective may affect the outcome of the analysis, the analysis itself does not change.

Thus, we apply the test previously relied upon by the Court to measure the constitutionality of gender-based discrimination. Because we conclude that the challenged statutory classification is not substantially related to an important objective, we need not decide whether classifications based upon gender are inherently suspect. *See Stanton v. Stanton*, 421 U.S. 7, 13 . . . (1975).

10. History provides numerous examples of legislative attempts to exclude women from particular areas simply because legislators believed women were less able than men to perform a particular function. In 1872, this Court remained unmoved by Myra Bradwell's argument that the Fourteenth Amendment prohibited a State from classifying her as unfit to practice law simply because she was a female. *Bradwell v. Illinois*, 16 Wall. 130 . . . (1872). In his concurring opinion, Justice Bradley described the reasons underlying the State's decision to determine which positions only men could fill:

> "It is the prerogative of the legislator to prescribe regulations founded on nature, reason, and experience for the due admission of qualified persons to professions and callings demanding special skill and confidence. This fairly belongs to the police power of the State; and, in my opinion, in view of the peculiar characteristics, destiny, and mission of woman, it is within the province of the legislature to ordain what offices, positions, and callings shall be filled and discharged by men, and shall receive the benefit of those energies and responsibilities, and that decision and firmness which are presumed to predominate in the sterner sex."
>
> *Id.*, 16 Wall., at 142.

cation is determined through reasoned analysis rather than through the mechanical application of traditional, often inaccurate, assumptions about the proper roles of men and women. The need for the requirement is amply revealed by reference to the broad range of statutes already invalidated by this Court, statutes that relied upon the simplistic, outdated assumption that gender could be used as a "proxy for other, more germane bases of classification," *Craig v. Boren*, 429 U.S. 190 . . . (1976), to establish a link between objective and classification.

Applying this framework, we now analyze the arguments advanced by the State to justify its refusal to allow males to enroll for credit in MUW's School of Nursing.

III

A

The State's primary justification for maintaining the single-sex admissions policy of MUW's School of Nursing is that it compensates for discrimination against women and, therefore, constitutes educational affirmative action. Pet. Brief 8. [13] As applied to the School of Nursing, we find the State's argument unpersuasive.

In limited circumstances, a gender-based classification favoring one sex can be justified if it intentionally and directly assists members of the sex that is disproportionately burdened. *See Schlesinger v. Ballard*, 419 U.S. 498 . . . (1975). However, we consistently have emphasized that "the mere recitation of a benign, compensatory purpose is not an automatic schield which protects against any inquiry into the actual purposes underlying a statutory scheme." *Weinberger v. Wisenfeld*, 420 U.S. 636, 648 . . . (1975). The same searching analysis must be made, regardless of whether the State's objective is to eliminate family controversy, *Reed v. Reed*, *supra*, to achieve administrative efficiency, *Frontiero v. Richardson*, *supra*, or to balance the burdens borne by males and females.

It is readily apparent that a State can evoke a compensatory purpose to justify an otherwise discriminatory classification only if members of the gender benefited by the classification actually suffer a disadvantage related to the classification. We considered such a situation in *Califano v. Webster*, 430 U.S. 313 . . . (1977), which involved a challenge to a statutory classification that allowed women to eliminate more low-earning years than men for purposes of computing Social Security retirement benefits. Although the effect of the classification was to allow women higher monthly benefits than were available to men with the same earning history, we upheld the statutory scheme, noting that it took into account that women "as such have been unfairly hindered from earning as much as men" and "work[ed] directly to remedy" the resulting economic disparity. *Id.*, at 318. . . .

* * *

In sharp contrast, Mississippi has made no showing that women lacked opportunities to obtain training in the field of nursing or to attain positions of leadership in that field when the MUW School of Nursing opened its door or that women currently are deprived of such opportunities. In fact, in 1970, the year before the School of Nursing's first class enrolled, women earned 94 percent of the nursing

---

In a similar vein, the Court in *Goesaert v. Cleary*, 335 U.S. 464, 466 . . . (1948), upheld a legislature's right to preclude women from bartending, except under limited circumstances, on the ground that the legislature could devise preventive measures against "moral and social problems" that result when women, but apparently not men, bartend. Similarly, the many protective labor laws enacted in the late nineteenth and early twentieth centuries often had as their objective the protection of weaker workers, which the laws assumed meant females. *See generally*, B. Brown, A. Freedman, H. Katz, & A. Price. *Women's Rights and the Law* 209–10 (1977).

13. In its Reply Brief, the State understandably retreated from its contention that MUW was founded to provide opportunities for women which were not available to men. Reply Brief 4. Apparently, the impetus for founding MUW came not from a desire to provide women with advantages superior to those offered men, but rather from a desire to provide white women in Mississippi access to state-supported higher learning. In 1856, Sally Reneau began agitating for a college for white women. Those initial efforts were unsuccessful, and, by 1870, Mississippi provided higher education only for white men and black men and women. E. Mayes, *History of Education in Mississippi* 178, 228, 245, 259, 266, 270 (1899) (hereinafter Mayes). *See also* S. Neilson, *The History of Mississippi State College for Women* 4–5 (unpublished manuscript, 1952) (hereinafter Neilson). In 1882, two years before MUW was chartered, the University of Mississippi opened its doors to women. However, the institution was in those early years not "extensively patronized by females: most of those who come being such as desire to qualify themselves to teach." Mayes, at 178. By 1890, the largest number of women in any class at the University had been 23, while nearly 350 women enrolled in the first session of MUW. Mayes, at 178, 253. Because the University did not solicit the attendance of women until after 1920, and did not accept women at all for a time between 1907 and 1920, most Mississippi women who attended college attended MUW. Neilson, at 86. Thus, in Mississippi, as elsewhere in the country, women's colleges were founded to provide some form of higher education for the academically disenfranchised. *See generally* II T. Woody, *A History of Women's Education in the United States* 137–223 (1929); L. Baker, *I'm Radcliffe! Fly Me! The Seven Sisters and the Failure of Women's Education* 22, 136–41 (1976).

baccalaureate degrees conferred in Mississippi and 98.6 percent of the degrees earned nationwide. . . . As one would expect, the labor force reflects the same predominance of women in nursing. When MUW's School of Nursing began operation, nearly 98 percent of all employed registered nurses were female. . . .

Rather than compensate for discriminatory barriers faced by women, MUW's policy of excluding males from admission to the School of Nursing tends to perpetuate the stereotyped view of nursing as an exclusively woman's job.[15] By assuring that Mississippi allots more openings in its state-supported nursing schools to women than it does to men, MUW's admissions policy lends credibility to the old view that women, not men, should become nurses, and makes the assumption that nursing is a field for women a self-fulfilling prophecy. *See Stanton v. Stanton*, 421 U.S. 7, 95 S.Ct. 1373, 43 L.Ed.2d 688 (1975). Thus, we conclude that, although the State recited a "benign, compensatory purpose," it failed to establish that the alleged objective is the actual purpose underlying the discriminatory classification.

The policy is invalid also because it fails the second part of the equal protection test, for the State has made no showing that the gender-based classification is substantially and directly related to its proposed compensatory objective. To the contrary, MUW's policy of permitting men to attend classes as auditors fatally undermines its claim that women, at least those in the School of Nursing, are adversely affected by the presence of men.

. . . The uncontroverted record reveals that admitting men to nursing classes does not affect teaching style, . . . that the presence of men in the classroom would not affect the performance of the female nursing students, . . . and that men in coeducational nursing schools do not dominate the classroom. . . . In sum, the record in this case is flatly inconsistent with the claim that excluding men from the School of Nursing is necessary to reach any of MUW's educational goals.

Thus, considering both the asserted interest and the relationship between the interest and the methods used by the State, we conclude that the State has fallen far short of establishing the "exceedingly persuasive justification" needed to sustain the gender-based classification. Accordingly, we hold that MUW's policy of denying males the right to enroll for credit in its School of Nursing violates the Equal Protection Clause of the Fourteenth Amendment.[17]

B

In an additional attempt to justify its exclusion of men from MUW's School of Nursing, the State contends that MUW is the direct beneficiary "of specific congressional legislation which, on its face, permits the institution to exist as it has in the past." . . . The argument is based upon the language of § 901(a) in Title IX of the Education Amendments of 1972, 20 U.S.C. § 1681(a). Although § 901(a) prohibits gender discrimination in education programs that receive federal financial assistance, subsection 5 exempts the admissions policies of undergraduate institutions "that traditionally and continually from [their] establishment [have] had a policy of admitting only students of one sex" from the general prohibition. *See* n. 5, *supra*. Arguing that Congress enacted Title IX in furtherance of its power to enforce the Fourteenth Amendment, a power granted by § 5 of that Amendment, the State would have us conclude that § 1681(a)(5) is but "a congressional limitation upon the broad prohibitions of the Equal Protection Clause of the Fourteenth Amendment." . . .

The argument requires little comment. Initially, it is far from clear that Congress intended, through § 1681(a)(5), to exempt MUW from any constitutional obligation. Rather, Congress apparently intended, at most, to exempt MUW from the requirements of Title IX.

Even if Congress envisioned a constitutional exemption, the State's argument would fail. Section 5 of the Fourteenth Amendment gives Congress broad

15. Officials of the American Nurses Association have suggested that excluding men from the field has depressed nurses' wages. Hearings Before the United States Equal Employment Opportunity Commission on Job Segregation and Wage Discrimination 510–11, 517–18, 523 (April 1980). To the extent the exclusion of men has that effect, MUW's admissions policy actually penalizes the very class the State purports to benefit. *Cf. Weinberger v. Wisenfeld, supra.*

17. Justice Powell's dissent suggests that a second objective is served by the gender-based classification in that Mississippi has elected to provide women a choice of educational environments. . . . Since any gender-based classification provides one class a benefit or choice not available to the other class, however, that argument begs the question. The issue is not whether the benefited class profits from the classification, but whether the State's decision to confer a benefit only upon one class by means of a discriminatory classification is substantially related to achieving a legitimate and substantial goal.

power indeed to enforce the command of the Amendment and "to secure to all persons the enjoyment of perfect equality of civil rights and the equal protection of the laws against State denial or invasion. . . ." *Ex parte Virginia*, 100 U.S. (10 Otto) 339, 346 . . . (1879). Congress' power under § 5, however, "is limited to adopting measures to enforce the guarantees of the Amendment; § 5 grants Congress no power to restrict, abrogate, or dilute these guarantees." *Katzenbach v. Morgan*, 384 U.S. 641, 651 n. 10 . . . (1966). Although we give deference to congressional decisions and classifications, neither Congress nor a State can validate a law that denies the rights guaranteed by the Fourteenth Amendment. . . .

* * *

IV

Because we conclude that the State's policy of excluding males from MUW's School of Nursing violates the Equal Protection Clause of the Fourteenth Amendment, we affirm the judgment of the Court of Appeals.

It is so ordered.

Chief Justice Burger, dissenting.

I agree generally with Justice Powell's dissenting opinion. I write separately, however, to emphasize that the Court's holding today is limited to the context of a professional nursing school. . . . n.7. . . . Since the Court's opinion relies heavily on its finding that women have traditionally dominated the nursing profession, . . . it suggests that a State might well be justified in maintaining, for example, the option of an all-women's business school or liberal arts program.

Justice Blackmun, dissenting.

* * *

While the Court purports to write narrowly, declaring that it does not decide the same issue with respect to "separate but equal" undergraduate institutions for females and males, *ante*, at . . . n.1, or with respect to units of MUW other than its School of Nursing, *ante*, at . . . n.7, there is inevitable spillover from the Court's ruling today. That ruling, it seems to me, places in constitutional jeopardy any state-supported educational institution that confines its student body in any area to members of one sex, even though the State elsewhere provides an equivalent program to the complaining applicant. The Court's reasoning does not stop with the School of Nursing of the Mississippi University for Women.

I hope that we do not lose all values that some think are worthwhile (and are not based on differences of race or religion) and relegate ourselves to needless conformity. The ringing words of the Equal Protection Clause of the Fourteenth Amendment—what Justice Powell aptly describes as its "liberating spirit," *post*, at 3345,—do not demand that price.

Justice Powell, with whom Justice Rehnquist joins, dissenting.

The Court's opinion bows deeply to conformity. Left without honor—indeed, held unconstitutional—is an element of diversity that has characterized much of American education and enriched much of American life. The Court in effect holds today that no State now may provide even a single institution of higher learning open only to women students. It gives no heed to the efforts of the State of Mississippi to provide abundant opportunities for young men and young women to attend coeducational institutions, and none to the preferences of the more than 40,000 young women who over the years have evidenced their approval of an all-women's college by choosing Mississippi University for Women (MUW) over seven coeducational universities within the State. The Court decides today that the Equal Protection Clause makes it unlawful for the State to provide women with a traditionally popular and respected choice of educational environment. It does so in a case instituted by one man, who represents no class, and whose primary concern is personal convenience.

It is undisputed that women enjoy complete equality of opportunity in Mississippi's public system of higher education. Of the State's eight universities and sixteen junior colleges, all except MUW are coeducational. At least two other Mississippi universities would have provided respondent with the nursing curriculum that he wishes to pursue.[1] No

1. "[T]wo other Mississippi universities offered coeducational programs leading to a Bachelor of Science in Nursing—the University of Southern Mississippi in Hattiesburg, 178 miles from Columbus and the University of Mississippi in Jackson, 147 miles from Columbus. . . ." Brief for Respondent 3. . . .

other male has joined in his complaint. The only groups with any personal acquaintance with MUW to file *amicus* briefs are female students and alumnae of MUW. And they have emphatically rejected respondent's arguments, urging that the State of Mississippi be allowed to continue offering the choice from which they have benefited.

Nor is respondent significantly disadvantaged by MUW's all-female tradition. His constitutional complaint is based upon a single asserted harm: that he must *travel* to attend the state-supported nursing schools that concededly are available to him. The Court characterizes this injury as one of "inconvenience." . . . This description is fair and accurate, though somewhat embarrassed by the fact that there is, of course, no constitutional right to attend a state-supported university in one's hometown. Thus the Court, to redress respondent's injury of inconvenience, must rest its invalidation of MUW's single-sex program on a mode of "sexual stereotype" reasoning that has no application whatever to the respondent or to the "wrong" of which he complains. . . .

I

Coeducation, historically, is a novel educational theory. From grade school through high school, college, and graduate and professional training, much of the nation's population during much of our history has been educated in sexually segregated classrooms. At the college level, for instance, until recently some of the most prestigious colleges and universities—including most of the Ivy League—had long histories of single-sex education. As Harvard, Yale, and Princeton remained all-male colleges well into the second half of this century, the "Seven Sister" institutions established a parallel standard of excellence for women's colleges. . . . Mount Holyoke, Smith, and Wellesley recently have made considered decisions to remain essentially single-sex institutions. . . . Barnard retains its independence from Columbia, its traditional coordinate institution. Harvard and Radcliffe maintained separate admissions policies as recently as 1975.

The sexual segregation of students has been a reflection of, rather than an imposition upon, the preference of those subject to the policy. It cannot be disputed, for example, that the highly qualified women attending the leading women's colleges could have earned admission to virtually any college of their choice.[3] Women attending such colleges have chosen to be there, usually expressing a preference for the special benefits of single-sex institutions. Similar decisions were made by the colleges that elected to remain open to women only.

The arguable benefits of single-sex colleges also continue to be recognized by students of higher education. The Carnegie Commission on Higher Education has reported that it "favor[s] the continuation of colleges for women. They provide an element of diversity . . . and [an environment in which women] generally . . . speak up more in their classes, . . . hold more positions of leadership on campus, . . . and have more role models and mentors among women teachers and administrators." Carnegie [Commission on Higher Education, Opportunities for Women in Higher Education] . . . quoted in K. Davidson, R. Ginsburg, & H. Kay, *Sex-Based Discrimination* 814 (1975 ed.). A 10-year empirical study by the Cooperative Institutional Research Program of the American Council of Education and the University of California, Los Angeles also has affirmed the distinctive benefits of single-sex colleges and universities. As summarized in A. Astin, *Four Critical Years* 232 (1977), the data established that

> [b]oth [male and female] single-sex colleges facilitate student involvement in several areas: academic, interaction with faculty, and verbal aggressiveness. . . . Men's and women's colleges also have a positive effect on intellectual self-esteem. Students at single-sex colleges are more satisfied than students at coeducational colleges with virtually all aspects of college life. . . . The only area where students are less satisfied is social life.[5]

3. It is true that historically many institutions of higher education—particularly in the East and South—were single-sex. To these extents, choices were by no means universally available to all men and women. But choices always were substantial, and the purpose of relating the experience of our country with single-sex colleges and universities is to document what should be obvious; generations of Americans, including scholars, have thought—wholly without regard to any discriminatory animus—that there were distinct advantages in this type of higher education.

5. In this Court the benefits of single-sex education have been asserted by the students and alumnae of MUW. One would expect the Court to regard their views as directly relevant to this case:

"[I]n the aspect of life known as courtship or mate-pairing, the American female remains in the role of the pursued sex, expected to adorn and groom herself to attract the male. Without comment on the equities of this social arrangement, it remains a sociological fact.

Despite the continuing expressions that single-sex institutions may offer singular advantages to their students, there is no doubt that coeducational institutions are far more numerous. But their numerical predominance does not establish—in any sense properly cognizable by a court—that individual preferences for single-sex education are misguided or illegitimate, or that a State may not provide its citizens with a choice.[6]

II

The issue in this case is whether a State transgresses the Constitution when—within the context of a public system that offers a diverse range of campuses, curricula, and educational alternatives—it seeks to accommodate the legitimate personal preferences of those desiring the advantages of an all-women's college. In my view, the Court errs seriously by assuming—without argument or discussion—that the equal protection standard generally applicable to sex discrimination is appropriate here. That standard was designed to free women from "archaic and overbroad generalizations. . . ." *Schlesinger v. Ballard*, 419 U.S. 498, 508 . . . (1975). In no previous case have we applied it to invalidate state efforts to *expand* women's choices. Nor are there prior sex discrimination decisions by this Court in which a male plaintiff, as in this case, had the choice of an equal benefit.

The cases cited by the Court therefore do not control the issue now before us. In most of them women were given no opportunity for the same benefit as men. Cases involving male plaintiffs are equally inapplicable. . . .

By applying heightened equal protection analysis to this case,[9] the Court frustrates the liberating spirit of the Equal Protection Clause. It forbids the States from providing women with an opportunity to choose the type of university they prefer. And yet it is these women whom the Court regards as the *victims* of an illegal, stereotyped perception of the role of women in our society. The Court reasons this way in a case in which no woman has complained, and the only complainant is a man who advances no claims on behalf of anyone else. His claim, it should be recalled, is not that he is being denied a substantive educational opportunity, or even the right to attend an all-male or a coeducational college. *See* Brief for Respondent 24.[10] It is *only* that the colleges open to him are located at inconvenient distances.

III

The Court views this case as presenting a serious equal protection claim of sex discrimination. I do not, and I would sustain Mississippi's right to continue MUW on a rational basis analysis. But I need not apply this "lowest tier" of scrutiny. I can accept for present purposes the standard applied by the Court: that there is a gender-based distinction that must serve an important governmental objective by means that are substantially related to its achievement. *E.g., Wengler v. Druggists Mutual Ins. Co.*, 446 U.S. 142, 150 . . . (1980). The record in this case reflects that MUW has a historical position in the State's educational system dating back to 1884. More than 2,000 women presently evidence their preference

"An institution of collegiate higher learning maintained exclusively for women is uniquely able to provide the education atmosphere in which some, but not all, women can best attain maximum learning potential. It can serve to overcome the historic repression of the past and can orient a woman to function and achieve in the still male dominated economy. It can free its students of the burden of playing the mating game while attending classes, thus giving academic rather than sexual emphasis. Consequently, many such institutions flourish and their graduates make significant contributions to the arts, professions and business." Brief for Mississippi University for Women Alumnae Assn. as *Amicus Curiae* 2–3.

6. "[T]he Constitution does not require that a classification keep abreast of the latest in educational opinion, especially when there remains a respectable opinion to the contrary. . . . Any other rule would mean that courts and not legislatures would determine all matters of public policy." *Williams v. McNair*, 316 F.Supp. 134, 137 (DSC 1970), *aff'd mem.*, 401 U.S. 951 . . . (1971).

9. Even the Court does not argue that the appropriate standard here is "strict scrutiny"—a standard that none of our "sex discrimination" cases ever has adopted. Sexual segregation in education differs from the tradition, typified by the decision in *Plessy v. Ferguson*, 163 U.S. 537 . . . (1896), of "separate but equal" *racial* segregation. It was characteristic of racial segregation that segregated facilities were offered, not as alternatives to increase the choices available to blacks, but as the *sole* alternative. MUW stands in sharp contrast. Of Mississippi's eight public universities and sixteen public junior colleges, only MUW considers sex as a criterion for admission. Women consequently are free to select a coeducational education environment for themselves if they so desire; their attendance of MUW is not a matter of coercion.

10. The Court says that "any gender-based classification provides one class a benefit or choice not available to the other class. . . ." It then states that the issue "is not whether the benefited class profits from the classification, but whether the state's decision to confer a benefit *only* upon *one* class by means of a discriminatory classification is substantially related to achieving a legitimate and substantial goal." . . . This is *not* the issue in this case. Hogan is not complaining about any benefit conferred upon women. Nor is he claiming discrimination because Mississippi offers no all-male college. As his brief states, at p. 24: "Joe Hogan does not ask to attend an all-male college which offers a Bachelor of Science in nursing; he asks only to attend MUW." And he asks this only for his personal convenience.

for MUW by having enrolled there. The choice is one that discriminates invidiously against no one. . . .

In arguing to the contrary, the Court suggests that the MUW is so operated as to "perpetuate the stereotyped view of nursing as an exclusively women's job." . . . [But] [t]he School of Nursing makes up only one part—a relatively small part—of MUW's diverse modern university campus and curriculum. The other departments on the MUW campus offer a typical range of degrees and a typical range of subjects. There is no indication that women suffer fewer opportunities at other Mississippi state campuses because of MUW's admission policy.

In sum, the practice of voluntarily chosen single-sex education is an honored tradition in our country, even if it now rarely exists in state colleges and universities. Mississippi's accommodation of such student choices is legitimate because it is completely consensual and is important because it permits students to decide for themselves the type of college education they think will benefit them most. Finally, Mississippi's policy is substantially related to its long-respected objective.

IV

A distinctive feature of America's tradition has been respect for diversity. This has been characteristic of the peoples from numerous lands who have built our country. It is the essence of our democratic system. At stake in this case as I see it is the preservation of a small aspect of this diversity. But that aspect is by no means insignificant, given our heritage of available choice between single-sex and coeducational institutions of higher learning. The Court answers that there is discrimination—not just that which may be tolerable, as for example between those candidates for admission able to contribute most to an educational institution and those able to contribute less—but discrimination of constitutional dimensions. But, having found "discrimination," the Court finds it difficult to identify the victims. It hardly can claim that women are discriminated against. A constitutional case is held to exist solely because one man found it inconvenient to travel to any of the other institutions made available to him by the State of Mississippi. In essence he insists that he has a right to attend a college in his home community. This simply is not a sex discrimination case. The Equal Protection Clause was never intended to be applied to this kind of case.[18]

NOTES AND QUESTIONS

1. Scope of the Decision

What standard of review does the Court use in *Hogan?* Does the dissent suggest a different standard in cases where males are the victims of discrimination? What does Justice Powell mean in asserting that a less rigorous standard should be applied because Hogan does not advance a "serious equal protection claim"? Is he saying that no one is guaranteed an equal right to attend professional school in his or her home town? Is that the issue?

2. Equality and Choice: The Puzzle Not Considered

For Joe Hogan, the practical consequence of the MUW admissions standard was to compel him to choose between his home and his vocation. But, while limiting his choices, the admissions policy also expanded the educational options of women, who were enabled to select a coeducational or single-sex course of instruction. Is it one thing to free men and women from gender-based rules premised on "archaic and overbroad generalizations" and something quite different to allow women to choose between two very different educational environments? Is that difference constitutionally relevant? Does it require, at a minimum, that there be a defensible educational rationale for the separation?

In this regard, does it matter that nursing, the field in question, is historically dominated by women? Would a similar challenge to, say, an all-female engineering school raise different questions? What about an all-female women's studies department? Single-sex social institutions? *See* Note, "Discrimination on Campus: A Critical Examination of Single-

---

18. . . . The Court . . . purports to decide this case "narrow[ly]." Normally and properly we decide only the question presented. It seems to me that in fact the issue properly before us is the single-sex policy of the University, and it is this issue that I have addressed in this dissent. The Court of Appeals so viewed this case, and unambiguously held that a single-sex state institution of higher education no longer is permitted by the Constitution. I see no principled way—in light of the Court's rationale—to reach a different result with respect to other MUW schools and departments. But given the Court's insistence that its decision applies only to the School of Nursing, it is my view that the Board and officials of MUW may continue to operate the remainder of the University on a single-sex basis without fear of personal liability. . . .

Sex College Social Organizations," 75 *Calif. L. Rev.* 2117 (1987).

3. *Single-Sex Education: The* Vorchheimer *Decision*

In *Vorchheimer v. School District of Philadelphia*, 532 F.2d 880 (3d Cir. 1976), *aff'd by an equally divided court*, 430 U.S. 703, 97 S.Ct. 1671, 51 L.Ed.2d 750 (1977), the Court held, without opinion, that neither Title IX nor the Constitution forbids a public school system from maintaining a limited number of single-sex high schools in which enrollment is voluntary and educational opportunities are "essentially equal." "We are not unsympathetic with [plaintiff's] desire to have an expanded freedom of choice, but its cost should not be overlooked. If she were to prevail, then all public single-sex schools would have to be abolished. The absence of these schools would stifle the ability of the local school board to continue with a respected education methodology." 532 F.2d at 888.

Is the argument persuasive? What is the impact of the *Vorchheimer* decision?

4. *Can Separate Be Equal?*

In assessing whether sex-separate schools are in fact equal, what facts are relevant: (a) the availability of courses desired by a student barred from admission by virtue of his or her sex (*see Allred v. Heaton*, 336 S.W.2d 251 (Tex.Civ.App. 1960), *cert denied*, 364 U.S. 517, 81 S.Ct. 293, 5 L.Ed.2d 265 (1960)); (b) the proximity of a given school to a student's residence (or family); (c) the expenditure per student at each school; (d) the "prestige" of each school; (e) the success of graduates in gaining admission to college? Would a careful investigation of these factors be likely to produce many examples of schools that were sex-separated and wholly equivalent?

Are schools that are segregated by sex inherently unequal? One commentator notes that "the problem with the *Vorchheimer* majority's theory of equal benefit is analogous to the problem with *Plessy v. Ferguson's* concept of 'separate but equal'." Note, "Single Sex Public Schools: The Last Bastion of 'Separate but Equal'?" 1977 *Duke L. J.* 259, 268. Is this assertion correct? Are all-female schools generally perceived as inferior?

Professor Freund thinks that sex-separate schools are defensible. He views legal assaults on separate schools as a quest for "a single standard of sameness . . . a doctrinaire equality," and Freund rejects the full application of the race-sex analogy:

> It is sometimes said that a rigid requirement of equality is no less proper for the sexes than for the races, and no less workable. But the moral dimensions of the concept of equality are clearly not the same in the two cases. . . . A school system offering a triple option based on race—all white, all-black, and mixed schools—would elevate freedom of choice over equal protection in an impermissible way. Are we prepared to pass that judgment as readily on a school system that offers a choice of boys', girls', and coeducational schools?

Freund, "The Equal Rights Amendment Is Not the Way," 6 *Harv. C.R.-C.L. Rev.* 234, 238, 240 (1971).

Is Professor Freund suggesting that society's views concerning race separation are clearer (or more fully developed) than its views concerning sex separation? If so, is the suggestion correct? How is it germane?

5. *Sex Separation and Racial Desegregation*

In a number of desegregation cases, school districts proposed to integrate racially while separating students according to sex. *See, e.g., United States v. Hinds County School Board*, 560 F.2d 619 (5th Cir. 1977) (prohibiting a district-wide plan of sex segregation); *Moore v. Tangipahoa Parish School Board*, 304 F.Supp. 244 (E.D.La. 1969) (authorizing sex segregation as a transitional measure). Should sex segregation in the context of a racial desegregation plan be treated differently from other sex-segregation situations? Is such a plan likely to be racially motivated, to reinforce racial stereotypes concerning the sexuality of blacks, or to cause psychological harm to black students? *See generally*, Note, "The Constitutionality of Sex Separation in School Desegregation Plans," 37 *U. Chi. L. Rev.* 296 (1970).

6. *Sex-Separateness and Liberation*

Some women scholars have argued that sex-separate educational institutions are needed in order to overcome the sex stereotyping perpetuated by men on women in coeducational institutions. *See, e.g., Tobias*, "How Coeducation Fails Women," in S. Anderson, ed., *Sex Differences in Education* 83 (1973). Might such an argument provide legal justification for sex-separate schools or even require that such schools be created? Might men advance a similar claim? Is the analogy to minority-controlled community schools, discussed in chapter 5, appropriate?

7. Title IX and Sex-Separate Education

In the version passed by the House of Representatives, Title IX required all single-sex schools, primary and secondary, public and private, receiving federal funds to become coeducational. The Senate version, however, which became law, exempted the admission policies of secondary schools and traditionally single-sex colleges. Why would Congress make such distinctions—and what is their constitutional relevance, if any?

E. Implementation Issues: The Private Right of Action and Beyond

One key concern with respect to any law is the process of its enforcement. Traditionally federal agencies were delegated exclusive enforcement responsibility, but this has not always been true. In antitrust law, for example, the idea of law suits filed by affected individuals—"private attorneys general"—have long been recognized. Because all federal agencies have too little staff to effectively address the range of disputes presented to them, private enforcement may serve as a useful supplement to official enforcement efforts.

Private Right of Action: *Cannon v. University of Chicago,* 441 U.S. 677, 99 S.Ct. 1946, 60 L.Ed.2d 560 (1979). An unsuccessful applicant for admissions to the medical school had brought suit under Title IX, claiming that her rejection was based on her sex. The Supreme Court read the legislation expansively, holding that Title IX implicitly authorizes a private right of action:

> Title IX explicitly confers a benefit on persons discriminated against on the basis of sex, and petitioner is clearly a member of that class for whose special benefit the statute was enacted. . . .
>
> [T]he history of Title IX rather plainly indicates that Congress intended to create such a remedy [noting that the statute was patterned after Title VI, which had already been construed as creating a private remedy]. . . . Finally, the very persistence . . . of the assumption that both Title VI and Title IX created a private right of action for the victims of illegal discrimination and the absence of legislative action to change that assumption provide further evidence that Congress at least acquiesces in, and apparently affirms, that assumption.

441 U.S. at 694, 702–703, 99 S.Ct. at 1961.

The Court dismissed the University of Chicago's argument that "it is unwise to subject admissions decisions . . . to judicial scrutiny at the behest of disappointed applicants on a case-by-case basis." This contention "is not a legal argument at all; it addresses a policy issue that Congress had already resolved." And "the fact that other provisions of a complex statutory scheme create express remedies has not been accepted as a sufficient reason for refusing to imply an otherwise appropriate remedy under a separate section. . . . Rather, the Court has generally avoided this type of 'excursion into extrapolation of legislative intent,' . . . unless there is other, more convincing evidence that Congress meant to exclude the remedy. . . ."

What are the consequences of the *Cannon* decision for the enforcement of Title IX? What remedy might a litigant seek? Would damages be appropriate? *See Lieberman v. University of Chicago,* 660 F.2d 1185 (7th Cir. 1981). What factors might deter individuals from taking advantage of this right?

What do you make—and what should the Court have made—of the university's concern that the prospect of case-by-case judicial review of admissions decisions undermines its capacity for self-governance? How similar is this contention to objections to due process advanced by educators in *Goss, Ingraham,* and *Horowitz,* discussed in chapter 3? To claims of institutional academic freedom? *See* chapter 2, *supra.*

Coverage of Title IX: In *North Haven Board of Education v. Bell,* 456 U.S. 512, 102 S.Ct. 1912, 72 L.Ed.2d 299 (1982), the Supreme Court ruled that Title IX applies to discrimination in employment, not just discrimination against students. Lower courts had earlier read the statutory language "no person" restrictively, as not including employees. But the Court declared that, since the language and legislative history did not explicitly or implicitly exclude employment discrimination, employees were covered.

Congress could have used the word "students" instead of "persons," said the Court, if that was its intention. And there was relevant legislative history: The sponsor of the measure, Indiana Senator Birch Bayh, had described the legislation as reaching "discrimination in employment within an institution, as a member of a faculty or whatever." *See* Brower, "Now You See It, Now You Don't: Title IX As An Alternate Remedy for Sex Discrimination in Educational Employment," 31 *N.Y.L. Sch. L. Rev.* 657 (1986).

Scope of the Remedy: In *Grove City College v. Bell,* 465 U.S. 555, 104 S.Ct. 1211, 79 L.Ed.2d 516 (1984), the justices limited the reach of Title IX. The issue was whether the federal government could cut off all federal assistance to an entire institution when only a particular program was discriminating in violation of Title IX. The Court, relying on the legislative history, declared that the federal government could terminate only those funds earmarked specifically for the discriminatory program. Title VI and Section 504 of the Rehabilitation Act were implicated since the relevant statutory language is virtually identical. *See Consolidated Rail Corp. v. Darrone,* 465 U.S. 624, 104 S.Ct. 1248, 79 L.Ed.2d 568 (1984) (§ 504).

The impact of *Grove City* on Title IX enforcement was significant. The Court's ruling allowed a university (or any other institution subject to Title IX) to discriminate in particular program areas (*e.g.* the engineering school or the athletic program)—indeed, any place except in a program where it received federal aid. On the other hand, a single instance of discrimination in one limited program would not trigger a university-wide sanction.

Within months of ruling, the *Grove City* decision prompted the Department of Education's Office of Civil Rights to close twenty-three civil rights investigations and to narrow the scope of eighteen others. A compliance action against the University of Maryland was dropped, for example, even though instances of discrimination by the athletic department had allegedly been documented. Since the only federal aid to that department was loan money received by athletes, and since there had been no discrimination in the disbursement of the loan funds, OCR declared that it could not proceed. *See* Griffin, "*Grove City College v. Bell:* Restricting the Scope of Title IX," 8 *Harv. Women's L. J.* 179 (1985); Mezey, "Gender Equality in Education: A Study of Policy-Making by the Burger Court," 20 *Wake Forest L. Rev.* 793 (1984).

Immediately after the ruling, there were attempts in Congress to reverse *Grove City* through legislation. But rewriting the law proved difficult. The 1984 Civil Rights Act would have replaced Title IX's "program or activity" language—the terms that the Court had construed—with the far more capacious term "recipient." Conservatives claimed the change would mean an enormous expansion of federal power, reaching even the corner grocer who accepted food stamps. The general counsel of the Office of Management and Budget argued the bill "would largely eliminate the remaining distinctions between federal and state, and federal and private, concerns." While the bill was overwhelmingly passed in the House of Representatives, it died in the Senate. Subsequently, various attempts at rewriting the relevant language failed in the Senate, largely because the measure was bottled up by an ancillary fight over the impact of the legislation on abortions performed in institutions receiving federal funding. *See generally* R. Salome, *Equal Education Under Law* 124–35 (1986).

In 1988 the Supreme Court's ruling was overturned by Congress. The Civil Rights Restoration Act of 1988, 20 U.S.C.A. § 1687, redefines "program or activity" in Title VI and Title IX: "a college, university, or other postsecondary institution, or a public system of higher education; or a local educational agency . . . any part of which is extended Federal financial assistance (constitutes a program or activity under the Act), except that such term does not include any operation of an entity which is controlled by a religious organization if the application of [Title IX] would not be consistent with the religious tenets of such organization." Section 1688 clarifies that the provision does not speak to the issue of abortion, neither requiring nor prohibiting its provision or financing.

Implementation: Surprisingly little attention has been paid to the implementation of Title IX by those groups who pressed for its passage. For a discussion of the politics of passage, *see* A. Fishel and J. Pottker, *National Politics and Sex Discrimination in Education* (1977). While the regulation of athletics has provoked dispute—and a body of case law almost as voluminous as that occasioned by hair-length regulations of a decade earlier—other issues have been little attended to. In some instances, as with allegations of sex bias in curricular materials, the Department of Education's decision not to regard the matter as appropriate for government action provides an explanation. In yet other situations, it may simply be the case that the advocacy groups that might mount litigation have other priorities. Whatever the explanation, one might surmise that the implementation of Title IX is at least as problematic as the implementation of statutory rights newly won by, for example, the disabled.

Another and deeper issue may be at work here. The law has defined gender issues in terms of discrimination, unjustified inequities of treatment. That definition of the problem is largely borrowed from the race context, where (as chapter 5 suggests) it clearly fits. With respect to gender, however, the critical issue may in fact be less one of equality, with its press toward sameness of outcome, than one of liberty. What may be central to the educational experiences of males and females is not the insistence that they behave identically but that they be offered the chance to develop what they perceive as their own potential. One can laud the substantial increase in women participating in athletic and vocational programs (and the more modest increase in males enrolled in "domestic survival" courses) as indications that stereotypes are beginning to erode, while not believing in parity as the necessarily appropriate outcome. Freedom to shape one's own identity coupled with the institutionalized resources to exercise that choice effectively: that, and not sex-sameness, may well make best personal sense—and best social policy sense. The exceptions to the nondiscrimination principle written into Title IX speak in part to this issue. If, however, liberty and not equality is properly the policy paradigm, a basic rethinking of the statutory framework and the constitutional standard is in order. *See generally* D. Kirp, M. Yudof, and M. Franks, *Gender Justice* (1986).

V. LIMITED-ENGLISH-PROFICIENT CHILDREN: ASSIMILATION OR CULTURAL IDENTITY?

A. Beyond *Lau:* The Development of Federal Bilingual Education Law

The Supreme Court in *Lau v. Nichols*, discussed in section I-B of this chapter, upheld the position of the Office of Civil Rights (OCR). OCR had asserted in a 1970 memorandum that Title VI of the 1964 Civil Rights Act included those having a "language deficiency" in the category "national origin." Because discrimination on the basis of national origin was proscribed, so too was discrimination on the basis of language deficiency. Furthermore, nondiscrimination with respect to this group implied not just equal treatment but rather some affirmative efforts to rectify the deficiency. For these students, "effective participation" constituted the entitlement.

This construction of Title VI was implicitly affirmed by Congress in the 1974 Equal Educational Opportunity Act, Section 204, which states: "No State shall deny equal educational opportunity to an individual on account of his or her race, color, sex, or national origin, by . . . (f) the failure by an educational agency to take appropriate action to overcome language barriers that impede equal participation by its students in the instructional program." 20 U.S.C. § 1703 (1976). What this provision requires—what groups are reached, what kinds of programs are called for, whether "equal participation" and "effective participation" are synonymous—has been the subject of policy debate. As the cases in this section note, it has also been the subject of litigation.

In 1975, OCR issued a memorandum expanding upon the *Lau* entitlement. That memo, *Task Force Findings Specifying Remedies for Eliminating Past Educational Practices Ruled Unlawful Under* Lau *v.* Nichols, outlined the procedures to be followed by school districts that enroll twenty or more limited-English-proficient students. In determining a student's primary language, the memo calls for an analysis of the child's first acquired language, the language most often spoken by the child, and the language most often spoken in the child's home. If in any of these circumstances a language other than English is used, then the child is treated as having a non-English primary language. Such students are then classified as monolingual speakers of a language other than English, predominant speakers of a language other than English, bilingual (equally fluent), predominantly English-speaking, and monolingual English-speaking. These classifications are supposed to determine the program that a school district adopts. For example, the monolingual (non-English-speaking) elementary or intermediate school student may be offered transitional bilingual education, bilingual-bicultural education, or multilingual-multicultural education. According to the OCR "*Lau* remedies," that child may not be enrolled in an English-as-a-second-language (ESL) course. More curricular flexibility is permitted at the secondary than the primary level and with respect to children who have a greater command of English. The OCR memorandum also addresses issues of curriculum, personnel, ethnic isolation, and the like. Instructional personnel, for instance, must be linguistically and culturally familiar with the background of students in the program. The OCR expectation is that "voluntary compliance plans . . . will be equally effective in ensuring equal educational opportunity." Neither the meaning of "equally effective" nor the mechanisms for enforcement are specified. The meaning of these provisions as well as their consistency with the law has been much debated.

The Bilingual Education Act, 20 U.S.C. § 880b, is a grants program, providing support for school districts enrolling sizable numbers of limited-English-proficient students. Because the program has received only limited funding, fewer than 10 percent of the estimated four million eligible children receive benefits from this program. As section B notes, questions concerning the efficacy of this undertaking have been raised.

The Reagan administration tried unsuccessfully to eliminate this program by proposing to consolidate it into a block grant to the states. In 1984, Congress weakened the bilingual requirements, giving the Department of Education permission to distribute up to 4 percent of bilingual funds to districts providing English-only instruction. For a detailed history, *see* Moran, "The Politics of Discretion: Federal Intervention in Bilingual Education," 76 *Cal. L. Rev.* 1249 (1988).

Martin Luther King Jr. Elementary School Children v. Michigan Board of Education

451 F.Supp. 1324 (E.D.Mich. 1978).

Joiner, District Judge.

Plaintiffs are fifteen black preschool or elementary school children residing at the Green Road Housing Project in Ann Arbor, Michigan, who previously attended, are currently attending, or will be eligible to attend the Martin Luther King, Jr., Elementary School. . . .

In this lawsuit the plaintiffs allege that in the process of determining the eligibility of all students for special education services . . . the defendants have failed to determine whether plaintiffs' learning difficulties stem from cultural, social, and economic deprivation and to establish a program which would enable plaintiffs to overcome the cultural, social, and economic deprivations which allegedly prevent them, in varying degrees, from making normal progress in school. Plaintiffs assert that these omissions constitute violations of . . . (III) their right to equal educational opportunity protected by 20 U.S.C. §§ 1703(f) and 1706. . . . [Other claims, based on federal and state constitutional arguments, are rejected by the court and not excerpted.]

. . . Plaintiffs are alleged to be culturally, socially, and economically deprived. . . . Five of the fifteen named plaintiffs have been found eligible to receive special education services for the handicapped as hereinafter explained. Four of these children have actually received services. Two children have been classified as "Learning Disabled." Two children have been classified as "Emotionally Impaired." The mother of the fifth child, who is also the mother of one of the learning disabled children, refused any further special services for her other child.

There is no separate category or discrete assistance in the program for handicapped for learning difficulties arising from cultural, social, and economic deprivation. Several other plaintiffs have been referred for an evaluation of their eligibility but these referrals have not resulted in any classification or access to services. . . .

In count III of the complaint plaintiffs allege that the defendants' previously described acts and omissions constitute a failure to take appropriate action to overcome language barriers in violation of 20 U.S.C. §§ 1703(f) . . . Section 1703(f) of Title 20 of the United States Code states:

> No State shall deny equal educational opportunity to an individual on account of his or her race, color, sex, or national origin, by—(f) the failure by an educational agency to take appropriate action to overcome language barriers that impede equal participation by its students in its instructional programs.

Plaintiffs assert that as a class of black economically disadvantaged children living in the social isolation of a housing project they speak a vernacular of English, referred to as "Black English," which is so different from the English commonly spoken in the public school as to constitute a language barrier which impedes their equal participation in King School's instructional programs.

In their attack on the legal sufficiency of this claim defendants present [as an issue for] resolution, . . . whether the term "language barrier" can be interpreted to include a child's inability to use standard English effectively because that child's native language is what plaintiffs have termed "Black English" as opposed to a foreign language such as Spanish. . . .

Federal Courts have not explicitly addressed the issue of whether the language barrier specified in § 1703(f) must be a foreign language barrier or may also include the barrier standard English presents to a black child with a "Black English" background. . . .

This section (f) requires a showing of two things. (1) The denial of educational opportunity must be on "account of" race, color, sex or national origin and, (2) the educational agency must fail to take action to overcome language barriers that are sufficiently severe so as to impede a student's equal participation in instructional programs. So the allegations in this case must be examined to determine the seriousness of the language barriers and the cause of the alleged denial of educational opportunities that results from the failure to take action to overcome the language barriers.

The statutory language places no limitations on the character or source of the language barrier except that it must be serious enough to "impede equal participation by . . . students in . . . instructional programs." Barring any more explicit legislative guidance to the contrary § 1703(f) applies to language barriers of appropriate severity encountered by students who speak "Black English" as well as to language barriers encountered by students who speak German.

The legislative history of this section does not provide a meaning more specific or limited in scope than the language of the statute. In his message to Congress President Nixon stated:

> School authorities must take appropriate action to overcome *whatever* language barriers might exist, in order to enable all students to participate equally in educational programs. This would establish, in effect, an educational bill of rights for Mexican-Americans, Puerto Ricans, Indians and others who start under language handicaps, and ensure at last that they too would have equal opportunity. [Emphasis added].

118 Cong. Rec. 8931 (1972). The President's list of persons covered by his proposal is not only merely illustrative but could well include students whose "language barrier" results from the use of some type of non-standard English. The report of the House Committee on Education and Labor simply paraphrases the statutory language and commends HEW for having initiated a compliance review of school districts throughout the country to ascertain whether they have fulfilled their obligation to remove language and cultural barriers under Title VI of the Civil Rights Act of 1964.

Paragraph 120 of the complaint contains an allegation that plaintiffs are all Black and economically disadvantaged and that the defendants have failed to take appropriate action to overcome language barriers. There is enough stated implicitly in this allegation as to causation to prevent this court from granting a motion to dismiss. In keeping with the terms of the statute this court holds that allegations of failure by an educational agency to take appropriate action to overcome language barriers of students which impede their equal participation in instructional programs when tied, as alleged, to race allege a violation of 20 U.S.C. § 1703(f). . . .

NOTES AND QUESTIONS

1. Martin Luther King Jr. Elementary School Children: *Scope of the Decision*

How does the court determine what constitutes "language barriers that impede equal participation"? Are you persuaded by the Court's treatment of the language of the statute and its legislative history that the statute was meant to encompass the "language barrier" of black English? Does one speak black English on "account of" race? *See* van Geel, "Law, Politics, and the Right to Be Taught English," 83 *Sch. Rev*. 245 (1975).

In a subsequent opinion, 473 F.Supp. 1371 (E.D. Mich. 1979), the court concluded that black English was indeed a distinct dialect that impedes equal participation and ordered the school district to prepare a plan to teach standard English to black English speakers. The district committed $42,000 to a teacher training course designed to steer students away from "she be gone" to "she is gone."

2. Who Is Entitled to Special Language Assistance?

Recall that the 1975 OCR guidelines call for some bilingual instruction to all children classified as "limited-English-speaking," even if they are predominantly English language speakers. Is this standard consistent with *Lau?* With the Equal Educational Opportunity Act? *See Aspira of New York, Inc. v. Board of Education*, 394 F.Supp. 1161 (S.D.N.Y. 1975).

One bilingual education proponent argues that "any child, irrespective of the language in which he is most proficient, is entitled to special language assistance if he can show that some language 'impediment' stemming from his linguistic background is causing '[in]effective' or '[un]equal' participation in a school district's educational program." Roos, "Bilingual Education: The Hispanic Response to Unequal Educational Opportunity," 42 *Law & Contemp. Probs.* 111, 119 (1978). If this reading of the law is correct, how might such a nexus be identified? A disproportionate number of students who come from homes in which English is not the primary language are also poor, have parents with limited educational backgrounds, and so on. How does one disentangle linguistic background from these other impediments to academic success? *See Otero v. Mesa County Valley School District No. 51*, 408 F.Supp. 162 (D. Colo. 1975), *vacated and remanded on other grounds*, 568 F.2d 1312 (10th Cir. 1977). Is it also appropriate to require a showing that some special language assistance will aid in overcoming the impediment? How likely is it that this can be established?

Castaneda v. Pickard

648 F.2d 989 (5th Cir. 1981).

Randall, Circuit Judge:

Plaintiffs, Mexican-American children and their parents who represent a class of others similarly situated, instituted this action against the Raymondville, Texas Independent School District (RISD) alleging that the district engaged in policies and practices of racial discrimination against Mexican-Americans which deprived the plaintiffs and their class of rights secured to them by the fourteenth amendment and 42 U.S.C. § 1983 (1976), Title VI of the Civil Rights Act of 1964, 42 U.S.C. § 2000d *et seq.* (1976), and the Equal Educational Opportunities Act of 1974, 20 U.S.C. § 1701 *et seq.* (1976). Specifically, plaintiffs charged that the school district unlawfully discriminated against them by using an ability grouping system for classroom assignments which was based on racially and ethnically discriminatory criteria and resulted in impermissible classroom segregation, by discriminating against Mexican-Americans in the hiring and promotion of faculty and administrators, and by failing to implement adequate bilingual education to overcome the linguistic barriers that impede the plaintiffs' equal participation in the educational program of the district. . . .

[T]he district court entered judgment in favor of the defendants based upon its determination that the policies and practices of the RISD, in the areas of hiring and promotion of faculty and administrators, ability grouping of students, and bilingual education did not violate any constitutional or statutory rights of the plaintiff class. From that judgment, the plaintiffs have brought this appeal. . . .

* * *

[W]e think it helpful to outline some of the basic demographic characteristics of the Raymondville school district. Raymondville is located in Willacy County, Texas. Willacy County is in the Rio Grande Valley; by conservative estimate based on census data, 77% of the population of the county is Mexican-American and almost all of the remaining 23% is "Anglo." The student population of RISD is about 85% Mexican-American.

Willacy County ranks 248th out of the 254 Texas counties in average family income. Approximately one-third of the population of Raymondville is composed of migrant farm workers. Three-quarters of the students in the Raymondville schools qualify for the federally funded free school lunch program. The district's assessed property valuation places it among the lowest 10% of all Texas counties in its per capita student expenditures. . . .

* * *

RISD currently operates a bilingual education program for all students in kindergarten through third grade. The language ability of each student entering the Raymondville program is assessed when he or she enters school. The language dominance test currently employed by the district is approved for this purpose by the TEA. The program of bilingual instruction offered students in the Raymondville schools has been developed with the assistance of expert consultants retained by the TEA and employs a group of materials developed by a regional educational center operated by the TEA. The articulated goal of the program is to teach students fundamental reading and writing skills in both Spanish and English by the end of the third grade.

Although the program's emphasis is on the development of language skills in the two languages, other cognitive and substantive areas are addressed, *e.g.*, mathematics skills are taught and tested in Spanish as well as English during these years. All of the teachers employed in the bilingual education program of the district have met the minimum state requirements to teach bilingual classes. However, only about half of these teachers are Mexican-American and native Spanish speakers; the other teachers in the program have been certified to teach bilingual classes following a 100 hour course designed by TEA to give them a limited Spanish vocabulary (700 words) and an understanding of the theory and methods employed in bilingual programs. Teachers in the bilingual program are assisted by classroom aides, most of whom are fluent in Spanish.

RISD does not offer a program of bilingual education after the third grade. In grades 4 and 5, although classroom instruction is only in English, Spanish-speaking teacher aides are used to assist students having language difficulties which may impair their ability to participate in classroom activities. For students in grades 4–12 having limited English proficiency or academic deficiencies in other areas, the RISD provides assistance in the form of a learning center operated at each school. This center provides a diagnostic/prescriptive program in which students' particular academic deficiencies, whether in language or other areas, are identified and addressed by special remedial programs. Approximately 1,000 of the district's students, almost one-third of the total enrollment, receive special assistance through small classes provided by these learning centers. The district also makes English as a Second Language classes and special tutoring in English available to all students in all grades; this program is especially designed to meet the needs of limited-English-speaking students who move into the district in grades above 3.

Plaintiffs claim that the bilingual education and language remediation programs offered by the Raymondville schools are educationally deficient and unsound and that RISD's failure to alter and improve these programs places the district in violation of Title VI and the Equal Educational Opportunities Act. The plaintiffs claim that the RISD programs fail to comport with the requirements of the "Lau Guidelines" promulgated in 1975 by the Department of Health, Education and Welfare. Specifically, plaintiffs contend that the articulated goal of the Raymondville program—to teach limited-English-speaking children to read and write in both English and Spanish at grade level—is improper because it overemphasizes the development of English language skills to the detriment of the child's overall cognitive development. Under the Lau Guidelines, plaintiffs argue, "pressing English on the child is not the first goal of language remediation." Plaintiffs criticize not only the premise and purpose of the RISD language programs but also particular aspects of the implementation of the program. Specifically, plaintiffs take issue with the tests the district employs to identify and assess limited-English-speaking children and the qualifications of the teachers and staff involved in the district's language remediation program. Plaintiffs contend that in both of these areas RISD falls short of standards established by the Lau Guidelines and thus has fallen out of compliance with Title VI and the EEOA.

We agree with the district court that RISD's program does not violate Title VI. Much of the plaintiffs' argument with regard to Title VI is based upon the premise that the Lau Guidelines are administrative regulations applicable to the RISD and thus should be given great weight by us in assessing the legal sufficiency of the district's programs. This premise is, however, flawed. . . .

* * *

Following the Supreme Court's decision in *Lau*, HEW developed the "Lau Guidelines" as a suggested compliance plan for school districts which, as a result of *Lau*, were in violation of Title VI because they failed to provide *any* English language assistance to students having limited English proficiency. Clearly, Raymondville is not culpable of such a failure. Under these circumstances, the fact that Raymondville provides (and long has provided) a program of language remediation which differs in some respects from these guidelines is, as the opinion of the Reviewing Authority for the OCR noted, "not in itself sufficient to rule that program unlawful in the first instance."

* * *

We must confess to serious doubts not only about the relevance of the Lau Guidelines to this case but also about the continuing vitality of the rationale of the Supreme Court's opinion in *Lau v. Nichols* which gave rise to those guidelines. *Lau* was written prior to *Washington v. Davis*, . . . in which the Court held that a discriminatory purpose, and not simply a disparate impact, must be shown to establish a violation of the Equal Protection Clause, and *University of California Regents v. Bakke*, . . . in which . . . a majority of the court interpreted Title VI to be coextensive with the Equal Protection Clause. Justice Brennan's opinion (in which Justices White, Marshall and Blackmun joined) in *Bakke* explicitly acknowledged that these developments raised serious questions about the vitality of *Lau*.

. . . Although the Supreme Court in *Bakke* did not expressly overrule *Lau*, as we noted above, we understand the clear import of *Bakke* to be that Title VI, like the Equal Protection Clause, is violated only by conduct animated by an intent to discriminate and not by conduct which, although benignly motivated, has a differential impact on persons of different races. Whatever the deficiencies of the RISD's program of language remediation may be, we do not think it can seriously be asserted that this program was intended or designed to discriminate against Mexican-American students in the district. . . .

Plaintiffs, however, do not base their legal challenge to the district's language program solely on Title VI. They also claim that the district's current program is unlawful under § 1703(f) of the EEOA which makes it unlawful for an educational agency to fail to take "appropriate action to overcome language barriers that impede equal participation by its students in its instructional programs." . . . [W]e have very little legislative history from which to glean the Congressional intent behind the EEOA's provisions. Thus, . . . we shall adhere closely to the plain language of § 1703(f) in defining the meaning of this provision. . . . [Section] 1703(f) does not contain language that explicitly incorporates an intent requirement nor . . . does this subsection employ words such as "discrimination" whose legal definition has been understood to incorporate an intent requirement. . . . [I]n *Morales v. Shannon*, . . . we assumed that the failure of an educational agency to undertake appropriate efforts to remedy the language deficiencies of its students, regardless of whether such a failure is motivated by an intent to discriminate against those students, would violate § 1703(f) and we think that such a construction of that subsection is most consistent with the plain meaning of the language employed in § 1703(f). Thus, although serious doubts exist about the continuing vitality of *Lau v. Nichols* as a judicial interpretation of the requirements of Title VI or the fourteenth amendment, the essential holding of *Lau*, *i.e.*, that schools are not free to ignore the need of limited-English-speaking children for language assistance to enable them to participate in the instructional program of the district, has now been legislated by Congress, acting pursuant to its power to enforce the fourteenth amendment, in § 1703(f). The difficult question presented by plaintiffs' challenge to the current language remediation programs in RISD is really whether Congress in enacting § 1703(f) intended to go beyond the essential requirement of *Lau*, that the schools do something, and impose, through the use of the term "appropriate action" a more specific obligation on state and local educational authorities.

* * *

We note that . . . Congress, in describing the remedial obligation it sought to impose on the states in the EEOA, did not specify that a state must provide a program of "bilingual education" to all limited-English-speaking students. We think Congress' use of the less specific term, "appropriate action," rather than "bilingual education," indicates that Congress intended to leave state and local educational authorities a substantial amount of latitude in choosing the programs and techniques they would use to meet their obligations under the EEOA. However, by including an obligation to address the problem of language barriers in the EEOA and granting limited-English-speaking students a private right of action to enforce that obligation in § 1706, Congress also must have intended to insure that schools made a genuine and good faith effort, consistent with local circumstances and resources, to remedy the language deficiencies of their students and deliberately placed on federal courts the difficult responsibility of determining whether that obligation had been met.

. . . Confronted, reluctantly, with this type of task in this case, we have attempted to devise a mode of analysis which will permit ourselves and the lower courts to fulfill the responsibility Congress has assigned to us without unduly substituting our educational values and theories for the educational and political decisions reserved to state or local school authorities or the expert knowledge of educators.

In a case such as this one . . ., we believe that the responsibility of the federal court is threefold. First, the court must examine carefully the evidence the record contains concerning the soundness of the educational theory or principles upon which the challenged program is based. This, of course, is not to be done with any eye toward discerning the relative merits of sound but competing bodies of expert educational opinion, for choosing between sound but competing theories is properly left to the educators and public officials charged with responsibility for directing the educational policy of a school system. The state of the art in the area of language remediation may well be such that respected authorities legitimately differ as to the best type of educational program for limited-English-speaking students and we do not believe that Congress in enacting § 1703(f) intended to make the resolutions of these differences the province of federal courts. The court's responsibility, insofar as educational theory is concerned, is only to ascertain that a school system is pursuing a program informed by an educational theory recognized as sound by some experts in the field or, at least, deemed a legitimate experimental strategy.

The court's second inquiry would be whether the programs and practices actually used by a school system are reasonably calculated to implement effectively the educational theory adopted by the school. We do not believe that it may fairly be said that a school system is taking appropriate action to remedy language barriers if, despite the adoption of a promising theory, the system fails to follow through with practices, resources and personnel necessary to transform the theory into reality.

Finally, a determination that a school system has adopted a sound program for alleviating the language barriers impeding the educational progress of some of its students and made bona fide efforts to make the program work does not necessarily end the court's inquiry into the appropriateness of the system's actions. If a school's program, although premised on a legitimate educational theory and implemented through the use of adequate techniques, fails, after being employed for a period of time sufficient to give the plan a legitimate trial, to produce results indicating that the language barriers confronting students are actually being overcome, that program may, at that point, no longer constitute appropriate action as far as that school is concerned. We do not believe Congress intended that under § 1703(f) a school would be free to persist in a policy which, although it may have been "appropriate" when adopted, in the sense that there were sound expectations for success and bona fide efforts to make the program work, has, in practice, proved a failure.

* * *

In this case, the plaintiffs' challenge . . . does not rest on an argument over the soundness of the educational policy being pursued by the district, but rather on the alleged inadequacy of the program actually implemented by the district. Plaintiffs contend that in three areas essential to the adequacy of a bilingual program—curriculum, staff and testing—Raymondville falls short. Plaintiffs contend that although RISD purports to offer a bilingual education program in grades K–3, the district's curriculum actually overemphasizes the development of reading and writing skills in English to the detriment of education in other areas such as mathematics and science, and that, as a result, children whose first language was Spanish emerge from the bilingual education program behind their classmates in these other areas. . . .

Even if we accept this allegation as true, however, we do not think that a school system which provides limited-English-speaking students with a curriculum, during the early part of their school career, which has, as its primary objective, the development of literacy in English, has failed to fulfill its obligations under § 1703(f), even if the result of such a program is an interim sacrifice of learning in other areas during this period. The language of § 1703(f) speaks in terms of taking action "to overcome language barriers" which impede the "equal participation" of limited-English-speaking children in the regular instructional program. We believe the statute clearly contemplates that provision of a program placing primary emphasis on the development of English language skills would constitute "appropriate action."

Limited-English-speaking students entering school face a task not encountered by students who are already proficient in English. Since the number of hours in any school day is limited, some of the time which limited-English-speaking children will spend learning English may be devoted to other subjects by students who entered school already proficient in English. In order to be able ultimately to participate equally with the students who entered school with an English language background, the limited-English-speaking students will have to acquire both English language proficiency comparable to that of the average native speakers and to recoup any deficits which they may incur in other areas of the curriculum as a result of this extra expenditure of time on English language development. We understand § 1703(f) to impose on educational agencies not only an obligation to overcome the direct obstacle to learning which the language barrier itself poses, but also a duty to provide limited-English-speaking-ability students with assistance in other areas of the curriculum where their equal participation may be impaired because of deficits incurred during participation in an agency's language remediation program. If no remedial action is taken to overcome the academic deficits that limited-English-speaking students may incur during a period of intensive language training, then the language barrier, although itself remedied, might, nevertheless, pose a lingering and indirect impediment to these students' equal participation in the regular instructional program. We also believe, however, that § 1703(f) leaves schools free to determine whether they wish to discharge these obligations simultaneously, by implementing a program designed to keep limited-English-speaking students at grade level in other areas of the curriculum by providing instruction in their native language at the same time that an English language development effort is pursued, or to address these problems in sequence, by focusing first on the development of English language skills and then later providing students with compensatory and supplemental education to remedy deficiencies in other areas which they may develop during this period. . . . Therefore, we disagree with plaintiffs' assertion that a school system which chooses to focus first on English language development and later provides students with an intensive remedial program to help them catch up in other areas of the curriculum has failed to fulfill its statutory obligation under § 1703(f).

. . . [W]e are more troubled by the plaintiffs' allegations that the district's implementation of the program has been severely deficient in the area of preparing its teachers for bilingual education. . . . We begin by noting that any school district that chooses to fulfill its obligations under § 1703 by means of a bilingual education program has undertaken a responsibility to provide teachers who are able competently to teach in such a program. The record in this case indicates that some of the teachers employed in the RISD bilingual program have a very limited command of Spanish, despite completion of the TEA course. . . .

The record in this case thus raises serious doubts about the actual language competency of the teachers employed in bilingual classrooms by RISD and about the degree to which the district is making a genuine effort to assess and improve the qualifications of its bilingual teachers. As in any educational program, qualified teachers are a critical component of the success of a language remediation program. A bilingual education program, however sound in theory, is clearly unlikely to have a significant impact on the language barriers confronting limited-English-speaking school children, if the teachers charged with day-to-day responsibility for educating these children are termed "qualified" despite the fact that they operate in the classroom under their own unremedied language disability. The use of Spanish-speaking aides may be an appropriate interim measure, but such aides cannot, RISD acknowledges, take the place of qualified bilingual teachers. The record in this case strongly suggests that the efforts RISD has made to overcome the language barriers confronting many of the teachers assigned to the bilingual education program are inadequate. On this record, we think a finding to the contrary would be clearly erroneous. Nor can there be any question that deficiencies in the in-service training of teachers for bilingual classrooms seriously undermine the promise of the district's bilingual education program. Until deficiencies in this aspect of the program's implementation are remedied, we do not think RISD can be deemed to be taking "appropriate action" to overcome the language disabilities of its students. Although we certainly hope and expect that RISD will attempt to hire teachers who are already qualified to teach in a bilingual classroom as positions become available, we are by no means suggesting that teachers already employed by the district should be replaced or that the district is limited to hiring only teachers who are already qualified to teach in a bilingual program. We are requiring only that RISD undertake further measures to improve the ability of any teacher, whether now or hereafter employed, to teach effectively in a bilingual classroom.

* * *

The third specific area in which plaintiffs claim that RISD programs are seriously deficient is in the testing and evaluation of students having limited English proficiency. . . .

. . . Plaintiffs contend, RISD apparently does not deny, and we agree that proper testing and evaluation is essential in determining the progress of students involved in a bilingual program and ultimately, in evaluating the program itself. In their brief, plaintiffs contend that RISD's testing program is inadequate because the limited-English-speaking students in the bilingual program are not tested in their own language to determine their progress in areas of the curriculum other than English language literacy skills. Although during the bilingual program Spanish-speaking students receive much of their instruction in these other areas in the Spanish language, the achievement level of these students is tested, in part, by the use of standardized English language achievement tests. No standardized Spanish language tests are used. Plaintiffs contend that testing the achievement levels of children, who are admittedly not yet literate in English and are receiving instruction in another language, through the use of an English language achievement test, does not meaningfully assess their achievement, any more than it does their ability, a contention with which we can scarcely disagree.

Valid testing of students' progress in these areas is, we believe, essential to measure the adequacy of a language remediation program. The progress of limited-English-speaking students in these other areas of the curriculum must be measured by means of a standardized test in their own language because no other device is adequate to determine their progress vis-a-vis that of their English-speaking counterparts. . . . [T]hese students cannot be permitted to incur irreparable academic deficits during this period. Only by measuring the actual progress of students in these areas during the language remediation program can it be determined that such irremediable deficiencies are not being incurred. . . .

Finally plaintiffs contend that test results indicate that the limited-English-speaking students who participate in the district's bilingual education program do not reach a parity of achievement with students who entered school already proficient in English at any time throughout the elementary grades and that since the district's language program has failed to establish such parity, it cannot be deemed "appropriate action" under § 1703(f). Although this question was raised at the district court level, no findings were made on this claim. While under some circumstances it may be proper for a court to examine the achievement scores of students involved in a language remediation program in order to determine whether this group appears on the whole to attain parity of participation with other students, we do not think that such an inquiry is, as yet, appropriate with regard to RISD. Such an inquiry may become proper after the inadequacies in the implementation of the RISD's program, which we have identified, have been corrected and the program has operated with the benefit of these improvements for a period of time sufficient to expect meaningful results.

To summarize, we affirm the district court's conclusion that RISD's bilingual education program is not violative of Title VI; however, we reverse the district court's judgment with respect to the other issues presented on appeal and we remand these issues for further proceedings not inconsistent with this opinion. . . .

NOTES AND QUESTIONS

1. **Castaneda:** ***Scope of the Decision***

Is the court correct to question the continuing vitality of *Lau*—to insist that Title VI, like the Fourteenth Amendment, requires a showing of intentional discrimination and not just discriminatory impact? *See Guardians Association v. Civil Service Commission*, chapter 5, *supra*.

How does the court read the statutory language that requires school districts to take "appropriate action to overcome language barriers"? Does the legislation require the court to become the arbiter of educational effectiveness—to assess "the soundness of educational theory," the relationship between theory and practice, and the success of the venture? Is this an appropriate judicial role? Is it consistent with the approach that the Supreme Court took to educational policy in *Rodriguez* (chapter 6) and *Rowley*, *supra?*

The court notes that "[l]ow test scores may well reflect many obstacles to learning other than language" and acknowledges, with becoming understatement, that "the process of delineating the causes . . . may well be a complicated one." Suppose the test scores of limited-English-proficient students start out, and remain, well below those of the native-language population. What remedy would then be appropriate? Section B, *infra*, discusses these policy questions in greater detail.

2. Monolingual Teachers and Limited English-Proficient Students

In *Teresa P. v. Berkeley Unified School District*, 724 F.Supp. 698 (N.D.Cal. 1989), a law reform group, the Multicultural Education Training and Advocacy Project (META), challenged the school district's approach to teaching limited-English-proficient students. The district offered transitional bilingual instruction for Spanish- and Cantonese-speaking elementary school children, and English as a Second Language (ESL) instruction to other language groups in elementary school and to all secondary school students. The ESL teachers were not bilingual. The California Education Department interprets federal law as mandating "equality of educational achievement," when limited-English-proficient and native English speakers are compared.

META argued that without any instruction in their native tongues, students would not develop their academic skills while learning English. The district court, following *Castaneda*, held that federal law "does not require school districts to adopt a specific educational theory or implement an ideal academic program"; instead, it leaves local officials "substantial latitude. . . ." *See also Gomez v. Illinois State Board of Education*, 811 F.2d 1030 (7th Cir. 1987). What is required is that the program be supported by a plausible pedagogical theory—of which, given the uncertain state of the art, there are many—and that it actually teach English to limited-English-proficient children. If the students do not suffer "permanent or irreparable" academic harm while learning English, courts will not intervene. Moreover, the court declared that specialized credentials for teachers are not required, for "good teachers are good teachers no matter what the educational challenge may be."

Berkeley enrolls 571 limited-English-proficient students, out of a total enrollment of approximately 8,000, and they are spread through the district's schools. No fewer than thirty-eight languages—among them Farsi, Samoan, and Armenian—are represented among the 571 students. What bearing, if any, should these facts have on the nature of the school district's legal obligation to provide bilingual instruction? *Compare Zambrano v. Oakland Unified School District*, No. 584503-9 (Alameda Superior Court, May 1, 1985), discussed in Moran, "Bilingual Education as a Status Conflict," 75 *Calif. L. Rev.* 321, 335–38 (1984).

3. *Language and Community*

The Hutterite community, which emigrated to the United States a century ago, still speaks Tyrolean German (a combination of sixteenth-century German and twentieth-century anglicizations); only the Hutterites speak this language. This language is retained for religious reasons, for reasons of cultural tradition, and to foster a separate sense of identity. Hutterite children growing up in the community speak only Tyrolean German.

To what remedy, if any, are the Hutterites entitled under Federal law: a bilingual program, a bilingual-bicultural program, a publicly run school operated by the community to preserve the children's sense of cultural identity? How, if at all, is *Wisconsin v. Yoder*, discussed in chapter 1, relevant? *See Deerfield Hutterian Association v. Ipswich Board of Education*, 468 F.Supp. 1219 (D.S.D. 1979).

4. *The Conflict with Desegregation*

Because special assistance for the limited-English-proficient requires some separation, such programs potentially conflict with desegregation decrees. For a discussion of the fit between bilingual instruction and desegregation, *see United States v. Texas*, 680 F.2d 356 (5th Cir. 1982); *Morgan v. Kerrigan*, 401 F.Supp. 216 (D.Mass. 1975), *aff'd*, 530 F.2d 401 (1st Cir. 1976); Roos, "Bilingual Education: The Hispanic Response to Unequal Educational Opportunity," 42 *Law & Contemp. Probs.* 111 (1978). *Compare Cintron v. Brentwood Union Free School District*, 455 F.Supp. 57 (E.D.N.Y. 1978). *See also* the discussion in chapter 5 of desegregation in tri-ethnic school districts.

B. Policy and Politics

1. Introduction: The Persisting Controversy. There is apparently very little about the education of limited-English-proficient students that could be described as uncontroversial. Should bilingual education be transitional? Should students be placed in the English language mainstream? Should the goal be the development of full academic competency? Is the goal to maintain (or in some instances to foster) competency in the students' native language and/or native culture? Debated too, as the cases suggest, are the techniques, which range from native language instruction to classes conducted entirely in English. The following excerpt speaks to the passions aroused by bilingualism:

> It came as a surprise to residents of San Diego when a county grand jury last year recommended that all

local school districts eliminate bilingual education, arguing that such programs are "impractical, expensive and, in a sense, un-American."

County supervisors eventually decided not to act on the suggestion. But even now, Jess D. Haro, chairman of the Chicano Federation, a local Hispanic civil rights group that strongly supports bilingual education, finds the episode rankling.

"The issue here is not simply bilingual education," he said. "There is a backlash, an attitude that minorities are getting too much for nothing, and that kind of racist, chauvinist thinking continues to see bilingual education as something wasteful and unpatriotic."

Perhaps no aspect of education policy in the United States excites political passions more than bilingual education. With thousands of jobs and several billion dollars in Federal and state funds at stake, bilingual education has become the center of a struggle that has divided educators, produced unlikely alliances and raised fundamental social issues.

One underlying issue is the "assimilation versus segregation" debate. Although many supporters of bilingual education say the "sink or swim" model of language education that prevailed in the first decades of this century should not apply today, they make it clear that they want newcomers brought into the nation's cultural mainstream.

"There is unanimity that these children should learn English," said James J. Lyons, legislative counsel for the National Association for Bilingual Education. "The real question is how to make sure they are learning other subjects while they learn English."

But those assurances have not convinced the most vocal critics of bilingual education. They argue that what they call the "bilingual lobby" has a hidden political agenda whose objective is to create unassimilated language-minority islands within America's English-speaking sea.

"What else can a guy like Lyons say when he has to go to Congress every year for new money?" asked Gerda Bikales, executive director of U.S. English, one of the most active of the groups opposed to bilingual education. "He can't very well go up on the Hill and say 'I'm against assimilation.' "

Those concerns are fed by the fact that some bilingual programs have, over the last decade or so, evolved into bicultural programs aimed at encouraging children to retain their native tongue and their ethnic identity. And both the proponents and the opponents of bilingual-education programs also say that lurking behind the debate is the explosive question of political power, with activists on each side accusing the other of trying to keep non-English speakers from participating fully in the nation's political and civic life.

"It's a question of empowerment, of bringing people into the process," Mr. Lyons said. "Bilingual education has effectively opened the schoolhouse door to hundreds of thousands of parents who historically have been locked out."

Opponents of current programs, on the other hand, see them as ploys designed to keep language minorities beholden to ethnic politicians who want to maintain their traditional control of voting blocs.

"Dependence on the home language tends to isolate the group and make it more manipulable," said Robert Rossier, a retired language teacher who is on the Department of Education's National Advisory and Coordinating Council on Bilingual Education. "Immigrants who learn English move closer culturally to the general society and even become assimilated, making political control difficult."

One sign of the complexity of the debate is the unusual political alliances it has created. The president of the American Federation of Teachers, Albert Shanker, a persistent critic of most education policies of the Reagan Administration, said last month, for example, that Secretary of Education William J. Bennett was "dead right" with his plan to give wider latitude to local school districts in choice of bilingual teaching methods.

"The fact is that there is no proven method" of bilingual education that guarantees English fluency, Mr. Shanker said. "And I don't think that Uncle Sam or anybody else ought to be shoving a particular message down anybody's throats."

At the same time, bilingual education also has disrupted traditional political coalitions, such as between blacks and Hispanics. In a study published last month, the Institute for Puerto Rican Policy said that "blacks in general have not been receptive to the introduction" of bilingual education and then offered reasons for the lack of support.

The study concluded, first of all, that many blacks believe that "bilingual programs in the schools would divert scarce funds away from much-needed compensatory programs for black children" at a time when the Administration is looking for budget cuts. In addition, the study noted, "blacks also found themselves in conflict with demands for bilingual education that require, by definition, a high degree of segregation of non-English-speaking students."

To some who advocate strengthening bilingual education, Mr. Shanker's endorsement of the Bennett plan came as no surprise. They argue that teachers' unions around the nation see bilingual programs as a threat to the jobs of their members, the vast majority of whom speak only English.

"Bilingual education is the political stepsister of community control in Mr. Shanker's view," Mr. Lyons said. "The two issues are locked together in his mind, and in this case he is trying to protect monolingual English-language teachers from parents."

Mr. Shanker has said that his primary concern is insuring that students receive an effective education. But there is no question that many teachers view bilingual education as a potentially threatening issue.

"We get letters from teachers saying 'I'm going to lose my job because I don't speak a foreign language, and I never thought I'd see that happen in America,' " said Ricardo Martinez, a policy analyst for the House Committee on Education and Labor in Washington. "That begins to build up a great resentment in the teachers' union."

The preoccupation over job assignments and qualifying procedures cuts two ways. Critics argue that many teachers hired for "bilingual" positions are unqualified for their jobs because of their limited command of English.

"Many so-called bilingual teachers are actually monolingual in their native tongue, as I found in my experience as a teacher in an inner-city school," said Eileen Gardner, education policy analyst for the conservative Heritage Foundation. "I was stunned to find groups of teachers who spoke Spanish exclusively and whose English was quite halting."

In turn, English-primary teachers are terrified to find that they may suddenly be required to learn, sometimes in mid-career, and teach in a new language. That leads some to fear they may be forced to make way for native speakers of foreign languages if they do not adapt.

"The growth of the school population is primarily among people who are not native English speakers, and there are teachers who fear they will be replaced," said Mrs. Bikales, of U.S. English. "There are also teachers who feel threatened because they have to take courses in Cambodian."

To the antibilingual activists, this smacks of patronage and the growth of a costly and inefficient "bilingual support" industry. They argue that the rise of bilingual education has created a demand for bilingual publishing materials, consultants, certifying boards and administrators, who they say have a vested interest in maintaining bilingual programs, even when they may not be needed.

"This thing is definitely seen as a pipeline to Federal money," Mrs. Bikales said. "The attitude is that 'this is our little pot of gold, our little preserve'."

"The game is to get large numbers of students in these programs and to maintain them there," Mr. Rossier said. "That is what creates the jobs and the political power."

"If schools are encouraged to experiment with other options and then move students into the mainstream as soon as possible, you will see a reduction in jobs for bilingual-education teachers," Dr. Gardner said.

For their part, backers of bilingual education charge the Reagan Administration is trying to strangle the program financially.

They say claims that bilingual education has failed result in part from the fact that there is not enough money to reach all the children who need such programs.

"That's because of the way the money is used," Mrs. Bikales retorted. "So much of the money goes to institutionalized things, such as support departments and Ph.D. candidates doing research. So much of it goes to training, evaluation and research that very little is left for the children."

More than twenty states have legislation promoting some form of bilingual education, but the debate is most heated in California, with its huge Hispanic and Asian populations.

"It's a big business in this state," Mr. Rossier said. "Chicano politicians see bilingual education as a big issue and feel it is going to control their political destinies for years."

"There is a tremendous amount of empire building going on," Mr. Rossier added. "These people want to continue this sort of thing and will do anything to hold on to what they've got."

Mr. Lyons, on the other hand, accuses the antibilingual lobby of trying to arouse "nativist passions in a lot of communities, not so much in the schools as on elected boards of education." In the process, he and other bilingual-education proponents say genuine pedagogical concerns end up being submerged by fear of foreigners and by political opportunism.

"It's an opportunity to scare the local yokels," Mr. Martinez said. "It makes good headlines everywhere."

But both sides agree that as the debate rages on, the problems continue to grow.

"In spite of all this discussion, people are moving into urban areas," Mr. Martinez said. "They show up on your doorstep, and you have to do something about it. There are hundreds of thousands of kids who can't understand English, so what are you going to do?"

Rohter, "The Politics of Bilingualism," *New York Times*, November 10, 1985, § 12, p. 46.

This debate has been carried out on the federal level, most notably by former Education Secretary William Bennett. In a 1985 address to the Association for a Better New York, published in 1 *La Raza L. Rev.* 213 (1986), Bennett argues that "we expect our schools to help teach all of our students English, the common language that will enable them to participate fully in our political, economic, and social life." While "pride in one's heritage is natural and commendable . . . the responsibility of the federal government must be to help ensure that local schools succeed in teaching non-English students English." That was the original purpose of the Bilingual Education Act, says Bennett, claiming that it has become so " 'perverted and politicized' that . . . English has been sort of thinned out and stretched out and in many cases banished into the mists and all of the courses tended to be taught in Spanish." Methods of instruction may well vary, Bennett declares, "but the goal of any method should be clear: Fluency in English." *See also*, R. Porter, *Forked Tongue* (1990).

Not surprisingly, many Hispanic scholars took strong exception. Replying in the same issue of *La Raza Law Journal* (1 *La Raza L. J.* 225 (1986)), Lori Orum and Raul Yzaguirre argue that Bennett is too narrow in his focus on English language instruction for those who don't speak the language—that the "total educational well-being of limited-English proficient children" is the government's responsibility.

It is not entirely clear that Bennett would disagree with this assessment; the real difference may be the fear, on the part of Orum and Yzaguirre, that Bennett is upsetting a delicate bipartisan consensus and would "substantially reduce the amount of federal support available for bilingual education." *See generally* Moran, "Bilingual Education as a Status Conflict," 75 *Calif. L. Rev.* 321 (1987). Of concern, too, is the perception that Bennett's position may give aid and comfort to those who promote the English-only cause, in schools as well as in the society generally. *See, e.g.*, Hernandez-Chavez, "Language Policy and Language Rights in the United States," in T. Kangas and J. Cummins, eds., *From Shame to Struggle: Language Policy and Language Rights* 42 (1989); K. Kahuta, *Mirror of Language: The Debate on Bilingualism* (1986); D. Lamm and G. Imhoff, *The Immigration Time Bomb: The Fragmenting of America* (1985); N. Glazer, *Ethnic Dilemmas* (1983); Tanton, "Bilingual Education: Is It Threatening to Divide the United States Along Language Lines?" *Vital Issues* 1 (Nov. 1984).

2. The Contribution of Research. Both Bennett, on the one side, and Orum and Yzaguirre on the other, call upon educational research to support their respective positions. To Bennett, "no research [has] established the superiority of [bilingual instruction] to any of the other possible educational methods, methods which placed greater emphasis on English. For there was—and is—no evidence of such superiority." *See also* Porter, *supra*. Orum and Yzaguirre see matters differently. While they note that the evidence is mixed, they are more inclined to fault the researchers than the bilingual programs.

This is familiar news. Three years after the Office of Civil Rights issued its memorandum specifying remedies that a school district might adopt to comply with *Lau*—the so-called *Lau* guidelines—a study prepared for HEW by the American Institutes for Research (AIR), *Education of the Impact of ESEA Title VII Spanish/English Bilingual Education Program* (1978), sharply criticized the program. It concluded: (1) in English, participation in a bilingual education project did not produce gains in achievement above what would be expected had the students been assigned to a traditional classroom; indeed, in several grades the non-participating students made slightly greater gains; (2) in mathematics, students participating in an ESEA Title VII project had achievement gains approximately equal to those of non-Title VII students; and (3) while Hispanic students showed improvement in Spanish reading, the extent to which such gains should be attributed to the program was not clear.

The AIR report in turn produced substantial critical reaction, mostly leveled at its methodology. The Center for Applied Linguistics, for example, notes: (1) the report aggregates very different programs and populations, thus cancelling out the positive effects of good programs; (2) the short (five-month) period between pre-test and post-test makes findings concerning the lack of achievement gains unreliable; (3) the "comparison groups" were never tested for comparability at the outset of the study, and they may have started with substantial differences in achievement.

More than a decade after the AIR Report, there is no consensus on the efficacy of bilingual instruction.

"The Social Science Evidence on Bilingual Education"

C. Rossell, J. Ross, 15 J. of Law & Educ. 385, 406, 411–14 (1986).

There are two characteristics of the research and writing on bilingual education which stand out. The first is that much of it consists of local evaluations with inadequate research designs. . . .

The second characteristic of the research is that, as is common with controversial social programs with egalitarian goals, the evaluators and those who review and integrate the research, are also passionate advocates of bilingual education for political or ideological reasons. The disgraceful treatment of linguistic minorities in this country . . . may have influenced many social scientists, bilingual education lawyers, and reviewers of the research to believe that any policy which ignores the mother tongue in favor of English is racist, and any policy which maintains the mother tongue, however inadequately, is equitable. This has created an atmosphere in which it is difficult for an academic to criticize current policy in this field. It has also created an atmosphere in which it is all too easy to interpret flawed studies as support for bilingual education and to reject or ignore competent, relevant studies with conflicting findings. . . .

Our discussion is centered on analyzing a program whose avowed goal is to "transition" non-English speaking students from their native tongue to English and to produce the highest English language achievement of which that student is capable. We are quite aware that is a politically-influenced goal which may not be a particularly desirable one. Indeed, if the issue were a purely pedagogical one, we would probably be discussing how best to bolster the linguistic advantage of speakers of other languages instead of how to transition them from potential bilingualism into assured monolingualism. But the supporters of transitional bilingual education have not disputed the goal of the program and thus our task is to evaluate whether it achieves that goal. In our conclusions we discuss other goals such as bilingual maintenance. . . .

We believe that the most thorough and intelligent review of the research to date is Baker and de Kanter[47] and Baker and Pelavin.[48] Unlike most other reviews of the research, they have taken the time to examine the details of each study and to assess each against the standards of the scientific model. Baker and de Kanter concluded that schools *can* improve the achievement level of language-minority children through special programs, but that the case for the effectiveness of transitional bilingual education is so weak that exclusive reliance on this instructional method is clearly not justified. This review has, of course, been subjected to much criticism as typically occurs when one departs from the conventional wisdom.[49]

If we only consider the studies which assess alternative second language programs and are of good methodological quality—characterized by random assignment to a treatment and control group, or statistical control for pretreatment differences between groups where random assignment is not possible—there is still—no consistent research support for transitional bilingual education as a superior instructional practice for improving the English language achievement of limited-English-proficient children. . . .*

* * *

In second language learning twenty-nine percent of the studies show transitional bilingual education to be superior, twenty-one percent show it to be inferior, and fifty percent show it to be no different

47. K. Baker & A. de Kanter, *Effectiveness of Bilingual Education: A Review of the Literature* (1981); K. Baker & A. de Kanter, "Federal Policy and the Effectiveness of Bilingual Education," in *Bilingual Education* 34 (K. Baker & A. de Kanter, eds., 1983); K. Baker and A. de Kanter, "An Answer from Research on Bilingual Education," 19 *Am. Educ.* 40 (1983); K. Baker & A. de Kanter, "Response to Evaluation and Incrementalism: The AIR Report and ESEA *Title VII*," 6 *Educ. Eval. & Pol. Anal.* 189 (1984).

48. *See* K. Baker & S. Pelavin, *Problems in Bilingual Education Evaluation* (1984) (Paper presented at annual meeting of American Educational Research Association, New Orleans, La.).

49. The Baker and de Kanter review has been subjected to several critiques [S. Seidner, *Political Expedience or Educational Research: An Analysis of Baker and de Kanter's Review of the Literature on Bilingual Education* (1981) (National Clearinghouse for Bilingual Education, Rosslyn, Va.); Willig, "The Effectiveness of Bilingual Education: Review of a Report," 6 *Nabe J.* 1 (1981–82); E. Hernandez-Chavez, et al., *The Federal Policy Towards Language and Education, Pendulum or Progress? A Response to the de Kanter/Baker Review* (1982) (California State Univ., Sacramento, Cal.); J. Yates, et al., *Baker de Kanter Review: Inappropriate Conclusions on the Efficacy of Bilingual Education* (Dec. 1982) (University of Texas, Austin, Tex.)]. The kindest thing that can be said of the Hernandez-Chavez, *et al.*, critique is that the document they describe bears no resemblance to the one we read. The main argument of the Seidner critique is that because bilingual education programs vary so much, anyone who attempts to draw negative policy conclusions from the program evaluations is a charlatan. . . .

The most thoughtful critique of Baker and de Kanter is Willig's. Although she characterizes Baker and de Kanter's conclusions inaccurately and criticizes them for failing to conduct a meta-analysis . . ., she does raise some important questions with regard to systematic biases in the program which make it difficult to evaluate. However, this still does not negate Baker and de Kanter's main conclusion that there is no evidence to support TBE.

* *See generally*, R. Porter, *Forked Tongue* (1990).

from submersion—doing nothing. Altogether, seventy-one percent show TBE to be no different or worse than the supposedly discredited submersion techniques. In math, seven percent of the studies show TBE to be superior, twenty-seven show it to be inferior, and sixty-seven percent show it to be no different from TBE. Altogether ninety-three percent of the studies show it to be no different or worse than the supposedly discredited submersion technique in developing math proficiency. . . .

* * *

Baker and de Kanter were not the first to discover the emperor has no clothes. How then to conclude, as so many have in and out of court, that transitional bilingual education is superior? One technique, used by Zappert and Cruz, is to simply redefine the word. As they argue:

> No significant difference should not be interpreted as a negative finding for bilingual education. . . . When one adds the fact that students in bilingual education classrooms learn two languages, their native language and a second language, one can conclude that a statistically non-significant finding demonstrates the positive advantages of bilingual education.

The main argument made for transitional bilingual education in the court decisions and the regulations, however, is that it produces *greater* English language achievement and content area mastery than doing nothing, not the same achievement. Doing nothing is assumed to be a fourteenth amendment violation that transitional bilingual education will *remedy*. . . .

. . . We think that the advocates of bilingual education may have made an unwarranted inferential leap from two undisputed findings of the research on second language learning: 1) children can transfer skills learned in one language to another language, and 2) older children are more "efficient" (i.e., faster) learners of languages (contrary to popular belief). Hence, when researchers observed that older learners who already knew how to read in their native tongue were acquiring a second language faster than younger learners, they erroneously argued that the causal variable was native tongue reading ability rather than age.

In fact, however, . . . there is absolutely no evidence that students can learn a second language *better* if they learn to read in their native tongue first. Indeed, the Canadian experiments in immersion and bilingual education show just the opposite. The later immersion English-Canadian students who had first learned to read in English were ultimately surpassed in French, when compared to the French native speakers, by the early immersion students who had first learned to read in French. . . . [W]e know of no educational theory that would suggest this process is cognitively different for non-English speakers learning English. . . . Virtually every analysis of second language learning has agreed that the length of time spent in language study is, all other things being equal, far and away the single greatest predictor of achievement in that language. . . . Rarely, however, is any of the vast body of research and theory on second language learning introduced into the bilingual education cases. The bilingual education advocates have effectively limited the focus of the testimony to compensatory education issues.

* * *

[O]ne of the most glaring deficiencies in the bilingual education court decisions is the failure of the courts to consider such promising alternatives to transitional bilingual education structured [as immersion in English]. The bilingual education advocates have limited the debate since *Lau* so that the controversy in any court case is over the violation. Once a violation is determined, typically only one remedy is considered desirable. The question then is the extent to which a school district has the resources to implement fully a transitional bilingual education program. Rarely, if ever, is structured immersion discussed as a viable alternative because the bilingual education advocates have effectively dismissed the Canadian experiments and prevented all but a few structured immersion experiments in this country.

* * *

What little good research there is suggests the advocates of transitional bilingual education have done a disservice to limited-English-proficient children by selling them half a loaf under the guise of a whole one. Contrary to the impression given by most court decisions, there is no consistent evidence that transitional bilingual education is the best way to improve the English language proficiency of limited-English-proficient children, nor the best way to make them or keep them bilingual. It seems to us that children who spend half their day being educated in their native tongue for three years and then all their time in the second language after that will not be very bilingual when they graduate many years later, and they will have lost one and one-half years of English language learning time.

One of the many serious limitations of the research on bilingual education and the programs themselves, however, is that no one looks at the future educational success of graduates of bilingual or immersion programs, as well as their life chances. It is quite possible, for example, that *maintenance* bilingual education, that is, bilingual education for an entire school career, reduces English language achievement in comparison to educating a child in the regular English language classroom or structured immersion, but increases life chances for these students. This is because it might produce greater native tongue ability resulting in greater economic gains in later life than would be predicted from the English language achievement of these students.

Even if this does not increase one's life chances in any material way, it certainly ought to do so in an intellectual sense. While there are problems . . . with the analyses that conclude bilingualism increases cognitive development, at the very least being able to converse in another language is a valuable skill. Rather than viewing limited-English-proficient children as a burden, perhaps we ought to view them as an opportunity to develop bilingual adults.

There are two elements of consumer protection, however, which are critical for the courts to consider if they are to adequately protect the rights of limited-English-proficient children. First, not every limited-English-proficient child will want to, or be able to, maintain their mother tongue. Nor should they be forced to do so by the courts and other policymakers. Second, children and their parents must be advised as to the probable consequences of being raised bilingually within the constraints of the normal school day. Such children will be like decathlon athletes and it is false advertising to promise them they will not only win the decathlon, but also come in first in each individual event against those who specialize in it. Unfortunately, that is what bilingual education advocates have been promising primarily because that is what the courts and other policymakers have been demanding.

Obviously, then, bilingual maintenance programs will be most successful in increasing life chances if . . . time in both languages is increased by either increasing the length of the normal school day and school year, or by cutting out non-academic subjects. In the latter case, such students would become academic specialists.

Of course, limited-English-proficient students in immersion programs could also benefit from an extended school day or year. There is no reason why the courts should not order "compensatory" education that truly compensates children for the time they have lost. If children are deficient in English, they should have more rather than the same amount or less of English language instruction. If English fluent children attend school for five hours, then limited-English-proficient children should attend it for six or seven. That is truly a remedy which compensates children for a fourteenth amendment violation.

Both a structured immersion and a bilingual maintenance curriculum should include a strong bicultural program in order to produce the greatest achievement gains and equal status intergroup contact. This is an area in which the courts have been reluctant to intervene, but one in which their involvement is greatly needed since it is the one issue which the school districts are most likely to ignore. . . .

* * *

This review has discussed the use of social science research in bilingual educational equity cases and the federal policymaking process and its policy implications. The court cases and OCR negotiations have been characterized by the mutual belief on the part of the plaintiffs and the defendants that transitional bilingual education is the best method of solving the English language achievement problems of limited-English-proficient children. The plaintiffs typically argue that its failure to do so in the defendant school district is a function of bad implementation. The school districts often contend that numbers are at the heart of the matter. They simply cannot afford to provide this "superior" instructional technique to every child who needs it.

The research, however, does not support transitional bilingual education as a superior instructional technique for increasing the English language achievement of limited-English-proficient children. Indeed, despite the general acceptance by the courts that submersion or doing nothing has failed, it fares no worse than transitional bilingual education.

We believe the most promising technique is structured immersion with bilingual, same ethnic group teachers, because this fulfills both the cognitive and psychological needs of limited-English-proficient children. There really need to be more planned variation experiments, however, before the courts would be willing to order such programs implemented. One area which the courts have almost completely ignored is the non-academic domain. Any special language program should be combined with a bicultural program and team learning to produce equal status contact and the greatest achievement gains for low achieving students.

The research does not support transitional bilingual education as a superior instructional technique for maintaining the mother tongue either. We would argue that the best way to do that is through a bilingual maintenance program composed of self-selected eager language learners willing to make the trade-offs that such an education will entail for the reward of being bilingual. This, however, is an educational and social policy concern, not a legal issue, and thus the courts will probably have little to say about it.

NOTES AND QUESTIONS

1. The Meaning of Equal Opportunity for Limited-English-Proficient Children

Consider again, in the light of the discussion of the research, the issue posed at the beginning of this section: What is the meaning of equal opportunity for children whose native language is not English? Bilingualism? Fluency in English? Pride in native culture? Acculturation? Suppose, as Rossell and Ross suggest, that there are trade-offs among these goals—that, for instance, a student who has maintained his or her native language through in-school instruction may be weaker in English than one instructed entirely in that language. But what if bilingualism brings an economic advantage? A cultural advantage? Which is the correct policy goal? Which is the goal set by the legislation?

2. The Research and the Judges

Though Rossell and Ross apply the calipers of social science to the research on bilingual education, they obviously do not have the last word on the subject. Partly, this is because of problems in research design; partly, it is due to the inherently politicized nature of the issue. How, if at all, should judges make use of such research? Is research, for instance, what underlies the willingness of the judge in *Teresa P.* to approve an instructional program that relies heavily on immersion as a pedagogical technique?

3. Research, Ideology, and Policy: The Complexities of Implementation

In "The Politics of Discretion: Federal Intervention in Bilingual Education," 76 *Calif. L. Rev.* 1249 (1988), Rachel Moran looks at the policy options available in this politically charged, research-deficient universe. In assessing Professor Moran's discussion of discretion-limiting and discretion-enhancing federal policy, recall the arguments developed by Richard Elmore in the first section of the chapter. Keep in mind, too, the feasibility of what Moran is proposing.

"The Politics of Discretion: Federal Intervention in Bilingual Education"

R. Moran, © 1988 by California Law Review, Inc. Reprinted from *California Law Review*, Vol. 76, pp. 1249, 1315–25, 1333–42, 1346–51. Reprinted by permission.

. . . Linguistic minority parents and community leaders, federal civil rights officials, and experts advocating native-language instruction—all have questioned the good faith and sensitivity of state and local educators. These groups have assumed that abuses of discretion are readily identifiable, that instances of misconduct arise through official malfeasance in an otherwise adequate school system, and that such wrongs can be ameliorated after the fact by limiting discretion. Under this view, discretion must be curbed to achieve corrective justice; that is, the wrongdoer must be punished and the victim's harm rectified through the constraints imposed.

Title VI and the EEOA [Equal Educational Opportunity Act] have been the primary vehicles for advancing the corrective justice rationale. The harshness of the potential sanctions reflects the moral egregiousness of the wrong. School officials are not being punished for a mere lapse of judgment; they are guilty of a serious abuse of discretion.

The corrective justice rationale underlying Title VI and the EEOA creates several difficulties in formulating appropriate bilingual education policy. First, the corrective justice perspective presumes sufficient certainty about effective teaching techniques for NEP [non-English-proficient] and LEP [limited-English-proficient] students to label some curricular choices as an abuse of discretion. Yet, because of ambiguity regarding the purposes of bilingual education and conflicting evidence on program effectiveness, it is often difficult to classify decisions as improper.

Second, the corrective justice approach emphasizes that bias or insensitivity has tainted school policy and practices in ways that have impaired the education of linguistic minority students. . . . [T]he proponents fail to consider whether even unbiased state and local decisionmaking processes exhibit systemic deficiencies that disadvantage NEP and LEP students.

Third, a corrective justice model narrowly focuses on retrospective reforms. This approach does not explicitly acknowledge the need for prospective policies to improve decisionmaking; rather, constraints are imposed only after past discrimination has been demonstrated and are intended to rectify some instance of official wrongdoing. . . .

To justify federal intervention, proponents of the corrective justice rationale have relied on an apparent consensus about the benefits of native-language instruction for NEP and LEP students. Based on this consensus, corrective justice advocates have established a presumption that other curricular choices are necessarily inferior and therefore discriminatory. Oddly enough, however, this view has coexisted with the Bilingual Education Act, which has recognized the considerable uncertainty associated with evaluating programs to educate linguistic minorities. Thus, the corrective justice perspective and the experimental orientation of the Act make diametrically opposite assumptions about the extent of pedagogical uncertainty. As a result, program requirements under the Bilingual Education Act have shifted according to which viewpoint was more powerful. For example, in 1974, civil rights advocates pressing for corrective justice moved to limit curricular choices under the Act.

When the highly influential AIR evaluation accentuated the uncertainties associated with the education of NEP and LEP children, these efforts to limit curricular choices under the Act failed.

The breakdown of pedagogical consensus deeply eroded the corrective justice rationale. First, pedagogical uncertainty undercut prescriptive devices, such as the *Lau* Guidelines, that forced state and local educators to adopt particular instructional techniques. More importantly, though, this uncertainty vitiated the moral force of federal intervention by making proof of wrongdoing more difficult. In the face of considerable uncertainty, federal policymakers could no longer easily identify a particular curricular choice as an abuse of discretion meriting strong federal sanctions. After all, there was at least some pedagogical authority for a wide array of instructional programs. . . .

* * *

Because the corrective justice approach makes state and local abuses the theoretical linchpin of federal intervention, it should require particularized determinations of wrongdoing before imposing constraints on discretion. Case-by-case evaluation, however, is extremely time-consuming and expensive. Impoverished, underrepresented linguistic minority communities do not command the resources necessary to undertake extensive policing. Overworked federal civil rights officials are also ill-equipped to shoulder this burden.

Consequently, OCR drafted the *Lau* Guidelines to simplify its policing obligations. Without regard to unique local circumstances, the Guidelines created standards for compliance with Title VI in school districts with significant numbers of NEP and LEP students. By divorcing remedies from specific instances of official wrongdoing, the Guidelines shifted the federal government's approach from rectifying particular abuses to alleviating systematic deficiencies in meeting linguistic minority students' needs. The Guidelines thus departed from a corrective justice rationale that treated wrongdoing as particularized misconduct; instead, they embraced a perspective that presupposed a systemic failure of state and local decisionmaking processes.

[T]he preoccupation with official wrongdoing under a corrective justice rationale fails to account fully for widespread structural inadequacies in local decisionmaking processes. . . .

. . . [A]dvocates of the corrective justice model have encountered obstacles to devising appropriate relief. First, there remains ambiguity about the primary purpose of relief: Is it to punish the wrongdoer, to compensate the victim, or to accomplish other desirable social objectives as well? For example, one possible sanction under Title VI and the EEOA is cutting off federal funds. Unfortunately, although such a sanction may punish the wrongdoer, it is unlikely to rectify the students' harms. If anything, such steps are apt to penalize, rather than benefit, the victims of past discrimination. Therefore, federal enforcement officers have created alternative devices, such as the *Lau* Guidelines, which are better calculated to meet NEP and LEP students' needs. These techniques, however, may not adequately punish the wrongdoer because although they constrain a school district's discretion, they also provide a substantial source of federal aid.

Even when a remedy is designed to compensate a class of victims, the courts have grappled with intractable difficulties in tailoring relief to fit the wrongdoing. When courts conclude that a school district has abused its discretion in designing the curriculum for NEP and LEP students, they typically find it impossible to discern the actual consequences of this misconduct. For example, if a district has not provided meaningful assistance to NEP and LEP students, how much has a child's educational development been hindered? How can this disadvantage be overcome? How long should a remedy be imposed to rectify these adverse consequences? . . .

In practice, courts generally have to rely on school districts to formulate programs that promise to provide meaningful access to the curriculum for all linguistic minority students. Although these plans must satisfy experts and attorneys who represent the interests of linguistic minority students, this process is still paradoxical from the standpoint of corrective justice. In effect, a district guilty of abusing its discretion is invited to exercise its discretion to craft the relief. Significantly, the school district's forte is making general educational policy, not doing corrective justice. In keeping with its organizational competency, a school district typically promulgates standards for meeting the needs of linguistic minority students as a whole; the plan does not attempt to classify victims based on the degree to which they have been injured by past discrimination. Thus, the remedial process ultimately fails to compensate commensurate with harm, instead promoting more general social objectives. . . .

* * *

Those who seek to constrain state and local discretion have assumed that school officials are unwilling to address fully NEP and LEP students' problems. By contrast, those who want to facilitate the exercise of state and local discretion have assumed that these officials are willing but unable to meet linguistic minority children's needs. Receptive to state and local educators' concerns about pedagogical uncertainties, some experts and federal officials in the educational bureaucracy have contended that school districts cannot work scholastic miracles with inadequate information, funding, and personnel. Under their view, devising a curriculum for NEP and LEP students requires school officials to weigh competing purposes and conflicting evidence about program effectiveness; state and local educators must inevitably exercise considerable discretion in fashioning a program. Precisely because the task is complex, decisionmakers need ample resources; yet, school districts often lack the data, financial support, and staff necessary to exercise discretion effectively. The federal government can provide resources to alleviate these impediments. The object of federal intervention under this revitalization rationale is not to do corrective justice, but to facilitate wise state and local policymaking. . . .

* * *

This goal of state and local revitalization stands in marked contrast to the corrective justice perspective. The corrective justice model presumes sufficient certainty to identify an abuse of discretion, but the revitalization approach asserts that there is so little certainty about the impact of bilingual education programs that it is counterproductive to promulgate hard-and-fast rules to limit state and local discretion. Moreover, while a corrective justice model treats instances of discrimination as particularized wrongdoing, a revitalization orientation treats resource limitations as a systemic problem for state and local officials. Finally, the corrective justice perspective adopts a retrospective orientation designed to remedy past wrongs; in contrast, the revitalization approach seeks prospective improvement of state and local decisionmaking processes. . . .

* * *

. . . Unfortunately, it is difficult to determine whether federal efforts have successfully enhanced the schools' ability to meet NEP and LEP students' needs because of pedagogical uncertainty. Ultimately, if there is no consensus about program objectives and efficacy, how can the federal government evaluate the soundness of state and local decisions?

The controversy that surrounded the AIR evaluation of federally funded programs illustrates the difficulties of measuring state and local performance under the revitalization approach. Without a clear consensus about program objectives, educational experts could not agree on the empirical measures to employ in evaluating "success." Those who considered the programs a means of promoting rapid English-acquisition emphasized English achievement test results. Others who treated the programs as a way of both promoting English-acquisition and preventing children from falling behind in other subjects examined results on both English achievement tests and achievement tests in other areas, such as mathematics. Those who viewed the programs as a means of enhancing a child's familiarity with and pride in native language and culture were concerned with native-language proficiency, self-esteem, and adjustment to school as well as academic achievement.

Even when experts agreed about the relevance of a particular program objective, they often disagreed about the appropriate methodology for assessing whether a program achieved the objective. . . .

* * *

The revitalization perspective presumes that state and local decisionmaking processes are sound, but their results are distorted by a lack of resources. . . . This view, however, overlooks a fundamental dilemma: Why do state and local policymakers consistently undersupport programs designed to meet NEP and LEP students' needs? A consistent failure to allocate sufficient resources to this group may well indicate problems in state and local decisionmaking processes.

Federal policymakers have tacitly acknowledged these underlying difficulties by insisting that the Bilingual Education Act remain a categorical grant-in-aid program, rather than being merged into a block grant program. The categorical grant earmarks funds for programs for NEP and LEP students; a block grant would permit state and local decisionmakers to allocate funds among a variety of other programs as well as those for linguistic minority children. . . .

The revitalization rationale raises other theoretical inconsistencies. If the federal government provides unconditional grants to state and local officials for a wide array of programs for NEP and LEP students, it merely enhances officials' ability to exercise discretion. If, however, the federal government offers funding with significant qualifications, it may influence and possibly control how state and local educators exercise their discretion. The revitalization perspective thus faces a perplexing problem: Can the federal government develop state and local capacity to exercise discretion without influencing unduly the substance of decisions? . . . [A]lthough designed to preserve state and local discretion, revitalization may in fact socialize officials to make decisions in accordance with federally acceptable values that limit state and local autonomy. . . .

* * *

. . . [B]ecause uncertainty about program objectives and effectiveness makes defining measures of "success" difficult, determining when state and local decisionmaking capacities have been restored sufficiently to permit withdrawal of federal support becomes speculative. This problem is aggravated because the revitalization approach makes no attempt to analyze why state and local decisionmakers have persistently underfunded programs for NEP and LEP students. Consequently, it is impossible to predict whether such programs will command adequate funding and staffing after federal support is withdrawn.

Whatever the approach adopted, national policymakers worry about the trade-off between the preservation of state and local autonomy and effective federal intervention on behalf of NEP and LEP students. Although federal policymakers have questioned the soundness of state and local decisionmaking regarding linguistic minority students, two important considerations have prompted them to be cautious about abrogating state and local discretion. First, state and local educators' sympathy for linguistic minority claims is typically secondary to a concern for their own decisionmaking prerogatives. . . . Second, federal decisionmakers are more certain about the measures needed to preserve state and local autonomy than they are about those necessary to promote linguistic minority students' educational achievement. Academics, lawyers, and government officials have long debated the merits of different approaches to federalism, and they consider themselves experts on how policy proposals will affect state and local autonomy. . . .

Even when federal policymakers find that involvement is entirely appropriate, their ongoing concern about preserving state and local discretion has often resulted in inattention to practical problems involved in implementing reforms. Federal intervention is merited where a consensus exists concerning national values, such as the elimination of racial or ethnic discrimination, or where the federal government is demonstrably better-equipped to execute a task, such as the coordination and dissemination of bilingual education research. Yet, even in these situations, implementation problems can stymie federal reform initiatives, leaving state and local discretion largely intact. . . .

* * *

To appreciate fully the trade-off between protecting state and local discretion and advancing the interests of linguistic minority students, federal decisionmakers must understand the nature of particular policy problems and the extent of federal intervention required. . . . To better address implementation concerns, federal policymakers must consider the variability of tasks that school districts face and the resulting richness of their bureaucratic structures. In this way, federal reformers can tailor both the degree and method of restricting local discretion to the particular characteristics of the problem addressed. . . .

* * *

Extensive federal regulations regarding curricular content and instructional methods make sense only where there is a high degree of consensus about program goals and effectiveness. Under these circumstances, a federal mandate can guide state and local officials without infringing on their ability to meet NEP and LEP students' needs. Moreover, such substantive rules can provide state and local officials with a welcome means of countering unjustified, parochial opposition. For example, if experts uniformly condemn harsh "no Spanish" rules and OCR declares such rules discriminatory under Title VI or the EEOA, state and local officials can refer to this federal action in resisting pressure to adopt such measures. . . .

* * *

In the face of substantial uncertainty regarding program objectives and effectiveness, comprehensive regulations are unworkable; they will accomplish little and merely limit state and local decisionmakers' ability to experiment and respond to new developments. Instead, the federal government should attempt to guarantee that state and local decisionmakers deal fairly with conflicts about program objectives. Federal policymakers can accomplish this task by establishing procedural rules that ensure that parents and community representatives have access to state and local decisionmaking processes and by providing for independent review of these parents' or representatives' complaints about exclusion. . . . To further guarantee procedural fairness, the federal government could require broader consultation with affected community groups as well as parental advisory councils, develop more specific guidelines about the consultative process, and create a mechanism to review the adequacy of parental and community involvement. These measures would ensure that state and local decisionmakers fully consider competing values in formulating programs for NEP and LEP students. . . .

* * *

In addition, the federal government should attempt to reduce uncertainty about program effectiveness through further research and evaluation. Before undertaking such an investigation, however, federal officials must ascertain whether the uncertainties in question are methodological in nature or derive from conflicting values. For example, research under the Bilingual Education Act was designed to identify instructional techniques that promote English acquisition and other academic skills for NEP and LEP students. Much of the debate on the subsequent findings addressed whether programs should promote English acquisition alone or maintain the child's native language and culture as well. These uncertainties about normative objectives are not susceptible to empirical resolution.

The federal government can also encourage the sound exercise of discretion by providing training for state and local personnel who make decisions in the face of uncertainty. . . .

. . . In the absence of clear consensus on the underlying objectives and pedagogical benefits of bilingual programs, the federal government will be able to promulgate few useful programmatic rules. Instead, it should rely on improving state and local decisionmaking processes. While procedural constraints may be somewhat burdensome, they nevertheless allow state and local officials to wield legitimate discretion. . . .

* * *

In a hierarchical school organization where high-level administrators formulate regulations that subordinates are expected to obey, federal intervention is appropriate if state and local elites consistently generate ill-advised policies or neglect to promulgate necessary regulations regarding linguistic minority students. Under these circumstances, state and local elites are abusing their formal discretion. Federal intervention is also proper when superiors generate adequate regulations that subordinates consistently disregard with impunity; here, state and local elites are improperly delegating informal discretion to lower-level officials. By contrast, federal intervention is inappropriate where state and local elites promptly amend erroneous policy mandates and successfully enforce compliance with applicable rules.

In a loosely coupled system, where success depends on sound choices made independently by a number of subordinates, it is appropriate for the federal government to intervene where state and local elites fail to foster conditions that enable subordinates to exercise their discretion wisely. Policymaking elites can promote these conditions by hiring qualified personnel, affording them the resources necessary to engage in informed, thoughtful decisionmaking, and providing feedback through reasonable monitoring and evaluation. By contrast, federal intervention is not appropriate simply because state and local elites delegate discretion to subordinates and refrain from promulgating regulations. Such action may be entirely proper when a school system confronts a high degree of pedagogical uncertainty. Nor is federal intervention necessary merely because state and local elites refuse to penalize every mistaken judgment by subordinates. Given the complexity of designing a classroom program for NEP and LEP students, even well-qualified teachers can select techniques that fail on occasion. Presumably, federal involvement is warranted only where subordinates' poor discretionary choices persist uncorrected on a significant scale.

In determining whether to intervene, federal policymakers should recognize that schools can operate hierarchically for some purposes, such as budgetary allocation, while delegating significant amounts of discretion to subordinates in other contexts, such as curriculum development. Where discretion is allocated hierarchically, federal reforms should focus on altering the behavior of high-level state and local officials. For example, state educational agencies and local school boards may determine how many NEP and LEP students will be in a classroom and how much money will be available for their special needs. Under these circumstances, federal agencies could make high-level state and local officials more generous by carefully earmarking funds for programs directed at LEP and NEP students. On the other hand, where subordinates enjoy considerable discretion in a loosely coupled system, federal reforms aimed solely at elite decisionmakers are apt to fail. For instance, classroom teachers may exercise substantial autonomy in deciding how to structure and implement their lesson plans. Where this is so, curricular reforms directed at classroom teachers are more likely to have a meaningful impact than reforms directed solely at state and local educational agencies. Such reforms might include training programs, workshops, or special grants to teachers of NEP and LEP students. . . .

[The parental participation policy] illustrates how federal policymakers can design initiatives that account for the variability of tasks that school districts perform and their corresponding bureaucratic features.

Attempts to increase parental participation in the educational decisionmaking process are complicated by the diverse situations that school districts face. Teachers and administrators have different attitudes toward parental involvement, and school decisionmaking processes operate in distinctive ways. Some districts have considerable experience in soliciting parental input, while others have taken few, if any, steps to encourage parental participation. Partly as a result of these different school practices, parents have varying levels of familiarity with school operations. Parents are also apt to harbor diverse expectations for their children's education. Their aspirations may differ significantly from those of school personnel. The strength of community organizations, which could support linguistic minority parents' efforts to participate, undoubtedly varies among districts. Under these circumstances, the federal government should not promulgate rigid requirements regarding parental participation but should experiment with different procedural reforms tailored to the characteristics of different school districts.

In districts where schools enjoy generally good relationships with parents, teachers and administrators are apt to share linguistic minority parents' vision of their participatory role in the educational process. State and local educators already may have taken steps to promote parental participation; linguistic minority parents are apt to voice their complaints through the schools' internal processes, rather than seeking external review through OCR or the federal courts. Partly as a result of this ongoing dialogue between school personnel and parents, they are likely to have common instructional goals for NEP and LEP students.

Under these circumstances, the federal government should facilitate state and local efforts to enhance parental involvement by providing supplementary resources and disseminating information about successful programs. Where state and local educational agencies generally have established policies conducive to parental participation, the federal government can provide incentives to principals and teachers to include linguistic minority parents fully in the decisionmaking process. Federal agencies can also provide teachers and school administrators with training to improve the solicitation of parental input. Finally, federal resources can assist state and local policy elites to construct effective systems for monitoring and evaluating parental participation programs.

In districts with a less positive history of school-parent relations, teachers, administrators, and parents probably have not reached a consensus about the appropriate role of parents in the educational process. In schools that have not made any significant attempts to seek parental input, linguistic minority parents are generally unfamiliar with school decisionmaking processes. Partly because of a continuing lack of contact, schools and parents may have quite different pedagogical objectives for NEP and LEP children. Under these circumstances, districts are apt to comply with rules regarding parental participation in a rigid, formalistic manner; parents are likely to voice their dissent through channels other than the schools' internal complaint mechanisms. For example, these linguistic minority parents will resort to lobbying, media campaigns, and litigation against the district.

The federal government faces a formidable task in ensuring meaningful parental participation in these districts. In selecting reform initiatives, federal officials should consider how intrusive they will appear to state and local decisionmakers. If federal reforms greatly enhance parents' ability to participate but fail to allay school officials' doubts about parental involvement, state and local educators will object that these reforms undermine the exercise of their professional judgment. To avoid such resistance, federal policymakers should build an official consensus about the value of parental participation while cultivating parents' capacity to get involved.

* * *

One useful technique may be to encourage state and local educational agencies to issue pronouncements that affirm the value of parental participation. . . .

* * *

Next, federal reforms should create strong incentives for teachers and school administrators to encourage parental involvement. The federal government could make funding available to districts willing to undertake a parental participation program. . . .

* * *

To overcome resistance among school staff, the federal government should present its proposals as peer-generated innovation rather than federal coercion. The federal government could promote the resocialization of teachers and school administrators through locally run workshops, conferences, and symposia on the benefits of parental participation and successful techniques to encourage it. . . .

* * *

In addition to focusing on school officials, federal policymakers must develop linguistic minority parents' skills to allow them to participate more fully in educational decisionmaking. . . .

In districts where linguistic minority parents have been poorly organized, federal policymakers must decide whether to focus exclusively on enhancing individual parents' participatory skills or whether to support the development of community organizations as well. The determination will turn in part on the characteristics of the linguistic minority population in the district. For instance, if linguistic minority parents are poorly organized because of rapid turnover in the population, an exclusive focus on individual parents may fail because newly arriving parents require a continual investment in expensive training and technical assistance, and departing parents derive few ongoing benefits from their brief participatory experience. . . .

* * *

In sum, then, even if a national consensus about the value of parental participation exists, there is no simple answer to how the federal government should promote such participation. Federal policymakers must undertake a closer analysis of the characteristics of school districts and the linguistic minority populations they serve to determine what types of measures are most likely to succeed. . . .

NOTES AND QUESTIONS

1. Parental Participation

What do you make of Professor Moran's complex prescription, both generally and in the particular instance of promoting parental participation? Is the federal government capable of the nuanced policy—attentive not only to differences concerning what is substantively known but also to differences in the bureaucratic capacities of school districts? Is Moran's focus on participation as a substitute for rules, in the face of limited substantive knowledge, likely to strengthen the quality of decision making? Politicize the process? If the prescription seems too complex, can you construct a simpler alternative strategy that fairly takes account of the variability that Professor Moran describes? Or, in this realm, is the only choice between a too-complex federal policy and an ineffectual federal policy?

VI. FEDERAL POLICY FOR THE 1990s: THE EXCELLENCE AGENDA

The major reform effort of the past decade has focused not on enhancing quality but on reversing what the National Commission on Excellence in Education termed "a rising tide of mediocrity that threatens our future as a nation and a people." *A Nation at Risk: The Imperative for Educational Reform* 1 (1983). The commission relied on eye-catching rhetoric to capture the public's attention: "If an unfriendly power had attempted to impose on America the mediocre educational performance that exists today, we might well have viewed it as an act of war." *Ibid.* at 5. Its report was followed by an armada of studies by, among others, the Education Commission of the States, the National Science Board, the Carnegie Foundation for the Advancement of Teaching, and the Twentieth Century Fund. What these studies had in common was the conviction that there was a crisis in American education, which, if left unattended, would leave the nation vulnerable to its economic and even military competitors. *See also* chapter 4, *supra*.

The following Congressional Research Service paper summarizes the leading national reports (pp. 817–28).

In these reports, excellence is the watchword of the day. Higher standards for students and teachers, stiffer academic requirements, reduction or elimination of electives, more mathematics and science, more homework, longer school days and school years, better school discipline and classroom management, more regular testing: These disparate ideas are lumped under a common rubric. The assumption of many of the commission proposals is that there should be a common curriculum, which transmits a common culture.

Missing from most of the reports is attention to the needs of the least well-off students. Indeed, "there is an implicit assumption that urban disadvantaged are no different from other students and to believe otherwise is anti-intellectual and anti-democratic." A.H. Passow, *Reforming Schools in the 1980s: A Critical Review of the National Reports* 86 (1984). In the discussion sparked by the reports, the needs of the disadvantaged were nowhere to be heard. On the contrary, the assertedly perilous state of American schooling was blamed, in some quarters, on a preoccupation with the least well-off and a corresponding inattention to the concerns of other students.

Although a federal commission first raised the excellence issue, the initiative has largely been taken by the states. *See* T. Timar and D. Kirp, *Managing Educational Excellence* (1988). In "Excellence in Education: The States Respond," a paper prepared in 1985 for the American Enterprise Institute, Denis Doyle and Terry Hartle analyzed this pattern:

> . . . Over the past twenty years—because of the Great Society—many observers had come to associate education reform, change and renewal with the federal government. The national government's penchant for distributing modest amounts of funds for clearly defined purposes had a significant impact on what schools did and how they did it. As well, the federal government's commitment to racial equality made its presence felt in a way that no pedagogically oriented program would have done. Change, insofar as it occurred, was purchased with federal funds; it was a top-down federal strategy, accomplished by rule, regulation, statute and appropriation. It was, as it were, trickled down reform.
>
> For the half century preceding the Great Society, education reform, change and renewal was associated not with the federal government, but with "lighthouse" schools and school districts, run by educators who assumed prominence by virtue of their high standards and independence. . . .
>
> * * *
>
> For more than a century before that, educational leadership was provided by individuals of great dis-

Table 7.1 Comparison Recommendations from Selected Education Reform Reports

	The National Commission on Excellence in Education	Twentieth Century Fund Task Force	Education Commission of the States Task Force on Education for Economic Growth	National Science Board Precollege Commission	Carnegie Foundation American High School Study
CURRICULUM	Significantly more time should be devoted to learning the "new basics"—English, mathematics, science, social studies, and computer sciences, and for the college-bound a foreign language. Rigorous programs should be provided to advance students' personnel, educational, and occupational goals, such as the fine and performing arts and vocational education. Elementary schools should provide a sound base in English language development and writing, computational and problem-solving skills, science, social studies, foreign language, and the arts. Foreign languages should be started in the elementary grades with 4–6 years of study.	The Federal Government should clearly state that the most important objective of elementary and secondary education in the United States is the development of literacy in the English language.	The school curriculum should be strengthened. States and communities should identify skills they expect the schools to impart. The academic experience should be more intense and more productive. Courses not only in mathematics and science, but also in all disciplines, must be enlivened and improved. The goal should be both richer substance and greater motivational power—elimination of "soft" non-essential courses, more enthusiastic involvement of students in learning, encouragement of mastery of skills beyond the basics, e.g., problem-solving, analysis, interpretation, and persuasive writing. Educators, business and labor leaders, and other interested parties should clearly identify the skills that the schools are expected to impart to students for effective employment and citizenship.	Schools should return to the basics of reading, writing, and arithmetic, but also should add the "new basics" of communication and higher problem-solving skills, scientific technological literacy, and computer literacy. Educational objectives should focus on mathematics, science, and technology for *all* students. New curricula should incorporate practical issues that will require the collection of data, communication of results, and formulation and testing of solutions. The goal would be to improve use and understanding of calculation and mathematical analysis, sharpen communication skills, develop problem-solving skills, impart scientific knowledge, develop a respect for science and mathematics, and stimulate interest in science, mathematics, and technical careers.	Each school should have clearly established goals that focus on the mastery of language, preparation for work and further education, and community service. In addition to English, social studies, science, and mathematics, the high school core should include foreign languages, the arts, non-western studies, technology, meaning of work, and importance of health. In the last two years of high school, students should enroll in a cluster of electives and explore career options. In elementary schools, the focus should be on communications skills. All high school students should complete a basic English course with an emphasis on writing, with enrollments limited to 20 students and no more than two such classes in the teacher's regular load. The high school core should stress the spoken word. Teachers should use a variety of teaching styles and encourage student participation.

Table 7.1 Comparison Recommendations from Selected Education Reform Reports (continued)

	The National Commission on Excellence in Education	Twentieth Century Fund Task Force	Education Commission of the States Task Force on Education for Economic Growth	National Science Board Precollege Commission	Carnegie Foundation American High School Study
High school graduation requirements	All students seeking a diploma should be required to complete (a) 4 years of English; (b) 3 years of mathematics; (c) 3 years of science; (d) 3 years of social studies; and (e) one-half year of computer science. For the college-bound, 2 years of foreign language in high school are strongly recommended.	No comparable provision	No comparable provision	High school students should complete at least (1) 3 years of mathematics, including one year of algebra; (2) 3 years of science and technology, including 1 semester of computer science. Steps should be taken to phase in requirements of four years of science and four years of mathematics.	Required courses in the student's core program should be increased from ½ to ⅔ of the total units for high school graduation. The core would include (a) 3 units of English; (b) 2 units of foreign language; (c) 2.5 units of history; (d) 1 unit of civics; (e) 2 units of science; (f) 2 units of mathematics; (g) ½ unit of technology; (h) ½ unit of health; (i) ½ unit seminar on work; and (j) ½ unit senior independent social issue project that draws upon their high school experiences. A "new Carnegie unit" service requirement involving school or community volunteer work should be added.

Time	Significantly more time should be devoted to learning the "new basics." School districts and State legislatures should strongly consider 7 hour school days, as well as a 200- to 220-day school year. Time available for learning should be expanded through better classroom management and organization of the school day. Additional instructional time should be found to meet the needs of slow learners, the gifted, and others who need more instructional diversity than can be provided in the conventional school day and year.	No comparable provision	Every state should increase the duration and intensity of academic learning time. Students should be introduced earlier to such critical subjects as science. Schools should examine each school year, especially the twelfth grade, to ensure that time is not wasted. Both States and localities should consider lengthening the school year and the school day by extending teachers' contracts. Learning time should be increased by establishing a wider range of learning opportunities beyond the normal school day and year.	School districts should explore lengthening the school year as a means of raising teacher pay. School time should be filled with purposeful and substantive content, and interruptions should be minimal. In grades K–6, 60 minutes per day should be spent on mathematics, and 30 minutes on science. A full year of mathematics and of science and technology should be required in grades 7 and 8. To provide more time for the study of mathematics, science, and technology, the school day, week, and/ or year must be substantially lengthened.	Class schedules should be arranged more flexibly to permit larger blocks of instructional time for certain courses. Greater use should be made of off-campus learning sites and part-time professionals. Large high schools (over 2,000 students) should be organized into smaller units, i.e., schools within a school.
Textbooks and instructional materials	Textbooks and tools of learning and teaching should be upgraded and updated to assure more rigorous content and to reflect current applications of technology, the best scholarship, and research findings. Funds should be made available to develop texts for the disadvantaged, learning disabled, and gifted and talented.	No comparable provision	No comparable provision	Secondary school students should be provided with course outlines. Textbooks and curriculum materials should be sufficient and up-to-date. Public and private support for educational television programs on science should be increased, and time should be provided by commercial stations as well as cable and local television stations.	Less reliance should be placed on textbooks and more on primary source materials. Technology, especially computers, should not be purchased until the district has a utilization plan and is confident that adequate software is available. Computer resources should be related to instructional objectives, and emphasis should be placed on the social importance of computers.

Table 7.1 Comparison Recommendations from Selected Education Reform Reports (continued)

	The National Commission on Excellence in Education	Twentieth Century Fund Task Force	Education Commission of the States Task Force on Education for Economic Growth	National Science Board Precollege Commission	Carnegie Foundation American High School Study
Textbook Adoption	In adopting textbooks, States and localities should evaluate texts on the basis of their capacity to present rigorous and challenging material clearly and require publishers to furnish data on effectiveness.	No comparable provision	No comparable provision	No comparable provision	States should ease their control over textbook selection and transfer more authority to the local level, with teachers having a far greater voice in selecting texts and materials.
Homework	Students in high schools should be assigned homework.	No comparable provision	States and local school districts should establish firm, explicit, and demanding requirements concerning homework.	Specific homework should be required regularly of all students, and the work should be suitably evaluated by a teacher.	No comparable provision
PROGRAMS FOR SPECIAL POPULATIONS	The Federal Government, in cooperation with States and localities, should help meet the needs of key groups of students such as the gifted and talented, socioeconomically disadvantaged, minority and language minority students, and the handicapped.	Federal efforts to provide special education programs for the poor and the handicapped should be continued. Federal programs for the disadvantaged and limited English speaking should be maintained.	Participation of young women and minorities should be increased in courses where they are under represented. Academically gifted students should be identified and challenged. Handicapped children should be specifically included in programs for education and economic growth.	Programs should be developed to identify and eliminate barriers to full educational opportunity for all youth. Schools should offer appropriate sequences of courses for students at various levels of ability.	Special arrangements and special programs should be provided for gifted students. Programs should be developed to accelerate these students. Federal funds for the education of the disadvantaged should be increased so that all eligible students may participate.
COLLEGE ENTRANCE REQUIREMENTS	Four-year colleges and universities should raise their admission standards in line with the recommended requirements for high school graduation.	No comparable provision	Colleges and universities should raise their entrance requirements.	Steps should be taken to phase in college entrance requirements of four years of science and four years of mathematics.	Each State should establish a School-College Coordination Panel to define minimum academic requirements needed for the transition from school to public higher education.

PERFORMANCE STANDARDS FOR STUDENTS	Grades should be reliable indicators of a students' readiness for further study.	No comparable provision	States and school systems should establish requirements concerning discipline, grades, and other matters.	No comparable provision	Expectations should be high, standards clear, evaluation fair, and students held accountable.
Standardized Tests	Standardized tests should be administered at major transition points from one level of schooling to another and particularly from high school to college or work. The purpose would be to certify credentials, identify the need for remedial work, and identify opportunities for enrichment.	No comparable provision	Effective programs should be established to monitor student progress through periodic testing of general achievement and specific skills. The testing program should be linked to a carefully designed program of remediation and enrichment for students who need special help.	Normed achievement measures should be used to assess student and teacher performance.	A new Student Achievement and Advisement Test (SAAT) should be developed. The achievement portion would be linked to the core curriculum and the advisement portion would be designed to help students make better informed choices.
Student Progress	Placement and grouping of students, as well as promotion and graduation policies, should be guided by the academic progress of students and their instructional needs, rather than by rigid adherence to age.	No comparable provision	Student progress should be measured by tests of general achievement and specific skills with promotion based on mastery, not age. States and local districts should establish firm, explicit, and demanding requirements concerning student grades.	Social promotions (i.e., based on chronological age and physical size) should be curtailed.	The English proficiency of all students should be assessed before students enter high school. Remedial programs should be provided for those who are deficient.
Student Absences and Failures	Attendance policies with clear incentives and sanctions should be used to reduce the amount of time lost through student absenteeism and tardiness.	No comparable provision	States, school systems, principals, teachers, and parents should work to reduce student absences and school failures. Efforts to deal with absenteeism and dropouts should include revitalizing course materials and making educational schedules flexible enough to accommodate students with special problems.	A clear attendance policy with sanctions should be adopted.	No comparable provision

Table 7.1 Comparison Recommendations from Selected Education Reform Reports (continued)

	The National Commission on Excellence in Education	Twentieth Century Fund Task Force	Education Commission of the States Task Force on Education for Economic Growth	National Science Board Precollege Commission	Carnegie Foundation American High School Study
Discipline	The burden on teachers to maintain discipline should be reduced by developing and enforcing firm and fair conduct codes, and by considering alternative rooms, programs, and schools for disruptive students.	No comparable provision	States and local school districts should establish firm, explicit, and demanding requirements concerning student discipline.	Schools and school districts should adopt rigorous discipline policies that reflect the district's goals and expectations. Rules should be applied consistently and impartially; and State laws modified to permit effective discipline in the schools.	School officials should support teachers in the maintenance of discipline on the basis of a clearly stated code of conduct.
TEACHERS	Teachers preparation should be improved, and teaching should be made a more rewarding profession.	A major Federal initiative should be undertaken that emphasizes the critical importance of quality teachers in America's schools.	States and school districts should improve methods for recruiting, training and paying teachers.	Programs should be started to improve knowledge and skills of in-service teachers, and States should take steps to raise the quality of new teachers.	Working conditions for teachers should be improved, teaching loads reduced, interruptions and extra duties minimized, preparation improved, and planning time of 60 minutes per day provided.
Teacher Preparation	Persons preparing to teach should be required to meet high educational standards, and to demonstrate competence in academic disciplines. Master teachers should be involved in designing teacher preparation programs. Resources should be used to solve the problem of a shortage of mathematics and science teachers.	No comparable provision	Every State and local school district, with the fullest participation of teachers, should drastically improve methods of training teachers. States, singly or in cooperation with one another, should establish better pre-service and in-service education programs for teachers.	States should require teachers to have computer skills. Liberal arts colleges should assume a greater role in training elementary and secondary mathematics and science teachers. The use of science museums in teacher training programs should be encouraged.	Efforts should be made to recruit outstanding students into teaching. High schools should establish cadet teacher programs. Prospective teachers should be chosen on the basis of grades and recommendations and should complete a core of common learning parallel to the proposed core curriculum. Their program should be for five years with the fifth year consisting of a professional education core curriculum and field experience.

Teacher Certification	Efforts should be made to have qualified persons with academic training in mathematics and science eligible to teach. Other areas of critical need, such as English, must also be addressed.	No comparable provision	Teacher certification processes should be changed to make it possible for qualified "outsiders" to serve in the schools.	Elementary teachers should have a comprehensive liberal arts education, and secondary teachers a major in their teaching area, with both having a limited number of effective education courses and an internship.	Credentialing should be based on recommendations and a written examination submitted to a Board of Examiners, the majority of whom are senior teachers. Staffing should be supplemented with lecturers, retirees, and joint appointments with industry.
Master Teachers	School boards, administrators, and teachers should cooperate to develop career ladders for teachers that distinguish among the beginning instructor, the experienced teacher, and the master teacher.	A national Masters Teacher Program should be established, funded by the Federal Government, that recognizes and rewards teaching excellence.	States should create career ladders for teachers.	State and local governments should provide opportunities for high quality teachers to move up in salary and status without leaving the classroom.	After credentialing, teachers should have the opportunity to pursue a career path, moving from associate teacher to senior teacher.
Teacher Salaries or Grants	Teacher salaries should be increased and made professionally competitive and market sensitive. School boards should adopt an 11-month contract for teachers. Teacher salaries should be performance based.	Master teachers would be awarded a grant of $40,000 per year for a period of 5 years. An incentive approach should be adopted to provide awards to teachers of exceptional merit; awards should be numerous enough to attract national attention and substantial enough to keep the master teachers in the classroom.	Every State and local school district, with the fullest participation of teachers, should drastically improve methods for paying teachers. Financial incentives for teachers should be keyed to differing responsibilities and to filling critical needs in certain subject areas.	Schools should explore means of adjusting pay in order to compete for and retain teachers in shortage areas. Stipends should be provided for summer institutes and other activities. Working conditions, salary levels, comparability, length of school day/ week/year, tenure provisions and promotion procedures should be reviewed as aspects of teacher pay.	The average salary for teachers should be raised by at least 25 percent beyond the rate of inflation. A base salary plus cost-of-living adjustments and merit increases should be provided. Competitive grant "Teacher Excellence Funds" should be established in every school. Travel funds and summer study grants should be provided for experienced teachers.

Table 7.1 Comparison Recommendations from Selected Education Reform Reports (continued)

	The National Commission on Excellence in Education	Twentieth Century Fund Task Force	Education Commission of the States Task Force on Education for Economic Growth	National Science Board Precollege Commission	Carnegie Foundation American High School Study
Teacher Performance	Salary, promotion, tenure, and retention decisions should be tied to an effective evaluation system that includes peer review so that superior teachers may be rewarded, average ones may be encouraged, and poor ones may be either improved or terminated. Master teachers should be involved in supervising teachers during their probationary years.	The master teacher proposal is designed to "pave the way for reconsideration of merit based personnel systems."	Boards of education and higher education officials should cooperate with teachers and administrators on ways to measure the effectiveness of teachers and reward outstanding performance. Procedures should be tightened for deciding which teachers to retain and dismiss.	Teachers should be objectively evaluated relative to salary, advancement, and retention of current position. Greater use should be made of special teachers qualified in the subject matter, and supervision provided as necessary.	Evaluation of teacher performance should be largely controlled by teachers judged to be outstanding in the classroom. A two-week professional development term should be added to the school year, with compensation.
LEADERSHIP AND MANAGEMENT	Citizens across the Nation should hold educators and elected officials responsible for providing the leadership necessary to achieve these reforms.	The executive and legislative branches of the Federal Government should emphasize the need for better schools and a better education for all young Americans.	Schools should use effective management techniques.	Administrative support should be provided for necessary equipment and materials, and class sizes should be reasonable and manageable.	No comparable provision
Principals	Principals and superintendents must play a crucial role in developing school and community support for reforms. Administrative burdens and related intrusions on the teacher should be reduced to add to the time available for teaching and learning.	No comparable provision	Principals should be in charge of educational programs. Pay should be related to responsibilities and effectiveness. States should set higher standards for recruiting, training, and monitoring the performance of principals.	Administrators should support better discipline, higher attendance, fewer classroom interruptions, higher expectations, more equipment and materials, and reasonable class sizes.	Principals should complete all requirements of a teacher and serve for two years as an administrative intern. Principals should have more control over budgets and staffing, and also be provided with a school improvement fund for staff and program development.
School Boards	School boards must consciously develop leadership skills at the school and district levels if the reforms are to be achieved.	No comparable provision	No comparable provision	School boards should work with national and State groups to develop goals and plans for implementing computer-managed instruction and technology by 1995.	Parents should become more involved in school board elections, and school boards should meet with representatives at least once a year.

Educators, Parents, and Citizens	The Commission calls upon educators, parents and citizens at all levels to assist in bringing about the reforms proposed in this report.	No comparable provision	No comparable provision	No comparable provision	Citizen participation in schools should be increased, and advisory councils and volunteer programs should be formed in all schools.
FISCAL SUPPORT	Citizens should provide the fiscal support and stability required to bring about the reforms.	The Federal Government must continue to help meet the special needs of poor and minority students while taking the lead in meeting the general and overwhelming need for educational quality.	Schools should make the best possible use of resources. More funds are needed from all sources for selective investments in efforts that promote quality.	State and local governments should bear most of the expense of elementary and secondary education, with Federal funds being used to address critical national issues.	Citizens, local school boards, State agencies and legislatures, and the Federal Government must work together to help bring excellence to the Nation's public schools.
Federal Government	(See "PROGRAMS FOR SPECIAL POPULATIONS.")	Categorial programs required by the Federal Government should be funded through the Federal Treasury. The Federal Government should fund the Master Teachers Program. The Federal Government has a responsibility to help overcome the unevenness of State efforts to fund education. School districts with substantial numbers of immigrant children should receive Federal impact aid. Federal funds now used for bilingual education should be used to teach non-English speaking children how to speak, read, and write English.	The Federal Government has an essential supporting role in financing education.	Federal funds should support (a) museum education activities in mathematics, science, and technology; and (b) a network of exemplary schools in mathematics, science, and technology, with 1,000 exemplary elementary and 1,000 similar secondary schools. The National Science Foundation should fund summer and inservice teacher training programs in mathematics, science, and technology, and also fund teacher training programs using information technologies. Federal support should continue funding for science television broadcasts.	Federal funds for the education of the disadvantaged should be increased to a level that will provide programs for all eligible students. Federal funds should be used to establish (a) ten Technology Resource Centers on university campuses; (b) regional networks to provide computerized library services to schools; (c) a National Film Library to secure and make available outstanding films and television programs; (d) a national network of residential science and mathematics academics; (e) a National Teacher's Service scholarship program; and (f) a expanded national survey to cover all high schools. A Federal school building and equipment loan fund should be started to update laboratories and rehabilitate schools.

Table 7.1 Comparison Recommendations from Selected Education Reform Reports (continued)

	The National Commission on Excellence in Education	Twentieth Century Fund Task Force	Education Commission of the States Task Force on Education for Economic Growth	National Science Board Precollege Commission	Carnegie Foundation American High School Study
States and Localities	State and local school officials, including school board members, governors, and legislators have the primary responsibility for financing and governing schools, and incorporating these reforms into educational policies and fiscal planning.	No comparable provision	States and localities have the chief responsibility for supporting the schools and making educational policy. States should continue efforts to secure more equitable distribution of educational resources. More human, financial, and institutional resources should be invested in education.	Each State should appoint a representative Governors' Council to develop and monitor educational goals and make recommendations for improving education. Each state should develop at least one regional resource center for mathematics and science teachers. The centers would encourage participation by business, educators, and government, and include assistance in technology instruction.	The overriding responsibility of States is to establish general standards and provide fiscal support. State education laws should be revised to eliminate confusing and inappropriate rules and regulations.

FEDERAL ROLE	The Federal Government's role includes several functions of national consequence that States and localities are unlikely to be able to meet: protecting the constitutional and civil rights of students and personnel; collecting data, statistics, and general information about education; supporting teacher training in these areas of shortage or key national needs; and providing student financial assistance and research and graduate training. Assistance should be provided with a minimum of administrative burden and intrusiveness. The Federal Government has the primary responsibility to identify the national interest in education and also to help fund and support efforts to protect and promote that interest.	The executive and legislative branches of the Federal Government are called upon to emphasize the need for better schools and a better education for young Americans. The Federal Government should promote and support proficiency in English for all children in the public schools, but especially for those who do not speak English, or have only a limited command of English. Federal attention and assistance should go to economically depressed localities with concentrations of immigrant and/or impoverished groups as well as those that already are making strong efforts to improve their educational performance. The Federal Government should emphasize programs to develop basic scientific literacy among all citizens and programs to provide advanced training in mathematics and science for secondary school students.	(See "Federal Government" under "FISCAL SUPPORT" above.)	The President should appoint a National Education Council consisting of representatives from a cross-section of national interests. This group would identify national educational goals and assessment mechanisms for every State, school district, and school; and monitor and report annually on the status of American education and its progress toward the goals. The Federal Government has a unique role in ensuring access to equal educational opportunity on its broadest sense. The National Science Foundation should develop and evaluate technology courses and programs. The National Science Foundation should establish a council to take the leadership role in curriculum evaluation and development for mathematics, science, and technology. Widely dispersed dissemination centers should test the new curriculum.	The Secretary of Education should name a National Commission on Computer Instruction to evaluate computer software. (See "Federal Government" under "FISCAL SUPPORT" above.)

Source: Congressional Research Service, 1984.

tinction . . . who conducted successful reform campaigns that changed the face of the nation. They achieved their objectives through exhortations to excellence, indefatigable campaigning for reform, and by convincing state legislatures and state school committees of the merits of their case. Implementation was accomplished largely through state rule, regulation and law.

Today we have come full circle. America again looks to committed reformers to enact major reform at the state and local level. . . .

There is no guarantee, of course, that real reform will occur, or that if it does, it will be lasting. The natural state for any organization, schools included, is a position of rest. And good education—as distinct from training—is by its nature a dynamic, tension-filled activity. Good education cannot exist in a moribund institution. If schools treat the need to restore excellence as business as usual—which they are inclined by temperament and experience to do—the prospects for reform will vanish, water into sand. Indeed, it is all too easy to write a scenario of missed opportunities and lost chances. One need only observe that we have the schools we want, even if they are not the schools we deserve. By any measure they have had substantial resources and flexibility; on balance they have been treated with generosity and respect. If our schools choose to give equal billing to driver education and trigonometry, to power volleyball and the Greek classics in translation, it is not because they are inadequately funded. It is because their values—and those of their constituents—point in that direction.

If the schools do not show progress, it will be state governments that must explain why. Today the states have the opportunity, the responsibility and the motive (economic growth) to change and improve education. They also have the competence and the moral authority to do so. . . .

* * *

. . . The greatest political triumph of the New Deal was to confer moral authority on the federal government as intervenor in domestic policy. . . .

* * *

But the modern welfare state, by reaching so far, overreached, and today there is widespread reaction to it. Not to the "safety net" nor to the authority of state intervention but to the level and nature of the intervention. The question is not "should we intervene?"—as it once was—but where and how should we intervene? What interventions are most likely to be successful? At present, the preferred locus of intervention is at the state and local level.

This reaction is not confined to the United States. In the great democracies the swing of the social and political pendulum is not surprising, it is to be expected. If the federal government is no longer viewed as the principal repository of political virtue, it is because moral authority in domestic politics is moving to the states.

In part this is a commentary on the federal government's success in dealing with the great moral issues of the twentieth century, economic and racial justice. . . . In part the shift in moral authority is also explained by the increasing institutional capacity of the states. The public's confidence in state government increases because they have something about which to be confident. . . .

Through federal budget policy [in the Reagan administration] the states have been starved, not into submission, but into self-reliance. One recent analysis called this the "major sleeper issue" of the Reagan presidency, "one likely to have a substantial and lasting impact." For education policy, the change is profound. . . .

* * *

Once having gained power and responsibility, the states will be reluctant to see it returned to the federal government. If anything, the process of "devolving" responsibility for education back to the states—for whatever reason—is likely to have enormous staying power. If state governments are to be small versions of Washington—with full or nearly full-time legislators, large and well qualified professional staffs, time, resources and energy to conduct oversight and foresight hearings—they will not willingly yield authority in those areas in which they have gained it, especially one where the constitutional responsibility is theirs.

As it is, the states have made extraordinary gains in education over the past several years. In part a response to the "rising tide" of reports, the reform impulse was also home grown. The problems enumerated in the reports and the sense of dismay they caused led states officials to take prompt, vigorous, and often comprehensive action. The states then, are to be commended for their enterprise and diligence. What remains to be seen is the pace, direction and impact of the reforms already adopted. . . .

Between the law and the impact falls the shadow. That shadow is what policy analysts call implementation—the process of moving from a policy decision to a program or policy operations . . . [but] nothing ever works as planned.

How the shadow of implementation falls is the result of many factors, some of which are within the control of elected officials: the design of the law, its flexibility, its scope and reach, the resources devoted to it and the oversight it receives.

Less susceptible to intervention is the attitude and enthusiasm of those who are called upon to act. And while a state legislature is more likely to be in tune with its local schools than the U.S. Congress, it is still an enormous distance from state house to school house. Similarly, state legislatures and governors (like the Congress and the President) cannot always control the events that come before it, many needing urgent attention. Nor can the states decisively influence federal policy actions that will shape their agenda. As we have suggested, how the federal government deals with the budget deficit has profound implications for the health of the states and the health of education reform.

Resource scarcity will also be an issue at the state level. When the state reform impulse passes, education will find itself in vigorous competition for funding, much as it already is at the national level. Education will compete with housing, with transportation, recreation and leisure. But the more pressing competition may be education versus education: preschool against vocational, higher against lower.

If the bottom line is not money, it is the values and character of the elected state officials. How they see the issues, what they choose to emphasize, their tolerance for conflict, and their willingness to continue to make tough choices are all unknown. Circumstances versus character is the most basic story of public policy making. It will continue to be. . . .

The following excerpt offers a contrasting appraisal of the era, and differing suggestions for future directions. As a matter of policy, which do you find more persuasive? What is the role of education law in these scenarios?

"Education Reform in the Reagan Era: False Paths, Broken Promises"

L. Botstein, *Social Policy* 3–11 (Spring 1988).

Since 1984, a particular view of America's educational ills, their origins, and likely remedies has gained official sanction. In retrospect, William Bennett may emerge as Reagan's single most influential and popular cabinet officer. He realized the potential inherent in the office of Secretary of Education to establish a national agenda for education. He set the terms of debate and utilized the research function to shape a seemingly "factual" basis for policy, all without committing the federal government to a greater share of the financial burden for education: for achieving improved teacher training, higher teacher salaries, effective compensatory programs, and smaller class sizes. By using research to lend prejudices and opinions about education the legitimation and aura of impartiality in the name of social science, Bennett has gained particular persuasive power for his views. . . .

Bennett's predecessor in the first Reagan Administration, Secretary Terrel Bell, had the shrewd sense to engineer *A Nation at Risk* in 1983, on the eve of the 1984 election, that gave Reagan the offensive on a subject that had not figured in the 1980 campaign and that might otherwise have become a liability. . . .

Bennett went further and exploited education brilliantly as an issue central to and symbolic of a conservative vision of America's present predicament and future. He satisfied the Republican right, shielded the Administration from responsibility for the state of education, and, most important, broadcast a view of education in American history, its role in democracy, and its potential as a social force in America, which, owing to Bennett's cabinet status, achieved influence over the formation of educational policy at the local and state levels. The most recent example was the December 1987 "official" Department of Education pamphlet, *James Madison High School: A Curriculum for American Students*. . . . Bennett's curriculum seeks to establish itself as the practical realization of the overdue need for serious national educational standards based on tradition.

What is so remarkable about the Reagan political achievement in education politics is that five years after *A Nation at Risk* there is no serious improvement in our schools, and yet the federal government has not only eluded responsibility for this lack of progress, but has taken credit for calling the failure of American schools to the public's attention and for setting the direction for change. Timothy Noah, writing in *Newsweek* in May 1988, glibly assumed that the federal role is merely to "set a high tone," since "real" improvements are a "local and state responsibility." This assumption remains unchallenged even though no other nation against which American pupils are so frequently negatively compared by Bennett and the press succeeds with a radically decentralized system like ours and without national governmental support. . . .

Precisely because Bennett effectively appropriated the neutral language of excellence and rigor, his views and the analysis upon which they rest have appealed not only to many educators, middle-class parents, and suburban white voters, but also to inner-city and minority constituents. One of Bennett's major achievements has been the recognition that the liberal attachment to constructs of compensatory education and celebration of diversity and tolerance—in the face of the miserable condition of schooling and schools, particularly in America's poorest regions and neighborhoods—were no longer convincing or compelling. . . .

Liberals displayed too great a penchant for making allowances, citing socioeconomic factors to excuse poor test scores and skills attainment among the poor and the disenfranchised. By the mid-1980s, this habit appeared as a form of tacit racism: nice-sounding apologetics that served only to perpetuate inequality and leave the educational establishment undisturbed. . . .

Bennett framed the issue as one of will, respect for tradition, and discipline, managing to pull the focus away from funding. He made it clear that those who did not measure up could not expect to succeed with high school diplomas that reflected few skills and passing grades awarded out of political pragmatism, not on account of competitive achievement. . . .

* * *

[A]n implicit Social Darwinism became respectable with regard to educational ability. Was it reasonable for the government to invest seriously in education across the board when the normal distribution of the population in terms of measurable educational ability was impervious to change? In short, investing in education may not really help those who do not show a talent for learning as measured by existing testing instruments and methods.

The difficulty, of course, is that while there will always be an elite and a remedial population, the *minimal* level attained by those at the low end can be raised and, with it, individual achievement and even the standards for the highest segment of the population. . . .

. . . [I]n the view of the Reagan Administration, the universal acceptance of proper standards, in the name of objective merit, must result inevitably in creating a sanctioned but unequal system of educational achievement. In this view, since the crux of equality lies in educational opportunities and not results, and since the school is a limited instrument, the educationally disenfranchised have no one but themselves to blame. This becomes just another hard fact of life that demands acknowledgment, liberal illusions notwithstanding. More money and programs will not solve the problem. Therefore, the social fact that the poor and the nonwhite populations do not achieve well enough by measurable standards in sufficient numbers cannot be held against the government.

Since excellence in education is, nevertheless, a national priority, one must, despite the inevitable inequalities, defend true standards and protect against the falsification of the credentialing process. It is this logic that permits Bennett to praise, in principle, the laudatory American intent to educate all citizens for democracy and, at the same time, declare that American education "is also less rigorous and productive" than that of other countries, without revealing a contradiction. His solutions are curricular changes with more testing and assessment, all without the obligation to engage, in either economic or pedagogical terms, the dramatic new strategies needed to make high educational attainment *actually* possible across social and economic barriers. The result is that, in the name of freedom and competition (all democratic virtues) as well as excellence, a static and inadequate definition of education and our decentralized and unequally funded system of delivering it become legitimated. Educational stratification along lines of class and race will remain unchanged, without any sense that something could or should have been done through the instrument of the federal government. . . .

* * *

The persistent failure of American schools, particularly for the poor and minority citizenry, as most observers agree, does not itself imply what the proper response should be. In particular, the new conservatism evident in the most influential educational critiques and Jeremiads utilizes the language and images of decline and unwittingly makes comparisons to an idealized American past during which far fewer Americans finished high school. It challenges implicitly . . . and explicitly . . . the post-World War II democratic goal of American schooling: to render excellence and equity compatible in reality. In the 1980s, the call for educational reform is not being framed, as it was in the late 1950s (when

America was concerned about Sputnik and Harvard's Conant studied the American high school), in terms of what might be achieved. Rather the discussion begins with a sense of what has been lost. Since this literature comes out of a reaction against the 1960s, after 20 years of rapid democratization of access to schooling and pressure for racial integration, a nagging question is never far from the surface: Can high standards—excellence—be reconciled with equity sufficiently to make the achievement of high standards and universal education plausible twin goals of public policy? Furthermore, the current literature advocating change in education confronts another post-1960s issue: How, in a democratic culture characterized by pluralism and diversity, can the concept of excellence in education, as a matter of public policy, avoid the necessity to assert what some might regard as an ethnocentric definition of the essential knowledge, culture, and skills appropriate to American democracy?

In other words, can notions of objectivity and excellence, in terms of measuring educational attainment, be established as absolutely valid in our democratic context? Can valid judgments on the priority of subject matters and skills be sustained in the face of social and ethnic diversity, political conflict, unfettered dissent, and influence peddling by small groups with respect to an educational system that is, by definition, decentralized and constantly politically vulnerable?

* * *

[The] *James Madison High School* curriculum is intended to be provocative in the political sense. It reveals where the appropriation of a strategy of educational reform based on a construct of nostalgia, cultural decline, and fear of pluralism on the part of the Reagan Administration can lead. The teaching of English that he recommends is American and British literature over two years, with one year required for world literature. The readings are to be used as "models" of good writing (as if style and argument were separable items). Charles Dickens and Mark Twain are Bennett's examples of normative style. . . . One senses a profound distrust of modernism.

Bennett's history curriculum talks of a "general survey" in which all American history is covered, already interpreted, defined, and categorized for the student. In Bennett's description of courses in politics and history, one recognizes a catechism, not merely a canon of materials and proper subjects. It is as if the young American needed less to learn how to reason and analyze than to identify and memorize a set of convenient facts and interpretive claims. . . .

Bennett's talk is all about heritage, about hammering into a younger generation, in a deeper sense than the general cultural ambiance already hints at, that their present and future cannot outstrip and exceed the past in quality and achievement: that they are in need of severe restrictive remediation in order to protect the society from deterioration and barbarism of which they are the representatives. It is as if the adult generation were exemplars of cultural understanding, and vulgarity were an exclusive characteristic of the young. There is no sense of the utility of education to effect cultural progress, change, and improvement, except perhaps in the areas of science and technology.

It is necessary, in the service of the future, to teach respect for traditions and an understanding of the past. But it is not necessary to write into a curriculum in the name of democracy a fear of modernity, of new cultural traditions in America, and fresh interpretations of how history might be understood and cast in the service of democracy. Bennett's proposal is more than a call for rigor. It seeks to impose a closed vision of culture and history on a new generation. Ironically, the very coherence and respect for certain cultural norms seemingly pressed for in the curriculum are neither shared nor upheld by the American adult community at large, much less by the intellectual, academic, and artistic community. It is as if the demographic changes of this century do not legitimate a new curriculum made up of not only the Western tradition, but other traditions as well. What role should be played by African, Asian, and Mexican history and culture, for example? Does not the global significance of the non-American world change the balance of what might be of interest and use to the next generation of Americans in the teaching of history and literature? . . .

In the name of objective standards and through the use of a *reductio ad absurdum* description of the dismantling by liberals of a so-called effective curricular consensus before 1960, Bennett seeks to legitimate an implicit judgment that perhaps only a small, elite number can succeed and, therefore, truly deserve to get a serious public education. Why, then, try to make a curriculum with high standards effective for all students? . . .

If American education is to effectively bring the habits of reason, inquiry, and literacy—of thinking and speaking—to bear on our public and private lives in a context of freedom in a world shaped by science and technology, then the diversity of our citizens, new concerns and issues, and the non-Western world constitute some of the new beginning points of a curriculum and of pedagogical strategies. The pupil must become active, not passive. Culture and tradition are not static objects of a museum, but essential instruments for the future. The politics of mythic cultural restoration in education in the name of excellence and standards will only lead to less educational attainment and to the tragic discrediting of our cultural continuities for future generations.

The task of real schooling for all Americans is more daunting and more expensive than we would like to admit. Without federal assistance, the number of teachers and their quality will not be assured. Neither will the required individual attention for all students. But most important, if we are now concerned about the ethical and political fiber of our citizenry, a substantial educational program that integrates modern life with cultural traditions, understanding, and knowledge in service of the power of judgment and the values of freedom and citizenship must be fashioned. One cannot merely preach an arbitrary canon and impose it in the name of quality. . . .

[T]he recognition of the diversity of culture and tradition must be reconciled with common aims of education. These aims include the teaching of a common culture. But that must be done by cultivating in reflective citizens the capacity for reasoned criticism and encouraging them to recognize and participate in the common cultural tradition. To achieve this, simplified definitions of cultural literacy, reductive tests, narrowly uniform and rigid survey curricula, passive classrooms, and a deep distrust of modernity, pluralism, and dissent, all cast in an antidemocratic context of cultural despair, cannot constitute effective bases for educational reform. Neither can a federal policy that refuses to assist materially.

Enormous resources will be needed to bring educational excellence to all citizens on an equitable basis. Only if excellence and equity are actually reconciled in our public educational system throughout the country can "character and intensity" . . . be developed. The active citizen who is vigilant about freedom, dignity, and the possibilities inherent in the future and who cherishes the traditions of culture justifies the institution of learning and keeps the promise of human progress from fading altogether from our consciousness.

VII. THE ROLE OF LAW: A CONCLUDING NOTE

As befits its title, this book has focused on the legalization (and, concomitantly, the centralization) of educational policy. These developments are not only important to this area of law. They are also the most significant developments in educational policy over the past two decades. As even a cursory review of the text will indicate, law touches all the vital—and some not so vital—policy matters concerning schooling. The education lawyer, while not yet a fixture in every school district, is rapidly becoming one.

As the reach of the law expands, distinctions between law and politics begin to blur. The standards against which decisions are made, the competencies of decision makers, the process of implementation—these are increasingly alike for all branches of government. What has diminished is dependency on professional expertise. In its place, there is increased reliance on various participatory devices and on procedures designed to assure reliability in decision making. The political and legal origins of these policymaking instrumentalities should be self-evident.

These are not inevitable developments. As studies of comparative education policymaking note, governments may choose to minimize the salience of an issue, to delimit both its political and legal ramifications. The British, for example, have behaved in just this manner with respect to race. In the face of a new and growing nonwhite population, they have sought, insofar as possible, to ignore the issue, hoping that such an approach would be self-confirming and that race would not become problematic. As a result, there have been few developments in the British discrimination law and fewer political initiatives. What has been done on behalf of racial minorities has been done largely surreptitiously. In this realm, the British, quite unlike the Americans, believe in doing good by stealth. *See* D. Kirp, *Doing Good By Doing Little: Race and Schooling in Britain* (1979).

As Americans, we are used to a different approach. Moreover, we are suspicious of the idea that neglect, at the policy level, may be the best way to address a problem. Almost by definition, problems beget policies, and policy begets law. "Doing good by stealth" becomes discredited as "benign neglect."

Which approach is the right one? There is no simple answer to this question. It bears remembering that law came to play such a prominent role in the shaping of educational policy because students who somehow differed from the norm were ignored or treated badly by educational institutions. They were compelled to attend public schools despite religious or political scruples, required once in school to defer to a governing regime that was more often authoritarian than communitarian, and subject to disciplinary action on the unchallengeable (and frequently arbitrary) judgment of the school administrator. If the students were black, they were consigned to separate schools; women students were treated in ways that reinforced sex-based stereotypes; the non-English-proficient were offered instruction in a language they could not understand; the handicapped were offered no instruction at all. Neither professional educators nor officials at the school district or state levels had the apparent inclination or the capacity to do much about these matters, which then became questions amenable to judicial resolution because no one else would address them, and because they could be treated as implicating constitutional values.

The actions of the courts, and then the federal government, embodied responses to these very real dilemmas. Yet if the hope was that these interventions would somehow resolve the problems of the schools, that lawyers would become the new heroes of the children's movement, this has not occurred. The dilemmas that confront the schools now appear more complex and the capacity of judicial or statutory directive to undo those dilemmas more limited than in 1974, when the first edition of this book was published. The legal and political solvents, if any, that should be applied to any given issue now appear to depend on myriad factors, including the tractability of the problem, the support that can be mustered for dealing with it, the antagonism that it arouses, the availability of resources, and—not least—the strength of the principled claim for intervention. Intervention always creates costs. Whether the benefits make those costs worthwhile—indeed just what one is to count as a benefit—is a question that depends in part on data. It is also and importantly an issue whose resolution turns on values and ideologies.

Some have argued for a radically reduced legal presence in the educational domain. In a 1988 address to the American Bar Association, then-Education Secretary William Bennett declared that "the excessive legalization of education in the last thirty years is . . . extreme:

> It's time to declare a broad consensus that the first purpose of education law is to enhance education—so that superintendents, principals, and teachers can do their job without consulting a lawyer at every turn. . . . Our schools are cracking under the weight of overregulation. They are spending too much money simply trying to comply with all the laws. . . . The excessive legalization of education is inhibiting bold, innovative educators who are willing to shoulder responsibilities and to accept the consequences. Worse still is the effect education law has on school officials who prefer to avoid taking on problems in their school. . . . [T]he presence of omnipresent, stultifying legal restrictions on education authority allows them to escape responsibility for their own failings by using the law as an excuse. . . . [E]ducational decisions should be made by educators, not lawyers.

While no one would argue with that last sentiment, it tells us little about how to strike the proper balance. If the rightness of legal intervention is no longer always so clearcut as it seemed a decade ago, it remains true that intervention by the courts and reliance on rights and procedures by the legislative and regulatory branches of the federal government sometimes makes good sense. It is difficult to imagine, for example, that the just claims of the handicapped will be realized without a substantial and persisting federal presence. And *laissez faire* creates its own costs: This much we have lately learned again as the reduced presence of the federal government has sometimes meant fewer educational opportunities for the least well off. These are not either–or matters. What is now needed is an understanding of the balance between law and politics, central and local authority, rule and discretion, stability and fluidity that can inform educational governance, policy, and law. This book does not assert a formula answer. It does provide the ingredients—the data, if you will —from which you may shape your own answers.

United States Constitution

Preamble

We the People of the United States, in Order to form a more perfect Union, establish Justice, insure domestic Tranquility, provide for the common defence, promote the general Welfare, and secure the Blessings of Liberty to ourselves and our Posterity, do ordain and establish this Constitution for the United States of America.

Article I

Section 1. All legislative Powers herein granted shall be vested in a Congress of the United States, which shall consist of a Senate and House of Representatives.

Section 2. The House of Representatives shall be composed of Members chosen every second Year by the People of the several States, and the Electors in each State shall have the Qualifications requisite for Electors of the most numerous Branch of the State Legislature.

No Person shall be a Representative who shall not have attained to the Age of twenty five Years, and been seven Years a Citizen of the United States, and who shall not, when elected, be an Inhabitant of that State in which he shall be chosen.

Representatives and direct Taxes shall be apportioned among the several States which may be included within this Union, according to their respective Numbers, which shall be determined by adding to the whole Number of free Persons, including those bound to Service for a Term of Years, and excluding Indians not taxed, three fifths of all other Persons. The actual Enumeration shall be made within three Years after the first Meeting of the Congress of the United States, and within every subsequent Term of ten Years, in such Manner as they shall by Law direct. The Number of Representatives shall not exceed one for every thirty Thousand, but each State shall have at Least one Representative; and until such enumeration shall be made, the State of New Hampshire shall be entitled to chuse three, Massachusetts eight, Rhode Island and Providence Plantations one, Connecticut five, New York six, New Jersey four, Pennsylvania eight, Delaware one, Maryland six, Virginia ten, North Carolina five, South Carolina five, and Georgia three.

When vacancies happen in the Representation from any State, the Executive Authority thereof shall issue Writs of Election to fill such Vacancies.

The House of Representatives shall chuse their Speaker and other Officers; and shall have the sole Power of Impeachment.

Section 3. The Senate of the United States shall be composed of two Senators from each State, chosen by the Legislature thereof, for six Years; and each Senator shall have one Vote.

Immediately after they shall be assembled in Consequence of the first Election, they shall be divided as equally as may be into three Classes. The Seats of the Senators of the first Class shall be vacated at the Expiration of the second Year, of the second Class at the Expiration of the fourth Year, and of the third Class at the Expiration of the sixth Year, so that one third may be chosen every second Year; and if Vacancies happen by Resignation, or otherwise, during the Recess of the Legislature of any State, the Executive thereof may make temporary Appointments until the next Meeting of the Legislature, which shall then fill such Vacancies.

No Person shall be a Senator who shall not have attained to the Age of thirty Years, and been nine Years a Citizen of the United States, and who shall not, when elected, be an Inhabitant of that State for which he shall be chosen.

The Vice President of the United States shall be President of the Senate, but shall have no Vote, unless they be equally divided.

The Senate shall chuse their other Officers, and also a President pro tempore, in the Absence of the Vice President, or when he shall exercise the Office of President of the United States.

The Senate shall have the sole Power to try all Impeachments. When sitting for that Purpose, they shall be on Oath or Affirmation. When the President of the United States is tried, the Chief Justice shall preside: And no Person shall be convicted without the Concurrence of two thirds of the Members present.

Judgment in Cases of Impeachment shall not extend further than to removal from Office, and disqualification to hold and enjoy any Office of honor, Trust or Profit under the United States: but the Party convicted shall nevertheless be liable and subject to Indictment, Trial, Judgment and Punishment, according to Law.

Section 4. The Times, Places and Manner of holding Elections for Senators and Representatives, shall be prescribed in each State by the Legislature thereof; but the Congress may at any time by Law make or alter such Regulations, except as to the Places of chusing Senators.

The Congress shall assemble at least once in every Year, and such Meeting shall be on the first Monday in December, unless they shall by Law appoint a different Day.

Section 5. Each House shall be the Judge of the Elections, Returns and Qualifications of its own Members, and a Majority of each shall constitute a Quorum to do Business; but a smaller Number may adjourn from day to day, and may be authorized to compel the Attendance of absent Members, in such Manner, and under such Penalties as each House may provide.

Each House may determine the Rules of its Proceedings, punish its Members for disorderly Behaviour, and, with the Concurrence of two thirds, expel a Member.

Each House shall keep a Journal of its Proceedings, and from time to time publish the same, excepting such Parts as may in their Judgment require Secrecy; and the Yeas and Nays of the Members of either House on any question shall, at the Desire of one fifth of those Present, be entered on the Journal.

Neither House, during the Session of Congress, shall, without the Consent of the other, adjourn for more than three days, nor to any other Place than that in which the two Houses shall be sitting.

Section 6. The Senators and Representatives shall receive a Compensation for their Services, to be ascertained by Law, and paid out of the Treasury of the United States. They shall in all Cases, except Treason, Felony and Breach of the Peace, be privileged from Arrest during their Attendance at the Session of their respective Houses, and in going to and returning from the same; and for any Speech or Debate in either House, they shall not be questioned in any other Place.

No Senator or Representative shall, during the Time for which he was elected, be appointed to any civil Office under the Authority of the United States, which shall have been created, or the Emoluments whereof shall have been encreased during such time; and no Person holding any Office under the United States, shall be a Member of either House during his Continuance in Office.

Section 7. All Bills for raising Revenue shall originate in the House of Representatives; but the Senate may propose or concur with Amendments as on other Bills.

Every Bill which shall have passed the House of Representatives and the Senate, shall, before it become a Law, be presented to the President of the United States: If he approve he shall sign it, but if not he shall return it, with his Objections to that House in which it shall have originated, who shall enter the Objections at large on their Journal, and proceed to reconsider it. If after such Reconsideration two thirds of that House shall agree to pass the Bill, it shall be sent, together with the Objections, to the other House, by which it shall likewise be reconsidered, and if approved by two thirds of that House, it shall become a Law. But in all such Cases the Votes of both Houses shall be determined by Yeas and Nays, and the Names of the Persons voting for and against the Bill shall be entered on the Journal of each House respectively. If any Bill shall not be returned by the President within ten Days (Sundays excepted) after it shall have been presented to him, the Same shall be a Law, in like Manner as if he had signed it, unless the Congress by their Adjournment prevent its Return, in which Case it shall not be a Law.

Every Order, Resolution, or Vote, to which the Concurrence of the Senate and House of Representatives may be necessary (except on a question of Adjournment) shall be presented to the President of the United States; and before the Same shall take Effect, shall be approved by him, or being disapproved by him, shall be repassed by two thirds of the Senate and House of Representatives, according to the Rules and Limitations prescribed in the Case of a Bill.

Section 8. The Congress shall have Power To lay and collect Taxes, Duties, Imposts and Excises, to pay the Debts and provide for the common Defence and general Welfare of the United States; but all Duties, Imposts and Excises shall be uniform throughout the United States;

To borrow Money on the credit of the United States;

To regulate Commerce with foreign Nations, and among the several States, and with the Indian Tribes;

To establish an uniform Rule of Naturalization, and uniform Laws on the subject of Bankruptcies throughout the United States;

To coin Money, regulate the Value thereof, and of foreign Coin, and fix the Standard of Weights and Measures;

To provide for the Punishment of counterfeiting the Securities and current Coin of the United States;

To establish Post Offices and post Roads;

To promote the Progress of Science and useful Arts, by securing for limited Times to Authors and Inventors the exclusive Right to their respective Writings and Discoveries;

To constitute Tribunals inferior to the supreme Court;

To define and punish Piracies and Felonies committed on the high Seas, and Offenses against the Law of Nations;

To declare War, grant Letters of Marque and Reprisal, and make Rules concerning Captures on Land and Water;

To raise and support Armies, but no Appropriation of Money to that Use shall be for a longer Term than two Years;

To provide and maintain a Navy;

To make Rules for the Government and Regulation of the land and naval Forces;

To provide for calling forth the Militia to execute the Laws of the Union, suppress Insurrections and repel Invasions;

To provide for organizing, arming, and disciplining, the Militia, and for governing such Part of them as may be employed in the Service of the United States, reserving to the States respectively, the Appointment of the Officers, and the Authority of training the Militia according to the discipline prescribed by Congress;

To exercise exclusive Legislation in all Cases whatsoever, over such District (not exceeding ten Miles square) as may, by Cession of particular States, and the Acceptance of Congress, become the Seat of the Government of the United States, and to exercise like Authority over all Places purchased by the Consent of the Legislature of the State in which the Same shall be, for the Erection of Forts, Magazines, Arsenals, dock-Yards, and other needful Buildings;—And

To make all Laws which shall be necessary and proper for carrying into Execution the foregoing Powers, and all other Powers vested by this Constitution in the Government of the United States, or in any Department or Officer thereof.

Section 9. The Migration or Importation of such Persons as any of the States now existing shall think proper to admit, shall not be prohibited by the Congress prior to the Year one thousand eight hundred and eight, but a Tax or duty may be imposed on such Importation, not exceeding ten dollars for each Person.

The Privilege of the Writ of Habeas Corpus shall not be suspended, unless when in Cases of Rebellion or Invasion the public Safety may require it.

No Bill of Attainder or ex post facto Law shall be passed.

No Capitation, or other direct, Tax shall be laid, unless in Proportion to the Census or Enumeration herein before directed to be taken.

No Tax or Duty shall be laid on Articles exported from any State.

No Preference shall be given by any Regulation of Commerce or Revenue to the Ports of one State over those of another: nor shall Vessels bound to, or from, one State, be obliged to enter, clear, or pay Duties in another.

No Money shall be drawn from the Treasury, but in Consequence of Appropriations made by Law; and a regular Statement and Account of the Receipts and Expenditures of all public Money shall be published from time to time.

No Title of Nobility shall be granted by the United States: And no Person holding any Office of Profit or Trust under them, shall, without the Consent of the Congress, accept of any present, Emolument, Office, or Title, of any kind whatever, from any King, Prince, or foreign State.

Section 10. No State shall enter into any Treaty, Alliance, or Confederation; grant Letters of Marque and Reprisal; coin Money; emit Bills of Credit; make any Thing but gold and silver Coin a Tender in Payment of Debts; pass any Bill of Attainder, ex post facto Law, or Law impairing the Obligation of Contracts, or grant any Title of Nobility.

No State shall, without the Consent of the Congress, lay any Imposts or Duties on Imports or Exports, except what may be absolutely necessary for executing it's inspection Laws: and the net Produce of all Duties and Imposts, laid by any State on Imports or Exports, shall be for the Use of the Treasury of the United States; and all such Laws shall be subject to the Revision and Controul of the Congress.

No State shall, without the Consent of Congress, lay any Duty of Tonnage, keep Troops, or Ships of War in time of Peace, enter into any Agreement or Compact with another State, or with a foreign Power, or engage in War, unless actually invaded, or in such imminent Danger as will not admit of delay.

Article II

Section 1. The executive Power shall be vested in a President of the United States of America. He shall hold his Office during the Term of four Years, and, together with the Vice President, chosen for the same Term, be elected, as follows:

Each State shall appoint, in such Manner as the Legislature thereof may direct, a Number of Electors, equal to the whole Number of Senators and Representatives to which the State may be entitled in the Congress: but no Senator or Representative, or Person holding an Office of Trust or Profit under the United States, shall be appointed an Elector.

The Electors shall meet in their respective States, and vote by Ballot for two Persons, of whom one at least shall not be an Inhabitant of the same State with themselves. And they shall make a List of all the Persons voted for, and of the Number of Votes for each; which List they shall sign and certify, and transmit sealed to the Seat of the Government of the United States, directed to the President of the Senate. The President of the Senate shall, in the Presence of the Senate and House of Representatives, open all the Certificates, and the Votes shall then be counted. The Person having the greatest Number of Votes shall be the President, if such Number be a Majority of the whole Number of Electors appointed; and if there be more than one who have such Majority, and have an equal Number of Votes, then the House of Representatives shall immediately chuse by Ballot one of them for President; and if no Person have a Majority, then from the five highest on the List the said House shall in like Manner chuse the President. But in chusing the President, the Votes shall be taken by States, the Representation from each State having one Vote; A quorum for this Purpose shall consist of a Member or Members from two thirds of the States, and a Majority of all the States shall be necessary to a Choice. In every Case, after the Choice of the President, the Person having the greatest Number of Votes of the Electors shall be the Vice President. But if there should remain two or more who have equal Votes, the Senate shall chuse from them by Ballot the Vice President.

The Congress may determine the Time of chusing the Electors, and the Day on which they shall give their Votes; which Day shall be the same throughout the United States.

No person except a natural born Citizen, or a Citizen of the United States, at the time of the Adoption of this Constitution, shall be eligible to the Office of President; neither shall any person be eligible to that Office who shall not have attained to the Age of thirty five Years, and been fourteen Years a Resident within the United States.

In Case of the Removal of the President from Office, or of his Death, Resignation, or Inability to discharge the Powers and Duties of the said Office, the same shall devolve on the Vice President, and the Congress may by Law provide for the Case of Removal, Death, Resignation or Inability, both of the President and Vice President, declaring what Officer shall then act as President, and such Officer shall act accordingly, until the Disability be removed, or a President shall be elected.

The President shall, at stated Times, receive for his Services, a Compensation, which shall neither be increased nor diminished during the Period for which he shall have been elected, and he shall not receive within that Period any other Emolument from the United States, or any of them.

Before he enter on the Execution of his Office, he shall take the following Oath or Affirmation: "I do solemnly swear (or affirm) that I will faithfully execute the Office of President of the United States, and will to the best of my Ability, preserve, protect and defend the Constitution of the United States."

Section 2. The President shall be Commander in Chief of the Army and Navy of the United States, and of the Militia of the several States, when called into the actual Service of the United States; he may require the Opinion, in writing, of the principal Officer in each of the executive Departments, upon any Subject relating to the Duties of their respective Offices, and he shall have Power to grant Reprieves and Pardons for Offenses against the United States, except in Cases of Impeachment.

He shall have Power, by and with the Advice and Consent of the Senate to make Treaties, provided two thirds of the Senators present concur; and he shall nominate, and by and with the Advice and Consent of the Senate, shall appoint Ambassadors, other public Ministers and Consuls, Judges of the supreme Court, and all other Officers of the United States, whose Appointments are not herein otherwise provided for, and which shall be established by Law: but the Congress may by Law vest the Appointment of such inferior Officers, as they think proper, in the President alone, in the Courts of Law, or in the Heads of Departments.

The President shall have Power to fill up all Vacancies that may happen during the Recess of the Senate, by granting Commissions which shall expire at the End of their next Session.

Section 3. He shall from time to time give to the Congress Information of the State of the Union, and recommend to their Consideration such Measures as he shall judge necessary and expedient; he may, on extraordinary Occasions, convene both Houses, or either of them, and in Case of Disagreement between them, with Respect to the Time of Adjournment, he may adjourn them to such Time as he shall think proper; he shall receive Ambassadors and other public Ministers; he shall take Care that the Laws be faithfully executed, and shall Commission all the Officers of the United States.

Section 4. The President, Vice President and all civil Officers of the United States, shall be removed from Office on Impeachment for, and Conviction of, Treason, Bribery, or other high Crimes and Misdemeanors.

Article III

Section 1. The judicial Power of the United States, shall be vested in one supreme Court, and in such inferior Courts as the Congress may from time to time ordain and establish. The Judges, both of the supreme and inferior Courts, shall hold their Offices during good Behaviour, and shall, at stated Times, receive for their Services, a Compensation, which shall not be diminished during their Continuance in Office.

Section 2. The judicial Power shall extend to all Cases, in Law and Equity, arising under this Constitution, the Laws of the United States, and Treaties made, or which shall be made, under their Authority;—to all Cases affecting Ambassadors, other public Ministers and Consuls;—to all Cases of admiralty and maritime Jurisdiction;—to Controversies to which the United States shall be a Party;—to Controversies between two or more States;—between a State and Citizens of another State;—between Citizens of different States;—between Citizens of the same State claiming Lands under Grants of different States, and between a State, or the Citizens thereof, and foreign States, Citizens or Subjects.

In all Cases affecting Ambassadors, other public Ministers and Consuls, and those in which a State shall be a Party, the supreme Court shall have original Jurisdiction. In all the other Cases before mentioned, the supreme Court shall have appellate Jurisdiction, both as to Law and Fact, with such Exceptions, and under such Regulations as the Congress shall make.

The Trial of all Crimes, except in Cases of Impeachment, shall be by Jury; and such Trial shall be held in the State where the said Crimes shall have been committed; but when not committed within any State, the Trial shall be at such Place or Places as the Congress may by Law have directed.

Section 3. Treason against the United States, shall consist only in levying War against them, or in adhering to their Enemies, giving them Aid and Comfort. No Person shall be convicted of Treason unless on the Testimony of two Witnesses to the same overt Act, or on Confession in open Court.

The Congress shall have Power to declare the Punishment of Treason, but no Attainder of Treason shall work Corruption of Blood, or Forfeiture except during the Life of the Person attainted.

Article IV

Section 1. Full Faith and Credit shall be given in each State to the public Acts, Records, and judicial Proceedings of every other State. And the Congress may by general Laws prescribe the Manner in which such Acts, Records and Proceedings shall be proved, and the Effect thereof.

Section 2. The Citizens of each State shall be entitled to all Privileges and Immunities of Citizens in the several States.

A Person charged in any State with Treason, Felony, or other Crime, who shall flee from Justice, and be found in another State, shall on Demand of the executive Authority of the State from which he fled, be delivered up, to be removed to the State having Jurisdiction of the Crime.

No Person held to Service or Labour in one State, under the Laws thereof, escaping into another, shall, in Consequence of any Law or Regulation therein, be discharged from such Service or Labour, but shall be delivered up on Claim of the Party to whom such Service or Labour may be due.

Section 3. New States may be admitted by the Congress into this Union; but no new State shall be formed or erected within the Jurisdiction of any other State; nor any State be formed by the Junction of two or more States, or Parts of States, without the Consent of the Legislatures of the States concerned as well as of the Congress.

The Congress shall have Power to dispose of and make all needful Rules and Regulations respecting the Territory or other Property belonging to the United States; and nothing in this Constitution shall be so construed as to Prejudice any Claims of the United States, or of any particular State.

Section 4. The United States shall guarantee to every State in this Union a Republican Form of Government, and shall protect each of them against Invasion; and on Application of the Legislature, or of the Executive (when the Legislature cannot be convened) against domestic Violence.

Article V

The Congress, whenever two thirds of both Houses shall deem it necessary, shall propose Amendments to this Constitution, or, on the Application of the Legislatures of two thirds of the several States, shall call a Convention for proposing Amendments, which, in either Case, shall be valid to all Intents and Purposes, as part of this Constitution, when ratified by the Legislatures of three fourths of the several States, or by Conventions in three fourths thereof, as the one or the other Mode of Ratification may be proposed by the Congress; Provided that no Amendment which may be made prior to the Year One thousand eight hundred and eight shall in any Manner affect the first and fourth Clauses in the Ninth Section of the first Article; and that no State, without its Consent, shall be deprived of its equal Suffrage in the Senate.

Article VI

All Debts contracted and Engagements entered into, before the Adoption of this Constitution, shall be as valid against the United States under this Constitution, as under the Confederation.

This Constitution, and the Laws of the United States which shall be made in Pursuance thereof; and all Treaties made, or which shall be made, under the Authority of the United States, shall be the supreme Law of the Land; and the Judges in every State shall be bound thereby, any Thing in the Constitution or Laws of any State to the Contrary notwithstanding.

The Senators and Representatives before mentioned, and the Members of the several State Legislatures, and all executive and judicial Officers, both of the United States and of the several States, shall be bound by Oath or Affirmation, to support this Constitution; but no religious Test shall ever be required as a Qualification to any Office or public Trust under the United States.

Article VII

The Ratification of the Conventions of nine States shall be sufficient for the Establishment of this Constitution between the States so ratifying the same.

Articles in addition to, and amendment of, the Constitution of the United States of America, proposed by Congress, and ratified by the several States, pursuant to the fifth Article of the original Constitution.

Amendment I [1791]

Congress shall make no law respecting an establishment of religion, or prohibiting the free exercise thereof; or abridging the freedom of speech, or of the press; or the right of the people peaceably to assembly, and to petition the Government for a redress of grievances.

Amendment II [1791]

A well regulated Militia, being necessary to the security of a free State, the right of the people to keep and bear Arms, shall not be infringed.

Amendment III [1791]

No Soldier shall, in time of peace be quartered in any house, without the consent of the Owner, nor in time of war, but in a manner to be prescribed by law.

Amendment IV [1791]

The right of the people to be secure in their persons, houses, papers, and effects, against unreasonable searches and seizures, shall not be violated, and no Warrants shall issue, but upon probable cause, supported by Oath or affirmation, and particularly describing the place to be searched, and the persons or things to be seized.

Amendment V [1791]

No person shall be held to answer for a capital, or otherwise infamous crime, unless on a presentment or indictment of a Grand Jury, except in cases arising in the land or naval forces, or in the Militia, when in actual service in time of War or public danger; nor shall any person be subject for the same offence to be twice put in jeopardy of life or limb; nor shall be compelled in any criminal case to be a witness against himself, nor be deprived of life, liberty, or property, without due process of law; nor shall private property be taken for public use, without just compensation.

Amendment VI [1791]

In all criminal prosecutions, the accused shall enjoy the right to a speedy and public trial, by an impartial jury of the State and district wherein the crime shall have been committed, which district shall have been previously ascertained by law, and to be informed of the nature and cause of the accusation; to be confronted with the witnesses against him; to have compulsory process for obtaining witnesses in his favor, and to have the Assistance of Counsel for his defence.

Amendment VII [1791]

In Suits at common law, where the value in controversy shall exceed twenty dollars, the right of trial by jury shall be preserved, and no fact tried by jury, shall be otherwise re-examined in any Court of the United States, than according to the rules of the common law.

Amendment VIII [1791]

Excessive bail shall not be required, nor excessive fines imposed, nor cruel and unusual punishments inflicted.

Amendment IX [1791]

The enumeration in the Constitution, of certain rights, shall not be construed to deny or disparage others retained by the people.

Amendment X [1791]

The powers not delegated to the United States by the Constitution, nor prohibited by it to the States, are reserved to the States respectively, or to the people.

Amendment XI [1798]

The Judicial power of the United States shall not be construed to extend to any suit in law or equity, commenced or prosecuted against one of the United States by Citizens of another State, or by Citizens or Subjects of any Foreign State.

Amendment XII [1804]

The Electors shall meet in their respective states and vote by ballot for President and Vice-President, one of whom, at least, shall not be an inhabitant of the same state with themselves; they shall name in their ballots the person voted for as President, and in distinct ballots the person voted for as Vice-President, and they shall make distinct lists of all persons voted for as President, and of all persons voted for as Vice-President, and of the number of votes for each, which lists they shall sign and certify, and transmit sealed to the seat of the government of the United States, directed to the President of the Senate;—The President of the Senate shall, in the presence of the Senate and House of Representatives, open all the certificates and the votes shall then be counted;—The person having the greatest Number of votes for President, shall be the President, if such number be a majority of the whole number of Electors appointed; and if no person have such majority, then from the persons having the highest numbers not exceeding three on the list of those voted for as President, the House of Representatives shall choose immediately, by ballot, the President. But in choosing the President, the votes shall be taken by states, the representation from each state having one vote; a quorum for this purpose shall consist of a member or members from two-thirds of the states, and a majority of all states shall be necessary to a choice. And if the House of Representatives shall not choose a President whenever the right of choice shall devolve upon them, before the fourth day of March next following, then the Vice-President shall act as President, as in the case of the death or other constitutional disability of the President—The person having the greatest number of votes as Vice-President, shall be the Vice-President, if such number be a majority of the whole number of Electors appointed, and if no person have a majority, then from the two highest numbers on the list, the Senate shall choose the Vice-President; a quorum for the purpose shall consist of two-thirds of the whole number of Senators, and a majority of the whole number shall be necessary to a choice. But no person constitutionally ineligible to the office of President shall be eligible to that of Vice-President of the United States.

Amendment XIII [1865]

Section 1. Neither slavery nor involuntary servitude, except as a punishment for crime whereof the party shall have been duly convicted, shall exist within the United States, or any place subject to their jurisdiction.

Section 2. Congress shall have power to enforce this article by appropriate legislation.

Amendment XIV [1868]

Section 1. All persons born or naturalized in the United States and subject to the jurisdiction thereof, are citizens of the United States and of the State wherein they reside. No State shall make or enforce any law which shall abridge the privileges or immunities of citizens of the United States; nor shall any State deprive any person of life, liberty, or property, without due process of law; nor deny to any person within its jurisdiction the equal protection of the laws.

Section 2. Representatives shall be apportioned among the several States according to their respective numbers, counting the whole number of persons in each State, excluding Indians not taxed. But when the right to vote at any election for the choice of electors for President and Vice President of the United States, Representatives in Congress, the Executive and Judicial officers of a State, or the members of the Legislature thereof, is denied to any of the male inhabitants of such State, being twenty-one years of age, and citizens of the United States, or in any way abridged, except for participation in rebellion, or other crime, the basis of representation therein shall be reduced in the proportion which the number of such male citizens shall bear to the whole number of male citizens twenty-one years of age in such State.

Section 3. No person shall be a Senator or Representative in Congress, or elector of President and Vice President, or hold any office, civil or military, under the United States, or under any State, who, having previously taken an oath, as a member of Congress, or as an officer of the United States, or as a member of any State legislature, or as an executive or judicial officer of any State, to support the Constitution of the United States, shall have engaged in insurrection or rebellion against the same, or given aid or comfort to the enemies thereof. But Congress may by a vote of two-thirds of each House, remove such disability.

Section 4. The validity of the public debt of the United States, authorized by law, including debts incurred for payment of pensions and bounties for services in suppressing insurrection or rebellion, shall not be questioned. But neither the United States nor any State shall assume or pay any debt or obligation incurred in aid of insurrection or rebellion against the United States, or any claim for the loss or emancipation of any slave; but all such debts, obligations and claims shall be held illegal and void.

Section 5. The Congress shall have power to enforce, by appropriate legislation, the provisions of this article.

Amendment XV [1870]

Section 1. The right of citizens of the United States to vote shall not be denied or abridged by the United States or by any State on account of race, color, or previous condition of servitude.

Section 2. The Congress shall have power to enforce this article by appropriate legislation.

Amendment XVI [1913]

The Congress shall have power to lay and collect taxes on incomes, from whatever source derived, without apportionment among the several States, and without regard to any census or enumeration.

Amendment XVII [1913]

The Senate of the United States shall be composed of two Senators from each State, elected by the people thereof, for six years; and each Senator shall have one vote. The electors in each State shall have the qualifications requisite for electors of the most numerous branch of the State legislatures.

When vacancies happen in the representation of any State in the Senate, the executive authority of such State shall issue writs of election to fill such vacancies: *Provided*, That the legislature of any State may empower the executive thereof to make temporary appointments until the people fill the vacancies by election as the legislature may direct.

This amendment shall not be so construed as to affect the election or term of any Senator chosen before it becomes valid as part of the Constitution.

Amendment XVIII [1919]

Section 1. After one year from the ratification of this article the manufacture, sale, or transportation of intoxicating liquors within, the importation thereof into, or the exportation thereof from the United States and all territory subject to the jurisdiction thereof for beverage purposes is hereby prohibited.

Section 2. The Congress and the several States shall have concurrent power to enforce this article by appropriate legislation.

Section 3. This article shall be inoperative unless it shall have been ratified as an amendment to the Constitution by the legislatures of the several States, as provided in the Constitution, within seven years from the date of the submission hereof to the States by the Congress.

Amendment XIX [1920]

The right of citizens of the United States to vote shall not be denied or abridged by the United States or by any State on account of sex.

Congress shall have power to enforce this article by appropriate legislation.

Amendment XX [1933]

Section 1. The terms of the President and Vice President shall end at noon on the 20th day of January, and the terms of Senators and Representatives at noon on the 3d day of January, of the years in which such terms would have ended if this article had not been ratified; and the terms of their successors shall then begin.

Section 2. The Congress shall assemble at least once in every year, and such meeting shall begin at noon on the 3d day of January, unless they shall by law appoint a different day.

Section 3. If, at the time fixed for the beginning of the term of the President, the President elect shall have died, the Vice President elect shall become President. If a President shall not have been chosen before the time fixed for the beginning of his term, or if the President elect shall have failed to qualify, then the Vice President elect shall act as President until a President shall have qualified; and the Congress may by law provide for the case wherein neither a President elect nor a Vice President elect shall have qualified, declaring who shall then act as President, or the manner in which one who is to act shall be selected, and such person shall act accordingly until a President or Vice President shall have qualified.

Section 4. The Congress may by law provide for the case of the death of any of the persons from whom the House of Representatives may choose a President whenever the right of choice shall have devolved upon them, and for the case of the death of any of the persons from whom the Senate may choose a Vice President whenever the right of choice shall have devolved upon them.

Section 5. Sections 1 and 2 shall take effect on the 15th day of October following the ratification of this article.

Section 6. This article shall be inoperative unless it shall have been ratified as an amendment to the Constitution by the legislatures of three-fourths of the several States within seven years from the date of its submission.

Amendment XXI [1933]

Section 1. The eighteenth article of amendment to the Constitution of the United States is hereby repealed.

Section 2. The transportation or importation into any State, Territory, or possession of the United States for delivery or use therein of intoxicating liquors, in violation of the laws thereof, is hereby prohibited.

Section 3. This article shall be inoperative unless it shall have been ratified as an amendment to the Constitution by conventions in the several States, as provided in the Constitution, within seven years from the date of the submission hereof to the States by the Congress.

Amendment XXII [1951]

Section 1. No person shall be elected to the office of the President more than twice, and no person who has held the office of President, or acted as President, for more than two years of a term to which some other person was elected President shall be elected to the office of President more than once. But this Article shall not apply to any person holding the office of President, when this Article was proposed by the Congress, and shall not prevent any person who may be holding the office of President, or acting as President, during the term within which this Article becomes operative from holding the office of President or acting as President during the remainder of such term.

Section 2. This article shall be inoperative unless it shall have been ratified as an amendment to the Constitution by the legislatures of three-fourths of the several States within seven years from the date of its submission to the States by the Congress.

Amendment XXIII [1961]

Section 1. The District constituting the seat of Government of the United States shall appoint in such manner as the Congress may direct:

A number of electors of President and Vice President equal to the whole number of Senators and Representatives in Congress to which the District would be entitled if it were a State, but in no event more than the least populous State; they shall be in addition to those appointed by the States, but they shall be considered, for the purposes of the election of President and Vice President, to be electors appointed by a State; and they shall meet in the District and perform such duties as provided by the twelfth article of amendment.

Section 2. The Congress shall have power to enforce this article by appropriate legislation.

Amendment XXIV [1964]

Section 1. The right of citizens of the United States to vote in any primary or other election for President or Vice President, for electors for President or Vice President, or for Senator or Representative in Congress, shall not be denied or abridged by the United States or any State by reason of failure to pay any poll tax or other tax.

Section 2. The Congress shall have power to enforce this article by appropriate legislation.

Amendment XXV [1967]

Section 1. In case of the removal of the President from office or of his death or resignation, the Vice President shall become President.

Section 2. Whenever there is a vacancy in the office of the Vice President, the President shall nominate a Vice President who shall take office upon confirmation by a majority vote of both Houses of Congress.

Section 3. Whenever the President transmits to the President pro tempore of the Senate and the Speaker of the House of Representatives his written declaration that he is unable to discharge the powers and duties of his office, and until he transmits to them a written declaration to the contrary, such powers and duties shall be discharged by the Vice President as Acting President.

Section 4. Whenever the Vice President and a majority of either the principal officers of the executive departments or of such other body as Congress may by law provide, transmit to the President pro tempore of the Senate and the Speaker of the House of Representatives their written declaration that the President is unable to discharge the powers and duties of his office, the Vice President shall immediately assume the powers and duties of the office as Acting President.

Thereafter, when the President transmits to the President pro tempore of the Senate and the Speaker of the House of Representatives his written declaration that no inability exists, he shall resume the powers and duties of his office unless the Vice President and a majority of either the principal officers of the executive department or of such other body as Congress may by law provide, transmit within four days to the President pro tempore of the Senate and the Speaker of the House of Representatives their written declaration that the President is unable to discharge the powers and duties of his office. Thereupon Congress shall decide the issue, assembling within forty-eight hours for that purpose if not in session. If the Congress, within twenty-one days after receipt of the latter written declaration, or, if Congress is not in session, within twenty-one days after Congress is required to assemble, determines by two-thirds vote of both Houses that the President is unable to discharge the powers and duties of his office, the Vice President shall continue to discharge the same as Acting President; otherwise, the President shall resume the powers and duties of his office.

Amendment XXVI [1971]

Section 1. The right of citizens of the United States, who are eighteen years of age or older, to vote shall not be denied or abridged by the United States or by any State on account of age.

Section 2. The Congress shall have power to enforce this article by appropriate legislation.

Index of Authors

Subject Index